UNIFORM CRIME REPORTS

for the United States

1996

SUMMARY

CRIME INDEX

CRIMES CLEARED

PERSONS ARRESTED

TOPICAL STUDY

LAW ENFORCEMENT PERSONNEL

APPENDICES

PRINTED ANNUALLY

Federal Bureau of Investigation
U.S. Department of Justice
Washington, D.C. 20535

ADVISORY:

Committee on Uniform Crime Records
International Association of Chiefs of Police;
Committee on Uniform Crime Reporting
National Sheriffs' Association;
Criminal Justice Information Services Advisory Policy Board

For sale by the U.S. Government Printing Office
Superintendent of Documents, Mail Stop: SSOP, Washington, DC 20402-9328
ISBN 0-16-049217-3

PREFACE

Each year *Crime in the United States* presents crime statistics for the Nation as a whole, as well as for regions, states, counties, cities, towns, and college and university campuses. These data are compiled from monthly law enforcement reports or individual crime incident records transmitted directly to the FBI or to centralized state agencies that then report to the FBI. The primary objective of the Uniform Crime Reporting (UCR) Program is to provide a reliable set of criminal justice statistics for law enforcement administration, operation, and management.

UCR crime statistics permit studies among neighboring jurisdictions and among those with similar populations and other common characteristics. In addition, a study of the nature and movement of crime over time allows researchers to theorize about the causes underlying changes and fluctuations and to hypothesize about possible effects on families and communities. A study of the crime data for a specific geographic locale enables researchers to assess the influence of crime on a particular district. For these reasons, UCR data are used not only by criminal justice agencies but by university researchers, sociologists, criminologists, community development organizations, tourism agencies, media, and many others. Each year the Uniform Crime Reporting Program strives to compile and present the facts and the many facets of crime in the United States in ways that will assist all students of crime data.

This current edition includes for the first time a presentation of the reported data on those Index crimes which are motivated by bias against individuals based upon race, religion, sexual orientation, or ethnicity. The hate crime data are extracts of those to be reported in the annual publication, *Hate Crime Statistics.* Produced since 1992, they provide an important additional perspective on the Nation's crime experience and are a positive addition to the historical crime report.

As the 21st century approaches, the Uniform Crime Reporting Program shares with state and local law enforcement an ever-increasing commitment to implement fully the National Incident-Based Reporting System (NIBRS). The foundation of the national system will be the thousands of automated records-management systems that are being developed within individual agencies across the Nation. Within the next few years, *information* may prove to be law enforcement's most important weapon. Many progressive computerized systems have the capacity not only to compile crime statistics but to link all associated criminal justice information systems. Good automated systems generate data that benefit officers in patrol cars as much as detectives and prosecutors. They also produce the statistical reports required for NIBRS.

The UCR staff continues to support and encourage law enforcement's efforts to develop computerized data collection systems through research, training, and technical assistance. Recently, Austin, Texas, became the first city with over 500,000 population to institute NIBRS reporting as part of a comprehensive, incident-based, automated records-management system. As more and more agencies, large and small, become part of NIBRS, the FBI will be able to offer more comprehensive national and regional crime statistics for use in law enforcement decisionmaking at all levels of government.

The Uniform Crime Reporting Program staff, now fully established in Clarksburg, West Virginia, is looking to the future with optimism and a commitment to maintain the high standards that have characterized the Program from its inception.

CRIME FACTORS

Each year when *Crime in the United States* is published, many entities—news media, tourism agencies, and other groups with an interest in crime in our Nation—use reported Crime Index figures to compile rankings of cities and counties. These rankings lead to simplistic and/or incomplete analyses which often create misleading perceptions adversely affecting cities and counties, along with their residents. Assessing criminality and law enforcement's response from jurisdiction to jurisdiction must encompass many elements, some of which, while having significant impact, are not readily measurable nor applicable pervasively among all locales. Geographic and demographic factors specific to each jurisdiction must be considered and applied if crime assessment is to approach completeness and accuracy. There are several sources of information which may assist the responsible researcher. The U.S. Bureau of the Census data, for example, can be utilized to better understand the makeup of a locale's population. The transience of the population, its racial and ethnic makeup, its composition by age and gender, education levels, and prevalent family structures are all key factors in assessing and comprehending the crime issue.

Local chambers of commerce, planning offices, or similar entities provide information regarding the economic and cultural makeup of cities and counties. Understanding a jurisdiction's industrial/economic base, its dependence upon neighboring jurisdictions, its transportation system, its economic dependence on nonresidents (such as tourists and convention attendees), its proximity to military installations, etc., all contribute to accurately gauging and interpreting the crime known to and reported by law enforcement.

The strength (personnel and other resources) and the aggressiveness of a jurisdiction's law enforcement agency are also key factors. While information pertaining to the number of sworn and civilian law enforcement employees can be found in this publication, assessment of the law enforcement emphases is, of course, much more difficult. For example, one city may report more crime than a comparable one, not because there is more crime, but rather because its law enforcement agency through proactive efforts identifies more offenses. Attitudes of the citizens toward crime and their crime reporting practices, especially concerning more minor offenses, have an impact on the volume of crimes known to police.

It is incumbent upon all data users to become as well educated as possible about how to categorize and quantify the nature and extent of crime in the United States and in any of the over 16,000 jurisdictions represented by law enforcement contributors to this Program. Valid assessments are possible only with careful study and analysis of the various unique conditions affecting each local law enforcement jurisdiction.

Historically, the causes and origins of crime have been the subjects of investigation by varied disciplines. Some factors which are known to affect the volume and type of crime occurring from place to place are:

Population density and degree of urbanization.

Variations in composition of the population, particularly youth concentration.

Stability of population with respect to residents' mobility, commuting patterns, and transient factors.

Modes of transportation and highway system.

Economic conditions, including median income, poverty level, and job availability.

Cultural factors and educational, recreational, and religious characteristics.

Family conditions with respect to divorce and family cohesiveness.

Climate.

Effective strength of law enforcement agencies.

Administrative and investigative emphases of law enforcement.

Policies of other components of the criminal justice system (i.e., prosecutorial, judicial, correctional, and probational).

Citizens' attitudes toward crime.

Crime reporting practices of the citizenry.

The Uniform Crime Reports give a nationwide view of crime based on statistics contributed by state and local law enforcement agencies. Population size is the only correlate of crime utilized in this publication. While the other factors listed above are of equal concern, no attempt is made to relate them to the data presented. *The reader is, therefore, cautioned against comparing statistical data of individual reporting units from cities, counties, metropolitan areas, states, or colleges and universities solely on the basis of their population coverage or student enrollment.*

Data users are cautioned against comparisons of crime trends presented in this report and those estimated by the National Crime Victimization Survey (NCVS), administered by the Bureau of Justice Statistics. Because of differences in methodology and crime coverage, the two programs examine the Nation's crime problem from somewhat different perspectives, and their results are not strictly comparable. The definitional and procedural differences can account for many of the apparent discrepancies in results from the two programs.

CONTENTS

SECTION I

Summary of the Uniform Crime Reporting (UCR) Program

The Uniform Crime Reporting Program is a nationwide, cooperative statistical effort of over 16,000 city, county, and state law enforcement agencies voluntarily reporting data on crimes brought to their attention. During 1996, law enforcement agencies active in the UCR Program represented nearly 252 million United States inhabitants or 95 percent of the total population as established by the Bureau of the Census. The coverage amounted to 97 percent of the United States population in Metropolitan Statistical Areas (MSAs), 90 percent of the population in cities outside metropolitan areas, and 87 percent of the rural population.

Since 1930, the FBI has administered the Program and issued periodic assessments of the nature and type of crime in the Nation. While the Program's primary objective is to generate a reliable set of criminal statistics for use in law enforcement administration, operation, and management, its data have over the years become one of the country's leading social indicators. The American public looks to Uniform Crime Reports for information on fluctuations in the level of crime, while criminologists, sociologists, legislators, municipal planners, the media, and other students of criminal justice use the statistics for varied research and planning purposes.

Historical Background

The International Association of Chiefs of Police (IACP), recognizing a need for national crime statistics, formed the Committee on Uniform Crime Records in the 1920s to develop a system of uniform police statistics. Establishing offenses known to law enforcement as the appropriate measure, the Committee evaluated various crimes on the basis of their seriousness, frequency of occurrence, pervasiveness in all geographic areas of the country, and likelihood of being reported to law enforcement. After studying state criminal codes and making an evaluation of the recordkeeping practices in use, the Committee in 1929 completed a plan for crime reporting which became the foundation of the Uniform Crime Reporting Program.

Seven offenses were chosen to serve as an Index for gauging fluctuations in the overall volume and rate of crime. Known collectively as the Crime Index, these offenses included the violent crimes of murder and nonnegligent manslaughter, forcible rape, robbery, and aggravated assault and the property crimes of burglary, larceny-theft, and motor vehicle theft. By congressional mandate, arson was added as the eighth Index offense in 1979.

During the early planning of the Program, it was recognized that the differences among criminal codes precluded a mere aggregation of state statistics to arrive at a national total. Further, because of the variances in punishment for the same offenses in different state codes, no distinction between felony and misdemeanor crimes was possible. To avoid these problems and provide nationwide uniformity in crime reporting, standardized offense definitions by which law enforcement agencies were to submit data without regard for local statutes were formulated. The definitions used by the Program are set forth in Appendix II of this publication.

In January 1930, 400 cities collectively representing 20 million inhabitants in 43 states began participating in the UCR Program. Congress enacted Title 28, Section 534, of the United States Code authorizing the Attorney General to gather crime information that same year. The Attorney General, in turn, designated the FBI to serve as the national clearinghouse for the data collected. Since that time, data based on uniform classifications and procedures for reporting have been obtained from the Nation's law enforcement agencies.

Advisory Groups

Providing vital links between local law enforcement and the FBI in the conduct of the UCR Program are the Criminal Justice Information Systems Committees of the IACP and the National Sheriffs' Association (NSA). The IACP, as it has since the Program began, represents the thousands of police departments nationwide. The NSA encourages sheriffs throughout the country to participate fully in the Program. Both committees serve in advisory capacities concerning the UCR Program's operation.

To function in an advisory capacity concerning UCR policy and provide suggestions on UCR data usage, a Data Providers' Advisory Policy Board (APB) was established in August 1988. The Board operated until 1993 when a new Board to address all FBI criminal justice information services was approved. The Board functions in an advisory capacity concerning UCR policy and on data collection and use. The UCR Subcommittee of the Board ensures continuing emphasis on UCR-related issues.

The Association of State Uniform Crime Reporting Programs and committees on UCR within individual state law enforcement associations are also active in promoting interest in the UCR Program. These organizations foster widespread and more intelligent use of uniform crime statistics and lend assistance to contributors when the needs arise.

Redesign of UCR

While throughout the years the UCR Program remained virtually unchanged in terms of the data collected and disseminated, a broad utility had evolved for UCR by the 1980s. Recognizing the need for improved statistics, law enforcement called for a thorough evaluative study that would modernize the UCR Program. The FBI concurred with the need for an updated

Program and lent its complete support, formulating a comprehensive three-phase redesign effort. The Bureau of Justice Statistics (BJS), the Department of Justice agency responsible for funding criminal justice information projects, agreed to underwrite the first two phases. Conducted by an independent contractor, these phases were structured to determine what, if any, changes should be made to the current Program. The third phase would involve implementation of the changes identified. Abt Associates Inc. of Cambridge, Massachusetts, overseen by the FBI, BJS, and a Steering Committee comprised of prestigious individuals representing a myriad of disciplines, commenced the first phase in 1982.

During the first phase, the historical evolution of the UCR Program was examined. All aspects of the Program, including the objectives and intended user audience, data items, reporting mechanisms, quality control, publications and user services, and relationships with other criminal justice data systems, were studied.

Early in 1984, a conference on the future of UCR, held in Elkridge, Maryland, launched the second phase of the study, which would examine potential futures for UCR and conclude with a set of recommended changes. Attendees at this conference reviewed work conducted during the first phase and discussed the potential changes that should be considered during phase two.

Findings from the first phase of the evaluation and input on alternatives for the future were also major topics of discussion at the seventh National UCR Conference in July 1984. Overlapping phases one and two was a survey of law enforcement agencies.

Phase two ended in early 1985 with the production of a draft, "Blueprint for the Future of the Uniform Crime Reporting Program." The study's Steering Committee reviewed the draft report at a March 1985 meeting and made various recommendations for revision. The Committee members, however, endorsed the report's concepts.

In April 1985, the phase two recommendations were presented at the eighth National UCR Conference. While various considerations for the final report were set forth, the overall concept for the revised Program was unanimously approved. The joint IACP/NSA Committee on UCR also issued a resolution endorsing the Blueprint.

The final report, the "Blueprint for the Future of the Uniform Crime Reporting Program," was released in the summer of 1985. It specifically outlined recommendations for an expanded, improved UCR Program to meet informational needs into the next century. There were three recommended areas of enhancement to the UCR Program. First, reporting of offenses and arrests would be made by means of an incident-based system. Second, collection of data would be accomplished on two levels. Agencies in level one would report important details about those offenses comprising the current Crime Index, their victims, and arrestees. Law enforcement agencies covering populations of over 100,000 and a sampling of smaller agencies would be included in level two, which would collect expanded detail on all significant offenses. The third proposal involved introducing a quality assurance program.

To begin implementation of NIBRS, the FBI awarded a contract to develop new offense definitions and data elements for the redesigned system. The work involved (a) revising the definitions of certain Index offenses, (b) identifying additional significant offenses to be reported, (c) refining definitions for both, and (d) developing data elements (incident details) for all UCR offenses in order to fulfill the requirements of incident-based reporting versus the current summary reporting.

Concurrent with the preparation of the data elements, the FBI studied the various state systems to select an experimental site for implementation of the redesigned Program. In view of its long-standing incident-based Program and well-established staff dedicated solely to UCR, the South Carolina Law Enforcement Division (SLED) was chosen. The SLED agreed to adapt its existing system to meet the requirements of the redesigned Program and collect data on both offenses and arrests relating to the newly defined offenses.

To assist SLED with the pilot project, offense definitions and data elements developed under the private contract were put at the staff's disposal. Also, FBI automated data processing personnel developed "Automated Data Capture Specifications" for use in adapting the state's data processing procedures to incorporate the revised system. The BJS supplied funding to facilitate software revisions needed at the state level. Testing of the new Program was completed in late 1987.

Following the completion of the pilot project conducted by SLED, the FBI produced a draft set of guidelines for an enhanced UCR Program. Law enforcement executives from around the country were then invited to a conference in Orange Beach, Alabama, where the guidelines were presented for final review.

During the conference, three overall endorsements were passed without dissent. First, that there be established a new, incident-based national crime reporting system; second, that the FBI manage this Program; and third, that an Advisory Policy Board composed of law enforcement executives be formed to assist in the direction and implementation of the new Program.

Information about the redesigned UCR Program, called the National Incident-Based Reporting System, or NIBRS, is contained in four documents produced subsequent to the Orange Beach Conference. Volume 1, *Data Collection Guidelines*, contains a system overview and descriptions of the offenses, offense codes, reports, data elements, and data values used in the system. Volume 2, *Data Submission Specifications*, is for the use of state and local systems personnel who are responsible for preparing magnetic tapes/floppy disks/etc., for submission to the FBI. Volume 3, *Approaches to Implementing an Incident-Based Reporting (IBR) System*, is for use by computer programmers, analysts, etc., responsible for developing a state or local IBR system which will meet NIBRS' reporting requirements. Volume 4, *Error Message Manual*, contains designations of mandatory and optional data elements, data element edits, and error messages.

A NIBRS edition of the *UCR Handbook* has been produced to assist law enforcement agency data contributors implementing NIBRS within their departments. This document is geared toward familiarizing local and state law enforcement personnel with the definitions, policies, and procedures of NIBRS. The book does not contain the technical coding and data transmission requirements presented in Volumes 1 through 4.

NIBRS will collect data on each single incident and arrest within 22 crime categories. For each offense known to police within these categories, incident, victim, property, offender, and arrestee information will be gathered when available. The goal of the redesign is to modernize crime information by collecting data presently maintained in law enforcement records; the enhanced UCR Program is, therefore, a by-product of current records systems. The integrity of UCR's long-running statistical series will, of course, be maintained.

It became apparent during the development of the prototype system that the level one and level two reporting proposed in the "Blueprint" might not be the most practical approach. Many state and local law enforcement administrators indicated that the collection of data on all pertinent offenses could be handled with more ease than could the extraction of selected ones. While "Limited" participation, equivalent to the "Blueprint's" level one, will remain an option, it appears that most reporting jurisdictions, upon implementation, will go immediately to "Full" participation, meeting all NIBRS data submission requirements.

Implementing NIBRS will be at a pace commensurate with the resources, abilities, and limitations of the contributing law enforcement agencies. The FBI was able to accept NIBRS data as of January 1989, and 10 state-level UCR Programs (Colorado, Idaho, Iowa, Massachusetts, Michigan, North Dakota, South Carolina, Utah, Vermont, and Virginia) and 3 individual law enforcement agencies in the state of Texas are now supplying data in the NIBRS format. An additional 25 state agencies, 8 local law enforcement agencies in states not having state-level programs, and 5 federal agencies (the Departments of Commerce, Interior, and Defense-Air Force, Federal Protective Service, and the FBI) have submitted test tapes or disks containing the expanded data. Eight other state agencies, agencies in the District of Columbia and Guam, and other federal agencies are in various stages of planning and development.

Recent Developments

CRIME IN THE UNITED STATES — A change has been made to this year's edition of *Crime in the United States.* Section II, "Crime Index Offenses Reported," has been expanded to include a presentation on hate crime statistics. Incidents motivated by bias involve the traditional offenses collected by the UCR Program; therefore, including current hate crime data in the publication will provide another perspective of crime in the Nation. The complete 1996 edition of *Hate Crime Statistics* is tentatively scheduled for release in the fall.

UCR RELOCATION — The UCR Program has completed the move to West Virginia. In Appendix VI, the new telephone numbers of each UCR unit are listed. The FBI headquarters' numbers will no longer transfer to the new site.

DATA USE BROCHURE — In early 1997, a brochure entitled *Uniform Crime Reporting Statistics: Their Proper Use* was published. As its title indicates, the purpose of this publication is to advise UCR data users about the proper employment of FBI-provided statistics. While UCR data are sometimes used to compile rankings of states, cities, counties, or colleges and universities, the FBI has long cautioned against such misleading analyses which lead to inaccurate perceptions of crime in these various locales. At the request of the CJIS Advisory Policy Board and law enforcement officials across the Nation, the UCR staff prepared the pamphlet addressing these issues in an effort to discourage the practice of ranking on the basis of crime data alone. It is available free upon request.

NIBRS IMPLEMENTATION — In 1995, the Bureau of Justice Statistics (BJS, U.S. Department of Justice), entered into a cooperative agreement with SEARCH, the National Consortium for Justice Information and Statistics, to identify impediments to NIBRS implementation. Under the joint direction of BJS and the FBI and guided by a Steering Committee, this project was initiated to (1) identify the most promising and cost effective approaches to encouraging wider and more rapid adoption of NIBRS, (2) identify the greatest impediments to full NIBRS participation, and (3) develop recommendations to address these obstacles.

As a first step in understanding agencies' problems with implementing NIBRS, the SEARCH project staff conducted a detailed survey of the Nation's 64 largest local law enforcement agencies. Next, representatives from the target agencies and their state UCR/NIBRS programs were invited to participate in regional focus groups hosted by SEARCH in five locations throughout the Nation.

Based upon survey data and information gained through the focus groups, several recommendations were formulated including: (1) the development of standard analytic methodologies that demonstrate how NIBRS data will be used in federal, state, and local reports; (2) intensive research into software and data input strategies; and (3) increased assistance to local agencies in upgrading their records management systems and implementing Incident-Based Reporting systems. The NIBRS Project Steering Committee, the UCR Subcommittee of the CJIS Advisory Policy Board, and the CJIS Advisory Policy Board have offered continued support to the project. Copies of the complete report are available in printed or in electronic format. SEARCH reports and other information are available on the World Wide Web Site located at http://www.nibrs.search.org

QUALITY ASSURANCE REVIEW OF UCR DATA — To further its goal to accurately, completely, and uniformly reflect local, state, and national crime statistics, UCR is implementing a Quality Assurance Review (QAR) for both summary and incident-based data. The purpose of the voluntary QAR is to increase the reliability and validity of crime statistics, achieve compliance with required procedures and correct errors within a system, and increase an agency's ability to report accurately with meaningful results. Designed to be a workable, supportive analysis of a system and its data, the QAR will focus on coding and classification procedures, clearances, property values, resubmission of errors, and arrests. The QAR staff began pilot reviews to assess its planned processes in June of 1997. This pilot review process will continue to be assessed and adjusted in order to best assist UCR's participating agencies in their objective of collecting accurate, dependable crime data.

CHART 2.1

CRIME CLOCK
1996

one
MURDER
every 27 minutes

one
FORCIBLE RAPE
every 6 minutes

one
ROBBERY
every 59 seconds

one
VIOLENT CRIME
every 19 seconds

one
AGGRAVATED ASSAULT
every 31 seconds

one
CRIME INDEX OFFENSE
every 2 seconds

one
PROPERTY CRIME
every 3 seconds

one
BURGLARY
every 13 seconds

one
LARCENY-THEFT
every 4 seconds

one
MOTOR VEHICLE THEFT
every 23 seconds

The Crime Clock should be viewed with care. Being the most aggregate representation of UCR data, it is designed to convey the annual reported crime experience by showing the relative frequency of occurrence of the Index Offenses. This mode of display should not be taken to imply a regularity in the commission of the Part I Offenses; rather, it represents the annual ratio of crime to fixed time intervals.

SECTION II
Crime Index Offenses Reported

CRIME INDEX TOTAL

DEFINITION

The Crime Index is composed of selected offenses used to gauge fluctuations in the overall volume and rate of crime reported to law enforcement. The offenses included are the violent crimes of murder and nonnegligent manslaughter, forcible rape, robbery, and aggravated assault and the property crimes of burglary, larceny-theft, motor vehicle theft, and arson.

TREND		
Year	*Number of offenses[1]*	*Rate per 100,000 inhabitants[1]*
1995	13,862,727	5,275.9
1996	13,473,614	5,078.9
Percent change	-2.8	-3.7

[1] Does not include arson. See page 61.

The Crime Index total dropped 3 percent to nearly 13.5 million offenses in 1996, the lowest annual serious crime count since 1986 and the fifth consecutive annual decline. The decrease in serious crime was also evident among the Nation's cities, collectively. Within the city population groups, the greatest decrease, 6 percent, was reported in cities having 1 million or more inhabitants. In the suburban and rural counties, decreases of 4 and 2 percent, respectively, were reported.

Five- and 10-year percent changes showed the 1996 national total was 7 percent lower than the 1992 level and virtually the same as the 1987 total.

By geographic region, the largest volume of Crime Index offenses was reported in the most populous Southern States, which accounted for 40 percent of the total. Following were the Western States with 24 percent, the Midwestern States with 21 percent, and the Northeastern States with 15 percent. Crime Index decreases in 1996 as compared to 1995 figures were recorded in the Western States, 8 percent; the Northeastern States, 7 percent; and the Midwestern States, 1 percent. In the South, the 1996 Index total increased 1 percent over the 1995 level. (See Tables 3 and 4.)

Crime Index offenses occurred most frequently in July and August and least often in February.

Table 2.1 — Crime Index Total by Month, 1992-1996
[Percent distribution]

Months	1992	1993	1994	1995	1996
January	8.3	8.0	7.6	8.1	8.1
February	7.8	6.9	7.1	7.2	7.6
March	8.2	8.1	8.2	8.1	8.0
April	8.0	7.9	8.1	7.8	8.0
May	8.3	8.2	8.5	8.4	8.5
June	8.4	8.6	8.5	8.5	8.5
July	9.0	9.1	9.1	9.0	9.1
August	9.0	9.2	9.4	9.3	9.1
September	8.4	8.4	8.5	8.5	8.4
October	8.5	8.6	8.8	8.8	8.7
November	8.0	8.1	8.3	8.2	7.9
December	8.1	9.1	7.9	8.1	8.1

Rate

Crime rates relate the incidence of crime to population. In 1996, there were an estimated 5,079 Crime Index offenses for each 100,000 in United States population, the lowest rate since 1984. The Crime Index rate was highest in the Nation's metropolitan areas and lowest in the rural counties. (See Tables 1 and 2.) The national 1996 Crime Index rate fell 4 percent from the 1995 rate, 10 percent from the 1992 level, and 8 percent from the 1987 rate.

Regionally, the Crime Index rates ranged from 5,727 in the South to 3,899 in the Northeast. Two-year percent changes (1996 versus 1995) showed rate declines in all four regions. (See Table 4.)

Nature

The Crime Index is composed of violent and property crime categories, and in 1996, 12 percent of the Index offenses reported to law enforcement were violent crimes and 88 percent, property crimes. Larceny-theft was the offense with the highest volume, while murder accounted for the fewest offenses. (See Chart 2.3.)

Property estimated in value at $15.5 billion was stolen in connection with all Crime Index offenses, with the greatest losses due to thefts of motor vehicles; televisions, radios, stereos, etc.; and jewelry and precious metals. Nationwide, law enforcement agencies recorded a 38-percent recovery rate for dollar losses in connection with stolen property. The highest recovery percentages were for stolen motor vehicles, consumable goods, livestock, clothing and furs, and firearms. (See Table 24.)

Law Enforcement Response

In 1996, law enforcement agencies nationwide recorded a 22-percent clearance rate for the collective Crime Index offenses and made an estimated 2.8 million arrests for Index crimes. Crimes can be cleared by arrest or by exceptional means when some element beyond law enforcement control precludes the placing of formal charges against the offender. The arrest of one person may clear several crimes, or several persons may be arrested in connection with the clearance of one offense.

The Index clearance rate has remained relatively stable throughout the past 10-year period. In both 1992 and 1987, the clearance rates were 21 percent.

Total Crime Index arrests, as well as those of adults, dropped 3 percent in 1996 when compared to 1995 figures. Juvenile arrests for Index crimes decreased 1 percent. By gender, arrests of males decreased 4 percent, and arrests of females showed virtually no change for the 2-year period. (See Tables 36 and 37.)

Between 1996 and 1995, declines in the number of persons arrested were recorded for each of the individual offenses composing the Index. Decreases ranged from 10 percent for murder to 1 percent for larceny-theft as shown in Table 36.

As in past years, arrests for larceny-theft, estimated at nearly 1.5 million in 1996, accounted for the highest volume of Crime Index arrests. (See Table 29.)

CRIME INDEX TOTAL
PERCENT CHANGE FROM 1992

CHART 2.2

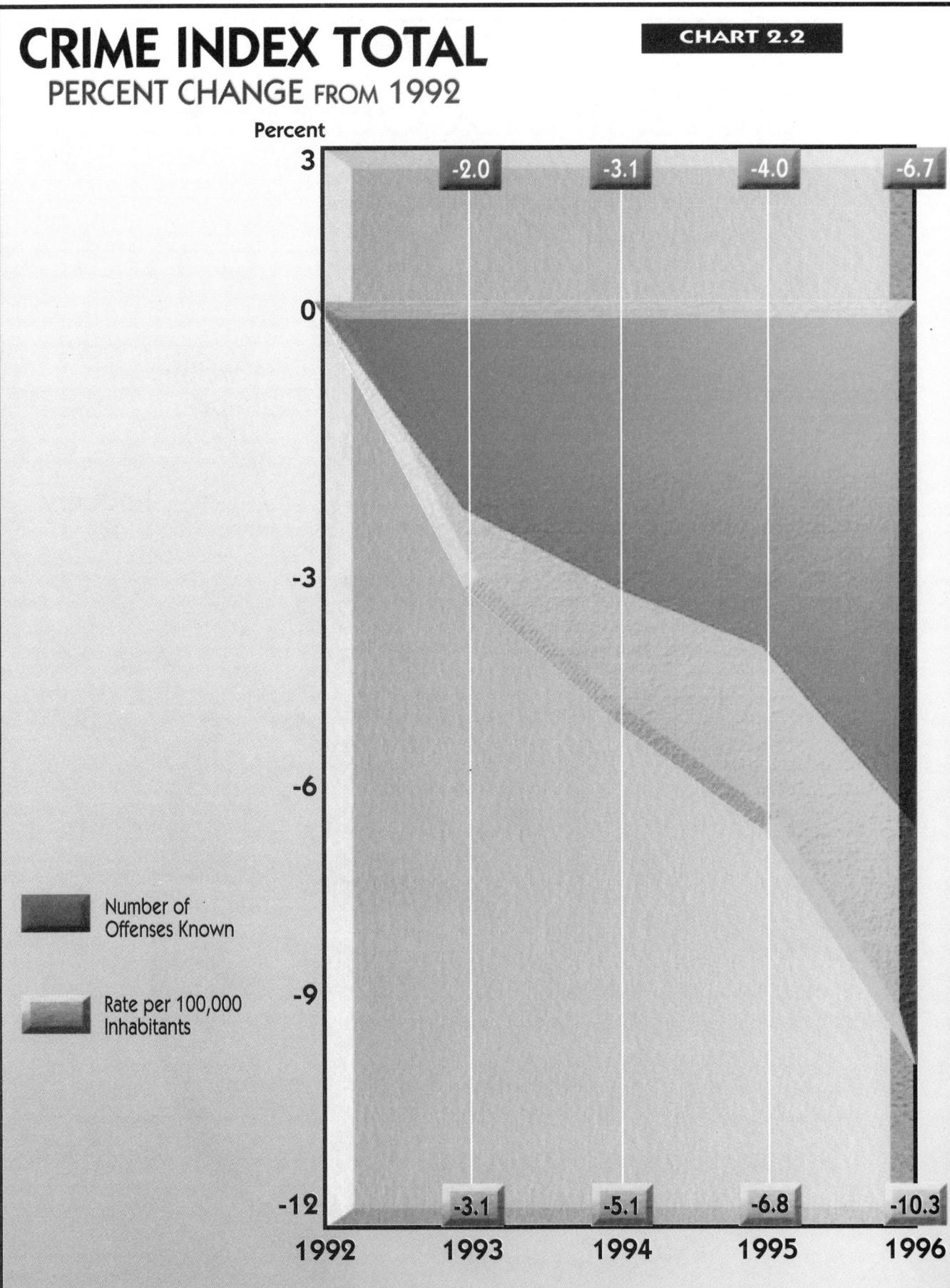

Percent

Number of
Offenses Known

Rate per 100,000
Inhabitants

	1992	1993	1994	1995	1996
Number of Offenses Known		-2.0	-3.1	-4.0	-6.7
Rate per 100,000 Inhabitants		-3.1	-5.1	-6.8	-10.3

CHART 2.3

CRIME INDEX OFFENSES
1996
Percent Distribution

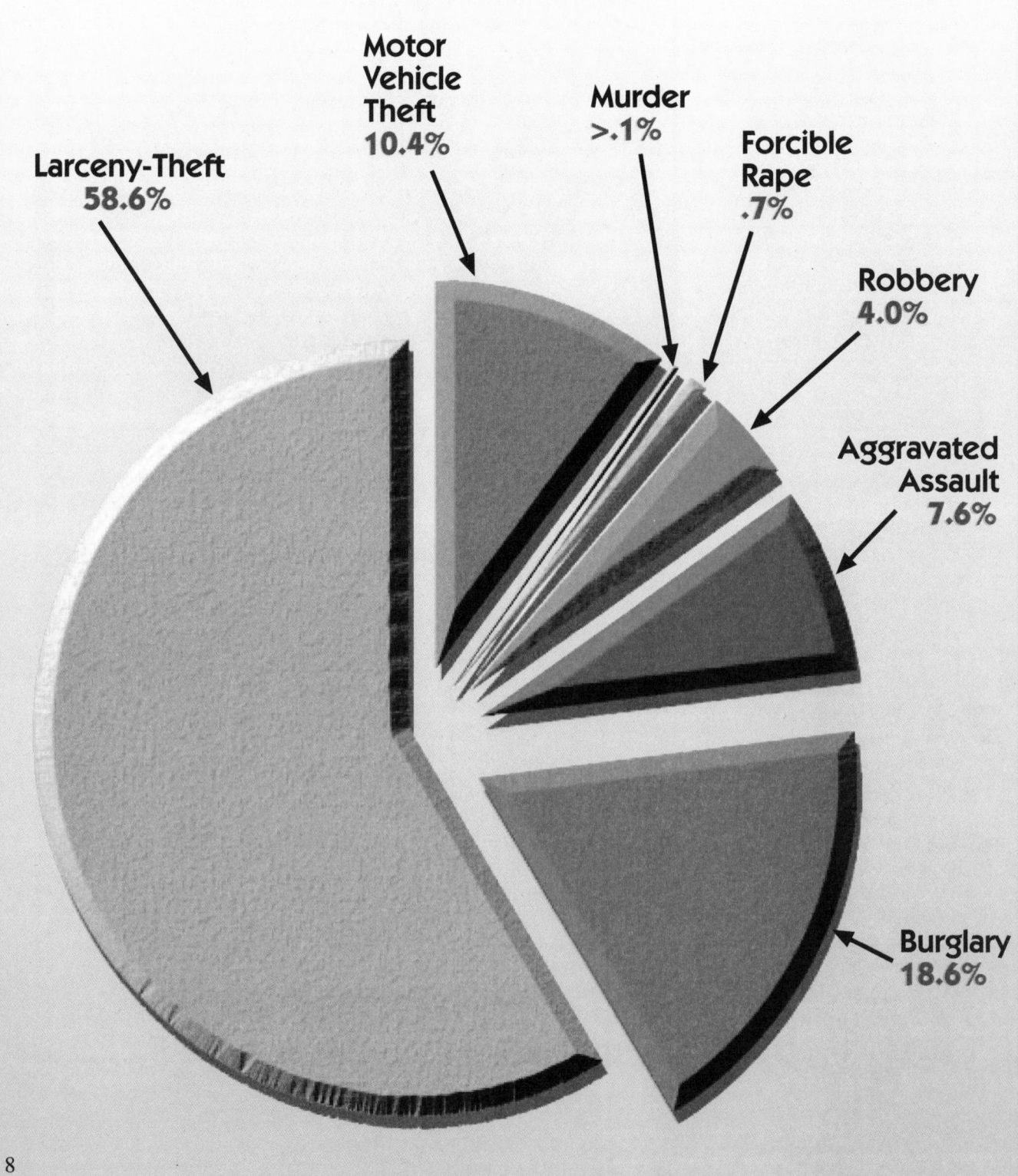

Motor
Vehicle
Theft
10.4%

Murder
>.1%

Forcible
Rape
.7%

Larceny-Theft
58.6%

Robbery
4.0%

Aggravated
Assault
7.6%

Burglary
18.6%

CHART 2.4
REGIONAL VIOLENT
AND PROPERTY CRIME RATES
1996
per 100,000 inhabitants

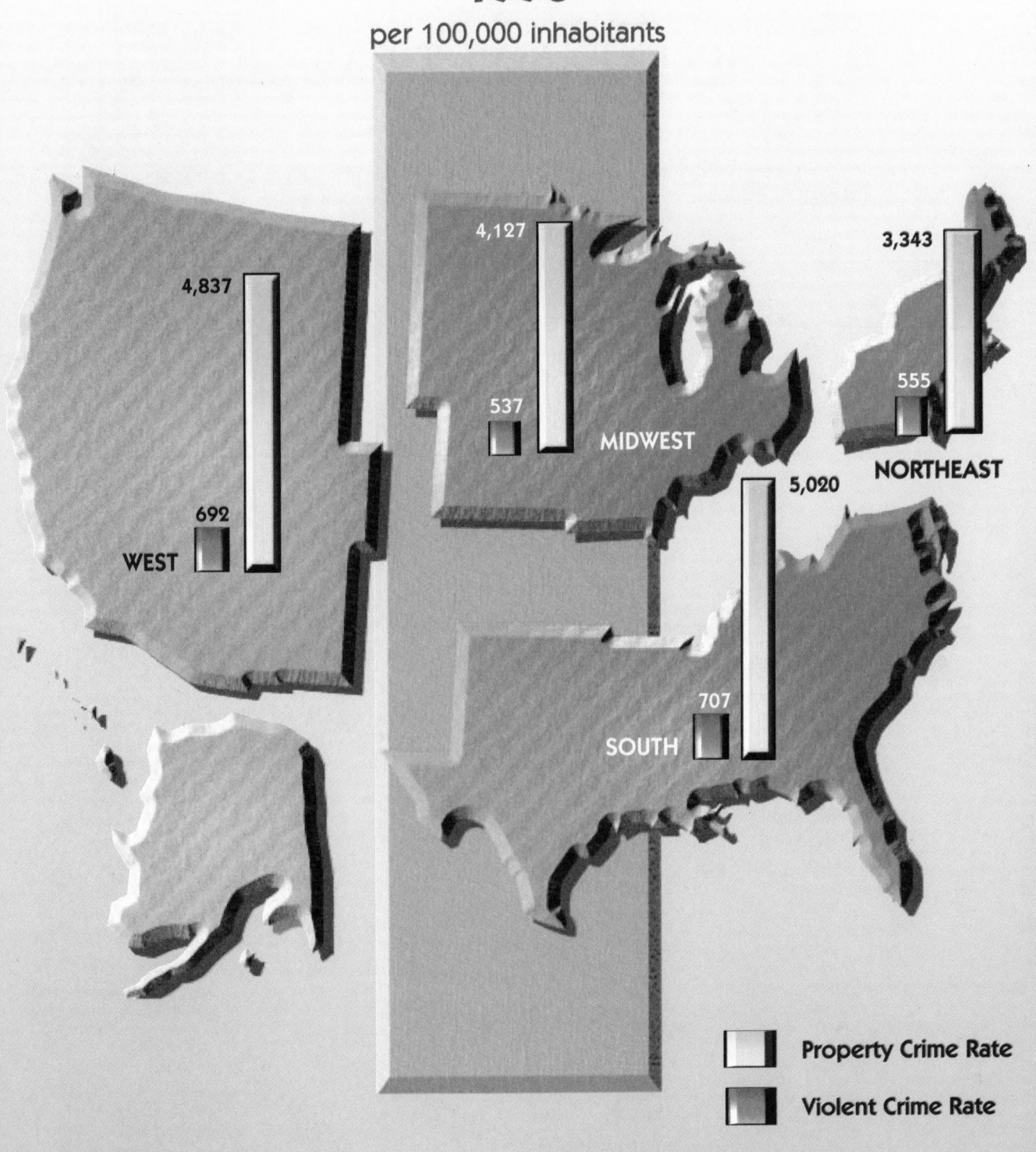

4,837 — WEST — 692

4,127 — MIDWEST — 537

3,343 — NORTHEAST — 555

5,020 — SOUTH — 707

Property Crime Rate

Violent Crime Rate

VIOLENT CRIME TOTAL

DEFINITION

Violent crime is composed of four offenses: murder and nonnegligent manslaughter, forcible rape, robbery, and aggravated assault. All violent crimes involve force or threat of force.

TREND		
Year	Number of offenses	Rate per 100,000 inhabitants
1995	1,798,792	684.6
1996	1,682,278	634.1
Percent change	-6.5	-7.4

An estimated 1.7 million violent crimes were reported to law enforcement in 1996. This number represents a decrease of 6 percent from the 1995 level and the lowest total recorded in the 1990s. The 1996 estimated total was 13 percent below the 1992 level, but 13 percent above that of 1987. From 1995 to 1996, violent crime decreased in the Nation's cities collectively by 7 percent; the suburban counties recorded an 8-percent drop; and the rural counties showed a 5-percent decline.

Regionally, the South, the most populous region, accounted for 39 percent of all violent crimes reported to law enforcement in 1996. Lesser volumes of 24 percent for the West, 20 percent for the Midwest, and 17 percent for the Northeast were recorded. All four regions experienced decreases in the number of violent crimes reported from 1995 to 1996. The Northeast and West registered 9-percent declines; the Midwest, 8 percent; and the South, 3 percent. (See Table 4.)

Violent crimes occurred most frequently in July and August. The lowest total was recorded in the month of February.

Table 2.2 — Violent Crime Total by Month, 1992-1996
[Percent distribution]

Months	1992	1993	1994	1995	1996
January	8.0	8.0	7.7	7.9	8.2
February	7.6	6.7	7.3	7.1	7.6
March	8.1	8.2	8.4	8.1	8.0
April	8.3	8.0	8.3	8.0	8.0
May	8.7	8.4	8.5	8.5	8.6
June	8.5	8.7	8.6	8.5	8.6
July	9.0	9.3	9.1	9.1	9.0
August	8.9	9.1	9.2	9.2	9.0
September	8.5	8.4	8.6	8.8	8.5
October	8.6	8.6	8.7	8.9	8.6
November	7.8	7.8	7.8	7.9	7.8
December	8.0	8.9	7.6	7.9	8.0

Rate

A violent crime rate of 634 per 100,000 inhabitants was registered nationally in 1996, the lowest rate since 1987. Two-, 5-, and 10-year trends show the 1996 rate was 7 percent lower than in 1995 and 16 percent below the 1992 rate. It was, however, 4 percent above the 1987 figure. The Nation's metropolitan areas collectively registered 715 offenses per 100,000 population. The rate in cities outside metropolitan areas was 461, and for rural counties, it was 222.

Geographically, the violent crime rate was 707 per 100,000 inhabitants in the South, 692 in the West, 555 in the Northeast, and 537 in the Midwest. All regions registered rate declines from their 1995 levels: the West, 10 percent; the Northeast and Midwest, 9 percent each; and the South, 4 percent. (See Table 4.)

Nature

Aggravated assaults accounted for 61 percent of the violent crimes reported to law enforcement during 1996. Robberies comprised 32 percent; forcible rapes, 6 percent; and murders, 1 percent.

While data concerning weapons used in connection with forcible rape are not collected, firearms were the weapons used in 29 percent of all murders, robberies, and aggravated assaults, collectively, in 1996. Knives or cutting instruments were used in 15 percent; other dangerous weapons in 26 percent; and personal weapons (hands, fists, feet, etc.) in 30 percent. The proportion of violent crimes committed with firearms has remained relatively constant in recent years.

Law Enforcement Response

The 1996 violent crime clearance rate was 47 percent, up from 45 percent in 1995. Among the violent offenses, the 1996 clearance rates ranged from 67 percent for murder to 27 percent for robbery. Over half of all forcible rapes (52 percent) and aggravated assaults (58 percent) were cleared.

There were an estimated 729,900 persons arrested for violent crimes in 1996. Violent crime arrests accounted for 5 percent of the arrests for all offenses and 26 percent of those for Index crimes. Males made up 85 percent of all violent crime arrestees; whites, 55 percent; and adults, 81 percent. (See Tables 38, 42, and 43.)

The total number of arrests for violent crimes show a 4-percent decline in the Nation and in cities from 1995 to 1996. Overall violent crime arrests dropped 5 percent in rural counties and 1 percent in suburban counties. Nationally, juvenile arrests (under age 18) decreased 6 percent, and adult arrests fell 3 percent. (For a breakdown on persons arrested by city, suburban, and rural areas, see Section IV, Persons Arrested.)

11

VIOLENT CRIME
PERCENT CHANGE FROM 1992

CHART 2.5

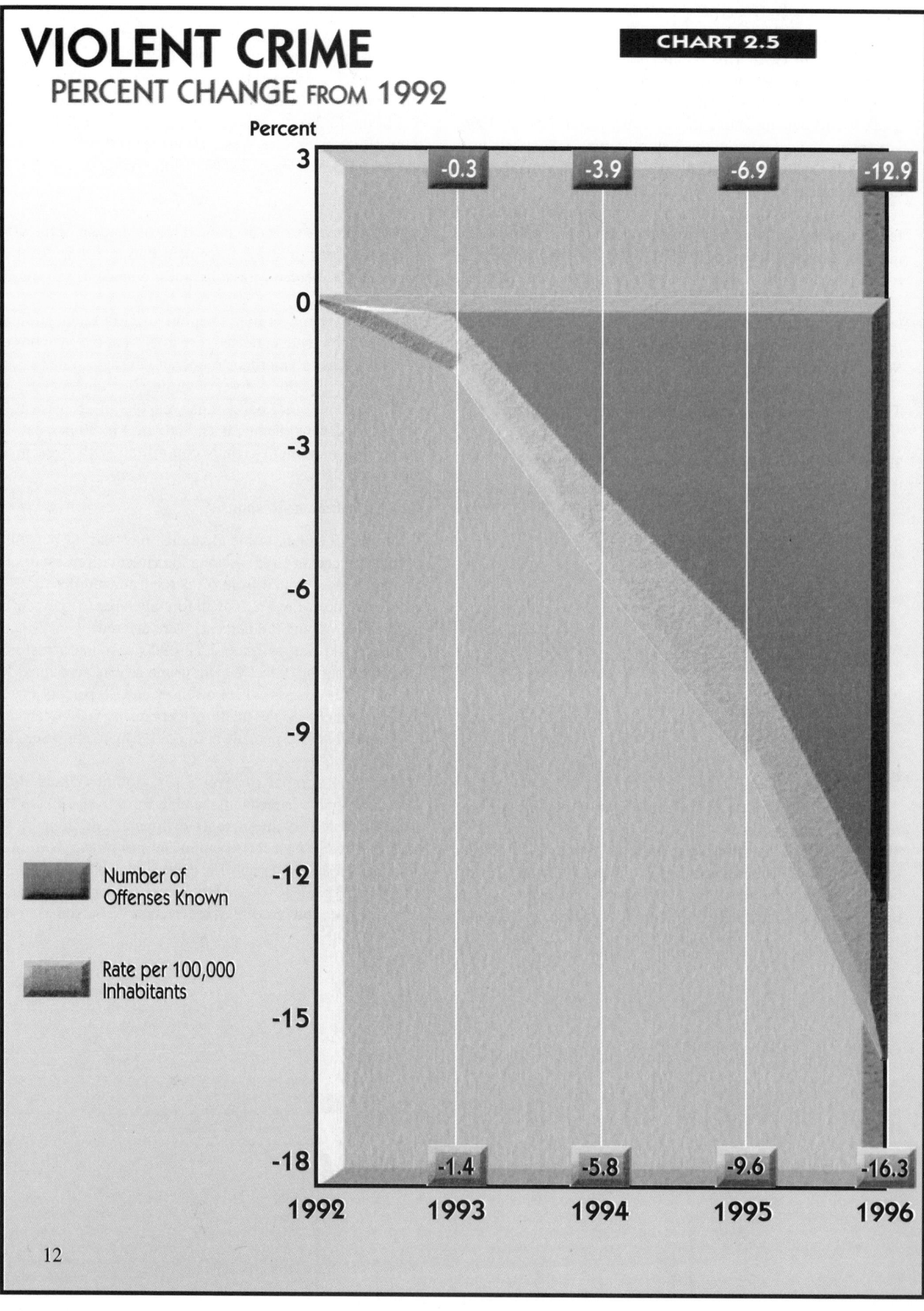

Percent

| | -0.3 | -3.9 | -6.9 | -12.9 |

Number of Offenses Known

Rate per 100,000 Inhabitants

| | -1.4 | -5.8 | -9.6 | -16.3 |

3

0

-3

-6

-9

-12

-15

-18

1992   1993   1994   1995   1996

MURDER AND NONNEGLIGENT MANSLAUGHTER

DEFINITION

Murder and nonnegligent manslaughter, as defined in the Uniform Crime Reporting Program, is the willful (nonnegligent) killing of one human being by another.

The classification of this offense, as for all other Crime Index offenses, is based solely on police investigation as opposed to the determination of a court, medical examiner, coroner, jury, or other judicial body. Not included in the count for this offense classification are deaths caused by negligence, suicide, or accident; justifiable homicides; and attempts to murder or assaults to murder, which are scored as aggravated assaults.

	TREND	
Year	Number of offenses	Rate per 100,000 inhabitants
1995	21,606	8.2
1996	19,645	7.4
Percent change	-9.1	-9.8

In 1996, the estimated number of persons murdered in the United States was 19,645. The 1996 figure was down 9 percent from the 1995 count, 17 percent from the 1992 total, and 2 percent from the 1987 level. (See Table 1.)

As compared to 1995 figures, murder volumes reported in 1996 dropped 10 percent in the Nation's cities, 9 percent in suburban counties, and 6 percent in rural counties. The greatest decrease—13 percent—was registered in cities with populations over 1 million and in cities with populations of 250,000 to 499,999.

When viewing the four regions of the Nation, the Southern States, the most populous region, accounted for 43 percent of the murders. The Western States reported 23 percent; the Midwestern States, 20 percent; and the Northeastern States, 14 percent. All regions showed declines in the number of murders reported from 1995 to 1996. The greatest drops were experienced in the Northeast and West, each with 13 percent. Decreases of 7 percent were recorded both in the South and Midwest. (See Tables 3 and 4.)

Monthly figures show that in 1996 most murders occurred in August while the fewest were committed in March and April. (See Table 2.3.)

Table 2.3 — Murder by Month, 1992-1996

[Percent distribution]

Months	1992	1993	1994	1995	1996
January	8.1	8.1	8.2	8.3	8.7
February	7.5	6.7	7.6	6.8	7.7
March	8.2	7.9	8.8	7.6	7.6
April	8.0	7.6	8.1	8.4	7.6
May	8.5	7.8	8.2	7.9	8.4
June	7.9	8.6	8.3	8.2	8.7
July	9.1	9.3	9.0	8.9	8.8
August	9.1	9.2	9.2	9.9	9.0
September	8.7	8.3	8.3	8.6	8.3
October	8.0	8.4	8.5	8.8	8.5
November	8.1	8.2	7.9	8.0	8.0
December	8.8	9.8	8.0	8.6	8.8

Rate

Down 10 percent from the 1995 rate, the national murder rate in 1996 was 7.4 per 100,000 inhabitants, the lowest since 1985. Five- and 10-year trends show the 1996 rate was 20 percent lower than in 1992 and 11 percent below the 1987 rate.

On a regional basis, the South averaged 9 murders per 100,000 people; the West, 8 per 100,000; the Midwest, 6 per 100,000, and the Northeast, 5 per 100,000. Compared to 1995 rates, murder rates in 1996 declined in all of the four geographic regions, with the West experiencing the greatest change, a 14-percent decrease, and the Midwest, the smallest, a 7-percent drop. (See Table 4.)

The Nation's metropolitan areas reported a 1996 murder rate of 8 victims per 100,000 inhabitants. In both the rural counties and cities outside metropolitan areas, the rate was 5 per 100,000.

Nature

Supplemental data were provided by contributing agencies for 15,848 of the estimated 19,645 murders in 1996. Submitted monthly, the data consist of the age, sex, and race of both victims and offenders; the types of weapons used; the relationships of victims to the offenders; and the circumstances surrounding the murders.

Based on this information, 77 percent of the murder victims in 1996 were males; and 87 percent were persons 18 years of age or older. Forty-three percent were ages 20 through 34. The percentages of whites and blacks murdered were equal at 49 percent, and other races accounted for the remainder.

Table 2.4 — Murder Victims by Race and Sex, 1996

Race of Victim	Sex of Victims			
	Total	Male	Female	Unknown
Total White Victims	7,647	5,596	2,048	3
Total Black Victims	7,638	6,201	1,434	3
Total Other Race Victims	425	310	115	—
Total Unknown Race	138	88	34	16
Total Victims[1]	15,848	12,195	3,631	22

[1] Total murder victims for whom supplemental data were received.

Supplemental data were also reported for 18,108 murder offenders in 1996. Of those for whom sex and age were reported, 90 percent of the offenders were males, and 86 percent were persons 18 years of age or older. Sixty-nine percent were ages 17 through 34. Of offenders for whom race was known, 52 percent were black, 45 percent were white, and the remainder were persons of other races.

Murder is most often intraracial among victims and offenders. In 1996, data based on incidents involving one victim and one offender show that 93 percent of the black murder victims were slain by black offenders, and 85 percent of the white murder victims were killed by white offenders. Likewise, males were most often slain by males (89 percent in single victim/single offender situations). These same data show, however, that 9 of every 10 female victims were murdered by males.

MURDER
PERCENT CHANGE FROM 1992

CHART 2.6

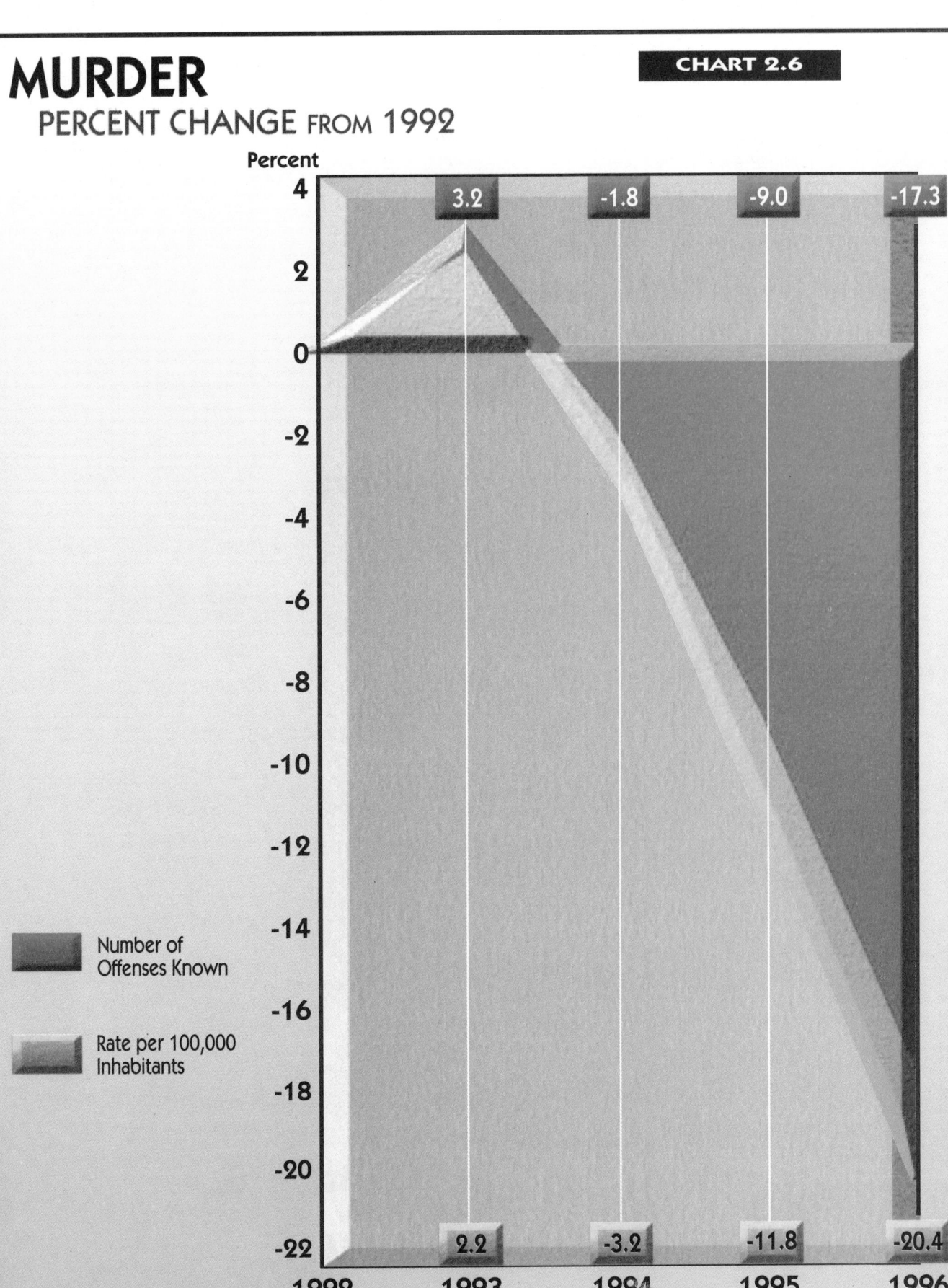

Percent

	1992	1993	1994	1995	1996
Number of Offenses Known		3.2	-1.8	-9.0	-17.3
Rate per 100,000 Inhabitants		2.2	-3.2	-11.8	-20.4

Number of
Offenses Known

Rate per 100,000
Inhabitants

15

Table 2.5 — Age, Sex, and Race of Murder Victims, 1996

Age	Total	Sex			Race			
		Male	Female	Unknown	White	Black	Other	Unknown
Total	15,848	12,195	3,631	22	7,647	7,638	425	138
Percent distribution[1]	100.0	76.9	22.9	.1	48.3	48.2	2.7	.9
Under 18[2]	1,960	1,385	572	3	973	907	57	23
Under 22[2]	4,366	3,511	852	3	1,923	2,295	113	35
18 and over[2]	13,669	10,661	3,003	5	6,564	6,659	364	82
Infant (under 1)	247	124	120	3	153	80	7	7
1 to 4	375	204	171	—	198	159	15	3
5 to 8	101	57	44	—	63	36	2	—
9 to 12	81	42	39	—	46	34	1	—
13 to 16	692	557	135	—	320	344	21	7
17 to 19	1,669	1,447	222	—	667	954	36	12
20 to 24	2,739	2,379	360	—	1,050	1,601	72	16
25 to 29	2,219	1,807	411	1	908	1,234	63	14
30 to 34	1,838	1,389	447	2	867	904	53	14
35 to 39	1,685	1,235	450	—	878	756	39	12
40 to 44	1,212	897	315	—	660	511	32	9
45 to 49	877	628	248	1	493	358	24	2
50 to 54	539	398	141	—	320	190	25	4
55 to 59	362	277	85	—	232	116	12	2
60 to 64	276	205	71	—	179	91	5	1
65 to 69	223	152	71	—	156	62	5	—
70 to 74	174	106	68	—	125	44	5	—
75 and over	320	142	177	1	222	92	4	2
Unknown	219	149	56	14	110	72	4	33

[1] Because of rounding, percentages may not add to total.
[2] Does not include unknown ages.

Table 2.6 — Age, Sex, and Race of Murder Offenders, 1996

Age	Total	Sex			Race			
		Male	Female	Unknown	White	Black	Other	Unknown
Total	18,108	12,000	1,331	4,777	5,977	6,874	337	4,920
Percent distribution[1]	100.0	66.3	7.4	26.4	33.0	38.0	1.9	27.2
Under 18[2]	1,683	1,559	124	—	677	931	63	12
Under 22[2]	4,911	4,567	344	—	1,965	2,781	133	32
18 and over[2]	10,676	9,488	1,182	6	4,998	5,349	268	61
Infant (under 1)	—	—	—	—	—	—	—	—
1 to 4	—	—	—	—	—	—	—	—
5 to 8	3	3	—	—	—	3	—	—
9 to 12	13	11	2	—	6	7	—	—
13 to 16	934	845	89	—	388	498	39	9
17 to 19	2,522	2,363	159	—	1,009	1,437	61	15
20 to 24	3,040	2,808	232	—	1,189	1,761	75	15
25 to 29	1,688	1,495	192	1	783	857	43	5
30 to 34	1,291	1,102	187	2	634	605	41	11
35 to 39	1,008	835	172	1	544	434	22	8
40 to 44	685	574	111	—	367	294	19	5
45 to 49	452	383	69	—	278	161	11	2
50 to 54	250	204	46	—	152	89	9	—
55 to 59	173	144	28	1	121	44	5	3
60 to 64	104	93	10	1	68	35	1	—
65 to 69	71	65	6	—	44	25	2	—
70 to 74	42	41	1	—	29	13	—	—
75 and over	83	81	2	—	63	17	3	—
Unknown	5,749	953	25	4,771	302	594	6	4,847

[1] Because of rounding, percentages may not add to total.
[2] Does not include unknown ages.

As in previous years, firearms were the weapons used in approximately 7 of every 10 murders committed in the Nation. Of those murders for which weapons were reported, 54 percent were by handguns, 4 percent by shotguns, and 3 percent by rifles. Other or unknown types of firearms accounted for another 6 percent of the total murders. Among the remaining weapons, knives or cutting instruments were employed in 14 percent of the murders; personal weapons (hands, fists, feet, etc.) in 6 percent; blunt objects (clubs, hammers, etc.) in 5 percent; and other dangerous weapons, such as poison, explosives, etc., in the remainder. (See Table 2.11.) A state-by-state breakdown of weapons used in connection with murder is shown in Table 20.

Table 2.7 — Victim/Offender Relationship by Age, 1996
[Single Victim/Single Offender]

Age of Victim	Age of Offender			
	Total	Under 18	18 and over	Unknown
Total	8,239	711	7,045	483
Under 18	1,053	252	748	53
18 and over	7,098	454	6,235	409
Unknown	88	5	62	21

Table 2.8 — Victim/Offender Relationship by Race and Sex, 1996
[Single Victim/Single Offender]

Race of Victim	Total	Race of Offender				Sex of Offender		
		White	Black	Other	Unknown	Male	Female	Unknown
White Victims	4,127	3,460	558	66	43	3,666	418	43
Black Victims	3,854	247	3,562	15	30	3,348	476	30
Other Race Victims	208	55	37	113	3	186	19	3
Unknown Race	50	9	17	2	22	27	1	22

Race of Victim	Total	Race of Offender				Sex of Offender		
		White	Black	Other	Unknown	Male	Female	Unknown
Male Victims	5,986	2,577	3,208	136	65	5,243	678	65
Female Victims	2,203	1,185	949	58	11	1,957	235	11
Unknown Sex	50	9	17	2	22	27	1	22

In 1996, over 50 percent of all murder victims knew their assailants: 13 percent were related and 38 percent were acquainted. Fifteen percent of the victims were murdered by strangers, while the relationships among victims and offenders were unknown for 35 percent of the murders. Among all female murder victims in 1996, 30 percent were slain by husbands or boyfriends. Three percent of the male victims were killed by wives or girlfriends.

Considering circumstances, arguments resulted in 31 percent of the murders during the year. Nineteen percent occurred as a result of felonious activities such as robbery, arson, etc., while less than 1 percent were suspected to have been the result of some felonious activity. Table 2.14 shows murder circumstances for the past 5 years (1992-1996).

Table 2.9 — Murder, Types of Weapons Used, 1996

[Percent distribution by region]

Region	Total all weapons[1]	Firearms	Knives or cutting instruments	Unknown or other dangerous weapons	Personal weapons (hands, fists, feet, etc.)[2]
Total	100.0	67.8	13.5	12.8	5.9
Northeastern States	100.0	61.9	17.1	13.5	7.5
Midwestern States	100.0	68.4	11.5	14.2	6.0
Southern States	100.0	69.2	13.7	11.5	5.6
Western States	100.0	67.5	13.2	13.5	5.8

[1] Because of rounding, percentages may not add to total.
[2] Pushed is included in personal weapons.

Table 2.10 — Murder Victims, Types of Weapons Used, 1992-1996

Weapons	1992	1993	1994	1995	1996
Total	22,716	23,180	22,084	20,232	15,848
Total Firearms	15,489	16,136	15,463	13,790	10,744
Handguns	12,580	13,212	12,775	11,282	8,594
Rifles	706	757	724	654	546
Shotguns	1,111	1,057	953	929	673
Other guns	42	37	19	29	20
Firearms, not stated	1,050	1,073	992	896	911
Knives or cutting instruments	3,296	2,967	2,802	2,557	2,142
Blunt objects (clubs, hammers, etc.)	1,040	1,022	912	918	733
Personal weapons (hands, fists, feet, etc.)[1]	1,131	1,151	1,165	1,201	939
Poison	13	9	10	14	8
Explosives	19	23	10	192	14
Fire	203	217	196	166	151
Narcotics	24	22	22	22	32
Drowning	29	23	25	30	24
Strangulation	314	331	287	237	243
Asphyxiation	115	111	113	137	92
Other weapons or weapons not stated	1,043	1,168	1,079	968	726

[1] Pushed is included in personal weapons.

Table 2.11 — Murder Victims, Types of Weapons Used, 1996

Age	Total	Firearms	Knives or cutting instruments	Blunt objects (clubs, hammers, etc.)	Personal weapons (hands, fists, feet, etc.)[1]	Poison	Explosives	Fire	Narcotics	Strangulation	Asphyxiation	Other weapon or weapon not stated[2]
Total	15,848	10,744	2,142	733	939	8	14	151	32	243	92	750
Percent distribution	100.0	67.8	13.5	4.6	5.9	.1	.1	1.0	.2	1.5	.6	4.7
Under 18[3]	1,960	1,084	137	66	393	4	2	53	8	21	39	153
Under 22[3]	4,366	3,120	336	102	438	4	3	61	11	42	42	207
18 and over[3]	13,669	9,543	1,979	653	538	4	12	95	24	216	52	553
Infant (under 1)	247	9	6	15	139	1	1	2	4	3	25	42
1 to 4	375	45	10	21	202	2	—	29	3	3	7	53
5 to 8	101	34	13	7	20	1	—	10	—	1	3	12
9 to 12	81	53	8	2	4	—	—	6	—	1	3	4
13 to 16	692	558	59	12	18	—	1	4	—	9	1	30
17 to 19	1,669	1,423	130	21	29	—	1	6	1	12	1	45
20 to 24	2,739	2,261	260	56	53	—	—	6	5	25	5	68
25 to 29	2,219	1,695	273	62	61	1	—	10	4	28	5	80
30 to 34	1,838	1,266	276	82	71	—	2	8	2	44	7	80
35 to 39	1,685	1,074	330	79	81	1	1	21	2	25	4	67
40 to 44	1,212	728	223	93	61	2	5	13	5	16	7	59
45 to 49	877	512	169	66	61	—	—	14	—	10	7	38
50 to 54	539	340	79	38	28	—	1	6	1	13	1	32
55 to 59	362	202	70	36	19	—	—	3	1	8	2	21
60 to 64	276	136	54	27	24	—	1	2	1	7	2	23
65 to 69	223	105	45	25	16	—	1	2	—	13	4	12
70 to 74	174	74	42	29	9	—	—	1	—	7	2	10
75 and over	320	112	69	48	35	—	1	5	3	12	5	30
Unknown	219	117	26	14	8	—	—	3	—	6	1	44

[1] Pushed is included in personal weapons.
[2] Includes drowning.
[3] Does not include unknown ages.

Table 2.12 — Murder Circumstances by Relationship,[1] 1996

Circumstances	Total	Husband	Wife	Mother	Father	Son	Daughter	Brother	Sister	Other Family	Acquaintance	Friend	Boyfriend	Girlfriend	Neighbor	Employee	Employer	Stranger	Unknown
Total[2]	15,848	206	679	107	125	261	207	98	19	283	4,797	478	163	424	162	8	12	2,321	5,498
Felony type total	3,018	4	13	6	8	33	25	4	2	35	868	58	2	19	31	1	5	901	1,003
Rape	68	—	—	—	—	—	1	—	—	2	24	2	—	2	2	—	—	11	24
Robbery	1,493	1	1	4	4	—	—	—	—	15	290	18	—	2	14	1	5	641	498
Burglary	117	1	1	—	—	—	—	2	—	2	26	1	—	2	4	—	—	46	32
Larceny–theft	26	—	—	—	—	—	—	—	—	—	11	1	—	—	—	—	—	11	3
Motor vehicle theft	23	1	1	1	1	—	—	—	—	—	8	—	—	1	—	—	—	8	4
Arson	95	—	4	—	—	8	5	—	—	4	12	1	1	—	5	—	—	18	35
Prostitution and commercialized vice	8	—	—	—	—	—	—	—	—	—	2	—	—	—	—	—	—	1	5
Other sex offenses	27	—	—	—	—	—	1	—	—	1	12	—	1	—	1	—	—	8	4
Narcotic drug laws	819	—	3	—	2	1	—	1	—	7	404	30	—	6	3	—	—	98	262
Gambling	12	—	—	—	—	—	—	—	—	—	8	1	—	—	—	—	—	—	2
Other – not specified	330	—	3	1	1	24	17	1	2	4	71	4	—	6	2	—	—	59	134
Suspected felony type	72	—	—	—	—	—	—	—	—	—	16	1	—	—	—	—	—	13	42
Other than felony type total	8,176	184	560	82	102	202	156	83	16	211	3,315	346	150	360	113	4	7	1,143	1,142
Romantic triangle	187	1	12	—	—	—	1	—	—	—	110	8	5	17	2	—	—	23	8
Child killed by babysitter	28	—	—	—	—	—	—	1	1	2	24	—	—	—	—	—	—	—	—
Brawl due to influence of alcohol	253	2	5	1	2	1	—	2	—	7	138	20	1	9	5	—	—	42	18
Brawl due to influence of narcotics	161	1	1	—	1	—	—	—	2	—	80	7	1	1	—	—	—	16	51
Argument over money or property	327	1	1	2	7	1	—	3	—	10	205	25	—	4	14	—	2	14	38
Other arguments	4,383	152	397	56	74	50	18	75	8	136	1,705	216	132	263	75	2	5	600	419
Gangland killings	83	—	—	—	—	—	—	—	—	1	36	1	—	1	—	—	—	17	28
Juvenile gang killings	855	—	—	—	—	—	—	—	—	—	427	—	—	—	1	—	—	226	199
Institutional killings	13	—	—	—	—	—	—	—	—	—	11	—	—	—	—	—	—	2	2
Sniper attack	8	—	—	—	—	—	—	—	—	—	—	—	—	—	—	—	—	4	2
Other – not specified	1,878	27	143	23	18	150	137	2	5	55	577	69	11	65	16	2	—	201	377
Unknown	4,582	18	106	19	15	26	26	11	1	37	598	73	11	45	18	3	—	264	3,311

[1] Relationship is that of victim to offender.
[2] Total murder victims for whom supplemental homicide data were received.

Table 2.13 — Murder Circumstances by Weapon, 1996

Circumstances	Total murder victims	Total firearms	Hand-guns	Rifles	Shot-guns	Other guns or type not stated	Knives or cutting instruments	Blunt objects (clubs, hammers, etc.)	Personal weapons (hands, fists, feet, etc.)	Poison	Pushed or thrown out window	Explo-sives	Fire	Narcotics	Drown-ing	Strangu-lation	Asphyxi-ation	Other
Total[1]	15,848	10,744	8,594	546	673	931	2,142	733	932	8	7	14	151	32	24	243	92	726
Felony type total	3,018	2,120	1,845	78	106	91	314	166	155	—	—	4	88	17	2	50	22	80
Rape	68	6	6	—	—	—	13	13	22	—	—	—	—	1	—	8	1	4
Robbery	1,493	1,087	943	36	52	56	190	96	54	—	—	1	2	—	—	20	12	31
Burglary	117	65	51	1	11	2	21	16	7	—	—	—	—	—	—	3	1	4
Larceny–theft	26	18	18	—	—	—	1	5	1	—	—	—	—	—	—	—	—	1
Motor vehicle theft	23	12	10	—	—	2	5	1	1	—	—	—	—	—	—	—	—	4
Arson	95	4	4	—	—	—	1	1	1	—	—	1	82	—	—	—	2	4
Prostitution and commercialized vice	8	6	6	—	—	—	1	—	1	—	—	—	—	—	—	—	—	—
Other sex offenses	27	3	3	—	—	—	4	2	13	—	—	—	—	—	—	3	—	2
Narcotic drug laws	819	685	608	25	27	25	52	17	20	—	—	2	3	15	1	9	2	13
Gambling	12	8	6	1	—	1	1	1	2	—	—	—	—	1	—	—	—	—
Other – not specified	330	226	190	15	16	5	25	15	33	—	—	—	1	1	1	7	4	17
Suspected felony type	72	41	31	2	1	7	7	3	4	—	—	1	2	—	3	—	2	9
Other than felony type total	8,176	5,483	4,285	365	440	393	1,317	334	611	6	3	2	39	13	14	80	43	231
Romantic triangle	187	134	103	11	18	2	36	7	5	—	—	—	1	—	—	2	—	2
Child killed by babysitter	28	2	2	—	—	—	—	3	20	—	—	—	—	—	—	—	1	2
Brawl due to influence of alcohol	253	130	100	12	9	9	76	16	16	—	—	—	—	—	—	7	—	8
Brawl due to influence of narcotics	161	132	95	5	10	22	16	5	4	—	—	—	—	1	—	1	—	2
Argument over money or property	327	240	190	10	25	15	53	16	13	—	—	—	—	—	—	2	—	3
Other arguments	4,383	2,856	2,262	197	270	127	936	200	213	—	2	2	23	3	2	49	8	89
Gangland killings	83	76	62	3	5	6	2	1	2	—	—	—	—	—	—	—	—	2
Juvenile gang killings	855	794	717	40	16	21	44	10	4	—	—	—	—	—	—	—	—	3
Institutional killings	13	—	—	—	—	—	9	—	4	—	—	—	—	—	—	—	—	—
Sniper attack	8	8	4	1	—	3	—	—	—	—	—	—	—	—	—	—	—	—
Other – not specified	1,878	1,111	750	86	87	188	145	76	330	6	1	—	15	9	12	19	34	120
Unknown	4,582	3,100	2,433	101	126	440	504	230	162	2	4	7	22	2	5	113	25	406

[1] Total murder victims for whom supplemental homicide data were received.

Table 2.14 — Murder Circumstances, 1992-1996

Circumstances	1992	1993	1994	1995	1996
Total[1]	22,716	23,180	22,084	20,232	15,848
Felony type total:	4,917	4,461	4,070	3,585	3,018
Rape	138	115	78	82	68
Robbery	2,266	2,305	2,076	1,872	1,493
Burglary	212	179	157	124	117
Larceny–theft	41	31	30	26	26
Motor vehicle theft	66	61	53	49	23
Arson	148	154	132	112	95
Prostitution and commercialized vice	32	18	14	9	8
Other sex offenses	34	28	41	30	27
Narcotic drug laws	1,302	1,295	1,239	1,031	819
Gambling	20	10	12	22	12
Other – not specified	658	265	238	228	330
Suspected felony type	280	145	136	113	72
Other than felony type total:	11,244	12,210	11,691	10,686	8,176
Romantic triangle	334	440	371	282	187
Child killed by babysitter	36	34	22	24	28
Brawl due to influence of alcohol	429	383	316	262	253
Brawl due to influence of narcotics	253	261	211	185	161
Argument over money or property	483	445	387	340	327
Other arguments	6,066	6,289	5,820	5,229	4,383
Gangland killings	137	142	111	88	83
Juvenile gang killings	813	1,145	1,157	1,158	855
Institutional killings	18	15	14	31	13
Sniper attack	33	7	2	14	8
Other – not specified	2,642	3,049	3,280	3,073	1,878
Unknown	6,275	6,364	6,187	5,848	4,582

[1] Total number of murder victims for whom supplemental homicide information was received.

Table 2.15 — Murder Circumstances by Victim Sex, 1996

Circumstances	Total murder victims[1]	Male	Female	Unknown
Total[1]	15,848	12,195	3,631	22
Felony type total:	3,018	2,438	579	1
Rape	68	8	60	—
Robbery	1,493	1,262	231	—
Burglary	117	71	46	—
Larceny–theft	26	25	1	—
Motor vehicle theft	23	19	4	—
Arson	95	54	41	—
Prostitution and commercialized vice	8	4	4	—
Other sex offenses	27	11	16	—
Narcotic drug laws	819	725	94	—
Gambling	12	12	—	—
Other – not specified	330	247	82	1
Suspected felony type	72	49	23	—
Other than felony type total:	8,176	6,171	2,002	3
Romantic triangle	187	139	48	—
Child killed by babysitter	28	16	12	—
Brawl due to influence of alcohol	253	224	29	—
Brawl due to influence of narcotics	161	149	12	—
Argument over money or property	327	302	25	—
Other arguments	4,383	3,248	1,134	1
Gangland killings	83	79	4	—
Juvenile gang killings	855	808	47	—
Institutional killings	13	13	—	—
Sniper attack	8	6	2	—
Other – not specified	1,878	1,187	689	2
Unknown	4,582	3,537	1,027	18

[1] Total number of murder victims for whom supplemental homicide information was received.

Law Enforcement Response

The clearance rate for murder is higher than for any other Crime Index offense. Law enforcement agencies nationwide recorded a 67-percent clearance rate in 1996. The most successful clearance rate, 79 percent, was reported in both cities with populations under 10,000 and in rural counties. Sixty-seven percent of murders in suburban counties and 66 percent of those in the Nation's cities were cleared. (See Table 25.)

Regionally, the highest murder clearance rate was registered in the Northeastern States, with 71 percent. Following were the Midwest and South, each with 69 percent, and the Western States with 61 percent.

The proportion of juvenile involvement, as measured by clearances, was lower for murder than for any other Index crime. Persons under 18 years of age accounted for 8 percent of the willful killings cleared by law enforcement nationally in 1996. Nine percent of clearances in cities nationwide and 7 percent in suburban counties involved only persons in this young age group. They accounted for 5 percent of clearances in rural counties.

Law enforcement agencies made an estimated 19,020 arrests for murder in 1996. Similar to the 1995 figures, 56 percent of the arrestees in 1996 were under 25 years of age, with the 18- to 24-year age group accounting for 41 percent of the total. (See Table 38.)

Ninety percent of those arrested for murder in 1996 were males and 10 percent, females. Blacks comprised 55 percent of the total; whites, 43 percent; and other races, the remainder.

Compared to the 1995 count, total arrests for murder decreased 10 percent. Arrests of persons age 18 and over also decreased 10 percent, and those of younger persons were down 14 percent. During the same 2-year period, arrests of males for murder were down 11 percent, and those of females were down 3 percent.

Long-term trends indicate the 1996 murder arrest total was 18 percent below the 1992 level and 4 percent lower than the 1987 figure.

Justifiable Homicide

Certain willful killings are classified as justifiable or excusable, based on law enforcement investigation. In Uniform Crime Reporting, justifiable homicide is defined as and limited to the killing of a felon by a law enforcement officer in the line of duty, or the killing of a felon by a private citizen during the commission of a felony. These offenses are tabulated independently and are not included in the murder counts.

In 1996, the total number of justifiable homicides decreased 12 percent. The justifiable homicide total was 580 in 1996 and 657 in 1995. Compared to the 1992 count of 769, the 1996 total was down 25 percent. Of justifiable homicides in 1996, 332 involved law enforcement officers and 248 were by private citizens. Data on weapons show that handguns were the weapons used most frequently in justifiable homicides. (See Tables 2.16 and 2.17.)

Table 2.16 — Justifiable Homicide by Weapon, Law Enforcement,[1] 1992-1996

Year	Total	Total fire-arms	Hand-guns	Rifles	Shot-guns	Fire-arms, type not stated	Knives or other cutting instru-ments	Other danger-ous weapons	Personal weapons
1992	418	411	357	22	21	11	4	1	2
1993	455	451	391	22	26	12	—	2	2
1994	462	460	404	21	29	6	—	1	1
1995	389	386	351	12	19	4	—	3	—
1996	332	327	300	10	10	7	3	1	1

[1] The killing of a felon by a law enforcement officer in the line of duty.

Table 2.17 — Justifiable Homicide by Weapon, Private Citizen,[1] 1992-1996

Year	Total	Total fire-arms	Hand-guns	Rifles	Shot-guns	Fire-arms, type not stated	Knives or other cutting instru-ments	Other danger-ous weapons	Personal weapons
1992	351	311	264	20	24	3	31	5	4
1993	357	313	254	15	33	11	28	9	7
1994	353	316	260	17	29	10	19	13	5
1995	268	230	179	18	25	8	24	10	4
1996	248	212	176	12	16	8	26	7	3

[1] The killing of a felon, during the commission of a felony, by a private citizen.

FORCIBLE RAPE

DEFINITION

Forcible rape, as defined in the Program, is the carnal knowledge of a female forcibly and against her will. Assaults or attempts to commit rape by force or threat of force are also included; however, statutory rape (without force) and other sex offenses are excluded.

TREND		
Year	Number of offenses	Rate per 100,000 inhabitants
1995	97,470	37.1
1996	95,769	36.1
Percent change............................	-1.7	-2.7

The 95,769 forcible rapes reported to law enforcement agencies across the Nation during 1996 represented the lowest total since 1989. The 1996 count was 2 percent lower than in 1995, and 12 percent below the 1992 level, but 5 percent higher than the 1987 volume.

Geographically, 39 percent of the forcible rape total in 1996 was accounted for by the most populous Southern States, 25 percent by the Midwestern States, 23 percent by the Western States, and 13 percent by the Northeastern States. Two-year trends show that forcible rapes declined 5 percent in the Midwest, and 3 percent in the West. Totals for the Northeast and the South remained virtually unchanged from the 1995 level. (See Tables 3 and 4.)

Monthly totals show the lowest volume occurred in December, while the largest number of forcible rapes was reported during the month of July. (See Table 2.18.)

Table 2.18 — Forcible Rape by Month, 1992-1996
[Percent distribution]

Months	1992	1993	1994	1995	1996
January	7.0	7.7	7.5	7.7	7.9
February	7.6	6.9	7.3	7.1	7.9
March	8.6	8.5	8.3	8.5	8.1
April	8.5	8.2	8.4	8.0	8.1
May	8.9	8.9	8.9	8.9	9.0
June	8.7	9.2	9.2	8.5	8.8
July	9.4	9.7	9.7	9.4	9.5
August	9.6	9.3	9.6	9.9	9.1
September	8.7	8.3	8.7	8.8	8.8
October	8.4	8.1	8.5	8.7	8.5
November	7.6	7.5	7.3	7.8	7.4
December	7.0	7.7	6.5	6.9	6.9

Rate

By Uniform Crime Reporting definition, the victims of forcible rape are always female, and in 1996, an estimated 71 of every 100,000 females in the country were reported rape victims. The 1996 female forcible rape rate was 1 percent lower than the 1995 rate and 15 percent lower than the 1992 rate.

The Nation's metropolitan areas recorded the highest forcible rape rate in 1996, 75 victims per 100,000 females. In cities outside metropolitan areas, the rate was 68 per 100,000 females, and in rural counties, it was 47 per 100,000 females. Although metropolitan areas record the highest rape rates, they have shown the only rate decline over the past 10 years (1987-1996), 10 percent. During this same period, the rate increased in cities outside metropolitan areas by 45 percent and in rural counties by 31 percent.

By region in 1996, the highest female rape rate was in the Southern States, which recorded 79 victims per 100,000 females. Following were the Midwestern States with a rate of 75; the

Western States with a rate of 73; and the Northeastern States with a rate of 49. Since 1995, forcible rape rates declined 4 percent in the Midwest, 3 percent in the West and 1 percent in the South. The Northeast's rate remained the same.

Over the last 10 years, female forcible rape rate decreases were recorded in two regions. Rates in the Northeast and West showed a 14- and 12-percent decreases, respectively, and those the Southern and Midwestern States increased 4 percent each.

Nature

Rapes by force constitute the greatest percentage of total forcible rapes, 87 percent of the 1996 incidents. The remainder were attempts or assaults to commit forcible rape. The number of rapes by force decreased 3 percent in 1996 from the 1995 volume, and attempts to rape decreased 4 percent.

As with all other Crime Index offenses, complaints of forcible rape made to law enforcement agencies are sometimes found to be false or baseless. In such cases, law enforcement agencies "unfound" the offenses and exclude them from crime counts. The "unfounded" rate, or percentage of complaints determined through investigation to be false, is higher for forcible rape than for any other Index crime. Eight percent of forcible rape complaints in 1996 were "unfounded," while the average for all Index crimes was 2 percent.

Law Enforcement Response

In 1996, over half of the forcible rapes reported to law enforcement nationwide were cleared by arrest or exceptional means. Rural and suburban county law enforcement clearance rates, each at 53 percent, were slightly higher than the city law enforcement clearance rate at 52 percent. (See Table 25.)

By geographic region, forcible rape clearance rates in 1996 were 57 percent in the South, 53 percent in the Northeast, 49 percent in the Midwest, and 46 percent in the West. (See Table 26.)

Of the total clearances for forcible rape in the country as a whole, 12 percent involved only persons under 18 years of age. The percentage of juvenile involvement varied by community type, ranging from 11 percent in the Nation's cities to 13 percent in rural counties. (See Table 28.)

Participating law enforcement agencies throughout the Nation made an estimated 33,050 arrests for forcible rape in 1996. Of the forcible rape arrestees, 44 percent were under age 25. Fifty-six percent of those arrested were white. (See Tables 29, 41, and 43.)

The national arrest total for forcible rape fell 2 percent from 1995 to 1996. Arrests also declined 2 percent both in the Nation's cities and rural counties and 1 percent in the suburban counties. (See Tables 36, 44, 50, and 56.)

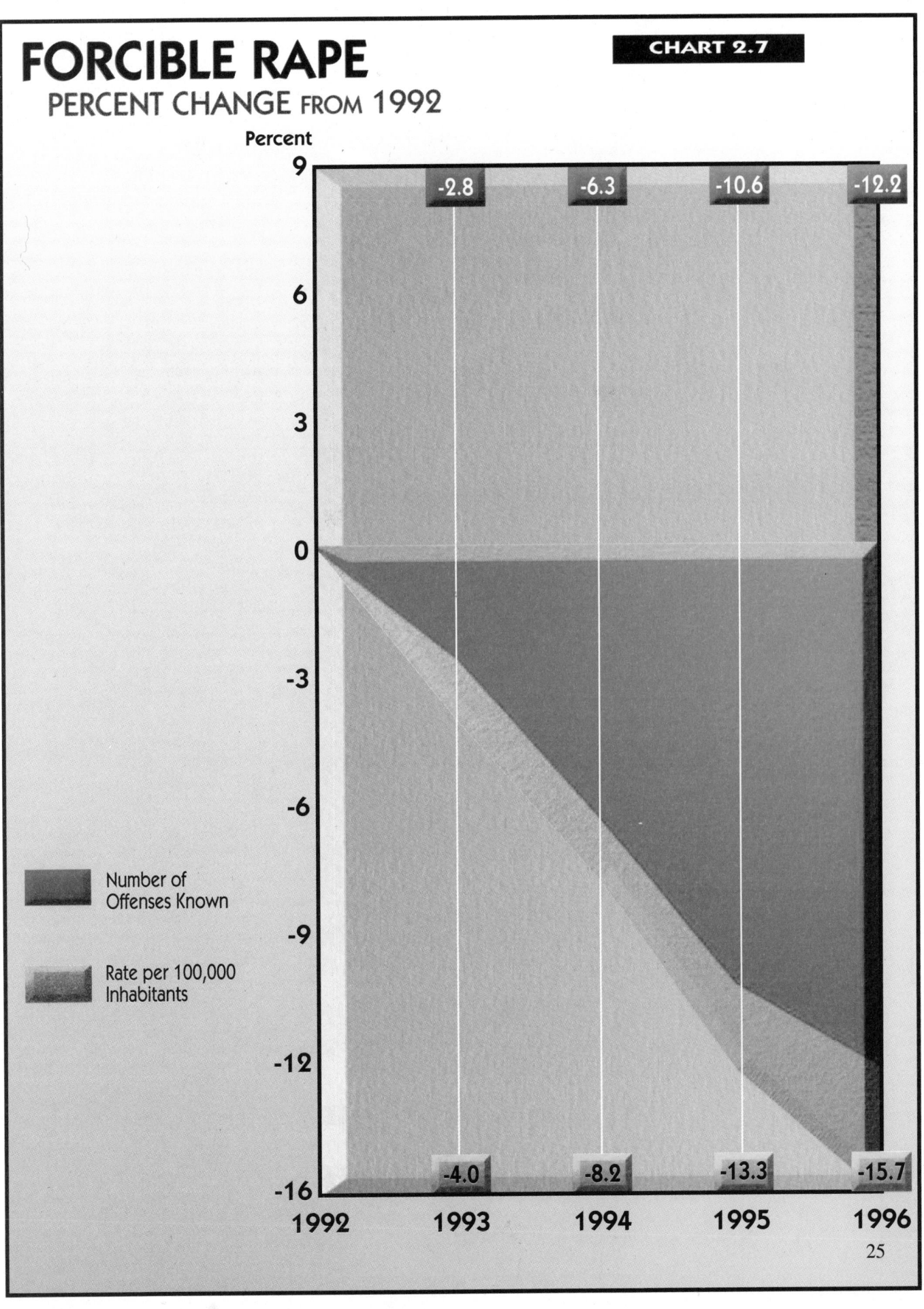

FORCIBLE RAPE
PERCENT CHANGE FROM 1992

CHART 2.7

Percent

9

-2.8   -6.3   -10.6   -12.2

6

3

0

-3

Number of
Offenses Known

-6

Rate per 100,000
Inhabitants

-9

-12

-4.0   -8.2   -13.3   -15.7

-16

1992   1993   1994   1995   1996

25

ROBBERY

DEFINITION

Robbery is the taking or attempting to take anything of value from the care, custody, or control of a person or persons by force or threat of force or violence and/or by putting the victim in fear.

Year	Number of offenses	Rate per 100,000 inhabitants
TREND		
1995	580,509	220.9
1996	537,050	202.4
Percent change	-7.5	-8.4

Nationally, the 1996 estimated robbery total, 537,050, was the lowest since 1987. The robbery volume for 1996 was down 7 percent from the 1995 national total and registered an 8-percent decrease in the Nation's cities. The largest decline—10 percent—was reported by cities with 1 million or more inhabitants. During the same period, the robbery volume dropped 6 percent in suburban counties and fell 2 percent in rural counties. (See Table 12.)

Regionally, the Southern States, the most populous area of the Nation, accounted for 35 percent of all reported robberies. The Western States followed with 24 percent, the Northeastern States with 22 percent, and the Midwestern States with 19 percent. (See Table 3.) Two-year trends show the number of robberies in 1996 was down in all regions as compared to 1995 figures. The Northeast and Midwest marked an 11-percent decrease, the West an 8-percent drop, and the South a 3-percent decline.

The national trend in the robbery volume, as well as the robbery rate, is presented in Chart 2.8 for the years 1992-1996. In 1996, the number of robbery offenses was 20 percent lower than in 1992 but 4 percent higher than in 1987.

Monthly volume figures for 1996 show robberies occurred most frequently in January and December and least often in April.

Table 2.19 — Robbery by Month, 1992-1996
[Percent distribution]

Months	1992	1993	1994	1995	1996
January	9.0	8.8	8.7	8.6	9.0
February	8.0	7.1	7.7	7.3	7.9
March	8.1	8.3	8.6	8.0	8.1
April	7.8	7.4	8.0	7.5	7.7
May	7.9	7.5	8.0	7.8	8.0
June	7.9	8.1	8.0	8.0	8.0
July	8.4	8.7	8.5	8.5	8.3
August	8.6	8.8	8.8	8.9	8.5
September	8.3	8.4	8.3	8.5	8.3
October	8.7	9.0	8.8	9.3	8.7
November	8.3	8.5	8.2	8.7	8.5
December	9.0	9.4	8.4	8.9	9.0

Rate

The national robbery rate in 1996 was 202 per 100,000 people, 8 percent lower than in 1995. In metropolitan areas, the 1996 rate was 244; in cities outside metropolitan areas, it was 72; and in the rural areas, it was 16. With 674 robberies per 100,000 inhabitants, the highest rate was recorded in cities with populations 1 million and over. (See Table 16.)

Robbery rates per 100,000 inhabitants declined in all regions from 1995 to 1996. The rates of 232 in the Northeast and 161 in the Midwest were down 11 percent. The West's rate of 219 was 9 percent lower than it was in 1995, and the South's rate of 203 was down 4 percent. (See Table 4.)

Nature

During 1996, losses estimated at nearly $500 million were attributed to robberies. The value of property stolen averaged $929 per robbery, up from $873 in 1995. Average dollar losses in 1996 ranged from $487 taken during robberies of gas or service stations to $4,207 per bank robbery. (See Table 23.) The impact of this violent crime on its victims cannot be measured in terms of monetary loss alone. While the object of a robbery is to obtain money or property, the crime always involves force or threat of force, and many victims suffer serious personal injury.

More than half (51 percent) of the offenses in this category during 1996 were robberies on streets or highways. Robberies of commercial and financial establishments accounted for 24 percent, and those occurring at residences, 11 percent. The remainder were miscellaneous types. All robbery types declined in 1996 as compared to 1995 totals, with the exception of bank robbery which increased by 14 percent. Among the remaining robbery types, decreases ranged from 11 percent for those committed on streets and highways to less than 1 percent for commercial house robberies. (See Table 23.)

Table 2.20 — Robbery, Percent Distribution, 1996
[By region]

	United States Total	Northeastern States	Midwestern States	Southern States	Western States
Total[1]	100.0	100.0	100.0	100.0	100.0
Street/highway	51.2	65.6	60.3	44.7	47.0
Commercial house	13.5	8.3	11.1	14.2	16.3
Gas or service station	2.4	2.5	3.0	2.2	2.5
Convenience store	5.9	4.5	4.1	7.6	5.5
Residence	10.6	7.7	9.8	14.1	8.8
Bank	2.0	1.3	1.7	1.6	3.0
Miscellaneous	14.4	10.3	10.1	15.6	17.0

[1] Because of rounding, percentages may not add to totals.

ROBBERY
PERCENT CHANGE FROM 1992

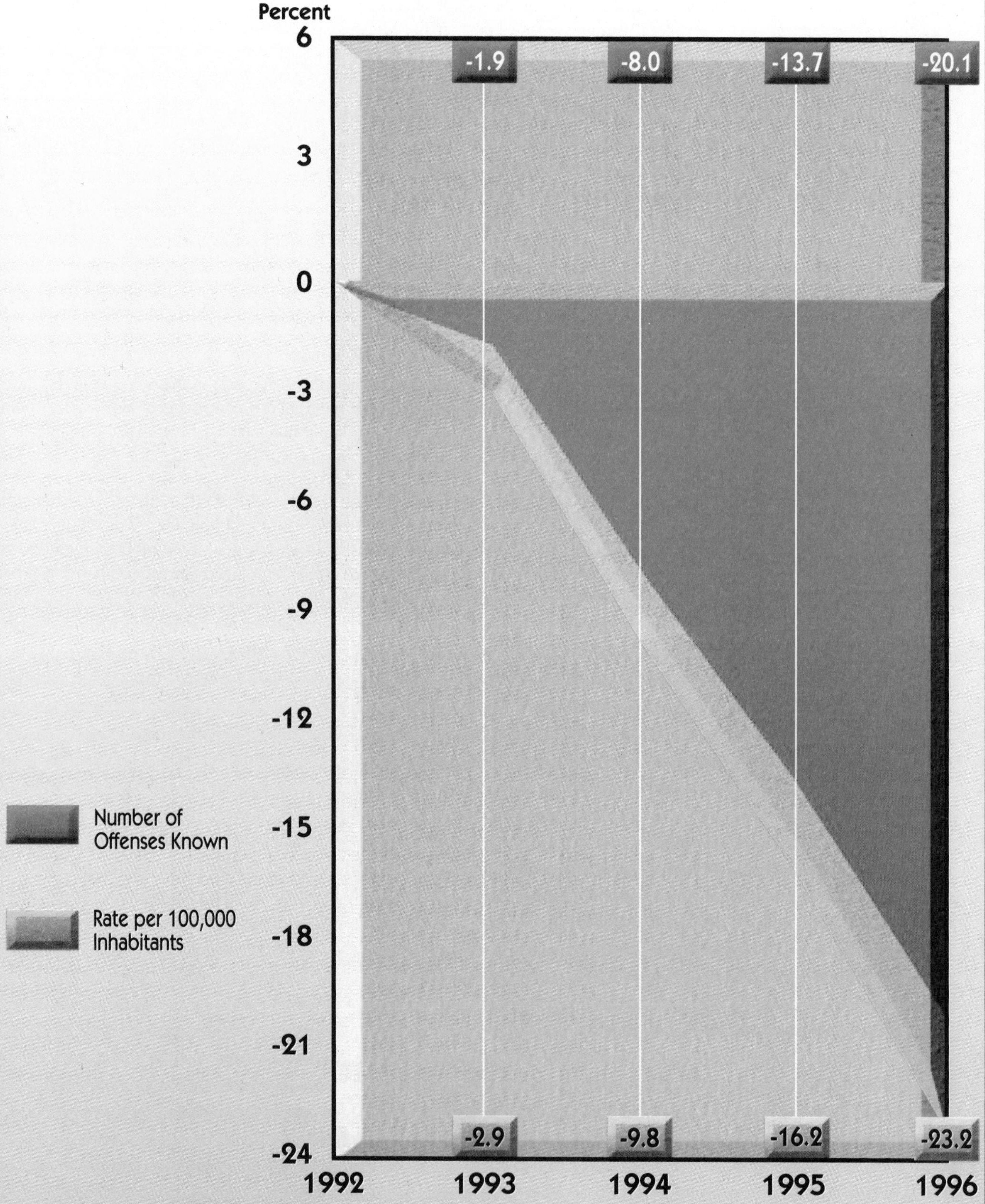

CHART 2.8

Percent

Year	Number of Offenses Known	Rate per 100,000 Inhabitants
1993	-1.9	-2.9
1994	-8.0	-9.8
1995	-13.7	-16.2
1996	-20.1	-23.2

Number of Offenses Known

Rate per 100,000 Inhabitants

Table 2.21 — Robbery, Percent Distribution, 1996

[By population group]

	Group I (57 cities, 250,000 and over; population 34,646,000)	Group II (133 cities, 100,000 to 249,999; population 19,427,000)	Group III (313 cities, 50,000 to 99,999; population 21,232,000)	Group IV (588 cities, 25,000 to 49,999; population 20,347,000)	Group V (1,446 cities, 10,000 to 24,999; population 22,764,000)	Group VI (5,399 cities, under 10,000; population 18,786,000)	County agencies (3,104 agencies; population 67,524,000)
Total[1]	100.0	100.0	100.0	100.0	100.0	100.0	100.0
Street/highway	59.7	52.0	48.2	40.5	35.6	29.6	33.3
Commercial house	12.0	14.0	13.7	13.7	14.4	15.3	17.9
Gas or service station	1.7	2.4	2.8	3.6	4.3	3.7	3.8
Convenience store	3.8	6.3	6.6	8.6	9.0	10.1	10.0
Residence	10.1	9.9	9.1	10.0	11.6	12.3	15.0
Bank	1.5	2.1	2.3	2.8	2.7	3.0	2.7
Miscellaneous	11.1	13.2	17.3	20.9	22.4	26.0	17.3

[1] Because of rounding, percentages may not add to total.

In 1996, firearms were the weapons used in 41 percent of all robberies. Strong-arm tactics were used in 39 percent, knives or cutting instruments in 9 percent, and other dangerous weapons were involved in the remainder. A comparison of 1995 and 1996 robbery totals by weapon show robberies committed using knives or other cutting instruments decreased 9 percent; those using strong-arm tactics decreased 8 percent; those with firearms declined 7 percent; and those with other dangerous weapons dropped 6 percent. A state-by-state breakdown of weapons used in robberies in 1996 is shown in Table 21.

Table 2.22 — Robbery, Types of Weapons Used, 1996

[Percent distribution by region]

Region	Total all weapons[1]	Armed			
		Firearms	Knives or cutting instruments	Other weapons	Strong-arm
Total	100.0	40.7	9.0	11.6	38.7
Northeastern States	100.0	32.2	11.1	19.1	37.6
Midwestern States	100.0	42.2	8.0	10.2	39.6
Southern States	100.0	42.6	7.5	9.0	36.1
Western States	100.0	38.5	9.7	9.2	42.6

[1] Because of rounding, percentages may not add to total.

Law Enforcement Response

The 1996 robbery clearance rate was 27 percent nationally. The highest robbery clearance rate—42 percent—was registered by rural county law enforcement agencies; suburban counties recorded a rate of 28 percent. In the Nation's cities collectively, it was 27 percent, with cities under 10,000 in population having the highest clearance rate, 37 percent. (See Table 25.) Regional robbery clearance percentages ranged from 29 percent in the Northeast to 25 percent in the West. (See Table 26.)

Persons under the age of 18, exclusively, were the offenders in 18 percent of all 1996 robbery clearances. This age group accounted for 17 percent of the suburban county clearances, 18 percent of those in the Nation's cities, and 12 percent of those in rural county agencies. (See Table 28.)

Nationwide, 7 percent fewer persons were arrested for robbery in 1996 than in 1995. For the 2-year period, juvenile arrests for robbery declined 8 percent; those of adults decreased 6 percent. Following the national trend, the number of robbery arrests dropped 7 percent both in the Nation's cities collectively and in rural counties. Suburban counties recorded a 2-percent decline.

Considering the 5-year period, 1992-1996, arrests of males and total arrests for robbery were down 12 and 10 percent, respectively, while arrests of females were up 2 percent. For the same timespan, arrests of persons 18 years of age and older decreased 17 percent, but juvenile arrests rose 7 percent.

Of all robbery arrestees in 1996, 65 percent were under 25 years of age, and 90 percent were males. Fifty-eight percent of those arrested were black, 40 percent were white, and the remainder were of other races.

ROBBERY Percent Change from 1992

CHART 2.9

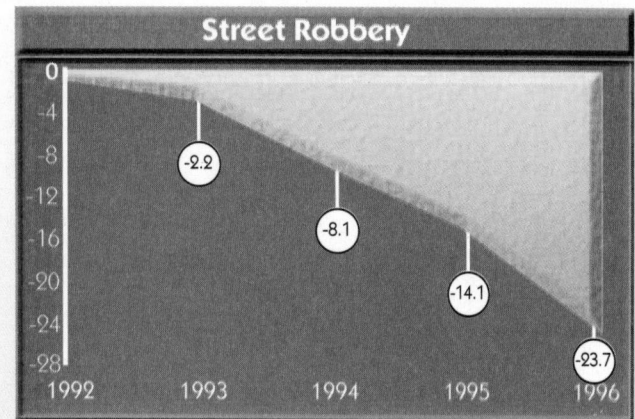

Street Robbery

1992	1993	1994	1995	1996
0	-2.2	-8.1	-14.1	-23.7

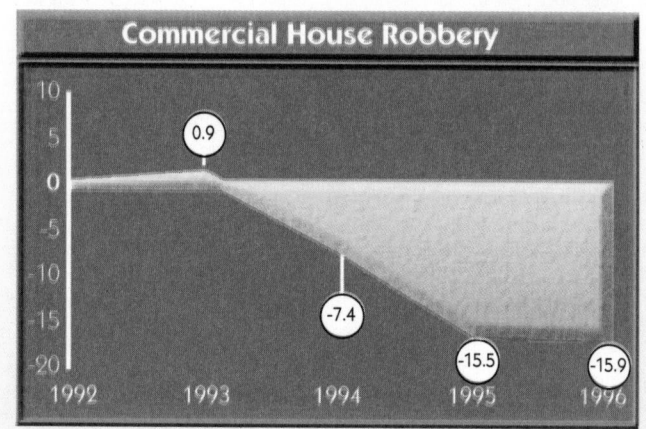

Commercial House Robbery

1992	1993	1994	1995	1996
	0.9	-7.4	-15.5	-15.9

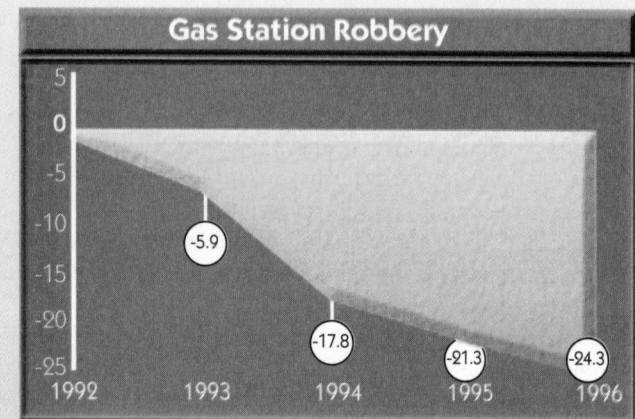

Gas Station Robbery

1992	1993	1994	1995	1996
	-5.9	-17.8	-21.3	-24.3

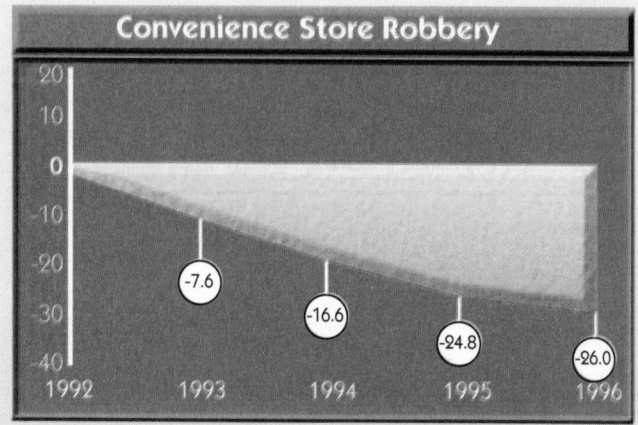

Convenience Store Robbery

1992	1993	1994	1995	1996
	-7.6	-16.6	-24.8	-26.0

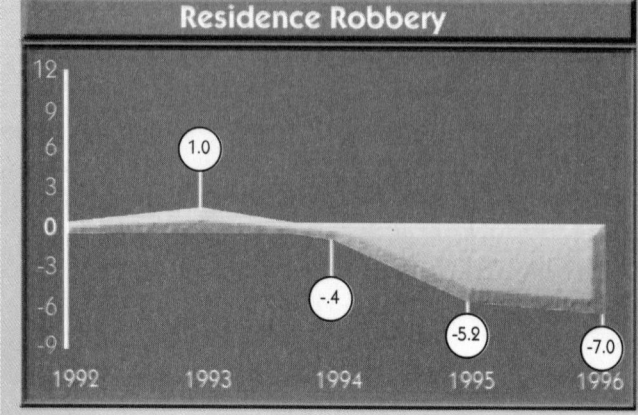

Residence Robbery

1992	1993	1994	1995	1996
	1.0	-.4	-5.2	-7.0

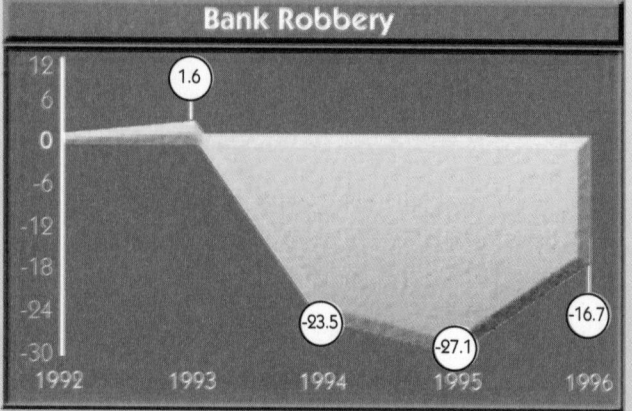

Bank Robbery

1992	1993	1994	1995	1996
	1.6	-23.5	-27.1	-16.7

AGGRAVATED ASSAULT

DEFINITION

Aggravated assault is an unlawful attack by one person upon another for the purpose of inflicting severe or aggravated bodily injury. This type of assault is usually accompanied by the use of a weapon or by means likely to produce death or great bodily harm. Attempts are included since it is not necessary that an injury result when a gun, knife, or other weapon is used which could and probably would result in serious personal injury if the crime were successfully completed.

	TREND	
Year	Number of offenses	Rate per 100,000 inhabitants
1995	1,099,207	418.3
1996	1,029,814	388.2
Percent change.........................	-6.3	-7.2

Aggravated assaults decreased in 1996, marking the third consecutive year of decline. Accounting for 61 percent of violent crimes in 1996, the total of 1,029,814 aggravated assaults represented a 6-percent drop for this offense.

Forty-one percent of the aggravated assault volume was accounted for by the Southern Region, the Nation's most populous area. Following were the Western Region with 24 percent, the Midwestern Region with 20 percent, and the Northeastern Region with 15 percent. All of the Nation's regions registered decreases in the number of reported aggravated assaults. (See Table 4.)

The 1996 monthly figures show that the greatest number of aggravated assaults was recorded during July while the lowest volume occurred during February and November.

Table 2.23 — Aggravated Assault by Month, 1992-1996
[Percent distribution]

Months	1992	1993	1994	1995	1996
January	7.3	7.5	7.2	7.6	7.8
February	7.3	6.5	7.0	7.0	7.5
March	8.0	8.1	8.3	8.1	8.0
April	8.7	8.3	8.5	8.3	8.2
May	9.2	8.9	8.8	8.8	8.9
June	8.9	9.1	8.9	8.8	9.0
July	9.4	9.6	9.5	9.4	9.3
August	9.1	9.2	9.4	9.4	9.2
September	8.6	8.3	8.9	8.9	8.6
October	8.5	8.5	8.7	8.7	8.5
November	7.6	7.4	7.7	7.5	7.5
December	7.4	8.6	7.3	7.4	7.6

The Nation's cities collectively experienced a decrease of 7 percent in the aggravated assault volume from 1995 to 1996. Among all city population groupings, decreases ranged from 9 percent in cities with populations from 50,000 to 99,999 to 4 percent in cities with 500,000 to 999,999 inhabitants. The number of aggravated assaults decreased 9 percent in suburban counties and 5 percent in the rural counties during the same 2-year period. (See Table 12.)

Five- and 10-year trends for the country as a whole show aggravated assaults 9 percent lower than in 1992 and 20 percent above the 1987 figure. (See Table 1.)

Rate

In 1996, there were 388 reported victims of aggravated assault for every 100,000 people nationwide, the lowest rate since 1989. The rate was 7 percent lower than in 1995 and 12 percent below the 1992 rate. The 1996 rate was, however, 11 percent higher than the 1987 rate.

Higher than the national average, the rate in metropolitan areas was 424 per 100,000 inhabitants in 1996. Cities outside metropolitan areas experienced a rate of 350 and rural counties, a rate of 177.

Regionally, the aggravated assault rate was 293 per 100,000 people in the Northeast, 331 in the Midwest, 428 in the West, and 454 in the South. Compared to 1995 rates, 1996 aggravated assault rates were down in all regions. The West marked an 11-percent decline, the Northeast and Midwest each recorded declines of 8 percent, and the South registered a 4-percent drop. (See Table 4.)

Nature

In 1996, 34 percent of the aggravated assaults were committed with blunt objects or other dangerous weapons. Personal weapons such as hands, fists, and feet were used in 26 percent of the assaults; firearms in 22 percent; and knives or cutting instruments in 18 percent.

When broken down by weapon, aggravated assaults in all four weapon categories decreased from the previous year's totals. Assault decreases were as follows: firearms, 10 percent; personal weapons (hands, fists, feet, etc.), 9 percent; knives or other cutting instruments, 7 percent; and other dangerous weapons, 3 percent. State-by-state totals for weapons used in assaults during 1996 are shown in Table 22.

Table 2.24 — Aggravated Assault, Types of Weapons Used, 1996
[Percent distribution by region]

Region	Total all weapons[1]	Firearms	Knives or cutting instruments	Other weapons (clubs, blunt objects, etc.)	Personal weapons
Total	100.0	22.0	18.1	34.4	25.5
Northeastern States	100.0	12.8	19.5	38.7	28.9
Midwestern States	100.0	25.0	19.1	36.6	19.3
Southern States	100.0	25.2	19.7	34.1	20.9
Western States	100.0	20.7	14.2	31.0	34.2

[1] Because of rounding, percentages may not add to total.

AGGRAVATED ASSAULT

PERCENT CHANGE FROM 1992

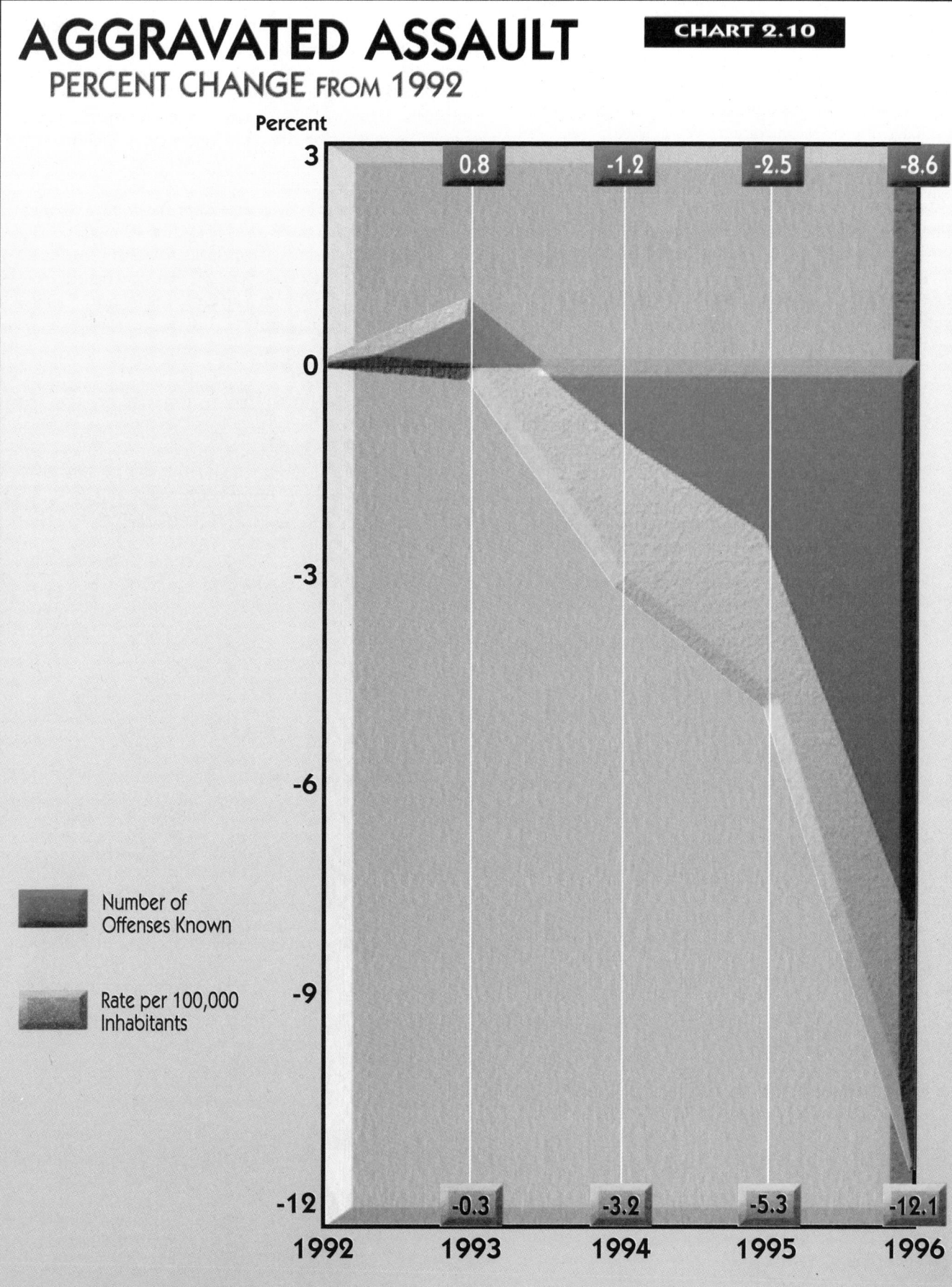

CHART 2.10

Percent

| | 0.8 | -1.2 | -2.5 | -8.6 |

Number of Offenses Known

Rate per 100,000 Inhabitants

| | -0.3 | -3.2 | -5.3 | -12.1 |

1992　1993　1994　1995　1996

33

Law Enforcement Response

During 1996, law enforcement agencies nationwide recorded a 58-percent aggravated assault clearance rate. The cities collectively reported 57 percent cleared, while the suburban and rural county law enforcement agencies cleared 61 and 65 percent, respectively. Among the city groupings, those with populations under 10,000 recorded the highest assault clearance rate, 67 percent. (See Table 25.)

Regional clearance percentages for aggravated assault were 59 percent in the Northeast, 58 percent in the West and South, and 55 percent in the Midwest.

Persons under age 18 were identified as the assailants in 12 percent of the clearances reported nationally, in cities, and in the suburban counties. Ten percent of the clearances reported in rural counties involved persons in this age group.

Seven of every 10 violent crime arrests were for aggravated assault. An estimated half a million individuals were arrested for this offense during 1996. Of these arrestees, 60 percent were white, 38 percent were black, and all other races comprised the remaining 2 percent. Eighty-two percent of the arrestees were males; 85 percent were adults.

Arrests for aggravated assault were down 3 percent in 1996 from the 1995 total. During this 2-year period, arrests of adults also were down 3 percent, and arrests of persons under age 18 decreased 4 percent. A 5-year comparison of 1992 and 1996 figures show increases of 4 percent for both total arrests and those of adults. Juvenile aggravated assault arrests increased 2 percent.

PROPERTY CRIME TOTAL

DEFINITION

Property crime includes the offenses of burglary, larceny-theft, motor vehicle theft, and arson. The object of the theft-type offenses is the taking of money or property, but there is no force or threat of force against the victims. Arson is included since it involves the destruction of property; its victims may be subjected to force.

	TREND	
Year	Number of offenses[1]	Rate per 100,000 inhabitants[1]
1995	12,063,935	4,591.3
1996	11,791,336	4,444.8
Percent change.........................	-2.3	-3.2

[1] Does not include arson. See page 61.

In 1996, property crime dropped to its lowest level since 1986, with nearly 12 million offenses representing a 2-percent decline from the previous year's level. Five- and 10-year trends show the 1996 volume was 6 percent lower than the 1992 level and was 2 percent lower than in 1987.

During 1996, 40 percent of all property crimes were recorded in the Southern States, the most populous region in the country. Following were the Western States with 24 percent, the Midwestern States with 22 percent, and the Northeastern States with 15 percent.

A comparison of 1995 and 1996 regional property crime volumes showed declines of 7 percent in the West and 6 percent in the Northeast. The volume of property crime increased 2 percent in the South and showed virtually no change in the Midwest. (See Table 4.)

The Nation's cities collectively recorded a 3-percent drop in property crime decrease, with the greatest decline, 5 percent, in cities with populations of 1 million or more. The suburban counties also experienced a 3-percent decline, and rural county law enforcement agencies recorded a decrease of 2 percent. (See Table 12.)

In 1996, monthly figures show most property crime occurred in July and August while the lowest count was recorded in February.

Table 2.25 — Property Crime Total by Month, 1992-1996
[Percent distribution]

Months	1992	1993	1994	1995	1996
January	8.4	8.0	7.6	8.1	8.1
February	7.8	6.9	7.1	7.2	7.6
March	8.2	8.1	8.2	8.2	8.0
April	8.0	7.9	8.0	7.8	8.0
May	8.2	8.1	8.5	8.4	8.5
June	8.4	8.6	8.5	8.5	8.4
July	9.0	9.1	9.2	9.0	9.1
August	9.1	9.2	9.4	9.3	9.1
September	8.4	8.4	8.5	8.5	8.4
October	8.5	8.6	8.8	8.8	8.7
November	8.0	8.1	8.3	8.2	7.9
December	8.1	9.1	7.9	8.1	8.1

Rate

There were an estimated 4,445 property crimes for every 100,000 United States inhabitants in 1996. The 1996 property crime rate was 3 percent lower than the 1995 rate, 9 percent below the 1992 rate, and 10 percent below the 1987 rate.

Geographically, 3 of 4 regions of the Nation registered property crime rate decreases in 1996 compared to the previous year's figures. With a rate of 4,837 per 100,000, the West showed the largest decline, 9 percent. The rate of 3,343 in the Northeast represented a 6-percent decrease; the rate of 4,127 in the Midwest represented a 1-percent decline. The South, with a rate of 5,020 per 100,000 inhabitants, recorded an increase of less than 1 percent.

Property crime rates for 1996 were 4,867 in cities outside metropolitan areas, 4,798 in metropolitan areas, and 1,828 in rural counties. By population group, the highest rate—7,877 per 100,000 inhabitants—was recorded in cities with populations from 250,000 to 499,999. (See Tables 2 and 16.)

Nature

The dollar value of property stolen in connection with property crimes in 1996 was estimated at over $15 billion. The average loss per offense in 1996 was $1,274, slightly more than the 1995 figure of $1,251.

In 1996, larceny-theft offenses accounted for 67 percent of all property crime. Burglary accounted for 21 percent and motor vehicle theft for 12 percent. Based on information from 11,250 law enforcement agencies who provided detailed arson data, nearly 77,000 arson offenses were reported in 1996. The average dollar loss of property damaged due to reported arsons was $10,280.

Law Enforcement Response

Property crimes generally have lower clearance rates than do violent crimes, and in 1996, the overall property crime clearance rate was 18 percent, as compared to 47 percent for violent crime. By region, property crime clearance rates of 19 percent were recorded in both the Northeast and South, the Midwest recorded 18 percent, and the West recorded 17 percent. (See Table 26.)

During 1996, 23 percent of the property crimes cleared nationwide by law enforcement involved only young people under age 18. The juvenile percentage was 24 percent in cities, 21 percent in the suburban counties, and 20 percent in the rural counties. (See Table 28.)

The estimated 2,045,600 persons arrested for property crimes in 1996 accounted for 13 percent of all arrestees. Property crime arrests in 1996 were 2 percent below the 1995 level, 6 percent lower than the 1992 total, and 1 percent below the 1987 figures. Compared to 1995 totals, arrests of juveniles fell by less than 1 percent, and arrests of adults for property crimes declined 3 percent nationwide. (See Tables 32, 34, and 36.)

In 1996, 72 percent of all property crime arrestees were males, 65 percent of the total were white, and 65 percent were over the age of 18.

PROPERTY CRIME
PERCENT CHANGE FROM 1992

CHART 2.11

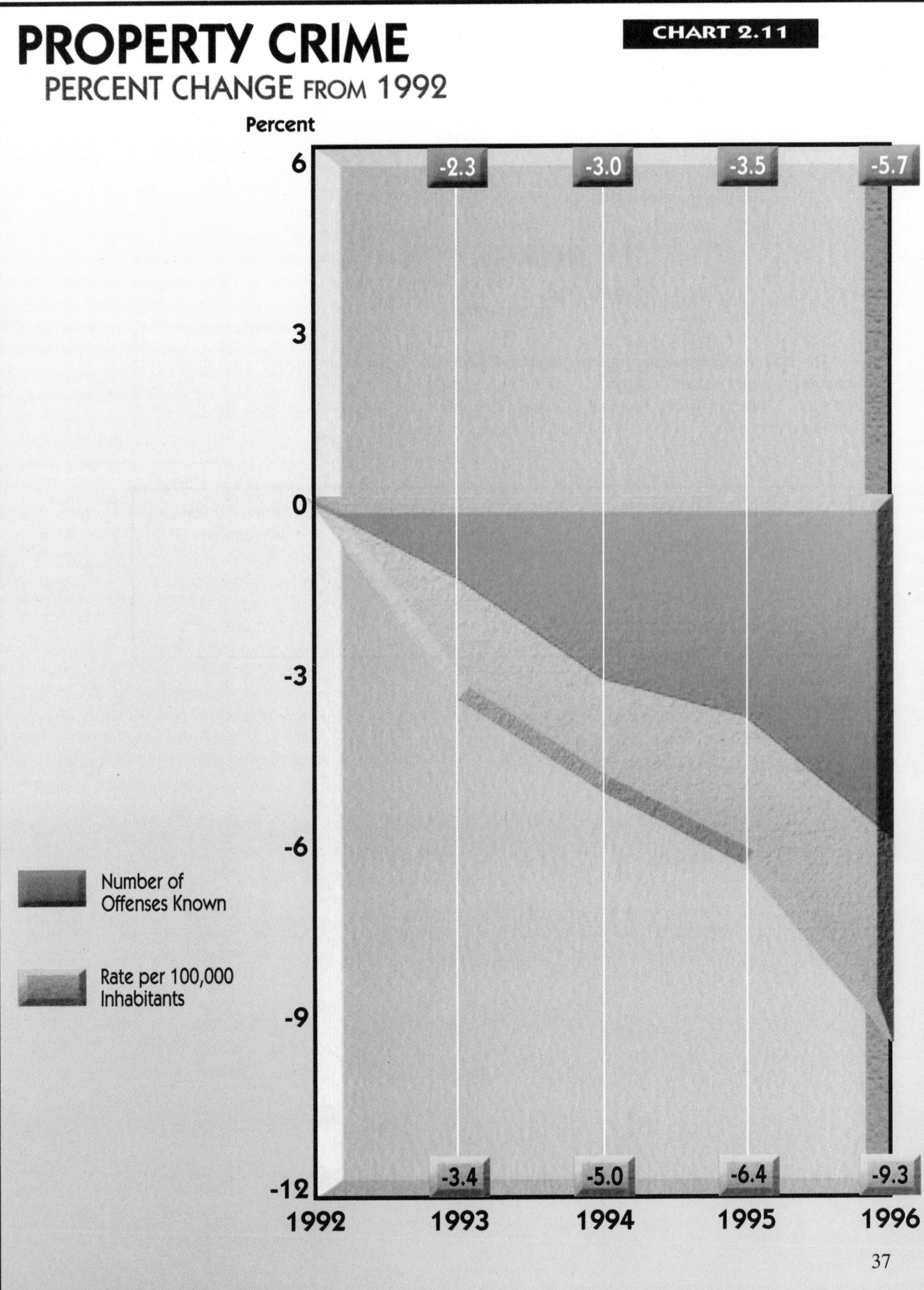

Percent

6   -2.3   -3.0   -3.5   -5.7

3

0

-3

-6

Number of
Offenses Known

Rate per 100,000
Inhabitants

-9

-12   -3.4   -5.0   -6.4   -9.3

1992   1993   1994   1995   1996

37

BURGLARY

DEFINITION

The Uniform Crime Reporting Program defines burglary as the unlawful entry of a structure to commit a felony or theft. The use of force to gain entry is not required to classify an offense as burglary. Burglary in this Program is categorized into three subclassifications: forcible entry, unlawful entry where no force is used, and attempted forcible entry.

TREND		
Year	Number of offenses	Rate per 100,000 inhabitants
1995	2,593,784	987.1
1996	2,501,524	943.0
Percent change.........................	-3.6	-4.5

During 1996, the estimated 2.5 million burglaries in the United States was the lowest total in more than two decades. Distribution figures for the regions showed that the highest burglary volume in 1996, 42 percent, occurred in the most populous Southern States. The Western States followed with 23 percent, the Midwestern States with 20 percent, and the Northeastern States with 14 percent. (See Table 3.)

In 1996, the greatest number of burglaries occurred during July while the lowest number took place in February. (See Table 2.26.)

Table 2.26 — Burglary by Month, 1992-1996
[Percent distribution]

Months	1992	1993	1994	1995	1996
January	8.6	8.3	7.9	8.4	8.3
February	7.7	6.9	7.1	7.2	7.6
March	8.2	8.2	8.2	8.2	7.8
April	7.8	7.7	8.0	7.7	7.8
May	8.2	8.0	8.5	8.4	8.3
June	8.1	8.4	8.3	8.3	8.2
July	9.0	9.0	9.2	9.0	9.1
August	9.0	9.1	9.4	9.2	9.0
September	8.4	8.5	8.6	8.5	8.6
October	8.3	8.4	8.6	8.8	8.8
November	8.2	8.1	8.4	8.3	8.0
December	8.3	9.3	7.9	8.1	8.5

The burglary volume dropped 4 percent nationwide during 1996 as compared to the 1995 total. By population group, the Nation's cities overall experienced a 4-percent decline; the largest decrease was in cities with populations of 1 million and over, which showed a 7-percent decline. Suburban and rural counties also recorded decreases, 6 percent and 3 percent, respectively. (See Table 12.)

Three of the four regions of the United States reported decreases in burglary volumes in 1996 as compared to the previous year's figures. The Northeastern States registered a 9-percent decline; the Western States, an 8-percent decrease; and the Midwestern States, a 2-percent decline. The Southern States recorded a 1-percent increase in burglary volumes. (See Table 4.)

Long-term national trends show burglary down 16 percent from the 1992 level and down 23 percent compared to the 1987 volume.

Rate

The burglary rate in 1996, lower than in any other year in more than two decades, was 943 per 100,000 inhabitants nationwide. The rate was 4 percent lower than in 1995, down 19 percent from the 1992 level, and 29 percent below the 1987 rate. In 1996, the burglary rate for every 100,000 in population was 993 in the metropolitan areas, 935 in the cities outside metropolitan areas, and 620 in the rural counties.

Looking at the Nation's regions, the burglary rate was 1,129 in the Southern States, 1,003 in the Western States, 817 in the Midwestern States, and 691 in the Northeastern States. A comparison of 1995 and 1996 rates showed declines of 10 percent in the West, 9 percent in the Northeast, 3 percent in the Midwest, and 1 percent in the South. (See Table 4.)

Nature

As in previous years, 2 of every 3 burglaries in 1996 were residential in nature. Sixty-six percent of all burglaries involved forcible entry, 26 percent were unlawful entries (without force), and the remainder were forcible entry attempts. Offenses for which time of occurrence was reported showed that 51 percent of burglaries happened during daytime hours and 49 percent at night. Fifty-nine percent of residential burglaries occurred during the daytime, and 65 percent of nonresidential burglaries occurred during nighttime hours.

Losses estimated at $3.3 billion in 1996 were suffered by burglary victims, and the average dollar loss per burglary was $1,332. The average loss for residential offenses was $1,350 and for nonresidential offenses, $1,296. Compared to 1995 losses, the 1996 average loss for both residential and nonresidential property increased.

Both residential and nonresidential burglary volumes declined 4 percent in 1996 from the previous year's figures. (See Table 23.)

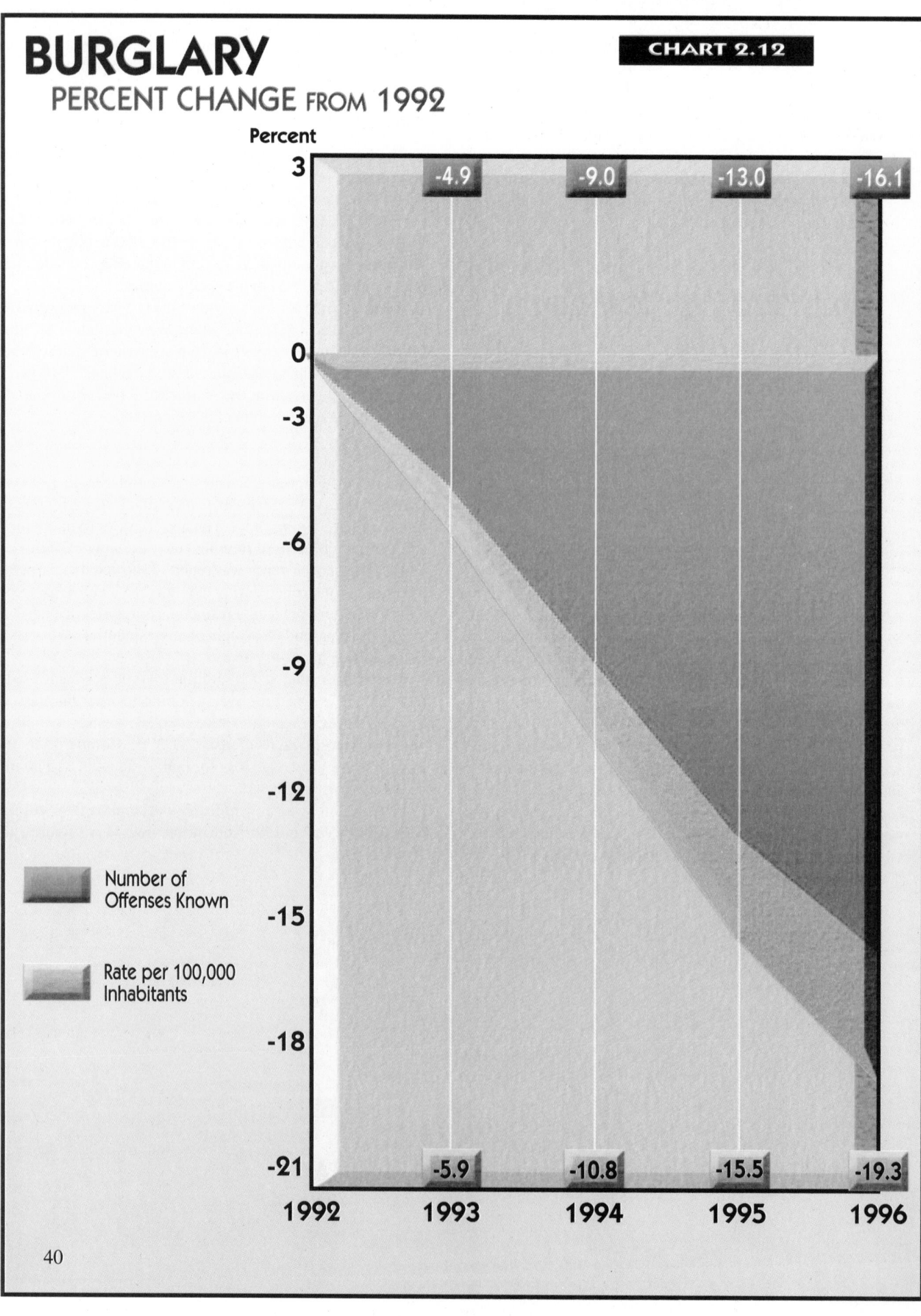

BURGLARY
PERCENT CHANGE FROM 1992

CHART 2.12

Percent

Year	Number of Offenses Known	Rate per 100,000 Inhabitants
1992	0	0
1993	-4.9	-5.9
1994	-9.0	-10.8
1995	-13.0	-15.5
1996	-16.1	-19.3

Number of Offenses Known

Rate per 100,000 Inhabitants

CHART 2.13

BURGLARY
Percent Change from 1992

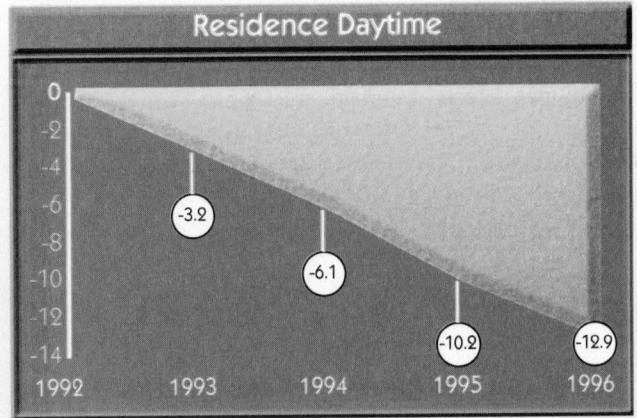

Residence Daytime

- 1993: -3.2
- 1994: -6.1
- 1995: -10.2
- 1996: -12.9

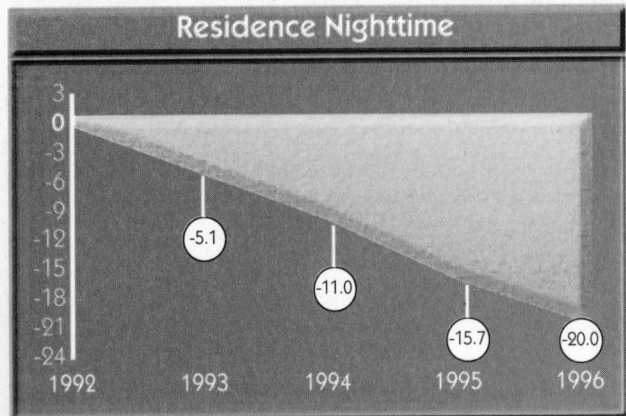

Residence Nighttime

- 1993: -5.1
- 1994: -11.0
- 1995: -15.7
- 1996: -20.0

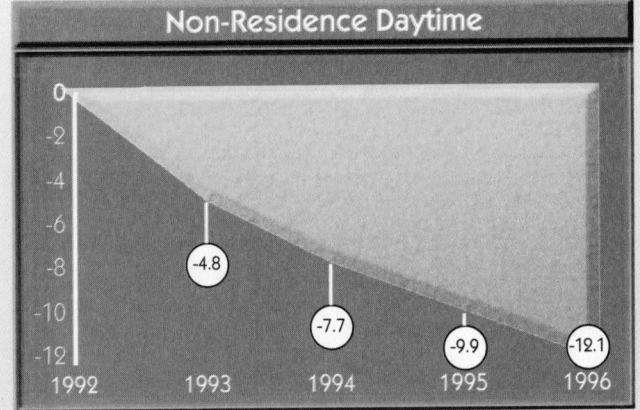

Non-Residence Daytime

- 1993: -4.8
- 1994: -7.7
- 1995: -9.9
- 1996: -12.1

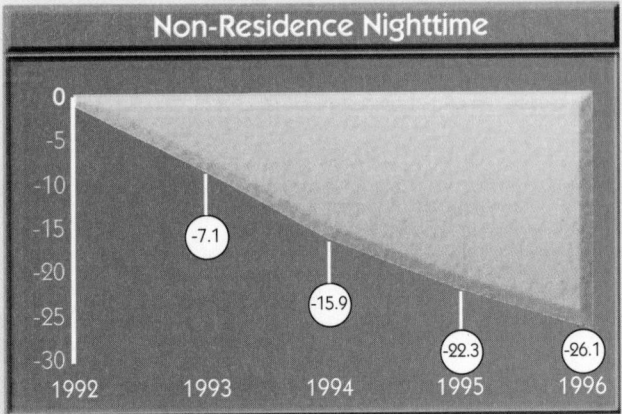

Non-Residence Nighttime

- 1993: -7.1
- 1994: -15.9
- 1995: -22.3
- 1996: -26.1

Law Enforcement Response

During 1996, a 14-percent clearance rate was recorded for burglaries brought to the attention of law enforcement agencies throughout the country. Regionally, in both the Northeast and South, the clearance rate was 15 percent; in the Midwest, it was 13 percent; and in the West, it was 12 percent. (See Table 26.)

Rural county law enforcement agencies cleared 18 percent of the burglaries in their jurisdictions. Agencies in suburban counties cleared 14 percent, and those in cities cleared 13 percent. (See Table 25.)

Adults were involved in 79 percent of all burglary offenses cleared; the remaining 21 percent involved only young people under 18 years of age. Persons under age 18 accounted for 20 percent of the burglary clearances in cities and 22 percent of those in both rural and suburban counties. The highest degree of juvenile involvement was recorded in the Nation's smallest cities (under 10,000 in population) where young persons under 18 years of age accounted for 28 percent of the clearances. (See Table 28.)

In the UCR Program, several persons may be arrested in connection with the clearance of one crime, or the arrest of one individual may clear numerous offenses. The latter is often true in cases of burglary for which an estimated 364,800 arrests were made in 1996.

Between 1995 and 1996, total burglary arrests were down 3 percent with arrests of adults down 6 percent. Arrests of persons under 18 years of age increased 3 percent. For the same 2-year time period, total burglary arrest trends showed a decrease of 4 percent in the Nation's cities. Arrests for burglary in rural counties remained unchanged from the 1995 total while a 1-percent increase was reported in suburban counties.

Eighty-nine percent of the burglary arrestees during 1996 were males, and 64 percent of the total were under 25 years of age. Among all burglary arrestees, whites accounted for 68 percent, blacks for 30 percent, and other races for the remainder.

42

LARCENY–THEFT

DEFINITION

Larceny-theft is the unlawful taking, carrying, leading, or riding away of property from the possession or constructive possession of another. It includes crimes such as shoplifting, pocket-picking, purse-snatching, thefts from motor vehicles, thefts of motor vehicle parts and accessories, bicycle thefts, etc., in which no use of force, violence, or fraud occurs. In the Uniform Crime Reporting Program, this crime category does not include embezzlement, confidence games, forgery, and worthless checks. Motor vehicle theft is also excluded from this category inasmuch as it is a separate Crime Index offense.

TREND		
Year	*Number of offenses*	*Rate per 100,000 inhabitants*
1995	7,997,710	3,043.8
1996	7,894,620	2,975.9
Percent change.........................	-1.3	-2.2

Estimated at nearly 7.9 million offenses during 1996, larceny-theft comprised 59 percent of the Crime Index total and 67 percent of the property crimes. Continuing the pattern of recent years, larceny-thefts were recorded most often during the months of July and August and least frequently in February.

Table 2.27 — Larceny–theft by Month, 1992-1996
[Percent distribution]

Months	1992	1993	1994	1995	1996
January	8.2	7.7	7.4	7.9	7.9
February	7.8	6.8	7.1	7.1	7.5
March	8.3	8.0	8.1	8.1	8.0
April	8.1	8.0	8.1	7.8	8.1
May	8.2	8.2	8.5	8.5	8.6
June	8.5	8.7	8.6	8.6	8.6
July	9.1	9.2	9.2	9.1	9.2
August	9.1	9.3	9.5	9.4	9.2
September	8.4	8.3	8.5	8.5	8.4
October	8.6	8.6	8.9	8.8	8.7
November	7.9	8.0	8.3	8.1	7.8
December	8.0	9.1	7.9	8.1	8.0

The Nation's most populous region, the Southern States, recorded 40 percent of the larceny-theft total. Both the Western States and Midwestern States recorded 23 percent, and the Northeastern States, 14 percent. (See Table 3.)

In 1996, the volume of larceny-thefts nationwide was 1 percent lower than the 1995 total. By community type, decreases of 2 percent were recorded both in cities collectively and suburban counties. A 1-percent decline was experienced in the rural counties. (See Table 12.)

In two of the four geographic regions, incidents of larceny-theft decreased from 1995 levels. The decreases were 6 percent in the West and 5 percent in the Northeast. The South recorded an increase of 2 percent, and the Midwest showed an increase of less than 1 percent. (See Table 4.)

An examination of long-term national trends indicated larceny was up 5 percent when compared to the 1987 total. However, there was virtually no change when compared to the 1992 level. (See Table 1.)

Rate

During 1996, the larceny-theft rate was 2,976 per 100,000 inhabitants in the United States. Two-, 5-, and 10-year trends show the rate was 2 percent below the 1995 rate, 4 percent lower than the rate in 1992, and 3 percent below the 1987 rate. The 1996 rate was 3,188 per 100,000 inhabitants of metropolitan areas; 3,695 per 100,000 population in cities outside metropolitan areas; and 1,083 per 100,000 people in the rural counties. (See Tables 1 and 2.)

By region, the 1996 larceny-theft rate per 100,000 inhabitants in the South increased 1 percent. The West recorded an 8-percent decline, and the Northeast marked a 5-percent drop. The Midwest's rate showed virtually no change from the 1995 level. The regional rates ranged from 2,181 per 100,000 people in the Northeast to 3,368 per 100,000 population in the South. (See Table 4.)

Nature

During 1996, the average value of property stolen due to larceny-theft was $532, down from $535 in 1995. When the average value was applied to the estimated number of larceny-thefts, the loss to victims nationally was over $4 billion for the year. This estimated dollar loss is considered conservative since many offenses in the larceny category never come to law enforcement attention, particularly if the value of the stolen goods is small. Losses under $50 and those over $200 jointly accounted for 77 percent of the thefts reported to law enforcement. The remainder involved losses ranging from $50 to $200.

Losses of goods and property reported stolen as a result of pocket-picking averaged $320; purse-snatching, $296; and shoplifting, $120. The average value loss due to thefts of motor vehicle accessories was $387 and for thefts of bicycles, $263. Thefts from buildings resulted in an average loss of $894; from motor vehicles, $518; and from coin-operated machines, $296. (See Table 23.)

Thefts of motor vehicle parts, accessories, and contents made up the largest portion of reported larcenies—36 percent. Also contributing to the high volume of thefts were shoplifting, accounting for 15 percent; thefts from buildings, 13 percent; and thefts of bicycles, 6 percent. The remainder was distributed among pocket-picking, purse-snatching, thefts from coin-operated machines, and all other types of larceny-thefts. Table 2.28 presents the distribution of larceny-theft by type and geographic region.

Table 2.28 — Larceny Analysis by Region, 1996
[Percent distribution]

	United States Total	North-eastern States	Mid-western States	Southern States	Western States
Total[1]	100.0	100.0	100.0	100.0	100.0
Pocket-picking	.4	1.1	.3	.3	.4
Purse-snatching	.6	1.0	.6	.5	.5
Shoplifting	15.4	15.5	14.4	14.5	17.1
From motor vehicles (except accessories)	25.3	23.6	23.5	23.1	30.4
Motor vehicle accessories	10.7	9.1	11.9	10.8	10.6
Bicycles	5.6	7.7	6.1	4.3	5.9
From buildings	12.7	16.9	15.9	9.9	12.5
From coin-operated machines	.6	.6	.5	.7	.6
All others	28.7	24.4	26.9	36.0	22.1

[1] Because of rounding, percentages may not add to total.

LARCENY-THEFT
PERCENT CHANGE FROM 1992

CHART 2.14

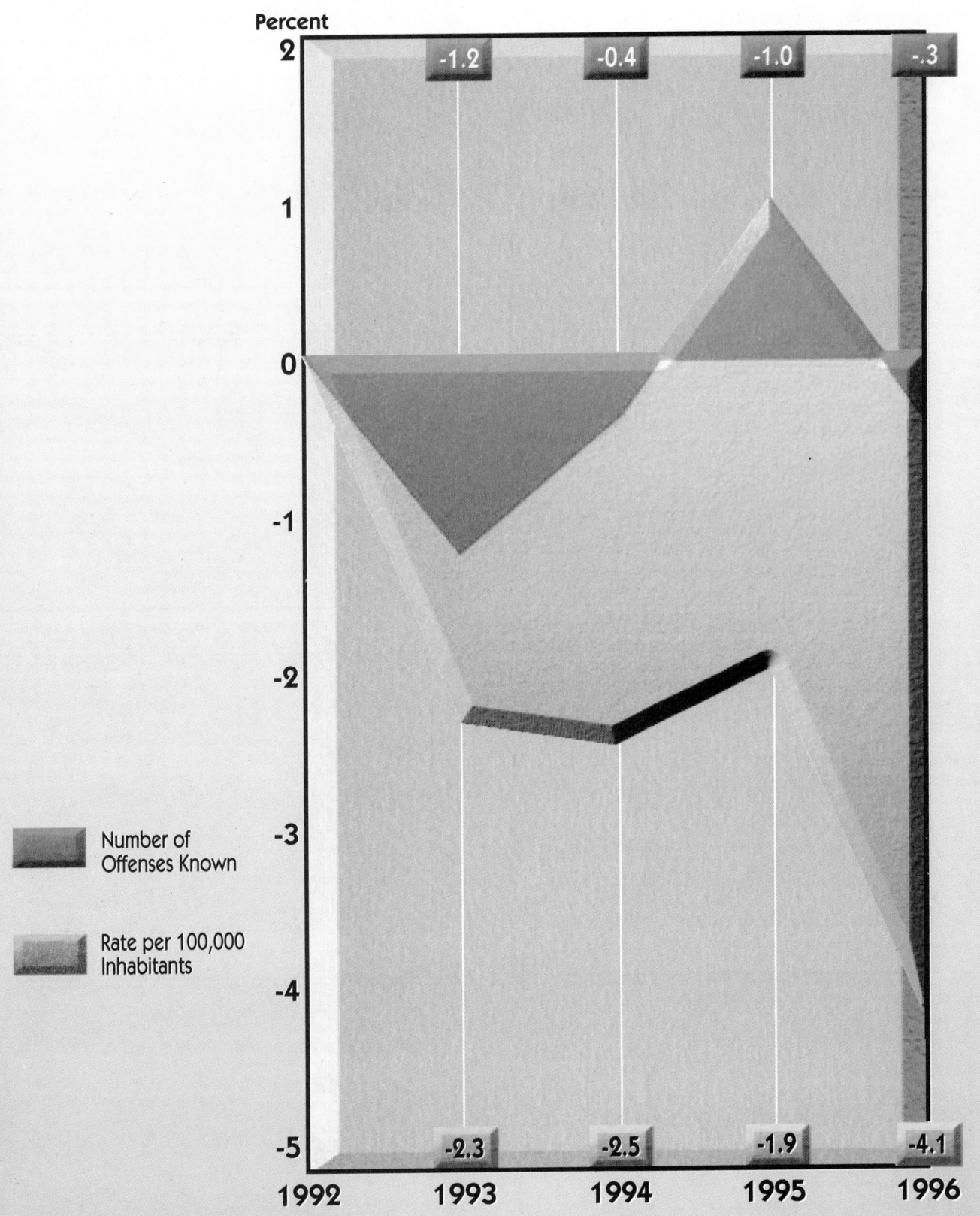

Percent

| | -1.2 | -0.4 | -1.0 | -.3 |

2

1

0

-1

-2

-3

Number of
Offenses Known

Rate per 100,000
Inhabitants

-4

-5

| | -2.3 | -2.5 | -1.9 | -4.1 |

| 1992 | 1993 | 1994 | 1995 | 1996 |

LARCENY/THEFT Percent Change from 1992

CHART 2.15

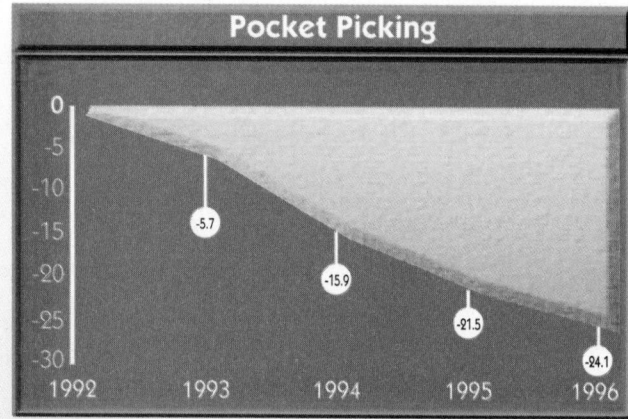

Pocket Picking

- 1992
- 1993: -5.7
- 1994: -15.9
- 1995: -21.5
- 1996: -24.1

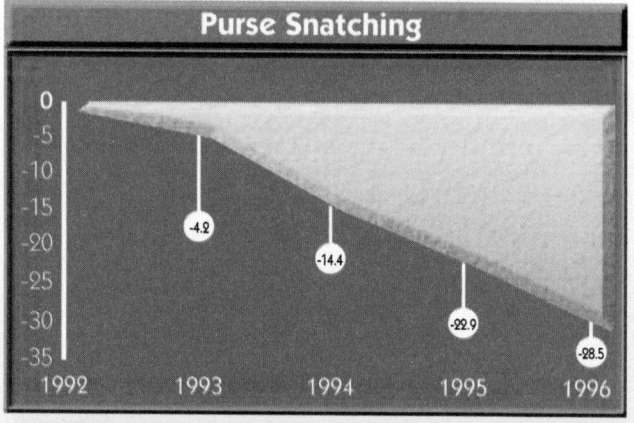

Purse Snatching

- 1992
- 1993: -4.2
- 1994: -14.4
- 1995: -22.9
- 1996: -28.5

Shoplifting

- 1992
- 1993: -4.9
- 1994: -6.7
- 1995: -5.6
- 1996: -5.6

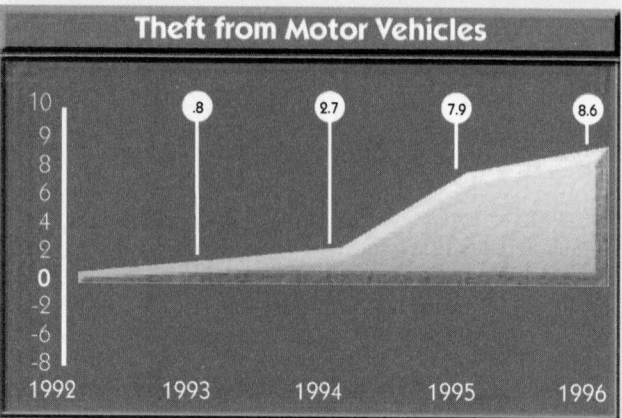

Theft from Motor Vehicles

- 1992
- 1993: .8
- 1994: 2.7
- 1995: 7.9
- 1996: 8.6

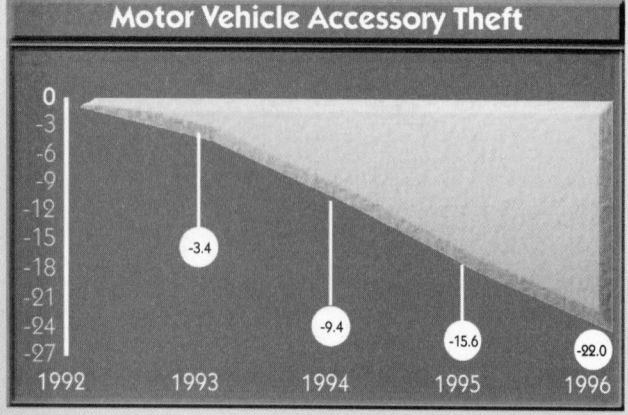

Motor Vehicle Accessory Theft

- 1992
- 1993: -3.4
- 1994: -9.4
- 1995: -15.6
- 1996: -22.0

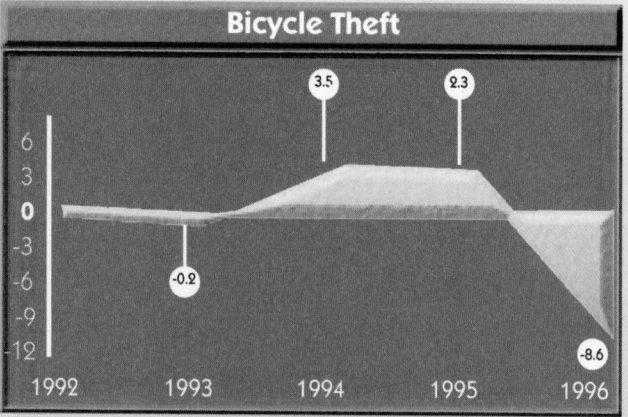

Bicycle Theft

- 1992
- 1993: -0.2
- 1994: 3.5
- 1995: 2.3
- 1996: -8.6

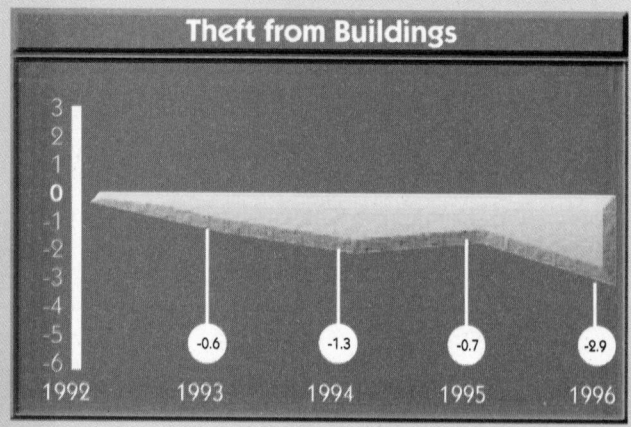

Theft from Buildings

- 1992
- 1993: -0.6
- 1994: -1.3
- 1995: -0.7
- 1996: -2.9

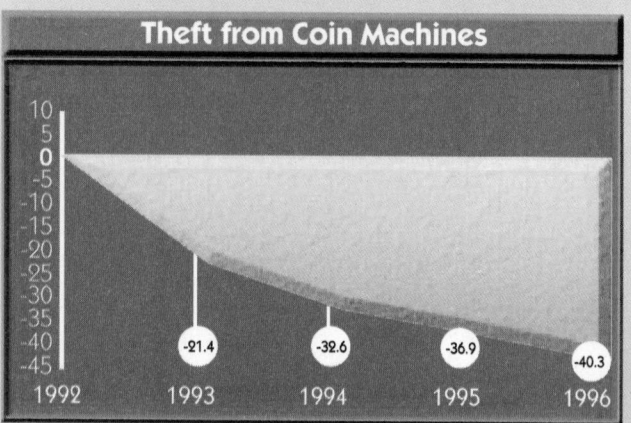

Theft from Coin Machines

- 1992
- 1993: -21.4
- 1994: -32.6
- 1995: -36.9
- 1996: -40.3

LARCENY-THEFT 1996

CHART 2.16

Percent Distribution by Type of Theft

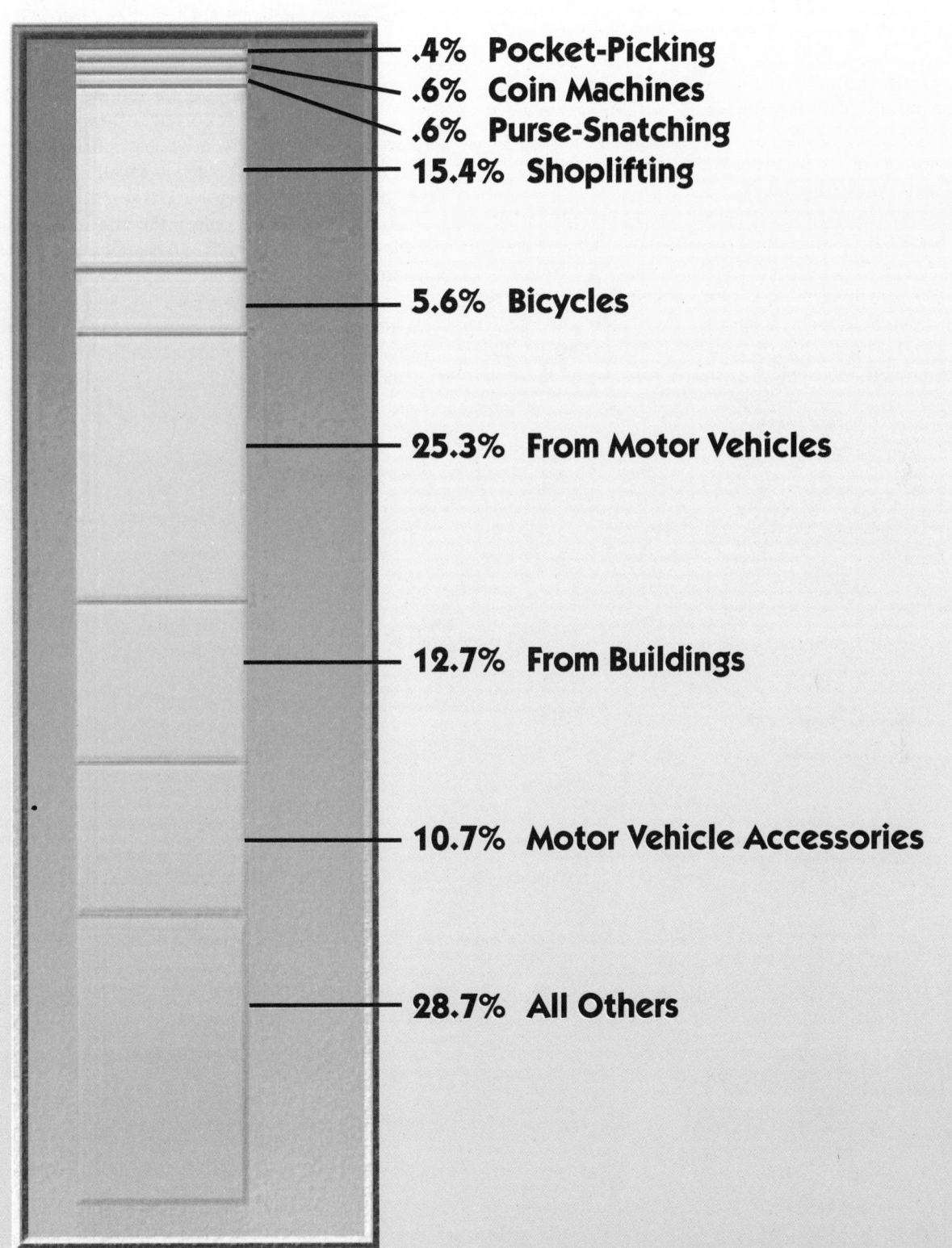

- .4% Pocket-Picking
- .6% Coin Machines
- .6% Purse-Snatching
- 15.4% Shoplifting
- 5.6% Bicycles
- 25.3% From Motor Vehicles
- 12.7% From Buildings
- 10.7% Motor Vehicle Accessories
- 28.7% All Others

Law Enforcement Response

In 1996, the national larceny-theft clearance rate was 20 percent, and in the Nation's cities, the rate was 21 percent. As in recent years, the highest rate, 26 percent, was reported by law enforcement agencies in cities from 10,000 to 24,999 in population. Agencies in rural counties reported a 20-percent clearance rate, and those in suburban counties recorded an 18-percent clearance rate.

A review of clearance rates by geographic region indicates that 21 percent of the larceny-thefts reported in the Northeast were cleared. Twenty percent of the reported larceny-thefts were cleared in both the South and the Midwest, and 19 percent were cleared in the West. (See Table 26.)

Twenty-four percent of the larceny-theft clearances in the Nation and 25 percent in cities involved only offenders under 18 years of age. Twenty-one percent of those in suburban counties and 19 percent of those in rural counties were accounted for by persons in this age group.

Between 1995 and 1996, the total number of persons arrested for larceny-theft fell 1 percent; arrests of males and those of adults declined 2 percent. During this same period, arrests of juveniles (persons under 18 years of age) increased less than 1 percent, and arrests of females increased 1 percent.

Considering the 5-year period, 1992-1996, larceny-theft arrests declined 2 percent. Arrests of males declined 5 percent; however, arrests of females increased 5 percent. During the same timespan, the number of arrests of adults dropped 6 percent while arrests of persons under the age of 18 were up 9 percent.

Larceny-theft not only comprised the largest portion of Crime Index offenses reported to law enforcement, but also accounted for 73 percent of arrests for property crimes in 1996 and 54 percent of total arrests for all Index crimes. Forty-seven percent of the larceny arrests were of persons under 21 years of age, and 34 percent of the arrestees were under 18. Females, who were arrested for this offense more often than for any other in 1996, comprised 34 percent of all larceny-theft arrestees.

Whites accounted for 65 percent of the total larceny-theft arrestees, blacks for 32 percent, and all other races for the remainder.

MOTOR VEHICLE THEFT

DEFINITION

Defined as the theft or attempted theft of a motor vehicle, this offense category includes the stealing of automobiles, trucks, buses, motorcycles, motorscooters, snowmobiles, etc. The definition excludes the taking of a motor vehicle for temporary use by those persons having lawful access.

	TREND	
Year	Number of offenses	Rate per 100,000 inhabitants
1995	1,472,441	560.4
1996	1,395,192	525.9
Percent change	-5.2	-6.2

During 1996, there were nearly 1.4 million thefts of motor vehicles nationwide, marking the lowest total for that offense since 1987. The regional distribution of thefts in 1996 showed 35 percent of the volume was in the Southern States, 28 percent in the Western States, 20 percent in the Midwestern States, and 17 percent in the Northeastern States. (See Table 3.)

An examination of the monthly distribution of motor vehicle thefts reveals the highest percentage of vehicles was stolen during the months of January and July, and the lowest percentage was stolen in February and April. (See Table 2.29.)

Table 2.29 — Motor Vehicle Theft by Month, 1992-1996
[Percent distribution]

Months	1992	1993	1994	1995	1996
January	8.8	8.5	8.2	8.6	8.7
February	7.9	7.3	7.4	7.5	8.0
March	8.2	8.2	8.5	8.2	8.2
April	7.8	7.8	8.0	7.8	8.0
May	8.1	7.9	8.2	8.2	8.2
June	8.2	8.4	8.3	8.1	8.1
July	8.8	8.9	8.9	8.6	8.7
August	8.9	8.9	9.1	9.0	8.6
September	8.2	8.4	8.4	8.4	8.2
October	8.6	8.6	8.8	8.9	8.6
November	8.3	8.3	8.4	8.5	8.2
December	8.2	8.8	7.8	8.3	8.5

In the Nation and in cities as a whole, motor vehicle thefts declined 5 percent from 1995 to 1996. Among city population groupings, the decreases ranged from 7 percent in cities 1 million and over in population and those with populations of 100,000 to 499,999 to less than 1 percent in cities with populations under 25,000. During the same 2-year period, a 6-percent decrease in the volume of motor vehicle thefts occurred in suburban counties, while rural counties registered virtually no change. (See Table 12.)

Geographically, decreases in motor vehicle thefts were recorded in the West, with 12 percent; in the Northeast, with 8 percent; and in the Midwest, with 1 percent. The South recorded virtually no change. (See Table 4.)

Chart 2.17 shows that the volume of motor vehicle thefts in 1996 declined 13 percent from the 1992 volume.

Rate

The 1996 national motor vehicle theft rate—526 per 100,000 inhabitants—was 6 percent lower than in 1995 and 17 percent below the 1992 rate. The 1996 rate was less than 1 percent below the 1987 rate.

For every 100,000 inhabitants living in metropolitan areas, there were 616 motor vehicle thefts reported in 1996. The rate in cities outside metropolitan areas was 238 and that in rural counties, 126. As in previous years, the highest rates were in the Nation's most heavily populated municipalities, indicating that this offense is primarily a large-city problem. For every 100,000 inhabitants in cities with populations over 250,000, the 1996 motor vehicle theft rate was 1,223. The Nation's smallest cities, those with fewer than 10,000 inhabitants, recorded a rate of 247 per 100,000.

Among all regions of the country, motor vehicle theft rates ranged from 666 per 100,000 inhabitants in the Western States to 443 in the Midwestern States. The Southern States' rate was 524, and the Northeastern States' rate was 472. All regions registered rate declines from 1995 to 1996. The West reported the greatest rate decrease, 13 percent. The Northeast reported a decrease of 9 percent; the Midwest, a decrease of 2 percent; and the South, a decrease of 1 percent. (See Table 4.)

An estimated average of 1 of every 147 registered motor vehicles was stolen nationwide during 1996. Regionally, this rate was greatest in the West where 1 of every 114 motor vehicles registered was stolen. The other three regions reported lesser rates—1 per 147 in the Northeast, 1 per 149 in the South, and 1 per 191 in the Midwest.

Nature

The estimated value of motor vehicles stolen nationwide in 1996 was nearly $7.5 billion. At the time of theft, the average value per vehicle was $5,372. The recovery percentage for the value of vehicles stolen was higher than for any other property type. Relating the value of vehicles stolen to the value of those recovered resulted in a 68-percent recovery rate for 1996. (See Tables 23 and 24.)

Seventy-eight percent of all motor vehicles reported stolen during the year were automobiles, 16 percent were trucks or buses, and the remainder were other types. (See Table 2.30.)

Table 2.30 — Motor Vehicle Theft, 1996
[Percent distribution by region]

Region	Total[1]	Autos	Trucks and buses	Other vehicles
Total	100.0	78.3	16.5	5.2
Northeastern States	100.0	90.4	5.9	3.7
Midwestern States	100.0	81.5	13.5	4.9
Southern States	100.0	75.5	18.3	6.2
Western States	100.0	72.5	22.4	5.1

[1] Because of rounding, percentages may not add to total.

MOTOR VEHICLE THEFT

CHART 2.17

PERCENT CHANGE FROM 1992

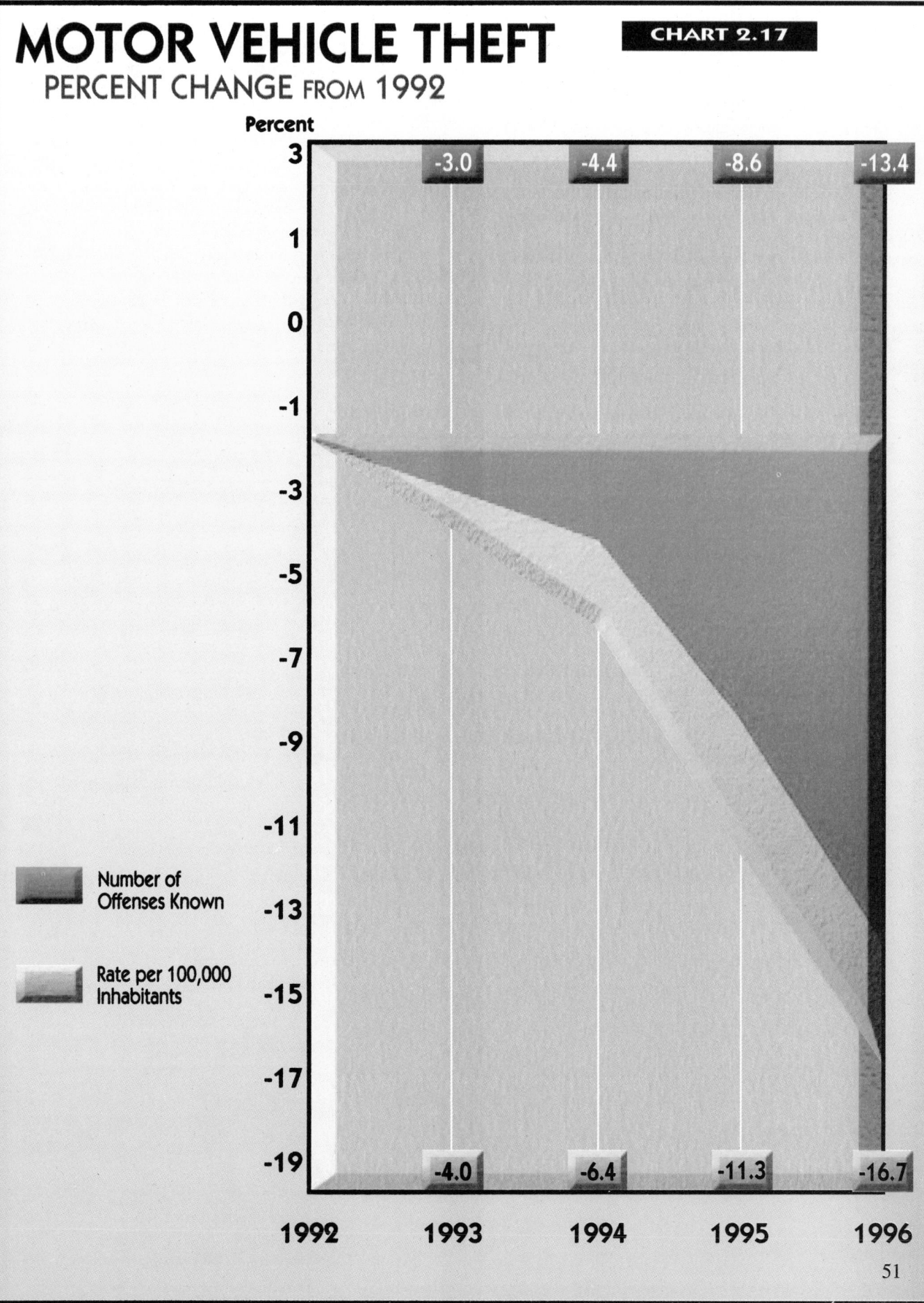

Percent

	1992	1993	1994	1995	1996
Number of Offenses Known		-3.0	-4.4	-8.6	-13.4
Rate per 100,000 Inhabitants		-4.0	-6.4	-11.3	-16.7

51

Law Enforcement Response

Law enforcement agencies nationwide recorded a 14-percent motor vehicle theft clearance rate for 1996. Those in cities cleared 13 percent; those in suburban counties cleared 16 percent; and rural county agencies cleared 32 percent. (See Table 25.)

Regional clearance percentages for motor vehicle theft were 18 percent for the Southern States, 16 percent for the Midwestern States, and 11 percent for both the Northeastern and Western States. (See Table 26.)

Persons in the under 18 age group accounted for 22 percent of the motor vehicle thefts cleared nationally. They comprised 23 percent of the clearances in cities, 22 percent in rural counties, and 19 percent in suburban counties. (See Table 28.)

An estimated 175,400 individuals were arrested for motor vehicle theft in 1996. Males accounted for 86 percent of those arrested. Fifty-seven percent of the arrestees were white, 40 percent were black, and the remainder were of other races.

When considering age of arrestees for the offense of motor vehicle theft, a large portion of arrests came from the younger segment of the Nation's population. In 1996, 59 percent of all persons arrested for this offense were under 21 years of age, and those under 18 comprised 42 percent of the total. Between 1995 and 1996, arrests of persons under age 18 were down 10 percent. Arrests of juvenile males decreased 10 percent, and those of young females decreased 8 percent.

Fifty-eight percent of motor vehicle theft arrests were for adults, a decline of 8 percent from the 1995 figure.

Total motor vehicle theft arrests in 1996 were down 9 percent from the previous year's total and 16 percent lower than in 1992. Compared to the 1987 level, however, the arrest total increased 2 percent.

ARSON

―――――― **DEFINITION** ――――――

Arson is defined by the Uniform Crime Reporting Program as any willful or malicious burning or attempt to burn, with or without intent to defraud, a dwelling house, public building, motor vehicle or aircraft, personal property of another, etc.

Only fires determined through investigation to have been willfully or maliciously set are classified as arsons. Fires of suspicious or unknown origins are excluded.

A total of 88,887 arson offenses was reported in 1996 by 11,453 law enforcement agencies across the Nation; these agencies furnished from 1 to 12 months of reports during the year. Among these reporting agencies, 11,250 provided the detailed information—type of structure, estimated monetary value of the property damaged, etc.—from which the tables on the accompanying pages were tabulated. Further information regarding arson offenses and trends is presented in Tables 12 through 15 and arson clearances in Tables 25 through 28. Since only 8,325 agencies covering 68 percent of the United States population submitted reports for all 12 months of the year, the data user should be aware that, while conservative indicators, the figures do not represent the Nation's total arson experience.

The number of arson offenses reported nationally and in the Nation's cities during 1996 decreased 3 percent from 1995 figures. While the number of arson offenses dropped in the Nation's cities collectively, changes among the population groupings ranged from an 11-percent decrease in cities with populations 100,000 to 249,999 to a 9-percent increase in cities with populations over 1 million. The rural counties showed a decline of 3 percent while the suburban counties registered an increase of 2 percent. (See Table 12.)

Regionally, the number of arson offenses decreased 15 percent in the Northeast and 1 percent each in the Midwest and West. The South recorded an increase of 2 percent in arson occurrences.

Nationally, the number of arsons involving structures declined 12 percent, and those involving all other property declined 7 percent. Mobile property registered a 6-percent increase in the number of arsons. (See Table 15.)

Table 2.31 — Arson Rate, Population Group, 1996
[8,325 agencies; 1996 estimated population 180,643,000; rate per 100,000 inhabitants]

Group	Rate
Total	44.3
Total cities	51.3
Group I (cities 250,000 and over)	83.9
(cities 1,000,000 and over)	90.0
(cities 500,000 to 999,999)	68.4
(cities 250,000 to 499,999)	89.9
Group II (cities 100,000 to 249,999)	50.4
Group III (cities 50,000 to 99,999)	40.6
Group IV (cities 25,000 to 49,999)	36.0
Group V (cities 10,000 to 24,999)	26.5
Group VI (cities under 10,000)	29.5
Suburban counties	33.3
Rural counties	18.9
Suburban area	31.0

It is recommended to use caution when viewing arson trend information. The percent change figures may have been influenced by improved arson reporting procedures. It is expected that year-to-year statistical comparability will improve as collection continues.

Rate

Since population coverage for arson data is lower than for the other Crime Index offenses, arson rates per 100,000 inhabitants are tabulated independently. Based only on figures from law enforcement agencies supplying 12 months of statistics for all Index crimes including arson the 1996 rates are shown in Table 2.31.

Arson rates ranged from 90 per 100,000 inhabitants in cities with populations over 1 million to 19 per 100,000 rural county inhabitants. The suburban counties and all cities collectively recorded rates of 33 and 51 per 100,000 inhabitants, respectively. Nationally, the 1996 arson rate was 44 per 100,000 population.

Geographically, the highest arson rate was registered in the Western States with 49 offenses per 100,000 population. Following were the Midwestern and Southern States each with rates of 43 per 100,000, and the Northeastern States with 40 per 100,000.

Nature

As in previous years, structures were the most frequent targets of arsonists in 1996 and comprised 48 percent of the reported incidents. Twenty-nine percent of the arsons were directed at mobile property (motor vehicles, trailers, etc.), while other types of property (crops, timber, etc.) accounted for 23 percent. (See Table 2.32.)

Table 2.32 — Arson, Type of Property, 1996
[11,250 agencies; 1996 estimated population 190,496,000]

Property classification	Number of offenses	Percent distribution[1]
Total	76,642	100.0
Total structure	37,047	48.3
Single occupancy residential	14,949	19.5
Other residential	6,758	8.8
Storage	3,073	4.0
Industrial/manufacturing	518	.7
Other commercial	3,861	5.0
Community/public	4,149	5.4
Other structure	3,739	4.9
Total mobile	22,162	28.9
Motor vehicles	20,926	27.3
Other mobile	1,236	1.6
Other	17,433	22.7

[1] Because of rounding, percentages may not add to total.

Fifty-nine percent of the structural arsons during the year involved residential property, with 40 percent of such offenses directed at single-family dwellings. Twenty percent of all targeted structural property was either uninhabited or abandoned at the time the arson occurred.

Motor vehicles comprised 94 percent of all mobile property at which arsons were directed.

Table 2.33 — Arson, Structures Not in Use, 1996
[11,250 agencies; 1996 estimated population 190,496,000]

Type of structure	Number of offenses	Percent not in use
Total	37,047	20.0
Single occupancy residential	14,949	25.0
Other residential	6,758	15.7
Storage	3,073	24.2
Industrial/manufacturing	518	26.3
Other commercial	3,861	15.3
Community/public	4,149	10.0
Other structure	3,739	19.8

The monetary value of property damaged due to reported arsons averaged $10,280 per incident in 1996. The overall average for all types of structures was $17,892. Mobile properties averaged $5,048 per incident, and other targets averaged $758.

Table 2.34 — Arson, Monetary Value of Property Damaged, 1996
[11,250 agencies; 1996 estimated population 190,496,000]

Property classification	Number of offenses	Average damage
Total	76,642	$10,280
Total structure	37,047	17,892
Single occupancy residential	14,949	14,032
Other residential	6,758	16,333
Storage	3,073	16,274
Industrial/manufacturing	518	119,273
Other commercial	3,861	38,121
Community/public	4,149	15,288
Other structure	3,739	5,480
Total mobile	22,162	5,048
Motor vehicles	20,926	4,723
Other mobile	1,236	10,553
Other	17,433	758

Law Enforcement Response

The 1996 arson clearance rate was 16 percent nationwide and in cities. Rural county agencies cleared 26 percent; and those in suburban counties, 16 percent. Law enforcement agencies in cities with fewer than 10,000 inhabitants showed the highest rate, clearing 26 percent of the arson offenses brought to their attention. (See Table 25.)

Regionally, the Southern States recorded an arson clearance rate of 20 percent; the Midwestern States, 16 percent; the Western States, 15 percent; and the Northeastern States, 14 percent.

Forty-five percent of all 1996 arson clearances involved only young people under age 18, a higher percentage of juvenile involvement than for any other Index crime. Persons in this age group accounted for 25 percent of the clearances for arsons of mobile property, 44 percent of structural arson clearances, and 61 percent of those of all other property. Juveniles were the offenders in 48 percent of the city, 41 percent of the suburban county, and 29 percent of the rural county arson clearances.

The accompanying tables show clearance data by type for the structural and mobile classifications. As shown in Table 2.35, the highest clearance rate, 29 percent, was recorded for arsons of community/public structures, while the lowest rate, 8 percent, was registered for motor vehicles.

Table 2.35 — Arson Offenses Cleared by Arrest,[1] 1996
[11,250 agencies; 1996 estimated population 190,496,000]

Property classification	Number of offenses	Percent cleared by arrest
Total	76,642	17.8
Total structure	37,047	22.5
Single occupancy residential	14,949	23.2
Other residential	6,758	24.2
Storage	3,073	19.2
Industrial/manufacturing	518	18.0
Other commercial	3,861	14.7
Community/public	4,149	29.2
Other structure	3,739	20.1
Total mobile	22,162	8.2
Motor vehicles	20,926	7.6
Other mobile	1,236	19.0
Other	17,433	19.8

[1] Includes offenses cleared by exceptional means.

An estimated 19,000 arrests for arson were made during 1996. Fifty-three percent of the arrestees were under 18 years of age and 70 percent were under 25. Males comprised 85 percent of all arson arrestees. Seventy-four percent of those arrested were white, 24 percent were black, and the remainder were of other races.

Table 2.36 — Arson Offenses Cleared by Arrest[1] of Persons under 18 Years of Age, 1996
[11,250 agencies; 1996 estimated population 190,496,000]

Property classification	Total clearances	Percent under 18
Total	13,605	45.5
Total structure	8,325	43.7
Single occupancy residential	3,473	37.1
Other residential	1,637	37.6
Storage	590	56.1
Industrial/manufacturing	93	29.0
Other commercial	568	36.1
Community/public	1,211	71.8
Other structure	753	40.6
Total mobile	1,820	24.7
Motor vehicles	1,585	23.0
Other mobile	235	36.2
Other	3,460	60.7

[1] Includes offenses cleared by exceptional means.

Trends for 1995 versus 1996 show arson arrests decreased 7 percent nationally and in cities. Decreases of 6 percent occurred in suburban counties and 4 percent in rural counties.

Nationwide, arrests of juveniles for arson were down 6 percent, and adult arrests dropped 8 percent from 1995 to 1996.

During the same period, male arrests decreased 6 percent, and female arrests fell 12 percent. The 1996 arson arrest total for all ages was 2 percent lower than in 1992 and 5 percent above the 1987 level.

HATE CRIME

DEFINITION

A hate crime, also known as a bias crime, is a criminal offense committed against a person, property, or society which is motivated, in whole or in part, by the offender's bias against a race, religion, ethnic/national origin group, or sexual-orientation group.

Background

In response to a growing concern about hate crimes, Congress, on April 23, 1990, enacted the Hate Crime Statistics Act of 1990. The Attorney General designated the FBI's Uniform Crime Reporting (UCR) Program to develop a hate crime data collection system for its voluntary law enforcement agency participants which would include data "about crimes that manifest evidence of prejudice based on race, religion, ethnicity, and sexual orientation." In September 1994, the Violent Crime Control and Law Enforcement Act amended the Hate Crime Statistics Act to add disabilities, both physical and mental, as factors that could be considered a basis for hate crimes. The disability bias data collection began in January 1997.

Hate crimes are not separate, distinct crimes, but rather traditional offenses motivated by the offender's bias; therefore, hate crime data can be collected by capturing additional information about offenses being reported to UCR. Included are the offenses of murder and nonnegligent manslaughter; forcible rape; aggravated assault, simple assault, and intimidation; robbery; burglary; larceny-theft; motor vehicle theft; arson; and destruction, damage, or vandalism of property.

Hate crime data are submitted to the FBI on a Quarterly Hate Crime Report which consists of a quarterly summary and an incident report for each bias incident. Agencies participating in the National Incident-Based Reporting System are able to include the hate crime data element in their submissions via magnetic tape.

The following statistics are a representation of the data received from law enforcement agencies that provided 1 to 12 months of hate crime reports during 1996. More detailed information concerning characteristics of hate crime can be found in the UCR annual publication *Hate Crime Statistics*.

Nature

In 1996, crimes against persons comprised 69 percent of the 10,702 offenses reported. Intimidation was the single most frequently reported hate crime among all offenses measured, accounting for 38 percent of the total. Of the crimes against persons, intimidation accounted for 56 percent, while simple assault and aggravated assault represented 24 percent and 20 percent, respectively. Destruction, damage, or vandalism was the most frequently reported offense of hate crime against property, accounting for 86 percent.

Table 2.37 — Number of Offenses, 1996

Circumstances	Offenses	Percent of total distribution[2]
Total	10,702	100.0
Crimes against persons:	**7,340**	**68.6**
Murder	12	.1
Forcible rape	11	.1
Aggravated assault	1,443	13.5
Simple assault	1,755	16.4
Intimidation	4,118	38.5
Other[1]	1	[3]
Crimes against property:	**3,345**	**31.3**
Robbery	154	1.4
Burglary	140	1.3
Larceny–theft	75	.7
Motor vehicle theft	7	.1
Arson	75	.7
Destruction/damage/vandalism	2,890	27.0
Other[1]	4	[3]
Crimes against society[1]	**17**	**.2**

[1] Includes offenses other than those listed that are collected in the National Incident-Based Reporting System.

[2] Because of rounding, percentages may not add to total.

[3] Less than one-tenth of 1 percent.

Racial bias continues to represent the largest percentage of bias-motivated offenses in 1996. Of the 10,702 reported offenses, 6,768 were motivated by racial bias; 1,497 by religious bias; 1,258 by sexual-orientation bias; and 1,179 by ethnic bias. (See Chart 2.18.)

CHART 2.18

BIAS MOTIVATION
1996
Percent Distribution

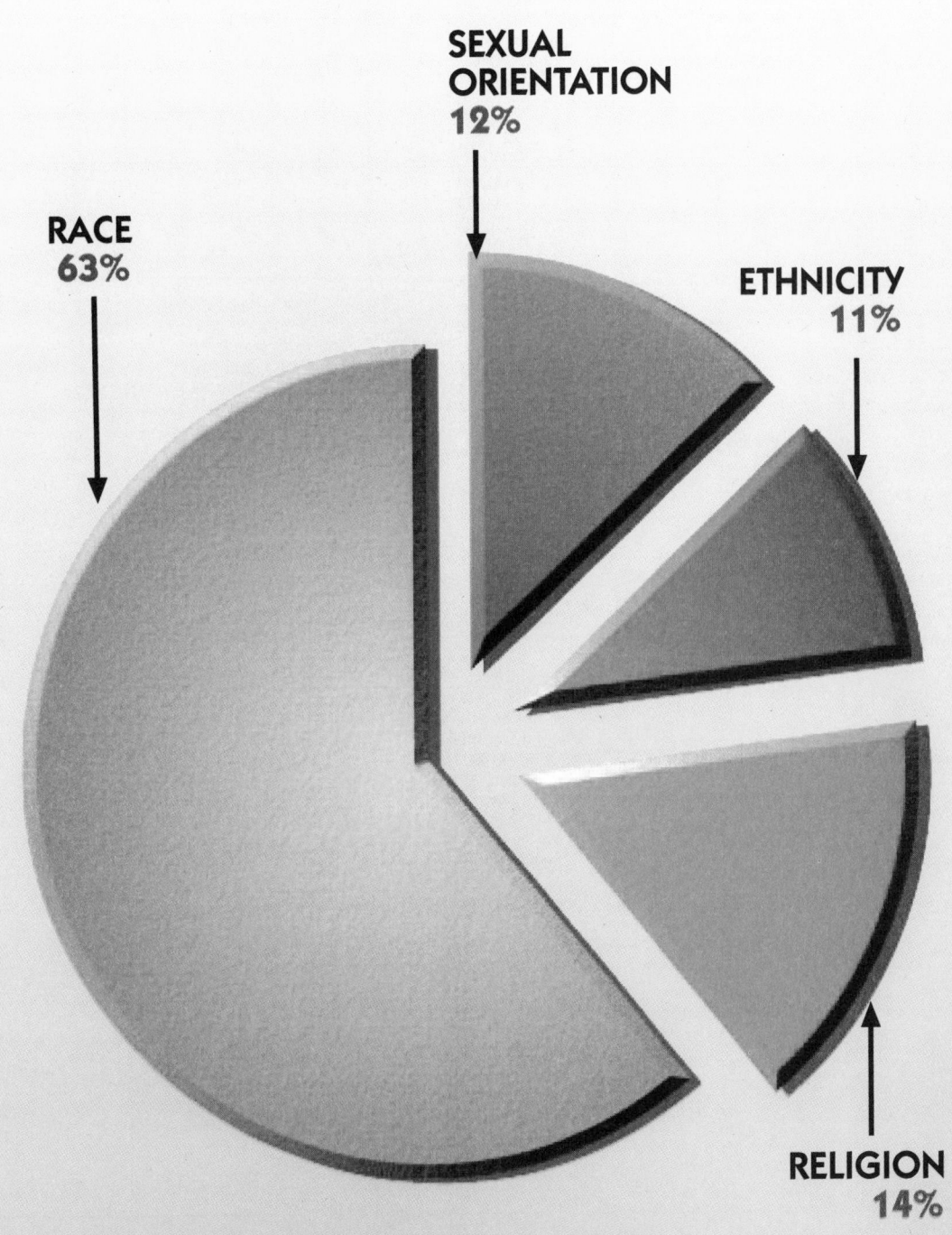

SEXUAL
ORIENTATION
12%

ETHNICITY
11%

RACE
63%

RELIGION
14%

Law Enforcement Participation

The law enforcement community recognizes that valid information is central to developing effective measures to deal with hate crime. Law enforcement participation in reporting bias-motivated crimes to UCR continues to grow each year as more agencies provide the needed information on their jurisdictions' experiences. Participation of individual law enforcement agencies has increased from 2,766 in 1991 to 11,355 in 1996.

Data for 1996 were supplied by 11,355 law enforcement agencies in 49 states and the District of Columbia and represented nearly 224 million United States inhabitants or approximately 84 percent of the Nation's population. (See Table 2.38.) Reports from these agencies, while not sufficient to allow valid national or regional measures of the volume and types of crimes motivated by hate, offer perspectives on the general nature of hate crime occurrences.

Table 2.38 — Agency Hate Crime, State, 1996

Participating states	Number of participating agencies	Population covered	Agencies submitting incident reports	Total number of incidents reported
Total	11,355	223,745,001	1,834	8,734
Alabama	289	4,165,994	0	0
Alaska	1	254,774	1	9
Arizona	81	4,253,428	19	250
Arkansas	191	2,504,563	1	1
California	718	31,861,494	256	2,052
Colorado	230	3,817,580	27	133
Connecticut	98	2,772,165	44	114
Delaware	50	725,000	9	67
District of Columbia	1	543,000	1	16
Florida	394	14,658,195	51	187
Georgia	2	413,123	2	28
Idaho	112	1,202,424	32	72
Illinois	114	5,407,993	114	333
Indiana	179	3,664,946	12	36
Iowa	231	2,841,077	25	43
Kansas	1	312,706	1	28
Kentucky	527	3,848,633	49	109
Louisiana	140	2,700,170	5	6
Maine	131	1,235,309	10	58
Maryland	148	5,071,690	37	387
Massachusetts	405	6,089,350	102	454
Michigan	485	7,958,039	159	485
Minnesota	307	4,651,132	58	268
Mississippi	129	1,716,566	3	3
Missouri	230	4,270,323	25	150
Montana	95	861,547	4	10
Nebraska	10	207,564	2	3
Nevada	4	1,169,351	3	44
New Hampshire	2	81,381	1	1
New Jersey	568	7,993,859	273	839
New Mexico	70	1,299,168	8	44
New York	499	17,645,588	40	903
North Carolina	83	2,888,221	19	34
North Dakota	101	640,486	1	1
Ohio	405	8,873,634	55	234
Oklahoma	293	3,299,915	27	83
Oregon	174	3,155,762	27	172
Pennsylvania	1,137	11,838,976	43	205
Rhode Island	46	990,000	11	40
South Carolina	340	3,677,033	24	42
South Dakota	32	255,844	2	3
Tennessee	191	2,908,259	13	33
Texas	915	19,031,043	88	350
Utah	124	1,988,036	25	59
Vermont	3	35,462	3	4
Virginia	409	6,674,610	32	92
Washington	230	5,469,395	62	198
West Virginia	22	179,467	3	4
Wisconsin	338	5,160,000	21	43
Wyoming	70	480,726	4	4

Crime Index Tabulations

This Section's tabular portions present data on crime in the United States as a whole; geographic divisions; individual states; Metropolitan Statistical Areas; cities, towns, and counties; and college and university campuses. Also furnished in the following tables are national averages for the value of property stolen in connection with Crime Index offenses; further breakdowns by type for the robbery, burglary, larceny-theft, and arson classifications; information on the types of weapons used; and data on the type and value of property stolen and recovered.

Although the total number of crimes occurring throughout the Nation is unknown, information on those reported to law enforcement gives a reliable indication of criminal activity. In reviewing the tables in this report, it must be remembered, however, that many factors can cause the volume and type of crime to vary from place to place. Even though population, one of these factors, is used in computing crime rates, all communities are affected to some degree by seasonal or transient populations. Since counts of current, permanent population are used in their construction, crime rates do not account for short-term population variables, such as an influx of day workers, tourists, shoppers, etc. A further discussion of various factors contributing to the amount of crime in a given area is presented on page *iv* of this publication.

National data can serve as a guide for the law enforcement administrator in analyzing the local crime count, as well as the performance of the jurisdiction's law enforcement agency. The analysis, however, should not end with a comparison based on data presented in this publication. It is only through an appraisal of local conditions that a true assessment of the community crime problem or the effectiveness of the law enforcement operation is possible.

National estimates of volume and rate per 100,000 inhabitants for all Crime Index offenses covering the past two decades are set forth in Table 1, "Index of Crime, United States, 1977-1996."

Table 2, "Index of Crime, United States, 1996," shows current year estimates for MSAs, rural counties, and cities and towns outside metropolitan areas. See Appendix III for the definitions of these community types.

Provided in Table 3, "Index of Crime, Regional Offense and Population Distribution, 1996," are data showing the geographical distribution of estimated Index crimes and population. When utilizing figures presented on a regional basis in this publication, the reader is cautioned to consider each region's proportion of the total United States population. For example, although the Southern States accounted for the largest volume of Crime Index offenses in 1996, they also represented the greatest regional population.

Note

The collection of statistics on arson as a Crime Index offense began in 1979. However, 1996 annual figures are not available for inclusion in tables presenting statistics for the total United States. Arson totals reported by individual law enforcement agencies are displayed in Tables 8 through 11. Two-year arson trends are shown in Tables 12 through 15.

Table 1. — Index of Crime, United States, 1977-1996

Population[1]	Crime Index total[2]	Modified Crime Index total[3]	Violent crime[4]	Property crime[4]	Murder and non-negligent man-slaughter	Forcible rape	Robbery	Aggravated assault	Burglary	Larceny–theft	Motor vehicle theft	Arson[3]
					Number of Offenses							
Population by year:												
1977-216,332,000	10,984,500		1,029,580	9,955,000	19,120	63,500	412,610	534,350	3,071,500	5,905,700	977,700	
1978-218,059,000	11,209,000		1,085,550	10,123,400	19,560	67,610	426,930	571,460	3,128,300	5,991,000	1,004,100	
1979-220,099,000	12,249,500		1,208,030	11,041,500	21,460	76,390	480,700	629,480	3,327,700	6,601,000	1,112,800	
1980-225,349,264	13,408,300		1,344,520	12,063,700	23,040	82,990	565,840	672,650	3,795,200	7,136,900	1,131,700	
1981-229,146,000	13,423,800		1,361,820	12,061,900	22,520	82,500	592,910	663,900	3,779,700	7,194,400	1,087,800	
1982-231,534,000	12,974,400		1,322,390	11,652,000	21,010	78,770	553,130	669,480	3,447,100	7,142,500	1,062,400	
1983-233,981,000	12,108,600		1,258,090	10,850,500	19,310	78,920	506,570	653,290	3,129,900	6,712,800	1,007,900	
1984-236,158,000	11,881,800		1,273,280	10,608,500	18,690	84,230	485,010	685,350	2,984,400	6,591,900	1,032,200	
1985-238,740,000	12,431,400		1,328,800	11,102,600	18,980	88,670	497,870	723,250	3,073,300	6,926,400	1,102,900	
1986-241,077,000	13,211,900		1,489,170	11,722,700	20,610	91,460	542,780	834,320	3,241,400	7,257,200	1,224,100	
1987-243,400,000	13,508,700		1,484,000	12,024,700	20,100	91,110	517,700	855,090	3,236,200	7,499,900	1,288,700	
1988-245,807,000	13,923,100		1,566,220	12,356,900	20,680	92,490	542,970	910,090	3,218,100	7,705,900	1,432,900	
1989-248,239,000	14,251,400		1,646,040	12,605,400	21,500	94,500	578,330	951,710	3,168,200	7,872,400	1,564,800	
1990-248,709,873	14,475,600		1,820,130	12,655,500	23,440	102,560	639,270	1,054,860	3,073,900	7,945,700	1,635,900	
1991-252,177,000	14,872,900		1,911,770	12,961,100	24,700	106,590	687,730	1,092,740	3,157,200	8,142,200	1,661,700	
1992-255,082,000	14,438,200		1,932,270	12,505,900	23,760	109,060	672,480	1,126,970	2,979,900	7,915,200	1,610,800	
1993-257,908,000	14,144,800		1,926,010	12,218,800	24,530	106,010	659,870	1,135,610	2,834,800	7,820,900	1,563,100	
1994-260,341,000	13,989,500		1,857,670	12,131,900	23,330	102,220	618,950	1,113,180	2,712,800	7,879,800	1,539,300	
1995-262,755,000[5]	13,862,700		1,798,790	12,063,900	21,610	97,470	580,510	1,099,210	2,593,800	7,997,700	1,472,400	
1996-265,284,000	13,473,600		1,682,280	11,791,300	19,650	95,770	537,050	1,029,810	2,501,500	7,894,600	1,395,200	
Percent change :												
number of offenses:												
1996/1995	-2.8		-6.5	-2.3	-9.1	-1.7	-7.5	-6.3	-3.6	-1.3	-5.2	
1996/1992	-6.7		-12.9	-5.7	-17.3	-12.2	-20.1	-8.6	-16.1	-.3	-13.4	
1996/1987	-.3		+13.4	-1.9	-2.2	+5.1	+3.7	+20.4	-22.7	+5.3	+8.3	
					Rate per 100,000 Inhabitants							
Year:												
1977	5,077.6		475.9	4,601.7	8.8	29.4	190.7	247.0	1,419.8	2,729.9	451.9	
1978	5,140.3		497.8	4,642.5	9.0	31.0	195.8	262.1	1,434.6	2,747.4	460.5	
1979	5,565.5		548.9	5,016.6	9.7	34.7	218.4	286.0	1,511.9	2,999.1	505.6	
1980	5,950.0		596.6	5,353.3	10.2	36.8	251.1	298.5	1,684.1	3,167.0	502.2	
1981	5,858.2		594.3	5,263.9	9.8	36.0	258.7	289.7	1,649.5	3,139.7	474.7	
1982	5,603.6		571.1	5,032.5	9.1	34.0	238.9	289.2	1,488.8	3,084.8	458.8	
1983	5,175.0		537.7	4,637.4	8.3	33.7	216.5	279.2	1,337.7	2,868.9	430.8	
1984	5,031.3		539.2	4,492.1	7.9	35.7	205.4	290.2	1,263.7	2,791.3	437.1	
1985	5,207.1		556.6	4,650.5	7.9	37.1	208.5	302.9	1,287.3	2,901.2	462.0	
1986	5,480.4		617.7	4,862.6	8.6	37.9	225.1	346.1	1,344.6	3,010.3	507.8	
1987	5,550.0		609.7	4,940.3	8.3	37.4	212.7	351.3	1,329.6	3,081.3	529.4	
1988	5,664.2		637.2	5,027.1	8.4	37.6	220.9	370.2	1,309.2	3,134.9	582.9	
1989	5,741.0		663.1	5,077.9	8.7	38.1	233.0	383.4	1,276.3	3,171.3	630.4	
1990	5,820.3		731.8	5,088.5	9.4	41.2	257.0	424.1	1,235.9	3,194.8	657.8	
1991	5,897.8		758.1	5,139.7	9.8	42.3	272.7	433.3	1,252.0	3,228.8	659.0	
1992	5,660.2		757.5	4,902.7	9.3	42.8	263.6	441.8	1,168.2	3,103.0	631.5	
1993	5,484.4		746.8	4,737.6	9.5	41.1	255.9	440.3	1,099.2	3,032.4	606.1	
1994	5,373.5		713.6	4,660.0	9.0	39.3	237.7	427.6	1,042.0	3,026.7	591.3	
1995[5]	5,275.9		684.6	4,591.3	8.2	37.1	220.9	418.3	987.1	3,043.8	560.4	
1996	5,078.9		634.1	4,444.8	7.4	36.1	202.4	388.2	943.0	2,975.9	525.9	
Percent change :												
rate per 100,000 inhabitants:												
1996/1995	-3.7		-7.4	-3.2	-9.8	-2.7	-8.4	-7.2	-4.5	-2.2	-6.2	
1996/1992	-10.3		-16.3	-9.3	-20.4	-15.7	-23.2	-12.1	-19.3	-4.1	-16.7	
1996/1987	-8.5		+4.0	-10.0	-10.8	-3.5	-4.8	+10.5	-29.1	-3.4	-.7	

[1] Populations are Bureau of the Census provisional estimates as of July 1, except 1980 and 1990 which are the decennial census counts.

[2] Because of rounding, the offenses may not add to total.

[3] Although arson data are included in the trend and clearance tables, sufficient data are not available to estimate totals for this offense.

[4] Violent crimes are offenses of murder, forcible rape, robbery, and aggravated assault. Property crimes are offenses of burglary, larceny–theft, and motor vehicle theft. Data are not included for the property crime of arson.

[5] The 1995 figures have been adjusted. See "Crime Trends," page 390 for details.

Complete data were not available for the states of Illinois, Kansas, Kentucky, and Montana; therefore, it was necessary that their crime counts be estimated. An aggregate Florida state total for 1996 was supplied by the Florida Department of Law Enforcement. See "Offense Estimation," pages 389-390 for details.

All rates were calculated on the offenses before rounding.

Table 2. — Index of Crime, United States, 1996

Area	Population[1]	Crime Index total	Modified Crime Index total[2]	Violent crime[3]	Property crime[3]	Murder and non-negligent man-slaughter	Forcible rape	Robbery	Aggra-vated assault	Burglary	Larceny-theft	Motor vehicle theft	Arson[2]
United States Total	**265,284,000**	13,473,614		**1,682,278**	**11,791,336**	**19,645**	**95,769**	**537,050**	**1,029,814**	**2,501,524**	**7,894,620**	**1,395,192**	
Rate per 100,000 inhabitants		5,078.9		634.1	4,444.8	7.4	36.1	202.4	388.2	943.0	2,975.9	525.9	
Metropolitan Statistical Area	**211,363,933**												
Area actually reporting[4] ...	90.1%	11,412,400		1,481,233	9,931,167	16,891	77,935	509,897	876,510	2,049,069	6,594,309	1,287,789	
Estimated totals	100.0%	11,650,725		1,510,225	10,140,500	17,156	80,541	515,967	896,561	2,098,367	6,739,198	1,302,935	
Rate per 100,000 inhabitants		5,512.2		714.5	4,797.6	8.1	38.1	244.1	424.2	992.8	3,188.4	616.4	
Cities outside metropolitan area	**21,885,070**												
Area actually reporting[4] ..	78.6%	1,032,477		89,380	943,097	881	6,769	13,900	67,830	181,097	716,185	45,815	
Estimated totals	100.0%	1,166,114		100,950	1,065,164	994	7,595	15,819	76,542	204,550	808,568	52,046	
Rate per 100,000 inhabitants		5,328.4		461.3	4,867.1	4.5	34.7	72.3	349.7	934.7	3,694.6	237.8	
Rural Counties	**32,034,997**												
Area actually reporting[4] ..	75.9%	580,082		61,765	518,317	1,290	6,813	4,643	49,019	173,958	308,703	35,656	
Estimated totals	100.0%	656,775		71,103	585,672	1,495	7,633	5,264	56,711	198,607	346,854	40,211	
Rate per 100,000 inhabitants		2,050.2		222.0	1,828.2	4.7	23.8	16.4	177.0	620.0	1,082.7	125.5	

[1] Populations are Bureau of the Census provisional estimates as of July 1, 1996, and are subject to change.

[2] Although arson data are included in the trend and clearance tables, sufficient data are not available to estimate totals for this offense.

[3] Violent crimes are offenses of murder, forcible rape, robbery, and aggravated assault. Property crimes are offenses of burglary, larceny-theft, and motor vehicle theft. Data are not included for the property crime of arson.

[4] The percentage representing area actually reporting will not coincide with the ratio between reported and estimated crime totals, since these data represent the sum of the calculations for individual states which have varying populations, portions reporting, and crime rates.

Complete data were not available for the states of Illinois, Kansas, Kentucky, and Montana; therefore, it was necessary that their crime counts be estimated. An aggregate Florida state total for 1996 was supplied by the Florida Department of Law Enforcement. See "Offense Estimation," pages 389-390 for details.

Table 3. — Index of Crime, Regional Offense and Population Distribution, 1996

Region	Population	Crime Index total	Modified Crime Index total[1]	Violent crime[2]	Property crime[2]	Murder and non-negligent man-slaughter	Forcible rape	Robbery	Aggra-vated assault	Burglary	Larceny-theft	Motor vehicle theft	Arson[1]
United States Total[3]	**100.0**	**100.0**		**100.0**	**100.0**	**100.0**	**100.0**	**100.0**	**100.0**	**100.0**	**100.0**	**100.0**	
Northeastern States	19.4	14.9		17.0	14.6	14.1	13.4	22.3	14.7	14.3	14.2	17.4	
Midwestern States	23.4	21.5		19.8	21.7	20.1	24.7	18.6	19.9	20.3	22.5	19.7	
Southern States	35.1	39.6		39.1	39.6	42.8	39.3	35.2	41.0	42.0	39.7	34.9	
Western States	22.1	24.0		24.1	24.0	23.0	22.6	23.8	24.3	23.5	23.5	27.9	

[1] Although arson data are included in the trend and clearance tables, sufficient data are not available to estimate totals for this offense.

[2] Violent crimes are offenses of murder, forcible rape, robbery, and aggravated assault. Property crimes are offenses of burglary, larceny-theft, and motor vehicle theft. Data are not included for the property crime of arson.

[3] Because of rounding, the percentages may not add to totals.

Complete data were not available for the states of Illinois, Kansas, Kentucky, and Montana; therefore, it was necessary that their crime counts be estimated. An aggregate Florida state total for 1996 was supplied by the Florida Department of Law Enforcement. See "Offense Estimation," pages 389-390 for details.

Table 4. — Index of Crime: Region, Geographic Division, and State, 1995-1996

Area	Year	Population[1]	Crime Index total		Modified Crime Index total[2]		Violent crime[3]		Property crime[3]		Murder and non-negligent manslaughter	
			Number	Rate per 100,000	Number	Rate per 100,000	Number	Rate per 100,000	Number	Rate per 100,000	Number	Rate per 100,000
United States Total [4,7,8]	**1995**	**262,755,000**	**13,862,727**	**5,275.9**			**1,798,792**	**684.6**	**12,063,935**	**4,591.3**	**21,606**	**8.2**
	1996	**265,284,000**	**13,473,614**	**5,078.9**			**1,682,278**	**634.1**	**11,791,336**	**4,444.8**	**19,645**	**7.4**
Percent change			**-2.8**	**-3.7**			**-6.5**	**-7.4**	**-2.3**	**-3.2**	**-9.1**	**-9.8**
Northeast	**1995**	**51,466,000**	**2,151,488**	**4,180.4**			**314,233**	**610.6**	**1,837,255**	**3,569.8**	**3,173**	**6.2**
	1996	**51,580,000**	**2,010,969**	**3,898.7**			**286,494**	**555.4**	**1,724,475**	**3,343.3**	**2,773**	**5.4**
Percent change			**-6.5**	**-6.7**			**-8.8**	**-9.0**	**-6.1**	**-6.3**	**-12.6**	**-12.9**
New England	1995	13,312,000	544,546	4,090.6			62,312	468.1	482,234	3,622.6	459	3.4
	1996	13,351,000	504,393	3,777.9			59,689	447.1	444,704	3,330.9	396	3.0
Percent change			-7.4	-7.6			-4.2	-4.5	-7.8	-8.1	-13.7	-11.8
Connecticut	1995	3,275,000	147,481	4,503.2			13,293	405.9	134,188	4,097.3	150	4.6
	1996	3,274,000	138,414	4,227.7			13,490	412.0	124,924	3,815.6	158	4.8
Percent change			-6.1	-6.1			+1.5	+1.5	-6.9	-6.9	+5.3	+4.3
Maine	1995	1,241,000	40,763	3,284.7			1,631	131.4	39,132	3,153.3	25	2.0
	1996	1,243,000	42,189	3,394.1			1,553	124.9	40,636	3,269.2	25	2.0
Percent change			+3.5	+3.3			-4.8	-4.9	+3.8	+3.7	—	—
Massachussetts	1995	6,074,000	263,710	4,341.6			41,739	687.2	221,971	3,654.4	217	3.6
	1996	6,092,000	233,758	3,837.1			39,122	642.2	194,636	3,194.9	157	2.6
Percent change			-11.4	-11.6			-6.3	-6.5	-12.3	-12.6	-27.6	-27.8
New Hampshire	1995	1,148,000	30,484	2,655.4			1,314	114.5	29,170	2,540.9	21	1.8
	1996	1,162,000	32,809	2,823.5			1,373	118.2	31,436	2,705.3	20	1.7
Percent change			+7.6	+6.3			+4.5	+3.2	+7.8	+6.5	-4.8	-5.6
Rhode Island	1995	990,000	42,021	4,244.5			3,643	368.0	38,378	3,876.6	33	3.3
	1996	990,000	39,536	3,993.5			3,437	347.2	36,099	3,646.4	25	2.5
Percent change			-5.9	-5.9			-5.7	-5.7	-5.9	-5.9	-24.2	-24.2
Vermont	1995	585,000	20,087	3,433.7			692	118.3	19,395	3,315.4	13	2.2
	1996	589,000	17,687	3,002.9			714	121.2	16,973	2,881.7	11	1.9
Percent change			-11.9	-12.5			+3.2	+2.5	-12.5	-13.1	-15.4	-13.6
Middle Atlantic	1995	38,153,000	1,606,942	4,211.8			251,921	660.3	1,355,021	3,551.5	2,714	7.1
	1996	38,229,000	1,506,576	3,940.9			226,805	593.3	1,279,771	3,347.6	2,377	6.2
Percent change			-6.2	-6.4			-10.0	-10.1	-5.6	-5.7	-12.4	-12.7
New Jersey	1995	7,945,000	373,708	4,703.7			47,652	599.8	326,056	4,103.9	409	5.1
	1996	7,988,000	346,116	4,332.9			42,459	531.5	303,657	3,801.4	338	4.2
Percent change			-7.4	-7.9			-10.9	-11.4	-6.9	-7.4	-17.4	-17.6
New York	1995	18,136,000	827,025	4,560.1			152,683	841.9	674,342	3,718.3	1,550	8.5
	1996	18,185,000	751,456	4,132.3			132,206	727.0	619,250	3,405.3	1,353	7.4
Percent change			-9.1	-9.4			-13.4	-13.6	-8.2	-8.4	-12.7	-12.9
Pennsylvania	1995	12,072,000	406,209	3,364.9			51,586	427.3	354,623	2,937.6	755	6.3
	1996	12,056,000	409,004	3,392.5			52,140	432.5	356,864	2,960.1	686	5.7
Percent change			+.7	+.8			+1.1	+1.2	+.6	+.8	-9.1	-9.5

See footnotes at end of table.

Table 4. — Index of Crime: Region, Geographic Division, and State, 1995-1996 — Continued

Forcible rape		Robbery		Aggravated assault		Burglary		Larceny–theft		Motor vehicle theft		Arson[2]	
Number	Rate per 100,000	Number	Rate per 100,000	Number	Rate per 100,000	Number	Rate per 100,000	Number	Rate per 100,000	Number	Rate per 100,000	Number	Rate per 100,000
97,470	**37.1**	**580,509**	**220.9**	**1,099,207**	**418.3**	**2,593,784**	**987.1**	**7,997,710**	**3,043.8**	**1,472,441**	**560.4**		
95,769	**36.1**	**537,050**	**202.4**	**1,029,814**	**388.2**	**2,501,524**	**943.0**	**7,894,620**	**2,975.9**	**1,395,192**	**525.9**		
-1.7	**-2.7**	**-7.5**	**-8.4**	**-6.3**	**-7.2**	**-3.6**	**-4.5**	**-1.3**	**-2.2**	**-5.2**	**-6.2**		
12,828	**24.9**	**133,944**	**260.3**	**164,288**	**319.2**	**390,180**	**758.1**	**1,181,573**	**2,295.8**	**265,502**	**515.9**		
12,830	**24.9**	**119,754**	**232.2**	**151,137**	**293.0**	**356,503**	**691.2**	**1,124,725**	**2,180.5**	**243,247**	**471.6**		
—	**—**	**-10.6**	**-10.8**	**-8.0**	**-8.2**	**-8.6**	**-8.8**	**-4.8**	**-5.0**	**-8.4**	**-8.6**		
3,565	26.8	16,108	121.0	42,180	316.9	106,270	798.3	313,059	2,351.7	62,905	472.5		
3,632	27.2	14,854	111.3	40,807	305.6	96,935	726.1	290,549	2,176.2	57,220	428.6		
+1.9	+1.5	-7.8	-8.0	-3.3	-3.6	-8.8	-9.0	-7.2	-7.5	-9.0	-9.3		
776	23.7	5,345	163.2	7,022	214.4	29,095	888.4	87,401	2,668.7	17,692	540.2		
755	23.1	5,552	169.6	7,025	214.6	27,574	842.2	81,328	2,484.1	16,022	489.4		
-2.7	-2.5	+3.9	+3.9	—	+.1	-5.2	-5.2	-6.9	-6.9	-9.4	-9.4		
265	21.4	334	26.9	1,007	81.1	9,015	726.4	28,444	2,292.0	1,673	134.8		
260	20.9	292	23.5	976	78.5	9,303	748.4	29,557	2,377.9	1,776	142.9		
-1.9	-2.3	-12.6	-12.6	-3.1	-3.2	+3.2	+3.0	+3.9	+3.7	+6.2	+6.0		
1,759	29.0	9,137	150.4	30,626	504.2	49,669	817.7	135,586	2,232.2	36,716	604.5		
1,767	29.0	7,778	127.7	29,420	482.9	42,896	704.1	119,562	1,962.6	32,178	528.2		
+.5	—	-14.9	-15.1	-3.9	-4.2	-13.6	-13.9	-11.8	-12.1	-12.4	-12.6		
333	29.0	314	27.4	646	56.3	4,806	418.6	22,698	1,977.2	1,666	145.1		
404	34.8	317	27.3	632	54.4	5,063	435.7	24,611	2,118.0	1,762	151.6		
+21.3	+20.0	+1.0	-.4	-2.2	-3.4	+5.3	+4.1	+8.4	+7.1	+5.8	+4.5		
267	27.0	914	92.3	2,429	245.4	9,234	932.7	24,780	2,503.0	4,364	440.8		
287	29.0	824	83.2	2,301	232.4	8,135	821.7	23,367	2,360.3	4,597	464.3		
+7.5	+7.4	-9.8	-9.9	-5.3	-5.3	-11.9	-11.9	-5.7	-5.7	+5.3	+5.3		
165	28.2	64	10.9	450	76.9	4,451	760.9	14,150	2,418.8	794	135.7		
159	27.0	91	15.4	453	76.9	3,964	673.0	12,124	2,058.4	885	150.3		
-3.6	-4.3	+42.2	+41.3	+.7	—	-10.9	-11.6	-14.3	-14.9	+11.5	+10.8		
9,263	24.3	117,836	308.9	122,108	320.0	283,910	744.1	868,514	2,276.4	202,597	531.0		
9,198	24.1	104,900	274.4	110,330	288.6	259,568	679.0	834,176	2,182.1	186,027	486.6		
-.7	-.8	-11.0	-11.2	-9.6	-9.8	-8.6	-8.7	-4.0	-4.1	-8.2	-8.4		
1,927	24.3	22,486	283.0	22,830	287.4	69,533	875.2	206,339	2,597.1	50,184	631.6		
1,976	24.7	18,838	235.8	21,307	266.7	63,259	791.9	193,961	2,428.2	46,437	581.3		
+2.5	+1.6	-16.2	-16.7	-6.7	-7.2	-9.0	-9.5	-6.0	-6.5	-7.5	-8.0		
4,290	23.7	72,492	399.7	74,351	410.0	146,562	808.1	425,184	2,344.4	102,596	565.7		
4,174	23.0	61,822	340.0	64,857	356.7	129,828	713.9	399,522	2,197.0	89,900	494.4		
-2.7	-3.0	-14.7	-14.9	-12.8	-13.0	-11.4	-11.7	-6.0	-6.3	-12.4	-12.6		
3,046	25.2	22,858	189.3	24,927	206.5	67,815	561.8	236,991	1,963.1	49,817	412.7		
3,048	25.3	24,240	201.1	24,166	200.4	66,481	551.4	240,693	1,996.5	49,690	412.2		
+.1	+.4	+6.0	+6.2	-3.1	-3.0	-2.0	-1.9	+1.6	+1.7	-.3	-.1		

Table 4. — Index of Crime: Region, Geographic Division, and State, 1995-1996 — Continued

Area	Year	Population[1]	Crime Index total		Modified Crime Index total[2]		Violent crime[3]		Property crime[3]		Murder and non-negligent manslaughter	
			Number	Rate per 100,000	Number	Rate per 100,000	Number	Rate per 100,000	Number	Rate per 100,000	Number	Rate per 100,000
Midwest[4]	**1995**	**61,804,000**	**2,936,313**	**4,751.0**			**363,105**	**587.5**	**2,573,208**	**4,163.5**	**4,242**	**6.9**
	1996	**62,082,000**	**2,895,531**	**4,664.0**			**333,121**	**536.6**	**2,562,410**	**4,127.5**	**3,957**	**6.4**
Percent change			**-1.4**	**-1.8**			**-8.3**	**-8.7**	**-.4**	**-.9**	**-6.7**	**-7.2**
East North Central[4]	1995	43,456,000	2,099,366	4,831.0			282,165	649.3	1,817,201	4,181.7	3,314	7.6
	1996	43,614,000	2,078,488	4,765.6			258,237	592.1	1,820,251	4,173.5	3,063	7.0
Percent change			-1.0	-1.4			-8.5	-8.8	+.2	-.2	-7.6	-7.9
Illinois[4]	1995	11,830,000	645,408	5,455.7			117,836	996.1	527,572	4,459.6	1,221	10.3
	1996	11,847,000	629,762	5,315.8			104,985	886.2	524,777	4,429.6	1,179	10.0
Percent change			-2.4	-2.6			-10.9	-11.0	-.5	-.7	-3.4	-2.9
Indiana	1995	5,803,000	268,768	4,631.5			30,451	524.7	238,317	4,106.8	466	8.0
	1996	5,841,000	262,742	4,498.2			31,366	537.0	231,376	3,961.2	420	7.2
Percent change			-2.2	-2.9			+3.0	+2.3	-2.9	-3.5	-9.9	-10.0
Michigan	1995	9,549,000	494,903	5,182.8			65,680	687.8	429,223	4,495.0	808	8.5
	1996	9,594,000	490,971	5,117.5			60,951	635.3	430,020	4,482.2	722	7.5
Percent change			-.8	-1.3			-7.2	-7.6	+.2	-.3	-10.6	-11.8
Ohio	1995	11,151,000	491,223	4,405.2			53,799	482.5	437,424	3,922.7	600	5.4
	1996	11,173,000	497,831	4,455.7			47,896	428.7	449,935	4,027.0	538	4.8
Percent change			+1.3	+1.1			-11.0	-11.2	+2.9	+2.7	-10.3	-11.1
Wisconsin	1995	5,123,000	199,064	3,885.7			14,399	281.1	184,665	3,604.6	219	4.3
	1996	5,160,000	197,182	3,821.4			13,039	252.7	184,143	3,568.7	204	4.0
Percent change			-.9	-1.7			-9.4	-10.1	-.3	-1.0	-6.8	-7.0
West North Central[4]	1995	18,348,000	836,947	4,561.5			80,940	441.1	756,007	4,120.4	928	5.1
	1996	18,468,000	817,043	4,424.1			74,884	405.5	742,159	4,018.6	894	4.8
Percent change			-2.4	-3.0			-7.5	-8.1	-1.8	-2.5	-3.7	-5.9
Iowa	1995	2,842,000	116,575	4,101.9			10,071	354.4	106,504	3,747.5	51	1.8
	1996	2,852,000	104,067	3,648.9			7,771	272.5	96,296	3,376.4	53	1.9
Percent change			-10.7	-11.0			-22.8	-23.1	-9.6	-9.9	+3.9	+5.6
Kansas[4]	1995	2,565,000	125,350	4,886.9			10,792	420.7	114,558	4,466.2	159	6.2
	1996	2,572,000	120,414	4,681.7			10,642	413.8	109,772	4,268.0	170	6.6
Percent change			-3.9	-4.2			-1.4	-1.6	-4.2	-4.4	+6.9	+6.5
Minnesota	1995	4,610,000	207,327	4,497.3			16,416	356.1	190,911	4,141.2	182	3.9
	1996	4,658,000	207,891	4,463.1			15,782	338.8	192,109	4,124.3	167	3.6
Percent change			+.3	-.8			-3.9	-4.9	+.6	-.4	-8.2	-7.7
Missouri	1995	5,324,000	272,617	5,120.5			35,339	663.8	237,278	4,456.8	469	8.8
	1996	5,359,000	272,450	5,084.0			31,669	590.9	240,781	4,493.0	433	8.1
Percent change			-.1	-.7			-10.4	-11.0	+1.5	+.8	-7.7	-8.0
Nebraska	1995	1,637,000	74,393	4,544.5			6,253	382.0	68,140	4,162.5	48	2.9
	1996	1,652,000	73,292	4,436.6			7,182	434.7	66,110	4,001.8	48	2.9
Percent change			-1.5	-2.4			+14.9	+13.8	-3.0	-3.9	—	—
North Dakota	1995	641,000	18,373	2,866.3			556	86.7	17,817	2,779.6	6	.9
	1996	644,000	17,189	2,669.1			541	84.0	16,648	2,585.1	14	2.2
Percent change			-6.4	-6.9			-2.7	-3.1	-6.6	-7.0	+133.3	+144.4
South Dakota	1995	729,000	22,312	3,060.6			1,513	207.5	20,799	2,853.1	13	1.8
	1996	732,000	21,740	2,969.9			1,297	177.2	20,443	2,792.8	9	1.2
Percent change			-2.6	-3.0			-14.3	-14.6	-1.7	-2.1	-30.8	-33.3

See footnotes at end of table.

66

Table 4. — Index of Crime: Region, Geographic Division, and State, 1995-1996 — Continued

Forcible rape		Robbery		Aggravated assault		Burglary		Larceny–theft		Motor vehicle theft		Arson[2]	
Number	Rate per 100,000	Number	Rate per 100,000	Number	Rate per 100,000	Number	Rate per 100,000	Number	Rate per 100,000	Number	Rate per 100,000	Number	Rate per 100,000
24,812	**40.1**	**112,350**	**181.8**	**221,701**	**358.7**	**519,928**	**841.3**	**1,774,505**	**2,871.2**	**278,775**	**451.1**		
23,664	**38.1**	**100,130**	**161.3**	**205,370**	**330.8**	**507,414**	**817.3**	**1,780,072**	**2,867.3**	**274,924**	**442.8**		
-4.6	**-5.0**	**-10.9**	**-11.3**	**-7.4**	**-7.8**	**-2.4**	**-2.9**	**+.3**	**-.1**	**-1.4**	**-1.8**		
18,189	41.9	90,183	207.5	170,479	392.3	368,058	847.0	1,233,720	2,839.0	215,423	495.7		
17,212	39.5	80,580	184.8	157,382	360.9	363,567	833.6	1,243,213	2,850.5	213,471	489.5		
-5.4	-5.7	-10.6	-10.9	-7.7	-8.0	-1.2	-1.6	+.8	+.4	-.9	-1.3		
4,313	36.5	39,139	330.8	73,163	618.5	108,555	917.6	357,143	3,019.0	61,874	523.0		
4,051	34.2	33,106	279.4	66,649	562.6	108,185	913.2	358,515	3,026.2	58,077	490.2		
-6.1	-6.3	-15.4	-15.5	-8.9	-9.0	-.3	-.5	+.4	+.2	-6.1	-6.3		
1,930	33.3	7,844	135.2	20,211	348.3	47,676	821.6	163,618	2,819.5	27,023	465.7		
1,992	34.1	7,249	124.1	21,705	371.6	45,782	783.8	160,777	2,752.6	24,817	424.9		
+3.2	+2.4	-7.6	-8.2	+7.4	+6.7	-4.0	-4.6	-1.7	-2.4	-8.2	-8.8		
5,917	62.0	17,885	187.3	41,070	430.1	86,872	909.7	280,712	2,939.7	61,639	645.5		
5,466	57.0	16,907	176.2	37,856	394.6	85,908	895.4	276,909	2,886.3	67,203	700.5		
-7.6	-8.1	-5.5	-5.9	-7.8	-8.3	-1.1	-1.6	-1.4	-1.8	+9.0	+8.5		
4,835	43.4	19,931	178.7	28,433	255.0	93,539	838.8	297,624	2,669.0	46,261	414.9		
4,617	41.3	18,336	164.1	24,405	218.4	93,336	835.4	311,071	2,784.1	45,528	407.5		
-4.5	-4.8	-8.0	-8.2	-14.2	-14.4	-.2	-.4	+4.5	+4.3	-1.6	-1.8		
1,194	23.3	5,384	105.1	7,602	148.4	31,416	613.2	134,623	2,627.8	18,626	363.6		
1,086	21.0	4,982	96.6	6,767	131.1	30,356	588.3	135,941	2,634.5	17,846	345.9		
-9.0	-9.9	-7.5	-8.1	-11.0	-11.7	-3.4	-4.1	+1.0	+.3	-4.2	-4.9		
6,623	36.1	22,167	120.8	51,222	279.2	151,870	827.7	540,785	2,947.4	63,352	345.3		
6,452	34.9	19,550	105.9	47,988	259.8	143,847	778.9	536,859	2,907.0	61,453	332.8		
-2.6	-3.3	-11.8	-12.3	-6.3	-6.9	-5.3	-5.9	-.7	-1.4	-3.0	-3.6		
619	21.8	1,507	53.0	7,894	277.8	21,527	757.5	78,645	2,767.2	6,332	222.8		
561	19.7	1,286	45.1	5,871	205.9	18,954	664.6	71,893	2,520.8	5,449	191.1		
-9.4	-9.6	-14.7	-14.9	-25.6	-25.9	-12.0	-12.3	-8.6	-8.9	-13.9	-14.2		
938	36.6	2,775	108.2	6,920	269.8	27,404	1,068.4	78,855	3,074.3	8,299	323.5		
1,096	42.6	2,476	96.3	6,900	268.3	25,239	981.3	78,145	3,038.3	6,388	248.4		
+16.8	+16.4	-10.8	-11.0	-.3	-.6	-7.9	-8.2	-.9	-1.2	-23.0	-23.2		
2,593	56.2	5,702	123.7	7,939	172.2	36,756	797.3	138,414	3,002.5	15,741	341.5		
2,327	50.0	5,385	115.6	7,903	169.7	35,515	762.5	138,671	2,977.1	17,923	384.8		
-10.3	-11.0	-5.6	-6.5	-.5	-1.5	-3.4	-4.4	+.2	-.8	+13.9	+12.7		
1,711	32.1	10,863	204.0	22,296	418.8	49,649	932.6	162,430	3,050.9	25,199	473.3		
1,566	29.2	9,142	170.6	20,528	383.1	47,919	894.2	168,870	3,151.1	23,992	447.7		
-8.5	-9.0	-15.8	-16.4	-7.9	-8.5	-3.5	-4.1	+4.0	+3.3	-4.8	-5.4		
317	19.4	1,067	65.2	4,821	294.5	10,344	631.9	52,044	3,179.2	5,752	351.4		
447	27.1	1,052	63.7	5,635	341.1	10,152	614.5	50,315	3,045.7	5,643	341.6		
+41.0	+39.7	-1.4	-2.3	+16.9	+15.8	-1.9	-2.8	-3.3	-4.2	-1.9	-2.8		
146	22.8	64	10.0	340	53.0	2,248	350.7	14,421	2,249.8	1,148	179.1		
155	24.1	71	11.0	301	46.7	1,991	309.2	13,433	2,085.9	1,224	190.1		
+6.2	+5.7	+10.9	+10.0	-11.5	-11.9	-11.4	-11.8	-6.9	-7.3	+6.6	+6.1		
299	41.0	189	25.9	1,012	138.8	3,942	540.7	15,976	2,191.5	881	120.9		
300	41.0	138	18.9	850	116.1	4,077	557.0	15,532	2,121.9	834	113.9		
+.3	—	-27.0	-27.0	-16.0	-16.4	+3.4	+3.0	-2.8	-3.2	-5.3	-5.8		

Table 4. — Index of Crime: Region, Geographic Division, and State, 1995-1996 — Continued

Area	Year	Population[1]	Crime Index total		Modified Crime Index total[2]		Violent crime[3]		Property crime[3]		Murder and non-negligent manslaughter	
			Number	Rate per 100,000	Number	Rate per 100,000	Number	Rate per 100,000	Number	Rate per 100,000	Number	Rate per 100,000
South[4,6]	1995	91,890,000	5,275,936	5,741.6			677,702	737.5	4,598,234	5,004.1	9,010	9.8
	1996	93,098,000	5,331,694	5,727.0			657,973	706.8	4,673,721	5,020.2	8,400	9.0
Percent change			+1.1	-.3			-2.9	-4.2	+1.6	+.3	-6.8	-8.2
South Atlantic[4]	1995	46,995,000	2,882,559	6,133.8			379,065	806.6	2,503,494	5,327.1	4,262	9.1
	1996	47,616,000	2,895,896	6,081.8			370,363	777.8	2,525,533	5,304.0	4,243	8.9
Percent change			+.5	-.8			-2.3	-3.6	+.9	-.4	-.4	-2.2
Delaware	1995	717,000	36,988	5,158.7			5,198	725.0	31,790	4,433.8	25	3.5
	1996	725,000	35,488	4,894.9			4,845	668.3	30,643	4,226.6	31	4.3
Percent change			-4.1	-5.1			-6.8	-7.8	-3.6	-4.7	+24.0	+22.9
District of Columbia[5]	1995	554,000	67,441	12,173.5			14,744	2,661.4	52,697	9,512.1	360	65.0
	1996	543,000	64,599	11,896.7			13,411	2,469.8	51,188	9,426.9	397	73.1
Percent change			-4.2	-2.3			-9.0	-7.2	-2.9	-.9	+10.3	+12.5
Florida[4]	1995	14,166,000	1,090,999	7,701.5			151,711	1,071.0	939,288	6,630.6	1,037	7.3
	1996	14,400,000	1,079,623	7,497.4			151,350	1,051.0	928,273	6,446.3	1,077	7.5
Percent change			-1.0	-2.7			-.2	-1.9	-1.2	-2.8	+3.9	+2.7
Georgia	1995	7,201,000	432,322	6,003.6			47,317	657.1	385,005	5,346.5	683	9.5
	1996	7,353,000	463,952	6,309.7			46,966	638.7	416,986	5,671.0	630	8.6
Percent change			+7.3	+5.1			-.7	-2.8	+8.3	+6.1	-7.8	-9.5
Maryland	1995	5,042,000	317,382	6,294.8			49,757	986.9	267,625	5,307.9	596	11.8
	1996	5,072,000	307,461	6,061.9			47,230	931.2	260,231	5,130.7	588	11.6
Percent change			-3.1	-3.7			-5.1	-5.6	-2.8	-3.3	-1.3	-1.7
North Carolina	1995	7,195,000	405,764	5,639.5			46,508	646.4	359,256	4,993.1	677	9.4
	1996	7,323,000	404,684	5,526.2			43,068	588.1	361,616	4,938.1	619	8.5
Percent change			-.3	-2.0			-7.4	-9.0	+.7	-1.1	-8.6	-9.6
South Carolina	1995	3,673,000	222,723	6,063.8			36,067	981.9	186,656	5,081.8	292	7.9
	1996	3,699,000	229,861	6,214.1			36,875	996.9	192,986	5,217.2	332	9.0
Percent change			+3.2	+2.5			+2.2	+1.5	+3.4	+2.7	+13.7	+13.9
Virginia	1995	6,618,000	264,005	3,989.2			23,921	361.5	240,084	3,627.7	503	7.6
	1996	6,675,000	264,882	3,968.3			22,782	341.3	242,100	3,627.0	500	7.5
Percent change			+.3	-.5			-4.8	-5.6	+.8	—	-.6	-1.3
West Virginia	1995	1,828,000	44,935	2,458.2			3,842	210.2	41,093	2,248.0	89	4.9
	1996	1,826,000	45,346	2,483.4			3,836	210.1	41,510	2,273.3	69	3.8
Percent change			+.9	+1.0			-.2	—	+1.0	+1.1	-22.5	-22.4
East South Central	1995	16,066,000	739,184	4,600.9			95,082	591.8	644,102	4,009.1	1,656	10.3
	1996	16,193,000	741,687	4,580.3			91,043	562.2	650,644	4,018.1	1,476	9.1
Percent change			+.3	-.4			-4.2	-5.0	+1.0	+.2	-10.9	-11.7
Alabama	1995	4,253,000	206,188	4,848.1			26,894	632.4	179,294	4,215.7	475	11.2
	1996	4,273,000	205,962	4,820.1			24,159	565.4	181,803	4,254.7	444	10.4
Percent change			-.1	-.6			-10.2	-10.6	+1.4	+.9	-6.5	-7.1
Kentucky[4]	1995	3,860,000	129,377	3,351.7			14,079	364.7	115,298	2,987.0	276	7.2
	1996	3,884,000	122,979	3,166.3			12,448	320.5	110,531	2,845.8	228	5.9
Percent change			-4.9	-5.5			-11.6	-12.1	-4.1	-4.7	-17.4	-18.1
Mississippi	1995	2,697,000	121,755	4,514.5			13,560	502.8	108,195	4,011.7	348	12.9
	1996	2,716,000	122,842	4,522.9			13,261	488.3	109,581	4,034.6	301	11.1
Percent change			+.9	+.2			-2.2	-2.9	+1.3	+.6	-13.5	-14.0
Tennessee	1995	5,256,000	281,864	5,362.7			40,549	771.5	241,315	4,591.2	557	10.6
	1996	5,320,000	289,904	5,449.3			41,175	774.0	248,729	4,675.4	503	9.5
Percent change			+2.9	+1.6			+1.5	+.3	+3.1	+1.8	-9.7	-10.4
West South Central[6]	1995	28,828,000	1,654,193	5,738.1			203,555	706.1	1,450,638	5,032.0	3,092	10.7
	1996	29,290,000	1,694,111	5,783.9			196,567	671.1	1,497,544	5,112.8	2,681	9.2
Percent change			+2.4	+.8			-3.4	-5.0	+3.2	+1.6	-13.3	-14.0
Arkansas	1995	2,484,000	116,521	4,690.9			13,741	553.2	102,780	4,137.7	259	10.4
	1996	2,510,000	117,951	4,699.2			13,161	524.3	104,790	4,174.9	219	8.7
Percent change			+1.2	+.2			-4.2	-5.2	+2.0	+.9	-15.4	-16.3
Louisiana	1995	4,342,000	289,873	6,676.0			43,741	1,007.4	246,132	5,668.6	740	17.0
	1996	4,351,000	297,556	6,838.8			40,426	929.1	257,130	5,909.7	762	17.5
Percent change			+2.7	+2.4			-7.6	-7.8	+4.5	+4.3	+3.0	+2.9
Oklahoma[6]	1995	3,278,000	183,463	5,596.8			21,770	664.1	161,693	4,932.7	400	12.2
	1996	3,301,000	186,602	5,652.9			19,710	597.1	166,892	5,055.8	223	6.8
Percent change			+1.7	+1.0			-9.5	-10.1	+3.2	+2.5	-44.3	-44.3
Texas	1995	18,724,000	1,064,336	5,684.3			124,303	663.9	940,033	5,020.5	1,693	9.0
	1996	19,128,000	1,092,002	5,708.9			123,270	644.4	968,732	5,064.5	1,477	7.7
Percent change			+2.6	+.4			-.8	-2.9	+3.1	+.9	-12.8	-14.4

See footnotes at end of table.

Table 4. — Index of Crime: Region, Geographic Division, and State, 1995-1996 — Continued

	Forcible rape		Robbery		Aggravated assault		Burglary		Larceny–theft		Motor vehicle theft		Arson[2]	
	Number	Rate per 100,000	Number	Rate per 100,000	Number	Rate per 100,000	Number	Rate per 100,000	Number	Rate per 100,000	Number	Rate per 100,000	Number	Rate per 100,000
	37,583	**40.9**	**195,143**	**212.4**	**435,966**	**474.4**	**1,044,918**	**1,137.1**	**3,066,121**	**3,336.7**	**487,195**	**530.2**		
	37,590	**40.4**	**189,253**	**203.3**	**422,730**	**454.1**	**1,050,622**	**1,128.5**	**3,135,724**	**3,368.2**	**487,375**	**523.5**		
	—	**-1.2**	**-3.0**	**-4.3**	**-3.0**	**-4.3**	**+.5**	**-.8**	**+2.3**	**+.9**	**—**	**-1.3**		
	18,667	39.7	115,741	246.3	240,395	511.5	559,772	1,191.1	1,680,341	3,575.6	263,381	560.4		
	18,735	39.3	111,715	234.6	235,670	494.9	562,273	1,180.8	1,701,816	3574.0	261,444	549.1		
	+.4	-1.0	-3.5	-4.8	-2.0	-3.2	+.4	-.9	+1.3	—	-.7	-2.0		
	575	80.2	1,425	198.7	3,173	442.5	6,491	905.3	22,329	3,114.2	2,970	414.2		
	454	62.6	1,304	179.9	3,056	421.5	5,830	804.1	21,665	2,988.3	3,148	434.2		
	-21.0	-21.9	-8.5	-9.5	-3.7	-4.7	-10.2	-11.2	-3.0	-4.0	+6.0	+4.8		
	292	52.7	6,864	1,239.0	7,228	1,304.7	10,185	1,838.4	32,319	5,833.8	10,193	1,839.9		
	260	47.9	6,444	1,186.7	6,310	1,162.1	9,828	1,809.9	31,385	5,779.9	9,975	1,837.0		
	-11.0	-9.1	-6.1	-4.2	-12.7	-10.9	-3.5	-1.6	-2.9	-.9	-2.1	-.2		
	6,887	48.6	42,485	299.9	101,302	715.1	215,657	1,522.4	612,311	4,322.4	111,320	785.8		
	7,508	52.1	41,643	289.2	101,122	702.2	219,056	1,521.2	605,448	4,204.5	103,769	720.6		
	+9.0	+7.2	-2.0	-3.6	-.2	-1.8	+1.6	-.1	-1.1	-2.7	-6.8	-8.3		
	2,539	35.3	14,777	205.2	29,318	407.1	76,324	1,059.9	264,872	3,678.3	43,809	608.4		
	2,357	32.1	15,100	205.4	28,879	392.8	81,968	1,114.8	288,803	3,927.7	46,215	628.5		
	-7.2	-9.1	+2.2	+.1	-1.5	-3.5	+7.4	+5.2	+9.0	+6.8	+5.5	+3.3		
	2,130	42.2	21,334	423.1	25,697	509.7	53,320	1,057.5	178,126	3,532.8	36,179	717.6		
	1,905	37.6	19,944	393.2	24,793	488.8	50,331	992.3	173,817	3,427.0	36,083	711.4		
	-10.6	-10.9	-6.5	-7.1	-3.5	-4.1	-5.6	-6.2	-2.4	-3.0	-.3	-.9		
	2,320	32.2	12,896	179.2	30,615	425.5	101,995	1,417.6	234,911	3,264.9	22,350	310.6		
	2,289	31.3	12,001	163.9	28,159	384.5	98,539	1,345.6	238,511	3,257.0	24,566	335.5		
	-1.3	-2.8	-6.9	-8.5	-8.0	-9.6	-3.4	-5.1	+1.5	-.2	+9.9	+8.0		
	1,737	47.3	6,461	175.9	27,577	750.8	46,083	1,254.6	126,416	3,441.8	14,157	385.4		
	1,821	49.2	6,361	172.0	28,361	766.7	47,487	1,283.8	129,650	3,505.0	15,849	428.5		
	+4.8	+4.0	-1.5	-2.2	+2.8	+2.1	+3.0	+2.3	+2.6	+1.8	+12.0	+11.2		
	1,799	27.2	8,718	131.7	12,901	194.9	39,388	595.2	181,333	2,740.0	19,363	292.6		
	1,783	26.7	8,181	122.6	12,318	184.5	39,255	588.1	184,237	2,760.1	18,608	278.8		
	-.9	-1.8	-6.2	-6.9	-4.5	-5.3	-.3	-1.2	+1.6	+.7	-3.9	-4.7		
	388	21.2	781	42.7	2,584	141.4	10,329	565.0	27,724	1,516.6	3,040	166.3		
	358	19.6	737	40.4	2,672	146.3	9,979	546.5	28,300	1,549.8	3,231	176.9		
	-7.7	-7.5	-5.6	-5.4	+3.4	+3.5	-3.4	-3.3	+2.1	+2.2	+6.3	+6.4		
	6,112	38.0	27,163	169.1	60,151	374.4	162,566	1,011.9	412,983	2,570.5	68,553	426.7		
	6,083	37.6	26,315	162.5	57,169	353.0	162,208	1,001.7	418,707	2,585.7	69,729	430.6		
	-.5	-1.1	-3.1	-3.9	-5.0	-5.7	-.2	-1.0	+1.4	+.6	+1.7	+.9		
	1,350	31.7	7,900	185.8	17,169	403.7	43,586	1,024.8	120,967	2,844.3	14,741	346.6		
	1,397	32.7	7,124	166.7	15,194	355.6	42,821	1,002.1	123,350	2,886.7	15,632	365.8		
	+3.5	+3.2	-9.8	-10.3	-11.5	-11.9	-1.8	-2.2	'+2.0	+1.5	+6.0	+5.5		
	1,231	31.9	4,001	103.7	8,571	222.0	28,389	735.5	76,906	1,992.4	10,003	259.1		
	1,230	31.7	3,643	93.8	7,347	189.2	26,736	688.4	73,653	1,896.3	10,142	261.1		
	-.1	-.6	-8.9	-9.5	-14.3	-14.8	-5.8	-6.4	-4.2	-4.8	+1.4	+.7		
	1,054	39.1	3,530	130.9	8,628	319.9	30,505	1,131.1	67,967	2,520.1	9,723	360.5		
	981	36.1	3,646	134.2	8,333	306.8	30,755	1,132.4	69,299	2,551.5	9,527	350.8		
	-6.9	-7.7	+3.3	+2.5	-3.4	-4.1	+.8	+.1	+2.0	+1.2	-2.0	-2.7		
	2,477	47.1	11,732	223.2	25,783	490.5	60,086	1,143.2	147,143	2,799.5	34,086	648.5		
	2,475	46.5	11,902	223.7	26,295	494.3	61,896	1,163.5	152,405	2,864.8	34,428	647.1		
	-.1	-1.3	+1.4	+.2	+2.0	+.8	+3.0	+1.8	+3.6	+2.3	+1.0	-.2		
	12,804	44.4	52,239	181.2	135,420	469.8	322,580	1,119.0	972,797	3,374.5	155,261	538.6		
	12,772	43.6	51,223	174.9	129,891	443.5	326,141	1,113.5	1,015,201	3,466.0	156,202	533.3		
	-.2	-1.8	-1.9	-3.5	-4.1	-5.6	+1.1	-.5	+4.4	+2.7	+.6	-1.0		
	925	37.2	3,122	125.7	9,435	379.8	24,763	996.9	69,935	2,815.4	8,082	325.4		
	1,046	41.7	2,864	114.1	9,032	359.8	23,925	953.2	73,010	2,908.8	7,855	312.9		
	+13.1	+12.1	-8.3	-9.2	-4.3	-5.3	-3.4	-4.4	+4.4	+3.3	-2.8	-3.8		
	1,855	42.7	11,662	268.6	29,484	679.0	53,481	1,231.7	166,667	3,838.5	25,984	598.4		
	1,805	41.5	12,036	276.6	25,823	593.5	56,379	1,295.8	173,271	3,982.3	27,480	631.6		
	-2.7	-2.8	+3.2	+3.0	-12.4	-12.6	+5.4	+5.2	+4.0	+3.7	+5.8	+5.5		
	1,461	44.6	3,788	115.6	16,121	491.8	41,694	1,271.9	103,727	3,164.3	16,272	496.4		
	1,545	46.8	3,519	106.6	14,423	436.9	41,447	1,255.6	109,506	3,317.4	15,939	482.9		
	+5.7	+4.9	-7.1	-7.8	-10.5	-11.2	-.6	-1.3	+5.6	+4.8	-2.0	-2.7		
	8,563	45.7	33,667	179.8	80,380	429.3	202,642	1,082.3	632,468	3,377.8	104,923	560.4		
	8,376	43.8	32,804	171.5	80,613	421.4	204,390	1,068.5	659,414	3,447.4	104,928	548.6		
	-2.2	-4.2	-2.6	-4.6	+.3	-1.8	+.9	-1.3	+4.3	+2.1	—	-2.1		

Table 4. — Index of Crime: Region, Geographic Division, and State, 1995-1996 — Continued

Area	Year	Population[1]	Crime Index total		Modified Crime Index total[2]		Violent crime[3]		Property crime[3]		Murder and non-negligent manslaughter	
			Number	Rate per 100,000	Number	Rate per 100,000	Number	Rate per 100,000	Number	Rate per 100,000	Number	Rate per 100,000
West[4,7]	1995	57,596,000	3,498,990	6,075.1			443,752	770.5	3,055,238	5,304.6	5,181	9.0
	1996	58,523,000	3,235,420	5,528.5			404,690	691.5	2,830,730	4,837.0	4,515	7.7
Percent change			-7.5	-9.0			-8.8	-10.3	-7.3	-8.8	-12.9	-14.4
Mountain[4,7]	1995	15,645,000	990,120	6,328.7			87,725	560.7	902,395	5,767.9	1,135	7.3
	1996	16,118,000	945,144	5,863.9			83,261	516.6	861,883	5,347.3	1,130	7.0
Percent change			-4.5	-7.3			-5.1	-7.9	-4.5	-7.3	-.4	-4.1
Arizona	1995	4,218,000	346,450	8,213.6			30,095	713.5	316,355	7,500.1	439	10.4
	1996	4,428,000	312,927	7,067.0			27,963	631.5	284,964	6,435.5	377	8.5
Percent change			-9.7	-14.0			-7.1	-11.5	-9.9	-14.2	-14.1	-18.3
Colorado	1995	3,747,000	202,199	5,396.3			16,494	440.2	185,705	4,956.1	216	5.8
	1996	3,823,000	195,681	5,118.5			15,463	404.5	180,218	4,714.0	180	4.7
Percent change			-3.2	-5.1			-6.3	-8.1	-3.0	-4.9	-16.7	-19.0
Idaho	1995	1,163,000	51,189	4,401.5			3,745	322.0	47,444	4,079.4	48	4.1
	1996	1,189,000	47,709	4,012.5			3,177	267.2	44,532	3,745.3	43	3.6
Percent change			-6.8	-8.8			-15.2	-17.0	-6.1	-8.2	-10.4	-12.2
Montana[4,7]	1995	870,000	41,737	4,797.4			1,491	171.4	40,246	4,626.0	35	4.0
	1996	879,000	39,499	4,493.6			1,415	161.0	38,084	4,332.7	34	3.9
Percent change			-5.4	-6.3			-5.1	-6.1	-5.4	-6.3	-2.9	-2.5
Nevada	1995	1,530,000	100,664	6,579.3			14,461	945.2	86,203	5,634.2	163	10.7
	1996	1,603,000	96,052	5,992.0			13,005	811.3	83,047	5,180.7	220	13.7
Percent change			-4.6	-8.9			-10.1	-14.2	-3.7	-8.0	+35.0	+28.0
New Mexico	1995	1,685,000	108,312	6,428.0			13,804	819.2	94,508	5,608.8	148	8.8
	1996	1,713,000	113,097	6,602.3			14,399	840.6	98,698	5,761.7	197	11.5
Percent change			+4.4	+2.7			+4.3	+2.6	+4.4	+2.7	+33.1	+30.7
Utah	1995	1,951,000	118,832	6,090.8			6,415	328.8	112,417	5,762.0	76	3.9
	1996	2,000,000	119,717	5,985.9			6,638	331.9	113,079	5,654.0	63	3.2
Percent change			+.7	-1.7			+3.5	+.9	+.6	-1.9	-17.1	-17.9
Wyoming	1995	480,000	20,737	4,320.2			1,220	254.2	19,517	4,066.0	10	2.1
	1996	481,000	20,462	4,254.1			1,201	249.7	19,261	4,004.4	16	3.3
Percent change			-1.3	-1.5			-1.6	-1.8	-1.3	-1.5	+60.0	+57.1
Pacific	1995	41,951,000	2,508,870	5,980.5			356,027	848.7	2,152,843	5,131.8	4,046	9.6
	1996	42,406,000	2,290,276	5,400.8			321,429	758.0	1,968,847	4,642.9	3,385	8.0
Percent change			-8.7	-9.7			-9.7	-10.7	-8.5	-9.5	-16.3	-16.7
Alaska	1995	604,000	34,753	5,753.8			4,656	770.9	30,097	4,982.9	55	9.1
	1996	607,000	33,084	5,450.4			4,417	727.7	28,667	4,722.7	45	7.4
Percent change			-4.8	-5.3			-5.1	-5.6	-4.8	-5.2	-18.2	-18.7
California	1995	31,589,000	1,841,984	5,831.1			305,154	966.0	1,536,830	4,865.1	3,531	11.2
	1996	31,878,000	1,660,131	5,207.8			274,996	862.7	1,385,135	4,345.1	2,916	9.1
Percent change			-9.9	-10.7			-9.9	-10.7	-9.9	-10.7	-17.4	-18.8
Hawaii	1995	1,187,000	85,447	7,198.6			3,509	295.6	81,938	6,902.9	56	4.7
	1996	1,184,000	77,961	6,584.5			3,322	280.6	74,639	6,304.0	40	3.4
Percent change			-8.8	-8.5			-5.3	-5.1	-8.9	-8.7	-28.6	-27.7
Oregon	1995	3,141,000	206,173	6,563.9			16,408	522.4	189,765	6,041.5	129	4.1
	1996	3,204,000	192,132	5,996.0			14,837	463.1	177,295	5,533.6	129	4.0
Percent change			-6.8	-8.6			-9.6	-11.4	-6.6	-8.4	—	-2.4
Washington	1995	5,431,000	340,513	6,269.8			26,300	484.3	314,213	5,785.5	275	5.1
	1996	5,533,000	326,968	5,909.4			23,857	431.2	303,111	5,478.2	255	4.6
Percent change			-4.0	-5.7			-9.3	-11.0	-3.5	-5.3	-7.3	-9.8
Puerto Rico[8]	1995		106,088				22,450		83,638		864	
	1996		99,788				20,147		79,641		868	
Percent change			-5.9				-10.3		-4.8		+.5	

[1] Populations are Bureau of the Census provisional estimates as of July 1 and are subject to change and may not add to totals due to rounding.

[2] Although arson data are included in the trend and clearance tables, sufficient data are not available to estimate totals for this offense.

[3] Violent crimes are offenses of murder, forcible rape, robbery, and aggravated assault. Property crimes are offenses of burglary, larceny–theft, and motor vehicle theft. Data are not included for the property crime of arson.

[4] Complete data were not available for the states of Illinois, Kansas, Kentucky, and Montana; therefore, it was necessary that their crime counts be estimated. An aggregate Florida state total for 1996 was supplied by the Florida Department of Law Enforcement. See "Offense Estimation," pages 389-390 for details.

[5] Includes offenses reported by the Zoological Police.

[6] The 1995 murder count includes the 168 victims of the bombing of the Alfred P. Murrah Federal Building in Oklahoma City.

[7] The 1995 figures have been adjusted. See "Crime Trends," page 390 for details.

[8] The 1996 Bureau of the Census population estimate for Puerto Rico was not available prior to publication; therefore, no population or rates per 100,000 inhabitants are provided. Data for Puerto Rico are not included in totals.

Offense totals are based on all reporting agencies and estimates for unreported areas.

	Forcible rape		Robbery		Aggravated assault		Burglary		Larceny–theft		Motor vehicle theft		Arson[2]	
	Number	Rate per 100,000	Number	Rate per 100,000	Number	Rate per 100,000	Number	Rate per 100,000	Number	Rate per 100,000	Number	Rate per 100,000	Number	Rate per 100,000
	22,247	**38.6**	**139,072**	**241.5**	**277,252**	**481.4**	**638,758**	**1,109.0**	**1,975,511**	**3,429.9**	**440,969**	**765.6**		
	21,685	**37.1**	**127,913**	**218.6**	**250,577**	**428.2**	**586,985**	**1,003.0**	**1,854,099**	**3,168.2**	**389,646**	**665.8**		
	-2.5	**-3.9**	**-8.0**	**-9.5**	**-9.6**	**-11.1**	**-8.1**	**-9.6**	**-6.1**	**-7.6**	**-11.6**	**-13.0**		
	6,349	40.6	20,430	130.6	59,811	382.3	172,071	1,099.8	633,321	4,048.1	97,003	620.0		
	6,617	41.1	20,874	129.5	54,640	339.0	166,698	1,034.2	604,060	3,747.7	91,125	565.4		
	+4.2	+1.2	+2.2	-.8	-8.6	-11.3	-3.1	-6.0	-4.6	-7.4	-6.1	-8.8		
	1,418	33.6	7,329	173.8	20,909	495.7	59,762	1,416.8	207,763	4,925.6	48,830	1,157.7		
	1,381	31.2	7,429	167.8	18,776	424.0	55,630	1,256.3	188,300	4,252.5	41,034	926.7		
	-2.6	-7.1	+1.4	-3.5	-10.2	-14.5	-6.9	-11.3	-9.4	-13.7	-16.0	-20.0		
	1,480	39.5	3,604	96.2	11,194	298.7	35,001	934.1	136,184	3,634.5	14,520	387.5		
	1,765	46.2	3,755	98.2	9,763	255.4	34,436	900.8	130,576	3,415.5	15,206	397.8		
	+19.3	+17.0	+4.2	+2.1	-12.8	-14.5	-1.6	-3.6	-4.1	-6.0	+4.7	+2.7		
	330	28.4	279	24.0	3,088	265.5	9,069	779.8	35,560	3,057.6	2,815	242.0		
	313	26.3	241	20.3	2,580	217.0	8,431	709.1	33,872	2,848.8	2,229	187.5		
	-5.2	-7.4	-13.6	-15.4	-16.5	-18.3	-7.0	-9.1	-4.7	-6.8	-20.8	-22.5		
	231	26.6	253	29.1	972	111.7	5,060	581.6	32,797	3,769.8	2,389	274.6		
	238	27.1	261	29.7	882	100.3	4,908	558.4	30,928	3,518.5	2,248	255.7		
	+3.0	+1.9	+3.2	+2.1	-9.3	-10.2	-3.0	-4.0	-5.7	-6.7	-5.9	-6.9		
	937	61.2	4,966	324.6	8,395	548.7	20,235	1,322.5	54,563	3,566.2	11,405	745.4		
	856	53.4	4,931	307.6	6,998	436.6	19,558	1,220.1	52,295	3,262.3	11,194	698.3		
	-8.6	-12.7	-.7	-5.2	-16.6	-20.4	-3.3	-7.7	-4.2	-8.5	-1.9	-6.3		
	954	56.6	2,604	154.5	10,098	599.3	24,383	1,447.1	61,478	3,648.5	8,647	513.2		
	1,088	63.5	2,782	162.4	10,332	603.2	23,586	1,376.9	65,139	3,802.6	9,973	582.2		
	+14.0	+12.2	+6.8	+5.1	+2.3	+.7	-3.3	-4.9	+6.0	+4.2	+15.3	+13.4		
	834	42.7	1,309	67.1	4,196	215.1	15,623	800.8	89,202	4,572.1	7,592	389.1		
	836	41.8	1,377	68.9	4,362	218.1	16,965	848.3	87,542	4,377.1	8,572	428.6		
	+.2	-2.1	+5.2	+2.7	+4.0	+1.4	+8.6	+5.9	-1.9	-4.3	+12.9	+10.2		
	165	34.4	86	17.9	959	199.8	2,938	612.1	15,774	3,286.3	805	167.7		
	140	29.1	98	20.4	947	196.9	3,184	662.0	15,408	3,203.3	669	139.1		
	-15.2	-15.4	+14.0	+14.0	-1.3	-1.5	+8.4	+8.2	-2.3	-2.5	-16.9	-17.1		
	15,898	37.9	118,642	282.8	217,441	518.3	466,687	1,112.5	1,342,190	3,199.4	343,966	819.9		
	15,068	35.5	107,039	252.4	195,937	462.1	420,287	991.1	1,250,039	2,947.8	298,521	704.0		
	-5.2	-6.3	-9.8	-10.7	-9.9	-10.8	-9.9	-10.9	-6.9	-7.9	-13.2	-14.1		
	485	80.3	937	155.1	3,179	526.3	5,055	836.9	21,891	3,624.3	3,151	521.7		
	398	65.6	710	117.0	3,264	537.7	5,118	843.2	20,557	3,386.7	2,992	492.9		
	-17.9	-18.3	-24.2	-24.6	+2.7	+2.2	+1.2	+.8	-6.1	-6.6	-5.0	-5.5		
	10,554	33.4	104,611	331.2	186,458	590.3	353,895	1,120.3	902,456	2,856.9	280,479	887.9		
	10,244	32.1	94,222	295.6	167,614	525.8	312,212	979.4	830,457	2,605.1	242,466	760.6		
	-2.9	-3.9	-9.9	-10.7	-10.1	-10.9	-11.8	-12.6	-8.0	-8.8	-13.6	-14.3		
	336	28.3	1,553	130.8	1,564	131.8	13,832	1,165.3	59,907	5,046.9	8,199	690.7		
	326	27.5	1,606	135.6	1,350	114.0	12,781	1,079.5	54,701	4,620.0	7,157	604.5		
	-3.0	-2.8	+3.4	+3.7	-13.7	-13.5	-7.6	-7.4	-8.7	-8.5	-12.7	-12.5		
	1,309	41.7	4,332	137.9	10,638	338.7	34,640	1,102.8	133,075	4,236.7	22,050	702.0		
	1,272	39.7	3,914	122.2	9,522	297.2	31,664	988.3	128,618	4,014.3	17,013	531.0		
	-2.8	-4.8	-9.6	-11.4	-10.5	-12.3	-8.6	-10.4	-3.3	-5.2	-22.8	-24.4		
	3,214	59.2	7,209	132.7	15,602	287.3	59,265	1,091.2	224,861	4,140.3	30,087	554.0		
	2,828	51.1	6,587	119.0	14,187	256.4	58,512	1,057.5	215,706	3,898.5	28,893	522.2		
	-12.0	-13.7	-8.6	-10.3	-9.1	-10.8	-1.3	-3.1	-4.1	-5.8	-4.0	-5.7		
	324		15,753		5,509		27,689		39,960		15,989			
	316		13,900		5,063		27,866		35,652		16,123			
	-2.5		-11.8		-8.1		+.6		-10.8		+.8			

Table 5. — Index of Crime, State, 1996

Area	Population	Crime Index total	Modified Crime Index total[1]	Violent crime[2]	Property crime[3]	Murder and non-negligent man-slaughter	Forcible rape	Robbery	Aggra-vated assault	Burglary	Larceny–theft	Motor vehicle theft	Arson[1]
ALABAMA													
Metropolitan Statistical Area	2,887,286												
Area actually reporting	99.6%	164,208		19,008	145,200	363	1,080	6,416	11,149	33,433	98,257	13,510	
Estimated totals	100.0%	164,766		19,068	145,698	363	1,083	6,433	11,189	33,530	98,618	13,550	
Cities outside metropolitan areas	603,124												
Area actually reporting	93.0%	29,269		3,570	25,699	53	190	545	2,782	5,446	18,885	1,368	
Estimated totals	100.0%	31,456		3,837	27,619	57	204	586	2,990	5,853	20,296	1,470	
Rural	782,590												
Area actually reporting	93.4%	9,094		1,171	7,923	22	103	98	948	3,210	4,142	571	
Estimated totals	100.0%	9,740		1,254	8,486	24	110	105	1,015	3,438	4,436	612	
State Total	**4,273,000**	**205,962**		**24,159**	**181,803**	**444**	**1,397**	**7,124**	**15,194**	**42,821**	**123,350**	**15,632**	
Rate per 100,000 inhabitants		4,820.1		565.4	4,254.7	10.4	32.7	166.7	355.6	1,002.1	2,886.7	365.8	
ALASKA													
Metropolitan Statistical Area	254,774												
Area actually reporting	100.0%	16,178		2,078	14,100	25	198	558	1,297	2,353	10,163	1,584	
Cities outside metropolitan areas	161,128												
Area actually reporting	66.6%	7,463		902	6,561	3	55	79	765	812	5,111	638	
Estimated totals	100.0%	11,209		1,356	9,853	5	83	119	1,149	1,219	7,676	958	
Rural	191,098												
Area actually reporting	100.0%	5,697		983	4,714	15	117	33	818	1,546	2,718	450	
State Total	**607,000**	**33,084**		**4,417**	**28,667**	**45**	**398**	**710**	**3,264**	**5,118**	**20,557**	**2,992**	
Rate per 100,000 inhabitants		5,450.4		727.7	4,722.7	7.4	65.6	117.0	537.7	843.2	3,386.7	492.9	
ARIZONA													
Metropolitan Statistical Area	3,747,461												
Area actually reporting	98.9%	281,916		25,388	256,528	361	1,261	7,148	16,618	49,895	167,456	39,177	
Estimated totals	100.0%	284,934		25,586	259,348	362	1,271	7,198	16,755	50,473	169,363	39,512	
Cities outside metropolitan areas	338,707												
Area actually reporting	89.8%	19,182		1,341	17,841	6	70	186	1,079	2,834	14,061	946	
Estimated totals	100.0%	21,356		1,493	19,863	7	78	207	1,201	3,155	15,655	1,053	
Rural	341,832												
Area actually reporting	78.7%	5,221		695	4,526	6	25	19	645	1,575	2,582	369	
Estimated totals	100.0%	6,637		884	5,753	8	32	24	820	2,002	3,282	469	
State Total	**4,428,000**	**312,927**		**27,963**	**284,964**	**377**	**1,381**	**7,429**	**18,776**	**55,630**	**188,300**	**41,034**	
Rate per 100,000 inhabitants		7,067.0		631.5	6,435.5	8.5	31.2	167.8	424.0	1,256.3	4,252.5	926.7	
ARKANSAS													
Metropolitan Statistical Area	1,204,110												
Area actually reporting	100.0%	75,344		8,761	66,583	116	724	2,177	5,744	13,602	47,618	5,363	
Cities outside metropolitan areas	500,249												
Area actually reporting	100.0%	29,443		3,185	26,258	46	173	603	2,363	6,213	18,528	1,517	
Rural	805,641												
Area actually reporting	100.0%	13,164		1,215	11,949	57	149	84	925	4,110	6,864	975	
State Total	**2,510,000**	**117,951**		**13,161**	**104,790**	**219**	**1,046**	**2,864**	**9,032**	**23,925**	**73,010**	**7,855**	
Rate per 100,000 inhabitants		4,699.2		524.3	4,174.9	8.7	41.7	114.1	359.8	953.2	2,908.8	312.9	
CALIFORNIA													
Metropolitan Statistical Area	30,806,175												
Area actually reporting	100.0%	1,614,420		268,752	1,345,668	2,867	9,911	93,493	162,481	300,242	806,405	239,021	
Cities outside metropolitan areas	442,563												
Area actually reporting	100.0%	27,003		3,213	23,790	25	159	555	2,474	5,753	16,007	2,030	
Rural	629,262												
Area actually reporting	100.0%	18,708		3,031	15,677	24	174	174	2,659	6,217	8,045	1,415	
State Total	**31,878,000**	**1,660,131**		**274,996**	**1,385,135**	**2,916**	**10,244**	**94,222**	**167,614**	**312,212**	**830,457**	**242,466**	
Rate per 100,000 inhabitants		5,207.8		862.7	4,345.1	9.1	32.1	295.6	525.8	979.4	2,605.1	760.6	

See footnotes at end of table.

Table 5. — Index of Crime, State, 1996 — Continued

Area	Population	Crime Index total	Modified Crime Index total[1]	Violent crime[2]	Property crime[3]	Murder and non-negligent man-slaughter	Forcible rape	Robbery	Aggra-vated assault	Burglary	Larceny–theft	Motor vehicle theft	Arson[1]
COLORADO													
Metropolitan Statistical													
Area	3,218,581												
Area actually reporting	96.9%	163,544		13,652	149,892	157	1,539	3,534	8,422	29,299	106,932	13,661	
Estimated totals	100.0%	169,389		14,087	155,302	161	1,584	3,652	8,690	30,189	111,041	14,072	
Cities outside metropolitan areas	286,839												
Area actually reporting	92.9%	17,622		817	16,805	7	111	77	622	2,449	13,731	625	
Estimated totals	100.0%	18,966		879	18,087	8	119	83	669	2,636	14,778	673	
Rural	317,580												
Area actually reporting	99.0%	7,255		492	6,763	11	61	20	400	1,595	4,711	457	
Estimated totals	100.0%	7,326		497	6,829	11	62	20	404	1,611	4,757	461	
State Total	**3,823,000**	**195,681**		**15,463**	**180,218**	**180**	**1,765**	**3,755**	**9,763**	**34,436**	**130,576**	**15,206**	
Rate per 100,000													
inhabitants		5,118.5		404.5	4,714.0	4.7	46.2	98.2	255.4	900.8	3,415.5	397.8	
CONNECTICUT													
Metropolitan Statistical													
Area	3,013,673												
Area actually reporting	100.0%	132,621		12,849	119,772	154	725	5,481	6,489	26,089	78,045	15,638	
Cities outside metropolitan areas	66,969												
Area actually reporting	100.0%	2,373		194	2,179	—	9	38	147	438	1,609	132	
Rural	193,358												
Area actually reporting	100.0%	3,420		447	2,973	4	21	33	389	1,047	1,674	252	
State Total	**3,274,000**	**138,414**		**13,490**	**124,924**	**158**	**755**	**5,552**	**7,025**	**27,574**	**81,328**	**16,022**	
Rate per 100,000													
inhabitants		4,227.7		412.0	3,815.6	4.8	23.1	169.6	214.6	842.2	2,484.1	489.4	
DELAWARE													
Metropolitan Statistical													
Area	601,197												
Area actually reporting	99.9%	29,362		3,812	25,550	21	368	1,157	2,266	4,498	18,068	2,984	
Estimated totals	100.0%	29,374		3,813	25,561	21	368	1,157	2,267	4,499	18,077	2,985	
Cities outside metropolitan areas	30,772												
Area actually reporting	100.0%	2,419		247	2,172	2	14	65	166	366	1,748	58	
Rural	93,031												
Area actually reporting	100.0%	3,695		785	2,910	8	72	82	623	965	1,840	105	
State Total	**725,000**	**35,488**		**4,845**	**30,643**	**31**	**454**	**1,304**	**3,056**	**5,830**	**21,665**	**3,148**	
Rate per 100,000													
inhabitants		4,894.9		668.3	4,226.6	4.3	62.6	179.9	421.5	804.1	2,988.3	434.2	
DISTRICT OF COLUMBIA[4]													
Metropolitan Statistical													
Area	543,000												
Area actually reporting	100.0%	64,599		13,411	51,188	397	260	6,444	6,310	9,828	31,385	9,975	
Cities outside metropolitan areas	NONE												
Rural	NONE												
State Total	**543,000**	**64,599**		**13,411**	**51,188**	**397**	**260**	**6,444**	**6,310**	**9,828**	**31,385**	**9,975**	
Rate per 100,000													
inhabitants		11,896.7		2,469.8	9,426.9	73.1	47.9	1,186.7	1,162.1	1,809.9	5,779.9	1,837.0	
FLORIDA[5]													
State Total	**14,400,000**	**1,079,623**		**151,350**	**928,273**	**1,077**	**7,508**	**41,643**	**101,122**	**219,056**	**605,448**	**103,769**	
Rate per 100,000													
inhabitants		7,497.4		1,051.0	6,446.3	7.5	52.1	289.2	702.2	1,521.2	4,204.5	720.6	

See footnotes at end of table.

Table 5. — Index of Crime, State, 1996 — Continued

Area	Population	Crime Index total	Modified Crime Index total[1]	Violent crime[2]	Property crime[3]	Murder and non-negligent man-slaughter	Forcible rape	Robbery	Aggra-vated assault	Burglary	Larceny-theft	Motor vehicle theft	Arson[1]
GEORGIA													
Metropolitan Statistical Area	5,010,645												
Area actually reporting	97.7%	350,917		34,523	316,394	468	1,758	13,022	19,275	59,017	217,629	39,748	
Estimated totals	100.0%	357,907		35,018	322,889	474	1,791	13,212	19,541	60,213	222,138	40,538	
Cities outside metropolitan areas	894,913												
Area actually reporting	95.0%	62,219		7,053	55,166	73	259	1,422	5,299	10,446	42,064	2,656	
Estimated totals	100.0%	65,515		7,427	58,088	77	273	1,497	5,580	10,999	44,292	2,797	
Rural	1,447,442												
Area actually reporting	93.9%	38,064		4,245	33,819	74	275	367	3,529	10,102	21,012	2,705	
Estimated totals	100.0%	40,530		4,521	36,009	79	293	391	3,758	10,756	22,373	2,880	
State Total	7,353,000	463,952		46,966	416,986	630	2,357	15,100	28,879	81,968	288,803	46,215	
Rate per 100,000 inhabitants		6,309.7		638.7	5,671.0	8.6	32.1	205.4	392.8	1,114.8	3,927.7	628.5	
HAWAII													
Metropolitan Statistical Area	878,044												
Area actually reporting	100.0%	60,059		2,748	57,311	27	222	1,421	1,078	9,026	41,915	6,370	
Cities outside metropolitan areas	40,475												
Area actually reporting	100.0%	2,875		86	2,789	2	14	30	40	517	2,147	125	
Rural	265,481												
Area actually reporting	100.0%	15,027		488	14,539	11	90	155	232	3,238	10,639	662	
State Total	1,184,000	77,961		3,322	74,639	40	326	1,606	1,350	12,781	54,701	7,157	
Rate per 100,000 inhabitants		6,584.5		280.6	6,304.0	3.4	27.5	135.6	114.0	1,079.5	4,620.0	604.5	
IDAHO													
Metropolitan Statistical Area	439,446												
Area actually reporting	100.0%	20,507		1,184	19,323	7	130	116	931	3,460	14,922	941	
Cities outside metropolitan areas	353,621												
Area actually reporting	99.0%	19,351		1,253	18,098	12	110	99	1,032	2,930	14,360	808	
Estimated totals	100.0%	19,541		1,265	18,276	12	111	100	1,042	2,959	14,501	816	
Rural	395,933												
Area actually reporting	98.9%	7,577		720	6,857	24	71	25	600	1,990	4,400	467	
Estimated totals	100.0%	7,661		728	6,933	24	72	25	607	2,012	4,449	472	
State Total	1,189,000	47,709		3,177	44,532	43	313	241	2,580	8,431	33,872	2,229	
Rate per 100,000 inhabitants		4,012.5		267.2	3,745.3	3.6	26.3	20.3	217.0	709.1	2,848.8	187.5	
ILLINOIS[5]													
State Total	11,847,000	629,762		104,985	524,777	1,179	4,051	33,106	66,649	108,185	358,515	58,077	
Rate per 100,000 inhabitants		5,315.8		886.2	4,429.6	10.0	34.2	279.4	562.6	913.2	3,026.2	490.2	
INDIANA													
Metropolitan Statistical Area	4,188,299												
Area actually reporting	82.8%	187,346		23,965	163,381	337	1,524	6,443	15,661	32,685	110,933	19,763	
Estimated totals	100.0%	211,061		25,985	185,076	353	1,667	6,798	17,167	36,383	126,919	21,774	
Cities outside metropolitan areas	595,163												
Area actually reporting	62.8%	21,235		1,988	19,247	15	98	236	1,639	2,962	15,092	1,193	
Estimated totals	100.0%	33,814		3,166	30,648	24	156	376	2,610	4,717	24,031	1,900	
Rural	1,057,538												
Area actually reporting	53.1%	9,491		1,177	8,314	23	90	40	1,024	2,487	5,220	607	
Estimated totals	100.0%	17,867		2,215	15,652	43	169	75	1,928	4,682	9,827	1,143	
State Total	5,841,000	262,742		31,366	231,376	420	1,992	7,249	21,705	45,782	160,777	24,817	
Rate per 100,000 inhabitants		4,498.2		537.0	3,961.2	7.2	34.1	124.1	371.6	783.8	2,752.6	424.9	

See footnotes at end of table.

Table 5. — Index of Crime, State, 1996 — Continued

Area	Population	Crime Index total	Modified Crime Index total[1]	Violent crime[2]	Property crime[3]	Murder and non-negligent man-slaughter	Forcible rape	Robbery	Aggra-vated assault	Burglary	Larceny-theft	Motor vehicle theft	Arson[1]
IOWA													
Metropolitan Statistical													
Area	1,255,805												
Area actually reporting	96.3%	63,783		5,435	58,348	38	383	1,110	3,904	10,344	44,293	3,711	
Estimated totals	100.0%	64,983		5,511	59,472	39	387	1,117	3,968	10,592	45,108	3,772	
Cities outside metropolitan areas	710,580												
Area actually reporting	84.4%	25,117		1,484	23,633	6	115	135	1,228	4,670	17,987	976	
Estimated totals	100.0%	29,764		1,758	28,006	7	136	160	1,455	5,534	21,315	1,157	
Rural	885,615												
Area actually reporting	86.4%	8,049		434	7,615	6	33	8	387	2,442	4,724	449	
Estimated totals	100.0%	9,320		502	8,818	7	38	9	448	2,828	5,470	520	
State Total	**2,852,000**	**104,067**		**7,771**	**96,296**	**53**	**561**	**1,286**	**5,871**	**18,954**	**71,893**	**5,449**	
Rate per 100,000													
inhabitants		3,648.9		272.5	3,376.4	1.9	19.7	45.1	205.9	664.6	2,520.8	191.1	
KANSAS[5]													
State Total	**2,572,000**	**120,414**		**10,642**	**109,772**	**170**	**1,096**	**2,476**	**6,900**	**25,239**	**78,145**	**6,388**	
Rate per 100,000													
inhabitants		4,681.7		413.8	4,268.0	6.6	42.6	96.3	268.3	981.3	3,038.3	248.4	
KENTUCKY[5]													
State Total	**3,884,000**	**122,979**		**12,448**	**110,531**	**228**	**1,230**	**3,643**	**7,347**	**26,736**	**73,653**	**10,142**	
Rate per 100,000													
inhabitants		3,166.3		320.5	2,845.8	5.9	31.7	93.8	189.2	688.4	1,896.3	261.1	
LOUISIANA													
Metropolitan Statistical													
Area	3,267,474												
Area actually reporting	96.6%	243,993		32,475	211,518	662	1,444	11,135	19,234	45,614	140,496	25,408	
Estimated totals	100.0%	250,701		33,239	217,462	670	1,477	11,284	19,808	46,824	144,754	25,884	
Cities outside metropolitan areas	397,518												
Area actually reporting	79.1%	24,101		3,171	20,930	26	134	485	2,526	4,512	15,579	839	
Estimated totals	100.0%	30,459		4,007	26,452	33	169	613	3,192	5,702	19,690	1,060	
Rural	686,008												
Area actually reporting	81.6%	13,375		2,594	10,781	48	130	113	2,303	3,143	7,201	437	
Estimated totals	100.0%	16,396		3,180	13,216	59	159	139	2,823	3,853	8,827	536	
State Total	**4,351,000**	**297,556**		**40,426**	**257,130**	**762**	**1,805**	**12,036**	**25,823**	**56,379**	**173,271**	**27,480**	
Rate per 100,000													
inhabitants		6,838.8		929.1	5,909.7	17.5	41.5	276.6	593.5	1,295.8	3,982.3	631.6	
MAINE													
Metropolitan Statistical													
Area	460,285												
Area actually reporting	100.0%	19,580		815	18,765	6	131	210	468	3,959	14,073	733	
Cities outside metropolitan areas	434,976												
Area actually reporting	98.8%	15,848		550	15,298	9	73	69	399	2,764	11,878	656	
Estimated totals	100.0%	16,034		557	15,477	9	74	70	404	2,796	12,017	664	
Rural	347,739												
Area actually reporting	100.0%	6,575		181	6,394	10	55	12	104	2,548	3,467	379	
State Total	**1,243,000**	**42,189**		**1,553**	**40,636**	**25**	**260**	**292**	**976**	**9,303**	**29,557**	**1,776**	
Rate per 100,000													
inhabitants		3,394.1		124.9	3,269.2	2.0	20.9	23.5	78.5	748.4	2,377.9	142.9	

See footnotes at end of table.

Table 5. — Index of Crime, State, 1996 — Continued

Area	Population	Crime Index total	Modified Crime Index total[1]	Violent crime[2]	Property crime[3]	Murder and non-negligent man-slaughter	Forcible rape	Robbery	Aggra-vated assault	Burglary	Larceny–theft	Motor vehicle theft	Arson[1]
MARYLAND													
Metropolitan Statistical Area	4,706,522												
Area actually reporting	99.9%	290,578		45,121	245,457	571	1,773	19,588	23,189	46,933	163,122	35,402	
Estimated totals	100.0%	290,715		45,138	245,577	571	1,773	19,595	23,199	46,952	163,211	35,414	
Cities outside metropolitan areas	98,635												
Area actually reporting	100.0%	9,584		1,159	8,425	6	56	247	850	1,662	6,386	377	
Rural	266,843												
Area actually reporting	100.0%	7,162		933	6,229	11	76	102	744	1,717	4,220	292	
State Total	**5,072,000**	**307,461**		**47,230**	**260,231**	**588**	**1,905**	**19,944**	**24,793**	**50,331**	**173,817**	**36,083**	
Rate per 100,000 inhabitants		6,061.9		931.2	5,130.7	11.6	37.6	393.2	488.8	992.3	3,427.0	711.4	
MASSACHUSETTS													
Metropolitan Statistical Area	5,793,412												
Area actually reporting	96.2%	214,928		36,225	178,703	150	1,615	7,611	26,849	38,973	108,945	30,785	
Estimated totals	100.0%	220,829		36,955	183,874	152	1,651	7,701	27,451	40,049	112,367	31,458	
Cities outside metropolitan areas	287,523												
Area actually reporting	88.7%	11,419		1,905	9,514	4	103	68	1,730	2,516	6,361	637	
Estimated totals	100.0%	12,879		2,149	10,730	5	116	77	1,951	2,838	7,174	718	
Rural	11,065												
Area actually reporting	100.0%	50		18	32	—	—	—	18	9	21	2	
State Total	**6,092,000**	**233,758**		**39,122**	**194,636**	**157**	**1,767**	**7,778**	**29,420**	**42,896**	**119,562**	**32,178**	
Rate per 100,000 inhabitants		3,837.1		642.2	3,194.9	2.6	29.0	127.7	482.9	704.1	1,962.6	528.2	
MICHIGAN													
Metropolitan Statistical Area	7,916,331												
Area actually reporting	90.9%	408,757		54,380	354,377	673	4,033	16,143	33,531	70,269	222,983	61,125	
Estimated totals	100.0%	440,866		57,099	383,767	692	4,274	16,718	35,415	74,837	244,347	64,583	
Cities outside metropolitan areas	621,723												
Area actually reporting	78.1%	17,255		954	16,301	1	249	76	628	1,948	13,516	837	
Estimated totals	100.0%	22,083		1,221	20,862	1	319	97	804	2,493	17,298	1,071	
Rural	1,055,946												
Area actually reporting	89.6%	25,102		2,356	22,746	26	782	82	1,466	7,684	13,674	1,388	
Estimated totals	100.0%	28,022		2,631	25,391	29	873	92	1,637	8,578	15,264	1,549	
State Total	**9,594,000**	**490,971**		**60,951**	**430,020**	**722**	**5,466**	**16,907**	**37,856**	**85,908**	**276,909**	**67,203**	
Rate per 100,000 inhabitants		5,117.5		635.3	4,482.2	7.5	57.0	176.2	394.6	895.4	2,886.3	700.5	
MINNESOTA													
Metropolitan Statistical Area	3,236,769												
Area actually reporting	99.8%	164,573		13,931	150,642	137	1,722	5,227	6,845	26,637	109,001	15,004	
Estimated totals	100.0%	164,921		13,946	150,975	137	1,725	5,231	6,853	26,683	109,266	15,026	
Cities outside metropolitan areas	544,942												
Area actually reporting	100.0%	25,408		963	24,445	10	290	117	546	3,433	19,567	1,445	
Rural	876,289												
Area actually reporting	100.0%	17,562		873	16,689	20	312	37	504	5,399	9,838	1,452	
State Total	**4,658,000**	**207,891**		**15,782**	**192,109**	**167**	**2,327**	**5,385**	**7,903**	**35,515**	**138,671**	**17,923**	
Rate per 100,000 inhabitants		4,463.1		338.8	4,124.3	3.6	50.0	115.6	169.7	762.5	2,977.1	384.8	

See footnotes at end of table.

Table 5. — Index of Crime, State, 1996 — Continued

Area	Population	Crime Index total	Modified Crime Index total[1]	Violent crime[2]	Property crime[3]	Murder and non-negligent man-slaughter	Forcible rape	Robbery	Aggra-vated assault	Burglary	Larceny–theft	Motor vehicle theft	Arson[1]
MISSISSIPPI													
Metropolitan Statistical Area	950,891												
Area actually reporting	68.1%	48,655		5,207	43,448	105	352	1,962	2,788	10,399	28,079	4,970	
Estimated totals	100.0%	56,532		5,814	50,718	132	429	2,075	3,178	12,535	32,660	5,523	
Cities outside metropolitan areas	654,447												
Area actually reporting	69.6%	35,144		3,147	31,997	69	263	849	1,966	8,245	21,637	2,115	
Estimated totals	100.0%	50,502		4,522	45,980	99	378	1,220	2,825	11,848	31,093	3,039	
Rural	1,110,662												
Area actually reporting	37.3%	5,895		1,091	4,804	26	65	131	869	2,376	2,068	360	
Estimated totals	100.0%	15,808		2,925	12,883	70	174	351	2,330	6,372	5,546	965	
State Total	**2,716,000**	**122,842**		**13,261**	**109,581**	**301**	**981**	**3,646**	**8,333**	**30,755**	**69,299**	**9,527**	
Rate per 100,000 inhabitants		4,522.9		488.3	4,034.6	11.1	36.1	134.2	306.8	1,132.4	2,551.5	350.8	
MISSOURI													
Metropolitan Statistical Area	3,648,247												
Area actually reporting	97.1%	224,491		26,984	197,507	352	1,238	8,719	16,675	37,109	138,907	21,491	
Estimated totals	100.0%	227,978		27,226	200,752	354	1,257	8,765	16,850	37,713	141,292	21,747	
Cities outside metropolitan areas	501,284												
Area actually reporting	88.8%	25,327		1,925	23,402	15	118	254	1,538	3,790	18,479	1,133	
Estimated totals	100.0%	28,507		2,167	26,340	17	133	286	1,731	4,266	20,799	1,275	
Rural	1,209,469												
Area actually reporting	50.5%	8,068		1,150	6,918	31	89	46	984	3,002	3,426	490	
Estimated totals	100.0%	15,965		2,276	13,689	62	176	91	1,947	5,940	6,779	970	
State Total	**5,359,000**	**272,450**		**31,669**	**240,781**	**433**	**1,566**	**9,142**	**20,528**	**47,919**	**168,870**	**23,992**	
Rate per 100,000 inhabitants		5,084.0		590.9	4,493.0	8.1	29.2	170.6	383.1	894.2	3,151.1	447.7	
MONTANA[5]													
State Total	**879,000**	**39,499**		**1,415**	**38,084**	**34**	**238**	**261**	**882**	**4,908**	**30,928**	**2,248**	
Rate per 100,000 inhabitants		4,493.6		161.0	4,332.7	3.9	27.1	29.7	100.3	558.4	3,518.5	255.7	
NEBRASKA													
Metropolitan Statistical Area	837,096												
Area actually reporting	100.0%	49,452		6,277	43,175	36	324	974	4,943	6,569	31,957	4,649	
Cities outside metropolitan areas	394,496												
Area actually reporting	98.4%	17,772		643	17,129	9	91	68	475	2,220	14,221	688	
Estimated totals	100.0%	18,059		653	17,406	9	92	69	483	2,256	14,451	699	
Rural	420,408												
Area actually reporting	96.9%	5,599		244	5,355	3	30	9	202	1,285	3,784	286	
Estimated totals	100.0%	5,781		252	5,529	3	31	9	209	1,327	3,907	295	
State Total	**1,652,000**	**73,292**		**7,182**	**66,110**	**48**	**447**	**1,052**	**5,635**	**10,152**	**50,315**	**5,643**	
Rate per 100,000 inhabitants		4,436.6		434.7	4,001.8	2.9	27.1	63.7	341.1	614.5	3,045.7	341.6	
NEVADA													
Metropolitan Statistical Area	1,367,552												
Area actually reporting	100.0%	88,274		12,129	76,145	213	780	4,858	6,278	17,856	47,502	10,787	
Cities outside metropolitan areas	48,936												
Area actually reporting	100.0%	2,456		250	2,206	1	32	18	199	451	1,644	111	
Rural	186,512												
Area actually reporting	100.0%	5,322		626	4,696	6	44	55	521	1,251	3,149	296	
State Total	**1,603,000**	**96,052**		**13,005**	**83,047**	**220**	**856**	**4,931**	**6,998**	**19,558**	**52,295**	**11,194**	
Rate per 100,000 inhabitants		5,992.0		811.3	5,180.7	13.7	53.4	307.6	436.6	1,220.1	3,262.3	698.3	

See footnotes at end of table.

Table 5. — Index of Crime, State, 1996 — Continued

Area	Population	Crime Index total	Modified Crime Index total[1]	Violent crime[2]	Property crime[3]	Murder and non-negligent man-slaughter	Forcible rape	Robbery	Aggra-vated assault	Burglary	Larceny–theft	Motor vehicle theft	Arson[1]
NEW HAMPSHIRE													
Metropolitan Statistical													
Area	683,195												
Area actually reporting	86.0%	18,031		765	17,266	9	216	239	301	2,635	13,428	1,203	
Estimated totals	100.0%	20,554		872	19,682	9	255	255	353	3,028	15,304	1,350	
Cities outside metropolitan areas	328,464												
Area actually reporting	74.0%	8,394		307	8,087	5	94	42	166	1,284	6,531	272	
Estimated totals	100.0%	11,349		415	10,934	7	127	57	224	1,736	8,830	368	
Rural	150,341												
Area actually reporting	92.7%	840		80	760	4	20	5	51	277	442	41	
Estimated totals	100.0%	906		86	820	4	22	5	55	299	477	44	
State Total	**1,162,000**	**32,809**		**1,373**	**31,436**	**20**	**404**	**317**	**632**	**5,063**	**24,611**	**1,762**	
Rate per 100,000													
inhabitants		2,823.5		118.2	2,705.3	1.7	34.8	27.3	54.4	435.7	2,118.0	151.6	
NEW JERSEY													
Metropolitan Statistical													
Area	7,988,000												
Area actually reporting	100.0%	346,116		42,459	303,657	338	1,976	18,838	21,307	63,259	193,961	46,437	
Cities outside metropolitan areas	NONE												
Rural	NONE												
State Total	**7,988,000**	**346,116**		**42,459**	**303,657**	**338**	**1,976**	**18,838**	**21,307**	**63,259**	**193,961**	**46,437**	
Rate per 100,000													
inhabitants		4,332.9		531.5	3,801.4	4.2	24.7	235.8	266.7	791.9	2,428.2	581.3	
NEW MEXICO													
Metropolitan Statistical													
Area	964,350												
Area actually reporting	68.6%	64,289		7,562	56,727	84	491	2,242	4,745	11,942	36,694	8,091	
Estimated totals	100.0%	69,831		8,726	61,105	123	592	2,279	5,732	13,280	39,494	8,331	
Cities outside metropolitan areas	446,301												
Area actually reporting	85.8%	29,075		3,298	25,777	30	255	381	2,632	6,228	18,724	825	
Estimated totals	100.0%	33,888		3,844	30,044	35	297	444	3,068	7,259	21,823	962	
Rural	302,349												
Area actually reporting	66.2%	6,208		1,211	4,997	26	132	39	1,014	2,017	2,530	450	
Estimated totals	100.0%	9,378		1,829	7,549	39	199	59	1,532	3,047	3,822	680	
State Total	**1,713,000**	**113,097**		**14,399**	**98,698**	**197**	**1,088**	**2,782**	**10,332**	**23,586**	**65,139**	**9,973**	
Rate per 100,000													
inhabitants		6,602.3		840.6	5,761.7	11.5	63.5	162.4	603.2	1,376.9	3,802.6	582.2	
NEW YORK													
Metropolitan Statistical													
Area	16,679,321												
Area actually reporting	99.0%	703,221		127,528	575,693	1,313	3,874	61,318	61,023	119,140	368,209	88,344	
Estimated totals	100.0%	708,140		127,914	580,226	1,316	3,890	61,443	61,265	119,918	371,588	88,720	
Cities outside metropolitan areas	650,213												
Area actually reporting	89.3%	21,911		1,898	20,013	8	130	255	1,505	3,851	15,615	547	
Estimated totals	100.0%	24,544		2,127	22,417	9	146	286	1,686	4,314	17,490	613	
Rural	855,466												
Area actually reporting	98.0%	18,403		2,122	16,281	27	135	91	1,869	5,486	10,239	556	
Estimated totals	100.0%	18,772		2,165	16,607	28	138	93	1,906	5,596	10,444	567	
State Total	**18,185,000**	**751,456**		**132,206**	**619,250**	**1,353**	**4,174**	**61,822**	**64,857**	**129,828**	**399,522**	**89,900**	
Rate per 100,000													
inhabitants		4,132.3		727.0	3,405.3	7.4	23.0	340.0	356.7	713.9	2,197.0	494.4	

See footnotes at end of table.

Table 5. — Index of Crime, State, 1996 — Continued

Area	Population	Crime Index total	Modified Crime Index total[1]	Violent crime[2]	Property crime[3]	Murder and non-negligent manslaughter	Forcible rape	Robbery	Aggravated assault	Burglary	Larceny–theft	Motor vehicle theft	Arson[1]
NORTH CAROLINA													
Metropolitan Statistical													
Area	4,876,036												
Area actually reporting	99.2%	295,808		32,369	263,439	432	1,685	9,847	20,405	66,305	177,801	19,333	
Estimated totals	100.0%	297,860		32,530	265,330	433	1,694	9,888	20,515	66,745	179,155	19,430	
Cities outside metropolitan areas	757,429												
Area actually reporting	97.0%	59,417		6,065	53,352	60	234	1,565	4,206	13,616	37,337	2,399	
Estimated totals	100.0%	61,283		6,255	55,028	62	241	1,614	4,338	14,044	38,510	2,474	
Rural	1,689,535												
Area actually reporting	96.5%	43,958		4,135	39,823	120	342	482	3,191	17,133	20,121	2,569	
Estimated totals	100.0%	45,541		4,283	41,258	124	354	499	3,306	17,750	20,846	2,662	
State Total	**7,323,000**	**404,684**		**43,068**	**361,616**	**619**	**2,289**	**12,001**	**28,159**	**98,539**	**238,511**	**24,566**	
Rate per 100,000 inhabitants		5,526.2		588.1	4,938.1	8.5	31.3	163.9	384.5	1,345.6	3,257.0	335.5	
NORTH DAKOTA													
Metropolitan Statistical													
Area	271,128												
Area actually reporting	99.4%	10,567		343	10,224	8	92	49	194	1,110	8,326	788	
Estimated totals	100.0%	10,627		347	10,280	8	93	49	197	1,115	8,373	792	
Cities outside metropolitan areas	149,788												
Area actually reporting	81.4%	3,688		101	3,587	2	37	14	48	303	3,051	233	
Estimated totals	100.0%	4,527		123	4,404	2	45	17	59	372	3,746	286	
Rural	223,084												
Area actually reporting	92.0%	1,873		66	1,807	4	16	5	41	464	1,209	134	
Estimated totals	100.0%	2,035		71	1,964	4	17	5	45	504	1,314	146	
State Total	**644,000**	**17,189**		**541**	**16,648**	**14**	**155**	**71**	**301**	**1,991**	**13,433**	**1,224**	
Rate per 100,000 inhabitants		2,669.1		84.0	2,585.1	2.2	24.1	11.0	46.7	309.2	2,085.9	190.1	
OHIO													
Metropolitan Statistical													
Area	9,073,282												
Area actually reporting	78.1%	373,461		41,061	332,400	472	3,726	16,675	20,188	71,183	222,402	38,815	
Estimated totals	100.0%	439,486		44,796	394,690	502	4,184	17,771	22,339	82,024	269,790	42,876	
Cities outside metropolitan areas	770,164												
Area actually reporting	60.0%	22,369		1,174	21,195	9	157	281	727	3,483	16,819	893	
Estimated totals	100.0%	37,258		1,956	35,302	15	262	468	1,211	5,801	28,014	1,487	
Rural	1,329,554												
Area actually reporting	56.0%	11,808		641	11,167	12	96	54	479	3,086	7,429	652	
Estimated totals	100.0%	21,087		1,144	19,943	21	171	97	855	5,511	13,267	1,165	
State Total	**11,173,000**	**497,831**		**47,896**	**449,935**	**538**	**4,617**	**18,336**	**24,405**	**93,336**	**311,071**	**45,528**	
Rate per 100,000 inhabitants		4,455.7		428.7	4,027.0	4.8	41.3	164.1	218.4	835.4	2,784.1	407.5	
OKLAHOMA													
Metropolitan Statistical													
Area	1,986,513												
Area actually reporting	100.0%	137,226		14,099	123,127	151	1,178	3,105	9,665	28,855	81,025	13,247	
Cities outside metropolitan areas	679,289												
Area actually reporting	100.0%	38,202		4,057	34,145	30	267	364	3,396	8,383	23,861	1,901	
Rural	635,198												
Area actually reporting	100.0%	11,174		1,554	9,620	42	100	50	1,362	4,209	4,620	791	
State Total	**3,301,000**	**186,602**		**19,710**	**166,892**	**223**	**1,545**	**3,519**	**14,423**	**41,447**	**109,506**	**15,939**	
Rate per 100,000 inhabitants		5,652.9		597.1	5,055.8	6.8	46.8	106.6	436.9	1,255.6	3,317.4	482.9	

See footnotes at end of table.

Table 5. — Index of Crime, State, 1996 — Continued

Area	Population	Crime Index total	Modified Crime Index total[1]	Violent crime[2]	Property crime[3]	Murder and non-negligent man-slaughter	Forcible rape	Robbery	Aggra-vated assault	Burglary	Larceny–theft	Motor vehicle theft	Arson[1]
OREGON													
Metropolitan Statistical													
Area	2,244,016												
Area actually reporting	97.8%	144,125		12,602	131,523	102	994	3,452	8,054	22,089	95,326	14,108	
Estimated totals	100.0%	146,928		12,733	134,195	103	1,010	3,494	8,126	22,506	97,349	14,340	
Cities outside metropolitan areas	445,469												
Area actually reporting	98.9%	30,929		1,122	29,807	11	126	318	667	5,161	23,007	1,639	
Estimated totals	100.0%	31,271		1,134	30,137	11	127	322	674	5,218	23,262	1,657	
Rural	514,515												
Area actually reporting	87.6%	12,200		849	11,351	13	118	86	632	3,450	7,011	890	
Estimated totals	100.0%	13,933		970	12,963	15	135	98	722	3,940	8,007	1,016	
State Total	**3,204,000**	**192,132**		**14,837**	**177,295**	**129**	**1,272**	**3,914**	**9,522**	**31,664**	**128,618**	**17,013**	
Rate per 100,000 inhabitants		5,996.6		463.1	5,533.6	4.0	39.7	122.2	297.2	988.3	4,014.3	531.0	
PENNSYLVANIA													
Metropolitan Statistical													
Area	10,217,690												
Area actually reporting	95.6%	355,847		47,428	308,419	633	2,514	23,553	20,728	56,284	205,906	46,229	
Estimated totals	100.0%	368,228		48,488	319,740	639	2,576	23,824	21,449	57,865	214,522	47,353	
Cities outside metropolitan areas	779,321												
Area actually reporting	82.5%	19,649		1,782	17,867	9	160	249	1,364	2,773	14,183	911	
Estimated totals	100.0%	23,827		2,161	21,666	11	194	302	1,654	3,363	17,198	1,105	
Rural	1,058,989												
Area actually reporting	100.0%	16,949		1,491	15,458	36	278	114	1,063	5,253	8,973	1,232	
State Total	**12,056,000**	**409,004**		**52,140**	**356,864**	**686**	**3,048**	**24,240**	**24,166**	**66,481**	**240,693**	**49,690**	
Rate per 100,000 inhabitants		3,392.5		432.5	2,960.1	5.7	25.3	201.1	200.4	551.4	1,996.5	412.2	
PUERTO RICO[6]													
Metropolitan Statistical													
Area													
Area actually reporting	100.0%	87,896		17,987	69,909	794	259	12,894	4,040	23,184	31,577	15,148	
Cities outside metropolitan areas													
Area actually reporting	100.0%	11,892		2,160	9,732	74	57	1,006	1,023	4,682	4,075	975	
Total		**99,788**		**20,147**	**79,641**	**868**	**316**	**13,900**	**5,063**	**27,866**	**35,652**	**16,123**	
RHODE ISLAND													
Metropolitan Statistical													
Area	910,980												
Area actually reporting	100.0%	36,158		3,101	33,057	24	254	767	2,056	7,423	21,178	4,456	
Cities outside metropolitan areas	79,020												
Area actually reporting	100.0%	3,346		316	3,030	1	26	56	233	709	2,181	140	
Rural													
Area actually reporting	100.0%	32		20	12	—	7	1	12	3	8	1	
State Total	**990,000**	**39,536**		**3,437**	**36,099**	**25**	**287**	**824**	**2,301**	**8,135**	**23,367**	**4,597**	
Rate per 100,000 inhabitants		3,993.5		347.2	3,646.4	2.5	29.0	83.2	232.4	821.7	2,360.3	464.3	
SOUTH CAROLINA													
Metropolitan Statistical													
Area	2,581,562												
Area actually reporting	99.9%	170,438		25,712	144,726	211	1,359	4,918	19,224	34,264	98,029	12,433	
Estimated totals	100.0%	170,589		25,729	144,860	211	1,360	4,921	19,237	34,288	98,130	12,442	
Cities outside metropolitan areas	325,914												
Area actually reporting	98.9%	24,717		4,800	19,917	48	142	740	3,870	4,442	14,299	1,176	
Estimated totals	100.0%	24,999		4,855	20,144	49	144	748	3,914	4,493	14,462	1,189	
Rural	791,524												
Area actually reporting	100.0%	34,273		6,291	27,982	72	317	692	5,210	8,706	17,058	2,218	
State Total	**3,699,000**	**229,861**		**36,875**	**192,986**	**332**	**1,821**	**6,361**	**28,361**	**47,487**	**129,650**	**15,849**	
Rate per 100,000 inhabitants		6,214.1		996.9	5,217.2	9.0	49.2	172.0	766.7	1,283.8	3,505.0	428.5	

See footnotes at end of table.

Table 5. — Index of Crime, State, 1996 — Continued

Area	Population	Crime Index total	Modified Crime Index total[1]	Violent crime[2]	Property crime[3]	Murder and non-negligent man-slaughter	Forcible rape	Robbery	Aggra-vated assault	Burglary	Larceny–theft	Motor vehicle theft	Arson[1]
SOUTH DAKOTA													
Metropolitan Statistical													
Area	245,957												
Area actually reporting	92.1%	10,796		822	9,974	2	174	110	536	1,824	7,775	375	
Estimated totals	100.0%	11,375		867	10,508	2	193	111	561	1,971	8,146	391	
Cities outside metropolitan areas	193,718												
Area actually reporting	71.9%	5,510		204	5,306	1	48	13	142	871	4,214	221	
Estimated totals	100.0%	7,660		283	7,377	1	67	18	197	1,211	5,859	307	
Rural	292,325												
Area actually reporting	53.0%	1,433		78	1,355	3	21	5	49	474	809	72	
Estimated totals	100.0%	2,705		147	2,558	6	40	9	92	895	1,527	136	
State Total	**732,000**	**21,740**		**1,297**	**20,443**	**9**	**300**	**138**	**850**	**4,077**	**15,532**	**834**	
Rate per 100,000 inhabitants		2,969.9		177.2	2,792.8	1.2	41.0	18.9	116.1	557.0	2,121.9	113.9	
TENNESSEE													
Metropolitan Statistical													
Area	3,594,699												
Area actually reporting	77.7%	207,901		31,853	176,048	361	1,844	10,860	18,788	41,403	105,552	29,093	
Estimated totals	100.0%	231,580		34,524	197,056	402	2,036	11,171	20,915	47,293	118,962	30,801	
Cities outside metropolitan areas	626,192												
Area actually reporting	73.0%	26,151		2,985	23,166	30	168	420	2,367	5,154	16,528	1,484	
Estimated totals	100.0%	35,838		4,091	31,747	41	230	576	3,244	7,063	22,650	2,034	
Rural	1,099,109												
Area actually reporting	46.3%	10,421		1,187	9,234	28	97	72	990	3,494	5,002	738	
Estimated totals	100.0%	22,486		2,560	19,926	60	209	155	2,136	7,540	10,793	1,593	
State Total	**5,320,000**	**289,904**		**41,175**	**248,729**	**503**	**2,475**	**11,902**	**26,295**	**61,896**	**152,405**	**34,428**	
Rate per 100,000 inhabitants		5,449.3		774.0	4,675.4	9.5	46.5	223.7	494.3	1,163.5	2,864.8	647.1	
TEXAS													
Metropolitan Statistical													
Area	16,077,676												
Area actually reporting	99.9%	991,854		112,125	879,729	1,296	7,539	31,744	71,546	179,742	599,336	100,651	
Estimated totals	100.0%	991,942		112,133	879,809	1,296	7,540	31,746	71,551	179,758	599,395	100,656	
Cities outside metropolitan areas	1,419,906												
Area actually reporting	99.6%	68,293		7,506	60,787	80	519	843	6,064	13,366	44,751	2,670	
Estimated totals	100.0%	68,490		7,528	60,962	80	520	845	6,083	13,405	44,879	2,678	
Rural	1,630,418												
Area actually reporting	99.4%	31,374		3,587	27,787	100	314	212	2,961	11,157	15,046	1,584	
Estimated totals	100.0%	31,570		3,609	27,961	101	316	213	2,979	11,227	15,140	1,594	
State Total	**19,128,000**	**1,092,002**		**123,270**	**968,732**	**1,477**	**8,376**	**32,804**	**80,613**	**204,390**	**659,414**	**104,928**	
Rate per 100,000 inhabitants		5,708.9		644.4	5,064.5	7.7	43.8	171.5	421.4	1,068.5	3,447.4	548.6	
UTAH													
Metropolitan Statistical													
Area	1,540,265												
Area actually reporting	99.4%	100,123		5,651	94,472	55	680	1,300	3,616	13,780	72,999	7,693	
Estimated totals	100.0%	100,679		5,681	94,998	55	683	1,305	3,638	13,857	73,414	7,727	
Cities outside metropolitan areas	245,735												
Area actually reporting	95.6%	12,735		569	12,166	5	88	49	427	1,852	9,825	489	
Estimated totals	100.0%	13,313		594	12,719	5	92	51	446	1,936	10,272	511	
Rural	214,000												
Area actually reporting	88.6%	5,074		322	4,752	3	54	19	246	1,039	3,417	296	
Estimated totals	100.0%	5,725		363	5,362	3	61	21	278	1,172	3,856	334	
State Total	**2,000,000**	**119,717**		**6,638**	**113,079**	**63**	**836**	**1,377**	**4,362**	**16,965**	**87,542**	**8,572**	
Rate per 100,000 inhabitants		5,985.9		331.9	5,654.0	3.2	41.8	68.9	218.1	848.3	4,377.1	428.6	

See footnotes at end of table.

Table 5. — Index of Crime, State, 1996 — Continued

Area	Population	Crime Index total	Modified Crime Index total[1]	Violent crime[2]	Property crime[3]	Murder and non-negligent man-slaughter	Forcible rape	Robbery	Aggra-vated assault	Burglary	Larceny–theft	Motor vehicle theft	Arson[1]
VERMONT													
Metropolitan Statistical													
Area	145,357												
Area actually reporting	76.1%	6,029		162	5,867	2	62	22	76	1,459	4,157	251	
Estimated totals	100.0%	7,370		188	7,182	2	72	22	92	1,662	5,219	301	
Cities outside metropolitan areas	203,176												
Area actually reporting	22.8%	1,590		95	1,495	1	14	15	65	238	1,153	104	
Estimated totals	100.0%	6,987		418	6,569	4	62	66	286	1,046	5,066	457	
Rural	240,467												
Area actually reporting	94.8%	3,158		103	3,055	5	24	3	71	1,191	1,744	120	
Estimated totals	100.0%	3,330		108	3,222	5	25	3	75	1,256	1,839	127	
State Total	**589,000**	**17,687**		**714**	**16,973**	**11**	**159**	**91**	**453**	**3,964**	**12,124**	**885**	
Rate per 100,000 inhabitants		3,002.9		121.2	2,881.7	1.9	27.0	15.4	76.9	673.0	2,058.4	150.3	
VIRGINIA													
Metropolitan Statistical													
Area	5,187,620												
Area actually reporting	100.0%	231,025		19,691	211,334	411	1,484	7,750	10,046	32,350	162,203	16,781	
Cities outside metropolitan areas	425,588												
Area actually reporting	99.9%	16,784		1,406	15,378	31	111	221	1,043	2,326	12,377	675	
Estimated totals	100.0%	16,799		1,407	15,392	31	111	221	1,044	2,328	12,388	676	
Rural	1,061,792												
Area actually reporting	100.0%	17,058		1,684	15,374	58	188	210	1,228	4,577	9,646	1,151	
State Total	**6,675,000**	**264,882**		**22,782**	**242,100**	**500**	**1,783**	**8,181**	**12,318**	**39,255**	**184,237**	**18,608**	
Rate per 100,000 inhabitants		3,968.3		341.3	3,627.0	7.5	26.7	122.6	184.5	588.1	2,760.1	278.8	
WASHINGTON													
Metropolitan Statistical													
Area	4,587,715												
Area actually reporting	99.9%	273,946		20,893	253,053	204	2,311	6,235	12,143	48,135	178,454	26,464	
Estimated totals	100.0%	274,360		20,915	253,445	204	2,315	6,242	12,154	48,198	178,743	26,504	
Cities outside metropolitan areas	435,133												
Area actually reporting	90.4%	32,163		1,661	30,502	16	271	250	1,124	4,789	24,417	1,296	
Estimated totals	100.0%	35,588		1,839	33,749	18	300	277	1,244	5,299	27,016	1,434	
Rural	510,152												
Area actually reporting	94.9%	16,154		1,047	15,107	31	202	65	749	4,760	9,441	906	
Estimated totals	100.0%	17,020		1,103	15,917	33	213	68	789	5,015	9,947	955	
State Total	**5,533,000**	**326,968**		**23,857**	**303,111**	**255**	**2,828**	**6,587**	**14,187**	**58,512**	**215,706**	**28,893**	
Rate per 100,000 inhabitants		5,909.4		431.2	5,478.2	4.6	51.1	119.0	256.4	1,057.5	3,898.5	522.2	
WEST VIRGINIA													
Metropolitan Statistical													
Area	762,957												
Area actually reporting	100.0%	26,107		2,027	24,080	28	203	563	1,233	5,076	17,199	1,805	
Cities outside metropolitan areas	279,890												
Area actually reporting	100.0%	8,945		629	8,316	11	64	113	441	1,509	6,349	458	
Rural	783,153												
Area actually reporting	100.0%	10,294		1,180	9,114	30	91	61	998	3,394	4,752	968	
State Total	**1,826,000**	**45,346**		**3,836**	**41,510**	**69**	**358**	**737**	**2,672**	**9,979**	**28,300**	**3,231**	
Rate per 100,000 inhabitants		2,483.4		210.1	2,273.3	3.8	19.6	40.4	146.3	546.5	1,549.8	176.9	

See footnotes at end of table.

Table 5. — Index of Crime, State, 1996 — Continued

Area	Population	Crime Index total	Modified Crime Index total[1]	Violent crime[2]	Property crime[3]	Murder and non-negligent man-slaughter	Forcible rape	Robbery	Aggra-vated assault	Burglary	Larceny–theft	Motor vehicle theft	Arson[1]
WISCONSIN													
Metropolitan Statistical Area	3,511,127												
Area actually reporting	100.0%	152,688		11,254	141,434	178	837	4,819	5,420	21,987	103,730	15,717	
Cities outside metropolitan areas	658,756												
Area actually reporting	99.5%	27,955		959	26,996	8	129	135	687	3,190	22,723	1,083	
Estimated totals	100.0%	28,092		964	27,128	8	130	136	690	3,206	22,834	1,088	
Rural	990,117												
Area actually reporting	100.0%	16,402		821	15,581	18	119	27	657	5,163	9,377	1,041	
State Total	**5,160,000**	**197,182**		**13,039**	**184,143**	**204**	**1,086**	**4,982**	**6,767**	**30,356**	**135,941**	**17,846**	
Rate per 100,000 inhabitants		3,821.4		252.7	3,568.7	4.0	21.0	96.6	131.1	588.3	2,634.5	345.9	
WYOMING													
Metropolitan Statistical Area	143,486												
Area actually reporting	100.0%	7,361		315	7,046	2	59	52	202	1,161	5,616	269	
Cities outside metropolitan areas	211,605												
Area actually reporting	99.2%	10,398		645	9,753	4	68	40	533	1,398	8,066	289	
Estimated totals	100.0%	10,485		650	9,835	4	69	40	537	1,410	8,134	291	
Rural	125,909												
Area actually reporting	85.7%	2,241		202	2,039	9	10	5	178	525	1,421	93	
Estimated totals	100.0%	2,616		236	2,380	10	12	6	208	613	1,658	109	
State Total	**481,000**	**20,462**		**1,201**	**19,261**	**16**	**140**	**98**	**947**	**3,184**	**15,408**	**669**	
Rate per 100,000 inhabitants		4,254.1		249.7	4,004.4	3.3	29.1	20.4	196.9	662.0	3,203.3	139.1	

[1] Although arson data were included in the trend and clearance tables, sufficient data are not available to estimate totals for this offense.

[2] Violent crimes are offenses of murder, forcible rape, robbery, and aggravated assault.

[3] Property crimes are offenses of burglary, larceny–theft, and motor vehicle theft. Data are not included for the property crime of arson.

[4] Includes offenses reported by the Zoological Police.

[5] Complete data were not available for the states of Illinois, Kansas, Kentucky, and Montana; therefore, it was necessary that their crime counts be estimated. An aggregate Florida state total for 1996 was supplied by the Florida Department of Law Enforcement. See "Offense Estimation," pages 389-390 for details.

[6] The 1996 Bureau of the Census population estimate for Puerto Rico was not available prior to publication; therefore, no population or rates per 100,0000 inhabitants are provided.

Offense totals are based on all reporting agencies and estimates for unreported areas.

Table 6. — Index of Crime, Metropolitan Statistical Areas, 1996

Metropolitan Statistical Area	Population	Crime Index total	Modified Crime Index total[1]	Violent crime[2]	Property crime[3]	Murder and non-negligent manslaughter	Forcible rape	Robbery	Aggravated assault	Burglary	Larceny-theft	Motor vehicle theft	Arson[1]
Abilene, Tx. M.S.A.	**126,875**												
(Includes Taylor County.)													
City of Abilene	114,523	5,971		598	5,373	7	66	126	399	1,120	4,008	245	
Total area actually reporting	100.0%	6,326		643	5,683	8	73	127	435	1,243	4,192	248	
Rate per 100,000 inhabitants		4,986.0		506.8	4,479.2	6.3	57.5	100.1	342.9	979.7	3,304.0	195.5	
Akron, Oh. M.S.A.	**675,300**												
(Includes Portage and Summit Counties.)													
City of Akron	223,303	16,007		2,345	13,662	14	194	811	1,326	2,866	8,763	2,033	
Total area actually reporting	78.1%	26,475		3,024	23,451	20	277	963	1,764	4,447	16,369	2,635	
Estimated total	100.0%	30,717		3,261	27,456	23	310	1,031	1,897	5,226	19,333	2,897	
Rate per 100,000 inhabitants		4,548.6		482.9	4,065.7	3.4	45.9	152.7	280.9	773.9	2,862.9	429.0	
Albany, Ga. M.S.A.	**121,907**												
(Includes Dougherty and Lee Counties.)													
City of Albany	84,485	3,136		516	2,620	6	52	101	357	627	1,662	331	
Total area actually reporting	99.3%	4,326		567	3,759	8	60	112	387	987	2,385	387	
Estimated total	100.0%	4,402		572	3,830	8	60	114	390	998	2,438	394	
Rate per 100,000 inhabitants		3,610.9		469.2	3141.7	6.6	49.2	93.5	319.9	818.7	1,999.9	323.2	
Albuquerque, N.M. M.S.A.	**669,120**												
(Includes Bernalillo, Sandoval, and Valencia Counties.)													
City of Albuquerque	426,736	48,253		6,267	41,986	70	375	1,998	3,824	9,037	25,961	6,988	
Total area actually reporting	78.2%	53,237		6,685	46,552	76	412	2,057	4,140	10,127	29,101	7,324	
Estimated total	100.0%	55,544		7,240	48,304	95	460	2,070	4,615	10,704	30,190	7,410	
Rate per 100,000 inhabitants		8,301.1		1,082.0	7,219.0	14.2	68.7	309.4	689.7	1,599.7	4,511.9	1,107.4	
Alexandria, La. M.S.A.	**127,528**												
(Includes Rapides Parish.)													
City of Alexandria	46,364	4,769		459	4,310	6	19	165	269	1,083	3,007	220	
Total area actually reporting	94.0%	7,873		752	7,121	11	40	179	522	2,071	4,637	413	
Estimated total	100.0%	8,402		819	7,583	12	42	189	576	2,158	4,980	445	
Rate per 100,000 inhabitants		6,588.4		642.2	5,946.1	9.4	32.9	148.2	451.7	1,692.2	3,905.0	348.9	
Allentown-Bethlehem-Easton, Pa. M.S.A.	**611,918**												
(Includes Carbon, Lehigh, and Northampton Counties, Pa.)													
City of:													
Allentown	105,372	7,443		652	6,791	6	49	321	276	1,513	4,670	608	
Bethlehem	72,843	2,905		311	2,594	2	16	93	200	489	1,913	192	
Easton	27,734	1,600		189	1,411	3	10	84	92	311	998	102	
Total area actually reporting	94.5%	21,293		1,686	19,607	11	121	587	967	3,633	14,634	1,340	
Estimated total	100.0%	22,227		1,766	20,461	12	126	607	1,021	3,752	15,284	1,425	
Rate per 100,000 inhabitants		3,632.3		288.6	3,343.7	2.0	20.6	99.2	166.9	613.2	2,497.7	232.9	
Altoona, Pa. M.S.A.	**131,854**												
(Includes Blair County.)													
City of Altoona	52,548	1,758		169	1,589	—	18	61	90	508	987	94	
Total area actually reporting	100.0%	3,507		270	3,237	1	35	71	163	845	2,192	200	
Rate per 100,000 inhabitants		2,659.8		204.8	2,455.0	.8	26.5	53.8	123.6	640.9	1,662.4	151.7	
Amarillo, Tx. M.S.A.	**205,075**												
(Includes Potter and Randall Counties.)													
City of Amarillo	171,770	14,088		1,428	12,660	11	71	334	1,012	2,116	9,857	687	
Total area actually reporting	100.0%	14,945		1,501	13,444	12	80	341	1,068	2,292	10,410	742	
Rate per 100,000 inhabitants		7,287.6		731.9	6,555.7	5.9	39.0	166.3	520.8	1,117.6	5,076.2	361.8	
Anchorage, Ak. M.S.A.	**254,774**												
(Includes Anchorage Borough.)													
Total area actually reporting	100.0%	16,178		2,078	14,100	25	198	558	1,297	2,353	10,163	1,584	
Rate per 100,000 inhabitants		6,349.9		815.6	5,534.3	9.8	77.7	219.0	509.1	923.6	3,989.0	621.7	
Ann Arbor, Mi. M.S.A.	**517,342**												
(Includes Lenawee, Livingston, and Washtenaw Counties.)													
City of Ann Arbor	109,939	4,696		409	4,287	1	37	113	258	804	3,283	200	
Total area actually reporting	93.5%	19,880		1,748	18,132	9	240	402	1,097	3,481	13,204	1,447	
Estimated total	100.0%	21,440		1,880	19,560	10	251	431	1,188	3,696	14,245	1,619	
Rate per 100,000 inhabitants		4,144.3		363.4	3,780.9	1.9	48.5	83.3	229.6	714.4	2,753.5	312.9	

See footnotes at end of table.

Table 6. — Index of Crime, Metropolitan Statistical Areas, 1996 — Continued

Metropolitan Statistical Area	Population	Crime Index total	Modified Crime Index total[1]	Violent crime[2]	Property crime[3]	Murder and non-negligent manslaughter	Forcible rape	Robbery	Aggravated assault	Burglary	Larceny–theft	Motor vehicle theft	Arson[1]
Anniston, Al. M.S.A.	**118,362**												
(Includes Calhoun County.)													
City of Anniston	27,553	4,377		660	3,717	10	26	135	489	1,087	2,365	265	
Total area actually reporting	100.0%	7,151		1,020	6,131	14	38	191	777	1,727	3,971	433	
Rate per 100,000 inhabitants		6,041.6		861.8	5,179.9	11.8	32.1	161.4	656.5	1,459.1	3,355.0	365.8	
Appleton-Oshkosh-Neenah,													
Wi. M.S.A.	**340,674**												
(Includes Calumet, Outagamie,													
and Winnebago Counties.)													
City of:													
Appleton	70,661	2,237		53	2,184	1	14	11	27	285	1,848	51	
Oshkosh	57,091	2,787		102	2,685	—	16	11	75	348	2,229	108	
Neenah	24,751	830		43	787	—	1	4	38	121	633	33	
Total area actually reporting	100.0%	10,165		307	9,858	4	50	40	213	1,286	8,234	338	
Rate per 100,000 inhabitants		2,983.8		90.1	2,893.7	1.2	14.7	11.7	62.5	377.5	2,417.0	99.2	
Asheville, N.C. M.S.A.	**210,821**												
(Includes Buncombe and													
Madison Counties.)													
City of Asheville	66,560	4,637		502	4,135	4	23	153	322	858	2,937	340	
Total area actually reporting	91.1%	7,512		813	6,699	11	51	187	564	1,793	4,388	518	
Estimated total	100.0%	8,189		867	7,322	12	55	198	602	1,979	4,788	555	
Rate per 100,000 inhabitants		3,884.3		411.2	3,473.1	5.7	26.1	93.9	285.6	938.7	2,271.1	263.3	
Athens, Ga. M.S.A.	**138,942**												
(Includes Clarke, Madison, and													
Oconee Counties.)													
City of Athens-Clarke County ...	93,168	7,660		723	6,937	12	58	192	461	1,105	5,358	474	
Total area actually reporting	84.3%	8,325		754	7,571	13	63	196	482	1,240	5,822	509	
Estimated total	100.0%	9,458		835	8,623	14	69	229	523	1,456	6,518	649	
Rate per 100,000 inhabitants		6,807.2		601.0	6,206.2	10.1	49.7	164.8	376.4	1,047.9	4,691.2	467.1	
Atlanta, Ga. M.S.A.	**3,471,906**												
(Includes Barrow, Bartow,													
Carroll, Cherokee, Clayton, Cobb,													
Coweta, De Kalb, Douglas,													
Fayette, Forsyth, Fulton, Gwinnett,													
Henry, Newton, Paulding, Pickens,													
Rockdale, Spalding, and													
Walton Counties.)													
City of Atlanta	413,123	70,521		13,699	56,822	196	392	4,805	8,306	10,471	37,104	9,247	
Total area actually reporting	98.2%	261,326		26,829	234,497	341	1,257	10,055	15,176	42,369	159,984	32,144	
Estimated total	100.0%	265,522		27,126	238,396	345	1,276	10,166	15,339	43,048	162,751	32,597	
Rate per 100,000 inhabitants		7,647.7		781.3	6,866.4	9.9	36.8	292.8	441.8	1,239.9	4,687.7	938.9	
Atlantic City-Cape May, N.J. M.S.A. ..	**333,478**												
(Includes Atlantic and													
Cape May Counties.)													
Total area actually reporting	100.0%	25,355		2,251	23,104	18	169	791	1,273	3,956	18,172	976	
Rate per 100,000 inhabitants		7,603.2		675.0	6,928.2	5.4	50.7	237.2	381.7	1,186.3	5,449.2	292.7	
Austin-San Marcos, Tx. M.S.A.	**1,003,297**												
(Includes Bastrop, Caldwell,													
Hays, Travis, and Williamson													
Counties.)													
City of:													
Austin	537,484	42,278		3,821	38,457	40	270	1,376	2,135	7,575	27,187	3,695	
San Marcos	32,284	1,497		157	1,340	—	23	25	109	259	1,016	65	
Total area actually reporting	100.0%	59,796		5,226	54,570	54	411	1,575	3,186	11,635	38,405	4,530	
Rate per 100,000 inhabitants		5,960.0		520.9	5,439.1	5.4	41.0	157.0	317.6	1,159.7	3,827.9	451.5	
Bakersfield, Ca. M.S.A.	**617,990**												
(Includes Kern County.)													
City of Bakersfield	193,777	12,584		1,122	11,462	25	37	482	578	2,874	7,456	1,132	
Total area actually reporting	100.0%	31,895		4,122	27,773	52	167	972	2,931	7,932	16,940	2,901	
Rate per 100,000 inhabitants		5,161.1		667.0	4,494.1	8.4	27.0	157.3	474.3	1,283.5	2,741.1	469.4	
Baltimore, Md. M.S.A.	**2,495,067**												
(Includes Baltimore City and													
Anne Arundel, Baltimore,													
Carroll, Harford, Howard, and													
Queen Anne's Counties.)													
City of Baltimore	716,446	85,982		19,507	66,475	328	641	10,393	8,145	14,802	40,522	11,151	
Total area actually reporting	100.0%	175,326		30,872	144,454	394	1,123	14,079	15,276	29,347	95,846	19,261	
Rate per 100,000 inhabitants		7,026.9		1,237.3	5,789.6	15.8	45.0	564.3	612.2	1,176.2	3,841.4	772.0	

See footnotes at end of table.

Table 6. — Index of Crime, Metropolitan Statistical Areas, 1996 — Continued

Metropolitan Statistical Area	Population	Crime Index total	Modified Crime Index total[1]	Violent crime[2]	Property crime[3]	Murder and non-negligent man-slaughter	Forcible rape	Robbery	Aggra-vated assault	Burglary	Larceny–theft	Motor vehicle theft	Arson[1]
Bangor, Me. M.S.A.	**67,255**												
(Includes part of Penobscot and Waldo Counties.)													
City of Bangor	32,080	2,088		36	2,052	1	8	9	18	298	1,688	66	
Total area actually reporting	100.0%	3,052		52	3,000	1	13	13	25	461	2,445	94	
Rate per 100,000 inhabitants		4,538.0		77.3	4,460.6	1.5	19.3	19.3	37.2	685.5	3,635.4	139.8	
Barnstable-Yarmouth, Ma. M.S.A. ...	**142,892**												
(Includes part of Barnstable County.)													
City of:													
Barnstable	42,937	2,371		764	1,607	1	23	21	719	482	1,014	111	
Yarmouth	22,517	837		82	755	—	5	6	71	258	475	22	
Total area actually reporting	100.0%	5,527		993	4,534	1	37	33	922	1,392	2,933	209	
Rate per 100,000 inhabitants		3,868.0		694.9	3,173.0	.7	25.9	23.1	645.2	974.2	2,052.6	146.3	
Baton Rouge, La. M.S.A.	**562,908**												
(Includes Ascension, East Baton Rouge, Livingston, and West Baton Rouge Parishes.)													
City of Baton Rouge[4]	229,501	27,361		3,398	23,963	71	118	1,210	1,999	5,577	15,179	3,207	
Total area actually reporting	100.0%	46,643		4,943	41,700	101	225	1,522	3,095	8,815	28,551	4,334	
Rate per 100,000 inhabitants		8,286.1		878.1	7,408.0	17.9	40.0	270.4	549.8	1,566.0	5,072.1	769.9	
Beaumont-Port Arthur, Tx. M.S.A. ...	**387,930**												
(Includes Hardin, Jefferson, and Orange Counties.)													
City of:													
Beaumont	119,715	10,309		1,252	9,057	15	203	420	614	1,958	6,362	737	
Port Arthur	61,194	4,125		629	3,496	5	21	153	450	1,067	1,952	477	
Total area actually reporting	100.0%	22,967		2,518	20,449	27	287	715	1,489	4,795	13,956	1,698	
Rate per 100,000 inhabitants		5,920.4		649.1	5,271.3	7.0	74.0	184.3	383.8	1,236.0	3,597.6	437.7	
Bellingham, Wa. M.S.A.	**150,574**												
(Includes Whatcom County.)													
City of Bellingham	59,149	4,725		192	4,533	1	22	64	105	603	3,781	149	
Total area actually reporting	100.0%	8,659		464	8,195	4	72	92	296	1,682	6,196	317	
Rate per 100,000 inhabitants		5,750.7		308.2	5,442.5	2.7	47.8	61.1	196.6	1,117.1	4,114.9	210.5	
Benton Harbor, Mi. M.S.A.	**163,380**												
(Includes Berrien County.)													
City of Benton Harbor	13,321	2,153		537	1,616	1	28	129	379	653	786	177	
Total area actually reporting	96.3%	8,893		1,125	7,768	5	105	218	797	1,862	5,369	537	
Estimated total	100.0%	9,171		1,148	8,023	5	107	223	813	1,900	5,555	568	
Rate per 100,000 inhabitants		5,613.3		702.7	4,910.6	3.1	65.5	136.5	497.6	1,162.9	3,400.0	347.7	
Bergen-Passaic, N.J. M.S.A.	**1,317,987**												
(Includes Bergen and Passaic Counties.)													
City of Passaic	56,636	3,750		790	2,960	2	25	370	393	785	1,627	548	
Total area actually reporting	100.0%	43,559		4,249	39,310	25	173	1,863	2,188	6,917	26,425	5,968	
Rate per 100,000 inhabitants		3,305.0		322.4	2,982.6	1.9	13.1	141.4	166.0	524.8	2,005.0	452.8	
Birmingham, Al. M.S.A.	**884,884**												
(Includes Blount, Jefferson, St. Clair, and Shelby Counties.)													
City of Birmingham	272,169	29,283		4,416	24,867	113	229	1,838	2,236	5,973	15,280	3,614	
Total area actually reporting	99.5%	52,243		6,882	45,361	160	362	2,628	3,732	10,246	29,500	5,615	
Estimated total	100.0%	52,491		6,909	45,582	160	363	2,636	3,750	10,289	29,660	5,633	
Rate per 100,000 inhabitants		5,932.0		780.8	5,151.2	18.1	41.0	297.9	423.8	1,162.8	3,351.9	636.6	
Bismarck, N.D. M.S.A.	**88,981**												
(Includes Burleigh and Morton Counties.)													
City of Bismarck	53,086	2,151		58	2,093	1	7	9	41	232	1,743	118	
Total area actually reporting	100.0%	2,919		120	2,799	1	28	10	81	303	2,322	174	
Rate per 100,000 inhabitants		3,280.5		134.9	3,145.6	1.1	31.5	11.2	91.0	340.5	2,609.5	195.5	
Boise, Id. M.S.A.	**365,009**												
(Includes Ada and Canyon Counties.)													
City of Boise	153,258	8,797		508	8,289	1	60	56	391	1,511	6,400	378	
Total area actually reporting	100.0%	17,299		966	16,333	5	113	89	759	2,935	12,599	799	
Rate per 100,000 inhabitants		4,739.3		264.7	4,474.7	1.4	31.0	24.4	207.9	804.1	3,451.7	218.9	

See footnotes at end of table.

Table 6. — Index of Crime, Metropolitan Statistical Areas, 1996 — Continued

Metropolitan Statistical Area	Population	Crime Index total	Modified Crime Index total[1]	Violent crime[2]	Property crime[3]	Murder and non-negligent man-slaughter	Forcible rape	Robbery	Aggra-vated assault	Burglary	Larceny–theft	Motor vehicle theft	Arson[1]
Boston, Ma.-N.H. M.S.A.	**3,443,191**												
(Includes part of Bristol, Essex, Middlesex, Norfolk, Plymouth, Suffolk, and Worcester Counties, MA; and part of Rockingham County, N.H.)													
City of Boston, Ma.	552,519	44,711		9,154	35,557	59	414	3,470	5,211	5,052	21,234	9,271	
Total area actually reporting	95.8%	125,932		19,530	106,402	95	872	5,195	13,368	19,803	67,229	19,370	
Estimated total	100.0%	129,745		20,001	109,744	97	894	5,253	13,757	20,499	69,440	19,805	
Rate per 100,000 inhabitants		3,768.2		580.9	3,187.3	2.8	26.0	152.6	399.5	595.3	2,016.7	575.2	
Boulder-Longmont, Co. M.S.A.	**261,000**												
(Includes Boulder County.)													
City of:													
Boulder	89,522	5,957		244	5,713	1	49	62	132	874	4,546	293	
Longmont	58,833	3,477		127	3,350	1	23	38	65	475	2,682	193	
Total area actually reporting	99.5%	13,422		610	12,812	3	130	128	349	2,169	9,958	685	
Estimated total	100.0%	13,507		617	12,890	3	131	130	353	2,182	10,017	691	
Rate per 100,000 inhabitants		5,175.1		236.4	4,938.7	1.1	50.2	49.8	135.2	836.0	3,837.9	264.8	
Brazoria, Tx. M.S.A.	**220,144**												
(Includes Brazoria County.)													
Total area actually reporting	99.6%	6,800		621	6,179	10	64	73	474	1,439	4,320	420	
Estimated total	100.0%	6,840		624	6,216	10	64	74	476	1,446	4,347	423	
Rate per 100,000 inhabitants		3,107.1		283.5	2,823.6	4.5	29.1	33.6	216.2	656.8	1,974.6	192.1	
Bremerton, Wa. M.S.A.	**228,229**												
(Includes Kitsap County.)													
City of Bremerton	43,822	2,639		278	2,361	2	44	82	150	500	1,683	178	
Total area actually reporting	100.0%	9,549		813	8,736	5	121	143	544	1,799	6,432	505	
Rate per 100,000 inhabitants		4,184.0		356.2	3,827.7	2.2	53.0	62.7	238.4	788.2	2,818.2	221.3	
Bridgeport, Ct. M.S.A.	**452,787**												
(Includes part of Fairfield and New Haven Counties.)													
City of Bridgeport	133,015	11,041		2,107	8,934	44	61	948	1,054	2,479	4,077	2,378	
Total area actually reporting	100.0%	21,466		2,602	18,864	49	121	1,120	1,312	4,649	10,687	3,528	
Rate per 100,000 inhabitants		4,740.9		574.7	4,166.2	10.8	26.7	247.4	289.8	1,026.8	2,360.3	779.2	
Brockton, Ma. M.S.A.	**250,799**												
(Includes part of Bristol, Norfolk, and Plymouth Counties.)													
City of Brockton	88,148	5,423		1,035	4,388	8	38	224	765	1,173	2,114	1,101	
Total area actually reporting	90.0%	8,801		1,453	7,348	11	65	258	1,119	1,736	4,106	1,506	
Estimated total	100.0%	9,466		1,535	7,931	11	69	268	1,187	1,857	4,492	1,582	
Rate per 100,000 inhabitants		3,774.3		612.0	3,162.3	4.4	27.5	106.9	473.3	740.4	1,791.1	630.8	
Brownsville-Harlingen-San Benito, Tx. M.S.A.	**309,053**												
(Includes Cameron County.)													
City of:													
Brownsville	117,511	9,868		1,151	8,717	11	22	231	887	1,328	6,911	478	
Harlingen	57,787	4,541		318	4,223	—	1	54	263	1,045	2,962	216	
San Benito	24,268	2,188		118	2,070	—	8	11	99	347	1,644	79	
Total area actually reporting	100.0%	19,248		1,760	17,488	19	33	335	1,373	3,705	12,876	907	
Rate per 100,000 inhabitants		6,228.1		569.5	5,658.6	6.1	10.7	108.4	444.3	1,198.8	4,166.3	293.5	
Bryan-College Station, Tx. M.S.A. .	**135,709**												
(Includes Brazos County.)													
City of:													
Bryan	63,235	4,520		503	4,017	6	43	83	371	915	2,799	303	
College Station	59,610	2,833		131	2,702	—	24	32	75	391	2,206	105	
Total area actually reporting	100.0%	8,475		660	7,815	7	77	121	455	1,546	5,836	433	
Rate per 100,000 inhabitants		6,245.0		486.3	5,758.6	5.2	56.7	89.2	335.3	1,139.2	4,300.4	319.1	

See footnotes at end of table.

Table 6. — Index of Crime, Metropolitan Statistical Areas, 1996 — Continued

Metropolitan Statistical Area	Population	Crime Index total	Modified Crime Index total[1]	Violent crime[2]	Property crime[3]	Murder and non-negligent man-slaughter	Forcible rape	Robbery	Aggra-vated assault	Burglary	Larceny-theft	Motor vehicle theft	Arson[1]
Buffalo-Niagara Falls, N.Y. M.S.A.	**1,192,353**												
(Includes Erie and Niagara Counties.)													
City of:													
Buffalo	313,238	26,644		4,532	22,112	60	272	2,624	1,576	6,298	11,314	4,500	
Niagara Falls	60,569	4,496		452	4,044	2	28	214	208	1,167	2,523	354	
Total area actually reporting	99.8%	54,319		6,416	47,903	71	412	3,232	2,701	11,127	30,101	6,675	
Estimated total	100.0%	54,415		6,424	47,991	71	412	3,235	2,706	11,142	30,167	6,682	
Rate per 100,000 inhabitants		4,563.7		538.8	4,024.9	6.0	34.6	271.3	226.9	934.5	2,530.0	560.4	
Casper, Wy. M.S.A.	**64,554**												
(Includes Natrona County.)													
City of Casper	49,708	3,149		125	3,024	—	17	22	86	595	2,299	130	
Total area actually reporting	100.0%	3,843		162	3,681	1	20	24	117	770	2,740	171	
Rate per 100,000 inhabitants		5,953.2		251.0	5,702.2	1.5	31.0	37.2	181.2	1,192.8	4,244.5	264.9	
Charleston-North Charleston, S.C. M.S.A.	**527,250**												
(Includes Berkeley, Charleston, and Dorchester Counties.)													
City of:													
Charleston	77,588	8,520		1,308	7,212	9	53	399	847	1,240	5,273	699	
North Charleston	68,366	10,781		1,792	8,989	11	85	431	1,265	1,759	6,014	1,216	
Total area actually reporting	99.7%	37,314		5,156	32,158	40	284	1,130	3,702	6,777	22,192	3,189	
Estimated total	100.0%	37,432		5,169	32,263	40	285	1,132	3,712	6,796	22,271	3,196	
Rate per 100,000 inhabitants		7,099.5		980.4	6,119.1	7.6	54.1	214.7	704.0	1,289.0	4,224.0	606.2	
Charleston, W.V. M.S.A.	**254,198**												
(Includes Kanawha and Putnam Counties.)													
City of Charleston	56,244	6,117		584	5,533	7	26	248	303	1,036	4,041	456	
Total area actually reporting	100.0%	10,724		873	9,851	13	63	318	479	2,026	6,891	934	
Rate per 100,000 inhabitants		4,218.8		343.4	3,875.3	5.1	24.8	125.1	188.4	797.0	2,710.9	367.4	
Charlotte-Gastonia-Rock Hill, N.C.-S.C. M.S.A.	**1,301,996**												
(Includes Cabarrus, Gaston, Lincoln, Mecklenburg, Rowan, and Union Counties, N.C.; and York County, S.C.)													
City of:													
Charlotte-Mecklenburg, N.C.	554,070	53,518		8,915	44,603	71	306	2,594	5,944	10,227	30,199	4,177	
Gastonia, N.C.	61,206	5,906		830	5,076	12	35	278	505	1,212	3,621	243	
Rock Hill, S.C.	47,454	3,367		628	2,739	3	26	99	500	503	2,111	125	
Total area actually reporting	99.5%	88,648		12,716	75,932	116	540	3,433	8,627	17,960	52,132	5,840	
Estimated total	100.0%	89,069		12,749	76,320	116	542	3,442	8,649	18,038	52,424	5,858	
Rate per 100,000 inhabitants		6,841.0		979.2	5,861.8	8.9	41.6	264.4	664.3	1,385.4	4,026.4	449.9	
Charlottesville, Va. M.S.A.	**143,311**												
(Includes Albemarle, Fluvanna, and Greene Counties and Charlottesville City.)													
City of Charlottesville	41,803	2,817		253	2,564	2	26	73	152	397	2,037	130	
Total area actually reporting	100.0%	5,812		401	5,411	2	43	100	256	882	4,274	255	
Rate per 100,000 inhabitants		4,055.5		279.8	3,775.7	1.4	30.0	69.8	178.6	615.4	2,982.3	177.9	
Cheyenne, Wy. M.S.A.	**78,932**												
(Includes Laramie County.)													
City of Cheyenne	54,195	2,762		89	2,673	1	20	22	46	276	2,327	70	
Total area actually reporting	100.0%	3,518		153	3,365	1	39	28	85	391	2,876	98	
Rate per 100,000 inhabitants		4,457.0		193.8	4,263.2	1.3	49.4	35.5	107.7	495.4	3,643.6	124.2	
Chico-Paradise, Ca. M.S.A.	**194,981**												
(Includes Butte County.)													
City of:													
Chico	44,262	2,809		242	2,567	2	43	60	137	544	1,850	173	
Paradise	26,763	894		68	826	1	1	5	61	229	551	46	
Total area actually reporting	100.0%	8,738		650	8,088	10	85	112	443	2,191	5,255	642	
Rate per 100,000 inhabitants		4,481.5		333.4	4,148.1	5.1	43.6	57.4	227.2	1,123.7	2,695.1	329.3	
Colorado Springs, Co. M.S.A.	**473,166**												
(Includes El Paso County.)													
City of Colorado Springs	331,020	20,523		1,595	18,928	12	238	453	892	3,304	14,248	1,376	
Total area actually reporting	99.9%	24,164		1,945	22,219	20	264	479	1,182	4,187	16,415	1,617	
Estimated total	100.0%	24,204		1,948	22,256	20	264	480	1,184	4,193	16,443	1,620	
Rate per 100,000 inhabitants		5,115.3		411.7	4,703.6	4.2	55.8	101.4	250.2	886.2	3,475.1	342.4	

See footnotes at end of table.

Metropolitan Statistical Area	Population	Crime Index total	Modified Crime Index total[1]	Violent crime[2]	Property crime[3]	Murder and non-negligent man-slaughter	Forcible rape	Robbery	Aggra-vated assault	Burglary	Larceny–theft	Motor vehicle theft	Arson[1]
Columbia, Mo. M.S.A.	**123,339**												
(Includes Boone County.)													
City of Columbia	75,207	5,055		403	4,652	3	33	96	271	490	3,969	193	
Total area actually reporting	100.0%	6,898		487	6,411	4	44	104	335	774	5,368	269	
Rate per 100,000 inhabitants		5,592.7		394.8	5,197.9	3.2	35.7	84.3	271.6	627.5	4,352.2	218.1	
Columbia, S.C. M.S.A.	**491,647**												
(Includes Lexington and Richland Counties.)													
City of Columbia	105,316	12,170		1,819	10,351	19	75	481	1,244	1,909	7,511	931	
Total area actually reporting	100.0%	32,026		4,637	27,389	48	273	1,171	3,145	6,380	18,392	2,617	
Rate per 100,000 inhabitants		6,514.0		943.2	5,570.9	9.8	55.5	238.2	639.7	1,297.7	3,740.9	532.3	
Columbus, Ga.-Al. M.S.A.	**287,397**												
(Includes Chattahoochee, Harris, and Muscogee Counties, Ga.; and Russell County, Al.)													
City of Columbus, Ga.	194,345	12,294		890	11,404	15	24	367	484	2,216	8,351	837	
Total area actually reporting	99.3%	15,046		1,247	13,799	17	56	428	746	2,882	9,886	1,031	
Estimated total	100.0%	15,221		1,259	13,962	17	57	432	753	2,906	10,008	1,048	
Rate per 100,000 inhabitants		5,296.2		438.1	4,858.1	5.9	19.8	150.3	262.0	1,011.1	3,482.3	364.7	
Columbus, Oh. M.S.A.	**1,430,860**												
(Includes Delaware, Fairfield, Franklin, Licking, Madison, and Pickaway Counties.)													
City of Columbus	640,297	61,083		6,216	54,867	89	571	3,318	2,238	13,013	34,244	7,610	
Total area actually reporting	86.2%	84,531		7,952	76,579	102	755	3,814	3,281	17,464	50,126	8,989	
Estimated total	100.0%	90,609		8,293	82,316	105	800	3,913	3,475	18,521	54,431	9,364	
Rate per 100,000 inhabitants		6,332.5		579.6	5,752.9	7.3	55.9	273.5	242.9	1,294.4	3,804.1	654.4	
Corpus Christi, Tx. M.S.A.	**391,941**												
(Includes Nueces and San Patricio Counties.)													
City of Corpus Christi	286,660	30,467		3,020	27,447	18	276	485	2,241	3,773	22,006	1,668	
Total area actually reporting	100.0%	33,608		3,335	30,273	23	299	510	2,503	4,651	23,811	1,811	
Rate per 100,000 inhabitants		8,574.8		850.9	7,723.9	5.9	76.3	130.1	638.6	1,186.7	6,075.1	462.1	
Cumberland, Md.-W.V. M.S.A.	**102,131**												
(Includes Allegany County, Md., and Mineral County, W.V.)													
City of Cumberland, Md.	24,215	1,458		208	1,250	—	10	9	189	249	960	41	
Total area actually reporting	100.0%	2,983		384	2,599	2	19	19	344	531	1,954	114	
Rate per 100,000 inhabitants		2,920.8		376.0	2,544.8	2.0	18.6	18.6	336.8	519.9	1,913.2	111.6	
Dallas, Tx. M.S.A.	**2,911,263**												
(Includes Collin, Dallas, Denton, Ellis, Henderson, Hunt, Kaufman, and Rockwall Counties.)													
City of Dallas	1,060,585	100,401		16,280	84,121	217	740	6,122	9,201	17,960	49,018	17,143	
Total area actually reporting	100.0%	184,871		22,835	162,036	285	1,280	7,459	13,811	33,114	105,876	23,046	
Rate per 100,000 inhabitants		6,350.2		784.4	5,565.8	9.8	44.0	256.2	474.4	1,137.4	3,636.8	791.6	
Danbury, Ct. M.S.A.	**163,802**												
(Includes part of Fairfield and Litchfield Counties.)													
City of Danbury	64,654	3,529		132	3,397	—	6	74	52	515	2,458	424	
Total area actually reporting	100.0%	5,246		189	5,057	—	13	82	94	883	3,674	500	
Rate per 100,000 inhabitants		3,202.6		115.4	3,087.3	—	7.9	50.1	57.4	539.1	2,243.0	305.2	
Danville, Va. M.S.A.	**112,019**												
(Includes Pittsylvania County and Danville City.)													
City of Danville	55,244	2,797		226	2,571	9	21	86	110	417	2,004	150	
Total area actually reporting	100.0%	3,487		303	3,184	16	34	99	154	616	2,355	213	
Rate per 100,000 inhabitants		3,112.9		270.5	2,842.4	14.3	30.4	88.4	137.5	549.9	2,102.3	190.1	
Dayton-Springfield, Oh. M.S.A.	**963,073**												
(Includes Clark, Greene, Miami, and Montgomery Counties.)													
City of:													
Dayton	179,680	17,841		2,026	15,815	38	201	1,085	702	3,720	8,859	3,236	
Springfield	70,837	7,458		1,405	6,053	8	94	288	1,015	1,215	4,361	477	
Total area actually reporting	77.5%	46,488		4,330	42,158	53	443	1,661	2,173	7,998	28,938	5,222	
Estimated total	100.0%	51,520		4,602	46,918	57	489	1,735	2,321	9,094	32,288	5,536	
Rate per 100,000 inhabitants		5,349.5		477.8	4,871.7	5.9	50.8	180.2	241.0	944.3	3,352.6	574.8	

See footnotes at end of table.

Metropolitan Statistical Area	Population	Crime Index total	Modified Crime Index total[1]	Violent crime[2]	Property crime[3]	Murder and non-negligent man-slaughter	Forcible rape	Robbery	Aggra-vated assault	Burglary	Larceny-theft	Motor vehicle theft	Arson[1]
Decatur, Al. M.S.A.	**139,638**												
(Includes Lawrence and Morgan Counties.)													
City of Decatur	53,135	3,772		258	3,514	5	23	94	136	759	2,596	159	
Total area actually reporting	99.6%	4,766		328	4,438	9	29	101	189	1,080	3,097	261	
Estimated total	100.0%	4,798		331	4,467	9	29	102	191	1,086	3,118	263	
Rate per 100,000 inhabitants		3,436.0		237.0	3,199.0	6.4	20.8	73.0	136.8	777.7	2,232.9	188.3	
Denver, Co. M.S.A.	**1,869,821**												
(Includes Adams, Arapahoe, Denver, Douglas, and Jefferson Counties.)													
City of Denver	516,224	34,314		3,832	30,482	64	358	1,327	2,083	7,788	17,269	5,425	
Total area actually reporting	95.2%	95,975		8,216	87,759	102	831	2,543	4,740	17,811	59,914	10,034	
Estimated total	100.0%	101,268		8,609	92,659	106	872	2,649	4,982	18,617	63,636	10,406	
Rate per 100,000 inhabitants		5,415.9		460.4	4,955.5	5.7	46.6	141.7	266.4	995.7	3,403.3	556.5	
Des Moines, Ia. M.S.A.	**419,768**												
(Includes Dallas, Polk, and Warren Counties.)													
City of Des Moines	195,455	15,157		926	14,231	19	100	321	486	1,794	11,226	1,211	
Total area actually reporting	100.0%	22,919		1,275	21,644	19	118	369	769	3,069	16,947	1,628	
Rate per 100,000 inhabitants		5,459.9		303.7	5,156.2	4.5	28.1	87.9	183.2	731.1	4,037.2	387.8	
Detroit, Mi. M.S.A.	**4,353,756**												
(Includes Lapeer, Macomb, Monroe, Oakland, St. Clair, and Wayne Counties.)													
City of Detroit	1,002,299	120,188		23,239	96,949	428	1,119	9,504	12,188	21,491	41,193	34,265	
Total area actually reporting	90.4%	245,627		34,470	211,157	505	2,108	11,836	20,021	39,021	122,113	50,023	
Estimated total	100.0%	264,784		36,087	228,697	517	2,238	12,190	21,142	41,659	134,897	52,141	
Rate per 100,000 inhabitants		6,081.7		828.9	5,252.9	11.9	51.4	280.0	485.6	956.9	3,098.4	1,197.6	
Dothan, Al. M.S.A.	**136,202**												
(Includes Dale and Houston Counties.)													
City of Dothan	56,505	2,922		250	2,672	9	25	132	84	687	1,829	156	
Total area actually reporting	98.1%	4,338		418	3,920	11	36	156	215	1,022	2,674	224	
Estimated total	100.0%	4,474		433	4,041	11	37	160	225	1,045	2,762	234	
Rate per 100,000 inhabitants		3,284.8		317.9	2,966.9	8.1	27.2	117.5	165.2	767.2	2,027.9	171.8	
Dover, De. M.S.A.	**126,645**												
(Includes Kent County.)													
City of Dover	29,515	2,660		250	2,410	—	22	84	144	257	1,961	192	
Total area actually reporting	99.9%	6,422		875	5,547	4	115	162	594	1,040	4,142	365	
Estimated total	100.0%	6,434		876	5,558	4	115	162	595	1,041	4,151	366	
Rate per 100,000 inhabitants		5,080.3		691.7	4,388.6	3.2	90.8	127.9	469.8	822.0	3,277.7	289.0	
Dubuque, Ia. M.S.A.	**88,988**												
(Includes Dubuque County.)													
City of Dubuque	59,563	2,335		174	2,161	1	31	15	127	396	1,698	67	
Total area actually reporting	100.0%	2,742		200	2,542	1	37	15	147	510	1,941	91	
Rate per 100,000 inhabitants		3,081.3		224.7	2,856.6	1.1	41.6	16.9	165.2	573.1	2,181.2	102.3	
Duluth-Superior, Mn.-Wi. M.S.A.	**245,507**												
(Includes St. Louis County, Mn., and Douglas County, Wi.)													
City of:													
Duluth, Mn.	85,663	4,960		303	4,657	3	65	67	168	794	3,465	398	
Superior, Wi.	27,968	1,955		68	1,887	1	13	18	36	324	1,464	99	
Total area actually reporting	100.0%	10,398		517	9,881	6	132	92	287	2,077	7,103	701	
Rate per 100,000 inhabitants		4,235.3		210.6	4,024.7	2.4	53.8	37.5	116.9	846.0	2,893.2	285.5	
Dutchess County, N.Y. M.S.A.	**261,693**												
(Includes Dutchess County.)													
Total area actually reporting	100.0%	7,625		943	6,682	7	46	246	644	1,378	4,955	349	
Rate per 100,000 inhabitants		2,913.7		360.3	2,553.4	2.7	17.6	94.0	246.1	526.6	1,893.4	133.4	
Eau Claire, Wi. M.S.A.	**144,116**												
(Includes Chippewa and Eau Claire Counties.)													
City of Eau Claire	59,372	2,945		195	2,750	4	16	21	154	453	2,202	95	
Total area actually reporting	100.0%	4,839		245	4,594	4	25	36	180	765	3,635	194	
Rate per 100,000 inhabitants		3,357.7		170.0	3,187.7	2.8	17.3	25.0	124.9	530.8	2,522.3	134.6	

See footnotes at end of table.

Table 6. — Index of Crime, Metropolitan Statistical Areas, 1996 — Continued

Metropolitan Statistical Area	Population	Crime Index total	Modified Crime Index total[1]	Violent crime[2]	Property crime[3]	Murder and non-negligent man-slaughter	Forcible rape	Robbery	Aggra-vated assault	Burglary	Larceny-theft	Motor vehicle theft	Arson[1]
Elkhart-Goshen, In. M.S.A.	**166,529**												
(Includes Elkhart County.)													
City of:													
Elkhart	45,533	4,958		250	4,708	6	26	149	69	939	3,457	312	
Goshen	25,737	1,570		140	1,430	3	9	18	110	176	1,184	70	
Total area actually reporting	100.0%	9,135		934	8,201	9	52	189	684	1,690	5,964	547	
Rate per 100,000 inhabitants		5,485.5		560.9	4,924.7	5.4	31.2	113.5	410.7	1,014.8	3,581.4	328.5	
El Paso, Tx. M.S.A.	**691,942**												
(Includes El Paso County.)													
City of El Paso	602,951	45,134		5,138	39,996	30	245	1,195	3,668	3,942	31,694	4,360	
Total area actually reporting	100.0%	48,303		5,614	42,689	37	319	1,245	4,013	4,532	33,555	4,602	
Rate per 100,000 inhabitants		6,980.8		811.3	6,169.4	5.3	46.1	179.9	580.0	655.0	4,849.4	665.1	
Enid, Ok. M.S.A.	**57,679**												
(Includes Garfield County.)													
City of Enid	46,455	4,085		384	3,701	4	31	57	292	722	2,725	254	
Total area actually reporting	100.0%	4,277		394	3,883	7	31	57	299	775	2,848	260	
Rate per 100,000 inhabitants		7,415.2		683.1	6,732.1	12.1	53.7	98.8	518.4	1,343.6	4,937.7	450.8	
Erie, Pa. M.S.A.	**280,400**												
(Includes Erie County.)													
City of Erie	108,432	5,532		669	4,863	6	68	336	259	1,019	3,458	386	
Total area actually reporting	100.0%	9,909		881	9,028	9	101	370	401	1,848	6,566	614	
Rate per 100,000 inhabitants		3,533.9		314.2	3,219.7	3.2	36.0	132.0	143.0	659.1	2,341.7	219.0	
Eugene-Springfield, Or. M.S.A.	**310,422**												
(Includes Lane County.)													
City of:													
Eugene	122,637	12,181		739	11,442	2	50	271	416	1,914	8,765	763	
Springfield	49,623	4,538		192	4,346	1	21	80	90	759	3,200	387	
Total area actually reporting	100.0%	21,413		1,281	20,132	11	125	411	734	3,913	14,726	1,493	
Rate per 100,000 inhabitants		6,898.0		412.7	6,485.4	3.5	40.3	132.4	236.5	1,260.5	4,743.9	481.0	
Fayetteville, N.C. M.S.A.	**296,617**												
(Includes Cumberland County.)													
City of Fayetteville	87,004	10,200		940	9,260	14	73	476	377	2,032	6,449	779	
Total area actually reporting	100.0%	21,189		1,743	19,446	37	170	709	827	5,087	12,768	1,591	
Rate per 100,000 inhabitants		7,143.6		587.6	6,555.9	12.5	57.3	239.0	278.8	1,715.0	4,304.5	536.4	
Fayetteville-Springdale-Rogers, Ar. M.S.A.	**248,090**												
(Includes Benton and Washington Counties.)													
City of:													
Fayetteville	50,362	3,301		173	3,128	2	37	23	111	467	2,557	104	
Springdale	37,401	1,526		67	1,459	—	12	8	47	202	1,168	89	
Rogers	31,169	1,728		70	1,658	—	17	8	45	202	1,393	63	
Total area actually reporting	100.0%	9,708		666	9,042	6	88	53	519	1,456	7,219	367	
Rate per 100,000 inhabitants		3,913.1		268.5	3,644.6	2.4	35.5	21.4	209.2	586.9	2,909.8	147.9	
Fitchburg-Leominster, Ma. M.S.A.	**136,511**												
(Includes part of Middlesex and Worcester Counties.)													
City of:													
Fitchburg	37,035	2,239		667	1,572	3	33	77	554	507	904	161	
Leominster	38,561	1,685		149	1,536	—	10	26	113	296	1,044	196	
Total area actually reporting	95.3%	5,346		1,031	4,315	3	59	117	852	1,145	2,754	416	
Estimated total	100.0%	5,519		1,053	4,466	3	60	120	870	1,176	2,854	436	
Rate per 100,000 inhabitants		4,042.9		771.4	3,271.5	2.2	44.0	87.9	637.3	861.5	2,090.7	319.4	
Flint, Mi. M.S.A.	**437,676**												
(Includes Genesee County.)													
City of Flint	139,588	16,054		3,325	12,729	40	182	937	2,166	4,141	6,340	2,248	
Total area actually reporting	97.4%	27,871		4,320	23,551	50	282	1,159	2,829	6,359	13,900	3,292	
Estimated total	100.0%	28,397		4,365	24,032	50	286	1,169	2,860	6,431	14,251	3,350	
Rate per 100,000 inhabitants		6,488.1		997.3	5,490.8	11.4	65.3	267.1	653.5	1,469.4	3,256.1	765.4	
Florence, Al. M.S.A.	**137,414**												
(Includes Colbert and Lauderdale Counties.)													
City of Florence	37,240	1,239		115	1,124	—	7	23	85	249	832	43	
Total area actually reporting	98.7%	3,898		261	3,637	3	13	38	207	718	2,804	115	
Estimated total	100.0%	3,995		272	3,723	3	14	41	214	735	2,866	122	
Rate per 100,000 inhabitants		2,907.3		197.9	2,709.3	2.2	10.2	29.8	155.7	534.9	2,085.7	88.8	

See footnotes at end of table.

Table 6. — Index of Crime, Metropolitan Statistical Areas, 1996 — Continued

Metropolitan Statistical Area	Population	Crime Index total	Modified Crime Index total[1]	Violent crime[2]	Property crime[3]	Murder and non-negligent man-slaughter	Forcible rape	Robbery	Aggra-vated assault	Burglary	Larceny–theft	Motor vehicle theft	Arson[1]
Florence, S.C. M.S.A.	**122,319**												
(Includes Florence County.)													
City of Florence	32,695	3,243		528	2,715	4	18	125	381	517	2,058	140	
Total area actually reporting	100.0%	6,651		1,118	5,533	14	58	189	857	1,359	3,879	295	
Rate per 100,000 inhabitants		5,437.4		914.0	4,523.4	11.4	47.4	154.5	700.6	1,111.0	3,171.2	241.2	
Fort Collins-Loveland, Co. M.S.A.	**222,043**												
(Includes Larimer County.)													
City of:													
Fort Collins	103,472	5,448		419	5,029	3	70	46	300	829	4,042	158	
Loveland	45,974	1,617		91	1,526	1	31	9	50	238	1,209	79	
Total area actually reporting	100.0%	9,116		585	8,531	4	132	68	381	1,401	6,808	322	
Rate per 100,000 inhabitants		4,105.5		263.5	3,842.0	1.8	59.4	30.6	171.6	631.0	3,066.1	145.0	
Fort Smith, Ar.-Ok. M.S.A.	**189,060**												
(Includes Crawford and Sebastian Counties, Ar., and Sequoyah County, Ok.)													
City of Fort Smith, Ar.	76,210	6,231		406	5,825	6	58	90	252	487	4,918	420	
Total area actually reporting	100.0%	9,210		733	8,477	12	69	101	551	1,242	6,633	602	
Rate per 100,000 inhabitants		4,871.5		387.7	4,483.8	6.3	36.5	53.4	291.4	656.9	3,508.4	318.4	
Fort Wayne, In. M.S.A.	**476,311**												
(Includes Adams, Allen, DeKalb, Huntington, Wells, and Whitley Counties.)													
City of Fort Wayne	186,196	13,966		1,069	12,897	13	121	499	436	1,927	9,407	1,563	
Total area actually reporting	83.1%	18,516		1,450	17,066	14	155	526	755	2,784	12,405	1,877	
Estimated total	100.0%	21,113		1,673	19,440	16	171	566	920	3,200	14,141	2,099	
Rate per 100,000 inhabitants		4,432.6		351.2	4,081.4	3.4	35.9	118.8	193.2	671.8	2,968.9	440.7	
Fort Worth-Arlington, Tx. M.S.A.	**1,621,158**												
(Includes Hood, Johnson, Parker, and Tarrant Counties.)													
City of:													
Fort Worth	470,254	38,902		4,984	33,918	68	319	1,692	2,905	7,917	21,481	4,520	
Arlington	298,632	21,312		2,478	18,834	17	156	618	1,687	3,395	13,165	2,274	
Total area actually reporting	100.0%	95,086		10,730	84,356	108	785	2,801	7,036	17,733	57,317	9,306	
Rate per 100,000 inhabitants		5,865.3		661.9	5,203.4	6.7	48.4	172.8	434.0	1,093.8	3,535.6	574.0	
Fresno, Ca. M.S.A.	**846,518**												
(Includes Fresno and Madera Counties.)													
City of Fresno	392,049	41,687		5,461	36,226	69	216	2,087	3,089	6,868	20,180	9,178	
Total area actually reporting	100.0%	64,507		8,831	55,676	105	360	2,633	5,733	11,709	31,013	12,954	
Rate per 100,000 inhabitants		7,620.3		1,043.2	6,577.1	12.4	42.5	311.0	677.2	1,383.2	3,663.6	1,530.3	
Gadsden, Al. M.S.A.	**101,188**												
(Includes Etowah County.)													
City of Gadsden	47,145	5,032		814	4,218	3	38	112	661	917	2,909	392	
Total area actually reporting	100.0%	6,526		879	5,647	5	45	124	705	1,198	3,971	478	
Rate per 100,000 inhabitants		6,449.4		868.7	5,580.7	4.9	44.5	122.5	696.7	1,183.9	3,924.4	472.4	
Galveston-Texas City, Tx. M.S.A.	**244,255**												
(Includes Galveston County.)													
City of:													
Galveston	61,641	6,066		1,093	4,973	11	62	265	755	911	3,380	682	
Texas City	43,361	4,984		575	4,409	7	34	116	418	1,456	2,545	408	
Total area actually reporting	100.0%	16,877		2,146	14,731	21	141	453	1,531	3,584	9,717	1,430	
Rate per 100,000 inhabitants		6,909.6		878.6	6,031.0	8.6	57.7	185.5	626.8	1,467.3	3,978.2	585.5	
Gary-Hammond, In. M.S.A.	**629,446**												
(Includes Lake and Porter Counties.)													
City of:													
Gary[4]	116,024	11,229		3,880	7,349	104	185	702	2,889	2,278	2,823	2,248	
Hammond	84,118	7,117		789	6,328	5	50	35	699	1,262	3,682	1,384	
Total area actually reporting	97.6%	33,244		6,634	26,610	114	285	1,223	5,012	4,927	16,358	5,325	
Estimated total	100.0%	33,933		6,687	27,246	114	288	1,230	5,055	4,997	16,874	5,375	
Rate per 100,000 inhabitants		5,390.9		1,062.4	4,328.6	18.1	45.8	195.4	803.1	793.9	2,680.8	853.9	
Glens Falls, N.Y. M.S.A.	**122,221**												
(Includes Warren and Washington Counties.)													
City of Glens Falls	13,573	949		156	793	1	1	7	147	185	603	5	
Total area actually reporting	97.6%	3,488		263	3,225	2	12	18	231	714	2,459	52	
Estimated total	100.0%	3,583		271	3,312	2	12	21	236	729	2,524	59	
Rate per 100,000 inhabitants		2,931.6		221.7	2,709.8	1.6	9.8	17.2	193.1	596.5	2,065.1	48.3	

See footnotes at end of table.

Table 6. — Index of Crime, Metropolitan Statistical Areas, 1996 — Continued

Metropolitan Statistical Area	Population	Crime Index total	Modified Crime Index total[1]	Violent crime[2]	Property crime[3]	Murder and non-negligent man-slaughter	Forcible rape	Robbery	Aggra-vated assault	Burglary	Larceny–theft	Motor vehicle theft	Arson[1]
Goldsboro, N.C. M.S.A.	**113,158**												
(Includes Wayne County.)													
City of Goldsboro	46,621	4,395		544	3,851	10	23	160	351	756	2,878	217	
Total area actually reporting	100.0%	6,743		757	5,986	17	34	190	516	1,561	4,081	344	
Rate per 100,000 inhabitants		5,958.9		669.0	5,289.9	15.0	30.0	167.9	456.0	1,379.5	3,606.5	304.0	
Grand Junction, Co. M.S.A.	**108,360**												
(Includes Mesa County.)													
City of Grand Junction	33,208	3,335		235	3,100	2	16	52	165	452	2,535	113	
Total area actually reporting	100.0%	5,099		338	4,761	7	37	56	238	830	3,721	210	
Rate per 100,000 inhabitants		4,705.6		311.9	4,393.7	6.5	34.1	51.7	219.6	766.0	3,433.9	193.8	
Grand Rapids-Muskegon-Holland, Mi. M.S.A.	**995,118**												
(Includes Allegan, Kent, Muskegon, and Ottawa Counties.)													
City of:													
Grand Rapids	192,358	14,600		2,443	12,157	20	101	675	1,647	3,033	8,051	1,073	
Muskegon	41,057	4,424		611	3,813	5	65	132	409	904	2,663	246	
Holland	31,882	1,548		125	1,423	—	22	7	96	138	1,218	67	
Total area actually reporting	90.0%	41,222		4,488	36,734	35	414	965	3,074	8,015	26,337	2,382	
Estimated total	100.0%	45,797		4,875	40,922	38	445	1,050	3,342	8,645	29,389	2,888	
Rate per 100,000 inhabitants		4,602.2		489.9	4,112.3	3.8	44.7	105.5	335.8	868.7	2,953.3	290.2	
Greeley, Co. M.S.A.	**150,697**												
(Includes Weld County.)													
City of Greeley	67,120	4,712		309	4,403	5	40	52	212	678	3,491	234	
Total area actually reporting	95.2%	7,426		543	6,883	8	66	61	408	1,312	5,145	426	
Estimated total	100.0%	7,853		575	7,278	8	69	70	428	1,377	5,445	456	
Rate per 100,000 inhabitants		5,211.1		381.6	4,829.6	5.3	45.8	46.5	284.0	913.8	3,613.2	302.6	
Green Bay, Wi. M.S.A.	**210,445**												
(Includes Brown County.)													
City of Green Bay	104,283	4,679		390	4,289	3	39	68	280	584	3,481	224	
Total area actually reporting	100.0%	8,007		465	7,542	3	57	80	325	1,058	6,114	370	
Rate per 100,000 inhabitants		3,804.8		221.0	3,583.8	1.4	27.1	38.0	154.4	502.7	2,905.3	175.8	
Greensboro-Winston-Salem-High Point, N.C. M.S.A.	**1,147,250**												
(Includes Alamance, Davidson, Davie, Forsythe, Guilford, Randolph, Stokes, and Yadkin Counties.)													
City of:													
Greensboro	203,186	16,393		1,927	14,466	23	95	710	1,099	3,228	10,190	1,048	
Winston-Salem	160,678	18,929		2,267	16,662	28	123	871	1,245	3,812	11,062	1,788	
High Point	74,791	7,884		906	6,978	12	37	300	557	1,990	4,519	469	
Total area actually reporting	99.8%	70,457		7,547	62,910	86	414	2,318	4,729	15,705	42,575	4,630	
Estimated total	100.0%	70,642		7,562	63,080	86	415	2,322	4,739	15,739	42,703	4,638	
Rate per 100,000 inhabitants		6,157.5		659.1	5,498.4	7.5	36.2	202.4	413.1	1,371.9	3,722.2	404.3	
Greenville, N.C. M.S.A.	**118,225**												
(Includes Pitt County.)													
City of Greenville	51,091	5,254		477	4,777	4	32	163	278	1,122	3,436	219	
Total area actually reporting	99.6%	8,359		866	7,493	10	52	217	587	2,037	5,089	367	
Estimated total	100.0%	8,394		869	7,525	10	52	218	589	2,043	5,113	369	
Rate per 100,000 inhabitants		7,100.0		735.0	6,365.0	8.5	44.0	184.4	498.2	1,728.1	4,324.8	312.1	
Greenville-Spartanburg-Anderson, S.C. M.S.A.	**882,948**												
(Includes Anderson, Cherokee, Greenville, Pickens, and Spartanburg Counties.)													
City of:													
Greenville	60,379	6,348		925	5,423	9	44	227	645	784	4,280	359	
Spartanburg	46,157	7,029		1,597	5,432	10	51	274	1,262	1,122	3,799	511	
Anderson	30,005	2,711		549	2,162	4	14	115	416	517	1,484	161	
Total area actually reporting	100.0%	56,172		9,570	46,602	71	463	1,491	7,545	11,110	31,974	3,518	
Rate per 100,000 inhabitants		6,361.9		1,083.9	5,278.0	8.0	52.4	168.9	854.5	1,258.3	3,621.3	398.4	
Hagerstown, Md. M.S.A.	**128,265**												
(Includes Washington County.)													
City of Hagerstown	39,016	2,077		270	1,807	—	15	68	187	372	1,298	137	
Total area actually reporting	100.0%	3,601		430	3,171	1	23	88	318	698	2,251	222	
Rate per 100,000 inhabitants		2,807.5		335.2	2,472.2	.8	17.9	68.6	247.9	544.2	1,755.0	173.1	

See footnotes at end of table.

Table 6. — Index of Crime, Metropolitan Statistical Areas, 1996 — Continued

Metropolitan Statistical Area	Population	Crime Index total	Modified Crime Index total[1]	Violent crime[2]	Property crime[3]	Murder and non-negligent man-slaughter	Forcible rape	Robbery	Aggra-vated assault	Burglary	Larceny–theft	Motor vehicle theft	Arson[1]
Harrisburg-Lebanon-Carlisle, Pa. M.S.A.	**610,869**												
(Includes Cumberland, Dauphin, Lebanon, and Perry Counties.)													
City of:													
Harrisburg	54,255	3,909		740	3,169	10	63	430	237	785	1,794	590	
Lebanon	25,523	998		102	896	2	11	58	31	128	736	32	
Carlisle	18,981	873		66	807	5	5	27	29	118	660	29	
Total area actually reporting	98.5%	19,414		1,810	17,604	24	179	779	828	2,938	13,160	1,506	
Estimated total	100.0%	19,659		1,830	17,829	24	180	784	842	2,969	13,332	1,528	
Rate per 100,000 inhabitants		3,218.2		299.6	2,918.6	3.9	29.5	128.3	137.8	486.0	2,182.5	250.1	
Hartford, Ct. M.S.A.	**1,047,972**												
(Includes all of Hartford Co., Ct., and part of Litchfield, Middlesex, New London, Tolland, and Windham Counties.)													
City of Hartford	124,223	13,188		2,132	11,056	20	94	1,089	929	2,072	7,036	1,948	
Total area actually reporting	100.0%	44,268		4,403	39,865	42	241	1,919	2,201	8,391	26,566	4,908	
Rate per 100,000 inhabitants		4,224.2		420.1	3,804.0	4.0	23.0	183.1	210.0	800.7	2,535.0	468.3	
Hickory-Morganton-Lenoir, N.C. M.S.A.	**316,701**												
(Includes Alexander, Burke, Caldwell, and Catawba Counties.)													
City of:													
Hickory	30,634	3,287		357	2,930	8	22	110	217	622	2,147	161	
Morganton	17,991	887		44	843	—	1	17	26	156	654	33	
Lenoir	15,169	1,095		110	985	—	4	30	76	247	701	37	
Total area actually reporting	99.6%	12,537		967	11,570	23	76	238	630	3,300	7,637	633	
Estimated total	100.0%	12,616		973	11,643	23	76	240	634	3,315	7,692	636	
Rate per 100,000 inhabitants		3,983.6		307.2	3,676.3	7.3	24.0	75.8	200.2	1,046.7	2,428.8	200.8	
Honolulu, Hi. M.S.A.	**878,044**												
(Includes Honolulu County.)													
Total area actually reporting	100.0%	60,059		2,748	57,311	27	222	1,421	1,078	9,026	41,915	6,370	
Rate per 100,000 inhabitants		6,840.1		313.0	6,527.1	3.1	25.3	161.8	122.8	1,028.0	4,773.7	725.5	
Houston, Tx. M.S.A.	**3,802,180**												
(Includes Chambers, Fort Bend, Harris, Liberty, Montgomery, and Waller Counties.)													
City of Houston	1,772,143	135,329		22,456	112,873	261	1,002	8,276	12,917	25,402	65,080	22,391	
Total area actually reporting	100.0%	219,044		32,659	186,385	373	1,708	10,509	20,069	43,336	111,903	31,146	
Rate per 100,000 inhabitants		5,761.0		859.0	4,902.1	9.8	44.9	276.4	527.8	1,139.8	2,943.1	819.2	
Huntsville, Al. M.S.A.	**320,176**												
(Includes Limestone and Madison Counties.)													
City of Huntsville	162,376	14,330		1,339	12,991	11	71	310	947	2,251	9,516	1,224	
Total area actually reporting	99.7%	17,873		1,730	16,143	23	99	338	1,270	2,977	11,732	1,434	
Estimated total	100.0%	17,918		1,734	16,184	23	99	339	1,273	2,985	11,762	1,437	
Rate per 100,000 inhabitants		5,596.3		541.6	5,054.7	7.2	30.9	105.9	397.6	932.3	3,673.6	448.8	
Indianapolis, In. M.S.A.[6]	**1,484,877**												
(Includes Boone, Hamilton, Hancock, Hendricks, Johnson, Madison, Marion, Morgan, and Shelby Counties.)													
City of Indianapolis[6]		37,917		7,418	30,499	114	424	2,600	4,280	7,797	16,842	5,860	
Total area actually reporting	81.2%	71,421		10,029	61,392	141	662	3,349	5,877	13,152	39,384	8,856	
Estimated total	100.0%	80,184		10,787	69,397	148	716	3,487	6,436	14,593	45,188	9,616	
Rate per 100,000 inhabitants		5,400.0		726.5	4,673.6	10.0	48.2	234.8	433.4	982.8	3,043.2	647.6	
Jackson, Mi. M.S.A.	**154,856**												
(Includes Jackson County.)													
City of Jackson	39,636	3,211		273	2,938	4	59	77	133	414	2,420	104	
Total area actually reporting	98.6%	6,762		708	6,054	11	122	111	464	978	4,740	336	
Estimated total	100.0%	6,862		717	6,145	11	123	113	470	992	4,806	347	
Rate per 100,000 inhabitants		4,431.2		463.0	3,968.2	7.1	79.4	73.0	303.5	640.6	3,103.5	224.1	

See footnotes at end of table.

Table 6. — Index of Crime, Metropolitan Statistical Areas, 1996 — Continued

Metropolitan Statistical Area	Population	Crime Index total	Modified Crime Index total[1]	Violent crime[2]	Property crime[3]	Murder and non-negligent man-slaughter	Forcible rape	Robbery	Aggra-vated assault	Burglary	Larceny–theft	Motor vehicle theft	Arson[1]
Jackson, Ms. M.S.A.	**419,232**												
(Includes Hinds, Madison, and Rankin Counties.)													
City of Jackson	196,619	20,466		2,366	18,100	67	209	1,309	781	4,924	9,744	3,432	
Total area actually reporting	83.3%	25,458		2,694	22,764	80	235	1,384	995	5,846	13,193	3,725	
Estimated total	100.0%	28,237		2,870	25,367	86	253	1,431	1,100	6,467	15,019	3,881	
Rate per 100,000 inhabitants		6,735.4		684.6	6,050.8	20.5	60.3	341.3	262.4	1,542.6	3,582.5	925.7	
Jackson, Tn. M.S.A.	**98,738**												
(Includes Chester and Madison Counties.)													
City of Jackson	55,600	6,256		817	5,439	16	38	239	524	1,147	3,534	758	
Total area actually reporting	100.0%	7,720		964	6,756	19	46	253	646	1,742	4,138	876	
Rate per 100,000 inhabitants		7,818.7		976.3	6,842.4	19.2	46.6	256.2	654.3	1,764.3	4,190.9	887.2	
Jacksonville, N.C. M.S.A.	**152,926**												
(Includes Onslow County.)													
City of Jacksonville	59,144	2,745		326	2,419	5	18	71	232	571	1,734	114	
Total area actually reporting	100.0%	6,027		455	5,572	7	43	114	291	1,645	3,564	363	
Rate per 100,000 inhabitants		3,941.1		297.5	3,643.6	4.6	28.1	74.5	190.3	1,075.7	2,330.5	237.4	
Janesville-Beloit, Wi. M.S.A.	**148,188**												
(Includes Rock County.)													
City of:													
Janesville	57,733	3,791		143	3,648	2	18	20	103	635	2,853	160	
Beloit	37,205	1,995		141	1,854	1	17	73	50	204	1,545	105	
Total area actually reporting	100.0%	6,955		339	6,616	3	45	96	195	1,102	5,193	321	
Rate per 100,000 inhabitants		4,693.4		228.8	4,464.6	2.0	30.4	64.8	131.6	743.6	3,504.3	216.6	
Jersey City, N.J. M.S.A.	**558,251**												
(Includes Hudson County.)													
City of Jersey City	228,424	16,704		3,791	12,913	26	91	1,859	1,815	3,425	5,994	3,494	
Total area actually reporting	100.0%	32,448		5,263	27,185	39	141	2,577	2,506	6,197	14,193	6,795	
Rate per 100,000 inhabitants		5,812.4		942.8	4,869.7	7.0	25.3	461.6	448.9	1,110.1	2,542.4	1,217.2	
Johnson City-Kingsport-Bristol, Tn.-Va. M.S.A.	**462,145**												
(Includes Carter, Hawkins, Sullivan, Unicoi, and Washington Counties, Tn., Bristol City and Scott and Washington Counties, Va.)													
City of:													
Johnson City, Tn.	53,017	3,446		385	3,061	3	36	57	289	463	2,417	181	
Kingsport, Tn.	39,553	1,828		239	1,589	2	23	24	190	364	1,108	117	
Bristol, Tn.	25,654	1,185		104	1,081	—	4	6	94	115	888	78	
Total area actually reporting	95.9%	12,625		1,430	11,195	14	135	115	1,166	2,439	8,001	755	
Estimated total	100.0%	13,282		1,501	11,781	15	140	124	1,222	2,586	8,392	803	
Rate per 100,000 inhabitants		2,874.0		324.8	2,549.2	3.2	30.3	26.8	264.4	559.6	1,815.9	173.8	
Johnstown, Pa. M.S.A.	**239,788**												
(Includes Cambria and Somerset Counties.)													
City of Johnstown	27,326	881		102	779	—	7	26	69	184	551	44	
Total area actually reporting	90.2%	3,395		402	2,993	5	30	36	331	850	1,920	223	
Estimated total	100.0%	4,044		457	3,587	5	33	50	369	933	2,372	282	
Rate per 100,000 inhabitants		1,686.5		190.6	1,495.9	2.1	13.8	20.9	153.9	389.1	989.2	117.6	
Jonesboro, Ar. M.S.A.	**75,086**												
(Includes Craighead County.)													
City of Jonesboro	51,375	2,883		227	2,656	4	22	69	132	699	1,817	140	
Total area actually reporting	100.0%	3,483		255	3,228	4	27	72	152	865	2,185	178	
Rate per 100,000 inhabitants		4,638.7		339.6	4,299.1	5.3	36.0	95.9	202.4	1,152.0	2,910.0	237.1	
Joplin, Mo. M.S.A.	**143,910**												
(Includes Jasper and Newton Counties.)													
City of Joplin	43,548	2,816		169	2,647	2	20	49	98	652	1,821	174	
Total area actually reporting	76.1%	5,057		307	4,750	3	34	59	211	1,076	3,416	258	
Estimated total	100.0%	5,954		370	5,584	4	39	68	259	1,252	4,007	325	
Rate per 100,000 inhabitants		4,137.3		257.1	3,880.2	2.8	27.1	47.3	180.0	870.0	2,784.4	225.8	

See footnotes at end of table.

Table 6. — Index of Crime, Metropolitan Statistical Areas, 1996 — Continued

Metropolitan Statistical Area	Population	Crime Index total	Modified Crime Index total[1]	Violent crime[2]	Property crime[3]	Murder and non-negligent man-slaughter	Forcible rape	Robbery	Aggra-vated assault	Burglary	Larceny–theft	Motor vehicle theft	Arson[1]
Kalamazoo-Battle Creek, Mi. M.S.A. ...	**447,168**												
(Includes Calhoun, Kalamazoo, and Van Buren Counties.)													
City of:													
Kalamazoo	82,485	6,379		1,141	5,238	8	48	234	851	1,055	3,797	386	
Battle Creek	77,415	5,154		707	4,447	8	43	196	460	982	3,228	237	
Total area actually reporting	81.9%	21,561		2,673	18,888	26	222	531	1,894	3,965	13,806	1,117	
Estimated total	100.0%	24,193		2,902	21,291	27	262	560	2,053	4,474	15,500	1,317	
Rate per 100,000 inhabitants		5,410.3		649.0	4,761.3	6.0	58.6	125.2	459.1	1,000.5	3,466.3	294.5	
Kenosha, WI. M.S.A.	**139,919**												
(Includes Kenosha County.)													
City of Kenosha	86,427	3,352		306	3,046	3	49	104	150	577	2,214	255	
Total area actually reporting	100.0%	5,080		374	4,706	5	62	113	194	856	3,512	338	
Rate per 100,000 inhabitants		3,630.7		267.3	3,363.4	3.6	44.3	80.8	138.7	611.8	2,510.0	241.6	
Killeen-Temple, Tx. M.S.A.	**298,882**												
(Includes Bell and Coryell Counties.)													
City of:													
Killeen	86,237	5,290		479	4,811	2	82	142	253	932	3,616	263	
Temple	54,212	3,625		293	3,332	1	12	80	200	553	2,556	223	
Total area actually reporting	100.0%	13,490		1,191	12,299	6	145	268	772	2,414	9,157	728	
Rate per 100,000 inhabitants		4,513.5		398.5	4,115.0	2.0	48.5	89.7	258.3	807.7	3,063.8	243.6	
Kokomo, In. M.S.A.	**100,878**												
(Includes Howard and Tipton Counties.)													
City of Kokomo	46,739	2,648		190	2,458	3	12	35	140	379	1,977	102	
Total area actually reporting	83.5%	3,209		248	2,961	3	20	37	188	513	2,320	128	
Estimated total	100.0%	3,765		294	3,471	3	23	45	223	598	2,698	175	
Rate per 100,000 inhabitants		3,732.2		291.4	3,440.8	3.0	22.8	44.6	221.1	592.8	2,674.5	173.5	
La Crosse, Wi.-Mn. M.S.A.	**122,041**												
(Includes La Crosse County, Wi., and Houston County, Mn.)													
City of La Crosse, Wi.	51,657	2,747		69	2,678	1	22	16	30	204	2,412	62	
Total area actually reporting	100.0%	4,098		204	3,894	1	30	16	157	310	3,490	94	
Rate per 100,000 inhabitants		3,357.9		167.2	3,190.7	.8	24.6	13.1	128.6	254.0	2,859.7	77.0	
Lafayette, In. M.S.A.	**169,310**												
(Includes Clinton and Tippecanoe Counties.)													
City of Lafayette	46,586	3,215		155	3,060	1	25	32	97	476	2,438	146	
Total area actually reporting	80.6%	6,197		263	5,934	3	47	37	176	737	4,962	235	
Estimated total	100.0%	7,414		362	7,052	3	54	53	252	901	5,818	333	
Rate per 100,000 inhabitants		4,378.9		213.8	4,165.1	1.8	31.9	31.3	148.8	532.2	3,436.3	196.7	
Lafayette, La. M.S.A.	**364,333**												
(Includes Acadia, Lafayette, St. Landry, and St. Martin Parishes.)													
City of Lafayette	103,134	8,483		845	7,638	8	75	247	515	1,375	5,589	674	
Total area actually reporting	99.4%	17,531		2,190	15,341	26	145	361	1,658	3,568	10,817	956	
Estimated total	100.0%	17,677		2,209	15,468	26	146	364	1,673	3,592	10,911	965	
Rate per 100,000 inhabitants		4,851.9		606.3	4,245.6	7.1	40.1	99.9	459.2	985.9	2,994.8	264.9	
Lake Charles, La. M.S.A.	**174,775**												
(Includes Calcasieu Parish.)													
City of Lake Charles	73,027	6,875		822	6,053	16	51	264	491	1,339	3,951	763	
Total area actually reporting	85.4%	14,132		1,549	12,583	21	86	385	1,057	2,755	8,673	1,155	
Estimated total	100.0%	15,908		1,775	14,133	23	93	420	1,239	3,047	9,823	1,263	
Rate per 100,000 inhabitants		9,102.0		1,015.6	8,086.4	13.2	53.2	240.3	708.9	1,743.4	5,620.4	722.6	
Lansing-East Lansing, Mi. M.S.A.	**440,606**												
(Includes Clinton, Eaton, and Ingham Counties.)													
City of:													
Lansing	120,821	9,744		1,649	8,095	10	172	343	1,124	1,607	5,952	536	
East Lansing	50,840	1,985		114	1,871	—	29	28	57	318	1,442	111	
Total area actually reporting	89.9%	20,356		2,321	18,035	12	296	468	1,545	3,349	13,612	1,074	
Estimated total	100.0%	22,403		2,494	19,909	13	310	506	1,665	3,631	14,978	1,300	
Rate per 100,000 inhabitants		5,084.6		566.0	4,518.5	3.0	70.4	114.8	377.9	824.1	3,399.4	295.0	
Laredo, Tx. M.S.A.	**169,720**												
(Includes Webb County.)													
City of Laredo	156,032	11,240		1,040	10,200	11	27	242	760	1,672	7,477	1,051	
Total area actually reporting	100.0%	11,802		1,100	10,702	11	30	249	810	1,855	7,765	1,082	
Rate per 100,000 inhabitants		6,953.8		648.1	6,305.7	6.5	17.7	146.7	477.3	1,093.0	4,575.2	637.5	

See footnotes at end of table.

Table 6. — Index of Crime, Metropolitan Statistical Areas, 1996 — Continued

Metropolitan Statistical Area	Population	Crime Index total	Modified Crime Index total[1]	Violent crime[2]	Property crime[3]	Murder and non-negligent man-slaughter	Forcible rape	Robbery	Aggra-vated assault	Burglary	Larceny–theft	Motor vehicle theft	Arson[1]
Las Vegas, Nv.-Az. M.S.A.	**1,182,509**												
(Includes Clark and Nye Counties, Nv., and Mohave County, Az.)													
City of Las Vegas, Nv.	831,303	56,943		8,409	48,534	161	475	3,650	4,123	11,656	28,952	7,926	
Total area actually reporting	100.0%	79,258		10,959	68,299	209	624	4,322	5,804	16,929	41,205	10,165	
Rate per 100,000 inhabitants		6,702.5		926.8	5,775.8	17.7	52.8	365.5	490.8	1,431.6	3,484.5	859.6	
Lawrence, Ma.-N.H. M.S.A.	**300,775**												
(Includes part of Essex County, Ma., and Rockingham County, N.H.)													
City of Lawrence, Ma.	63,648	5,553		1,247	4,306	2	17	291	937	1,241	1,295	1,770	
Total area actually reporting	86.1%	10,393		1,476	8,917	3	81	327	1,065	1,919	4,457	2,541	
Estimated total	100.0%	11,497		1,523	9,974	3	98	334	1,088	2,091	5,278	2,605	
Rate per 100,000 inhabitants		3,822.5		506.4	3,316.1	1.0	32.6	111.0	361.7	695.2	1,754.8	866.1	
Lawton, Ok. M.S.A.	**119,176**												
(Includes Comanche County.)													
City of Lawton	87,213	7,351		676	6,675	7	59	183	427	1,833	4,439	403	
Total area actually reporting	100.0%	7,966		753	7,213	7	61	192	493	1,988	4,762	463	
Rate per 100,000 inhabitants		6,684.2		631.8	6,052.4	5.9	51.2	161.1	413.7	1,668.1	3,995.8	388.5	
Lewiston-Auburn, Me. M.S.A.	**104,126**												
(Includes part of Androscoggin County.)													
City of:													
Lewiston	37,475	2,618		71	2,547	1	11	34	25	579	1,932	36	
Auburn	23,419	995		18	977	—	3	12	3	203	727	47	
Total area actually reporting	100.0%	4,640		105	4,535	1	18	47	39	1,030	3,366	139	
Rate per 100,000 inhabitants		4,456.1		100.8	4,355.3	1.0	17.3	45.1	37.5	989.2	3,232.6	133.5	
Lima, Oh. M.S.A.	**156,843**												
(Includes Allen and Auglaize Counties.)													
City of Lima	44,656	3,461		506	2,955	5	40	205	256	905	1,907	143	
Total area actually reporting	79.9%	5,690		757	4,933	7	54	235	461	1,296	3,416	221	
Estimated total	100.0%	6,962		830	6,132	7	62	257	504	1,477	4,356	299	
Rate per 100,000 inhabitants		4,438.8		529.2	3,909.6	4.5	39.5	163.9	321.3	941.7	2,777.3	190.6	
Lincoln, Ne. M.S.A.	**229,780**												
(Includes Lancaster County.)													
City of Lincoln	206,704	14,349		1,215	13,134	3	83	142	987	1,877	10,742	515	
Total area actually reporting	100.0%	15,568		1,234	14,334	4	87	145	998	2,029	11,764	541	
Rate per 100,000 inhabitants		6,775.2		537.0	6,238.1	1.7	37.9	63.1	434.3	883.0	5,119.7	235.4	
Little Rock-North Little Rock, Ar. M.S.A.	**550,543**												
(Includes Faulkner, Lonoke, Pulaski, and Saline Counties.)													
City of:													
Little Rock	182,799	21,016		2,757	18,259	29	166	837	1,725	3,382	13,253	1,624	
North Little Rock	63,642	6,223		715	5,508	15	99	293	308	1,085	3,903	520	
Total area actually reporting	100.0%	39,955		4,516	35,439	58	385	1,288	2,785	6,895	25,649	2,895	
Rate per 100,000 inhabitants		7,257.4		820.3	6,437.1	10.5	69.9	234.0	505.9	1,252.4	4,658.9	525.8	
Longview-Marshall, Tx. M.S.A.	**212,123**												
(Includes Gregg, Harrison, and Upshur Counties.)													
City of:													
Longview	76,254	6,119		521	5,598	8	69	176	268	994	4,020	584	
Marshall	24,275	2,190		237	1,953	6	24	56	151	404	1,346	203	
Total area actually reporting	100.0%	12,194		1,104	11,090	23	120	272	689	2,330	7,740	1,020	
Rate per 100,000 inhabitants		5,748.6		520.5	5,228.1	10.8	56.6	128.2	324.8	1,098.4	3,648.8	480.9	
Los Angeles-Long Beach, Ca. M.S.A.	**9,280,355**												
(Includes Los Angeles County.)													
City of:													
Los Angeles	3,498,139	235,260		62,840	172,420	711	1,463	25,189	35,477	35,865	95,069	41,486	
Long Beach	440,023	26,308		5,069	21,239	95	158	2,431	2,385	5,003	11,671	4,565	
Total area actually reporting	100.0%	505,071		118,600	386,471	1,401	3,034	46,172	67,993	87,318	208,611	90,542	
Rate per 100,000 inhabitants		5,442.4		1,278.0	4,164.4	15.1	32.7	497.5	732.7	940.9	2,247.9	975.6	

See footnotes at end of table.

Table 6. — Index of Crime, Metropolitan Statistical Areas, 1996 — Continued

Metropolitan Statistical Area	Population	Crime Index total	Modified Crime Index total[1]	Violent crime[2]	Property crime[3]	Murder and non-negligent man-slaughter	Forcible rape	Robbery	Aggra-vated assault	Burglary	Larceny–theft	Motor vehicle theft	Arson[1]
Lowell, Ma.-N.H. M.S.A.	**281,080**												
(Includes part of Middlesex County, Ma., and Hillsborough County, N.H.)													
City of Lowell, Ma.	96,863	4,724		1,018	3,706	5	43	143	827	816	1,920	970	
Total area actually reporting	92.9%	8,271		1,355	6,916	6	61	173	1,115	1,385	4,036	1,495	
Estimated total	100.0%	8,800		1,400	7,400	6	67	179	1,148	1,474	4,385	1,541	
Rate per 100,000 inhabitants		3,130.8		498.1	2,632.7	2.1	23.8	63.7	408.4	524.4	1,560.1	548.2	
Lubbock, Tx. M.S.A.	**239,119**												
(Includes Lubbock County.)													
City of Lubbock	202,403	12,948		2,066	10,882	15	126	276	1,649	2,456	7,472	954	
Total area actually reporting	100.0%	14,735		2,216	12,519	15	140	288	1,773	2,762	8,732	1,025	
Rate per 100,000 inhabitants		6,162.2		926.7	5,235.5	6.3	58.5	120.4	741.5	1,155.1	3,651.7	428.7	
Lynchburg, Va. M.S.A.	**206,695**												
(Includes Lynchburg and Bedford Cities and Amherst, Bedford, and Campbell Counties.)													
City of Lynchburg	67,738	3,401		471	2,930	6	24	102	339	509	2,233	188	
Total area actually reporting	100.0%	6,171		743	5,428	12	42	130	559	966	4,102	360	
Rate per 100,000 inhabitants		2,985.6		359.5	2,626.1	5.8	20.3	62.9	270.4	467.4	1,984.6	174.2	
Macon, Ga. M.S.A.	**320,386**												
(Includes Bibb, Houston, Jones, Peach, and Twiggs Counties.)													
City of Macon	113,802	14,011		924	13,087	18	77	382	447	2,452	9,195	1,440	
Total area actually reporting	99.9%	22,832		1,565	21,267	25	131	515	894	4,062	15,346	1,859	
Estimated total	100.0%	22,849		1,566	21,283	25	131	515	895	4,064	15,358	1,861	
Rate per 100,000 inhabitants		7,131.7		488.8	6,642.9	7.8	40.9	160.7	279.4	1,268.5	4,793.6	580.9	
Madison, Wi. M.S.A.	**389,020**												
(Includes Dane County.)													
City of Madison	197,572	9,096		772	8,324	1	75	299	397	1,389	6,294	641	
Total area actually reporting	100.0%	15,922		1,145	14,777	2	103	328	712	2,223	11,686	868	
Rate per 100,000 inhabitants		4,092.8		294.3	3,798.5	.5	26.5	84.3	183.0	571.4	3,004.0	223.1	
Manchester, N.H. M.S.A.	**170,019**												
(Includes part of Hillsborough, Merrimack, and Rockingham Counties.)													
City of Manchester	99,036	5,129		238	4,891	1	55	137	45	837	3,629	425	
Total area actually reporting	85.0%	6,174		267	5,907	2	56	144	65	1,015	4,413	479	
Estimated total	100.0%	6,846		295	6,551	2	66	148	79	1,120	4,913	518	
Rate per 100,00 inhabitants		4,026.6		173.5	3,853.1	1.2	38.8	87.0	46.5	658.7	2,889.7	304.7	
Mansfield, Oh. M.S.A.	**176,681**												
(Includes Crawford and Richland Counties.)													
City of Mansfield	53,531	5,017		1,141	3,876	1	57	119	964	970	2,706	200	
Total area actually reporting	93.3%	8,562		1,259	7,303	4	66	154	1,035	1,711	5,310	282	
Estimated total	100.0%	9,039		1,286	7,753	4	69	162	1,051	1,779	5,663	311	
Rate per 100,000 inhabitants		5,116.0		727.9	4,388.1	2.3	39.1	91.7	594.9	1,006.9	3,205.2	176.0	
McAllen-Edinburg-Mission, Tx. M.S.A.	**479,830**												
(Includes Hidalgo County.)													
City of:													
McAllen	99,188	10,697		546	10,151	5	23	148	370	1,475	7,730	946	
Edinburg	37,967	3,107		234	2,873	—	21	42	171	443	2,214	216	
Mission	40,005	2,474		65	2,409	2	9	17	37	619	1,540	250	
Total area actually reporting	100.0%	31,461		2,512	28,949	36	151	519	1,806	7,334	18,825	2,790	
Rate per 100,000 inhabitants		6,556.7		523.5	6,033.2	7.5	31.5	108.2	376.4	1,528.5	3,923.3	581.5	
Medford-Ashland, Or. M.S.A.	**168,566**												
(Includes Jackson County.)													
City of:													
Medford	54,622	4,604		251	4,353	5	16	33	197	607	3,546	200	
Ashland	17,599	885		16	869	3	6	5	2	107	727	35	
Total area actually reporting	100.0%	8,922		532	8,390	12	53	63	404	1,341	6,642	407	
Rate per 100,000 inhabitants		5,292.9		315.6	4,977.3	7.1	31.4	37.4	239.7	795.5	3,940.3	241.4	

See footnotes at end of table.

Table 6. — Index of Crime, Metropolitan Statistical Areas, 1996 — Continued

Metropolitan Statistical Area	Population	Crime Index total	Modified Crime Index total[1]	Violent crime[2]	Property crime[3]	Murder and non-negligent man-slaughter	Forcible rape	Robbery	Aggra-vated assault	Burglary	Larceny–theft	Motor vehicle theft	Arson[1]
Memphis, Tn.-Ar.-Ms. M.S.A.	**1,084,720**												
(Includes Fayette, Shelby, and Tipton Counties, Tn., Crittenden County, Ar., and DeSoto County, Ms.)													
City of Memphis, Tn.	631,626	70,281		12,535	57,746	161	789	5,970	5,615	16,634	26,828	14,284	
Total area actually reporting	76.5%	79,495		13,609	65,886	178	838	6,297	6,296	18,576	32,205	15,105	
Estimated total	100.0%	85,285		14,278	71,007	193	899	6,358	6,828	20,293	35,187	15,527	
Rate per 100,000 inhabitants		7,862.4		1,316.3	6,546.1	17.8	82.9	586.1	629.5	1,870.8	3,243.9	1,431.4	
Merced, Ca. M.S.A.	**199,641**												
(Includes Merced County.)													
City of Merced	61,205	4,923		563	4,360	3	25	131	404	889	3,035	436	
Total area actually reporting	100.0%	10,821		1,269	9,552	8	74	208	979	2,922	5,582	1,048	
Rate per 100,000 inhabitants		5,420.2		635.6	4,784.6	4.0	37.1	104.2	490.4	1,463.6	2,796.0	524.9	
Middlesex-Somerset-Hunterdon, N.J. M.S.A.	**1,080,068**												
(Includes Hunterdon, Middlesex, and Somerset Counties.)													
Total area actually reporting	100.0%	32,264		2,474	29,790	10	103	1,007	1,354	5,771	20,898	3,121	
Rate per 100,000 inhabitants		2,987.2		229.1	2,758.2	.9	9.5	93.2	125.4	534.3	1,934.9	289.0	
Milwaukee-Waukesha, Wi. M.S.A.	**1,468,452**												
(Includes Milwaukee, Ozaukee, Washington, and Waukesha Counties.)													
City of:													
Milwaukee	627,139	49,623		5,974	43,649	130	281	3,353	2,210	7,622	25,948	10,079	
Waukesha	61,060	1,902		104	1,798	—	10	30	64	282	1,400	116	
Total area actually reporting	100.0%	76,460		6,970	69,490	138	362	3,704	2,766	10,808	46,893	11,789	
Rate per 100,000 inhabitants		5,206.8		474.6	4,732.2	9.4	24.7	252.2	188.4	736.0	3,193.4	802.8	
Minneapolis-St. Paul, Mn.-Wi. M.S.A.	**2,743,403**												
(Includes Anoka, Carver, Chicago, Dakota, Hennepin, Isanti, Ramsey, Scott, Sherburne, Washington, and Wright Counties, Mn., and Pierce and St. Croix Counties, Wi.)													
City of:													
Minneapolis, Mn.	361,595	40,826		6,808	34,018	83	516	3,242	2,967	7,678	20,690	5,650	
St. Paul, Mn.	267,292	20,704		2,437	18,267	26	234	875	1,302	4,127	11,504	2,636	
Total area actually reporting	100.0%	146,666		12,854	133,812	123	1,448	5,036	6,247	23,670	96,198	13,944	
Rate per 100,000 inhabitants		5,346.1		468.5	4,877.6	4.5	52.8	183.6	227.7	862.8	3,506.5	508.3	
Mobile, Al. M.S.A.	**518,683**												
(Includes Baldwin and Mobile Counties.)													
City of Mobile	207,106	19,512		2,185	17,327	51	119	1,283	732	4,404	10,990	1,933	
Total area actually reporting	100.0%	32,217		3,864	28,353	80	236	1,676	1,872	7,448	18,098	2,807	
Rate per 100,000 inhabitants		6,211.3		745.0	5,466.3	15.4	45.5	323.1	360.9	1,435.9	3,489.2	541.2	
Modesto, Ca. M.S.A.	**412,542**												
(Includes Stanislaus County.)													
City of Modesto	178,865	12,840		1,267	11,573	12	80	421	754	2,701	7,100	1,772	
Total area actually reporting	100.0%	27,662		3,661	24,001	28	179	711	2,743	6,266	14,365	3,370	
Rate per 100,000 inhabitants		6,705.3		887.4	5,817.8	6.8	43.4	172.3	664.9	1,518.9	3,482.1	816.9	
Monmouth-Ocean, N.J. M.S.A.	**1,045,938**												
(Includes Monmouth and Ocean Counties.)													
Total area actually reporting	100.0%	34,315		2,537	31,778	15	221	743	1,558	6,012	24,004	1,762	
Rate per 100,000 inhabitants		3,280.8		242.6	3,038.2	1.4	21.1	71.0	149.0	574.8	2,295.0	168.5	
Monroe, La. M.S.A.	**147,662**												
(Includes Ouachita Parish.)													
City of Monroe	57,524	8,228		1,217	7,011	6	54	177	980	1,454	5,060	497	
Total area actually reporting	99.1%	13,321		1,521	11,800	9	74	218	1,220	2,475	8,603	722	
Estimated total	100.0%	13,410		1,532	11,878	9	74	220	1,229	2,490	8,661	727	
Rate per 100,000 inhabitants		9,081.6		1,037.5	8,044.0	6.1	50.1	149.0	832.3	1,686.3	5,865.4	492.3	
Montgomery, Al. M.S.A.	**319,432**												
(Includes Autauga, Elmore, and Montgomery Counties.)													
City of Montgomery	197,972	13,202		1,589	11,613	31	80	627	851	3,376	7,111	1,126	
Total area actually reporting	100.0%	17,653		2,071	15,582	46	134	729	1,162	4,373	9,839	1,370	
Rate per 100,000 inhabitants		5,526.4		648.3	4,878.0	14.4	41.9	228.2	363.8	1,369.0	3,080.2	428.9	

See footnotes at end of table.

Table 6. — Index of Crime, Metropolitan Statistical Areas, 1996 — Continued

Metropolitan Statistical Area	Population	Crime Index total	Modified Crime Index total[1]	Violent crime[2]	Property crime[3]	Murder and non-negligent man-slaughter	Forcible rape	Robbery	Aggra-vated assault	Burglary	Larceny–theft	Motor vehicle theft	Arson[1]
Muncie, In. M.S.A.	**121,088**												
(Includes Delaware County.)													
City of Muncie	72,511	3,856		595	3,261	9	25	168	393	755	2,295	211	
Total area actually reporting	100.0%	5,139		630	4,509	12	32	172	414	991	3,269	249	
Rate per 100,000 inhabitants		4,244.0		520.3	3,723.7	9.9	26.4	142.0	341.9	818.4	2,699.7	205.6	
Myrtle Beach, S.C. M.S.A.	**154,331**												
(Includes Horry County.)													
City of Myrtle Beach	28,314	5,062		499	4,563	2	24	163	310	1,071	3,185	307	
Total area actually reporting	100.0%	16,283		1,887	14,396	13	85	364	1,425	3,549	9,701	1,146	
Rate per 100,000 inhabitants		10,550.7		1,222.7	9,328.0	8.4	55.1	235.9	923.3	2,299.6	6,285.8	742.6	
Nashua, N.H. M.S.A.	**163,947**												
(Includes part of Hillsborough County.)													
City of Nashua	81,381	2,836		89	2,747	2	24	23	40	365	2,171	211	
Total area actually reporting	98.6%	4,487		164	4,323	3	48	33	80	596	3,464	263	
Estimated total	100.0%	4,549		166	4,383	3	49	33	81	606	3,510	267	
Rate per 100,000 inhabitants		2,774.7		101.3	2,673.4	1.8	29.9	20.1	49.4	369.6	2,140.9	162.9	
Nashville, Tn. M.S.A.	**1,099,939**												
(Includes Cheatham, Davidson, Dickson, Robertson, Rutherford, Sumner, Williamson, and Wilson Counties.)													
City of Nashville	530,059	59,467		10,021	49,446	89	487	2,910	6,535	8,025	33,195	8,226	
Total area actually reporting	77.2%	74,629		11,681	62,948	101	585	3,094	7,901	10,814	43,067	9,067	
Estimated total	100.0%	83,528		12,643	70,885	114	646	3,227	8,656	12,776	48,392	9,717	
Rate per 100,000 inhabitants		7,593.9		1,149.4	6,444.4	10.4	58.7	293.4	787.0	1,161.5	4,399.5	883.4	
Nassau-Suffolk, N.Y. M.S.A.	**2,626,078**												
(Includes Nassau and Suffolk Counties.)													
Total area actually reporting	99.9%	76,072		5,590	70,482	60	150	2,274	3,106	11,376	50,656	8,450	
Estimated total	100.0%	76,116		5,593	70,523	60	150	2,275	3,108	11,383	50,687	8,453	
Rate per 100,000 inhabitants		2,898.5		213.0	2,685.5	2.3	5.7	86.6	118.4	433.5	1,930.1	321.9	
Newark, N.J. M.S.A.	**1,954,570**												
(Includes Essex, Morris, Sussex, Union, and Warren Counties.)													
City of Newark	261,909	34,437		8,761	25,676	92	179	4,219	4,271	5,991	11,693	7,992	
Total area actually reporting	100.0%	101,956		16,995	84,961	160	591	8,395	7,849	18,606	46,982	19,373	
Rate per 100,000 inhabitants		5,216.3		869.5	4,346.8	8.2	30.2	429.5	401.6	951.9	2,403.7	991.2	
New Bedford, Ma. M.S.A.	**175,565**												
(Includes part of Bristol and Plymouth Counties.)													
City of New Bedford	95,420	4,567		1,006	3,561	2	69	214	721	1,143	1,602	816	
Total area actually reporting	97.6%	7,537		1,469	6,068	4	74	242	1,149	1,873	3,175	1,020	
Estimated total	100.0%	7,649		1,483	6,166	4	75	244	1,160	1,893	3,240	1,033	
Rate per 100,000 inhabitants		4,356.8		844.7	3,512.1	2.3	42.7	139.0	660.7	1,078.2	1,845.5	588.4	
Newburgh, N.Y.-Pa. M.S.A.	**356,256**												
(Includes Orange County, N.Y., and Pike County, Pa.)													
City of Newburgh, N.Y.	25,727	2,051		367	1,684	7	20	138	202	565	965	154	
Total area actually reporting	97.7%	10,812		1,223	9,589	18	62	247	896	2,101	6,938	550	
Estimated total	100.0%	11,070		1,245	9,825	18	63	254	910	2,140	7,115	570	
Rate per 100,000 inhabitants		3,107.3		349.5	2,757.8	5.1	17.7	71.3	255.4	600.7	1,997.2	160.0	
New Haven-Meriden, Ct. M.S.A.	**561,102**												
(Includes part of Middlesex and New Haven Counties.)													
City of:													
New Haven	119,566	15,036		2,616	12,420	22	120	1,207	1,267	2,936	7,139	2,345	
Meriden	56,910	3,117		152	2,965	2	1	66	83	883	1,872	210	
Total area actually reporting	100.0%	31,613		3,356	28,257	31	157	1,529	1,639	6,188	18,022	4,047	
Rate per 100,000 inhabitants		5,634.1		598.1	5,036.0	5.5	28.0	272.5	292.1	1,102.8	3,211.9	721.3	
New London-Norwich, Ct.-R.I. M.S.A.	**302,242**												
(Includes part of Middlesex, New London, and Windham Counties, Ct., and Washington County, R.I.)													
City of:													
New London, Ct.	22,784	1,133		126	1,007	—	5	38	83	164	733	110	
Norwich, Ct.	35,492	1,399		169	1,230	3	25	44	97	328	792	110	
Total area actually reporting	100.0%	8,265		755	7,510	6	105	147	497	1,686	5,276	548	
Rate per 100,000 inhabitants		2,734.6		249.8	2,484.8	2.0	34.7	48.6	164.4	557.8	1,745.6	181.3	

See footnotes at end of table.

Metropolitan Statistical Area	Population	Crime Index total	Modified Crime Index total[1]	Violent crime[2]	Property crime[3]	Murder and non-negligent man-slaughter	Forcible rape	Robbery	Aggra-vated assault	Burglary	Larceny–theft	Motor vehicle theft	Arson[1]
New Orleans, La. M.S.A.	**1,319,922**												
(Includes Jefferson, Orleans, Plaquemines, St. Bernard, St. Charles, St. James, St. John the Baptist, and St. Tammany Parishes.)													
City of New Orleans	488,300	53,919		11,021	42,898	351	390	5,700	4,580	9,954	22,774	10,170	
Total area actually reporting	94.5%	105,155		17,086	88,069	416	637	7,394	8,639	18,232	54,524	15,313	
Estimated total	100.0%	109,127		17,502	91,625	421	659	7,489	8,933	18,992	57,010	15,623	
Rate per 100,000 inhabitants		8,267.7		1,326.0	6,941.7	31.9	49.9	567.4	676.8	1,438.9	4,319.2	1,183.6	
New York, N.Y. M.S.A.	**8,618,741**												
(Includes Bronx, Kings, New York, Putnam, Queens, Richmond, Rockland, and Westchester Counties, N.Y.)													
City of New York	7,339,594	382,555		98,659	283,896	983	2,332	49,670	45,674	61,270	162,246	60,380	
Total area actually reporting	99.9%	421,750		102,702	319,048	1,030	2,466	51,443	47,763	67,401	186,822	64,825	
Estimated total	100.0%	422,024		102,726	319,298	1,030	2,467	51,451	47,778	67,443	187,010	64,845	
Rate per 100,000 inhabitants		4,896.6		1,191.9	3,704.7	12.0	28.6	597.0	554.4	782.5	2,169.8	752.4	
Norfolk-Virginia Beach-Newport News, Va.-N.C. M.S.A.	**1,559,640**												
(Includes Gloucester, Isle of Wight, James City, Mathews, and York Counties; Chesapeake, Hampton, Newport News, Poquoson, Portsmouth, Suffolk, Virginia Beach, and Williamsburg Cities, Va.; and Currituck County, N.C.)													
City of:													
Norfolk, Va.	245,956	18,854		2,332	16,522	61	142	1,079	1,050	2,766	12,053	1,703	
Virginia Beach, Va.	439,851	20,819		1,075	19,744	20	127	455	473	3,063	15,688	993	
Newport News, Va.	182,487	9,829		1,176	8,653	27	110	363	676	1,224	6,850	579	
Total area actually reporting	100.0%	83,257		7,910	75,347	164	612	3,225	3,909	12,501	57,149	5,697	
Rate per 100,000 inhabitants		5,338.2		507.2	4,831.1	10.5	39.2	206.8	250.6	801.5	3,664.2	365.3	
Oakland, Ca. M.S.A.	**2,213,427**												
(Includes Alameda and Contra Costa Counties.)													
City of Oakland	372,145	39,174		8,168	31,006	93	322	3,622	4,131	6,058	19,878	5,070	
Total area actually reporting	100.0%	138,346		19,283	119,063	213	818	7,679	10,573	22,633	80,176	16,254	
Rate per 100,000 inhabitants		6,250.3		871.2	5,379.1	9.6	37.0	346.9	477.7	1,022.5	3,622.3	734.3	
Odessa-Midland, Tx. M.S.A.	**246,977**												
(Includes Ector and Midland Counties.)													
City of:													
Odessa	98,630	6,748		1,105	5,643	14	35	128	928	1,198	4,136	309	
Midland	100,087	4,966		377	4,589	4	58	80	235	1,030	3,273	286	
Total area actually reporting	100.0%	13,738		1,590	12,148	19	122	227	1,222	2,671	8,788	689	
Rate per 100,000 inhabitants		5,562.5		643.8	4,918.7	7.7	49.4	91.9	494.8	1,081.5	3,558.2	279.0	
Oklahoma City, Ok. M.S.A.	**1,021,052**												
(Includes Canadian, Cleveland, Logan, McClain, Oklahoma, and Pottawatomie Counties.)													
City of Oklahoma City	469,632	57,100		5,308	51,792	67	477	1,478	3,286	10,690	35,957	5,145	
Total area actually reporting	100.0%	84,260		7,227	77,033	87	686	1,863	4,591	16,657	53,369	7,007	
Rate per 100,000 inhabitants		8,252.3		707.8	7,544.5	8.5	67.2	182.5	449.6	1,631.4	5,226.9	686.3	
Olympia, Wa. M.S.A.	**193,891**												
(Includes Thurston County.)													
City of Olympia	41,136	3,041		161	2,880	1	29	45	86	472	2,222	186	
Total area actually reporting	99.7%	8,649		494	8,155	8	103	102	281	1,942	5,679	534	
Estimated total	100.0%	8,690		496	8,194	8	103	103	282	1,948	5,708	538	
Rate per 100,000 inhabitants		4,481.9		255.8	4,226.1	4.1	53.1	53.1	145.4	1,004.7	2,943.9	277.5	
Omaha, Ne.-Ia. M.S.A.	**673,237**												
(Includes Cass, Douglas, Sarpy, and Washington Counties, Ne., and Pottawatomie County, Ia.)													
City of Omaha, Ne.	350,607	26,939		4,742	22,197	27	207	782	3,726	3,552	14,999	3,646	
Total area actually reporting	96.2%	33,398		5,026	28,372	31	233	827	3,935	4,505	19,804	4,063	
Estimated total	100.0%	33,952		5,074	28,878	32	236	829	3,977	4,662	20,117	4,099	
Rate per 100,000 inhabitants		5,043.1		753.7	4,289.4	4.8	35.1	123.1	590.7	692.5	2,988.1	608.8	

See footnotes at end of table.

Metropolitan Statistical Area	Population	Crime Index total	Modified Crime Index total[1]	Violent crime[2]	Property crime[3]	Murder and non-negligent man-slaughter	Forcible rape	Robbery	Aggra-vated assault	Burglary	Larceny–theft	Motor vehicle theft	Arson[1]
Orange County, Ca. M.S.A.	**2,579,317**												
(Includes Orange County.)													
Total area actually reporting	100.0%	102,748		12,002	90,746	111	492	4,494	6,905	19,261	56,976	14,509	
Rate per 100,000 inhabitants		3,983.5		465.3	3,518.2	4.3	19.1	174.2	267.7	746.7	2,209.0	562.5	
Philadelphia, Pa.-N.J. M.S.A.	**4,966,719**												
(Includes Bucks, Chester, Delaware, Montgomery, and Philadelphia Counties, Pa., and Burlington, Camden, Gloucester, and Salem Counties, N.J.)													
City of Philadelphia, Pa.	1,528,403	105,766		23,367	82,399	414	704	15,485	6,764	16,204	43,064	23,131	
Total area actually reporting	98.2%	227,581		36,211	191,370	505	1,416	19,902	14,388	36,048	117,834	37,488	
Estimated total	100.0%	229,998		36,418	193,580	506	1,428	19,955	14,529	36,357	119,516	37,707	
Rate per 100,000 inhabitants		4,630.8		733.2	3,897.5	10.2	28.8	401.8	292.5	732.0	2,406.3	759.2	
Phoenix-Mesa, Az. M.S.A.	**2,687,593**												
(Includes Maricopa and Pinal Counties.)													
City of:													
Phoenix	1,139,793	108,749		10,529	98,220	186	460	3,757	6,126	19,559	60,565	18,096	
Mesa	340,818	25,735		2,459	23,276	18	110	506	1,825	3,883	15,582	3,811	
Total area actually reporting	98.9%	205,541		17,808	187,733	266	831	5,430	11,281	37,335	120,092	30,306	
Estimated total	100.0%	207,756		17,954	189,802	267	838	5,467	11,382	37,759	121,491	30,552	
Rate per 100,000 inhabitants		7,730.2		668.0	7,062.2	9.9	31.2	203.4	423.5	1,404.9	4,520.4	1,136.8	
Pine Bluff, Ar. M.S.A.	**85,983**												
(Includes Jefferson County.)													
City of Pine Bluff	59,317	6,405		1,563	4,842	18	84	346	1,115	1,713	2,303	826	
Total area actually reporting	100.0%	7,155		1,661	5,494	20	92	356	1,193	1,952	2,646	896	
Rate per 100,000 inhabitants		8,321.4		1,931.8	6,389.6	23.3	107.0	414.0	1,387.5	2,270.2	3,077.4	1,042.1	
Pittsburgh, Pa. M.S.A.	**2,409,583**												
(Includes Allegheny, Beaver, Bulter, Fayette, Washington, and Westmoreland Counties.)													
City of Pittsburgh	354,308	18,764		2,848	15,916	47	206	1,565	1,030	3,049	10,057	2,810	
Total area actually reporting	94.3%	60,418		6,980	53,438	81	534	2,531	3,834	10,225	36,421	6,792	
Estimated total	100.0%	64,218		7,306	56,912	83	554	2,614	4,055	10,710	39,065	7,137	
Rate per 100,000 inhabitants		2,665.1		303.2	2,361.9	3.4	23.0	108.5	168.3	444.5	1,621.2	296.2	
Pittsfield, Ma. M.S.A.	**97,317**												
(Includes part of Berkshire County.)													
City of Pittsfield	46,828	1,488		134	1,354	—	3	29	102	400	869	85	
Total area actually reporting	90.0%	2,073		216	1,857	—	4	32	180	507	1,243	107	
Estimated total	100.0%	2,331		248	2,083	—	6	36	206	554	1,393	136	
Rate per 100,000 inhabitants		2,395.3		254.8	2,140.4	—	6.2	37.0	211.7	569.3	1,431.4	139.7	
Pocatello, Id. M.S.A.	**74,437**												
(Includes Bannock County.)													
City of Pocatello	52,087	2,295		177	2,118	—	14	23	140	374	1,642	102	
Total area actually reporting	100.0%	3,208		218	2,990	2	17	27	172	525	2,323	142	
Rate per 100,000 inhabitants		4,309.7		292.9	4,016.8	2.7	22.8	36.3	231.1	705.3	3,120.8	190.8	
Portland, Me. M.S.A.	**237,494**												
(Includes part of Cumberland and York Counties.)													
City of Portland	61,968	4,691		457	4,234	1	63	103	290	989	3,014	231	
Total area actually reporting	100.0%	10,546		635	9,911	2	97	145	391	2,169	7,288	454	
Rate per 100,000 inhabitants		4,440.5		267.4	4,173.2	.8	40.8	61.1	164.6	913.3	3,068.7	191.2	
Portland-Vancouver, Or.-Wa. M.S.A.	**1,742,641**												
(Includes Clackamas, Columbia, Multnomah, Washington, and Yamhill Counties, Or., and Clark County, Wa.)													
City of:													
Portland, Or.	467,906	50,306		7,835	42,471	51	402	2,057	5,325	7,142	28,823	6,506	
Vancouver, Wa.	53,689	4,988		571	4,417	3	73	126	369	916	2,961	540	
Total area actually reporting	97.4%	104,635		11,110	93,525	74	816	3,006	7,214	16,397	65,219	11,909	
Estimated total	100.0%	107,255		11,232	96,023	75	831	3,045	7,281	16,787	67,110	12,126	
Rate per 100,000 inhabitants		6,154.7		644.5	5,510.2	4.3	47.7	174.7	417.8	963.3	3,851.1	695.8	

See footnotes at end of table.

Table 6. — Index of Crime, Metropolitan Statistical Areas, 1996 — Continued

Metropolitan Statistical Area	Population	Crime Index total	Modified Crime Index total[1]	Violent crime[2]	Property crime[3]	Murder and non-negligent man-slaughter	Forcible rape	Robbery	Aggra-vated assault	Burglary	Larceny–theft	Motor vehicle theft	Arson[1]
Portsmouth-Rochester, N.H.-Me. M.S.A.	**278,260**												
(Includes part of York County, Me. and Rockingham and Strafford Counties, N.H.)													
City of:													
Portsmouth, N.H.	20,024	904		54	850	1	9	18	26	88	700	62	
Rochester, N.H.	27,616	915		28	887	3	5	5	15	108	734	45	
Total area actually reporting	94.2%	6,921		272	6,649	6	67	53	146	1,005	5,337	307	
Estimated total	100.0%	7,347		291	7,056	6	74	56	155	1,071	5,653	332	
Rate per 100,000 inhabitants		2,640.3		104.6	2,535.8	2.2	26.6	20.1	55.7	384.9	2,031.6	119.3	
Providence-Fall River-Warwick, R.I.-Ma. M.S.A.	**951,344**												
(Includes part of Bristol, Kent, Newport, Providence, and Washington Counties, R.I., and part of Bristol County, Ma.)													
City of:													
Providence, R.I.	149,805	13,106		1,033	12,073	16	77	445	495	2,934	6,720	2,419	
Fall River, Ma.	90,179	4,440		636	3,804	3	29	93	511	913	2,240	651	
Warwick, R.I.	85,711	3,425		245	3,180	1	19	29	196	461	2,397	322	
Total area actually reporting	100.0%	38,187		3,366	34,821	25	264	797	2,280	7,712	22,423	4,686	
Rate per 100,000 inhabitants		4,014.0		353.8	3,660.2	2.6	27.8	83.8	239.7	810.6	2,357.0	492.6	
Provo-Orem, Ut. M.S.A.	**305,042**												
(Includes Utah County.)													
City of:													
Provo	92,787	3,507		166	3,341	1	45	20	100	533	2,604	204	
Orem	77,990	4,144		78	4,066	1	17	16	44	426	3,510	130	
Total area actually reporting	100.0%	13,749		474	13,275	3	103	51	317	1,870	10,785	620	
Rate per 100,000 inhabitants		4,507.2		155.4	4,351.9	1.0	33.8	16.7	103.9	613.0	3,535.6	203.3	
Pueblo, Co. M.S.A.	**133,494**												
(Includes Pueblo County.)													
City of Pueblo	105,059	7,371		1,386	5,985	12	74	196	1,104	1,348	4,305	332	
Total area actually reporting	100.0%	8,342		1,415	6,927	13	79	199	1,124	1,589	4,971	367	
Rate per 100,000 inhabitants		6,249.0		1,060.0	5,189.0	9.7	59.2	149.1	842.0	1,190.3	3,723.8	274.9	
Racine, Wi. M.S.A.	**184,485**												
(Includes Racine County.)													
City of Racine	87,334	6,228		657	5,571	12	17	316	312	1,167	3,744	660	
Total area actually reporting	100.0%	8,913		737	8,176	12	27	348	350	1,597	5,771	808	
Rate per 100,000 inhabitants		4,831.3		399.5	4,431.8	6.5	14.6	188.6	189.7	865.7	3,128.2	438.0	
Raleigh-Durham-Chapel Hill, N.C. M.S.A.	**999,006**												
(Includes Chatham, Durham, Franklin, Johnston, Orange, and Wake Counties.)													
City of:													
Raleigh	245,176	17,080		2,109	14,971	25	90	732	1,262	3,139	10,456	1,376	
Durham	148,571	16,838		1,689	15,149	41	84	810	754	4,226	9,400	1,523	
Chapel Hill	48,281	2,705		220	2,485	1	9	61	149	448	1,937	100	
Total area actually reporting	99.3%	60,202		5,664	54,538	99	270	1,999	3,296	12,992	37,212	4,334	
Estimated total	100.0%	60,704		5,703	55,001	99	272	2,010	3,322	13,085	37,560	4,356	
Rate per 100,000 inhabitants		6,076.4		570.9	5,505.6	9.9	27.2	201.2	332.5	1,309.8	3,759.7	436.0	
Rapid City, S.D. M.S.A.	**87,902**												
(Includes Pennington County.)													
City of Rapid City	58,487	3,824		212	3,612	1	35	43	133	557	2,947	108	
Total area actually reporting	100.0%	4,834		295	4,539	1	71	44	179	796	3,608	135	
Rate per 100,000 inhabitants		5,499.3		335.6	5,163.7	1.1	80.8	50.1	203.6	905.6	4,104.6	153.6	
Reading, Pa. M.S.A.	**344,751**												
(Includes Berks County.)													
City of Reading	78,270	8,139		971	7,168	11	36	491	433	2,038	4,530	600	
Total area actually reporting	97.3%	14,042		1,350	12,692	15	64	555	716	2,971	8,758	963	
Estimated total	100.0%	14,296		1,372	12,924	15	65	561	731	3,003	8,935	986	
Rate per 100,000 inhabitants		4,146.8		398.0	3,748.8	4.4	18.9	162.7	212.0	871.1	2,591.7	286.0	
Redding, Ca. M.S.A.	**162,294**												
(Includes Shasta County.)													
City of Redding	73,942	4,453		520	3,933	5	57	98	360	943	2,677	313	
Total area actually reporting	100.0%	7,322		1,231	6,091	9	89	145	988	1,600	3,976	515	
Rate per 100,000 inhabitants		4,511.6		758.5	3,753.1	5.5	54.8	89.3	608.8	985.9	2,449.9	317.3	

See footnotes at end of table.

Metropolitan Statistical Area	Population	Crime Index total	Modified Crime Index total[1]	Violent crime[2]	Property crime[3]	Murder and non-negligent man-slaughter	Forcible rape	Robbery	Aggra-vated assault	Burglary	Larceny-theft	Motor vehicle theft	Arson[1]
Reno, Nv. M.S.A.	311,282												
(Includes Washoe County.)													
City of Reno	159,559	10,854		1,123	9,731	12	113	507	491	1,676	7,330	725	
Total area actually reporting	100.0%	17,027		1,706	15,321	14	173	609	910	3,007	11,169	1,145	
Rate per 100,000 inhabitants		5,470.0		548.1	4,921.9	4.5	55.6	195.6	292.3	966.0	3,588.1	367.8	
Richland-Kennewick-Pasco, Wa. M.S.A.	178,118												
(Includes Benton and Franklin Counties.)													
City of:													
Richland	37,010	1,443		74	1,369	1	18	9	46	205	1,108	56	
Kennewick	49,810	3,142		172	2,970	—	25	42	105	452	2,366	152	
Pasco	24,051	2,004		157	1,847	2	18	33	104	244	1,416	187	
Total area actually reporting	100.0%	8,278		516	7,762	7	78	88	343	1,282	5,996	484	
Rate per 100,000 inhabitants		4,647.5		289.7	4,357.8	3.9	43.8	49.4	192.6	719.7	3,366.3	271.7	
Richmond-Petersburg, Va. M.S.A.	933,862												
(Includes Colonial Heights, Hopewell, Petersburg, and Richmond Cities, and Charles City, Chesterfield, Dinwiddie, Goochland, Hanover, Henrico, New Kent, Powhatan, and Prince George Counties.)													
City of:													
Richmond	204,881	19,771		3,383	16,388	112	143	1,545	1,583	4,022	10,338	2,028	
Petersburg	41,701	3,362		534	2,828	6	27	199	302	654	1,876	298	
Total area actually reporting	100.0%	50,944		5,571	45,373	149	303	2,287	2,832	8,646	33,083	3,644	
Rate per 100,000 inhabitants		5,455.2		596.6	4,858.6	16.0	32.4	244.9	303.3	925.8	3,542.6	390.2	
Riverside-San Bernardino, Ca. M.S.A.	2,933,494												
(Includes Riverside and San Bernardino Counties.)													
City of:													
Riverside	245,081	15,493		3,169	12,324	18	115	874	2,162	2,894	7,121	2,309	
San Bernardino	184,303	16,970		3,233	13,737	42	79	1,281	1,831	3,544	7,201	2,992	
Total area actually reporting	100.0%	163,120		23,896	139,224	295	974	7,187	15,440	40,642	73,634	24,948	
Rate per 100,000 inhabitants		5,560.6		814.6	4,746.0	10.1	33.2	245.0	526.3	1,385.4	2,510.1	850.5	
Roanoke, Va. M.S.A.	232,888												
(Includes Roanoke and Salem Cities, and Botetourt and Roanoke Counties.)													
City of Roanoke	98,456	6,217		577	5,640	15	42	273	247	933	4,396	311	
Total area actually reporting	100.0%	9,202		750	8,452	17	57	304	372	1,302	6,713	437	
Rate per 100,000 inhabitants		3,951.3		322.0	3,629.2	7.3	24.5	130.5	159.7	559.1	2,882.5	187.6	
Rochester, Mn. M.S.A.	115,157												
(Includes Olmsted County.)													
City of Rochester	77,278	3,595		292	3,303	5	53	60	174	476	2,682	145	
Total area actually reporting	100.0%	4,186		328	3,858	5	63	62	198	597	3,055	206	
Rate per 100,000 inhabitants		3,635.0		284.8	3,350.2	4.3	54.7	53.8	171.9	518.4	2,652.9	178.9	
Rochester, N.Y. M.S.A.	1,091,510												
(Includes Genesee, Livingston, Monroe, Ontario, Orleans, and Wayne Counties.)													
City of Rochester	231,372	20,928		2,270	18,658	53	119	1,360	738	4,474	11,491	2,693	
Total area actually reporting	99.3%	46,434		3,373	43,061	60	235	1,673	1,405	7,855	31,208	3,998	
Estimated total	100.0%	46,665		3,392	43,273	60	236	1,679	1,417	7,891	31,367	4,015	
Rate per 100,000 inhabitants		4,275.3		310.8	3,964.5	5.5	21.6	153.8	129.8	722.9	2,873.7	367.8	
Rocky Mount, N.C. M.S.A.	145,314												
(Includes Edgecombe and Nash Counties.)													
City of Rocky Mount	53,797	5,216		558	4,658	10	19	232	297	1,225	3,210	223	
Total area actually reporting	99.1%	8,369		808	7,561	14	40	308	446	2,150	5,031	380	
Estimated total	100.0%	8,462		815	7,647	14	40	310	451	2,167	5,096	384	
Rate per 100,000 inhabitants		5,823.3		560.9	5,262.4	9.6	27.5	213.3	310.4	1,491.3	3,506.9	264.3	
Sacramento, Ca. M.S.A.	1,461,970												
(Includes El Dorado, Placer, and Sacramento Counties.)													
City of Sacramento	379,283	33,780		3,707	30,073	43	154	1,874	1,636	7,148	16,842	6,083	
Total area actually reporting	100.0%	91,798		10,246	81,552	101	497	3,644	6,004	19,270	45,797	16,485	
Rate per 100,000 inhabitants		6,279.1		700.8	5,578.2	6.9	34.0	249.3	410.7	1,318.1	3,132.6	1,127.6	

See footnotes at end of table.

Table 6. — Index of Crime, Metropolitan Statistical Areas, 1996 — Continued

Metropolitan Statistical Area	Population	Crime Index total	Modified Crime Index total[1]	Violent crime[2]	Property crime[3]	Murder and non-negligent man-slaughter	Forcible rape	Robbery	Aggra-vated assault	Burglary	Larceny–theft	Motor vehicle theft	Arson[1]
Saginaw-Bay City-Midland, Mi. M.S.A.	**406,429**												
(Includes Bay, Midland, and Saginaw Counties.)													
City of:													
Saginaw	71,334	5,694		1,505	4,189	15	91	319	1,080	1,665	2,166	358	
Bay City	38,784	2,230		291	1,939	1	29	46	215	343	1,438	158	
Midland	39,975	1,130		85	1,045	2	16	6	61	105	907	33	
Total area actually reporting	93.4%	16,585		2,527	14,058	20	244	453	1,810	3,239	9,902	917	
Estimated total	100.0%	17,819		2,631	15,188	21	252	476	1,882	3,409	10,726	1,053	
Rate per 100,000 inhabitants		4,384.3		647.3	3,736.9	5.2	62.0	117.1	463.1	838.8	2,639.1	259.1	
St. Cloud, Mn. M.S.A.	**160,029**												
(Includes Benton and Stearns Counties.)													
City of St. Cloud	51,794	3,482		194	3,288	—	66	44	84	505	2,577	206	
Total area actually reporting	100.0%	5,234		245	4,989	4	77	55	109	789	3,904	296	
Rate per 100,000 inhabitants		3,270.7		153.1	3,117.6	2.5	48.1	34.4	68.1	493.0	2,439.6	185.0	
Salem, Or. M.S.A.	**317,128**												
(Includes Marion and Polk Counties.)													
City of Salem	119,822	10,732		394	10,338	7	94	191	102	1,282	8,310	746	
Total area actually reporting	99.0%	20,661		883	19,778	11	162	294	416	2,846	15,441	1,491	
Estimated total	100.0%	20,844		892	19,952	11	163	297	421	2,873	15,573	1,506	
Rate per 100,000 inhabitants		6,572.7		281.3	6,291.5	3.5	51.4	93.7	132.8	905.9	4,910.6	474.9	
Salinas, Ca. M.S.A.	**356,919**												
(Includes Monterey County.)													
City of Salinas	121,517	7,554		1,359	6,195	9	54	412	884	1,031	4,339	825	
Total area actually reporting	100.0%	16,802		2,390	14,412	23	101	640	1,626	3,082	10,064	1,266	
Rate per 100,000 inhabitants		4,707.5		669.6	4,037.9	6.4	28.3	179.3	455.6	863.5	2,819.7	354.7	
Salt Lake City-Ogden, Ut. M.S.A.	**1,235,223**												
(Includes Davis, Salt Lake, and Weber Counties.)													
City of:													
Salt Lake City	180,180	22,283		1,501	20,782	20	152	591	738	3,015	14,898	2,869	
Ogden	71,030	6,434		382	6,052	5	57	102	218	927	4,719	406	
Total area actually reporting	99.2%	86,374		5,177	81,197	52	577	1,249	3,299	11,910	62,214	7,073	
Estimated total	100.0%	86,930		5,207	81,723	52	580	1,254	3,321	11,987	62,629	7,107	
Rate per 100,000 inhabitants		7,037.6		421.5	6,616.1	4.2	47.0	101.5	268.9	970.4	5,070.3	575.4	
San Angelo, Tx. M.S.A.	**105,374**												
(Includes Tom Green County.)													
City of San Angelo	92,346	5,275		453	4,822	2	37	39	375	739	3,923	160	
Total area actually reporting	100.0%	5,729		617	5,112	3	53	43	518	826	4,116	170	
Rate per 100,000 inhabitants		5,436.8		585.5	4,851.3	2.8	50.3	40.8	491.6	783.9	3,906.1	161.3	
San Antonio, Tx. M.S.A.	**1,495,941**												
(Includes Bexar, Comal, Guadalupe, and Wilson Counties.)													
City of San Antonio	1,021,477	87,710		4,741	82,969	117	637	2,350	1,637	13,685	60,488	8,796	
Total area actually reporting	100.0%	105,923		6,406	99,517	140	764	2,555	2,947	17,261	72,518	9,738	
Rate per 100,000 inhabitants		7,080.7		428.2	6,652.5	9.4	51.1	170.8	197.0	1,153.9	4,847.7	651.0	
San Diego, Ca. M.S.A.	**2,669,512**												
(Includes San Diego County.)													
City of San Diego	1,168,364	61,574		10,149	51,425	80	368	2,998	6,703	8,608	31,688	11,129	
Total area actually reporting	100.0%	123,434		18,954	104,480	166	815	5,466	12,507	21,871	62,014	20,595	
Rate per 100,000 inhabitants		4,623.8		710.0	3,913.8	6.2	30.5	204.8	468.5	819.3	2,323.0	771.5	
San Francisco, Ca. M.S.A.	**1,669,334**												
(Includes Marin, San Francisco, and San Mateo Counties.)													
City of San Francisco	745,127	56,592		9,886	46,706	82	298	5,539	3,967	7,079	31,062	8,565	
Total area actually reporting	100.0%	89,837		13,377	76,460	96	476	6,627	6,178	11,676	53,033	11,751	
Rate per 100,000 inhabitants		5,381.6		801.3	4,580.3	5.8	28.5	397.0	370.1	699.4	3,176.9	703.9	
San Jose, Ca. M.S.A.	**1,579,373**												
(Includes Santa Clara County.)													
City of San Jose	830,374	34,287		6,075	28,212	40	341	1,098	4,596	4,700	19,793	3,719	
Total area actually reporting	100.0%	63,496		8,877	54,619	48	543	1,742	6,544	8,922	39,993	5,704	
Rate per 100,000 inhabitants		4,020.3		562.1	3,458.3	3.0	34.4	110.3	414.3	564.9	2,532.2	361.2	

See footnotes at end of table.

Metropolitan Statistical Area	Population	Crime Index total	Modified Crime Index total[1]	Violent crime[2]	Property crime[3]	Murder and non-negligent man-slaughter	Forcible rape	Robbery	Aggra-vated assault	Burglary	Larceny–theft	Motor vehicle theft	Arson[1]
San Luis Obispo-Atascadero-													
Paso Robles, Ca. M.S.A.	**226,883**												
(Includes San Luis Obispo													
County.)													
City of:													
San Luis Obispo	40,880	1,966		233	1,733	—	17	14	202	360	1,304	69	
Atascadero	24,575	870		58	812	—	5	8	45	270	506	36	
Paso Robles	17,694	871		108	763	—	14	13	81	159	559	45	
Total area actually reporting	100.0%	7,846		909	6,937	5	78	69	757	1,556	5,093	288	
Rate per 100,000 inhabitants		3,458.2		400.6	3,057.5	2.2	34.4	30.4	333.7	685.8	2,244.8	126.9	
Santa Barbara-Santa Maria-													
Lompoc, Ca. M.S.A.	**385,898**												
(Includes Santa Barbara County.)													
City of:													
Santa Barbara	86,843	4,659		599	4,060	1	40	105	453	1,002	2,844	214	
Santa Maria	66,869	3,853		422	3,431	4	33	117	268	730	2,526	175	
Lompoc	42,105	1,781		193	1,588	3	10	58	122	415	1,099	74	
Total area actually reporting	100.0%	15,000		1,734	13,266	12	127	317	1,278	3,641	8,981	644	
Rate per 100,000 inhabitants		3,887.0		449.3	3,437.7	3.1	32.9	82.1	331.2	943.5	2,327.3	166.9	
Santa Cruz-Watsonville, Ca.													
M.S.A.	**238,309**												
(Includes Santa Cruz County.)													
City of:													
Santa Cruz	49,185	4,160		577	3,583	2	12	103	460	600	2,752	231	
Watsonville	32,547	2,473		558	1,915	6	10	87	455	378	1,383	154	
Total area actually reporting	100.0%	13,324		1,774	11,550	10	71	276	1,417	2,170	8,596	784	
Rate per 100,000 inhabitants		5,591.1		744.4	4,846.6	4.2	29.8	115.8	594.6	910.6	3,607.1	329.0	
Santa Rosa, Ca. M.S.A.	**416,018**												
(Includes Sonoma County.)													
City of Santa Rosa	118,625	6,905		663	6,242	2	81	170	410	920	4,901	421	
Total area actually reporting	100.0%	17,559		1,862	15,697	17	173	326	1,346	3,520	11,208	969	
Rate per 100,000 inhabitants		4,220.7		447.6	3,773.2	4.1	41.6	78.4	323.5	846.1	2,694.1	232.9	
Savannah, Ga. M.S.A.	**287,285**												
(Includes Bryan, Chatham, and													
Effingham Counties.)													
City of Savannah	146,534	13,089		1,417	11,672	22	63	849	483	2,158	8,427	1,087	
Total area actually reporting	90.9%	19,622		2,001	17,621	26	97	989	889	3,354	12,766	1,501	
Estimated total	100.0%	20,982		2,098	18,884	27	104	1,028	939	3,613	13,602	1,669	
Rate per 100,000 inhabitants		7,303.5		730.3	6,573.3	9.4	36.2	357.8	326.9	1,257.6	4,734.7	581.0	
Sheboygan, Wi. M.S.A.	**108,669**												
(Includes Sheboygan County.)													
City of Sheboygan	51,140	2,599		88	2,511	—	15	12	61	405	2,020	86	
Total area actually reporting	100.0%	3,931		150	3,781	1	21	18	110	606	3,040	135	
Rate per 100,000 inhabitants		3,617.4		138.0	3,479.4	.9	19.3	16.6	101.2	557.7	2,797.5	124.2	
Sherman-Denison, Tx. M.S.A.	**101,232**												
(Includes Grayson County.)													
City of:													
Sherman	32,825	2,604		259	2,345	2	55	54	148	388	1,838	119	
Denison	22,374	1,631		170	1,461	1	8	37	124	262	1,146	53	
Total area actually reporting	100.0%	5,487		497	4,990	5	69	100	323	1,011	3,732	247	
Rate per 100,000 inhabitants		5,420.2		491.0	4,929.3	4.9	68.2	98.8	319.1	998.7	3,686.6	244.0	
Shreveport-Bossier City, La. M.S.A.	**381,518**												
(Includes Bossier, Caddo,													
and Webster Parishes.)													
City of:													
Shreveport	199,418	23,658		2,490	21,168	51	134	729	1,576	4,185	15,454	1,529	
Bossier City	54,872	3,804		465	3,339	5	24	82	354	569	2,548	222	
Total area actually reporting	100.0%	31,535		3,416	28,119	69	186	845	2,316	5,787	20,299	2,033	
Rate per 100,000 inhabitants		8,265.7		895.4	7,370.3	18.1	48.8	221.5	607.0	1,516.8	5,320.6	532.9	
Sioux City, Ia.-Ne. M.S.A.	**120,152**												
(Includes Woodbury County, Ia.,													
and Dakota County, Ne.)													
City of Sioux City, Ia.	83,407	6,403		604	5,799	—	33	66	505	994	4,405	400	
Total area actually reporting	97.4%	7,303		660	6,643	1	43	69	547	1,181	4,994	468	
Estimated total	100.0%	7,400		664	6,736	1	43	70	550	1,195	5,069	472	
Rate per 100,000 inhabitants		6,158.9		552.6	5,606.2	.8	35.8	58.3	457.8	994.6	4,218.8	392.8	

See footnotes at end of table.

Metropolitan Statistical Area	Population	Crime Index total	Modified Crime Index total[1]	Violent crime[2]	Property crime[3]	Murder and non-negligent man-slaughter	Forcible rape	Robbery	Aggra-vated assault	Burglary	Larceny-theft	Motor vehicle theft	Arson[1]
Sioux Falls, S.D. M.S.A.	**158,055**												
(Includes Lincoln and Minnehaha Counties.)													
City of Sioux Falls	110,891	5,354		473	4,881	1	82	65	325	864	3,808	209	
Total area actually reporting	87.7%	5,962		527	5,435	1	103	66	357	1,028	4,167	240	
Estimated total	100.0%	6,541		572	5,969	1	122	67	382	1,175	4,538	256	
Rate per 100,000 inhabitants		4,138.4		361.9	3,776.5	.6	77.2	42.4	241.7	743.4	2,871.2	162.0	
South Bend, In. M.S.A.	**259,385**												
(Includes St. Joseph County.)													
City of South Bend	106,718	10,822		1,022	9,800	22	93	512	395	2,880	6,185	735	
Total area actually reporting	82.8%	13,760		1,133	12,627	22	104	538	469	3,390	8,373	864	
Estimated total	100.0%	15,827		1,292	14,535	23	114	559	596	3,601	9,919	1,015	
Rate per 100,000 inhabitants		6,101.7		498.1	5,603.6	8.9	44.0	215.5	229.8	1,388.3	3,824.0	391.3	
Spokane, Wa. M.S.A.	**409,949**												
(Includes Spokane County.)													
City of Spokane	199,636	16,286		1,308	14,978	15	89	346	858	3,032	11,101	845	
Total area actually reporting	100.0%	26,027		1,800	24,227	20	145	449	1,186	5,198	17,639	1,390	
Rate per 100,000 inhabitants		6,348.8		439.1	5,909.8	4.9	35.4	109.5	289.3	1,268.0	4,302.7	339.1	
Springfield, Ma. M.S.A.[7]	**509,784**												
(Includes part of Franklin, Hampden, and Hampshire Counties.)													
City of Springfield	150,421			3,424		12	99	531	2,782	3,206	3,477		
Total area actually reporting	98.1%	23,574		5,661	17,913	19	230	750	4,662	5,599	9,827	2,487	
Estimated total	100.0%	23,831		5,693	18,138	19	232	754	4,688	5,646	9,976	2,516	
Rate per 100,000 inhabitants		4,674.7		1,116.7	3,558.0	3.7	45.5	147.9	919.6	1,107.5	1,956.9	493.5	
Springfield, Mo. M.S.A.	**321,225**												
(Includes Christian, Greene, and Webster Counties.)													
City of Springfield	152,024	11,505		795	10,710	4	76	173	542	2,182	7,851	677	
Total area actually reporting	100.0%	14,575		1,045	13,530	4	105	195	741	2,950	9,682	898	
Rate per 100,000 inhabitants		4,537.3		325.3	4,212.0	1.2	32.7	60.7	230.7	918.4	3,014.1	279.6	
Stamford-Norwalk, Ct. M.S.A.	**331,522**												
(Includes part of Fairfield County.)													
City of:													
Stamford	107,165	4,955		441	4,514	6	18	212	205	704	3,332	478	
Norwalk	78,685	4,464		276	4,188	5	14	169	88	852	3,017	319	
Total area actually reporting	100.0%	12,365		824	11,541	13	46	416	349	2,102	8,431	1,008	
Rate per 100,000 inhabitants		3,729.8		248.6	3,481.2	3.9	13.9	125.5	105.3	634.0	2,543.1	304.1	
State College, Pa. M.S.A.	**129,871**												
(Includes Centre County.)													
City of State College	61,686	1,487		45	1,442	1	7	12	25	138	1,279	25	
Total area actually reporting	100.0%	3,685		166	3,519	3	32	18	113	529	2,903	87	
Rate per 100,000 inhabitants		2,837.4		127.8	2,709.6	2.3	24.6	13.9	87.0	407.3	2,235.3	67.0	
Stockton-Lodi, Ca. M.S.A.	**525,533**												
(Includes San Joaquin County.)													
City of:													
Stockton	225,799	19,401		3,115	16,286	46	123	1,313	1,633	3,418	9,815	3,053	
Lodi	53,168	3,126		353	2,773	3	18	57	275	361	2,110	302	
Total area actually reporting	100.0%	33,798		4,322	29,476	66	209	1,602	2,445	6,254	18,363	4,859	
Rate per 100,000 inhabitants		6,431.2		822.4	5,608.8	12.6	39.8	304.8	465.2	1,190.0	3,494.2	924.6	
Sumter, S.C. M.S.A.	**107,716**												
(Includes Sumter County.)													
City of Sumter	43,181	2,807		518	2,289	5	22	141	350	640	1,381	268	
Total area actually reporting	100.0%	6,334		1,260	5,074	9	57	222	972	1,645	2,863	566	
Rate per 100,000 inhabitants		5,880.3		1,169.7	4,710.5	8.4	52.9	206.1	902.4	1,527.2	2,657.9	525.5	
Syracuse, N.Y. M.S.A.	**755,856**												
(Includes Cayuga, Madison, Onondaga, and Oswego Counties.)													
City of Syracuse	160,033	10,999		1,398	9,601	15	62	579	742	2,821	5,940	840	
Total area actually reporting	99.6%	26,742		2,169	24,573	19	151	744	1,255	5,915	17,423	1,235	
Estimated total	100.0%	26,843		2,177	24,666	19	151	747	1,260	5,931	17,493	1,242	
Rate per 100,000 inhabitants		3,551.3		288.0	3,263.3	2.5	20.0	98.8	166.7	784.7	2,314.3	164.3	
Tacoma, Wa. M.S.A.	**661,776**												
(Includes Pierce County.)													
City of Tacoma	189,568	20,143		2,785	17,358	20	137	792	1,836	3,284	11,255	2,819	
Total area actually reporting	99.6%	45,597		4,881	40,716	45	307	1,226	3,303	8,008	27,587	5,121	
Estimated total	100.0%	45,781		4,891	40,890	45	309	1,229	3,308	8,036	27,715	5,139	
Rate per 100,000 inhabitants		6,917.9		739.1	6,178.8	6.8	46.7	185.7	499.9	1,214.3	4,188.0	776.5	

See footnotes at end of table.

Table 6. — Index of Crime, Metropolitan Statistical Areas, 1996 — Continued

Metropolitan Statistical Area	Population	Crime Index total	Modified Crime Index total[1]	Violent crime[2]	Property crime[3]	Murder and non-negligent man-slaughter	Forcible rape	Robbery	Aggra-vated assault	Burglary	Larceny–theft	Motor vehicle theft	Arson[1]
Texarkana, Tx.-Texarkana, Ar. M.S.A.	**126,958**												
(Includes Bowie County, Tx., and Miller County, Ar.)													
City of:													
Texarkana, Tx.	33,784	2,856		349	2,507	6	23	72	248	591	1,772	144	
Texarkana, Ar.	23,454	2,697		276	2,421	4	29	72	171	366	1,953	102	
Total area actually reporting	100.0%	7,342		805	6,537	14	67	163	561	1,423	4,779	335	
Rate per 100,000 inhabitants		5,783.0		634.1	5,148.9	11.0	52.8	128.4	441.9	1,120.8	3,764.2	263.9	
Toledo, Oh. M.S.A.	**617,844**												
(Includes Fulton, Lucas, and Wood Counties.)													
City of Toledo	324,610	27,488		2,635	24,853	30	277	1,297	1,031	5,597	16,218	3,038	
Total area actually reporting	94.4%	36,609		3,044	33,565	36	333	1,375	1,300	7,128	22,991	3,446	
Estimated total	100.0%	38,008		3,123	34,885	36	341	1,399	1,347	7,327	24,026	3,532	
Rate per 100,000 inhabitants		6,151.7		505.5	5,646.2	5.8	55.2	226.4	218.0	1,185.9	3,888.7	571.7	
Trenton, N.J. M.S.A.	**332,922**												
(Includes Mercer County.)													
City of Trenton	85,338	6,347		1,325	5,022	14	160	462	689	1,364	2,572	1,086	
Total area actually reporting	100.0%	14,449		1,717	12,732	16	198	615	888	2,812	7,968	1,952	
Rate per 100,000 inhabitants		4,340.1		515.7	3,824.3	4.8	59.5	184.7	266.7	844.6	2,393.4	586.3	
Tucson, Az. M.S.A.	**794,894**												
(Includes Pima County.)													
City of Tucson	472,385	46,385		5,199	41,186	46	282	1,288	3,583	6,710	28,460	6,016	
Total area actually reporting	99.0%	61,869		6,396	55,473	75	377	1,557	4,387	9,249	38,391	7,833	
Estimated total	100.0%	62,428		6,432	55,996	75	379	1,566	4,412	9,356	38,745	7,895	
Rate per 100,000 inhabitants		7,853.6		809.2	7,044.5	9.4	47.7	197.0	555.0	1,177.0	4,874.2	993.2	
Tulsa, Ok. M.S.A.	**752,889**												
(Includes Creek, Osage, Rogers, Tulsa, and Wagoner Counties.)													
City of Tulsa	379,798	27,373		4,428	22,945	31	304	868	3,225	6,131	12,545	4,269	
Total area actually reporting	100.0%	39,699		5,576	34,123	46	395	986	4,149	9,105	19,576	5,442	
Rate per 100,000 inhabitants		5,272.9		740.6	4,532.3	6.1	52.5	131.0	551.1	1,209.3	2,600.1	722.8	
Tuscaloosa, Al. M.S.A.	**159,053**												
(Includes Tuscaloosa County.)													
City of Tuscaloosa	80,818	11,949		904	11,045	5	50	340	509	1,346	9,322	377	
Total area actually reporting	100.0%	15,453		1,288	14,165	10	63	386	829	2,155	11,399	611	
Rate per 100,000 inhabitants		9,715.6		809.8	8,905.8	6.3	39.6	242.7	521.2	1,354.9	7,166.8	384.1	
Tyler, Tx. M.S.A.	**165,414**												
(Includes Smith County.)													
City of Tyler	83,467	6,405		630	5,775	9	54	191	376	952	4,466	357	
Total area actually reporting	100.0%	9,335		950	8,385	15	114	210	611	1,662	6,187	536	
Rate per 100,000 inhabitants		5,643.4		574.3	5,069.1	9.1	68.9	127.0	369.4	1,004.8	3,740.3	324.0	
Utica-Rome, N.Y. M.S.A.	**314,233**												
(Includes Herkimer and Oneida Counties.)													
City of:													
Utica	64,150	3,266		198	3,068	8	25	116	49	637	2,199	232	
Rome	44,271	1,061		56	1,005	1	7	26	22	267	675	63	
Total area actually reporting	96.8%	9,391		745	8,646	11	64	172	498	1,886	6,354	406	
Estimated total	100.0%	9,515		755	8,760	11	64	175	505	1,905	6,440	415	
Rate per 100,000 inhabitants		3,028.0		240.3	2,787.7	3.5	20.4	55.7	160.7	606.2	2,049.4	132.1	
Vallejo-Fairfield-Napa, Ca. M.S.A.	**489,406**												
(Includes Napa and Solano Counties.)													
City of:													
Vallejo	113,069	8,996		1,564	7,432	15	59	523	967	1,658	4,901	873	
Fairfield	84,967	5,366		677	4,689	3	40	192	442	907	3,269	513	
Napa	64,346	2,724		259	2,465	—	23	53	183	389	1,894	182	
Total area actually reporting	100.0%	24,696		3,414	21,282	22	184	928	2,280	4,685	14,435	2,162	
Rate per 100,000 inhabitants		5,046.1		697.6	4,348.5	4.5	37.6	189.6	465.9	957.3	2,949.5	441.8	
Ventura, Ca. M.S.A.	**712,727**												
(Includes Ventura County.)													
City of Ventura	97,657	4,111		407	3,704	6	26	148	227	952	2,355	397	
Total area actually reporting	100.0%	23,178		2,902	20,276	33	148	874	1,847	4,563	13,400	2,313	
Rate per 100,000 inhabitants		3,252.0		407.2	2,844.8	4.6	20.8	122.6	259.1	640.2	1,880.1	324.5	

See footnotes at end of table.

Table 6. — Index of Crime, Metropolitan Statistical Areas, 1996 — Continued

Metropolitan Statistical Area	Population	Crime Index total	Modified Crime Index total[1]	Violent crime[2]	Property crime[3]	Murder and non-negligent man-slaughter	Forcible rape	Robbery	Aggra-vated assault	Burglary	Larceny–theft	Motor vehicle theft	Arson[1]
Victoria, Tx. M.S.A.	**82,679**												
(Includes Victoria County.)													
City of Victoria	63,056	3,912		597	3,315	2	29	60	506	748	2,394	173	
Total area actually reporting	100.0%	4,523		662	3,861	2	42	70	548	940	2,712	209	
Rate per 100,000 inhabitants		5,470.6		800.7	4,669.9	2.4	50.8	84.7	662.8	1,136.9	3,280.2	252.8	
Vineland-Millville-Bridgeton,													
N.J. M.S.A.	**140,274**												
(Includes Cumberland County.)													
City of:													
Vineland	55,253	3,416		408	3,008	2	26	174	206	719	2,056	233	
Millville	26,809	1,688		221	1,467	—	28	58	135	437	963	67	
Bridgeton	19,239	1,747		328	1,419	2	13	93	220	420	911	88	
Total area actually reporting	100.0%	7,842		1,098	6,744	5	87	341	665	1,852	4,398	494	
Rate per 100,000 inhabitants		5,590.5		782.8	4,807.7	3.6	62.0	243.1	474.1	1,320.3	3,135.3	352.2	
Visalia-Tulare-Porterville, Ca.													
M.S.A.	**348,130**												
(Includes Tulare County.)													
City of:													
Visalia	86,282	5,927		632	5,295	7	28	175	422	922	3,668	705	
Tulare	39,111	3,052		556	2,496	1	14	95	446	485	1,608	403	
Porterville	32,388	2,129		159	1,970	—	17	33	109	381	1,336	253	
Total area actually reporting	100.0%	17,901		2,376	15,525	22	110	429	1,815	3,508	9,831	2,186	
Rate per 100,000 inhabitants		5,142.0		682.5	4,459.5	6.3	31.6	123.2	521.4	1,007.7	2,823.9	627.9	
Waco, Tx. M.S.A.	**205,205**												
(Includes McLennan County.)													
City of Waco	110,213	11,553		1,352	10,201	14	92	386	860	2,092	6,832	1,277	
Total area actually reporting	100.0%	15,297		1,621	13,676	16	110	439	1,056	2,844	9,352	1,480	
Rate per 100,000 inhabitants		7,454.5		789.9	6,664.6	7.8	53.6	213.9	514.6	1,385.9	4,557.4	721.2	
Washington, D.C.-Md.-Va.-W.V.													
M.S.A.	**4,503,120**												
(Includes District of Columbia,													
Calvert, Charles, Frederick,													
Montgomery, and Prince Georges													
Counties, Md.; Alexandria, Fairfax,													
Falls Church, Fredericksburg,													
Manassas, and Manassas Park Cities,													
and Arlington, Clarke, Culpeper,													
Fairfax, Fauquier, King George,													
Loudoun, Prince William,													
Spotsylvania, Stafford, and Warren													
Counties, Va.; and Berkeley and													
Jefferson Counties, W.V.)													
City of Washington, D.C.	543,000	64,557		13,411	51,146	397	260	6,444	6,310	9,828	31,343	9,975	
Total area actually reporting	99.9%	245,374		30,597	214,777	621	1,243	13,450	15,283	33,507	149,310	31,960	
Estimated total	100.0%	245,453		30,607	214,846	621	1,243	13,454	15,289	33,518	149,361	31,967	
Rate per 100,000 inhabitants		5,450.7		679.7	4,771.0	13.8	27.6	298.8	339.5	744.3	3,316.8	709.9	
Waterbury, Ct. M.S.A.	**182,623**												
(Includes part of Litchfield and													
New Haven Counties.)													
City of Waterbury	103,490	7,952		657	7,295	13	39	245	360	1,930	4,396	969	
Total area actually reporting	100.0%	9,889		726	9,163	13	44	269	400	2,311	5,735	1,117	
Rate per 100,000 inhabitants		5,415.0		397.5	5,017.4	7.1	24.1	147.3	219.0	1,265.4	3,140.3	611.6	
Waterloo-Cedar Falls, Ia. M.S.A.	**124,706**												
(Includes Black Hawk County.)													
City of:													
Waterloo	67,078	5,117		450	4,667	2	40	151	257	1,099	3,293	275	
Cedar Falls	34,182	1,287		112	1,175	—	6	14	92	135	999	41	
Total area actually reporting	100.0%	6,942		594	6,348	2	53	170	369	1,416	4,599	333	
Rate per 100,000 inhabitants		5,566.7		476.3	5,090.4	1.6	42.5	136.3	295.9	1,135.5	3,687.9	267.0	
Wausau, Wi. M.S.A.	**141,562**												
(Includes Marathon County.)													
City of Wausau	39,395	1,574		77	1,497	2	15	11	49	199	1,215	83	
Total area actually reporting	100.0%	3,896		172	3,724	2	36	14	120	541	2,988	195	
Rate per 100,000 inhabitants		2,752.2		121.5	2,630.6	1.4	25.4	9.9	84.8	382.2	2,110.7	137.7	

See footnotes at end of table.

Table 6. — Index of Crime, Metropolitan Statistical Areas, 1996 — Continued

Metropolitan Statistical Area	Population	Crime Index total	Modified Crime Index total[1]	Violent crime[2]	Property crime[3]	Murder and non-negligent man-slaughter	Forcible rape	Robbery	Aggra-vated assault	Burglary	Larceny-theft	Motor vehicle theft	Arson[1]
Wheeling, W.V.-Oh. M.S.A.	**158,505**												
(Includes Marshall and Ohio Counties, W.V., and Belmont County, Oh.)													
City of Wheeling, W.V.	34,042	1,455		157	1,298	1	11	37	108	362	866	70	
Total area actually reporting	93.5%	2,964		250	2,714	1	25	50	174	767	1,805	142	
Estimated total	100.0%	3,379		274	3,105	1	28	57	188	826	2,112	167	
Rate per 100,000 inhabitants		2,131.8		172.9	1,958.9	.6	17.7	36.0	118.6	521.1	1,332.5	105.4	
Wichita Falls, Tx. M.S.A.	**137,375**												
(Includes Archer and Wichita Counties.)													
City of Wichita Falls	101,755	6,704		878	5,826	9	81	152	636	1,020	4,436	370	
Total area actually reporting	100.0%	7,532		944	6,588	11	88	154	691	1,258	4,925	405	
Rate per 100,000 inhabitants		5,482.8		687.2	4,795.6	8.0	64.1	112.1	503.0	915.7	3,585.1	294.8	
Wilmington, N.C. M.S.A.	**200,322**												
(Includes Brunswick and New Hanover Counties.)													
City of Wilmington	64,892	7,180		701	6,479	4	40	240	417	1,562	4,361	556	
Total area actually reporting	99.6%	13,223		1,233	11,990	17	65	296	855	3,361	7,809	820	
Estimated total	100.0%	13,283		1,237	12,046	17	65	297	858	3,372	7,851	823	
Rate per 100,000 inhabitants		6,630.8		617.5	6,013.3	8.5	32.4	148.3	428.3	1,683.3	3,919.2	410.8	
Worcester, Ma.-Ct. M.S.A.	**481,332**												
(Includes part of Windham County, Ct., and Hampden and Worcester Counties, Ma.)													
City of Worcester, Ma.	166,782	10,043		1,563	8,480	7	108	410	1,038	2,230	5,137	1,113	
Total area actually reporting	97.2%	16,091		2,777	13,314	7	162	461	2,147	3,421	8,368	1,525	
Estimated total	100.0%	16,444		2,820	13,624	7	164	466	2,183	3,486	8,573	1,565	
Rate per 100,000 inhabitants		3,416.4		585.9	2,830.5	1.5	34.1	96.8	453.5	724.2	1,781.1	325.1	
Yakima, Wa. M.S.A.	**214,123**												
(Includes Yakima County.)													
City of Yakima	64,179	7,508		547	6,961	7	50	115	375	1,351	4,950	660	
Total area actually reporting	98.8%	15,024		1,037	13,987	16	154	175	692	3,526	9,164	1,297	
Estimated total	100.0%	15,213		1,047	14,166	16	156	178	697	3,555	9,296	1,315	
Rate per 100,000 inhabitants		7,104.8		489.0	6,615.8	7.5	72.9	83.1	325.5	1,660.3	4,341.4	614.1	
Yuba City, Ca. M.S.A.	**137,105**												
(Includes Sutter and Yuba Counties.)													
City of Yuba	32,902	2,606		290	2,316	1	23	33	233	525	1,622	169	
Total area actually reporting	100.0%	7,304		1,023	6,281	7	57	106	853	1,673	4,041	567	
Rate per 100,000 inhabitants		5,327.3		746.1	4,581.2	5.1	41.6	77.3	622.2	1,220.2	2,947.4	413.6	
San Juan, Puerto Rico M.S.A.[8]													
Total area actually reporting	100.0%	60,848		13,443	47,405	629	178	10,167	2,469	14,536	20,554	12,315	
Aguadilla, Puerto Rico M.S.A.[8]													
Total area actually reporting	100.0%	3,709		482	3,227	21	10	231	220	1,325	1,652	250	
Arecibo, Puerto Rico M.S.A.[8]													
Total area actually reporting	100.0%	3,836		509	3,327	15	14	283	197	1,469	1,298	560	
Caguas, Puerto Rico M.S.A.[8]													
Total area actually reporting	100.0%	7,720		1,749	5,971	57	23	1,226	443	2,363	2,448	1,160	
Mayaguez, Puerto Rico M.S.A.[8]													
Total area actually reporting	100.0%	5,029		589	4,440	13	17	271	288	1,636	2,570	234	
Ponce, Puerto Rico M.S.A.[8]													
Total area actually reporting	100.0%	6,754		1,215	5,539	59	17	716	423	1,855	3,055	629	

[1] Although arson data are included in the trend and clearance tables, sufficient data are not available to estimate totals for this offense.

[2] Violent crimes are offenses of murder, forcible rape, robbery, and aggravated assault.

[3] Property crimes are offenses of burglary, larceny–theft, and motor vehicle theft. Data are not included for the property crime of arson.

[4] Due to reporting changes or annexations, figures are not comparable to previous years.

[5] Aggravated assault figures for 1996 are not comparable to 1995. See "Crime Trends," page 390 for details.

[6] Indianapolis/Marion County, Indiana is a unified city-county government with a total population of 777,458.

[7] Motor vehicle theft data furnished by the police department were not in accordance with national Uniform Crime Reporting guidelines; therefore, the figures were excluded from the motor vehicle theft, violent crime, and Crime Index total categories.

[8] The 1996 Bureau of the Census population estimate for Puerto Rico was not available prior to publication; therefore, no population or rates per 100,000 inhabitants are provided.

Complete data were not available for the states of Illinois, Kansas, Kentucky, Montana, and Vermont; therefore, it was necessary that their crime counts be estimated. An aggregate Florida state total for 1996 was supplied by the Florida Department of Law Enforcement. See "Offense Estimation," pages 389-390 for details.

Table 7. — Offense Analysis, United States, 1992-1996

Classification	1992	1993	1994	1995	1996
Murder	23,760	24,530	23,330	21,600	19,650
Forcible Rape	109,060	106,010	102,220	97,460	95,770
Robbery:					
Total	672,480	659,870	618,950	580,550	537,050
Street/highway	374,157	360,799	337,758	315,413	275,096
Commercial house	79,717	82,385	76,130	71,463	72,247
Gas or service station	16,752	15,391	13,436	13,428	13,101
Convenience store	35,312	34,817	31,831	30,023	31,591
Residence	67,619	67,914	67,389	62,973	57,134
Bank	11,121	11,856	8,961	9,175	10,734
Miscellaneous	87,802	86,708	83,446	78,077	77,147
Burglary:					
Total	2,979,900	2,834,800	2,712,800	2,595,000	2,501,500
Residence (dwelling):	1,972,919	1,883,907	1,814,172	1,735,881	1,663,227
Night	629,462	591,404	556,647	530,365	492,576
Day	863,812	827,731	805,992	763,977	699,749
Unknown	479,645	464,772	451,533	441,539	470,902
Nonresidence (store, office, etc.):	1,006,981	950,893	898,628	859,120	838,274
Night	469,929	440,653	400,856	374,504	373,591
Day	258,914	242,340	242,758	235,745	200,334
Unknown	278,138	267,900	255,014	248,871	264,349
Larceny–theft (except motor vehicle theft):					
Total	7,915,200	7,820,900	7,879,800	8,000,600	7,894,600
By type:					
Pocket-picking	78,194	72,775	63,716	51,100	35,210
Purse-snatching	74,858	68,447	60,476	51,150	46,533
Shoplifting	1,253,766	1,200,910	1,178,223	1,204,567	1,212,885
From motor vehicles (except accessories)	1,792,386	1,827,643	1,865,813	1,940,333	1,996,699
Motor vehicle accessories	1,107,131	1,090,850	1,014,214	964,368	843,235
Bicycles	468,584	478,485	496,637	500,627	438,421
From buildings	1,106,809	1,028,997	1,026,961	1,004,010	1,005,722
From coin-operated machines	72,087	61,686	53,147	49,689	47,474
All others	1,961,384	1,991,106	2,120,612	2,234,756	2,268,421
By value:					
Over $200	2,844,553	2,865,453	2,946,988	3,061,607	3,039,421
$50 to $200	1,874,226	1,829,138	1,845,866	1,864,188	1,847,336
Under $50	3,196,421	3,126,309	3,086,946	3,074,805	3,007,843
Motor Vehicle Theft	1,610,800	1,563,100	1,539,300	1,472,700	1,395,200

Note: Because of rounding, offenses may not add to total.

Table 8. — Number of Offenses Known to the Police, Cities and Towns 10,000 and over in Population, 1996

* Arson is shown only if 12 months of arson data were received. Dashes (—) indicate zero data. The Modified Crime Index total is the sum of the Crime Index offenses, including arson.

City by State	Population	Crime Index total	Modified* Crime Index total	Murder and non-negligent man-slaughter	Forcible rape	Robbery	Aggravated assault	Burglary	Larceny–theft	Motor vehicle theft	Arson*
ALABAMA											
Alabaster	17,480	44		—	—	1	3	4	33	3	
Albertville	17,365	60		—	1	1	12	6	28	12	
Alexander City	15,287	1,011		—	3	23	68	178	719	20	
Anniston	27,553	4,377	4,395	10	26	135	489	1,087	2,365	265	18
Athens	18,943	698	700	1	8	5	55	82	515	32	2
Auburn	36,320	2,010		1	8	8	79	318	1,541	55	
Bessemer	32,228	3,400	3,438	8	31	210	473	754	1,560	364	38
Birmingham	272,169	29,283	29,529	113	229	1,838	2,236	5,973	15,280	3,614	246
Cullman	18,311	760	762	—	9	4	47	98	564	38	2
Daphne	14,663	717		—	4	4	24	120	549	16	
Decatur	53,135	3,772		5	23	94	136	759	2,596	159	
Dothan	56,505	2,922		9	25	132	84	687	1,829	156	
Enterprise	21,543	754		6	14	19	18	230	431	36	
Eufaula	13,899	776		1	1	13	6	100	638	17	
Fairfield	12,544	1,842		—	9	78	95	284	1,209	167	
Fairhope	10,657	602		—	4	21	54	133	366	24	
Florence	37,240	1,239		—	7	23	85	249	832	43	
Fort Payne	12,918	667		—	1	5	15	174	434	38	
Gadsden	47,145	5,032		3	38	112	661	917	2,909	392	
Gardendale	10,042	520		—	—	7	13	67	404	29	
Hartselle	11,813	370		—	2	1	7	54	277	29	
Homewood	24,174	1,730	1,733	—	6	85	31	188	1,284	136	3
Hoover	42,500	2,429	2,432	2	8	50	19	220	1,912	218	3
Hueytown	15,622	356		—	1	5	23	48	242	37	
Huntsville	162,376	14,330	14,392	11	71	310	947	2,251	9,516	1,224	62
Jacksonville	11,127	455		1	—	13	9	123	295	14	
Jasper	14,026	1,156	1,164	1	6	17	97	172	736	127	8
Leeds	10,154	526	527	2	—	12	31	58	389	34	1
Madison	20,499	598		—	3	4	42	104	404	41	
Mobile	207,106	19,512	19,652	51	119	1,283	732	4,404	10,990	1,933	140
Montgomery	197,972	13,202	13,283	31	80	627	851	3,376	7,111	1,126	81
Mountain Brook	20,400	457		1	—	20	9	81	316	30	
Muscle Shoals	10,367	572		—	—	2	1	24	541	4	
Northport	20,487	739		—	3	23	88	110	490	25	
Opelika	24,121	1,726		4	11	40	339	286	996	50	
Oxford	10,555	1,390		—	3	33	194	230	809	121	
Ozark	13,373	634		—	3	19	63	115	411	23	
Pelham	12,202	447	448	—	—	9	18	45	345	30	1
Phenix City	29,282	1,691		2	16	42	169	375	951	136	
Prattville	24,426	1,339		3	15	43	86	269	869	54	
Prichard	33,688	3,867		14	27	236	615	959	1,537	479	
Saraland	12,389	184		—	3	2	1	8	165	5	
Scottsboro	14,793	380		—	—	1	11	56	294	18	
Selma	24,961	3,326		9	31	120	513	560	1,888	205	
Sheffield	10,408	772	778	—	3	5	19	140	588	17	6
Sylacauga	14,014	888		—	8	15	94	149	583	39	
Talladega	19,428	913		1	7	25	17	201	613	49	
Troy	14,170	1,065	1,069	2	4	23	32	178	792	34	4
Tuscaloosa	80,818	11,949		5	50	340	509	1,346	9,322	377	
Tuskegee	12,297	1,186		5	11	23	197	376	538	36	
Vestavia Hills	20,108	302		—	1	12	3	52	196	38	
ALASKA											
Anchorage	254,774	16,178	16,265	25	198	558	1,297	2,353	10,163	1,584	87
Fairbanks	34,377	2,593	2,597	3	23	59	325	265	1,706	212	4

112

City by State	Population	Crime Index total	Modified* Crime Index total	Murder and non-negligent man-slaughter	Forcible rape	Robbery	Aggravated assault	Burglary	Larceny-theft	Motor vehicle theft	Arson*
ARIZONA											
Apache Junction	23,203	1,326	1,335	—	3	14	99	269	837	104	9
Bullhead City	29,529	2,487	2,509	3	2	34	164	587	1,499	198	22
Casa Grande	22,913	2,950	2,964	2	17	32	207	386	2,084	222	14
Chandler	129,554	8,550	8,627	2	29	143	254	1,796	5,210	1,116	77
Flagstaff	55,100	5,231	5,257	1	10	65	242	575	4,161	177	26
Gilbert	55,498	3,007	3,022	1	11	43	167	782	1,740	263	15
Glendale	183,029	13,480	13,558	11	51	301	858	2,277	7,883	2,099	78
Kingman	17,323	1,736	1,749	1	8	13	124	390	1,128	72	13
Lake Havasu City	34,657	1,716	1,726	1	2	11	53	278	1,257	114	10
Mesa	340,818	25,735	25,862	18	110	506	1,825	3,883	15,582	3,811	127
Nogales	22,088	1,176	1,184	1	1	37	114	315	490	218	8
Paradise Valley	14,977	570	573	—	1	1	6	314	209	39	3
Payson	10,653	602	602	—	4	4	12	56	505	21	—
Peoria	76,214	3,407	3,421	3	14	42	98	808	2,156	286	14
Phoenix	1,139,793	108,749	109,028	186	460	3,757	6,126	19,559	60,565	18,096	279
Prescott	33,017	2,000	2,016	—	19	15	80	214	1,603	69	16
Prescott Valley	14,291	781	782	—	7	4	40	125	574	31	1
Scottsdale	165,644	9,737	9,795	8	23	133	281	1,786	6,455	1,051	58
Sierra Vista	41,585	1,418	1,421	—	3	13	31	167	1,062	142	3
Surprise	10,207	491	491	—	—	2	2	136	323	28	—
Tempe	156,788	14,031	14,083	3	35	321	512	2,047	9,169	1,944	52
Tucson	472,385	46,385	46,667	46	282	1,288	3,583	6,710	28,460	6,016	282
ARKANSAS											
Arkadelphia	10,724	276	276	—	1	3	3	24	239	6	—
Benton	22,399	1,339	1,345	1	9	6	96	162	980	85	6
Bentonville	13,822	709	709	—	6	2	11	68	619	3	—
Blytheville	17,737	2,962	2,987	5	17	86	288	865	1,548	153	25
Cabot	12,029	423	423	—	2	1	32	50	307	31	—
Camden	14,554	1,220	1,221	2	11	35	175	220	699	78	1
Conway	34,734	2,278	2,288	1	22	32	71	213	1,830	109	10
El Dorado	24,433	1,855	1,867	1	12	52	266	440	967	117	12
Fayetteville	50,362	3,301	3,306	2	37	23	111	467	2,557	104	5
Forrest City	13,650	1,745	1,752	3	3	51	356	310	970	52	7
Fort Smith	76,210	6,231	6,239	6	58	90	252	487	4,918	420	8
Harrison	11,132	582	584	—	3	2	8	46	500	23	2
Hope	10,313	762	766	—	6	13	23	235	457	28	4
Hot Springs	36,471	3,762	3,776	7	26	137	88	913	2,389	202	14
Jacksonville	30,270	1,905	1,911	1	14	37	143	354	1,254	102	6
Jonesboro	51,375	2,883	2,889	4	22	69	132	699	1,817	140	6
Little Rock	182,799	21,016	21,170	29	166	837	1,725	3,382	13,253	1,624	154
Magnolia	12,040	782	783	—	4	13	56	203	463	43	1
Mountain Home	10,242	192	192	2	—	—	4	16	163	7	—
North Little Rock	63,642	6,223	6,246	15	99	293	308	1,085	3,903	520	23
Paragould	21,752	649	651	—	3	2	6	123	468	47	2
Pine Bluff	59,317	6,405	6,457	18	84	346	1,115	1,713	2,303	826	52
Rogers	31,169	1,728	1,728	—	17	8	45	202	1,393	63	—
Russellville	23,782	1,700	1,707	—	6	14	62	272	1,243	103	7
Searcy	18,493	972	974	1	3	9	13	39	846	61	2
Sherwood	20,927	904	904	1	6	14	39	103	665	76	—
Springdale	37,401	1,526	1,527	—	12	8	47	202	1,168	89	1
Stuttgart	10,484	691	692	2	3	14	71	120	441	40	1
Texarkana	23,454	2,697	2,708	4	29	72	171	366	1,953	102	11
Van Buren	17,284	959	959	—	1	3	6	153	760	36	—
West Helena	10,125	242	243	2	3	22	4	130	59	22	1
West Memphis	28,155	2,443	2,454	13	32	209	227	754	909	299	11

Table 8. — Number of Offenses Known to the Police, Cities and Towns 10,000 and over in Population, 1996 — Continued

City by State	Population	Crime Index total	Modified* Crime Index total	Murder and non-negligent man-slaughter	Forcible rape	Robbery	Aggravated assault	Burglary	Larceny-theft	Motor vehicle theft	Arson*
CALIFORNIA											
Agoura Hills	25,724	670	671	—	2	16	39	162	376	75	1
Alameda	79,790	4,323	4,356	3	22	199	220	590	2,908	381	33
Albany	17,116	637	644	1	2	58	25	114	373	64	7
Alhambra	85,611	3,618	3,634	4	14	257	181	758	1,637	767	16
Anaheim	286,146	14,670	14,745	14	81	978	998	2,698	7,550	2,351	75
Antioch	74,057	3,090	3,111	7	22	127	358	692	1,512	372	21
Apple Valley	52,733	2,785	2,795	5	14	71	134	991	1,243	327	10
Arcadia	51,373	2,378	2,383	—	4	119	76	489	1,459	231	5
Arcata	15,670	995	1,011	—	6	11	41	173	719	45	16
Arroyo Grande	15,362	546	552	—	5	7	31	75	413	15	6
Artesia	15,808	767	779	—	1	59	104	154	297	152	12
Arvin	10,305	367	385	—	3	29	17	98	176	44	18
Atascadero	24,575	870	894	—	5	8	45	270	506	36	24
Atwater	23,698	1,282	1,290	—	6	25	156	454	540	101	8
Auburn	12,034	518	518	—	12	7	40	98	333	28	—
Avenal	12,272	334	344	1	5	4	84	96	133	11	10
Azusa	43,706	1,808	1,817	4	13	93	129	390	844	335	9
Bakersfield	193,777	12,584	12,727	25	37	482	578	2,874	7,456	1,132	143
Baldwin Park	73,797	1,848	1,855	12	17	125	181	638	286	589	7
Banning	23,784	1,126	1,138	2	9	33	329	416	232	105	12
Barstow	20,135	1,765	1,771	5	10	81	105	382	991	191	6
Beaumont	10,794	470	472	1	5	19	69	147	174	55	2
Bell	36,194	937	941	3	3	169	89	198	186	289	4
Bell Gardens	43,035	1,762	1,774	5	5	239	170	409	446	488	12
Bellflower	67,615	4,135	4,163	7	25	330	579	785	1,454	955	28
Belmont	25,509	640	640	—	6	9	28	78	482	37	—
Benicia	27,409	843	852	—	3	10	77	168	547	38	9
Berkeley	101,250	10,333	10,374	8	32	492	555	1,502	6,683	1,061	41
Beverly Hills	33,599	2,402	2,407	—	7	138	84	493	1,531	149	5
Brawley	22,137	1,207	1,220	—	—	29	86	376	639	77	13
Brea	35,164	1,900	1,909	1	8	30	63	264	1,308	226	9
Buena Park	73,704	3,154	3,201	3	19	157	159	602	1,506	708	47
Burbank	101,082	4,161	4,171	4	19	169	264	611	2,219	875	10
Burlingame	28,041	1,271	1,275	—	9	33	56	143	899	131	4
Calabasas	76,256	494	495	—	4	20	44	112	285	29	1
Calexico	24,613	1,746	1,760	5	1	87	94	353	933	273	14
Camarillo	57,540	1,212	1,219	—	—	26	63	236	777	110	7
Campbell	37,844	1,526	1,545	—	10	39	81	197	1,098	101	19
Capitola	10,108	1,172	1,174	1	1	13	46	85	984	42	2
Carlsbad	66,391	3,120	3,131	3	18	76	196	676	1,770	381	11
Carpinteria	13,850	410	411	—	4	5	56	158	169	18	1
Carson	91,304	4,402	4,453	19	37	291	796	801	1,597	861	51
Cathedral City	35,227	1,748	1,753	2	10	57	301	464	709	205	5
Ceres	30,358	2,181	2,188	—	13	46	204	434	1,285	199	7
Cerritos	55,564	3,833	3,855	1	11	183	227	719	1,781	911	22
Chico	44,262	2,809	2,861	2	43	60	137	544	1,850	173	52
Chino	65,701	3,360	3,461	2	8	118	508	606	1,562	556	101
Chino Hills	45,597	1,399	1,410	—	3	19	43	332	847	155	11
Chula Vista	151,377	8,822	8,864	5	37	399	653	1,451	4,591	1,686	42
Claremont	34,609	1,428	1,431	1	3	42	52	348	804	178	3
Clearlake	13,219	1,162	1,174	—	5	14	168	409	492	74	12
Clovis	61,138	3,643	3,682	2	17	44	107	592	2,382	499	39
Coachella	18,872	636	644	3	—	46	106	169	216	96	8
Colton	41,825	2,675	2,695	12	23	172	147	629	1,092	600	20
Commerce	12,531	1,580	1,590	4	2	100	138	182	750	404	10
Compton	97,849	5,515	5,533	72	39	827	735	1,283	1,351	1,208	18
Concord	113,479	7,302	7,326	4	38	167	437	1,186	4,780	690	24
Corcoran	13,988	588	588	5	3	11	100	122	304	43	—

City by State	Population	Crime Index total	Modified* Crime Index total	Murder and non-negligent man-slaughter	Forcible rape	Robbery	Aggravated assault	Burglary	Larceny–theft	Motor vehicle theft	Arson*
CALIFORNIA — Continued											
Corona	94,219	4,816	4,840	4	18	198	389	1,156	2,264	787	24
Coronado	22,140	643	645	2	2	10	12	128	422	67	2
Costa Mesa	99,827	5,413	5,424	1	22	158	194	892	3,531	615	11
Covina	45,277	2,003	2,018	7	25	81	82	390	981	437	15
Cudahy	23,367	798	801	1	4	74	204	90	202	223	3
Culver City	39,844	1,807	1,807	4	3	183	45	253	991	328	—
Cupertino	43,297	1,373	1,388	—	10	27	68	217	991	60	15
Cypress	47,078	1,622	1,634	—	8	70	80	305	903	256	12
Daly City	95,373	2,936	2,941	—	14	170	144	277	1,790	541	5
Dana Point	33,930	1,223	1,231	—	6	24	132	252	743	66	8
Danville	39,259	685	688	—	5	13	22	159	472	14	3
Davis	48,960	2,767	2,783	—	7	17	39	293	2,233	178	16
Delano	28,077	2,062	2,071	—	8	58	109	474	1,084	329	9
Desert Hot Springs	14,610	1,312	1,318	2	6	56	153	399	552	144	6
Diamond Bar	59,663	1,720	1,727	2	7	76	176	351	757	351	7
Dinuba	13,745	675	684	—	5	6	88	213	296	67	9
Dixon	11,734	585	596	—	7	8	32	126	376	36	11
Downey	101,309	4,785	4,823	7	33	318	232	932	2,078	1,185	38
Duarte	22,772	792	794	1	6	41	101	186	341	116	2
Dublin	26,511	731	732	—	—	16	47	117	478	73	1
East Palo Alto	26,212	1,401	1,428	1	12	176	160	275	541	236	27
El Cajon	93,976	5,353	5,392	5	33	210	629	1,038	2,596	842	39
El Centro	38,127	2,285	2,301	3	12	80	236	868	918	168	16
El Cerrito	22,860	1,596	1,607	—	8	109	50	223	1,027	179	11
El Monte	106,149	4,597	4,666	9	43	572	658	854	1,608	853	69
El Segundo	15,806	951	956	—	3	34	52	152	551	159	5
Escondido	118,003	6,857	6,902	7	50	215	547	1,079	3,943	1,016	45
Eureka	27,604	2,995	3,015	1	23	59	167	362	2,069	314	20
Fairfield	84,967	5,366	5,433	3	40	192	442	907	3,269	513	67
Fillmore	12,575	320	323	—	1	4	41	71	176	27	3
Folsom	40,166	1,145	1,147	—	6	10	22	188	826	93	2
Fontana	105,211	5,430	5,460	16	72	414	845	1,143	1,447	1,493	30
Foster City	29,891	619	623	1	2	7	22	91	461	35	4
Fountain Valley	56,255	2,258	2,266	—	2	68	60	325	1,494	309	8
Fremont	186,186	7,769	7,813	3	32	186	591	1,306	4,689	962	44
Fresno	392,049	41,687	42,801	69	216	2,087	3,089	6,868	20,180	9,178	1,114
Fullerton	118,524	5,246	5,260	5	26	201	253	930	3,110	721	14
Galt	13,054	517	521	—	3	15	55	90	279	75	4
Gardena	54,238	2,895	2,904	6	22	475	290	556	957	589	9
Garden Grove	150,062	6,478	6,520	5	34	309	498	1,229	3,245	1,158	42
Gilroy	34,098	2,190	2,229	1	9	98	342	382	1,214	144	39
Glendale	181,019	6,966	7,015	14	16	344	347	1,135	4,044	1,066	49
Glendora	52,695	1,409	1,421	1	7	53	87	266	848	147	12
Grand Terrace	11,787	486	486	—	—	15	8	109	222	132	—
Grover Beach	12,305	496	500	—	1	3	32	101	339	20	4
Hanford	34,461	2,263	2,297	3	6	47	303	278	1,356	270	34
Hawaiian Gardens	13,410	820	822	1	6	96	65	295	207	150	2
Hawthorne	76,399	5,766	5,845	14	32	635	917	823	2,377	968	79
Hayward	117,233	7,876	7,975	12	28	370	408	1,253	4,438	1,367	99
Hemet	42,205	3,437	3,463	2	18	115	262	1,227	1,408	405	26
Hercules	19,893	606	609	—	5	16	59	100	359	67	3
Hermosa Beach	19,126	830	835	—	2	26	33	184	466	119	5
Hesperia	59,971	2,800	2,834	5	18	105	173	731	1,323	445	34
Highland	39,772	2,358	2,378	8	18	149	117	759	976	331	20
Hillsborough	11,387	87	87	—	—	—	1	32	53	1	—
Hollister	22,310	982	1,000	—	16	19	114	211	539	83	18
Huntington Beach	191,911	7,305	7,336	—	26	194	391	1,629	4,161	904	31
Huntington Park	56,504	3,268	3,280	4	10	459	191	593	834	1,177	12

City by State	Population	Crime Index total	Modified* Crime Index total	Murder and non-negligent man-slaughter	Forcible rape	Robbery	Aggravated assault	Burglary	Larceny–theft	Motor vehicle theft	Arson*
CALIFORNIA — Continued											
Indio	40,015	1,839	1,857	2	22	139	253	564	510	349	18
Inglewood	111,650	6,241	6,286	27	61	952	903	1,082	1,851	1,365	45
Irvine	127,410	4,090	4,123	1	22	65	186	837	2,647	332	33
La Canada-Flintridge	20,115	402	407	—	3	20	29	106	204	40	5
Lafayette	24,337	622	624	—	—	21	16	137	413	35	2
Laguna Niguel	57,487	982	995	2	5	18	88	222	589	58	13
Laguna Beach	24,262	1,126	1,127	—	9	10	73	247	721	66	1
Laguna Hills	48,989	982	991	—	4	28	56	217	592	85	9
La Habra	54,426	2,311	2,320	1	13	92	378	404	1,157	266	9
Lake Elsinore	23,048	1,815	1,819	5	7	57	194	478	823	251	4
Lake Forest	60,745	1,279	1,291	—	9	29	112	255	756	118	12
Lakewood	80,545	3,831	3,850	2	17	228	396	653	1,716	819	19
La Mesa	55,088	2,693	2,705	2	7	101	129	496	1,505	453	12
La Mirada	47,001	1,273	1,276	2	7	60	178	250	514	262	3
Lancaster	120,881	5,947	6,003	12	58	308	1,005	1,455	2,338	771	56
La Palma	16,235	626	628	—	2	25	24	112	331	132	2
La Puente	39,581	1,416	1,425	6	13	120	310	249	477	241	9
La Quinta	17,485	972	978	1	5	7	77	353	482	47	6
La Verne	33,577	1,002	1,014	5	1	18	58	175	611	134	12
Lawndale	29,321	1,403	1,415	5	13	151	284	285	426	239	12
Lemoore	15,340	783	787	—	8	15	53	139	496	72	4
Livermore	64,262	1,957	1,981	—	15	41	127	357	1,281	136	24
Lodi	53,168	3,126	3,134	3	18	57	275	361	2,110	302	8
Loma Linda	18,739	988	991	1	6	25	15	199	456	286	3
Lomita	21,000	669	673	—	—	55	115	153	250	96	4
Lompoc	42,105	1,781	1,802	3	10	58	122	415	1,099	74	21
Long Beach	440,023	26,308	26,499	95	158	2,431	2,385	5,003	11,671	4,565	191
Los Alamitos	12,183	467	474	—	5	22	16	131	224	69	7
Los Altos	28,605	523	523	—	3	14	27	120	350	9	—
Los Angeles	3,498,139	235,258	238,851	709	1,463	25,189	35,477	35,865	95,069	41,486	3,593
Los Banos	18,191	834	837	—	12	14	83	220	463	42	3
Los Gatos	29,643	833	843	—	2	11	40	188	555	37	10
Lynwood	65,729	3,373	3,409	20	27	382	767	639	787	751	36
Madera	34,193	2,925	2,930	8	32	142	383	533	1,396	431	5
Malibu	11,639	537	542	1	5	11	62	103	296	59	5
Manhattan Beach	33,761	1,699	1,704	2	6	60	68	359	1,040	164	5
Manteca	44,808	2,387	2,406	3	14	34	97	362	1,498	379	19
Marina	15,651	742	752	1	3	34	45	185	431	43	10
Martinez	33,152	1,430	1,436	3	7	21	34	268	875	222	6
Marysville	13,364	1,304	1,305	1	6	27	230	224	677	139	1
Maywood	27,737	804	807	4	5	94	114	102	319	166	3
Menlo Park	30,178	1,442	1,451	—	6	54	54	186	1,084	58	9
Merced	61,205	4,923	5,079	3	25	131	404	889	3,035	436	156
Millbrae	21,164	577	580	—	3	21	56	77	342	78	3
Mill Valley	13,377	472	475	—	—	9	19	73	352	19	3
Milpitas	56,722	2,440	2,442	2	23	66	139	350	1,606	254	2
Mission Viejo	85,004	1,993	2,010	1	4	32	146	438	1,244	128	17
Modesto	178,865	12,840	13,014	12	80	421	754	2,701	7,100	1,772	174
Monrovia	39,314	1,421	1,424	8	10	94	75	262	743	229	3
Montclair	28,949	2,781	2,786	2	11	144	134	413	1,545	532	5
Montebello	62,393	3,255	3,292	7	20	241	331	419	1,476	761	37
Monterey	30,236	2,015	2,018	2	10	41	109	358	1,425	70	3
Monterey Park	58,744	2,232	2,235	1	9	226	100	403	922	571	3
Moorpark	29,429	505	513	1	7	11	39	148	267	32	8
Moraga	16,422	327	328	—	3	4	10	69	229	12	1
Moreno Valley	141,292	8,733	8,762	13	52	418	709	2,280	4,216	1,045	29
Morgan Hill	27,148	1,179	1,205	—	9	14	27	225	839	65	26
Mountain View	66,748	3,113	3,139	—	13	102	306	326	2,174	192	26

City by State	Population	Crime Index total	Modified* Crime Index total	Murder and non-negligent man-slaughter	Forcible rape	Robbery	Aggravated assault	Burglary	Larceny-theft	Motor vehicle theft	Arson*
CALIFORNIA — Continued											
Murrieta	33,537	749	751	1	9	13	43	171	421	91	2
Napa	64,346	2,724	2,742	—	23	53	183	389	1,894	182	18
National City	58,356	4,092	4,106	8	33	300	333	619	1,754	1,045	14
Newark	40,130	2,239	2,250	5	11	53	115	233	1,641	181	11
Newport Beach	71,672	3,164	3,177	—	20	46	174	788	1,891	245	13
Norco	24,988	1,017	1,020	—	5	28	82	174	574	154	3
Norwalk	102,176	4,388	4,429	14	26	329	807	710	1,516	986	41
Novato	49,489	1,509	1,515	—	16	36	150	336	874	97	6
Oakdale	13,960	885	894	—	7	12	81	176	553	56	9
Oakland	372,145	39,174	39,579	93	322	3,622	4,131	6,058	19,878	5,070	405
Oceanside	148,308	7,197	7,224	10	75	330	824	1,737	3,309	912	27
Ontario	136,742	8,907	9,028	17	44	504	860	1,479	4,292	1,711	121
Orange	118,445	4,086	4,125	1	30	177	354	878	2,019	627	39
Orinda	17,662	384	384	—	1	11	4	84	264	20	—
Oroville	13,305	963	963	—	2	17	11	284	540	109	—
Oxnard	147,937	7,910	7,934	16	57	460	849	1,255	4,332	941	24
Pacifica	40,068	1,131	1,141	—	14	27	218	128	648	96	10
Pacific Grove	16,755	502	506	—	3	5	54	144	276	20	4
Palmdale	104,894	5,311	5,352	6	38	260	837	1,231	2,246	693	41
Palm Desert	26,932	2,525	2,533	2	10	43	106	732	1,505	127	8
Palm Springs	40,198	2,889	2,927	4	18	136	331	658	1,414	328	38
Palo Alto	57,734	3,303	3,322	1	6	65	66	346	2,668	151	19
Palos Verdes Estates	14,142	188	189	—	2	5	3	76	92	10	1
Paradise	26,763	894	900	1	1	5	61	229	551	46	6
Paramount	52,951	3,649	3,671	5	13	297	527	668	1,332	807	22
Pasadena	136,077	7,423	7,512	14	40	521	603	1,365	4,142	738	89
Paso Robles	17,694	871	876	—	14	13	81	159	559	45	5
Perris	30,787	2,094	2,107	5	16	88	254	552	870	309	13
Petaluma	46,609	1,721	1,744	2	21	25	233	263	1,089	88	23
Pico Rivera	63,455	2,410	2,431	12	19	232	485	360	794	508	21
Piedmont	11,745	349	353	—	—	9	2	67	221	50	4
Pinole	18,716	1,276	1,290	1	10	63	135	218	671	178	14
Pittsburg	52,775	2,206	2,212	2	16	103	178	537	1,112	258	6
Placentia	43,613	1,161	1,180	3	2	48	89	274	606	139	19
Pleasant Hill	32,084	1,816	1,824	—	5	38	60	377	1,212	124	8
Pleasanton	58,502	1,811	1,816	2	3	22	41	236	1,387	120	5
Pomona	145,916	7,789	7,824	19	47	545	926	1,697	3,039	1,516	35
Porterville	32,888	2,129	2,130	—	17	33	109	381	1,336	253	1
Port Hueneme	23,295	771	777	—	9	32	63	187	429	51	6
Rancho Cucamonga	116,431	4,828	4,855	8	14	157	191	990	2,531	937	27
Rancho Mirage	10,502	521	521	—	4	8	26	159	297	27	—
Rancho Palos Verdes	44,456	751	755	1	1	30	78	200	351	90	4
Red Bluff	13,473	1,095	1,109	2	8	24	123	144	760	34	14
Redding	73,942	4,453	4,479	5	57	98	360	943	2,677	313	26
Redlands	65,443	3,600	3,620	3	27	136	257	626	1,833	718	20
Redondo Beach	65,149	2,944	2,951	—	16	131	189	601	1,632	375	7
Redwood City	68,749	2,788	2,807	3	12	92	250	375	1,749	307	19
Reedley	17,122	813	820	—	13	32	129	136	424	79	7
Rialto	84,707	3,441	3,459	6	17	299	275	950	993	901	18
Richmond	89,194	7,635	7,726	34	67	555	1,036	1,428	3,576	939	91
Ridgecrest	29,815	1,120	1,187	1	11	11	119	266	656	56	67
Riverbank	12,188	630	633	—	3	11	64	131	330	91	3
Riverside	245,081	15,493	15,782	18	115	874	2,162	2,894	7,121	2,309	289
Rocklin	26,590	852	861	—	3	13	43	163	562	68	9
Rohnert Park	39,095	1,800	1,809	1	12	30	92	720	847	98	9
Rosemead	52,763	2,176	2,192	7	15	211	304	492	717	430	16
Roseville	53,772	2,908	2,916	—	8	62	194	582	1,670	392	8
Sacramento	379,283	33,780	33,950	43	154	1,874	1,636	7,148	16,842	6,083	170

117

Table 8. — Number of Offenses Known to the Police, Cities and Towns 10,000 and over in Population, 1996 — Continued

City by State	Population	Crime Index total	Modified* Crime Index total	Murder and non-negligent man-slaughter	Forcible rape	Robbery	Aggravated assault	Burglary	Larceny-theft	Motor vehicle theft	Arson*
CALIFORNIA — Continued											
Salinas	121,517	7,554	7,608	9	54	412	884	1,031	4,339	825	54
San Anselmo	12,265	322	323	—	2	3	11	98	198	10	1
San Bernardino	184,303	16,970	17,119	42	79	1,281	1,831	3,544	7,201	2,992	149
San Bruno	41,129	1,510	1,526	—	6	32	47	160	1,108	157	16
San Carlos	28,474	612	614	—	3	15	33	107	410	44	2
San Clemente	45,791	1,360	1,374	1	7	41	168	247	793	103	14
San Diego	1,168,364	61,573	61,825	79	368	2,998	6,703	8,608	31,688	11,129	252
San Dimas	36,151	1,089	1,100	—	13	34	135	237	541	129	11
San Fernando	23,324	1,197	1,198	2	9	97	86	225	533	245	1
San Francisco	745,127	56,592	57,044	82	298	5,539	3,967	7,079	31,062	8,565	452
San Gabriel	38,522	1,555	1,560	1	3	137	151	415	604	244	5
Sanger	18,195	905	914	1	1	32	132	174	395	170	9
San Jacinto	21,013	655	656	2	7	27	74	281	144	120	1
San Jose	830,374	34,287	34,942	40	341	1,098	4,596	4,700	19,793	3,719	655
San Juan Capistrano	29,505	957	966	1	3	20	111	153	602	67	9
San Leandro	70,478	5,172	5,200	6	21	305	278	764	3,073	725	28
San Luis Obispo	40,880	1,966	2,034	—	17	14	202	360	1,304	69	68
San Marino	13,700	247	249	—	—	13	2	78	136	18	2
San Pablo	27,262	2,356	2,362	10	22	192	332	386	1,113	301	6
San Rafael	49,336	2,158	2,172	1	18	68	192	345	1,327	207	14
San Ramon	40,470	1,080	1,092	—	5	14	25	171	804	61	12
Santa Ana	294,963	13,213	13,589	46	62	1,178	945	1,822	6,501	2,659	376
Santa Barbara	86,843	4,659	4,666	1	40	105	453	1,002	2,844	214	7
Santa Clara	95,906	4,480	4,502	—	19	77	337	555	3,135	357	22
Santa Clarita	125,435	3,255	3,295	2	19	83	492	716	1,550	393	40
Santa Cruz	49,185	4,160	4,187	2	12	103	460	600	2,752	231	27
Santa Fe Springs	16,518	1,910	1,911	5	6	139	57	334	979	390	1
Santa Maria	66,869	3,853	3,867	4	33	117	268	730	2,526	175	14
Santa Monica	88,284	7,374	7,453	3	44	438	442	1,038	4,469	940	79
Santa Paula	26,059	1,283	1,288	3	6	65	78	299	730	102	5
Santa Rosa	118,625	6,905	6,954	2	81	170	410	920	4,901	421	49
Saratoga	30,279	480	480	—	2	6	36	112	312	12	—
Seal Beach	25,286	778	780	1	1	18	94	122	440	102	2
Seaside	32,642	1,410	1,423	5	4	65	214	190	853	79	13
Sierra Madre	11,654	140	141	—	—	3	6	35	82	14	1
Simi Valley	108,469	2,401	2,435	1	12	38	105	460	1,532	253	34
South El Monte	22,407	1,001	1,009	2	5	95	150	181	411	157	8
South Gate	93,214	3,774	3,800	7	17	478	320	673	1,072	1,207	26
South Lake Tahoe	22,430	1,310	1,314	—	8	31	105	338	750	78	4
South Pasadena	25,192	731	749	—	3	56	25	190	322	135	18
South San Francisco	57,380	2,018	2,036	2	16	74	135	204	1,304	283	18
Stanton	30,567	1,549	1,570	2	7	72	202	387	638	241	21
Stockton	225,799	19,401	19,512	46	123	1,313	1,633	3,418	9,815	3,053	111
Suisun City	27,748	951	970	—	9	32	53	255	513	89	19
Sunnyvale	121,284	3,488	3,506	—	29	80	122	420	2,522	315	18
Temecula	40,208	1,569	1,576	—	11	43	134	384	846	151	7
Temple City	34,214	819	826	1	11	50	147	227	284	99	7
Thousand Oaks	112,559	2,547	2,619	3	9	64	156	447	1,616	252	72
Torrance	140,185	7,054	7,080	3	31	317	281	1,385	3,826	1,211.	26
Tracy	45,372	1,954	1,960	—	13	17	86	381	1,206	251	6
Tulare	39,111	3,052	3,122	1	14	95	446	485	1,608	403	70
Turlock	47,019	3,739	3,802	4	28	79	206	776	2,210	436	63
Tustin	59,311	2,735	2,757	3	12	66	94	609	1,637	314	22
Twenty-Nine Palms	13,696	721	728	—	10	27	54	245	319	66	7
Twin Cities	20,402	694	695	—	3	11	10	157	459	54	1
Ukiah	14,767	904	910	—	11	21	41	226	579	26	6
Union City	56,170	2,860	2,877	—	13	151	164	505	1,720	307	17
Upland	62,705	4,246	4,278	3	22	135	281	1,058	2,169	578	32

Table 8. — Number of Offenses Known to the Police, Cities and Towns 10,000 and over in Population, 1996 — Continued

City by State	Population	Crime Index total	Modified* Crime Index total	Murder and non-negligent man-slaughter	Forcible rape	Robbery	Aggravated assault	Burglary	Larceny–theft	Motor vehicle theft	Arson*
CALIFORNIA — Continued											
Vacaville	84,188	3,071	3,106	2	19	74	306	540	1,893	237	35
Vallejo	113,069	8,996	9,055	15	59	523	967	1,658	4,901	873	59
Ventura	97,657	4,111	4,147	6	26	148	227	952	2,355	397	36
Victorville	50,835	3,855	3,866	6	24	194	184	927	1,800	720	11
Visalia	86,282	5,927	5,945	7	28	175	422	922	3,668	705	18
Walnut	32,804	889	899	—	1	31	135	239	368	115	10
Walnut Creek	62,912	3,102	3,126	1	4	44	106	555	2,231	161	24
Watsonville	32,547	2,473	2,480	6	10	87	455	378	1,383	154	7
West Covina	104,766	4,968	5,010	6	24	273	265	806	2,689	905	42
West Hollywood	34,932	3,037	3,055	2	11	270	312	394	1,517	531	18
Westminster	80,885	4,394	4,427	9	20	220	175	792	2,330	848	33
West Sacramento	30,530	2,023	2,046	3	21	75	497	509	625	293	23
Whittier	80,948	3,220	3,237	4	13	196	214	592	1,737	464	17
Windsor	13,795	414	417	2	5	8	50	66	248	35	3
Woodland	43,406	1,522	1,542	1	15	30	221	301	759	195	20
Yorba Linda	62,371	1,115	1,124	1	4	14	56	204	731	105	9
Yuba City	32,902	2,606	2,619	1	23	33	233	525	1,622	169	13
Yucaipa	37,077	1,442	1,464	—	9	24	86	424	742	157	22
Yucca Valley	14,362	749	762	1	5	13	54	248	363	65	13
COLORADO											
Arvada	99,804	3,797	3,821	1	17	55	132	612	2,769	211	24
Aurora	262,168	15,982	16,061	11	193	559	866	2,589	10,366	1,398	79
Boulder	89,522	5,957	5,986	1	49	62	132	874	4,546	293	29
Broomfield	28,678	1,050	1,069	1	4	7	43	205	733	57	19
Canon City	14,636	876	876	—	6	5	26	93	713	33	—
Castle Rock	12,597	224	226	—	2	1	5	35	173	8	2
Colorado Springs	331,020	20,523	20,675	12	238	453	892	3,304	14,248	1,376	152
Commerce City	18,522	1,950	1,958	3	7	29	134	262	1,345	170	8
Denver	516,224	34,314	34,694	64	358	1,327	2,083	7,788	17,269	5,425	380
Englewood	34,218	2,438	2,477	2	21	46	111	347	1,649	262	39
Federal Heights	10,697	723	726	1	2	15	13	77	564	51	3
Fort Collins	103,472	5,448	5,490	3	70	46	300	829	4,042	158	42
Fort Morgan	10,417	584	595	—	2	4	11	66	485	16	11
Fountain	12,849	649	657	3	8	4	50	87	462	35	8
Golden	14,621	636	651	1	4	9	12	106	470	34	15
Grand Junction	33,208	3,335	3,360	2	16	52	165	452	2,535	113	25
Greeley	67,120	4,712		5	40	52	212	678	3,491	234	28
Lafayette	18,064	928	956	—	6	4	47	124	718	29	28
Lakewood	131,786	7,595	7,631	4	54	179	394	1,209	5,193	562	36
Littleton	39,544	1,517	1,537	—	10	14	78	257	1,052	106	20
Longmont	58,833	3,477	3,497	1	23	38	65	475	2,682	193	20
Loveland	45,974	1,617	1,631	1	31	9	50	238	1,209	79	14
Montrose	10,431	1,085	1,093	—	7	5	26	178	831	38	8
Northglenn	28,744	1,752	1,759	—	16	26	62	190	1,343	115	7
Pueblo	105,059	7,371	7,423	12	74	196	1,104	1,348	4,305	332	52
Sterling	10,772	547	555	1	6	—	14	83	420	23	8
Thornton	65,960	4,569	4,569	2	18	45	204	689	3,312	299	—
Wheat Ridge	32,299	1,730	1,764	3	12	41	20	306	1,200	148	34
CONNECTICUT											
Ansonia	18,150	554	555	—	6	21	53	104	319	51	1
Avon	13,946	250	250	—	—	5	—	66	171	8	—
Berlin	16,798	422	422	—	5	1	—	80	295	41	—
Bethel	17,800	293	299	—	1	5	19	63	196	9	6
Bloomfield	19,498	752	753	—	8	27	58	123	453	83	1
Branford	27,939	684	685	—	2	12	1	87	526	56	1
Bridgeport	133,015	11,041	11,519	44	61	948	1,054	2,479	4,077	2,378	478
Bristol	60,628	1,973	1,982	—	20	39	175	453	1,098	188	9

Table 8. — Number of Offenses Known to the Police, Cities and Towns 10,000 and over in Population, 1996 — Continued

City by State	Population	Crime Index total	Modified* Crime Index total	Murder and non-negligent man-slaughter	Forcible rape	Robbery	Aggravated assault	Burglary	Larceny–theft	Motor vehicle theft	Arson*
CONNECTICUT — Continued											
Brookfield	14,321	248	251	—	1	—	5	41	191	10	3
Cheshire	25,996	469	471	—	—	1	—	119	332	17	2
Clinton	13,154	278	282	—	—	1	9	66	194	8	4
Coventry	10,228	142	142	—	—	2	9	43	82	6	—
Cromwell	12,658	362	362	—	1	8	3	47	267	36	—
Danbury	64,654	3,529	3,569	—	6	74	52	515	2,458	424	40
Darien	18,464	351	354	—	1	4	2	59	243	42	3
Derby	12,051	537	538	—	8	8	17	134	303	67	1
East Hampton	10,742	204	204	—	—	1	4	32	158	9	—
East Hartford	50,495	2,287	2,305	—	5	111	108	478	1,208	377	18
East Haven Town	26,462	1,119	1,120	1	1	30	6	191	724	166	1
East Windsor	10,086	308	310	—	1	4	10	56	202	35	2
Enfield	45,570	1,351	1,358	1	2	22	11	249	939	127	7
Fairfield	54,211	2,037	2,041	—	3	26	19	484	1,256	249	4
Farmington	20,625	715	716	—	2	8	4	125	509	67	1
Glastonbury	27,925	561	563	—	6	4	2	114	419	16	2
Greenwich	59,310	1,178	1,181	—	8	28	32	161	870	79	3
Groton Town	35,139	977	980	—	48	17	35	109	704	64	3
Guilford	20,088	482	482	—	1	5	15	97	348	16	—
Hamden	53,072	2,354	2,354	2	14	73	21	280	1,647	317	—
Hartford	124,223	13,188	13,291	20	94	1,089	929	2,072	7,036	1,948	103
Madison Town	15,672	255	256	1	1	1	7	59	168	18	1
Manchester	51,249	2,937	3,002	2	28	74	81	655	1,952	145	65
Meriden	56,910	3,117	3,118	2	1	66	83	883	1,872	210	1
Middletown	42,601	1,955	1,958	2	2	31	27	287	1,446	160	3
Milford	49,076	2,410	2,422	2	25	31	46	379	1,695	232	12
Monroe	17,144	240	242	—	—	3	3	56	167	11	2
Naugatuck	30,958	788	789	—	4	19	24	150	535	56	1
New Britain	69,865	4,902	4,908	3	22	252	359	1,179	2,482	605	6
New Canaan	18,128	266	266	—	1	—	—	70	180	15	—
New Haven	119,566	15,036	15,138	22	120	1,207	1,267	2,936	7,139	2,345	102
Newington	29,232	902	905	—	3	10	15	116	694	64	3
New London	22,784	1,133	1,136	—	5	38	83	164	733	110	3
New Milford	24,713	580	581	—	4	—	8	93	443	32	1
Newtown	21,086	327	331	—	1	3	8	104	192	19	4
North Branford	13,154	245	245	—	—	1	1	49	172	22	—
North Haven	22,518	941	946	1	1	16	18	132	684	89	5
Norwalk	78,685	4,464	4,473	5	14	169	88	852	3,017	319	9
Norwich	35,492	1,399	1,407	3	25	44	97	328	792	110	8
Orange	12,985	556	558	—	—	10	6	95	418	27	2
Plainfield	14,521	204	204	—	1	2	18	51	113	19	—
Plainville	17,406	521	522	—	—	16	7	94	325	79	1
Plymouth	12,118	275	279	1	1	1	5	93	146	28	4
Ridgefield Town	21,228	164	167	—	—	—	1	51	110	2	3
Rocky Hill	16,565	523	526	—	2	8	1	62	384	66	3
Seymour	14,460	307	309	—	2	1	27	78	176	23	2
Shelton	36,893	706	706	1	2	13	7	184	397	102	—
Simsbury	22,039	291	295	—	—	5	—	79	197	10	4
Southington	38,550	1,084	1,087	4	9	18	11	220	741	81	3
South Windsor	22,108	421	423	—	5	4	10	79	283	40	2
Stamford	107,165	4,955	5,007	6	18	212	205	704	3,332	478	52
Stonington	16,835	454	454	1	1	2	5	66	363	16	—
Stratford	50,121	1,868	1,882	—	11	52	19	426	1,129	231	14
Suffield	11,436	150	151	—	1	—	5	27	97	20	1
Torrington	33,778	726	727	—	1	3	26	136	500	60	1
Trumbull	32,490	1,181	1,191	1	—	12	8	144	875	141	10
Vernon	30,341	698	699	—	1	30	32	114	472	49	1
Wallingford	41,321	1,313	1,314	—	—	9	31	246	909	118	1

City by State	Population	Crime Index total	Modified* Crime Index total	Murder and non-negligent man-slaughter	Forcible rape	Robbery	Aggravated assault	Burglary	Larceny-theft	Motor vehicle theft	Arson*
CONNECTICUT — Continued											
Waterbury	103,490	7,952	7,962	13	39	245	360	1,930	4,396	969	10
Waterford	17,844	921	924	—	4	12	23	122	727	33	3
Watertown	20,971	624	625	—	1	1	10	106	450	56	1
West Hartford	60,161	2,164	2,170	3	5	83	37	397	1,445	194	6
West Haven	52,831	2,973	2,983	1	10	78	61	506	1,767	550	10
Westport	24,771	800	803	1	3	3	21	142	563	67	3
Wethersfield	25,672	628	632	1	2	22	23	103	404	73	4
Willimantic	15,413	1,023	1,024	—	2	30	95	198	653	45	1
Wilton	16,225	240	242	1	1	—	—	78	155	5	2
Windsor	27,840	735	740	2	3	16	6	82	561	65	5
Windsor Locks	12,367	282	283	—	—	4	9	49	178	42	1
Wolcott	13,865	304	304	—	—	4	2	71	214	13	—
DELAWARE											
Dover	29,515	2,660	2,669	—	22	84	144	257	1,961	192	9
Newark	27,991	1,484	1,504	1	12	45	64	177	1,105	80	20
DISTRICT OF COLUMBIA											
Washington	543,000	64,557	64,719	397	260	6,444	6,310	9,828	31,343	9,975	162
FLORIDA[1]											
Altamonte Springs	37,443	3,126		1	21	89	72	390	2,220	333	
Boca Raton	68,550	2,889		2	11	66	85	776	1,583	366	
Clearwater	103,036	7,577	7,607	2	62	215	876	1,353	4,763	306	30
Cocoa Beach	12,454	1,008		—	1	12	56	143	757	39	
Coconut Creek	30,613	1,259		1	8	9	45	342	703	151	
Crestview	14,900	637		2	7	18	58	82	455	15	
Daytona Beach	66,715	7,685		15	90	338	903	1,695	3,931	713	
Eustis	15,590	509		—	2	13	47	73	341	33	
Fort Lauderdale	168,059	25,487	25,557	34	96	1,186	1,268	4,744	15,125	3,034	70
Fort Myers	52,105	7,074		9	57	405	883	1,355	3,308	1,057	
Haines City	12,857	958		—	5	41	88	216	517	91	
Hialeah	200,339	18,210	18,301	12	63	887	1,051	2,894	9,123	4,180	91
Hialeah Gardens	14,853	904		—	2	16	34	215	457	180	
Hollywood	128,996	12,535	12,552	10	56	502	590	2,411	7,545	1,421	17
Jacksonville	690,367	59,534	59,976	85	681	2,792	6,207	13,171	31,852	4,746	442
Jupiter	28,455	1,577		—	7	22	59	380	1,023	86	
Kissimmee	37,572	3,908		1	21	142	407	735	2,376	226	
Lady Lake	14,951	226		—	2	2	31	66	109	16	
Margate	48,969	2,295		1	7	60	113	471	1,374	269	
Melbourne	70,202	6,171		4	38	148	537	1,172	3,930	342	
Miami	384,976	52,918	53,150	124	201	5,139	6,526	9,804	23,431	7,693	232
Miami Beach	93,041	16,841		9	41	650	885	2,420	10,834	2,002	
New Port Richey	15,575	1,212		—	12	22	75	221	837	45	
Opa Locka	16,866	2,899		9	21	221	429	641	1,236	342	
Orlando	182,616	24,055	24,128	13	165	1,080	2,744	4,418	13,444	2,191	73
Pinellas Park	46,511	3,056		—	3	46	160	536	2,136	175	
Pompano Beach	78,144	9,496		12	47	449	776	2,386	4,476	1,350	
Punta Gorda	12,488	429		—	—	10	17	70	309	23	
St. Augustine	13,520	1,453		1	9	40	112	189	1,053	49	
St. Petersburg	246,229	23,843	24,095	26	166	1,380	3,156	4,535	12,373	2,207	252
Sanford	35,564	3,823		3	29	158	358	825	2,155	295	
Sarasota	56,153	5,774		2	36	297	560	1,043	3,533	303	
South Daytona	12,710	455		—	1	12	22	211	193	16	
Stuart	12,991	1,187		1	8	44	116	199	779	40	
Tallahassee	138,001	14,018	14,040	10	95	363	1,094	2,157	9,505	794	22
Tampa	294,670	42,873	43,100	43	264	2,671	5,711	7,373	20,787	6,024	227
Titusville	42,376	2,767		7	30	71	282	619	1,599	159	
Vero Beach	18,718	1,476		1	14	19	81	262	1,028	71	

See footnotes at end of table.

Table 8. — Number of Offenses Known to the Police, Cities and Towns 10,000 and over in Population, 1996 — Continued

City by State	Population	Crime Index total	Modified* Crime Index total	Murder and non-negligent man-slaughter	Forcible rape	Robbery	Aggravated assault	Burglary	Larceny–theft	Motor vehicle theft	Arson*
GEORGIA											
Americus	18,144	1,281	1,291	3	2	23	6	188	1,017	42	10
Athens-Clarke County	93,168	7,660	7,695	12	58	192	461	1,105	5,358	474	35
Atlanta	413,123	70,521	70,760	196	392	4,805	8,306	10,471	37,104	9,247	239
Bainbridge	11,704	1,325	1,325	3	6	32	141	241	847	55	—
Brunswick	18,472	2,254	2,265	1	17	90	270	438	1,356	82	11
Carrollton	17,866	1,701	1,705	—	20	51	88	224	1,214	104	4
Cartersville	13,970	883	884	—	7	10	82	193	547	44	1
College Park	23,417	4,246	4,252	11	22	182	239	670	2,155	967	6
Columbus	194,345	12,294	12,302	15	24	367	484	2,216	8,351	837	8
Cordele	12,399	1,215		2	1	43	212	171	743	43	
Covington	11,859	1,317	1,317	2	4	38	86	126	986	75	—
Dalton	23,323	1,697	1,702	2	9	34	137	224	1,185	106	5
Douglas	11,963	1,990	1,991	—	7	30	284	275	1,334	60	1
Douglasville	14,253	1,669	1,677	1	8	22	107	99	1,306	126	8
Dublin	18,681	1,437	1,437	—	12	48	81	250	993	53	—
Duluth	13,133	456	456	—	1	9	8	115	296	27	—
East Point	33,983	4,799	4,871	5	42	202	131	1,076	2,525	818	72
Fitzgerald	10,450	811	811	2	3	16	55	121	578	36	—
Forest Park	17,062	2,613	2,619	2	8	105	147	376	1,651	324	6
Gainesville	20,297	2,511	2,514	—	9	38	153	297	1,845	169	3
Griffin	23,350	3,227	3,241	4	14	71	304	560	2,002	272	14
Hinesville	28,148	2,019	2,019	—	11	43	58	298	1,550	59	—
Jesup	10,507	809	809	—	3	11	99	166	493	37	—
Kennesaw	10,849	388	388	—	2	2	13	65	303	3	—
La Grange	28,173	3,026	3,045	1	8	70	161	488	2,121	177	19
Lawrenceville	22,148	1,142	1,150	—	—	7	52	176	816	91	8
Lilburn	10,433	578	578	—	1	7	6	75	450	39	—
Macon	113,802	14,011	14,061	18	77	382	447	2,452	9,195	1,440	50
Marietta	52,413	6,502	6,517	2	31	164	428	864	4,293	720	15
Milledgeville	19,151	1,115	1,117	—	5	26	84	147	817	36	2
Moultrie	16,051	1,607	1,613	3	12	68	78	279	1,094	73	6
Newnan	15,938	1,441	1,442	3	1	45	47	271	985	89	1
Peachtree City	26,140	411	417	1	1	—	5	49	323	32	6
Perry	10,636	715	716	1	—	8	1	64	630	11	1
Powder Springs	10,990	232	232	—	—	5	16	35	152	24	—
Riverdale	10,599	1,610	1,610	2	4	49	30	147	1,243	135	—
Rome	32,515	3,779	3,805	3	6	99	472	700	2,370	129	26
Roswell	57,227	2,805	2,808	4	3	62	54	359	2,091	232	3
St. Marys	11,962	895	897	—	6	7	41	112	700	29	2
Savannah	146,534	13,089	13,187	22	63	849	483	2,158	8,427	1,087	98
Smyrna	33,774	3,022	3,022	1	10	96	90	352	2,196	277	—
Snellville	15,063	658	658	—	1	6	5	62	561	23	—
Statesboro	19,063	1,332	1,333	1	8	32	27	222	993	49	1
Thomasville	19,170	1,735	1,742	1	4	52	31	314	1,245	88	7
Tifton	15,296	1,714	1,715	5	7	49	108	221	1,261	63	1
Union City	11,274	1,607	1,607	—	5	42	11	167	1,166	216	—
Valdosta	46,678	4,298	4,305	4	28	110	305	604	2,996	251	7
Vidalia	12,046	1,070	1,072	1	1	35	99	145	760	29	2
Warner Robins	49,707	3,183	3,183	3	34	73	123	572	2,183	195	—
Waycross	18,309	1,762	1,772	3	4	37	43	184	1,454	37	10
HAWAII											
Hilo	40,475	2,875	2,889	2	14	30	40	517	2,147	125	14
Honolulu	878,044	60,059	60,352	27	222	1,421	1,078	9,026	41,915	6,370	293
IDAHO											
Blackfoot	11,296	671	672	—	7	1	31	96	500	36	1
Boise	153,258	8,797	8,878	1	60	56	391	1,511	6,400	378	81
Caldwell	25,154	1,673	1,681	—	12	8	88	148	1,338	79	8

Table 8. — Number of Offenses Known to the Police, Cities and Towns 10,000 and over in Population, 1996 — Continued

City by State	Population	Crime Index total	Modified* Crime Index total	Murder and non-negligent man-slaughter	Forcible rape	Robbery	Aggravated assault	Burglary	Larceny–theft	Motor vehicle theft	Arson*
IDAHO — Continued											
Coeur d'Alene	29,863	2,708		—	13	20	192	420	1,949	114	
Idaho Falls	52,395	2,929	2,942	2	21	13	191	362	2,247	93	13
Lewiston	31,583	1,755	1,763	1	6	10	48	263	1,371	56	8
Meridian	15,285	815		—	1	3	23	156	608	24	
Moscow	19,842	831	834	—	10	1	22	67	715	16	3
Nampa	37,078	2,570	2,592	—	16	12	63	297	2,096	86	22
Pocatello	52,087	2,295		—	14	23	140	374	1,642	102	
Post Falls	10,889	888	893	—	3	4	16	168	671	26	5
Rexburg	15,222	450	451	—	2	1	13	21	403	10	1
Twin Falls	33,127	2,931		3	16	22	136	554	2,037	163	
ILLINOIS[1,2]											
Aurora	113,220			26		226	567	1,241	3,964	357	61
Chicago	2,754,118			789		26,860	37,097	40,475	119,492	34,091	1,560
Naperville	101,980			2		16	49	407	2,235	106	8
Peoria	113,790			11		448	1,736	2,086	6,480	964	127
Rockford	144,421			31		750	879	3,401	8,422	1,387	48
Springfield	106,794			7		452	1,008	2,359	5,697	363	33
INDIANA											
Bedford	14,382	888	891	2	2	5	100	102	625	52	3
Beech Grove	13,233	556	560	—	3	3	9	99	386	56	4
Bloomington[3]	63,527	2,759	2,770	—	27	28	69	398	2,052	185	11
Carmel	31,896	1,009	1,011	—	4	3	69	92	797	44	2
Clarksville	21,919	2,337	2,342	—	13	24	13	156	1,955	176	5
Crawfordsville	14,486	955	958	—	3	5	25	172	725	25	3
Crown Point	18,305	358	360	—	2	1	78	28	229	20	2
Decatur	10,012	285	285	—	—	2	35	24	210	14	—
Dyer	12,113	304	304	—	—	—	30	23	235	16	—
Elkhart	45,533	4,958		6	26	149	69	939	3,457	312	
Evansville	131,455	7,405	7,460	7	41	166	566	1,439	4,733	453	55
Fort Wayne	186,196	13,966	14,052	13	121	499	436	1,927	9,407	1,563	86
Franklin	15,574	808	808	—	8	3	1	134	644	18	—
Gary[3]	116,024	11,229	11,846	104	185	702	2,889	2,278	2,823	2,248	617
Goshen	25,737	1,570	1,580	3	9	18	110	176	1,184	70	10
Greenfield	13,226	223	224	—	1	1	—	21	191	9	1
Greenwood	30,801	1,234	1,235	—	5	4	38	85	1,044	58	1
Griffith	18,830	781	783	1	1	15	113	55	449	147	2
Hammond	84,118	7,117	7,207	5	50	35	699	1,262	3,682	1,384	90
Highland	22,962	1,094	1,094	—	4	14	64	73	790	149	—
Huntington	17,204	805	812	—	7	5	183	98	494	18	7
Indianapolis[4]		37,917	38,242	114	424	2,600	4,280	7,797	16,842	5,860	325
Jasper	11,022	322	322	1	—	—	27	22	260	12	—
Kokomo	46,739	2,648	2,670	3	12	35	140	379	1,977	102	22
Lafayette	46,586	3,215	3,234	1	25	32	97	476	2,438	146	19
Lake Station	14,399	604	605	1	—	9	25	56	438	75	1
La Porte	23,267	1,203	1,203	3	5	13	48	146	920	68	—
Lawrence	27,596	1,341	1,344	1	8	56	98	242	809	127	3
Logansport	17,130	1,288	1,291	—	8	4	203	137	892	44	3
Marion	32,811	3,621	3,625	2	15	53	704	388	2,314	145	4
Martinsville	12,531	606	608	2	3	5	19	73	478	26	2
Merrillville	28,079	1,207	1,208	—	6	21	78	75	828	199	1
Michigan City	34,423	3,160	3,182	2	21	115	65	504	2,026	427	22
Muncie	72,511	3,856	3,873	9	25	168	393	755	2,295	211	17
Munster	20,716	712	716	—	—	13	46	46	539	68	4
New Albany	38,506	2,416	2,456	1	8	28	416	397	1,450	116	40
New Castle	19,005	1,192	1,192	—	3	2	4	232	896	55	—
New Haven	11,143	280	280	—	3	11	9	50	159	48	—
Plainfield	15,875	555	556	—	9	4	8	76	435	23	1
Portage	31,526	1,145	1,152	1	9	6	25	131	825	148	7

See footnotes at end of table.

Table 8. — Number of Offenses Known to the Police, Cities and Towns 10,000 and over in Population, 1996 — Continued

City by State	Population	Crime Index total	Modified* Crime Index total	Murder and non-negligent man-slaughter	Forcible rape	Robbery	Aggravated assault	Burglary	Larceny–theft	Motor vehicle theft	Arson*
INDIANA — Continued											
Schererville	24,864	750	751	—	4	5	26	55	585	75	1
Seymour	17,569	1,073	1,078	—	8	1	52	117	859	36	5
South Bend	106,718	10,822	10,937	22	93	512	395	2,880	6,185	735	115
Speedway	12,443	1,232		—	10	19	11	57	1,037	98	
Valparaiso	26,341	1,034	1,044	1	2	6	84	111	789	41	10
Vincennes	20,094	1,262	1,267	—	3	5	20	309	884	41	5
Wabash	12,439	233	235	1	2	2	10	42	164	12	2
Warsaw	13,133	662	662	—	8	6	7	75	540	26	—
West Lafayette	25,159	866	866	—	8	3	34	67	736	18	—
IOWA											
Ames	46,940	1,516	1,524	—	11	2	25	146	1,272	60	8
Ankeny	21,379	711	715	1	1	3	3	78	589	36	4
Bettendorf	30,888	1,150	1,165	—	2	17	68	182	839	42	15
Boone	12,780	400	408	1	1	—	—	42	342	14	8
Burlington	27,796	2,427	2,437	—	17	30	122	534	1,635	89	10
Cedar Falls	34,182	1,287	1,296	—	6	14	92	135	999	41	9
Davenport	97,752	8,348	8,408	4	55	271	1,130	1,376	5,035	477	60
Des Moines	195,455	15,157	15,276	19	100	321	486	1,794	11,226	1,211	119
Dubuque	59,563	2,335	2,378	1	31	15	127	396	1,698	67	43
Fort Dodge	25,504	2,135	2,147	—	15	35	105	341	1,527	112	12
Fort Madison	12,500	611	614	—	—	3	2	96	488	22	3
Indianola	12,655	346	346	1	—	—	7	51	272	15	—
Keokuk	12,644	932	936	1	9	7	167	231	470	47	4
Marion	22,733	738	747	—	—	3	3	91	629	12	9
Marshalltown	25,140	1,310	1,322	—	3	8	80	213	957	49	12
Mason City	29,050	2,134	2,145	—	10	12	228	550	1,273	61	11
Muscatine	24,130	1,226	1,235	—	10	6	98	481	590	41	9
Oskaloosa	11,157	396	399	—	2	1	16	83	266	28	3
Ottumwa	24,829	1,211	1,221	1	—	5	66	186	925	28	10
Sioux City	83,407	6,403	6,453	—	33	66	505	994	4,405	400	50
Spencer	11,231	249	249	—	1	—	3	17	217	11	—
Waterloo	67,078	5,117	5,178	2	40	151	257	1,099	3,293	275	61
West Des Moines	37,545	1,783	1,797	—	—	13	73	279	1,332	86	14
KANSAS[1]											
Topeka	121,495	15,394		17	89	533	863	3,563	9,659	670	
Wichita	312,706	24,881		24	227	823	1,298	5,193	14,936	2,380	
KENTUCKY[1]											
Bowling Green	46,127	3,783		4	39	96	479	643	2,303	219	
Lexington	241,150	15,328	15,405	14	122	579	1,283	2,893	9,522	915	77
Louisville	274,506	21,030	21,418	63	131	1,812	1,379	4,830	9,484	3,331	388
Madisonville	19,126	1,419	1,422	1	2	22	307	174	841	72	3
Owensboro	54,443	2,912	2,920	1	15	51	31	532	2,160	122	8
Radcliff	20,174	973	975	1	17	35	45	219	627	29	2
LOUISIANA											
Abbeville	11,891	694	694	2	4	12	88	127	457	4	—
Alexandria	46,364	4,769	4,769	6	19	165	269	1,083	3,007	220	—
Bastrop	14,824	1,322	1,323	2	10	39	143	310	777	41	1
Baton Rouge[3]	229,501	27,361	27,623	71	118	1,210	1,999	5,577	15,179	3,207	262
Bogalusa	15,039	1,541	1,549	3	11	39	121	305	1,003	59	8
Bossier City	54,872	3,804	3,817	5	24	82	354	569	2,548	222	13
Crowley	14,607	834	834	—	1	8	87	132	580	26	—
De Ridder	10,277	268		—	1	3	13	18	229	4	—
Gretna	17,515	1,536	1,539	4	14	106	125	295	837	155	3
Hammond	17,800	4,190	4,199	5	23	120	119	675	2,978	270	9
Jennings	11,975	967	970	2	6	14	143	130	659	13	3
Kenner	73,498	5,737	5,737	7	18	170	522	779	3,537	704	—

See footnotes at end of table.

Table 8. — Number of Offenses Known to the Police, Cities and Towns 10,000 and over in Population, 1996 — Continued

City by State	Population	Crime Index total	Modified* Crime Index total	Murder and non-negligent man-slaughter	Forcible rape	Robbery	Aggravated assault	Burglary	Larceny–theft	Motor vehicle theft	Arson*
LOUISIANA — Continued											
Lafayette	103,134	8,483	8,516	8	75	247	515	1,375	5,589	674	33
Lake Charles	73,027	6,875	6,924	16	51	264	491	1,339	3,951	763	49
Minden	13,928	489	490	1	2	4	76	98	283	25	1
Monroe	57,524	8,228	8,228	6	54	177	980	1,454	5,060	497	—
Morgan City	14,048	831	833	1	11	41	57	197	485	39	2
Natchitoches	16,901	1,433	1,433	—	18	46	165	297	860	47	—
New Iberia	33,938	1,353	1,353	2	9	31	45	360	836	70	—
New Orleans	488,300	53,919		351	390	5,700	4,580	9,954	22,774	10,170	
Opelousas	19,465	1,490		3	13	26	135	346	920	47	
Pineville	12,112	929	931	—	4	3	15	277	597	33	2
Ruston	20,289	1,952	1,958	—	1	30	178	374	1,317	52	6
Shreveport	199,418	23,658	23,853	51	134	729	1,576	4,185	15,454	1,529	195
Slidell	29,915	2,719	2,719	2	7	36	253	349	1,924	148	—
Thibodaux	14,329	796	800	2	5	27	88	168	485	21	4
West Monroe	14,468	1,537	1,542	1	10	15	89	142	1,202	78	5
Westwego	11,018	1,071	1,075	1	7	48	71	231	637	76	4
MAINE											
Auburn	23,419	995	997	—	3	12	3	203	727	47	2
Augusta	19,817	1,476	1,488	1	10	14	47	263	1,076	65	12
Bangor	32,080	2,088	2,101	1	8	9	18	298	1,688	66	13
Biddeford	20,464	1,368	1,396	1	12	8	10	294	999	44	28
Brunswick	21,126	625	631	—	2	4	5	104	477	33	6
Gorham	11,979	307	308	1	—	1	17	81	199	8	1
Lewiston	37,475	2,618	2,631	1	11	34	25	579	1,932	36	13
Orono	10,615	217	217	—	1	—	—	35	177	4	—
Portland	61,968	4,691	4,800	1	63	103	290	989	3,014	231	109
Presque Isle	10,058	318	319	—	—	1	6	27	279	5	1
Saco	15,422	854	858	—	2	7	11	199	614	21	4
Sanford	20,829	842	842	—	—	3	7	120	663	49	—
Scarborough	12,649	515	515	—	2	1	13	90	396	13	—
South Portland	22,650	1,421		—	1	6	13	98	1,264	39	
Waterville	16,272	884	888	2	2	6	13	93	740	28	4
Westbrook	15,774	617	624	—	6	8	6	133	433	31	7
Windham	13,155	400	402	—	1	4	6	93	274	22	2
York	11,607	295	295	—	—	—	3	69	215	8	—
MARYLAND											
Aberdeen	13,634	878	886	1	3	26	57	130	622	39	8
Annapolis	35,631	2,965	3,012	4	12	205	277	612	1,683	172	47
Baltimore	716,446	85,982	86,401	328	641	10,393	8,145	14,802	40,522	11,151	419
Bel Air	10,049	630	631	—	4	8	7	69	519	23	1
Cambridge	11,825	1,013	1,017	—	6	29	117	198	625	38	4
Cumberland	24,215	1,458	1,464	—	10	9	189	249	960	41	6
Easton	11,119	792	799	4	4	29	55	117	549	34	7
Frederick	47,244	2,733	2,750	1	15	106	585	279	1,631	116	17
Greenbelt	20,983	1,549	1,549	2	7	85	47	148	998	262	—
Hagerstown	39,016	2,077	2,130	—	15	68	187	372	1,298	137	53
Hyattsville	14,723	1,094		—	2	87	15	153	712	125	
Laurel	21,851	1,363		—	11	71	50	150	931	150	
Salisbury	22,496	3,026	3,049	1	17	122	331	584	1,819	152	23
Takoma Park (Montgomery County)	12,915	556		—	6	48	18	72	303	109	
Takoma Park (Prince George's County)	5,171	556		3	2	59	10	86	292	104	
Westminster	14,702	1,054	1,070	—	3	26	57	150	778	40	16
MASSACHUSETTS											
Abington	14,735	344		1	2	3	89	103	112	34	
Acton	18,582	303		—	—	1	17	52	209	24	
Acushnet	10,099	334	340	—	2	2	74	76	152	28	6
Agawam	27,804	654	680	—	6	6	66	101	414	61	26

Table 8. — Number of Offenses Known to the Police, Cities and Towns 10,000 and over in Population, 1996 — Continued

City by State	Population	Crime Index total	Modified* Crime Index total	Murder and non-negligent man-slaughter	Forcible rape	Robbery	Aggravated assault	Burglary	Larceny–theft	Motor vehicle theft	Arson*
MASSACHUSETTS — Continued											
Andover	30,965	861	874	—	1	2	11	121	642	84	13
Arlington	46,408	518	532	—	2	9	28	110	326	43	14
Ashland	12,544	133	135	—	2	1	36	39	51	4	2
Athol	11,964	463	469	—	9	4	167	134	134	15	6
Auburn	15,679	379		—	2	1	16	49	289	22	
Barnstable	42,937	2,371	2,377	1	23	21	719	482	1,014	111	6
Bedford	13,511	118	118	—	1	1	1	11	93	11	—
Belchertown	10,948	114	118	—	2	—	3	21	83	5	4
Belmont	25,705	257	264	—	1	4	21	33	174	24	7
Beverly	39,081	1,177	1,180	—	5	13	20	463	589	87	3
Billerica	39,107	684	692	—	2	2	77	99	401	103	8
Boston	552,519	44,711	45,329	59	414	3,470	5,211	5,052	21,234	9,271	618
Bourne	17,083	798	808	1	2	6	172	191	381	45	10
Braintree	34,958	1,437	1,437	—	9	21	107	185	898	217	—
Brockton	88,148	5,423	5,454	8	38	224	765	1,173	2,114	1,101	31
Brookline	56,533	1,953	1,957	—	7	42	172	274	1,229	229	4
Burlington	24,229	1,036	1,042	—	2	12	37	107	733	145	6
Cambridge	100,725	4,968	5,003	1	35	226	387	799	2,973	547	35
Canton	19,143	301	304	1	1	—	14	51	215	19	3
Carver	11,294	246	246	—	—	3	9	49	170	15	—
Charlton	10,006	113	129	—	1	—	23	27	55	7	16
Chelmsford	33,673	827	828	—	2	5	53	109	576	82	1
Chelsea[3]	25,942	2,216		3	17	147	386	394	783	486	
Chicopee	55,487	2,554	2,612	4	34	44	1,011	684	739	38	58
Clinton	13,814	365	367	—	2	9	66	53	209	26	2
Concord	17,755	272	274	—	4	—	14	21	223	10	2
Danvers	25,677	1,058	1,061	1	5	3	21	120	780	128	3
Dartmouth	28,775	1,529	1,534	—	2	15	246	323	836	107	5
Dedham	24,570	535	543	—	—	10	7	52	335	131	8
Dennis	14,743	616	616	—	2	1	49	182	362	20	—
Dracut	26,614	748	757	—	11	10	50	142	370	165	9
Duxbury	14,818	92	96	—	—	—	1	23	61	7	4
East Bridgewater	11,842	267	267	—	4	2	16	47	172	26	—
Easthampton	16,080	141	144	—	3	3	31	23	80	1	3
East Longmeadow	13,768	478	479	—	—	11	22	95	313	37	1
Everett	34,426	1,847	1,866	—	6	33	459	363	513	473	19
Fairhaven	17,055	690	700	2	1	7	80	237	320	43	10
Fall River	90,179	4,440	4,440	3	29	93	511	913	2,240	651	—
Falmouth	29,738	1,523	1,542	—	13	9	96	539	776	90	19
Fitchburg	37,035	2,239	2,264	3	33	77	554	507	904	161	25
Foxborough	15,119	315	319	2	4	—	5	62	215	27	4
Framingham	67,580	1,992	2,004	1	24	47	255	458	1,124	83	12
Franklin	26,034	427		—	7	3	33	62	308	14	
Gardner	20,501	552		—	6	9	37	103	381	16	
Gloucester	29,342	695	730	—	4	1	104	171	358	57	35
Grafton	13,620	193		—	—	—	56	33	82	22	
Greenfield	18,996	1,044	1,044	—	15	5	246	203	532	43	—
Harvard	12,882	46	46	—	—	—	1	16	28	1	—
Harwich	10,926	394	394	—	3	1	30	146	203	11	—
Haverhill	53,408	2,909	2,939	—	35	49	280	879	1,233	433	30
Hingham	21,140	331	344	—	1	2	31	61	216	20	13
Holbrook	11,404	207	213	—	2	3	12	72	91	27	6
Holden	15,284	202	210	—	3	1	48	35	105	10	8
Holliston	13,439	111	114	—	1	—	3	31	73	3	3
Holyoke	40,710	2,837	2,882	3	41	117	69	497	1,708	402	45
Hudson	17,918	355	361	—	—	—	36	60	242	17	6
Hull	11,160	231	233	—	4	1	26	61	120	19	2
Ipswich	12,609	198	199	—	1	—	10	59	119	9	1

See footnotes at end of table.

City by State	Population	Crime Index total	Modified* Crime Index total	Murder and non-negligent man-slaughter	Forcible rape	Robbery	Aggravated assault	Burglary	Larceny-theft	Motor vehicle theft	Arson*
MASSACHUSETTS — Continued											
Lawrence	63,648	5,553	5,553	2	17	291	937	1,241	1,295	1,770	—
Leicester	10,647	162	175	—	—	—	10	29	106	17	13
Leominster	38,561	1,685	1,690	—	10	26	113	296	1,044	196	5
Longmeadow	15,933	265		—	—	1	4	39	214	7	
Lowell	96,863	4,724	4,778	5	43	143	827	816	1,920	970	54
Ludlow	19,386	393	405	—	7	—	56	94	210	26	12
Lynn	78,972	5,353	5,394	6	23	234	955	960	1,902	1,273	41
Malden	52,239	1,767	1,793	1	12	56	372	397	608	321	26
Mansfield	17,513	507	510	—	5	2	162	97	198	43	3
Marblehead	21,211	333		—	—	1	6	29	293	4	
Marlborough	33,558	714	727	—	8	5	49	108	502	42	13
Marshfield	22,964	500	500	—	2	3	36	81	350	28	—
Medfield	10,878	86	86	—	4	—	4	26	47	5	—
Medford	56,139	1,786	1,792	2	5	23	309	300	935	212	6
Medway	10,258	130	130	—	—	—	16	39	70	5	—
Melrose	27,453	452	457	—	5	10	3	75	320	39	5
Methuen	41,308	1,535	1,598	1	12	17	66	137	873	429	63
Middleboro	19,055	588		1	4	1	42	105	358	77	
Milford	26,497	221	227	—	2	3	2	60	116	38	6
Millbury	12,777	218	220	—	3	—	78	55	65	17	2
Milton	26,575	288	289	—	—	7	7	45	201	28	1
Natick	31,725	791	791	—	5	8	21	83	609	65	—
Needham	28,470	320	321	—	—	2	20	32	249	17	1
New Bedford	95,420	4,567	4,659	2	69	214	721	1,143	1,602	816	92
Newton	86,078	1,571	1,578	—	6	13	100	309	984	159	7
North Adams	15,615	895	911	1	14	6	293	203	349	29	16
Northampton	29,121	847	865	—	6	8	67	115	568	83	18
North Andover	24,209	357	363	—	1	3	14	35	259	45	6
North Attleboro	26,472	1,089	1,095	—	5	9	80	63	809	123	6
Northborough	12,463	246	254	—	—	2	9	29	191	15	8
Northbridge	13,972	371	375	—	4	—	98	73	185	11	4
North Reading	12,477	130	131	1	—	—	7	39	60	23	1
Norton	15,080	305	330	—	2	1	60	52	159	31	25
Norwood	29,650	420		—	5	1	15	53	307	39	
Oxford	13,153	388	392	—	3	4	100	90	156	35	4
Palmer	12,415	395	397	—	6	1	76	104	181	27	2
Peabody	48,397	1,517	1,518	1	2	20	54	281	990	169	1
Pembroke	15,510	468		—	3	—	110	95	236	24	
Pepperell	10,497	193	193	—	—	2	7	40	139	5	—
Pittsfield	46,828	1,488	1,536	—	3	29	102	400	869	85	48
Plymouth	48,647	1,333	1,376	1	12	18	103	264	862	73	43
Quincy	84,748	2,897	2,950	3	25	50	191	610	1,637	381	53
Randolph	31,088	651	651	1	6	14	16	195	333	86	—
Raynham	10,429	586	588	—	—	8	50	44	393	91	2
Reading	23,437	178	179	—	1	—	5	39	115	18	1
Revere	42,195	2,559	2,583	3	12	60	218	546	1,068	652	24
Salem	37,812	1,707	1,723	—	8	31	18	233	1,226	191	16
Sandwich	16,472	225		—	1	2	7	45	166	4	
Saugus	27,138	1,516		1	6	15	178	179	836	301	
Scituate	17,903	167	183	—	—	—	2	39	117	9	16
Seekonk	13,791	926	928	—	1	8	102	105	612	98	2
Sharon	16,029	114	115	—	1	—	5	11	91	6	1
Somerset	18,664	412	423	—	2	1	43	51	290	25	11
Somerville	69,521	2,791	2,796	2	6	108	378	432	1,243	622	5
Southbridge	18,615	556	566	—	6	10	219	137	169	15	10
South Hadley	17,267	367	370	—	1	2	77	63	213	11	3
Spencer	12,166	202	203	—	4	2	8	56	104	28	1
Springfield[3]	150,421			12	99	531	2,782	3,206	3,477		

See footnotes at end of table.

Table 8. — Number of Offenses Known to the Police, Cities and Towns 10,000 and over in Population, 1996 — Continued

City by State	Population	Crime Index total	Modified* Crime Index total	Murder and non-negligent man-slaughter	Forcible rape	Robbery	Aggravated assault	Burglary	Larceny-theft	Motor vehicle theft	Arson*
MASSACHUSETTS — Continued											
Stoneham	23,088	432	432	—	3	5	26	82	268	48	—
Stoughton	27,662	553	554	—	7	8	22	115	319	82	1
Sudbury	14,929	141	141	—	1	—	6	20	113	1	—
Swampscott	14,497	315	315	—	2	2	13	69	200	29	—
Swansea	16,292	560	583	—	—	4	117	86	268	85	23
Taunton	52,058	1,805	1,832	2	5	47	202	352	939	258	27
Tewksbury	28,351	656	659	1	3	10	16	85	450	91	3
Uxbridge	10,882	250	252	—	9	3	85	51	89	13	2
Wakefield	25,813	369	372	—	5	7	9	109	198	41	3
Walpole	20,880	331	332	1	1	2	61	35	218	13	1
Waltham	55,253	1,397	1,399	1	5	20	126	214	910	121	2
Ware	10,148	169	171	1	3	2	26	52	76	9	2
Wareham	20,513	920	939	—	5	13	57	267	526	52	19
Watertown	31,701	1,009	1,010	—	2	14	121	96	713	63	1
Webster	16,923	603	613	—	5	8	33	133	379	45	10
Wellesley	27,495	346	356	—	2	2	12	93	224	13	10
Westfield	38,507	899	910	—	11	8	159	204	459	58	11
Westford	17,044	106		—	—	1	7	9	87	2	
Weston	10,604	114	114	—	—	1	5	43	61	4	—
Westport	14,644	157	173	—	—	3	13	34	93	14	16
West Springfield	28,367	1,832	1,851	—	14	21	142	255	1,128	272	19
Westwood	12,972	173	174	—	1	1	1	23	132	15	1
Wilbraham	13,015	281	287	—	—	2	32	72	153	22	6
Wilmington	18,353	534	534	1	2	4	71	104	284	68	—
Winchester	21,073	379	379	—	—	—	8	63	275	33	—
Winthrop	18,105	247	255	—	4	4	85	42	65	47	8
Woburn	36,680	1,148		1	3	10	34	150	764	183	
Worcester	166,782	10,048	10,143	7	108	412	1,038	2,231	5,139	1,113	95
Yarmouth	22,517	837	837	—	5	6	71	258	475	22	—
MICHIGAN											
Albion	10,301	857	863	—	12	21	112	140	532	40	6
Allen Park	30,468	1,149	1,161	—	3	26	44	212	689	175	12
Alpena	11,401	502	508	—	4	2	15	63	393	25	6
Ann Arbor	109,939	4,696	4,741	1	37	113	258	804	3,283	200	45
Auburn Hills	19,078	1,088	1,091	—	9	16	67	174	745	77	3
Battle Creek	77,415	5,154	5,203	8	43	196	460	982	3,228	237	49
Bay City	38,784	2,230	2,254	1	29	46	215	343	1,438	158	24
Bedford Township	10,125	305	309	—	4	6	20	103	153	19	4
Benton Harbor	13,321	2,153	2,203	1	28	129	379	653	786	177	50
Benton Township	17,718	2,265	2,276	—	25	45	151	411	1,525	108	11
Berkley	16,731	332	334	—	2	3	10	46	254	17	2
Berrien Springs-Oronoko	12,123	360	364	—	2	2	12	52	279	13	4
Beverly Hills	10,988	213	213	—	—	2	5	29	172	5	—
Big Rapids	12,704	533	535	—	19	9	19	55	413	18	2
Birmingham	20,716	670	673	—	4	9	3	66	561	27	3
Bloomfield Township	43,849	1,419	1,422	—	4	18	36	151	1,124	86	3
Bridgeport Township	13,157	290	294	2	1	6	41	67	156	17	4
Canton Township	58,889	2,133		1	33	14	69	242	1,562	212	
Chesterfield Township	26,743	929	931	—	—	4	25	91	755	54	2
Clawson	14,404	449	450	—	—	3	22	46	344	34	1
Clinton Township	88,650	2,635	2,648	1	81	46	225	287	1,589	406	13
Davison Township	15,143	395	396	—	1	1	13	86	276	18	1
Dearborn	87,075	7,289	7,304	1	11	170	440	598	4,788	1,281	15
Detroit	1,002,299	120,188	121,999	428	1,119	9,504	12,188	21,491	41,193	34,265	1,811
De Witt Township	10,784	322	323	—	3	6	10	83	204	16	1
East Grand Rapids	10,348	321	322	—	1	3	9	43	260	5	1
East Lansing	50,840	1,985	2,010	—	29	28	57	318	1,442	111	25
Emmett Township	11,110	674	679	2	8	9	43	140	442	30	5

City by State	Population	Crime Index total	Modified* Crime Index total	Murder and non-negligent man-slaughter	Forcible rape	Robbery	Aggravated assault	Burglary	Larceny–theft	Motor vehicle theft	Arson*
MICHIGAN — Continued											
Farmington	10,391	388	388	—	2	8	21	58	283	16	—
Farmington Hills	79,959	2,837	2,844	1	11	37	128	482	1,942	236	7
Flint	139,588	16,054	16,269	40	182	937	2,166	4,141	6,340	2,248	215
Fraser	14,229	531	533	—	3	5	9	37	430	47	2
Garden City	31,349	933	937	2	1	23	37	158	646	66	4
Genesee Township	24,871	1,063	1,078	2	8	22	120	219	578	114	15
Grand Blanc Township	26,213	954	955	1	4	10	47	204	620	68	1
Grand Haven	12,988	684	688	—	7	5	16	48	585	23	4
Grand Rapids	192,358	14,600	14,698	20	101	675	1,647	3,033	8,051	1,073	98
Grandville	17,124	705	707	1	4	3	12	171	489	25	2
Grosse Ile Township	10,095	110	111	—	1	—	5	17	82	5	1
Grosse Pointe Park	12,731	396	397	—	—	17	5	17	295	62	1
Grosse Pointe Woods	17,728	304	304	—	—	5	—	17	257	25	—
Hamburg Township	13,505	281	283	—	3	—	13	46	200	19	2
Hamtramck	16,653	2,085	2,088	2	15	105	186	473	749	555	3
Harper Woods	14,409	1,685	1,688	—	1	36	28	94	1,210	316	3
Highland Park	20,258	2,899	2,927	16	38	233	401	511	920	780	28
Holland	31,882	1,548	1,562	—	22	7	96	138	1,218	67	14
Huron Township	10,783	349	352	1	1	2	14	82	174	75	3
Jackson	39,636	3,211	3,242	4	59	77	133	414	2,420	104	31
Kalamazoo	82,485	6,379	6,447	8	48	234	851	1,055	3,797	386	68
Kalamazoo Township	21,654	924	927	—	12	17	44	128	655	68	3
Kentwood	40,306	2,219	2,224	—	23	36	74	399	1,559	128	5
Lansing	120,821	9,744	9,812	10	172	343	1,124	1,607	5,952	536	68
Lincoln Park	40,866	2,668	2,681	1	2	94	115	425	1,645	386	13
Lincoln Township	14,409	367	372	—	6	3	29	56	262	11	5
Livonia	101,450	3,422		2	22	65	150	507	2,271	405	
Madison Heights	32,243	2,035	2,058	—	3	38	74	218	1,405	297	23
Marquette	22,424	699	700	—	7	1	13	61	603	14	1
Melvindale	10,938	522	523	—	6	15	18	105	292	86	1
Midland	39,975	1,130	1,142	2	16	6	61	105	907	33	12
Monroe	23,657	864	872	3	10	16	61	104	617	53	8
Mount Clemens	19,087	1,148	1,161	—	22	53	98	170	720	85	13
Mount Morris Township	26,013	1,521	1,537	1	20	65	134	416	654	231	16
Mount Pleasant	24,106	832	844	—	7	3	35	93	670	24	12
Mundy Township	11,882	529	529	—	2	4	13	102	391	17	—
Muskegon	41,057	4,424	4,466	5	65	132	409	904	2,663	246	42
Niles	12,521	746	750	1	11	15	48	117	519	35	4
Northville Township	17,871	528	531	—	3	5	14	75	391	40	3
Norton Shores	22,288	944	951	—	2	15	38	144	692	53	7
Novi	39,080	1,774	1,777	1	14	10	48	167	1,429	105	3
Oak Park	32,184	1,921	1,927	2	18	61	165	238	1,001	436	6
Oscoda Township	14,730	436	437	—	6	1	17	126	259	27	1
Pittsfield Township	18,239	1,449	1,460	—	9	13	40	153	1,072	162	11
Plymouth Township	24,411	603	607	1	3	5	24	82	434	54	4
Portage	42,964	2,223	2,232	1	11	15	54	293	1,761	88	9
Port Huron	33,718	1,707	1,741	—	26	33	163	303	1,078	104	34
Redford Township	56,150	2,544	2,559	1	13	100	105	453	1,478	394	15
River Rouge	10,697	1,060	1,075	3	11	33	149	210	517	137	15
Romulus	23,229	1,885	1,898	3	15	37	92	276	953	509	13
Roseville	52,123	2,586	2,588	2	11	48	102	153	1,957	313	2
Royal Oak	69,136	2,363	2,373	2	14	31	81	318	1,692	225	10
Saginaw	71,334	5,694	5,825	15	91	319	1,080	1,665	2,166	358	131
Saginaw Township	38,904	1,415	1,427	—	3	28	49	160	1,125	50	12
Sault Ste. Marie	14,981	591	596	—	3	3	1	79	464	41	5
Shelby Township	50,232	1,423	1,430	4	5	4	47	183	1,057	123	7
Southfield	80,611	6,638	6,651	2	30	123	830	755	3,777	1,121	13
Southgate	29,899	1,932	1,951	—	16	15	258	130	1,310	203	19

Table 8. — Number of Offenses Known to the Police, Cities and Towns 10,000 and over in Population, 1996 — Continued

City by State	Population	Crime Index total	Modified* Crime Index total	Murder and non-negligent man-slaughter	Forcible rape	Robbery	Aggravated assault	Burglary	Larceny-theft	Motor vehicle theft	Arson*
MICHIGAN — Continued											
Sterling Heights	120,737	4,621	4,642	1	10	36	223	438	3,506	407	21
Sturgis	10,529	408	418	—	5	1	21	46	312	23	10
Sumpter Township	11,242	323	324	—	2	3	12	92	172	42	1
Taylor	69,247	5,636	5,683	—	26	130	379	1,079	3,130	892	47
Thomas Township	11,324	359	362	—	1	—	8	32	309	9	3
Traverse City	15,857	846	852	—	6	6	25	90	688	31	6
Trenton	20,002	494	495	—	4	4	19	73	363	31	1
Troy	79,843	3,485	3,500	3	12	32	96	381	2,671	290	15
Van Buren Township	21,689	717	717	—	—	8	28	77	507	97	—
Walker	19,029	1,134	1,141	—	6	14	49	123	886	56	7
Wayne	19,489	1,231	1,249	2	12	40	113	197	712	155	18
Westland	86,099	4,068	4,111	1	55	76	239	647	2,485	565	43
White Lake Township	23,337	708	710	—	14	4	55	91	507	37	2
Woodhaven	12,048	565	574	—	3	6	22	52	436	46	9
Ypsilanti	23,849	2,089	2,108	3	27	139	241	392	1,030	257	19
MINNESOTA											
Albert Lea	18,237	699	699	—	6	5	16	102	537	33	—
Andover	20,396	631	638	—	6	1	16	107	445	56	7
Anoka	17,018	1,011	1,023	1	9	13	28	150	766	44	12
Apple Valley	40,580	1,417	1,439	—	8	15	28	163	1,163	40	22
Austin	22,186	1,066	1,068	—	12	4	36	153	798	63	2
Bemidji	12,613	1,389	1,391	—	16	17	38	126	1,071	121	2
Blaine	42,787	2,643	2,654	—	11	25	36	252	2,205	114	11
Bloomington	86,882	5,486	5,510	—	37	99	94	469	4,391	396	24
Brainerd	13,802	1,229	1,234	—	16	5	24	180	918	86	5
Brooklyn Center	28,106	2,494	2,502	—	23	57	42	245	1,914	213	8
Brooklyn Park	59,956	3,520	3,539	—	38	85	210	666	2,291	230	19
Burnsville	56,177	3,148	3,164	—	26	24	34	352	2,485	227	16
Champlin	20,960	465	466	—	6	6	18	69	342	24	1
Chanhassen	15,431	345	347	—	4	1	3	38	284	15	2
Chaska	13,762	533	538	—	2	3	13	53	446	16	5
Cloquet	11,261	509	518	1	4	2	18	63	385	36	9
Columbia Heights	18,536	1,302	1,312	1	13	29	53	273	827	106	10
Coon Rapids	63,606	2,874	2,887	—	21	20	61	454	2,145	173	13
Cottage Grove	27,362	769	773	—	9	8	36	110	589	17	4
Crystal	23,347	1,026	1,029	3	3	20	38	154	734	74	3
Duluth	85,663	4,960	4,980	3	65	67	168	794	3,465	398	20
Eagan	58,126	1,996	2,008	—	22	18	27	254	1,485	190	12
Eden Prairie	48,895	1,418	1,435	—	11	16	18	150	1,179	44	17
Edina	47,442	1,491	1,497	—	6	17	20	236	1,161	51	6
Elk River	13,378	573	573	—	1	1	10	89	425	47	—
Fairmont	11,314	562	564	—	6	—	8	86	450	12	2
Faribault	18,245	1,188	1,204	2	13	13	23	225	842	70	16
Fergus Falls	12,734	577	578	—	16	1	9	74	442	35	1
Fridley	26,758	1,816	1,825	—	30	14	51	180	1,396	145	9
Golden Valley	21,045	848	851	2	10	13	21	195	550	57	3
Ham Lake	10,601	499	518	—	4	2	10	134	301	48	19
Hastings	16,696	590	591	—	4	4	15	66	472	29	1
Hibbing	18,014	368	370	1	4	—	6	77	269	11	2
Hopkins	16,056	787	799	—	10	12	32	107	560	66	12
Hutchinson	12,803	714	717	—	8	1	17	61	604	23	3
Inver Grove Heights	24,988	1,113	1,125	—	10	13	34	197	789	70	12
Lakeville	34,088	908	920	—	5	1	15	97	745	45	12
Lino Lakes	11,898	306	307	—	4	3	15	34	219	31	1
Mankato	32,028	2,310	2,315	—	8	14	30	351	1,820	87	5
Maple Grove	47,580	1,311	1,318	1	6	13	29	177	1,021	64	7
Maplewood	34,229	2,788	2,791	—	14	38	29	268	2,271	168	3
Marshall	12,432	453	454	—	12	1	13	58	339	30	1

City by State	Population	Crime Index total	Modified* Crime Index total	Murder and non-negligent man-slaughter	Forcible rape	Robbery	Aggravated assault	Burglary	Larceny–theft	Motor vehicle theft	Arson*
MINNESOTA — Continued											
Mendota Heights	10,991	281	282	—	1	1	6	40	222	11	1
Minneapolis	361,595	40,826	41,319	83	516	3,242	2,967	7,678	20,690	5,650	493
Minnetonka	51,789	1,771	1,779	—	5	14	21	361	1,305	65	8
Moorhead	33,730	1,463	1,468	—	6	5	39	146	1,205	62	5
Mound	10,205	273	277	—	2	6	9	41	199	16	4
Mounds View	13,248	631	638	—	3	1	44	70	477	36	7
New Brighton	22,036	889	897	—	11	4	12	138	671	53	8
New Hope	21,558	653	658	—	5	19	20	69	505	35	5
New Ulm	13,816	446	450	—	6	2	7	78	336	17	4
Northfield	16,266	698	700	—	3	1	10	118	531	35	2
North Mankato	11,621	388	388	—	4	2	1	18	348	15	—
North St. Paul	12,905	497	503	—	3	9	8	58	396	23	6
Oakdale	23,907	969	973	—	5	7	31	127	758	41	4
Owatonna	20,532	746	753	1	5	3	10	64	611	52	7
Plymouth	61,340	1,885	1,898	—	13	13	26	280	1,457	96	13
Prior Lake	13,544	482	484	—	1	4	13	53	373	38	2
Ramsey	16,012	550	551	1	7	—	9	77	400	56	1
Red Wing	16,055	854	857	—	13	2	14	120	661	44	3
Richfield	35,115	1,734	1,756	—	22	66	55	307	1,122	162	22
Robbinsdale	14,329	704	707	—	6	21	15	140	460	62	3
Rochester	77,278	3,595	3,610	5	53	60	174	476	2,682	145	15
Rosemount	10,058	276	276	—	—	—	2	34	226	14	—
Roseville	33,733	2,426	2,434	—	9	19	29	221	2,018	130	8
St. Cloud	51,794	3,482	3,502	—	66	44	84	505	2,577	206	20
St. Louis Park	43,336	1,817	1,826	—	12	29	36	271	1,353	116	9
St. Paul	267,292	20,704	21,010	26	234	875	1,302	4,127	11,504	2,636	306
Savage	14,154	464	469	—	2	1	24	68	340	29	5
Shakopee	13,307	746	752	1	5	2	24	59	579	76	6
Shoreview	27,489	471	479	1	1	3	12	50	371	33	8
South Lake Minnetonka	11,099	205	214	—	5	—	3	35	152	10	9
South St. Paul	19,959	919	928	—	14	13	36	112	679	65	9
Stillwater	16,273	621	625	—	5	6	17	102	466	25	4
Vadnais Heights	13,518	339	341	—	2	1	9	28	269	30	2
West St. Paul	19,234	1,257	1,259	—	16	20	14	94	1,003	110	2
White Bear Lake	24,975	991	996	—	2	6	10	153	732	88	5
Willmar	18,865	1,132	1,141	—	33	7	41	162	797	92	9
Winona	26,140	1,436	1,437	1	1	9	8	222	1,128	67	1
Woodbury	29,734	1,054	1,061	—	6	2	24	175	813	34	7
Worthington	10,524	367	367	—	7	1	17	47	276	19	—
MISSISSIPPI											
Biloxi	48,665	6,096		2	28	171	1,338	772	3,502	283	
Greenville	45,174	5,842	5,915	12	70	167	298	1,612	3,479	204	73
Greenwood	19,115	1,950		8	11	45	26	451	1,283	126	
Gulfport	66,839	5,588	5,639	8	29	142	105	1,192	3,734	378	51
Indianola	12,284	1,337	1,346	2	12	28	47	478	755	15	9
Jackson	196,619	20,466	20,550	67	209	1,309	781	4,924	9,744	3,432	84
Long Beach	17,101	663	665	—	3	6	9	118	504	23	2
Madison	12,471	258	258	—	1	2	3	10	240	2	—
McComb	12,344	1,011	1,012	2	4	40	144	228	539	54	1
Moss Point	18,290	1,221	1,243	4	17	42	79	385	613	81	22
Natchez	19,619	1,749	1,755	3	10	31	75	236	1,353	41	6
Oxford	10,268	500	501	—	—	11	20	101	335	33	1
Pascagoula	29,554	2,509	2,527	3	11	93	78	557	1,623	144	18
Picayune	12,205	726		3	1	21	42	118	513	28	2
Ridgeland	14,335	1,381	1,381	1	3	24	31	93	1,166	63	—
Starkville	19,876	1,189	1,192	—	11	19	74	179	856	50	3
Tupelo	33,567	3,203	3,206	3	10	77	73	872	1,938	230	3
Vicksburg[3]	28,617	2,979	2,981	5	32	50	338	460	1,823	271	2

See footnotes at end of table.

Table 8. — Number of Offenses Known to the Police, Cities and Towns 10,000 and over in Population, 1996 — Continued

City by State	Population	Crime Index total	Modified* Crime Index total	Murder and non-negligent man-slaughter	Forcible rape	Robbery	Aggravated assault	Burglary	Larceny-theft	Motor vehicle theft	Arson*
MISSOURI											
Arnold	20,390	714	716	—	4	13	88	81	504	24	2
Ballwin	22,232	386	386	—	2	3	21	61	283	16	—
Bellefontaine Neighbors	10,935	627	629	—	2	15	19	53	478	60	2
Belton	21,008	761	761	—	7	4	32	90	595	33	—
Berkeley	12,889	996	1,008	—	5	36	65	179	536	175	12
Blue Springs	41,558	2,020	2,023	—	7	26	71	236	1,590	90	3
Bridgeton	18,048	1,482	1,482	2	5	40	31	135	1,114	155	—
Carthage	11,231	567	567	—	2	7	10	82	452	14	—
Chesterfield	42,946	1,172	1,179	1	—	11	32	134	965	29	7
Clayton	13,914	741	742	—	—	14	8	179	510	30	1
Columbia	75,207	5,055	5,079	3	33	96	271	490	3,969	193	24
Crestwood	11,334	661	661	—	1	6	6	22	602	24	—
Creve Coeur	12,255	596	596	—	3	8	13	51	478	43	—
Excelsior Springs	11,152	621	623	—	12	7	7	106	469	20	2
Farmington	12,346	734	734	—	5	2	11	57	620	39	—
Ferguson	22,932	1,234	1,236	1	5	41	69	203	736	179	2
Florissant	52,186	1,506	1,511	1	4	31	26	192	1,146	106	5
Fulton	10,641	519	519	—	3	4	21	59	416	16	—
Gladstone	28,099	970	983	1	4	31	54	126	689	65	13
Grandview	25,762	962	975	—	10	29	61	231	527	104	13
Hannibal	18,380	966	978	1	7	15	88	186	643	26	12
Hazelwood	16,033	1,120	1,124	—	10	23	57	167	717	146	4
Independence	113,382	8,771	8,840	1	26	124	436	1,229	6,213	742	69
Jefferson City	37,496	1,888	1,894	1	9	27	49	209	1,534	59	6
Jennings	16,234	1,292	1,304	2	4	65	74	273	620	254	12
Joplin	43,548	2,816	2,825	2	20	49	98	652	1,821	174	9
Kansas City	448,474	52,300	52,726	104	412	2,881	5,488	8,947	28,124	6,344	426
Kennett	11,417	1,064	1,064	—	3	7	45	137	648	224	—
Kirksville	17,550	680	681	—	4	1	1	96	551	27	1
Kirkwood	28,717	764	769	—	6	20	23	104	572	39	5
Lebanon	10,536	676	676	1	5	3	27	106	479	55	—
Lees Summit	47,748	1,774	1,784	1	5	21	32	348	1,267	100	10
Liberty	22,096	822	829	—	5	12	21	108	648	28	7
Maplewood	10,393	673	680	1	3	21	52	60	475	61	7
Marshall	12,606	331	331	1	—	1	1	47	273	8	—
Maryland Heights	26,429	1,459	1,460	—	2	9	88	140	1,130	90	1
Maryville	10,670	284	284	—	1	—	5	35	237	6	—
Mexico	11,394	265	267	1	—	2	17	62	174	9	2
Moberly	12,773	783	784	—	5	12	70	122	549	25	1
O'Fallon	20,367	923	926	—	7	13	24	129	714	36	3
Overland	18,595	957	960	1	—	13	18	112	770	43	3
Park Hills	13,289	184	185	—	1	2	34	7	119	21	1
Poplar Bluff	17,592	1,403	1,413	—	5	18	64	205	1,058	53	10
Raytown	30,398	1,295	1,299	—	9	42	22	197	887	138	4
Richmond Heights	10,612	1,294	1,297	—	—	18	34	37	1,149	56	3
Rolla	15,002	935	938	—	3	13	36	162	691	30	3
St. Ann	14,923	1,815	1,815	—	6	30	16	94	1,560	109	—
St. Charles	57,203	2,386	2,414	1	21	42	147	380	1,666	129	28
St. Louis	374,041	56,588	57,372	166	269	4,086	5,682	9,887	29,228	7,270	784
St. Peters	47,119	2,124	2,154	—	2	21	82	211	1,740	68	30
Sedalia	20,565	1,332	1,332	—	5	6	71	272	911	67	—
Sikeston	18,202	1,255	1,262	—	5	32	82	177	913	46	7
Springfield	152,024	11,505	11,608	4	76	173	542	2,182	7,851	677	103
University City	41,403	2,750	2,758	3	16	93	67	462	1,922	187	8
Warrensburg	16,894	745	748	—	3	5	12	107	596	22	3
Washington	11,506	624	632	—	1	3	28	86	498	8	8
Webster Groves	23,410	401	401	1	1	13	15	59	284	28	—

Table 8. — Number of Offenses Known to the Police, Cities and Towns 10,000 and over in Population, 1996 — Continued

City by State	Population	Crime Index total	Modified* Crime Index total	Murder and non-negligent man-slaughter	Forcible rape	Robbery	Aggravated assault	Burglary	Larceny–theft	Motor vehicle theft	Arson*
MONTANA[1]											
NEBRASKA											
Beatrice	12,548	798	808	—	5	3	17	90	651	32	10
Bellevue	42,011	1,708	1,719	1	7	11	15	189	1,361	124	11
Columbus	20,880	589	596	—	4	4	11	78	464	28	7
Fremont	24,179	1,081	1,083	—	1	7	50	139	858	26	2
Grand Island	41,882	3,279	3,281	1	12	15	94	355	2,680	122	2
Hastings	23,366	1,143	1,146	—	2	3	13	180	900	45	3
Kearney	26,684	1,329	1,337	1	7	2	52	152	1,060	55	8
La Vista	10,823	392	392	—	1	3	3	17	356	12	—
Lincoln	206,704	14,349	14,403	3	83	142	987	1,877	10,742	515	54
Norfolk	22,835	1,143	1,147	1	25	7	11	91	961	47	4
Omaha	350,607	26,939	27,192	27	207	782	3,726	3,552	14,999	3,646	253
Papillion	11,009	400	401	—	—	—	1	34	358	7	1
Scottsbluff	14,320	954	961	—	1	2	31	108	781	31	7
South Sioux City	10,468	490	490	1	4	1	9	57	372	46	—
NEVADA											
Boulder City	14,402	418	425	1	—	2	25	87	277	26	7
Elko	20,445	913	921	—	22	6	39	159	631	56	8
Henderson	112,217	5,028	5,061	7	81	122	112	1,028	3,033	645	33
Las Vegas Metropolitan Police Department Jurisdiction	831,303	56,943	57,322	161	475	3,650	4,123	11,656	28,952	7,926	379
North Las Vegas	71,002	6,170	6,293	28	51	426	866	1,340	2,522	937	123
Reno	159,559	10,854	10,883	12	113	507	491	1,676	7,330	725	29
Sparks	66,272	3,806		1	48	88	162	665	2,605	237	
NEW HAMPSHIRE											
Bedford	13,110	238	240	—	—	2	3	40	191	2	2
Berlin	11,127	173	173	—	3	1	11	24	121	13	—
Claremont	13,601	719	721	1	8	4	14	137	536	19	2
Concord	36,993	1,670	1,688	4	26	18	13	215	1,336	58	18
Derry	30,897	875	899	—	33	10	10	183	551	88	24
Dover	25,437	806	812	—	5	5	16	63	687	30	6
Durham	12,332	199	205	—	6	2	13	24	152	2	6
Exeter	13,026	216	219	—	3	1	1	30	174	7	3
Goffstown	15,259	368	377	1	—	3	7	46	296	15	9
Hampton	12,813	615	622	—	8	7	21	88	452	39	7
Hudson	20,382	460	471	—	3	4	8	57	360	28	11
Keene	22,396	931	948	—	15	4	40	138	699	35	17
Lebanon	12,739	738	739	—	—	4	20	70	631	13	1
Manchester	99,036	5,129	5,147	1	55	137	45	837	3,629	425	18
Merrimack	23,123	342	345	—	—	2	6	43	280	11	3
Milford	12,308	413	418	1	19	1	22	40	326	4	5
Nashua	81,381	2,836	2,859	2	24	23	40	365	2,171	211	23
Portsmouth	20,024	904	915	1	9	18	26	88	700	62	11
Rochester	27,616	915	919	3	5	5	15	108	734	45	4
Somersworth	12,026	650	651	—	5	2	4	86	518	35	1
NEW JERSEY											
Aberdeen Township	17,922	584	590	—	9	8	24	129	380	34	6
Asbury Park	15,770	1,588	1,590	2	23	139	140	309	816	159	2
Atlantic City	36,950	9,871	10,070	11	48	440	363	859	7,825	325	199
Barnegat Township	12,667	251	264	1	2	3	17	45	163	20	13
Bayonne	62,931	1,701	1,704	1	5	113	111	276	906	289	3
Beachwood	10,088	370	370	—	—	6	5	67	276	16	—
Belleville	34,915	1,419	1,428	—	8	61	104	303	666	277	9
Bellmawr	12,408	378	379	—	2	13	16	64	264	19	1
Bergenfield	25,149	434	434	—	—	9	15	73	321	16	—
Berkeley Heights	12,357	99	99	—	—	4	1	16	64	14	—

See footnotes at end of table.

Table 8. — Number of Offenses Known to the Police, Cities and Towns 10,000 and over in Population, 1996 — Continued

City by State	Population	Crime Index total	Modified* Crime Index total	Murder and non-negligent man-slaughter	Forcible rape	Robbery	Aggravated assault	Burglary	Larceny–theft	Motor vehicle theft	Arson*
NEW JERSEY — Continued											
Berkeley Township	38,640	887	900	1	10	12	44	165	615	40	13
Bernards Township	18,589	221	223	—	—	—	7	25	181	8	2
Bloomfield	45,984	1,836	1,846	—	4	96	62	318	881	475	10
Branchburg Township	11,766	201	201	—	—	4	3	38	149	7	—
Brick Township	68,829	1,819	1,830	—	7	17	89	330	1,326	50	11
Bridgeton	19,239	1,747	1,755	2	13	93	220	420	911	88	8
Bridgewater Township	35,138	952	952	1	—	25	13	94	710	109	—
Brigantine	12,123	572	574	1	5	4	37	133	377	15	2
Burlington Township	12,815	819	821	—	1	19	43	141	537	78	2
Camden	83,746	10,565	10,932	28	102	1,279	1,180	2,781	3,497	1,698	367
Carteret	19,333	621	622	—	5	29	18	144	343	82	1
Cedar Grove Township	12,299	335	343	—	6	3	40	72	182	32	8
Cherry Hill Township	72,663	3,413	3,425	1	5	67	65	597	2,244	434	12
Cinnaminson Township	15,006	381	384	1	—	11	7	91	216	55	3
Clark Township	15,090	274	275	—	—	2	5	37	213	17	1
Cliffside Park	21,057	391	391	—	1	12	14	71	230	63	—
Clifton	74,788	2,597	2,599	1	11	105	72	470	1,474	464	2
Clinton Township	11,129	120	121	—	2	1	—	43	71	3	1
Collingswood	14,504	641	647	—	2	24	21	125	393	76	6
Cranford Township	23,348	476	476	—	2	9	9	57	367	32	—
Delran Township	13,560	450	450	—	3	14	9	59	319	46	—
Denville Township	14,384	181	181	—	4	2	9	13	142	11	—
Deptford Township	25,447	1,754	1,757	2	—	42	36	226	1,253	195	3
Dover	14,651	388	388	1	4	8	17	64	255	39	—
Dover Township	79,078	3,300	3,325	1	19	65	116	649	2,259	191	25
Dumont	17,542	322	322	—	—	2	20	53	241	6	—
East Brunswick Township	45,618	1,249	1,255	—	4	18	25	159	974	69	6
East Hanover Township	10,337	388	388	—	—	4	16	25	294	49	—
East Orange	73,621	5,671	5,740	15	58	763	588	1,075	2,035	1,137	69
East Windsor Township	23,098	453	465	1	6	5	17	69	318	37	12
Eatontown	13,154	820	821	—	4	8	15	61	705	27	1
Edison Township	92,897	3,228	3,260	1	11	98	186	500	1,866	566	32
Egg Harbor Township	25,258	1,512	1,522	—	9	31	62	237	1,102	71	10
Elizabeth	107,427	9,209	9,238	13	54	795	325	1,768	4,382	1,872	29
Elmwood Park	17,999	697	702	—	2	22	10	81	515	67	5
Englewood	25,153	1,029	1,029	3	4	55	62	226	541	138	—
Evesham Township	36,339	878	884	—	—	12	18	242	538	68	6
Ewing Township	35,325	1,428	1,438	1	8	38	35	327	802	217	10
Fair Lawn	31,514	648	648	—	2	20	22	101	468	35	—
Fairview	10,680	251	251	—	—	8	7	70	115	51	—
Florence Township	10,563	205	211	1	1	6	11	49	122	15	6
Fort Lee	32,407	1,228	1,236	3	2	21	61	95	866	180	8
Franklin Lakes	10,427	129	129	—	—	—	—	38	90	1	—
Franklin Township (Gloucester County)	15,267	533	536	—	2	8	30	136	313	44	3
Franklin Township (Somerset County)	46,240	1,614	1,631	—	7	42	42	359	1,039	125	17
Freehold	11,720	618	620	1	5	42	42	83	423	22	2
Freehold Township	25,991	891	891	—	—	9	6	64	750	62	—
Galloway Township	24,011	777	780	—	5	11	67	153	493	48	3
Garfield	26,723	991	994	1	4	32	27	206	569	152	3
Glassboro	17,568	1,078	1,083	1	12	35	34	177	761	58	5
Glen Rock	11,471	131	136	—	—	—	1	15	104	11	5
Gloucester City	12,495	339	339	1	3	11	11	55	221	37	—
Gloucester Township	56,368	2,361	2,385	1	24	74	132	378	1,484	268	24
Hackensack	37,838	2,058	2,067	2	9	95	106	187	1,394	265	9
Haddonfield	11,705	303	305	—	—	3	4	50	225	21	2
Haddon Township	15,543	581	585	—	—	17	19	82	404	59	4
Hamilton Township (Atlantic County)	16,477	1,301	1,309	1	15	21	81	232	883	68	8
Hamilton Township (Mercer County)	89,445	2,424	2,431	—	13	67	65	490	1,559	230	7

134

Table 8. — Number of Offenses Known to the Police, Cities and Towns 10,000 and over in Population, 1996 — Continued

City by State	Population	Crime Index total	Modified* Crime Index total	Murder and non-negligent man-slaughter	Forcible rape	Robbery	Aggravated assault	Burglary	Larceny–theft	Motor vehicle theft	Arson*
NEW JERSEY — Continued											
Hammonton	12,441	295	302	—	—	7	16	41	204	27	7
Hanover Township	12,015	217	217	1	—	1	6	19	178	12	—
Harrison	13,311	689	689	1	—	33	32	115	323	185	—
Hasbrouck Heights	11,844	340	340	—	1	5	1	38	236	59	—
Hawthorne	18,268	354	354	—	6	4	13	23	281	27	—
Hazlet Township	23,116	326	328	—	3	6	17	40	230	30	2
Highland Park	13,030	362	362	—	—	3	10	41	294	14	—
Hillsborough Township	31,137	518	520	—	2	8	4	118	375	11	2
Hillsdale	10,028	76	76	—	—	1	1	10	59	5	—
Hillside Township	21,709	1,438	1,440	1	13	95	63	237	759	270	2
Hoboken	33,717	2,119	2,119	3	1	52	107	277	1,145	534	—
Holmdel Township	12,129	254	256	—	1	4	12	33	198	6	2
Hopatcong	16,214	289	291	—	4	—	14	36	230	5	2
Hopewell Township	11,975	210	211	—	—	—	14	33	158	5	1
Howell Township	41,012	818	821	—	4	9	31	173	555	46	3
Irvington	62,271	6,718	6,727	9	66	805	673	1,747	1,695	1,723	9
Jackson Township	34,410	1,492	1,500	1	4	3	25	200	1,222	37	8
Jefferson Township	18,564	229	231	—	1	1	9	57	146	15	2
Jersey City	228,424	16,704	16,839	26	91	1,859	1,815	3,425	5,994	3,494	135
Keansburg	11,866	511	515	—	24	3	70	68	329	17	4
Kearny	36,204	2,077	2,085	—	7	74	82	391	1,201	322	8
Lacey Township	22,924	612	619	—	—	5	16	99	474	18	7
Lakewood	46,643	2,734	2,767	2	20	121	135	526	1,694	236	33
Lawrence Township	26,646	1,561	1,564	—	2	28	24	211	1,040	256	3
Lincoln Park	11,202	184	184	—	—	—	3	24	153	4	—
Linden	36,951	2,031	2,034	1	6	89	67	274	1,229	365	3
Lindenwold	18,677	1,050	1,059	1	5	58	54	271	501	160	9
Little Egg Harbor Township	13,803	493	499	—	7	3	27	104	336	16	6
Little Falls Township	11,924	524	527	—	—	6	23	57	347	91	3
Little Ferry	10,048	266	266	—	1	1	5	43	151	65	—
Livingston Township	27,156	976	976	—	1	11	17	92	734	121	—
Lodi	22,841	714	718	—	1	13	42	109	447	102	4
Long Branch	28,173	2,011	2,013	—	15	111	116	409	1,248	112	2
Lower Township	21,428	749	755	1	12	1	41	148	512	34	6
Lyndhurst Township	19,169	556	563	—	2	15	8	63	370	98	7
Madison	15,929	267	267	—	—	4	5	53	192	13	—
Mahwah Township	18,795	408	409	—	3	4	4	50	334	13	1
Manalapan Township	28,103	356	358	—	2	6	23	64	248	13	2
Manchester Township	37,249	421	433	—	4	1	36	88	277	15	12
Mantua Township	10,619	402	404	—	2	8	9	59	310	14	2
Manville	10,594	188	188	1	—	5	5	27	142	8	—
Maple Shade Township	19,770	905	907	1	3	13	28	158	533	169	2
Maplewood Township	22,096	982	984	—	2	47	34	148	499	252	2
Marlboro Township	29,427	460	462	—	4	2	16	113	310	15	2
Medford Township	21,124	373	378	—	3	3	14	59	282	12	5
Metuchen	13,145	327	328	—	2	3	7	72	216	27	1
Middlesex	13,505	269	270	—	1	3	16	24	213	12	1
Middle Township	15,201	587	591	—	5	15	31	116	387	33	4
Middletown Township	71,726	1,031	1,034	—	2	5	28	107	842	47	3
Millburn Township	19,011	1,215	1,216	—	—	24	11	76	1,011	93	1
Millville	26,809	1,688	1,698	—	28	58	135	437	963	67	10
Monroe Township (Gloucester County)	28,154	958	964	—	1	15	13	228	614	87	6
Monroe Township (Middlesex County)	23,311	385	391	—	—	1	17	60	282	25	6
Montclair	38,504	2,064	2,066	1	10	80	109	373	1,081	410	2
Montgomery Township	10,388	230	234	—	2	1	6	66	145	10	4
Montville Township	16,246	300	300	—	1	1	3	77	189	29	—
Moorestown Township	16,585	658	663	—	2	15	24	102	462	53	5
Morristown	16,580	1,142	1,149	—	11	77	46	145	799	64	7

Table 8. — Number of Offenses Known to the Police, Cities and Towns 10,000 and over in Population, 1996 — Continued

City by State	Population	Crime Index total	Modified* Crime Index total	Murder and non-negligent man-slaughter	Forcible rape	Robbery	Aggravated assault	Burglary	Larceny–theft	Motor vehicle theft	Arson*
NEW JERSEY — Continued											
Morris Township	20,779	306	306	—	2	1	14	51	225	13	—
Mount Holly	10,947	748	757	—	13	62	45	200	379	49	9
Mount Laurel Township	31,151	925	929	—	3	17	21	174	590	120	4
Mount Olive Township	22,165	375	380	—	8	4	25	70	255	13	5
Neptune Township	29,609	1,709	1,713	—	2	50	70	340	1,127	120	4
Newark	261,909	34,437	34,594	92	179	4,219	4,271	5,991	11,693	7,992	157
New Brunswick	41,704	3,421	3,431	—	2	274	129	799	1,949	268	10
New Milford	16,201	423	424	—	2	1	20	72	319	9	1
New Providence	12,171	143	148	—	1	—	3	6	125	8	5
North Arlington	14,261	450	451	—	—	14	12	59	323	42	1
North Bergen Township	50,561	2,255	2,257	2	5	69	62	395	1,179	543	2
North Brunswick Township	32,773	1,064	1,069	1	4	33	37	175	701	113	5
North Hanover Township	10,283	60	60	—	—	—	1	16	41	2	—
North Plainfield	19,485	845	845	—	4	31	16	100	619	75	—
Nutley	27,654	655	661	—	1	16	58	151	328	101	6
Oakland	12,268	131	137	—	—	2	3	14	104	8	6
Ocean City	15,180	1,523	1,525	—	1	17	26	315	1,148	16	2
Ocean Township (Monmouth County)	26,358	962	967	—	6	16	20	169	704	47	5
Old Bridge	59,159	1,303	1,323	1	3	28	33	215	916	107	20
Orange	30,540	3,257	3,278	7	19	325	190	684	1,295	737	21
Palisades Park	15,283	289	291	—	—	4	12	74	154	45	2
Paramus	25,408	3,370	3,383	1	7	53	79	184	2,558	488	13
Parsippany-Troy Hills Township	50,494	1,139	1,143	—	25	15	50	329	610	110	4
Passaic	56,636	3,750	3,758	2	25	370	393	785	1,627	548	8
Paterson	139,759	8,448	8,500	7	48	805	774	1,948	3,486	1,380	52
Pemberton Township	32,255	923	936	1	—	31	63	326	410	92	13
Pennsauken	36,396	2,101	2,113	—	—	137	86	500	983	395	12
Pennsville Township	14,194	384	387	—	—	4	12	40	316	12	3
Pequannock Township	13,375	221	222	—	2	8	9	23	162	17	1
Perth Amboy	40,897	2,519	2,546	3	—	126	180	650	1,269	291	27
Phillipsburg	16,013	439	442	1	—	7	11	83	314	23	3
Pine Hill	10,682	281	287	—	2	5	5	81	156	32	6
Piscataway Township	49,327	1,167	1,170	—	4	30	77	204	778	74	3
Plainfield	45,268	3,185	3,223	6	9	302	233	843	1,434	358	38
Plainsboro Township	14,886	302	303	—	2	5	8	36	239	12	1
Pleasantville	17,253	1,243	1,250	1	10	103	170	296	584	79	7
Point Pleasant	18,758	357	359	—	3	3	6	57	281	7	2
Pompton Lakes	11,119	202	202	2	—	4	5	31	152	8	—
Princeton	11,985	719	719	—	2	7	11	143	543	13	—
Princeton Township	13,636	241	241	—	2	3	3	37	187	9	—
Rahway	26,033	1,084	1,086	2	3	55	27	179	703	115	2
Ramsey	14,666	312	312	—	—	—	9	28	255	20	—
Randolph Township	20,802	310	312	—	—	—	9	13	280	8	2
Raritan Township	16,070	354	354	—	—	1	15	65	262	11	—
Readington Township	13,789	194	195	—	1	2	7	40	135	9	1
Red Bank	10,299	542	543	1	—	12	19	32	470	8	1
Ridgefield	10,225	258	258	—	—	3	11	27	178	39	—
Ridgefield Park	12,648	257	258	—	3	4	3	45	174	28	1
Ridgewood	24,874	305	307	—	2	11	7	42	230	13	2
Ringwood	13,378	129	129	—	1	3	3	23	97	2	—
River Edge	11,014	219	219	—	—	6	5	24	170	14	—
Rockaway Township	20,384	1,033	1,038	—	1	11	17	83	845	76	5
Roselle	20,789	873	879	1	7	35	41	187	478	124	6
Roselle Park	13,043	376	376	1	2	10	20	106	203	34	—
Roxbury Township	21,277	414	416	—	3	1	15	89	280	26	2
Rutherford	17,908	312	313	—	—	6	19	40	164	83	1
Saddle Brook Township	13,956	370	370	1	—	8	4	57	258	42	—
Sayreville	36,790	941	956	—	4	33	64	197	546	97	15

Table 8. — Number of Offenses Known to the Police, Cities and Towns 10,000 and over in Population, 1996 — Continued

City by State	Population	Crime Index total	Modified* Crime Index total	Murder and non-negligent man-slaughter	Forcible rape	Robbery	Aggravated assault	Burglary	Larceny–theft	Motor vehicle theft	Arson*
NEW JERSEY — Continued											
Scotch Plains Township	21,829	411	412	—	1	15	10	74	276	35	1
Secaucus	15,532	1,121	1,122	—	1	15	24	43	808	230	1
Somers Point	11,612	448	448	—	1	7	22	134	269	15	—
Somerville	12,322	552	555	1	1	24	14	91	397	24	3
South Brunswick Township	27,016	697	705	—	5	5	14	174	443	56	8
South Orange	16,722	1,076	1,078	—	3	42	20	178	442	391	2
South Plainfield	21,203	827	829	—	1	16	13	71	672	54	2
South River	14,003	344	352	—	5	8	36	61	219	15	8
Sparta Township	15,597	172	172	1	—	3	5	45	111	7	—
Springfield	13,844	414	416	—	1	6	2	53	234	118	2
Stafford Township	13,795	649	654	—	1	—	17	119	478	34	5
Summit	20,405	608	608	—	—	6	9	79	446	68	—
Teaneck Township	39,707	1,014	1,034	1	10	30	55	214	629	75	20
Tenafly	13,429	161	165	—	—	—	3	65	87	6	4
Tinton Falls	13,389	326	327	—	3	6	18	40	247	12	1
Totowa	10,487	594	594	—	2	11	14	45	448	74	—
Trenton	85,338	6,347	6,361	14	160	462	689	1,364	2,572	1,086	14
Union City	56,906	2,896	2,900	5	20	231	153	662	1,237	588	4
Union Township	51,608	2,452	2,456	—	10	93	114	395	1,375	465	4
Ventnor City	10,904	538	538	—	3	7	11	101	397	19	—
Vernon Township	21,829	400	401	—	—	2	12	81	283	22	1
Verona	13,874	248	250	—	1	5	5	39	152	46	2
Vineland	55,253	3,416	3,437	2	26	174	206	719	2,056	233	21
Voorhees Township	25,731	1,273	1,282	2	2	34	24	173	909	129	9
Waldwick	10,029	101	101	—	—	1	3	15	76	6	—
Wallington	10,598	329	330	—	—	7	7	95	181	39	1
Wall Township	21,295	310	313	2	4	6	20	76	184	18	3
Wanaque	10,235	173	175	—	—	1	11	34	114	13	2
Warren Township	11,703	178	180	—	1	1	6	39	122	9	2
Washington Township (Gloucester County)	44,240	1,546	1,555	—	8	36	50	288	1,041	123	9
Washington Township (Morris County)	16,238	200	203	—	—	—	4	32	156	8	3
Waterford Township	11,460	291	291	—	3	3	22	51	197	15	—
Wayne Township	49,655	2,443	2,444	—	11	22	46	117	1,782	465	1
Weehawken Township	12,932	645	648	—	3	19	16	101	321	185	3
West Caldwell	10,636	246	247	—	—	1	3	19	210	13	1
West Deptford Township	20,430	801	811	—	3	13	25	184	520	56	10
Westfield	29,651	522	523	2	—	2	6	84	399	29	1
West Milford Township	26,850	457	460	—	1	3	13	100	315	25	3
West New York	36,945	1,872	1,882	1	7	99	88	444	887	346	10
West Orange	39,902	1,637	1,644	1	1	59	67	319	743	447	7
West Paterson	11,491	311	313	—	—	7	4	47	212	41	2
West Windsor Township	16,555	515	516	—	—	2	4	59	398	52	1
Westwood	10,413	175	175	—	—	—	8	21	131	15	—
Willingboro Township	37,349	1,460	1,470	—	6	71	48	318	840	177	10
Winslow Township	31,522	1,112	1,124	1	7	36	108	262	607	91	12
Woodbridge Township	97,512	3,787	3,803	1	16	98	189	532	2,345	606	16
Woodbury	10,683	824	829	—	2	32	38	119	596	37	5
Wyckoff	16,135	135	135	—	—	—	2	21	106	6	—
NEW MEXICO											
Alamogordo	30,684	1,587	1,590	1	20	15	79	176	1,243	53	3
Albuquerque[3]	426,736	48,253	48,441	70	375	1,998	3,824	9,037	25,961	6,988	188
Artesia	12,161	565	568	—	—	6	30	205	312	12	3
Deming	13,883	1,050	1,050	—	2	19	64	281	632	52	—
Farmington	39,530	3,149	3,176	3	36	52	213	573	2,189	83	27
Gallup	20,676	2,814	2,823	5	24	70	217	263	2,107	128	9
Hobbs	30,771	2,155	2,171	2	24	37	236	484	1,341	31	16
Las Cruces	73,576	6,717	6,741	5	50	124	423	1,179	4,462	474	24
Las Vegas	16,146	1,831	1,854	1	8	31	358	416	950	67	23

See footnotes at end of table.

Table 8. — Number of Offenses Known to the Police, Cities and Towns 10,000 and over in Population, 1996 — Continued

City by State	Population	Crime Index total	Modified* Crime Index total	Murder and non-negligent man-slaughter	Forcible rape	Robbery	Aggravated assault	Burglary	Larceny-theft	Motor vehicle theft	Arson*
NEW MEXICO — Continued											
Portales	12,717	738	741	1	5	1	22	310	381	18	3
Rio Rancho	42,971	1,309	1,326	3	18	21	50	333	820	64	17
Roswell	49,085	4,866	4,889	11	38	62	370	1,170	3,105	110	23
Silver City	11,917	691	704	2	2	4	14	207	449	13	13
NEW YORK											
Albany	104,919	8,130	8,180	11	46	491	584	2,087	4,355	556	50
Amherst Town	107,331	2,749	2,752	—	7	59	32	265	2,211	175	3
Amsterdam	20,082	629		—	8	11	41	176	382	11	
Blooming Grove Town	11,898	214	218	—	1	—	1	80	121	11	4
Brighton Town	34,843	1,189	1,191	—	3	24	10	158	926	68	2
Buffalo	313,238	26,644		60	272	2,624	1,576	6,298	11,314	4,500	
Camillus Town and Village	23,891	507	509	—	1	5	26	75	388	12	2
Canandaigua	11,214	268	269	—	4	—	9	35	212	8	1
Carmel Town	29,142	377	380	—	—	2	10	54	286	25	3
Cicero Town	23,890	332	333	—	—	2	11	42	270	7	1
Clay Town	54,936	668	677	—	—	4	1	138	523	2	9
Corning	11,813	774	777	—	5	4	54	98	600	13	3
Cortlandt Town	28,688	267	268	—	—	4	32	54	172	5	1
Dewitt Town	22,049	992	999	—	1	14	7	165	772	33	7
Dobbs Ferry Village	10,238	153	153	1	—	2	15	17	101	17	—
Eastchester Town	18,744	355	355	4	1	8	8	35	230	69	—
East Greenbush Town	14,233	401	404	—	1	7	16	53	309	15	3
East Hampton Town	14,147	656	657	—	2	2	6	194	425	27	1
Fallsburg Town	10,781	338	342	—	2	4	9	178	127	18	4
Floral Park Village	16,414	167	168	—	2	9	8	43	88	17	1
Freeport Village	39,934	1,623	1,633	2	9	108	111	246	924	223	10
Fulton	13,019	671	677	—	6	11	13	117	505	19	6
Garden City Village	22,018	591		—	3	4	7	50	437	90	
Gates Town	28,904	1,262	1,264	—	4	38	7	194	893	126	2
Geddes Town	11,081	341	341	—	1	1	4	66	253	16	—
Glens Falls	13,573	949		1	1	7	147	185	603	5	
Goshen	11,629	69	69	—	—	—	8	9	47	5	—
Greece Town	91,127	3,123		—	11	43	17	303	2,483	266	
Harrison Town	23,383	452	453	—	3	5	3	57	307	77	1
Haverstraw Town	23,535	607	607	—	3	6	92	94	390	22	—
Hempstead Village	44,768	2,450	2,475	6	17	260	598	320	905	344	25
Irondequoit Town	52,969	2,709	2,721	—	7	67	32	321	2,147	135	12
Ithaca	29,266	1,487		1	7	46	19	280	1,086	48	
Kent Town	13,329	243	245	—	—	—	4	55	175	9	2
Kingston	23,440	1,056	1,064	2	9	30	27	121	798	69	8
Lockport	25,728	1,444	1,448	—	11	42	230	266	812	83	4
Long Beach	34,245	802	804	—	3	23	64	141	467	104	2
Lynbrook Village	19,611	301	302	—	—	11	7	45	195	43	1
Mamaroneck Town	11,534	239	239	—	—	4	2	28	159	46	—
Mamaroneck Village	17,674	642	642	—	2	7	42	97	380	114	—
Manlius Town	35,250	474	476	—	3	3	10	86	365	7	2
Massena Village	11,876	135		—	1	4	16	27	85	2	
Middletown	24,817	1,041	1,054	—	5	35	86	196	686	33	13
Mount Pleasant Town	25,334	443	448	1	4	6	33	63	280	56	5
Mount Vernon	65,919	3,715	3,733	9	22	430	322	893	1,410	629	18
Newburgh	25,727	2,051	2,085	7	20	138	202	565	965	154	34
Newburgh Town	24,328	1,136	1,139	—	4	15	25	150	899	43	3
New Castle Town	16,835	173	175	1	—	—	5	28	128	11	2
New Hartford Town and Village	21,996	1,086	1,091	—	1	5	3	68	985	24	5
New Paltz Town and Village	16,755	329	330	—	2	5	70	53	189	10	1
New Rochelle	66,821	2,677	2,686	2	10	103	84	398	1,754	326	9
New Windsor Town	23,195	626		—	2	5	54	106	433	26	

Table 8. — Number of Offenses Known to the Police, Cities and Towns 10,000 and over in Population, 1996 — Continued

City by State	Population	Crime Index total	Modified* Crime Index total	Murder and non-negligent man-slaughter	Forcible rape	Robbery	Aggravated assault	Burglary	Larceny–theft	Motor vehicle theft	Arson*
NEW YORK — Continued											
New York	7,339,594	382,555		983	2,332	49,670	45,674	61,270	162,246	60,380	
Niagara Falls	60,569	4,496	4,549	2	28	214	208	1,167	2,523	354	53
Niskayuna Town	19,261	486	489	—	—	7	28	77	361	13	3
North Castle Town	10,173	178	178	—	—	2	2	33	131	10	—
North Greenbush Town	11,011	275	276	—	2	1	27	60	181	4	1
North Tonawanda	32,962	858	864	—	—	12	12	147	651	36	6
Ogdensburg	13,185	689	689	—	—	—	8	133	534	14	—
Ogden Town	17,101	392		—	1	5	12	94	268	12	
Oneida	11,217	513	515	—	—	4	9	94	394	12	2
Oneonta	13,068	578	579	—	9	4	24	125	400	16	1
Orangetown Town	35,227	969	970	1	2	16	30	160	716	44	1
Ossining Village	22,732	810	812	—	6	32	45	179	487	61	2
Oswego	18,730	742	742	—	1	8	8	141	544	40	—
Peekskill	20,406	696	697	—	2	46	59	125	418	46	1
Port Chester Village	24,694	697	697	—	—	31	49	101	462	54	—
Port Washington Village	14,941	377	381	3	—	5	4	27	305	33	4
Ramapo Town	66,819	1,401	1,405	1	2	21	22	285	1,024	46	4
Riverhead Town	23,270	932	937	3	—	19	146	289	446	29	5
Rochester	231,372	20,928	21,208	53	119	1,360	738	4,474	11,491	2,693	280
Rome	44,271	1,061	1,077	1	7	26	22	267	675	63	16
Rotterdam Town	28,714	1,031	1,035	—	3	17	1	117	857	36	4
Rye	15,020	273	273	—	—	2	3	27	220	21	—
Saratoga Springs	26,139	1,590	1,597	—	11	25	292	247	983	32	7
Scarsdale Village	16,980	287	287	—	—	3	1	31	218	34	—
Schodack Town	10,462	204	204	—	—	—	8	50	138	8	—
Shawangunk Town	10,193	154	154	—	—	—	32	26	91	5	—
Southampton Town	37,543	1,703	1,711	1	3	27	96	448	1,059	69	8
Southold Town	17,965	747	750	—	2	16	8	228	478	15	3
Spring Valley Village	23,122	1,425	1,428	3	5	100	93	209	914	101	3
Stony Point Town	12,957	122	122	—	—	1	5	18	96	2	—
Suffern Village	11,372	227	227	—	1	7	6	38	162	13	—
Syracuse	160,033	10,999	11,105	15	62	579	742	2,821	5,940	840	106
Tarrytown Village	10,378	264	265	—	1	5	13	53	164	28	1
Troy	52,651	3,226	3,234	2	25	155	101	822	1,929	192	8
Ulster Town	12,466	700	700	1	1	5	35	51	587	20	—
Utica	64,150	3,266	3,288	8	25	116	49	637	2,199	232	22
Wallkill Town	23,275	501	504	—	—	3	19	54	407	18	3
Webster Town and Village	37,509	733	736	—	4	4	9	86	595	35	3
White Plains	49,814	2,569	2,573	1	7	65	64	138	2,131	163	4
Yonkers	183,650	8,210	8,266	13	34	639	418	1,381	4,125	1,600	56
Yorktown Town	33,844	735	736	—	1	9	11	73	622	19	1
NORTH CAROLINA											
Albemarle	17,856	1,419	1,430	2	8	25	81	393	857	53	11
Archdale	11,786	263	267	1	1	8	4	65	167	17	4
Asheboro	19,121	1,683	1,684	2	11	26	72	308	1,176	88	1
Asheville	66,560	4,637	4,646	4	23	153	322	858	2,937	340	9
Boone	14,219	642	644	—	4	5	29	82	497	25	2
Burlington	45,371	2,646	2,658	—	6	92	247	337	1,865	99	12
Carrboro	14,255	895	898	1	6	28	25	144	651	40	3
Cary	62,949	2,341	2,359	—	4	40	59	354	1,776	108	18
Chapel Hill	48,281	2,705	2,722	1	9	61	149	448	1,937	100	17
Charlotte-Mecklenburg	554,070	53,518	53,957	71	306	2,594	5,944	10,227	30,199	4,177	439
Concord	31,999	1,907	1,919	—	11	48	84	343	1,341	80	12
Durham	148,571	16,838	16,909	41	84	810	754	4,226	9,400	1,523	71
Eden	16,373	1,111	1,112	—	2	26	48	270	717	48	1
Elizabeth City	17,685	1,241	1,246	1	5	42	88	242	814	49	5
Fayetteville	87,004	10,200	10,258	14	73	476	377	2,032	6,449	779	58

City by State	Population	Crime Index total	Modified* Crime Index total	Murder and non-negligent man-slaughter	Forcible rape	Robbery	Aggravated assault	Burglary	Larceny–theft	Motor vehicle theft	Arson*
NORTH CAROLINA — Continued											
Garner	17,727	1,059	1,060	—	4	21	23	114	837	60	1
Gastonia	61,206	5,906	5,966	12	35	278	505	1,212	3,621	243	60
Goldsboro	46,621	4,395	4,406	10	23	160	351	756	2,878	217	11
Graham	11,373	808	811	1	4	22	101	185	459	36	3
Greensboro	203,186	16,393	16,472	23	95	710	1,099	3,228	10,190	1,048	79
Greenville	51,091	5,254	5,269	4	32	163	278	1,122	3,436	219	15
Havelock	21,876	490	496	—	—	13	32	116	312	17	6
Henderson	16,609	1,994	2,001	4	7	74	228	422	1,172	87	7
Hickory	30,634	3,287	3,303	8	22	110	217	622	2,147	161	16
High Point	74,791	7,884	7,941	12	37	300	557	1,990	4,519	469	57
Jacksonville	59,144	2,745	2,752	5	18	71	232	571	1,734	114	7
Kannapolis	31,758	982	992	2	5	31	47	197	642	58	10
Kernersville	13,651	927	933	—	8	16	47	149	636	71	6
Kings Mountain	10,582	1,023	1,031	—	6	24	74	219	656	44	8
Kinston	26,129	2,590	2,595	5	8	97	157	627	1,577	119	5
Laurinburg	13,580	1,121	1,133	2	2	36	75	270	676	60	12
Lenoir	15,169	1,095	1,102	—	4	30	76	247	701	37	7
Lexington	19,208	1,563	1,578	2	9	49	85	329	979	110	15
Lumberton	19,873	2,054	2,061	1	3	56	143	528	1,212	111	7
Matthews	15,433	701	713	—	5	13	38	114	506	25	12
Monroe	20,122	1,638	1,644	5	2	42	107	288	1,125	69	6
Mooresville	12,374	762	769	1	5	15	82	109	539	11	7
Morganton	17,991	887	890	—	1	17	26	156	654	33	3
New Bern	18,736	2,279	2,285	1	8	63	133	529	1,480	65	6
Newton	11,370	776	779	—	1	11	32	168	515	49	3
Raleigh	245,176	17,080	17,164	25	90	732	1,262	3,139	10,456	1,376	84
Reidsville	12,831	938	939	2	3	13	110	194	597	19	1
Roanoke Rapids	17,155	1,269	1,277	1	4	33	41	173	963	54	8
Rockingham	10,118	930	933	2	4	11	90	156	635	32	3
Rocky Mount	53,797	5,216	5,252	10	19	232	297	1,225	3,210	223	36
Salisbury	28,794	2,075	2,086	4	21	69	132	383	1,353	113	11
Sanford	16,821	2,576	2,587	1	7	66	111	376	1,926	89	11
Shelby	16,352	1,978	1,990	5	4	106	185	457	1,135	86	12
Statesville	18,851	2,555	2,567	3	10	96	241	528	1,574	103	12
Tarboro	11,185	911	911	—	1	24	70	220	583	13	—
Thomasville	18,302	1,278	1,282	—	5	43	82	336	763	49	4
Washington	10,146	1,115	1,120	2	3	41	39	313	665	52	5
Wilmington	64,892	7,180	7,222	4	40	240	417	1,562	4,361	556	42
Wilson	40,237	4,099	4,099	6	27	152	297	1,341	2,043	233	—
Winston-Salem	160,678	18,929	19,090	28	123	871	1,245	3,812	11,062	1,788	161
NORTH DAKOTA											
Bismarck	53,086	2,151	2,152	1	7	9	41	232	1,743	118	1
Jamestown	15,509	494	496	—	6	6	1	47	414	20	2
Mandan	15,975	627	628	—	18	1	39	43	475	51	1
Minot	35,684	1,714	1,724	1	13	7	18	139	1,430	106	10
West Fargo	13,899	380	383	—	7	1	16	67	266	23	3
Williston	12,867	337	339	—	6	—	5	20	286	20	2
OHIO											
Akron	223,303	16,007	16,113	14	194	811	1,326	2,866	8,763	2,033	106
Amherst	11,170	457	457	—	3	5	—	47	386	16	—
Ashland	21,246	719	719	—	2	—	5	66	621	25	—
Athens	21,153	580	582	—	8	9	12	46	477	28	2
Aurora	10,756	264	264	—	1	—	2	29	219	13	—
Barberton	27,960	1,563	1,575	2	15	31	187	260	970	98	12
Beavercreek	37,979	1,751	1,788	1	7	21	14	212	1,426	70	37
Bedford	14,690	496	496	1	4	10	10	25	371	75	—
Bedford Heights	11,903	455	455	—	4	6	24	82	269	70	—

Table 8. — Number of Offenses Known to the Police, Cities and Towns 10,000 and over in Population, 1996 — Continued

City by State	Population	Crime Index total	Modified* Crime Index total	Murder and non-negligent man-slaughter	Forcible rape	Robbery	Aggravated assault	Burglary	Larceny–theft	Motor vehicle theft	Arson*
OHIO — Continued											
Bellefontaine	12,723	520	520	—	4	2	11	112	370	21	—
Berea	18,914	545	548	1	6	10	16	62	415	35	3
Bexley	13,469	495	496	—	1	23	3	59	374	35	1
Bowling Green	28,030	979	981	1	6	11	26	112	789	34	2
Brecksville	12,614	147	147	—	1	1	2	27	109	7	—
Brooklyn	11,168	720	720	—	—	17	4	17	561	121	—
Bucyrus	13,282	899	902	—	1	4	11	235	627	21	3
Canton	84,725	7,796	7,881	10	84	461	812	1,691	3,931	807	85
Centerville	21,879	684	688	—	2	6	3	100	538	35	4
Chillicothe	22,439	1,788	1,811	—	5	16	53	253	1,389	72	23
Cincinnati	360,457	27,455	28,132	32	315	1,774	1,800	5,687	16,025	1,822	677
Cleveland	496,049	37,409	38,033	103	643	4,062	2,823	7,708	13,441	8,629	624
Cleveland Heights	51,805	1,146		3	1	26	2	131	801	182	
Columbus	640,297	61,083	61,894	89	571	3,318	2,238	13,013	34,244	7,610	811
Conneaut	13,296	376	376	—	—	5	8	84	267	12	—
Dayton	179,680	17,841	18,078	38	201	1,085	702	3,720	8,859	3,236	237
Delaware	21,996	948	955	—	17	12	14	145	713	47	7
Delhi Township	31,142	716	718	—	4	4	5	49	640	14	2
Dover	12,084	398	398	—	3	3	2	30	345	15	—
Dublin	21,895	906	906	—	2	14	7	189	657	37	—
Eastlake	21,008	471	472	—	—	8	18	65	357	23	1
East Liverpool	14,310	670	671	1	7	11	9	159	443	40	1
Englewood	11,347	636	638	—	2	3	7	49	540	35	2
Euclid	53,590	2,175	2,184	—	17	96	40	443	1,239	340	9
Fairborn	30,117	1,474	1,475	1	9	16	29	183	1,120	116	1
Fairfield	41,152	2,266	2,281	—	8	23	134	368	1,611	122	15
Franklin	11,508	511	512	—	2	7	18	113	334	37	1
Fremont	18,247	1,455	1,459	4	7	31	50	212	1,103	48	4
Gahanna	31,168	897	901	1	3	16	23	189	643	22	4
Girard	11,527	321		—	—	8	5	55	227	26	
Goshen Township	13,069	233	237	1	7	—	8	53	144	20	4
Grove City	22,826	941	941	—	6	16	20	100	753	46	—
Hamilton	65,326	5,244	5,286	4	80	225	634	1,111	2,778	412	42
Hilliard	16,828	693	701	—	5	12	10	128	522	16	8
Huber Heights	40,932	1,708	1,723	1	29	33	20	240	1,251	134	15
Jackson Township	33,015	1,502	1,508	—	6	33	30	176	1,178	79	6
Kent	28,858	1,264	1,274	—	6	31	60	221	855	91	10
Kettering	59,735	2,794	2,808	—	21	39	26	484	2,003	221	14
Lakewood	57,426	1,443	1,454	—	8	52	18	161	1,047	157	11
Lebanon	11,720	654	656	—	5	13	20	112	474	30	2
Liberty Township	13,535	531	532	—	4	24	12	98	334	59	1
Lima	44,656	3,461	3,500	5	40	205	256	905	1,907	143	39
Lorain	71,371	1,939	1,959	3	50	81	99	399	1,160	147	20
Loveland	12,211	309	312	—	1	1	7	29	257	14	3
Madison Township (Lake County)	18,482	625	631	—	8	4	20	118	416	59	6
Mansfield	53,531	5,017	5,062	1	57	119	964	970	2,706	200	45
Marietta	15,252	674	679	1	10	4	14	83	551	11	5
Marion	34,831	2,259	2,279	—	21	48	40	393	1,670	87	20
Mason	13,368	426	428	—	1	2	2	51	354	16	2
Mentor	50,377	1,860	1,884	—	6	22	32	195	1,509	96	24
Miamisburg	18,235	917	919	—	7	8	19	163	635	85	2
Middletown	48,837	3,116	3,131	2	23	62	61	643	2,209	116	15
Montgomery	10,163	248	249	—	—	5	—	23	215	5	1
Newark	45,551	2,578	2,592	2	43	61	173	457	1,687	155	14
New Philadelphia	16,740	523	525	—	1	11	5	59	434	13	2
Niles	21,501	1,295	1,295	—	4	31	132	143	836	149	—
North Ridgeville	22,562	301	303	—	4	5	7	72	196	17	2
Norton	11,858	414	415	—	—	3	21	76	297	17	1

Table 8. — Number of Offenses Known to the Police, Cities and Towns 10,000 and over in Population, 1996 — Continued

City by State	Population	Crime Index total	Modified* Crime Index total	Murder and non-negligent man-slaughter	Forcible rape	Robbery	Aggravated assault	Burglary	Larceny–theft	Motor vehicle theft	Arson*
OHIO — Continued											
Norwalk	15,301	477	478	—	—	1	8	92	365	11	1
Norwood	22,518	1,571	1,572	3	18	56	19	219	1,196	60	1
Oregon	18,392	1,149	1,154	—	5	10	34	166	883	51	5
Oxford	19,578	763		—	4	2	15	183	541	18	
Perkins Township	11,108	573	573	—	5	8	11	55	480	14	—
Perrysburg	13,875	373	373	—	1	3	16	59	285	9	—
Perry Township	31,200	968	975	—	1	28	67	210	594	68	7
Piqua	20,913	1,401	1,412	—	10	21	24	187	1,106	53	11
Portsmouth	24,058	1,882	1,888	—	15	48	60	474	1,191	94	6
Reading	11,827	329	329	—	2	9	4	44	239	31	—
Reynoldsburg	29,067	1,044	1,052	—	8	30	6	166	784	50	8
Salem	12,922	56	56	—	—	1	3	10	33	9	—
Seven Hills	12,117	110	110	—	—	1	5	21	72	11	—
Shaker Heights	30,742	980	987	—	5	69	8	215	585	98	7
Sharonville	14,057	1,018	1,021	—	8	20	43	99	809	39	3
Sheffield Lake[3]	10,278	256	259	—	2	1	68	34	137	14	3
Shelby	10,248	393	397	—	3	4	4	101	271	10	4
Solon	20,600	410	412	—	1	3	19	38	315	34	2
Springdale	10,700	1,465	1,466	—	2	26	2	75	1,299	61	1
Springfield	70,837	7,458	7,515	8	94	288	1,015	1,215	4,361	477	57
Springfield Township (Hamilton County)	39,644	1,125	1,131	1	6	29	74	178	788	49	6
Stow	30,376	788	801	—	7	8	4	68	680	21	13
Streetsboro	10,681	338	343	—	—	5	5	46	268	14	5
Sylvania	18,822	488	488	—	1	5	8	90	384	—	—
Sylvania Township	23,350	1,309	1,311	2	5	8	68	178	949	99	2
Tallmadge	15,413	642	649	—	6	12	17	106	456	45	7
Tiffin	18,647	1,018		1	2	6	20	222	732	35	
Toledo	324,610	27,488	28,094	30	277	1,297	1,031	5,597	16,218	3,038	606
Trotwood	30,045	2,499	2,530	2	20	63	92	286	1,795	241	31
Troy	20,534	1,025	1,030	—	8	12	12	157	794	42	5
Twinsburg	12,520	249	254	—	4	1	12	51	169	12	5
Union Township (Butler County)	40,875	1,534	1,553	1	9	13	35	326	1,114	36	19
Union Township (Clermont County)	34,352	2,179	2,197	1	15	38	8	244	1,769	104	18
University Heights	14,347	340	345	—	5	17	15	37	252	14	5
Upper Arlington	36,313	797	815	1	13	11	7	97	646	22	18
Vandalia	14,085	553	559	—	1	5	6	81	428	32	6
Van Wert	11,558	674	679	—	18	1	45	126	459	25	5
Vermilion	11,438	299	299	—	2	—	4	40	245	8	—
Wadsworth	16,943	387	395	—	—	1	6	56	305	11	8
Warrensville Heights	15,839	784	791	—	10	50	70	162	350	142	7
Washington Court House	13,364	446	446	—	5	13	3	126	262	37	—
West Carrollton	14,477	623	628	—	4	12	29	106	378	94	5
Westerville	35,054	1,101	1,121	—	4	14	15	151	881	36	20
Westlake	30,563	553	556	—	3	7	11	101	385	46	3
Whitehall	21,229	2,015	2,055	—	9	67	412	271	1,142	114	40
Wickliffe	13,872	341	343	—	1	5	16	37	248	34	2
Wilmington	11,640	830	836	—	5	7	18	64	694	42	6
Worthington	15,140	584	586	—	4	12	6	108	427	27	2
Xenia	24,211	1,361	1,363	—	7	27	22	136	1,117	52	2
Youngstown	92,360	6,368	6,697	61	62	410	824	1,769	2,176	1,066	329
OKLAHOMA											
Ada	16,063	953	968	—	7	7	73	192	620	54	15
Altus	22,596	1,491	1,510	—	8	14	193	274	962	40	19
Ardmore	23,906	2,751		1	9	34	229	525	1,839	114	
Bartlesville	34,083	1,724		—	9	17	132	257	1,244	65	
Bethany	20,230	1,039		1	11	10	84	222	624	87	
Bixby	10,892	221	231	—	1	—	7	42	147	24	10
Broken Arrow	66,545	1,913		—	10	14	94	518	1,098	179	

See footnotes at end of table.

City by State	Population	Crime Index total	Modified* Crime Index total	Murder and non-negligent man-slaughter	Forcible rape	Robbery	Aggravated assault	Burglary	Larceny–theft	Motor vehicle theft	Arson*
OKLAHOMA — Continued											
Chickasha	15,356	1,397	1,413	1	8	31	150	295	860	52	16
Claremore	15,773	786	802	—	6	2	24	129	574	51	16
Del City	24,065	1,262		—	12	36	24	289	803	98	
Duncan	22,460	1,280	1,293	—	5	17	49	257	908	44	13
Durant	13,408	1,051	1,052	1	5	9	33	206	708	89	1
Edmond	62,031	2,151	2,174	—	13	33	49	500	1,389	167	23
Elk City	10,727	492	492	—	6	1	8	123	332	22	—
El Reno	16,007	902		4	7	32	72	184	536	67	
Enid	46,455	4,085	4,119	4	31	57	292	722	2,725	254	34
Guthrie	10,736	792	809	1	8	13	40	201	495	34	17
Lawton	87,213	7,351	7,390	7	59	183	427	1,833	4,439	403	39
McAlester	17,852	809	811	1	8	8	53	187	507	45	2
Miami	13,580	940	948	—	5	1	52	164	685	33	8
Midwest City	54,178	3,625		—	24	59	150	791	2,280	321	
Moore	43,154	1,849	1,855	1	16	32	146	416	1,074	164	6
Muskogee	39,476	3,362		4	38	71	280	907	1,793	269	
Mustang	11,729	334	336	—	2	1	13	68	237	13	2
Norman	88,441	4,547	4,560	3	33	61	125	926	3,097	302	13
Oklahoma City	469,632	57,100	57,523	67	477	1,478	3,286	10,690	35,957	5,145	423
Okmulgee	13,753	1,029	1,040	2	6	17	113	182	631	78	11
Owasso	13,152	518	519	—	6	3	30	91	354	34	1
Ponca City	26,413	1,676	1,712	—	27	16	99	348	1,107	79	36
Sand Springs	16,713	854	883	—	6	12	50	145	535	106	29
Sapulpa	18,729	1,206	1,207	1	6	12	49	222	782	134	1
Shawnee	28,246	2,145	2,152	1	9	34	94	465	1,381	161	7
Stillwater	38,008	1,737	1,749	—	17	19	98	352	1,190	61	12
Tahlequah	11,553	634	638	—	3	7	14	105	477	28	4
Tulsa	379,798	27,373	27,613	31	304	868	3,225	6,131	12,545	4,269	240
The Village	11,006	1,005	1,007	—	4	11	17	134	801	38	2
Weatherford	10,292	330	330	—	4	2	6	81	226	11	—
Woodward	12,389	633	636	2	8	2	58	225	313	25	3
Yukon	21,975	908	915	—	7	3	16	129	731	22	7
OREGON											
Albany	32,999	2,854	2,873	2	11	27	32	314	2,262	206	19
Ashland	17,599	885	889	3	6	5	2	107	727	35	4
Astoria	10,577	606	610	—	6	4	15	153	387	41	4
Baker	10,102	841	845	—	—	2	35	194	579	31	4
Beaverton	61,636	3,094	3,111	—	20	54	107	372	2,299	242	17
Bend	24,866	3,238	3,251	—	12	29	86	433	2,530	148	13
Canby	10,231	503	508	—	1	4	2	50	418	28	5
Coos Bay	17,978	1,257	1,262	—	9	8	11	236	935	58	5
Corvallis	48,012	2,600	2,614	1	11	22	44	400	2,022	100	14
Dallas	11,083	394	395	—	3	3	5	57	309	17	1
Eugene	122,637	12,181	12,278	2	50	271	416	1,914	8,765	763	97
Forest Grove	16,112	807	818	—	6	2	20	132	608	39	11
Gladstone	11,210	683	689	—	3	13	9	87	450	121	6
Grants Pass	20,066	2,045	2,054	1	7	23	35	304	1,537	138	9
Gresham	81,598	4,385		1	40	93	150	780	2,563	758	
Hermiston	11,478	688	691	—	4	3	9	134	485	53	3
Keizer	27,998	1,521	1,531	—	4	21	18	242	1,145	91	10
Klamath Falls	19,546	1,230	1,235	2	17	35	73	287	719	97	5
La Grande	13,189	555	557	—	2	4	13	77	441	18	2
Lake Oswego	34,400	1,088	1,101	—	6	8	33	191	806	44	13
Lebanon	12,231	1,048	1,053	1	2	10	18	123	842	52	5
McMinnville	21,068	1,475	1,491	1	13	14	16	205	1,124	102	16
Medford	54,622	4,604	4,654	5	16	33	197	607	3,546	200	50
Milwaukie	21,189	1,092	1,101	—	2	33	30	177	702	148	9

143

City by State	Population	Crime Index total	Modified* Crime Index total	Murder and non-negligent man-slaughter	Forcible rape	Robbery	Aggravated assault	Burglary	Larceny-theft	Motor vehicle theft	Arson*
OREGON — Continued											
North Bend	10,341	522	524	—	2	11	9	63	405	32	2
Ontario	10,739	1,039	1,049	—	1	9	39	132	808	50	10
Oregon City	16,713	1,675	1,698	—	3	37	36	261	1,191	147	23
Pendleton	16,293	857	863	1	5	9	13	163	614	52	6
Portland	467,906	50,306	50,805	51	402	2,057	5,325	7,142	28,823	6,506	499
Roseburg	18,327	1,870	1,880	—	8	32	35	274	1,434	87	10
Salem	119,822	10,732	10,784	7	94	191	102	1,282	8,310	746	52
Springfield	49,623	4,538	4,573	1	21	80	90	759	3,200	387	35
The Dalles	10,637	821	824	—	3	13	10	156	596	43	3
Tigard	36,865	3,056	3,072	1	6	55	35	375	2,395	189	16
Tualatin	19,184	1,351	1,355	2	8	29	20	219	970	103	4
West Linn	19,278	421	423	—	5	1	31	69	291	24	2
Woodburn	14,485	1,109	1,117	1	8	15	27	132	828	98	8
PENNSYLVANIA											
Abington Township	57,211	1,837	1,839	2	5	44	27	147	1,387	225	2
Allentown	105,372	7,443	7,493	6	49	321	276	1,513	4,670	608	50
Altoona	52,548	1,758	1,807	—	18	61	90	508	987	94	49
Aston Township	15,316	318	324	1	1	5	27	35	209	40	6
Baldwin Borough	21,373	212	212	—	2	—	4	40	145	21	—
Bensalem Township	57,686	3,053	3,068	1	22	64	42	445	1,905	574	15
Berwick	10,835	235	240	—	3	7	17	30	156	22	5
Bethel Park	34,297	382	382	1	1	3	13	37	284	43	—
Bethlehem	72,843	2,905	2,920	2	16	93	200	489	1,913	192	15
Bloomsburg Town	12,331	358	359	—	4	2	7	49	279	17	1
Brentwood	10,529	115	115	—	2	—	25	16	61	11	—
Bristol	10,816	431	431	—	3	13	29	50	266	70	—
Bristol Township	58,032	2,759	2,770	3	18	82	123	435	1,745	353	11
Butler	16,900	621	621	1	2	9	13	79	474	43	—
Butler Township	26,403	470		—	1	2	9	27	417	14	
Caln Township	12,185	517		—	3	16	59	45	340	54	
Carlisle	18,981	873	877	5	5	27	29	118	660	29	4
Center Township	10,909	143		—	—	—	11	50	73	9	
Cheltenham Township	35,473	1,995	1,996	2	7	85	24	191	1,326	360	1
Chester	39,479	5,165	5,281	9	72	533	1,385	831	1,514	821	116
Coal Township	10,077	193	193	1	1	—	7	23	150	11	—
Coatesville	11,841	566	577	2	4	52	50	96	279	83	11
Colebrookdale Township	12,804	146	146	—	1	—	16	8	117	4	—
Columbia	11,538	446	453	—	2	12	44	75	249	64	7
Cranberry Township	15,046	273	273	—	—	4	5	24	213	27	—
Cumru Township	19,269	512	512	—	—	2	6	92	387	25	—
Darby	11,057	605	607	—	5	57	117	101	249	76	2
Darby Township	11,126	279	279	1	1	12	16	42	168	39	—
Doylestown Township	14,736	241	241	—	—	1	19	16	184	21	—
Dunmore	14,843	300	300	—	1	4	24	20	241	10	—
East Hempfield Township	18,890	616	616	—	3	6	13	98	474	22	—
East Lampeter Township	12,187	690	692	—	2	10	5	89	548	36	2
East Norriton Township	13,532	458	458	—	—	2	12	51	355	38	—
Easton	27,734	1,600	1,606	3	10	84	92	311	998	102	6
Elizabethtown	10,340	285	287	—	2	4	4	21	246	8	2
Elizabeth Township	14,942	227	227	—	—	—	43	34	138	12	—
Emmaus	12,149	337		—	—	6	13	33	271	14	
Erie	108,432	5,532	5,581	6	68	336	259	1,019	3,458	386	49
Exeter Township	17,531	608	610	2	5	7	41	75	451	27	2
Falls Township	35,548	1,195	1,205	—	7	24	56	253	669	186	10
Franklin Park	10,296	61	61	—	—	1	1	14	43	2	—
Greensburg	16,650	522		—	2	1	89	30	376	24	
Greenville	10,282	178	180	—	1	3	5	38	124	7	2
Hampden Township	20,705	622	626	—	2	9	28	65	493	25	4

City by State	Population	Crime Index total	Modified* Crime Index total	Murder and non-negligent man-slaughter	Forcible rape	Robbery	Aggravated assault	Burglary	Larceny–theft	Motor vehicle theft	Arson*
PENNSYLVANIA — Continued											
Hampton Township	15,811	176	176	—	—	—	22	12	136	6	—
Hanover	14,941	726	728	—	2	7	9	63	627	18	2
Harrisburg	54,255	3,909	3,929	10	63	430	237	785	1,794	590	20
Harrison Township	11,946	390	390	—	2	5	57	25	280	21	—
Hatfield Township	21,083	448	452	—	3	—	9	56	349	31	4
Haverford Township	50,635	950	951	—	1	15	29	108	710	87	1
Hazleton	24,671	590	592	—	4	3	9	139	387	48	2
Hilltown Township	10,746	380		—	1	3	4	32	312	28	
Hopewell Township	13,482	209	210	—		5	12	17	157	18	1
Horsham Township	22,240	451	454	—	1	5	10	74	307	54	3
Indiana	14,953	399	400	—	1	—	12	57	307	22	1
Jefferson	10,063	139	139	1	1	2	9	27	79	20	
Johnstown	27,326	881	896	—	7	26	69	184	551	44	15
Kingston	13,809	340	340	—	1	2	7	25	292	13	—
Lansdowne	11,664	265	266	—	—	10	17	38	172	28	1
Lebanon	25,523	998	1,002	2	11	58	31	128	736	32	4
Lower Allen Township	15,493	411	411	—	2	21	12	38	323	15	—
Lower Gwynedd Township	10,113	277	280	—	2	6	6	64	154	45	3
Lower Makefield Township	25,479	537		—	2	2	18	100	385	30	
Lower Merion Township	58,920	2,173	2,173	2	4	51	9	207	1,510	390	—
Lower Moreland Township	11,951	290	290	—	—	—	6	49	190	45	—
Lower Providence Township	19,655	431	431	—	1	1	6	67	319	37	—
Lower Salford Township	10,902	202		—	—	—	26	26	147	3	
Lower Southampton Township	20,172	617	618	—	4	7	14	89	435	68	1
Manheim Township	29,334	1,085	1,091	—	4	17	43	150	826	45	6
Manor Township	17,388	308	309	1	—	—	8	42	247	10	1
Marple Township	23,486	533	535	—	1	4	34	62	370	62	2
McCandless	29,235	285	286	—	1	1	10	24	235	14	1
McKeesport	25,128	1,096	1,105	—	7	71	50	284	563	121	9
Meadville	14,186	571	573	—	6	8	21	63	455	18	2
Millcreek Township	47,558	1,291	1,307	1	4	14	27	243	930	72	16
Montgomery Township	12,370	719	719	—	2	9	11	44	581	72	—
Moon Township	19,940	420	420	—	4	2	2	73	307	32	—
Morrisville	10,267	306	306	—	1	17	5	41	184	58	—
Mountaintop Regional	16,143	57	57	—	—	—	1	6	47	3	—
Mount Lebanon	33,888	309	313	—	—	6	14	35	250	4	4
Muhlenberg Township	12,834	736	737	—	2	11	27	98	541	57	1
Murrysville	18,473	338	340	—	3	1	5	38	280	11	2
Nanticoke	11,986	305	305	1	1	4	—	44	249	6	—
Nazareth Area	10,356	150	150	—	—	1	2	16	130	1	*
Nether Providence Township	13,437	251	251	—	1	1	19	21	180	29	—
Newberry Township	12,657	313	313	—	1	—	2	39	248	23	—
New Castle	27,806	1,437	1,488	1	17	68	51	349	815	136	51
New Kensington	16,152	594	594	—	4	32	157	98	247	56	—
Newtown Township (Delaware County)	11,542	183	184	1	2	1	3	33	129	14	1
Norristown	32,079	2,737		8	35	179	305	531	1,299	380	
Northern York Regional	55,885	1,454	1,466	—	6	16	15	95	1,280	42	12
Oil City	11,813	419	423	—	4	4	13	57	329	12	4
Palmer Township	15,199	537	538	—	2	—	9	26	487	11	1
Patton Township	10,126	222	224	—	2	—	3	21	190	6	2
Penn Hills	52,291	973	984	—	4	35	46	127	600	161	11
Pennridge Regional	29,750	234	236	—	—	1	9	29	180	15	2
Penn Township (Westmoreland County)	16,195	74	74	—	3	2	7	11	50	1	—
Peters Township	14,693	238	244	—	—	1	7	36	173	21	6
Philadelphia	1,528,403	105,766	108,447	414	704	15,485	6,764	16,204	43,064	23,131	2,681
Phoenixville	15,658	385	385	—	5	13	25	35	264	43	—
Pine Township	14,879	205	205	—	1	1	4	27	147	25	—
Pittsburgh	354,308	18,764	19,012	47	206	1,565	1,030	3,049	10,057	2,810	248

Table 8. — Number of Offenses Known to the Police, Cities and Towns 10,000 and over in Population, 1996 — Continued

City by State	Population	Crime Index total	Modified* Crime Index total	Murder and non-negligent man-slaughter	Forcible rape	Robbery	Aggravated assault	Burglary	Larceny-theft	Motor vehicle theft	Arson*
PENNSYLVANIA — Continued											
Plains Township	11,160	307	309	—	—	5	40	47	188	27	2
Plymouth Township	16,208	957		—	3	14	74	103	630	133	
Pottstown	23,137	1,455	1,461	—	18	46	166	232	903	90	6
Pottsville	16,607	449	451	—	3	6	20	47	348	25	2
Radnor Township	29,155	570	571	—	2	8	7	56	463	34	1
Reading	78,270	8,139	8,196	11	36	491	433	2,038	4,530	600	57
Richland Township	14,154	362	364	—	5	1	75	34	230	17	2
Robinson Township	10,999	342	343	—	—	2	17	35	251	37	1
Ross Township	34,010	692	695	—	—	6	14	70	513	89	3
Rostraver Township	11,398	567	569	—	3	6	16	35	478	29	2
Saint Marys City	22,826	289		—	—	1	39	37	201	11	
Salisbury Township	13,610	389	389	—	—	4	2	34	328	21	—
Scott Township	17,386	209		—	—	2	6	34	136	31	
Shaler Township	31,014	313	314	—	—	2	8	36	243	24	1
Sharon	17,189	841		—	5	19	58	132	576	51	
Southern	11,938	175	176	—	1	1	1	36	129	7	1
South Fayette Township	10,490	142	144	—	3	—	11	14	106	8	2
South Park Township	14,515	105	107	—	—	3	6	29	58	9	2
South Whitehall Township	18,547	701		—	1	9	21	93	563	14	
Springfield Township (Delaware County)	24,540	1,060	1,063	1	3	12	71	67	742	164	3
Spring Township	19,196	280	281	—	2	2	2	64	197	13	1
State College	61,686	1,487	1,490	1	7	12	25	138	1,279	25	3
Stroud Township	10,764	652	653	—	2	10	15	71	522	32	1
Sunbury	11,565	633	637	—	16	2	109	118	360	28	4
Susquehanna Township	18,929	812	816	1	9	21	16	86	603	76	4
Swatara Township	19,970	1,216	1,216	—	1	45	29	130	884	127	—
Towamencin Township	14,388	322	324	—	1	1	12	47	245	16	2
Tredyffrin Township	28,471	803	805	—	1	7	17	66	673	39	2
Upper Chichester Township	15,240	673	680	—	3	17	42	62	456	93	7
Upper Dublin Township	24,406	446	447	—	—	4	12	99	318	13	1
Upper Gwynedd Township	12,388	304	305	—	1	5	4	32	228	34	1
Upper Merion Township	26,126	2,546	2,550	—	1	16	23	163	1,903	440	4
Upper Perkiomen	11,239	199	199	—	—	1	52	25	106	15	—
Upper Providence Township	10,876	102	102	—	—	—	12	16	63	11	—
Upper St. Clair Township	20,001	151	151	—	—	1	3	19	111	17	—
Upper Southampton Township	16,328	315		—	—	2	2	65	230	16	
Uwchlan Township	13,202	253	258	1	—	5	19	57	161	10	5
Warminster Township	33,349	1,027	1,027	—	9	15	35	136	754	78	—
Warren	10,778	265	267	—	2	—	5	47	199	12	2
Warrington Township	12,360	285	285	—	5	2	6	48	204	20	—
Warwick Township	11,802	68	68	—	—	—	—	10	55	3	—
Washington Township	11,291	159	161	—	2	—	11	18	116	12	2
West Chester	18,872	763		—	7	35	32	115	435	139	
West Deer Township	11,547	149	149	—	—	—	—	17	122	10	—
West Goshen Township	18,365	601	605	1	3	4	30	55	469	39	4
West Hempfield Township	13,144	374	374	—	—	7	10	72	255	30	—
West Hills Regional	19,696	66	66	—	—	—	21	11	34	—	—
West Mifflin	23,382	867	869	3	2	32	45	85	560	140	2
West Norriton Township	15,447	505	505	—	2	7	33	48	370	45	—
Westtown Township	28,913	327	327	—	—	1	11	30	277	8	—
West Whiteland Township	12,597	716	719	—	2	6	6	56	575	71	3
Whitehall	14,085	60	60	—	—	1	2	6	45	6	—
Whitehall Township	23,137	1,236	1,260	—	2	28	29	149	926	102	24
Whitpain Township	15,919	357	358	—	2	1	9	34	267	44	1
Wilkinsburg	20,310	1,072		4	13	108	91	297	390	169	
Williamsport	31,863	2,116	2,122	3	13	83	36	392	1,501	88	6

146

City by State	Population	Crime Index total	Modified* Crime Index total	Murder and non-negligent man-slaughter	Forcible rape	Robbery	Aggravated assault	Burglary	Larceny-theft	Motor vehicle theft	Arson*
PENNSYLVANIA — Continued											
Windsor Township	10,305	153	154	—	—	1	3	25	117	7	1
Yeadon	12,097	498	504	—	2	31	8	55	295	107	6
York Township	24,532	672	677	1	4	2	19	85	518	43	5
RHODE ISLAND											
Barrington	15,780	483	502	—	2	2	16	155	305	3	19
Bristol	21,533	365	365	—	1	2	17	67	255	23	—
Burrillville	16,739	284	286	—	4	1	6	81	180	12	2
Central Falls	15,103	782	792	—	17	31	107	183	319	125	10
Coventry	31,185	826	845	2	4	1	28	158	594	39	19
Cranston	76,780	2,392	2,406	1	26	30	59	423	1,534	319	14
Cumberland	29,953	707	708	—	—	3	117	107	436	44	1
East Greenwich	11,902	224	226	—	2	3	7	40	164	8	2
East Providence	49,707	1,102	1,105	—	4	10	14	197	722	155	3
Johnston	27,379	681	690	—	2	7	22	146	433	71	9
Lincoln	18,613	686	687	—	—	3	15	103	506	59	1
Middletown	19,825	617	620	—	8	6	20	107	452	24	3
Narragansett	14,931	450	450	1	1	3	29	102	299	15	—
Newport	24,044	2,115	2,157	—	12	47	187	501	1,281	87	42
North Kingstown	23,704	553	557	—	1	5	26	111	391	19	4
North Providence	33,102	742	754	—	7	21	39	165	425	85	12
North Smithfield	10,826	239	239	—	1	—	44	39	133	22	—
Pawtucket	68,517	3,137	3,172	—	27	110	153	857	1,583	407	35
Portsmouth	17,172	301	310	—	3	3	9	46	226	14	9
Providence	149,805	13,106	13,509	16	77	445	495	2,934	6,720	2,419	403
Scituate	10,102	125	127	—	1	—	5	30	82	7	2
Smithfield	19,767	313	318	—	1	1	11	65	211	24	5
South Kingstown	24,547	525	527	—	3	2	12	113	374	21	2
Tiverton	14,580	265	268	1	3	—	17	48	181	15	3
Warren	11,334	388	392	—	7	3	14	56	296	12	4
Warwick	85,711	3,425	3,458	1	19	29	196	461	2,397	322	33
Westerly	21,530	367	367	—	2	1	2	81	266	15	—
West Warwick	29,364	1,264	1,264	1	3	7	407	170	616	60	—
Woonsocket	40,465	1,196	1,210	1	5	42	99	248	698	103	14
SOUTH CAROLINA											
Aiken	25,166	1,910	1,913	2	8	51	70	302	1,354	123	3
Anderson	30,005	2,711	2,720	4	14	115	416	517	1,484	161	9
Beaufort	10,845	1,321	1,327	1	8	41	92	146	987	46	6
Bennettsville	10,589	1,023	1,029	3	8	39	166	185	584	38	6
Cayce	10,594	1,012	1,014	—	3	24	77	153	547	208	2
Charleston	77,588	8,520	8,540	9	53	399	847	1,240	5,273	699	20
Clemson	11,221	522	522	—	9	8	71	101	314	19	—
Columbia	105,316	12,170	12,203	19	75	481	1,244	1,909	7,511	931	33
Conway	11,158	1,201	1,203	1	3	21	131	177	788	80	2
Easley	19,840	973	973	—	5	20	69	149	684	46	—
Florence	32,695	3,243	3,267	4	18	125	381	517	2,058	140	24
Gaffney	16,114	942	946	1	9	37	169	155	516	55	4
Georgetown	10,006	1,021	1,026	3	4	34	74	213	660	33	5
Goose Creek	27,715	702	710	—	4	11	37	144	471	35	8
Greenville	60,379	6,348	6,367	9	44	227	645	784	4,280	359	19
Greenwood	23,383	2,845	2,851	7	14	70	678	492	1,288	296	6
Greer	12,119	1,270	1,274	—	10	34	117	181	841	87	4
Hanahan	13,008	595	597	—	7	10	41	186	321	30	2
Hartsville	10,308	1,190	1,190	—	3	52	164	231	676	64	—
Irmo	12,916	239	239	—	1	8	8	50	156	16	—
Lancaster	10,060	1,211	1,221	—	10	28	181	171	784	37	10
Laurens	10,382	816	818	5	3	28	145	177	422	36	2

Table 8. — Number of Offenses Known to the Police, Cities and Towns 10,000 and over in Population, 1996 — Continued

City by State	Population	Crime Index total	Modified* Crime Index total	Murder and non-negligent man-slaughter	Forcible rape	Robbery	Aggravated assault	Burglary	Larceny–theft	Motor vehicle theft	Arson*
SOUTH CAROLINA — Continued											
Mauldin	13,252	546	547	—	2	2	58	89	387	8	1
Mount Pleasant	34,753	1,678	1,686	—	4	17	87	168	1,335	67	8
Myrtle Beach	28,314	5,062	5,066	2	24	163	310	1,071	3,185	307	4
Newberry	10,682	625	625	—	4	12	97	69	440	3	—
North Augusta	17,786	955	957	3	5	24	44	153	644	82	2
North Charleston	68,366	10,781	10,813	11	85	431	1,265	1,759	6,014	1,216	32
Orangeburg	13,892	1,478	1,483	2	11	56	197	257	886	69	5
Rock Hill	47,454	3,367	3,387	3	26	99	500	503	2,111	125	20
Simpsonville	13,084	310	311	—	2	1	30	38	226	13	1
Spartanburg	46,157	7,029	7,059	10	51	274	1,262	1,122	3,799	511	30
Summerville	22,731	1,767	1,771	1	13	24	113	248	1,249	119	4
Sumter	43,181	2,807	2,812	5	22	141	350	640	1,381	268	5
Union	10,224	561	563	—	2	24	125	100	289	21	2
West Columbia	12,205	1,314	1,316	—	12	48	123	226	812	93	2
SOUTH DAKOTA											
Aberdeen	25,473	1,084	1,088	—	17	1	38	152	846	30	4
Brookings	17,503	505	505	—	2	2	3	83	393	22	—
Mitchell	14,143	647	649	—	2	1	13	91	514	26	2
Pierre	13,794	627	636	—	7	2	22	85	496	15	9
Rapid City	58,487	3,824	3,835	1	35	43	133	557	2,947	108	11
Sioux Falls	110,891	5,354	5,405	1	82	65	325	864	3,808	209	51
Vermillion	10,536	465	465	—	9	2	7	49	382	16	—
Yankton	13,812	481		—	3	8	68	380	22		
TENNESSEE											
Athens	14,201	1,181	1,182	—	6	28	67	201	809	70	1
Bartlett	33,686	1,116	1,120	—	4	16	50	167	784	95	4
Brentwood	21,840	557	557	—	4	5	9	61	462	16	—
Bristol	25,654	1,185	1,187	—	4	6	94	115	888	78	2
Brownsville	10,740	947	947	4	19	36	116	300	389	83	—
Chattanooga	156,524	14,688	14,814	21	86	556	1,482	2,668	8,665	1,210	126
Clarksville	94,696	5,439	5,439	8	86	115	328	2,102	2,385	415	—
Cleveland	34,662	1,833	1,839	1	12	43	180	412	1,030	155	6
Collierville	20,090	752	756	—	3	6	23	93	581	46	4
Columbia	35,884	2,811	2,829	4	32	68	258	447	1,904	98	18
Franklin	26,032	1,609	1,613	—	11	24	150	140	1,203	81	4
Gallatin	21,543	1,669	1,675	—	5	20	190	211	1,141	102	6
Germantown	36,819	891	891	—	2	9	19	128	673	60	—
Goodlettsville	12,252	1,734	1,735	1	2	29	59	149	1,340	154	1
Greeneville	14,452	845	845	—	6	11	9	235	512	72	—
Hendersonville	37,651	1,465	1,465	3	2	10	42	404	1,004	—	—
Humboldt	11,028	1,114	1,117	—	6	18	111	223	660	96	3
Jackson	55,600	6,256	6,284	16	38	239	524	1,147	3,534	758	28
Johnson City	53,017	3,446	3,478	3	36	57	289	463	2,417	181	32
Kingsport	39,553	1,828	1,842	2	23	24	190	364	1,108	117	14
Knoxville	174,054	10,767	10,874	23	67	593	844	2,341	5,304	1,595	107
La Vergne	11,335	620	623	—	6	9	123	81	342	59	3
Lawrenceburg	11,919	885	885	—	1	7	54	203	586	34	—
Maryville	23,097	672	674	—	8	8	7	132	480	37	2
McMinnville	12,437	1,054	1,055	2	8	7	74	213	676	74	1
Memphis	631,626	70,281	70,901	161	789	5,970	5,615	16,634	26,828	14,284	620
Millington	17,558	889	889	1	5	23	84	255	439	82	—
Morristown	22,635	1,847	1,859	—	6	9	272	204	1,201	155	12
Nashville	530,059	59,467		89	487	2,910	6,535	8,025	33,195	8,226	
Oak Ridge	28,998	1,553	1,560	—	6	28	47	219	1,163	90	7
Red Bank	12,147	725	731	—	3	7	80	125	453	57	6
Sevierville	10,489	605	610	—	6	1	53	92	402	51	5
Shelbyville	16,118	687	689	3	3	21	64	171	388	37	2

Table 8. — Number of Offenses Known to the Police, Cities and Towns 10,000 and over in Population, 1996 — Continued

City by State	Population	Crime Index total	Modified* Crime Index total	Murder and non-negligent man-slaughter	Forcible rape	Robbery	Aggravated assault	Burglary	Larceny-theft	Motor vehicle theft	Arson*
TENNESSEE — Continued											
Smyrna	17,331	1,072	1,079	—	7	20	33	173	774	65	7
Springfield	14,415	1,496	1,496	1	5	30	171	158	1,064	67	—
Union City	11,123	1,322	1,328	1	6	15	73	358	843	26	6
TEXAS											
Abilene	114,523	5,971	5,995	7	66	126	399	1,120	4,008	245	24
Alamo	10,910	597	600	—	—	7	17	175	358	40	3
Alice	21,198	1,259	1,278	1	6	10	101	260	792	89	19
Allen	28,296	953	953	—	7	1	24	159	736	26	—
Alvin	22,415	866	868	1	7	11	51	147	603	46	2
Amarillo	171,770	14,088	14,175	11	71	334	1,012	2,116	9,857	687	87
Andrews	11,169	457	458	1	1	1	20	85	339	10	1
Angleton	19,448	716	720	1	9	9	47	102	501	47	4
Arlington	298,632	21,312	21,372	17	156	618	1,687	3,395	13,165	2,274	60
Athens	11,543	758	759	1	1	4	55	221	443	33	1
Austin	537,484	42,278	42,726	40	270	1,376	2,135	7,575	27,187	3,695	448
Azle	10,035	507	508	—	1	3	28	56	411	8	1
Balch Springs	19,657	1,326		2	18	19	62	249	869	107	
Bay City	19,660	1,439	1,443	—	7	40	77	278	989	48	4
Baytown	70,207	4,163	4,187	6	25	91	206	595	2,736·	504	24
Beaumont	119,715	10,309	10,362	15	203	420	614	1,958	6,362	737	53
Bedford	46,675	1,729	1,734	1	13	31	99	329	1,152	104	5
Beeville	13,006	865	867	1	7	3	61	219	559	15	2
Bellaire	15,266	489	490	—	—	19	31	101	304	34	1
Belton	14,510	447	447	—	7	6	19	86	285	44	—
Benbrook	21,851	423	426	1	10	11	6	84	285	26	3
Big Spring	23,964	1,151	1,161	3	13	11	92	237	742	53	10
Borger	15,524	613	616	—	7	9	45	102	421	29	3
Brenham	13,062	1,027	1,032	1	11	12	192	167	621	23	5
Brownsville	117,511	9,868	9,882	11	22	231	887	1,328	6,911	478	14
Brownwood	19,541	1,730	1,738	1	14	15	109	373	1,156	62	8
Bryan	63,235	4,520	4,532	6	43	83	371	915	2,799	303	12
Burkburnett	10,711	233	239	1	—	1	6	71	152	2	6
Burleson	18,872	717	722	—	2	9	18	116	532	40	5
Canyon	12,235	216	217	—	2	4	5	14	186	5	1
Carrollton	97,897	3,781	3,810	1	15	65	268	659	2,425	348	29
Cedar Hill	25,815	829	831	1	1	7	21	195	538	66	2
Cleburne	24,160	1,408	1,419	—	5	8	59	157	1,133	46	11
Clute	10,136	552	552	—	2	3	33	112	379	23	—
College Station	59,610	2,833	2,838	—	24	32	75	391	2,206	105	5
Colleyville	19,305	288	288	—	—	1	9	36	234	8	—
Conroe	32,150	2,337	2,346	3	14	65	168	287	1,613	187	9
Converse	11,847	226	227	—	4	3	19	74	108	18	1
Coppell	25,309	698	703	—	—	8	20	140	502	28	5
Copperas Cove	29,576	1,321	1,330	—	8	15	52	263	922	61	9
Corpus Christi	286,660	30,467	30,683	18	276	485	2,241	3,773	22,006	1,668	216
Corsicana	23,840	1,718	1,737	2	24	40	64	314	1,182	92	19
Dallas	1,060,585	100,401	102,088	217	740	6,122	9,201	17,960	49,018	17,143	1,687
Deer Park	31,021	681	685	—	8	11	47	162	410	43	4
Del Rio	36,814	2,020	2,024	—	—	36	137	417	1,332	98	4
Denison	22,374	1,631	1,649	1	8	37	124	262	1,146	53	18
Denton	72,034	3,817	3,845	3	35	83	257	583	2,646	210	28
DeSoto	36,183	1,506	1,520	1	9	13	63	342	967	111	14
Dickinson	10,849	559	561	1	2	7	30	98	378	43	2
Donna	15,068	1,093	1,104	2	2	14	41	267	673	94	11
Dumas	14,171	444	445	1	10	6	38	44	327	18	1
Duncanville	37,777	1,989	1,998	1	11	45	164	280	1,291	197	9

Table 8. — Number of Offenses Known to the Police, Cities and Towns 10,000 and over in Population, 1996 — Continued

City by State	Population	Crime Index total	Modified* Crime Index total	Murder and non-negligent man-slaughter	Forcible rape	Robbery	Aggravated assault	Burglary	Larceny-theft	Motor vehicle theft	Arson*
TEXAS — Continued											
Eagle Pass	25,943	1,617	1,620	—	2	3	34	316	1,197	65	3
Edinburg	37,967	3,107	3,129	—	21	42	171	443	2,214	216	22
El Campo	10,834	641	644	2	13	11	31	139	413	32	3
El Paso	602,951	45,134	45,310	30	245	1,195	3,668	3,942	31,694	4,360	176
Ennis	14,885	550	568	1	5	10	66	113	332	23	18
Euless	41,593	1,674	1,688	1	15	25	92	304	1,105	132	14
Farmers Branch	25,509	1,270	1,274	1	1	28	60	235	788	157	4
Flower Mound	29,045	626	628	—	1	2	28	171	410	14	2
Forest Hill	12,581	917	924	—	15	43	63	142	559	95	7
Fort Worth	470,254	38,902	39,266	68	319	1,692	2,905	7,917	21,481	4,520	364
Freeport	12,589	575	581	—	6	7	57	107	355	43	6
Friendswood	29,570	547	557	—	6	5	18	104	383	31	10
Frisco	11,226	383	383	—	1	1	17	92	253	19	—
Gainesville	14,740	547	551	1	3	9	22	95	377	40	4
Galena Park	10,638	275	276	—	1	5	28	69	153	19	1
Galveston	61,641	6,066	6,111	11	62	265	755	911	3,380	682	45
Garland	201,336	9,562	9,640	14	63	210	490	1,786	6,150	849	78
Gatesville	12,464	180	183	—	2	1	12	57	96	12	3
Georgetown	18,315	653	660	—	3	4	31	130	458	27	7
Grand Prairie	112,930	6,882	6,887	3	50	147	956	1,068	3,734	924	5
Grapevine	38,175	1,219	1,224	—	12	12	50	196	867	82	5
Greenville	23,553	2,365	2,423	2	12	78	177	500	1,496	100	58
Groves	17,522	936	936	1	3	11	16	138	723	44	—
Haltom City	35,881	1,905	1,911	—	40	38	172	435	1,047	173	6
Harker Heights	18,575	799	800	1	11	11	61	120	572	23	1
Harlingen	57,787	4,541	4,551	—	1	54	263	1,045	2,962	216	10
Henderson	12,235	1,341	1,341	1	9	22	208	143	883	75	—
Hereford	15,458	691	692	—	2	7	58	105	500	19	1
Hewitt	10,863	190	190	1	3	4	5	54	113	10	—
Highland Village	10,167	126	126	—	—	1	1	21	100	3	—
Houston	1,772,143	135,329	137,082	261	1,002	8,276	12,917	25,402	65,080	22,391	1,753
Humble	13,631	1,566	1,572	—	4	22	62	180	1,001	297	6
Huntsville	30,177	1,327	1,331	—	8	40	156	200	852	71	4
Hurst	36,694	2,192	2,209	1	27	42	145	250	1,614	113	17
Irving	170,960	9,483	9,548	8	65	202	529	1,480	6,342	857	65
Jacinto City	10,494	401	401	—	1	15	13	103	230	39	—
Jacksonville	13,062	891	892	2	12	14	55	152	633	23	1
Keller	19,587	288	289	—	3	1	4	85	186	9	1
Kerrville	19,767	870	877	2	11	19	42	122	632	42	7
Kilgore	11,823	976	980	4	5	13	61	128	723	42	4
Killeen	86,237	5,290	5,471	2	82	142	253	932	3,616	263	181
Kingsville	26,757	1,585	1,592	4	13	12	98	268	1,138	52	7
Lake Jackson	26,106	900	902	—	5	3	3	70	775	44	2
La Marque	15,386	902	904	1	2	18	19	195	605	62	2
Lamesa	10,994	447	450	—	2	3	93	97	240	12	3
Lancaster	24,351	1,315	1,335	1	17	28	74	207	888	100	20
La Porte	32,183	1,122	1,123	1	18	14	66	322	643	58	1
Laredo	156,032	11,240	11,322	11	27	242	760	1,672	7,477	1,051	82
League City	38,613	1,299	1,300	—	3	11	20	215	991	59	1
Leon Valley	10,783	684			5	4	17	78	538	42	
Levelland	15,105	509	512	—	3	—	11	69	404	22	3
Lewisville	53,230	3,546	3,555	—	22	46	71	548	2,588	271	9
Live Oak	11,403	367	368	3	5	3	26	32	264	34	1
Lockhart	10,347	603	603	1	8	12	104	112	351	15	—
Longview	76,254	6,119	6,160	8	69	176	268	994	4,020	584	41
Lubbock	202,403	12,948	13,044	15	126	276	1,649	2,456	7,472	954	96
Lufkin	32,952	2,270	2,275	5	10	65	174	372	1,545	99	5
Mansfield	19,973	791	796	1	3	6	77	162	505	37	5

City by State	Population	Crime Index total	Modified* Crime Index total	Murder and non-negligent man-slaughter	Forcible rape	Robbery	Aggravated assault	Burglary	Larceny-theft	Motor vehicle theft	Arson*
TEXAS — Continued											
Marshall	24,275	2,190	2,198	6	24	56	151	404	1,346	203	8
McAllen	99,188	10,697	10,744	5	23	148	370	1,475	7,730	946	47
McKinney	27,606	1,793	1,797	1	19	36	135	243	1,262	97	4
Mercedes	14,927	512	516	1	5	5	97	170	197	37	4
Mesquite	117,795	6,452	6,580	3	8	64	363	564	4,781	669	128
Midland	100,087	4,966	4,984	4	58	80	235	1,030	3,273	286	18
Mineral Wells	15,245	924	935	—	8	2	81	199	593	41	11
Mission	40,005	2,474	2,479	2	9	17	37	619	1,540	250	5
Missouri City	47,171	1,687	1,703	1	17	57	57	546	913	96	16
Mount Pleasant	13,411	919	923	1	5	8	168	125	560	52	4
Nacogdoches	33,051	1,279	1,298	2	12	36	240	198	743	48	19
Nederland	17,616	922	922	—	4	13	8	125	739	33	—
New Braunfels	32,423	2,084	2,090	1	10	26	72	355	1,554	66	6
North Richland Hills	57,734	2,410	2,416	1	12	36	80	457	1,613	211	6
Odessa	98,630	6,748	6,811	14	35	128	928	1,198	4,136	309	63
Orange	20,712	1,803	1,809	2	11	66	154	362	1,114	94	6
Palestine	19,046	1,632	1,638	—	21	35	228	260	1,037	51	6
Pampa	20,351	949	949	1	4	15	57	173	653	46	—
Paris	25,551	2,666	2,678	4	10	38	449	342	1,737	86	12
Pasadena	134,568	7,278	7,371	9	63	189	642	1,408	3,983	984	93
Pearland	25,953	868	869	—	9	11	45	139	595	69	1
Pecos	12,141	352	352	—	1	3	24	76	238	10	—
Pharr	38,068	3,152	3,162	3	22	55	311	602	1,823	336	10
Plainview	23,235	1,315	1,333	—	11	10	91	313	867	23	18
Plano	163,817	8,318	8,329	—	49	97	423	1,443	5,918	388	11
Port Arthur	61,194	4,125	4,200	5	21	153	450	1,067	1,952	477	75
Portland	14,197	376	378	—	1	2	6	73	279	15	2
Port Lavaca	12,021	629	635	1	—	4	39	157	394	34	6
Port Neches	14,043	524	524	—	5	2	20	87	383	27	—
Richardson	81,906	3,768	3,788	4	20	67	162	594	2,724	197	20
Richmond	13,125	648	650	1	3	17	43	130	415	39	2
Rio Grande City	10,791	682	689	—	1	2	64	134	433	48	7
Robstown	13,834	648	648	—	1	10	59	248	288	42	—
Rockwall	14,253	504	505	—	6	5	21	87	357	28	1
Rosenberg	22,404	1,689	1,758	3	20	70	125	315	1,043	113	69
Round Rock	43,125	1,437	1,442	—	14	26	52	255	1,014	76	5
Rowlett	32,307	1,127	1,145	2	3	12	44	264	767	35	18
San Angelo	92,346	5,275		2	37	39	375	739	3,923	160	
San Antonio	1,021,477	87,710	88,601	117	637	2,350	1,637	13,685	60,488	8,796	891
San Benito	24,268	2,188	2,191	—	8	11	99	347	1,644	79	3
San Juan	13,624	850	851	1	6	14	37	244	470	78	1
San Marcos	32,284	1,497	1,500	—	23	25	109	259	1,016	65	3
Schertz	13,211	446	451	1	3	5	21	86	320	10	5
Seagoville	10,425	569	569	—	6	7	51	107	351	47	—
Seguin	20,675	1,522	1,522	1	7	33	44	283	1,103	51	—
Sherman	32,825	2,604	2,614	2	55	54	148	388	1,838	119	10
Snyder	12,655	431	433	1	5	1	31	74	306	13	2
Socorro	27,639	535	537	—	—	—	85	116	285	49	2
South Houston	15,329	953	954	1	—	38	44	189	543	138	1
Southlake	12,848	357	357	—	1	5	21	73	252	5	—
Stafford	10,959	838	841	4	10	26	26	134	532	106	3
Stephenville	14,789	763	765	—	3	2	22	88	620	28	2
Sugar Land	32,130	1,831	1,837	1	5	37	88	275	1,352	73	6
Sulphur Springs	15,128	695	695	—	7	12	85	126	422	43	—
Sweetwater	12,467	609	610	1	6	7	54	130	391	20	1
Taylor	12,614	737	741	1	1	11	74	131	487	32	4
Temple	54,212	3,625	3,663	1	12	80	200	553	2,556	223	38
Terrell	13,561	973	978	1	—	23	55	201	622	71	5

City by State	Population	Crime Index total	Modified* Crime Index total	Murder and non-negligent man-slaughter	Forcible rape	Robbery	Aggravated assault	Burglary	Larceny–theft	Motor vehicle theft	Arson*
TEXAS — Continued											
Texarkana	33,784	2,856	2,893	6	23	72	248	591	1,772	144	37
Texas City	43,361	4,984	5,010	7	34	116	418	1,456	2,545	408	26
The Colony	27,555	766	772	—	11	7	16	143	566	23	6
Tyler	83,467	6,405	6,440	9	54	191	376	952	4,466	357	35
Universal City	14,192	696	698	—	5	7	44	90	528	22	2
University Park	23,234	534	541	—	—	12	7	63	421	31	7
Uvalde	16,249	778	781	—	—	3	76	174	505	20	3
Vernon	12,211	364	375	—	—	8	24	111	206	15	11
Victoria	63,056	3,912	3,927	2	29	60	506	748	2,394	173	15
Vidor	11,818	551	555	2	—	4	31	98	390	26	4
Village	12,900	177	177	—	—	9	4	59	100	5	—
Waco	110,213	11,553	11,638	14	92	386	860	2,092	6,832	1,277	85
Watauga	24,124	595	597	—	5	6	18	134	421	11	2
Waxahachie	20,398	1,170	1,173	3	2	32	50	173	837	73	3
Weatherford	18,645	743	747	—	2	7	30	127	541	36	4
Weslaco	26,211	2,422	2,426	2	7	37	103	512	1,428	333	4
West University Place	14,415	211	212	—	—	12	4	47	136	12	1
White Settlement	17,174	872	878	1	3	9	63	127	603	66	6
Wichita Falls	101,755	6,704	6,742	9	81	152	636	1,020	4,436	370	38
Wylie	10,342	367	371	—	4	2	20	65	264	12	4
UTAH											
American Fork	19,071	881	881	—	3	3	53	93	686	43	—
Bountiful	38,863	1,123	1,123	1	9	4	42	163	857	47	—
Brigham City	17,418	1,337	1,342	—	14	13	46	237	975	52	5
Cedar City	16,506	941	942	—	1	5	33	124	716	62	1
Centerville	14,442	570	572	—	—	1	6	222	324	17	2
Clearfield	24,470	670	672	—	9	10	20	82	523	26	2
Farmington	10,649	280	285	—	1	—	14	32	210	23	5
Kaysville	17,682	388	392	—	3	1	8	62	297	17	4
Layton	56,005	2,160	2,173	2	17	4	70	305	1,605	157	13
Lehi	11,074	452	452	—	4	2	17	106	299	24	—
Logan	37,817	1,717	1,724	—	7	2	22	253	1,407	26	7
Midvale	12,665	1,145	1,152	3	10	9	55	151	822	95	7
Murray	34,972	4,037	4,050	2	19	48	73	450	3,244	201	13
North Ogden	13,710	257	257	1	—	—	4	33	215	4	—
Ogden	71,030	6,434	6,449	5	57	102	218	927	4,719	406	15
Orem	77,990	4,144	4,146	1	17	16	44	426	3,510	130	2
Payson	11,359	607	607	—	6	2	13	105	432	49	—
Pleasant Grove	21,804	814	822	—	5	—	14	111	634	50	8
Provo	92,787	3,507	3,540	1	45	20	100	533	2,604	204	33
St. George	40,827	2,163	2,171	2	16	8	78	279	1,668	112	8
Salt Lake City	180,180	22,283	22,360	20	152	591	738	3,015	14,898	2,869	77
Sandy	89,524	4,011	4,018	1	9	34	134	679	2,989	165	7
South Jordan	17,726	685	686	—	3	4	26	111	485	56	1
South Ogden	13,597	661	664	—	3	2	21	102	506	27	3
South Salt Lake	11,735	3,198	3,202	—	13	59	156	361	2,254	355	4
Spanish Fork	14,173	757	763	—	2	1	9	137	584	24	6
Springville	16,521	750	755	—	6	1	16	103	614	10	5
Tooele	15,510	862	862	—	3	2	24	121	669	43	—
West Jordan	52,388	2,886	2,896	—	11	16	53	446	2,195	165	10
VERMONT[1]											
Brattleboro	12,786	755	756	1	4	10	35	107	556	42	1
Burlington	38,726	3,338	3,345	2	26	22	24	818	2,328	118	7
Essex	17,234	606	607	—	9	—	6	85	474	32	1
VIRGINIA											
Alexandria	114,996	7,143	7,157	7	45	318	266	945	4,615	947	14
Alexandria State Police		5		—	—	1	1	—	1	2	
Blacksburg	35,891	897	907	2	2	8	42	142	661	40	10

See footnotes at end of table.

Table 8. — Number of Offenses Known to the Police, Cities and Towns 10,000 and over in Population, 1996 — Continued

City by State	Population	Crime Index total	Modified* Crime Index total	Murder and non-negligent man-slaughter	Forcible rape	Robbery	Aggravated assault	Burglary	Larceny-theft	Motor vehicle theft	Arson*
VIRGINIA — Continued											
Bristol	18,407	673	684	—	4	11	54	94	479	31	11
Bristol State Police		2		—	—	—	—	1	1	—	
Charlottesville	41,803	2,817	2,831	2	26	73	152	397	2,037	130	14
Chesapeake	183,965	8,463	8,576	13	49	284	458	1,529	5,596	534	113
Chesapeake State Police		12	13	—	—	—	2	2	6	2	1
Christiansburg	17,860	704	711	2	4	1	30	126	521	20	7
Colonial Heights	16,755	1,119	1,132	1	2	25	12	67	978	34	13
Danville	55,244	2,797	2,817	9	21	86	110	417	2,004	150	20
Fairfax City	21,041	1,216	1,216	2	2	18	47	142	928	77	—
Fredericksburg	22,575	684	687	1	8	22	51	51	508	43	3
Fredericksburg State Police		6		—	—	—	2	—	4	—	
Front Royal	13,672	612	616	—	5	4	9	64	480	50	4
Hampton	142,248	7,167	7,223	10	56	323	203	962	5,151	462	56
Hampton State Police		13	13	—	—	3	—	—	6	4	—
Harrisonburg	33,890	1,414	1,416	3	12	27	33	172	1,095	72	2
Harrisonburg State Police		2		—	—	—	1	—	1	—	
Herndon	18,173	819	820	1	5	26	15	73	644	55	1
Hopewell	24,911	1,895	1,895	1	13	58	390	228	1,162	43	—
Hopewell State Police		1		—	—	—	—	—	1	—	
Leesburg	20,147	809	810	—	6	19	37	80	631	36	1
Lynchburg	67,738	3,401	3,437	6	24	102	339	509	2,233	188	36
Lynchburg State Police		1		—	—	—	—	—	1	—	
Manassas	32,470	1,274	1,277	2	11	25	57	154	911	114	3
Martinsville	16,114	1,027	1,031	2	8	26	68	164	695	64	4
Newport News	182,487	9,829	9,926	27	110	363	676	1,224	6,850	579	97
Newport News State Police		6	6	—	—	—	2	—	3	1	—
Norfolk	245,956	18,854	18,974	61	142	1,079	1,050	2,766	12,053	1,703	120
Norfolk State Police		15	15	—	—	—	2	—	5	8	—
Petersburg	41,701	3,362	3,368	6	27	199	302	654	1,876	298	6
Petersburg State Police		4	4	—	—	—	1	—	3	—	
Poquoson	11,902	199	200	1	1	3	33	30	125	6	1
Portsmouth	105,404	8,582	8,649	23	57	532	454	1,605	5,040	871	67
Portsmouth State Police		4	4	—	—	—	—	—	4	—	5
Pulaski	10,068	353	358	—	2	3	22	37	281	8	5
Radford	16,084	377	379	1	4	4	29	86	235	18	2
Richmond	204,881	19,771	19,942	112	143	1,545	1,583	4,022	10,338	2,028	171
Richmond State Police		10	10	—	—	—	—	—	6	4	—
Roanoke	98,456	6,217	6,259	15	42	273	247	933	4,396	311	42
Roanoke State Police		2	2	—	—	—	—	—	2	—	—
Salem	24,671	768	771	1	7	13	6	55	642	44	3
Staunton	25,306	920	928	2	4	9	50	102	732	21	8
Staunton State Police		1		—	—	—	—	—	1	—	
Suffolk	55,952	3,316	3,338	5	30	112	251	532	2,158	228	22
Suffolk State Police		1		—	—	—	—	—	1	—	
Vienna	16,083	416	418	—	1	7	10	45	336	17	2
Virginia Beach	439,851	20,819	21,041	20	127	455	473	3,063	15,688	993	222
Virginia Beach State Police		13	13	—	—	—	3	—	4	6	—
Waynesboro	19,100	897	906	1	11	14	79	128	604	60	9
Waynesboro State Police		1		—	—	—	—	—	—	1	
Williamsburg	12,795	532	532	—	2	13	34	25	424	34	—
Williamsburg State Police		1		—	—	—	—	—	—	1	
Winchester	24,241	2,031	2,048	3	11	36	111	269	1,539	62	17
Winchester State Police		6	6	—	1	1	—	—	4	—	
WASHINGTON											
Aberdeen	17,450	1,828	1,841	1	16	16	31	190	1,513	61	13
Anacortes	13,327	715	725	—	6	4	15	86	582	22	10
Auburn	37,780	3,644	3,670	3	40	71	98	478	2,549	405	26
Bellevue	87,234	5,341	5,378	3	28	59	96	602	4,158	395	37

City by State	Population	Crime Index total	Modified* Crime Index total	Murder and non-negligent man-slaughter	Forcible rape	Robbery	Aggravated assault	Burglary	Larceny–theft	Motor vehicle theft	Arson*
WASHINGTON — Continued											
Bellingham	59,149	4,725	4,757	1	22	64	105	603	3,781	149	32
Bonney Lake	10,590	413	414	—	3	3	8	68	310	21	1
Bothell	13,508	973	985	1	6	13	15	132	721	85	12
Bremerton	43,822	2,639	2,649	2	44	82	150	500	1,683	178	10
Burien	29,695	2,259	2,274	—	25	55	92	298	1,388	401	15
Centralia	13,084	1,647	1,655	1	12	18	50	203	1,281	82	8
Des Moines	19,479	1,403	1,411	1	17	37	44	277	823	204	8
Edmonds	31,419	1,522	1,527	—	8	21	20	299	1,040	134	5
Ellensburg	13,977	795	798	—	5	3	37	102	624	24	3
Federal Way	75,390	6,272	6,307	3	70	182	172	960	4,086	799	35
Kelso	12,678	1,264	1,273	2	21	20	12	224	890	95	9
Kennewick	49,810	3,142	3,167	—	25	42	105	452	2,366	152	25
Kent	42,587	5,648	5,704	2	34	141	114	1,106	3,500	751	56
Kirkland	43,757	2,110	2,123	—	15	30	61	281	1,580	143	13
Lacey	23,598	1,225	1,233	2	26	26	22	247	829	73	8
Longview	33,867	2,880	2,926	2	12	25	89	643	1,900	209	46
Lynnwood	31,644	3,112	3,139	—	14	41	35	294	2,496	232	27
Marysville	12,129	766	773	1	15	12	18	124	541	55	7
Mercer Island	21,690	308	310	1	1	1	8	52	235	10	2
Moses Lake	13,982	1,688	1,693	6	22	12	90	180	1,319	59	5
Mountlake Terrace	20,344	927	943	—	5	16	33	128	635	110	16
Mount Vernon	21,414	2,017	2,037	—	13	18	26	208	1,685	67	20
Oak Harbor	19,371	666	679	—	8	8	16	80	538	16	13
Olympia	41,136	3,041	3,072	1	29	45	86	472	2,222	186	31
Pasco	24,051	2,004	2,009	2	18	33	104	244	1,416	187	5
Port Angeles	19,581	1,063	1,084	1	18	13	25	212	757	37	21
Puyallup	27,851	2,529	2,556	3	8	27	45	205	2,035	206	27
Redmond	41,173	1,614	1,628	—	16	14	13	199	1,294	78	14
Renton	45,077	4,246	4,270	2	32	127	95	664	2,744	582	24
Richland	37,010	1,443	1,473	1	18	9	46	205	1,108	56	30
Sea Tac	24,965	2,332	2,347	3	43	72	95	466	1,256	397	15
Seattle	539,591	55,636	55,886	37	261	1,963	2,282	7,855	36,883	6,355	250
Shoreline	49,110	2,237	2,248	—	19	28	53	394	1,483	260	11
Spokane	199,636	16,286	16,327	15	89	346	858	3,032	11,101	845	41
Sunnyside	13,262	1,095	1,102	2	9	11	95	192	706	80	7
Tacoma	189,568	20,143	20,268	20	137	792	1,836	3,284	11,255	2,819	125
Tukwila	13,028	3,727	3,732	2	20	114	102	360	2,806	323	5
Tumwater	11,921	787	792	1	5	10	17	169	517	68	5
Vancouver	53,689	4,988	5,015	3	73	126	369	916	2,961	540	27
Walla Walla	30,226	2,634	2,663	1	32	24	230	421	1,831	95	29
Wenatchee	24,137	2,235	2,251	—	17	30	64	281	1,765	78	16
Yakima	64,179	7,508	7,537	7	50	115	375	1,351	4,950	660	29
WEST VIRGINIA											
Beckley	18,492	1,355	1,366	1	5	32	105	181	956	75	11
Bluefield	12,620	294	301	1	—	16	37	75	155	10	7
Charleston	56,244	6,117	6,168	7	26	248	303	1,036	4,041	456	51
Clarksburg	17,716	560	561	1	10	7	14	71	433	24	1
Fairmont	20,671	522	527	1	6	10	10	105	367	23	5
Huntington	53,905	3,534	3,589	4	73	92	143	735	2,301	186	55
Martinsburg	14,953	997	998	—	—	9	23	85	839	41	1
Morgantown	26,575	1,281	1,294	1	13	11	72	249	869	66	13
Moundsville	10,824	436	437	—	1	5	19	113	271	27	1
Parkersburg	33,173	1,758	1,787	—	20	21	58	370	1,208	81	29
St. Albans	10,846	313	315	—	1	3	2	55	224	28	2
South Charleston	13,438	527	527	—	1	7	9	51	409	50	—
Vienna	11,053	385	386	—	2	—	1	13	358	11	1
Weirton	21,528	360	366	—	1	7	13	72	245	22	6
Wheeling	34,042	1,455	1,462	1	11	37	108	362	866	70	7

Table 8. — Number of Offenses Known to the Police, Cities and Towns 10,000 and over in Population, 1996 — Continued

City by State	Population	Crime Index total	Modified* Crime Index total	Murder and non-negligent man-slaughter	Forcible rape	Robbery	Aggravated assault	Burglary	Larceny–theft	Motor vehicle theft	Arson*
WISCONSIN											
Appleton	70,661	2,237	2,251	1	14	11	27	285	1,848	51	14
Ashwaubenon	17,535	991	995	—	3	2	13	58	886	29	4
Baraboo	10,417	558	558	—	—	3	18	39	479	19	—
Beaver Dam	15,051	647	652	—	1	3	25	48	555	15	5
Beloit	37,205	1,995	2,012	1	17	73	50	204	1,545	105	17
Brookfield	37,378	1,458	1,489	2	2	16	6	106	1,253	73	31
Brown Deer	12,079	530	534	—	—	14	4	53	419	40	4
Caledonia	22,926	437	441	—	2	3	6	104	298	24	4
Cedarburg	10,824	177	177	—	1	1	1	13	158	3.	—
Chippewa Falls	13,581	410	413	—	1	4	7	65	321	12	3
Cudahy	18,543	736	753	—	6	4	22	116	527	61	17
De Pere	19,165	623	623	—	1	6	12	104	471	29	—
Eau Claire	59,372	2,945	2,975	4	16	21	154	453	2,202	95	30
Everest	14,328	518	524	—	1	2	12	65	409	29	6
Fitchburg	17,304	818	818	—	5	9	22	95	660	27	—
Fond du Lac	39,943	2,185	2,187	2	10	5	27	119	1,945	77	2
Fort Atkinson	11,372	383	387	—	—	—	2	36	338	7	4
Fox Valley	15,623	485	486	—	—	—	1	54	422	8	1
Franklin	22,059	534	539	—	11	7	21	86	375	34	5
Germantown	16,479	426	428	—	3	2	4	62	337	18	2
Glendale	13,406	1,020	1,020	—	2	25	6	62	866	59	—
Grand Chute	14,973	1,054	1,054	—	6	6	9	54	948	31	—
Green Bay	104,283	4,679	4,710	3	39	68	280	584	3,481	224	31
Greendale	14,848	749	749	1	—	4	5	7	716	16	—
Greenfield	32,542	1,313	1,317	—	4	21	9	153	998	128	4
Janesville	57,733	3,791	3,815	2	18	20	103	635	2,853	160	24
Kaukauna	12,092	283	284	1	—	1	9	43	223	6	1
Kenosha	86,427	3,352	3,369	3	49	104	150	577	2,214	255	17
La Crosse	51,657	2,747	2,759	1	22	16	30	204	2,412	62	12
Madison	197,572	9,096	9,154	1	75	299	397	1,389	6,294	641	58
Manitowoc	33,582	1,560	1,561	—	8	3	26	191	1,276	56	1
Marinette	12,453	452	456	1	5	1	5	57	365	18	4
Marshfield	19,933	790	791	—	6	1	3	118	631	31	1
Menasha	15,795	576	580	—	2	1	9	42	508	14	4
Menasha Town	14,621	288	292	—	—	—	1	65	208	14	4
Menomonee Falls	28,884	827	832	—	—	8	4	144	612	59	5
Menomonie	15,157	947	952	—	2	2	2	106	801	34	5
Mequon	21,807	183	184	—	—	1	2	40	129	11	1
Merrill	10,286	501	504	—	1	1	7	37	441	14	3
Middleton	14,670	453	453	—	3	1	2	58	369	20	—
Milwaukee	627,139	49,623	50,220	130	281	3,353	2,210	7,622	25,948	10,079	597
Monroe	10,709	339	339	—	6	2	7	36	273	15	—
Mount Pleasant	21,961	890	894	—	4	15	16	150	637	68	4
Muskego	20,276	231	232	—	2	—	3	42	172	12	1
Neenah	24,751	830	834	—	1	4	38	121	633	33	4
New Berlin	36,483	719	732	1	1	1	29	143	512	32	13
Oak Creek	19,593	704	711	1	3	10	4	62	578	46	7
Oconomowoc	11,956	357	358	—	1	2	11	47	276	20	1
Onalaska	12,878	333	333	—	—	—	27	6	293	7	—
Oshkosh	57,091	2,787	2,794	—	16	11	75	348	2,229	108	7
Pewaukee Township	10,043	170	170	—	3	—	2	24	133	8	—
Platteville	10,367	254	254	—	3	1	3	22	224	1	—
Pleasant Prairie	13,549	411	414	1	1	3	7	44	347	8	3
Plover	11,955	224	224	—	1	1	7	34	172	9	—
Port Washington	10,102	295	296	—	1	1	4	19	259	11	1
Racine	87,334	6,228	6,270	12	17	316	312	1,167	3,744	660	42
River Falls	11,696	568	568	—	1	1	7	27	519	13	—
Sheboygan	51,140	2,599	2,625	—	15	12	61	405	2,020	86	26

Table 8. — Number of Offenses Known to the Police, Cities and Towns 10,000 and over in Population, 1996 — Continued

City by State	Population	Crime Index total	Modified* Crime Index total	Murder and non-negligent man-slaughter	Forcible rape	Robbery	Aggravated assault	Burglary	Larceny–theft	Motor vehicle theft	Arson*
WISCONSIN — Continued											
Shorewood	13,729	549	549	—	1	16	3	44	463	22	—
South Milwaukee	20,516	856	863	1	4	13	4	158	642	34	7
Stevens Point	21,594	1,452	1,453	—	7	10	53	239	1,106	37	1
Stoughton	10,477	453	453	—	—	1	12	77	350	13	—
Sun Prairie	17,674	713	722	—	8	—	19	93	579	14	9
Superior	27,968	1,955	1,975	1	13	18	36	324	1,464	99	20
Two Rivers	13,389	475	476	—	4	1	14	69	373	14	1
Watertown	21,002	739	747	—	12	5	9	114	568	31	8
Waukesha	61,060	1,902	1,906	—	10	30	64	282	1,400	116	4
Wausau	39,395	1,574	1,592	2	15	11	49	199	1,215	83	18
Wauwatosa	48,425	2,454	2,454	—	1	63	29	339	1,798	224	—
West Allis	62,198	3,103	3,133	2	5	61	78	394	2,241	322	30
West Bend	27,633	1,355	1,360	—	1	5	30	77	1,207	35	5
Whitefish Bay	14,282	292	292	—	—	4	1	22	249	16	—
Whitewater	13,877	325	329	—	3	2	8	41	261	10	4
Wisconsin Rapids	18,626	993	994	—	4	—	15	184	759	31	1
WYOMING											
Casper	49,708	3,149	3,193	—	17	22	86	595	2,299	130	44
Cheyenne	54,195	2,762		1	20	22	46	276	2,327	70	
Evanston	12,117	665	665	—	4	2	18	99	520	22	—
Gillette	18,957	1,124		—	3	4	91	101	893	32	
Green River	13,573	495		2	1	—	13	51	420	8	
Riverton	10,165	709		—	1	5	27	95	552	29	
Rock Springs	20,355	1,263		—	10	8	102	197	906	40	
Sheridan	14,953	599	602	—	7	4	27	66	468	27	3

[1] Complete data were not available for the states of Illinois, Kansas, Kentucky, Montana, and Vermont; therefore, it was necessary that their crime counts be estimated. An aggregate Florida state total for 1996 was supplied by the Florida Department of Law Enforcement. See "Offense Estimation," pages 389-390 for details.

[2] Forcible rape figures furnished by the state-level Uniform Crime Reporting (UCR) Program administered by the Illinois Department of State Police were not in accordance with national UCR guidelines. Therefore, the figures are excluded from the forcible rape, Crime Index total, and Modified Crime Index total categories.

[3] Due to reporting changes or annexations, figures are not comparable to previous years.

[4] Indianapolis/Marion County, Indiana is a unified city-county government with a total population of 777,458.

Table 9. — Number of Offenses Known to the Police, Universities and Colleges, 1996

*Arson is shown only if 12 months of arson data were received. Dashes (—) indicate zero data.

University/College	Student enrollment[1]	Violent[2] crime total	Violent Crime				Property[3] crime total	Property Crime			
			Murder and non-negligent man-slaughter	Forcible rape	Robbery	Aggravated assault		Burglary	Larceny-theft	Motor vehicle theft	Arson*
ALABAMA											
Alabama State University	5,037	9	—	—	5	4	168	7	159	2	
Auburn University:											
Main Campus	21,226	4	—	—	2	2	317	10	305	2	
Montgomery	6,148	—	—	—	—	—	46	1	43	2	
Jacksonville State University	7,553	3	—	—	1	2	85	8	76	1	
Livingston State University	4	1	—	—	—	1	19	—	19	—	
Talladega College	976	2	—	—	—	2	22	—	22	—	
Troy State University	6,458	2	—	—	—	2	102	8	92	2	1
University of Alabama:											
Huntsville	7,492	—	—	—	—	—	73	—	73	—	—
Tuscaloosa	4	9	—	1	3	5	466	28	435	3	—
University of Montevallo	3,282	—	—	—	—	—	9	—	9	—	
University of North Alabama	5,221	—	—	—	—	—	52	12	38	2	—
University of South Alabama	12,386	14	—	2	8	4	216	20	196	—	—
ALASKA											
University of Alaska, Fairbanks	7,703	20	—	7	1	12	95	1	93	1	—
ARIZONA											
Arizona State University:											
Main Campus	42,189	51	—	3	10	38	1,584	632	907	45	2
West	4,681	—	—	—	—	—	44	13	30	1	—
Arizona Western College	5,647	4	—	—	—	4	76	8	65	3	—
Central Arizona College	4,369	2	—	1	—	1	95	13	81	1	—
Northern Arizona University	19,242	18	—	2	2	14	507	57	446	4	6
Pima Community College	27,960	1	—	—	—	1	159	34	108	17	—
University of Arizona	35,306	10	—	—	3	7	1,105	157	902	46	10
Yavapai College	4,953	2	—	2	—	—	45	2	43	—	1
ARKANSAS											
Arkansas State University	9,631	9	—	—	2	7	238	49	185	4	—
Henderson State University	4,033	1	—	—	—	1	53	7	46	—	2
University of Arkansas:											
Fayetteville	14,495	3	—	—	1	2	255	68	182	5	3
Little Rock	11,451	3	—	—	—	3	118	11	100	7	1
Medical Sciences	1,864	5	—	—	1	4	196	15	178	3	—
Monticello	2,394	—	—	—	—	—	23	5	18	—	—
Pine Bluff	3,823	28	—	—	2	26	143	49	84	10	—
University of Central Arkansas	9,192	4	—	1	—	3	132	17	114	1	1
CALIFORNIA											
Allen Hancock College	7,384	—	—	—	—	—	52	4	47	1	2
Cabrillo Community College	12,212	1	—	—	—	1	62	13	48	1	—
California State Polytechnic University:											
Pomona	16,304	4	—	—	1	3	359	27	287	45	—
San Luis Obispo	15,440	3	—	1	1	1	393	32	354	7	1
California State University:											
Bakersfield	5,086	4	—	—	1	3	51	10	41	—	7
Chico	14,232	2	—	1	1	—	280	15	262	3	3
Dominiguez Hills	9,744	1	—	—	—	1	105	46	52	7	1
Fresno	17,293	20	—	—	7	13	482	59	338	85	5
Fullerton	22,097	15	—	1	1	13	394	19	326	49	2
Hayward	12,567	3	—	—	—	3	148	7	133	8	—
Long Beach	26,277	6	—	1	2	3	372	39	283	50	1
Los Angeles	18,244	13	—	2	5	6	363	63	257	43	1
Monterey Bay	4	22	—	—	—	22	127	45	80	2	—
Northridge	24,310	16	—	3	1	12	442	40	363	39	—
Sacramento	22,726	7	—	2	2	3	321	23	267	31	1
San Bernardino	11,864	3	—	1	1	1	244	42	184	18	—
San Jose	4	14	—	3	2	9	373	33	330	10	5
San Marcos	2,736	—	—	—	—	—	20	1	19	—	—
Stanislaus	5,877	4	—	1	—	3	94	3	84	7	—
College of the Sequoias	8,483	2	—	—	—	2	90	39	47	4	—
Contra Costa Community College	6,710	21	—	—	9	12	299	22	255	22	

See footnotes at end of table.

Table 9. — Number of Offenses Known to the Police, Universities and Colleges, 1996 — Continued

University/College	Student enrollment[1]	Violent[2] crime total	Murder and non-negligent man-slaughter	Forcible rape	Robbery	Aggravated assault	Property[3] crime total	Burglary	Larceny–theft	Motor vehicle theft	Arson*
CALIFORNIA — Continued											
El Camino College	21,763	3	—	1	1	1	283	32	224	27	2
Foothill-De Anza College	35,807	—	—	—	—	—	144	16	123	5	—
Fresno Community College	16,962	9	—	—	2	7	257	11	214	32	—
Humboldt State University	7,049	5	—	1	—	4	268	11	254	3	—
Kings River Community College	6,065	—	—	—	—	—	56	3	50	3	—
Los Angeles City College	15,433	10	—	—	9	1	95	13	68	14	—
Marin Community College	11,708	6	—	—	1	5	170	14	152	4	1
Pasadena Community College	21,787	3	—	—	2	1	178	12	151	15	—
San Bernardino Community College	9,878	4	—	1	2	1	161	14	132	15	—
San Diego State University	28,372	19	3	4	4	8	559	34	454	71	—
San Francisco State University	26,260	9	—	1	6	2	441	42	357	42	9
San Jose/Evergreen Community College	9,524	3	—	—	—	3	79	15	64	—	5
Santa Rosa Junior College	20,869	2	—	1	1	—	89	11	77	1	—
Sonoma State University	6,611	1	—	—	—	1	174	21	150	3	3
University of California:											
Berkeley	29,634	25	—	2	15	8	1,319	56	1,237	26	3
Davis	22,442	3	—	—	2	1	1,151	85	1,033	33	3
Hastings College of Law	1,234	—	—	—	—	—	16	1	15	—	—
Irvine	17,073	15	—	3	—	12	766	68	652	46	2
Lawrence Livermore Laboratory	[4]	—	—	—	—	—	1	—	1	—	—
Los Angeles	35,110	27	1	3	13	10	1,400	388	896	116	3
Riverside	8,590	49	—	2	2	45	432	186	204	42	—
Sacramento	3,744	4	—	—	2	2	257	23	217	17	—
San Diego	17,774	8	—	2	2	4	632	66	504	62	2
San Francisco	3,729	7	—	—	—	7	523	33	487	3	2
Santa Barbara	17,834	4	—	1	2	1	519	45	471	3	9
Santa Cruz	10,117	5	—	2	1	2	210	33	175	2	—
West Valley College	10,550	4	—	1	2	1	86	17	64	5	—
COLORADO											
Arapahoe Community College	7,601	1	—	—	—	1	35	2	33	—	—
Auraria Higher Education Center	[4]	18	—	—	1	17	365	24	330	11	—
Colorado School of Mines	3,677	2	—	—	—	2	51	8	40	3	—
Colorado State University	27,130	15	—	5	—	10	507	36	462	9	13
Fort Lewis College	4,015	—	—	—	—	—	34	1	33	—	—
Pikes Peak Community College	8,992	—	—	—	—	—	32	2	30	—	1
Red Rocks Community College	6,964	—	—	—	—	—	36	4	32	—	1
University of Colorado:											
Boulder	27,862	8	—	3	1	4	740	88	640	12	8
Colorado Springs	6,606	—	—	—	—	—	81	5	76	—	—
Health Sciences Center	2,500	2	—	1	—	1	146	12	134	—	1
University of Northern Colorado	12,226	4	—	—	—	4	198	23	172	3	3
University of Southern Colorado	5,182	1	—	1	—	—	53	14	39	—	—
CONNECTICUT											
Central Connecticut State University	11,959	3	—	—	1	2	113	3	93	17	—
Eastern Connecticut State University	4,523	3	—	—	—	3	128	4	124	—	—
Southern Connecticut State University	11,652	—	—	—	—	—	131	17	106	8	—
University of Connecticut:											
Health Center	[4]	1	—	—	—	1	127	11	112	4	—
Storrs, Avery Point, and Hartford	[4]	11	—	—	2	9	436	68	350	18	4
Western Connecticut State University	5,583	1	—	—	—	1	104	16	84	4	2
Yale University	10,916	13	—	—	9	4	714	124	579	11	—
DELAWARE											
University of Delaware	21,585	22	—	1	4	17	583	55	514	14	11
FLORIDA[5]											
Florida International University	26,547	15	—	1	3	11	555	100	390	65	—
Santa Fe Community College	12,640	2	—	—	—	2	89	1	83	5	—
University of South Florida:											
St. Petersburg	[4]	1	—	—	—	1	33	7	23	3	—
Sarasota	[4]	3	—	1	—	2	53	8	45	—	—
University of West Florida	7,801	2	—	—	1	1	96	16	79	1	—

See footnotes at end of table.

158

Table 9. — Number of Offenses Known to the Police, Universities and Colleges, 1996 — Continued

University/College	Student enrollment[1]	Violent[2] crime total	Violent Crime				Property[3] crime total	Property Crime			
			Murder and non-negligent man-slaughter	Forcible rape	Robbery	Aggravated assault		Burglary	Larceny–theft	Motor vehicle theft	Arson*
GEORGIA											
Abraham Baldwin Agricultural College	2,751	—	—	—	—	—	51	4	46	1	4
Agnes Scott College	595	1	—	—	—	1	55	6	43	6	—
Albany State College	3,062	—	—	—	—	—	40	15	25	—	—
Armstrong State College	2,830	—	—	—	—	—	62	2	60	—	—
Augusta College	5,651	—	—	—	—	—	50	5	43	2	—
Berry College	1,701	—	—	—	—	—	81	—	81	—	—
Brunswick College	1,912	—	—	—	—	—	18	2	15	1	—
Clark Atlanta University	5,193	14	—	1	9	4	253	29	222	2	—
Clayton State College	4,903	—	—	—	—	—	69	1	67	1	—
Columbus College	5,526	1	—	—	—	1	41	6	34	1	—
Dalton College	3,003	—	—	—	—	—	10	—	10	—	—
Emory University	10,899	3	—	2	—	1	587	22	558	7	—
Fort Valley State College	2,823	—	—	—	—	—	80	4	75	1	—
Georgia College	5,655	1	—	1	—	—	81	4	74	3	1
Georgia Institute of Technology	12,901	10	—	2	7	1	1,263	201	951	111	—
Georgia Southern University	14,138	2	—	—	2	—	307	4	303	—	—
Georgia Southwestern College	2,532	3	—	—	—	3	33	2	31	—	—
Georgia State University	23,730	10	—	—	6	4	511	11	497	3	—
Gordon College	2,157	—	—	—	—	—	1	—	1	—	—
Kennesaw State University	11,901	—	—	—	—	—	56	3	53	—	—
Medical College of Georgia	2,546	1	—	1	—	—	199	1	186	12	1
Mercer University	5,160	—	—	—	—	—	85	1	80	4	—
Middle Georgia College	2,168	—	—	—	—	—	45	4	41	—	—
Morehouse College	2,992	11	—	—	7	4	162	21	132	9	—
Morris-Brown College	1,894	12	—	—	2	10	176	27	143	6	—
North Georgia College	2,877	—	—	—	—	—	9	—	9	—	—
Savannah State College	2,759	5	—	1	—	4	130	12	114	4	—
South Georgia College	1,267	—	—	—	—	—	23	6	17	—	—
University of Georgia	29,469	7	—	4	1	2	169	19	141	9	—
Valdosta State University	9,126	2	—	—	1	1	244	42	199	3	—
Wesleyan College	424	—	—	—	—	—	27	1	26	—	—
West Georgia College	8,306	1	—	1	—	—	163	38	122	3	—
ILLINOIS[5]											
INDIANA											
Ball State University	20,390	8	—	4	2	2	640	96	535	9	—
Indiana State University	11,641	14	—	2	2	10	406	11	375	20	—
Indiana University:											
Bloomington	35,594	23	—	2	5	16	840	115	707	18	—
Gary	5,639	—	—	—	—	—	40	1	35	4	—
Indianapolis	26,766	5	—	—	5	—	610	7	582	21	1
New Albany	5,464	—	—	—	—	—	29	—	29	—	—
Purdue University	36,172	9	1	4	—	4	868	13	847	8	3
IOWA											
Iowa State University	24,990	—	—	—	—	—	504	73	429	2	1
University of Iowa	27,671	14	—	2	1	11	578	102	469	7	—
University of Northern Iowa	12,956	6	—	1	—	5	139	5	133	1	4
KANSAS[5]											
KENTUCKY[5]											
LOUISIANA											
Louisiana State University:											
Baton Rouge	26,010	19	—	1	4	14	866	142	706	18	—
Medical Center	3,217	—	—	—	—	—	110	1	109	—	—
Shreveport	4,237	3	—	—	—	3	14	—	14	—	—
Louisiana Tech. University	9,947	4	—	—	2	2	247	42	203	2	—
McNeese State University	8,701	5	—	—	1	4	120	42	72	6	2
Northeast Louisiana University	11,379	6	—	—	—	6	282	21	261	—	—
Northwestern State University	8,761	5	—	—	1	4	171	53	118	—	—
Southeastern Louisiana University	13,818	1	—	—	—	1	217	31	178	8	—
Southern University and A&M College,											
Baton Rouge	[4]	14	—	1	3	10	306	70	211	25	—
University of Southwestern Lousiana	16,789	11	—	2	1	8	353	96	255	2	8
MAINE											
University of Maine:											
Farmington	2,338	1	—	1	—	—	33	14	18	1	1

See footnotes at end of table.

Table 9. — Number of Offenses Known to the Police, Universities and Colleges, 1996 — Continued

University/College	Student enrollment[1]	Violent[2] crime total	Murder and non-negligent man-slaughter	Forcible rape	Robbery	Aggravated assault	Property[3] crime total	Burglary	Larceny–theft	Motor vehicle theft	Arson*
MAINE — Continued											
Orono	11,001	3	—	1	1	1	207	9	197	1	5
University of Southern Maine	9,628	2	—	—	—	2	113	3	109	1	—
MARYLAND											
Bowie State University	4,896	7	—	—	2	5	65	34	31	—	—
Coppin State University	3,380	2	—	—	1	1	49	3	44	2	1
Frostburg State University	5,443	6	—	1	—	5	98	7	90	1	—
Morgan State University	5,766	31	—	1	13	17	210	55	151	4	—
St. Mary's College	1,565	1	—	1	—	—	67	7	60	—	—
Salisbury State University	6,048	4	—	—	—	4	273	19	249	5	—
Towson State University	14,551	5	—	1	—	4	365	75	286	4	—
University of Baltimore	5,204	4	—	—	3	1	162	6	149	7	—
University of Maryland:											
Baltimore City	5,609	20	—	—	14	6	514	11	490	13	—
Baltimore County	10,315	2	—	1	—	1	212	36	170	6	1
College Park	32,493	49	—	4	15	30	1,114	169	881	64	8
Eastern Shore	2,925	12	—	2	1	9	121	27	94	—	—
MASSACHUSETTS											
Boston College	14,713	7	—	3	1	3	306	5	300	1	
Boston University	29,072	23	—	2	9	12	749	66	661	22	
Brandeis University	4,008	10	—	6	2	2	108	4	103	1	
Emerson College	3,409	3	—	—	1	2	70	4	66	—	
Framingham State College	5,149	5	—	—	—	5	50	3	46	1	
Massachusetts College of Art	2,145	2	—	1	1	—	53	1	52	—	
Massachusetts Institute of Technology	9,774	13	—	3	2	8	746	18	704	24	
North Adams State College	1,775	4	—	—	—	4	45	5	39	1	
Northeastern University	25,086	16	—	1	9	6	391	33	351	7	
Tufts University:											
Medford	8,324	8	—	1	—	7	153	9	141	3	
Suffolk	4	—	—	—	—	—	69	—	69	—	
Worcester	4	—	—	—	—	—	11	1	10	—	
University of Massachusetts:											
Amherst	24,825	15	—	5	4	6	790	205	571	14	1
Worcester	637	1	—	—	—	1	116	3	111	2	
Wentworth Institute of Technology	2,799	—	—	—	—	—	90	9	81	—	
MICHIGAN											
Central Michigan University	23,390	6	—	3	—	3	386	3	379	4	3
Delta College	11,114	1	—	—	1	—	45	1	44	—	1
Eastern Michigan University	23,321	24	—	4	5	15	521	19	497	5	20
Ferris State University	10,258	7	—	3	2	2	303	6	294	3	2
Grand Valley State University	13,553	2	—	—	1	1	142	4	137	1	2
Hope College	2,825	—	—	—	—	—	156	6	150	—	3
Lansing Community College	16,816	2	—	—	2	—	200	9	191	—	1
Macomb Community College	25,809	1	—	—	—	1	104	5	97	2	—
Michigan State University	40,254	55	1	6	14	34	1,391	252	1,107	32	—
Michigan Technological University	6,460	2	—	2	—	—	113	1	111	1	3
Northern Michigan University	7,898	2	—	1	—	1	210	2	206	2	—
Oakland Community College	26,324	2	—	—	—	2	79	—	77	2	—
Oakland University	13,165	1	—	—	—	1	150	6	138	6	3
Saginaw Valley State University	7,037	4	—	—	2	2	84	2	81	1	—
University of Michigan:											
Ann Arbor	36,543	19	—	3	4	12	2,002	132	1,836	34	18
Flint	6,236	—	—	—	—	—	74	1	72	1	1
Western Michigan University	25,673	14	—	4	2	8	548	5	532	11	19
MINNESOTA											
University of Minnesota:											
Duluth	9,417	—	—	—	—	—	179	2	175	2	—
Twin Cities	51,478	16	—	4	6	6	1,087	59	1,022	6	7
MISSISSIPPI											
Hinds Community College	9,183	1	—	—	1	—	43	15	22	6	—
Itawamba Community College	3,088	—	—	—	—	—	54	35	17	2	—
Jackson State University	6,224	8	—	—	5	3	310	43	252	15	—

See footnotes at end of table.

Table 9. — Number of Offenses Known to the Police, Universities and Colleges, 1996 — Continued

University/College	Student enrollment[1]	Violent[2] crime total	Violent Crime				Property[3] crime total	Property Crime			
			Murder and non-negligent man-slaughter	Forcible rape	Robbery	Aggravated assault		Burglary	Larceny–theft	Motor vehicle theft	Arson*
MISSISSIPPI — Continued											
Mississippi State University	14,152	25	—	—	2	23	207	6	199	2	—
University of Mississippi Medical Center	1,817	—	—	—	—	—	208	9	186	13	—
MISSOURI											
Lincoln University	3,512	1	—	—	—	1	59	4	53	2	1
University of Missouri:											
Columbia	22,175	13	—	1	3	9	613	91	519	3	4
St. Louis	15,588	1	—	—	1	—	174	9	156	9	—
Washington University	11,655	4	—	—	2	2	321	26	290	5	—
MONTANA[5]											
NEBRASKA											
University of Nebraska:											
Kearney	7,584	1	—	—	—	1	99	12	87	—	—
Lincoln	23,854	5	—	2	2	1	629	49	574	6	—
NEVADA											
University of Nevada:											
Las Vegas	18,954	23	—	—	4	19	309	59	223	27	1
Reno	12,379	11	—	—	1	10	253	120	128	5	3
NEW HAMPSHIRE											
University of New Hampshire	15,394	5	—	3	1	1	232	29	201	2	8
NEW JERSEY											
Brookdale Community College	12,257	1	—	—	—	1	98	1	97	—	—
Essex County College	8,735	3	—	—	3	—	30	—	26	4	—
Kean College	11,387	9	—	3	1	5	242	23	201	18	—
Middlesex County College	11,767	—	—	—	—	—	81	—	79	2	—
Monmouth University	4,422	3	—	1	—	2	83	1	81	1	—
Montclair State University	12,748	16	—	—	2	14	226	14	186	26	1
New Jersey Institute of Technology	7,504	6	—	—	1	5	129	28	96	5	—
Rowan College	8,936	6	1	2	2	1	179	8	165	6	—
Rutgers University:											
Camden	4,833	5	—	—	1	4	90	5	80	5	—
Newark	9,477	1	—	—	—	1	407	17	385	5	2
New Brunswick	33,464	21	—	7	7	7	687	49	617	21	1
Stockton State College	5,683	3	—	2	—	1	110	30	76	4	—
The College of New Jersey	6,946	3	—	2	1	—	112	15	90	7	—
University of Medicine and Dentistry:											
Camden	[4]	—	—	—	—	—	9	—	9	—	—
Newark	4,020	26	—	3	6	17	528	27	494	7	—
Piscataway	[4]	—	—	—	—	—	49	1	47	1	—
William Paterson College	9,669	2	—	—	—	2	100	12	87	1	1
NEW MEXICO											
Eastern New Mexico University	3,854	1	—	—	—	1	78	40	35	3	2
New Mexico Highlands University	15,643	4	—	—	—	4	75	4	70	1	—
New Mexico State University	24,572	8	—	4	—	4	521	37	435	49	11
NEW YORK											
Cornell University	[4]	13	—	1	4	8	568	92	474	2	—
Ithaca College	5,688	2	—	1	—	1	150	3	147	—	—
Rensselaer Polytechnic Institute	6,520	4	—	1	1	2	284	26	253	5	—
Syracuse University	18,971	1	—	—	—	1	351	—	351	—	—
NORTH CAROLINA											
Appalachian State University	12,236	9	—	—	2	7	242	4	233	5	1
Barton College	1,465	—	—	—	—	—	6	1	4	1	—
Davidson College	1,614	3	—	—	—	3	67	5	62	—	—
Duke University	11,352	28	—	—	14	14	998	64	919	15	2
East Carolina University	18,076	27	—	4	5	18	372	14	354	4	1
Elizabeth City State University	2,099	4	—	—	1	3	39	21	17	1	1
Fayetteville State University	4,109	9	—	—	4	5	86	30	52	4	—

See footnotes at end of table.

Table 9. — Number of Offenses Known to the Police, Universities and Colleges, 1996 — Continued

University/College	Student enrollment[1]	Violent[2] crime total	Violent Crime				Property[3] crime total	Property Crime			
			Murder and non-negligent man-slaughter	Forcible rape	Robbery	Aggravated assault		Burglary	Larceny–theft	Motor vehicle theft	Arson*
NORTH CAROLINA — Continued											
Mars Hill College	1,325	1	—	1	—	—	24	4	20	—	—
Methodist College	1,907	3	—	—	—	3	50	9	39	2	—
North Carolina Agricultural and Technical State University	8,136	24	—	3	11	10	315	92	208	15	3
North Carolina Central University	5,692	16	—	1	9	6	219	24	188	7	8
North Carolina School of the Arts	644	—	—	—	—	—	43	7	36	—	—
North Carolina State University at Raleigh	28,223	18	—	—	7	11	784	70	696	18	5
Pembroke State University	3,017	2	—	—	1	1	45	6	38	1	—
University of North Carolina:											
Chapel Hill	24,565	17	—	—	4	13	642	40	594	8	9
Charlotte	15,648	12	—	2	5	5	397	62	327	8	3
Greensboro	12,658	23	—	4	4	15	291	59	229	3	4
Wilmington	8,472	4	—	2	1	1	385	24	359	2	—
Wake Forest University	5,728	6	—	—	2	4	193	38	154	1	1
Western Carolina University	6,790	11	—	4	—	7	140	24	115	1	—
Winston-Salem State University	2,915	4	—	—	—	4	27	6	21	—	—
OHIO											
Bowling Green State University	17,669	3	—	2	—	1	451	26	422	3	—
Cuyahoga Community College	24,079	1	—	—	—	1	201	38	159	4	—
Kent State University, Main Campus	21,413	2	—	—	1	1	304	9	294	1	—
Lakeland Community College	8,698	—	—	—	—	—	32	—	32	—	—
Marietta College	1,318	1	—	1	—	—	41	7	34	—	1
Miami University	15,624	4	—	2	—	2	469	1	468	—	—
Ohio State University, Main Campus	49,542	25	—	3	13	9	1,644	266	1,343	35	10
Ohio University	19,461	8	—	3	1	4	294	1	291	2	6
University of Cincinnati	28,758	19	—	1	8	10	989	114	864	11	5
University of Toledo	23,107	5	—	—	1	4	339	24	311	4	6
Youngstown State University	13,979	4	—	—	2	2	144	4	135	5	2
OKLAHOMA											
Cameron University	6,081	—	—	—	—	—	29	1	27	1	—
East Central University	4,501	1	—	—	—	1	12	2	10	—	—
Murray State College	1,601	—	—	—	—	—	9	1	8	—	—
Northeastern Oklahoma State University	8,994	7	—	1	—	6	93	7	82	4	—
Oklahoma State University:											
Main Campus	18,807	1	—	1	—	—	329	84	236	9	1
Okmulgee	2,175	2	—	—	—	2	45	4	40	1	—
Rogers State College	[4]	1	—	—	—	1	33	2	29	2	—
Seminole Junior College	1,622	—	—	—	—	—	22	3	19	—	—
Southeastern Oklahoma State University	4,004	—	—	—	—	—	32	7	25	—	—
Tulsa Junior College	18,604	—	—	—	—	—	79	—	79	—	—
University of Central Oklahoma	16,076	10	—	—	2	8	135	9	119	7	—
University of Oklahoma:											
Health Science Center	2,971	—	—	—	—	—	52	1	47	4	—
Norman	22,043	12	—	1	1	10	577	140	422	15	1
PENNSYLVANIA											
Bloomsburg University	7,277	1	—	1	—	—	51	5	45	1	—
California University	6,215	—	—	—	—	—	87	1	85	1	1
Clarion University	5,637	4	—	2	—	2	84	—	84	—	1
East Stroudsburg University	5,527	2	—	1	—	1	78	—	77	1	—
Edinboro University	7,484	1	—	—	—	1	105	2	101	2	—
Elizabethtown College	1,797	1	—	—	—	1	37	3	34	—	—
Indiana University	13,814	11	—	5	3	3	194	25	167	2	—
Kutztown University	7,916	4	—	1	—	3	103	4	97	2	—
Lehigh University	6,447	7	—	1	1	5	150	—	149	1	—
Millersville University	7,417	10	—	2	—	8	116	7	109	—	—
Moravian College	1,840	1	—	—	—	1	34	1	32	1	—
Pennsylvania State University:											
Altoona	2,468	—	—	—	—	—	48	1	47	—	3
Behrend	3,090	—	—	—	—	—	51	—	50	1	—
Mont Alto	1,111	—	—	—	—	—	16	3	12	1	—
University Park	38,294	5	1	—	—	4	742	48	689	5	1

See footnotes at end of table.

Table 9. — Number of Offenses Known to the Police, Universities and Colleges, 1996 — Continued

University/College	Student enrollment[1]	Violent[2] crime total	Violent Crime				Property[3] crime total	Property Crime			
			Murder and non-negligent man-slaughter	Forcible rape	Robbery	Aggravated assault		Burglary	Larceny–theft	Motor vehicle theft	Arson*
PENNSYLVANIA — Continued											
Shippensburg University	6,603	1	—	—	—	1	92	3	87	2	1
Slippery Rock University	7,563	1	—	—	1	—	122	3	119	—	—
University of Pittsburgh, Bradford	1,340	—	—	—	—	—	35	3	32	—	—
West Chester University	11,168	7	—	—	1	6	142	1	140	1	3
RHODE ISLAND											
Brown University	7,801	8	—	4	1	3	363	33	328	2	5
University of Rhode Island	14,151	5	—	1	—	4	265	18	243	4	2
SOUTH CAROLINA											
Clemson University	16,290	18	—	4	—	14	372	14	348	10	9
Francis Marion University	3,898	1	—	—	—	1	89	4	85	—	—
Lander University	2,779	4	—	2	—	2	46	8	38	—	—
Medical University of South Carolina	2,256	4	—	—	2	2	451	30	416	5	—
South Carolina State University	4,693	26	—	—	9	17	165	53	110	2	2
Trident Technical College	9,623	1	—	—	—	1	58	—	58	—	—
University of South Carolina:											
Coastal Carolina	4,542	2	—	—	1	1	134	34	98	2	—
Columbia	26,754	9	1	5	1	2	670	13	635	22	1
Spartanburg	3,443	4	—	3	—	1	47	1	44	2	—
Winthrop University	5,164	2	—	—	2	—	96	4	92	—	—
SOUTH DAKOTA											
South Dakota State University	9,707	—	—	—	—	—	41	15	26	—	—
TENNESSEE											
East Tennessee State University	11,439	4	—	—	2	2	151	4	144	3	1
Middle Tennessee State University	17,120	4	—	1	2	1	233	23	207	3	—
University of Tennessee:											
Knoxville	25,914	19	—	2	8	9	661	37	624	—	4
Martin	5,608	4	—	—	—	4	126	3	120	3	—
TEXAS											
Alamo Community College	[4]	1	—	—	—	1	351	7	328	16	—
Alvin Community College	3,645	—	—	—	—	—	14	—	13	1	—
Amarillo College	6,724	—	—	—	—	—	37	7	29	1	—
Angelo State University	6,276	1	—	1	—	—	72	8	64	—	—
Austin College	1,123	1	—	—	1	—	28	1	25	2	—
Baylor University	12,241	4	—	1	1	2	234	19	211	4	—
Baylor University Medical Center	1,126	4	—	—	3	1	271	7	254	10	1
Central Texas College	14,547	—	—	—	—	—	53	2	50	1	1
College of the Mainland	4,034	3	—	—	—	3	41	—	39	2	1
Eastfield College	8,722	3	1	—	1	1	73	11	60	2	3
East Texas State University, Commerce	7,752	2	—	1	—	1	155	27	125	3	—
Grayson County Junior College	3,092	—	—	—	—	—	20	4	16	—	—
Hardin-Simmons University	2,133	1	—	—	—	1	45	15	30	—	—
Houston Baptist University	2,130	—	—	—	—	—	17	—	17	—	—
Lamar University, Beaumont	9,787	5	—	—	1	4	146	31	112	3	—
Laredo Community College	7,019	—	—	—	—	—	81	4	74	3	—
McLennan Community College	5,435	—	—	—	—	—	19	—	19	—	—
Midwestern State University	5,828	3	—	—	—	3	84	24	57	3	—
North Lake College	6,196	—	—	—	—	—	24	—	23	1	—
Paris Junior College	2,617	—	—	—	—	—	50	29	21	—	—
Prairie View A&M University	5,849	20	—	8	1	11	267	87	160	20	3
Rice University	4,139	5	—	1	1	3	184	3	177	4	—
Richland College	12,069	1	—	—	—	1	90	3	86	1	—
Southern Methodist University	9,014	2	—	1	—	1	165	3	154	8	1
South Plains College	5,671	—	—	—	—	—	18	9	9	—	1
Southwestern University	1,238	—	—	—	—	—	42	15	25	2	—
Southwest Texas State University	20,889	7	—	3	1	3	333	45	277	11	1
Stephen F. Austin State University	12,206	12	—	1	1	10	185	24	160	1	—
Sul Ross State University	3,145	—	—	—	—	—	73	28	42	3	—
Tarleton State University	6,460	—	—	—	—	—	60	8	51	1	1
Texas A&M International University	1,964	—	—	—	—	—	21	—	21	—	—
Texas A&M University:											
College Station	42,018	8	—	2	4	2	693	83	600	10	2

See footnotes at end of table.

Table 9. — Number of Offenses Known to the Police, Universities and Colleges, 1996 — Continued

University/College	Student enrollment[1]	Violent[2] crime total	Violent Crime				Property[3] crime total	Property Crime			
			Murder and non-negligent man-slaughter	Forcible rape	Robbery	Aggravated assault		Burglary	Larceny–theft	Motor vehicle theft	Arson*
TEXAS — Continued											
Corpus Christi	5,152	—	—	—	—	—	52	1	50	1	—
Galveston	1,237	1	—	—	—	1	17	5	12	—	—
Kingsville	6,545	—	—	—	—	—	132	44	87	1	1
Texas Christian University	6,706	4	—	3	1	—	93	19	72	2	—
Texas College Osteo. Med.	416	—	—	—	—	—	38	2	36	—	—
Texas Southern University	10,078	16	—	2	8	6	217	40	161	16	—
Texas State Technical College:											
Amarillo	498	—	—	—	—	—	1	—	1	—	—
Harlingen	2,888	1	—	—	—	1	40	8	32	—	—
Waco	3,430	5	—	—	1	4	306	66	227	13	1
Texas Tech University:											
Health Science Center	1,430	1	—	—	—	1	109	2	105	2	—
Lubbock	24,083	3	—	1	1	1	411	11	400	—	1
Texas Woman's University	10,090	1	—	1	—	—	105	6	94	5	—
Trinity University	2,478	—	—	—	—	—	136	48	88	—	2
University of Houston:											
Central Campus	33,022	7	—	—	3	4	516	10	489	17	1
Clearlake	7,228	—	—	—	—	—	37	—	36	1	—
Downtown Campus	7,715	5	—	—.	1	4	68	6	58	4	—
University of North Texas	25,605	3	—	1	1	1	300	27	267	6	—
University of Texas:											
Arlington	23,373	6	—	3	1	2	322	25	281	16	1
Austin	47,957	12	2	—	1	9	616	13	592	11	—
Brownsville and Texas Southmost College	7,770	2	—	—	1	1	93	1	84	8	—
Dallas	8,487	—	—	—	—	—	59	1	57	1	—
El Paso	17,196	5	—	3	—	2	258	12	221	25	1
Health Science Center, San Antonio	2,790	—	—	—	—	—	87	2	84	1	—
Health Science Center, Tyler	3,183	1	—	—	—	1	22	—	22	—	—
Houston	[4]	3	—	2	—	1	323	2	318	3	—
Medical Branch	2,327	2	—	1	1	—	322	4	314	4	—
Pan American	15,104	—	—	—	—	—	120	2	110	8	—
Permian Basin	2,315	1	—	—	—	1	33	4	28	1	—
San Antonio	17,579	4	1	2	—	1	223	16	207	—	2
Southwestern Medical School	1,700	1	—	—	—	1	215	3	207	5	—
Tyler	3,917	1	—	—	—	1	32	4	27	1	—
West Texas State University	6,633	4	—	1	1	2	101	2	99	—	—
UTAH											
Brigham Young University	31,511	6	—	—	—	6	465	9	452	4	2
College of Eastern Utah	3,135	—	—	—	—	—	33	6	26	1	—
Salt Lake Community College	18,534	1	—	—	1	—	153	5	144	4	—
Southern Utah University	4,754	11	—	3	—	8	71	28	42	1	—
University of Utah	26,906	11	—	1	2	8	688	19	642	27	15
Utah State University	20,371	—	—	—	—	—	195	7	186	2	3
Utah Valley State College	13,293	2	—	—	—	2	144	6	137	1	—
Weber State University	14,230	2	—	—	—	2	124	6	113	5	—
VERMONT[5]											
VIRGINIA											
Christopher Newport College	4,705	—	—	—	—	—	60	—	60	—	—
Clinch Valley College	1,839	4	—	2	—	2	10	4	6	—	—
College of William and Mary	7,547	4	—	3	—	1	300	9	291	—	—
George Mason University	21,774	5	—	1	4	—	558	65	488	5	3
Hampton University	5,769	15	—	—	1	14	124	3	120	1	1
James Madison University	11,680	7	—	—	—	7	182	35	147	—	1
Longwood College	3,351	5	—	2	2	1	98	—	97	1	—
Mary Washington College	3,727	5	—	—	1	4	124	21	102	1	—
Norfolk State University	8,667	17	—	—	6	11	166	22	144	—	1
Northern Virginia Community College	37,655	5	—	—	—	5	220	5	214	1	—
Old Dominion University	16,490	18	—	1	10	7	419	6	405	8	—
Radford University	9,105	12	—	4	—	8	196	17	177	2	2
Thomas Nelson Community College	7,483	—	—	—	—	—	32	—	32	—	—
University of Richmond	4,258	8	—	2	—	6	144	5	138	1	—
University of Virginia	21,421	12	—	1	6	5	587	26	558	3	—

See footnotes at end of table.

Table 9. — Number of Offenses Known to the Police, Universities and Colleges, 1996 — Continued

University/College	Student enrollment[1]	Violent[2] crime total	Violent Crime				Property[3] crime total	Property Crime			
			Murder and non-negligent man-slaughter	Forcible rape	Robbery	Aggravated assault		Burglary	Larceny–theft	Motor vehicle theft	Arson*
VIRGINIA — Continued											
Virginia Commonwealth University	21,523	9	—	—	4	5	733	16	711	6	1
Virginia Military Institute	1,179	1	—	—	—	1	18	1	17	—	
Virginia Polytechnic Institute and State University	25,842	20	—	3	3	14	367	22	340	5	6
Virginia State University	4,007	14	—	—	2	12	113	30	82	1	—
Virginia Western Community College	6,136	—	—	—	—	—	28	—	28	—	—
WASHINGTON											
Central Washington University	8,468	1	—	1	—	—	279	26	252	1	1
Eastern Washington University	8,360	3	—	—	1	2	67	1	66	—	—
University of Washington	33,719	10	—	—	2	8	909	96	791	22	4
Washington State University:											
Pullman	19,314	5	—	1	—	4	381	41	337	3	1
Vancouver	[4]	—	—	—	—	—	3	—	3	—	—
Western Washington University	10,598	—	—	—	—	—	275	18	249	8	—
WEST VIRGINIA											
Concord College	2,623	—	—	—	—	—	20	8	12	—	—
Glenville State College	2,269	—	—	—	—	—	15	—	15	—	1
Marshall University	12,659	7	—	2	2	3	210	8	201	1	2
West Liberty State College	2,381	—	—	—	—	—	38	4	34	—	—
West Virginia State College	4,519	1	—	1	—	—	45	9	35	1	—
West Virginia Tech	2,697	1	—	—	—	1	12	1	11	—	—
West Virginia University	22,500	3	—	2	—	1	357	41	306	10	1
WISCONSIN											
University of Wisconsin:											
Eau Claire	10,395	1	—	1	—	—	156	7	148	1	7
Green Bay	5,712	1	—	1	—	—	68	2	65	1	—
La Crosse	8,663	2	—	—	—	2	124	11	113	—	—
Madison	39,361	6	—	1	1	4	829	37	771	21	13
Milwaukee	22,604	6	—	4	1	1	339	5	333	1	—
Oshkosh	10,611	2	—	2	—	—	128	3	124	1	13
Parkside	5,050	1	—	—	—	1	74	2	71	1	—
Platteville	5,305	3	—	1	—	2	54	1	52	1	4
Stout	7,512	—	—	—	—	—	165	24	140	1	—
Whitewater	10,850	—	—	—	—	—	173	9	157	7	2
WYOMING											
University of Wyoming	12,022	—	—	—	—	—	235	10	224	1	—

[1] The student enrollment figures provided by the United States Department of Education are for the 1994-1995 school year. The 1996 figures were not available at the time of this publication. The enrollment figure includes full-time and part-time students. See Appendix I for details.

[2] Violent crimes are offenses of murder, forcible rape, robbery, and aggravated assault.

[3] Property crimes are offenses of burglary, larceny–theft, and motor vehicle theft. Data are not included for the property crime of arson.

[4] Student enrollment figures were not available.

[5] Complete data were not available for the states of Illinois, Kansas, Kentucky, Montana, and Vermont; therefore, it was necessary that their crime counts be estimated. An aggregate Florida state total for 1996 was supplied by the Florida Department of Law Enforcement. See "Offense Estimation," pages 389-390 for details.

NOTE: Caution should be exercised in making any inter-campus comparisons or ranking schools, as university/college crime statistics are affected by a variety of factors. These include: demographic characteristics of the surrounding community, ratio of male to female students, number of on-campus residents, accessibility of outside visitors, size of enrollment, etc.

Table 10. — Number of Offenses Known to the Police, Suburban Counties, 1996

[The data shown in this table do not reflect county totals but are the number of offenses reported by the sheriff's office, county police department, or state police.]

*Arson is shown only if 12 months of arson data were received. Dashes (—) indicate zero data. The Modified Crime Index total is the sum of the Crime Index offenses, including arson.

County by State	Crime Index total	Modified* Crime Index total	Murder and non-negligent man-slaughter	Forcible rape	Robbery	Aggravated assault	Burglary	Larceny–theft	Motor vehicle theft	Arson*
ALABAMA										
Autauga	192	194	4	4	4	11	79	71	19	2
Baldwin	887		2	25	9	52	274	474	51	
Calhoun	665		2	6	7	51	249	323	27	
Colbert	180		3	—	1	13	78	75	10	
Dale	160		—	4	2	21	50	79	4	
Elmore	702		5	14	9	27	219	387	41	
Etowah	362		1	3	1	2	132	205	18	
Houston	305		1	3	1	19	101	154	26	
Jefferson	6,192	6,264	17	47	166	477	1,604	3,415	466	72
Lauderdale	389		—	2	2	54	111	197	23	
Lawrence	34		1	—	—	12	9	12	—	
Limestone	218		2	1	1	24	74	89	27	
Madison	1,934	1,935	9	16	18	193	450	1,145	103	1
Mobile	3,165	3,170	7	31	61	213	967	1,720	166	5
Montgomery	937		2	13	21	104	192	543	62	
Morgan	470		3	1	6	31	237	132	60	
Russell	382		—	8	6	17	112	215	24	
St. Clair	489		4	9	4	49	127	256	40	
Shelby	222		3	5	9	17	56	90	42	
Tuscaloosa	2,223		5	9	20	220	658	1,110	201	
ARIZONA										
Maricopa	6,374	6,385	22	24	75	394	1,241	3,843	775	11
Mohave	2,072	2,098	5	5	15	95	825	988	139	26
Pima	12,159	12,236	22	85	189	619	2,075	7,558	1,611	77
Pinal	1,886	1,887	6	23	19	179	543	923	193	1
Yuma	1,155	1,155	—	4	7	96	397	575	76	—
ARKANSAS										
Benton	804	812	2	13	7	67	185	490	40	8
Craighead	353	357	—	5	1	13	117	183	34	4
Crawford	409	415	1	1	—	95	160	110	42	6
Crittenden	682	690	3	1	15	127	227	253	56	8
Faulkner	523	524	3	—	—	27	199	252	42	1
Jefferson	579	583	2	8	8	52	190	259	60	4
Lonoke	107	107	—	—	—	—	33	43	31	—
Miller	383	383	—	4	5	53	88	213	20	—
Pulaski	2,813	2,842	6	56	59	251	634	1,627	180	29
Sebastian	258	259	—	1	—	20	67	153	17	1
Washington	643	645	2	2	1	189	167	247	35	2
CALIFORNIA										
Alameda	3,949	3,986	8	25	223	431	746	1,826	690	37
Alameda Highway Patrol	143	143	—	1	—	4	10	38	90	—
Butte	2,950	3,081	6	36	26	210	1,044	1,604	24	131
Butte Highway Patrol	328	328	—	—	—	3	2	56	267	—
Contra Costa	5,424	5,469	9	54	176	396	1,482	3,303	4	45
Contra Costa Highway Patrol	622	622	—	—	—	3	1	40	578	—
El Dorado	2,417	2,435	2	23	20	269	733	1,360	10	18
El Dorado Highway Patrol	191	191	—	—	2	—	—	6	183	—
Fresno	7,456	7,465	16	48	158	1,135	1,943	2,866	1,290	9
Fresno Highway Patrol	284	284	—	—	—	4	4	20	256	—
Kern	14,330	15,505	26	103	378	1,940	3,859	6,852	1,172	1,175
Kern Highway Patrol	146	146	—	—	—	1	—	43	102	—
Los Angeles	37,057	37,539	165	279	3,222	9,106	7,207	10,582	6,496	482
Los Angeles Highway Patrol	821	821	—	—	6	430	29	111	245	—
Madera	1,903	1,990	3	15	30	249	617	974	15	87
Madera Highway Patrol	281	281	—	—	—	—	—	13	268	—
Marin	1,441	1,448	1	9	23	158	289	945	16	7
Marin Highway Patrol	79	79	—	—	—	—	—	11	68	—
Merced	2,479	2,482	4	28	25	196	1,060	1,158	8	3
Merced Highway Patrol	386	386	—	—	—	4	—	14	368	—
Monterey	2,547	2,581	4	21	48	78	758	1,616	22	34
Monterey Highway Patrol	137	137	—	—	—	—	—	7	130	—
Napa	514	520	—	7	7	45	178	274	3	6
Napa Highway Patrol	64	64	—	—	—	—	—	18	46	—

Table 10. — Number of Offenses Known to the Police, Suburban Counties, 1996 — Continued

County by State	Crime Index total	Modified* Crime Index total	Murder and non-negligent man-slaughter	Forcible rape	Robbery	Aggravated assault	Burglary	Larceny-theft	Motor vehicle theft	Arson*
CALIFORNIA — Continued										
Orange	3,535	3,587	9	13	77	440	845	1,796	355	52
Orange Highway Patrol	146	146	—	1	2	58	13	41	31	—
Riverside	17,640	17,752	42	98	325	1,734	4,905	8,514	2,022	112
Riverside Highway Patrol	57	57	—	—	—	6	—	5	46	—
Sacramento	32,940	33,074	51	251	1,578	3,187	8,586	18,970	317	134
Sacramento Highway Patrol	9,668	9,669	—	1	5	9	56	786	8,811	1
San Bernardino	11,471	11,580	41	76	317	884	3,981	4,515	1,657	109
San Bernardino Highway Patrol	94	94	—	—	—	19	8	19	48	—
San Diego	21,155	21,329	42	184	817	2,449	5,847	9,013	2,803	174
San Diego Highway Patrol	194	194	—	1	2	7	15	58	111	—
San Joaquin	4,847	4,903	14	37	132	261	1,385	2,942	76	56
San Joaquin Highway Patrol	841	841	—	—	—	—	3	120	718	—
San Luis Obispo	1,625	1,634	5	29	10	252	460	866	3	9
San Luis Obispo Highway Patrol	95	95	—	—	—	2	—	20	73	—
San Mateo	2,685	2,697	2	9	45	65	263	2,051	250	12
San Mateo Highway Patrol	21	21	—	—	—	1	—	1	19	—
Santa Barbara	3,217	3,235	4	37	24	339	1,181	1,616	16	18
Santa Barbara Highway Patrol	146	146	—	—	—	1	—	34	111	—
Santa Clara	3,289	3,294	4	59	41	312	662	2,028	183	5
Santa Clara Highway Patrol	104	104	—	1	—	3	3	17	80	—
Santa Cruz	4,212	4,241	1	43	68	391	964	2,730	15	29
Santa Cruz Highway Patrol	388	388	—	—	—	1	—	64	323	—
Shasta	1,798	1,856	4	22	28	314	546	836	48	58
Shasta Highway Patrol	168	168	—	—	—	—	2	39	127	—
Solano	673	689	2	12	17	93	259	282	8	16
Solano Highway Patrol	100	100	—	—	—	—	—	11	89	—
Sonoma	4,094	4,153	9	48	74	425	1,088	2,424	26	59
Sonoma Highway Patrol	327	327	—	—	—	9	—	93	225	—
Stanislaus	5,732	5,972	12	43	131	1,297	1,798	2,168	283	240
Stanislaus Highway Patrol	511	511	—	—	1	3	—	51	456	—
Sutter	1,039	1,041	4	9	11	137	270	581	27	2
Sutter Highway Patrol	63	63	—	—	—	—	—	1	62	—
Tulare	3,819	4,349	12	40	103	533	1,140	1,991	—	530
Tulare Highway Patrol	675	675	—	—	—	2	—	56	617	—
Ventura	1,653	1,693	3	18	24	197	435	854	122	40
Ventura Highway Patrol	15	15	—	—	—	—	—	3	12	—
Yolo	486	497	2	7	5	86	163	215	8	11
Yolo Highway Patrol	59	59	—	—	1	—	6	9	43	—
Yuba	2,063	2,081	1	19	34	249	630	1,124	6	18
Yuba Highway Patrol	171	171	—	—	—	1	—	10	160	—
COLORADO										
Adams	3,913	3,942	6	40	58	252	767	2,318	472	29
Arapahoe	3,593	3,619	1	16	41	35	816	2,479	205	26
Boulder	1,057	1,080	—	37	15	54	348	507	96	23
Douglas	1,710	1,745	—	17	7	99	323	1,194	70	35
El Paso	2,431	2,440	5	16	19	219	680	1,309	183	9
Jefferson	4,511	4,555	—	27	42	89	876	3,208	269	44
Larimer	1,304	1,317	—	24	12	18	256	922	72	13
Mesa	1,564	1,580	4	18	4	64	339	1,041	94	16
Pueblo	909	910	1	4	3	20	227	619	35	1
Weld	1,213		2	20	3	73	367	620	128	
DELAWARE										
Kent State Police	2,217	2,220	4	69	44	332	606	1,052	110	3
New Castle State Police	7,442	7,452	7	55	381	491	645	5,197	666	10
FLORIDA[1]										
Alachua	7,268		2	83	183	928	1,685	3,854	533	
Collier	10,326		4	85	282	873	2,485	5,921	676	
Escambia	13,509		17	153	438	1,941	3,022	7,264	674	
Hillsborough	38,356		28	217	1,041	3,016	7,305	23,223	3,526	
Leon	3,170		5	47	96	454	967	1,402	199	
Manatee	12,111		11	75	370	1,555	2,827	6,591	682	
Marion	6,406		9	107	79	1,237	1,886	2,777	311	
Orange	43,078		34	272	1,964	3,883	8,700	24,454	3,771	
Polk	16,617		15	155	297	1,595	4,952	7,871	1,732	

See footnotes at end of table.

Table 10. — Number of Offenses Known to the Police, Suburban Counties, 1996 — Continued

County by State	Crime Index total	Modified* Crime Index total	Murder and non-negligent man-slaughter	Forcible rape	Robbery	Aggravated assault	Burglary	Larceny–theft	Motor vehicle theft	Arson*
GEORGIA										
Barrow	681	685	—	3	7	30	209	373	59	4
Bartow	1,026	1,026	3	4	4	121	471	220	203	—
Bryan	308	310	1	2	6	10	77	191	21	2
Catoosa	956	959	1	7	6	25	138	680	99	3
Chatham Police Department	3,488	3,498	3	21	85	265	705	2,185	224	10
Chattahoochee	45	47	—	—	—	12	27	4	2	2
Cherokee	2,045	2,060	1	5	10	80	497	1,303	149	15
Clayton Police Department	11,670	11,714	4	71	255	411	2,336	7,193	1,400	44
Cobb Police Department	16,248	16,296	7	96	314	513	2,795	10,762	1,761	48
Columbia	2,377	2,384	2	3	24	47	335	1,821	145	7
Coweta	1,448	1,452	3	9	24	111	348	831	122	4
Dade	188	188	—	—	9	7	27	123	22	—
DeKalb Police Department	50,011	50,248	48	196	2,227	896	9,027	29,722	7,895	237
Dougherty	39	39	—	—	—	1	10	26	2	—
Dougherty Police Department	545	545	—	7	4	5	165	342	22	—
Douglas	2,198	2,210	3	9	26	101	393	1,424	242	12
Fayette	726	727	—	—	2	9	184	490	41	1
Forsyth	2,866	2,881	1	5	12	199	519	1,900	230	15
Fulton Police Department	5,194	5,236	9	75	152	360	905	2,223	1,470	42
Gwinnett Police Department	19,678	19,791	5	102	325	587	2,985	14,049	1,625	113
Harris	179	183	—	5	—	18	60	77	19	4
Houston	1,642	1,642	1	8	14	164	247	1,137	71	—
Jones	308	311	—	—	3	27	90	178	10	3
Lee	450	456	2	1	6	11	160	241	29	6
McDuffie	425	425	—	2	3	32	74	281	33	—
Newton	956	956	1	4	8	37	274	537	95	—
Oconee	310	310	1	1	3	16	85	179	25	—
Paulding	1,512	1,525	1	13	6	45	307	995	145	13
Peach	299	301	—	3	2	63	80	137	14	2
Pickens	213	213	—	2	—	45	82	78	6	—
Richmond	13,973	13,987	35	102	712	654	3,384	7,155	1,931	14
Rockdale	2,402		1	24	28	103	438	1,656	152	
Twiggs	99	99	—	—	—	—	54	44	1	—
Walton	1,249	1,249	1	5	3	235	278	593	134	—
IDAHO										
Ada	1,960	1,983	2	7	4	77	416	1,359	95	23
Bannock	218	223	2	—	2	17	41	144	12	5
Canyon	903	910	2	14	3	56	261	488	79	7
ILLINOIS[1]										
INDIANA										
Allen	2,215	2,217	1	16	8	23	471	1,524	172	2
Allen State Police	130	131	—	2	—	16	21	78	13	1
Boone	74	74	—	—	1	1	24	44	4	—
Boone State Police	29	29	—	—	—	6	6	10	7	—
Dearborn	405	406	—	1	—	183	101	108	12	1
Dearborn State Police	107	108	—	—	—	23	26	44	14	1
Elkhart	2,343	2,355	—	13	20	460	546	1,156	148	12
Elkhart State Police	209	209	—	2	2	18	23	153	11	—
Hancock	503	507	2	1	6	1	156	318	19	4
Hancock State Police	20	20	—	—	—	2	1	12	5	—
Harrison	460		—	—	9	59	183	193	16	
Harrison State Police	120	121	—	3	—	23	43	45	6	1
Howard	519	530	—	6	2	40	125	321	25	11
Howard State Police	24	24	—	1	—	3	8	11	1	—
Huntington	167	169	—	—	1	28	71	67	—	2
Huntington State Police	22	22	—	—	—	3	6	8	5	—
Lake	697	697	—	3	4	76	119	326	169	—
Lake State Police	269	270	—	1	2	53	3	93	117	1
Marion[2]	18,360	18,459	18	143	532	620	3,405	11,748	1,894	99
Marion State Police	386	386	—	3	7	86	8	154	128	—
Porter	1,059	1,062	—	3	7	30	163	756	100	3
Porter State Police	71	72	—	—	6	26	3	28	8	1
St. Joseph	2,745	2,753	—	10	24	39	481	2,097	94	8
St. Joseph State Police	170	171	—	1	2	35	26	78	28	1
Scott	265	265	1	4	3	16	40	167	34	—

See footnotes at end of table.

Table 10. — Number of Offenses Known to the Police, Suburban Counties, 1996 — Continued

County by State	Crime Index total	Modified* Crime Index total	Murder and non-negligent man-slaughter	Forcible rape	Robbery	Aggravated assault	Burglary	Larceny–theft	Motor vehicle theft	Arson*
INDIANA — Continued										
Scott State Police	31	32	—	1	—	6	6	12	6	1
Tippecanoe	1,092	1,099	1	7	2	8	158	866	50	7
Tippecanoe State Police	126	126	—	2	—	28	20	64	12	—
Vanderburgh	981	984	1	6	10	96	90	755	23	3
Vanderburgh State Police	99	99	—	—	—	12	7	74	6	—
Warrick	555	563	3	5	3	5	69	452	18	8
Warrick State Police	39	40	3	—	1	6	5	19	5	1
IOWA										
Black Hawk	314	314	—	1	5	12	158	127	11	—
Dallas	224	224	—	—	—	11	54	154	5	—
Dubuque	328	332	—	5	—	20	105	177	21	4
Johnson	464	465	2	1	—	50	130	255	26	1
Linn	567	572	2	—	1	82	160	279	43	5
Polk	1,521	1,535	1	13	11	95	336	911	154	14
Scott	469	469	—	2	2	14	136	302	13	—
Warren	374	379	—	—	—	29	107	224	14	5
Woodbury	255	255	—	6	1	24	85	135	4	—
KANSAS¹										
KENTUCKY¹										
Boone	275		—	2	5	23	49	177	19	
Boone Police Department	800		1	15	5	44	164	522	49	
Jefferson Police Department	14,380		12	98	471	2,279	3,238	7,160	1,122	
LOUISIANA										
Acadia	756	756	—	3	7	66	219	449	12	—
Ascension	1,442		8	6	20	89	239	1,029	51	
Bossier	1,025	1,028	3	4	10	209	154	622	23	3
Caddo	1,999	1,999	3	21	13	4	629	1,211	118	—
Calcasieu	6,931	6,954	5	35	121	544	1,368	4,480	378	23
East Baton Rouge	12,199	12,229	15	66	239	366	1,949	8,704	860	30
Jefferson	28,650	28,846	25	133	1,086	1,941	4,495	17,490	3,480	196
Lafayette	1,808	1,821	2	23	32	169	513	1,004	65	13
Lafourche	2,111	2,114	5	6	45	97	350	1,475	133	3
Livingston	1,088	1,111	6	19	12	197	523	310	21	23
Ouachita	3,429	3,433	2	9	25	121	842	2,292	138	4
Plaquemines	677	680	2	4	10	93	187	330	51	3
Rapides	2,170	2,171	5	17	11	238	711	1,029	159	1
St. Charles	2,281	2,291	1	17	67	355	452	1,243	146	10
St. James	494		—	2	8	63	87	326	8	
St. Landry	1,058	1,060	6	12	16	106	268	605	45	2
St. Martin	617		4	10	7	11	203	361	21	
St. Tammany	4,077	4,096	10	37	53	270	952	2,466	289	19
Terrebonne	3,943	3,960	2	24	71	418	1,015	2,166	247	17
West Baton Rouge	752	757	—	9	10	64	77	545	47	5
MAINE										
Androscoggin	379	379	—	—	1	2	115	236	25	—
Androscoggin State Police	49	49	—	1	—	—	21	23	4	—
Cumberland	577	579	—	9	4	12	228	282	42	2
Cumberland State Police	150	150	—	—	—	5	55	80	10	—
MARYLAND										
Allegany	110	110	—	—	1	9	26	73	1	—
Allegany State Police	547	553	1	2	4	75	100	332	33	6
Anne Arundel Police Department	19,179	19,288	12	73	565	951	3,379	12,596	1,603	109
Anne Arundel State Police	161	161	—	1	1	43	11	87	18	—
Baltimore County Police Department	44,729	45,132	34	274	2,427	4,673	6,858	25,743	4,720	403
Baltimore County	8	8	—	—	—	—	—	8	—	—
Baltimore County State Police	102	102	—	—	—	12	1	70	19	—
Calvert	1,004	1,004	—	5	7	98	223	634	37	—
Calvert State Police	561	574	1	5	2	88	110	326	29	13
Carroll	23	23	—	—	—	1	4	18	—	—
Carroll State Police	1,960	1,984	1	27	31	173	438	1,183	107	24
Cecil	529	529	1	3	8	70	158	255	34	—
Cecil State Police	1,042	1,069	—	6	13	161	287	515	60	27

See footnotes at end of table.

169

Table 10. — Number of Offenses Known to the Police, Suburban Counties, 1996 — Continued

County by State	Crime Index total	Modified* Crime Index total	Murder and non-negligent man-slaughter	Forcible rape	Robbery	Aggravated assault	Burglary	Larceny–theft	Motor vehicle theft	Arson*
MARYLAND — Continued										
Charles	4,696	4,696	11	38	111	448	772	2,923	393	—
Charles State Police	80	124	—	3	1	11	10	48	7	44
Frederick	1,089	1,089	2	9	10	105	191	718	54	—
Frederick State Police	1,093	1,118	1	15	11	61	164	782	59	25
Harford	3,524	3,524	3	37	63	209	871	2,105	236	—
Harford State Police	756	809	1	5	22	39	163	449	77	53
Howard Police Department	8,978	8,978	5	33	248	336	1,278	6,297	781	—
Howard State Police	70	104	—	1	3	10	2	48	6	34
Montgomery	11	11	—	—	—	11	—	—	—	—
Montgomery Police Department	33,837	34,209	12	154	983	1,016	4,581	23,881	3,210	372
Montgomery State Police	44	44	—	—	—	16	2	22	4	—
Prince George's	634	634	—	1	—	633	—	—	—	—
Prince George's Police Department	49,748	50,205	132	296	3,466	3,413	7,953	24,208	10,280	457
Prince George's State Police	181	181	—	1	6	39	—	98	37	—
Queen Anne's	433	433	—	1	3	15	113	286	15	—
Queen Anne's State Police	432	448	—	2	4	44	79	269	34	16
Washington	981	981	—	5	12	57	223	632	52	—
Washington State Police	460	488	1	3	8	62	91	266	29	28
MASSACHUSETTS										
Barnstable State Police	18		—	—	—	9	—	7	2	
Berkshire State Police	122		—	—	—	28	29	60	5	
Bristol State Police	83		—	—	—	24	—	9	50	
Essex State Police	44		—	—	—	8	3	7	26	
Hampden State Police	49		—	—	—	17	4	21	7	
Hampshire State Police	43		—	—	—	11	10	15	7	
Middlesex State Police	24		—	—	2	6	—	1	15	
Norfolk State Police	23		—	—	—	9	—	6	8	
Plymouth State Police	80		—	—	—	25	—	12	43	
Suffolk State Police	267		—	—	5	22	22	186	32	
MIGHIGAN										
Allegan	1,164	1,175	—	9	6	75	335	670	69	11
Allegan State Police	669	683	—	24	4	53	232	325	31	14
Bay	766	770	—	4	8	24	170	492	68	4
Bay State Police	624	639	—	23	7	55	111	396	32	15
Berrien	831		2	8	12	75	231	464	39	
Berrien State Police	707	714	1	22	6	58	150	418	52	7
Calhoun	252	255	—	5	1	33	92	115	6	3
Calhoun State Police	300	303	2	24	4	21	82	158	9	3
Clinton	348	349	—	7	—	12	95	222	12	1
Clinton State Police	55	57	—	—	—	6	19	29	1	2
Eaton	2,321	2,330	—	10	27	99	276	1,790	119	9
Eaton State Police	102	105	—	7	—	5	23	55	12	3
Genesee	920	924	—	6	13	77	185	560	79	4
Genesee State Police	514	520	—	30	5	40	149	256	34	6
Ingham	1,593	1,609	—	28	11	90	328	1,033	103	16
Ingham State Police	209	212	—	12	4	9	16	157	11	3
Kent	4,362	4,387	5	26	21	245	905	2,932	228	25
Kent State Police	698	703	—	9	5	20	130	498	36	5
Lapeer	416	419	—	1	2	16	107	263	27	3
Lapeer State Police	185	191	—	18	2	14	53	79	19	6
Lenawee	751	761	1	6	1	35	180	475	53	10
Lenawee State Police	278	278	—	14	2	21	73	150	18	—
Livingston	854	857	—	8	3	27	199	541	76	3
Livingston State Police	740	747	—	19	1	39	172	468	41	7
Macomb	2,061		1	26	10	89	310	1,483	142	
Macomb State Police	159	163	—	6	2	18	24	92	17	4
Midland	442	446	—	14	4	29	133	249	13	4
Midland State Police	36	36	—	4	—	—	9	22	1	—
Monroe	3,146	3,181	2	28	23	118	554	2,170	251	35
Monroe State Police	469	493	—	8	6	30	117	275	33	24
Oakland	6,890	6,986	2	104	40	407	1,114	4,898	325	96
Oakland State Police	443	448	—	22	—	24	166	202	29	5
Saginaw	1,715		—	21	11	147	197	1,233	106	
Saginaw State Police	525	541	—	34	8	59	93	299	32	16
St. Clair	2,343	2,363	1	26	16	104	587	1,433	176	20
St. Clair State Police	345	350	—	10	2	23	106	179	25	5

Table 10. — Number of Offenses Known to the Police, Suburban Counties, 1996 — Continued

County by State	Crime Index total	Modified* Crime Index total	Murder and non-negligent man-slaughter	Forcible rape	Robbery	Aggravated assault	Burglary	Larceny– theft	Motor vehicle theft	Arson*
MICHIGAN — Continued										
Van Buren	853	856	—	10	3	43	285	408	104	3
Van Buren State Police	972	987	2	20	5	92	353	435	65	15
Washtenaw	3,464	3,507	3	70	97	239	858	1,775	422	43
Washtenaw State Police	306	320	1	14	9	47	78	121	36	14
Wayne	62	62	—	1	1	13	4	41	2	—
Wayne State Police	183	190	—	20	23	47	12	62	19	7
MINNESOTA										
Anoka	591	600	—	5	1	19	169	318	79	9
Benton	231	232	1	4	1	3	66	129	27	1
Carver	444	444	—	9	1	10	88	300	36	—
Chisago	1,259	1,260	—	12	7	31	249	851	109	1
Clay	153	153	1	8	2	14	30	83	15	—
Dakota	247	249	—	4	1	21	61	126	34	2
Hennepin	233	234	—	9	1	14	62	117	30	1
Houston	108	109	—	5	—	6	11	77	9	1
Isanti	401	405	—	15	2	14	125	174	71	4
Olmsted	485	487	—	9	2	18	101	299	56	2
Polk	221	223	1	3	—	12	88	96	21	2
Ramsey	311	316	1	3	1	5	30	256	15	5
St. Louis	1,021	1,034	—	26	1	24	459	444	67	13
Scott	287	287	—	6	3	11	44	197	26	—
Sherburne	656	656	—	8	1	20	155	408	64	—
Stearns	671	674	—	3	2	4	165	463	34	3
Washington	1,414	1,418	—	5	3	21	324	965	96	4
Wright	1,241	1,243	—	16	5	15	249	875	81	2
MISSISSIPPI										
Hinds	601	601	2	9	10	12	244	263	61	—
Madison	603	625	5	12	12	57	185	259	73	22
Rankin	1,006	1,015	3	9	7	42	329	553	63	9
MISSOURI										
Andrew	142	142	2	—	—	11	29	95	5	—
Boone	1,062	1,071	1	10	5	43	179	757	67	9
Buchanan	284	287	—	—	2	26	85	154	17	3
Cass	687	694	4	7	4	132	166	319	55	7
Christian	495	498	—	3	2	3	204	261	22	3
Clay	170	173	1	2	1	21	72	63	10	3
Franklin	1,616	1,689	2	9	3	141	690	660	111	73
Greene	1,428	1,430	—	14	12	98	330	867	107	2
Jackson	718	726	2	7	11	34	211	413	40	8
Jasper	514	514	1	7	—	44	191	240	31	—
Jefferson	3,607	3,687	7	20	16	170	864	2,175	355	80
Platte	468	468	1	3	2	37	125	283	17	—
Ray	163	165	1	2	—	29	53	69	9	2
St. Charles	2,114	2,127	—	13	10	103	408	1,451	129	13
St. Louis County Police Department	15,120	15,204	15	57	215	622	1,876	11,190	1,145	84
Webster	224	229	—	3	2	18	83	102	16	5
MONTANA[1]										
NEBRASKA										
Dakota	138	139	—	—	1	—	34	85	18	1
Dakota State Patrol	1	1	—	—	—	1	—	—	—	—
Douglas	1,665	1,675	2	9	21	133	218	1,172	110	10
Douglas State Patrol	12	12	—	—	—	7	—	5	—	—
Lancaster	571	579	1	2	1	8	103	438	18	8
Lancaster State Patrol	14	14	—	—	—	2	—	10	2	—
Sarpy	861	872	1	7	2	23	168	615	45	11
Sarpy State Patrol	4	4	—	—	—	—	—	4	—	—
Washington	141	144	—	—	1	2	31	97	10	3
Washington State Patrol	4	4	—	—	—	3	—	1	—	—
NEVADA										
Nye	879	894	1	—	4	108	351	400	15	15
Washoe	2,103	2,110	1	12	13	247	546	1,106	178	7

See footnotes at end of table.

Table 10. — Number of Offenses Known to the Police, Suburban Counties, 1996 — Continued

County by State	Crime Index total	Modified* Crime Index total	Murder and non-negligent man-slaughter	Forcible rape	Robbery	Aggravated assault	Burglary	Larceny–theft	Motor vehicle theft	Arson*
NEW HAMPSHIRE										
Rockingham State Police	30	32	—	3	3	6	13	4	1	2
Strafford State Police	12	12	—	1	—	1	6	3	1	—
NEW JERSEY										
Atlantic State Police	1,000	1,007	—	6	15	50	98	786	45	7
Bergen State Police	248	248	—	1	1	17	15	147	67	—
Burlington State Police	680	700	4	10	10	51	149	385	71	20
Camden State Police	49	49	—	1	2	12	4	27	3	—
Cape May State Police	465	466	—	3	4	31	136	250	41	1
Cumberland State Police	991	1,025	1	20	16	104	276	468	106	34
Essex Police Department	453	471	2	10	95	43	24	185	94	18
Essex State Police	61	64	—	1	8	14	2	28	8	3
Gloucester State Police	14	14	—	—	—	6	—	6	2	—
Hudson State Police	27	27	—	1	3	5	—	18	—	—
Hunterdon State Police	214	219	—	—	4	12	56	119	23	5
Mercer State Police	210	210	—	2	—	6	16	159	27	—
Middlesex State Police	111	112	—	—	8	10	2	77	14	1
Monmouth State Police	271	271	—	1	1	22	46	173	28	—
Morris State Police	46	47	—	—	3	11	4	17	11	1
Ocean State Police	115	122	—	—	—	11	12	87	5	7
Passaic State Police	30	30	—	—	—	5	1	7	17	—
Salem State Police	428	434	1	5	3	44	117	223	35	6
Somerset State Police	20	20	—	—	—	2	2	12	4	—
Sussex State Police	503	506	—	5	2	41	146	261	48	3
Union State Police	41	41	—	—	2	5	5	18	11	—
Warren State Police	303	308	—	8	6	18	107	142	22	5
NEW MEXICO										
Sandoval	260	262	3	7	1	70	70	103	6	2
NEW YORK										
Albany State Police	401		—	3	5	24	89	272	8	
Broome State Police	801		—	6	3	27	179	554	32	
Cayuga State Police	496		1	3	1	65	95	316	15	
Herkimer State Police	376	384	—	3	3	23	159	177	11	8
Livingston	767	768	1	5	2	6	138	588	27	1
Livingston State Police	115	116	—	1	—	35	18	59	2	1
Madison	130	130	—	—	2	21	25	82	—	—
Madison State Police	519	524	—	7	4	34	172	297	5	5
Montgomery	444	445	—	1	—	13	59	349	22	1
Montgomery State Police	174	174	—	—	—	12	42	112	8	—
Nassau	23,870	24,085	10	71	805	921	3,156	15,226	3,681	215
Niagara	1,423		2	12	18	28	324	864	175	
Niagara State Police	423	428	1	2	2	20	82	268	48	5
Oneida	993	996	—	19	7	169	256	532	10	3
Oneida State Police	903	915	2	4	4	89	224	558	22	12
Onondaga	2,896		1	35	52	62	592	2,048	106	
Onondaga State Police	1,053		—	2	10	26	212	780	23	
Ontario	1,173	1,179	—	5	6	14	226	863	59	6
Ontario State Police	501	504	—	3	3	15	71	399	10	3
Orange	40	40	—	—	1	19	3	15	2	—
Orange State Police	1,179		6	8	19	114	212	727	93	
Orleans	264	264	—	6	4	23	50	176	5	—
Orleans State Police	119	120	—	—	—	23	29	64	3	1
Oswego	751	782	—	8	4	11	247	461	20	31
Oswego State Police	883		1	5	3	102	251	508	13	
Putnam	327	328	—	3	3	16	103	175	27	1
Putnam State Police	212	214	—	—	3	15	43	134	17	2
Rensselaer	550	569	1	7	2	31	132	354	23	19
Rensselaer State Police	633	634	1	13	3	47	183	370	16	1
Rockland	99		—	1	—	7	3	86	2	
Rockland State Police	54	59	1	1	—	7	4	19	22	5
Saratoga	1,175	1,184	—	4	5	50	344	735	37	9
Saratoga State Police	698	702	1	10	9	42	173	443	20	4
Schenectady State Police	89	90	—	—	—	6	24	53	6	1
Schoharie	61	61	—	—	—	1	25	33	2	—
Schoharie State Police	265	273	—	—	1	13	109	138	4	8
Tioga	225	229	1	—	—	8	74	139	3	4

County by State	Crime Index total	Modified* Crime Index total	Murder and non-negligent man-slaughter	Forcible rape	Robbery	Aggravated assault	Burglary	Larceny–theft	Motor vehicle theft	Arson*
NEW YORK — Continued										
Tioga State Police	135	135	1	1	1	6	42	81	3	—
Warren	1,133	1,139	1	5	6	26	217	851	27	6
Warren State Police	221	222	—	2	2	3	33	173	8	1
Washington	376		—	1	—	5	110	258	2	
Washington State Police	178	179	—	—	1	32	54	91	—	1
Wayne	704	711	—	12	3	21	158	489	21	7
Wayne State Police	585	589	1	5	4	28	130	395	22	4
Westchester	485	485	2	3	13	52	33	349	33	—
Westchester State Police	597	607	1	3	11	92	109	337	44	10
NORTH CAROLINA										
Alamance	1,248	1,256	1	4	15	58	400	683	87	8
Alexander	545	548	—	1	7	23	200	275	39	3
Brunswick	1,176	1,190	11	2	12	38	548	481	84	14
Buncombe	2,469	2,488	7	24	29	222	858	1,174	155	19
Burke	1,421	1,429	4	13	21	77	487	722	97	8
Cabarrus	1,043	1,046	—	4	5	28	357	627	22	3
Caldwell	1,411	1,428	8	10	10	73	482	743	85	17
Catawba	1,817	1,825	—	16	12	42	702	965	80	8
Chatham	1,032	1,041	5	7	8	61	340	558	53	9
Cumberland	8,981	9,107	23	88	192	325	2,631	5,001	721	126
Currituck	561	561	—	—	3	45	187	303	23	—
Davidson	2,103	2,128	2	19	15	154	793	996	124	25
Davie	576	579	—	8	4	40	161	327	36	3
Durham	1,539	1,543	—	1	8	198	364	855	113	4
Edgecombe	876	882	1	10	15	43	338	421	48	6
Forsyth	3,885	3,953	2	19	45	315	919	2,414	171	68
Franklin	907	916	4	8	9	55	241	521	69	9
Gaston	2,527	2,565	6	24	34	289	845	1,192	137	38
Guilford	3,583	3,604	1	28	38	243	1,002	2,125	146	21
Johnston	1,918	1,927	3	13	15	29	684	1,004	170	9
Lincoln	1,284	1,305	—	4	18	25	385	787	65	21
Nash	1,012	1,012	3	8	21	18	283	614	65	—
New Hanover	2,689	2,695	—	15	19	294	692	1,555	114	6
Onslow	3,001	3,016	2	24	43	50	968	1,677	237	15
Orange	891	892	3	3	13	22	383	423	44	1
Pitt	1,801	1,830	3	12	27	171	712	787	89	29
Randolph	2,291	2,297	3	10	9	128	663	1,379	99	6
Rowan	1,668	1,682	—	17	16	106	583	859	87	14
Stokes	935	942	2	8	3	92	304	453	73	7
Union	2,049	2,057	6	13	34	44	646	1,238	68	8
Wake	3,257	3,295	7	26	47	198	1,035	1,657	287	38
Wayne	1,899	1,904	6	10	17	133	680	944	109	5
Yadkin	550	557	1	3	—	15	162	337	32	7
NORTH DAKOTA										
Burleigh	55	56	—	—	—	—	17	35	3	1
Cass	165	171	—	2	1	13	34	92	23	6
Morton	86	86	—	3	—	1	11	69	2	—
OHIO										
Ashtabula	1,469	1,490	3	15	10	16	392	950	83	21
Auglaize	369	369	1	6	2	15	120	207	18	—
Clermont	1,374	1,396	1	40	10	30	392	832	69	22
Columbiana	426	427	—	3	1	1	67	311	43	1
Delaware	767	772	—	2	1	24	347	359	34	5
Franklin	4,527	4,553	8	45	142	73	937	2,836	486	26
Fulton	392	400	—	1	2	3	133	235	18	8
Greene	410	410	—	3	—	10	101	276	20	—
Hamilton	8,209	8,264	3	68	135	77	1,078	6,403	445	55
Jefferson	356	356	—	—	—	—	108	221	27	—
Lake	718	721	—	4	10	23	132	522	27	3
Licking	1,031	1,032	1	3	1	89	284	583	70	1
Lorain	1,221	1,240	—	8	16	185	519	429	64	19
Lucas	1,692	1,692	1	25	21	37	427	1,110	71	—
Miami	687	687	2	6	3	16	181	404	75	—
Pickaway	864	874	—	7	3	6	325	503	20	10
Portage	1,494	1,494	4	26	11	30	340	968	115	—

Table 10. — Number of Offenses Known to the Police, Suburban Counties, 1996 — Continued

County by State	Crime Index total	Modified* Crime Index total	Murder and non-negligent man-slaughter	Forcible rape	Robbery	Aggravated assault	Burglary	Larceny-theft	Motor vehicle theft	Arson*
OHIO — Continued										
Richland	1,175	1,182	3	3	12	46	269	817	25	7
Stark	3,074	3,109	2	29	68	81	976	1,703	215	35
Trumbull	258	258	—	—	—	3	86	129	40	—
Wood	594	598	1	7	4	14	132	384	52	4
OKLAHOMA										
Canadian	178	178	—	4	—	5	74	82	13	—
Cleveland	336	336	3	9	1	4	154	141	24	—
Comanche	586	597	—	2	9	66	154	296	59	11
Creek	710		2	3	4	121	255	235	90	
Garfield	150	171	3	—	—	2	46	93	6	21
Logan	464	470	—	5	5	25	172	230	27	6
McClain	179	182	3	1	3	31	53	75	13	3
Oklahoma	342		1	1	—	44	150	120	26	
Osage	285	285	1	7	1	52	98	101	25	—
Pottawatomie	674	688	2	4	5	93	236	295	39	14
Rogers	717	721	3	1	2	19	238	408	46	4
Sequoyah	371	376	4	3	2	19	183	114	46	5
Tulsa	1,695	1,744	4	19	38	280	360	772	222	49
Wagoner	679	704	1	12	6	54	290	266	50	25
OREGON										
Clackamas	9,095	9,131	4	48	123	134	1,538	6,155	1,093	36
Clackamas State Police	38	60	—	1	1	3	2	18	13	22
Columbia	387	390	—	1	1	11	117	220	37	3
Columbia State Police	11	12	—	1	—	4	3	1	2	1
Jackson	1,925	1,933	1	18	10	154	387	1,235	120	8
Jackson State Police	159	167	1	5	1	21	51	62	18	8
Lane	2,430	2,437	5	25	27	134	791	1,236	212	7
Lane State Police	254	280	2	13	6	34	47	125	27	26
Marion	4,130	4,140	—	29	49	135	729	2,800	388	10
Marion State Police	179	206	1	4	2	50	4	93	25	27
Multnomah	1,058	1,074	2	15	9	103	200	634	95	16
Multnomah State Police	55	60	—	1	1	4	1	42	6	5
Polk	545	554	—	10	2	18	144	326	45	9
Polk State Police	21	23	—	—	—	4	—	17	—	2
Yamhill	1,016	1,027	1	11	6	147	250	516	85	11
Yamhill State Police	11	13	—	—	—	3	2	4	2	2
PENNSYLVANIA										
Allegheny State Police	110	110	1	1	4	38	9	47	10	—
Beaver	19	20	—	—	—	7	1	11	—	1
Beaver State Police	204	212	2	6	2	17	57	96	24	8
Berks State Police	631	655	2	5	11	23	180	341	69	24
Blair State Police	567	573	1	8	4	22	158	324	50	6
Bucks State Police	713	720	—	3	12	68	122	444	64	7
Butler State Police	1,066	1,078	1	7	5	33	268	645	107	12
Cambria	1		—	—	—	1	—	—	—	
Cambria State Police	261	267	1	4	2	22	89	104	39	6
Carbon State Police	359	366	—	10	—	14	121	188	26	7
Centre	1		—	—	—	1	—	—	—	
Centre State Police	735	764	—	17	2	43	263	378	32	29
Chester Detective	18	18	—	8	—	4	—	6	—	—
Chester State Police	1,792	1,812	3	16	25	102	525	969	152	20
Columbia State Police	147	150	—	1	—	6	37	86	17	3
Cumberland State Police	685	699	1	17	8	39	200	372	48	14
Dauphin	88	88	—	4	5	2	1	75	1	—
Dauphin State Police	961	961	1	16	11	103	172	588	70	—
Delaware State Police	1,148	1,154	—	8	14	66	152	737	171	6
Erie State Police	2,016	2,026	1	20	15	50	473	1,346	111	10
Fayette State Police	2,587	2,757	3	37	45	96	789	1,235	382	170
Lackawanna State Police	372	374	1	7	4	37	124	158	41	2
Lancaster	2	2	—	—	—	—	—	2	—	—
Lancaster State Police	1,173	1,199	—	10	16	40	404	606	97	26
Lebanon Detective	3	3	—	2	—	—	—	1	—	—
Lebanon State Police	378	378	—	5	1	13	99	229	31	—
Lehigh State Police	1,377	1,400	—	8	18	49	286	936	80	23
Luzerne State Police	808	846	1	5	3	108	203	441	47	38

Table 10. — Number of Offenses Known to the Police, Suburban Counties, 1996 — Continued

County by State	Crime Index total	Modified* Crime Index total	Murder and non-negligent man-slaughter	Forcible rape	Robbery	Aggravated assault	Burglary	Larceny-theft	Motor vehicle theft	Arson*
PENNSYLVANIA — Continued										
Lycoming State Police	931	946	—	13	12	85	229	541	51	15
Mercer State Police	447	451	—	4	6	23	130	245	39	4
Montgomery State Police	605	621	—	7	6	66	108	368	50	16
Northampton State Police	378	388	—	3	4	28	91	222	30	10
Perry State Police	501	504	—	8	8	35	150	260	40	3
Philadelphia State Police	10	10	—	—	—	—	—	7	3	—
Pike State Police	781	781	—	11	4	50	316	347	53	—
Somerset State Police	725	736	3	3	3	38	332	283	63	11
Washington State Police	867	911	—	9	14	41	298	400	105	44
Westmoreland Detective	79	79	—	—	—	1	—	78	—	—
Westmoreland State Police	2,416	2,485	4	33	36	117	627	1,334	265	69
Wyoming State Police	341	346	1	5	4	35	91	166	39	5
York State Police	788	804	—	8	7	44	229	433	67	16
RHODE ISLAND										
Hope Valley	179	180	—	16	2	54	26	73	8	1
Chepachet/Lincoln Woods	137	139	1	8	1	12	15	84	16	2
Wickford	111	111	—	5	—	11	33	59	3	—
SOUTH CAROLINA										
Aiken	3,603	3,605	5	49	87	279	1,184	1,684	315	2
Anderson	6,369	6,386	8	62	103	835	1,605	3,289	467	17
Berkeley	4,126	4,147	5	46	57	436	962	2,263	357	21
Charleston	4,608	4,621	9	41	109	557	1,188	2,308	396	13
Cherokee	1,416	1,423	6	7	23	323	326	649	82	7
Cherokee State Police	1	1	—	—	—	1	—	—	—	—
Dorchester	2,617	2,626	2	22	45	243	636	1,473	196	9
Edgefield	585	589	1	4	10	83	194	244	49	4
Florence	2,363	2,388	8	31	34	366	628	1,194	102	25
Florence State Police	1	1	—	—	—	—	—	1	—	—
Greenville	12,090	12,178	22	113	305	1,437	2,904	6,516	793	88
Horry	8	8	—	—	—	—	2	6	—	—
Horry Police Department	7,233	7,244	10	55	128	814	1,682	3,935	609	11
Lexington	6,013	6,028	12	62	157	623	1,803	2,923	433	15
Pickens	1,284	1,290	1	18	6	107	342	747	63	6
Richland	8,665	8,681	15	108	399	906	1,911	4,368	958	16
Spartanburg	10,823	10,879	8	88	278	1,591	2,202	5,966	690	56
Sumter	3,488	3,513	4	35	79	604	994	1,474	298	42
York	3,230	3,272	2	39	40	367	796	1,829	157	42
SOUTH DAKOTA										
Minnehaha	382	386	—	20	1	25	126	181	29	4
Pennington	888	890	—	30	1	42	183	605	27	2
TENNESSEE										
Madison	1,042	1,045	3	6	14	92	321	522	84	3
Marion	527		6	7	11	114	42	328	19	
Montgomery	1,017		—	—	—	195	268	510	44	
Robertson	495	495	1	5	8	21	157	295	8	—
Sullivan	1,549		3	42	4	133	419	843	105	
Sumner	1,088	1,099	3	12	4	126	372	506	65	11
Washington	623	628	3	5	1	46	225	304	39	5
TEXAS										
Archer	81	84	—	5	—	5	32	33	6	3
Bastrop	752	760	2	3	9	87	298	310	43	8
Bell	1,268	1,306	2	23	7	139	317	690	90	38
Bexar	5,506	5,639	7	32	68	586	1,227	3,160	426	133
Bowie	797	797	3	9	6	62	253	409	55	—
Brazoria	1,533	1,544	7	21	18	169	560	652	106	11
Brazos	421	426	1	8	2	7	157	231	15	5
Caldwell	228	230	—	5	1	3	60	152	7	2
Cameron	1,188	1,193	7	—	22	90	627	392	50	5
Chambers	529	530	3	10	9	21	115	322	49	1
Collin	661	667	1	13	3	54	219	313	58	6
Comal	942		6	22	3	52	305	525	29	
Coryell	102	119	—	—	—	12	41	46	3	17
Dallas	479	507	5	3	17	111	125	184	34	28

County by State	Crime Index total	Modified* Crime Index total	Murder and non-negligent man-slaughter	Forcible rape	Robbery	Aggravated assault	Burglary	Larceny–theft	Motor vehicle theft	Arson*
TEXAS — Continued										
Denton	625	625	1	3	3	38	164	381	35	—
Ector	1,177	1,177	1	10	14	17	294	782	59	—
Ellis	976	976	—	17	11	81	397	433	37	—
El Paso	1,897	1,911	7	70	46	226	413	989	146	14
Fort Bend	2,089	2,122	9	20	49	204	695	983	129	33
Galveston	1,208	1,226	1	17	21	229	343	512	85	18
Grayson	1,002	1,009	1	6	8	30	325	563	69	7
Gregg	557	560	—	8	11	75	154	259	50	3
Guadalupe	1,223	1,223	2	19	8	250	367	518	59	—
Hardin	375	376	—	2	—	30	127	179	37	1
Harris	38,617	39,127	56	378	1,297	4,325	8,930	18,888	4,743	510
Harrison	910	940	3	1	5	32	310	513	46	30
Hays	1,060	1,066	1	10	5	45	334	599	66	6
Henderson	1,033	1,039	2	13	3	65	404	490	56	6
Hidalgo	5,471	5,568	19	55	162	566	2,448	1,840	381	97
Hood	792	798	—	6	3	39	240	477	27	6
Hunt	940	955	—	10	2	87	423	363	55	15
Jefferson	692	699	—	16	13	12	197	392	62	7
Johnson	1,030	1,031	4	23	2	67	372	506	56	1
Kaufman	924	946	—	13	6	53	319	463	70	22
Liberty	908	911	4	14	7	36	436	350	61	3
Lubbock	847	853	—	11	5	78	170	525	58	6
McLennan	958	962	1	1	12	58	318	514	54	4
Midland	631	634	—	19	4	36	127	414	31	3
Montgomery	5,918	5,996	6	55	62	517	1,615	3,221	442	78
Nueces	236	239	1	11	2	31	62	118	11	3
Orange	974	986	1	13	11	75	290	525	59	12
Parker	879	879	4	21	3	55	295	455	46	—
Potter	269	273	1	1	2	22	65	151	27	4
Randall	329	333	—	6	1	29	89	185	19	4
Rockwall	171	172	—	4	1	22	48	88	8	1
San Patricio	361	362	—	—	—	19	112	216	14	1
Smith	2,346	2,454	5	58	14	202	621	1,277	169	108
Tarrant	1,361	1,378	2	9	13	132	457	674	74	17
Taylor	242	248	1	7	2	32	80	118	2	6
Tom Green	372	376	1	15	3	142	77	124	10	4
Travis	3,986	4,007	2	35	46	185	1,156	2,307	255	21
Upshur	333	339	1	11	1	14	119	145	42	6
Victoria	611	614	—	13	10	42	192	318	36	3
Waller	126	128	—	1	1	3	58	53	10	2
Webb	363	364	—	3	5	32	155	147	21	1
Wichita	162	168	1	2	1	22	47	76	13	6
Williamson	2,159	2,176	—	25	14	104	616	1,289	111	17
Wilson	250	250	1	—	1	15	124	109	—	—
UTAH										
Davis	389	389	—	9	4	29	124	188	35	—
Salt Lake	21,435	21,499	11	173	222	880	2,845	15,862	1,442	64
Utah	808	820	1	12	3	31	156	554	51	12
Weber	1,025	1,026	1	5	5	15	195	735	69	1
VERMONT[1]										
VIRGINIA										
Albemarle Police Department	1,958	1,997	—	12	18	70	346	1,415	97	39
Albemarle State Police	6		—	—	1	—	—	4	1	
Amherst	677	679	1	3	7	70	84	461	51	2
Amherst State Police	6		—	—	—	—	1	3	2	
Arlington	9,673	9,712	3	43	311	230	793	7,028	1,265	39
Arlington State Police	8	8	—	—	—	1	—	1	6	—
Bedford	741	741	1	7	3	40	159	494	37	—
Bedford State Police	14	14	—	—	—	1	—	9	4	—
Botetourt	316	317	—	2	3	13	77	210	11	1
Botetourt State Police	7	7	—	—	—	1	—	6	—	—
Campbell	820	825	2	5	9	50	161	530	63	5
Campbell State Police	6	6	—	—	—	—	1	4	1	—
Charles City	41	41	—	—	1	6	16	18	—	—
Charles City State Police	5		—	—	—	—	2	2	1	
Chesterfield Police Department	8,669	8,736	7	47	159	100	1,325	6,615	416	67

See footnotes at end of table.

County by State	Crime Index total	Modified* Crime Index total	Murder and non-negligent man-slaughter	Forcible rape	Robbery	Aggravated assault	Burglary	Larceny–theft	Motor vehicle theft	Arson*
VIRGINIA — Continued										
Chesterfield State Police	30	30	—	—	1	7	—	18	4	—
Clarke	187	188	—	2	—	1	51	129	4	1
Culpeper	384	401	3	3	8	37	58	259	16	17
Culpeper State Police	17	17	1	—	—	2	1	11	2	—
Dinwiddie	386	389	—	2	5	15	83	267	14	3
Dinwiddie State Police	9	10	—	—	—	—	1	4	4	1
Fairfax Police Department	26,678	26,870	14	87	487	335	1,942	21,707	2,106	192
Fairfax State Police	29	29	—	—	—	4	2	21	2	—
Fauquier	760	765	—	12	9	28	216	450	45	5
Fauquier State Police	25	25	—	—	—	—	5	18	2	—
Fluvanna	187	191	—	2	—	6	67	103	9	4
Fluvanna State Police	1	—	—	—	—	—	—	1	—	—
Gloucester	496	499	—	6	3	17	97	353	20	3
Gloucester State Police	12	12	—	—	—	—	1	11	—	—
Goochland	209	209	1	1	1	9	104	75	18	—
Goochland State Police	16	18	—	—	—	—	—	13	3	2
Greene	242	243	—	2	2	23	46	156	13	1
Greene State Police	2	—	—	—	—	—	—	—	2	—
Hanover	1,302	1,307	—	4	17	36	145	1,066	34	5
Hanover State Police	29	29	—	—	2	5	—	15	7	—
Henrico Police Department	10,691	10,778	17	43	234	257	1,643	7,894	603	87
Henrico State Police	21	21	—	—	—	—	—	17	4	—
Isle of Wight	591	592	1	6	6	39	107	389	43	1
Isle of Wight State Police	2	2	—	—	—	—	—	2	—	—
James City Police Department	1,031	1,035	1	16	12	39	124	792	47	4
James City State Police	4	4	—	—	—	—	—	4	—	—
King George	321	325	2	3	7	31	73	179	26	4
King George State Police	20	20	—	1	—	3	5	7	4	—
Loudoun	2,459	2,460	1	9	22	80	319	1,950	78	1
Loudoun State Police	22	22	—	—	—	1	4	14	3	—
Mathews	77	77	—	1	1	9	14	39	13	—
New Kent	272	275	1	7	2	9	54	175	24	3
New Kent State Police	17	17	1	—	—	1	3	8	4	—
Pittsylvania State Police	39	39	—	—	—	—	—	16	23	—
Powhatan	197	198	2	2	4	3	48	123	15	1
Powhatan State Police	20	20	—	—	—	12	1	7	—	—
Prince George Police Department	603	604	1	6	9	25	143	387	32	1
Prince George State Police	7	7	—	—	—	2	—	3	2	—
Prince William State Police	38	38	1	—	4	4	3	23	3	—
Roanoke Police Department	1,668	1,675	1	6	14	99	218	1,265	65	7
Scott	239	243	1	7	1	25	70	120	15	4
Scott State Police	6	7	—	—	—	2	—	2	2	1
Spotsylvania	1,939	1,940	2	11	22	59	235	1,501	109	1
Spotsylvania State Police	63	63	—	—	—	6	3	46	8	—
Stafford	1,943	1,976	4	19	29	55	230	1,484	122	33
Stafford State Police	27	27	—	—	—	5	1	18	3	—
Washington	567	569	2	7	2	48	112	362	34	2
Washington State Police	14	14	—	—	—	—	1	—	9	4
York	1,672	1,690	1	6	25	81	166	1,296	97	18
York State Police	5	6	—	—	—	1	—	2	2	1
WASHINGTON										
Benton	958	961	3	11	2	46	210	644	42	3
Clark	5,610	5641	3	81	194	324	1,365	3,053	590	31
Franklin	277	279	1	4	2	26	63	159	22	2
Island	758	762	3	5	2	29	238	443	38	4
King	16,373	16,585	12	226	281	505	3,322	10,050	1,977	212
Kitsap	5,487	5,541	3	66	46	359	1,041	3,698	274	54
Pierce	20,211	20,308	22	141	371	1,363	4,073	12,370	1,871	97
Snohomish	6,834		13	186	91	301	1,869	3,563	811	
Spokane	9,174	9,193	5	53	100	292	2,102	6,088	534	19
Thurston	3,159	3,174	4	39	18	138	958	1,810	192	15
Whatcom	2,197	2,220	1	40	14	97	825	1,126	94	23
Yakima	3,663	3,721	6	79	24	106	1,509	1,626	313	58
WEST VIRGINIA										
Brooke	73	74	—	1	1	2	32	34	3	1
Cabell	786	786	2	—	17	13	144	547	63	—
Cabell State Police	277	277	—	1	1	25	65	161	24	—

Table 10. — Number of Offenses Known to the Police, Suburban Counties, 1996 — Continued

County by State	Crime Index total	Modified* Crime Index total	Murder and non-negligent man-slaughter	Forcible rape	Robbery	Aggravated assault	Burglary	Larceny–theft	Motor vehicle theft	Arson*
WEST VIRGINIA — Continued										
Hancock	270	273	2	1	4	36	63	141	23	3
Hancock State Police	7	8	1	—	—	1	1	3	1	1
Kanawha	1,626	1,626	4	10	37	84	503	780	208	—
Kanawha State Police	579	581	1	9	1	35	79	373	81	2
Marshall	102	102	—	—	1	4	60	32	5	—
Marshall State Police	18	18	—	1	—	1	8	5	3	—
Mineral	41	42	—	2	—	3	11	19	6	1
Mineral State Police	145	145	—	1	—	33	41	54	16	—
Ohio	105	105	—	—	2	26	20	54	3	—
Ohio State Police	31	31	—	—	—	—	6	23	2	—
Putnam	537	540	—	3	10	6	116	371	31	3
Putnam State Police	214	214	—	9	—	36	34	125	10	—
Wayne	115	115	—	—	—	14	46	39	16	—
Wayne State Police	319	321	—	4	4	58	80	127	46	2
Wood	328	328	—	4	—	7	92	214	11	—
Wood State Police	82	83	1	—	—	2	36	41	2	1
WISCONSIN										
Brown	1,608	1,612	—	12	4	19	309	1,178	86	4
Calumet	190	192	—	5	—	11	36	129	9	2
Chippewa	428	428	—	—	—	4	81	310	33	—
Dane	1,404	1,424	1	4	8	194	276	841	80	20
Douglas	383	383	1	3	—	3	178	174	24	—
Eau Claire	380	384	—	5	8	8	97	231	31	4
Kenosha	1,001	1,014	1	12	6	33	197	689	63	13
La Crosse	328	329	—	1	—	82	35	204	6	1
Marathon	601	601	—	11	—	46	114	386	44	—
Milwaukee	108	108	—	—	4	5	—	86	13	—
Outagamie	428	429	1	1	2	22	83	302	17	1
Ozaukee	225	225	—	—	1	3	58	153	10	—
Pierce	317	317	1	2	—	5	102	183	24	—
Racine	761	762	—	2	8	8	111	595	37	1
Rock	629	631	—	10	1	32	185	364	37	2
St. Croix	554	558	—	3	5	35	120	343	48	4
Sheboygan	736	742	—	4	3	26	141	525	37	6
Washington	767	779	—	3	4	17	150	554	39	12
Waukesha	901	909	—	2	1	76	118	653	51	8
Winnebago	467	467	1	2	3	7	108	320	26	—
WYOMING										
Laramie	722	724	—	19	6	38	106	529	24	2
Natrona	489	497	1	2	2	20	128	305	31	8

[1] Complete data were not available for the states of Illinois, Kansas, Kentucky, Montana, and Vermont; therefore, it was necessary that their crime counts be estimated. An aggregate Florida state total for 1996 was supplied by the Florida Department of Law Enforcement. See "Offense Estimation," pages 389-390 for details.

[2] Indianapolis/Marion County, Indiana, is a unified city-county government with a total population of 777,458.

Table 11. — Number of Offenses Known to the Police, Rural Counties 25,000 and over in Population, 1996

[The data shown in this table do not reflect county totals but are the number of offenses reported by the sheriff's office, county police department, or state police.]
* Arson is shown only if 12 months of arson data were received. Dashes (—) indicate zero data. The Modified Crime Index total is the sum of the Crime Index offenses, including arson.

County by State	Crime Index total	Modified* Crime Index total	Murder and non-negligent man-slaughter	Forcible rape	Robbery	Aggravated assault	Burglary	Larceny–theft	Motor vehicle theft	Arson*
ALABAMA										
Cullman	1,258	1,272	—	10	8	84	324	701	131	14
De Kalb	270		—	4	1	1	101	158	5	
Jackson	457	471	2	5	4	6	197	190	53	14
Lee	1,053		1	2	7	87	419	499	38	
Marshall	141		—	3	—	11	59	64	4	
Talladega	26		—	—	—	1	10	13	2	
Walker	71		—	1	1	4	23	28	14	
ARIZONA										
Apache	250	250	1	3	1	40	76	120	9	—
Cochise	1,330	1,336	1	2	11	115	477	587	137	6
Navajo	535	545	—	5	—	63	183	249	35	10
Yavapai	2,505	2,516	4	12	7	325	719	1,292	146	11
ARKANSAS										
Baxter	171	171	1	—	1	13	19	124	13	—
Garland	288	290	3	5	1	4	94	149	32	2
Independence	1,292	1,301	3	10	2	55	189	979	54	9
Pope	489	494	4	3	—	4	167	293	18	5
White	864	875	1	12	9	31	297	430	84	11
CALIFORNIA										
Calaveras	1,000	1,018	2	8	3	107	422	456	2	18
Calaveras Highway Patrol	71	71	—	—	—	1	—	18	52	
Humboldt	1,512	1,520	2	22	19	195	658	581	35	8
Humboldt Highway Patrol	172	172	—	—	—	4	2	6	160	—
Imperial	967	982	4	8	16	147	336	448	8	15
Imperial Highway Patrol	87	87	—	—	—	1	—	8	78	—
Kings	858	869	1	4	13	125	329	377	9	11
Kings Highway Patrol	112	112	—	—	—	1	—	12	99	—
Lake	977	977	2	16	16	123	511	308	1	—
Lake Highway Patrol	97	97	—	1	—	4	—	9	83	—
Mendocino	1,209	1,232	4	24	21	235	527	391	7	23
Mendocino Highway Patrol	112	112	—	—	—	3	—	22	87	—
Nevada	2,037	2,041	2	11	12	340	536	1,086	50	4
Nevada Highway Patrol	111	112	—	—	—	5	1	13	92	1
Tehama	800	828	1	4	9	149	245	380	12	28
Tehama Highway Patrol	74	74	—	—	—	5	—	5	64	—
Tuolumne	1,812	1,824	1	14	9	345	656	786	1	12
Tuolumne Highway Patrol	118	118	—	—	—	—	—	4	114	—
DELAWARE										
Sussex State Police	3,695	3,704	8	72	82	623	965	1,840	105	9
FLORIDA[1]										
Columbia	2,178		—	17	31	295	503	1,205	127	
Monroe	3,881		1	22	37	361	752	2,499	209	
Putnam	3,116		1	56	39	487	985	1,519	29	
Sumter	849		1	9	6	114	337	337	45	
GEORGIA										
Floyd Police Department	564	572	2	18	5	49	256	222	12	8
Glynn Police Department	3,548	3,560	1	17	73	308	517	2,436	196	12
Gordon	864	864	1	—	1	25	217	513	107	—
Hall	3,318	3,337	1	19	21	262	735	1,920	360	19
Liberty	589	589	3	11	8	26	150	338	53	—
Lowndes	1,284		2	9	15	45	218	924	71	
Murray	470	470	3	—	—	—	146	284	37	
Troup	1,015		1	11	2	29	140	787	45	
Whitfield	1,943	1,966	—	18	14	90	539	1,147	135	23

See footnotes at end of table.

Table 11. — Number of Offenses Known to the Police, Rural Counties 25,000 and over in Population, 1996 — Continued

County by State	Crime Index total	Modified* Crime Index total	Murder and non-negligent man-slaughter	Forcible rape	Robbery	Aggravated assault	Burglary	Larceny–theft	Motor vehicle theft	Arson*
HAWAII										
Hawaii Police Department	3,980	4,000	6	31	31	93	1,064	2,571	184	20
Kauai Police Department	2,977	2,987	4	20	13	25	590	2,242	83	10
Maui Police Department	8,070	8,086	1	39	111	114	1,584	5,826	395	16
IDAHO										
Bingham	300	300	1	4	1	9	56	189	40	—
Bonneville	763	764	2	7	3	72	160	474	45	—
Kootenai	1,088	1,091	4	11	4	97	368	561	43	3
ILLINOIS[1]										
INDIANA										
Bartholomew	264	267	2	5	2	8	62	178	7	3
Bartholomew State Police	27	27	—	2	—	2	3	14	6	—
Benton State Police	12	12	—	1	—	4	1	4	2	—
Blackford State Police	8	8	—	—	—	2	4	1	1	—
Brown State Police	17	17	—	1	—	1	3	11	1	—
Carroll State Police	33	33	—	—	—	9	8	13	3	—
Cass State Police	26	26	—	—	—	11	5	8	2	—
Crawford State Police	49	49	—	—	—	10	19	15	5	—
Daviess State Police	37	37	—	—	—	5	9	20	3	—
Decatur State Police	29	30	—	2	1	10	6	10	—	1
DuBois State Police	70	70	—	2	—	8	13	46	1	—
Fayette State Police	25	25	—	—	—	7	7	9	2	—
Fountain State Police	32	32	—	—	—	7	14	8	3	—
Franklin State Police	54	55	—	—	—	11	15	26	2	1
Fulton State Police	19	19	—	—	—	5	2	9	3	—
Gibson State Police	58	58	—	2	1	10	10	27	8	—
Grant	426	434	—	3	1	41	116	241	24	8
Grant State Police	20	22	—	—	—	4	1	14	1	2
Greene State Police	44	44	—	4	—	10	9	16	5	—
Henry	637	641	—	3	—	3	178	423	30	4
Henry State Police	28	28	—	—	1	5	4	15	3	—
Jackson State Police	118	119	—	2	—	22	27	55	12	1
Jasper State Police	24	24	—	—	—	2	2	17	3	—
Jay State Police	13	13	—	—	—	5	2	4	2	—
Jefferson State Police	34	34	—	1	—	6	11	15	1	—
Jennings State Police	50	51	—	2	—	8	12	22	6	1
Knox State Police	50	52	—	1	1	10	11	22	5	2
Kosciusko State Police	68	68	—	2	1	20	10	31	4	—
La Grange	179	179	1	—	—	38	49	78	13	—
La Grange State Police	88	88	—	—	—	19	13	50	6	—
La Porte	1,110	1,114	—	5	5	37	270	743	50	4
La Porte State Police	77	77	—	—	1	22	2	41	11	—
Lawrence	353	355	4	—	1	28	105	207	8	2
Lawrence State Police	40	40	—	1	1	8	10	16	4	—
Marshall State Police	59	59	—	—	—	17	8	26	8	—
Martin State Police	12	12	1	—	—	6	1	4	—	—
Miami State Police	56	56	—	—	—	12	19	16	9	—
Montgomery State Police	30	30	1	—	—	4	4	13	8	—
Newton State Police	26	26	—	—	—	7	3	9	7	—
Noble State Police	104	104	1	1	—	19	40	34	9	—
Orange State Police	50	51	2	4	—	2	21	16	5	1
Owen State Police	40	40	2	—	—	10	19	5	4	—
Parke State Police	25	26	1	2	—	4	6	12	—	1
Perry State Police	40	40	2	3	—	4	15	15	1	—
Pike State Police	32	32	—	—	—	10	6	12	4	—
Pulaski State Police	9	9	—	—	—	4	3	1	1	—
Putnam State Police	93	94	—	2	1	22	28	32	8	1
Randolph State Police	5	5	—	—	—	2	—	3	—	—
Ripley State Police	173	174	1	1	1	22	52	82	14	1

See footnotes at end of table.

Table 11. — Number of Offenses Known to the Police, Rural Counties 25,000 and over in Population, 1996 — Continued

County by State	Crime Index total	Modified* Crime Index total	Murder and non-negligent man-slaughter	Forcible rape	Robbery	Aggravated assault	Burglary	Larceny–theft	Motor vehicle theft	Arson*
INDIANA — Continued										
Rush State Police	12	12	—	—	—	—	1	11	—	—
Spencer State Police	49	49	1	—	1	6	15	25	1	—
Starke State Police	34	34	—	3	—	16	1	11	3	—
Steuben State Police	64	64	—	2	—	6	16	34	6	—
Sullivan State Police	67	67	1	1	—	34	7	23	1	—
Switzerland State Police	56	56	—	1	—	13	23	18	1	—
Union State Police	22	22	—	1	—	5	8	8	—	—
Wabash State Police	18	18	—	2	—	2	3	7	4	—
Warren State Police	24	25	—	1	1	4	6	10	2	1
Washington State Police	27	27	—	1	—	8	9	7	2	—
Wayne	600	602	—	—	—	11	125	427	37	2
Wayne State Police	48	48	—	2	—	12	7	25	2	—
White State Police	51	51	—	—	2	8	10	27	4	—
KANSAS¹										
KENTUCKY¹										
LOUISIANA										
Avoyelles	533		1	25	5	253	70	179	—	
Iberia	786	786	4	5	9	37	141	548	42	—
Tangipahoa	1,808		3	6	42	452	268	976	61	
Vermilion	442	443	1	9	3	30	146	248	5	1
Vernon	952	953	1	8	6	153	179	573	32	1
MAINE										
Aroostook	120	121	—	—	—	3	50	64	3	1
Aroostook State Police	432	435	—	8	2	5	165	219	33	3
Hancock	343	343	—	—	—	5	98	226	14	—
Hancock State Police	157	157	1	3	—	—	54	95	4	—
Kennebec	411	411	—	7	—	4	167	212	21	—
Kennebec State Police	332	332	2	1	2	2	105	175	45	—
Penobscot	916	918	—	4	3	9	300	543	57	2
Penobscot State Police	269	269	1	8	1	11	92	129	27	—
Somerset	446	446	—	—	—	11	197	213	25	—
Somerset State Police	114	114	2	1	—	1	39	64	7	—
Waldo	157	161	—	—	—	3	71	77	6	4
Waldo State Police	35	35	—	1	—	—	13	17	4	—
York	461	463	—	5	1	8	225	188	34	2
York State Police	209	209	1	—	1	3	117	77	10	—
MARYLAND										
Garrett	267	267	—	1	—	8	65	186	7	—
Garrett State Police	298	305	1	2	2	32	77	172	12	7
St. Mary's	2,203	2,221	3	18	33	211	513	1,367	58	18
St. Mary's State Police	403	419	—	11	12	42	89	229	20	16
Wicomico	1,173	1,173	1	4	19	81	243	808	17	—
Wicomico State Police	536	559	2	6	7	53	129	287	52	23

See footnotes at end of table.

Table 11. — Number of Offenses Known to the Police, Rural Counties 25,000 and over in Population, 1996 — Continued

County by State	Crime Index total	Modified* Crime Index total	Murder and non-negligent man-slaughter	Forcible rape	Robbery	Aggravated assault	Burglary	Larceny–theft	Motor vehicle theft	Arson*
MICHIGAN										
Barry	312	315	—	2	2	17	92	172	27	3
Barry State Police	683	687	2	31	3	49	240	318	40	4
Cass	490	493	—	6	3	29	194	241	17	3
Cass State Police	117	120	—	15	3	9	33	48	9	3
Grand Traverse	1,271	1,286	—	16	6	55	180	980	34	15
Grand Traverse State Police	482	484	—	5	1	20	96	337	23	2
Hillsdale	335	339	—	5	1	29	98	181	21	4
Hillsdale State Police	215	220	—	21	1	22	65	96	10	5
Isabella	327	333	1	3	—	17	72	203	31	6
Isabella State Police	403	406	—	6	—	20	119	233	25	3
Mecosta	568	572	—	14	1	36	174	328	15	4
Mecosta State Police	118	118	—	15	—	10	32	53	8	—
Montcalm	582	590	1	23	4	37	183	301	33	8
Montcalm State Police	466	471	—	31	2	20	143	246	24	5
Newaygo	340	342	—	14	—	31	119	155	21	2
Newaygo State Police	538	549	—	14	4	28	233	242	17	11
Shiawassee	444	448	—	8	2	60	112	236	26	4
Shiawassee State Police	255	263	2	5	2	13	53	169	11	8
Tuscola	363	365	—	10	4	21	108	182	38	2
Tuscola State Police	297	300	2	21	1	23	72	148	30	3
MINNESOTA										
Beltrami	550	553	—	15	4	11	168	302	50	3
Crow Wing	900	903	1	12	2	22	338	445	80	3
Itasca	650	652	—	1	—	11	250	343	45	2
Otter Tail	734	738	—	8	—	11	270	394	51	4
MISSISSIPPI										
Lauderdale	558	562	2	3	15	45	236	232	25	4
MISSOURI										
Cole	478	481	1	5	2	29	113	306	22	3
Pulaski	135	137	—	—	9	59	53	4	10	2
MONTANA[1]										
NEVADA										
Carson City	1,802	1,806	—	11	25	184	373	1,120	89	4
Douglas	949	952	1	3	14	36	195	651	49	3
NEW HAMPSHIRE										
Hillsboro State Police	30	31	—	6	—	5	5	13	1	1
NEW MEXICO										
McKinley	383	397	—	7	1	54	105	179	37	14
San Juan	1,278	1,281	4	14	9	117	397	675	62	3
NEW YORK										
Allegany State Police	376		—	8	—	20	177	166	5	
Clinton State Police	1,287	1,293	1	6	1	265	348	643	23	6
Delaware State Police	449		1	4	3	26	161	246	8	
Franklin State Police	465	473	3	7	1	55	166	215	18	8
Greene State Police	693		3	3	2	178	201	280	26	
St. Lawrence	538	540	—	4	2	32	159	321	20	2
St. Lawrence State Police	676	686	2	6	2	59	234	350	23	10
Steuben State Police	686	689	1	8	5	38	196	428	10	3
Sullivan	678	682	—	8	10	77	258	291	34	4
Sullivan State Police	889	906	1	9	5	136	277	441	20	17
Tompkins	659	660	—	5	11	4	190	426	23	1
Tompkins State Police	282		1	2	1	20	56	195	7	
Ulster State Police	1,052	1,069	5	6	9	245	283	466	38	17
Wyoming	573	576	—	3	5	46	297	198	24	3
Wyoming State Police	104	104	—	1	—	50	27	26	—	—

See footnotes at end of table.

Table 11. — Number of Offenses Known to the Police, Rural Counties 25,000 and over in Population, 1996 — Continued

County by State	Crime Index total	Modified* Crime Index total	Murder and non-negligent man-slaughter	Forcible rape	Robbery	Aggravated assault	Burglary	Larceny–theft	Motor vehicle theft	Arson*
NORTH CAROLINA										
Beaufort	871	877	2	11	14	39	346	417	42	6
Carteret	907	914	2	8	7	19	320	498	53	7
Cleveland	1,983	1,990	1	14	29	107	726	1,001	105	7
Columbus	1,268	1,286	5	20	13	105	477	552	96	18
Duplin	960	963	5	6	9	97	431	365	47	3
Halifax	1,238	1,254	6	7	22	58	560	523	62	16
Harnett	2,630	2,648	5	19	25	187	916	1,254	224	18
Haywood	817	829	—	4	—	62	328	380	43	12
Henderson	1,254	1,265	—	20	12	31	475	661	55	11
Iredell	1,575	1,594	3	13	20	105	543	777	114	19
Jackson	568	575	—	3	5	36	301	200	23	7
Lee	883	892	1	4	3	50	283	488	54	9
Lenoir	1,041	1,050	2	8	11	109	358	499	54	9
McDowell	662	673	2	2	2	40	241	331	44	11
Moore	1,235	1,260	—	11	16	111	507	514	76	25
Pender	788	791	1	—	5	18	337	373	54	3
Person	549	556	—	4	4	22	193	300	26	7
Richmond	1,018	1,043	2	10	12	60	408	457	69	25
Robeson	1,641	1,654	15	8	17	188	774	561	78	13
Rockingham	1,616	1,626	1	7	16	150	550	778	114	10
Rutherford	1,123	1,146	1	8	14	72	424	544	60	23
Sampson	1,488	1,496	5	13	17	133	600	618	102	8
Stanly	547	548	2	—	7	17	209	274	38	1
Surry	1,188	1,197	1	9	11	110	367	583	107	9
Vance	1,112	1,129	3	7	16	20	489	506	71	17
Wilkes	1,031	1,051	2	7	8	99	367	472	76	20
OHIO										
Ashland	145	147	—	1	—	15	60	57	12	2
Coshocton	523	533	—	—	2	5	79	422	15	10
Darke	331	332	—	12	—	8	162	125	24	1
Huron	373	373	—	—	—	16	153	170	34	—
Logan	408	409	—	6	—	13	118	255	16	1
Marion	1,001	1,007	—	9	12	6	208	700	66	6
Muskingum	1,175	1,183	—	8	7	41	259	817	43	8
Preble	602	609	2	12	3	98	168	285	34	7
Ross	947	947	2	1	11	6	263	572	92	—
Seneca	340	341	3	7	1	5	130	171	23	1
Shelby	365	365	—	4	—	21	61	262	17	—
Tuscarawas	428	428	—	3	4	29	124	234	34	—
OREGON										
Benton	461	467	—	6	2	48	118	258	29	6
Benton State Police	125	127	—	—	2	7	5	104	7	2
Coos	809	811	5	15	4	16	210	509	50	2
Coos State Police	28	31	—	1	—	5	4	16	2	3
Deschutes	1,444	1,454	1	5	5	11	303	1,044	75	10
Deschutes State Police	94	100	—	6	—	5	20	47	16	6
Josephine	1,170	1,177	2	7	10	38	367	636	110	7
Josephine State Police	116	122	—	5	2	36	18	31	24	6
Klamath	1,189	1,192	2	4	16	28	336	728	75	3
Klamath State Police	65	71	—	10	3	17	8	21	6	6
Linn	1,767	1,774	—	10	11	91	586	959	110	7
Linn State Police	17	19	—	3	—	7	2	4	1	2

Table 11. — Number of Offenses Known to the Police, Rural Counties 25,000 and over in Population, 1996 — Continued

County by State	Crime Index total	Modified* Crime Index total	Murder and non-negligent man-slaughter	Forcible rape	Robbery	Aggravated assault	Burglary	Larceny–theft	Motor vehicle theft	Arson*
PENNSYLVANIA										
Adams State Police	619	625	1	16	6	54	158	337	47	6
Armstrong State Police	605	615	1	14	4	14	163	351	58	10
Bedford State Police	670	679	4	9	1	21	183	413	39	9
Bradford State Police	541	541	—	11	3	19	210	262	36	—
Clarion State Police	420	424	—	9	—	10	138	245	18	4
Clearfield State Police	653	663	—	8	2	23	217	356	47	10
Crawford State Police	912	926	2	8	10	36	393	388	75	14
Franklin State Police	1,287	1,295	3	14	16	56	327	774	97	8
Greene State Police	581	612	2	11	3	34	184	281	66	31
Huntingdon State Police	494	498	—	4	3	37	154	267	29	4
Indiana State Police	1,066	1,094	—	15	7	275	212	488	69	28
Lawrence State Police	645	652	1	7	8	52	185	320	72	7
Monroe State Police	1,429	1,432	3	20	21	85	488	727	85	3
Northumberland State Police	345	352	—	7	1	30	66	211	30	7
Schuylkill State Police	883	913	2	11	8	78	198	503	83	30
Snyder State Police	446	449	—	3	1	15	90	315	22	3
Susquehanna State Police	362	366	3	19	3	15	126	160	36	4
Tioga State Police	372	376	2	7	—	5	145	195	18	4
Venango State Police	778	798	—	15	3	20	284	428	28	20
Wayne State Police	803	803	2	19	3	59	264	369	87	—
RHODE ISLAND										
Portsmouth	32	32	—	7	1	12	3	8	1	—
SOUTH CAROLINA										
Beaufort	6,023	6,036	—	49	103	406	1,335	3,783	347	13
Chesterfield	865	870	1	7	6	157	286	337	71	5
Colleton	1,475	1,495	8	8	37	274	386	650	112	20
Darlington	2,046	2,057	4	20	49	270	596	893	214	11
Georgetown	1,655	1,664	5	15	21	260	352	899	103	9
Greenwood	1,619		2	14	29	296	397	821	60	
Kershaw	1,510	1,513	4	6	25	151	384	844	96	3
Lancaster	1,883	1,891	3	19	37	138	460	1,121	105	8
Laurens	1,855	1,871	4	17	34	390	460	869	81	16
Oconee	1,368	1,372	3	7	8	160	364	762	64	4
Orangeburg	3,010	3,030	4	35	117	478	785	1,367	224	20
Williamsburg	927	945	5	10	20	186	254	335	117	18
TENNESSEE										
Bradley	858	859	2	7	8	90	241	439	71	1
Hamblen	404	405	1	6	3	10	117	236	31	1
McMinn	703	705	3	2	10	41	236	359	52	2
Monroe	468	476	1	6	3	47	170	201	40	8
TEXAS										
Anderson	481	481	5	2	4	19	224	206	21	—
Angelina	731	734	2	5	9	21	192	457	45	3
Cass	283	284	1	11	4	24	117	110	16	1
Nacogdoches	410	413	2	2	—	67	143	175	21	3
Polk	581	582	2	1	7	33	238	275	25	1
Rusk	658	661	—	12	7	67	240	274	58	3
Starr	675	677	—	8	9	126	338	170	24	2
Van Zandt	662		—	5	4	113	266	199	75	
Walker	725	733	1	2	8	80	252	355	27	8
Wise	495	497	—	5	1	34	171	269	15	2
UTAH										
Cache	789	790		5	1	7	90	655	31	1
VERMONT[1]										

See footnotes at end of table.

Table 11. — Number of Offenses Known to the Police, Rural Counties 25,000 and over in Population, 1996 — Continued

County by State	Crime Index total	Modified* Crime Index total	Murder and non-negligent man-slaughter	Forcible rape	Robbery	Aggravated assault	Burglary	Larceny–theft	Motor vehicle theft	Arson*
VIRGINIA										
Accomack	300	300	1	7	17	25	73	143	34	—
Accomack State Police	31	32	—	—	1	—	1	17	12	1
Augusta	886	890	5	5	10	27	221	545	73	4
Augusta State Police	32	32	—	1	—	1	1	17	12	—
Buchanan	256	256	—	—	1	15	89	130	21	—
Buchanan State Police	77	86	—	2	1	5	27	35	7	9
Carroll	315	318	—	2	6	23	100	155	29	3
Carroll State Police	13	13	—	—	—	—	—	10	3	—
Franklin	495	496	3	2	2	12	111	316	49	1
Franklin State Police	6	6	—	—	—	—	—	3	3	—
Frederick	1,396	1,397	1	13	5	30	264	1,014	69	1
Frederick State Police	22	22	—	1	—	—	5	13	3	—
Halifax	432	435	4	3	7	63	110	227	18	3
Halifax State Police	28	28	—	—	1	1	—	12	14	—
Henry	1,848	1,858	1	12	57	91	601	915	171	10
Henry State Police	8	8	—	—	—	—	—	6	2	—
Rockingham	469	472	1	8	1	6	168	270	15	3
Rockingham State Police	44	44	—	—	—	—	5	10	29	—
Tazewell	505	510	1	6	1	118	96	264	19	5
Tazewell State Police	31	31	1	—	—	2	8	14	6	—
WASHINGTON										
Chelan	1,347	1,348	—	11	7	59	311	909	50	1
Clallam	708	714	—	10	1	57	147	466	27	6
Cowlitz	1,189	1,198	3	7	8	50	385	630	106	9
Douglas	660	664	2	7	2	32	200	390	27	4
Grant	1,389	1,389	4	21	7	64	567	625	101	—
Grays Harbor	484	490	2	4	7	43	172	216	40	6
Lewis	1,584	1,590	3	34	4	48	463	954	78	6
Mason	1,833	1,844	2	19	3	79	688	921	121	11
Skagit	1,444	1,452	1	9	11	13	345	1,027	38	8
WEST VIRGINIA										
Berkeley	777	778	1	—	6	24	144	567	35	1
Berkeley State Police	562	566	—	7	11	69	100	314	61	4
Fayette	199	201	1	—	3	5	79	91	20	2
Fayette State Police	403	405	—	1	1	59	114	200	28	2
Harrison	245	246	2	3	4	25	77	121	13	1
Harrison State Police	124	125	—	—	1	1	45	57	20	1
Jefferson	191	193	—	—	3	6	47	116	19	2
Jefferson State Police	365	366	1	1	4	4	92	245	18	1
Logan	115	121	—	1	5	8	44	42	15	6
Logan State Police	384	384	—	2	2	15	112	184	69	—
Marion	170	173	—	1	3	8	49	82	27	3
Marion State Police	67	67	—	—	1	1	22	27	16	—
McDowell	52	52	—	—	—	11	12	26	3	—
McDowell State Police	42	59	2	—	2	10	9	10	9	17
Mercer	549	549	—	—	—	52	210	223	64	—
Mercer State Police	228	231	1	8	5	17	58	112	27	3
Mingo	55	55	—	—	1	3	4	25	22	—
Mingo State Police	180	188	2	2	1	30	52	56	37	8
Monongalia	312	314	—	3	1	—	91	197	20	2
Monongalia State Police	314	314	—	4	1	5	134	122	48	—
Raleigh	1,386	1,397	8	—	8	358	235	689	88	11
Raleigh State Police	367	367	1	—	4	54	103	168	37	—

Table 11. — Number of Offenses Known to the Police, Rural Counties 25,000 and over in Population, 1996 — Continued

County by State	Crime Index total	Modified* Crime Index total	Murder and non-negligent man-slaughter	Forcible rape	Robbery	Aggravated assault	Burglary	Larceny–theft	Motor vehicle theft	Arson*
WISCONSIN										
Barron	408	409	—	2	—	22	136	225	23	1
Clark	374	375	—	2	—	5	121	216	30	1
Columbia	497	499	2	2	3	17	91	347	35	2
Dodge	281	282	1	3	2	12	64	174	25	1
Fond Du Lac	385	389	—	1	1	14	73	273	23	4
Grant	376	380	—	12	—	34	126	192	12	4
Jefferson	475	480	1	5	—	26	65	323	55	5
Manitowoc	460	460	—	1	—	18	123	276	42	—
Marinette	535	540	2	1	2	5	221	272	32	5
Polk	369	373	—	2	—	6	164	164	33	4
Portage	584	585	—	9	—	22	148	361	44	1
Sauk	652	653	1	4	1	23	106	480	37	1
Shawano	632	632	1	5	1	10	181	397	37	—
Waupaca	610	611	1	7	1	9	254	302	36	1
Wood	535	542	1	2	—	7	192	307	26	7
STATE AGENCIES										
Alaska State Police	5,697	5,751	15	117	33	818	1,546	2,718	450	54
Arizona Department of Public Safety	32	32	—	—	—	15	—	17	—	—
Connecticut State Police	8,861	8,904	11	55	85	1,006	2,712	4,337	655	43
OTHER AGENCIES										
American Samoa	571	584	4	17	7	142	259	136	6	13
Guam	7,994	8,007	15	168	107	231	2,202	4,526	745	13
United States Department of the Interior:										
Bureau of Indian Affairs	5,317	5,480	51	266	41	1,642	1,430	1,369	518	163
Bureau of Land Management	335	411	12	—	1	11	22	259	30	76
Bureau of Reclamation	14	14	—	—	1	—	—	9	4	—
National Park Service	5,827	5,991	23	40	146	299	677	4,465	177	164
U.S. Fish and Wildlife Service	612	744	7	3	2	11	202	349	38	132

[1] Complete data for 1996 were not received for the states of Florida, Illinois, Kansas, Kentucky, Montana, and Vermont. See "Offense Estimation," pages 389-390 for details.

Table 12. — Crime Trends, Offenses Known to the Police, Population Group, 1995-1996

[1996 estimated population]

Population group	Crime Index total	Modified Crime Index total[1]	Violent crime[2]	Property crime[3]	Murder and non-negligent man-slaughter	Forcible rape	Robbery	Aggravated assault	Burglary	Larceny–theft	Motor vehicle theft	Arson[1]
TOTAL ALL AGENCIES: 11,020 agencies; population 220,886,000:												
1995	11,888,644	11,975,674	1,580,309	10,308,335	19,293	81,317	531,866	947,833	2,217,144	6,780,486	1,310,705	87,030
1996	11,484,447	11,569,173	1,468,549	10,015,898	17,413	79,069	491,885	880,182	2,118,455	6,654,542	1,242,901	84,726
Percent change	-3.4	-3.4	-7.1	-2.8	-9.7	-2.8	-7.5	-7.1	-4.5	-1.9	-5.2	-2.6
TOTAL CITIES: 7,785 cities; population 151,579,000:												
1995	9,737,867	9,807,485	1,337,381	8,400,486	15,814	62,055	487,001	772,511	1,699,881	5,584,250	1,116,355	69,618
1996	9,407,948	9,475,187	1,243,781	8,164,167	14,218	60,948	449,413	719,202	1,626,489	5,478,639	1,059,039	67,239
Percent change	-3.4	-3.4	-7.0	-2.8	-10.1	-1.8	-7.7	-6.9	-4.3	-1.9	-5.1	-3.4
GROUP I												
64 cities, 250,000 and over; population 46,674,000:												
1995	3,957,249	3,988,299	721,952	3,235,297	9,631	26,293	309,236	376,792	675,910	1,953,212	606,175	31,050
1996	3,778,750	3,810,447	669,799	3,108,951	8,587	25,602	283,210	352,400	641,240	1,897,255	570,456	31,697
Percent change	-4.5	-4.5	-7.2	-3.9	-10.8	-2.6	-8.4	-6.5	-5.1	-2.9	-5.9	+2.1
10 cities, 1,000,000 and over; population 22,285,000:												
1995	1,698,749	1,711,107	367,731	1,331,018	4,796	8,945	166,591	187,399	280,744	758,761	291,513	12,358
1996	1,596,336	1,609,792	337,006	1,259,330	4,186	8,825	150,211	173,784	260,519	727,903	270,908	13,456
Percent change	-6.0	-5.9	-8.4	-5.4	-12.7	-1.3	-9.8	-7.3	-7.2	-4.1	-7.1	+8.9
17 cities, 500,000 to 999,999; population 10,967,000:												
1995	959,302	966,966	146,625	812,677	1,956	7,232	61,915	75,522	163,046	520,913	128,718	7,664
1996	933,999	941,140	139,950	794,049	1,890	6,900	58,813	72,347	157,995	510,120	125,934	7,141
Percent change	-2.6	-2.7	-4.6	-2.3	-3.4	-4.6	-5.0	-4.2	-3.1	-2.1	-2.2	-6.8
37 cities, 250,000 to 499,999; population 13,423,000:												
1995	1,299,198	1,310,226	207,596	1,091,602	2,879	10,116	80,730	113,871	232,120	673,538	185,944	11,028
1996	1,248,415	1,259,515	192,843	1,055,572	2,511	9,877	74,186	106,269	222,726	659,232	173,614	11,100
Percent change	-3.9	-3.9	-7.1	-3.3	-12.8	-2.4	-8.1	-6.7	-4.0	-2.1	-6.6	+.7
GROUP II												
147 cities, 100,000 to 249,999; population 21,674,000:												
1995	1,621,072	1,633,587	206,641	1,414,431	2,493	10,534	73,262	120,352	304,028	928,612	181,791	12,515
1996	1,556,398	1,567,582	191,597	1,364,801	2,203	10,159	67,618	111,617	287,832	907,006	169,963	11,184
Percent change	-4.0	-4.0	-7.3	-3.5	-11.6	-3.6	-7.7	-7.3	-5.3	-2.3	-6.5	-10.6
GROUP III												
320 cities, 50,000 to 99,999; population 21,769,000:												
1995	1,273,929	1,282,464	149,553	1,124,376	1,429	8,412	47,064	92,648	229,671	762,191	132,514	8,535
1996	1,222,856	1,230,654	137,721	1,085,135	1,309	8,464	43,283	84,665	218,303	739,986	126,846	7,798
Percent change	-4.0	-4.0	-7.9	-3.5	-8.4	+.6	-8.0	-8.6	-4.9	-2.9	-4.3	-8.6
GROUP IV												
590 cities, 25,000 to 49,999; population 20,446,000:												
1995	1,038,061	1,044,834	101,647	936,414	880	6,495	27,757	66,515	183,915	667,775	84,724	6,773
1996	1,015,634	1,022,330	95,778	919,856	824	6,401	26,117	62,436	176,601	662,248	81,007	6,696
Percent change	-2.2	-2.2	-5.8	-1.8	-6.4	-1.4	-5.9	-6.1	-4.0	-.8	-4.4	-1.1

See footnotes at end of table.

Table 12. — Crime Trends, Offenses Known to the Police, Population Group, 1995-1996 — Continued

Population group	Crime Index total	Modified Crime Index total[1]	Violent crime[2]	Property crime[3]	Murder and non-negligent man-slaughter	Forcible rape	Robbery	Aggravated assault	Burglary	Larceny–theft	Motor vehicle theft	Arson[1]
GROUP V												
1,436 cities, 10,000 to 24,999; population 22,582,000:												
1995	1,015,386	1,021,201	89,606	925,780	810	6,029	19,507	63,260	171,893	685,776	68,111	5,815
1996	1,009,995	1,015,311	85,273	924,722	732	6,108	19,324	59,109	168,727	688,081	67,914	5,316
Percent change	-.5	-.6	-4.8	-.1	-9.6	+1.3	-.9	-6.6	-1.8	+.3	-.3	-8.6
GROUP VI												
5,228 cities under 10,000; population 18,434,000:												
1995	832,170	837,100	67,982	764,188	571	4,292	10,175	52,944	134,464	586,684	43,040	4,930
1996	824,315	828,863	63,613	760,702	563	4,214	9,861	48,975	133,786	584,063	42,853	4,548
Percent change	-.9	-1.0	-6.4	-.5	-1.4	-1.8	-3.1	-7.5	-.5	-.4	-.4	-7.7
SUBURBAN COUNTIES												
1,108 agencies; population 46,151,000:												
1995	1,634,073	1,647,362	186,134	1,447,939	2,337	13,480	40,798	129,519	360,432	924,060	163,447	13,289
1996	1,570,040	1,583,529	170,736	1,399,304	2,126	12,692	38,501	117,417	339,543	906,722	153,039	13,489
Percent change	-3.9	-3.9	-8.3	-3.4	-9.0	-5.8	-5.6	-9.3	-5.8	-1.9	-6.4	+1.5
RURAL COUNTIES[4]												
2,127 agencies; population 23,155,000:												
1995	516,704	520,827	56,794	459,910	1,142	5,782	4,067	45,803	156,831	272,176	30,903	4,123
1996	506,459	510,457	54,032	452,427	1,069	5,429	3,971	43,563	152,423	269,181	30,823	3,998
Percent change	-2.0	-2.0	-4.9	-1.6	-6.4	-6.1	-2.4	-4.9	-2.8	-1.1	-.3	-3.0
SUBURBAN AREA[5]												
5,452 agencies; population 87,516,000:												
1995	3,386,739	3,410,885	333,654	3,053,085	3,525	22,766	78,266	229,097	650,933	2,097,395	304,757	24,146
1996	3,286,230	3,309,809	309,803	2,976,427	3,248	21,918	74,383	210,254	618,291	2,068,643	289,493	23,579
Percent change	-3.0	-3.0	-7.1	-2.5	-7.9	-3.7	-5.0	-8.2	-5.0	-1.4	-5.0	-2.3

[1] The number of agency reports used in arson trends is less than used in compiling trends for other Crime Index offenses. It is not necessary to report arson by property classification to be included in this table. The Modified Crime Index total is the sum of the Crime Index offenses, including arson.

[2] Violent crimes are offenses of murder, forcible rape, robbery, and aggravated assault.

[3] Property crimes are offenses of burglary, larceny–theft, and motor vehicle theft. Data are not included for the property crime of arson.

[4] Includes state police agencies with no county breakdowns.

[5] Includes suburban city and county law enforcement agencies within metropolitan areas. Excludes central cities. Suburban cities and counties are also included in other groups.

Forcible rape figures furnished by the state-level Uniform Crime Reporting (UCR) Program administered by the Illinois State Police were not in accordance with national UCR guidelines and were excluded from the forcible rape, violent crime, Crime Index total, and Modified Crime Index total categories.

Complete data for 1996 were not available for the states of Florida, Illinois, Kansas, Kentucky, and Montana. See "Offense Estimation," pages 389-390 for details.

Table 13. — Crime Trends, Offenses Known to the Police, Suburban and Nonsuburban Cities,[1] Population Group, 1995-1996

[1996 estimated population]

Population group	Crime Index total	Modified Crime Index total[2]	Violent crime[3]	Property crime[4]	Murder and non-negligent man-slaughter	Forcible rape	Robbery	Aggravated assault	Burglary	Larceny-theft	Motor vehicle theft	Arson[2]
Suburban Cities												
TOTAL SUBURBAN CITIES; 4,344 cities; population 41,365,000:												
1995	1,752,666	1,763,523	147,520	1,605,146	1,188	9,286	37,468	99,578	290,501	1,173,335	141,310	10,857
1996	1,716,190	1,726,280	139,067	1,577,123	1,122	9,226	35,882	92,837	278,748	1,161,921	136,454	10,090
Percent change	-2.1	-2.1	-5.7	-1.7	-5.6	-.6	-4.2	-6.8	-4.0	-1.0	-3.4	-7.1
GROUP IV												
418 cities, 25,000 to 49,999; population 14,295,000:												
1995	625,599	629,743	58,773	566,826	483	3,538	17,755	36,997	109,245	395,805	61,776	4,144
1996	605,136	609,102	55,429	549,707	458	3,444	16,545	34,982	103,261	388,716	57,730	3,966
Percent change	-3.3	-3.3	-5.7	-3.0	-5.2	-2.7	-6.8	-5.4	-5.5	-1.8	-6.5	-4.3
GROUP V												
1,037 cities, 10,000 to 24,999; population 16,299,000:												
1995	635,203	638,885	53,243	581,960	438	3,551	12,960	36,294	105,513	425,830	50,617	3,682
1996	626,779	630,139	50,094	576,685	397	3,579	12,848	33,270	101,885	424,776	50,024	3,360
Percent change	-1.3	-1.4	-5.9	-.9	-9.4	+.8	-.9	-8.3	-3.4	-.2	-1.2	-8.7
GROUP VI												
2,889 cities under 10,000; population 10,771,000:												
1995	491,864	494,895	35,504	456,360	267	2,197	6,753	26,287	75,743	351,700	28,917	3,031
1996	484,275	487,039	33,544	450,731	267	2,203	6,489	24,585	73,602	348,429	28,700	2,764
Percent change	-1.5	-1.6	-5.5	-1.2	—	+.3	-3.9	-6.5	-2.8	-.9	-.8	-8.8
Nonsuburban Cities												
TOTAL NONSUBURBAN CITIES: 2,910 cities; population 20,096,000:												
1995	1,132,951	1,139,612	111,715	1,021,236	1,073	7,530	19,971	83,141	199,771	766,900	54,565	6,661
1996	1,133,754	1,140,224	105,597	1,028,157	997	7,497	19,420	77,683	200,366	772,471	55,320	6,470
Percent change	+.1	+.1	-5.5	+.7	-7.1	-.4	-2.8	-6.6	+.3	+.7	+1.4	-2.9
GROUP IV												
172 cities, 25,000 to 49,999; population 6,151,000:												
1995	412,462	415,091	42,874	369,588	397	2,957	10,002	29,518	74,670	271,970	22,948	2,629
1996	410,498	413,228	40,349	370,149	366	2,957	9,572	27,454	73,340	273,532	23,277	2,730
Percent change	-.5	-.4	-5.9	+.2	-7.8	—	-4.3	-7.0	-1.8	+.6	+1.4	+3.8
GROUP V												
399 cities, 10,000 to 24,999; population 6,283,000:												
1995	380,183	382,316	36,363	343,820	372	2,478	6,547	26,966	66,380	259,946	17,494	2,133
1996	383,216	385,172	35,179	348,037	335	2,529	6,476	25,839	66,842	263,305	17,890	1,956
Percent change	+.8	+.7	-3.3	+1.2	-9.9	+2.1	-1.1	-4.2	+.7	+1.3	+2.3	-8.3
GROUP VI												
2,339 cities under 10,000; population 7,662,000:												
1995	340,306	342,205	32,478	307,828	304	2,095	3,422	26,657	58,721	234,984	14,123	1,899
1996	340,040	341,824	30,069	309,971	296	2,011	3,372	24,390	60,184	235,634	14,153	1,784
Percent change	-.1	-.1	-7.4	+.7	-2.6	-4.0	-1.5	-8.5	+2.5	+.3	+.2	-6.1

[1] Suburban places are within Metropolitan Statistical Areas (MSAs) and include suburban city and county law enforcement agencies within the metropolitan area. Central cities are excluded. Nonsuburban places are outside MSAs.

[2] The number of agencies used in arson trends is less than used in compiling trends for other Crime Index offenses. It is not necessary to report arson by property classification to be included in this table. The Modified Crime Index total is the sum of the Crime Index offenses, including arson.

[3] Violent crimes are offenses of murder, forcible rape, robbery, and aggravated assault.

[4] Property crimes are offenses of burglary, larceny–theft, and motor vehicle theft. Data are not included for the property crime of arson.

Forcible rape figures furnished by the state-level Uniform Crime Reporting (UCR) Program administered by the Illinois State Police were not in accordance with national UCR guidelines and were excluded from the forcible rape, violent crime, Crime Index total, and Modified Crime Index total categories.

Complete data for 1996 were not available for the states of Florida, Illinois, Kansas, Kentucky, and Montana. See "Offense Estimation," pages 389-390 for details.

Table 14. — Crime Trends, Offenses Known to the Police, Suburban and Nonsuburban Counties, Population Group, 1995-1996

[1996 estimated population]

Population group	Crime Index total	Modified Crime Index total[1]	Violent crime[2]	Property crime[3]	Murder and non-negligent man-slaughter	Forcible rape	Robbery	Aggravated assault	Burglary	Larceny–theft	Motor vehicle theft	Arson[1]
Suburban Counties[4]												
100,000 and over												
106 counties; population 26,837,000:												
1995	1,128,768	1,137,632	133,753	995,015	1,574	8,357	34,991	88,831	232,052	645,756	117,207	8,864
1996	1,063,895	1,073,015	120,695	943,200	1,418	7,628	32,804	78,845	214,288	622,723	106,189	9,120
Percent change	-5.7	-5.7	-9.8	-5.2	-9.9	-8.7	-6.3	-11.2	-7.7	-3.6	-9.4	+2.9
25,000 to 99,999												
325 counties; population 16,643,000:												
1995	386,178	389,199	38,896	347,282	557	3,718	4,270	30,351	103,300	219,298	24,684	3,021
1996	389,616	392,730	36,838	352,778	552	3,668	4,219	28,399	101,188	226,232	25,358	3,114
Percent change	+.9	+.9	-5.3	+1.6	-.9	-1.3	-1.2	-6.4	-2.0	+3.2	+2.7	+3.1
Under 25,000												
677 counties; population 2,672,000:												
1995	119,127	120,531	13,485	105,642	206	1,405	1,537	10,337	25,080	59,006	21,556	1,404
1996	116,529	117,784	13,203	103,326	156	1,396	1,478	10,173	24,067	57,767	21,492	1,255
Percent change	-2.2	-2.3	-2.1	-2.2	-24.3	-.6	-3.8	-1.6	-4.0	-2.1	-.3	-10.6
Nonsuburban counties[4]												
25,000 and over												
241 counties; population 9,518,000:												
1995	213,223	214,803	22,055	191,168	407	1,986	2,088	17,574	64,006	115,438	11,724	1,580
1996	210,865	212,328	21,680	189,185	353	1,943	2,012	17,372	62,257	114,746	12,182	1,463
Percent change	-1.1	-1.2	-1.7	-1.0	-13.3	-2.2	-3.6	-1.1	-2.7	-.6	+3.9	-7.4
10,000 to 24,999												
577 counties; population 9,218,000:												
1995	172,970	174,190	20,289	152,681	406	1,774	1,180	16,929	55,151	87,967	9,563	1,220
1996	169,639	170,814	18,941	150,698	432	1,761	1,124	15,624	53,775	87,030	9,893	1,175
Percent change	-1.9	-1.9	-6.6	-1.3	+6.4	-.7	-4.7	-7.7	-2.5	-1.1	+3.5	-3.7
Under 10,000												
1,199 counties; population 3,809,000:												
1995	96,867	97,880	10,740	86,127	264	1,588	530	8,358	28,667	49,832	7,628	1,013
1996	94,514	95,669	9,765	84,749	229	1,372	564	7,600	27,796	50,215	6,738	1,155
Percent change	-2.4	-2.3	-9.1	-1.6	-13.3	-13.6	+6.4	-9.1	-3.0	+.8	-11.7	+14.0

[1] The number of agencies used in arson trends is less than used in compiling trends for other Crime Index offenses. It is not necessary to report arson by property classification to be included in this table. The Modified Crime Index total is the sum of the Crime Index offenses, including arson.

[2] Violent crimes are offenses of murder, forcible rape, robbery, and aggravated assault.

[3] Property crimes are offenses of burglary, larceny–theft, and motor vehicle theft. Data are not included for the property crime of arson.

[4] Offenses include sheriffs' and county law enforcement agencies. State police offenses are not included.

Forcible rape figures furnished by the state-level Uniform Crime Reporting (UCR) Program administered by the Illinois State Police were not in accordance with national UCR guidelines and were excluded from the forcible rape, violent crime, Crime Index total, and Modified Crime Index total categories.

Complete data for 1996 were not available for the states of Florida, Illinois, Kansas, Kentucky, and Montana. See "Offense Estimation," pages 389-390 for details.

Table 15. — Crime Trends, Offenses Known Breakdown, Population Group, 1995-1996

[1996 estimated population]

Population group	Forcible rape — Rape by force	Forcible rape — Assault to rape–attempts	Robbery — Firearm	Robbery — Knife or cutting instrument	Robbery — Other weapon	Robbery — Strong-armed	Aggravated assault — Firearm	Aggravated assault — Knife or cutting instrument	Aggravated assault — Other weapon	Aggravated assault — Hands, fists, feet, etc.	Burglary — Forcible entry	Burglary — Unlawful entry	Burglary — Attempted forcible entry	Motor vehicle theft — Autos	Motor vehicle theft — Trucks and buses	Motor vehicle theft — Other vehicles	Arson[1] — Structure	Arson[1] — Mobile	Arson[1] — Other
TOTAL ALL AGENCIES: 11,012 agencies; population 220,550,000:																			
1995	70,644	10,370	215,185	48,424	60,627	206,402	213,867	170,201	310,533	251,312	1,459,476	564,673	187,650	1,027,248	209,464	70,770	42,489	21,236	19,518
1996	68,832	9,957	199,242	44,172	56,918	190,452	192,375	157,986	299,911	227,746	1,388,623	550,338	173,910	971,558	203,807	64,139	37,564	22,497	18,202
Percent change	-2.6	-4.0	-7.6	-8.8	-6.1	-7.7	-10.0	-7.2	3.4	-9.4	-1.6	-2.5	-7.3	-5.4	-2.7	-9.4	-11.6	+5.9	-6.7
TOTAL CITIES: 7,779 cities; population 151,295,000:																			
1995	53,535	8,241	195,181	44,638	56,128	189,857	178,827	144,917	255,038	191,954	1,116,542	423,682	155,046	890,953	172,768	49,642	34,167	16,796	15,119
1996	52,603	8,087	180,231	40,795	52,278	175,040	161,936	135,256	246,677	173,283	1,063,511	415,441	142,712	843,135	168,911	43,868	29,945	17,407	13,690
Percent change	-1.7	-1.9	-7.7	-8.6	-6.9	-7.8	-9.4	-6.7	-3.3	-9.7	-4.7	-1.9	-8.0	-5.4	-2.2	-11.6	-12.4	+3.6	-9.5
GROUP I																			
64 cities, 250,000 and over; population 46,674,000:																			
1995	22,559	3,734	130,548	28,429	39,312	110,947	103,042	76,883	132,844	64,023	462,295	145,689	67,926	488,068	99,283	18,824	14,568	8,813	4,926
1996	21,822	3,780	119,081	26,241	35,990	101,898	95,901	72,311	129,117	55,071	442,166	139,804	59,270	455,389	99,374	15,693	12,759	9,622	4,861
Percent change	-3.3	+1.2	-8.8	-7.7	-8.5	-8.2	-6.9	-5.9	-2.8	-14.0	-4.4	-4.0	-12.7	-6.7	+.1	-16.6	-12.4	+9.2	-1.3
10 cities, 1,000,000 and over; population 22,285,000:																			
1995	7,598	1,347	69,271	16,723	27,577	53,020	49,178	39,913	66,035	32,273	173,372	67,550	39,822	238,504	46,558	6,451	4,489	3,727	1,750
1996	7,303	1,522	60,831	15,661	25,388	48,331	45,305	37,648	64,110	26,721	164,273	61,973	34,273	217,003	47,935	5,970	4,425	4,404	1,811
Percent change	-3.9	+13.0	-12.2	-6.4	-7.9	-8.8	-7.9	-5.7	-2.9	-17.2	-5.2	-8.3	-13.9	-9.0	+3.0	-7.5	-1.4	+18.2	+3.5
17 cities, 500,000 to 999,999; population 10,967,000:																			
1995	6,249	983	27,594	5,150	4,975	24,196	19,696	14,359	27,640	13,827	122,643	29,377	11,026	103,288	19,443	5,987	4,155	2,343	1,044
1996	5,913	987	26,237	4,792	4,731	23,053	18,750	14,161	27,994	11,442	118,399	28,476	11,120	100,016	20,797	5,121	3,182	2,429	926
Percent change	-5.4	+.4	-4.9	-7.0	-4.9	-4.7	-4.8	-1.4	+1.3	-17.2	-3.5	-3.1	+.9	-3.2	+7.0	-14.5	-23.4	+3.7	-11.3
37 cities, 250,000 to 499,999; population 13,423,000:																			
1995	8,712	1,404	33,683	6,556	6,760	33,731	34,168	22,611	39,169	17,923	166,280	48,762	17,078	146,276	33,282	6,386	5,924	2,743	2,132
1996	8,606	1,271	32,013	5,788	5,871	30,514	31,846	20,502	37,013	16,908	159,494	49,355	13,877	138,370	30,642	4,602	5,152	2,789	2,124
Percent change	-1.2	-9.5	-5.0	-11.7	-13.2	-9.5	-6.8	-9.3	-5.5	-5.7	-4.1	+1.2	-18.7	-5.4	-7.9	-27.9	-13.0	+1.7	-.4
GROUP II																			
146 cities, 100,000 to 249,999; population 21,451,000:																			
1995	8,911	1,402	28,819	7,048	6,756	29,663	31,014	21,753	41,659	24,760	205,137	70,663	25,016	143,192	28,386	8,053	6,547	2,965	2,567
1996	8,741	1,224	26,934	5,994	6,498	27,381	26,087	19,800	39,980	24,424	194,370	68,382	22,214	135,561	26,041	6,328	5,054	2,672	2,030
Percent change	-1.9	-12.7	-6.5	-15.0	-3.8	-7.7	-15.9	-9.0	-4.0	-1.4	-5.2	-3.2	-11.2	-5.3	-8.3	-21.4	-22.8	-9.9	-20.9
GROUP III																			
320 cities, 50,000 to 99,999; population 21,769,000:																			
1995	7,479	933	16,740	4,126	4,312	21,886	17,594	16,582	31,171	27,301	148,724	61,190	19,757	107,735	17,915	6,864	4,152	2,143	2,114
1996	7,456	1,008	15,568	3,757	4,139	19,819	16,034	15,042	29,580	24,009	138,861	58,964	20,478	102,991	17,378	6,477	3,625	2,173	1,901
Percent change	-.3	+8.0	-7.0	-8.9	-4.0	-9.4	-8.9	-9.3	-5.1	-12.1	-6.6	-3.6	+3.6	-4.4	-3.0	-5.6	-12.7	+1.4	-10.1

See footnotes at end of table.

Table 15. — Crime Trends, Offenses Known Breakdown, Population Group, 1995-1996 — Continued

Population group	Forcible rape — Rape by force	Forcible rape — Assault to rape—attempts	Robbery — Firearm	Robbery — Knife or cutting instrument	Robbery — Other weapon	Robbery — Strong-armed	Aggravated assault — Firearm	Aggravated assault — Knife or cutting instrument	Aggravated assault — Other weapon	Aggravated assault — Hands, fists, feet, etc.	Burglary — Forcible entry	Burglary — Unlawful entry	Burglary — Attempted forcible entry	Motor vehicle theft — Autos	Motor vehicle theft — Trucks and buses	Motor vehicle theft — Other vehicles	Arson[1] — Structure	Arson[1] — Mobile	Arson[1] — Other
Group IV																			
590 cities, 25,000 to 49,999; population 20,446,000:																			
1995	5,692	781	9,250	2,492	2,743	13,180	10,894	11,038	19,684	24,828	114,676	53,206	15,608	66,806	11,712	5,796	3,228	1,260	2,202
1996	5,637	738	8,861	2,383	2,798	11,967	9,578	10,411	19,455	22,889	107,508	53,407	14,958	63,930	11,066	5,518	3,155	1,352	2,099
Percent change	-1.0	-5.5	-4.2	-4.4	+2.0	-9.2	-12.1	-5.7	-1.2	-7.8	-6.3	+.4	-4.2	-4.3	-5.5	-4.8	-2.3	+7.3	-4.7
Group V																			
1,433 cities, 10,000 to 24,999; population 22,533,000:																			
1995	5,260	736	6,469	1,677	2,051	9,185	9,751	10,797	17,917	24,341	106,818	49,089	15,160	53,056	8,952	5,742	2,999	973	1,767
1996	5,378	700	6,542	1,569	1,925	9,154	8,402	10,386	16,950	22,820	103,032	50,119	14,586	53,128	8,782	5,459	2,776	949	1,513
Percent change	+2.2	-4.9	+1.1	-6.4	-6.1	-.3	-13.8	-3.8	-5.4	-6.2	-3.5	+2.1	-3.8	+.1	-1.9	-4.9	-7.4	-2.5	-14.4
Group VI																			
5,226 cities under 10,000; population 18,422,000:																			
1995	3,634	655	3,355	866	954	4,996	6,532	7,864	11,763	26,701	78,892	43,845	11,579	32,096	6,520	4,363	2,673	642	1,543
1996	3,569	637	3,245	851	928	4,821	5,934	7,306	11,595	24,070	77,574	44,765	11,206	32,136	6,270	4,393	2,576	639	1,286
Percent change	-1.8	-2.7	-3.3	-1.7	-2.7	-3.5	-9.2	-7.1	-1.4	-9.9	-1.7	+2.1	-3.2	+.1	-3.8	+.7	-3.6	-.5	-16.7
Suburban Counties																			
1,107 agencies; population 46,104,000:																			
1995	11,893	1,568	18,431	3,398	3,995	14,946	26,410	19,030	44,272	39,712	235,945	99,781	24,223	117,959	30,729	14,572	5,845	3,645	3,624
1996	11,288	1,390	17,410	3,015	4,158	13,890	22,275	16,652	41,903	36,512	221,383	94,144	23,537	109,979	29,227	13,619	5,357	4,208	3,784
Percent change	-5.1	-11.4	-5.5	-11.3	+4.1	-7.1	-15.7	-12.5	-5.4	-8.1	-6.2	-5.6	-2.8	-6.8	-4.9	-6.5	-8.3	+15.4	+4.4
Rural Counties																			
2,126 agencies; population 23,150,000:																			
1995	5,216	561	1,573	388	504	1,599	8,630	6,254	11,223	19,646	106,989	41,210	8,381	18,336	5,967	6,556	2,477	795	775
1996	4,941	480	1,601	362	482	1,522	8,164	6,078	11,331	17,951	103,729	40,753	7,661	18,444	5,669	6,652	2,262	882	728
Percent change	-5.3	-14.4	+1.8	-6.7	-4.4	-4.8	-5.4	-2.8	+1.0	-8.6	-3.0	-1.1	-8.6	+.6	-5.0	+1.5	-8.7	+10.9	-6.1
Suburban Area[2]																			
5,447 agencies; population 87,413,000:																			
1995	19,959	2,735	31,482	6,457	7,607	32,490	40,196	33,763	71,523	82,999	409,657	189,076	50,546	229,492	49,331	24,961	11,006	5,526	7,322
1996	19,343	2,506	29,965	6,003	7,639	30,511	34,365	30,150	68,483	76,525	384,757	182,444	48,942	218,190	46,667	23,377	10,242	6,081	6,996
Percent change	-3.1	-8.4	-4.8	-7.0	+.4	-6.1	-14.5	-10.7	-4.3	-7.8	-6.1	-3.5	-3.2	-4.9	-5.4	-6.3	-6.9	+10.0	-4.5

[1] The number of agency reports used in arson trends is less than used in compiling trends for other Crime Index offenses.

[2] Includes suburban city and county law enforcement agencies within metropolitan areas. Excludes central cities. Suburban cities and counties are also included in other groups.

Forcible rape figures furnished by the state-level Uniform Crime Reporting (UCR) Program administered by the Illinois State Police were not in accordance with national UCR guidelines and were excluded from the forcible rape categories.

Complete data for 1996 were not available for the states of Florida, Illinois, Kansas, Kentucky, and Montana. See "Offense Estimation," pages 389-390 for details.

Table 16. — Crime Rates, Offenses Known to the Police, Population Group, 1996

[1996 estimated population. Rate: Number of crimes per 100,000 inhabitants]

Population group	Crime Index total	Modified Crime Index total[1]	Violent crime[2]	Property crime[3]	Murder and non-negligent man-slaughter	Forcible rape	Robbery	Aggravated assault	Burglary	Larceny–theft	Motor vehicle theft	Arson[1]
TOTAL ALL AGENCIES: 10,296 agencies; population 213,316,000:												
Number of offenses known ..	11,447,543		1,476,611	9,970,932	17,387	80,527	495,238	883,459	2,114,375	6,612,894	1,243,663	
Rate	5,366.5		692.2	4,674.3	8.2	37.8	232.2	414.2	991.2	3,100.0	583.0	
TOTAL CITIES: 7,250 cities; population 146,951,000:												
Number of offenses known ..	9,337,157		1,243,941	8,093,216	14,176	62,102	450,273	717,390	1,615,164	5,422,985	1,055,067	
Rate	6,353.9		846.5	5,507.4	9.6	42.3	306.4	488.2	1,099.1	3,690.3	718.0	
GROUP I												
65 cities, 250,000 and over; population 47,046,000:												
Number of offenses known ...	3,819,169		679,212	3,139,957	8,680	27,169	286,832	356,531	647,298	1,917,133	575,526	
Rate	8,117.9		1,443.7	6,674.2	18.4	57.7	609.7	757.8	1,375.9	4,075.0	1,223.3	
10 cities, 1,000,000 and over; population 22,285,000:												
Number of offenses known ...	1,597,581		338,251	1,259,330	4,186	10,070	150,211	173,784	260,519	727,903	270,908	
Rate	7,168.9		1,517.8	5,651.0	18.8	45.2	674.0	779.8	1,169.0	3,266.3	1,215.7	
17 cities 500,000 to 999,999; population 10,967,000:												
Number of offenses known ...	933,999		139,950	794,049	1,890	6,900	58,813	72,347	157,995	510,120	125,934	
Rate	8,516.7		1,276.1	7,240.6	17.2	62.9	536.3	659.7	1,440.7	4,651.6	1,148.3	
38 cities, 250,000 to 499,999; population 13,795,000:												
Number of offenses known ...	1,287,589		201,011	1,086,578	2,604	10,199	77,808	110,400	228,784	679,110	178,684	
Rate	9,333.9		1,457.2	7,876.7	18.9	73.9	564.0	800.3	1,658.5	4,922.9	1,295.3	
GROUP II												
147 cities, 100,000 to 249,999; population 21,655,000:												
Number of offenses known ...	1,558,278		192,181	1,366,097	2,174	10,382	67,224	112,401	287,633	909,686	168,778	
Rate	7,195.9		887.5	6,308.5	10.0	47.9	310.4	519.1	1,328.3	4,200.8	779.4	
GROUP III												
305 cities, 50,000 to 99,999; population 20,750,000:												
Number of offenses known ...	1,181,912		133,694	1,048,218	1,276	8,153	42,005	82,260	212,168	713,202	122,848	
Rate	5,695.9		644.3	5,051.6	6.1	39.3	202.4	396.4	1,022.5	3,437.1	592.0	
GROUP IV												
561 cities, 25,000 to 49,999; population 19,486,000:												
Number of offenses known ...	989,949		93,892	896,057	787	6,266	25,389	61,450	172,689	643,431	79,937	
Rate	5,080.3		481.8	4,598.4	4.0	32.2	130.3	315.4	886.2	3,302.0	410.2	

See footnotes at end of table.

Table 16. — Crime Rates, Offenses Known to the Police, Population Group, 1996 — Continued

[1996 estimated population. Rate: Number of crimes per 100,000 inhabitants]

Population group	Crime Index total	Modified Crime Index total[1]	Violent crime[2]	Property crime[3]	Murder and non-negligent man-slaughter	Forcible rape	Robbery	Aggravated assault	Burglary	Larceny–theft	Motor vehicle theft	Arson[1]
GROUP V												
1,342 cities, 10,000 to 24,999; population 21,087,000:												
Number of offenses known ...	981,093		82,974	898,119	712	5,946	18,969	57,347	164,441	667,474	66,204	
Rate	4,652.6		393.5	4,259.1	3.4	28.2	90.0	272.0	779.8	3,165.3	314.0	
GROUP VI												
4,830 cities under 10,000; population 16,926,000:												
Number of offenses known ...	806,756		61,988	744,768	547	4,186	9,854	47,401	130,935	572,059	41,774	
Rate	4,766.3		366.2	4,400.1	3.2	24.7	58.2	280.0	773.6	3,379.7	246.8	
SUBURBAN COUNTIES												
1,053 agencies; population 44,438,000:												
Number of offenses known ...	1,615,399		179,474	1,435,925	2,168	13,028	41,025	123,253	350,101	927,548	158,276	
Rate	3,635.2		403.9	3,231.3	4.9	29.3	92.3	277.4	787.8	2,087.3	356.2	
RURAL COUNTIES[4]												
1,993 agencies; population 21,927,000:												
Number of offenses known ...	494,987		53,196	441,791	1,043	5,397	3,940	42,816	149,110	262,361	30,320	
Rate	2,257.4		242.6	2,014.8	4.8	24.6	18.0	195.3	680.0	1,196.5	138.3	
SUBURBAN AREA[5]												
5,045 agencies; population 82,781,000:												
Number of offenses known ...	3,280,553		314,958	2,965,595	3,252	22,063	76,360	213,283	621,890	2,051,841	291,864	
Rate	3,962.9		380.5	3,582.5	3.9	26.7	92.2	257.6	751.2	2,478.6	352.6	

[1] Arson rates are not presented in this table because fewer agencies furnished complete reports for arson than for the other seven Crime Index offenses. Independently tabulated arson rates appear on page 54 of this publication.

[2] Violent crimes are offenses of murder, forcible rape, robbery, and aggravated assault.

[3] Property crimes are offenses of burglary, larceny–theft, and motor vehicle theft. Data are not included for the property crime of arson.

[4] Includes state police agencies with no county breakdown.

[5] Includes suburban city and county law enforcement agencies within metropolitan areas. Excludes central cities. Suburban cities and counties are also included in other groups. Population figures were rounded to the nearest thousand. All rates were calculated on the population before rounding.

Forcible rape figures furnished by the state-level Uniform Crime Reporting (UCR) Program administered by the Illinois State Police were not in accordance with national UCR guidelines. See Appendix 1 for details.

Complete data for 1996 were not available for the states of Florida, Illinois, Kansas, Kentucky, Montana, and Vermont. See "Offense Estimation," pages 389-390 for details.

Table 17. — Crime Rates, Offenses Known to the Police, Suburban and Nonsuburban Cities,[1] Population Group, 1996

[1996 estimated population. Rate: Number of crimes per 100,000 inhabitants]

Population group	Crime Index total	Modified Crime Index total[2]	Violent crime[3]	Property crime[4]	Murder and non-negligent man-slaughter	Forcible rape	Robbery	Aggravated assault	Burglary	Larceny–theft	Motor vehicle theft	Arson[2]
Suburban Cities												
TOTAL SUBURBAN CITIES: 3,992 cities; population 38,343,000:												
Number of offenses known ..	1,665,154		135,484	1,529,670	1,084	9,035	35,335	90,030	271,789	1,124,293	133,588	
Rate	4,342.8		353.3	3,989.4	2.8	23.6	92.2	234.8	708.8	2,932.2	348.4	
GROUP IV												
396 cities, 25,000 to 49,999; population 13,597,000:												
Number of offenses known ...	589,167		54,566	534,601	439	3,406	16,297	34,424	101,153	376,243	57,205	
Rate	4,333.1		401.3	3,931.8	3.2	25.0	119.9	253.2	743.9	2,767.1	420.7	
GROUP V												
957 cities, 10,000 to 24,999; population 15,035,000:												
Number of offenses known ...	603,979		48,061	555,918	391	3,456	12,540	31,674	98,549	408,740	48,629	
Rate	4,017.0		319.7	3,697.4	2.6	23.0	83.4	210.7	655.4	2,718.5	323.4	
GROUP VI												
2,639 cities, under 10,000; population 9,711,000:												
Number of offenses known ...	472,008		32,857	439,151	254	2,173	6,498	23,932	72,087	339,310	27,754	
Rate	4,860.8		338.4	4,522.4	2.6	22.4	66.9	246.5	742.4	3,494.2	285.8	
Nonsuburban Cities												
TOTAL NONSUBURBAN CITIES: 2,741 cities; population 19,156,000:												
Number of offenses known ..	1,112,644		103,370	1,009,274	962	7,363	18,877	76,168	196,276	758,671	54,327	
Rate	5,808.2		539.6	5,268.6	5.0	38.4	98.5	397.6	1,024.6	3,960.4	283.6	
GROUP IV												
165 cities, 25,000 to 49,999; population 5,889,000:												
Number of offenses known ...	400,782		39,326	361,456	348	2,860	9,092	27,026	71,536	267,188	22,732	
Rate	6,805.4		667.8	6,137.6	5.9	48.6	154.4	458.9	1,214.7	4,536.9	386.0	
GROUP V												
385 cities, 10,000 to 24,999; population 6,051,000:												
Number of offenses known ...	377,114		34,913	342,201	321	2,490	6,429	25,673	65,892	258,734	17,575	
Rate	6,231.8		576.9	5,654.8	5.3	41.1	106.2	424.2	1,088.9	4,275.5	290.4	
GROUP VI												
2,191 cities under 10,000; population 7,216,000:												
Number of offenses known ...	334,748		29,131	305,617	293	2,013	3,356	23,469	58,848	232,749	14,020	
Rate	4,639.2		403.7	4,235.5	4.1	27.9	46.5	325.3	815.6	3,225.6	194.3	

[1] Suburban places are within Metropolitan Statistical Areas (MSAs) and include suburban city and county law enforcement agencies within the metropolitan area. Central cities are excluded. Nonsuburban places are outside MSAs.

[2] Arson rates are not presented in this table because fewer agencies furnished complete reports for arson than for the seven Crime Index offenses. Independently tabulated arson rates appear on page 54 of the publication.

[3] Violent crimes are offenses of murder, forcible rape, robbery, and aggravated assault.

[4] Property crimes are offenses of burglary, larceny–theft, and motor vehicle theft. Data are not included for the property crime of arson.

Population figures were rounded to the nearest thousand. All rates were calculated on the population before rounding.

Forcible rape figures furnished by the state-level Uniform Crime Reporting (UCR) Program administered by the Illinois State Police were not in accordance with national UCR guidelines. See Appendix I for details.

Complete data for 1996 were not available for the states of Florida, Illinois, Kansas, Kentucky, Montana, and Vermont. See "Offense Estimation," pages 389-390 for details.

Table 18. — Crime Rates, Offenses Known to the Police, Suburban and Nonsuburban Counties, Population Group, 1996

[1996 estimated population. Rate: Number of crimes per 100,000 inhabitants]

Population group	Crime Index total	Modified Crime Index total[1]	Violent crime[2]	Property crime[3]	Murder and non-negligent man-slaughter	Forcible rape	Robbery	Aggravated assault	Burglary	Larceny–theft	Motor vehicle theft	Arson[1]
Suburban Counties[4]												
100,000 and over												
102 counties; population 26,106,000:												
Number of offenses known ...	1,107,888		128,911	978,977	1,466	7,974	34,913	84,558	226,108	642,192	110,677	
Rate	4,243.8		493.8	3,750.0	5.6	30.5	133.7	323.9	866.1	2,459.9	423.9	
25,000 to 99,999												
307 counties; population 15,712,000:												
Number of offenses known ...	383,487		36,375	347,112	539	3,656	4,149	28,031	99,838	222,058	25,216	
Rate	2,440.7		231.5	2,209.2	3.4	23.3	26.4	178.4	635.4	1,413.3	160.5	
Under 25,000												
644 counties; population 2,619,000:												
Number of offenses known ...	124,024		14,188	109,836	163	1,398	1,963	10,664	24,155	63,298	22,383	
Rate	4,734.8		541.7	4,193.2	6.2	53.4	74.9	407.1	922.2	2,416.5	854.5	
Nonsuburban Counties[4]												
25,000 and over												
234 counties; population 9,222,000:												
Number of offenses known ...	210,413		21,858	188,555	358	1,972	2,052	17,476	62,354	114,001	12,200	
Rate	2,281.7		237.0	2,044.7	3.9	21.4	22.3	189.5	676.2	1,236.2	132.3	
10,000 to 24,999												
547 counties; population 8,697,000:												
Number of offenses known ...	163,456		18,159	145,297	414	1,722	1,064	14,959	51,963	83,768	9,566	
Rate	1,879.5		208.8	1,670.7	4.8	19.8	12.2	172.0	597.5	963.2	110.0	
Under 10,000												
1,111 counties; population 3,603,000:												
Number of offenses known ...	92,101		9,593	82,508	220	1,364	555	7,454	27,139	48,739	6,630	
Rate	2,556.4		266.3	2,290.1	6.1	37.9	15.4	206.9	753.3	1,352.8	184.0	

[1] Arson rates are not presented in this table because fewer agencies furnished complete reports for arson than for the other seven Crime Index offenses. Independently tabulated arson rates appear on page 54 of this publication.

[2] Violent crimes are offenses of murder, forcible rape, robbery, and aggravated assault.

[3] Property crimes are offenses of burglary, larceny–theft, and motor vehicle theft. Data are not included for the property crime of arson.

[4] Offenses include sheriffs' and county law enforcement agencies. State police offenses are not included.

Population figures were rounded to the nearest thousand. All rates were calculated on the population before rounding.

Forcible rape figures furnished by the state-level Uniform Crime Reporting (UCR) Program administered by the Illinois State Police were not in accordance with national UCR guidelines. See Appendix I for details.

Complete data for 1996 were not available for the states of Florida, Illinois, Kansas, Kentucky, Montana, and Vermont. See "Offense Estimation," pages 389-390 for details.

Table 19. — Crime Rates, Offenses Known Breakdown, Population Group, 1996

[1996 estimated population. Rate: Number of crimes per 100,000 inhabitants]

Population group	Forcible rape — Rape by force	Forcible rape — Assault to rape—attempts	Robbery — Firearm	Robbery — Knife or cutting instrument	Robbery — Other weapon	Robbery — Strong-armed	Aggravated assault — Firearm	Aggravated assault — Knife or cutting instrument	Aggravated assault — Other weapon	Aggravated assault — Hands, fists, feet, etc.	Burglary — Forcible entry	Burglary — Unlawful entry	Burglary — Attempted forcible entry	Motor vehicle theft — Autos	Motor vehicle theft — Trucks and buses	Motor vehicle theft — Other vehicles	Arson[1] — Structure	Arson[1] — Mobile	Other
TOTAL ALL AGENCIES: 10,238 agencies; population 212,532,000: Number of offenses known	70,027	10,162	201,015	44,249	57,282	191,309	193,923	159,044	302,834	224,823	1,386,737	546,119	172,999	970,886	204,294	63,987			
Rate	32.9	4.8	94.6	20.8	27.0	90.0	91.2	74.8	142.5	105.8	652.5	257.0	81.4	456.8	96.1	30.1			
TOTAL CITIES: 7,211 cities; population 146,520,000: Number of offenses known	53,545	8,310	180,842	40,743	52,514	175,095	162,293	135,236	247,169	170,597	1,057,869	410,535	141,637	840,191	185,181	43,540			
Rate	36.5	5.7	123.4	27.8	35.8	119.5	110.8	92.3	168.7	116.4	722.0	280.2	96.7	573.4	126.4	29.7			
GROUP I																			
65 cities, 250,000 and over; population 47,046,000: Number of offenses known	23,116	4,053	120,572	26,422	36,419	103,419	96,779	72,815	130,309	56,628	446,270	141,018	60,010	459,729	99,865	15,932			
Rate	49.1	8.6	256.3	56.2	77.4	219.8	205.7	154.8	277.0	120.4	948.6	299.7	127.6	977.2	212.3	33.9			
10 cities, 1,000,000 and over; population 22,285,000: Number of offenses known	8,333	1,737	60,831	15,661	25,388	48,331	45,305	37,648	64,110	26,721	164,273	61,973	34,273	217,003	47,935	5,970			
Rate	37.4	7.8	273.0	70.3	113.9	216.9	203.3	168.9	287.7	119.9	737.1	278.1	153.8	973.8	215.1	26.8			
17 cities, 500,000 to 999,999; population 10,967,000: Number of offenses known	5,913	987	26,237	4,792	4,731	23,053	18,750	14,161	27,994	11,442	118,399	28,476	11,120	100,016	20,797	5,121			
Rate	53.9	9.0	239.2	43.7	43.1	210.2	171.0	129.1	255.3	104.3	1,079.6	259.7	101.4	912.0	189.6	46.7			
38 cities, 250,000 to 499,999; population 13,795,000: Number of offenses known	8,870	1,329	33,504	5,969	6,300	32,035	32,724	21,006	38,205	18,465	163,598	50,569	14,617	142,710	31,133	4,841			
Rate	64.3	9.6	242.9	43.3	45.7	232.2	237.2	152.3	277.0	133.9	1,185.9	366.6	106.0	1,034.5	225.7	35.1			
GROUP II																			
146 cities, 100,000 to 249,999; population 21,432,000: Number of offenses known	8,940	1,248	26,681	5,980	6,491	27,261	26,234	19,904	40,262	24,675	194,227	68,427	22,113	134,379	26,039	6,327			
Rate	41.7	5.8	124.5	27.9	30.3	127.2	122.4	92.9	187.9	115.1	906.3	319.3	103.2	627.0	121.5	29.5			
GROUP III																			
305 cities, 50,000 to 99,999; population 20,750,000: Number of offenses known	7,175	978	15,188	3,636	4,039	19,142	15,463	14,651	29,029	23,117	135,334	56,948	19,886	99,816	16,786	6,246			
Rate	34.6	4.7	73.2	17.5	19.5	92.3	74.5	70.6	139.9	111.4	652.2	274.4	95.8	481.0	80.9	30.1			

See footnotes at end of table.

Table 19. — Crime Rates, Offenses Known Breakdown, Population Group, 1996 — Continued

Population group	Forcible rape — Rape by force	Forcible rape — Assault to rape—attempts	Robbery — Firearm	Robbery — Knife or cutting instrument	Robbery — Other weapon	Robbery — Strong-armed	Aggravated assault — Firearm	Aggravated assault — Knife or cutting instrument	Aggravated assault — Other weapon	Aggravated assault — Hands, fists, feet, etc.	Burglary — Forcible entry	Burglary — Unlawful entry	Burglary — Attempted forcible entry	Motor vehicle theft — Autos	Motor vehicle theft — Trucks and buses	Motor vehicle theft — Other vehicles	Arson[1] — Structure	Arson[1] — Mobile	Arson[1] — Other
GROUP IV																			
560 cities, 25,000 to 49,999; population 19,457,000:																			
Number of offenses known	5,538	717	8,709	2,314	2,750	11,523	9,462	10,262	19,411	22,237	105,509	51,902	14,721	63,438	10,913	5,442			
Rate	28.5	3.7	44.8	11.9	14.1	59.2	48.6	52.7	99.8	114.3	542.3	266.8	75.7	326.0	56.1	28.0			
GROUP V																			
1,337 cities, 10,000 to 24,999; population 21,010,000:																			
Number of offenses known	5,238	682	6,460	1,546	1,903	8,928	8,440	10,335	16,775	21,428	100,973	48,491	14,097	51,688	8,686	5,293			
Rate	24.9	3.2	30.7	7.4	9.1	42.5	40.2	49.2	79.8	102.0	480.6	230.8	67.1	246.0	41.3	25.2			
GROUP VI																			
4,798 cities under 10,000; population 16,825,000:																			
Number of offenses known	3,538	632	3,232	845	912	4,822	5,915	7,269	11,383	22,512	75,556	43,749	10,810	31,141	6,180	4,300			
Rate	21.0	3.8	19.2	5.0	5.4	28.7	35.2	43.2	67.7	133.8	449.1	260.0	64.2	185.1	36.7	25.6			
SUBURBAN COUNTIES																			
1,047 agencies; population 44,234,000:																			
Number of offenses known	11,569	1,372	18,581	3,150	4,303	14,697	23,435	17,770	44,227	37,194	227,828	95,703	23,934	112,602	30,225	13,916			
Rate	26.2	3.1	42.0	7.1	9.7	33.2	53.0	40.2	100.0	84.1	515.1	216.4	54.1	254.6	68.3	31.5			
RURAL COUNTIES																			
1,980 agencies; population 21,778,000:																			
Number of offenses known	4,913	480	1,592	356	465	1,517	8,195	6,038	11,438	17,032	101,040	39,881	7,428	18,093	5,600	6,531			
Rate	22.6	2.2	7.3	1.6	2.1	7.0	37.6	27.7	52.5	78.2	464.0	183.1	34.1	83.1	25.7	30.0			
SUBURBAN AREA[2]																			
5,022 agencies; population 82,463,000:																			
Number of offenses known	19,480	2,462	31,078	6,104	7,747	30,982	35,494	31,182	70,386	75,054	387,980	181,521	48,597	218,905	47,408	23,399			
Rate	23.6	3.0	37.7	7.4	9.4	37.6	43.0	37.8	85.4	91.0	470.5	220.1	58.9	265.5	57.5	28.4			

[1] Arson rates are not presented in this table because fewer agencies furnished complete reports for arson than for the other seven Crime Index offenses. Independently tabulated arson rates appear on page 54 of this publication.
[2] Includes suburban city and county law enforcement agencies within metropolitan areas. Excludes central cities. Suburban cities and counties are also included in other groups.
Population figures were rounded to the nearest thousand. All rates were calculated on the population before rounding.
Forcible rape figures furnished by the state-level Uniform Crime Reporting (UCR) Program administered by the Illinois State Police were not in accordance with national UCR guidelines. See Appendix I for details.
Complete data for 1996 were not available for the states of Florida, Illinois, Kansas, Kentucky, Montana, and Vermont. See "Offense Estimation," pages 389-390 for details.

Table 20. — Murder, State, Types of Weapons, 1996

State	Total murders[1]	Total firearms	Handguns	Rifles	Shotguns	Firearms (type unknown)	Knives or cutting instruments	Other weapons	Hands, fists, feet, etc.
Alabama	424	308	265	23	19	1	63	37	16
Alaska	40	27	24	—	3	—	6	5	2
Arizona	359	270	223	16	13	18	44	24	21
Arkansas	216	155	116	14	18	7	26	25	10
California	2,916	2,061	1,872	95	86	8	342	357	156
Colorado	169	87	66	7	6	8	36	31	15
Connecticut	158	109	87	3	3	16	17	18	14
Delaware	29	15	9	3	2	1	4	5	5
District of Columbia[2]									
Florida[2,3]	263	163				163	39	39	22
Georgia	610	445	378	21	29	17	79	56	30
Hawaii	38	16	10	1	4	1	5	8	9
Idaho	42	28	14	8	4	2	5	5	4
Illinois[2]	765	585	513	4	7	61	72	62	46
Indiana	294	200	161	7	10	22	38	35	21
Iowa	44	27	21	1	1	4	5	6	6
Kansas[2]									
Kentucky[2]	219	146	98	12	17	19	39	20	14
Louisiana	704	547	453	25	23	46	70	59	28
Maine	25	11	5	—	5	1	7	4	3
Maryland	578	424	398	3	14	9	69	67	18
Massachusetts	155	75	23	5	4	43	50	29	1
Michigan	695	480	225	39	31	185	79	107	29
Minnesota	133	71	58	5	3	5	25	23	14
Mississippi	178	136	107	6	10	13	21	15	6
Missouri	384	264	204	19	14	27	54	53	13
Montana[2]									
Nebraska	19	9	7	2	—	—	3	5	2
Nevada	215	130	118	3	5	4	37	35	13
New Hampshire	19	9	4	2	3	—	4	2	4
New Jersey	332	164	157	1	2	4	62	62	44
New Mexico	136	76	54	7	13	2	32	22	6
New York[2]	305	168	125	12	19	12	72	42	23
North Carolina	615	397	318	26	48	5	82	97	39
North Dakota	7	3	1	1	1	—	2	1	1
Ohio	459	300	270	7	12	11	38	87	34
Oklahoma	214	136	99	10	21	6	28	34	16
Oregon	116	59	50	1	6	2	18	29	10
Pennsylvania	665	493	438	19	22	14	71	67	34
Rhode Island	25	13	9	2	—	2	4	5	3
South Carolina	329	224	160	8	25	31	41	44	20
South Dakota	6	3	—	1	1	1	2	—	1
Tennessee	385	279	243	9	21	6	52	22	32
Texas	1,476	962	689	73	89	111	235	195	84
Utah	62	35	24	—	3	8	10	9	8
Vermont[2]	8	5	3	1	1	—	2	1	1
Virginia	490	322	250	18	29	25	78	56	34
Washington	238	129	105	12	9	3	40	60	9
West Virginia	67	45	27	5	11	2	6	12	4
Wisconsin	193	108	98	4	4	2	26	46	13
Wyoming	16	14	8	4	2	—	1	—	1

[1] Total number of murders for which supplemental homicide data were received.

[2] Complete data were not available for the states of Illinois, Kansas, Kentucky, Montana, Vermont, nor the District of Columbia, and New York City; therefore, it was necessary that their crime counts be estimated. An aggregate Florida state total for 1996 was supplied by the Florida Department of Law Enforcement. See "Offense Estimation," pages 389-390 for details.

[3] Firearm breakdowns were not provided by the state of Florida.

Table 21. — Robbery, State, Types of Weapons, 1996

State	Total robberies[1]	Firearms	Knives or cutting instruments	Other weapons	Strong-armed	Agency count	Population
Alabama	7,057	3,284	571	577	2,625	277	4,168,000
Alaska	670	260	71	53	286	26	546,000
Arizona	7,272	2,866	699	730	2,977	79	4,174,000
Arkansas	2,843	1,342	206	234	1,061	178	2,378,000
California	94,032	37,125	9,109	8,609	39,189	714	31,705,000
Colorado	3,563	1,264	328	506	1,465	180	3,550,000
Connecticut	4,604	1,665	436	373	2,130	97	2,639,000
Delaware	1,124	461	54	72	537	49	371,000
District of Columbia	6,444	2,746	446	339	2,913	2	543,000
Florida[2]	24,848	10,151	2,031	2,288	10,378	94	6,107,000
Georgia	14,168	7,322	777	1,651	4,418	430	6,386,000
Hawaii	1,606	134	125	30	1,317	5	1,184,000
Idaho	240	83	27	32	98	105	1,171,000
Illinois[2]	28,752	12,045	3,065	2,640	11,002	6	3,334,000
Indiana	5,361	2,649	391	344	1,977	206	3,401,000
Iowa	1,006	235	108	191	472	166	2,233,000
Kansas[2]	1,356	563	129	138	526	2	434,000
Kentucky[2]	3,077	1,355	312	159	1,251	10	1,037,000
Louisiana	11,130	7,027	549	621	2,933	123	3,438,000
Maine	288	52	26	28	182	149	1,224,000
Maryland	19,891	10,365	1,489	1,362	6,675	138	5,017,000
Massachusetts	7,542	1,720	1,319	1,010	3,493	242	4,971,000
Michigan	15,940	7,409	945	2,792	4,794	450	7,870,000
Minnesota	5,203	1,550	447	436	2,770	299	4,602,000
Mississippi	2,125	1,216	92	199	618	56	906,000
Missouri	8,878	3,794	573	769	3,742	189	4,110,000
Montana[2]							
Nebraska	1,035	387	109	61	478	238	1,548,000
Nevada	4,931	2,014	470	420	2,027	31	1,593,000
New Hampshire	271	63	36	27	145	76	927,000
New Jersey	18,811	5,616	1,827	1,372	9,996	515	7,988,000
New Mexico	2,477	1,207	337	180	753	49	1,012,000
New York	59,367	24,102	6,515	5,731	23,019	470	14,025,000
North Carolina	11,868	5,339	822	1,153	4,554	457	7,177,000
North Dakota	23	2	7	3	11	41	355,000
Ohio	15,081	5,845	862	1,250	7,124	275	7,025,000
Oklahoma	3,519	1,294	308	248	1,669	292	3,301,000
Oregon	3,728	1,126	391	326	1,885	183	2,838,000
Pennsylvania	21,330	9,980	1,295	979	9,076	677	9,322,000
Rhode Island	748	177	8	64	499	44	990,000
South Carolina	6,344	2,613	558	789	2,384	213	3,658,000
South Dakota	128	52	10	11	55	59	505,000
Tennessee	11,044	6,737	694	736	2,877	103	2,846,000
Texas	32,787	13,991	3,035	3,548	12,213	907	19,074,000
Utah	1,320	454	99	210	557	113	1,939,000
Vermont[2]							
Virginia	7,947	3,614	453	1,059	2,821	338	640,000
Washington	6,191	1,935	600	499	3,157	206	5,198,000
West Virginia	737	268	51	54	364	298	1,826,000
Wisconsin	4,981	2,500	371	315	1,795	331	5,143,000
Wyoming	84	23	16	7	38	50	397,000

[1] The number of robberies for which breakdowns were received for 12 months of 1996.

[2] Complete data were not available for the states of Illinois, Kansas, Kentucky, Montana, and Vermont; therefore, it was necessary that their crime counts be estimated. An aggregate Florida state total for 1996 was supplied by the Florida Department of Law Enforcement. See "Offense Estimation," pages 389-390 for details.

Table 22. — Aggravated Assault, State, Types of Weapons, 1996

State	Total aggravated assaults[1]	Firearms	Knives or cutting instruments	Other weapons	Personal weapons	Agency count	Population
Alabama	14,867	4,117	2,635	4,431	3,684	277	4,168,000
Alaska	2,808	635	585	693	895	26	546,000
Arizona	17,839	5,976	2,664	4,868	4,331	79	4,174,000
Arkansas	8,845	2,579	1,468	1,993	2,805	178	2,378,000
California	167,164	30,853	21,269	51,945	63,097	714	31,705,000
Colorado	9,234	2,289	1,914	2,971	2,060	180	3,550,000
Connecticut	5,971	624	917	1,999	2,431	97	2,639,000
Delaware	2,302	448	466	1,090	298	49	371,000
District of Columbia	6,310	1,308	1,601	2,583	818	2	543,000
Florida[2]	54,614	12,835	10,431	22,255	9,093	94	6,107,000
Georgia	25,699	6,994	5,008	8,275	5,422	430	6,386,000
Hawaii	1,350	164	155	292	739	5	1,184,000
Idaho	2,512	766	601	807	338	105	1,171,000
Illinois[2]	41,336	12,260	9,524	17,589	1,963	6	3,334,000
Indiana	12,299	2,118	1,399	3,244	5,538	206	3,401,000
Iowa	4,600	528	742	1,354	1,976	166	2,233,000
Kansas[2]	2,161	593	338	1,002	228	2	434,000
Kentucky[2]	5,873	1,241	667	1,501	2,464	10	1,037,000
Louisiana	20,678	6,391	3,996	6,909	3,382	123	3,438,000
Maine	959	29	128	258	544	149	1,224,000
Maryland	24,539	5,017	4,945	10,590	3,987	138	5,017,000
Massachusetts	26,729	1,670	3,951	10,892	10,216	242	4,971,000
Michigan	34,167	9,074	6,354	15,334	3,405	450	7,870,000
Minnesota	7,585	1,872	2,104	1,828	1,781	299	4,602,000
Mississippi	3,197	1,163	515	836	683	56	906,000
Missouri	17,986	5,390	3,024	6,230	3,342	189	4,110,000
Montana[2]							
Nebraska	5,540	795	634	1,451	2,660	238	1,548,000
Nevada	6,891	1,500	1,048	2,244	2,099	31	1,593,000
New Hampshire	492	48	84	128	232	76	927,000
New Jersey	21,307	3,271	4,459	6,659	6,918	515	7,988,000
New Mexico	7,384	2,418	1,386	2,302	1,278	49	1,012,000
New York	59,511	13,703	12,018	19,374	14,416	470	14,025,000
North Carolina	27,759	8,295	5,320	8,032	6,112	457	7,177,000
North Dakota	190	14	33	82	61	41	355,000
Ohio	16,655	3,780	3,262	4,899	4,714	275	7,025,000
Oklahoma	14,423	2,811	2,201	4,890	4,521	292	3,301,000
Oregon	9,043	1,746	1,410	2,932	2,955	183	2,838,000
Pennsylvania	18,854	3,883	2,800	4,236	7,935	677	9,322,000
Rhode Island	2,301	248	418	960	675	44	990,000
South Carolina	28,066	6,896	6,610	10,274	4,286	213	3,658,000
South Dakota	729	143	209	178	199	59	505,000
Tennessee	19,894	6,691	3,610	6,579	3,014	103	2,846,000
Texas	80,455	19,800	17,243	26,260	17,152	907	19,074,000
Utah	4,040	777	720	1,605	938	113	1,939,000
Vermont[2]							
Virginia	11,823	1,884	2,354	3,148	4,437	338	640,000
Washington	13,346	2,867	2,498	4,161	3,820	206	5,198,000
West Virginia	2,672	371	413	507	1,381	298	1,826,000
Wisconsin	6,759	939	1,026	1,676	3,118	331	5,143,000
Wyoming	753	96	135	210	312	50	397,000

[1] The number of aggravated assaults for which breakdowns were received for 12 months of 1996.

[2] Complete data were not available for the states of Illinois, Kansas, Kentucky, Montana, and Vermont; therefore, it was necessary that their crime counts be estimated. An aggregate Florida state total for 1996 was supplied by the Florida Department of Law Enforcement. See "Offense Estimation," pages 389-390 for details.

Table 23. — Offense Analysis, 1996, and Percent Change from 1995

[11,040 agencies; 1996 estimated population 204,726,000]

Classification	Number of offenses 1996	Percent change over 1995	Percent distribution[1]	Average value
MURDER	14,326	-12.3	—	$125
FORCIBLE RAPE	71,135	-2.9	—	25
ROBBERY:				
Total	**377,335**	**-7.1**	**100.0**	**929**
Street/highway	193,284	-11.1	51.2	667
Commercial house	50,761	-.4	13.5	1,477
Gas or service station	9,205	-3.8	2.4	487
Convenience store	22,196	-1.5	5.9	567
Residence	40,143	-1.9	10.6	1,133
Bank	7,542	+14.2	2.0	4,207
Miscellaneous	54,204	-6.4	14.4	969
BURGLARY:				
Total	**1,867,756**	**-4.2**	**100.0**	**1,332**
Residence (dwelling):	1,241,856	-4.1	66.5	1,350
Night	367,784	-5.1	19.7	1,392
Day	522,471	-3.0	28.0	1,318
Unknown	351,601	-4.6	18.8	1,355
Nonresidence (store, office, etc.):	625,900	-4.3	33.5	1,296
Night	278,943	-4.9	14.9	1,197
Day	149,580	-2.5	8.0	1,167
Unknown	197,377	-4.6	10.6	1,533
LARCENY–THEFT (EXCEPT MOTOR VEHICLE THEFT):				
Total	**5,977,516**	**-1.8**	**100.0**	**532**
By type:				
Pocket-picking	26,660	-3.3	.4	320
Purse-snatching	35,233	-7.3	.6	296
Shoplifting	918,354	—	15.4	120
From motor vehicles (except accessories)	1,511,831	+.7	25.3	518
Motor vehicle accessories	638,468	-7.6	10.7	387
Bicycles	331,957	-10.6	5.6	263
From buildings	761,498	-2.2	12.7	894
From coin-operated machines	35,946	-5.3	.6	296
All others	1,717,569	-.1	28.7	723
By value:				
Over $200	2,303,402	-1.8	38.5	1,289
$50 to $200	1,398,518	-2.1	23.4	118
Under $50	2,275,596	-1.6	38.1	20
MOTOR VEHICLE THEFT	1,092,014	-2.7	—	5,372

[1] Because of rounding, percentages may not add to total.

Complete data were not available for the states of Illinois, Kansas, Kentucky, and Montana; therefore, it was necessary that their crime counts be estimated. An aggregate Florida state total for 1996 was supplied by the Florida Department of Law Enforcement. See "Offense Estimation," pages 389-390 for details.

Table 24. — Type and Value of Property Stolen and Recovered, 1996

[11,040 agencies; 1996 estimated population 204,726,000]

Type of property	Value of property		Percent recovered
	Stolen	Recovered	
Total[1]	**$11,895,212,000**	**$4,516,443,000**	**38.0**
Currency, notes, etc.	733,562,000	52,399,000	7.1
Jewelry and precious metals	865,771,000	44,924,000	5.2
Clothing and furs	247,125,000	39,274,000	15.9
Locally stolen motor vehicles	5,960,766,000	4,032,359,000	67.6
Office equipment	471,516,000	29,640,000	6.3
Televisions, radios, stereos, etc.	885,476,000	41,857,000	4.7
Firearms	99,349,000	10,832,000	10.9
Household goods	181,068,000	11,352,000	6.3
Consumable goods	71,489,000	18,984,000	26.6
Livestock	14,015,000	2,299,000	16.4
Miscellaneous	2,365,074,000	232,524,000	9.8

[1] All totals and percentages calculated before rounding.

Complete data were not available for the states of Illinois, Kansas, Kentucky, and Montana; therefore, it was necessary that their crime counts be estimated. An aggregate Florida state total for 1996 was supplied by the Florida Department of Law Enforcement. See "Offense Estimation," pages 389-390 for details.

SECTION III

Crime Index Offenses Cleared

For UCR purposes, law enforcement agencies clear or solve an offense when at least one person is arrested, charged with the commission of the offense, and turned over to the court for prosecution. Clearances recorded in 1996 may be for offenses which occurred in prior years. Several crimes may be cleared by the arrest of one person, or the arrest of many persons may clear only one offense. Law enforcement agencies may clear a crime by exceptional means when some element beyond law enforcement control precludes the placing of formal charges against the offender. Examples of circumstances allowing such clearances are the death of the offender (suicide, justifiably killed by police or private citizen, etc.); the victim's refusal to cooperate with prosecution after the offender has been identified; or the denial of extradition because the offender committed another crime in a different jurisdiction and is being prosecuted there. In all exceptional clearance cases, law enforcement must have identified the offender, have enough evidence to support arrest, and know the offender's location.

Law enforcement agencies nationwide recorded a 22-percent Crime Index clearance rate for 1996. Collectively, 47 percent of violent crimes were cleared. Among the violent offenses, the clearance rates were 67 percent for murder, 52 percent for forcible rape, 27 percent for robbery, and 58 percent for aggravated assault. Clearances for crimes against persons (murder, forcible rape, and aggravated assault) are generally higher than for property crimes as crimes against persons are often given more intensive investigative efforts, and the victims and/or witnesses can frequently identify the perpetrators.

The overall property crime clearance rate was 18 percent. Twenty percent of the larceny-thefts, 14 percent each of motor vehicle thefts and burglaries, and 16 percent of arsons were cleared during the year.

When considering the Modified Crime Index total which includes arson, the overall clearance rate was 22 percent.

The highest total Crime Index clearance rates geographically were registered in both the Northeastern and Southern States, each with 23 percent. The Midwestern and Western States each recorded a 21-percent clearance rate. For violent crime, the highest clearance rate, 49 percent, was recorded in the South. In the West, the rate was 47 percent, while the Midwest and Northeast each registered a 46-percent rate. Property crime clearance rates were 19 percent each in the Northeast and South, 18 percent in the Midwest, and 17 percent in the West.

By community type, rural county law enforcement agencies recorded the highest clearance rate for Crime Index offenses brought to their attention, 24 percent. City agencies solved 22 percent of total crimes reported and suburban county agencies, 21 percent. Cities with 10,000 to 24,999 inhabitants registered the highest total Crime Index and property crime clearance rates, 27 percent and 24 percent, respectively. The highest violent crime clearance rate—62 percent—was recorded both in cities with populations under 10,000 and in the rural counties. (See Table 25.)

Clearances Involving Only Persons under 18 Years of Age

Involvement of juveniles in crime can be measured by the number of crimes in which they have been identified as the offenders. Even though no physical arrest may have been made, a clearance by arrest is recorded when an offender under 18 years of age is cited to appear in juvenile court or before other juvenile authorities. Since the juvenile clearance percentages shown in this publication indicate only those offenses where no adults were involved, they should be considered a slight underestimation of juvenile involvement in crime. Juveniles (persons under 18 years of age) account for 26 percent of the United States population, according to 1996 Bureau of the Census estimates.

Twenty-one percent of the Crime Index offenses cleared by law enforcement during 1996 involved only young people under age 18. Persons in this age group accounted for 13 percent of the violent crime clearances and 23 percent of those for property crimes. Murder showed the lowest percentage of juvenile involvement, 8 percent, while the highest percentage was shown for arson, 45 percent.

Geographically, the Midwestern States recorded the largest percentage of Crime Index offense involvement by the under 18 age group—25 percent. Juveniles alone were the offenders in 23 percent of the clearances in the Western States, 20 percent of those in the Northeastern States, and 17 percent of those in the Southern States.

CHART 3.1

CRIMES CLEARED
by ARREST
1996

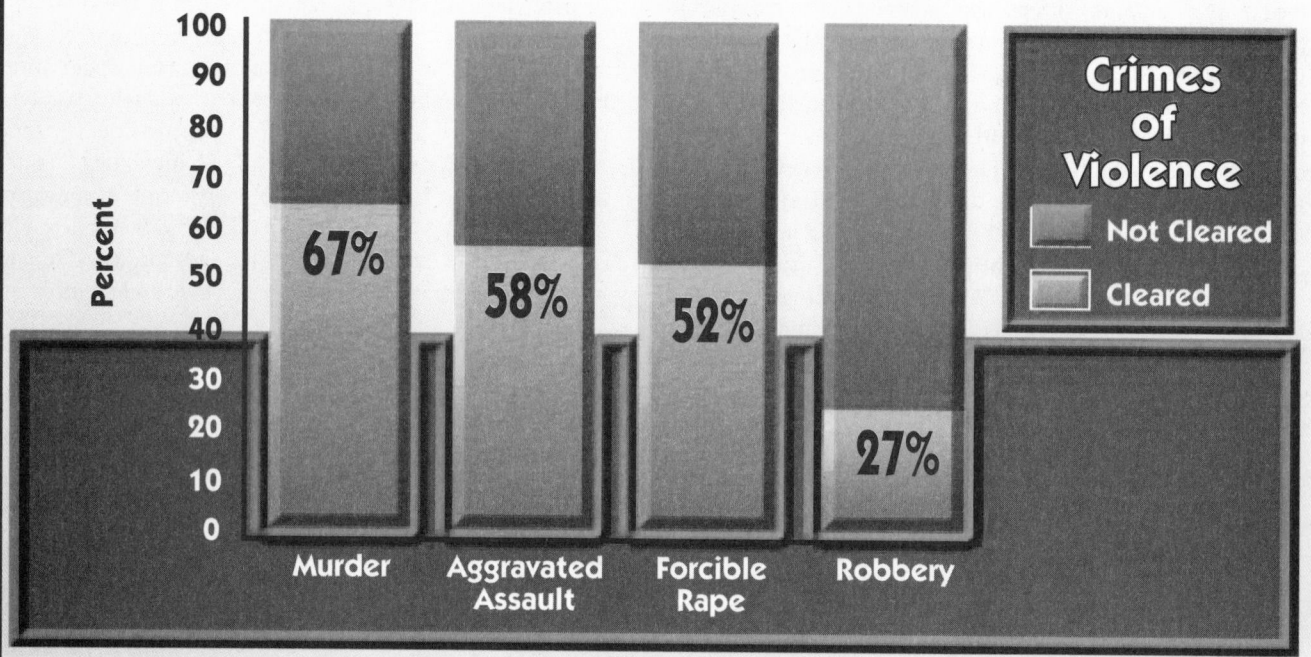

Crimes of Violence

- Not Cleared
- Cleared

Murder — 67%
Aggravated Assault — 58%
Forcible Rape — 52%
Robbery — 27%

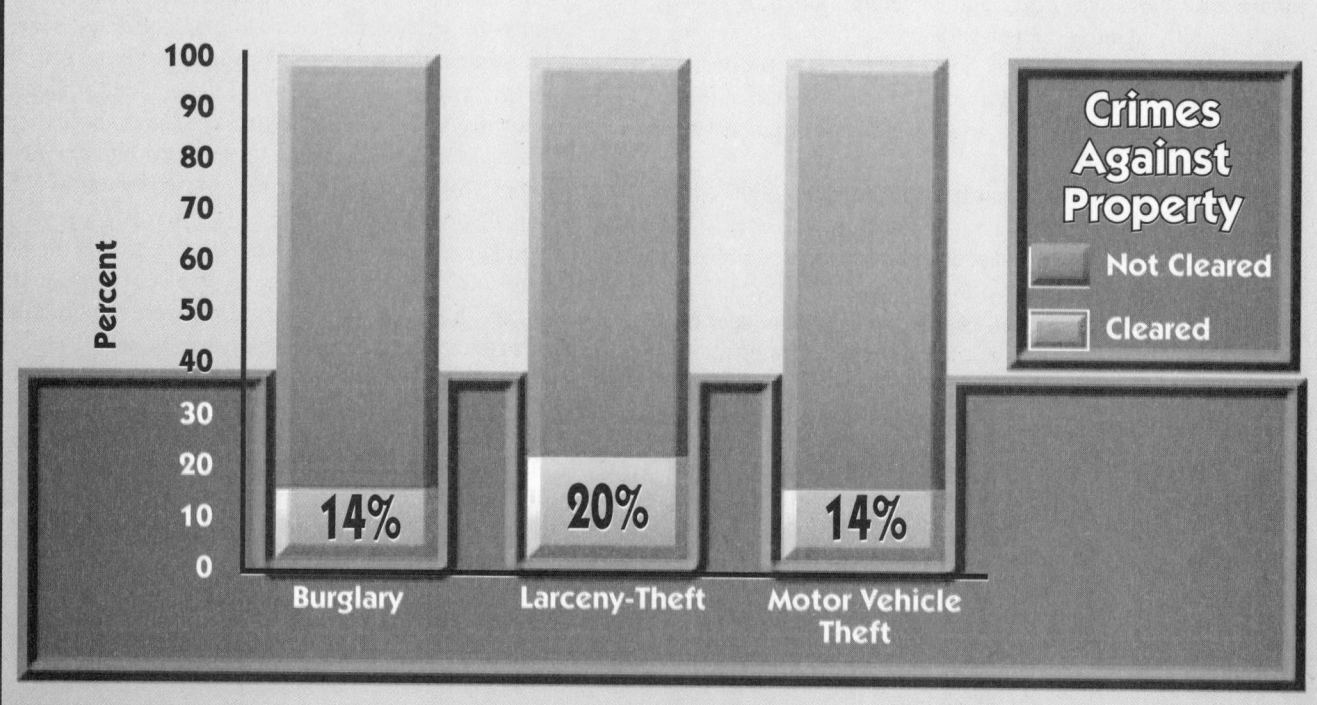

Crimes Against Property

- Not Cleared
- Cleared

Burglary — 14%
Larceny-Theft — 20%
Motor Vehicle Theft — 14%

Table 25. — Offenses Known and Percent Cleared by Arrest,[1] Population Group, 1996

[1996 estimated population]

Population group	Crime Index total	Modified Crime Index total[2]	Violent crime[3]	Property crime[4]	Murder and non-negligent man-slaughter	Forcible rape	Robbery	Aggravated assault	Burglary	Larceny–theft	Motor vehicle theft	Arson[2]
TOTAL ALL AGENCIES: 11,015 agencies; population 206,926,000:												
Offenses known	10,419,304	10,500,544	1,293,408	9,125,896	15,487	73,349	429,368	775,204	1,910,140	6,083,637	1,132,119	81,240
Percent cleared by arrest ..	21.8	21.7	47.4	18.1	66.9	51.9	26.9	58.0	13.8	20.3	14.0	16.5
TOTAL CITIES: 7,809 cities; population 141,427,000:												
Offenses known	8,462,172	8,525,590	1,085,069	7,377,103	12,466	56,489	389,065	627,049	1,452,130	4,969,366	955,607	63,418
Percent cleared by arrest ..	21.8	21.8	45.9	18.3	65.7	51.5	26.6	57.0	13.3	20.7	13.1	16.0
GROUP I												
56 cities, 250,000 and over; population 41,176,000:												
Offenses known	3,254,008	3,282,876	564,144	2,689,864	7,374	23,383	241,680	291,707	548,157	1,635,030	506,677	28,868
Percent cleared by arrest ...	19.0	18.9	40.9	14.4	60.5	52.7	24.3	53.3	11.4	16.7	10.1	12.0
9 cities, 1,000,000 and over; population 19,531,000:												
Offenses known	1,337,532	1,349,428	272,260	1,065,272	3,397	8,825	123,351	136,687	220,044	608,411	236,817	11,896
Percent cleared by arrest ...	19.1	19.0	41.3	13.4	63.1	52.9	25.2	54.6	11.3	16.1	8.4	9.0
15 cities, 500,000 to 999,999; population 9,739,000:												
Offenses known	832,187	838,438	126,364	705,823	1,765	5,949	54,645	64,005	137,249	451,081	117,493	6,251
Percent cleared by arrest ...	18.5	18.4	39.3	14.7	54.7	53.6	22.3	52.1	12.3	16.3	11.4	11.2
32 cities, 250,000 to 499,999; population 11,907,000:												
Offenses known	1,084,289	1,095,010	165,520	918,769	2,212	8,609	63,684	91,015	190,864	575,538	152,367	10,721
Percent cleared by arrest ...	19.3	19.3	41.5	15.3	61.0	51.9	24.2	52.1	11.0	17.8	11.7	15.7
GROUP II												
129 cities, 100,000 to 249,999; population 18,777,000:												
Offenses known	1,283,412	1,293,213	155,554	1,127,858	1,846	8,690	54,238	90,780	235,696	748,970	143,192	9,801
Percent cleared by arrest ...	21.4	21.3	47.9	17.7	73.3	52.8	28.8	58.3	13.5	19.9	13.1	16.6
GROUP III												
311 cities, 50,000 to 99,999; population 21,128,000:												
Offenses known	1,149,289	1,157,190	129,898	1,019,391	1,239	8,032	40,462	80,165	204,791	694,798	119,802	7,901
Percent cleared by arrest ...	22.5	22.4	47.3	19.3	67.6	47.5	28.1	56.7	12.8	22.3	12.7	16.9
GROUP IV												
569 cities, 25,000 to 49,999; population 19,668,000:												
Offenses known	960,026	966,660	88,953	871,073	761	6,146	24,470	57,576	166,333	628,200	76,540	6,634
Percent cleared by arrest ...	23.6	23.5	52.4	20.6	74.1	48.6	31.6	61.4	13.9	23.0	15.7	17.8

See footnotes at end of table.

Table 25. — Offenses Known and Percent Cleared by Arrest,[1] Population Group, 1996 — Continued

Population group	Crime Index total	Modified Crime Index total[2]	Violent crime[3]	Property crime[4]	Murder and non-negligent man-slaughter	Forcible rape	Robbery	Aggravated assault	Burglary	Larceny–theft	Motor vehicle theft	Arson[2]
GROUP V												
1,411 cities, 10,000 to 24,999; population 22,199,000:												
Offenses known	990,278	995,761	83,232	907,046	699	5,968	18,589	57,976	164,159	676,287	66,600	5,483
Percent cleared by arrest	26.6	26.5	55.2	23.9	78.4	51.3	35.1	61.8	16.2	25.9	22.9	24.0
GROUP VI												
5,333 cities under 10,000; population 18,479,000:												
Offenses known	825,159	829,890	63,288	761,871	547	4,270	9,626	48,845	132,994	586,081	42,796	4,731
Percent cleared by arrest	25.0	25.0	61.7	21.9	79.0	55.0	36.8	66.9	16.9	22.5	29.0	25.6
SUBURBAN COUNTIES												
1,086 agencies; population 43,197,000:												
Offenses known	1,470,828	1,484,616	156,873	1,313,955	1,979	11,547	36,478	106,869	311,769	855,714	146,472	13,788
Percent cleared by arrest	20.8	20.7	52.8	16.9	67.3	53.1	28.3	60.8	14.2	18.1	16.3	16.0
RURAL COUNTIES												
2,120 agencies; population 22,301,000:												
Offenses known	486,304	490,338	51,466	434,838	1,042	5,313	3,825	41,286	146,241	258,557	30,040	4,034
Percent cleared by arrest	24.3	24.3	62.3	19.8	79.3	52.6	42.1	65.0	17.7	19.6	31.7	26.3
SUBURBAN AREA[5]												
5,423 agencies; population 83,739,000:												
Offenses known	3,134,847	3,158,845	290,285	2,844,562	3,033	20,481	70,246	196,525	579,895	1,986,075	278,592	23,998
Percent cleared by arrest	22.3	22.3	53.7	19.1	69.7	52.7	30.2	61.9	14.5	20.7	17.1	17.9

[1] Includes offenses cleared by exceptional means.

[2] The number of agency reports used in arson clearance rates is less than used in compiling clearance rates for other Crime Index offenses. It is not necessary to report clearances by detailed property classification to be included in this table. The Modified Crime Index total is the sum of the Crime Index offenses, including arson.

[3] Violent crimes are offenses of murder, forcible rape, robbery, and aggravated assault.

[4] Property crimes are offenses of burglary, larceny–theft, and motor vehicle theft. Data are not included for the property crime of arson.

[5] Includes suburban city and county law enforcement agencies within metropolitan areas. Excludes central cities. Suburban cities and counties are also included in other groups.

Forcible rape figures furnished by the state-level Uniform Crime Reporting (UCR) Program administered by the Illinois State Police were not in accordance with national UCR guidelines and were excluded from the forcible rape, violent crime, Crime Index total, and Modified Crime Index total categories.

Complete data were not available for the states of Illinois, Kansas, Kentucky, and Montana; therefore, it was necessary that their crime counts be estimated. An aggregate Florida state total for 1996 was supplied by the Florida Department of Law Enforcement. See "Offense Estimation," pages 389-390 for details.

Table 26. — Offenses Known and Percent Cleared by Arrest,[1] Geographic Region and Division, 1996

[1996 estimated population]

Geographic region/division	Crime Index total	Modified Crime Index total[2]	Violent crime[3]	Property crime[4]	Murder and non-negligent man-slaughter	Forcible rape	Robbery	Aggravated assault	Burglary	Larceny–theft	Motor vehicle theft	Arson[2]
TOTAL												
11,015 agencies;												
population 206,926,000:												
Offenses known	10,419,304	10,500,544	1,293,408	9,125,896	15,487	73,349	429,368	775,204	1,910,140	6,083,637	1,132,119	81,240
Percent cleared by arrest ...	21.8	21.7	47.4	18.1	66.9	51.9	26.9	58.0	13.8	20.3	14.0	16.5
NEW ENGLAND												
705 agencies;												
population 11,879,000:												
Offenses known	465,610	470,409	56,525	409,085	377	3,295	14,415	38,438	89,567	265,417	54,101	4,799
Percent cleared by arrest	22.1	22.0	50.4	18.2	70.8	48.0	27.4	59.1	14.9	20.0	15.0	9.7
MIDDLE ATLANTIC												
2,139 agencies;												
population 36,707,000:												
Offenses known	1,416,253	1,426,258	219,005	1,197,248	2,289	8,720	101,804	106,192	244,599	774,542	178,107	10,005
Percent cleared by arrest	22.7	22.7	44.8	18.7	70.7	54.5	28.7	58.9	15.0	21.8	10.0	16.0
Northeast												
2,844 agencies;												
population 48,586,000:												
Offenses known	1,881,863	1,896,667	275,530	1,606,333	2,666	12,015	116,219	144,630	334,166	1,039,959	232,208	14,804
Percent cleared by arrest ...	22.6	22.5	46.0	18.6	70.7	52.7	28.5	59.0	15.0	21.3	11.1	13.9
EAST NORTH CENTRAL												
1,377 agencies;												
population 23,996,000:												
Offenses known	1,162,619	1,173,106	125,809	1,036,810	1,590	10,740	41,651	71,828	205,640	698,545	132,625	10,487
Percent cleared by arrest	19.7	19.7	41.9	17.0	66.7	46.3	24.0	51.1	12.3	19.0	14.2	15.1
WEST NORTH CENTRAL												
1,094 agencies;												
population 13,820,000:												
Offenses known	599,070	603,547	52,966	546,104	568	4,418	13,310	34,670	98,945	400,704	46,455	4,477
Percent cleared by arrest	23.8	23.8	54.6	20.8	76.9	56.6	30.6	63.2	13.7	22.4	22.0	19.5
Midwest												
2,471 agencies;												
population 37,816,000:												
Offenses known	1,761,689	1,776,653	178,775	1,582,914	2,158	15,158	54,961	106,498	304,585	1,099,249	179,080	14,964
Percent cleared by arrest ...	21.1	21.1	45.6	18.3	69.4	49.3	25.6	55.0	12.7	20.2	16.3	16.4
SOUTH ATLANTIC												
2,116 agencies;												
population 32,860,000:												
Offenses known	1,785,048	1,795,380	216,457	1,568,591	3,140	11,017	69,412	132,888	336,675	1,076,845	155,071	10,332
Percent cleared by arrest	22.2	22.2	48.2	18.6	66.6	57.2	27.4	57.9	15.4	19.6	19.2	20.8
EAST SOUTH CENTRAL												
236 agencies;												
population 5,480,000:												
Offenses known	359,187	361,296	50,621	308,566	655	3,049	16,718	30,199	74,531	191,567	42,468	2,109
Percent cleared by arrest	23.5	23.5	49.6	19.2	71.0	52.0	24.8	62.7	13.6	22.1	15.9	24.2
WEST SOUTH CENTRAL												
1,539 agencies;												
population 27,810,000:												
Offenses known	1,605,111	1,617,968	183,300	1,421,811	2,548	12,235	47,765	120,752	308,287	963,203	150,321	12,857
Percent cleared by arrest	22.8	22.7	50.3	19.2	70.3	58.5	28.7	57.6	14.5	21.1	16.8	18.7

See footnotes at end of table.

Table 26. — Offenses Known and Percent Cleared by Arrest,[1] Geographic Region and Division, 1996 — Continued

Geographic region/division	Crime Index total	Modified Crime Index total[2]	Violent crime[3]	Property crime[4]	Murder and non-negligent man-slaughter	Forcible rape	Robbery	Aggravated assault	Burglary	Larceny–theft	Motor vehicle theft	Arson[2]
South												
3,891 agencies; population 66,150,000:												
Offenses known	3,749,346	3,774,644	450,378	3,298,968	6,343	26,301	133,895	283,839	719,493	2,231,615	347,860	25,298
Percent cleared by arrest ...	22.6	22.6	49.2	19.0	68.5	57.2	27.6	58.2	14.9	20.5	17.8	20.0
MOUNTAIN												
659 agencies; population 13,779,000:												
Offenses known	827,949	832,612	74,140	753,809	995	5,626	19,318	48,201	147,798	522,063	83,948	4,663
Percent cleared by arrest	20.6	20.6	43.3	18.4	57.0	37.0	23.8	51.6	11.0	21.2	13.7	18.9
PACIFIC												
1,150 agencies; population 40,595,000:												
Offenses known	2,198,457	2,219,968	314,585	1,883,872	3,325	14,249	104,975	192,036	404,098	1,190,751	289,023	21,511
Percent cleared by arrest	20.7	20.6	48.1	16.1	61.9	49.9	25.4	60.1	12.6	18.7	10.4	13.6
WEST												
1,809 agencies; population 54,374,000:												
Offenses known	3,026,406	3,052,580	388,725	2,637,681	4,320	19,875	124,293	240,237	551,896	1,712,814	372,971	26,174
Percent cleared by arrest ...	20.7	20.6	47.2	16.8	60.7	46.3	25.2	58.4	12.2	19.5	11.1	14.6

[1] Includes offenses cleared by exceptional means.

[2] The number of agency reports used in arson clearance rates is less than used in compiling clearance rates for other Crime Index offenses. It is not necessary to report clearances by detailed property classification to be included in this table. The Modified Crime Index total is the sum of the Crime Index offenses, including arson.

[3] Violent crimes are offenses of murder, forcible rape, robbery, and aggravated assault.

[4] Property crimes are offenses of burglary, larceny–theft, and motor vehicle theft. Data are not included for the property crime of arson.

Forcible rape figures furnished by the state-level Uniform Crime Reporting (UCR) Program administered by the Illinois State Police were not in accordance with national UCR guidelines and were excluded from the forcible rape, violent crime, Crime Index total, and Modified Crime Index total categories.

Complete data were not available for the states of Illinois, Kansas, Kentucky, and Montana; therefore, it was necessary that their crime counts be estimated. An aggregate Florida state total for 1996 was supplied by the Florida Department of Law Enforcement. See "Offense Estimation," pages 389–390 for details.

Table 27. — Offenses Known Breakdown and Percent Cleared by Arrest,[1] Population Group, 1996

[1996 estimated population]

Population group	Forcible rape — Rape by force	Forcible rape — Assault to rape-attempts	Robbery — Firearm	Robbery — Knife or cutting instrument	Robbery — Other weapon	Robbery — Strong-armed	Aggravated assault — Firearm	Aggravated assault — Knife or cutting instrument	Aggravated assault — Other weapon	Aggravated assault — Hands, fists, feet, etc.	Burglary — Forcible entry	Burglary — Unlawful entry	Burglary — Attempted forcible entry	Motor vehicle theft — Autos	Motor vehicle theft — Trucks and buses	Motor vehicle theft — Other vehicles	Arson[2] — Structure	Arson[2] — Mobile	Arson[2] — Other
TOTAL ALL AGENCIES: 11,008 agencies; population 206,816,000: Offenses known	63,999	9,313	181,385	37,626	39,510	171,966	174,593	134,546	251,265	219,377	1,269,402	498,292	141,108	878,401	193,188	59,977	37,685	22,821	18,309
Percent cleared by arrest	52.2	49.4	20.7	30.0	38.6	29.8	41.9	64.7	58.1	65.2	13.2	16.0	11.3	14.4	11.8	15.2	21.5	7.9	18.7
TOTAL CITIES: 7,804 cities; population 141,364,000: Offenses known	48,957	7,503	163,213	34,380	35,221	157,394	146,447	113,976	203,897	167,372	966,601	372,989	111,583	753,828	160,522	40,867	29,907	17,546	13,812
Percent cleared by arrest	51.9	49.4	20.3	29.7	39.8	29.3	39.8	64.4	57.8	64.4	12.5	15.9	11.1	13.4	10.9	14.5	21.1	7.4	18.0
GROUP I																			
56 cities, 250,000 and over; population 41,176,000: Offenses known	19,927	3,456	109,057	21,036	20,418	91,169	83,322	56,571	97,000	54,814	398,347	116,940	32,870	395,052	97,131	14,494	12,614	9,743	4,842
Percent cleared by arrest	53.3	49.2	17.7	28.8	45.5	26.4	36.5	64.1	57.3	60.4	10.3	15.6	11.1	10.6	8.0	10.1	18.0	5.2	13.8
9 cities, 1,000,000 and over; population 19,531,000: Offenses known	7,303	1,522	56,557	11,811	10,860	44,123	40,164	27,162	39,759	29,602	157,918	50,475	11,651	179,840	51,144	5,833	4,425	4,404	1,811
Percent cleared by arrest	54.2	46.7	16.2	31.8	63.0	25.8	30.1	65.0	64.6	64.7	9.1	17.7	14.0	9.0	6.4	6.7	16.1	3.8	10.7
15 cities, 500,000 to 999,999; population 9,739,000: Offenses known	5,118	831	24,474	4,418	4,284	21,469	16,254	12,286	25,205	10,260	103,305	24,464	9,480	93,363	19,258	4,872	2,877	2,337	875
Percent cleared by arrest	53.6	53.2	19.1	24.6	25.8	24.6	47.3	62.2	51.2	50.1	11.2	17.5	10.7	11.7	10.8	7.8	16.2	4.7	12.1
32 cities, 250,000 to 499,999; population 11,907,000: Offenses known	7,506	1,103	28,026	4,807	5,274	25,577	26,904	17,123	32,036	14,952	137,124	42,001	11,739	121,849	26,729	3,789	5,312	3,002	2,156
Percent cleared by arrest	52.2	49.7	19.4	25.0	25.3	29.0	39.7	63.8	53.2	58.7	10.9	12.0	8.6	12.0	9.1	18.3	20.5	7.7	17.0
GROUP II																			
129 cities, 100,000 to 249,999; population 18,777,000: Offenses known	7,648	1,042	22,188	5,212	5,473	22,625	26,167	16,515	33,370	20,636	160,760	56,642	18,294	115,764	22,184	5,244	5,000	2,659	1,982
Percent cleared by arrest	53.4	48.2	24.6	28.4	32.3	30.6	34.6	64.5	59.1	65.7	12.7	15.9	12.5	13.4	11.6	12.5	20.7	7.2	20.1
GROUP III																			
311 cities, 50,000 to 99,999; population 21,128,000: Offenses known	7,091	941	14,586	3,496	3,907	18,473	14,945	14,065	27,566	23,589	130,306	54,803	19,682	97,618	16,142	6,042	3,662	2,169	1,971
Percent cleared by arrest	47.4	47.9	23.9	30.7	28.9	30.7	43.2	61.7	54.4	64.9	12.6	14.7	9.0	13.0	11.1	12.3	21.8	8.0	18.6
GROUP IV																			
568 cities, 25,000 to 49,999; population 19,642,000: Offenses known	5,420	714	8,143	2,255	2,612	11,431	8,353	9,735	18,182	21,156	100,860	50,822	14,480	60,835	10,281	5,338	3,113	1,326	2,105
Percent cleared by arrest	48.7	48.2	25.9	32.0	31.7	35.5	51.1	65.2	59.7	64.6	13.5	15.4	11.1	15.9	15.3	14.7	21.0	11.0	18.0

See footnotes at end of table.

Table 27. — Offenses Known Breakdown and Percent Cleared by Arrest,[1] Population Group, 1996 — Continued

Population group	Forcible rape		Robbery				Aggravated assault				Burglary			Motor vehicle theft			Arson[2]		
	Rape by force	Assault to rape—attempts	Firearm	Knife or cutting instrument	Other weapon	Strong-armed	Firearm	Knife or cutting instrument	Other weapon	Hands, fists, feet, etc.	Forcible entry	Unlawful entry	Attempted forcible entry	Autos	Trucks and buses	Other vehicles	Structure	Mobile	Other
GROUP V																			
1,410 cities, 10,000 to 24,999; population 22,176,000:																			
Offenses known	5,259	694	6,136	1,537	1,892	8,945	7,947	10,011	16,343	22,570	99,661	49,145	14,754	52,370	8,559	5,385	2,856	977	1,567
Percent cleared by arrest ...	51.5	50.3	30.2	36.8	33.7	38.8	56.9	66.3	58.6	66.7	16.3	17.4	12.2	23.1	22.9	23.0	27.5	14.8	24.4
GROUP VI																			
5,330 cities under 10,000; population 18,465,000:																			
Offenses known	3,612	656	3,103	844	919	4,751	5,713	7,079	11,436	24,607	76,667	44,637	11,503	32,189	6,225	4,364	2,662	672	1,345
Percent cleared by arrest ...	55.0	55.2	32.1	40.3	39.7	38.8	62.8	68.8	62.3	69.5	17.4	17.5	11.3	29.8	28.2	23.6	28.9	20.7	22.1
SUBURBAN COUNTIES																			
1,085 agencies; population 43,156,000:																			
Offenses known	10,205	1,334	16,639	2,900	3,826	13,090	20,302	14,851	36,589	35,061	203,073	86,470	21,957	106,497	27,216	12,615	5,508	4,381	3,753
Percent cleared by arrest ...	53.6	48.9	22.6	31.3	27.8	35.0	48.2	65.3	58.8	68.3	13.9	15.4	11.3	17.1	13.7	15.6	21.2	7.5	18.7
RURAL COUNTIES																			
2,119 agencies; population 22,296,000:																			
Offenses known	4,837	476	1,533	346	463	1,482	7,844	5,719	10,779	16,944	99,728	38,833	7,568	18,076	5,450	6,495	2,270	894	744
Percent cleared by arrest ...	52.9	50.4	38.7	42.2	39.5	46.2	64.1	68.9	61.3	66.4	17.7	18.4	14.0	36.4	31.0	19.2	28.5	20.0	31.0
SUBURBAN AREA[3]																			
5,417 agencies; population 83,634,000:																			
Offenses known	18,004	2,442	28,184	5,772	7,177	28,983	31,164	27,589	61,817	74,624	359,378	172,203	47,259	212,105	43,835	22,130	10,420	6,276	7,026
Percent cleared by arrest ...	53.2	49.2	24.3	32.4	29.8	35.8	50.7	65.9	59.2	68.2	14.3	16.0	11.0	17.5	15.1	16.5	22.9	9.2	18.9

[1] Includes offenses cleared by exceptional means.

[2] The number of agency reports used in arson clearance rates is less than used in compiling clearance rates for other Crime Index offenses.

[3] Includes suburban city and county law enforcement agencies within metropolitan areas. Excludes central cities. Suburban cities and counties are also included in other groups.

Forcible rape figures furnished by the state-level Uniform Crime Reporting (UCR) Program administered by the Illinois State Police were not in accordance with national UCR guidelines and were excluded from the forcible rape, violent crime, Crime Index total, and Modified Crime Index total categories.

Complete data were not available for the states of Illinois, Kansas, Kentucky, and Montana; therefore, it was necessary that their crime counts be estimated. An aggregate Florida state total for 1996 was supplied by the Florida Department of Law Enforcement. See "Offense Estimation," pages 389-390 for details.

Table 28. — Offenses Cleared by Arrest[1] of Persons Under 18 Years of Age, 1996

[1996 estimated population]

Population group	Crime Index total	Modified Crime Index total[2]	Violent crime[3]	Property crime[4]	Murder and non-negligent man-slaughter	Forcible rape	Robbery	Aggravated assault	Burglary	Larceny–theft	Motor vehicle theft	Arson[2]
TOTAL ALL AGENCIES: **10,921 agencies;** **population 196,293,000:**												
Total clearances:	2,164,758	2,178,021	567,577	1,597,181	9,540	36,246	99,900	421,891	251,354	1,194,284	151,543	13,263
Percent under 18	20.6	20.8	12.8	23.4	8.1	11.7	18.2	11.7	20.6	24.1	22.2	45.5
TOTAL CITIES: 7,755 cities; **population 132,250,000:**												
Total clearances	1,749,610	1,759,648	454,488	1,295,122	7,427	27,486	88,064	331,511	182,893	993,519	118,710	10,038
Percent under 18	21.1	21.3	13.1	24.0	8.7	11.5	18.5	11.9	20.2	24.8	22.9	48.2
GROUP I												
54 cities, 250,000 and over; population 33,293,000:												
Total clearances	538,287	541,728	188,197	350,090	3,731	11,056	43,502	129,908	54,547	248,935	46,608	3,441
Percent under 18	17.2	17.4	11.8	20.2	8.6	10.4	17.7	10.1	16.1	20.2	24.8	44.1
8 cities, 1,000,000 and over; population 12,191,000:												
Total clearances	180,153	181,227	72,664	107,489	1,511	3,467	16,413	51,273	17,285	74,423	15,781	1,074
Percent under 18	15.9	16.1	10.0	19.9	7.1	7.8	17.9	7.8	14.5	20.8	21.7	41.2
14 cities, 500,000 to 999,999; population 9,196,000:												
Total clearances	148,508	149,188	46,912	101,596	870	3,125	11,696	31,221	16,349	72,195	13,052	680
Percent under 18	15.7	15.8	13.0	17.0	9.3	14.8	17.7	11.1	15.0	16.3	23.6	38.4
32 cities, 250,000 to 499,999; population 11,907,000:												
Total clearances	209,626	211,313	68,621	141,005	1,350	4,464	15,393	47,414	20,913	102,317	17,775	1,687
Percent under 18	19.4	19.7	12.9	22.6	9.8	9.4	17.4	11.9	18.4	22.4	28.5	48.4
GROUP II												
127 cities, 100,000 to 249,999; population 18,474,000:												
Total clearances	271,132	272,738	75,574	195,558	1,335	4,347	15,739	54,153	31,312	145,912	18,334	1,606
Percent under 18	18.9	19.1	12.0	21.6	8.9	9.3	16.9	10.8	16.6	22.7	21.3	48.0
GROUP III												
308 cities, 50,000 to 99,999; population 20,896,000:												
Total clearances	256,918	258,240	61,122	195,796	833	3,787	11,291	45,211	26,037	154,631	15,128	1,322
Percent under 18	23.5	23.6	14.2	26.4	9.7	11.1	20.5	13.0	21.2	27.6	23.2	48.3

See footnotes at end of table.

Table 28. — Offenses Cleared by Arrest[1] of Persons Under 18 Years of Age, 1996 — Continued

Population group	Crime Index total	Modified Crime Index total[2]	Violent crime[3]	Property crime[4]	Murder and non-negligent man-slaughter	Forcible rape	Robbery	Aggravated assault	Burglary	Larceny-theft	Motor vehicle theft	Arson[2]
GROUP IV												
557 cities, 25,000 to 49,999; population 19,284,000:												
Total clearances	221,681	222,858	45,479	176,202	558	2,953	7,573	34,395	22,534	142,085	11,583	1,177
Percent under 18	24.2	24.3	14.8	26.6	7.7	13.6	20.7	13.7	22.0	27.8	20.8	51.1
GROUP V												
1,393 cities, 10,000 to 24,999; population 21,901,000:												
Total clearances	256,701	257,992	45,277	211,424	539	3,002	6,420	35,316	26,049	170,664	14,711	1,291
Percent under 18	23.8	24.0	15.0	25.7	7.4	13.9	21.0	14.2	23.5	26.5	20.2	52.0
GROUP VI												
5,316 cities under 10,000; population 18,401,000:												
Total clearances	204,891	206,092	38,839	166,052	431	2,341	3,539	32,528	22,414	131,292	12,346	1,201
Percent under 18	24.7	24.9	15.2	26.9	10.0	15.5	19.1	14.8	28.1	27.1	22.5	53.2
SUBURBAN COUNTIES												
1,069 agencies; population 42,276,000:												
Total clearances	299,954	302,128	81,856	218,098	1,312	6,033	10,271	64,240	43,183	151,396	23,519	2,174
Percent under 18	18.7	18.8	12.1	21.2	6.6	11.7	16.8	11.5	21.6	21.4	18.9	40.8
RURAL COUNTIES												
2,097 agencies; population 21,767,000:												
Total clearances	115,194	116,245	31,233	83,961	801	2,727	1,565	26,140	25,278	49,369	9,314	1,051
Percent under 18	17.5	17.6	10.2	20.2	5.5	13.5	11.8	9.9	22.0	18.8	22.3	29.1
SUBURBAN AREA[5]												
5,375 agencies; population 82,320,000:												
Total clearances	686,996	691,233	153,798	533,198	2,090	10,626	21,017	120,065	82,593	404,014	46,591	4,237
Percent under 18	21.3	21.4	14.0	23.4	6.9	12.8	19.5	13.3	22.5	24.0	19.4	47.4

[1] Includes offenses cleared by exceptional means.

[2] The number of agency reports used in arson clearance rates is less than those used in compiling clearance rates for other Crime Index offenses. It is not necessary to report clearances by detailed property classification to be included in this table. The Modified Crime Index total is the sum of the Crime Index offenses, including arson.

[3] Violent crimes are offenses of murder, forcible rape, robbery, and aggravated assault.

[4] Property crimes are offenses of burglary, larceny-theft, and motor vehicle theft. Data are not included for the property crime of arson.

[5] Includes suburban city and county law enforcement agencies within metropolitan areas. Excludes central cities. Suburban cities and counties are also included in other groups.

Forcible rape figures furnished by the state-level Uniform Crime Reporting (UCR) Program administered by the Illinois State Police were not in accordance with national UCR guidelines and were excluded from the forcible rape, violent crime, Crime Index total, and Modified Crime Index total categories.

Complete data were not available for the states of Illinois, Kansas, Kentucky, and Montana; therefore, it was necessary that their crime counts be estimated. An aggregate Florida state total for 1996 was supplied by the Florida Department of Law Enforcement. See "Offense Estimation," pages 389-390 for details.

SECTION IV

Persons Arrested

Primarily a gauge of law enforcement's response to crime, arrest counts also provide definitive data concerning the age, sex, and race of perpetrators. Arrest practices, policies, and enforcement emphases vary from place to place and even within a community from time to time as, for example, during a local police campaign against residential burglary. While the practices for certain unlawful conduct such as drunkenness, disorderly conduct, vagrancy, and related violations may differ among agencies, those for robbery, burglary, and other serious crime arrests are more likely to be uniform and consistent throughout all jurisdictions. The Program's procedures require that an arrest be counted on each separate occasion a person is taken into custody, notified, or cited. Annual arrest figures do not measure the number of individuals arrested since one person may be arrested several times during the year for the same or different offenses.

Law enforcement agencies throughout the country in 1996 made an estimated 15.2 million arrests nationwide for all criminal infractions except traffic violations. Among the specific crime categories, the highest arrest counts were for drug abuse violations, larceny-thefts, and driving under the influence, with approximately 1.5 million arrests each. Simple assaults accounted for 1.3 million arrests in 1996. (See Table 29.)

When the overall arrest volume was related to the total United States population, the rate was 5,838 arrests per 100,000 inhabitants. Among the city population groupings, those cities with more than 250,000 inhabitants recorded the highest rate, 7,700, while those with populations from 25,000 to 49,999 recorded the lowest rate, 5,426. (See Table 31.) For suburban county agencies overall, the arrest rate was 4,206, and for rural county law enforcement, it was 4,312 per 100,000 inhabitants. By region, the arrest rates per 100,000 population registered 4,995 in the Northeast, 5,717 in the West, 6,169 in the South, and 6,382 in the Midwest. (See Tables 30 and 31.)

Because of reporting problems at the state levels, only limited arrest statistics were provided from Kentucky and Illinois. No arrest data were available for the District of Columbia, Florida, and Vermont. Due to NIBRS conversion efforts, arrest data were not received from contributing law enforcement agencies in Kansas and Montana. Therefore, tables showing the age, sex, or race of persons arrested contain limited or no data for these states. Arrest totals were, however, estimated for inclusion in Table 29, "Total Estimated Arrests, United States, 1996."

Arrest Trends

The national total number of arrests for all offenses except traffic violations increased 1 percent in 1996 as compared to the 1995 volume. Violent crime arrests showed a 4-percent decline, Crime Index arrests fell 3 percent, and those for property crimes decreased 2 percent.

For the 2-year period, 1995 and 1996, juvenile arrests rose 3 percent, while adult arrests showed virtually no change. Violent crime arrests decreased 3 percent for adults and 6 percent for juveniles. During the same timespan, property crime arrests declined 3 percent for adults and less than 1 percent for juveniles. (See Table 36.)

Two-year trends in total arrests show no change in cities, but indicate a 3-percent increase both in the suburban and rural counties. (See Tables 44, 50, and 56.)

Over the 5-year period, 1992-1996, data show total arrests were up 7 percent. Juvenile arrests increased 21 percent, and adult arrests rose 4 percent for the same timeframe. (See Table 34.) Total Crime Index and property crime arrests declined 5 and 6 percent, respectively. Violent crime arrests decreased 1 percent during the period.

For the decade, 1987-1996, arrests for all offenses were up 16 percent. Crime Index arrests rose 5 percent; and those for violent crimes, 29 percent. During the same timeframe, however, property crime arrests declined 1 percent.

In 1996, the drug abuse violation arrest total was 1 percent above the 1995 level, 37 percent higher than in 1992, and 58 percent higher than in 1987. The following table shows the types of drugs involved in violations resulting in arrests during 1996 by geographic region.

Table 4.1 — Arrests for Drug Abuse Violations, 1996
[Percent distribution]

	United States total	North-eastern States	Mid-western States	Southern States	Western States
Total[1]	100.0	100.0	100.0	100.0	100.0
Sale/manufacture:	24.9	35.2	25.8	20.2	20.7
Heroin or cocaine and their derivatives	14.2	26.8	7.5	11.9	9.5
Marijuana	6.3	6.8	8.1	5.9	5.7
Synthetic or manufactured drugs	.6	.5	.4	.8	.6
Other dangerous nonnarcotic drugs	3.7	1.2	9.8	1.6	4.8
Possession:	75.1	64.8	74.2	79.8	79.3
Heroin or cocaine and their derivatives	25.6	29.2	15.8	22.9	29.1
Marijuana	36.3	32.4	44.8	49.3	24.9
Synthetic or manufactured drugs	1.4	.7	1.3	2.0	1.5
Other dangerous nonnarcotic drugs	11.9	2.5	12.4	5.6	23.9

[1] Because of rounding, percentages may not add to total.

Age

During 1996, 6 percent of all persons arrested nationally were under the age of 15; 19 percent were under 18; 32 percent were under 21; and 45 percent were under 25. Persons in the under-25 age group accounted for 47 percent of arrests in the cities, 41 percent in the suburban counties, and 40 percent in the rural counties. (See Tables 41, 47, 53, and 59.)

Age distribution figures for persons arrested for Crime Index offenses showed 31 percent were under the age of 18; 45 percent, under 21; and 56 percent, under 25. The under-25 age group was also responsible for 46 percent of the violent crime arrests and 59 percent of property crime arrests in 1996.

The offense resulting in the most arrests of persons under age 18 was larceny-theft, while adults were most often arrested for driving under the influence. (See Table 38.)

Sex

Males comprised 79 percent of the persons arrested in the Nation during 1996. (See Table 42.) They accounted for 76 percent of Index crime arrests, 85 percent of those for violent crimes, and 72 percent of the property crime arrests. Men were most often arrested for drug abuse violations and driving under the influence, which jointly accounted for 20 percent of all male arrests.

Continuing with 1996 figures, larceny-theft was the crime for which females were most often arrested. This single offense accounted for 74 percent of arrests of women for Index crimes and 16 percent of all female arrests. Fifty-seven percent of all female larceny-theft arrestees were under 25 years of age.

Comparing 1995 and 1996 arrests by gender, virtually no change was recorded in the number of male arrests from 1995 to 1996, and a 3-percent rise in female arrests was registered for the same period. (See Table 37.) Arrests of males rose 5 percent, and those of females were up 16 percent for the 5-year period from 1992 to 1996.

Race

Race distribution figures for the total number of arrests in the United States during 1996 showed 67 percent of the arrestees were white, 31 percent were black, and the remainder were of other races. (See Table 43.) Whites accounted for 62 percent of the Index crime arrests, 55 percent of the arrests for violent crimes, and 65 percent of those for property crimes.

Table 29. — Total Estimated Arrests,[1] United States, 1996

Total[2]	15,168,100		
		Embezzlement	15,700
		Stolen property; buying, receiving, possessing	151,100
Murder and nonnegligent manslaughter	19,020	Vandalism	320,900
Forcible rape	33,050	Weapons; carrying, possessing, etc.	216,200
Robbery	156,270	Prostitution and commercialized vice	99,000
Aggravated assault	521,570	Sex offenses (except forcible rape and prostitution)	95,800
Burglary	364,800	Drug abuse violations	1,506,200
Larceny–theft	1,486,300	Gambling	21,000
Motor vehicle theft	175,400	Offenses against family and children	149,800
Arson	19,000	Driving under the influence	1,467,300
		Liquor laws	677,400
Violent crime[3]	729,900	Drunkenness	718,700
Property crime[4]	2,045,600	Disorderly conduct	842,600
		Vagrancy	27,800
Crime Index total[5]	2,775,500	All other offenses	3,786,700
Other assaults	1,329,000	Suspicion (not included in totals)	4,900
Forgery and counterfeiting	121,600	Curfew and loitering law violations	185,100
Fraud	465,000	Runaways	195,700

[1] Arrest totals are based on all reporting agencies and estimates for unreported areas.

[2] Because of rounding, figures may not add to total.

[3] Violent crimes are offenses of murder, forcible rape, robbery, and aggravated assault.

[4] Property crimes are offenses of burglary, larceny–theft, motor vehicle theft, and arson.

[5] Includes arson.

Table 30. — Arrests, Number and Rate, Regions, 1996

[Rate: Number of arrests per 100,000 inhabitants]

Offense charged	United States Total (9,666 agencies; population 189,927,000)	Northeast (2,165 agencies; population 40,190,000)	Midwest (2,094 agencies; population 37,198,000)	South (3,768 agencies; population 60,270,000)	West (1,639 agencies; population 52,269,000)
TOTAL	**11,088,352**	**2,007,557**	**2,373,969**	**3,718,348**	**2,988,478**
Rate	**5,838.2**	**4,995.2**	**6,382.0**	**6,169.5**	**5,717.5**
Murder and nonnegligent manslaughter	14,447	2,244	3,456	5,157	3,590
Rate	7.6	5.6	9.3	8.6	6.9
Forcible rape	24,347	4,750	5,792	8,145	5,660
Rate	12.8	11.8	15.6	13.5	10.8
Robbery	121,781	40,476	18,287	29,711	33,307
Rate	64.1	100.7	49.2	49.3	63.7
Aggravated assault	387,571	71,164	61,793	113,156	141,458
Rate	204.1	177.1	166.1	187.7	270.6
Burglary	264,193	43,661	41,444	88,720	90,368
Rate	139.1	108.6	111.4	147.2	172.9
Larceny–theft	1,096,488	176,081	237,482	369,204	313,721
Rate	577.3	438.1	638.4	612.6	600.2
Motor vehicle theft	132,023	20,186	30,913	34,457	46,467
Rate	69.5	50.2	83.1	57.2	88.9
Arson	13,755	2,329	3,155	4,045	4,226
Rate	7.2	5.8	8.5	6.7	8.1
Violent crime[1]	548,146	118,634	89,328	156,169	184,015
Rate	288.6	295.2	240.1	259.1	352.1
Property crime[2]	1,506,459	242,257	312,994	496,426	454,782
Rate	793.2	602.8	841.4	823.7	870.1
Crime Index total[3]	2,054,605	360,891	402,322	652,595	638,797
Rate	1,081.8	898.0	1,081.6	1,082.8	1,222.1
Other assaults	972,984	162,561	220,560	367,139	222,724
Rate	512.3	404.5	592.9	609.2	426.1
Forgery and counterfeiting	88,355	14,819	13,054	37,043	23,439
Rate	46.5	36.9	35.1	61.5	44.8
Fraud	324,776	66,052	49,384	185,143	24,197
Rate	171.0	164.4	132.8	307.2	46.3
Embezzlement	11,449	794	1,818	6,076	2,761
Rate	6.0	2.0	4.9	10.1	5.3
Stolen property; buying, receiving, possessing	111,066	24,886	24,246	26,744	35,190
Rate	58.5	61.9	65.2	44.4	67.3
Vandalism	234,215	51,061	60,412	57,442	65,300
Rate	123.3	127.1	162.4	95.3	124.9
Weapons; carrying, possessing, etc.	161,158	23,749	34,516	54,557	48,336
Rate	84.9	59.1	92.8	90.5	92.5
Prostitution and commercialized vice	81,036	18,046	20,778	14,296	27,916
Rate	42.7	44.9	55.9	23.7	53.4
Sex offenses (except forcible rape and prostitution)	70,619	11,960	14,446	18,804	25,409
Rate	37.2	29.8	38.8	31.2	48.6
Drug abuse violations	1,128,647	265,924	201,453	304,805	356,465
Rate	594.3	661.7	541.6	505.7	682.0
Gambling	16,984	7,451	4,120	3,224	2,189
Rate	8.9	18.5	11.1	5.3	4.2
Offenses against family and children	103,800	24,960	36,783	29,934	12,123
Rate	54.7	62.1	98.9	49.7	23.2
Driving under the influence	1,013,932	117,672	203,075	345,308	347,877
Rate	533.9	292.8	545.9	572.9	665.5
Liquor laws	491,176	108,603	150,090	95,692	136,791
Rate	258.6	270.2	403.5	158.8	261.7
Drunkenness	522,869	26,124	40,354	328,879	127,512
Rate	275.3	65.0	108.5	545.7	244.0
Disorderly conduct	626,918	176,106	224,230	147,548	79,034
Rate	330.1	438.2	602.8	244.8	151.2
Vagrancy	21,735	6,680	2,104	4,684	8,267
Rate	11.4	16.6	5.7	7.8	15.8
All other offenses (except traffic)	2,767,751	496,757	602,366	947,818	720,810
Rate	1,457.3	1,236.0	1,619.4	1,572.6	1,379.0
Suspicion (not included in totals)	4,859	1,159	1,215	1,895	590
Rate	2.6	2.9	3.3	3.1	1.1
Curfew and loitering law violations	142,433	25,493	34,730	34,760	47,450
Rate	75.0	63.4	93.4	57.7	90.8
Runaways	141,844	16,968	33,128	55,857	35,891
Rate	74.7	42.2	89.1	92.7	68.7

[1] Violent crimes are offenses of murder, forcible rape, robbery, and aggravated assault.
[2] Property crimes are offenses of burglary, larceny–theft, motor vehicle theft, and arson.
[3] Includes arson.
Population figures were rounded to the nearest thousand. All rates were calculated before rounding.

Table 31. — Arrests, Number and Rate, Population Group, 1996

[Rate: Number of arrests per 100,000 inhabitants]

Offense charged	Total (9,666 agencies; population 189,927,000)	Cities — Total cities (6,917 cities; population 132,725,000)	Cities — Group I (50 cities, 250,000 and over; population 39,932,000)	Cities — Group II (123 cities, 100,000 to 249,999; population 18,051,000)	Cities — Group III (284 cities, 50,000 to 99,999; population 19,251,000)	Cities — Group IV (540 cities, 25,000 to 49,999; population 18,696,000)	Cities — Group V (1,293 cities, 10,000 to 24,999; population 20,328,000)	Cities — Group VI (4,627 cities, under 10,000; population 16,466,000)	Counties — Suburban counties[1] (913 agencies; population 37,056,000)	Counties — Rural counties (1,836 agencies; population 20,146,000)	Suburban area[2] (4,845 agencies; population 77,866,000)
TOTAL	11,088,352	8,660,982	3,074,699	1,179,059	1,097,690	1,014,476	1,159,674	1,135,384	1,558,644	868,726	3,717,622
Rate	5,838.2	6,525.5	7,699.8	6,531.7	5,701.8	5,426.2	5,704.7	6,895.5	4,206.2	4,312.1	4,774.4
Murder and nonnegligent manslaughter	14,447	11,386	6,761	1,789	1,016	683	643	494	1,963	1,098	3,088
Rate	7.6	8.6	16.9	9.9	5.3	3.7	3.2	3.0	5.3	5.5	4.0
Forcible rape	24,347	18,602	7,860	2,697	2,436	1,883	2,048	1,678	3,599	2,146	7,329
Rate	12.8	14.0	19.7	14.9	12.7	10.1	10.1	10.2	9.7	10.7	9.4
Robbery	121,781	108,840	61,828	15,413	11,705	8,486	7,209	4,199	10,558	2,383	25,557
Rate	64.1	82.0	154.8	85.4	60.8	45.4	35.5	25.5	28.5	11.8	32.8
Aggravated assault	387,571	306,949	127,335	49,076	40,488	33,974	29,927	26,149	56,613	24,009	118,777
Rate	204.1	231.3	318.9	271.9	210.3	181.7	147.2	158.8	152.8	119.2	152.5
Burglary	264,193	196,436	59,366	33,225	29,752	24,736	25,533	23,824	41,348	26,409	89,709
Rate	139.1	148.0	148.7	184.1	154.5	132.3	125.6	144.7	111.6	131.1	115.2
Larceny–theft	1,096,488	936,989	263,010	137,280	144,951	135,605	147,864	108,279	118,419	41,080	374,379
Rate	577.3	706.0	658.6	760.5	752.9	725.3	727.4	657.6	319.6	203.9	480.8
Motor vehicle theft	132,023	107,127	54,063	14,345	12,117	8,501	9,541	8,560	17,851	7,045	35,672
Rate	69.5	80.7	135.4	79.5	62.9	45.5	46.9	52.0	48.2	35.0	45.8
Arson	13,755	10,452	3,040	1,422	1,529	1,395	1,565	1,501	2,067	1,236	5,124
Rate	7.2	7.9	7.6	7.9	7.9	7.5	7.7	9.1	5.6	6.1	6.6
Violent crime[3]	548,146	445,777	203,784	68,975	55,645	45,026	39,827	32,520	72,733	29,636	154,751
Rate	288.6	335.9	510.3	382.1	289.0	240.8	195.9	197.5	196.3	147.1	198.7
Property crime[4]	1,506,459	1,251,004	379,479	186,272	188,349	170,237	184,503	142,164	179,685	75,770	504,884
Rate	793.2	942.6	950.3	1,031.9	978.4	910.6	907.6	863.4	484.9	376.1	648.4
Crime Index total[5]	2,054,605	1,696,781	583,263	255,247	243,994	215,263	224,330	174,684	252,418	105,406	659,635
Rate	1,081.8	1,278.4	1,460.6	1,414.0	1,267.4	1,151.4	1,103.5	1,060.9	681.2	523.2	847.1
Other assaults	972,984	756,522	271,003	114,372	93,224	83,567	100,768	93,588	139,627	76,835	315,903
Rate	512.3	570.0	678.7	633.6	484.2	447.0	495.7	568.4	376.8	381.4	405.7
Forgery and counterfeiting	88,355	68,273	20,600	10,475	9,402	8,593	10,483	8,720	13,473	6,609	30,659
Rate	46.5	51.4	51.6	58.0	48.8	46.0	51.6	53.0	36.4	32.8	39.4
Fraud	324,776	190,335	58,717	21,112	23,126	25,784	32,168	29,428	83,092	51,349	134,787
Rate	171.0	143.4	147.0	117.0	120.1	137.9	158.2	178.7	224.2	254.9	173.1
Embezzlement	11,449	8,903	1,722	2,155	1,854	1,079	1,215	878	1,782	764	3,789
Rate	6.0	6.7	4.3	11.9	9.6	5.8	6.0	5.3	4.8	3.8	4.9
Stolen property; buying, receiving, possessing	111,066	89,704	26,947	15,106	13,842	12,748	11,869	9,192	15,288	6,074	40,769
Rate	58.5	67.6	67.5	83.7	71.9	68.2	58.4	55.8	41.3	30.1	52.4

See footnotes at end of table.

Table 31. — Arrests, Number and Rate, Population Group, 1996 — Continued

Offense charged	Total (9,666 agencies; population 189,927,000)	Total cities (6,917 cities, population 132,725,000)	Cities						Counties		Suburban area[2] (4,845 agencies; population 77,866,000)
			Group I (50 cities, 250,000 and over; population 39,932,000)	Group II (123 cities, 100,000 to 249,999; population 18,051,000)	Group III (284 cities, 50,000 to 99,999; population 19,251,000)	Group IV (540 cities, 25,000 to 49,999; population 18,696,000)	Group V (1,293 cities, 10,000 to 24,999; population 20,328,000)	Group VI (4,627 cities, under 10,000; population 16,466,000)	Suburban counties[1] (913 agencies; population 37,056,000)	Rural counties (1,836 agencies; population 20,146,000)	
Vandalism	234,215	188,637	60,720	24,137	23,725	23,651	28,658	27,746	28,813	16,765	81,610
Rate	123.3	142.1	152.1	133.7	123.2	126.5	141.0	168.5	77.8	83.2	104.8
Weapons; carrying, possessing, etc.	161,158	131,030	55,129	20,259	16,249	13,193	13,204	12,996	20,509	9,619	47,653
Rate	84.9	98.7	138.1	112.2	84.4	70.6	65.0	78.9	55.3	47.7	61.2
Prostitution and commercialized vice	81,036	77,427	59,996	9,387	4,277	2,274	1,131	362	3,389	220	6,740
Rate	42.7	58.3	150.2	52.0	22.2	12.2	5.6	2.2	9.1	1.1	8.7
Sex offenses (except forcible rape and prostitution)	70,619	53,666	23,352	7,323	6,859	5,573	5,739	4,820	11,296	5,657	22,133
Rate	37.2	40.4	58.5	40.6	35.6	29.8	28.2	29.3	30.5	28.1	28.4
Drug abuse violations	1,128,647	906,626	430,395	132,466	99,580	89,703	78,684	75,798	153,318	68,703	332,284
Rate	594.3	683.1	1,077.8	733.8	517.3	479.8	387.1	460.3	413.7	341.0	426.7
Gambling	16,984	15,781	12,778	890	820	525	393	375	728	475	1,488
Rate	8.9	11.9	32.0	4.9	4.3	2.8	1.9	2.3	2.0	2.4	1.9
Offenses against family and children	103,800	60,007	13,179	5,242	8,827	11,980	12,473	8,306	32,206	11,587	54,079
Rate	54.7	45.2	33.0	29.0	45.9	64.1	61.4	50.4	86.9	57.5	69.5
Driving under the influence	1,013,932	619,273	119,220	70,543	83,232	91,247	117,802	137,229	221,172	173,487	451,051
Rate	533.9	466.6	298.6	390.8	432.3	488.1	579.5	833.4	596.9	861.1	579.3
Liquor laws	491,176	402,602	132,911	34,647	42,054	42,009	68,831	82,150	47,508	41,066	155,384
Rate	258.6	303.3	332.8	191.9	218.4	224.7	338.6	498.9	128.2	203.8	199.6
Drunkenness	522,869	435,346	107,265	64,986	66,050	58,962	66,924	71,159	54,659	32,864	172,139
Rate	275.3	328.0	268.6	360.0	343.1	315.4	329.2	432.2	147.5	163.1	221.1
Disorderly conduct	626,918	557,596	207,900	57,258	65,192	56,772	82,542	87,932	40,863	28,459	187,609
Rate	330.1	420.1	520.6	317.2	338.6	303.7	406.0	534.0	110.3	141.3	240.9
Vagrancy	21,735	20,016	12,164	2,250	1,468	1,569	1,129	1,436	1,248	471	4,408
Rate	11.4	15.1	30.5	12.5	7.6	8.4	5.6	8.7	3.4	2.3	5.7
All other offenses (except traffic)	2,767,751	2,138,529	784,855	300,895	260,586	240,459	268,818	282,916	408,460	220,762	929,688
Rate	1,457.3	1,611.3	1,965.5	1,666.9	1,353.6	1,286.2	1,322.4	1,718.2	1,102.3	1,095.8	1,194.0
Suspicion (not included in totals)	4,859	4,138	—	358	608	602	1,087	1,483	445	276	2,179
Rate	2.6	3.1		2.0	3.2	3.2	5.3	9.0	1.2	1.4	2.8
Curfew and loitering law violations	142,433	134,737	64,748	12,499	13,711	14,067	16,377	13,335	5,806	1,890	34,934
Rate	75.0	101.5	162.1	69.2	71.2	75.2	80.6	81.0	15.7	9.4	44.9
Runaways	141,844	109,191	27,835	17,810	19,618	15,458	16,136	12,334	22,989	9,664	50,880
Rate	74.7	82.3	69.7	98.7	101.9	82.7	79.4	74.9	62.0	48.0	65.3

[1] Includes only suburban county law enforcement agencies.
[2] Includes suburban city and county law enforcement agencies within metropolitan areas. Excludes central cities. Suburban cities and counties are also included in other groups.
[3] Violent crimes are offenses of murder, forcible rape, robbery, and aggravated assault.
[4] Property crimes are offenses of burglary, larceny–theft, motor vehicle theft, and arson.
[5] Includes arson.
Population figures were rounded to the nearest thousand. All rates were calculated before rounding.

Table 32. — Total Arrest Trends, 1987-1996

[7,423 agencies; 1996 estimated population 167,886,000; 1987 estimated population 155,141,000]

Offense charged	Number of persons arrested								
	Total all ages			Under 18 years of age			18 years of age and over		
	1987	1996	Percent change	1987	1996	Percent change	1987	1996	Percent change
TOTAL	**8,574,732**	**9,974,944**	**+16.3**	**1,398,050**	**1,892,312**	**+35.4**	**7,176,682**	**8,082,632**	**+12.6**
Murder and nonnegligent manslaughter	13,966	13,446	-3.7	1,355	2,039	+50.5	12,611	11,407	-9.5
Forcible rape	24,850	21,752	-12.5	3,782	3,680	-2.7	21,068	18,072	-14.2
Robbery	102,316	113,089	+10.5	23,229	36,569	+57.4	79,087	76,520	-3.2
Aggravated assault	241,498	345,644	+43.1	29,705	50,560	+70.2	211,793	295,084	+39.3
Burglary	288,483	236,266	-18.1	98,707	87,233	-11.6	189,776	149,033	-21.5
Larceny–theft	960,888	993,209	+3.4	295,785	336,774	+13.9	665,103	656,435	-1.3
Motor vehicle theft	118,058	120,989	+2.5	46,143	50,212	+8.8	71,915	70,777	-1.6
Arson	11,747	12,291	+4.6	4,823	6,553	+35.9	6,924	5,738	-17.1
Violent crime[1]	382,630	493,931	+29.1	58,071	92,848	+59.9	324,559	401,083	+23.6
Property crime[2]	1,379,176	1,362,755	-1.2	445,458	480,772	+7.9	933,718	881,983	-5.5
Crime Index total[3]	1,761,806	1,856,686	+5.4	503,529	573,620	+13.9	1,258,277	1,283,066	+2.0
Other assaults	536,527	873,030	+62.7	77,415	154,762	+99.9	459,112	718,268	+56.4
Forgery and counterfeiting	60,987	79,477	+30.3	5,500	5,644	+2.6	55,487	73,833	+33.1
Fraud	226,009	285,131	+26.2	17,227	18,187	+5.6	208,782	266,944	+27.9
Embezzlement	8,684	10,252	+18.1	745	862	+15.7	7,939	9,390	+18.3
Stolen property; buying, receiving, possessing	98,190	99,302	+1.1	24,764	26,773	+8.1	73,426	72,529	-1.2
Vandalism	179,704	212,045	+18.0	73,826	93,139	+26.2	105,878	118,906	+12.3
Weapons; carrying, possessing, etc.	133,580	147,202	+10.2	21,049	35,670	+69.5	112,531	111,532	-.9
Prostitution and commercialized vice	85,588	76,754	-10.3	1,779	1,048	-41.1	83,809	75,706	-9.7
Sex offenses (except forcible rape and prostitution)	67,289	64,386	-4.3	10,636	11,493	+8.1	56,653	52,893	-6.6
Drug abuse violations	654,426	1,030,888	+57.5	61,358	142,922	+132.9	593,068	887,966	+49.7
Gambling	19,558	16,040	-18.0	677	2,121	+213.3	18,881	13,919	-26.3
Offenses against family and children	36,530	80,571	+120.6	2,063	4,400	+113.3	34,467	76,171	+121.0
Driving under the influence	1,111,391	887,181	-20.2	15,627	11,318	-27.6	1,095,764	875,863	-20.1
Liquor laws	389,570	436,193	+12.0	103,068	97,967	-4.9	286,502	338,226	+18.1
Drunkenness	602,428	480,261	-20.3	17,558	15,637	-10.9	584,870	464,624	-20.6
Disorderly conduct	480,196	554,081	+15.4	72,598	139,781	+92.5	407,598	414,300	+1.6
Vagrancy	30,763	20,303	-34.0	2,160	2,553	+18.2	28,603	17,750	-37.9
All other offenses (except traffic)	1,922,653	2,504,296	+30.3	217,618	293,550	+34.9	1,705,035	2,210,746	+29.7
Suspicion (not included in totals)	6,110	3,768	-38.3	2,149	1,440	-33.0	3,961	2,328	-41.2
Curfew and loitering law violations	62,316	132,747	+113.0	62,316	132,747	+113.0	—	—	—
Runaways	106,537	128,118	+20.3	106,537	128,118	+20.3	—	—	—

[1] Violent crimes are offenses of murder, forcible rape, robbery, and aggravated assault.
[2] Property crimes are offenses of burglary, larceny–theft, motor vehicle theft, and arson.
[3] Includes arson.

Table 33. — Total Arrest Trends, Sex, 1987-1996

[7,423 agencies; 1996 estimated population 167,886,000; 1987 estimated population 155,141,000]

Offense charged	Males						Females					
	Total			Under 18			Total			Under 18		
	1987	1996	Percent change	1987	1996	Percent change	1987	1996	Percent change	1987	1996	Percent change
TOTAL	7,061,872	7,918,554	+12.1	1,083,664	1,411,148	+30.2	1,512,860	2,056,390	+35.9	314,386	481,164	+53.0
Murder and nonnegligent manslaughter ...	12,247	12,062	-1.5	1,244	1,907	+53.3	1,719	1,384	-19.5	111	132	+18.9
Forcible rape	24,551	21,505	-12.4	3,689	3,625	-1.7	299	247	-17.4	93	55	-40.9
Robbery	93,885	101,998	+8.6	21,585	33,001	+52.9	8,431	11,091	+31.6	1,644	3,568	+117.0
Aggravated assault	209,782	284,004	+35.4	25,135	40,320	+60.4	31,716	61,640	+94.3	4,570	10,240	+124.1
Burglary	264,041	209,076	-20.8	91,054	78,327	-14.0	24,442	27,190	+11.2	7,653	8,906	+16.4
Larceny–theft	663,264	655,775	-1.1	215,278	222,730	+3.5	297,624	337,434	+13.4	80,507	114,044	+41.7
Motor vehicle theft	106,604	104,562	-1.9	41,206	42,634	+3.5	11,454	16,427	+43.4	4,937	7,578	+53.5
Arson	10,144	10,431	+2.8	4,334	5,800	+33.8	1,603	1,860	+16.0	489	753	+54.0
Violent crime[1]	340,465	419,569	+23.2	51,653	78,853	+52.7	42,165	74,362	+76.4	6,418	13,995	+118.1
Property crime[2]	1,044,053	979,844	-6.1	351,872	349,491	-.7	335,123	382,911	+14.3	93,586	131,281	+40.3
Crime Index total[3]	1,384,518	1,399,413	+1.1	403,525	428,344	+6.2	377,288	457,273	+21.2	100,004	145,276	+45.3
Other assaults	454,944	695,386	+52.9	59,537	111,388	+87.1	81,583	177,644	+117.7	17,878	43,374	+142.6
Forgery and counterfeiting	39,931	51,372	+28.7	3,696	3,551	-3.9	21,056	28,105	+33.5	1,804	2,093	+16.0
Fraud	127,472	168,385	+32.1	12,811	13,696	+6.9	98,537	116,746	+18.5	4,416	4,491	+1.7
Embezzlement	5,355	5,633	+5.2	477	473	-.8	3,329	4,619	+38.8	268	389	+45.1
Stolen property; buying, receiving, possessing	86,771	84,867	-2.2	22,415	23,395	+4.4	11,419	14,435	+26.4	2,349	3,378	+43.8
Vandalism	160,482	182,709	+13.9	67,202	82,856	+23.3	19,222	29,336	+52.6	6,624	10,283	+55.2
Weapons; carrying, possessing, etc.	123,403	135,565	+9.9	19,550	32,621	+66.9	10,177	11,637	+14.3	1,499	3,049	+103.4
Prostitution and commercialized vice	29,335	30,657	+4.5	567	496	-12.5	56,253	46,097	-18.1	1,212	552	-54.5
Sex offenses (except forcible rape and prostitution)	62,263	59,062	-5.1	9,950	10,589	+6.4	5,026	5,324	+5.9	686	904	+31.8
Drug abuse violations	554,554	857,057	+54.5	53,151	124,758	+134.7	99,872	173,831	+74.1	8,207	18,164	+121.3
Gambling	16,811	13,834	-17.7	651	2,059	+216.3	2,747	2,206	-19.7	26	62	+138.5
Offenses against family and children	30,037	61,308	+104.1	1,270	2,753	+116.8	6,493	19,263	+196.7	793	1,647	+107.7
Driving under the influence	983,915	756,935	-23.1	13,484	9,490	-29.6	127,476	130,246	+2.2	2,143	1,828	-14.7
Liquor laws	320,504	352,456	+10.0	75,298	68,908	-8.5	69,066	83,737	+21.2	27,770	29,059	+4.6
Drunkenness	547,595	422,605	-22.8	14,751	12,998	-11.9	54,833	57,656	+5.1	2,807	2,639	-6.0
Disorderly conduct	389,340	437,824	+12.5	58,934	106,269	+80.3	90,856	116,257	+28.0	13,664	33,512	+145.3
Vagrancy	27,324	16,168	-40.8	1,791	2,185	+22.0	3,439	4,135	+20.2	369	368	-.3
All other offenses (except traffic)	1,624,731	2,039,086	+25.5	172,017	226,087	+31.4	297,922	465,210	+56.2	45,601	67,463	+47.9
Suspicion (not included in totals)	5,094	2,941	-42.3	1,727	1,097	-36.5	1,016	827	-18.6	422	343	-18.7
Curfew and loitering law violations	47,039	93,756	+99.3	47,039	93,756	+99.3	15,277	38,991	+155.2	15,277	38,991	+155.2
Runaways	45,548	54,476	+19.6	45,548	54,476	+19.6	60,989	73,642	+20.7	60,989	73,642	+20.7

[1] Violent crimes are offenses of murder, forcible rape, robbery, and aggravated assault.

[2] Property crimes are offenses of burglary, larceny–theft, motor vehicle theft, and arson.

[3] Includes arson.

Table 34. — Total Arrest Trends, 1992-1996

[8,081 agencies; 1996 estimated population 175,560,000; 1992 estimated population 169,507,000]

Offense charged	Number of persons arrested								
	Total all ages			Under 18 years of age			18 years of age and over		
	1992	1996	Percent change	1992	1996	Percent change	1992	1996	Percent change
TOTAL	**9,660,919**	**10,314,768**	**+6.8**	**1,611,137**	**1,957,184**	**+21.5**	**8,049,782**	**8,357,584**	**+3.8**
Murder and nonnegligent manslaughter	16,824	13,745	-18.3	2,541	2,074	-18.4	14,283	11,671	-18.3
Forcible rape	25,825	22,455	-13.0	4,036	3,768	-6.6	21,789	18,687	-14.2
Robbery	130,010	116,485	-10.4	35,003	37,414	+6.9	95,007	79,071	-16.8
Aggravated assault	350,025	363,252	+3.8	51,861	52,766	+1.7	298,164	310,486	+4.1
Burglary	290,704	246,959	-15.0	97,540	91,194	-6.5	193,164	155,765	-19.4
Larceny–theft	1,036,949	1,019,251	-1.7	315,942	343,316	+8.7	721,007	675,935	-6.3
Motor vehicle theft	147,133	123,488	-16.1	64,029	50,925	-20.5	83,104	72,563	-12.7
Arson	13,107	12,802	-2.3	6,350	6,783	+6.8	6,757	6,019	-10.9
Violent crime[1]	522,684	515,937	-1.3	93,441	96,022	+2.8	429,243	419,915	-2.2
Property crime[2]	1,487,893	1,402,500	-5.7	483,861	492,218	+1.7	1,004,032	910,282	-9.3
Crime Index total[3]	2,010,577	1,918,437	-4.6	577,302	588,240	+1.9	1,433,275	1,330,197	-7.2
Other assaults	743,465	903,086	+21.5	123,304	159,334	+29.2	620,161	743,752	+19.9
Forgery and counterfeiting	66,608	81,319	+22.1	5,227	5,658	+8.2	61,381	75,661	+23.3
Fraud	279,682	298,713	+6.8	11,217	18,145	+61.8	268,465	280,568	+4.5
Embezzlement	8,860	10,935	+23.4	501	911	+81.8	8,359	10,024	+19.9
Stolen property; buying, receiving, possessing	111,270	104,157	-6.4	29,783	28,156	-5.5	81,487	76,001	-6.7
Vandalism	216,694	216,477	-.1	97,720	95,414	-2.4	118,974	121,063	+1.8
Weapons; carrying, possessing, etc.	177,302	151,815	-14.4	40,865	36,969	-9.5	136,437	114,846	-15.8
Prostitution and commercialized vice	76,565	78,212	+2.2	956	1,052	+10.0	75,609	77,160	+2.1
Sex offenses (except forcible rape and prostitution)	74,467	66,131	-11.2	13,852	11,737	-15.3	60,615	54,394	-10.3
Drug abuse violations	780,038	1,069,877	+37.2	67,958	149,174	+119.5	712,080	920,703	+29.3
Gambling	14,449	16,554	+14.6	1,471	2,188	+48.7	12,978	14,366	+10.7
Offenses against family and children	69,609	93,037	+33.7	3,044	5,077	+66.8	66,565	87,960	+32.1
Driving under the influence	1,064,083	937,550	-11.9	9,624	11,738	+22.0	1,054,459	925,812	-12.2
Liquor laws	351,948	456,215	+29.6	80,002	102,995	+28.7	271,946	353,220	+29.9
Drunkenness	554,896	494,025	-11.0	12,744	16,201	+27.1	542,152	477,824	-11.9
Disorderly conduct	554,652	580,937	+4.7	103,346	148,730	+43.9	451,306	432,207	-4.2
Vagrancy	27,496	20,307	-26.1	3,100	2,656	-14.3	24,396	17,651	-27.6
All other offenses (except traffic)	2,290,706	2,548,586	+11.3	241,569	304,411	+26.0	2,049,137	2,244,175	+9.5
Suspicion (not included in totals)	9,734	4,299	-55.8	4,579	1,329	-71.0	5,155	2,970	-42.4
Curfew and loitering law violations	62,336	134,887	+116.4	62,336	134,887	+116.4	—	—	—
Runaways	125,216	133,511	+6.6	125,216	133,511	+6.6	—	—	—

[1] Violent crimes are offenses of murder, forcible rape, robbery, and aggravated assault.

[2] Property crimes are offenses of burglary, larceny–theft, motor vehicle theft, and arson.

[3] Includes arson.

Table 35. — Total Arrest Trends, Sex, 1992-1996

[8,081 agencies; 1996 estimated population 175,560,000; 1992 estimated population 169,507,000]

Offense charged	Males						Females					
	Total			Under 18			Total			Under 18		
	1992	1996	Percent change	1992	1996	Percent change	1992	1996	Percent change	1992	1996	Percent change
TOTAL	**7,833,058**	**8,190,819**	**+4.6**	**1,244,698**	**1,460,581**	**+17.3**	**1,827,861**	**2,123,949**	**+16.2**	**366,439**	**496,603**	**+35.5**
Murder and nonnegligent manslaughter ...	15,228	12,347	-18.9	2,396	1,940	-19.0	1,596	1,398	-12.4	145	134	-7.6
Forcible rape	25,525	22,200	-13.0	3,970	3,710	-6.5	300	255	-15.0	66	58	-12.1
Robbery	118,834	105,075	-11.6	31,953	33,766	+5.7	11,176	11,410	+2.1	3,050	3,648	+19.6
Aggravated assault	299,777	298,540	-.4	43,523	42,094	-3.3	50,248	64,712	+28.8	8,338	10,672	+28.0
Burglary	262,602	218,563	-16.8	88,474	81,821	-7.5	28,102	28,396	+1.0	9,066	9,373	+3.4
Larceny–theft	706,549	673,982	-4.6	223,426	227,632	+1.9	330,400	345,269	+4.5	92,516	115,684	+25.0
Motor vehicle theft	131,053	106,826	-18.5	56,078	43,271	-22.8	16,080	16,662	+3.6	7,951	7,654	-3.7
Arson	11,356	10,889	-4.1	5,662	6,025	+6.4	1,751	1,913	+9.3	688	758	+10.2
Violent crime[1]	459,364	438,162	-4.6	81,842	81,510	-.4	63,320	77,775	+22.8	11,599	14,512	+25.1
Property crime[2]	1,111,560	1,010,260	-9.1	373,640	358,749	-4.0	376,333	392,240	+4.2	110,221	133,469	+21.1
Crime Index total[3]	1,570,924	1,448,422	-7.8	455,482	440,259	-3.3	439,653	470,015	+6.9	121,820	147,981	+21.5
Other assaults	614,641	718,951	+17.0	92,555	114,875	+24.1	128,824	184,135	+42.9	30,749	44,459	+44.6
Forgery and counterfeiting	42,800	52,633	+23.0	3,325	3,568	+7.3	23,808	28,686	+20.5	1,902	2,090	+9.9
Fraud	160,050	174,214	+8.8	8,243	13,663	+65.8	119,632	124,499	+4.1	2,974	4,482	+50.7
Embezzlement	5,225	6,030	+15.4	273	508	+86.1	3,635	4,905	+34.9	228	403	+76.8
Stolen property; buying, receiving, possessing	97,419	89,076	-8.6	26,639	24,643	-7.5	13,851	15,081	+8.9	3,144	3,513	+11.7
Vandalism	192,156	186,656	-2.9	89,232	84,941	-4.8	24,538	29,821	+21.5	8,488	10,473	+23.4
Weapons; carrying, possessing, etc.	164,066	139,892	-14.7	37,974	33,847	-10.9	13,236	11,923	-9.9	2,891	3,122	+8.0
Prostitution and commercialized vice	25,141	31,112	+23.8	451	497	+10.2	51,424	47,100	-8.4	505	555	+9.9
Sex offenses (except forcible rape and prostitution)	68,468	60,733	-11.3	12,852	10,811	-15.9	5,999	5,398	-10.0	1,000	926	-7.4
Drug abuse violations	651,938	890,334	+36.6	60,767	130,210	+114.3	128,100	179,543	+40.2	7,191	18,964	+163.7
Gambling	12,480	14,268	+14.3	1,397	2,126	+52.2	1,969	2,286	+16.1	74	62	-16.2
Offenses against family and children	57,010	71,999	+26.3	1,939	3,183	+64.2	12,599	21,038	+67.0	1,105	1,894	+71.4
Driving under the influence	920,350	799,884	-13.1	8,290	9,859	+18.9	143,733	137,666	-4.2	1,334	1,879	+40.9
Liquor laws	284,064	367,742	+29.5	57,468	72,473	+26.1	67,884	88,473	+30.3	22,534	30,522	+35.4
Drunkenness	495,017	434,676	-12.2	10,605	13,407	+26.4	59,879	59,349	-.9	2,139	2,794	+30.6
Disorderly conduct	446,697	458,347	+2.6	82,268	112,937	+37.3	107,955	122,590	+13.6	21,078	35,793	+69.8
Vagrancy	24,859	16,225	-34.7	2,643	2,266	-14.3	2,637	4,082	+54.8	457	390	-14.7
All other offenses (except traffic)	1,899,660	2,077,405	+9.4	192,202	234,288	+21.9	391,046	471,181	+20.5	49,367	70,123	+42.0
Suspicion (not included in totals)	7,967	3,461	-56.6	3,515	1,058	-69.9	1,767	838	-52.6	1,064	271	-74.5
Curfew and loitering law violations	45,762	95,254	+108.2	45,762	95,254	+108.2	16,574	39,633	+139.1	16,574	39,633	+139.1
Runaways	54,331	56,966	+4.8	54,331	56,966	+4.8	70,885	76,545	+8.0	70,885	76,545	+8.0

[1] Violent crimes are offenses of murder, forcible rape, robbery, and aggravated assault.

[2] Property crimes are offenses of burglary, larceny–theft, motor vehicle theft, and arson.

[3] Includes arson.

Table 36. — Total Arrest Trends, 1995-1996

[8,275 agencies; 1996 estimated population 175,898,000; 1995 estimated population 174,157,000]

Offense charged	Number of persons arrested											
	Total all ages			Under 15 years of age			Under 18 years of age			18 years of age and over		
	1995	1996	Percent change	1995	1996	Percent change	1995	1996	Percent change	1995	1996	Percent change
TOTAL	10,300,741	10,370,655	+.7	636,579	632,328	-.7	1,905,868	1,958,361	+2.8	8,394,873	8,412,294	+.2
Murder and nonnegligent manslaughter ...	15,571	13,937	-10.5	270	244	-9.6	2,464	2,109	-14.4	13,107	11,828	-9.8
Forcible rape	23,238	22,741	-2.1	1,407	1,291	-8.2	3,807	3,796	-.3	19,431	18,945	-2.5
Robbery	125,376	116,884	-6.8	11,669	10,214	-12.5	41,176	37,713	-8.4	84,200	79,171	-6.0
Aggravated assault	379,250	368,802	-2.8	17,750	17,108	-3.6	56,101	53,877	-4.0	323,149	314,925	-2.5
Burglary	254,025	247,417	-2.6	34,186	34,510	+.9	88,252	91,129	+3.3	165,773	156,288	-5.7
Larceny–theft	1,025,672	1,011,799	-1.4	149,826	143,264	-4.4	339,506	341,092	+.5	686,166	670,707	-2.3
Motor vehicle theft	137,591	125,678	-8.7	16,353	13,796	-15.6	57,921	52,359	-9.6	79,670	73,319	-8.0
Arson	13,826	12,873	-6.9	4,898	4,566	-6.8	7,285	6,835	-6.2	6,541	6,038	-7.7
Violent crime[1]	543,435	522,364	-3.9	31,096	28,857	-7.2	103,548	97,495	-5.8	439,887	424,869	-3.4
Property crime[2]	1,431,114	1,397,767	-2.3	205,263	196,136	-4.4	492,964	491,415	-.3	938,150	906,352	-3.4
Crime Index total[3]	1,974,549	1,920,131	-2.8	236,359	224,993	-4.8	596,512	588,910	-1.3	1,378,037	1,331,221	-3.4
Other assaults	903,655	907,422	+.4	63,952	65,607	+2.6	155,128	159,836	+3.0	748,527	747,586	-.1
Forgery and counterfeiting	80,124	80,948	+1.0	742	695	-6.3	5,892	5,705	-3.2	74,232	75,243	+1.4
Fraud	289,501	295,985	+2.2	4,590	5,358	+16.7	17,296	18,272	+5.6	272,205	277,713	+2.0
Embezzlement	9,959	10,928	+9.7	66	56	-15.2	849	902	+6.2	9,110	10,026	+10.1
Stolen property; buying, receiving, possession	113,917	103,401	-9.2	8,238	7,554	-8.3	29,934	28,143	-6.0	83,983	75,258	-10.4
Vandalism	225,114	218,661	-2.9	46,509	43,170	-7.2	99,987	96,078	-3.9	125,127	122,583	-2.0
Weapons; carrying, possessing, etc.	173,731	153,735	-11.5	12,207	11,057	-9.4	41,008	37,483	-8.6	132,723	116,252	-12.4
Prostitution and commercialized vice	78,503	78,171	-.4	152	130	-14.5	1,000	1,054	+5.4	77,503	77,117	-.5
Sex offenses (except forcible rape and prostitution)	64,599	66,261	+2.6	5,732	5,934	+3.5	11,156	11,804	+5.8	53,443	54,457	+1.9
Drug abuse violations	1,058,757	1,070,642	+1.1	23,688	25,177	+6.3	140,909	149,506	+6.1	917,848	921,136	+.4
Gambling	16,560	16,602	+.3	321	274	-14.6	1,972	2,169	+10.0	14,588	14,433	-1.1
Offenses against family and children	94,066	94,201	+.1	1,186	1,662	+40.1	3,980	5,141	+29.2	90,086	89,060	-1.1
Driving under the influence	912,573	941,794	+3.2	250	308	+23.2	9,771	11,774	+20.5	902,802	930,020	+3.0
Liquor laws	400,836	456,053	+13.8	8,970	11,266	+25.6	84,379	101,742	+20.6	316,457	354,311	+12.0
Drunkenness	498,566	489,958	-1.7	2,135	2,260	+5.9	14,554	16,086	+10.5	484,012	473,872	-2.1
Disorderly conduct	564,189	581,011	+3.0	46,284	49,969	+8.0	136,404	148,186	+8.6	427,785	432,825	+1.2
Vagrancy	20,249	20,522	+1.3	552	545	-1.3	2,746	2,551	-7.1	17,503	17,971	+2.7
All other offenses (except traffic)	2,569,311	2,595,831	+1.0	82,988	84,244	+1.5	300,409	304,621	+1.4	2,268,902	2,291,210	+1.0
Suspicion (not included in totals)	3,974	4,367	+9.9	371	358	-3.5	1,319	1,333	+1.1	2,655	3,034	+14.3
Curfew and loitering law violations	112,258	135,912	+21.1	32,158	37,509	+16.6	112,258	135,912	+21.1	—	—	—
Runaways	139,724	132,486	-5.2	59,500	54,560	-8.3	139,724	132,486	-5.2	—	—	—

[1] Violent crimes are offenses of murder, forcible rape, robbery, and aggravated assault.

[2] Property crimes are offenses of burglary, larceny–theft, motor vehicle theft, and arson.

[3] Includes arson.

Table 37. — Total Arrest Trends, Sex, 1995-1996

[8,275 agencies; 1996 estimated population 175,898,000; 1995 estimated population 174,157,000]

Offense charged	Males						Females					
	Total			Under 18			Total			Under 18		
	1995	1996	Percent change	1995	1996	Percent change	1995	1996	Percent change	1995	1996	Percent change
TOTAL	8,223,945	8,239,213	+.2	1,437,879	1,463,009	+1.7	2,076,796	2,131,442	+2.6	467,989	495,352	+5.8
Murder and nonnegligent manslaughter ...	14,110	12,516	-11.3	2,327	1,972	-15.3	1,461	1,421	-2.7	137	137	—
Forcible rape	22,960	22,493	-2.0	3,730	3,743	+.3	278	248	-10.8	77	53	-31.2
Robbery	113,419	105,487	-7.0	37,268	34,051	-8.6	11,957	11,397	-4.7	3,908	3,662	-6.3
Aggravated assault	314,582	302,629	-3.8	45,404	42,868	-5.6	64,668	66,173	+2.3	10,697	11,009	+2.9
Burglary	225,059	219,026	-2.7	79,385	81,809	+3.1	28,966	28,391	-2.0	8,867	9,320	+5.1
Larceny–theft	687,011	670,877	-2.3	230,621	227,000	-1.6	338,661	340,922	+.7	108,885	114,092	+4.8
Motor vehicle theft	119,098	108,666	-8.8	49,413	44,499	-9.9	18,493	17,012	-8.0	8,508	7,860	-7.6
Arson	11,666	10,965	-6.0	6,412	6,081	-5.2	2,160	1,908	-11.7	873	754	-13.6
Violent crime[1]	465,071	443,125	-4.7	88,729	82,634	-6.9	78,364	79,239	+1.1	14,819	14,861	+.3
Property crime[2]	1,042,834	1,009,534	-3.2	365,831	359,389	-1.8	388,280	388,233	[3]	127,133	132,026	+3.8
Crime Index total[4]	1,507,905	1,452,659	-3.7	454,560	442,023	-2.8	466,644	467,472	+.2	141,952	146,887	+3.5
Other assaults	727,605	723,464	-.6	112,567	115,354	+2.5	176,050	183,958	+4.5	42,561	44,482	+4.5
Forgery and counterfeiting	51,032	52,505	+2.9	3,808	3,611	-5.2	29,092	28,443	-2.2	2,084	2,094	+.5
Fraud	170,440	173,308	+1.7	12,822	13,717	+7.0	119,061	122,677	+3.0	4,474	4,555	+1.8
Embezzlement	5,597	6,018	+7.5	492	494	+.4	4,362	4,910	+12.6	357	408	+14.3
Stolen property; buying, receiving, possessing	97,749	88,333	-9.6	26,311	24,563	-6.6	16,168	15,068	-6.8	3,623	3,580	-1.2
Vandalism	194,757	188,322	-3.3	89,221	85,465	-4.2	30,357	30,339	-.1	10,766	10,613	-1.4
Weapons; carrying, possessing, etc.	159,987	141,592	-11.5	37,688	34,323	-8.9	13,744	12,143	-11.6	3,320	3,160	-4.8
Prostitution and commercialized vice	29,910	31,217	+4.4	517	504	-2.5	48,593	46,954	-3.4	483	550	+13.9
Sex offenses (except forcible rape and prostitution)	59,495	60,973	+2.5	10,345	10,897	+5.3	5,104	5,288	+3.6	811	907	+11.8
Drug abuse violations	880,907	891,206	+1.2	123,574	130,408	+5.5	177,850	179,436	+.9	17,335	19,098	+10.2
Gambling	14,147	14,306	+1.1	1,910	2,106	+10.3	2,413	2,296	-4.8	62	63	+1.6
Offenses against family and children	75,004	72,908	-2.8	2,507	3,223	+28.6	19,062	21,293	+11.7	1,473	1,918	+30.2
Driving under the influence	781,518	803,028	+2.8	8,264	9,877	+19.5	131,055	138,766	+5.9	1,507	1,897	+25.9
Liquor laws	325,931	367,847	+12.9	60,160	71,634	+19.1	74,905	88,206	+17.8	24,219	30,108	+24.3
Drunkenness	439,319	430,895	-1.9	12,241	13,317	+8.8	59,247	59,063	-.3	2,313	2,769	+19.7
Disorderly conduct	446,196	458,492	+2.8	104,447	112,479	+7.7	117,993	122,519	+3.8	31,957	35,707	+11.7
Vagrancy	16,316	16,424	+.7	2,433	2,191	-9.9	3,933	4,098	+4.2	313	360	+15.0
All other offenses (except traffic)	2,101,428	2,113,328	+.6	235,310	234,435	-.4	467,883	482,503	+3.1	65,099	70,186	+7.8
Suspicion (not included in totals)	3,287	3,524	+7.2	1,047	1,062	+1.4	687	843	+22.7	272	271	-.4
Curfew and loitering law violations	78,981	95,892	+21.4	78,981	95,892	+21.4	33,277	40,020	+20.3	33,277	40,020	+20.3
Runaways	59,721	56,496	-5.4	59,721	56,496	-5.4	80,003	75,990	-5.0	80,003	75,990	-5.0

[1] Violent crimes are offenses of murder, forcible rape, robbery, and aggravated assault.

[2] Property crimes are offenses of burglary, larceny–theft, motor vehicle theft, and arson.

[3] Less than one-tenth of 1 percent.

[4] Includes arson.

Table 38. — Total Arrests, Distribution by Age, 1996

[9,666 agencies; 1996 estimated population 189,927,000]

Offense charged	Total all ages	Ages under 15	Ages under 18	Ages 18 and over	Under 10	10-12	13-14	15	16	17	18	19	20	21
TOTAL	11,093,211	679,449	2,103,658	8,989,553	32,450	151,551	495,448	418,656	494,000	511,553	526,435	499,616	438,551	398,610
Percent distribution[1]	100.0	6.1	19.0	81.0	.3	1.4	4.5	3.8	4.5	4.6	4.7	4.5	4.0	3.6
Murder and nonnegligent manslaughter	14,447	257	2,172	12,275	17	16	224	359	651	905	1,076	1,103	887	858
Forcible rape	24,347	1,423	4,128	20,219	61	346	1,016	751	888	1,066	1,128	1,060	977	982
Robbery	121,781	10,525	39,037	82,744	266	1,882	8,377	8,100	9,883	10,529	9,787	7,917	6,133	4,955
Aggravated assault	387,571	18,122	56,894	330,677	1,000	4,366	12,756	10,626	13,358	14,788	15,415	15,173	14,075	14,210
Burglary	264,193	36,859	97,809	166,384	2,487	9,110	25,262	19,548	20,896	20,506	19,133	14,146	10,524	8,346
Larceny–theft	1,096,488	155,287	370,607	725,881	7,749	43,132	104,406	70,042	74,988	70,290	62,161	48,537	36,677	30,830
Motor vehicle theft	132,023	14,473	54,813	77,210	199	1,706	12,568	13,403	14,190	12,747	10,082	7,393	5,594	4,433
Arson	13,755	4,887	7,302	6,453	922	1,623	2,342	965	797	653	532	405	334	272
Violent crime[2]	548,146	30,327	102,231	445,915	1,344	6,610	22,373	19,836	24,780	27,288	27,406	25,253	22,072	21,005
Percent distribution[1]	100.0	5.5	18.7	81.3	.2	1.2	4.1	3.6	4.5	5.0	5.0	4.6	4.0	3.8
Property crime[3]	1,506,459	211,506	530,531	975,928	11,357	55,571	144,578	103,958	110,871	104,196	91,908	70,481	53,129	43,881
Percent distribution[1]	100.0	14.0	35.2	64.8	.8	3.7	9.6	6.9	7.4	6.9	6.1	4.7	3.5	2.9
Crime Index total[4]	2,054,605	241,833	632,762	1,421,843	12,701	62,181	166,951	123,794	135,651	131,484	119,314	95,734	75,201	64,886
Percent distribution[1]	100.0	11.8	30.8	69.2	.6	3.0	8.1	6.0	6.6	6.4	5.8	4.7	3.7	3.2
Other assaults	972,984	70,276	171,366	801,618	3,791	19,503	46,982	32,258	34,417	34,415	32,152	31,686	30,599	32,334
Forgery and counterfeiting	88,355	755	6,238	82,117	28	115	612	905	1,780	2,798	4,230	4,422	4,176	3,786
Fraud	324,776	5,452	18,872	305,904	95	799	4,558	4,964	3,416	5,040	8,861	11,968	12,632	13,424
Embezzlement	11,449	63	958	10,491	4	11	48	57	326	512	739	697	652	586
Stolen property; buying, receiving, possessing	111,066	8,099	30,189	80,877	187	1,439	6,473	6,214	7,504	8,372	8,695	7,062	5,572	4,691
Vandalism	234,215	46,353	103,333	130,882	4,660	13,595	28,098	18,616	20,332	18,032	14,673	10,551	7,962	7,231
Weapons; carrying, possessing, etc.	161,158	11,684	39,363	121,795	600	2,542	8,542	7,646	9,485	10,548	10,907	9,575	7,830	7,314
Prostitution and commercialized vice	81,036	140	1,104	79,932	10	16	114	153	263	548	1,433	1,966	2,141	2,341
Sex offenses (except forcible rape and prostitution)	70,619	6,343	12,660	57,959	589	1,811	3,943	2,188	1,999	2,130	2,255	2,082	1,855	1,932
Drug abuse violations	1,128,647	26,705	158,447	970,200	296	2,951	23,458	29,232	44,199	58,311	69,436	63,717	53,749	47,443
Gambling	16,984	297	2,263	14,721	5	34	258	422	678	866	855	838	692	627
Offenses against family and children	103,800	1,879	5,850	97,950	165	369	1,345	1,191	1,385	1,395	2,286	2,358	2,597	2,853
Driving under the influence ...	1,013,932	341	12,814	1,001,118	120	34	187	549	3,481	8,443	18,622	24,030	26,401	36,276
Liquor laws	491,176	12,363	112,553	378,623	194	994	11,175	17,787	33,088	49,315	68,095	66,400	50,683	14,602
Drunkenness	522,869	2,414	17,111	505,758	103	216	2,095	2,768	4,313	7,616	13,686	14,174	13,528	17,591
Disorderly conduct	626,918	53,726	159,951	466,967	1,766	11,887	40,073	32,114	36,642	37,469	34,721	29,899	26,020	26,540
Vagrancy	21,735	622	2,873	18,862	15	92	515	568	721	962	1,396	1,113	842	740
All other offenses (except traffic)	2,767,751	92,240	329,070	2,438,681	4,791	17,544	69,905	65,774	80,702	90,354	113,767	121,156	115,252	113,244
Suspicion	4,859	436	1,604	3,255	18	82	336	339	391	438	312	188	167	169
Curfew and loitering law violations	142,433	39,315	142,433	—	940	5,927	32,448	33,302	40,132	29,684	—	—	—	—
Runaways	141,844	58,113	141,844	—	1,372	9,409	47,332	37,815	33,095	12,821	—	—	—	—

See footnotes at end of table.

Table 38. — Total Arrests, Distribution by Age, 1996 — Continued

Offense charged	Age											
	22	23	24	25-29	30-34	35-39	40-44	45-49	50-54	55-59	60-64	65 and over
TOTAL	**361,283**	**346,222**	**341,152**	**1,543,234**	**1,485,916**	**1,273,836**	**819,962**	**467,540**	**228,682**	**119,917**	**65,842**	**72,755**
Percent distribution[1]	**3.3**	**3.1**	**3.1**	**13.9**	**13.4**	**11.5**	**7.4**	**4.2**	**2.1**	**1.1**	**.6**	**.7**
Murder and nonnegligent manslaughter	786	638	593	2,008	1,473	1,092	703	441	250	139	88	140
Forcible rape	794	734	788	3,652	3,521	2,827	1,705	940	469	266	193	183
Robbery	4,043	3,715	3,217	14,994	12,419	8,480	4,217	1,769	630	250	116	102
Aggravated assault	13,216	13,268	12,928	60,377	57,758	48,171	30,325	17,053	8,577	4,436	2,531	3,164
Burglary	7,143	6,500	6,121	27,927	26,468	20,410	11,282	5,052	1,882	743	311	396
Larceny–theft	26,689	24,750	24,298	115,927	115,457	100,072	65,201	35,994	16,906	8,851	5,279	8,252
Motor vehicle theft	3,669	3,316	3,171	13,392	10,941	7,931	3,984	1,953	730	299	156	166
Arson	266	230	233	888	1,043	843	610	339	211	112	71	64
Violent crime[2]	18,839	18,355	17,526	81,031	75,171	60,570	36,950	20,203	9,926	5,091	2,928	3,589
Percent distribution[1]	3.4	3.3	3.2	14.8	13.7	11.0	6.7	3.7	1.8	.9	.5	.7
Property crime[3]	37,767	34,796	33,823	158,134	153,909	129,256	81,077	43,338	19,729	10,005	5,817	8,878
Percent distribution[1]	2.5	2.3	2.2	10.5	10.2	8.6	5.4	2.9	1.3	.7	.4	.6
Crime Index total[4]	56,606	53,151	51,349	239,165	229,080	189,826	118,027	63,541	29,655	15,096	8,745	12,467
Percent distribution[1]	2.8	2.6	2.5	11.6	11.1	9.2	5.7	3.1	1.4	.7	.4	.6
Other assaults	31,114	31,006	31,955	150,547	148,873	124,722	75,360	40,418	19,387	9,813	5,356	6,296
Forgery and counterfeiting	3,815	3,710	3,533	16,360	14,983	11,103	6,532	3,216	1,195	567	241	248
Fraud	13,177	13,189	13,218	61,070	54,214	44,752	28,453	16,189	7,461	3,526	1,720	2,050
Embezzlement	528	479	432	1,916	1,579	1,209	818	426	228	106	56	40
Stolen property; buying, receiving, possessing	3,803	3,442	3,188	13,692	11,921	8,936	5,226	2,548	1,046	520	277	258
Vandalism	6,254	5,604	5,276	21,817	19,336	15,133	8,460	4,451	2,012	963	519	640
Weapons; carrying, possessing, etc.	6,428	5,785	5,186	20,289	15,914	12,582	8,419	5,190	2,771	1,617	909	1,079
Prostitution and commercialized vice	2,466	2,726	2,933	17,105	18,325	14,163	7,400	3,614	1,563	815	427	514
Sex offenses (except forcible rape and prostitution)	1,789	1,717	1,760	8,897	9,716	8,910	6,170	4,059	2,624	1,662	1,064	1,467
Drug abuse violations	41,816	39,448	38,118	169,822	161,707	136,473	82,704	40,348	14,849	6,117	2,531	1,922
Gambling	523	425	483	1,878	1,785	1,620	1,359	1,121	871	629	482	533
Offenses against family and children	3,026	3,247	3,555	17,826	20,405	18,180	11,166	5,622	2,458	1,145	608	618
Driving under the influence	36,126	36,422	37,324	174,457	175,240	159,047	112,280	73,617	40,858	23,332	13,430	13,656
Liquor laws	10,862	9,082	8,471	33,155	32,115	30,071	22,629	14,661	8,292	4,752	2,519	2,234
Drunkenness	16,014	15,456	15,401	73,490	84,392	86,137	64,225	41,725	23,028	12,900	7,335	6,676
Disorderly conduct	22,523	20,128	19,089	77,287	69,980	60,156	37,689	20,945	10,377	5,375	2,985	3,253
Vagrancy	677	603	536	2,614	2,802	2,787	2,137	1,166	666	371	210	202
All other offenses (except traffic)	103,588	100,460	99,197	441,293	413,043	347,634	220,653	124,556	59,270	30,579	16,409	18,580
Suspicion	148	142	148	554	506	395	255	127	71	32	19	22
Curfew and loitering law violations	—	—	—	—	—	—	—	—	—	—	—	—
Runaways	—	—	—	—	—	—	—	—	—	—	—	—

[1] Because of rounding, the percentages may not add to total.
[2] Violent crimes are offenses of murder, forcible rape, robbery, and aggravated assault.
[3] Property crimes are offenses of burglary, larceny–theft, motor vehicle theft, and arson.
[4] Includes arson.

Table 39. — Male Arrests, Distribution by Age, 1996

[9,666 agencies; 1996 estimated population 189,927,000]

Offense charged	Total all ages	Ages under 15	Ages under 18	Ages 18 and over	Under 10	10-12	13-14	15	16	17	18	19	20	21
TOTAL	8,803,292	482,943	1,570,417	7,232,875	26,910	113,904	342,129	301,811	374,389	411,274	435,940	412,385	361,507	329,792
Percent distribution[1]	100.0	5.5	17.8	82.2	.3	1.3	3.9	3.4	4.3	4.7	5.0	4.7	4.1	3.7
Murder and nonnegligent manslaughter	12,965	226	2,030	10,935	16	14	196	329	612	863	1,000	1,029	820	786
Forcible rape	24,066	1,393	4,065	20,001	61	335	997	740	875	1,057	1,118	1,056	970	976
Robbery	109,912	9,178	35,256	74,656	247	1,651	7,280	7,235	9,086	9,757	9,151	7,401	5,634	4,593
Aggravated assault	318,279	14,056	45,370	272,909	891	3,546	9,619	8,231	10,790	12,293	13,118	12,838	11,846	11,908
Burglary	234,208	32,569	87,888	146,320	2,185	8,014	22,370	17,561	18,966	18,792	17,548	12,924	9,491	7,526
Larceny–theft	726,006	102,828	246,361	479,645	5,974	29,708	67,146	45,880	49,958	47,695	42,891	32,972	24,373	19,992
Motor vehicle theft	114,125	11,659	46,562	67,563	187	1,412	10,060	11,220	12,298	11,385	9,157	6,779	5,101	4,005
Arson	11,703	4,329	6,484	5,219	847	1,422	2,060	849	722	584	486	365	288	224
Violent crime[2]	465,222	24,853	86,721	378,501	1,215	5,546	18,092	16,535	21,363	23,970	24,387	22,324	19,270	18,263
Percent distribution[1]	100.0	5.3	18.6	81.4	.3	1.2	3.9	3.6	4.6	5.2	5.2	4.8	4.1	3.9
Property crime[3]	1,086,042	151,385	387,295	698,747	9,193	40,556	101,636	75,510	81,944	78,456	70,082	53,040	39,253	31,747
Percent distribution[1]	100.0	13.9	35.7	64.3	.8	3.7	9.4	7.0	7.5	7.2	6.5	4.9	3.6	2.9
Crime Index total[4]	1,551,264	176,238	474,016	1,077,248	10,408	46,102	119,728	92,045	103,307	102,426	94,469	75,364	58,523	50,010
Percent distribution[1]	100.0	11.4	30.6	69.4	.7	3.0	7.7	5.9	6.7	6.6	6.1	4.9	3.8	3.2
Other assaults	775,102	49,963	123,716	651,386	3,265	14,810	31,888	22,429	25,007	26,317	25,178	24,877	24,384	25,938
Forgery and counterfeiting	57,060	432	3,949	53,111	17	69	346	576	1,095	1,846	2,813	2,923	2,727	2,529
Fraud	189,374	3,965	14,147	175,227	66	586	3,313	3,921	2,572	3,689	5,647	7,327	7,419	7,851
Embezzlement	6,331	41	530	5,801	1	8	32	38	175	276	390	370	335	318
Stolen property; buying, receiving, possessing	94,868	6,904	26,389	68,479	169	1,249	5,486	5,395	6,637	7,453	7,820	6,325	4,910	4,149
Vandalism	201,857	41,114	91,995	109,862	4,299	12,205	24,610	16,511	18,187	16,183	13,164	9,337	6,920	6,276
Weapons; carrying, possessing, etc.	148,478	10,377	36,036	112,442	564	2,253	7,560	6,891	8,796	9,972	10,395	9,130	7,452	6,927
Prostitution and commercialized vice	32,445	69	526	31,919	7	13	49	62	126	269	470	635	810	827
Sex offenses (except forcible rape and prostitution)	64,938	5,790	11,669	53,269	523	1,636	3,631	2,018	1,862	1,999	2,050	1,852	1,650	1,748
Drug abuse violations	939,767	21,594	138,103	801,664	240	2,335	19,019	25,288	38,958	52,263	62,147	56,963	47,826	41,948
Gambling	14,648	285	2,194	12,454	5	33	247	407	662	840	814	794	640	582
Offenses against family and children	80,549	1,094	3,667	76,882	101	261	732	723	866	984	1,712	1,795	1,999	2,216
Driving under the influence ...	864,226	257	10,775	853,451	101	28	128	425	2,877	7,216	16,107	20,967	23,226	31,646
Liquor laws	395,446	7,014	79,290	316,156	133	544	6,337	11,425	23,375	37,476	53,215	53,062	41,355	12,599
Drunkenness	459,345	1,683	14,135	445,210	87	156	1,440	2,140	3,578	6,734	12,403	12,821	12,289	16,097
Disorderly conduct	494,381	38,700	121,406	372,975	1,502	8,959	28,239	23,675	28,544	30,487	28,886	24,783	21,486	22,120
Vagrancy	17,365	486	2,434	14,931	12	76	398	472	613	863	1,220	970	738	606
All other offenses (except traffic)	2,250,707	66,734	252,944	1,997,763	3,710	13,620	49,404	48,463	62,921	74,826	96,778	101,926	96,680	95,261
Suspicion	3,888	337	1,243	2,645	17	66	254	267	294	345	262	164	138	144
Curfew and loitering law violations	100,618	26,137	100,618	—	764	4,164	21,209	22,953	28,993	22,535	—	—	—	—
Runaways	60,635	23,729	60,635	—	919	4,731	18,079	15,687	14,944	6,275	—	—	—	—

See footnotes at end of table.

Table 39. — Male Arrests, Distribution by Age, 1996 — Continued

Offense charged	22	23	24	25-29	30-34	35-39	40-44	45-49	50-54	55-59	60-64	65 and over
TOTAL	295,867	281,533	274,848	1,220,803	1,154,565	1,000,724	661,296	388,710	193,635	103,402	57,008	60,860
Percent distribution[1]	3.4	3.2	3.1	13.9	13.1	11.4	7.5	4.4	2.2	1.2	.6	.7
Murder and nonnegligent manslaughter	728	588	545	1,788	1,245	904	585	377	203	125	84	128
Forcible rape	786	724	782	3,614	3,480	2,777	1,678	934	466	266	191	183
Robbery	3,699	3,407	2,914	13,354	10,845	7,377	3,707	1,588	571	222	102	91
Aggravated assault	11,011	10,965	10,694	49,354	46,361	38,910	25,031	14,447	7,395	3,898	2,272	2,861
Burglary	6,321	5,725	5,345	24,111	22,928	17,561	9,680	4,353	1,590	627	261	329
Larceny–theft	17,089	15,604	15,183	73,889	75,645	67,284	44,907	24,883	11,036	5,702	3,276	4,919
Motor vehicle theft	3,233	2,938	2,751	11,350	9,191	6,672	3,423	1,744	655	267	145	152
Arson	209	191	186	721	790	645	470	265	178	88	61	52
Violent crime[2]	16,224	15,684	14,935	68,110	61,931	49,968	31,001	17,346	8,635	4,511	2,649	3,263
Percent distribution[1]	3.5	3.4	3.2	14.6	13.3	10.7	6.7	3.7	1.9	1.0	.6	.7
Property crime[3]	26,852	24,458	23,465	110,071	108,554	92,162	58,480	31,245	13,459	6,684	3,743	5,452
Percent distribution[1]	2.5	2.3	2.2	10.1	10.0	8.5	5.4	2.9	1.2	.6	.3	.5
Crime Index total[4]	43,076	40,142	38,400	178,181	170,485	142,130	89,481	48,591	22,094	11,195	6,392	8,715
Percent distribution[1]	2.8	2.6	2.5	11.5	11.0	9.2	5.8	3.1	1.4	.7	.4	.6
Other assaults	25,071	25,040	25,818	121,894	119,703	101,782	62,761	34,105	16,406	8,438	4,628	5,363
Forgery and counterfeiting	2,505	2,466	2,277	10,351	9,361	7,050	4,326	2,186	855	408	191	143
Fraud	7,357	7,270	7,366	33,117	30,696	25,390	16,707	9,909	4,553	2,247	1,142	1,229
Embezzlement	275	236	233	1,041	910	710	473	245	128	65	39	33
Stolen property; buying, receiving, possessing	3,265	2,936	2,615	11,295	9,662	7,242	4,308	2,151	906	466	209	220
Vandalism	5,400	4,779	4,388	17,770	15,459	12,266	6,915	3,724	1,678	816	442	528
Weapons; carrying, possessing, etc.	6,079	5,444	4,800	18,626	14,209	11,124	7,574	4,765	2,526	1,510	860	1,021
Prostitution and commercialized vice	971	1,039	1,116	6,094	6,168	5,235	3,364	2,246	1,297	751	406	490
Sex offenses (except forcible rape and prostitution)	1,602	1,529	1,590	7,943	8,747	8,194	5,768	3,896	2,563	1,639	1,043	1,455
Drug abuse violations	36,556	34,011	32,424	138,438	124,689	105,433	65,441	33,675	12,771	5,378	2,263	1,701
Gambling	474	383	438	1,539	1,429	1,250	1,071	909	711	529	419	472
Offenses against family and children	2,363	2,519	2,769	14,037	15,767	14,014	9,064	4,688	2,051	937	477	474
Driving under the influence	31,466	31,744	32,388	149,940	145,726	131,514	93,811	63,365	36,016	20,900	12,201	12,434
Liquor laws	9,469	7,913	7,442	28,749	27,615	25,814	19,684	13,052	7,476	4,356	2,350	2,005
Drunkenness	14,549	14,009	13,794	64,490	71,337	73,556	56,026	37,465	21,112	12,071	6,880	6,311
Disorderly conduct	18,561	16,529	15,378	60,301	52,653	46,307	30,053	17,199	8,772	4,624	2,576	2,747
Vagrancy	543	471	399	1,821	1,996	2,158	1,730	976	603	344	181	175
All other offenses (except traffic)	86,160	82,959	81,099	354,734	327,555	279,236	182,521	105,469	51,057	26,703	14,293	15,332
Suspicion	125	114	114	442	398	319	218	94	60	25	16	12
Curfew and loitering law violations	—	—	—	—	—	—	—	—	—	—	—	—
Runaways	—	—	—	—	—	—	—	—	—	—	—	—

[1] Because of rounding, the percentages may not add to total.
[2] Violent crimes are offenses of murder, forcible rape, robbery, and aggravated assault.
[3] Property crimes are offenses of burglary, larceny–theft, motor vehicle theft, and arson.
[4] Includes arson.

Table 40. — Female Arrests, Distribution by Age, 1996

[9,666 agencies; 1996 estimated population 189,927,000]

Offense charged	Total all ages	Ages under 15	Ages under 18	Ages 18 and over	Under 10	10-12	13-14	15	16	17	18	19	20	21
TOTAL	2,289,919	196,506	533,241	1,756,678	5,540	37,647	153,319	116,845	119,611	100,279	90,495	87,231	77,044	68,818
Percent distribution[1]	100.0	8.6	23.3	76.7	.2	1.6	6.7	5.1	5.2	4.4	4.0	3.8	3.4	3.0
Murder and nonnegligent manslaughter	1,482	31	142	1,340	1	2	28	30	39	42	76	74	67	72
Forcible rape	281	30	63	218	—	11	19	11	13	9	10	4	7	6
Robbery	11,869	1,347	3,781	8,088	19	231	1,097	865	797	772	636	516	499	362
Aggravated assault	69,292	4,066	11,524	57,768	109	820	3,137	2,395	2,568	2,495	2,297	2,335	2,229	2,302
Burglary	29,985	4,290	9,921	20,064	302	1,096	2,892	1,987	1,930	1,714	1,585	1,222	1,033	820
Larceny–theft	370,482	52,459	124,246	246,236	1,775	13,424	37,260	24,162	25,030	22,595	19,270	15,565	12,304	10,838
Motor vehicle theft	17,898	2,814	8,251	9,647	12	294	2,508	2,183	1,892	1,362	925	614	493	428
Arson	2,052	558	818	1,234	75	201	282	116	75	69	46	40	46	48
Violent crime[2]	82,924	5,474	15,510	67,414	129	1,064	4,281	3,301	3,417	3,318	3,019	2,929	2,802	2,742
Percent distribution[1]	100.0	6.6	18.7	81.3	.2	1.3	5.2	4.0	4.1	4.0	3.6	3.5	3.4	3.3
Property crime[3]	420,417	60,121	143,236	277,181	2,164	15,015	42,942	28,448	28,927	25,740	21,826	17,441	13,876	12,134
Percent distribution[1]	100.0	14.3	34.1	65.9	.5	3.6	10.2	6.8	6.9	6.1	5.2	4.1	3.3	2.9
Crime Index total[4]	503,341	65,595	158,746	344,595	2,293	16,079	47,223	31,749	32,344	29,058	24,845	20,370	16,678	14,876
Percent distribution[1]	100.0	13.0	31.5	68.5	.5	3.2	9.4	6.3	6.4	5.8	4.9	4.0	3.3	3.0
Other assaults	197,882	20,313	47,650	150,232	526	4,693	15,094	9,829	9,410	8,098	6,974	6,809	6,215	6,396
Forgery and counterfeiting	31,295	323	2,289	29,006	11	46	266	329	685	952	1,417	1,499	1,449	1,257
Fraud	135,402	1,487	4,725	130,677	29	213	1,245	1,043	844	1,351	3,214	4,641	5,213	5,573
Embezzlement	5,118	22	428	4,690	3	3	16	19	151	236	349	327	317	268
Stolen property; buying, receiving, possessing	16,198	1,195	3,800	12,398	18	190	987	819	867	919	875	737	662	542
Vandalism	32,358	5,239	11,338	21,020	361	1,390	3,488	2,105	2,145	1,849	1,509	1,214	1,042	955
Weapons; carrying, possessing, etc.	12,680	1,307	3,327	9,353	36	289	982	755	689	576	512	445	378	387
Prostitution and commercialized vice	48,591	71	578	48,013	3	3	65	91	137	279	963	1,331	1,331	1,514
Sex offenses (except forcible rape and prostitution)	5,681	553	991	4,690	66	175	312	170	137	131	205	230	205	184
Drug abuse violations	188,880	5,111	20,344	168,536	56	616	4,439	3,944	5,241	6,048	7,289	6,754	5,923	5,495
Gambling	2,336	12	69	2,267	—	1	11	15	16	26	41	44	52	45
Offenses against family and children	23,251	785	2,183	21,068	64	108	613	468	519	411	574	563	598	637
Driving under the influence	149,706	84	2,039	147,667	19	6	59	124	604	1,227	2,515	3,063	3,175	4,630
Liquor laws	95,730	5,349	33,263	62,467	61	450	4,838	6,362	9,713	11,839	14,880	13,338	9,328	2,003
Drunkenness	63,524	731	2,976	60,548	16	60	655	628	735	882	1,283	1,353	1,239	1,494
Disorderly conduct	132,537	15,026	38,545	93,992	264	2,928	11,834	8,439	8,098	6,982	5,835	5,116	4,534	4,420
Vagrancy	4,370	136	439	3,931	3	16	117	96	108	99	176	143	104	134
All other offenses (except traffic)	517,044	25,506	76,126	440,918	1,081	3,924	20,501	17,311	17,781	15,528	16,989	19,230	18,572	17,983
Suspicion	971	99	361	610	1	16	82	72	97	93	50	24	29	25
Curfew and loitering law violations	41,815	13,178	41,815	—	176	1,763	11,239	10,349	11,139	7,149	—	—	—	—
Runaways	81,209	34,384	81,209	—	453	4,678	29,253	22,128	18,151	6,546	—	—	—	—

See footnotes at end of table.

Table 40. — Female Arrests, Distribution by Age, 1996 — Continued

Offense charged	Age											
	22	23	24	25-29	30-34	35-39	40-44	45-49	50-54	55-59	60-64	65 and over
TOTAL	65,416	64,689	66,304	322,431	331,351	273,112	158,666	78,830	35,047	16,515	8,834	11,895
Percent distribution[1]	2.9	2.8	2.9	14.1	14.5	11.9	6.9	3.4	1.5	.7	.4	.5
Murder and nonnegligent manslaughter	58	50	48	220	228	188	118	64	47	14	4	12
Forcible rape	8	10	6	38	41	50	27	6	3	—	2	—
Robbery	344	308	303	1,640	1,574	1,103	510	181	59	28	14	11
Aggravated assault	2,205	2,303	2,234	11,023	11,397	9,261	5,294	2,606	1,182	538	259	303
Burglary	822	775	776	3,816	3,540	2,849	1,602	699	292	116	50	67
Larceny–theft	9,600	9,146	9,115	42,038	39,812	32,788	20,294	11,111	5,870	3,149	2,003	3,333
Motor vehicle theft	436	378	420	2,042	1,750	1,259	561	209	75	32	11	14
Arson	57	39	47	167	253	198	140	74	33	24	10	12
Violent crime[2]	2,615	2,671	2,591	12,921	13,240	10,602	5,949	2,857	1,291	580	279	326
Percent distribution[1]	3.2	3.2	3.1	15.6	16.0	12.8	7.2	3.4	1.6	.7	.3	.4
Property crime[3]	10,915	10,338	10,358	48,063	45,355	37,094	22,597	12,093	6,270	3,321	2,074	3,426
Percent distribution[1]	2.6	2.5	2.5	11.4	10.8	8.8	5.4	2.9	1.5	.8	.5	.8
Crime Index total[4]	13,530	13,009	12,949	60,984	58,595	47,696	28,546	14,950	7,561	3,901	2,353	3,752
Percent distribution[1]	2.7	2.6	2.6	12.1	11.6	9.5	5.7	3.0	1.5	.8	.5	.7
Other assaults	6,043	5,966	6,137	28,653	29,170	22,940	12,599	6,313	2,981	1,375	728	933
Forgery and counterfeiting	1,310	1,244	1,256	6,009	5,622	4,053	2,206	1,030	340	159	50	105
Fraud	5,820	5,919	5,852	27,953	23,518	19,362	11,746	6,280	2,908	1,279	578	821
Embezzlement	253	243	199	875	669	499	345	181	100	41	17	7
Stolen property; buying, receiving, possessing	538	506	573	2,397	2,259	1,694	918	397	140	54	68	38
Vandalism	854	825	888	4,047	3,877	2,867	1,545	727	334	147	77	112
Weapons; carrying, possessing, etc.	349	341	386	1,663	1,705	1,458	845	425	245	107	49	58
Prostitution and commercialized vice	1,495	1,687	1,817	11,011	12,157	8,928	4,036	1,368	266	64	21	24
Sex offenses (except forcible rape and prostitution)	187	188	170	954	969	716	402	163	61	23	21	12
Drug abuse violations	5,260	5,437	5,694	31,384	37,018	31,040	17,263	6,673	2,078	739	268	221
Gambling	49	42	45	339	356	370	288	212	160	100	63	61
Offenses against family and children	663	728	786	3,789	4,638	4,166	2,102	934	407	208	131	144
Driving under the influence	4,660	4,678	4,936	24,517	29,514	27,533	18,469	10,252	4,842	2,432	1,229	1,222
Liquor laws	1,393	1,169	1,029	4,406	4,500	4,257	2,945	1,609	816	396	169	229
Drunkenness	1,465	1,447	1,607	9,000	13,055	12,581	8,199	4,260	1,916	829	455	365
Disorderly conduct	3,962	3,599	3,711	16,986	17,327	13,849	7,636	3,746	1,605	751	409	506
Vagrancy	134	132	137	793	806	629	407	190	63	27	29	27
All other offenses (except traffic)	17,428	17,501	18,098	86,559	85,488	68,398	38,132	19,087	8,213	3,876	2,116	3,248
Suspicion	23	28	34	112	108	76	37	33	11	7	3	10
Curfew and loitering law violations	—	—	—	—	—	—	—	—	—	—	—	—
Runaways	—	—	—	—	—	—	—	—	—	—	—	—

[1] Because of rounding, the percentages may not add to total.
[2] Violent crimes are offenses of murder, forcible rape, robbery, and aggravated assault.
[3] Property crimes are offenses of burglary, larceny–theft, motor vehicle theft, and arson.
[4] Includes arson.

Table 41. — Total Arrests of Persons under 15, 18, 21, and 25 Years of Age, 1996

[9,666 agencies; 1996 estimated population 189,927,000]

Offense charged	Total all ages	Number of persons arrested				Percent of total all ages			
		Under 15	Under 18	Under 21	Under 25	Under 15	Under 18	Under 21	Under 25
TOTAL	**11,093,211**	**679,449**	**2,103,658**	**3,568,260**	**5,015,527**	**6.1**	**19.0**	**32.2**	**45.2**
Murder and nonnegligent manslaughter	14,447	257	2,172	5,238	8,113	1.8	15.0	36.3	56.2
Forcible rape	24,347	1,423	4,128	7,293	10,591	5.8	17.0	30.0	43.5
Robbery	121,781	10,525	39,037	62,874	78,804	8.6	32.1	51.6	64.7
Aggravated assault	387,571	18,122	56,894	101,557	155,179	4.7	14.7	26.2	40.0
Burglary	264,193	36,859	97,809	141,612	169,722	14.0	37.0	53.6	64.2
Larceny–theft	1,096,488	155,287	370,607	517,982	624,549	14.2	33.8	47.2	57.0
Motor vehicle theft	132,023	14,473	54,813	77,882	92,471	11.0	41.5	59.0	70.0
Arson	13,755	4,887	7,302	8,573	9,574	35.5	53.1	62.3	69.6
Violent crime[1]	548,146	30,327	102,231	176,962	252,687	5.5	18.7	32.3	46.1
Property crime[2]	1,506,459	211,506	530,531	746,049	896,316	14.0	35.2	49.5	59.5
Crime Index total[3]	2,054,605	241,833	632,762	923,011	1,149,003	11.8	30.8	44.9	55.9
Other assaults	972,984	70,276	171,366	265,803	392,212	7.2	17.6	27.3	40.3
Forgery and counterfeiting	88,355	755	6,238	19,066	33,910	.9	7.1	21.6	38.4
Fraud	324,776	5,452	18,872	52,333	105,341	1.7	5.8	16.1	32.4
Embezzlement	11,449	63	958	3,046	5,071	.6	8.4	26.6	44.3
Stolen property; buying, receiving, possessing	111,066	8,099	30,189	51,518	66,642	7.3	27.2	46.4	60.0
Vandalism	234,215	46,353	103,333	136,519	160,884	19.8	44.1	58.3	68.7
Weapons; carrying, possessing, etc.	161,158	11,684	39,363	67,675	92,388	7.3	24.4	42.0	57.3
Prostitution and commercialized vice	81,036	140	1,104	6,644	17,110	.2	1.4	8.2	21.1
Sex offenses (except forcible rape and prostitution)	70,619	6,343	12,660	18,852	26,050	9.0	17.9	26.7	36.9
Drug abuse violations	1,128,647	26,705	158,447	345,349	512,174	2.4	14.0	30.6	45.4
Gambling	16,984	297	2,263	4,648	6,706	1.7	13.3	27.4	39.5
Offenses against family and children	103,800	1,879	5,850	13,091	25,772	1.8	5.6	12.6	24.8
Driving under the influence	1,013,932	341	12,814	81,867	228,015	[4]	1.3	8.1	22.5
Liquor laws	491,176	12,363	112,553	297,731	340,748	2.5	22.9	60.6	69.4
Drunkenness	522,869	2,414	17,111	58,499	122,961	.5	3.3	11.2	23.5
Disorderly conduct	626,918	53,726	159,951	250,591	338,871	8.6	25.5	40.0	54.1
Vagrancy	21,735	622	2,873	6,224	8,780	2.9	13.2	28.6	40.4
All other offenses (except traffic)	2,767,751	92,240	329,070	679,245	1,095,734	3.3	11.9	24.5	39.6
Suspicion	4,859	436	1,604	2,271	2,878	9.0	33.0	46.7	59.2
Curfew and loitering law violations	142,433	39,315	142,433	142,433	142,433	27.6	100.0	100.0	100.0
Runaways	141,844	58,113	141,844	141,844	141,844	41.0	100.0	100.0	100.0

[1] Violent crimes are offenses of murder, forcible rape, robbery, and aggravated assault.

[2] Property crimes are offenses of burglary, larceny–theft, motor vehicle theft, and arson.

[3] Includes arson.

[4] Less than one-tenth of 1 percent.

Table 42. — Total Arrests, Distribution by Sex, 1996

[9,666 agencies; 1996 estimated population 189,927,000]

Offense charged	Number of persons arrested			Percent male	Percent female	Percent distribution[1]		
	Total	Male	Female			Total	Male	Female
TOTAL	**11,093,211**	**8,803,292**	**2,289,919**	**79.4**	**20.6**	**100.0**	**100.0**	**100.0**
Murder and nonnegligent manslaughter	14,447	12,965	1,482	89.7	10.3	.1	.1	.1
Forcible rape	24,347	24,066	281	98.8	1.2	.2	.3	[2]
Robbery	121,781	109,912	11,869	90.3	9.7	1.1	1.2	.5
Aggravated assault	387,571	318,279	69,292	82.1	17.9	3.5	3.6	3.0
Burglary	264,193	234,208	29,985	88.7	11.3	2.4	2.7	1.3
Larceny–theft	1,096,488	726,006	370,482	66.2	33.8	9.9	8.2	16.2
Motor vehicle theft	132,023	114,125	17,898	86.4	13.6	1.2	1.3	.8
Arson	13,755	11,703	2,052	85.1	14.9	.1	.1	.1
Violent crime[3]	548,146	465,222	82,924	84.9	15.1	4.9	5.3	3.6
Property crime[4]	1,506,459	1,086,042	420,417	72.1	27.9	13.6	12.3	18.4
Crime Index total[5]	2,054,605	1,551,264	503,341	75.5	24.5	18.5	17.6	22.0
Other assaults	972,984	775,102	197,882	79.7	20.3	8.8	8.8	8.6
Forgery and counterfeiting	88,355	57,060	31,295	64.6	35.4	.8	.6	1.4
Fraud	324,776	189,374	135,402	58.3	41.7	2.9	2.2	5.9
Embezzlement	11,449	6,331	5,118	55.3	44.7	.1	.1	.2
Stolen property; buying, receiving, possessing	111,066	94,868	16,198	85.4	14.6	1.0	1.1	.7
Vandalism	234,215	201,857	32,358	86.2	13.8	2.1	2.3	1.4
Weapons; carrying, possessing, etc.	161,158	148,478	12,680	92.1	7.9	1.5	1.7	.6
Prostitution and commercialized vice	81,036	32,445	48,591	40.0	60.0	.7	.4	2.1
Sex offenses (except forcible rape and prostitution)	70,619	64,938	5,681	92.0	8.0	.6	.7	.2
Drug abuse violations	1,128,647	939,767	188,880	83.3	16.7	10.2	10.7	8.2
Gambling	16,984	14,648	2,336	86.2	13.8	.2	.2	.1
Offenses against family and children	103,800	80,549	23,251	77.6	22.4	.9	.9	1.0
Driving under the influence	1,013,932	864,226	149,706	85.2	14.8	9.1	9.8	6.5
Liquor laws	491,176	395,446	95,730	80.5	19.5	4.4	4.5	4.2
Drunkenness	522,869	459,345	63,524	87.9	12.1	4.7	5.2	2.8
Disorderly conduct	626,918	494,381	132,537	78.9	21.1	5.7	5.6	5.8
Vagrancy	21,735	17,365	4,370	79.9	20.1	.2	.2	.2
All other offenses (except traffic)	2,767,751	2,250,707	517,044	81.3	18.7	24.9	25.6	22.6
Suspicion	4,859	3,888	971	80.0	20.0	[2]	[2]	[2]
Curfew and loitering law violations	142,433	100,618	41,815	70.6	29.4	1.3	1.1	1.8
Runaways	141,844	60,635	81,209	42.7	57.3	1.3	.7	3.5

[1] Because of rounding, the percentages may not add to total.

[2] Less than one-tenth of 1 percent.

[3] Violent crimes are offenses of murder, forcible rape, robbery, and aggravated assault.

[4] Property crimes are offenses of burglary, larceny–theft, motor vehicle theft, and arson.

[5] Includes arson.

231

Table 43. — Total Arrests, Distribution by Race, 1996

[9,661 agencies; 1996 estimated population 189,885,000]

Offense charged	Total arrests					Percent distribution[1]				
	Total	White	Black	American Indian or Alaskan Native	Asian or Pacific Islander	Total	White	Black	American Indian or Alaskan Native	Asian or Pacific Islander
TOTAL	11,072,832	7,404,170	3,400,338	139,290	129,034	100.0	66.9	30.7	1.3	1.2
Murder and nonnegligent manslaughter	14,439	6,176	7,928	119	216	100.0	42.8	54.9	.8	1.5
Forcible rape	24,317	13,637	10,124	266	290	100.0	56.1	41.6	1.1	1.2
Robbery	121,673	48,412	70,828	651	1,782	100.0	39.8	58.2	.5	1.5
Aggravated assault	387,090	230,785	147,463	3,929	4,913	100.0	59.6	38.1	1.0	1.3
Burglary	263,774	179,063	78,473	2,853	3,385	100.0	67.9	29.8	1.1	1.3
Larceny–theft	1,094,186	709,109	351,993	13,707	19,377	100.0	64.8	32.2	1.3	1.8
Motor vehicle theft	131,892	74,618	53,022	1,579	2,673	100.0	56.6	40.2	1.2	2.0
Arson	13,739	10,175	3,297	132	135	100.0	74.1	24.0	1.0	1.0
Violent crime[2]	547,519	299,010	236,343	4,965	7,201	100.0	54.6	43.2	.9	1.3
Property crime[3]	1,503,591	972,965	486,785	18,271	25,570	100.0	64.7	32.4	1.2	1.7
Crime Index total[4]	2,051,110	1,271,975	723,128	23,236	32,771	100.0	62.0	35.3	1.1	1.6
Other assaults	971,267	606,019	340,930	13,071	11,247	100.0	62.4	35.1	1.3	1.2
Forgery and counterfeiting	88,063	56,461	29,547	511	1,544	100.0	64.1	33.6	.6	1.8
Fraud	324,121	204,054	115,980	1,470	2,617	100.0	63.0	35.8	.5	.8
Embezzlement	11,434	7,216	3,985	59	174	100.0	63.1	34.9	.5	1.5
Stolen property; buying, receiving, possessing	110,834	63,893	44,647	870	1,424	100.0	57.6	40.3	.8	1.3
Vandalism	233,952	171,124	56,725	3,220	2,883	100.0	73.1	24.2	1.4	1.2
Weapons; carrying, possessing, etc.	161,016	93,430	64,534	1,152	1,900	100.0	58.0	40.1	.7	1.2
Prostitution and commercialized vice	81,022	47,809	31,065	528	1,620	100.0	59.0	38.3	.7	2.0
Sex offenses (except forcible rape and prostitution) .	70,546	52,136	16,691	791	928	100.0	73.9	23.7	1.1	1.3
Drug abuse violations	1,127,114	681,008	433,352	5,600	7,154	100.0	60.4	38.4	.5	.6
Gambling	16,982	7,711	8,588	66	617	100.0	45.4	50.6	.4	3.6
Offenses against family and children	102,944	67,531	32,561	1,129	1,723	100.0	65.6	31.6	1.1	1.7
Driving under the influence	1,011,470	876,558	104,793	16,867	13,252	100.0	86.7	10.4	1.7	1.3
Liquor laws	489,219	395,689	78,178	12,007	3,345	100.0	80.9	16.0	2.5	.7
Drunkenness	522,159	423,358	84,362	12,450	1,989	100.0	81.1	16.2	2.4	.4
Disorderly conduct	625,861	390,499	223,234	8,052	4,076	100.0	62.4	35.7	1.3	.7
Vagrancy	21,719	11,800	9,416	422	81	100.0	54.3	43.4	1.9	.4
All other offenses (except traffic)	2,763,311	1,758,183	938,754	34,429	31,945	100.0	63.6	34.0	1.2	1.2
Suspicion	4,843	3,272	1,492	56	23	100.0	67.6	30.8	1.2	.5
Curfew and loitering law violations	142,135	103,664	34,756	1,655	2,060	100.0	72.9	24.5	1.2	1.4
Runaways	141,710	110,780	23,620	1,649	5,661	100.0	78.2	16.7	1.2	4.0

See footnotes at end of table.

Table 43. — Total Arrests, Distribution by Race, 1996 — Continued

Offense charged	Arrests under 18					Percent distribution[1]				
	Total	White	Black	American Indian or Alaskan Native	Asian or Pacific Islander	Total	White	Black	American Indian or Alaskan Native	Asian or Pacific Islander
TOTAL	2,099,997	1,462,863	573,498	25,515	38,121	100.0	69.7	27.3	1.2	1.8
Murder and nonnegligent manslaughter	2,171	849	1,248	14	60	100.0	39.1	57.5	.6	2.8
Forcible rape	4,123	2,279	1,772	38	34	100.0	55.3	43.0	.9	.8
Robbery	39,012	15,432	22,578	193	809	100.0	39.6	57.9	.5	2.1
Aggravated assault	56,791	32,775	22,594	576	846	100.0	57.7	39.8	1.0	1.5
Burglary	97,634	71,885	22,861	1,305	1,583	100.0	73.6	23.4	1.3	1.6
Larceny–theft	369,771	260,972	94,522	5,371	8,906	100.0	70.6	25.6	1.5	2.4
Motor vehicle theft	54,755	31,647	20,876	815	1,417	100.0	57.8	38.1	1.5	2.6
Arson	7,289	5,836	1,290	81	82	100.0	80.1	17.7	1.1	1.1
Violent crime[2]	102,097	51,335	48,192	821	1,749	100.0	50.3	47.2	.8	1.7
Property crime[3]	529,449	370,340	139,549	7,572	11,988	100.0	69.9	26.4	1.4	2.3
Crime Index total[4]	631,546	421,675	187,741	8,393	13,737	100.0	66.8	29.7	1.3	2.2
Other assaults	171,111	106,615	59,906	1,942	2,648	100.0	62.3	35.0	1.1	1.5
Forgery and counterfeiting	6,225	4,829	1,242	63	91	100.0	77.6	20.0	1.0	1.5
Fraud	18,864	9,940	8,238	82	604	100.0	52.7	43.7	.4	3.2
Embezzlement	957	599	344	2	12	100.0	62.6	35.9	.2	1.3
Stolen property; buying, receiving, possessing	30,127	18,179	11,111	306	531	100.0	60.3	36.9	1.0	1.8
Vandalism	103,207	82,357	18,057	1,272	1,521	100.0	79.8	17.5	1.2	1.5
Weapons; carrying, possessing, etc.	39,331	24,877	13,480	356	618	100.0	63.3	34.3	.9	1.6
Prostitution and commercialized vice	1,104	650	412	25	17	100.0	58.9	37.3	2.3	1.5
Sex offenses (except forcible rape and prostitution)	12,644	8,812	3,589	112	131	100.0	69.7	28.4	.9	1.0
Drug abuse violations	158,161	98,396	57,221	1,093	1,451	100.0	62.2	36.2	.7	.9
Gambling	2,263	334	1,916	1	12	100.0	14.8	84.7	[5]	.5
Offenses against family and children	5,796	4,344	1,253	50	149	100.0	74.9	21.6	.9	2.6
Driving under the influence	12,775	11,651	725	251	148	100.0	91.2	5.7	2.0	1.2
Liquor laws	112,191	101,943	6,284	2,989	975	100.0	90.9	5.6	2.7	.9
Drunkenness	17,098	15,066	1,557	366	109	100.0	88.1	9.1	2.1	.6
Disorderly conduct	159,814	100,900	56,113	1,429	1,372	100.0	63.1	35.1	.9	.9
Vagrancy	2,869	1,823	1,002	21	23	100.0	63.5	34.9	.7	.8
All other offenses (except traffic)	328,465	234,209	84,564	3,450	6,242	100.0	71.3	25.7	1.1	1.9
Suspicion	1,604	1,220	367	8	9	100.0	76.1	22.9	.5	.6
Curfew and loitering law violations	142,135	103,664	34,756	1,655	2,060	100.0	72.9	24.5	1.2	1.4
Runaways	141,710	110,780	23,620	1,649	5,661	100.0	78.2	16.7	1.2	4.0

See footnotes at end of table.

Table 43. — Total Arrests, Distribution by Race, 1996 — Continued

Offense charged	Arrests 18 and over					Percent distribution[1]				
	Total	White	Black	American Indian or Alaskan Native	Asian or Pacific Islander	Total	White	Black	American Indian or Alaskan Native	Asian or Pacific Islander
TOTAL	8,972,835	5,941,307	2,826,840	113,775	90,913	100.0	66.2	31.5	1.3	1.0
Murder and nonnegligent manslaughter	12,268	5,327	6,680	105	156	100.0	43.4	54.5	.9	1.3
Forcible rape	20,194	11,358	8,352	228	256	100.0	56.2	41.4	1.1	1.3
Robbery	82,661	32,980	48,250	458	973	100.0	39.9	58.4	.6	1.2
Aggravated assault	330,299	198,010	124,869	3,353	4,067	100.0	59.9	37.8	1.0	1.2
Burglary	166,140	107,178	55,612	1,548	1,802	100.0	64.5	33.5	.9	1.1
Larceny–theft	724,415	448,137	257,471	8,336	10,471	100.0	61.9	35.5	1.2	1.4
Motor vehicle theft	77,137	42,971	32,146	764	1,256	100.0	55.7	41.7	1.0	1.6
Arson	6,450	4,339	2,007	51	53	100.0	67.3	31.1	.8	.8
Violent crime[2]	445,422	247,675	188,151	4,144	5,452	100.0	55.6	42.2	.9	1.2
Property crime[3]	974,142	602,625	347,236	10,699	13,582	100.0	61.9	35.6	1.1	1.4
Crime Index total[4]	1,419,564	850,300	535,387	14,843	19,034	100.0	59.9	37.7	1.0	1.3
Other assaults	800,156	499,404	281,024	11,129	8,599	100.0	62.4	35.1	1.4	1.1
Forgery and counterfeiting	81,838	51,632	28,305	448	1,453	100.0	63.1	34.6	.5	1.8
Fraud	305,257	194,114	107,742	1,388	2,013	100.0	63.6	35.3	.5	.7
Embezzlement	10,477	6,617	3,641	57	162	100.0	63.2	34.8	.5	1.5
Stolen property; buying, receiving, possessing	80,707	45,714	33,536	564	893	100.0	56.6	41.6	.7	1.1
Vandalism	130,745	88,767	38,668	1,948	1,362	100.0	67.9	29.6	1.5	1.0
Weapons; carrying, possessing, etc.	121,685	68,553	51,054	796	1,282	100.0	56.3	42.0	.7	1.1
Prostitution and commercialized vice	79,918	47,159	30,653	503	1,603	100.0	59.0	38.4	.6	2.0
Sex offenses (except forcible rape and prostitution)	57,902	43,324	13,102	679	797	100.0	74.8	22.6	1.2	1.4
Drug abuse violations	968,953	582,612	376,131	4,507	5,703	100.0	60.1	38.8	.5	.6
Gambling	14,719	7,377	6,672	65	605	100.0	50.1	45.3	.4	4.1
Offenses against family and children	97,148	63,187	31,308	1,079	1,574	100.0	65.0	32.2	1.1	1.6
Driving under the influence	998,695	864,907	104,068	16,616	13,104	100.0	86.6	10.4	1.7	1.3
Liquor laws	377,028	293,746	71,894	9,018	2,370	100.0	77.9	19.1	2.4	.6
Drunkenness	505,061	408,292	82,805	12,084	1,880	100.0	80.8	16.4	2.4	.4
Disorderly conduct	466,047	289,599	167,121	6,623	2,704	100.0	62.1	35.9	1.4	.6
Vagrancy	18,850	9,977	8,414	401	58	100.0	52.9	44.6	2.1	.3
All other offenses (except traffic)	2,434,846	1,523,974	854,190	30,979	25,703	100.0	62.6	35.1	1.3	1.1
Suspicion	3,239	2,052	1,125	48	14	100.0	63.4	34.7	1.5	.4
Curfew and loitering law violations	—	—	—	—	—	—	—	—	—	—
Runaways	—	—	—	—	—	—	—	—	—	—

[1] Because of rounding, the percentages may not add to total.
[2] Violent crimes are offenses of murder, forcible rape, robbery, and aggravated assault.
[3] Property crimes are offenses of burglary, larceny–theft, motor vehicle theft, and arson.
[4] Includes arson.
[5] Less than one-tenth of 1 percent.

Table 44. — City Arrest Trends, 1995-1996

[5,882 agencies; 1996 estimated population 123,259,000; 1995 estimated population 122,073,000]

Offense charged	Number of persons arrested								
	Total all ages			Under 18 years of age			18 years of age and over		
	1995	1996	Percent change	1995	1996	Percent change	1995	1996	Percent change
TOTAL	8,140,604	8,140,494	[1]	1,617,872	1,651,097	+2.1	6,522,732	6,489,397	-.5
Murder and nonnegligent manslaughter	12,504	11,067	-11.5	2,094	1,819	-13.1	10,410	9,248	-11.2
Forcible rape	18,005	17,571	-2.4	3,061	3,033	-.9	14,944	14,538	-2.7
Robbery	113,167	104,995	-7.2	38,034	34,542	-9.2	75,133	70,453	-6.2
Aggravated assault	302,585	293,681	-2.9	47,231	44,838	-5.1	255,354	248,843	-2.5
Burglary	192,019	185,181	-3.6	66,113	67,881	+2.7	125,906	117,300	-6.8
Larceny–theft	885,729	870,043	-1.8	298,843	299,440	+.2	586,886	570,603	-2.8
Motor vehicle theft	112,276	102,345	-8.8	48,000	43,217	-10.0	64,276	59,128	-8.0
Arson	10,606	9,833	-7.3	5,946	5,500	-7.5	4,660	4,333	-7.0
Violent crime[2]	446,261	427,314	-4.2	90,420	84,232	-6.8	355,841	343,082	-3.6
Property crime[3]	1,200,630	1,167,402	-2.8	418,902	416,038	-.7	781,728	751,364	-3.9
Crime Index total[4]	1,646,891	1,594,716	-3.2	509,322	500,270	-1.8	1,137,569	1,094,446	-3.8
Other assaults	714,881	710,955	-.5	128,224	129,986	+1.4	586,657	580,969	-1.0
Forgery and counterfeiting	62,718	63,493	+1.2	4,864	4,793	-1.5	57,854	58,700	+1.5
Fraud	180,725	181,011	+.2	15,625	16,569	+6.0	165,100	164,442	-.4
Embezzlement	7,690	8,492	+10.4	746	787	+5.5	6,944	7,705	+11.0
Stolen property; buying, receiving, possessing	92,275	83,960	-9.0	25,556	24,033	-6.0	66,719	59,927	-10.2
Vandalism	182,080	176,401	-3.1	81,497	78,012	-4.3	100,583	98,389	-2.2
Weapons; carrying, possessing, etc.	141,647	125,558	-11.4	35,360	32,004	-9.5	106,287	93,554	-12.0
Prostitution and commercialized vice	74,693	74,867	+.2	949	989	+4.2	73,744	73,878	+.2
Sex offenses (except forcible rape and prostitution)	49,309	50,714	+2.8	8,501	8,950	+5.3	40,808	41,764	+2.3
Drug abuse violations	858,344	865,027	+.8	120,348	126,906	+5.4	737,996	738,121	[1]
Gambling	15,032	15,589	+3.7	1,903	2,113	+11.0	13,129	13,476	+2.6
Offenses against family and children	53,214	54,176	+1.8	3,258	4,126	+26.6	49,956	50,050	+.2
Driving under the influence	555,965	567,519	+2.1	6,424	7,584	+18.1	549,541	559,935	+1.9
Liquor laws	331,106	375,401	+13.4	64,841	77,541	+19.6	266,265	297,860	+11.9
Drunkenness	416,421	406,735	-2.3	12,563	13,721	+9.2	403,858	393,014	-2.7
Disorderly conduct	503,530	519,618	+3.2	123,866	134,346	+8.5	379,664	385,272	+1.5
Vagrancy	19,074	19,144	+.4	2,524	2,235	-11.5	16,550	16,909	+2.2
All other offenses (except traffic)	2,018,404	2,015,781	-.1	254,896	254,795	[4]	1,763,508	1,760,986	-.1
Suspicion (not included in totals)	3,466	3,740	+7.9	1,191	1,119	-6.0	2,275	2,621	+15.2
Curfew and loitering law violations	106,767	128,920	+20.7	106,767	128,920	+20.7	—	—	—
Runaways	109,838	102,417	-6.8	109,838	102,417	-6.8	—	—	—

[1] Less than one-tenth of 1 percent.

[2] Violent crimes are offenses of murder, forcible rape, robbery, and aggravated assault.

[3] Property crimes are offenses of burglary, larceny–theft, motor vehicle theft, and arson.

[4] Includes arson.

Table 45. — City Arrest Trends, Sex, 1995-1996

[5,882 agencies; 1996 estimated population 123,259,000; 1995 estimated population 122,073,000]

Offense charged	Males						Females					
	Total			Under 18			Total			Under 18		
	1995	1996	Percent change	1995	1996	Percent change	1995	1996	Percent change	1995	1996	Percent change
TOTAL	6,483,766	6,454,921	-.4	1,219,147	1,231,881	+1.0	1,656,838	1,685,573	+1.7	398,725	419,216	+5.1
Murder and nonnegligent manslaughter ...	11,414	10,013	-12.3	1,998	1,708	-14.5	1,090	1,054	-3.3	96	111	+15.6
Forcible rape	17,808	17,384	-2.4	3,000	2,992	-.3	197	187	-5.1	61	41	-32.8
Robbery	102,279	94,620	-7.5	34,384	31,129	-9.5	10,888	10,375	-4.7	3,650	3,413	-6.5
Aggravated assault	249,682	239,429	-4.1	38,066	35,436	-6.9	52,903	54,252	+2.5	9,165	9,402	+2.6
Burglary	169,487	162,967	-3.8	59,327	60,716	+2.3	22,532	22,214	-1.4	6,786	7,165	+5.6
Larceny–theft	587,491	571,445	-2.7	200,397	196,603	-1.9	298,238	298,598	+.1	98,446	102,837	+4.5
Motor vehicle theft	97,283	88,676	-8.8	41,103	36,934	-10.1	14,993	13,669	-8.8	6,897	6,283	-8.9
Arson	8,909	8,342	-6.4	5,240	4,886	-6.8	1,697	1,491	-12.1	706	614	-13.0
Violent crime[1]	381,183	361,446	-5.2	77,448	71,265	-8.0	65,078	65,868	+1.2	12,972	12,967	[2]
Property crime[3]	863,170	831,430	-3.7	306,067	299,139	-2.3	337,460	335,972	-.4	112,835	116,899	+3.6
Crime Index total[4]	1,244,353	1,192,876	-4.1	383,515	370,404	-3.4	402,538	401,840	-.2	125,807	129,866	+3.2
Other assaults	575,471	567,042	-1.5	92,651	93,408	+.8	139,410	143,913	+3.2	35,573	36,578	+2.8
Forgery and counterfeiting	40,050	41,542	+3.7	3,099	3,002	-3.1	22,668	21,951	-3.2	1,765	1,791	+1.5
Fraud	113,093	114,489	+1.2	11,846	12,619	+6.5	67,632	66,522	-1.6	3,779	3,950	+4.5
Embezzlement	4,242	4,595	+8.3	431	434	+.7	3,448	3,897	+13.0	315	353	+12.1
Stolen property; buying, receiving, possessing	79,121	71,597	-9.5	22,477	20,981	-6.7	13,154	12,363	-6.0	3,079	3,052	-.9
Vandalism	157,260	151,602	-3.6	72,473	69,335	-4.3	24,820	24,799	-.1	9,024	8,677	-3.8
Weapons; carrying, possessing, etc.	130,382	115,541	-11.4	32,463	29,240	-9.9	11,265	10,017	-11.1	2,897	2,764	-4.6
Prostitution and commercialized vice	27,436	29,160	+6.3	488	463	-5.1	47,257	45,707	-3.3	461	526	+14.1
Sex offenses (except forcible rape and prostitution)	45,056	46,334	+2.8	7,866	8,258	+5.0	4,253	4,380	+3.0	635	692	+9.0
Drug abuse violations	715,117	721,396	+.9	106,126	111,230	+4.8	143,227	143,631	+.3	14,222	15,676	+10.2
Gambling	12,854	13,449	+4.6	1,846	2,056	+11.4	2,178	2,140	-1.7	57	57	[2]
Offenses against family and children	38,751	37,772	-2.5	2,036	2,527	+24.1	14,463	16,404	+13.4	1,222	1,599	+30.9
Driving under the influence	472,639	479,750	+1.5	5,417	6,362	+17.4	83,326	87,769	+5.3	1,007	1,222	+21.4
Liquor laws	271,304	305,070	+12.4	46,665	55,022	+17.9	59,802	70,331	+17.6	18,176	22,519	+23.9
Drunkenness	367,075	357,785	-2.5	10,572	11,363	+7.5	49,346	48,950	-.8	1,991	2,358	+18.4
Disorderly conduct	398,339	410,856	+3.1	95,036	102,197	+7.5	105,191	108,762	+3.4	28,830	32,149	+11.5
Vagrancy	15,308	15,307	[2]	2,244	1,956	-12.8	3,766	3,837	+1.9	280	279	-.4
All other offenses (except traffic)	1,654,077	1,644,251	-.6	200,058	196,517	-1.8	364,327	371,530	+2.0	54,838	58,278	+6.3
Suspicion (not included in totals)	2,860	2,985	+4.4	947	871	-8.0	606	755	+24.6	244	248	+1.6
Curfew and loitering law violations	75,197	91,049	+21.1	75,197	91,049	+21.1	31,570	37,871	+20.0	31,570	37,871	+20.0
Runaways	46,641	43,458	-6.8	46,641	43,458	-6.8	63,197	58,959	-6.7	63,197	58,959	-6.7

[1] Violent crimes are offenses of murder, forcible rape, robbery, and aggravated assault.

[2] Less than one-tenth of 1 percent.

[3] Property crimes are offenses of burglary, larceny–theft, motor vehicle theft, and arson.

[4] Includes arson.

Table 46. — City Arrests, Distribution by Age, 1996

[6,917 agencies; 1996 estimated population 132,725,000]

Offense charged	Total all ages	Ages under 15	Ages under 18	Ages 18 and over	Under 10	10-12	13-14	15	16	17	18	19	20	21
TOTAL	8,665,120	580,687	1,766,971	6,898,149	27,327	129,943	423,417	354,253	411,057	420,974	417,369	393,814	343,465	310,538
Percent distribution[1]	100.0	6.7	20.4	79.6	.3	1.5	4.9	4.1	4.7	4.9	4.8	4.5	4.0	3.6
Murder and nonnegligent manslaughter	11,386	215	1,868	9,518	13	12	190	310	561	782	856	908	733	693
Forcible rape	18,602	1,131	3,255	15,347	54	276	801	592	710	822	821	788	745	749
Robbery	108,840	9,798	35,638	73,202	253	1,760	7,785	7,492	8,919	9,429	8,557	6,951	5,393	4,316
Aggravated assault	306,949	15,078	47,164	259,785	783	3,618	10,677	8,883	11,079	12,124	12,252	12,192	11,316	11,473
Burglary	196,436	28,311	72,426	124,010	1,916	6,980	19,415	14,564	15,093	14,458	12,696	9,510	7,078	5,804
Larceny–theft	936,989	138,136	324,023	612,966	6,961	38,788	92,387	61,487	64,682	59,718	51,824	40,188	30,473	25,617
Motor vehicle theft	107,127	11,913	45,094	62,033	170	1,413	10,330	10,941	11,612	10,628	8,209	5,979	4,486	3,510
Arson	10,452	4,011	5,874	4,578	764	1,344	1,903	769	619	475	362	275	239	176
Violent crime[2]	445,777	26,222	87,925	357,852	1,103	5,666	19,453	17,277	21,269	23,157	22,486	20,839	18,187	17,231
Percent distribution[1]	100.0	5.9	19.7	80.3	.2	1.3	4.4	3.9	4.8	5.2	5.0	4.7	4.1	3.9
Property crime[3]	1,251,004	182,371	447,417	803,587	9,811	48,525	124,035	87,761	92,006	85,279	73,091	55,952	42,276	35,107
Percent distribution[1]	100.0	14.6	35.8	64.2	.8	3.9	9.9	7.0	7.4	6.8	5.8	4.5	3.4	2.8
Crime Index total[4]	1,696,781	208,593	535,342	1,161,439	10,914	54,191	143,488	105,038	113,275	108,436	95,577	76,791	60,463	52,338
Percent distribution[1]	100.0	12.3	31.6	68.4	.6	3.2	8.5	6.2	6.7	6.4	5.6	4.5	3.6	3.1
Other assaults	756,522	58,122	138,753	617,769	3,116	16,233	38,773	26,125	27,219	27,287	25,122	25,136	24,212	25,669
Forgery and counterfeiting	68,273	654	5,206	63,067	21	102	531	766	1,495	2,291	3,267	3,503	3,285	2,943
Fraud	190,335	5,219	16,896	173,439	76	767	4,376	4,738	2,892	4,047	6,313	7,680	7,723	7,794
Embezzlement	8,903	48	835	8,068	4	8	36	47	288	452	625	591	562	487
Stolen property; buying, receiving, possessing	89,704	7,117	25,709	63,995	172	1,285	5,660	5,314	6,298	6,980	6,992	5,640	4,374	3,733
Vandalism	188,637	38,456	83,889	104,748	3,785	11,274	23,397	15,432	16,139	13,862	11,231	8,252	6,309	5,835
Weapons; carrying, possessing, etc.	131,030	9,980	33,464	97,566	498	2,138	7,344	6,537	8,067	8,880	9,131	7,995	6,553	6,030
Prostitution and commercialized vice	77,427	123	1,030	76,397	10	15	98	142	242	523	1,381	1,895	2,055	2,245
Sex offenses (except forcible rape and prostitution)	53,666	4,884	9,553	44,113	461	1,411	3,012	1,662	1,457	1,550	1,652	1,538	1,370	1,507
Drug abuse violations	906,626	22,559	133,868	772,758	253	2,419	19,887	25,071	37,533	48,705	55,617	50,620	42,641	37,506
Gambling	15,781	272	2,148	13,633	4	31	237	406	648	822	808	792	640	585
Offenses against family and children	60,007	1,546	4,678	55,329	136	296	1,114	938	1,111	1,083	1,657	1,588	1,706	1,799
Driving under the influence	619,273	262	8,412	610,861	108	25	129	383	2,273	5,494	11,763	15,146	16,471	22,801
Liquor laws	402,602	9,814	85,859	316,743	150	773	8,891	13,766	25,012	37,267	52,696	52,388	40,397	12,329
Drunkenness	435,346	2,088	14,622	420,724	89	173	1,826	2,388	3,672	6,474	10,934	11,433	11,051	14,498
Disorderly conduct	557,596	48,524	144,373	413,223	1,545	10,679	36,300	29,020	32,922	33,907	31,398	27,187	23,671	24,139
Vagrancy	20,016	511	2,520	17,496	13	78	420	491	632	886	1,298	1,024	782	693
All other offenses (except traffic)	2,138,529	77,899	274,507	1,864,022	3,914	14,626	59,359	55,438	67,022	74,148	89,609	94,448	89,052	87,451
Suspicion	4,138	370	1,379	2,759	10	71	289	292	335	382	298	167	148	156
Curfew and loitering law violations	134,737	37,186	134,737	—	908	5,619	30,659	31,494	37,997	28,060	—	—	—	—
Runaways	109,191	46,460	109,191	—	1,140	7,729	37,591	28,765	24,528	9,438	—	—	—	—

See footnotes at end of table.

Table 46. — City Arrests, Distribution by Age, 1996 — Continued

Offense charged	Age											
	22	23	24	25-29	30-34	35-39	40-44	45-49	50-54	55-59	60-64	65 and over
TOTAL	279,216	265,550	259,620	1,179,102	1,130,740	970,805	624,893	355,461	172,660	90,201	49,482	55,233
Percent distribution[1]	3.2	3.1	3.0	13.6	13.0	11.2	7.2	4.1	2.0	1.0	.6	.6
Murder and nonnegligent manslaughter	643	522	481	1,571	1,116	820	500	295	161	86	53	80
Forcible rape	600	557	594	2,846	2,733	2,119	1,279	708	352	190	137	129
Robbery	3,555	3,283	2,844	13,329	11,106	7,588	3,765	1,543	553	229	101	89
Aggravated assault	10,654	10,610	10,373	48,295	45,156	37,345	23,222	12,919	6,474	3,317	1,875	2,312
Burglary	5,027	4,659	4,458	21,481	21,003	16,433	9,215	4,065	1,492	569	227	293
Larceny–theft	22,216	20,547	20,236	97,314	98,011	85,645	56,262	30,948	14,418	7,483	4,571	7,213
Motor vehicle theft	2,960	2,663	2,545	10,729	8,880	6,350	3,167	1,547	537	227	120	124
Arson	177	170	170	659	773	589	437	230	159	73	48	41
Violent crime[2]	15,452	14,972	14,292	66,041	60,111	47,872	28,766	15,465	7,540	3,822	2,166	2,610
Percent distribution[1]	3.5	3.4	3.2	14.8	13.5	10.7	6.5	3.5	1.7	.9	.5	.6
Property crime[3]	30,380	28,039	27,409	130,183	128,667	109,017	69,081	36,790	16,606	8,352	4,966	7,671
Percent distribution[1]	2.4	2.2	2.2	10.4	10.3	8.7	5.5	2.9	1.3	.7	.4	.6
Crime Index total[4]	45,832	43,011	41,701	196,224	188,778	156,889	97,847	52,255	24,146	12,174	7,132	10,281
Percent distribution[1]	2.7	2.5	2.5	11.6	11.1	9.2	5.8	3.1	1.4	.7	.4	.6
Other assaults	24,802	24,665	25,001	118,065	114,108	94,691	56,872	30,017	14,078	7,042	3,744	4,545
Forgery and counterfeiting	2,915	2,832	2,644	12,541	11,499	8,516	5,035	2,416	886	426	166	193
Fraud	7,263	7,190	7,216	33,982	30,373	25,151	15,903	9,049	3,919	1,839	904	1,140
Embezzlement	421	370	343	1,474	1,148	896	572	293	152	74	27	33
Stolen property; buying, receiving, possessing	3,044	2,645	2,533	10,849	9,398	7,053	4,135	1,991	825	390	208	185
Vandalism	5,048	4,575	4,320	17,763	15,665	12,264	6,797	3,561	1,549	714	392	473
Weapons; carrying, possessing, etc.	5,322	4,707	4,165	16,358	12,464	9,652	6,464	3,923	2,072	1,215	688	827
Prostitution and commercialized vice	2,370	2,625	2,820	16,509	17,579	13,543	7,007	3,387	1,426	725	385	445
Sex offenses (except forcible rape and prostitution)	1,393	1,361	1,337	6,916	7,515	6,818	4,720	3,018	1,948	1,235	741	1,044
Drug abuse violations	32,912	30,999	29,729	135,173	129,016	108,878	66,800	32,605	11,974	4,915	1,946	1,427
Gambling	499	407	462	1,754	1,669	1,509	1,236	1,026	781	551	433	481
Offenses against family and children	1,882	1,897	2,049	9,872	11,029	10,119	5,924	3,007	1,333	659	358	450
Driving under the influence	22,403	22,372	22,851	107,137	106,491	96,590	67,442	44,449	24,511	13,873	8,112	8,449
Liquor laws	9,272	7,779	7,340	28,961	28,447	27,018	20,516	13,378	7,648	4,329	2,258	1,987
Drunkenness	13,164	12,713	12,635	60,953	70,030	72,071	53,766	35,122	19,570	11,014	6,184	5,586
Disorderly conduct	20,361	18,139	17,033	68,617	61,126	52,236	32,651	18,016	8,842	4,582	2,512	2,713
Vagrancy	627	558	503	2,402	2,564	2,581	1,992	1,088	632	353	205	194
All other offenses (except traffic)	79,561	76,592	74,811	333,099	311,433	263,999	168,998	96,753	46,315	24,069	13,073	14,759
Suspicion	125	113	127	453	408	331	216	107	53	22	14	21
Curfew and loitering law violations	—	—	—	—	—	—	—	—	—	—	—	—
Runaways	—	—	—	—	—	—	—	—	—	—	—	—

[1] Because of rounding, the percentages may not add to total.

[2] Violent crimes are offenses of murder, forcible rape, robbery, and aggravated assault.

[3] Property crimes are offenses of burglary, larceny–theft, motor vehicle theft, and arson.

[4] Includes arson.

Table 47. — City Arrests of Persons under 15, 18, 21, and 25 Years of Age, 1996

[6,917 agencies; estimated population 132,725,000]

Offense charged	Total all ages	Number of persons arrested				Percent of total all ages			
		Under 15	Under 18	Under 21	Under 25	Under 15	Under 18	Under 21	Under 25
TOTAL	8,665,120	580,687	1,766,971	2,921,619	4,036,543	6.7	20.4	33.7	46.6
Murder and nonnegligent manslaughter	11,386	215	1,868	4,365	6,704	1.9	16.4	38.3	58.9
Forcible rape	18,602	1,131	3,255	5,609	8,109	6.1	17.5	30.2	43.6
Robbery	108,840	9,798	35,638	56,539	70,537	9.0	32.7	51.9	64.8
Aggravated assault	306,949	15,078	47,164	82,924	126,034	4.9	15.4	27.0	41.1
Burglary	196,436	28,311	72,426	101,710	121,658	14.4	36.9	51.8	61.9
Larceny–theft	936,989	138,136	324,023	446,508	535,124	14.7	34.6	47.7	57.1
Motor vehicle theft	107,127	11,913	45,094	63,768	75,446	11.1	42.1	59.5	70.4
Arson	10,452	4,011	5,874	6,750	7,443	38.4	56.2	64.6	71.2
Violent crime[1]	445,777	26,222	87,925	149,437	211,384	5.9	19.7	33.5	47.4
Property crime[2]	1,251,004	182,371	447,417	618,736	739,671	14.6	35.8	49.5	59.1
Crime Index total[3]	1,696,781	208,593	535,342	768,173	951,055	12.3	31.6	45.3	56.1
Other assaults	756,522	58,122	138,753	213,223	313,360	7.7	18.3	28.2	41.4
Forgery and counterfeiting	68,273	654	5,206	15,261	26,595	1.0	7.6	22.4	39.0
Fraud	190,335	5,219	16,896	38,612	68,075	2.7	8.9	20.3	35.8
Embezzlement	8,903	48	835	2,613	4,234	.5	9.4	29.3	47.6
Stolen property; buying, receiving, possessing	89,704	7,117	25,709	42,715	54,670	7.9	28.7	47.6	60.9
Vandalism	188,637	38,456	83,889	109,681	129,459	20.4	44.5	58.1	68.6
Weapons; carrying, possessing, etc.	131,030	9,980	33,464	57,143	77,367	7.6	25.5	43.6	59.0
Prostitution and commercialized vice	77,427	123	1,030	6,361	16,421	.2	1.3	8.2	21.2
Sex offenses (except forcible rape and prostitution)	53,666	4,884	9,553	14,113	19,711	9.1	17.8	26.3	36.7
Drug abuse violations	906,626	22,559	133,868	282,746	413,892	2.5	14.8	31.2	45.7
Gambling	15,781	272	2,148	4,388	6,341	1.7	13.6	27.8	40.2
Offenses against family and children	60,007	1,546	4,678	9,629	17,256	2.6	7.8	16.0	28.8
Driving under the influence	619,273	262	8,412	51,792	142,219	[4]	1.4	8.4	23.0
Liquor laws	402,602	9,814	85,859	231,340	268,060	2.4	21.3	57.5	66.6
Drunkenness	435,346	2,088	14,622	48,040	101,050	.5	3.4	11.0	23.2
Disorderly conduct	557,596	48,524	144,373	226,629	306,301	8.7	25.9	40.6	54.9
Vagrancy	20,016	511	2,520	5,624	8,005	2.6	12.6	28.1	40.0
All other offenses (except traffic)	2,138,529	77,899	274,507	547,616	866,031	3.6	12.8	25.6	40.5
Suspicion	4,138	370	1,379	1,992	2,513	8.9	33.3	48.1	60.7
Curfew and loitering law violations	134,737	37,186	134,737	134,737	134,737	27.6	100.0	100.0	100.0
Runaways	109,191	46,460	109,191	109,191	109,191	42.5	100.0	100.0	100.0

[1] Violent crimes are offenses of murder, forcible rape, robbery, and aggravated assault.

[2] Property crimes are offenses of burglary, larceny–theft, motor vehicle theft, and arson.

[3] Includes arson.

[4] Less than one-tenth of 1 percent.

Table 48. — City Arrests, Distribution by Sex, 1996

[6,917 agencies; 1996 estimated population 132,725,000]

Offense charged	Number of persons arrested			Percent male	Percent female	Percent distribution[1]		
	Total	Male	Female			Total	Male	Female
TOTAL	**8,665,120**	**6,864,722**	**1,800,398**	**79.2**	**20.8**	**100.0**	**100.0**	**100.0**
Murder and nonnegligent manslaughter	11,386	10,295	1,091	90.4	9.6	.1	.1	.1
Forcible rape	18,602	18,395	207	98.9	1.1	.2	.3	[2]
Robbery	108,840	98,080	10,760	90.1	9.9	1.3	1.4	.6
Aggravated assault	306,949	250,457	56,492	81.6	18.4	3.5	3.6	3.1
Burglary	196,436	173,129	23,307	88.1	11.9	2.3	2.5	1.3
Larceny–theft	936,989	614,957	322,032	65.6	34.4	10.8	9.0	17.9
Motor vehicle theft	107,127	92,780	14,347	86.6	13.4	1.2	1.4	.8
Arson	10,452	8,859	1,593	84.8	15.2	.1	.1	.1
Violent crime[3]	445,777	377,227	68,550	84.6	15.4	5.1	5.5	3.8
Property crime[4]	1,251,004	889,725	361,279	71.1	28.9	14.4	13.0	20.1
Crime Index total[5]	1,696,781	1,266,952	429,829	74.7	25.3	19.6	18.5	23.9
Other assaults	756,522	602,732	153,790	79.7	20.3	8.7	8.8	8.5
Forgery and counterfeiting	68,273	44,444	23,829	65.1	34.9	.8	.6	1.3
Fraud	190,335	119,748	70,587	62.9	37.1	2.2	1.7	3.9
Embezzlement	8,903	4,830	4,073	54.3	45.7	.1	.1	.2
Stolen property; buying, receiving, possessing	89,704	76,487	13,217	85.3	14.7	1.0	1.1	.7
Vandalism	188,637	162,238	26,399	86.0	14.0	2.2	2.4	1.5
Weapons; carrying, possessing, etc.	131,030	120,642	10,388	92.1	7.9	1.5	1.8	.6
Prostitution and commercialized vice	77,427	30,155	47,272	38.9	61.1	.9	.4	2.6
Sex offenses (except forcible rape and prostitution)	53,666	48,960	4,706	91.2	8.8	.6	.7	.3
Drug abuse violations	906,626	756,339	150,287	83.4	16.6	10.5	11.0	8.3
Gambling	15,781	13,621	2,160	86.3	13.7	.2	.2	.1
Offenses against family and children	60,007	42,198	17,809	70.3	29.7	.7	.6	1.0
Driving under the influence	619,273	523,361	95,912	84.5	15.5	7.1	7.6	5.3
Liquor laws	402,602	326,426	76,176	81.1	18.9	4.6	4.8	4.2
Drunkenness	435,346	382,473	52,873	87.9	12.1	5.0	5.6	2.9
Disorderly conduct	557,596	440,506	117,090	79.0	21.0	6.4	6.4	6.5
Vagrancy	20,016	16,002	4,014	79.9	20.1	.2	.2	.2
All other offenses (except traffic)	2,138,529	1,741,561	396,968	81.4	18.6	24.7	25.4	22.0
Suspicion	4,138	3,274	864	79.1	20.9	[2]	[2]	[2]
Curfew and loitering law violations	134,737	95,288	39,449	70.7	29.3	1.6	1.4	2.2
Runaways	109,191	46,485	62,706	42.6	57.4	1.3	.7	3.5

[1] Because of rounding, the percentages may not add to total.

[2] Less than one-tenth of 1 percent.

[3] Violent crimes are offenses of murder, forcible rape, robbery, and aggravated assault.

[4] Property crimes are offenses of burglary, larceny–theft, motor vehicle theft, and arson.

[5] Includes arson.

240

Table 49. — City Arrests, Distribution by Race, 1996

[6,913 agencies; 1996 estimated population 132,693,000]

Offense charged	Total arrests					Percent distribution[1]				
	Total	White	Black	American Indian or Alaskan Native	Asian or Pacific Islander	Total	White	Black	American Indian or Alaskan Native	Asian or Pacific Islander
TOTAL	8,650,628	5,546,450	2,893,226	104,614	106,338	100.0	64.1	33.4	1.2	1.2
Murder and nonnegligent manslaughter	11,379	4,184	6,937	64	194	100.0	36.8	61.0	.6	1.7
Forcible rape	18,591	9,524	8,645	167	255	100.0	51.2	46.5	.9	1.4
Robbery	108,756	41,999	64,562	546	1,649	100.0	38.6	59.4	.5	1.5
Aggravated assault	306,673	173,051	126,705	2,615	4,302	100.0	56.4	41.3	.9	1.4
Burglary	196,184	125,328	66,398	1,714	2,744	100.0	63.9	33.8	.9	1.4
Larceny–theft	935,126	598,079	307,796	12,173	17,078	100.0	64.0	32.9	1.3	1.8
Motor vehicle theft	107,045	56,605	46,832	1,174	2,434	100.0	52.9	43.7	1.1	2.3
Arson	10,442	7,383	2,847	100	112	100.0	70.7	27.3	1.0	1.1
Violent crime[2]	445,399	228,758	206,849	3,392	6,400	100.0	51.4	46.4	.8	1.4
Property crime[3]	1,248,797	787,395	423,873	15,161	22,368	100.0	63.1	33.9	1.2	1.8
Crime Index total[4]	1,694,196	1,016,153	630,722	18,553	28,768	100.0	60.0	37.2	1.1	1.7
Other assaults	755,643	445,043	291,142	10,004	9,454	100.0	58.9	38.5	1.3	1.3
Forgery and counterfeiting	68,010	42,564	23,701	382	1,363	100.0	62.6	34.8	.6	2.0
Fraud	190,019	111,447	75,571	826	2,175	100.0	58.7	39.8	.4	1.1
Embezzlement	8,889	5,439	3,267	47	136	100.0	61.2	36.8	.5	1.5
Stolen property; buying, receiving, possessing	89,545	48,714	38,948	628	1,255	100.0	54.4	43.5	.7	1.4
Vandalism	188,441	132,548	50,888	2,484	2,521	100.0	70.3	27.0	1.3	1.3
Weapons; carrying, possessing, etc.	130,925	71,884	56,664	785	1,592	100.0	54.9	43.3	.6	1.2
Prostitution and commercialized vice	77,421	45,166	30,158	518	1,579	100.0	58.3	39.0	.7	2.0
Sex offenses (except forcible rape and prostitution)	53,624	38,112	14,192	528	792	100.0	71.1	26.5	1.0	1.5
Drug abuse violations	905,454	514,299	381,389	3,884	5,882	100.0	56.8	42.1	.4	.6
Gambling	15,781	6,953	8,263	54	511	100.0	44.1	52.4	.3	3.2
Offenses against family and children	59,727	39,488	17,932	742	1,565	100.0	66.1	30.0	1.2	2.6
Driving under the influence	617,834	533,893	67,112	10,066	6,763	100.0	86.4	10.9	1.6	1.1
Liquor laws	400,765	315,058	72,903	10,015	2,789	100.0	78.6	18.2	2.5	.7
Drunkenness	434,690	347,015	75,532	10,510	1,633	100.0	79.8	17.4	2.4	.4
Disorderly conduct	556,685	336,222	210,103	6,646	3,714	100.0	60.4	37.7	1.2	.7
Vagrancy	20,002	10,610	8,914	403	75	100.0	53.0	44.6	2.0	.4
All other offenses (except traffic)	2,135,336	1,303,304	780,109	24,868	27,055	100.0	61.0	36.5	1.2	1.3
Suspicion	4,123	2,700	1,393	12	18	100.0	65.5	33.8	.3	.4
Curfew and loitering law violations	134,440	97,227	34,004	1,402	1,807	100.0	72.3	25.3	1.0	1.3
Runaways	109,078	82,611	20,319	1,257	4,891	100.0	75.7	18.6	1.2	4.5

See footnotes at end of table.

Table 49. — City Arrests, Distribution by Race, 1996 — Continued

Offense charged	Arrests under 18					Percent distribution[1]				
	Total	White	Black	American Indian or Alaskan Native	Asian or Pacific Islander	Total	White	Black	American Indian or Alaskan Native	Asian or Pacific Islander
TOTAL	1,763,863	1,195,749	514,714	20,042	33,358	100.0	67.8	29.2	1.1	1.9
Murder and nonnegligent manslaughter	1,867	677	1,125	9	56	100.0	36.3	60.3	.5	3.0
Forcible rape	3,252	1,629	1,570	24	29	100.0	50.1	48.3	.7	.9
Robbery	35,618	13,781	20,900	174	763	100.0	38.7	58.7	.5	2.1
Aggravated assault	47,116	26,112	19,832	422	750	100.0	55.4	42.1	.9	1.6
Burglary	72,310	50,878	19,386	804	1,242	100.0	70.4	26.8	1.1	1.7
Larceny–theft	323,263	226,723	83,879	4,794	7,867	100.0	70.1	25.9	1.5	2.4
Motor vehicle theft	45,056	24,443	18,707	615	1,291	100.0	54.3	41.5	1.4	2.9
Arson	5,867	4,572	1,160	63	72	100.0	77.9	19.8	1.1	1.2
Violent crime[2]	87,853	42,199	43,427	629	1,598	100.0	48.0	49.4	.7	1.8
Property crime[3]	446,496	306,616	123,132	6,276	10,472	100.0	68.7	27.6	1.4	2.3
Crime Index total[4]	534,349	348,815	166,559	6,905	12,070	100.0	65.3	31.2	1.3	2.3
Other assaults	138,561	83,268	51,579	1,461	2,253	100.0	60.1	37.2	1.1	1.6
Forgery and counterfeiting	5,193	3,939	1,116	56	82	100.0	75.9	21.5	1.1	1.6
Fraud	16,891	8,548	7,677	74	592	100.0	50.6	45.5	.4	3.5
Embezzlement	834	511	310	2	11	100.0	61.3	37.2	.2	1.3
Stolen property; buying, receiving, possessing	25,654	14,795	10,125	254	480	100.0	57.7	39.5	1.0	1.9
Vandalism	83,795	65,244	16,214	993	1,344	100.0	77.9	19.3	1.2	1.6
Weapons; carrying, possessing, etc.	33,436	20,642	12,018	239	537	100.0	61.7	35.9	.7	1.6
Prostitution and commercialized vice	1,030	591	399	23	17	100.0	57.4	38.7	2.2	1.7
Sex offenses (except forcible rape and prostitution)	9,542	6,290	3,071	61	120	100.0	65.9	32.2	.6	1.3
Drug abuse violations	133,639	79,334	52,303	849	1,153	100.0	59.4	39.1	.6	.9
Gambling	2,148	266	1,873	1	8	100.0	12.4	87.2	5	.4
Offenses against family and children	4,640	3,352	1,122	34	132	100.0	72.2	24.2	.7	2.8
Driving under the influence	8,379	7,605	532	171	71	100.0	90.8	6.3	2.0	.8
Liquor laws	85,516	76,801	5,578	2,337	800	100.0	89.8	6.5	2.7	.9
Drunkenness	14,609	12,801	1,414	296	98	100.0	87.6	9.7	2.0	.7
Disorderly conduct	144,252	89,590	52,287	1,115	1,260	100.0	62.1	36.2	.8	.9
Vagrancy	2,516	1,527	956	10	23	100.0	60.7	38.0	.4	.9
All other offenses (except traffic)	273,982	190,968	74,914	2,500	5,600	100.0	69.7	27.3	.9	2.0
Suspicion	1,379	1,024	344	2	9	100.0	74.3	24.9	.1	.7
Curfew and loitering law violations	134,440	97,227	34,004	1,402	1,807	100.0	72.3	25.3	1.0	1.3
Runaways	109,078	82,611	20,319	1,257	4,891	100.0	75.7	18.6	1.2	4.5

See footnotes at end of table.

Table 49. — City Arrests, Distribution by Race, 1996 — Continued

Offense charged	Arrests 18 and over					Percent distribution[1]				
	Total	White	Black	American Indian or Alaskan Native	Asian or Pacific Islander	Total	White	Black	American Indian or Alaskan Native	Asian or Pacific Islander
TOTAL	6,886,765	4,350,701	2,378,512	84,572	72,980	100.0	63.2	34.5	1.2	1.1
Murder and nonnegligent manslaughter	9,512	3,507	5,812	55	138	100.0	36.9	61.1	.6	1.5
Forcible rape	15,339	7,895	7,075	143	226	100.0	51.5	46.1	.9	1.5
Robbery	73,138	28,218	43,662	372	886	100.0	38.6	59.7	.5	1.2
Aggravated assault	259,557	146,939	106,873	2,193	3,552	100.0	56.6	41.2	.8	1.4
Burglary	123,874	74,450	47,012	910	1,502	100.0	60.1	38.0	.7	1.2
Larceny–theft	611,863	371,356	223,917	7,379	9,211	100.0	60.7	36.6	1.2	1.5
Motor vehicle theft	61,989	32,162	28,125	559	1,143	100.0	51.9	45.4	.9	1.8
Arson	4,575	2,811	1,687	37	40	100.0	61.4	36.9	.8	.9
Violent crime[2]	357,546	186,559	163,422	2,763	4,802	100.0	52.2	45.7	.8	1.3
Property crime[3]	802,301	480,779	300,741	8,885	11,896	100.0	59.9	37.5	1.1	1.5
Crime Index total[4]	1,159,847	667,338	464,163	11,648	16,698	100.0	57.5	40.0	1.0	1.4
Other assaults	617,082	361,775	239,563	8,543	7,201	100.0	58.6	38.8	1.4	1.2
Forgery and counterfeiting	62,817	38,625	22,585	326	1,281	100.0	61.5	36.0	.5	2.0
Fraud	173,128	102,899	67,894	752	1,583	100.0	59.4	39.2	.4	.9
Embezzlement	8,055	4,928	2,957	45	125	100.0	61.2	36.7	.6	1.6
Stolen property; buying, receiving, possessing	63,891	33,919	28,823	374	775	100.0	53.1	45.1	.6	1.2
Vandalism	104,646	67,304	34,674	1,491	1,177	100.0	64.3	33.1	1.4	1.1
Weapons; carrying, possessing, etc.	97,489	51,242	44,646	546	1,055	100.0	52.6	45.8	.6	1.1
Prostitution and commercialized vice	76,391	44,575	29,759	495	1,562	100.0	58.4	39.0	.6	2.0
Sex offenses (except forcible rape and prostitution)	44,082	31,822	11,121	467	672	100.0	72.2	25.2	1.1	1.5
Drug abuse violations	771,815	434,965	329,086	3,035	4,729	100.0	56.4	42.6	.4	.6
Gambling	13,633	6,687	6,390	53	503	100.0	49.1	46.9	.4	3.7
Offenses against family and children	55,087	36,136	16,810	708	1,433	100.0	65.6	30.5	1.3	2.6
Driving under the influence	609,455	526,288	66,580	9,895	6,692	100.0	86.4	10.9	1.6	1.1
Liquor laws	315,249	238,257	67,325	7,678	1,989	100.0	75.6	21.4	2.4	.6
Drunkenness	420,081	334,214	74,118	10,214	1,535	100.0	79.6	17.6	2.4	.4
Disorderly conduct	412,433	246,632	157,816	5,531	2,454	100.0	59.8	38.3	1.3	.6
Vagrancy	17,486	9,083	7,958	393	52	100.0	51.9	45.5	2.2	.3
All other offenses (except traffic)	1,861,354	1,112,336	705,195	22,368	21,455	100.0	59.8	37.9	1.2	1.2
Suspicion	2,744	1,676	1,049	10	9	100.0	61.1	38.2	.4	.3
Curfew and loitering law violations	—	—	—	—	—	—	—	—	—	—
Runaways	—	—	—	—	—	—	—	—	—	—

[1] Because of rounding, the percentages may not add to total.
[2] Violent crimes are offenses of murder, forcible rape, robbery, and aggravated assault.
[3] Property crimes are offenses of burglary, larceny–theft, motor vehicle theft, and arson.
[4] Includes arson.
[5] Less than one-tenth of 1 percent.

Table 50. — Suburban County Arrest Trends, 1995-1996

[774 agencies; 1996 estimated population 34,676,000; 1995 estimated population 34,280,000]

Offense charged	Number of persons arrested								
	Total all ages			Under 18 years of age			18 years of age and over		
	1995	1996	Percent change	1995	1996	Percent change	1995	1996	Percent change
TOTAL	1,390,935	1,434,115	+3.1	197,141	213,114	+8.1	1,193,794	1,221,001	+2.3
Murder and nonnegligent manslaughter	1,934	1,863	-3.7	259	197	-23.9	1,675	1,666	-.5
Forcible rape	3,287	3,267	-.6	475	506	+6.5	2,812	2,761	-1.8
Robbery	9,948	9,777	-1.7	2,685	2,727	+1.6	7,263	7,050	-2.9
Aggravated assault	53,834	53,353	-.9	6,674	6,880	+3.1	47,160	46,473	-1.5
Burglary	38,227	38,445	+.6	13,599	14,243	+4.7	24,628	24,202	-1.7
Larceny–theft	102,861	105,316	+2.4	30,540	31,647	+3.6	72,321	73,669	+1.9
Motor vehicle theft	18,152	16,862	-7.1	6,966	6,451	-7.4	11,186	10,411	-6.9
Arson	2,037	1,910	-6.2	966	924	-4.3	1,071	986	-7.9
Violent crime[1]	69,003	68,260	-1.1	10,093	10,310	+2.2	58,910	57,950	-1.6
Property crime[2]	161,277	162,533	+.8	52,071	53,265	+2.3	109,206	109,268	+.1
Crime Index total[3]	230,280	230,793	+.2	62,164	63,575	+2.3	168,116	167,218	-.5
Other assaults	120,701	127,024	+5.2	19,401	21,691	+11.8	101,300	105,333	+4.0
Forgery and counterfeiting	11,270	11,762	+4.4	683	592	-13.3	10,587	11,170	+5.5
Fraud	64,294	65,888	+2.5	838	1,007	+20.2	63,456	64,881	+2.2
Embezzlement	1,629	1,715	+5.3	80	97	+21.3	1,549	1,618	+4.5
Stolen property; buying, receiving, possessing	15,755	14,075	-10.7	3,317	3,079	-7.2	12,438	10,996	-11.6
Vandalism	27,316	26,860	-1.7	12,132	12,034	-.8	15,184	14,826	-2.4
Weapons; carrying, possessing, etc.	21,864	19,241	-12.0	4,264	4,195	-1.6	17,600	15,046	-14.5
Prostitution and commercialized vice	3,579	3,124	-12.7	41	54	+31.7	3,538	3,070	-13.2
Sex offenses (except forcible rape and prostitution)	10,211	10,434	+2.2	1,725	1,827	+5.9	8,486	8,607	+1.4
Drug abuse violations	140,227	143,428	+2.3	15,120	16,489	+9.1	125,107	126,939	+1.5
Gambling	999	678	-32.1	47	41	-12.8	952	637	-33.1
Offenses against family and children	31,287	30,253	-3.3	473	696	+47.1	30,814	29,557	-4.1
Driving under the influence	206,227	211,399	+2.5	1,671	2,013	+20.5	204,556	209,386	+2.4
Liquor laws	35,676	43,355	+21.5	9,966	13,430	+34.8	25,710	29,925	+16.4
Drunkenness	50,801	52,861	+4.1	1,297	1,667	+28.5	49,504	51,194	+3.4
Disorderly conduct	35,255	36,084	+2.4	8,108	9,256	+14.2	27,147	26,828	-1.2
Vagrancy	790	923	+16.8	153	217	+41.8	637	706	+10.8
All other offenses (except traffic)	357,762	377,123	+5.4	30,649	34,059	+11.1	327,113	343,064	+4.9
Suspicion (not included in totals)	258	410	+58.9	80	175	+118.8	178	235	+32.0
Curfew and loitering law violations	3,980	5,326	+33.8	3,980	5,326	+33.8	—	—	—
Runaways	21,032	21,769	+3.5	21,032	21,769	+3.5	—	—	—

[1] Violent crimes are offenses of murder, forcible rape, robbery, and aggravated assault.

[2] Property crimes are offenses of burglary, larceny–theft, motor vehicle theft, and arson.

[3] Includes arson.

Table 51. — Suburban County Arrest Trends, Sex, 1995-1996

[774 agencies; 1996 estimated population 34,676,000; 1995 estimated population 34,280,000]

Offense charged	Males						Females					
	Total			Under 18			Total			Under 18		
	1995	1996	Percent change	1995	1996	Percent change	1995	1996	Percent change	1995	1996	Percent change
TOTAL	1,117,935	1,145,180	+2.4	149,320	160,296	+7.4	273,000	288,935	+5.8	47,821	52,818	+10.4
Murder and nonnegligent manslaughter ...	1,731	1,627	-6.0	232	175	-24.6	203	236	+16.3	27	22	-18.5
Forcible rape	3,239	3,225	-.4	466	496	+6.4	48	42	-12.5	9	10	+11.1
Robbery	9,078	8,935	-1.6	2,469	2,503	+1.4	870	842	-3.2	216	224	+3.7
Aggravated assault	45,569	44,831	-1.6	5,522	5,627	+1.9	8,265	8,522	+3.1	1,152	1,253	+8.8
Burglary	34,070	34,596	+1.5	12,278	12,971	+5.6	4,157	3,849	-7.4	1,321	1,272	-3.7
Larceny–theft	70,910	71,724	+1.1	21,970	22,501	+2.4	31,951	33,592	+5.1	8,570	9,146	+6.7
Motor vehicle theft	15,748	14,593	-7.3	5,905	5,472	-7.3	2,404	2,269	-5.6	1,061	979	-7.7
Arson	1,745	1,637	-6.2	844	825	-2.3	292	273	-6.5	122	99	-18.9
Violent crime[1]	59,617	58,618	-1.7	8,689	8,801	+1.3	9,386	9,642	+2.7	1,404	1,509	+7.5
Property crime[2]	122,473	122,550	+.1	40,997	41,769	+1.9	38,804	39,983	+3.0	11,074	11,496	+3.8
Crime Index total[3]	182,090	181,168	-.5	49,686	50,570	+1.8	48,190	49,625	+3.0	12,478	13,005	+4.2
Other assaults	96,912	100,781	+4.0	14,373	16,030	+11.5	23,789	26,243	+10.3	5,028	5,661	+12.6
Forgery and counterfeiting	7,168	7,401	+3.3	480	398	-17.1	4,102	4,361	+6.3	203	194	-4.4
Fraud	34,224	33,793	-1.3	536	674	+25.7	30,070	32,095	+6.7	302	333	+10.3
Embezzlement	998	984	-1.4	48	51	+6.3	631	731	+15.8	32	46	+43.8
Stolen property; buying, receiving, possessing	13,602	12,108	-11.0	2,924	2,712	-7.3	2,153	1,967	-8.6	393	367	-6.6
Vandalism	23,926	23,369	-2.3	11,046	10,735	-2.8	3,390	3,491	+3.0	1,086	1,299	+19.6
Weapons; carrying, possessing, etc.	20,103	17,746	-11.7	3,933	3,878	-1.4	1,761	1,495	-15.1	331	317	-4.2
Prostitution and commercialized vice	2,343	1,945	-17.0	27	37	+37.0	1,236	1,179	-4.6	14	17	+21.4
Sex offenses (except forcible rape and prostitution)	9,597	9,768	+1.8	1,619	1,698	+4.9	614	666	+8.5	106	129	+21.7
Drug abuse violations	115,465	117,957	+2.2	12,881	14,065	+9.2	24,762	25,471	+2.9	2,239	2,424	+8.3
Gambling	850	575	-32.4	46	36	-21.7	149	103	-30.9	1	5	+400.0
Offenses against family and children	28,173	26,918	-4.5	287	478	+66.6	3,114	3,335	+7.1	186	218	+17.2
Driving under the influence	178,631	182,404	+2.1	1,411	1,691	+19.8	27,596	28,995	+5.1	260	322	+23.8
Liquor laws	27,924	33,820	+21.1	6,971	9,342	+34.0	7,752	9,535	+23.0	2,995	4,088	+36.5
Drunkenness	44,722	46,548	+4.1	1,076	1,380	+28.3	6,079	6,313	+3.8	221	287	+29.9
Disorderly conduct	27,716	27,825	+.4	6,099	6,887	+12.9	7,539	8,259	+9.6	2,009	2,369	+17.9
Vagrancy	683	744	+8.9	136	160	+17.6	107	179	+67.3	17	57	+235.3
All other offenses (except traffic)	290,848	305,866	+5.2	23,781	26,014	+9.4	66,914	71,257	+6.5	6,868	8,045	+17.1
Suspicion (not included in totals)	221	358	+62.0	67	157	+134.3	37	52	+40.5	13	18	+38.5
Curfew and loitering law violations	2,793	3,797	+35.9	2,793	3,797	+35.9	1,187	1,529	+28.8	1,187	1,529	+28.8
Runaways	9,167	9,663	+5.4	9,167	9,663	+5.4	11,865	12,106	+2.0	11,865	12,106	+2.0

[1] Violent crimes are offenses of murder, forcible rape, robbery, and aggravated assault.

[2] Property crimes are offenses of burglary, larceny–theft, motor vehicle theft, and arson.

[3] Includes arson.

245

Table 52. — Suburban County Arrests, Distribution by Age, 1996

[913 agencies; 1996 estimated population 37,056,000]

Offense charged	Total all ages	Ages under 15	Ages under 18	Ages 18 and over	Age									
					Under 10	10-12	13-14	15	16	17	18	19	20	21
TOTAL	1,559,089	70,334	231,865	1,327,224	3,482	15,384	51,468	45,602	56,437	59,492	67,722	65,798	58,800	55,701
Percent distribution[1]	100.0	4.5	14.9	85.1	.2	1.0	3.3	2.9	3.6	3.8	4.3	4.2	3.8	3.6
Murder and nonnegligent manslaughter	1,963	24	204	1,759	1	2	21	39	63	78	151	143	98	108
Forcible rape	3,599	188	581	3,018	7	43	138	116	111	166	197	165	136	141
Robbery	10,558	653	2,919	7,639	11	113	529	533	831	902	988	792	581	517
Aggravated assault	56,613	2,353	7,329	49,284	172	592	1,589	1,370	1,645	1,961	2,088	2,067	1,872	1,884
Burglary	41,348	5,262	15,528	25,820	328	1,253	3,681	3,265	3,442	3,559	3,647	2,657	1,978	1,512
Larceny–theft	118,419	13,202	35,392	83,027	555	3,262	9,385	6,610	7,768	7,812	7,300	6,042	4,417	3,749
Motor vehicle theft	17,851	1,773	6,811	11,040	19	187	1,567	1,695	1,823	1,520	1,306	1,009	777	655
Arson	2,067	629	987	1,080	108	202	319	136	113	109	95	68	49	57
Violent crime[2]	72,733	3,218	11,033	61,700	191	750	2,277	2,058	2,650	3,107	3,424	3,167	2,687	2,650
Percent distribution[1]	100.0	4.4	15.2	84.8	.3	1.0	3.1	2.8	3.6	4.3	4.7	4.4	3.7	3.6
Property crime[3]	179,685	20,866	58,718	120,967	1,010	4,904	14,952	11,706	13,146	13,000	12,348	9,776	7,221	5,973
Percent distribution[1]	100.0	11.6	32.7	67.3	.6	2.7	8.3	6.5	7.3	7.2	6.9	5.4	4.0	3.3
Crime Index total[4]	252,418	24,084	69,751	182,667	1,201	5,654	17,229	13,764	15,796	16,107	15,772	12,943	9,908	8,623
Percent distribution[1]	100.0	9.5	27.6	72.4	.5	2.2	6.8	5.5	6.3	6.4	6.2	5.1	3.9	3.4
Other assaults	139,627	9,098	23,530	116,097	505	2,531	6,062	4,494	5,037	4,901	4,347	4,064	3,941	4,101
Forgery and counterfeiting	13,473	65	673	12,800	3	10	52	89	198	321	613	594	581	544
Fraud	83,092	158	1,233	81,859	13	16	129	169	328	578	1,573	2,619	3,046	3,615
Embezzlement	1,782	13	102	1680	—	2	11	6	30	53	89	89	73	72
Stolen property; buying, receiving, possessing	15,288	750	3,343	11,945	12	119	619	685	905	1,003	1,211	1,000	866	652
Vandalism	28,813	5,350	12,817	15,996	560	1,524	3,266	2,221	2,658	2,588	1,963	1,374	928	851
Weapons; carrying, possessing, etc.	20,509	1,330	4,520	15,989	61	315	954	875	1,064	1,251	1,311	1,140	907	900
Prostitution and commercialized vice	3,389	11	56	3,333	—	1	10	6	19	20	48	66	83	87
Sex offenses (except forcible rape and prostitution)	11,296	959	1,982	9,314	74	261	624	330	325	368	377	330	306	264
Drug abuse violations	153,318	3,023	17,818	135,500	26	367	2,630	3,101	4,839	6,855	9,511	8,782	7,389	6,713
Gambling	728	13	58	670	1	1	11	8	18	19	21	17	16	24
Offenses against family and children	32,206	237	801	31,405	21	56	160	181	185	198	400	527	619	692
Driving under the influence ...	221,172	40	2,120	219,052	4	6	30	84	551	1,445	3,581	4,790	5,472	7,700
Liquor laws	47,508	1,268	14,590	32,918	16	107	1,145	2,163	4,416	6,743	8,419	7,391	5,327	1,185
Drunkenness	54,659	248	1,755	52,904	7	33	208	285	461	761	1,712	1,755	1,528	1,883
Disorderly conduct	40,863	3,516	10,210	30,653	144	880	2,492	2,102	2,396	2,196	1,951	1,618	1,382	1,396
Vagrancy	1,248	80	244	1,004	2	7	71	42	64	58	66	68	45	35
All other offenses (except traffic)	408,460	10,228	37,282	371,178	633	2,077	7,518	7,234	9,288	10,532	14,752	16,622	16,368	16,357
Suspicion	445	58	185	260	7	10	41	43	43	41	5	9	15	7
Curfew and loitering law violations	5,806	1,542	5,806	—	19	202	1,321	1,315	1,676	1,273	—	—	—	—
Runaways	22,989	8,263	22,989	—	173	1,205	6,885	6,405	6,140	2,181	—	—	—	—

See footnotes at end of table.

246

Table 52. — Suburban County Arrests, Distribution by Age, 1996 — Continued

Offense charged	Age											
---	22	23	24	25-29	30-34	35-39	40-44	45-49	50-54	55-59	60-64	65 and over
TOTAL	51,837	51,679	52,093	236,247	230,036	194,610	122,972	69,482	33,727	17,453	9,280	9,787
Percent distribution[1]	3.3	3.3	3.3	15.2	14.8	12.5	7.9	4.5	2.2	1.1	.6	.6
Murder and nonnegligent manslaughter	108	74	74	278	211	166	124	85	53	33	19	34
Forcible rape	112	120	122	486	498	426	289	151	66	47	28	34
Robbery	400	329	299	1,330	1,081	700	356	173	58	15	11	9
Aggravated assault	1,749	1,821	1,754	8,578	8,927	7,659	4,982	2,848	1,397	731	417	510
Burglary	1,295	1,052	982	4,071	3,538	2,637	1,317	638	250	121	51	74
Larceny–theft	3,299	2,986	2,901	13,824	13,052	10,922	6,670	3,812	1,821	1,007	489	736
Motor vehicle theft	513	474	465	1,989	1,537	1,169	603	289	138	54	28	34
Arson	49	31	30	140	167	154	97	63	26	24	13	17
Violent crime[2]	2,369	2,344	2,249	10,672	10,717	8,951	5,751	3,257	1,574	826	475	587
Percent distribution[1]	3.3	3.2	3.1	14.7	14.7	12.3	7.9	4.5	2.2	1.1	.7	.8
Property crime[3]	5,156	4,543	4,378	20,024	18,294	14,882	8,687	4,802	2,235	1,206	581	861
Percent distribution[1]	2.9	2.5	2.4	11.1	10.2	8.3	4.8	2.7	1.2	.7	.3	.5
Crime Index total[4]	7,525	6,887	6,627	30,696	29,011	23,833	14,438	8,059	3,809	2,032	1,056	1,448
Percent distribution[1]	3.0	2.7	2.6	12.2	11.5	9.4	5.7	3.2	1.5	.8	.4	.6
Other assaults	3,848	3,993	4,351	20,695	22,373	19,281	11,643	6,553	3,272	1,657	944	1,034
Forgery and counterfeiting	586	574	625	2,608	2,363	1,769	1,016	533	210	90	54	40
Fraud	3,713	3,753	3,730	16,880	14,851	12,202	7,588	4,245	2,101	983	448	512
Embezzlement	87	78	66	297	298	216	146	78	48	19	20	4
Stolen property; buying, receiving, possessing	530	535	447	2,035	1,857	1,355	750	380	147	90	38	52
Vandalism	713	661	578	2,561	2,362	1,815	1,022	571	287	154	68	88
Weapons; carrying, possessing, etc.	782	754	689	2,634	2,259	1,831	1,146	737	414	231	121	133
Prostitution and commercialized vice	90	99	109	560	714	589	373	210	127	81	40	57
Sex offenses (except forcible rape and prostitution)	266	236	291	1,366	1,540	1,420	998	698	452	280	221	269
Drug abuse violations	5,894	5,747	5,620	24,039	22,832	19,099	11,050	5,266	1,972	807	428	351
Gambling	14	11	16	79	74	70	69	65	60	56	40	38
Offenses against family and children	799	975	1,102	5,894	7,068	6,031	3,884	1,966	825	350	175	98
Driving under the influence	7,960	8,388	8,579	39,665	39,011	34,543	24,525	15,814	8,865	4,994	2,665	2,500
Liquor laws	833	698	586	2,255	1,968	1,645	1,170	665	342	211	113	110
Drunkenness	1,770	1,780	1,716	7,899	8,969	8,843	6,468	4,175	2,032	1,088	666	620
Disorderly conduct	1,285	1,114	1,207	4,989	4,976	4,449	2,813	1,645	851	437	263	277
Vagrancy	28	35	24	164	164	162	114	52	24	13	5	5
All other offenses (except traffic)	15,102	15,344	15,722	70,882	67,289	55,422	33,744	17,757	7,880	3,874	1,912	2,151
Suspicion	12	17	8	49	57	35	15	13	9	6	3	—
Curfew and loitering law violations	—	—	—	—	—	—	—	—	—	—	—	—
Runaways	—	—	—	—	—	—	—	—	—	—	—	—

[1] Because of rounding, the percentages may not add to total.
[2] Violent crimes are offenses of murder, forcible rape, robbery, and aggravated assault.
[3] Property crimes are offenses of burglary, larceny–theft, motor vehicle theft, and arson.
[4] Includes arson.

Table 53. — Suburban County Arrests of Persons under 15, 18, 21, and 25 Years of Age, 1996

[913 agencies; 1996 estimated population 37,056,000]

Offense charged	Total all ages	Number of persons arrested				Percent of total all ages			
		Under 15	Under 18	Under 21	Under 25	Under 15	Under 18	Under 21	Under 25
TOTAL	1,559,089	70,334	231,865	424,185	635,495	4.5	14.9	27.2	40.8
Murder and nonnegligent manslaughter	1,963	24	204	596	960	1.2	10.4	30.4	48.9
Forcible rape	3,599	188	581	1,079	1,574	5.2	16.1	30.0	43.7
Robbery	10,558	653	2,919	5,280	6,825	6.2	27.6	50.0	64.6
Aggravated assault	56,613	2,353	7,329	13,356	20,564	4.2	12.9	23.6	36.3
Burglary	41,348	5,262	15,528	23,810	28,651	12.7	37.6	57.6	69.3
Larceny–theft	118,419	13,202	35,392	53,151	66,086	11.1	29.9	44.9	55.8
Motor vehicle theft	17,851	1,773	6,811	9,903	12,010	9.9	38.2	55.5	67.3
Arson	2,067	629	987	1,199	1,366	30.4	47.8	58.0	66.1
Violent crime[1]	72,733	3,218	11,033	20,311	29,923	4.4	15.2	27.9	41.1
Property crime[2]	179,685	20,866	58,718	88,063	108,113	11.6	32.7	49.0	60.2
Crime Index total[3]	252,418	24,084	69,751	108,374	138,036	9.5	27.6	42.9	54.7
Other assaults	139,627	9,098	23,530	35,882	52,175	6.5	16.9	25.7	37.4
Forgery and counterfeiting	13,473	65	673	2,461	4,790	.5	5.0	18.3	35.6
Fraud	83,092	158	1,233	8,471	23,282	.2	1.5	10.2	28.0
Embezzlement	1,782	13	102	353	656	.7	5.7	19.8	36.8
Stolen property; buying, receiving, possessing	15,288	750	3,343	6,420	8,584	4.9	21.9	42.0	56.1
Vandalism	28,813	5,350	12,817	17,082	19,885	18.6	44.5	59.3	69.0
Weapons; carrying, possessing, etc.	20,509	1,330	4,520	7,878	11,003	6.5	22.0	38.4	53.6
Prostitution and commercialized vice	3,389	11	56	253	638	.3	1.7	7.5	18.8
Sex offenses (except forcible rape and prostitution)	11,296	959	1,982	2,995	4,052	8.5	17.5	26.5	35.9
Drug abuse violations	153,318	3,023	17,818	43,500	67,474	2.0	11.6	28.4	44.0
Gambling	728	13	58	112	177	1.8	8.0	15.4	24.3
Offenses against family and children	32,206	237	801	2,347	5,915	.7	2.5	7.3	18.4
Driving under the influence	221,172	40	2,120	15,963	48,590	[4]	1.0	7.2	22.0
Liquor laws	47,508	1,268	14,590	35,727	39,029	2.7	30.7	75.2	82.2
Drunkenness	54,659	248	1,755	6,750	13,899	.5	3.2	12.3	25.4
Disorderly conduct	40,863	3,516	10,210	15,161	20,163	8.6	25.0	37.1	49.3
Vagrancy	1,248	80	244	423	545	6.4	19.6	33.9	43.7
All other offenses (except traffic)	408,460	10,228	37,282	85,024	147,549	2.5	9.1	20.8	36.1
Suspicion	445	58	185	214	258	13.0	41.6	48.1	58.0
Curfew and loitering law violations	5,806	1,542	5,806	5,806	5,806	26.6	100.0	100.0	100.0
Runaways	22,989	8,263	22,989	22,989	22,989	35.9	100.0	100.0	100.0

[1] Violent crimes are offenses of murder, forcible rape, robbery, and aggravated assault.

[2] Property crimes are offenses of burglary, larceny–theft, motor vehicle theft, and arson.

[3] Includes arson.

[4] Less than one-tenth of 1 percent.

Table 54. — Suburban County Arrests, Distribution by Sex, 1996

[913 agencies; 1996 estimated population 37,056,000]

Offense charged	Number of persons arrested			Percent male	Percent female	Percent distribution[1]		
	Total	Male	Female			Total	Male	Female
TOTAL	**1,559,089**	**1,240,370**	**318,719**	**79.6**	**20.4**	**100.0**	**100.0**	**100.0**
Murder and nonnegligent manslaughter	1,963	1,714	249	87.3	12.7	.1	.1	.1
Forcible rape	3,599	3,549	50	98.6	1.4	.2	.3	[2]
Robbery	10,558	9,650	908	91.4	8.6	.7	.8	.3
Aggravated assault	56,613	47,512	9,101	83.9	16.1	3.6	3.8	2.9
Burglary	41,348	37,255	4,093	90.1	9.9	2.7	3.0	1.3
Larceny–theft	118,419	79,913	38,506	67.5	32.5	7.6	6.4	12.1
Motor vehicle theft	17,851	15,463	2,388	86.6	13.4	1.1	1.2	.7
Arson	2,067	1,771	296	85.7	14.3	.1	.1	.1
Violent crime[3]	72,733	62,425	10,308	85.8	14.2	4.7	5.0	3.2
Property crime[4]	179,685	134,402	45,283	74.8	25.2	11.5	10.8	14.2
Crime Index total[5]	252,418	196,827	55,591	78.0	22.0	16.2	15.9	17.4
Other assaults	139,627	110,797	28,830	79.4	20.6	9.0	8.9	9.0
Forgery and counterfeiting	13,473	8,432	5,041	62.6	37.4	.9	.7	1.6
Fraud	83,092	43,295	39,797	52.1	47.9	5.3	3.5	12.5
Embezzlement	1,782	1,032	750	57.9	42.1	.1	.1	.2
Stolen property; buying, receiving, possessing	15,288	13,157	2,131	86.1	13.9	1.0	1.1	.7
Vandalism	28,813	25,079	3,734	87.0	13.0	1.8	2.0	1.2
Weapons; carrying, possessing, etc.	20,509	18,903	1,606	92.2	7.8	1.3	1.5	.5
Prostitution and commercialized vice	3,389	2,150	1,239	63.4	36.6	.2	.2	.4
Sex offenses (except forcible rape and prostitution)	11,296	10,585	711	93.7	6.3	.7	.9	.2
Drug abuse violations	153,318	126,165	27,153	82.3	17.7	9.8	10.2	8.5
Gambling	728	622	106	85.4	14.6	[2]	.1	[2]
Offenses against family and children	32,206	28,602	3,604	88.8	11.2	2.1	2.3	1.1
Driving under the influence	221,172	190,816	30,356	86.3	13.7	14.2	15.4	9.5
Liquor laws	47,508	37,109	10,399	78.1	21.9	3.0	3.0	3.3
Drunkenness	54,659	48,119	6,540	88.0	12.0	3.5	3.9	2.1
Disorderly conduct	40,863	31,598	9,265	77.3	22.7	2.6	2.5	2.9
Vagrancy	1,248	975	273	78.1	21.9	.1	.1	.1
All other offenses (except traffic)	408,460	331,434	77,026	81.1	18.9	26.2	26.7	24.2
Suspicion	445	388	57	87.2	12.8	[2]	[2]	[2]
Curfew and loitering law violations	5,806	4,128	1,678	71.1	28.9	.4	.3	.5
Runaways	22,989	10,157	12,832	44.2	55.8	1.5	.8	4.0

[1] Because of rounding, the percentages may not add to total.

[2] Less than one-tenth of 1 percent.

[3] Violent crimes are offenses of murder, forcible rape, robbery, and aggravated assault.

[4] Property crimes are offenses of burglary, larceny–theft, motor vehicle theft, and arson.

[5] Includes arson.

Table 55. — Suburban County Arrests, Distribution by Race, 1996

[913 agencies; 1996 estimated population 37,056,000]

Offense charged	Total arrests					Percent distribution[1]				
	Total	White	Black	American Indian or Alaskan Native	Asian or Pacific Islander	Total	White	Black	American Indian or Alaskan Native	Asian or Pacific Islander
TOTAL	1,554,260	1,173,706	363,141	8,774	8,639	100.0	75.5	23.4	.6	.6
Murder and nonnegligent manslaughter	1,963	1,333	593	23	14	100.0	67.9	30.2	1.2	.7
Forcible rape	3,581	2,540	1,000	26	15	100.0	70.9	27.9	.7	.4
Robbery	10,535	5,295	5,123	45	72	100.0	50.3	48.6	.4	.7
Aggravated assault	56,446	41,083	14,525	387	451	100.0	72.8	25.7	.7	.8
Burglary	41,212	32,532	8,185	209	286	100.0	78.9	19.9	.5	.7
Larceny–theft	118,024	79,367	36,716	616	1,325	100.0	67.2	31.1	.5	1.1
Motor vehicle theft	17,810	12,240	5,381	78	111	100.0	68.7	30.2	.4	.6
Arson	2,058	1,746	281	15	16	100.0	84.8	13.7	.7	.8
Violent crime[2]	72,525	50,251	21,241	481	552	100.0	69.3	29.3	.7	.8
Property crime[3]	179,104	125,885	50,563	918	1,738	100.0	70.3	28.2	.5	1.0
Crime Index total[4]	251,629	176,136	71,804	1,399	2,290	100.0	70.0	28.5	.6	.9
Other assaults	138,852	102,951	34,266	954	681	100.0	74.1	24.7	.7	.5
Forgery and counterfeiting	13,453	9,033	4,264	50	106	100.0	67.1	31.7	.4	.8
Fraud	82,768	55,854	26,423	221	270	100.0	67.5	31.9	.3	.3
Embezzlement	1,781	1,139	624	6	12	100.0	64.0	35.0	.3	.7
Stolen property; buying, receiving, possessing	15,232	10,619	4,402	93	118	100.0	69.7	28.9	.6	.8
Vandalism	28,754	24,439	3,938	195	182	100.0	85.0	13.7	.7	.6
Weapons; carrying, possessing, etc.	20,477	14,283	5,915	82	197	100.0	69.8	28.9	.4	1.0
Prostitution and commercialized vice	3,381	2,473	862	9	37	100.0	73.1	25.5	.3	1.1
Sex offenses (except forcible rape and prostitution)	11,266	9,222	1,908	62	74	100.0	81.9	16.9	.6	.7
Drug abuse violations	153,033	113,240	38,742	520	531	100.0	74.0	25.3	.3	.3
Gambling	726	443	250	7	26	100.0	61.0	34.4	1.0	3.6
Offenses against family and children	31,660	19,373	12,166	52	69	100.0	61.2	38.4	.2	.2
Driving under the influence	220,402	199,679	18,296	1,194	1,233	100.0	90.6	8.3	.5	.6
Liquor laws	47,441	43,144	3,569	457	271	100.0	90.9	7.5	1.0	.6
Drunkenness	54,640	47,845	5,938	558	299	100.0	87.6	10.9	1.0	.5
Disorderly conduct	40,759	31,352	8,824	387	196	100.0	76.9	21.6	.9	.5
Vagrancy	1,246	821	411	11	3	100.0	65.9	33.0	.9	.2
All other offenses (except traffic)	407,527	286,289	117,077	2,304	1,857	100.0	70.3	28.7	.6	.5
Suspicion	445	361	42	40	2	100.0	81.1	9.4	9.0	.4
Curfew and loitering law violations	5,806	5,063	676	29	38	100.0	87.2	11.6	.5	.7
Runaways	22,982	19,947	2,744	144	147	100.0	86.8	11.9	.6	.6

See footnotes at end of table.

Table 55. — Suburban County Arrests, Distribution by Race, 1996 — Continued

Offense charged	Arrests under 18					Percent distribution[1]				
	Total	White	Black	American Indian or Alaskan Native	Asian or Pacific Islander	Total	White	Black	American Indian or Alaskan Native	Asian or Pacific Islander
TOTAL	231,425	180,281	47,725	1,499	1,920	100.0	77.9	20.6	.6	.8
Murder and nonnegligent manslaughter	204	117	84	1	2	100.0	57.4	41.2	.5	1.0
Forcible rape	579	407	167	2	3	100.0	70.3	28.8	.3	.5
Robbery	2,914	1,430	1,451	7	26	100.0	49.1	49.8	.2	.9
Aggravated assault	7,278	4,982	2,175	53	68	100.0	68.5	29.9	.7	.9
Burglary	15,476	12,624	2,617	82	153	100.0	81.6	16.9	.5	1.0
Larceny–theft	35,330	25,048	9,554	231	497	100.0	70.9	27.0	.7	1.4
Motor vehicle theft	6,793	4,716	1,962	43	72	100.0	69.4	28.9	.6	1.1
Arson	981	870	93	10	8	100.0	88.7	9.5	1.0	.8
Violent crime[2]	10,975	6,936	3,877	63	99	100.0	63.2	35.3	.6	.9
Property crime[3]	58,580	43,258	14,226	366	730	100.0	73.8	24.3	.6	1.2
Crime Index total[4]	69,555	50,194	18,103	429	829	100.0	72.2	26.0	.6	1.2
Other assaults	23,477	16,739	6,425	164	149	100.0	71.3	27.4	.7	.6
Forgery and counterfeiting	673	554	106	5	8	100.0	82.3	15.8	.7	1.2
Fraud	1,230	801	419	3	7	100.0	65.1	34.1	.2	.6
Embezzlement	102	70	31	—	1	100.0	68.6	30.4	—	1.0
Stolen property; buying, receiving, possessing	3,341	2,454	827	23	37	100.0	73.5	24.8	.7	1.1
Vandalism	12,788	11,198	1,413	87	90	100.0	87.6	11.0	.7	.7
Weapons; carrying, possessing, etc.	4,517	3,207	1,212	29	69	100.0	71.0	26.8	.6	1.5
Prostitution and commercialized vice	56	44	11	1	—	100.0	78.6	19.6	1.8	—
Sex offenses (except forcible rape and prostitution)	1,977	1,589	376	8	4	100.0	80.4	19.0	.4	.2
Drug abuse violations	17,769	13,676	3,949	70	74	100.0	77.0	22.2	.4	.4
Gambling	58	17	39	—	2	100.0	29.3	67.2	—	3.4
Offenses against family and children	785	681	93	5	6	100.0	86.8	11.8	.6	.8
Driving under the influence	2,115	2,010	90	6	9	100.0	95.0	4.3	.3	.4
Liquor laws	14,577	13,849	543	109	76	100.0	95.0	3.7	.7	.5
Drunkenness	1,755	1,613	117	15	10	100.0	91.9	6.7	.9	.6
Disorderly conduct	10,204	7,221	2,799	127	57	100.0	70.8	27.4	1.2	.6
Vagrancy	244	201	35	8	—	100.0	82.4	14.3	3.3	—
All other offenses (except traffic)	37,229	28,986	7,702	234	307	100.0	77.9	20.7	.6	.8
Suspicion	185	167	15	3	—	100.0	90.3	8.1	1.6	—
Curfew and loitering law violations	5,806	5,063	676	29	38	100.0	87.2	11.6	.5	.7
Runaways	22,982	19,947	2,744	144	147	100.0	86.8	11.9	.6	.6

See footnotes at end of table.

Table 55. — Suburban County Arrests, Distribution by Race, 1996 — Continued

Offense charged	Arrests 18 and over					Percent distribution[1]				
	Total	White	Black	American Indian or Alaskan Native	Asian or Pacific Islander	Total	White	Black	American Indian or Alaskan Native	Asian or Pacific Islander
TOTAL	**1,322,835**	**993,425**	**315,416**	**7,275**	**6,719**	**100.0**	**75.1**	**23.8**	**.5**	**.5**
Murder and nonnegligent manslaughter	1,759	1,216	509	22	12	100.0	69.1	28.9	1.3	.7
Forcible rape	3,002	2,133	833	24	12	100.0	71.1	27.7	.8	.4
Robbery	7,621	3,865	3,672	38	46	100.0	50.7	48.2	.5	.6
Aggravated assault	49,168	36,101	12,350	334	383	100.0	73.4	25.1	.7	.8
Burglary	25,736	19,908	5,568	127	133	100.0	77.4	21.6	.5	.5
Larceny–theft	82,694	54,319	27,162	385	828	100.0	65.7	32.8	.5	1.0
Motor vehicle theft	11,017	7,524	3,419	35	39	100.0	68.3	31.0	.3	.4
Arson	1,077	876	188	5	8	100.0	81.3	17.5	.5	.7
Violent crime[2]	61,550	43,315	17,364	418	453	100.0	70.4	28.2	.7	.7
Property crime[3]	120,524	82,627	36,337	552	1,008	100.0	68.6	30.1	.5	.8
Crime Index total[4]	182,074	125,942	53,701	970	1,461	100.0	69.2	29.5	.5	.8
Other assaults	115,375	86,212	27,841	790	532	100.0	74.7	24.1	.7	.5
Forgery and counterfeiting	12,780	8,479	4,158	45	98	100.0	66.3	32.5	.4	.8
Fraud	81,538	55,053	26,004	218	263	100.0	67.5	31.9	.3	.3
Embezzlement	1,679	1,069	593	6	11	100.0	63.7	35.3	.4	.7
Stolen property; buying, receiving, possessing	11,891	8,165	3,575	70	81	100.0	68.7	30.1	.6	.7
Vandalism	15,966	13,241	2,525	108	92	100.0	82.9	15.8	.7	.6
Weapons; carrying, possessing, etc.	15,960	11,076	4,703	53	128	100.0	69.4	29.5	.3	.8
Prostitution and commercialized vice	3,325	2,429	851	8	37	100.0	73.1	25.6	.2	1.1
Sex offenses (except forcible rape and prostitution)	9,289	7,633	1,532	54	70	100.0	82.2	16.5	.6	.8
Drug abuse violations	135,264	99,564	34,793	450	457	100.0	73.6	25.7	.3	.3
Gambling	668	426	211	7	24	100.0	63.8	31.6	1.0	3.6
Offenses against family and children	30,875	18,692	12,073	47	63	100.0	60.5	39.1	.2	.2
Driving under the influence	218,287	197,669	18,206	1,188	1,224	100.0	90.6	8.3	.5	.6
Liquor laws	32,864	29,295	3,026	348	195	100.0	89.1	9.2	1.1	.6
Drunkenness	52,885	46,232	5,821	543	289	100.0	87.4	11.0	1.0	.5
Disorderly conduct	30,555	24,131	6,025	260	139	100.0	79.0	19.7	.9	.5
Vagrancy	1,002	620	376	3	3	100.0	61.9	37.5	.3	.3
All other offenses (except traffic)	370,298	257,303	109,375	2,070	1,550	100.0	69.5	29.5	.6	.4
Suspicion	260	194	27	37	2	100.0	74.6	10.4	14.2	.8
Curfew and loitering law violations	—	—	—	—	—	—	—	—	—	—
Runaways	—	—	—	—	—	—	—	—	—	—

[1] Because of rounding, the percentages may not add to total.

[2] Violent crimes are offenses of murder, forcible rape, robbery, and aggravated assault.

[3] Property crimes are offenses of burglary, larceny–theft, motor vehicle theft, and arson.

[4] Includes arson.

252

Table 56. — Rural County Arrest Trends, 1995-1996

[1,619 agencies; 1996 estimated population 17,963,000; 1995 estimated population 17,805,000]

Offense charged	Number of persons arrested								
	Total all ages			Under 18 years of age			18 years of age and over		
	1995	1996	Percent change	1995	1996	Percent change	1995	1996	Percent change
TOTAL	**769,202**	**796,046**	**+3.5**	**90,855**	**94,150**	**+3.6**	**678,347**	**701,896**	**+3.5**
Murder and nonnegligent manslaughter	1,133	1,007	-11.1	111	93	-16.2	1,022	914	-10.6
Forcible rape	1,946	1,903	-2.2	271	257	-5.2	1,675	1,646	-1.7
Robbery	2,261	2,112	-6.6	457	444	-2.8	1,804	1,668	-7.5
Aggravated assault	22,831	21,768	-4.7	2,196	2,159	-1.7	20,635	19,609	-5.0
Burglary	23,779	23,791	+.1	8,540	9,005	+5.4	15,239	14,786	-3.0
Larceny–theft	37,082	36,440	-1.7	10,123	10,005	-1.2	26,959	26,435	-1.9
Motor vehicle theft	7,163	6,471	-9.7	2,955	2,691	-8.9	4,208	3,780	-10.2
Arson	1,183	1,130	-4.5	373	411	+10.2	810	719	-11.2
Violent crime[1]	28,171	26,790	-4.9	3,035	2,953	-2.7	25,136	23,837	-5.2
Property crime[2]	69,207	67,832	-2.0	21,991	22,112	+.6	47,216	45,720	-3.2
Crime Index total[3]	97,378	94,622	-2.8	25,026	25,065	+.2	72,352	69,557	-3.9
Other assaults	68,073	69,443	+2.0	7,503	8,159	+8.7	60,570	61,284	+1.2
Forgery and counterfeiting	6,136	5,693	-7.2	345	320	-7.2	5,791	5,373	-7.2
Fraud	44,482	49,086	+10.4	833	696	-16.4	43,649	48,390	+10.9
Embezzlement	640	721	+12.7	23	18	-21.7	617	703	+13.9
Stolen property; buying, receiving, possessing	5,887	5,366	-8.9	1,061	1,031	-2.8	4,826	4,335	-10.2
Vandalism	15,718	15,400	-2.0	6,358	6,032	-5.1	9,360	9,368	+.1
Weapons; carrying, possessing, etc.	10,220	8,936	-12.6	1,384	1,284	-7.2	8,836	7,652	-13.4
Prostitution and commercialized vice	231	180	-22.1	10	11	+10.0	221	169	-23.5
Sex offenses (except forcible rape and prostitution)	5,079	5,113	+.7	930	1,027	+10.4	4,149	4,086	-1.5
Drug abuse violations	60,186	62,187	+3.3	5,441	6,111	+12.3	54,745	56,076	+2.4
Gambling	529	335	-36.7	22	15	-31.8	507	320	-36.9
Offenses against family and children	9,565	9,772	+2.2	249	319	+28.1	9,316	9,453	+1.5
Driving under the influence	150,381	162,876	+8.3	1,676	2,177	+29.9	148,705	160,699	+8.1
Liquor laws	34,054	37,297	+9.5	9,572	10,771	+12.5	24,482	26,526	+8.3
Drunkenness	31,344	30,362	-3.1	694	698	+.6	30,650	29,664	-3.2
Disorderly conduct	25,404	25,309	-.4	4,430	4,584	+3.5	20,974	20,725	-1.2
Vagrancy	385	455	+18.2	69	99	+43.5	316	356	+12.7
All other offenses (except traffic)	193,145	202,927	+5.1	14,864	15,767	+6.1	178,281	187,160	+5.0
Suspicion (not included in totals)	250	217	-13.2	48	39	-18.8	202	178	-11.9
Curfew and loitering law violations	1,511	1,666	+10.3	1,511	1,666	+10.3	—	—	—
Runaways	8,854	8,300	-6.3	8,854	8,300	-6.3	—	—	—

[1] Violent crimes are offenses of murder, forcible rape, robbery, and aggravated assault.

[2] Property crimes are offenses of burglary, larceny–theft, motor vehicle theft, and arson.

[3] Includes arson.

Table 57. — Rural County Arrest Trends, Sex, 1995-1996

[1,619 agencies; 1996 estimated population 17,963,000; 1995 estimated population 17,805,000]

Offense charged	Males						Females					
	Total			Under 18			Total			Under 18		
	1995	1996	Percent change	1995	1996	Percent change	1995	1996	Percent change	1995	1996	Percent change
TOTAL	622,244	639,112	+2.7	69,412	70,832	+2.0	146,958	156,934	+6.8	21,443	23,318	+8.7
Murder and nonnegligent manslaughter ...	965	876	-9.2	97	89	-8.2	168	131	-22.0	14	4	-71.4
Forcible rape	1,913	1,884	-1.5	264	255	-3.4	33	19	-42.4	7	2	-71.4
Robbery	2,062	1,932	-6.3	415	419	+1.0	199	180	-9.5	42	25	-40.5
Aggravated assault	19,331	18,369	-5.0	1,816	1,805	-.6	3,500	3,399	-2.9	380	354	-6.8
Burglary	21,502	21,463	-.2	7,780	8,122	+4.4	2,277	2,328	+2.2	760	883	+16.2
Larceny–theft	28,610	27,708	-3.2	8,254	7,896	-4.3	8,472	8,732	+3.1	1,869	2,109	+12.8
Motor vehicle theft	6,067	5,397	-11.0	2,405	2,093	-13.0	1,096	1,074	-2.0	550	598	+8.7
Arson	1,012	986	-2.6	328	370	+12.8	171	144	-15.8	45	41	-8.9
Violent crime[1]	24,271	23,061	-5.0	2,592	2,568	-.9	3,900	3,729	-4.4	443	385	-13.1
Property crime[2]	57,191	55,554	-2.9	18,767	18,481	-1.5	12,016	12,278	+2.2	3,224	3,631	+12.6
Crime Index total[3]	81,462	78,615	-3.5	21,359	21,049	-1.5	15,916	16,007	+.6	3,667	4,016	+9.5
Other assaults	55,222	55,641	+.8	5,543	5,916	+6.7	12,851	13,802	+7.4	1,960	2,243	+14.4
Forgery and counterfeiting	3,814	3,562	-6.6	229	211	-7.9	2,322	2,131	-8.2	116	109	-6.0
Fraud	23,123	25,026	+8.2	440	424	-3.6	21,359	24,060	+12.6	393	272	-30.8
Embezzlement	357	439	+23.0	13	9	-30.8	283	282	-.4	10	9	-10.0
Stolen property; buying, receiving, possessing	5,026	4,628	-7.9	910	870	-4.4	861	738	-14.3	151	161	+6.6
Vandalism	13,571	13,351	-1.6	5,702	5,395	-5.4	2,147	2,049	-4.6	656	637	-2.9
Weapons; carrying, possessing, etc.	9,502	8,305	-12.6	1,292	1,205	-6.7	718	631	-12.1	92	79	-14.1
Prostitution and commercialized vice	131	112	-14.5	2	4	+100.0	100	68	-32.0	8	7	-12.5
Sex offenses (except forcible rape and prostitution)	4,842	4,871	+.6	860	941	+9.4	237	242	+2.1	70	86	+22.9
Drug abuse violations	50,325	51,853	+3.0	4,567	5,113	+12.0	9,861	10,334	+4.8	874	998	+14.2
Gambling	443	282	-36.3	18	14	-22.2	86	53	-38.4	4	1	-75.0
Offenses against family and children	8,080	8,218	+1.7	184	218	+18.5	1,485	1,554	+4.6	65	101	+55.4
Driving under the influence	130,248	140,874	+8.2	1,436	1,824	+27.0	20,133	22,002	+9.3	240	353	+47.1
Liquor laws	26,703	28,957	+8.4	6,524	7,270	+11.4	7,351	8,340	+13.5	3,048	3,501	+14.9
Drunkenness	27,522	26,562	-3.5	593	574	-3.2	3,822	3,800	-.6	101	124	+22.8
Disorderly conduct	20,141	19,811	-1.6	3,312	3,395	+2.5	5,263	5,498	+4.5	1,118	1,189	+6.4
Vagrancy	325	373	+14.8	53	75	+41.5	60	82	+36.7	16	24	+50.0
All other offenses (except traffic)	156,503	163,211	+4.3	11,471	11,904	+3.8	36,642	39,716	+8.4	3,393	3,863	+13.9
Suspicion (not included in totals)	206	181	-12.1	33	34	+3.0	44	36	-18.2	15	5	-66.7
Curfew and loitering law violations	991	1,046	+5.5	991	1,046	+5.5	520	620	+19.2	520	620	+19.2
Runaways	3,913	3,375	-13.7	3,913	3,375	-13.7	4,941	4,925	-.3	4,941	4,925	-.3

[1] Violent crimes are offenses of murder, forcible rape, robbery, and aggravated assault.

[2] Property crimes are offenses of burglary, larceny–theft, motor vehicle theft, and arson.

[3] Includes arson.

Table 58. — Rural County Arrests, Distribution by Age, 1996

[1,836 agencies; 1996 estimated population 20,146,000]

Offense charged	Total all ages	Ages under 15	Ages under 18	Ages 18 and over	Under 10	10-12	13-14	15	16	17	18	19	20	21
TOTAL	869,002	28,428	104,822	764,180	1,641	6,224	20,563	18,801	26,506	31,087	41,344	40,004	36,286	32,371
Percent distribution[1]	100.0	3.3	12.1	87.9	.2	.7	2.4	2.2	3.1	3.6	4.8	4.6	4.2	3.7
Murder and nonnegligent manslaughter	1,098	18	100	998	3	2	13	10	27	45	69	52	56	57
Forcible rape	2,146	104	292	1,854	—	27	77	43	67	78	110	107	96	92
Robbery	2,383	74	480	1,903	2	9	63	75	133	198	242	174	159	122
Aggravated assault	24,009	691	2,401	21,608	45	156	490	373	634	703	1,075	914	887	853
Burglary	26,409	3,286	9,855	16,554	243	877	2,166	1,719	2,361	2,489	2,790	1,979	1,468	1,030
Larceny–theft	41,080	3,949	11,192	29,888	233	1,082	2,634	1,945	2,538	2,760	3,037	2,307	1,787	1,464
Motor vehicle theft	7,045	787	2,908	4,137	10	106	671	767	755	599	567	405	331	268
Arson	1,236	247	441	795	50	77	120	60	65	69	75	62	46	39
Violent crime[2]	29,636	887	3,273	26,363	50	194	643	501	861	1,024	1,496	1,247	1,198	1,124
Percent distribution[1]	100.0	3.0	11.0	89.0	.2	.7	2.2	1.7	2.9	3.5	5.0	4.2	4.0	3.8
Property crime[3]	75,770	8,269	24,396	51,374	536	2,142	5,591	4,491	5,719	5,917	6,469	4,753	3,632	2,801
Percent distribution[1]	100.0	10.9	32.2	67.8	.7	2.8	7.4	5.9	7.5	7.8	8.5	6.3	4.8	3.7
Crime Index total[4]	105,406	9,156	27,669	77,737	586	2,336	6,234	4,992	6,580	6,941	7,965	6,000	4,830	3,925
Percent distribution[1]	100.0	8.7	26.2	73.8	.6	2.2	5.9	4.7	6.2	6.6	7.6	5.7	4.6	3.7
Other assaults	76,835	3,056	9,083	67,752	170	739	2,147	1,639	2,161	2,227	2,683	2,486	2,446	2,564
Forgery and counterfeiting	6,609	36	359	6,250	4	3	29	50	87	186	350	325	310	299
Fraud	51,349	75	743	50,606	6	16	53	57	196	415	975	1,669	1,863	2,015
Embezzlement	764	2	21	743	—	1	1	4	8	7	25	17	17	27
Stolen property; buying, receiving, possessing	6,074	232	1,137	4,937	3	35	194	215	301	389	492	422	332	306
Vandalism	16,765	2,547	6,627	10,138	315	797	1,435	963	1,535	1,582	1,479	925	725	545
Weapons; carrying, possessing, etc.	9,619	374	1,379	8,240	41	89	244	234	354	417	465	440	370	384
Prostitution and commercialized vice	220	6	18	202	—	—	6	5	2	5	4	5	3	9
Sex offenses (except forcible rape and prostitution)	5,657	500	1,125	4,532	54	139	307	196	217	212	226	214	179	161
Drug abuse violations	68,703	1,123	6,761	61,942	17	165	941	1,060	1,827	2,751	4,308	4,315	3,719	3,224
Gambling	475	12	57	418	—	2	10	8	12	25	26	29	36	18
Offenses against family and children	11,587	96	371	11,216	8	17	71	72	89	114	229	243	272	362
Driving under the influence	173,487	39	2,282	171,205	8	3	28	82	657	1,504	3,278	4,094	4,458	5,775
Liquor laws	41,066	1,281	12,104	28,962	28	114	1,139	1,858	3,660	5,305	6,980	6,621	4,959	1,088
Drunkenness	32,864	78	734	32,130	7	10	61	95	180	381	1,040	986	949	1,210
Disorderly conduct	28,459	1,686	5,368	23,091	77	328	1,281	992	1,324	1,366	1,372	1,094	967	1,005
Vagrancy	471	31	109	362	—	7	24	35	25	18	32	21	15	12
All other offenses (except traffic)	220,762	4,113	17,281	203,481	244	841	3,028	3,102	4,392	5,674	9,406	10,086	9,832	9,436
Suspicion	276	8	40	236	1	1	6	4	13	15	9	12	4	6
Curfew and loitering law violations	1,890	587	1,890	—	13	106	468	493	459	351	—	—	—	—
Runaways	9,664	3,390	9,664	—	59	475	2,856	2,645	2,427	1,202	—	—	—	—

See footnotes at end of table.

255

Table 58. — Rural County Arrests, Distribution by Age, 1996 — Continued

Offense charged	22	23	24	25-29	30-34	35-39	40-44	45-49	50-54	55-59	60-64	65 and over
TOTAL	**30,230**	**28,993**	**29,439**	**127,885**	**125,140**	**108,421**	**72,097**	**42,597**	**22,295**	**12,263**	**7,080**	**7,735**
Percent distribution[1]	**3.5**	**3.3**	**3.4**	**14.7**	**14.4**	**12.5**	**8.3**	**4.9**	**2.6**	**1.4**	**.8**	**.9**
Murder and nonnegligent manslaughter	35	42	38	159	146	106	79	61	36	20	16	26
Forcible rape	82	57	72	320	290	282	137	81	51	29	28	20
Robbery	88	103	74	335	232	192	96	53	19	6	4	4
Aggravated assault	813	837	801	3,504	3,675	3,167	2,121	1,286	706	388	239	342
Burglary	821	789	681	2,375	1,927	1,340	750	349	140	53	33	29
Larceny–theft	1,174	1,217	1,161	4,789	4,394	3,505	2,269	1,234	667	361	219	303
Motor vehicle theft	196	179	161	674	524	412	214	117	55	18	8	8
Arson	40	29	33	89	103	100	76	46	26	15	10	6
Violent crime[2]	1,018	1,039	985	4,318	4,343	3,747	2,433	1,481	812	443	287	392
Percent distribution[1]	3.4	3.5	3.3	14.6	14.7	12.6	8.2	5.0	2.7	1.5	1.0	1.3
Property crime[3]	2,231	2,214	2,036	7,927	6,948	5,357	3,309	1,746	888	447	270	346
Percent distribution[1]	2.9	2.9	2.7	10.5	9.2	7.1	4.4	2.3	1.2	.6	.4	.5
Crime Index total[4]	3,249	3,253	3,021	12,245	11,291	9,104	5,742	3,227	1,700	890	557	738
Percent distribution[1]	3.1	3.1	2.9	11.6	10.7	8.6	5.4	3.1	1.6	.8	.5	.7
Other assaults	2,464	2,348	2,603	11,787	12,392	10,750	6,845	3,848	2,037	1,114	668	717
Forgery and counterfeiting	314	304	264	1,211	1,121	818	481	267	99	51	21	15
Fraud	2,201	2,246	2,272	10,208	8,990	7,399	4,962	2,895	1,441	704	368	398
Embezzlement	20	31	23	145	133	97	100	55	28	13	9	3
Stolen property; buying, receiving, possessing	229	262	208	808	666	528	341	177	74	40	31	21
Vandalism	493	368	378	1,493	1,309	1,054	641	319	176	95	59	79
Weapons; carrying, possessing, etc.	324	324	332	1,297	1,191	1,099	809	530	285	171	100	119
Prostitution and commercialized vice	6	2	4	36	32	31	20	17	10	9	2	12
Sex offenses (except forcible rape and prostitution)	130	120	132	615	661	672	452	343	224	147	102	154
Drug abuse violations	3,010	2,702	2,769	10,610	9,859	8,496	4,854	2,477	903	395	157	144
Gambling	10	7	5	45	42	41	54	30	30	22	9	14
Offenses against family and children	345	375	404	2,060	2,308	2,030	1,358	649	300	136	75	70
Driving under the influence	5,763	5,662	5,894	27,655	29,738	27,914	20,313	13,354	7,482	4,465	2,653	2,707
Liquor laws	757	605	545	1,939	1,700	1,408	943	618	302	212	148	137
Drunkenness	1,080	963	1,050	4,638	5,393	5,223	3,991	2,428	1,426	798	485	470
Disorderly conduct	877	875	849	3,681	3,878	3,471	2,225	1,284	684	356	210	263
Vagrancy	22	10	9	48	74	44	31	26	10	5	—	3
All other offenses (except traffic)	8,925	8,524	8,664	37,312	34,321	28,213	17,911	10,046	5,075	2,636	1,424	1,670
Suspicion	11	12	13	52	41	29	24	7	9	4	2	1
Curfew and loitering law violations	—	—	—	—	—	—	—	—	—	—	—	—
Runaways	—	—	—	—	—	—	—	—	—	—	—	—

[1] Because of rounding, the percentages may not add to total.

[2] Violent crimes are offenses of murder, forcible rape, robbery, and aggravated assault.

[3] Property crimes are offenses of burglary, larceny–theft, motor vehicle theft, and arson.

[4] Includes arson.

Table 59. — Rural County Arrests of Persons under 15, 18, 21, and 25 Years of Age, 1996

[1,836 agencies; 1996 estimated population 20,146,000]

Offense charged	Total all ages	Number of persons arrested				Percent of total all ages			
		Under 15	Under 18	Under 21	Under 25	Under 15	Under 18	Under 21	Under 25
TOTAL	869,002	28,428	104,822	222,456	343,489	3.3	12.1	25.6	39.5
Murder and nonnegligent manslaughter	1,098	18	100	277	449	1.6	9.1	25.2	40.9
Forcible rape	2,146	104	292	605	908	4.8	13.6	28.2	42.3
Robbery	2,383	74	480	1,055	1,442	3.1	20.1	44.3	60.5
Aggravated assault	24,009	691	2,401	5,277	8,581	2.9	10.0	22.0	35.7
Burglary	26,409	3,286	9,855	16,092	19,413	12.4	37.3	60.9	73.5
Larceny–theft	41,080	3,949	11,192	18,323	23,339	9.6	27.2	44.6	56.8
Motor vehicle theft	7,045	787	2,908	4,211	5,015	11.2	41.3	59.8	71.2
Arson	1,236	247	441	624	765	20.0	35.7	50.5	61.9
Violent crime[1]	29,636	887	3,273	7,214	11,380	3.0	11.0	24.3	38.4
Property crime[2]	75,770	8,269	24,396	39,250	48,532	10.9	32.2	51.8	64.1
Crime Index total[3]	105,406	9,156	27,669	46,464	59,912	8.7	26.2	44.1	56.8
Other assaults	76,835	3,056	9,083	16,698	26,677	4.0	11.8	21.7	34.7
Forgery and counterfeiting	6,609	36	359	1,344	2,525	.5	5.4	20.3	38.2
Fraud	51,349	75	743	5,250	13,984	.1	1.4	10.2	27.2
Embezzlement	764	2	21	80	181	.3	2.7	10.5	23.7
Stolen property; buying, receiving, possessing	6,074	232	1,137	2,383	3,388	3.8	18.7	39.2	55.8
Vandalism	16,765	2,547	6,627	9,756	11,540	15.2	39.5	58.2	68.8
Weapons; carrying, possessing, etc.	9,619	374	1,379	2,654	4,018	3.9	14.3	27.6	41.8
Prostitution and commercialized vice	220	6	18	30	51	2.7	8.2	13.6	23.2
Sex offenses (except forcible rape and prostitution)	5,657	500	1,125	1,744	2,287	8.8	19.9	30.8	40.4
Drug abuse violations	68,703	1,123	6,761	19,103	30,808	1.6	9.8	27.8	44.8
Gambling	475	12	57	148	188	2.5	12.0	31.2	39.6
Offenses against family and children	11,587	96	371	1,115	2,601	.8	3.2	9.6	22.4
Driving under the influence	173,487	39	2,282	14,112	37,206	[4]	1.3	8.1	21.4
Liquor laws	41,066	1,281	12,104	30,664	33,659	3.1	29.5	74.7	82.0
Drunkenness	32,864	78	734	3,709	8,012	.2	2.2	11.3	24.4
Disorderly conduct	28,459	1,686	5,368	8,801	12,407	5.9	18.9	30.9	43.6
Vagrancy	471	31	109	177	230	6.6	23.1	37.6	48.8
All other offenses (except traffic)	220,762	4,113	17,281	46,605	82,154	1.9	7.8	21.1	37.2
Suspicion	276	8	40	65	107	2.9	14.5	23.6	38.8
Curfew and loitering law violations	1,890	587	1,890	1,890	1,890	31.1	100.0	100.0	100.0
Runaways	9,664	3,390	9,664	9,664	9,664	35.1	100.0	100.0	100.0

[1] Violent crimes are offenses of murder, forcible rape, robbery, and aggravated assault.

[2] Property crimes are offenses of burglary, larceny–theft, motor vehicle theft, and arson.

[3] Includes arson.

[4] Less than one-tenth of 1 percent.

Table 60. — Rural County Arrests, Distribution by Sex, 1996

[1,836 agencies; 1996 estimated population 20,146,000]

Offense charged	Number of persons arrested			Percent male	Percent female	Percent distribution[1]		
	Total	Male	Female			Total	Male	Female
TOTAL	**869,002**	**698,200**	**170,802**	**80.3**	**19.7**	**100.0**	**100.0**	**100.0**
Murder and nonnegligent manslaughter	1,098	956	142	87.1	12.9	.1	.1	.1
Forcible rape	2,146	2,122	24	98.9	1.1	.3	.3	[2]
Robbery	2,383	2,182	201	91.6	8.4	.3	.3	.1
Aggravated assault	24,009	20,310	3,699	84.6	15.4	2.8	2.9	2.2
Burglary	26,409	23,824	2,585	90.2	9.8	3.0	3.4	1.5
Larceny–theft	41,080	31,136	9,944	75.8	24.2	4.7	4.5	5.8
Motor vehicle theft	7,045	5,882	1,163	83.5	16.5	.8	.8	.7
Arson	1,236	1,073	163	86.8	13.2	.1	.2	.1
Violent crime[3]	29,636	25,570	4,066	86.3	13.7	3.4	3.7	2.4
Property crime[4]	75,770	61,915	13,855	81.7	18.3	8.7	8.9	8.1
Crime Index total[5]	105,406	87,485	17,921	83.0	17.0	12.1	12.5	10.5
Other assaults	76,835	61,573	15,262	80.1	19.9	8.8	8.8	8.9
Forgery and counterfeiting	6,609	4,184	2,425	63.3	36.7	.8	.6	1.4
Fraud	51,349	26,331	25,018	51.3	48.7	5.9	3.8	14.6
Embezzlement	764	469	295	61.4	38.6	.1	.1	.2
Stolen property; buying, receiving, possessing	6,074	5,224	850	86.0	14.0	.7	.7	.5
Vandalism	16,765	14,540	2,225	86.7	13.3	1.9	2.1	1.3
Weapons; carrying, possessing, etc.	9,619	8,933	686	92.9	7.1	1.1	1.3	.4
Prostitution and commercialized vice	220	140	80	63.6	36.4	[2]	[2]	[2]
Sex offenses (except forcible rape and prostitution)	5,657	5,393	264	95.3	4.7	.7	.8	.2
Drug abuse violations	68,703	57,263	11,440	83.3	16.7	7.9	8.2	6.7
Gambling	475	405	70	85.3	14.7	.1	.1	[2]
Offenses against family and children	11,587	9,749	1,838	84.1	15.9	1.3	1.4	1.1
Driving under the influence	173,487	150,049	23,438	86.5	13.5	20.0	21.5	13.7
Liquor laws	41,066	31,911	9,155	77.7	22.3	4.7	4.6	5.4
Drunkenness	32,864	28,753	4,111	87.5	12.5	3.8	4.1	2.4
Disorderly conduct	28,459	22,277	6,182	78.3	21.7	3.3	3.2	3.6
Vagrancy	471	388	83	82.4	17.6	.1	.1	[2]
All other offenses (except traffic)	220,762	177,712	43,050	80.5	19.5	25.4	25.5	25.2
Suspicion	276	226	50	81.9	18.1	[2]	[2]	[2]
Curfew and loitering law violations	1,890	1,202	688	63.6	36.4	.2	.2	.4
Runaways	9,664	3,993	5,671	41.3	58.7	1.1	.6	3.3

[1] Because of rounding, the percentages may not add to total.

[2] Less than one-tenth of 1 percent.

[3] Violent crimes are offenses of murder, forcible rape, robbery, and aggravated assault.

[4] Property crimes are offenses of burglary, larceny–theft, motor vehicle theft, and arson.

[5] Includes arson.

Table 61. — Rural County Arrests, Distribution by Race, 1996

[1,835 agencies; 1996 estimated population 20,135,000]

Offense charged	Total arrests					Percent distribution[1]				
	Total	White	Black	American Indian or Alaskan Native	Asian or Pacific Islander	Total	White	Black	American Indian or Alaskan Native	Asian or Pacific Islander
TOTAL	867,944	684,014	143,971	25,902	14,057	100.0	78.8	16.6	3.0	1.6
Murder and nonnegligent manslaughter	1,097	659	398	32	8	100.0	60.1	36.3	2.9	.7
Forcible rape	2,145	1,573	479	73	20	100.0	73.3	22.3	3.4	.9
Robbery	2,382	1,118	1,143	60	61	100.0	46.9	48.0	2.5	2.6
Aggravated assault	23,971	16,651	6,233	927	160	100.0	69.5	26.0	3.9	.7
Burglary	26,378	21,203	3,890	930	355	100.0	80.4	14.7	3.5	1.3
Larceny–theft	41,036	31,663	7,481	918	974	100.0	77.2	18.2	2.2	2.4
Motor vehicle theft	7,037	5,773	809	327	128	100.0	82.0	11.5	4.6	1.8
Arson	1,239	1,046	169	17	7	100.0	84.4	13.6	1.4	.6
Violent crime[2]	29,595	20,001	8,253	1,092	249	100.0	67.6	27.9	3.7	.8
Property crime[3]	75,690	59,685	12,349	2,192	1,464	100.0	78.9	16.3	2.9	1.9
Crime Index total[4]	105,285	79,686	20,602	3,284	1,713	100.0	75.7	19.6	3.1	1.6
Other assaults	76,772	58,025	15,522	2,113	1,112	100.0	75.6	20.2	2.8	1.4
Forgery and counterfeiting	6,600	4,864	1,582	79	75	100.0	73.7	24.0	1.2	1.1
Fraud	51,334	36,753	13,986	423	172	100.0	71.6	27.2	.8	.3
Embezzlement	764	638	94	6	26	100.0	83.5	12.3	.8	3.4
Stolen property; buying, receiving, possession	6,057	4,560	1,297	149	51	100.0	75.3	21.4	2.5	.8
Vandalism	16,757	14,137	1,899	541	180	100.0	84.4	11.3	3.2	1.1
Weapons; carrying, possessing, etc.	9,614	7,263	1,955	285	111	100.0	75.5	20.3	3.0	1.2
Prostitution and commercialized vice	220	170	45	1	4	100.0	77.3	20.5	.5	1.8
Sex offenses (except forcible rape and prostitution)	5,656	4,802	591	201	62	100.0	84.9	10.4	3.6	1.1
Drug abuse violations	68,627	53,469	13,221	1,196	741	100.0	77.9	19.3	1.7	1.1
Gambling	475	315	75	5	80	100.0	66.3	15.8	1.1	16.8
Offenses against family and children	11,557	8,670	2,463	335	89	100.0	75.0	21.3	2.9	.8
Driving under the influence	173,234	142,986	19,385	5,607	5,256	100.0	82.5	11.2	3.2	3.0
Liquor laws	41,013	37,487	1,706	1,535	285	100.0	91.4	4.2	3.7	.7
Drunkenness	32,829	28,498	2,892	1,382	57	100.0	86.8	8.8	4.2	.2
Disorderly conduct	28,417	22,925	4,307	1,019	166	100.0	80.7	15.2	3.6	.6
Vagrancy	471	369	91	8	3	100.0	78.3	19.3	1.7	.6
All other offenses (except traffic)	220,448	168,590	41,568	7,257	3,033	100.0	76.5	18.9	3.3	1.4
Suspicion	275	211	57	4	3	100.0	76.7	20.7	1.5	1.1
Curfew and loitering law violations	1,889	1,374	76	224	215	100.0	72.7	4.0	11.9	11.4
Runaways	9,650	8,222	557	248	623	100.0	85.2	5.8	2.6	6.5

See footnotes at end of table.

259

Table 61. — Rural County Arrests, Distribution by Race, 1996 — Continued

Offense charged	Arrests under 18					Percent distribution[1]				
	Total	White	Black	American Indian or Alaskan Native	Asian or Pacific Islander	Total	White	Black	American Indian or Alaskan Native	Asian or Pacific Islander
TOTAL	**104,709**	**86,833**	**11,059**	**3,974**	**2,843**	**100.0**	**82.9**	**10.6**	**3.8**	**2.7**
Murder and nonnegligent manslaughter	100	55	39	4	2	100.0	55.0	39.0	4.0	2.0
Forcible rape	292	243	35	12	2	100.0	83.2	12.0	4.1	.7
Robbery	480	221	227	12	20	100.0	46.0	47.3	2.5	4.2
Aggravated assault	2,397	1,681	587	101	28	100.0	70.1	24.5	4.2	1.2
Burglary	9,848	8,383	858	419	188	100.0	85.1	8.7	4.3	1.9
Larceny–theft	11,178	9,201	1,089	346	542	100.0	82.3	9.7	3.1	4.8
Motor vehicle theft	2,906	2,488	207	157	54	100.0	85.6	7.1	5.4	1.9
Arson	441	394	37	8	2	100.0	89.3	8.4	1.8	.5
Violent crime[2]	3,269	2,200	888	129	52	100.0	67.3	27.2	3.9	1.6
Property crime[3]	24,373	20,466	2,191	930	786	100.0	84.0	9.0	3.8	3.2
Crime Index total[4]	27,642	22,666	3,079	1,059	838	100.0	82.0	11.1	3.8	3.0
Other assaults	9,073	6,608	1,902	317	246	100.0	72.8	21.0	3.5	2.7
Forgery and counterfeiting	359	336	20	2	1	100.0	93.6	5.6	.6	.3
Fraud	743	591	142	5	5	100.0	79.5	19.1	.7	.7
Embezzlement	21	18	3	—	—	100.0	85.7	14.3	—	—
Stolen property; buying, receiving, possessing	1,132	930	159	29	14	100.0	82.2	14.0	2.6	1.2
Vandalism	6,624	5,915	430	192	87	100.0	89.3	6.5	2.9	1.3
Weapons; carrying, possessing, etc.	1,378	1,028	250	88	12	100.0	74.6	18.1	6.4	.9
Prostitution and commercialized vice	18	15	2	1	—	100.0	83.3	11.1	5.6	—
Sex offenses (except forcible rape and prostitution)	1,125	933	142	43	7	100.0	82.9	12.6	3.8	.6
Drug abuse violations	6,753	5,386	969	174	224	100.0	79.8	14.3	2.6	3.3
Gambling	57	51	4	—	2	100.0	89.5	7.0	—	3.5
Offenses against family and children	371	311	38	11	11	100.0	83.8	10.2	3.0	3.0
Driving under the influence	2,281	2,036	103	74	68	100.0	89.3	4.5	3.2	3.0
Liquor laws	12,098	11,293	163	543	99	100.0	93.3	1.3	4.5	.8
Drunkenness	734	652	26	55	1	100.0	88.8	3.5	7.5	.1
Disorderly conduct	5,358	4,089	1,027	187	55	100.0	76.3	19.2	3.5	1.0
Vagrancy	109	95	11	3	—	100.0	87.2	10.1	2.8	—
All other offenses (except traffic)	17,254	14,255	1,948	716	335	100.0	82.6	11.3	4.1	1.9
Suspicion	40	29	8	3	—	100.0	72.5	20.0	7.5	—
Curfew and loitering law violations	1,889	1,374	76	224	215	100.0	72.7	4.0	11.9	11.4
Runaways	9,650	8,222	557	248	623	100.0	85.2	5.8	2.6	6.5

See footnotes at end of table.

Table 61. — Rural County Arrests, Distribution by Race, 1996 — Continued

Offense charged	Arrests 18 and over					Percent distribution[1]				
	Total	White	Black	American Indian or Alaskan Native	Asian or Pacific Islander	Total	White	Black	American Indian or Alaskan Native	Asian or Pacific Islander
TOTAL	**763,235**	**597,181**	**132,912**	**21,928**	**11,214**	**100.0**	**78.2**	**17.4**	**2.9**	**1.5**
Murder and nonnegligent manslaughter	997	604	359	28	6	100.0	60.6	36.0	2.8	.6
Forcible rape	1,853	1,330	444	61	18	100.0	71.8	24.0	3.3	1.0
Robbery	1,902	897	916	48	41	100.0	47.2	48.2	2.5	2.2
Aggravated assault	21,574	14,970	5,646	826	132	100.0	69.4	26.2	3.8	.6
Burglary	16,530	12,820	3,032	511	167	100.0	77.6	18.3	3.1	1.0
Larceny–theft	29,858	22,462	6,392	572	432	100.0	75.2	21.4	1.9	1.4
Motor vehicle theft	4,131	3,285	602	170	74	100.0	79.5	14.6	4.1	1.8
Arson	798	652	132	9	5	100.0	81.7	16.5	1.1	.6
Violent crime[2]	26,326	17,801	7,365	963	197	100.0	67.6	28.0	3.7	.7
Property crime[3]	51,317	39,219	10,158	1,262	678	100.0	76.4	19.8	2.5	1.3
Crime Index total[4]	77,643	57,020	17,523	2,225	875	100.0	73.4	22.6	2.9	1.1
Other assaults	67,699	51,417	13,620	1,796	866	100.0	75.9	20.1	2.7	1.3
Forgery and counterfeiting	6,241	4,528	1,562	77	74	100.0	72.6	25.0	1.2	1.2
Fraud	50,591	36,162	13,844	418	167	100.0	71.5	27.4	.8	.3
Embezzlement	743	620	91	6	26	100.0	83.4	12.2	.8	3.5
Stolen property; buying, receiving, possessing	4,925	3,630	1,138	120	37	100.0	73.7	23.1	2.4	.8
Vandalism	10,133	8,222	1,469	349	93	100.0	81.1	14.5	3.4	.9
Weapons; carrying, possessing, etc.	8,236	6,235	1,705	197	99	100.0	75.7	20.7	2.4	1.2
Prostitution and commercialized vice	202	155	43	—	4	100.0	76.7	21.3	—	2.0
Sex offenses (except forcible rape and prostitution)	4,531	3,869	449	158	55	100.0	85.4	9.9	3.5	1.2
Drug abuse violations	61,874	48,083	12,252	1,022	517	100.0	77.7	19.8	1.7	.8
Gambling	418	264	71	5	78	100.0	63.2	17.0	1.2	18.7
Offenses against family and children	11,186	8,359	2,425	324	78	100.0	74.7	21.7	2.9	.7
Driving under the influence	170,953	140,950	19,282	5,533	5,188	100.0	82.4	11.3	3.2	3.0
Liquor laws	28,915	26,194	1,543	992	186	100.0	90.6	5.3	3.4	.6
Drunkenness	32,095	27,846	2,866	1,327	56	100.0	86.8	8.9	4.1	.2
Disorderly conduct	23,059	18,836	3,280	832	111	100.0	81.7	14.2	3.6	.5
Vagrancy	362	274	80	5	3	100.0	75.7	22.1	1.4	.8
All other offenses (except traffic)	203,194	154,335	39,620	6,541	2,698	100.0	76.0	19.5	3.2	1.3
Suspicion	235	182	49	1	3	100.0	77.4	20.9	.4	1.3
Curfew and loitering law violations	—	—	—	—	—	—	—	—	—	—
Runaways	—	—	—	—	—	—	—	—	—	—

[1] Because of rounding, the percentages may not add to total.
[2] Violent crimes are offenses of murder, forcible rape, robbery, and aggravated assault.
[3] Property crimes are offenses of burglary, larceny–theft, motor vehicle theft, and arson.
[4] Includes arson.

Table 62. — Suburban Area[1] Arrest Trends, 1995-1996

[3,978 agencies; 1996 estimated population 67,129,000; 1995 estimated population 66,501,000]

Offense charged	Number of persons arrested								
	Total all ages			Under 18 years of age			18 years of age and over		
	1995	1996	Percent change	1995	1996	Percent change	1995	1996	Percent change
TOTAL	**3,020,561**	**3,093,410**	**+2.4**	**573,569**	**602,037**	**+5.0**	**2,446,992**	**2,491,373**	**+1.8**
Murder and nonnegligent manslaughter	2,873	2,683	-6.6	414	331	-20.0	2,459	2,352	-4.4
Forcible rape	6,033	6,011	-.4	975	1,058	+8.5	5,058	4,953	-2.1
Robbery	21,673	21,125	-2.5	6,872	6,709	-2.4	14,801	14,416	-2.6
Aggravated assault	103,246	101,106	-2.1	15,417	15,496	+.5	87,829	85,610	-2.5
Burglary	76,479	75,958	-.7	29,634	30,614	+3.3	46,845	45,344	-3.2
Larceny–theft	302,464	302,342	[2]	104,925	105,691	+.7	197,539	196,651	-.4
Motor vehicle theft	34,041	30,996	-8.9	14,337	13,012	-9.2	19,704	17,984	-8.7
Arson	4,550	4,373	-3.9	2,720	2,579	-5.2	1,830	1,794	-2.0
Violent crime[3]	133,825	130,925	-2.2	23,678	23,594	-.4	110,147	107,331	-2.6
Property crime[4]	417,534	413,669	-.9	151,616	151,896	+.2	265,918	261,773	-1.6
Crime Index total[5]	551,359	544,594	-1.2	175,294	175,490	+.1	376,065	369,104	-1.9
Other assaults	252,877	259,245	+2.5	48,724	52,271	+7.3	204,153	206,974	+1.4
Forgery and counterfeiting	24,551	24,885	+1.4	1,924	1,790	-7.0	22,627	23,095	+2.1
Fraud	101,644	104,238	+2.6	2,043	2,326	+13.9	99,601	101,912	+2.3
Embezzlement	3,098	3,293	+6.3	223	249	+11.7	2,875	3,044	+5.9
Stolen property; buying, receiving, possessing	37,317	34,254	-8.2	10,192	9,696	-4.9	27,125	24,558	-9.5
Vandalism	69,322	67,658	-2.4	35,541	34,726	-2.3	33,781	32,932	-2.5
Weapons; carrying, possessing, etc.	46,649	40,842	-12.4	11,672	10,873	-6.8	34,977	29,969	-14.3
Prostitution and commercialized vice	5,483	5,195	-5.3	81	112	+38.3	5,402	5,083	-5.9
Sex offenses (except forcible rape and prostitution)	18,396	18,714	+1.7	3,548	3,784	+6.7	14,848	14,930	+.6
Drug abuse violations	277,027	283,161	+2.2	40,280	42,878	+6.4	236,747	240,283	+1.5
Gambling	1,564	1,225	-21.7	155	142	-8.4	1,409	1,083	-23.1
Offenses against family and children	47,482	46,082	-2.9	1,671	2,215	+32.6	45,811	43,867	-4.2
Driving under the influence	385,525	397,282	+3.0	3,770	4,677	+24.1	381,755	392,605	+2.8
Liquor laws	108,694	128,027	+17.8	31,511	40,112	+27.3	77,183	87,915	+13.9
Drunkenness	135,948	137,501	+1.1	4,694	5,903	+25.8	131,254	131,598	+.3
Disorderly conduct	138,747	142,174	+2.5	39,769	43,967	+10.6	98,978	98,207	-.8
Vagrancy	3,396	3,458	+1.8	664	630	-5.1	2,732	2,828	+3.5
All other offenses (except traffic)	740,690	779,737	+5.3	91,021	98,351	+8.1	649,669	681,386	+4.9
Suspicion (not included in totals)	1,651	1,808	+9.5	487	494	+1.4	1,164	1,314	+12.9
Curfew and loitering law violations	26,138	28,803	+10.2	26,138	28,803	+10.2	—	—	—
Runaways	44,654	43,042	-3.6	44,654	43,042	-3.6	—	—	—

[1] Includes suburban city and county law enforcement agencies within metropolitan areas. Excludes central cities. Suburban cities and counties are also included in other groups.

[2] Less than one-tenth of 1 percent.

[3] Violent crimes are offenses of murder, forcible rape, robbery, and aggravated assault.

[4] Property crimes are offenses of burglary, larceny–theft, motor vehicle theft, and arson.

[5] Includes arson.

Table 63. — Suburban Area[1] Arrest Trends, Sex, 1995-1996

[3,978 agencies; 1996 estimated population 67,129,000; 1995 estimated population 66,501,000]

Offense charged	Males						Females					
	Total			Under 18			Total			Under 18		
	1995	1996	Percent change	1995	1996	Percent change	1995	1996	Percent change	1995	1996	Percent change
TOTAL	2,405,481	2,449,099	+1.8	433,923	453,190	+4.4	615,080	644,311	+4.8	139,646	148,847	+6.6
Murder and nonnegligent manslaughter ...	2,559	2,357	-7.9	377	301	-20.2	314	326	+3.8	37	30	-18.9
Forcible rape	5,960	5,948	-.2	958	1,042	+8.8	73	63	-13.7	17	16	-5.9
Robbery	19,732	19,278	-2.3	6,352	6,208	-2.3	1,941	1,847	-4.8	520	501	-3.7
Aggravated assault	87,148	84,581	-2.9	12,763	12,647	-.9	16,098	16,525	+2.7	2,654	2,849	+7.3
Burglary	68,070	67,942	-.2	26,731	27,755	+3.8	8,409	8,016	-4.7	2,903	2,859	-1.5
Larceny–theft	202,938	201,729	-.6	73,774	73,507	-.4	99,526	100,613	+1.1	31,151	32,184	+3.3
Motor vehicle theft	29,267	26,700	-8.8	11,992	10,904	-9.1	4,774	4,296	-10.0	2,345	2,108	-10.1
Arson	3,928	3,801	-3.2	2,397	2,317	-3.3	622	572	-8.0	323	262	-18.9
Violent crime[2]	115,399	112,164	-2.8	20,450	20,198	-1.2	18,426	18,761	+1.8	3,228	3,396	+5.2
Property crime[3]	304,203	300,172	-1.3	114,894	114,483	-.4	113,331	113,497	+.1	36,722	37,413	+1.9
Crime Index total[4]	419,602	412,336	-1.7	135,344	134,681	-.5	131,757	132,258	+.4	39,950	40,809	+2.2
Other assaults	201,468	204,553	+1.5	35,994	38,586	+7.2	51,409	54,692	+6.4	12,730	13,685	+7.5
Forgery and counterfeiting	15,385	15,539	+1.0	1,284	1,159	-9.7	9,166	9,346	+2.0	640	631	-1.4
Fraud	54,830	54,563	-.5	1,333	1,553	+16.5	46,814	49,675	+6.1	710	773	+8.9
Embezzlement	1,764	1,841	+4.4	135	151	+11.9	1,334	1,452	+8.8	88	98	+11.4
Stolen property; buying, receiving, possessing	31,771	28,970	-8.8	8,974	8,381	-6.6	5,546	5,284	-4.7	1,218	1,315	+8.0
Vandalism	60,693	59,133	-2.6	31,930	31,068	-2.7	8,629	8,525	-1.2	3,611	3,658	+1.3
Weapons; carrying, possessing, etc.	43,016	37,779	-12.2	10,834	10,088	-6.9	3,633	3,063	-15.7	838	785	-6.3
Prostitution and commercialized vice	3,343	3,013	-9.9	50	76	+52.0	2,140	2,182	+2.0	31	36	+16.1
Sex offenses (except forcible rape and prostitution)	17,398	17,674	+1.6	3,321	3,515	+5.8	998	1,040	+4.2	227	269	+18.5
Drug abuse violations	229,727	234,693	+2.2	34,351	36,400	+6.0	47,300	48,468	+2.5	5,929	6,478	+9.3
Gambling	1,336	1,058	-20.8	146	135	-7.5	228	167	-26.8	9	7	-22.2
Offenses against family and children	40,918	39,023	-4.6	1,044	1,441	+38.0	6,564	7,059	+7.5	627	774	+23.4
Driving under the influence	328,792	337,000	+2.5	3,179	3,943	+24.0	56,733	60,282	+6.3	591	734	+24.2
Liquor laws	85,329	99,727	+16.9	22,298	28,272	+26.8	23,365	28,300	+21.1	9,213	11,840	+28.5
Drunkenness	119,442	120,602	+1.0	3,909	4,874	+24.7	16,506	16,899	+2.4	785	1,029	+31.1
Disorderly conduct	109,824	111,697	+1.7	30,591	33,575	+9.8	28,923	30,477	+5.4	9,178	10,392	+13.2
Vagrancy	2,919	2,888	-1.1	584	514	-12.0	477	570	+19.5	80	116	+45.0
All other offenses (except traffic)	599,712	627,494	+4.6	70,410	75,262	+6.9	140,978	152,243	+8.0	20,611	23,089	+12.0
Suspicion (not included in totals)	1,414	1,515	+7.1	412	431	+4.6	237	293	+23.6	75	63	-16.0
Curfew and loitering law violations	18,667	20,498	+9.8	18,667	20,498	+9.8	7,471	8,305	+11.2	7,471	8,305	+11.2
Runaways	19,545	19,018	-2.7	19,545	19,018	-2.7	25,109	24,024	-4.3	25,109	24,024	-4.3

[1] Includes suburban city and county law enforcement agencies within metropolitan areas. Excludes central cities. Suburban cities and counties are also included in other groups.

[2] Violent crimes are offenses of murder, forcible rape, robbery, and aggravated assault.

[3] Property crimes are offenses of burglary, larceny–theft, motor vehicle theft, and arson.

[4] Includes arson.

Table 64. — Suburban Area[1] Arrests, Distribution by Age, 1996

[4,845 agencies; 1996 estimated population 77,866,000]

Offense charged	Total all ages	Ages under 15	Ages under 18	Ages 18 and over	Under 10	10-12	13-14	15	16	17	18	19	20	21
TOTAL	3,719,801	235,294	729,221	2,990,580	11,450	53,160	170,684	144,278	172,402	177,247	187,574	173,532	147,998	133,231
Percent distribution[2]	100.0	6.3	19.6	80.4	.3	1.4	4.6	3.9	4.6	4.8	5.0	4.7	4.0	3.6
Murder and nonnegligent manslaughter	3,088	54	388	2,700	1	4	49	72	118	144	217	217	164	182
Forcible rape	7,329	397	1,304	6,025	14	88	295	254	271	382	375	367	291	301
Robbery	25,557	1,923	8,000	17,557	49	336	1,538	1,586	2,156	2,335	2,314	1,791	1,349	1,102
Aggravated assault	118,777	5,952	18,453	100,324	384	1,504	4,064	3,466	4,282	4,753	4,844	4,554	4,159	4,199
Burglary	89,709	13,220	36,195	53,514	846	3,173	9,201	7,492	7,736	7,747	7,412	5,277	3,799	2,920
Larceny–theft	374,379	53,244	131,430	242,949	2,383	14,415	36,446	24,702	27,361	26,123	23,506	18,140	13,110	11,039
Motor vehicle theft	35,672	3,954	14,990	20,682	54	450	3,450	3,750	3,984	3,302	2,648	1,957	1,411	1,200
Arson	5,124	2,040	3,016	2,108	311	693	1,036	391	319	266	212	139	102	104
Violent crime[3]	154,751	8,326	28,145	126,606	448	1,932	5,946	5,378	6,827	7,614	7,750	6,929	5,963	5,784
Percent distribution[2]	100.0	5.4	18.2	81.8	.3	1.2	3.8	3.5	4.4	4.9	5.0	4.5	3.9	3.7
Property crime[4]	504,884	72,458	185,631	319,253	3,594	18,731	50,133	36,335	39,400	37,438	33,778	25,513	18,422	15,263
Percent distribution[2]	100.0	14.4	36.8	63.2	.7	3.7	9.9	7.2	7.8	7.4	6.7	5.1	3.6	3.0
Crime Index total[5]	659,635	80,784	213,776	445,859	4,042	20,663	56,079	41,713	46,227	45,052	41,528	32,442	24,385	21,047
Percent distribution[2]	100.0	12.2	32.4	67.6	.6	3.1	8.5	6.3	7.0	6.8	6.3	4.9	3.7	3.2
Other assaults	315,903	25,240	62,273	253,630	1,405	6,842	16,993	11,874	12,796	12,363	10,796	9,951	9,404	9,863
Forgery and counterfeiting	30,659	251	2,202	28,457	13	36	202	321	639	991	1,637	1,686	1,501	1,279
Fraud	134,787	450	2,943	131,844	46	63	341	397	774	1,322	3,192	4,616	5,247	6,051
Embezzlement	3,789	24	299	3490	1	4	19	16	98	161	253	216	199	169
Stolen property; buying, receiving, possessing	40,769	3,129	11,614	29,155	67	574	2,488	2,421	2,952	3,112	3,346	2,641	2,104	1,698
Vandalism	81,610	18,544	41,084	40,526	1,804	5,444	11,296	7,411	8,043	7,086	5,492	3,759	2,560	2,245
Weapons; carrying, possessing, etc.	47,653	4,122	12,689	34,964	180	959	2,983	2,457	2,893	3,217	3,247	2,734	2,211	2,004
Prostitution and commercialized vice	6,740	32	139	6,601	—	5	27	21	36	50	115	145	154	188
Sex offenses (except forcible rape and prostitution)	22,133	2,182	4,488	17,645	192	612	1,378	769	736	801	780	680	577	576
Drug abuse violations	332,284	8,890	50,939	281,345	104	1,005	7,781	9,397	14,036	18,616	24,247	21,084	17,060	14,780
Gambling	1,488	38	194	1,294	2	7	29	31	61	64	72	63	44	45
Offenses against family and children	54,079	867	2,858	51,221	57	181	629	621	720	650	1,009	1,092	1,223	1,324
Driving under the influence ...	451,051	143	5,413	445,638	49	18	76	211	1,421	3,638	8,093	10,578	11,557	15,921
Liquor laws	155,384	4,841	48,438	106,946	72	378	4,391	7,535	14,382	21,680	28,051	25,744	18,198	3,917
Drunkenness	172,139	1,066	7,125	165,014	38	87	941	1,253	1,973	2,833	5,287	5,269	4,821	6,107
Disorderly conduct	187,609	19,660	55,213	132,396	764	4,661	14,235	11,166	12,514	11,873	10,436	8,709	7,185	7,437
Vagrancy	4,408	270	938	3,470	9	39	222	198	218	252	278	235	180	157
All other offenses (except traffic)	929,688	35,564	120,145	809,543	1,976	7,205	26,383	24,191	29,109	31,281	39,604	41,816	39,314	38,353
Suspicion	2,179	190	637	1,542	11	34	145	150	154	143	111	72	74	70
Curfew and loitering law violations	34,934	9,751	34,934	—	132	1,400	8,219	8,217	9,892	7,074	—	—	—	—
Runaways	50,880	19,256	50,880	—	486	2,943	15,827	13,908	12,728	4,988	—	—	—	—

See footnotes at end of table.

Table 64. — Suburban Area[1] Arrests, Distribution by Age, 1996 — Continued

Offense charged	22	23	24	25-29	30-34	35-39	40-44	45-49	50-54	55-59	60-64	Over 64
TOTAL	**120,171**	**115,861**	**114,720**	**515,294**	**494,497**	**416,698**	**263,949**	**148,772**	**73,980**	**38,564**	**20,979**	**24,760**
Percent distribution[2]	**3.2**	**3.1**	**3.1**	**13.9**	**13.3**	**11.2**	**7.1**	**4.0**	**2.0**	**1.0**	**.6**	**.7**
Murder and nonnegligent manslaughter	149	113	126	441	334	251	178	129	75	48	29	47
Forcible rape	244	211	242	1,011	1,011	836	528	277	132	84	49	66
Robbery	873	753	661	3,094	2,507	1,662	867	344	135	51	27	27
Aggravated assault	3,769	3,943	3,752	17,884	17,811	14,940	9,429	5,322	2,623	1,352	774	969
Burglary	2,532	2,137	1,996	8,516	7,785	5,722	2,998	1,430	533	225	98	134
Larceny–theft	9,323	8,458	8,177	38,409	36,956	31,394	19,975	11,315	5,489	3,010	1,799	2,849
Motor vehicle theft	966	868	830	3,633	2,925	2,160	1,101	521	242	102	55	63
Arson	92	71	78	290	323	271	175	106	56	39	21	29
Violent crime[3]	5,035	5,020	4,781	22,430	21,663	17,689	11,002	6,072	2,965	1,535	879	1,109
Percent distribution[2]	3.3	3.2	3.1	14.5	14.0	11.4	7.1	3.9	1.9	1.0	.6	.7
Property crime[4]	12,913	11,534	11,081	50,848	47,989	39,547	24,249	13,372	6,320	3,376	1,973	3,075
Percent distribution[2]	2.6	2.3	2.2	10.1	9.5	7.8	4.8	2.6	1.3	.7	.4	.6
Crime Index total[5]	17,948	16,554	15,862	73,278	69,652	57,236	35,251	19,444	9,285	4,911	2,852	4,184
Percent distribution[2]	2.7	2.5	2.4	11.1	10.6	8.7	5.3	2.9	1.4	.7	.4	.6
Other assaults	9,133	9,313	9,583	45,986	47,721	40,482	24,342	13,162	6,501	3,341	1,865	2,187
Forgery and counterfeiting	1,330	1,241	1,237	5,659	5,193	3,730	2,127	1,072	412	186	89	78
Fraud	5,950	6,046	5,917	27,153	23,618	19,141	11,927	6,653	3,233	1,521	691	888
Embezzlement	193	155	148	621	559	400	277	142	93	31	27	7
Stolen property; buying, receiving, possessing	1,326	1,222	1,101	4,851	4,320	3,204	1,767	842	356	184	82	111
Vandalism	1,854	1,756	1,578	6,426	5,685	4,197	2,348	1,302	609	305	172	238
Weapons; carrying, possessing, etc.	1,737	1,577	1,423	5,623	4,679	3,792	2,480	1,503	874	504	256	320
Prostitution and commercialized vice	181	189	210	1,198	1,407	1,184	716	406	196	138	68	106
Sex offenses (except forcible rape and prostitution)	543	506	571	2,597	2,891	2,638	1,882	1,203	795	532	383	491
Drug abuse violations	12,629	11,843	11,373	49,119	45,313	37,059	21,151	9,654	3,464	1,390	628	551
Gambling	36	28	34	163	147	123	125	101	102	85	62	64
Offenses against family and children	1,451	1,577	1,831	9,447	11,081	9,578	6,041	3,106	1,321	604	290	246
Driving under the influence	16,117	16,512	16,860	78,690	78,932	70,956	49,908	32,251	18,043	10,035	5,596	5,589
Liquor laws	2,726	2,118	1,841	6,597	5,556	4,719	3,233	1,895	1,042	606	324	379
Drunkenness	5,613	5,313	5,328	24,379	27,663	27,249	20,102	12,876	6,867	3,908	2,181	2,051
Disorderly conduct	6,218	5,466	5,313	21,615	19,813	16,952	10,521	5,974	3,149	1,597	934	1,077
Vagrancy	127	109	108	513	533	462	393	181	86	49	25	34
All other offenses (except traffic)	34,990	34,268	34,336	151,098	139,471	113,416	69,220	36,928	17,517	8,615	4,444	6,153
Suspicion	69	68	66	281	263	180	138	77	35	22	10	6
Curfew and loitering law violations	—	—	—	—	—	—	—	—	—	—	—	—
Runaways	—	—	—	—	—	—	—	—	—	—	—	—

[1] Includes suburban city and county law enforcement agencies within metropolitan areas. Excludes central cities. Suburban cities and counties are also included in other groups.

[2] Because of rounding, the percentages may not add to total.

[3] Violent crimes are offenses of murder, forcible rape, robbery, and aggravated assault.

[4] Property crimes are offenses of burglary, larceny–theft, motor vehicle theft, and arson.

[5] Includes arson.

Table 65. — Suburban Area[1] Arrests of Persons under 15, 18, 21, and 25 Years of Age, 1996

[4,845 agencies; 1996 estimated population 77,866,000]

Offense charged	Total all ages	Number of persons arrested				Percent of total all ages			
		Under 15	Under 18	Under 21	Under 25	Under 15	Under 18	Under 21	Under 25
TOTAL	3,719,801	235,294	729,221	1,238,325	1,722,308	6.3	19.6	33.3	46.3
Murder and nonnegligent manslaughter	3,088	54	388	986	1,556	1.7	12.6	31.9	50.4
Forcible rape	7,329	397	1,304	2,337	3,335	5.4	17.8	31.9	45.5
Robbery	25,557	1,923	8,000	13,454	16,843	7.5	31.3	52.6	65.9
Aggravated assault	118,777	5,952	18,453	32,010	47,673	5.0	15.5	26.9	40.1
Burglary	89,709	13,220	36,195	52,683	62,268	14.7	40.3	58.7	69.4
Larceny–theft	374,379	53,244	131,430	186,186	223,183	14.2	35.1	49.7	59.6
Motor vehicle theft	35,672	3,954	14,990	21,006	24,870	11.1	42.0	58.9	69.7
Arson	5,124	2,040	3,016	3,469	3,814	39.8	58.9	67.7	74.4
Violent crime[2]	154,751	8,326	28,145	48,787	69,407	5.4	18.2	31.5	44.9
Property crime[3]	504,884	72,458	185,631	263,344	314,135	14.4	36.8	52.2	62.2
Crime Index total[4]	659,635	80,784	213,776	312,131	383,542	12.2	32.4	47.3	58.1
Other assaults	315,903	25,240	62,273	92,424	130,316	8.0	19.7	29.3	41.3
Forgery and counterfeiting	30,659	251	2,202	7,026	12,113	.8	7.2	22.9	39.5
Fraud	134,787	450	2,943	15,998	39,962	.3	2.2	11.9	29.6
Embezzlement	3,789	24	299	967	1,632	.6	7.9	25.5	43.1
Stolen property; buying, receiving, possessing	40,769	3,129	11,614	19,705	25,052	7.7	28.5	48.3	61.4
Vandalism	81,610	18,544	41,084	52,895	60,328	22.7	50.3	64.8	73.9
Weapons; carrying, possessing, etc.	47,653	4,122	12,689	20,881	27,622	8.7	26.6	43.8	58.0
Prostitution and commercialized vice	6,740	32	139	553	1,321	.5	2.1	8.2	19.6
Sex offenses (except forcible rape and prostitution)	22,133	2,182	4,488	6,525	8,721	9.9	20.3	29.5	39.4
Drug abuse violations	332,284	8,890	50,939	113,330	163,955	2.7	15.3	34.1	49.3
Gambling	1,488	38	194	373	516	2.6	13.0	25.1	34.7
Offenses against family and children	54,079	867	2,858	6,182	12,365	1.6	5.3	11.4	22.9
Driving under the influence	451,051	143	5,413	35,641	101,051	[5]	1.2	7.9	22.4
Liquor laws	155,384	4,841	48,438	120,431	131,033	3.1	31.2	77.5	84.3
Drunkenness	172,139	1,066	7,125	22,502	44,863	.6	4.1	13.1	26.1
Disorderly conduct	187,609	19,660	55,213	81,543	105,977	10.5	29.4	43.5	56.5
Vagrancy	4,408	270	938	1,631	2,132	6.1	21.3	37.0	48.4
All other offenses (except traffic)	929,688	35,564	120,145	240,879	382,826	3.8	12.9	25.9	41.2
Suspicion	2,179	190	637	894	1,167	8.7	29.2	41.0	53.6
Curfew and loitering law violations	34,934	9,751	34,934	34,934	34,934	27.9	100.0	100.0	100.0
Runaways	50,880	19,256	50,880	50,880	50,880	37.8	100.0	100.0	100.0

[1] Includes suburban city and county law enforcement agencies within metropolitan areas. Excludes central cities. Suburban cities and counties are also included in other groups.

[2] Violent crimes are offenses of murder, forcible rape, robbery, and aggravated assault.

[3] Property crimes are offenses of burglary, larceny–theft, motor vehicle theft, and arson.

[4] Includes arson.

[5] Less than one-tenth of 1 percent.

266

Table 66. — Suburban Area[1] Arrests, Distribution by Sex, 1996

[4,845 agencies; 1996 estimated population 77,866,000]

Offense charged	Number of persons arrested			Percent male	Percent female	Percent distribution[2]		
	Total	Male	Female			Total	Male	Female
TOTAL	3,719,801	2,933,919	785,882	78.9	21.1	100.0	100.0	100.0
Murder and nonnegligent manslaughter	3,088	2,722	366	88.1	11.9	.1	.1	[3]
Forcible rape	7,329	7,241	88	98.8	1.2	.2	.2	[3]
Robbery	25,557	23,265	2,292	91.0	9.0	.7	.8	.3
Aggravated assault	118,777	98,922	19,855	83.3	16.7	3.2	3.4	2.5
Burglary	89,709	80,296	9,413	89.5	10.5	2.4	2.7	1.2
Larceny–theft	374,379	247,988	126,391	66.2	33.8	10.1	8.5	16.1
Motor vehicle theft	35,672	30,740	4,932	86.2	13.8	1.0	1.0	.6
Arson	5,124	4,433	691	86.5	13.5	.1	.2	.1
Violent crime[4]	154,751	132,150	22,601	85.4	14.6	4.2	4.5	2.9
Property crime[5]	504,884	363,457	141,427	72.0	28.0	13.6	12.4	18.0
Crime Index total[6]	659,635	495,607	164,028	75.1	24.9	17.7	16.9	20.9
Other assaults	315,903	248,968	66,935	78.8	21.2	8.5	8.5	8.5
Forgery and counterfeiting	30,659	19,076	11,583	62.2	37.8	.8	.7	1.5
Fraud	134,787	71,178	63,609	52.8	47.2	3.6	2.4	8.1
Embezzlement	3,789	2,122	1,667	56.0	44.0	.1	.1	.2
Stolen property; buying, receiving, possessing	40,769	34,588	6,181	84.8	15.2	1.1	1.2	.8
Vandalism	81,610	71,208	10,402	87.3	12.7	2.2	2.4	1.3
Weapons; carrying, possessing, etc.	47,653	44,027	3,626	92.4	7.6	1.3	1.5	.5
Prostitution and commercialized vice	6,740	3,783	2,957	56.1	43.9	.2	.1	.4
Sex offenses (except forcible rape and prostitution)	22,133	20,881	1,252	94.3	5.7	.6	.7	.2
Drug abuse violations	332,284	275,811	56,473	83.0	17.0	8.9	9.4	7.2
Gambling	1,488	1,300	188	87.4	12.6	[3]	[3]	[3]
Offenses against family and children	54,079	45,424	8,655	84.0	16.0	1.5	1.5	1.1
Driving under the influence	451,051	382,132	68,919	84.7	15.3	12.1	13.0	8.8
Liquor laws	155,384	121,102	34,282	77.9	22.1	4.2	4.1	4.4
Drunkenness	172,139	150,849	21,290	87.6	12.4	4.6	5.1	2.7
Disorderly conduct	187,609	147,029	40,580	78.4	21.6	5.0	5.0	5.2
Vagrancy	4,408	3,621	787	82.1	17.9	.1	.1	.1
All other offenses (except traffic)	929,688	745,990	183,698	80.2	19.8	25.0	25.4	23.4
Suspicion	2,179	1,813	366	83.2	16.8	.1	.1	[3]
Curfew and loitering law violations	34,934	24,981	9,953	71.5	28.5	.9	.9	1.3
Runaways	50,880	22,429	28,451	44.1	55.9	1.4	.8	3.6

[1] Includes suburban city and county law enforcement agencies within metropolitan areas. Excludes central cities. Suburban cities and counties are also included in other groups.

[2] Because of rounding, the percentages may not add to total.

[3] Less than one-tenth of 1 percent.

[4] Violent crimes are offenses of murder, forcible rape, robbery, and aggravated assault.

[5] Property crimes are offenses of burglary, larceny–theft, motor vehicle theft, and arson.

[6] Includes arson.

Table 67. — Suburban Area[1] Arrests, Distribution by Race, 1996

[4,842 agencies; 1996 estimated population 77,866,000]

Offense charged	Total arrests					Percent distribution[2]				
	Total	White	Black	American Indian or Alaskan Native	Asian or Pacific Islander	Total	White	Black	American Indian or Alaskan Native	Asian or Pacific Islander
TOTAL	3,709,973	2,849,937	813,638	20,313	26,085	100.0	76.8	21.9	.5	.7
Murder and nonnegligent manslaughter	3,088	1,999	1,032	27	30	100.0	64.7	33.4	.9	1.0
Forcible rape	7,309	5,061	2,149	48	51	100.0	69.2	29.4	.7	.7
Robbery	25,523	12,878	12,324	111	210	100.0	50.5	48.3	.4	.8
Aggravated assault	118,537	84,907	31,818	724	1,088	100.0	71.6	26.8	.6	.9
Burglary	89,529	69,576	18,893	388	672	100.0	77.7	21.1	.4	.8
Larceny–theft	373,598	260,034	106,547	2,124	4,893	100.0	69.6	28.5	.6	1.3
Motor vehicle theft	35,615	24,988	10,070	214	343	100.0	70.2	28.3	.6	1.0
Arson	5,114	4,335	703	27	49	100.0	84.8	13.7	.5	1.0
Violent crime[3]	154,457	104,845	47,323	910	1,379	100.0	67.9	30.6	.6	.9
Property crime[4]	503,856	358,933	136,213	2,753	5,957	100.0	71.2	27.0	.5	1.2
Crime Index total[5]	658,313	463,778	183,536	3,663	7,336	100.0	70.4	27.9	.6	1.1
Other assaults	314,947	232,846	77,919	2,004	2,178	100.0	73.9	24.7	.6	.7
Forgery and counterfeiting ...	30,536	21,045	9,067	123	301	100.0	68.9	29.7	.4	1.0
Fraud	134,428	93,109	40,204	333	782	100.0	69.3	29.9	.2	.6
Embezzlement	3,786	2,530	1,215	9	32	100.0	66.8	32.1	.2	.8
Stolen property; buying, receiving, possessing	40,650	26,892	13,144	205	409	100.0	66.2	32.3	.5	1.0
Vandalism	81,462	68,876	11,541	430	615	100.0	84.5	14.2	.5	.8
Weapons; carrying, possessing, etc.	47,578	33,801	13,108	202	467	100.0	71.0	27.6	.4	1.0
Prostitution and commercialized vice	6,732	5,011	1,607	30	84	100.0	74.4	23.9	.4	1.2
Sex offenses (except forcible rape and prostitution)	22,080	18,107	3,668	117	188	100.0	82.0	16.6	.5	.9
Drug abuse violations	331,571	249,457	79,518	1,149	1,447	100.0	75.2	24.0	.3	.4
Gambling	1,486	797	644	8	37	100.0	53.6	43.3	.5	2.5
Offenses against family and children	53,477	36,940	16,192	152	193	100.0	69.1	30.3	.3	.4
Driving under the influence ...	449,654	407,645	36,476	2,529	3,004	100.0	90.7	8.1	.6	.7
Liquor laws	154,296	141,131	10,693	1,329	1,143	100.0	91.5	6.9	.9	.7
Drunkenness	172,008	151,898	17,603	1,805	702	100.0	88.3	10.2	1.0	.4
Disorderly conduct	187,126	144,057	40,864	1,009	1,196	100.0	77.0	21.8	.5	.6
Vagrancy	4,399	3,091	1,267	26	15	100.0	70.3	28.8	.6	.3
All other offenses (except traffic)	927,552	673,338	244,319	4,684	5,211	100.0	72.6	26.3	.5	.6
Suspicion	2,165	1,496	611	44	14	100.0	69.1	28.2	2.0	.6
Curfew and loitering law violations	34,901	30,185	4,240	168	308	100.0	86.5	12.1	.5	.9
Runaways	50,826	43,907	6,202	294	423	100.0	86.4	12.2	.6	.8

See footnotes at end of table.

Table 67. — Suburban Area[1] Arrests, Distribution by Race, 1996 — Continued

Offense charged	Arrests under 18					Percent distribution[2]				
	Total	White	Black	American Indian or Alaskan Native	Asian or Pacific Islander	Total	White	Black	American Indian or Alaskan Native	Asian or Pacific Islander
TOTAL	727,989	581,141	135,480	4,016	7,352	100.0	79.8	18.6	.6	1.0
Murder and nonnegligent manslaughter	388	227	152	3	6	100.0	58.5	39.2	.8	1.5
Forcible rape	1,301	902	382	9	8	100.0	69.3	29.4	.7	.6
Robbery	7,991	4,035	3,825	32	99	100.0	50.5	47.9	.4	1.2
Aggravated assault	18,387	12,794	5,270	113	210	100.0	69.6	28.7	.6	1.1
Burglary	36,128	29,343	6,275	156	354	100.0	81.2	17.4	.4	1.0
Larceny–theft	131,198	98,173	30,053	835	2,137	100.0	74.8	22.9	.6	1.6
Motor vehicle theft	14,963	10,720	3,895	112	236	100.0	71.6	26.0	.7	1.6
Arson	3,010	2,670	295	16	29	100.0	88.7	9.8	.5	1.0
Violent crime[3]	28,067	17,958	9,629	157	323	100.0	64.0	34.3	.6	1.2
Property crime[4]	185,299	140,906	40,518	1,119	2,756	100.0	76.0	21.9	.6	1.5
Crime Index total[5]	213,366	158,864	50,147	1,276	3,079	100.0	74.5	23.5	.6	1.4
Other assaults	62,192	45,631	15,719	334	508	100.0	73.4	25.3	.5	.8
Forgery and counterfeiting	2,191	1,795	348	17	31	100.0	81.9	15.9	.8	1.4
Fraud	2,938	2,131	768	7	32	100.0	72.5	26.1	.2	1.1
Embezzlement	298	209	86	—	3	100.0	70.1	28.9	—	1.0
Stolen property; buying, receiving, possessing	11,587	8,022	3,326	72	167	100.0	69.2	28.7	.6	1.4
Vandalism	41,008	36,040	4,420	195	353	100.0	87.9	10.8	.5	.9
Weapons; carrying, possessing, etc.	12,678	9,619	2,833	60	166	100.0	75.9	22.3	.5	1.3
Prostitution and commercialized vice	139	111	24	2	2	100.0	79.9	17.3	1.4	1.4
Sex offenses (except forcible rape and prostitution)	4,479	3,565	882	11	21	100.0	79.6	19.7	.2	.5
Drug abuse violations	50,838	40,861	9,435	214	328	100.0	80.4	18.6	.4	.6
Gambling	194	54	137	—	3	100.0	27.8	70.6	—	1.5
Offenses against family and children	2,833	2,376	437	8	12	100.0	83.9	15.4	.3	.4
Driving under the influence	5,396	5,091	253	26	26	100.0	94.3	4.7	.5	.5
Liquor laws	48,314	45,708	1,890	350	366	100.0	94.6	3.9	.7	.8
Drunkenness	7,124	6,604	412	74	34	100.0	92.7	5.8	1.0	.5
Disorderly conduct	55,179	42,018	12,431	284	446	100.0	76.1	22.5	.5	.8
Vagrancy	938	758	164	13	3	100.0	80.8	17.5	1.4	.3
All other offenses (except traffic)	119,933	97,067	21,222	608	1,036	100.0	80.9	17.7	.5	.9
Suspicion	637	525	104	3	5	100.0	82.4	16.3	.5	.8
Curfew and loitering law violations	34,901	30,185	4,240	168	308	100.0	86.5	12.1	.5	.9
Runaways	50,826	43,907	6,202	294	423	100.0	86.4	12.2	.6	.8

See footnotes at end of table.

Table 67. — Suburban Area[1] Arrests, Distribution by Race, 1996 — Continued

Offense charged	Arrests 18 and over					Percent distribution[2]				
	Total	White	Black	American Indian or Alaskan Native	Asian or Pacific Islander	Total	White	Black	American Indian or Alaskan Native	Asian or Pacific Islander
TOTAL	2,981,984	2,268,796	678,158	16,297	18,733	100.0	76.1	22.7	.5	.6
Murder and nonnegligent manslaughter	2,700	1,772	880	24	24	100.0	65.6	32.6	.9	.9
Forcible rape	6,008	4,159	1,767	39	43	100.0	69.2	29.4	.6	.7
Robbery	17,532	8,843	8,499	79	111	100.0	50.4	48.5	.5	.6
Aggravated assault	100,150	72,113	26,548	611	878	100.0	72.0	26.5	.6	.9
Burglary	53,401	40,233	12,618	232	318	100.0	75.3	23.6	.4	.6
Larceny–theft	242,400	161,861	76,494	1,289	2,756	100.0	66.8	31.6	.5	1.1
Motor vehicle theft	20,652	14,268	6,175	102	107	100.0	69.1	29.9	.5	.5
Arson	2,104	1,665	408	11	20	100.0	79.1	19.4	.5	1.0
Violent crime[3]	126,390	86,887	37,694	753	1,056	100.0	68.7	29.8	.6	.8
Property crime[4]	318,557	218,027	95,695	1,634	3,201	100.0	68.4	30.0	.5	1.0
Crime Index total[5]	444,947	304,914	133,389	2,387	4,257	100.0	68.5	30.0	.5	1.0
Other assaults	252,755	187,215	62,200	1,670	1,670	100.0	74.1	24.6	.7	.7
Forgery and counterfeiting	28,345	19,250	8,719	106	270	100.0	67.9	30.8	.4	1.0
Fraud	131,490	90,978	39,436	326	750	100.0	69.2	30.0	.2	.6
Embezzlement	3,488	2,321	1,129	9	29	100.0	66.5	32.4	.3	.8
Stolen property; buying, receiving, possessing	29,063	18,870	9,818	133	242	100.0	64.9	33.8	.5	.8
Vandalism	40,454	32,836	7,121	235	262	100.0	81.2	17.6	.6	.6
Weapons; carrying, possessing, etc.	34,900	24,182	10,275	142	301	100.0	69.3	29.4	.4	.9
Prostitution and commercialized vice	6,593	4,900	1,583	28	82	100.0	74.3	24.0	.4	1.2
Sex offenses (except forcible rape and prostitution)	17,601	14,542	2,786	106	167	100.0	82.6	15.8	.6	.9
Drug abuse violations	280,733	208,596	70,083	935	1,119	100.0	74.3	25.0	.3	.4
Gambling	1,292	743	507	8	34	100.0	57.5	39.2	.6	2.6
Offenses against family and children	50,644	34,564	15,755	144	181	100.0	68.2	31.1	.3	.4
Driving under the influence	444,258	402,554	36,223	2,503	2,978	100.0	90.6	8.2	.6	.7
Liquor laws	105,982	95,423	8,803	979	777	100.0	90.0	8.3	.9	.7
Drunkenness	164,884	145,294	17,191	1,731	668	100.0	88.1	10.4	1.0	.4
Disorderly conduct	131,947	102,039	28,433	725	750	100.0	77.3	21.5	.5	.6
Vagrancy	3,461	2,333	1,103	13	12	100.0	67.4	31.9	.4	.3
All other offenses (except traffic)	807,619	576,271	223,097	4,076	4,175	100.0	71.4	27.6	.5	.5
Suspicion	1,528	971	507	41	9	100.0	63.5	33.2	2.7	.6
Curfew and loitering law violations	—	—	—	—	—	—	—	—	—	—
Runaways	—	—	—	—	—	—	—	—	—	—

[1] Includes suburban city and county law enforcement agencies within metropolitan areas. Excludes central cities. Suburban cities and counties are also included in other groups.

[2] Because of rounding, the percentages may not add to total.

[3] Violent crimes are offenses of murder, forcible rape, robbery, and aggravated assault.

[4] Property crimes are offenses of burglary, larceny–theft, motor vehicle theft, and arson.

[5] Includes arson.

Table 68. — Police Disposition of Juvenile Offenders Taken into Custody, 1996

[1996 estimated population]

Population group	Total[1]	Handled within department and released	Referred to juvenile court jurisdiction	Referred to welfare agency	Referred to other police agency	Referred to criminal or adult court
TOTAL ALL AGENCIES: 8,062 agencies; population 165,572,000						
Number	1,315,578	307,016	903,014	12,228	11,800	81,520
Percent[2]	100.0	23.3	68.6	.9	.9	6.2
TOTAL CITIES: 5,823 cities; population 117,558,000						
Number	1,104,909	260,638	758,365	10,291	9,359	66,256
Percent[2]	100.0	23.6	68.6	.9	.8	6.0
GROUP I						
46 cities, 250,000 and over; population 37,889,000						
Number	270,777	68,725	185,767	3,020	2,505	10,760
Percent[2]	100.0	25.4	68.6	1.1	.9	4.0
GROUP II						
107 cities, 100,000 to 249,999; population 15,684,000						
Number	146,979	35,023	100,580	2,221	1,892	7,263
Percent[2]	100.0	23.8	68.4	1.5	1.3	4.9
GROUP III						
250 cities, 50,000 to 99,999; population 16,967,000						
Number	160,770	35,982	115,275	953	624	7,936
Percent[2]	100.0	22.4	71.7	.6	.4	4.9
GROUP IV						
464 cities, 25,000 to 49,999; population 16,114,000						
Number	161,047	37,488	112,108	1,609	1,966	7,876
Percent[2]	100.0	23.3	69.6	1.0	1.2	4.9
GROUP V						
1,088 cities, 10,000 to 24,999; population 17,132,000						
Number	189,526	41,852	129,307	1,235	1,324	15,808
Percent[2]	100.0	22.1	68.2	.7	.7	8.3
GROUP VI						
3,868 cities under 10,000; population 13,770,000						
Number	175,810	41,568	115,328	1,253	1,048	16,613
Percent[2]	100.0	23.6	65.6	.7	.6	9.4
SUBURBAN COUNTIES						
1,461 agencies; population 15,717,000						
Number	63,024	11,099	44,601	1,155	518	5,651
Percent[2]	100.0	17.6	70.8	1.8	.8	9.0
RURAL COUNTIES						
778 agencies; population 32,297,000						
Number	147,645	35,279	100,048	782	1,923	9,613
Percent[2]	100.0	23.9	67.8	.5	1.3	6.5
SUBURBAN AREA[3]						
4,205 agencies; population 74,256,000						
Number	541,290	138,296	354,762	3,220	4,551	40,461
Percent[2]	100.0	25.5	65.5	.6	.8	7.5

[1] Includes all offenses except traffic and neglect cases.

[2] Because of rounding, the percentages may not add to total.

[3] Includes suburban city and county law enforcement agencies within metropolitan areas. Excludes central cities. Suburban cities and counties are also included in other groups.

Table 69. — Arrests by State, 1996

[1996 estimated population] Dashes indicate zero data.

State	Total[1] all classes	Crime[2] Index total	Violent[3] crime	Property[4] crime	Murder and non-negligent man-slaughter	Forcible rape	Robbery	Aggra-vated assault	Burglary	Larceny-theft	Motor vehicle theft	Arson	Other assaults	Forgery and counter-feiting	Fraud
ALABAMA: 272 agencies; population 4,121,000															
Under 18	18,217	7,706	1,021	6,685	49	51	401	520	1,051	5,195	404	35	1,597	70	138
Total all ages	215,361	37,032	10,980	26,052	402	456	2,042	8,080	3,845	20,472	1,586	149	30,344	2,044	13,006
ALASKA: 25 agencies; population 538,000															
Under 18	5,791	2,574	259	2,315	4	18	54	183	486	1,658	153	18	579	10	11
Total all ages	34,180	6,835	1,520	5,315	28	113	164	1,215	852	3,983	452	28	4,608	75	171
ARIZONA: 79 agencies; population 4,173,000															
Under 18	68,974	18,607	2,083	16,524	45	38	470	1,530	2,772	11,935	1,554	263	5,050	129	111
Total all ages	299,937	57,689	9,025	48,664	253	252	1,617	6,903	5,969	39,197	3,109	389	29,061	1,524	1,848
ARKANSAS: 178 agencies; population 2,375,000															
Under 18	21,473	7,349	874	6,475	39	67	272	496	1,244	4,898	292	41	935	156	115
Total all ages	198,776	25,427	5,279	20,148	227	444	923	3,685	3,243	16,156	632	117	8,351	2,045	17,949
CALIFORNIA: 672 agencies; population 31,195,000															
Under 18	268,835	99,432	21,227	78,205	382	480	8,558	11,807	22,111	42,822	11,912	1,360	22,587	879	990
Total all ages	1,573,555	370,478	146,092	224,386	2,492	3,134	25,398	115,068	61,140	130,242	30,766	2,238	77,007	13,706	11,855
COLORADO: 161 agencies; population 2,827,000															
Under 18	40,182	10,203	799	9,404	18	67	195	519	1,069	7,678	467	190	2,207	149	192
Total all ages	217,716	30,057	5,211	24,846	113	454	590	4,054	2,469	20,716	1,379	282	19,037	1,167	2,979
CONNECTICUT: 93 agencies; population 2,528,000															
Under 18	27,006	8,545	1,376	7,169	16	62	432	866	1,483	4,873	718	95	2,127	29	80
Total all ages	154,446	30,937	6,365	24,572	115	308	1,609	4,333	4,197	18,599	1,596	180	12,113	849	3,043
DELAWARE: 49 agencies; population 371,000															
Under 18	5,485	2,114	384	1,730	3	25	106	250	253	1,382	92	3	833	25	83
Total all ages	26,667	7,246	1,789	5,457	19	155	397	1,218	794	4,468	186	9	4,552	551	1,634
DISTRICT OF COLUMBIA[6]:															
FLORIDA[6]:															
GEORGIA: 400 agencies; population 4,505,000															
Under 18	34,004	11,397	1,260	10,137	18	63	378	801	2,012	7,360	693	72	2,687	200	248
Total all ages	250,064	47,301	9,816	37,485	246	395	1,875	7,300	5,930	29,385	1,920	250	19,687	4,520	10,304
HAWAII: 5 agencies; population 1,184,000															
Under 18	17,334	4,468	463	4,005	12	16	299	136	496	3,050	452	7	1,338	8	45
Total all ages	65,258	12,397	1,488	10,909	51	128	678	631	1,381	8,021	1,472	35	5,110	424	608
IDAHO: 107 agencies; population 1,171,000															
Under 18	24,513	7,120	381	6,739	1	11	45	324	858	5,422	359	100	1,533	118	56
Total all ages	78,229	12,766	1,372	11,394	29	83	117	1,143	1,474	9,188	603	129	6,620	445	780
ILLINOIS[6]: 1 agency population 2,754,000															
Under 18	68,630	13,669	3,444	10,225	165	159	1,201	1,919	1,265	5,933	2,965	62	8,143	18	44
Total all ages	301,870	59,323	12,685	46,638	767	457	3,279	8,182	4,350	33,548	8,566	174	45,539	363	703
INDIANA: 110 agencies; population 3,294,000															
Under 18	38,458	10,862	1,968	8,894	15	38	206	1,709	961	6,821	992	120	1,980	60	56
Total all ages	162,253	31,567	8,283	23,284	123	178	852	7,130	2,609	18,198	2,282	195	9,933	907	2,098

See footnotes at end of table.

Table 69. — Arrests by State, 1996 — Continued

Embezzlement	Stolen property; buying, receiving, possessing	Vandalism	Weapons; carrying, possessing, etc.	Prostitution and commercialized vice	Sex offenses (except forcible rape and prostitution)	Drug abuse violations	Gambling	Offenses against family and children	Driving under the influence	Liquor laws	Drunkenness[5]	Disorderly conduct	Vagrancy	All other offenses (except traffic)	Suspicion	Curfew and loitering law violations	Runaways
1	435	462	477	2	33	1,475	20	45	185	874	146	1,131	50	2,028	—	262	1,080
30	2,347	3,220	2,381	263	409	14,647	119	1,160	18,919	7,986	12,477	5,183	412	62,040	—	262	1,080
—	19	344	118	3	77	379	2	3	61	425	—	85	—	1,032	—	69	—
7	39	907	490	185	313	1,619	7	162	4,373	1,281	2	808	—	12,229	—	69	—
27	807	3,529	878	42	334	5,094	7	167	432	6,100	—	4,045	63	6,599	—	9,122	7,831
208	3,009	9,754	3,981	2,460	2,238	24,348	39	1,920	32,398	25,135	—	22,179	759	64,434	—	9,122	7,831
1	452	430	367	7	79	1,291	19	41	286	644	427	1,463	23	3,997	214	1,949	1,228
29	2,286	1,304	2,527	235	501	11,640	143	1,219	18,656	3,727	20,413	8,592	1,106	68,585	864	1,949	1,228
91	6,184	14,740	8,855	290	2,245	24,393	141	15	1,806	5,862	5,728	7,934	576	37,763	—	20,434	7,890
1,435	23,117	27,584	31,281	17,393	15,724	252,974	1,681	679	199,536	32,120	117,728	15,359	4,146	331,428	—	20,434	7,890
7	171	2,131	574	2	254	2,034	3	40	537	4,604	37	2,827	14	7,584	—	3,271	3,341
175	487	5,947	2,535	1,178	1,218	12,950	17	1,651	29,599	17,676	880	16,013	1,889	65,648	1	3,271	3,341
9	129	1,727	486	6	187	3,012	2	158	112	536	4	3,641	43	5,562	6	155	450
101	390	4,106	1,898	550	686	16,479	36	2,016	9,489	1,844	15	21,837	120	47,325	7	155	450
—	161	235	89	1	55	439	4	4	—	386	8	575	7	429	—	37	—
1	392	664	342	146	214	1,764	16	100	146	1,589	392	1,602	197	5,082	—	37	—
11	369	681	572	7	332	2,651	76	120	510	1,455	164	2,917	19	6,985	30	764	1,809
222	2,441	2,048	2,946	283	1,837	24,522	255	3,240	32,538	7,340	6,896	19,313	164	61,279	355	764	1,809
—	27	532	77	5	74	772	2	149	67	309	—	116	—	3,457	—	693	5,195
63	275	1,071	432	385	367	3,470	310	1,865	4,733	1,163	—	904	—	25,790	3	693	5,195
19	207	1,115	239	1	95	861	2	35	303	2,033	4	596	—	5,348	—	1,932	2,896
128	423	1,768	703	7	326	3,991	13	434	11,176	5,412	307	2,208	21	25,873	—	1,932	2,896
2	149	3,873	1,907	93	295	11,056	1,023	34	27	1,030	—	17,039	—	10,228	—	—	—
4	634	11,129	6,240	7,780	2,137	52,903	2,647	541	2,894	3,331	—	66,909	—	38,793	—	—	—
1	366	1,250	312	8	131	1,853	16	290	123	2,500	346	1,575	13	7,213	25	3,380	6,098
8	946	2,037	1,758	1,355	865	11,047	87	1,170	16,088	8,359	15,618	4,647	26	44,144	115	3,380	6,098

Table 69. — Arrests by State, 1996 — Continued

State	Total[1] all classes	Crime[2] Index total	Violent[3] crime	Property[4] crime	Murder and non-negligent man-slaughter	Forcible rape	Robbery	Aggra-vated assault	Burglary	Larceny-theft	Motor vehicle theft	Arson	Other assaults	Forgery and counter-feiting	Fraud
IOWA: 172 agencies; population 2,304,000															
Under 18	19,183	6,264	627	5,637	4	15	84	524	852	4,273	387	125	1,655	100	56
Total all ages	89,972	16,072	3,120	12,952	27	77	282	2,734	1,802	10,281	685	184	7,854	696	1,734
KANSAS[6]:															
KENTUCKY[6]: 10 agencies; population 765,000															
Under 18	9,044	3,730	646	3,084	7	15	219	405	620	1,963	481	20	286	43	41
Total all ages	56,688	12,414	4,192	8,222	64	117	885	3,126	1,699	5,446	1,038	39	3,104	956	3,392
LOUISIANA: 107 agencies; population 2,666,000															
Under 18	33,272	11,708	1,679	10,029	72	86	320	1,201	2,178	7,318	445	88	3,625	70	31
Total all ages	177,083	41,893	9,962	31,931	418	445	1,372	7,727	6,127	24,236	1,366	202	19,585	1,591	2,090
MAINE: 150 agencies; population 1,223,000															
Under 18	12,801	5,090	237	4,853	1	18	88	130	1,095	3,415	250	93	1,303	43	39
Total all ages	54,319	10,838	895	9,943	15	75	189	616	2,099	7,175	525	144	6,977	244	1,357
MARYLAND: 129 agencies; population 4,025,000															
Under 18	48,856	17,542	3,656	13,886	147	112	1,403	1,994	2,633	8,240	2,818	195	7,432	65	70
Total all ages	242,128	52,481	12,711	39,770	625	610	4,007	7,469	7,780	26,104	5,527	359	32,648	847	3,124
MASSACHUSETTS: 263 agencies; population 5,034,000															
Under 18	23,230	7,931	2,597	5,334	15	85	570	1,927	1,416	3,300	569	49	1,349	24	32
Total all ages	155,962	33,587	14,224	19,363	93	584	1,747	11,800	4,362	13,321	1,554	126	13,398	483	372
MICHIGAN: 443 agencies; population 7,888,000															
Under 18	51,552	18,081	2,946	15,135	113	278	863	1,692	2,762	10,752	1,409	212	3,295	90	467
Total all ages	378,119	61,867	20,573	41,294	1,220	1,673	3,646	14,034	7,779	29,842	2,998	675	34,749	1,277	6,357
MINNESOTA: 283 agencies; population 4,209,000															
Under 18	65,992	18,773	1,817	16,956	27	148	551	1,091	1,815	12,958	1,995	188	4,952	356	494
Total all ages	221,193	38,720	6,395	32,325	145	782	1,382	4,086	3,697	24,872	3,470	286	20,665	2,383	10,710
MISSISSIPPI: 55 agencies; population 632,000															
Under 18	9,486	2,392	226	2,166	8	17	82	119	617	1,441	86	22	1,046	35	17
Total all ages	51,625	8,419	1,393	7,026	84	123	316	870	1,824	4,744	416	42	5,764	565	1,036
MISSOURI: 162 agencies; population 3,092,000															
Under 18	39,412	13,248	1,751	11,497	59	109	651	932	1,524	8,740	1,095	138	4,378	136	91
Total all ages	272,065	48,464	9,877	38,587	338	619	2,527	6,393	5,011	29,919	3,306	351	31,067	1,751	2,802
MONTANA[6]:															
NEBRASKA: 234 agencies; population 1,187,000															
Under 18	14,511	4,280	140	4,140	2	6	41	91	484	3,334	256	66	1,687	78	55
Total all ages	59,007	8,718	800	7,918	15	82	125	578	962	6,428	437	91	7,047	670	1,917
NEVADA: 30 agencies; population 1,569,000															
Under 18	22,092	6,077	621	5,456	27	39	323	232	1,333	3,631	420	72	2,217	20	48
Total all ages	123,823	21,073	3,608	17,465	174	290	1,387	1,757	4,185	11,722	1,456	102	15,462	443	1,629
NEW HAMPSHIRE: 74 agencies; population 885,000															
Under 18	9,610	2,361	129	2,232	2	25	60	42	277	1,826	90	39	959	17	14
Total all ages	34,735	4,912	539	4,373	12	104	131	292	551	3,618	153	51	4,666	134	375

See footnotes at end of table.

Table 69. — Arrests by State, 1996 — Continued

Embezzlement	Stolen property; buying, receiving, possessing	Vandalism	Weapons; carrying, possessing, etc.	Prostitution and commercialized vice	Sex offenses (except forcible rape and prostitution)	Drug abuse violations	Gambling	Offenses against family and children	Driving under the influence	Liquor laws	Drunkenness[5]	Disorderly conduct	Vagrancy	All other offenses (except traffic)	Suspicion	Curfew and loitering law violations	Runaways
15	47	1,096	86	4	44	749	—	7	268	2,459	236	1,257	—	2,532	—	1,240	1,068
139	123	2,160	600	254	234	6,570	5	257	12,051	9,312	6,603	4,633	127	18,240	—	1,240	1,068
17	477	277	158	8	26	808	21	5	51	523	147	550	26	1,259	—	72	519
154	1,185	958	964	380	260	6,663	85	872	4,403	1,276	4,728	2,541	26	11,736	—	72	519
7	713	1,343	500	5	176	2,197	23	133	131	556	128	3,299	117	5,453	22	1,324	1,711
27	2,644	3,575	2,034	359	1,024	14,993	166	1,143	10,757	1,996	5,668	11,786	843	51,687	187	1,324	1,711
—	137	947	89	5	77	727	—	4	153	728	16	272	—	2,505	—	100	566
14	434	1,971	310	47	319	3,789	3	217	7,984	2,496	34	1,959	—	14,660	—	100	566
37	66	2,279	1,284	28	371	7,983	79	80	148	910	18	1,814	25	6,710	96	592	1,227
509	381	4,038	4,023	1,630	1,407	32,952	223	2,150	17,913	4,166	24	5,420	397	75,633	343	592	1,227
1	641	1,009	307	32	62	2,814	2	199	144	1,291	464	1,913	58	3,914	48	101	894
9	2,383	2,630	1,293	2,615	981	22,262	183	3,113	15,431	4,244	8,901	10,977	363	31,294	448	101	894
125	1,816	2,316	1,050	39	349	3,845	27	8	676	3,876	24	2,381	84	7,822	—	2,387	2,794
1,357	8,738	6,423	6,572	3,628	1,899	33,398	372	2,798	46,506	20,315	503	20,228	389	115,562	—	2,387	2,794
—	1,146	4,191	1,116	29	210	3,215	8	30	506	8,712	—	7,063	20	5,592	—	6,502	3,077
2	2,747	7,521	2,665	1,176	743	14,025	59	714	33,348	25,189	—	15,779	91	35,077	—	6,502	3,077
10	66	99	132	3	56	764	24	33	63	285	88	1,045	11	2,103	3	1024	187
276	350	330	439	19	284	4,239	206	864	5,740	1,939	3,073	4,047	19	12,753	52	1024	187
20	379	2,132	742	32	337	2,816	21	125	241	1,304	42	1,494	141	6,654	59	1,937	3,083
79	1,960	7,470	4,717	1,723	1,995	22,692	155	3,068	15,873	5,811	1,454	11,104	597	103,811	452	1,937	3,083
8	211	1,374	152	—	57	685	—	19	284	1,730	—	593	—	2,189	—	591	518
28	601	2,456	636	13	313	4,128	12	979	8,617	6,556	—	2,908	—	12,299	—	591	518
27	532	794	421	27	123	1,238	23	113	76	1,302	35	625	72	3,218	3	3,879	1,222
383	1,946	1,629	1,977	3,458	1,017	8,753	87	1,080	7,473	4,989	681	3,525	1,266	41,842	9	3,879	1,222
2	238	446	17	2	38	570	—	—	94	651	227	209	21	1,955	110	77	1,602
10	515	850	126	62	251	2,756	8	106	5,074	2,263	2,001	944	88	7,805	110	77	1,602

Table 69. — Arrests by State, 1996 — Continued

State	Total[1] all classes	Crime[2] Index total	Violent[3] crime	Property[4] crime	Murder and non-negligent man-slaughter	Forcible rape	Robbery	Aggra-vated assault	Burglary	Larceny-theft	Motor vehicle theft	Arson	Other assaults	Forgery and counter-feiting	Fraud
NEW JERSEY: 537 agencies; population 7,657,000															
Under 18	84,973	22,775	5,256	17,519	52	155	2,113	2,936	3,238	12,846	1,140	295	8,139	76	180
Total all ages	396,784	71,757	20,032	51,725	349	910	5,654	13,119	9,166	39,845	2,172	542	38,249	1,335	5,654
NEW MEXICO: 46 agencies; population 1,005,000															
Under 18	15,450	4,855	440	4,415	12	14	97	317	485	3,689	211	30	1,247	44	61
Total all ages	87,259	14,172	2,181	11,991	72	85	339	1,685	1,210	10,131	607	43	6,766	451	556
NEW YORK: 330 agencies; population 12,604,000															
Under 18	105,731	30,697	12,953	17,744	142	236	8,796	3,779	3,203	12,731	1,634	176	7,870	323	11,198
Total all ages	824,639	129,002	54,426	74,576	1,136	1,568	24,240	27,482	13,212	53,983	6,930	451	45,745	8,818	45,802
NORTH CAROLINA: 457 agencies; population 7,177,000															
Under 18	56,032	18,687	3,413	15,274	71	92	979	2,271	3,925	10,288	860	201	7,173	260	975
Total all ages	505,310	85,957	26,880	59,077	697	771	4,034	21,378	15,429	40,752	2,388	508	56,358	4,667	53,197
NORTH DAKOTA: 48 agencies; population 396,000															
Under 18	6,120	1,333	40	1,293	1	7	3	29	137	1,046	101	9	330	24	20
Total all ages	21,205	2,422	154	2,268	6	25	11	112	252	1,833	170	13	1,001	114	4,711
OHIO: 251 agencies; population 6,426,000															
Under 18	81,029	19,975	3,188	16,787	48	244	1,302	1,594	2,912	11,583	1,976	316	7,667	149	117
Total all ages	377,034	61,789	17,420	44,369	329	1,113	4,065	11,913	7,418	32,502	3,840	609	35,241	2,052	6,179
OKLAHOMA: 292 agencies; population 3,301,000															
Under 18	30,715	12,782	1,314	11,468	29	70	378	837	1,909	7,965	1,319	275	1,239	137	126
Total all ages	153,537	29,659	6,525	23,134	216	445	965	4,899	4,253	16,016	2,417	448	8,127	1,432	2,603
OREGON: 182 agencies; population 2,740,000															
Under 18	45,755	13,810	1,056	12,754	20	56	343	637	1,665	9,712	1,113	264	2,843	166	171
Total all ages	159,691	39,300	4,304	34,996	147	298	1,343	2,516	3,885	27,430	3,221	460	16,801	1,930	1,464
PENNSYLVANIA: 676 agencies; population 9,322,000															
Under 18	97,297	21,866	4,813	17,053	58	191	1,986	2,578	3,032	10,993	2,676	352	6,319	165	294
Total all ages	346,773	71,812	19,744	52,068	511	1,095	6,698	11,440	8,995	35,596	6,753	724	36,204	2,843	8,334
RHODE ISLAND: 42 agencies; population 936,000															
Under 18	9,128	2,861	474	2,387	1	12	65	396	394	1,707	218	68	913	18	35
Total all ages	41,058	8,046	2,409	5,637	13	106	208	2,082	1,079	3,944	503	111	5,209	113	1,115
SOUTH CAROLINA: 241 agencies; population 3,658,000															
Under 18	29,729	10,999	1,797	9,202	36	85	415	1,261	2,178	6,425	515	84	3,998	114	363
Total all ages	215,578	39,827	11,917	27,910	324	625	1,736	9,232	5,787	20,792	1,115	216	25,835	2,453	35,103
SOUTH DAKOTA: 59 agencies; population 505,000															
Under 18	10,427	2,821	199	2,622	2	30	37	130	369	2,070	133	50	511	64	28
Total all ages	32,960	5,602	686	4,916	9	89	63	525	747	3,915	193	61	2,667	198	807
TENNESSEE: 100 agencies; population 2,069,000															
Under 18	23,810	7,736	944	6,792	31	34	244	635	895	5,091	736	70	1,354	53	78
Total all ages	160,461	33,093	8,090	25,003	206	335	1,159	6,390	3,159	19,550	2,115	179	12,519	1,873	8,881
TEXAS: 848 agencies; population 16,601,000															
Under 18	212,368	57,578	7,196	50,382	217	439	2,291	4,249	9,649	35,835	4,360	538	16,259	577	594
Total all ages	1,020,750	165,474	33,827	131,647	1,157	2,316	7,094	23,260	20,737	100,021	9,917	972	88,004	7,610	13,581

See footnotes at end of table.

Table 69. — Arrests by State, 1996 — Continued

Embezzlement	Stolen property; buying, receiving, possessing	Vandalism	Weapons; carrying, possessing, etc.	Prostitution and commercialized vice	Sex offenses (except forcible rape and prostitution)	Drug abuse violations	Gambling	Offenses against family and children	Driving under the influence	Liquor laws	Drunkenness[5]	Disorderly conduct	Vagrancy	All other offenses (except traffic)	Suspicion	Curfew and loitering law violations	Runaways
5	3,106	5,660	1,827	20	435	10,240	14	27	258	3,531	—	9,631	273	10,092	—	3,080	5,604
92	9,374	10,261	5,699	2,316	1,977	56,075	470	16,911	24,486	11,688	—	36,114	2,619	93,023	—	3,080	5,604
14	249	407	331	9	16	1,363	1	127	261	1,906	68	503	—	2,686	3	813	486
175	889	792	850	365	141	6,185	2	1,710	12,595	5,680	763	2,131	6	31,586	145	813	486
11	1,451	5,273	2,002	100	811	13,477	315	246	158	2,382	—	8,548	736	17,672	—	—	2,461
320	7,808	16,294	10,338	9,148	5,064	135,316	6,449	1,162	24,031	66,337	—	50,589	3,011	256,944	—	—	2,461
237	1,400	2,915	1,485	12	315	4,326	20	87	1,020	1,440	—	3,073	18	10,691	—	109	1,789
2,270	6,676	11,004	7,967	914	2,547	35,658	426	7,057	71,411	9,714	—	15,152	169	132,268	—	109	1,789
—	50	261	32	2	27	142	—	49	26	1,160	1	328	—	1,233	—	485	617
5	72	388	75	2	83	640	2	67	1,992	3,209	323	840	—	4,157	—	485	617
6	2,050	3,398	1,087	25	338	4,738	109	2,038	307	3,502	364	4,534	45	19,559	129	6,171	4,721
26	6,291	5,973	4,725	2,697	2,105	33,030	535	22,860	24,049	18,815	15,478	22,362	711	100,971	253	6,171	4,721
67	555	777	449	14	124	1,604	—	101	348	885	792	465	—	2,980	—	4,001	3,269
666	2,120	1,438	2,580	187	981	14,360	33	1,096	21,658	4,573	27,882	2,791	—	24,081	—	4,001	3,269
2	155	2,786	487	20	290	2,400	4	19	260	5,439	—	1,209	—	6,999	—	4,685	4,010
74	585	5,274	2,245	930	1,303	15,493	25	630	20,449	14,785	—	4,802	—	24,906	—	4,685	4,010
4	921	5,873	1,306	26	458	4,186	17	77	350	6,700	360	13,207	75	8,615	—	21,930	4,548
148	3,401	13,164	3,571	2,779	2,311	25,474	257	978	29,296	18,470	15,130	50,700	414	35,009	—	21,930	4,548
9	161	832	218	5	59	581	—	93	24	238	8	589	30	1,200	361	50	843
100	581	1,785	514	529	371	3,773	45	457	1,881	1,261	43	2,986	65	10,697	594	50	843
4	633	1,704	722	19	207	2,904	5	23	170	1,028	141	2,495	—	2,615	—	90	1,495
72	2,410	4,682	3,149	1,026	855	20,841	319	1,423	15,326	10,028	10,553	14,856	360	24,875	—	90	1,495
13	101	431	87	1	22	448	—	83	63	1,752	43	361	—	1,860	—	511	1,227
39	187	683	182	16	130	1,788	2	266	4,187	6,857	237	1,889	11	5,473	1	511	1,227
6	86	635	444	6	57	1,611	60	37	130	767	211	1,539	129	4,816	8	2,194	1,853
111	191	2,082	3,039	1,172	468	12,479	509	1,009	14,427	3,285	17,181	5,551	137	38,352	55	2,194	1,853
66	288	7,776	3,108	66	889	13,425	109	222	689	5,501	5,669	18,004	75	29,752	25	17,833	33,863
396	911	13,926	13,544	6,277	5,361	78,440	551	4,841	75,497	24,286	168,801	40,460	837	260,218	39	17,833	33,863

Table 69. — Arrests by State, 1996 — Continued

State	Total[1] all classes	Crime[2] Index total	Violent[3] crime	Property[4] crime	Murder and non-negligent man-slaughter	Forcible rape	Robbery	Aggra-vated assault	Burglary	Larceny-theft	Motor vehicle theft	Arson	Other assaults	Forgery and counter-feiting	Fraud
UTAH: 112 agencies; population 1,840,000															
Under 18	36,408	11,486	760	10,726	9	36	152	563	981	8,685	931	129	2,493	188	89
Total all ages	120,600	23,581	2,244	21,337	66	154	403	1,621	1,863	17,848	1,433	193	9,124	1,183	707
VERMONT[6]:															
VIRGINIA: 333 agencies; population 6,177,000															
Under 18	55,592	15,285	1,568	13,717	57	89	637	785	2,087	10,069	1,349	212	4,889	224	286
Total all ages	375,677	56,303	11,417	44,886	417	790	2,635	7,575	6,518	34,643	3,273	452	43,335	5,230	14,523
WASHINGTON: 189 agencies; population 3,747,000															
Under 18	47,544	20,155	1,700	18,455	29	131	471	1,069	2,846	14,355	1,055	199	5,827	220	50
Total all ages	208,713	47,667	6,559	41,108	157	651	1,253	4,498	5,659	33,286	1,850	313	31,972	2,003	1,503
WEST VIRGINIA: 296 agencies; population 1,826,000															
Under 18	7,881	2,656	151	2,505	9	10	47	85	472	1,790	218	25	661	35	80
Total all ages	70,538	10,069	1,391	8,678	55	118	271	947	1,595	6,419	561	103	8,926	659	4,720
WISCONSIN: 331 agencies; population 5,143,000															
Under 18	144,403	31,573	2,291	29,282	96	148	803	1,244	3,674	22,426	2,857	325	5,647	452	502
Total all ages	459,506	67,778	9,335	58,443	477	697	2,055	6,106	6,817	46,144	4,966	516	24,797	2,643	11,366
WYOMING: 31 agencies; population 281,000															
Under 18	5,323	1,309	67	1,242	1	1	6	59	91	1,083	57	11	207	21	1
Total all ages	20,107	2,782	411	2,371	8	18	18	367	281	1,957	119	14	1,156	88	97

[1] Does not include traffic arrests.

[2] Includes arson.

[3] Violent crime includes offenses of murder, forcible rape, robbery, and aggravated assault.

[4] Property crime includes offenses of burglary, larceny–theft, motor vehicle theft, and arson.

[5] Drunkenness is not considered a crime in some states; therefore, the figures vary widely from state to state.

[6] Complete data were not available for the states of Illinois, Kansas, Kentucky, Montana, Vermont, and the District of Columbia; therefore, it was necessary that their crime counts be estimated. An aggregate Florida state total for 1996 was supplied by the Florida Department of Law Enforcement. See "Offense Estimation," pages 389-390 for details.

NOTE: Direct comparisons of arrest totals listed in this table should not be made with prior years' issues. Some Part II offenses are not considered crimes in some states; therefore, figures may vary widely.

Table 69. — Arrests by State, 1996 — Continued

Embezzlement	Stolen property; buying, receiving, possessing	Vandalism	Weapons; carrying, possessing, etc.	Prostitution and commercialized vice	Sex offenses (except forcible rape and prostitution)	Drug abuse violations	Gambling	Offenses against family and children	Driving under the influence	Liquor laws	Drunkenness[5]	Disorderly conduct	Vagrancy	All other offenses (except traffic)	Suspicion	Curfew and loitering law violations	Runaways
2	265	2,523	551	28	295	2,044	—	61	185	3,555	134	1,715	15	7,679	207	2,109	784
18	693	3,671	1,252	772	968	11,114	1	1,378	7,410	12,602	6,029	4,739	36	32,187	242	2,109	784
40	385	2,612	1,195	8	377	3,493	16	204	348	2,360	712	1,788	—	12,281	—	4,005	5,084
1,176	1,794	6,869	7,287	1,195	2,326	27,261	154	2,971	28,100	11,103	42,334	8,567	2	106,058	—	4,005	5,084
12	1,267	2,900	637	32	258	2,338	—	18	241	4,273	13	775	38	6,272	32	181	2,005
82	3,682	6,679	2,497	780	1,719	14,707	7	486	15,495	13,315	159	4,863	132	58,703	76	181	2,005
3	109	394	142	3	24	424	—	10	145	374	264	190	3	1,117	—	504	743
137	616	1,304	1,335	210	330	4,346	19	789	9,817	2,684	8,457	1,687	15	13,171	—	504	743
18	997	6,724	2,214	26	1,529	4,759	48	460	512	13,667	29	24,002	51	29,519	223	11,526	9,925
131	1,947	14,172	6,346	2,134	3,942	21,232	244	4,063	37,470	42,336	138	72,931	152	123,839	394	11,526	9,925
1	15	100	34	1	12	223	—	11	35	1,008	13	536	2	1,301	—	262	231
13	45	224	93	3	75	861	—	128	2,640	2,633	963	1,503	12	6,184	114	262	231

SECTION V

Drugs in America: 1980-1995

The Nation experienced its highest level of illicit drug activity in 1995 when measured by the total number of reported drug arrests since 1980. This study examines the national drug arrest trend for 1980-1995 using reported drug abuse violations arrest figures from local, county, and state law enforcement agencies participating in the Uniform Crime Reporting Program. Additionally, the study looks at the change in the profile of drug arrestees that has occurred during this same period.

The illegal drug trade confronting the Nation has steadily increased during the period under consideration. The total impact of drug abuse on society is immeasurable, and the cost to law enforcement alone is astronomical. According to the Office of National Drug Control Policy, federal law enforcement agencies expend $16 billion annually to combat this problem. Trends for overall drug arrests indicate that this social ill shows no signs of abating.

In 1995, the Nation recorded its highest drug arrest total; an estimated 1.5 million people were arrested for either the sale and/or manufacture or possession of illegal narcotics. Furthermore, Table 5.1 shows that since 1980, the number of arrests for all drug types rose substantially, with those of heroin/cocaine showing the highest increase, 741 percent. In comparing arrests for specific drug types from 1990 to 1995, marijuana arrests have increased 80 percent and heroin/cocaine arrests 6 percent. These two drug categories account for more than eight out of every 10 drug arrests.

Regionally, when examining the year 1995 over 1990, the South, the most populous region, registered a 55-percent increase in total drug arrests. This region accounts for 34 percent of the Nation's total drug arrests in 1995. During this same time period, the other three regions also registered increases in drug arrests: 37 percent in the Midwest, 36 percent in the Northeast, and 18 percent in the West. (See Table 5.2.)

Table 5.2

Percent Changes in Estimated Number of Drug Arrests by Region, United States, 1995 over 1990

Year	Total	Northeast	Midwest	South	West
1990	1,089,500	252,250	131,901	323,756	381,593
1995	1,476,100	342,544	181,216	501,351	450,979
Percent Change	35.5	35.8	37.4	54.9	18.2

The majority of arrests for the offense of drug abuse violations by type are for possession. Table 5.3 shows that while the percent of sale/manufacture drug arrests peaked in 1990, arrests for possession constituted three out of every four drug arrests in 1995. This pattern is consistent with the historical trend.

Table 5.3

Percent Distribution of Total Drug Arrests by Sale/Manufacture and Possession, United States, 1980, 1985, 1990, and 1995

Year	Total	Sale/ Manufacture	Possession
1980	100.0	22.6	77.4
1985	100.0	23.7	76.3
1990	100.0	31.9	68.1
1995	100.0	24.9	75.1

Table 5.1

Percent Changes in the Estimated Number of Drug Arrests by Type, United States, 1995 over 1980, 1985, and 1990

Drug Type	1995/1980	1995/1985	1995/1990
Total	154.1	81.9	35.5
Heroin/Cocaine	741.5	163.1	5.7
Marijuana	48.8	30.6	79.8
Synthetic	50.6	69.3	39.3
Other	153.6	120.8	57.4

Charts 5.1 to 5.5 show 1980-1995 national drug arrest trends by drug type. An analysis of these charts indicates that marijuana arrests dominated the first part of the decade, but toward the end of the decade, these arrests were outstripped by heroin/cocaine arrests. However, in the 1990s the pendulum is swinging the other way as the number of marijuana arrests is again increasing.

ESTIMATED DRUG ARRESTS
UNITED STATES FROM 1980 - 1995

CHART 5.1

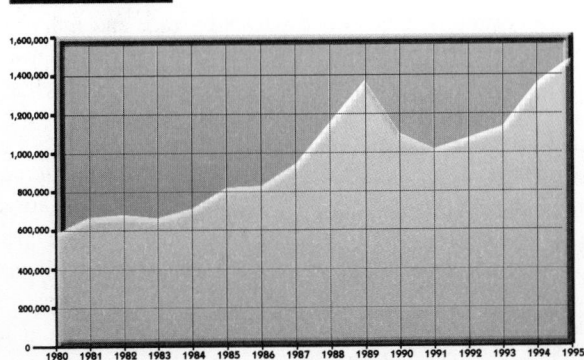

ESTIMATED HEROIN/COCAINE ARRESTS UNITED STATES FROM 1980 - 1995

CHART 5.2

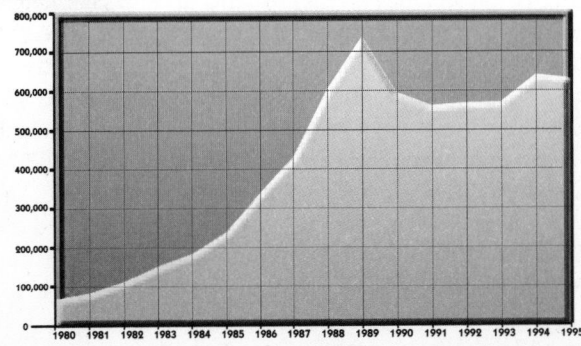

ESTIMATED MARIJUANA ARRESTS UNITED STATES FROM 1980 - 1995

CHART 5.3

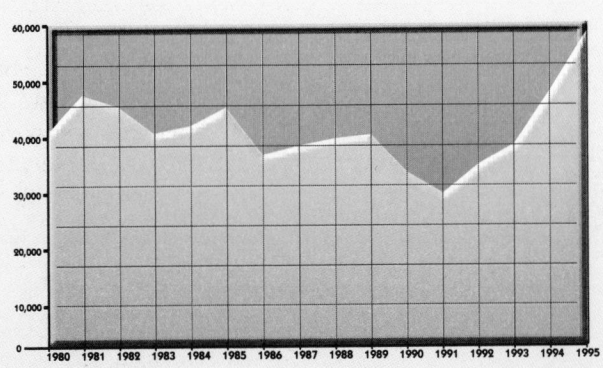

ESTIMATED SYNTHETIC DRUG ARRESTS
UNITED STATES FROM 1980 - 1995

CHART 5.4

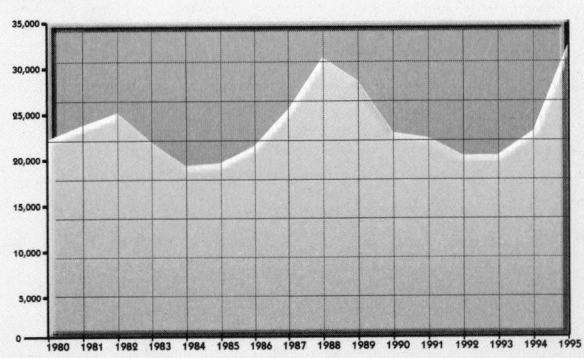

ESTIMATED OTHER DRUG ARRESTS
UNITED STATES FROM 1980 - 1995

CHART 5.5

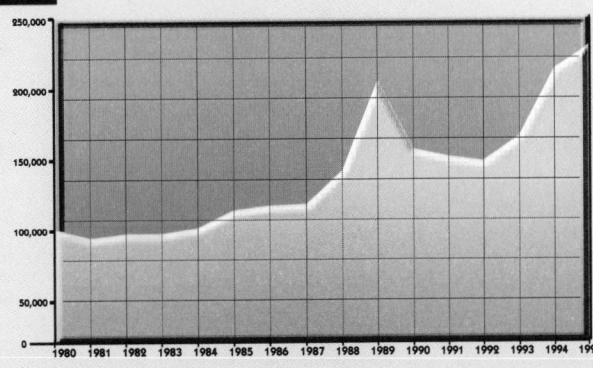

281

Between the years 1980 and 1995, the profile of drug arrestees in the United States has changed somewhat. Arrests of juveniles and adults for drug abuse violations have increased significantly during this same time period (see Chart 5.6 and Chart 5.7); however, the percent involving juveniles has fallen. In 1980, arrests of persons under 18 accounted for 19 percent of total drug arrestees; in 1995 the total declined to 13 percent. When considering the percent change in the number of juvenile and adult drug arrests from 1980 to 1995, adult arrests jumped 173 percent and juvenile arrests rose 73 percent. It should be noted, however, that when examining 1995 versus 1990, the number of juvenile arrests for drug violations has increased at a faster rate than that of adults. During this period, juvenile drug arrests increased 132 percent, versus a 28-percent increase for adults. This overall increase in juvenile drug arrests was influenced by a 278-percent rise in marijuana arrests.

Considering race distribution figures of drug arrestees in 1995, blacks constituted 39 percent of the total, up from 24 percent in 1980 (see Table 5.4). In 1995 whites made up 60 percent of all drug arrestees, down from the 75 percent in 1980. The percent distribution of persons arrested in other racial groups has remained relatively stable.

Further examination of drug arrests by race and individual drug type reveals that from 1990 to 1995 all racial groups experienced a substantial increase in the number of marijuana arrests. Increases were 98 percent for blacks, 69 percent for whites, and 96 percent for other races. Arrests for involvement with heroin/cocaine have also risen when comparing 1995 numbers with 1990 numbers, though less markedly. The number of white arrestees increased 4 percent and, that for blacks, 1 percent. The number of arrests for heroin/cocaine for all other races has increased 34 percent for those same years. (See Table 5.5.)

Although the age and racial composition of drug arrestees have changed, the gender distribution of arrestees has remained constant with males accounting for 84 percent of persons arrested.

Table 5.4
Percent Distribution of Total Drug Arrests by Race,
United States, 1980, 1985, 1990, and 1995

Year	Total	White	Black	Indian	Asian
1980	100.0	74.7	24.5	.4	.4
1985	100.0	67.8	31.2	.4	.6
1990	100.0	58.0	41.2	.3	.4
1995	100.0	59.9	39.1	.4	.6

Table 5.5
Percent Changes in the Estimated Number
of Heroin/Cocaine and Marijuana Arrests
by Race, United States, 1995 over 1990

Race	Heroin/Cocaine	Marijuana
White	3.6	69.1
Black	1.3	97.7
Other	34.4	95.6

ESTIMATED ADULT DRUG ARRESTS
UNITED STATES FROM 1980 - 1995

CHART 5.6

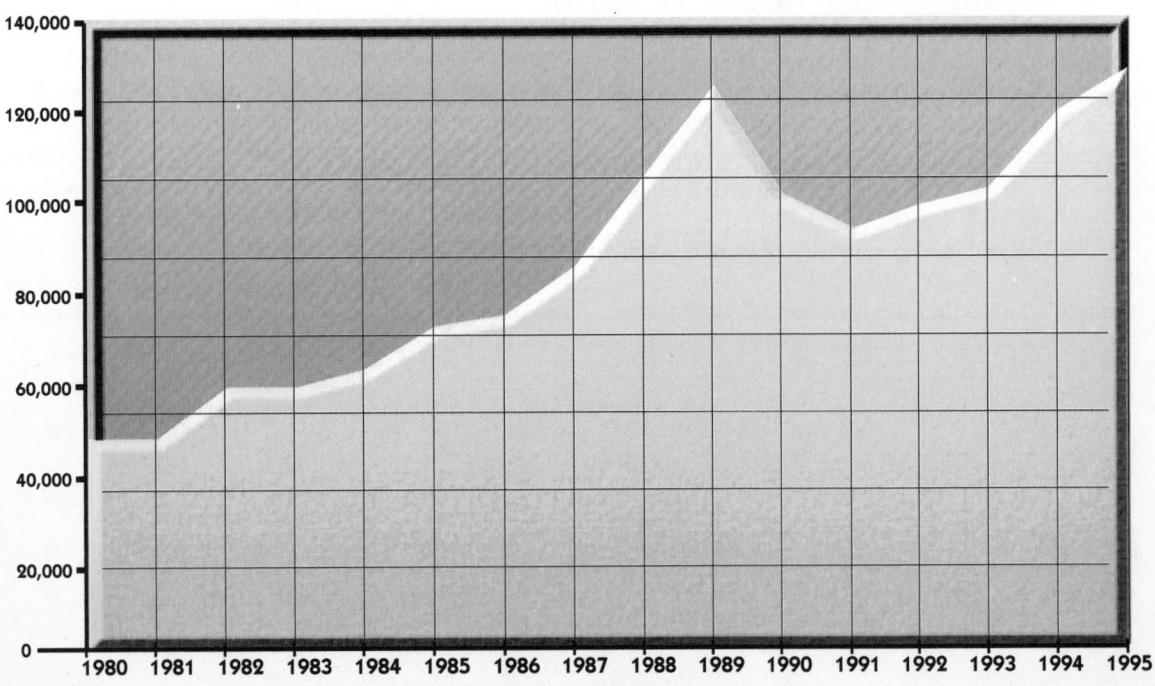

ESTIMATED JUVENILE DRUG ARRESTS
UNITED STATES FROM 1980 - 1995

CHART 5.7

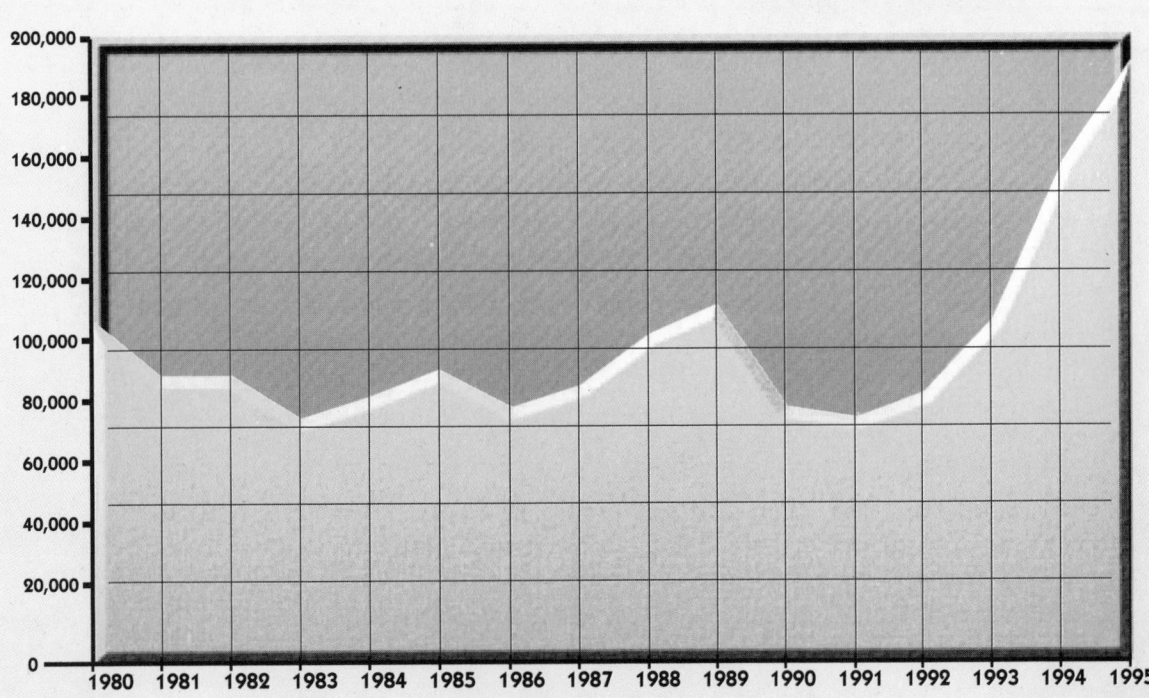

Summary

The majority of arrests for drug abuse violations during the 1980s were for marijuana. However, when comparing the number of drug abuse violation arrests in 1990 to that in 1980, the number of marijuana arrests decreased 17 percent while the number of heroin/cocaine arrests increased 696 percent. During the 1990s, marijuana appears to be the fastest growing drug category with arrests increasing 80 percent between 1990 and 1995, while heroin/cocaine arrests have increased 6 percent.

On a regional basis, the more populous South has replaced the West as the region in the country during the 1990s with the highest number of drug violation arrests.

During the past decade and a half, the age and racial composition of drug arrestees has also shown a change. Adults are more frequently arrested than are juveniles; the number of adult arrests is up 173 percent, while the number of juvenile arrests increased 73 percent. Current 1995 figures show juveniles constituted only 13 percent of total drug arrests; a decline of 32 percent from the 1980 level. However, a year-to-year analysis of juveniles arrested for drug abuse violations during the 1990s shows a rise in the number of persons under 18 being arrested in this category. The racial distribution of drug arrestees has also changed. In 1995, nonwhites accounted for 40 percent of drug arrests compared to 25 percent in 1980. Finally, the age and racial makeup of the marijuana arrestee has also undergone a change. From 1990 to 1995, the number of persons under the age of 18 arrested for marijuana increased 278 percent. Additionally, during the 1990s the number of nonwhite persons arrested for marijuana violations also increased. Specifically, arrests for blacks were up 98 percent and other races, up 96 percent. The number of marijuana arrests for whites increased 96 percent.

SECTION VI

Law Enforcement Personnel

The Nation's law enforcement community employed an average of 2.4 full-time officers for every 1,000 inhabitants as of October 31, 1996. Including full-time civilians, the overall law enforcement employee rate was 3.3 per 1,000 inhabitants according to 13,025 city, county, and state police agencies reporting in 1996. These agencies collectively employed 595,170 officers and 234,668 civilians giving law enforcement service to nearly 249 million U.S. inhabitants. A listing of reported full-time law enforcement officers and civilian employees by state is shown in Table 77.

Varying demographic and other jurisdictional characteristics greatly affect the requirements for law enforcement service from one locale to another. The needs of a community having a highly mobile or seasonal population, for example, may be very different from those of a city whose population is relatively stable. Similarly, a small community situated between two large cities may require a greater number of law enforcement personnel than a community of the same size which has no urban centers nearby.

The functions of law enforcement are also significantly diverse throughout the Nation. In certain areas, sheriffs' responsibilities are limited almost exclusively to civil functions and/or the administration of the county jail facilities. Likewise, the responsibilities of state police and highway patrol agencies vary from one jurisdiction to another.

In view of these differing service requirements and responsibilities, care should be used when attempting any comparison of law enforcement employee rates. The rates presented in the following tables represent national averages; they should be viewed as guides or indicators, not as recommended or desirable police strengths. Adequate personnel for a specific locale can be determined only after careful study and analysis of the various conditions affecting service requirements in that jurisdiction.

The Nation's cities collectively reported an average of 3.0 law enforcement employees per 1,000 inhabitants. The highest average among the city groups, 4.0 employees per 1,000 population, was recorded in cities with over 250,000 inhabitants. Rural and suburban county law enforcement agencies averaged full-time law enforcement employee rates of 4.3 and 3.8 per 1,000 population, respectively. (See Table 74.)

Regionally, the law enforcement employee rate was 3.4 per 1,000 inhabitants in both the South and the Northeast, 2.7 in the Midwest, and 2.5 in the West. (See Table 70.)

Sworn Personnel

Rates based solely on sworn law enforcement personnel (excluding civilians) showed the national average for all cities was 2.3 officers per 1,000 inhabitants. By city population grouping, the rates ranged from 1.8 for cities with populations of 25,000 to 99,999 to 3.1 in cities with 250,000 or more inhabitants. Suburban county law enforcement agencies averaged 2.3 officers per 1,000 population, while agencies in rural counties averaged 2.8. (See Table 74.)

Geographically, the highest rates of sworn officers to population were recorded in the Northeastern States where there were 2.8 officers per 1,000 inhabitants. Following were the Southern States with 2.6, the Midwestern States with 2.2, and the Western States with 1.8.

Males comprised 90 percent of all sworn employees nationally and in cities. Ninety-three percent of sworn officers in rural counties and 88 percent in suburban counties were males. (See Table 74.)

Civilian Employees

Civilians made up 28 percent of the total United States law enforcement employee force in 1996. They represented 22 percent of the police employees in cities, 37 percent in rural counties, and 38 percent of the suburban county law enforcement strength. Sixty-two percent of all civilian employees were females.

Law Enforcement Officers Killed and Assaulted

Fifty-five law enforcement officers were feloniously slain in the line of duty during 1996, 19 fewer than in 1995. Accidents occurring while performing official duties claimed the lives of an additional 45 officers in 1996. The 1996 total for officers accidentally killed was 12 lower than the 1995 total of 57.

Extensive data on line-of-duty deaths and assaults on city, county, state, and federal officers can be found in the Uniform Crime Reporting publication, *Law Enforcement Officers Killed and Assaulted.*

Table 70. — Full-time Law Enforcement Employees,[1] Number and Rate per 1,000 Inhabitants, Geographic Region and Division by Population Group, October 31, 1996

[1996 estimated population]

Geographic region/division	Total (9,907 cities; population 166,590,000)	Group I (65 cities, 250,000 and over; population 47,047,000)	Group II (144 cities, 100,000 to 249,999; population 21,226,000)	Group III (359 cities, 50,000 to 99,999; population 24,492,000)	Group IV (682 cities, 25,000 to 49,999; population 23,614,000)	Group V (1,699 cities, 10,000 to 24,999; population 26,735,000)	Group VI (6,958 cities, under 10,000; population 23,477,000)
TOTAL: 9,907 cities; population 166,590,000:							
Number of employees	501,823	188,190	53,486	56,323	53,979	63,298	86,547
Average number of employees per 1,000 inhabitants	3.0	4.0	2.5	2.3	2.3	2.4	3.7
New England: 712 cities; population 11,829,000:							
Number of employees	31,214	2,926	4,233	6,186	6,170	6,746	4,953
Average number of employees per 1,000 inhabitants	2.6	5.3	3.7	2.5	2.2	2.2	2.8
Middle Atlantic: 1,473 cities; population 27,136,000:							
Number of employees	100,464	59,555	3,091	7,550	9,390	11,172	9,706
Average number of employees per 1,000 inhabitants	3.7	6.1	3.2	2.5	2.4	2.1	2.3
NORTHEAST: 2,185 cities; population 38,965,000:							
Number of employees	131,678	62,481	7,324	13,736	15,560	17,918	14,659
Average number of employees per 1,000 inhabitants	3.4	6.0	3.4	2.5	2.4	2.2	2.4
East North Central: 1,918 cities; population 29,675,000:							
Number of employees	84,909	30,694	6,748	9,707	10,421	13,495	13,844
Average number of employees per 1,000 inhabitants	2.9	4.7	2.4	2.1	2.1	2.2	3.0
West North Central: 873 cities; population 11,419,000:							
Number of employees	27,859	7,610	2,864	2,919	3,464	4,587	6,415
Average number of employees per 1,000 inhabitants	2.4	3.6	2.2	1.7	1.9	2.1	2.8
MIDWEST: 2,791 cities; population 41,094,000:							
Number of employees	112,768	38,304	9,612	12,626	13,885	18,082	20,259
Average number of employees per 1,000 inhabitants	2.7	4.4	2.4	2.0	2.0	2.2	2.9
South Atlantic: 1,667 cities; population 19,337,000:							
Number of employees	75,483	17,497	11,457	10,046	6,992	9,630	19,861
Average number of employees per 1,000 inhabitants	3.9	4.3	3.1	3.2	3.0	3.3	6.1
East South Central: 808 cities; population 8,372,000:							
Number of employees	27,231	5,584	3,896	1,610	3,165	5,051	7,925
Average number of employees per 1,000 inhabitants	3.3	3.3	2.9	2.8	3.0	2.9	4.1
West South Central: 1,140 cities; population 19,764,000:							
Number of employees	57,070	22,225	6,754	5,339	4,691	6,508	11,553
Average number of employees per 1,000 inhabitants	2.9	3.0	2.4	2.3	2.3	2.5	4.4
SOUTH: 3,615 cities; population 47,473,000:							
Number of employees	159,784	45,306	22,107	16,995	14,848	21,189	39,339
Average number of employees per 1,000 inhabitants	3.4	3.4	2.8	2.8	2.8	2.9	5.0
Mountain: 554 cities; population 11,087,000:							
Number of employees	29,143	11,937	3,593	3,559	2,500	2,275	5,279
Average number of employees per 1,000 inhabitants	2.6	2.8	2.3	1.9	2.2	2.4	4.2
Pacific: 762 cities; population 27,972,000:							
Number of employees	68,450	30,162	10,850	9,407	7,186	3,834	7,011
Average number of employees per 1,000 inhabitants	2.4	2.9	1.9	2.0	2.0	2.1	4.7
WEST: 1,316 cities; population 39,059,000:							
Number of employees	97,593	42,099	14,443	12,966	9,686	6,109	12,290
Average number of employees per 1,000 inhabitants	2.5	2.8	2.0	1.9	2.0	2.2	4.5

Suburban and County

Suburban:[2] 6,059 agencies; population 101,447,000:		County: 3,118 agencies; population 82,134,000:	
Number of employees	335,002	Number of employees	328,015
Average number of employees per 1,000 inhabitants	3.3	Average number of employees per 1,000 inhabitants	4.0

[1]Includes civilians.

[2]Includes suburban city and county law enforcement agencies within metropolitan areas. Excludes central cities. Suburban cities and counties are also included in other groups. Population figures were rounded to the nearest thousand. All rates were calculated before rounding.

Table 71. — Full-time Law Enforcement Officers, Number and Rate per 1,000 Inhabitants, Geographic Region and Division by Population Group, October 31, 1996

[1996 estimated population]

Geographic region/division	Total (9,907 cities; population 166,590,000)	Population group					
		Group I (65 cities, 250,000 and over; population 47,047,000)	Group II (144 cities, 100,000 to 249,999; population 21,226,000)	Group III (359 cities, 50,000 to 99,999; population 24,492,000)	Group IV (682 cities, 25,000 to 49,999; population 23,614,000)	Group V (1,699 cities, 10,000 to 24,999; population 26,735,000)	Group VI (6,958 cities, under 10,000; population 23,477,000)
TOTAL: 9,907 cities; population 166,590,000:							
Number of officers	**390,590**	**145,312**	**40,790**	**43,744**	**42,278**	**50,616**	**67,850**
Average number of officers per 1,000 inhabitants	**2.3**	**3.1**	**1.9**	**1.8**	**1.8**	**1.9**	**2.9**
New England: 712 cities; population 11,829,000:							
Number of officers	25,862	2,218	3,574	5,326	5,268	5,632	3,844
Average number of officers per 1,000 inhabitants	2.2	4.0	3.1	2.1	1.9	1.8	2.1
Middle Atlantic: 1,473 cities; population 27,136,000:							
Number of officers	81,548	46,845	2,637	6,319	7,850	9,507	8,390
Average number of officers per 1,000 inhabitants	3.0	4.8	2.7	2.1	2.0	1.8	2.0
NORTHEAST: 2,185 cities; population 38,965,000:							
Number of officers	**107,410**	**49,063**	**6,211**	**11,645**	**13,118**	**15,139**	**12,234**
Average number of officers per 1,000 inhabitants	**2.8**	**4.7**	**2.9**	**2.1**	**2.0**	**1.8**	**2.0**
East North Central: 1,918 cities; population 29,675,000:							
Number of officers	68,564	25,216	5,443	7,716	8,168	10,757	11,264
Average number of officers per 1,000 inhabitants	2.3	3.8	2.0	1.7	1.6	1.7	2.4
West North Central: 873 cities; population 11,419,000:							
Number of officers	21,659	5,569	2,162	2,348	2,691	3,667	5,222
Average number of officers per 1,000 inhabitants	1.9	2.6	1.7	1.4	1.4	1.7	2.3
MIDWEST: 2,791 cities; population 41,094,000:							
Number of officers	**90,223**	**30,785**	**7,605**	**10,064**	**10,859**	**14,424**	**16,486**
Average number of officers per 1,000 inhabitants	**2.2**	**3.5**	**1.9**	**1.6**	**1.6**	**1.7**	**2.4**
South Atlantic: 1,667 cities; population 19,337,000:							
Number of officers	58,218	13,463	8,803	7,622	5,394	7,548	15,388
Average number of officers per 1,000 inhabitants	3.0	3.3	2.4	2.4	2.3	2.6	4.8
East South Central: 808 cities; population 8,372,000:							
Number of officers	20,889	4,188	2,877	1,254	2,442	3,970	6,158
Average number of officers per 1,000 inhabitants	2.5	2.5	2.2	2.2	2.3	2.3	3.2
West South Central: 1,140 cities; population 19,764,000:							
Number of officers	43,357	16,960	5,324	4,098	3,496	5,027	8,452
Average number of officers per 1,000 inhabitants	2.2	2.3	1.9	1.8	1.7	1.9	3.2
SOUTH: 3,615 cities; population 47,473,000:							
Number of officers	. **122,464**	**34,611**	**17,004**	**12,974**	**11,332**	**16,545**	**29,998**
Average number of officers per 1,000 inhabitants	**2.6**	**2.6**	**2.2**	**2.2**	**2.1**	**2.3**	**3.8**
Mountain: 554 cities; population 11,087,000:							
Number of officers	21,200	8,636	2,562	2,576	1,828	1,685	3,913
Average number of officers per 1,000 inhabitants	1.9	2.0	1.6	1.4	1.6	1.8	3.1
Pacific: 762 cities; population 27,972,000:							
Number of officers	49,293	22,217	7,408	6,485	5,141	2,823	5,219
Average number of officers per 1,000 inhabitants	1.8	2.1	1.3	1.3	1.4	1.6	3.5
WEST: 1,316 cities; population 39,059,000:							
Number of officers	**70,493**	**30,853**	**9,970**	**9,061**	**6,969**	**4,508**	**9,132**
Average number of officers per 1,000 inhabitants	**1.8**	**2.1**	**1.4**	**1.4**	**1.5**	**1.6**	**3.3**

Suburban and County

Suburban: [1] 6,059 agencies; population 101,447,000:		County: 3,118 agencies; population 82,134,000:	
Number of officers	229,452	Number of officers	204,580
Average number of officers per 1,000 inhabitants	2.3	Average number of officers per 1,000 inhabitants	2.5

[1] Includes suburban city and county law enforcement agencies within metropolitan areas. Excludes central cities. Suburban cities and counties are also included in other groups. Population figures were rounded to the nearest thousand. All rates were calculated before rounding.

Table 72. — Full-time Law Enforcement Employees, October 31, 1996

[Range in rate per 1,000 inhabitants]

Rate range		Total[1] (9,216 cities; population 166,590,000)	Group I (65 cities, 250,000 and over; population 47,047,000)	Group II (144 cities, 100,000 to 249,999; population 21,226,000)	Group III (359 cities, 50,000 to 99,999; population 24,492,000)	Group IV (682 cities, 25,000 to 49,999; population 23,614,000)	Group V (1,699 cities, 10,000 to 24,999; population 26,735,000)	Group VI (6,267 cities, under 10,000; population 23,477,000)
.1-.5	Number	111	—	—	1	1	15	94
	Percent	1.2	—	—	.3	.1	.9	1.5
.6-1.0	Number	398	—	1	1	13	46	337
	Percent	4.3	—	.7	.3	1.9	2.7	5.4
1.1-1.5	Number	1,031	—	7	38	79	165	742
	Percent	11.2	—	4.9	10.6	11.6	9.7	11.8
1.6-2.0	Number	1,807	8	39	120	204	395	1,041
	Percent	19.6	12.3	27.1	33.4	29.9	23.2	16.6
2.1-2.5	Number	1,804	10	40	93	191	490	980
	Percent	19.6	15.4	27.8	25.9	28.0	28.8	15.6
2.6-3.0	Number	1,344	15	25	56	96	284	868
	Percent	14.6	23.1	17.4	15.6	14.1	16.7	13.9
3.1-3.5	Number	875	15	20	27	57	140	616
	Percent	9.5	23.1	13.9	7.5	8.4	8.2	9.8
3.6-4.0	Number	569	1	5	9	24	91	439
	Percent	6.2	1.5	3.5	2.5	3.5	5.4	7.0
4.1-4.5	Number	366	6	5	10	9	37	299
	Percent	4.0	9.2	3.5	2.8	1.3	2.2	4.8
4.6-5.0	Number	220	3	2	3	4	24	184
	Percent	2.4	4.6	1.4	.8	.6	1.4	2.9
5.1 and over	Number	691	7	—	1	4	12	667
	Percent	7.5	10.8	—	.3	.6	.7	10.6
Total		9,216	65	144	359	682	1,699	6,267
Percent[2]		100.0	100.0	100.0	100.0	100.0	100.0	100.0

[1]The number of agencies used to compile these figures differs from the other Law Enforcement Employee tables because small agencies with no resident population are excluded from this table.

[2]Because of rounding, percentages may not add to total.

Table 73. — Full-time Law Enforcement Officers, October 31, 1996

[Range in rate per 1,000 inhabitants]

Rate range		Total[1] (9,216 cities; population 166,590,000)	Group I (65 cities, 250,000 and over; population 47,047,000)	Group II (144 cities, 100,000 to 249,999; population 21,226,000)	Group III (359 cities, 50,000 to 99,999; population 24,492,000)	Group IV (682 cities, 25,000 to 49,999; population 23,614,000)	Group V (1,699 cities, 10,000 to 24,999; population 26,735,000)	Group VI (6,267 cities, under 10,000; population 23,477,000)
.1-.5	Number	133	—	—	1	3	21	108
	Percent	1.4	—	—	.3	.4	1.2	1.7
.6-1.0	Number	534	—	6	19	41	75	393
	Percent	5.8	—	4.2	5.3	6.0	4.4	6.3
1.1-1.5	Number	1,892	8	45	122	212	413	1,092
	Percent	20.5	12.3	31.3	34.0	31.1	24.3	17.4
1.6-2.0	Number	2,430	16	42	115	242	611	1,404
	Percent	26.4	24.6	29.2	32.0	35.5	36.0	22.4
2.1-2.5	Number	1,670	14	26	61	117	334	1,118
	Percent	18.1	21.5	18.1	17.0	17.2	19.7	17.8
2.6-3.0	Number	967	12	18	30	43	143	721
	Percent	10.5	18.5	12.5	8.4	6.3	8.4	11.5
3.1-3.5	Number	542	4	4	6	18	65	445
	Percent	5.9	6.2	2.8	1.7	2.6	3.8	7.1
3.6-4.0	Number	310	4	3	2	2	23	276
	Percent	3.4	6.2	2.1	.6	.3	1.4	4.4
4.1-4.5	Number	201	3	—	3	3	10	182
	Percent	2.2	4.6	—	.8	.4	.6	2.9
4.6-5.0	Number	133	2	—	—	—	2	129
	Percent	1.4	3.1	—	—	—	.1	2.1
5.1 and over	Number	404	2	—	—	1	2	399
	Percent	4.4	3.1	—	—	.1	.1	6.4
Total		9,216	65	144	359	682	1,699	6,267
Percent[2]		100.0	100.0	100.0	100.0	100.0	100.0	100.0

[1]The number of agencies used to compile these figures differs from the other Law Enforcement Officer tables because small agencies with no resident population are excluded from this table.

[2]Because of rounding, percentages may not add to total.

Table 74. — Law Enforcement Employees, Percent Male and Female, October 31, 1996

[1996 estimated population]

Population group	Total police employees			Police officers (sworn)			Civilian employees		
	Total	Percent male	Percent female	Total	Percent male	Percent female	Total	Percent male	Percent female
TOTAL AGENCIES: 13,025 agencies; population 248,724,000:	829,838	75.1	24.9	595,170	89.9	10.1	234,668	37.6	62.4
TOTAL CITIES: 9,907 cities; population 166,590,000:	501,823	76.7	23.3	390,590	89.9	10.1	111,233	30.2	69.8
GROUP I 65 cities, 250,000 and over; population 47,047,000:	188,190	72.8	27.2	145,312	84.8	15.2	42,878	32.0	68.0
10 cities, 1,000,000 and over; population 22,285,000:	107,311	72.7	27.3	83,841	83.9	16.1	23,470	32.6	67.4
17 cities, 500,000 to 999,999; population 10,967,000:	38,242	73.9	26.1	29,363	86.1	13.9	8,879	33.4	66.6
38 cities, 250,000 to 499,999; population 13,796,000:	42,637	72.2	27.8	32,108	86.1	13.9	10,529	29.7	70.3
GROUP II 144 cities, 100,000 to 249,999; population 21,226,000:	53,486	74.8	25.2	40,790	90.1	9.9	12,696	25.5	74.5
GROUP III 359 cities, 50,000 to 99,999; population 24,492,000:	56,323	77.6	22.4	43,744	92.4	7.6	12,579	26.4	73.6
GROUP IV 682 cities, 25,000 to 49,999; population 23,614,000:	53,979	78.9	21.1	42,278	93.5	6.5	11,701	26.4	73.6
GROUP V 1,699 cities, 10,000 to 24,999; population 26,735,000:	63,298	81.0	19.0	50,616	94.4	5.6	12,682	27.5	72.5
GROUP VI 6,958 cities, under 10,000; population 23,477,000:	86,547	81.0	19.0	67,850	93.3	6.7	18,697	36.2	63.8
SUBURBAN COUNTIES 832 agencies; population 53,272,000:	202,741	71.9	28.1	125,103	88.2	11.8	77,638	45.6	54.4
RURAL COUNTIES 2,286 agencies; population 28,862,000:	125,274	74.2	25.8	79,477	92.8	7.2	45,797	41.9	58.1
SUBURBAN AREA[1] 6,059 agencies; population 101,447,000:	335,002	75.3	24.7	229,452	90.6	9.4	105,550	42.0	58.0

[1]Includes suburban city and county law enforcement agencies within metropolitan areas. Excludes central cities. Suburban cities and counties are also included in other groups.

Table 75. — Civilian Law Enforcement Employees, Percent of Total, Population Group, October 31, 1996

[1996 estimated population]

Population group	Percent civilian employees	Population group	Percent civilian employees
TOTAL AGENCIES: 13,025 agencies; population 248,724,000:	28.3	GROUP IV 682 cities, 25,000 to 49,999; population 23,614,000:	21.7
TOTAL CITIES: 9,907 cities; population 166,590,000:	22.2	GROUP V 1,699 cities, 10,000 to 24,999; population 26,735,000:	20.0
GROUP I 65 cities, 250,000 and over; population 47,047,000:	22.8	GROUP VI 6,958 cities, under 10,000; population 23,477,000:	21.6
10 cities, 1,000,000 and over; population 22,285,000:	21.9		
17 cities, 500,000 to 999,999; population 10,967,000:	23.2	SUBURBAN COUNTIES 832 agencies; population 53,272,000:	38.3
38 cities, 250,000 to 499,999; population 13,796,000:	24.7		
GROUP II 144 cities, 100,000 to 249,999; population 21,226,000:	23.7	RURAL COUNTIES 2,286 agencies; population 28,862,000:	36.6
GROUP III 359 cities, 50,000 to 99,999; population 24,492,000:	22.3	SUBURBAN AREA[1] 6,059 agencies; population 101,447,000:	31.5

[1]Includes suburban city and county law enforcement agencies within metropolitan areas. Excludes central cities. Suburban cities and counties are also included in other groups.

Table 76. — Full-time State Law Enforcement Employees, October 31, 1996

State	Number of law enforcement employees					State	Number of law enforcement employees				
	TOTAL	Officers		Civilians			TOTAL	Officers		Civilians	
		Male	Female	Male	Female			Male	Female	Male	Female
ALABAMA:						**MONTANA:**					
Department of Public Safety ..	1,171	553	11	190	417	Highway Patrol	264	188	16	21	39
Other state agencies	216	174	7	5	30	Other state agencies	219	184	2	5	28
ALASKA:						**NEBRASKA:**					
State Police	531	299	18	71	143	State Patrol	592	466	20	32	74
ARIZONA:						**NEVADA:**					
Department of Public Safety ..	1,656	899	65	305	387	Highway Patrol	523	333	23	51	116
Other state agencies	60	27	1	22	10	**NEW HAMPSHIRE:**					
ARKANSAS:						State Police	388	260	27	37	64
State Police	737	491	22	77	147	**NEW JERSEY:**					
CALIFORNIA:						State Police	3,580	2,574	76	400	530
Highway Patrol	9,726	6,136	572	1,193	1,825	**NEW MEXICO:**					
Other state agencies	815	590	159	15	51	State Police	558	423	12	27	96
COLORADO:						**NEW YORK:**					
State Police	796	542	25	67	162	State Police	4,665	3,652	313	250	450
Other state agencies	432	366	38	15	13	Other state agencies	95	50	2	39	4
CONNECTICUT:						**NORTH CAROLINA:**					
State Police	1,522	921	65	248	288	Highway Patrol	1,716	1,326	12	217	161
DELAWARE:						Other state agencies	1,052	616	73	123	240
State Police	739	496	44	81	118	**NORTH DAKOTA:**					
Other state agencies	141	101	9	9	22	Highway Patrol	182	114	3	35	30
FLORIDA:						**OHIO:**					
Highway Patrol	2,091	1,474	178	138	301	State Highway Patrol	2,331	1,241	111	443	536
Other state agencies	112	37	7	56	12	**OKLAHOMA:**					
GEORGIA:						Department of Public Safety ...	1,283	734	9	254	286
Department of Public Safety ..	2,015	842	34	417	722	Other state agencies	53	49	3	—	1
Other state agencies	1,627	875	107	265	380	**OREGON:**					
IDAHO:						State Police	1,083	731	50	104	198
State Police	207	151	6	14	36	Other state agencies	54	35	8	—	11
Other state agencies	77	60	4	3	10	**PENNSYLVANIA:**					
ILLINOIS:						State Police	5,430	4,049	160	550	671
State Police	3,705	1,858	172	633	1,042	Other state agencies	133	112	11	3	7
Other state agencies	676	514	36	60	66	**RHODE ISLAND:**					
INDIANA:						State Police	234	179	14	25	16
State Police	1,920	1,182	62	273	403	Other state agencies	59	40	6	5	8
IOWA:						**SOUTH CAROLINA:**					
Department of Public Safety ..	849	559	30	103	157	Highway Patrol	1,091	883	22	54	132
Other state agencies	26	22	3	—	1	Other state agencies	697	373	77	77	170
KANSAS:						**SOUTH DAKOTA:**					
Highway Patrol	737	423	5	182	127	Highway Patrol	225	143	2	62	18
Other state agencies	392	225	11	53	103	**TENNESSEE:**					
KENTUCKY:						Department of Public Safety ...	1,726	815	50	185	676
State Police	1,674	931	24	376	343	**TEXAS:**					
Other state agencies	527	378	21	30	98	Department of Public Safety ...	6,604	2,669	128	1,186	2,621
LOUISIANA:						**UTAH:**					
State Police	1,391	839	20	180	352	Highway Patrol	415	362	17	14	22
MAINE:						Other state agencies	26	19	6	—	1
State Police	433	289	15	77	52	**VERMONT:**					
Other state agencies	132	35	2	39	56	State Police	372	267	15	16	74
MARYLAND:						**VIRGINIA:**					
State Police	2,249	1,384	134	357	374	State Police	2,287	1,621	63	196	407
Other state agencies	1,578	938	163	283	194	Other state agencies	298	240	23	1	34
MASSACHUSETTS:						**WASHINGTON:**					
State Police	2,607	2,079	225	154	149	State Patrol	1,968	881	41	599	447
MICHIGAN:						**WEST VIRGINIA:**					
State Police	3,094	1,818	284	478	514	State Police	980	639	17	97	227
Other state agencies	35	31	3	—	1	Other state agencies	119	108	1	—	10
MINNESOTA:						**WISCONSIN:**					
Highway Patrol	649	443	31	113	62	State Patrol	656	429	67	72	88
MISSISSIPPI:						Other state agencies	261	209	18	15	19
Highway Safety Patrol	822	515	8	91	208	**WYOMING:**					
MISSOURI:						Highway Patrol	289	150	1	75	63
State Highway Patrol	2,123	1,023	33	574	493						

NOTE: The responsibilities of the various state police, highway patrol, and department of public safety agencies range from full law enforcement duties to traffic patrol only. Any comparison of the data from state to state must take these factors and those on page iv into consideration.

Table 77. — Full-time Law Enforcement Employees, State, 1996

[1996 estimated population]

State	Total employees	Officers Male	Officers Female	Civilians Male	Civilians Female
ALABAMA: 327 agencies; Population 4,271,000:	13,956	8,638	717	1,734	2,867
ALASKA: 37 agencies; Population 606,000:	1,758	1,029	81	178	470
ARIZONA: 99 agencies; Population 4,417,000:	15,578	8,130	879	3,036	3,533
ARKANSAS: 192 agencies; Population 2,505,000:	7,190	4,530	392	894	1,374
CALIFORNIA: 468 agencies; Population 28,898,000:	94,528	57,189	7,049	9,976	20,314
COLORADO: 229 agencies; Population 3,771,000:	12,795	7,936	1,069	1,132	2,658
CONNECTICUT: 98 agencies; Population 2,772,000:	9,207	6,923	534	590	1,160
DELAWARE: 42 agencies; Population 550,000:	2,008	1,438	147	141	282
DISTRICT OF COLUMBIA: 2 agencies; Population 543,000:	4,391	2,738	894	251	508
FLORIDA: 340 agencies; Population 13,772,000:	55,364	29,346	3,920	8,717	13,381
GEORGIA: 598 agencies; Population 6,493,000:	27,945	17,140	2,322	3,224	5,259
HAWAII: 5 agencies; Population 1,184,000:	3,292	2,388	203	201	500
IDAHO: 107 agencies; Population 1,181,000:	2,904	1,966	142	134	662
ILLINOIS: 738 agencies; Population 11,797,000:	42,466	28,705	3,681	3,717	6,363
INDIANA: 212 agencies; Population 5,285,000:	13,945	8,496	676	2,089	2,684
IOWA: 234 agencies; Population 2,850,000:	6,589	4,336	369	582	1,302
KANSAS: 323 agencies; Population 2,492,000:	8,826	5,761	436	978	1,651
KENTUCKY: 381 agencies; Population 3,795,000:	9,148	6,223	612	1,046	1,267
LOUISIANA: 207 agencies; Population 4,254,000:	17,575	11,734	2,181	1,240	2,420
MAINE: 134 agencies; Population 1,237,000:	2,669	1,919	99	311	340
MARYLAND: 120 agencies; Population 4,962,000:	17,336	11,771	1,653	1,534	2,378
MASSACHUSETTS: 309 agencies; Population 6,011,000:	18,733	14,745	1,131	1,247	1,610
MICHIGAN: 563 agencies; Population 9,536,000:	26,442	17,600	2,301	2,746	3,795
MINNESOTA: 275 agencies; Population 4,518,000:	10,588	6,746	631	1,201	2,010
MISSISSIPPI: 191 agencies; Population 2,436,000:	6,745	4,305	274	843	1,323
MISSOURI: 293 agencies; Population 5,245,000:	15,684	10,125	973	1,791	2,795
MONTANA: 98 agencies; Population 877,000:	2,290	1,382	75	315	518
NEBRASKA: 159 agencies; Population 1,635,000:	4,231	2,803	275	292	861
NEVADA: 34 agencies; Population 1,595,000:	5,666	3,493	427	374	1,372
NEW HAMPSHIRE: 113 agencies; Population 946,000:	2,736	1,952	122	214	448
NEW JERSEY: 531 agencies; Population 7,636,000:	35,236	26,429	1,569	2,442	4,796
NEW MEXICO: 75 agencies; Population 1,352,000:	4,327	2,883	230	348	866
NEW YORK: 360 agencies; Population 15,668,000:	73,834	51,034	7,173	5,236	10,391
NORTH CAROLINA: 503 agencies; Population 7,308,000:	23,411	15,297	1,732	2,649	3,733
NORTH DAKOTA: 98 agencies; Population 640,000:	1,407	968	66	130	243
OHIO: 502 agencies; Population 10,595,000:	29,401	18,428	1,998	3,912	5,063
OKLAHOMA: 290 agencies; Population 3,299,000:	9,669	6,114	464	1,400	1,691
OREGON: 166 agencies; Population 3,186,000:	7,135	4,797	441	396	1,501
PENNSYLVANIA: 692 agencies; Population 7,830,000:	24,294	18,546	2,121	1,371	2,256
RHODE ISLAND: 43 agencies; Population 979,000:	2,881	2,217	128	239	297
SOUTH CAROLINA: 249 agencies; Population 3,696,000:	10,890	7,468	711	977	1,734
SOUTH DAKOTA: 104 agencies; Population 716,000:	1,681	1,047	48	268	318
TENNESSEE: 266 agencies; Population 4,960,000:	16,287	9,844	968	2,192	3,283
TEXAS: 923 agencies; Population 19,123,000:	68,089	39,074	4,146	10,784	14,085
UTAH: 121 agencies; Population 1,982,000:	5,111	3,296	231	651	933
VERMONT: 50 agencies; Population 353,000:	1,108	793	51	77	187
VIRGINIA: 270 agencies; Population 6,672,000:	18,593	13,164	1,419	1,107	2,903
WASHINGTON: 228 agencies; Population 5,292,000:	12,552	7,941	733	1,420	2,458
WEST VIRGINIA: 237 agencies; Population 1,518,000:	4,001	2,824	113	498	566
WISCONSIN: 323 agencies; Population 5,012,000:	15,527	10,380	1,305	1,245	2,597
WYOMING: 66 agencies; Population 474,000:	1,819	1,154	73	170	422

Table 78. — Number of Full-time Law Enforcement Employees, Cities, October 31, 1996

City	Total police employees	Total officers	Total civilians	City	Total police employees	Total officers	Total civilians
ALABAMA				**ALABAMA — Continued**			
Abbeville	14	10	4	Fairfield	65	51	14
Adamsville	18	13	5	Fairhope	20	19	1
Alabaster	33	27	6	Falkville	4	4	—
Albertville	41	32	9	Fayette	11	11	—
Alexander City	60	45	15	Flomaton	10	6	4
Aliceville	11	7	4	Florence	113	87	26
Andalusia	39	30	9	Foley	36	27	9
Anniston	126	96	30	Fort Payne	45	34	11
Arab	30	23	7	Fultondale	19	15	4
Ardmore	16	6	10	Gadsden	162	110	52
Argo	5	4	1	Gardendale	28	22	6
Ariton	4	1	3	Geneva	16	12	4
Ashford	11	6	5	Glencoe	8	5	3
Ashland	12	9	3	Goodwater	3	3	—
Athens	44	34	10	Gordo	4	4	—
Atmore	26	23	3	Graysville	11	7	4
Attalla	26	21	5	Greenville	37	30	7
Auburn	79	67	12	Grove Hill	6	6	—
Bay Minette	23	18	5	Guin	4	4	—
Bayou La Batre	17	12	5	Gulf Shores	33	24	9
Bear Creek	3	3	—	Guntersville	36	25	11
Bessemer	123	104	19	Gurley	4	4	—
Birmingham	1,158	901	257	Haleyville	17	12	5
Blountsville	7	7	—	Hamilton	14	13	1
Boaz	30	24	6	Hanceville	13	8	5
Brantley	6	5	1	Hartford	13	9	4
Brewton	24	20	4	Hartselle	28	24	4
Bridgeport	8	4	4	Headland	12	9	3
Brighten	10	5	5	Heflin	9	8	1
Brundidge	11	7	4	Helena	12	8	4
Butler	12	7	5	Hokes Bluff	6	6	—
Calera	14	10	4	Hollywood	4	2	2
Camden	13	8	5	Homewood	90	65	25
Camp Hill	5	5	—	Hoover	146	114	32
Centre	11	7	4	Hueytown	32	26	6
Centreville	5	5	—	Huntsville	474	347	127
Chatom	6	6	—	Hurtsboro	4	4	—
Cherokee	3	3	—	Irondale	36	29	7
Chickasaw	20	20	—	Jackson	24	19	5
Childersburg	17	13	4	Jacksonville	26	20	6
Citronelle	11	7	4	Jasper	61	41	20
Clanton	25	24	1	Jemison	4	4	—
Clayton	3	3	—	Killen	4	4	—
Columbiana	12	8	4	Kimberly	4	4	—
Cottonwood	2	2	—	Lafayette	18	14	4
Courtland	6	5	1	Lanett	31	25	6
Creola	11	9	2	Leeds	28	22	6
Cullman	49	41	8	Lexington	3	3	—
Dadeville	11	11	—	Lincoln	12	8	4
Daleville	18	13	5	Linden	7	7	—
Daphne	46	29	17	Lineville	11	7	4
Decatur	145	117	28	Lipscomb	10	6	4
Demopolis	29	20	9	Livingston	12	7	5
Dora	8	4	4	Louisville	4	4	—
Dothan	190	120	70	Loxley	6	6	—
East Brewton	7	5	2	Luverne	16	12	4
Eclectic	8	4	4	Madison	52	38	14
Elba	20	16	4	McIntosh	6	6	—
Enterprise	63	50	13	Midfield	16	12	4
Eufaula	49	33	16	Midland City	9	5	4
Eutaw	12	8	4	Millbrook	21	15	6
Evergreen	21	16	5	Mobile	641	456	185

Table 78. — Number of Full-time Law Enforcement Employees, Cities, October 31, 1996 — Continued

City	Total police employees	Total officers	Total civilians	City	Total police employees	Total officers	Total civilians
ALABAMA — Continued				**ALABAMA — Continued**			
Monroeville	27	22	5	Tuscumbia	23	19	4
Montevallo	16	11	5	Tuskegee	56	45	11
Montgomery	621	462	159	Valley	27	20	7
Moody	13	12	1	Vance	2	2	—
Morris	3	3	—	Vestavia Hills	47	45	2
Moulton	9	9	—	Warrior	14	10	4
Moundville	7	4	3	Weaver	10	9	1
Mountain Brook	62	47	15	Wetumpka	22	17	5
Mount Vernon	7	6	1	Winfield	9	9	—
Muscle Shoals	34	34	—	York	12	9	3
Napier Field	1	1	—				
New Brockton	4	4	—	**ALASKA**			
New Hope	6	6	—	Anchorage	464	319	145
Newton	8	4	4	Bethel	18	11	7
Northport	60	49	11	Bristol Bay Borough	11	5	6
Notasulga	8	4	4	Cordova	10	5	5
Oneonta	16	15	1	Craig	9	4	5
Opelika	104	78	26	Dillingham	19	6	13
Opp	26	20	6	Fairbanks	50	34	16
Orange Beach	29	21	8	Haines	10	5	5
Oxford	41	33	8	Homer	21	10	11
Ozark	45	37	8	Juneau	74	45	29
Pelham	56	46	10	Kenai	24	16	8
Pell City	27	25	2	Ketchikan	32	23	9
Phenix City	79	62	17	Klawock	2	2	—
Phil Campbell	6	6	—	Kodiak	35	18	17
Pickensville	2	1	1	North Pole	11	7	4
Piedmont	18	14	4	North Slope Borough	84	45	39
Pleasant Grove	19	14	5	Palmer	27	13	14
Prattville	61	55	6	Petersburg	14	7	7
Priceville	4	4	—	Seward	21	9	12
Prichard	111	81	30	Skagway	4	4	—
Rainbow City	24	18	6	Soldotna	12	10	2
Rainsville	15	11	4	Togiak	3	3	—
Ranburne	3	2	1	Wasilla	16	12	4
Red Bay	12	8	4	Wrangell	12	7	5
Reform	4	4	—				
Roanoke	27	22	5	**ARIZONA**			
Robertsdale	12	8	4	Apache Junction	68	46	22
Russellville	23	19	4	Benson	18	11	7
Samson	11	7	4	Bisbee	22	16	6
Saraland	37	30	7	Buckeye	22	15	7
Satsuma	14	10	4	Bullhead City	104	68	36
Scottsboro	63	37	26	Camp Verde	25	16	9
Selma	111	69	42	Casa Grande	74	50	24
Shorter	7	4	3	Chandler	261	193	68
Somerville	3	3	—	Chino Valley	21	13	8
Southside	12	7	5	Clarkdale	8	8	—
Springville	4	4	—	Coolidge	25	19	6
Stevenson	10	6	4	Cottonwood	33	20	13
Sumiton	12	7	5	Eagar	9	7	2
Summerdale	5	4	1	El Mirage	18	14	4
Sylacauga	42	37	5	Flagstaff	112	76	36
Talladega	57	44	13	Florence	20	14	6
Tallassee	21	16	5	Gilbert	110	79	31
Tarrant City	23	18	5	Glendale	340	244	96
Thorsby	3	3	—	Globe	36	28	8
Town Creek	4	4	—	Goodyear	35	28	7
Trinity	3	3	—	Hayden	8	6	2
Troy	57	44	13	Holbrook	23	18	5
Trussville	30	25	5	Huachuca City	9	4	5
Tuscaloosa	258	201	57	Jerome	3	3	—
				Kearny	12	8	4

City	Total police employees	Total officers	Total civilians	City	Total police employees	Total officers	Total civilians
ARIZONA — Continued				**ARKANSAS — Continued**			
Kingman	57	39	18	Dardanelle	11	8	3
Lake Havasu City	79	58	21	De Queen	13	10	3
Mammoth	6	6	—	Dermott	15	8	7
Marana	47	37	10	Des Arc	4	4	—
Mesa	925	614	311	De Witt	16	11	5
Miami	11	8	3	Dumas	19	14	5
Nogales	74	57	17	Earle	9	8	1
Paradise Valley	39	30	9	Elaine	1	1	—
Payson	33	24	9	El Dorado	65	51	14
Peoria	119	85	34	England	10	6	4
Phoenix	3,140	2,255	885	Eudora	13	7	6
Pinetop-Lakeside	24	16	8	Eureka Springs	17	10	7
Prescott	83	54	29	Farmington	6	5	1
Prescott Valley	38	28	10	Fayetteville	116	79	37
Quartzsite	6	5	1	Fordyce	14	10	4
Safford	20	17	3	Forrest City	40	30	10
St. Johns	9	8	1	Fort Smith	176	138	38
San Luis	24	18	6	Greenbrier	7	4	3
Scottsdale	408	270	138	Green Forest	7	5	2
Sedona	26	18	8	Greenwood	8	8	—
Show Low	32	21	11	Gurdon	5	4	1
Sierra Vista	60	41	19	Hamburg	7	6	1
Snowflake-Taylor	13	11	2	Hampton	5	5	—
Somerton	19	14	5	Harrison	39	30	9
South Tucson	32	22	10	Hazen	9	5	4
Springerville	7	6	1	Heber Springs	19	12	7
Superior	13	9	4	Helena	20	16	4
Surprise	27	25	2	Hope	27	21	6
Tempe	383	263	120	Horseshoe Bend	9	7	2
Thatcher	10	9	1	Hot Springs	106	86	20
Tolleson	21	14	7	Hoxie	8	6	2
Tombstone	7	6	1	Jacksonville	76	58	18
Tucson	1,071	813	258	Jonesboro	88	77	11
Wickenburg	15	9	6	Judsonia	5	4	1
Willcox	14	9	5	Kensett	4	4	—
Winslow	32	23	9	Lake Village	14	9	5
Youngtown	15	9	6	Lincoln	6	6	—
Yuma	168	115	53	Little Rock	622	544	78
				Lonoke	12	7	5
ARKANSAS				Lowell	8	7	1
Alma	12	6	6	Magnolia	24	18	6
Arkadelphia	25	19	6	Malvern	27	20	7
Ashdown	13	11	2	Marianna	18	13	5
Bald Knob	9	5	4	Marion	13	12	1
Barling	9	8	1	Marked Tree	11	8	3
Beebe	11	6	5	Maumelle	40	21	19
Benton	47	36	11	McGehee	17	10	7
Bentonville	40	29	11	Mena	13	13	—
Berryville	9	8	1	Monticello	21	16	5
Blytheville	64	47	17	Morrilton	28	17	11
Booneville	11	7	4	Mountain Home	26	19	7
Brinkley	16	11	5	Mountain View	7	6	1
Bryant	19	12	7	Nashville	11	10	1
Bull Shoals	3	3	—	Newport	23	17	6
Cabot	30	22	8	North Little Rock	218	184	34
Camden	39	27	12	Osceola	42	25	17
Carlisle	8	4	4	Ozark	7	5	2
Clarksville	17	13	4	Paragould	36	31	5
Conway	99	82	17	Paris	12	7	5
Corning	12	8	4	Piggott	7	6	1
Crossett	19	12	7	Pine Bluff	163	143	20
Danville	7	6	1	Pocahontas	19	14	5

Table 78. — Number of Full-time Law Enforcement Employees, Cities, October 31, 1996 — Continued

City	Total police employees	Total officers	Total civilians	City	Total police employees	Total officers	Total civilians
ARKANSAS — Continued				**CALIFORNIA — Continued**			
Prairie Grove	7	6	1	Brentwood	25	19	6
Prescott	8	8	—	Brisbane	19	15	4
Rogers	90	61	29	Broadmoor	11	9	2
Russellville	51	44	7	Buena Park	143	89	54
Searcy	46	33	13	Burbank	243	159	84
Sheridan	8	7	1	Burlingame	64	45	19
Sherwood	73	63	10	Calexico	47	30	17
Siloam Springs	41	25	16	California City	15	10	5
Smackover	5	4	1	Calipatria	6	5	1
Springdale	98	70	28	Calistoga	13	10	3
Stamps	4	3	1	Camarillo	57	49	8
Star City	7	5	2	Campbell	58	42	16
Stuttgart	31	20	11	Capitola	27	22	5
Texarkana	114	73	41	Carlsbad	108	80	28
Trumann	20	15	5	Carmel	24	15	9
Van Buren	37	29	8	Cathedral City	71	46	25
Waldron	6	6	—	Ceres	49	35	14
Walnut Ridge	14	9	5	Chico	117	74	43
Warren	23	14	9	Chino	97	74	23
West Fork	3	3	—	Chowchilla	18	12	6
West Helena	24	18	6	Chula Vista	260	180	80
West Memphis	89	68	21	Claremont	59	40	19
Wynne	20	19	1	Clayton	13	10	3
				Clearlake	33	21	12
CALIFORNIA				Cloverdale	15	11	4
Adelanto	30	22	8	Clovis	108	77	31
Alameda	165	105	60	Coachella	32	29	3
Albany	32	27	5	Coalinga	27	19	8
Alhambra	143	90	53	Colma	18	14	4
Alturas	9	8	1	Colton	77	62	15
American Canyon	90	72	18	Colusa	10	9	1
Anaheim	566	399	167	Compton	182	130	52
Anderson	23	15	8	Concord	210	156	54
Angels Camp	6	5	1	Corcoran	23	18	5
Antioch	124	88	36	Corning	18	14	4
Arcadia	94	71	23	Corona	181	125	56
Arcata	30	22	8	Coronado	57	39	18
Arroyo Grande	32	23	9	Costa Mesa	210	147	63
Arvin	17	11	6	Cotati	18	12	6
Atascadero	34	25	9	Covina	82	54	28
Atherton	30	23	7	Crescent City	13	12	1
Atwater	31	23	8	Culver City	162	118	44
Auburn	27	19	8	Cypress	83	56	27
Azusa	85	57	28	Daly City	144	110	34
Bakersfield	348	259	89	Danville	32	27	5
Baldwin Park	108	73	35	Davis	71	52	19
Banning	37	29	8	Delano	45	36	9
Barstow	62	44	18	Del Rey Oaks	5	5	—
Bear Valley Springs	10	6	4	Dinuba	23	17	6
Beaumont	23	17	6	Dixon	19	17	2
Bell	47	35	12	Dos Palos	7	7	—
Bell Gardens	69	51	18	Downey	162	117	45
Belmont	44	30	14	Dublin	37	32	5
Belvedere	9	9	—	East Palo Alto	56	46	10
Benicia	50	35	15	El Cajon	187	124	63
Berkeley	312	196	116	El Centro	70	48	22
Beverly Hills	187	129	58	El Cerrito	39	34	5
Bishop	20	13	7	El Monte	165	132	33
Blue Lake	3	3	—	El Segundo	86	64	22
Blythe	35	22	13	Emeryville	49	33	16
Brawley	34	24	10	Escalon	10	8	2
Brea	125	101	24	Escondido	210	143	67

Table 78. — Number of Full-time Law Enforcement Employees, Cities, October 31, 1996 — Continued

City	Total police employees	Total officers	Total civilians	City	Total police employees	Total officers	Total civilians
CALIFORNIA — Continued				**CALIFORNIA — Continued**			
Etna	1	1	—	Lakeport	14	12	2
Eureka	78	50	28	Lake Shastina	4	4	—
Exeter	15	14	1	La Mesa	83	61	22
Fairfax	15	11	4	La Palma	30	24	6
Fairfield	162	101	61	La Verne	55	41	14
Farmersville	11	10	1	Lemoore	28	22	6
Ferndale	3	3	—	Lincoln	16	10	6
Firebaugh	15	10	5	Lindsay	26	18	8
Folsom	52	40	12	Livermore	103	69	34
Fontana	160	114	46	Livingston	25	18	7
Fort Bragg	18	14	4	Lodi	108	77	31
Fortuna	21	15	6	Lompoc	61	46	15
Foster City	56	42	14	Long Beach	1,307	844	463
Fountain Valley	87	65	22	Los Alamitos	30	24	6
Fowler	9	9	—	Los Altos	42	27	15
Fremont	288	190	98	Los Angeles	12,204	9,148	3,056
Fresno	777	512	265	Los Banos	38	27	11
Fullerton	219	148	71	Los Gatos	62	41	21
Galt	26	18	8	Madera	68	51	17
Gardena	106	86	20	Mammoth Lakes	17	15	2
Garden Grove	233	167	66	Manhattan Beach	90	60	30
Gilroy	87	53	34	Manteca	73	50	23
Glendale	334	226	108	Maricopa	4	3	1
Glendora	78	54	24	Marina	35	28	7
Gonzales	13	11	2	Martinez	49	37	12
Grass Valley	27	19	8	Marysville	39	26	13
Greenfield	12	11	1	Maywood	33	24	9
Gridley	18	12	6	Menlo Park	67	47	20
Grover Beach	26	19	7	Merced	114	81	33
Guadalupe	9	8	1	Millbrae	32	26	6
Gustine	10	9	1	Mill Valley	32	21	11
Half Moon Bay	14	12	2	Milpitas	113	82	31
Hanford	57	41	16	Modesto	314	225	89
Hawaiian Gardens	24	19	5	Monrovia	82	60	22
Hawthorne	137	97	40	Montclair	75	53	22
Hayward	256	157	99	Montebello	140	92	48
Healdsburg	26	15	11	Monterey	76	58	18
Hemet	70	53	17	Monterey Park	125	76	49
Hercules	24	20	4	Moraga	13	12	1
Hermosa Beach	48	33	15	Moreno Valley	172	130	42
Hillsborough	34	27	7	Morgan Hill	43	29	14
Hollister	30	24	6	Morro Bay	24	18	6
Holtville	9	7	2	Mountain View	118	85	33
Hughson	7	5	2	Mount Shasta	14	9	5
Huntington Beach	360	223	137	Murrieta	34	26	8
Huntington Park	103	68	35	Napa	122	75	47
Huron	13	9	4	National City	94	71	23
Imperial	14	11	3	Nevada City	10	9	1
Indio	70	48	22	Newark	71	51	20
Inglewood	291	203	88	Newman	12	11	1
Ione	5	4	1	Newport Beach	201	130	71
Irvine	191	133	58	Novato	82	60	22
Irwindale	27	21	6	Oakdale	30	22	8
Isleton	4	4	—	Oakland	1,024	626	398
Jackson	11	9	2	Oceanside	236	162	74
Kensington	9	9	—	Ontario	351	218	133
Kerman	15	13	2	Orange	225	148	77
King City	16	14	2	Orinda	15	13	2
Kingsburg	18	13	5	Orland	9	8	1
Lafayette	14	13	1	Oroville	34	24	10
Laguna Beach	79	47	32	Oxnard	269	174	95
La Habra	108	73	35	Pacifica	50	38	12

Table 78. — Number of Full-time Law Enforcement Employees, Cities, October 31, 1996 — Continued

City	Total police employees	Total officers	Total civilians	City	Total police employees	Total officers	Total civilians
CALIFORNIA — Continued				**CALIFORNIA — Continued**			
Pacific Grove	39	29	10	Santa Barbara	214	138	76
Palm Springs	121	80	41	Santa Clara	183	144	39
Palo Alto	167	100	67	Santa Cruz	122	89	33
Palos Verdes Estates	33	23	10	Santa Fe Springs	11	—	11
Paradise	29	21	8	Santa Maria	110	82	28
Parlier	14	13	1	Santa Monica	381	198	183
Pasadena	334	224	110	Santa Paula	38	29	9
Paso Robles	38	31	7	Santa Rosa	247	163	84
Patterson	16	14	2	Sausalito	26	21	5
Petaluma	83	63	20	Scotts Valley	29	21	8
Piedmont	27	20	7	Seal Beach	49	33	16
Pinole	48	27	21	Seaside	48	38	10
Pismo Beach	30	19	11	Sebastopol	18	14	4
Pittsburg	82	69	13	Selma	34	22	12
Placentia	67	51	16	Shafter	19	14	5
Placerville	21	15	6	Sierra Madre	22	15	7
Pleasant Hill	62	42	20	Signal Hill	46	31	15
Pleasanton	104	75	29	Simi Valley	169	112	57
Pomona	298	167	131	Soledad	18	14	4
Porterville	65	41	24	Sonoma	17	13	4
Port Hueneme	28	21	7	Sonora	17	13	4
Rancho Cucamonga	108	81	27	South Gate	125	89	36
Red Bluff	39	25	14	South Lake Tahoe	72	52	20
Redding	151	101	50	South Pasadena	48	33	15
Redlands	108	75	33	South San Francisco	109	74	35
Redondo Beach	153	102	51	Stallion Springs	3	3	—
Redwood City	122	85	37	Stockton	541	369	172
Reedley	33	23	10	Suisun City	34	25	9
Rialto	151	103	48	Sunnyvale	186	125	61
Richmond	259	184	75	Susanville	19	18	1
Ridgecrest	40	28	12	Sutter Creek	6	5	1
Rio Dell	7	7	—	Taft	16	10	6
Rio Vista	12	11	1	Tiburon	16	14	2
Ripon	19	13	6	Torrance	319	241	78
Riverside	474	323	151	Tracy	65	42	23
Rocklin	43	28	15	Trinidad	3	2	1
Rohnert Park	82	53	29	Tulare	67	47	20
Roseville	120	71	49	Tulelake	4	4	—
Ross	9	9	—	Turlock	84	53	31
Sacramento	1,044	638	406	Tustin	127	89	38
St. Helena	17	12	5	Twin Cities	42	31	11
Salinas	181	144	37	Ukiah	30	25	5
San Anselmo	23	17	6	Union City	88	66	22
San Bernardino	421	260	161	Upland	120	86	34
San Bruno	54	45	9	Vacaville	140	85	55
San Carlos	45	33	12	Vallejo	202	137	65
Sand City	7	6	1	Ventura	186	118	68
San Diego	2,784	2,002	782	Vernon	76	56	20
San Fernando	56	40	16	Visalia	128	87	41
San Francisco	2,416	2,020	396	Walnut Creek	103	75	28
San Gabriel	67	54	13	Waterford	12	11	1
Sanger	28	20	8	Watsonville	67	58	9
San Jacinto	35	26	9	Weed	13	9	4
San Jose	1,706	1,300	406	West Covina	156	114	42
San Leandro	136	92	44	Westminster	145	100	45
San Luis Obispo	80	55	25	Westmoreland	4	4	—
San Marino	31	26	5	West Sacramento	77	54	23
San Mateo	133	101	32	Wheatland	4	4	—
San Pablo	45	36	9	Whittier	177	128	49
San Rafael	100	73	27	Williams	8	7	1
San Ramon	39	34	5	Willits	21	14	7
Santa Ana	596	377	219	Willows	10	9	1

Table 78. — Number of Full-time Law Enforcement Employees, Cities, October 31, 1996 — Continued

City	Total police employees	Total officers	Total civilians	City	Total police employees	Total officers	Total civilians
CALIFORNIA — Continued				**COLORADO — Continued**			
Winters	11	10	1	Fowler	2	2	—
Woodlake	12	11	1	Frederick	4	4	—
Woodland	79	54	25	Frisco	10	9	1
Yreka	21	14	7	Fruita	11	10	1
Yuba City	68	43	25	Georgetown	4	4	—
				Gilcrest	2	2	—
COLORADO				Glendale	39	28	11
Alamosa	24	21	3	Glenwood Springs	26	22	4
Alma	2	1	1	Golden	43	31	12
Antonito	3	3	—	Grand Junction	124	74	50
Arvada	187	127	60	Greeley	163	94	69
Aspen	35	26	9	Greenwood Village	69	50	19
Aurora	708	487	221	Gunnison	23	14	9
Avon	13	12	1	Haxtun	3	3	—
Basalt	8	7	1	Holly	4	3	1
Bayfield	3	3	—	Holyoke	4	4	—
Berthoud	5	4	1	Hotchkiss	2	2	—
Black Hawk	27	18	9	Idaho Springs	9	8	1
Blue River	1	1	—	Ignacio	6	6	—
Boulder	189	130	59	Johnstown	5	5	—
Breckenridge	25	18	7	Kersey	2	2	—
Brighton	42	30	12	Kremmling	5	5	—
Broomfield	65	48	17	Lafayette	33	26	7
Brush	13	11	2	La Junta	19	16	3
Burlington	9	8	1	Lakewood	320	212	108
Calahan	2	2	—	Lamar	26	21	5
Canon City	37	28	9	Las Animas	9	7	2
Carbondale	13	11	2	La Veta	2	2	—
Castle Rock	29	23	6	Limon	6	5	1
Cedaredge	4	4	—	Littleton	76	58	18
Center	13	8	5	Longmont	120	94	26
Central City	16	14	2	Louisville	32	26	6
Cherry Hills Village	23	21	2	Loveland	108	71	37
Colorado Springs	720	498	222	Manitou Springs	20	15	5
Columbine Valley	3	3	—	Manzanola	1	1	—
Commerce City	66	46	20	Meeker	3	3	—
Cortez	37	24	13	Milliken	4	4	—
Craig	27	19	8	Minturn	6	5	1
Crested Butte	7	6	1	Monte Vista	19	14	5
Cripple Creek	30	17	13	Montrose	34	28	6
Dacono	7	6	1	Monument	7	7	—
De Beque	1	1	—	Mountain View	2	2	—
Del Norte	5	4	1	Mount Crested Butte	6	6	—
Delta	16	12	4	New Castle	4	4	—
Denver	1,600	1,408	192	Northglenn	66	49	17
Dillon	6	5	1	Olathe	5	4	1
Durango	55	33	22	Pagosa Springs	6	6	—
Eagle	7	6	1	Palisade	7	6	1
Eaton	6	5	1	Palmer Lake	4	4	—
Edgewater	18	16	2	Paonia	4	3	1
Elizabeth	4	4	—	Parachute	6	4	2
Empire	1	1	—	Parker	29	20	9
Englewood	98	67	31	Platteville	4	4	—
Erie	8	6	2	Pueblo	234	185	49
Estes Park	25	15	10	Rangely	9	5	4
Evans	21	18	3	Ridgway	2	2	—
Federal Heights	31	23	8	Rifle	20	14	6
Florence	11	7	4	Rocky Ford	9	8	1
Fort Collins	184	120	64	Salida	17	16	1
Fort Lupton	22	13	9	Sheridan	24	16	8
Fort Morgan	35	27	8	Silt	4	4	—
Fountain	29	20	9	Silverthorne	15	13	2

City	Total police employees	Total officers	Total civilians	City	Total police employees	Total officers	Total civilians
COLORADO — Continued				**CONNECTICUT — Continued**			
Snowmass Village	11	8	3	Newington	55	43	12
Springfield	4	4	—	New London	95	80	15
Steamboat Springs	31	20	11	New Milford	55	43	12
Sterling	36	23	13	Newtown	45	36	9
Telluride	12	10	2	North Branford	26	21	5
Thornton	136	106	30	North Haven	55	46	9
Trinidad	28	19	9	Norwalk	201	175	26
Vail	50	31	19	Norwich	106	91	15
Walsenburg	19	13	6	Old Saybrook	25	23	2
Westminster	178	125	53	Orange	50	39	11
Wheat Ridge	90	63	27	Plainfield	19	17	2
Windsor	10	9	1	Plainville	38	31	7
Woodland Park	23	16	7	Plymouth	23	19	4
Wray	11	7	4	Putnam	19	15	4
Yuma	8	7	1	Ridgefield Town	42	37	5
				Rocky Hill	38	31	7
CONNECTICUT				Seymour	30	28	2
Ansonia	39	34	5	Shelton	50	46	4
Avon	37	30	7	Simsbury	39	33	6
Berlin	48	39	9	Southington	64	58	6
Bethel	37	31	6	South Windsor	43	34	9
Bloomfield	57	47	10	Stamford	306	281	25
Branford	46	42	4	Stonington	42	33	9
Bridgeport	483	398	85	Stratford	115	101	14
Bristol	119	111	8	Suffield	18	13	5
Brookfield	33	27	6	Thomaston	14	12	2
Canton	18	13	5	Torrington	73	67	6
Cheshire	52	44	8	Trumbull	80	69	11
Clinton	27	24	3	Vernon	62	48	14
Coventry	15	11	4	Wallingford	88	70	18
Cromwell	27	21	6	Waterbury	362	312	50
Danbury	155	149	6	Waterford	53	46	7
Darien	58	51	7	Watertown	43	36	7
Derby	27	25	2	West Hartford	138	119	19
East Hampton	15	13	2	West Haven	130	114	16
East Hartford	155	123	32	Weston	15	14	1
East Haven Town	54	50	4	Westport	73	66	7
Easton	17	14	3	Wethersfield	53	43	10
East Windsor	28	21	7	Willimantic	43	39	4
Enfield	108	88	20	Wilton	42	40	2
Fairfield	112	105	7	Windsor	60	51	9
Farmington	56	41	15	Windsor Locks	27	20	7
Glastonbury	66	49	17	Winchester	25	21	4
Granby	16	11	5	Wolcott	32	23	9
Greenwich	175	158	17	Woodbridge	31	25	6
Groton	38	32	6				
Groton Long Point	5	5	—	**DELAWARE**			
Groton Town	71	65	6	Bethany Beach	10	9	1
Guilford	41	35	6	Blades	1	1	—
Hamden	119	98	21	Bridgeville	5	4	1
Hartford	599	461	138	Camden-Wyoming	7	6	1
Madison Town	41	32	9	Clayton	1	1	—
Manchester	146	111	35	Dagsboro	2	2	—
Meriden	129	123	6	Delmar	12	11	1
Middlebury	11	9	2	Dewey Beach	7	6	1
Middletown	114	93	21	Dover	100	80	20
Milford	122	108	14	Ellendale	2	2	—
Monroe	45	36	9	Elsmere	14	13	1
Naugatuck	59	51	8	Felton	2	2	—
New Britain	179	154	25	Fenwick Island	8	7	1
New Canaan	49	45	4	Frankford	1	1	—
New Haven	529	421	108	Frederica	3	3	—

Table 78. — Number of Full-time Law Enforcement Employees, Cities, October 31, 1996 — Continued

City	Total police employees	Total officers	Total civilians	City	Total police employees	Total officers	Total civilians
DELAWARE — Continued				**FLORIDA — Continued**			
Georgetown	12	12	—	Coral Gables	208	148	60
Greenwood	7	5	2	Coral Springs	239	157	82
Harrington	13	11	2	Crescent City	8	7	1
Laurel	10	9	1	Crestview	33	25	8
Lewes	9	9	—	Cross City	5	5	—
Milford	33	25	8	Crystal River	21	19	2
Millsboro	10	9	1	Davenport	8	7	1
Milton	7	7	—	Davie	157	126	31
Newark	64	49	15	Daytona Beach	316	237	79
New Castle	15	13	2	Daytona Beach Shores	37	29	8
Newport	7	7	—	De Funiak Springs	14	13	1
Ocean View	3	3	—	De Land	75	54	21
Rehoboth Beach	23	17	6	Delray Beach	210	145	65
Seaford	27	21	6	Dundee	13	9	4
Selbyville	5	5	—	Dunnellon	9	7	2
Smyrna	20	15	5	Eagle Lake	6	6	—
South Bethany	6	6	—	Eatonville	12	11	1
Wilmington	287	230	57	Edgewater	41	31	10
				Edgewood	13	12	1
DISTRICT OF COLUMBIA				Eustis	48	36	12
Washington	4,369	3,611	758	Fellesmere	9	8	1
				Fernandina Beach	37	28	9
FLORIDA				Flagler Beach	10	10	—
Alachua	18	14	4	Florida City	33	24	9
Altamonte Springs	120	88	32	Fort Lauderdale	709	444	265
Altha	1	1	—	Fort Meade	22	16	6
Apalachicola	8	7	1	Fort Myers	220	154	66
Apopka	60	52	8	Fort Pierce	133	98	35
Arcadia	30	23	7	Fort Walton Beach	66	53	13
Atlantis	17	11	6	Frostproof	15	10	5
Auburndale	36	27	9	Fruitland Park	9	8	1
Avon Park	29	23	6	Gainesville	370	249	121
Bal Harbour	28	21	7	Golden Beach	19	18	1
Bartow	67	48	19	Graceville	10	6	4
Bay Harbor Islands	26	21	5	Greenacres City	81	39	42
Belleair	15	10	5	Green Cove Springs	20	15	5
Belleair Beach	8	7	1	Groveland	12	8	4
Belle Glade	66	54	12	Gulf Breeze	18	16	2
Belleview	17	14	3	Gulfport	36	30	6
Biscayne Park	7	7	—	Gulf Stream	10	10	—
Blountstown	12	7	5	Haines City	51	38	13
Boca Raton	229	144	85	Hallandale	121	85	36
Bonifay	10	6	4	Havana	12	8	4
Bowling Green	5	5	—	Hialeah	428	322	106
Boynton Beach	160	126	34	Hialeah Gardens	37	26	11
Bradenton	108	87	21	Highland Beach	11	11	—
Bradenton Beach	9	8	1	High Springs	13	8	5
Bunnell	9	8	1	Hillsboro Beach	16	13	3
Cape Coral	186	126	60	Holly Hill	30	23	7
Casselberry	71	52	19	Hollywood	457	302	155
Cedar Grove	7	6	1	Holmes Beach	20	11	9
Center Hill	5	5	—	Homestead	111	86	25
Chattahoochee	11	10	1	Howey-in-the-Hills	4	4	—
Chiefland	13	10	3	Indialantic	12	9	3
Chipley	10	9	1	Indian Harbour Beach	22	15	7
Clearwater	384	257	127	Indian River Shores	20	19	1
Clermont	25	17	8	Indian Shores	13	12	1
Clewiston	23	15	8	Inverness	19	17	2
Cocoa	88	66	22	Jacksonville	2,362	1,394	968
Cocoa Beach	43	32	11	Jacksonville Beach	75	54	21
Coconut Creek	85	59	26	Juno Beach	16	13	3
Coleman	2	2	—	Jupiter	107	83	24

City	Total police employees	Total officers	Total civilians	City	Total police employees	Total officers	Total civilians
FLORIDA — Continued				**FLORIDA — Continued**			
Jupiter Inlet Colony	5	5	—	Ocoee	45	37	8
Jupiter Island	19	15	4	Okeechobee	24	18	6
Kenneth City	16	14	2	Opa Locka	57	41	16
Key Biscayne	34	24	10	Orange City	25	16	9
Key West	107	83	24	Orange Park	28	21	7
Kissimmee	141	91	50	Orlando	859	609	250
Lady Lake	27	21	6	Ormond Beach	83	59	24
Lake Alfred	16	12	4	Oviedo	54	40	14
Lake City	42	31	11	Pahokee	19	13	6
Lake Clarke Shores	10	10	—	Palatka	41	35	6
Lake Hamilton	9	6	3	Palm Bay	175	113	62
Lake Helen	6	5	1	Palm Beach	119	71	48
Lakeland	315	219	96	Palm Beach Gardens	108	83	25
Lake Mary	30	21	9	Palm Beach Shores	8	7	1
Lake Park	36	28	8	Palmetto	38	29	9
Lake Wales	53	42	11	Palm Springs	36	24	12
Lake Worth	127	89	38	Panama City	117	85	32
Lantana	35	27	8	Panama City Beach	49	37	12
Largo	191	131	60	Parker	8	7	1
Lauderdale-by-the-Sea	19	16	3	Parkland	26	24	2
Leesburg	71	53	18	Pembroke Pines	241	185	56
Lighthouse Point	39	31	8	Pensacola	211	161	50
Longboat Key	26	20	6	Perry	25	23	2
Longwood	40	35	5	Pinellas Park	111	78	33
Lynn Haven	30	23	7	Plantation	258	170	88
Madison	12	11	1	Plant City	79	56	23
Maitland	48	33	15	Pompano Beach	290	233	57
Manalapan	13	9	4	Ponce Inlet	13	8	5
Mangonia Park	16	15	1	Port Orange	82	63	19
Margate	154	102	52	Port Richey	16	11	5
Marianna	24	17	7	Port St. Joe	17	12	5
Mascotte	8	7	1	Port St. Lucie	159	109	50
Medley	38	31	7	Punta Gorda	39	27	12
Melbourne	188	140	48	Quincy	41	31	10
Melbourne Beach	9	8	1	Redington Beach	9	8	1
Melbourne Village	3	3	—	Riviera Beach	133	97	36
Mexico Beach	4	4	—	Rockledge	47	36	11
Miami	1,427	1,027	400	Royal Palm Beach	57	42	15
Miami Beach	500	344	156	St. Augustine	56	46	10
Miami Shores	40	32	8	St. Augustine Beach	12	10	2
Miami Springs	51	40	11	St. Cloud	48	35	13
Miccosukee	27	18	9	St. Petersburg Beach	44	30	14
Milton	22	16	6	St. Petersburg	717	505	212
Miramar	137	114	23	Sanford	113	90	23
Monticello	14	10	4	Sanibel	36	24	12
Mount Dora	32	24	8	Sarasota	250	187	63
Mulberry	14	10	4	Satellite Beach	25	18	7
Naples	116	79	37	Sea Ranch Lakes	11	8	3
Neptune Beach	23	17	6	Sebastian	40	28	12
New Smyrna Beach	61	46	15	Sebring	34	27	7
Niceville	25	20	5	Seminole Tribal	75	56	19
North Bay Village	31	24	7	Sewall's Point	7	7	—
North Lauderdale	65	52	13	Sneads	8	6	2
North Miami	159	117	42	South Bay	18	12	6
North Miami Beach	158	91	67	South Daytona	32	23	9
North Palm Beach	45	36	9	South Miami	54	45	9
North Port	47	28	19	South Palm Beach	10	10	—
Oak Hill	4	4	—	Springfield	20	15	5
Oakland	5	5	—	Starke	26	20	6
Oakland Park	111	81	30	Stuart	56	42	14
Ocala	204	146	58	Sunrise	189	136	53
Ocean Ridge	16	11	5	Surfside	30	23	7

City	Total police employees	Total officers	Total civilians	City	Total police employees	Total officers	Total civilians
FLORIDA — Continued				**GEORGIA — Continued**			
Sweetwater	28	22	6	Blythe	1	1	—
Tallahassee	478	328	150	Boston	4	4	—
Tampa	1,200	915	285	Bowdon	13	9	4
Tarpon Springs	58	44	14	Braselton	1	1	—
Tavares	29	22	7	Bremen	16	14	2
Temple Terrace	64	45	19	Brooklet	3	3	—
Tequesta	21	16	5	Brunswick	31	26	5
Titusville	109	78	31	Buchanan	5	5	—
Treasure Island	25	20	5	Buena Vista	6	6	—
Umatilla	7	6	1	Butler	5	5	—
Valparaiso	13	9	4	Byron	16	10	6
Venice	70	46	24	Cairo	24	21	3
Vero Beach	87	61	26	Calhoun	36	35	1
Virginia Gardens	6	5	1	Camilla	21	16	5
Waldo	7	7	—	Canton	24	21	3
Wauchula	13	11	2	Carrollton	66	54	12
Webster	3	3	—	Cartersville	51	42	9
West Melbourne	23	21	2	Cave Spring	3	3	—
West Miami	18	13	5	Cedartown	23	21	2
West Palm Beach	338	233	105	Chamblee	43	32	11
White Springs	5	3	2	Chatsworth	18	13	5
Wildwood	18	13	5	Chickamauga	5	5	—
Williston	16	11	5	Clarkesville	5	5	—
Wilton Manors	40	30	10	Clarkston	16	14	2
Windermere	10	9	1	Claxton	8	8	—
Winter Garden	44	34	10	Clayton	9	8	1
Winter Haven	102	73	29	Cleveland	8	8	—
Winter Park	101	75	26	Cochran	16	15	1
Winter Springs	57	40	17	Cohutta	1	1	—
Zephyrhills	35	25	10	College Park	99	80	19
Zolfo Springs	1	1	—	Collins	2	1	1
				Colquitt	5	4	1
GEORGIA				Columbus	485	383	102
Abbeville	4	4	—	Comer	3	3	—
Acworth	33	23	10	Commerce	19	13	6
Adairsville	11	9	2	Conyers	51	38	13
Adel	21	18	3	Coolidge	7	5	2
Alamo	3	2	1	Cordele	33	26	7
Albany	227	200	27	Cornelia	19	17	2
Alma	23	17	6	Covington	56	51	5
Alpharetta	70	49	21	Cumming	13	9	4
Americus	58	46	12	Cuthbert	15	7	8
Arcade	4	3	1	Dacula	1	1	—
Arlington	3	3	—	Dallas	16	12	4
Ashburn	11	10	1	Dalton	80	65	15
Athens-Clarke County	249	198	51	Damascus	1	1	—
Atlanta	1,967	1,467	500	Danielsville	1	1	—
Attapulgus	2	1	1	Darien	6	6	—
Auburn	9	8	1	Dawson	20	15	5
Austell	17	12	5	Decatur	59	45	14
Avondale Estates	12	11	1	Demorest	4	4	—
Bainbridge	45	33	12	Dillard	2	2	—
Baldwin	4	4	—	Doerun	5	4	1
Ball Ground	2	2	—	Doraville	52	36	16
Barnesville	17	14	3	Douglas	42	34	8
Barwick	2	2	—	Dublin	53	44	9
Baxley	24	19	5	Duluth	41	30	11
Berlin	1	1	—	East Dublin	9	8	1
Blackshear	9	8	1	East Ellijay	7	5	2
Blakely	22	17	5	Eastman	18	14	4
Bloomingdale	10	9	1	East Point	130	99	31
Blue Ridge	7	6	1	Eatonton	12	11	1

Table 78. — Number of Full-time Law Enforcement Employees, Cities, October 31, 1996 — Continued

City	Total police employees	Total officers	Total civilians	City	Total police employees	Total officers	Total civilians
GEORGIA — Continued				**GEORGIA — Continued**			
Edison	4	4	—	Lakeland	7	6	1
Elberton	24	20	4	Lake Park	3	3	—
Ellaville	5	5	—	Lavonia	13	12	1
Emerson	3	2	1	Lawrenceville	58	44	14
Eton	3	3	—	Leary	1	1	—
Euharlee	3	2	1	Leesburg	7	7	—
Fairburn	23	17	6	Lenox	1	1	—
Fairmount	3	3	—	Leslie	4	4	—
Fayetteville	38	32	6	Lilburn	29	21	8
Fitzgerald	34	29	5	Lincolnton	4	4	—
Folkston	6	6	—	Lithonia	14	10	4
Forest Park	93	49	44	Loganville	16	11	5
Forsyth	20	16	4	Lookout Mountain	8	7	1
Fort Gaines	6	4	2	Louisville	8	8	—
Fort Oglethorpe	25	20	5	Lumber City	7	4	3
Fort Valley	38	34	4	Lumpkin	5	5	—
Franklin Springs	3	2	1	Macon	320	288	32
Gainesville	83	71	12	Madison	15	14	1
Garden City	25	23	2	Manchester	20	14	6
Georgetown	3	2	1	Marietta	145	121	24
Gibson	1	1	—	Maysville	2	2	—
Glennville	13	8	5	McCaysville	4	4	—
Glenwood	3	2	1	McDonough	18	17	1
Gordon	8	5	3	McIntyre	2	2	—
Grantville	5	5	—	McRae	10	7	3
Gray	8	7	1	Meigs	6	6	—
Greenville	8	7	1	Metter	12	11	1
Griffin	95	77	18	Milan	1	1	—
Grovetown	16	13	3	Milledgeville	58	36	22
Hagan	1	1	—	Millen	11	11	—
Hahira	8	5	3	Molena	1	1	—
Hamilton	1	1	—	Monroe	37	31	6
Hampton	11	10	1	Montezuma	20	16	4
Hapeville	47	39	8	Monticello	17	12	5
Harlem	13	8	5	Morrow	29	26	3
Harrison	2	1	1	Morven	2	2	—
Hawkinsville	11	10	1	Moultrie	54	44	10
Hazlehurst	17	12	5	Mountain City	2	2	—
Helen	12	8	4	Muscogee City	15	14	1
Helena	3	3	—	Nahunta	2	2	—
Hephzibah	4	4	—	Nashville	16	12	4
Hiawassee	4	3	1	Nelson	1	1	—
Hilltonia	1	1	—	Newington	1	1	—
Hinesville	67	60	7	Newnan	44	39	5
Hiram	5	5	—	Nicholls	3	1	2
Hoboken	2	1	1	Norcross	32	25	7
Hogansville	14	9	5	Oakwood	8	7	1
Holly Springs	6	6	—	Ochlocknee	3	2	1
Homerville	8	7	1	Ocilla	17	12	5
Hoschton	2	2	—	Oglethorpe	5	4	1
Ivey	2	2	—	Omega	3	3	—
Jackson	21	13	8	Oxford	4	4	—
Jasper	10	10	—	Palmetto	11	10	1
Jefferson	15	13	2	Patterson	3	3	—
Jeffersonville	5	4	1	Pavo	3	2	1
Jesup	28	26	2	Peachtree City	44	41	3
Jonesboro	10	9	1	Pearson	4	4	—
Kennesaw	47	26	21	Pelham	19	15	4
Kingsland	27	24	3	Pembroke	7	6	1
Lafayette	21	17	4	Perry	37	28	9
La Grange	89	75	14	Pinehurst	2	2	—
Lake City	18	16	2	Pine Mountain	6	6	—

Table 78. — Number of Full-time Law Enforcement Employees, Cities, October 31, 1996 — Continued

City	Total police employees	Total officers	Total civilians	City	Total police employees	Total officers	Total civilians
GEORGIA — Continued				**GEORGIA — Continued**			
Pineview	1	1	—	Valdosta	110	97	13
Plains	4	4	—	Vidalia	37	30	7
Pooler	16	14	2	Vienna	7	7	—
Port Wentworth	18	16	2	Villa Rica	24	18	6
Powder Springs	23	18	5	Warner Robins	112	95	17
Preston	1	1	—	Warrenton	7	7	—
Quitman	20	15	5	Washington	16	15	1
Reidsville	11	6	5	Watkinsville	5	5	—
Remerton	5	5	—	Waverly Hall	3	2	1
Reynolds	3	3	—	Waycross	68	48	20
Richland	7	5	2	Waynesboro	23	17	6
Richmond Hill	17	14	3	West Point	18	13	5
Rincon	9	7	2	Whigham	2	2	—
Ringgold	5	5	—	Willacoochee	3	3	—
Roberta	3	3	—	Winder	34	30	4
Rockmart	15	14	1	Woodbine	6	6	—
Rome	95	83	12	Woodland	1	1	—
Rossville	12	9	3	Woodstock	30	25	5
Roswell	141	94	47	Wrens	14	13	1
Royston	13	10	3	Zebulon	5	5	—
St. Marys	32	29	3				
Sandersville	32	21	11	**HAWAII**			
Sardis	4	4	—	Hilo	237	133	104
Savannah	507	416	91	Honolulu	2,251	1,815	436
Screven	1	1	—				
Senoia	6	6	—	**IDAHO**			
Shellman	3	3	—	Aberdeen	9	6	3
Shiloh	1	1	—	American Falls	10	8	2
Smyrna	120	88	32	Bellevue	4	4	—
Snellville	33	26	7	Blackfoot	22	19	3
Soperton	9	6	3	Boise	255	213	42
Sparks	1	1	—	Bonners Ferry	8	7	1
Sparta	15	8	7	Buhl	10	8	2
Springfield	7	6	1	Caldwell	46	35	11
Statham	3	3	—	Cascade	7	6	1
Stone Mountain	22	17	5	Chubbuck	24	16	8
Stone Mountain Park	30	20	10	Coeur d'Alene	62	52	10
Summerville	22	19	3	Emmett	12	11	1
Suwanee	18	13	5	Filer	5	5	—
Swainsboro	24	16	8	Firth	1	1	—
Sycamore	1	1	—	Fruitland	8	7	1
Sylvania	14	10	4	Garden City	28	21	7
Sylvester	19	15	4	Glenns Ferry	3	3	—
Talbottom	4	4	—	Gooding	6	6	—
Tallapoosa	13	11	2	Grangeville	5	5	—
Tallulah Falls	2	1	1	Hailey	10	9	1
Temple	4	4	—	Heyburn	6	5	1
Tennille	2	2	—	Homedale	6	6	—
Thomaston	44	35	9	Idaho Falls	118	83	35
Thomasville	53	47	6	Jerome	14	13	1
Tifton	57	46	11	Kamiah	4	4	—
Tignall	4	3	1	Kellogg	9	8	1
Toccoa	27	21	6	Ketchum	16	11	5
Trenton	6	6	—	Kimberly	6	6	—
Trion	7	7	—	Lewiston	62	45	17
Tunnel Hill	5	5	—	McCall	13	10	3
Twin City	4	4	—	Meridian	31	27	4
Tybee Island	23	16	7	Montpelier	6	6	—
Tyrone	12	10	2	Moscow	42	30	12
Union City	52	39	13	Mountain Home	30	23	7
Union Point	11	8	3	Nampa	71	50	21
Uvalda	1	1	—	New Plymouth	4	4	—

Table 78. — Number of Full-time Law Enforcement Employees, Cities, October 31, 1996 — Continued

City	Total police employees	Total officers	Total civilians	City	Total police employees	Total officers	Total civilians
IDAHO — Continued				**ILLINOIS — Continued**			
Orofino	8	7	1	Bellwood	61	47	14
Osburn	3	3	—	Belvidere	31	29	2
Parma	4	4	—	Bensenville	50	40	10
Payette	12	11	1	Benton	10	5	5
Pinehurst	3	3	—	Berkeley	19	15	4
Pocatello	109	83	26	Berwyn	108	83	25
Ponderay	3	3	—	Bethalto	20	14	6
Post Falls	39	24	15	Bloomingdale	63	46	17
Preston	5	5	—	Bloomington	111	94	17
Priest River	6	5	1	Blue Island	50	34	16
Rexburg	31	27	4	Blue Mound	2	2	—
Rigby	7	7	—	Bolingbrook	112	79	33
Rupert	14	13	1	Bourbonnais	25	19	6
St. Anthony	8	8	—	Bradley	29	22	7
St. Maries	5	5	—	Braidwood	13	9	4
Salmon	7	6	1	Breese	8	5	3
Sandpoint	23	15	8	Bridgeport	3	3	—
Shelley	6	6	—	Bridgeview	57	44	13
Soda Springs	8	7	1	Brighton	4	3	1
Spirit Lake	3	3	—	Broadview	44	36	8
Twin Falls	65	49	16	Brookfield	34	27	7
Wallace	4	4	—	Brooklyn	2	2	—
Weiser	10	9	1	Buda	1	1	—
Wendell	5	5	—	Buffalo Grove	84	72	12
Wilder	3	3	—	Bull Valley	2	2	—
				Bunker Hill	4	3	1
ILLINOIS				Burbank	55	46	9
Abingdon	8	4	4	Burnham	13	9	4
Addison	78	59	19	Burr Ridge	24	21	3
Albany	1	1	—	Byron	6	5	1
Albion	3	3	—	Cahokia	42	31	11
Aledo	8	7	1	Cairo	18	13	5
Alexis	1	1	—	Calumet City	104	77	27
Algonquin	31	25	6	Calumet Park	27	22	5
Alsip	51	40	11	Cambridge	1	1	—
Altamont	5	5	—	Camp Point	2	2	—
Alton	85	71	14	Canton	30	21	9
Amboy	2	2	—	Carbon Cliff	3	3	—
Andalusia	3	3	—	Carbondale	77	60	17
Anna	8	8	—	Carlinville	16	11	5
Annawan	1	1	—	Carlyle	7	6	1
Antioch	26	18	8	Carmi	9	8	1
Arcola	5	5	—	Carol Stream	76	54	22
Arlington Heights	140	104	36	Carpentersville	52	47	5
Arthur	5	4	1	Carrier Mills	2	2	—
Ashland	1	1	—	Carrollton	6	6	—
Astoria	1	1	—	Carterville	5	5	—
Atkinson	1	1	—	Carthage	3	3	—
Atlanta	3	3	—	Cary	30	23	7
Auburn	8	4	4	Casey	8	7	1
Aurora	312	242	70	Caseyville	11	7	4
Avon	1	1	—	Central City	4	4	—
Bannockburn	7	7	—	Centralia	35	28	7
Barrington	41	28	13	Centreville	17	14	3
Barrington Hills	24	16	8	Champaign	145	115	30
Bartlett	56	42	14	Channahon	14	12	2
Bartonville	13	9	4	Charleston	38	30	8
Batavia	44	37	7	Chatham	12	10	2
Beardstown	12	8	4	Chenoa	3	3	—
Bedford Park	35	29	6	Cherry Valley	13	13	—
Beecher	6	6	—	Chester	11	8	3
Belleville	92	78	14	Chicago	15,687	13,032	2,655

Table 78. — Number of Full-time Law Enforcement Employees, Cities, October 31, 1996 — Continued

City	Total police employees	Total officers	Total civilians	City	Total police employees	Total officers	Total civilians
ILLINOIS — Continued				**ILLINOIS — Continued**			
Chicago Heights	117	86	31	Energy	3	3	—
Chicago Ridge	31	27	4	Enfield	1	1	—
Chillicothe	13	9	4	Equality	2	2	—
Christopher	5	5	—	Erie	3	3	—
Cicero	154	113	41	Essex	2	2	—
Clarendon Hills	13	13	—	Eureka	4	4	—
Clinton	16	12	4	Evanston	198	143	55
Coal City	10	6	4	Evergreen Park	67	57	10
Coal Valley	7	6	1	Fairbury	6	6	—
Cobden	3	3	—	Fairfield	15	11	4
Collinsville	45	35	10	Fairmont City	14	9	5
Colona	5	5	—	Fairview	1	1	—
Columbia	17	11	6	Fairview Heights	48	37	11
Cordova	2	2	—	Farmer City	7	4	3
Coulterville	2	2	—	Farmington	7	4	3
Country Club Hills	37	27	10	Fisher	3	3	—
Countryside	28	22	6	Flora	16	11	5
Crest Hill	23	19	4	Flossmoor	23	17	6
Crestwood	4	3	1	Ford Heights	7	4	3
Crete	17	13	4	Forest Park	52	38	14
Creve Coeur	10	9	1	Forest View	11	8	3
Crystal Lake	65	48	17	Fox Lake	24	18	6
Cuba	2	2	—	Fox River Grove	10	10	—
Dallas City	2	2	—	Frankfort	21	19	2
Danvers	1	1	—	Franklin Park	68	54	14
Danville	84	67	17	Freeburg	7	6	1
Darien	45	30	15	Freeport	68	51	17
Decatur	153	147	6	Fulton	7	6	1
Deerfield	50	37	13	Galena	11	9	2
De Kalb	63	52	11	Galesburg	72	51	21
DePue	3	3	—	Galva	4	4	—
De Soto	3	3	—	Geneseo	17	11	6
Des Plaines	119	99	20	Geneva	39	28	11
Divernon	2	2	—	Genoa	10	9	1
Dixmoor	8	6	2	Germantown	2	2	—
Dixon	28	24	4	Gibson City	11	7	4
Dolton	53	48	5	Gifford	1	1	—
Downers Grove	93	69	24	Gilberts	1	1	—
Dupo	5	5	—	Gillespie	10	7	3
Du Quoin	13	9	4	Gilman	2	2	—
Durand	2	2	—	Girard	4	4	—
Dwight	10	8	2	Glasford	1	1	—
Earlville	3	3	—	Glen Carbon	18	13	5
East Alton	17	11	6	Glencoe	44	35	9
East Carondelet	1	1	—	Glendale Heights	77	53	24
East Dubuque	7	7	—	Glen Ellyn	42	35	7
East Dundee	13	12	1	Glenview	94	68	26
East Galesburg	1	1	—	Glenwood	24	17	7
East Hazel Crest	10	9	1	Golf	2	2	—
East Moline	50	37	13	Grafton	3	3	—
East Peoria	46	35	11	Granite City	64	53	11
East St. Louis	125	92	33	Grant Park	7	6	1
Edwardsville	39	29	10	Grayslake	28	19	9
Effingham	37	26	11	Grayville	7	3	4
Elburn	7	6	1	Greenfield	3	3	—
Eldorado	11	7	4	Green Rock	4	4	—
Elgin	198	151	47	Greenup	4	4	—
Elizabeth	2	2	—	Green Valley	1	1	—
Elk Grove Village	110	96	14	Greenville	14	10	4
Elmhurst	89	68	21	Gridley	1	1	—
Elmwood Park	48	37	11	Gurnee	64	45	19
El Paso	3	3	—	Hamilton	4	4	—

Table 78. — Number of Full-time Law Enforcement Employees, Cities, October 31, 1996 — Continued

City	Total police employees	Total officers	Total civilians	City	Total police employees	Total officers	Total civilians
ILLINOIS — Continued				**ILLINOIS — Continued**			
Hampton	3	3	—	Lansing	76	59	17
Hampshire	6	6	—	La Salle	21	17	4
Hanover	1	1	—	Lebanon	11	7	4
Hanover Park	65	47	18	Leland Grove	5	5	—
Harrisburg	14	13	1	Lemont	25	23	2
Hartford	6	5	1	Le Roy	4	4	—
Harvard	21	17	4	Lewistown	3	3	—
Harvey	102	66	36	Libertyville	50	38	12
Harwood Heights	32	24	8	Lincoln	28	27	1
Havana	9	9	—	Lincolnshire	28	18	10
Hawthorn Woods	9	8	1	Lincolnwood	46	34	12
Hazel Crest	39	29	10	Lindenhurst	14	12	2
Hebron	2	2	—	Lisle	53	39	14
Henry	4	4	—	Litchfield	19	14	5
Herrin	17	13	4	Livingston	2	2	—
Herscher	2	2	—	Lockport	26	22	4
Hickory Hills	33	27	6	Lombard	83	66	17
Highland	23	17	6	London Mills	1	1	—
Highland Park	74	58	16	Loves Park	33	24	9
Highwood	13	9	4	Lynwood	17	13	4
Hillsboro	8	8	—	Lyons	29	23	6
Hillside	38	30	8	Mackinaw	1	1	—
Hinckley	4	4	—	Macomb	26	25	1
Hinsdale	37	27	10	Madison	15	12	3
Hodgkins	16	15	1	Mahomet	6	6	—
Hoffman Estates	116	92	24	Manhattan	6	6	—
Holiday Hills	2	2	—	Manito	4	4	—
Homer	1	1	—	Manteno	9	9	—
Hometown	5	1	4	Marengo	17	13	4
Homewood	46	36	10	Marion	26	19	7
Hoopeston	14	9	5	Marissa	5	5	—
Huntley	13	12	1	Markham	37	30	7
Indian Head Park	12	9	3	Maroa	3	3	—
Island Lake	17	12	5	Marquette Heights	5	5	—
Itasca	38	27	11	Marseilles	8	8	—
Jacksonville	42	35	7	Marshall	9	8	1
Jerome	6	6	—	Martinsville	3	3	—
Jerseyville	18	12	6	Maryville	11	7	4
Johnsburg	9	8	1	Mascoutah	11	10	1
Johnston City	5	5	—	Mason City	4	4	—
Joliet	280	224	56	Matteson	48	36	12
Jonesboro	3	3	—	Mattoon	46	40	6
Justice	37	29	8	Maywood	70	61	9
Kankakee	93	68	25	McCook	20	14	6
Kenilworth	14	11	3	McCullom Lake	1	1	—
Kewanee	25	19	6	McHenry	47	35	12
Kildeer	7	7	—	McLeansboro	5	5	—
Kincaid	1	1	—	Melrose Park	77	58	19
Kirkland	3	3	—	Mendota	15	13	2
Knoxville	4	4	—	Meredosia	3	3	—
Lacon	1	1	—	Metamora	5	5	—
La Grange	36	27	9	Metropolis	21	16	5
La Grange Park	29	24	5	Midlothian	28	22	6
Lake Bluff	14	13	1	Milan	16	12	4
Lake Forest	62	45	17	Milledgeville	2	2	—
Lake-in-the-Hills	31	24	7	Millstadt	5	5	—
Lakemoor	6	6	—	Minier	2	2	—
Lake Villa	11	10	1	Minonk	2	2	—
Lakewood	4	4	—	Minooka	10	9	1
Lake Zurich	51	34	17	Mokena	22	21	1
La Moille	1	1	—	Moline	105	79	26
Lanark	2	2	—	Momence	9	9	—

Table 78. — Number of Full-time Law Enforcement Employees, Cities, October 31, 1996 — Continued

City	Total police employees	Total officers	Total civilians	City	Total police employees	Total officers	Total civilians
ILLINOIS — Continued				**ILLINOIS—Continued**			
Monee	6	6	—	Palestine	3	3	—
Monmouth	26	18	8	Palmyra	1	1	—
Montgomery	19	13	6	Palos Heights	26	24	2
Monticello	8	7	1	Palos Hills	36	30	6
Morris	26	20	6	Palos Park	14	12	2
Morrison	7	7	—	Pana	14	10	4
Morton	23	18	5	Paris	17	13	4
Morton Grove	66	46	20	Park City	13	8	5
Mound City	3	3	—	Park Forest	48	38	10
Mount Carmel	17	12	5	Park Ridge	65	53	12
Mount Carroll	3	3	—	Pawnee	8	4	4
Mount Morris	7	4	3	Paxton	6	6	—
Mount Olive	4	3	1	Pecatonica	3	3	—
Mount Prospect	97	78	19	Pekin	60	50	10
Mount Pulaski	4	4	—	Peoria	275	222	53
Mount Sterling	9	4	5	Peoria Heights	14	11	3
Mount Vernon	51	40	11	Peotone	12	7	5
Mount Zion	10	9	1	Peru	23	20	3
Moweaqua	2	2	—	Petersburg	5	5	—
Mundelein	47	35	12	Phoenix	8	3	5
Murphysboro	18	12	6	Pinckneyville	9	6	3
Naperville	229	147	82	Pittsfield	6	6	—
Nashville	7	6	1	Plainfield	21	19	2
Nauvoo	1	1	—	Plano	15	13	2
Neoga	2	2	—	Plymouth	1	1	—
Neponset	1	1	—	Polo	4	4	—
New Athens	4	4	—	Pontiac	24	20	4
New Baden	4	4	—	Pontoon Beach	17	11	6
New Lenox	24	23	1	Port Byron	3	3	—
Newman	1	1	—	Posen	12	10	2
Newton	7	6	1	Princeton	14	13	1
Niles	67	52	15	Prophetstown	5	4	1
Nokomis	6	3	3	Prospect Heights	29	23	6
Normal	72	58	14	Quincy	91	76	15
Norridge	48	37	11	Rantoul	37	31	6
North Aurora	19	17	2	Raymond	1	1	—
Northbrook	84	60	24	Red Bud	4	4	—
North Chicago	70	52	18	Richmond	6	5	1
Northfield	27	21	6	Richton Park	27	22	5
Northlake	29	27	2	Ridgway	3	3	—
North Pekin	1	1	—	Riverdale	48	36	12
North Riverside	39	30	9	River Forest	41	31	10
Oak Brook	53	39	14	River Grove	25	19	6
Oakbrook Terrace	20	17	3	Riverside	22	18	4
Oak Forest	51	39	12	Robbins	10	5	5
Oak Lawn	140	97	43	Robinson	14	12	2
Oak Park	147	115	32	Rochelle	24	19	5
Oblong	1	1	—	Rochester	7	7	—
O'Fallon	41	29	12	Rockdale	5	5	—
Ogden	1	1	—	Rock Falls	25	18	7
Oglesby	11	8	3	Rockford	304	272	32
Okawville	3	3	—	Rock Island	113	84	29
Old Shawneetown	1	1	—	Rockton	9	8	1
Olney	18	12	6	Rolling Meadows	72	51	21
Olympia Fields	20	18	2	Romeoville	43	33	10
Oregon	7	7	—	Roodhouse	4	4	—
Orion	3	3	—	Roscoe	10	9	1
Orland Hills	15	14	1	Roselle	48	37	11
Orland Park	106	83	23	Rosemont	78	65	13
Oswego	22	19	3	Rossville	2	2	—
Ottawa	37	29	8	Round Lake	10	9	1
Palatine	116	88	28	Round Lake Beach	39	33	6

City	Total police employees	Total officers	Total civilians	City	Total police employees	Total officers	Total civilians
ILLINOIS — Continued				**ILLINOIS — Continued**			
Round Lake Heights	3	3	—	Tower Lakes	2	2	—
Round Lake Park	13	11	2	Tremont	4	3	1
Roxana	6	5	1	Trenton	3	3	—
Royalton	3	3	—	Troy	18	13	5
Rushville	4	4	—	Tuscola	8	7	1
St. Anne	4	4	—	University Park	25	18	7
St. Charles	61	49	12	Urbana	59	47	12
St. Francisville	1	1	—	Vandalia	17	12	5
Salem	19	14	5	Venice	12	7	5
Sandwich	17	11	6	Vernon Hills	57	37	20
Sauget	9	9	—	Vienna	2	2	—
Sauk Village	23	17	6	Villa Grove	4	4	—
Savanna	8	7	1	Villa Park	53	38	15
Schaumburg	190	136	54	Virden	8	4	4
Schiller Park	36	29	7	Wamac	2	2	—
Seneca	7	4	3	Warren	4	4	—
Sesser	6	5	1	Warrensburg	1	1	—
Shawneetown	4	4	—	Warrenville	23	18	5
Shelbyville	8	7	1	Washburn	1	1	—
Sherman	4	4	—	Washington	20	13	7
Shiloh	7	7	—	Washington Park	11	7	4
Shorewood	16	14	2	Waterloo	9	8	1
Silvis	19	12	7	Watseka	16	11	5
Skokie	138	105	33	Wauconda	28	17	11
Sleepy Hollow	6	5	1	Waukegan	189	141	48
Smithton	4	4	—	Wayne	4	4	—
Somonauk	3	3	—	Westchester	47	36	11
South Barrington	13	12	1	West Chicago	48	40	8
South Beloit	13	9	4	West City	8	4	4
South Chicago Heights	12	7	5	West Dundee	16	14	2
South Elgin	27	20	7	Western Springs	25	20	5
South Holland	49	38	11	West Frankfort	19	14	5
South Jacksonville	7	6	1	Westmont	52	37	15
South Pekin	2	2	—	West Salem	1	1	—
South Roxana	6	5	1	Wheaton	90	66	24
Sparta	14	10	4	Wheeling	78	55	23
Springfield	308	258	50	White Hall	4	4	—
Spring Grove	8	7	1	Williamsfield	1	1	—
Spring Valley	12	8	4	Williamsville	2	2	—
Staunton	10	7	3	Willowbrook	29	25	4
Steger	16	13	3	Willow Springs	16	12	4
Sterling	38	27	11	Wilmette	61	43	18
Stickney	21	16	5	Wilmington	18	11	7
Stockton	3	3	—	Winchester	3	3	—
Stone Park	31	20	11	Winfield	19	17	2
Stonington	1	1	—	Winnebago	2	2	—
Streamwood	65	48	17	Winnetka	38	27	11
Streator	25	20	5	Winthrop Harbor	14	9	5
Sugar Grove	7	6	1	Witt	1	1	—
Sullivan	9	7	2	Wood Dale	49	32	17
Summit	34	29	5	Woodhull	1	1	—
Sumner	2	2	—	Woodridge	62	46	16
Swansea	21	17	4	Wood River	26	18	8
Sycamore	30	21	9	Woodstock	39	27	12
Tampico	1	1	—	Worth	26	24	2
Taylorville	25	19	6	Wyoming	1	1	—
Thomasboro	2	2	—	Yorkville	13	13	—
Thornton	10	9	1	Zeigler	5	4	1
Tinley Park	80	62	18	Zion	56	41	15
Tolono	2	2	—				
Tonica	1	1	—	**INDIANA**			
Toulon	1	1	—	Alexandria	14	10	4

Table 78. — Number of Full-time Law Enforcement Employees, Cities, October 31, 1996 — Continued

City	Total police employees	Total officers	Total civilians	City	Total police employees	Total officers	Total civilians
INDIANA — Continued				**INDIANA — Continued**			
Anderson	170	127	43	Long Beach	5	5	—
Angola	17	13	4	Lowell	17	12	5
Austin	4	4	—	Madison	34	25	9
Batesville	12	8	4	Marion	84	75	9
Bedford	39	31	8	Martinsville	22	17	5
Beech Grove	36	27	9	Merrillville	55	46	9
Berne	6	5	1	Monticello	12	10	2
Bloomington	86	64	22	Mooresville	23	15	8
Bluffton	24	17	7	Mount Vernon	16	15	1
Boonville	11	11	—	Muncie	119	118	1
Brazil	15	11	4	Munster	45	35	10
Brownsburg	29	22	7	Nappanee	18	13	5
Burns Harbor	9	5	4	New Albany	74	58	16
Carmel	78	65	13	New Castle	39	36	3
Charlestown	13	9	4	New Chicago	4	1	3
Chesterfield	7	7	—	New Haven	22	16	6
Chesterton	21	15	6	Noblesville	47	38	9
Clarksville	41	33	8	North Manchester	15	11	4
Clinton	14	9	5	North Vernon	16	14	2
Connersville	38	36	2	Plainfield	33	31	2
Corydon	7	7	—	Plymouth	26	21	5
Crawfordsville	40	28	12	Portage	53	39	14
Crown Point	35	28	7	Portland	18	14	4
Culver	4	4	—	Rensselaer	13	9	4
Decatur	20	16	4	Rushville	19	13	6
Delphi	12	8	4	Schererville	48	39	9
Dunkirk	8	4	4	Sellersburg	16	11	5
Dyer	27	21	6	Seymour	41	29	12
Elkhart	132	103	29	South Bend	322	253	69
Evansville	305	276	29	Speedway	38	30	8
Fairmount	9	5	4	Tell City	16	11	5
Fort Wayne	467	383	84	Terre Haute	141	119	22
Fowler	4	4	—	Trail Creek	4	4	—
Franklin	35	26	9	Union City	7	7	—
Garrett	15	10	5	Valparaiso	53	37	16
Gary	309	234	75	Vincennes	32	27	5
Gas City	15	11	4	Wabash	32	25	7
Georgetown	3	3	—	Warsaw	43	34	9
Goshen	53	47	6	West Lafayette	50	39	11
Greendale	13	9	4	West Terre Haute	9	5	4
Greenfield	30	24	6	Whitestown	1	1	—
Greenwood	63	46	17	Winchester	15	11	4
Griffith	35	27	8	**IOWA**			
Hagerstown	5	5	—	Adel	6	6	—
Hammond	265	211	54	Albia	8	7	1
Hartford City	16	12	4	Algona	15	10	5
Highland	46	39	7	Altoona	16	15	1
Hobart	63	49	14	Ames	68	49	19
Huntingburg	9	8	1	Anamosa	6	5	1
Huntington	39	32	7	Ankeny	30	24	6
Indianapolis	1,275	1,013	262	Atlantic	14	12	2
Jasonville	4	4	—	Audubon	2	2	—
Jasper	24	17	7	Bedford	2	2	—
Kendallville	20	15	5	Belle Plaine	4	4	—
Kingsford Heights	3	3	—	Belmond	4	4	—
Kokomo	148	105	43	Bettendorf	52	40	12
Kouts	3	3	—	Bloomfield	7	7	—
Lafayette	109	82	27	Boone	16	15	1
Lake Station	24	19	5	Burlington	55	41	14
La Porte	43	39	4	Camanche	7	7	—
Lawrence	45	41	4	Carlisle	5	5	—
Logansport	48	38	10				

City	Total police employees	Total officers	Total civilians	City	Total police employees	Total officers	Total civilians
IOWA — Continued				**IOWA — Continued**			
Carroll	18	13	5	Mason City	61	45	16
Carter Lake	7	6	1	Missouri Valley	7	7	—
Cedar Falls	47	44	3	Monticello	8	5	3
Cedar Rapids	228	181	47	Mount Pleasant	16	14	2
Centerville	17	12	5	Mount Vernon	5	5	—
Chariton	8	7	1	Muscatine	45	37	8
Charles City	18	13	5	Nevada	8	7	1
Cherokee	10	9	1	New Hampton	6	6	—
Clarinda	15	10	5	Newton	34	29	5
Clarion	6	6	—	Norwalk	10	8	2
Clear Lake	18	13	5	Oelwein	16	11	5
Clinton	58	49	9	Onawa	4	4	—
Clive	19	15	4	Orange City	5	5	—
Coralville	27	25	2	Osage	6	6	—
Council Bluffs	110	98	12	Osceola	9	8	1
Cresco	7	7	—	Oskaloosa	19	18	1
Creston	16	12	4	Ottumwa	44	36	8
Davenport	193	154	39	Palo	1	1	—
Decorah	17	12	5	Pella	14	12	2
Denison	16	12	4	Perry	15	11	4
Des Moines	463	334	129	Pleasant Hill	10	10	—
De Witt	8	8	—	Red Oak	13	9	4
Dubuque	87	81	6	Rock Rapids	3	3	—
Dyersville	9	5	4	Rock Valley	4	4	—
Eagle Grove	7	7	—	Sac City	5	5	—
Eldora	6	6	—	Sergeant Bluff	7	7	—
Eldridge	6	6	—	Sheldon	11	7	4
Emmetsburg	7	6	1	Shenandoah	13	10	3
Estherville	11	11	—	Sioux Center	6	6	—
Evansdale	7	6	1	Sioux City	153	125	28
Fairfield	19	13	6	Spencer	26	19	7
Forest City	8	8	—	Spirit Lake	7	6	1
Fort Dodge	47	43	4	Storm Lake	21	17	4
Fort Madison	25	20	5	Story City	5	5	—
Garner	5	5	—	Tama	5	5	—
Glenwood	14	12	2	Tipton	5	5	—
Grinnell	17	16	1	Urbandale	43	36	7
Grundy Center	4	4	—	Vinton	7	7	—
Guttenberg	5	3	2	Washington	10	10	—
Hampton	13	8	5	Waterloo	131	121	10
Harlan	9	8	1	Waukee	7	6	1
Hawarden	4	4	—	Waukon	6	6	—
Hiawatha	7	7	—	Waverly	15	14	1
Humboldt	7	7	—	Webster City	19	13	6
Independence	19	13	6	West Burlington	9	8	1
Indianola	18	16	2	West Des Moines	61	48	13
Iowa City	83	62	21	West Union	5	5	—
Iowa Falls	15	11	4	Williamsburg	5	5	—
Jefferson	8	8	—	Windsor Heights	11	10	1
Johnston	10	9	1	Winterset	7	7	—
Keokuk	38	28	10				
Knoxville	15	11	4	**KANSAS**			
Lamoni	3	3	—	Abilene	26	14	12
Le Claire	6	6	—	Andover	13	9	4
Le Mars	14	13	1	Anthony	5	5	—
Lenox	3	3	—	Arcadia	1	1	—
Leon	4	3	1	Argonia	1	1	—
Lisbon	1	1	—	Arkansas City	31	24	7
Manchester	13	9	4	Arma	5	5	—
Maquoketa	16	11	5	Atchison	24	23	1
Marion	39	31	8	Attica	1	1	—
Marshalltown	60	43	17	Augusta	27	21	6

Table 78. — Number of Full-time Law Enforcement Employees, Cities, October 31, 1996 — Continued

City	Total police employees	Total officers	Total civilians	City	Total police employees	Total officers	Total civilians
KANSAS — Continued				**KANSAS — Continued**			
Baldwin City	7	6	1	Goodland	11	9	2
Basehor	3	3	—	Grandview Plaza	3	3	—
Baxter Springs	12	9	3	Great Bend	43	32	11
Belle Plaine	4	4	—	Halstead	5	5	—
Belleville	5	5	—	Harper	3	3	—
Beloit	12	8	4	Hays	40	26	14
Blue Rapids	2	2	—	Haysville	24	15	9
Bonner Springs	21	18	3	Herington	9	5	4
Buhler	3	3	—	Hesston	5	4	1
Burden	1	1	—	Hiawatha	7	6	1
Burlingame	3	3	—	Highland	2	2	—
Burlington	9	7	2	Hill City	4	4	—
Burrton	1	1	—	Hillsboro	4	4	—
Caldwell	4	4	—	Hoisington	10	7	3
Caney	9	5	4	Holcomb	4	3	1
Carbondale	2	2	—	Holton	6	6	—
Cawker City	1	1	—	Holyrood	1	1	—
Cedar Vale	1	1	—	Hope	1	1	—
Chanute	19	17	2	Horton	6	6	—
Chapman	2	2	—	Hoxie	2	2	—
Chase	1	1	—	Hugoton	7	6	1
Cheney	3	3	—	Humboldt	5	5	—
Cherokee	1	1	—	Hutchinson	95	65	30
Cherryvale	6	6	—	Independence	29	21	8
Chetopa	5	5	—	Inman	2	2	—
Cimarron	3	3	—	Iola	27	18	9
Clay Center	7	7	—	Junction City	68	49	19
Clearwater	6	6	—	Kansas City	476	364	112
Coffeyville	34	25	9	Kingman	10	6	4
Colby	16	11	5	Kinsley	4	4	—
Columbus	8	7	1	Kiowa	1	1	—
Colwich	4	2	2	La Crosse	3	3	—
Concordia	29	11	18	La Cygne	1	1	—
Conway Springs	4	4	—	Lake Quivira	2	2	—
Council Grove	6	6	—	Lansing	11	10	1
Derby	36	26	10	Larned	13	9	4
Dodge City	43	31	12	Lawrence	130	116	14
Eastborough	7	7	—	Leavenworth	79	58	21
Edna	1	1	—	Leawood	66	50	16
Edwardsville	13	12	1	Lebo	2	2	—
El Dorado	29	24	5	Lenexa	99	59	40
Elkhart	3	3	—	Liberal	34	30	4
Ellinwood	5	5	—	Lindsborg	6	5	1
Ellis	4	4	—	Louisburg	6	6	—
Ellsworth	5	5	—	Lyndon	3	3	—
Elwood	2	2	—	Lyons	8	7	1
Emporia	56	46	10	Maize	5	4	1
Enterprise	1	1	—	Marion	3	3	—
Erie	3	3	—	Marquette	1	1	—
Eudora	5	5	—	Marysville	7	6	1
Fairway	8	7	1	McLouth	1	1	—
Florence	1	1	—	McPherson	26	22	4
Fort Scott	20	14	6	Meade	3	3	—
Fredonia	8	7	1	Medicine Lodge	4	4	—
Frontenac	10	6	4	Melvern	1	1	—
Galena	12	12	—	Merriam	28	25	3
Garden City	89	59	30	Minneapolis	5	5	—
Garden Plain	2	2	—	Mission	23	21	2
Gardner	16	14	2	Moundridge	3	3	—
Garnett	14	9	5	Mound Valley	2	2	—
Girard	5	5	—	Mount Hope	2	2	—
Goddard	4	4	—	Mulberry	1	1	—

City	Total police employees	Total officers	Total civilians	City	Total police employees	Total officers	Total civilians
KANSAS — Continued				**KANSAS — Continued**			
Mulvane	15	11	4	Wellsville	4	4	—
Neodesha	8	7	1	Westwood	8	7	1
Newton	32	27	5	Wichita	765	572	193
North Newton	1	1	—	Wilson	1	1	—
Norton	5	5	—	Winfield	25	20	5
Oakley	11	6	5	Yates Center	3	3	—
Oberlin	4	4	—				
Olathe	141	112	29	**KENTUCKY**			
Osage City	7	7	—	Adairville	1	1	—
Osawatomie	18	16	2	Albany	8	5	3
Osborne	3	3	—	Alexandria	9	9	—
Oswego	5	5	—	Allen	1	1	—
Ottawa	28	24	4	Anchorage	14	10	4
Overbrook	1	1	—	Ashland	57	50	7
Overland Park	231	175	56	Auburn	2	2	—
Oxford	2	2	—	Audubon Park	8	7	1
Paola	18	12	6	Augusta	2	2	—
Park City	13	12	1	Barbourville	15	12	3
Parsons	30	23	7	Bardstown	21	17	4
Peabody	2	2	—	Bardwell	2	2	—
Pittsburg	40	31	9	Barlow	2	2	—
Plainville	4	4	—	Beattyville	5	5	—
Pleasanton	2	2	—	Beaver Dam	4	4	—
Prairie Village	50	40	10	Bellefonte	1	1	—
Pratt	20	14	6	Bellevue	11	10	1
Roeland Park	16	14	2	Benham	2	2	—
Rose Hill	6	6	—	Benton	8	7	1
Rossville	1	1	—	Berea	25	19	6
Russell	17	8	9	Bloomfield	3	2	1
Sabetha	5	5	—	Bowling Green	120	92	28
St. Francis	6	5	1	Brandenburg	4	4	—
St. George	1	1	—	Brodhead	1	1	—
St. John	4	4	—	Brooksville	2	2	—
St. Marys	5	5	—	Brownsville	1	1	—
Salina	94	72	22	Burgin	2	2	—
Scott City	11	6	5	Burkesville	7	4	3
Scranton	2	2	—	Burnside	4	4	—
Sedan	2	2	—	Cadiz	5	5	—
Sedgwick	3	3	—	Calhoun	2	2	—
Seneca	5	5	—	Calvert City	5	4	1
Shawnee	82	66	16	Campbellsburg	1	1	—
Silver Lake	2	2	—	Campbellsville	15	14	1
Smith Center	3	3	—	Campton	1	1	—
South Hutchinson	7	6	1	Caneyville	1	1	—
Spearville	1	1	—	Carlisle	7	6	1
Spring Hill	6	6	—	Carrollton	10	10	—
Stafford	4	4	—	Catlettsburg	7	7	—
Sterling	5	5	—	Cave City	6	6	—
Stockton	5	5	—	Central City	9	9	—
Tonganoxie	5	5	—	Clarkson	1	1	—
Topeka	353	272	81	Clay	2	2	—
Towanda	1	1	—	Clay City	3	3	—
Udall	2	2	—	Clinton	4	4	—
Ulysses	9	8	1	Cloverport	2	2	—
Valley Center	13	8	5	Cold Spring	6	6	—
Valley Falls	2	2	—	Columbia	9	9	—
Wa Keeney	5	5	—	Corbin	23	17	6
Wakefield	1	1	—	Covington	130	106	24
Wamego	11	6	5	Crab Orchard	2	2	—
Waterville	1	1	—	Crittenden	1	1	—
Waverly	1	1	—	Crofton	1	1	—
Wellington	17	13	4	Cumberland	11	8	3

Table 78. — Number of Full-time Law Enforcement Employees, Cities, October 31, 1996 — Continued

City	Total police employees	Total officers	Total civilians	City	Total police employees	Total officers	Total civilians
KENTUCKY — Continued				**KENTUCKY — Continued**			
Cynthiana	19	15	4	La Center	2	2	—
Danville	32	26	6	La Grange	10	9	1
Dawson Springs	9	5	4	Lakeside Park	8	7	1
Dayton	8	8	—	Lancaster	8	8	—
Devondale	3	3	—	Land-between-the-Lakes	39	33	6
Dixie Police Authority	9	9	—	Lawrenceburg	19	15	4
Dry Ridge	4	4	—	Lebanon	22	15	7
Earlington	2	2	—	Lebanon Junction	4	4	—
Edgewood	11	11	—	Leitchfield	12	12	—
Edmonton	6	6	—	Lewisburg	1	1	—
Elizabethtown	50	38	12	Lewisport	2	2	—
Elkhorn City	5	5	—	Lexington	553	403	150
Elkton	7	7	—	Liberty	8	6	2
Elsmere	11	10	1	Livermore	1	1	—
Eminence	6	6	—	London	22	19	3
Erlanger	37	28	9	Lone Oak	1	1	—
Eubank	1	1	—	Louisa	10	6	4
Evarts	5	5	—	Louisville	861	652	209
Falmouth	14	10	4	Loyall	1	1	—
Flatwoods	15	10	5	Ludlow	9	8	1
Fleming-Neon	3	3	—	Lynch	2	2	—
Flemingsburg	7	7	—	Madisonville	57	47	10
Florence	55	51	4	Manchester	13	10	3
Fort Mitchell	12	12	—	Marion	7	7	—
Fort Thomas	23	22	1	Martin	4	4	—
Fort Wright	9	9	—	Mayfield	36	29	7
Frankfort	62	56	6	Maysville	29	23	6
Franklin	26	18	8	McKee	1	1	—
Fulton	15	11	4	Middlesboro	26	22	4
Gamaliel	2	2	—	Millersburg	1	1	—
Georgetown	47	43	4	Monticello	11	7	4
Glasgow	36	27	9	Morehead	27	19	8
Grayson	11	9	2	Morganfield	14	8	6
Greensburg	9	5	4	Morgantown	6	6	—
Greenup	4	4	—	Mortons Gap	2	2	—
Greenville	8	8	—	Mount Sterling	20	14	6
Guthrie	5	5	—	Mount Vernon	5	5	—
Hardinsburg	3	3	—	Mount Washington	8	8	—
Harlan	16	11	5	Muldraugh	3	3	—
Harrodsburg	26	17	9	Munfordville	3	3	—
Hartford	4	4	—	Murray	35	29	6
Hawesville	1	1	—	New Castle	1	1	—
Hazard	29	23	6	New Haven	2	2	—
Henderson	62	54	8	Newport	53	43	10
Hickman	9	5	4	Nicholasville	40	31	9
Highland Heights	8	8	—	Northfield	1	1	—
Hillview	14	14	—	Nortonville	2	2	—
Hindman	2	2	—	Oak Grove	7	7	—
Hodgenville	8	8	—	Olive Hill	4	4	—
Hopkinsville	62	56	6	Owensboro	100	86	14
Horse Cave	5	5	—	Owenton	3	3	—
Hustonville	1	1	—	Owingsville	4	4	—
Independence	17	16	1	Paducah	85	74	11
Indian Hills	5	5	—	Paintsville	18	12	6
Inez	2	1	1	Paris	26	18	8
Irvine	8	8	—	Park City	1	1	—
Irvington	4	4	—	Park Hills	6	5	1
Jackson	11	10	1	Pembroke	1	1	—
Jamestown	4	4	—	Perryville	1	1	—
Jeffersontown	52	45	7	Pewee Valley	4	4	—
Jenkins	6	5	1	Pikeville	24	18	6
Junction City	4	4	—	Pineville	8	8	—

Table 78. — Number of Full-time Law Enforcement Employees, Cities, October 31, 1996 — Continued

City	Total police employees	Total officers	Total civilians	City	Total police employees	Total officers	Total civilians
KENTUCKY — Continued				**LOUISIANA — Continued**			
Pioneer Village	4	4	—	Baldwin	7	6	1
Pippa Passes	4	4	—	Ball	5	4	1
Prestonsburg	9	9	—	Bastrop	55	49	6
Princeton	15	14	1	Baton Rouge	767	664	103
Prospect	7	7	—	Bernice	5	5	—
Providence	11	9	2	Berwick	10	10	—
Raceland	5	5	—	Blanchard	3	3	—
Radcliff	42	32	10	Bogalusa	51	41	10
Ravenna	2	2	—	Bossier City	175	124	51
Richmond	55	43	12	Breaux Bridge	22	22	—
Russell	12	12	—	Brusly	5	5	—
Russell Springs	5	5	—	Cheneyville	3	3	—
Russellville	31	23	8	Church Point	15	15	—
St. Matthews	35	29	6	Clinton	5	5	—
Salyersville	6	5	1	Covington	36	28	8
Science Hill	1	1	—	Crowley	31	30	1
Scottsville	17	13	4	Cullen	4	4	—
Sebree	1	1	—	Delcambre	9	9	—
Shelbyville	18	17	1	Denham Springs	36	31	5
Shepherdsville	10	10	—	De Ridder	25	24	1
Shively	26	21	5	Duson	3	3	—
Silver Grove	1	1	—	Erath	10	8	2
Somerset	32	29	3	Eunice	37	30	7
Southgate	6	6	—	Farmerville	12	12	—
South Shore	3	3	—	Ferriday	14	7	7
Springfield	11	7	4	Franklin	25	24	1
Stamping Ground	2	2	—	Franklinton	14	14	—
Stanford	7	7	—	Golden Meadow	6	5	1
Stanton	6	6	—	Gonzales	30	30	—
Sturgis	5	5	—	Gramercy	4	4	—
Taylor Mill	8	7	1	Grand Isle	12	12	—
Taylorsville	3	3	—	Gretna	82	69	13
Tompkinsville	9	7	2	Gueydan	5	5	—
Uniontown	2	2	—	Hammond	86	64	22
Vanceburg	4	4	—	Harahan	28	28	—
Versailles	25	18	7	Harrisonburg	1	1	—
Villa Hills	9	8	1	Haynesville	6	6	—
Vine Grove	7	6	1	Iota	3	3	—
Walton	4	4	—	Iowa	8	8	—
Warsaw	4	4	—	Jackson	4	4	—
West Buechel	9	9	—	Jeanerette	20	14	6
West Liberty	10	6	4	Jena	5	5	—
West Point	6	4	2	Jennings	40	38	2
Wheelwright	1	1	—	Jonesboro	15	14	1
Whitesburg	5	5	—	Kenner	170	125	45
Wickliffe	1	1	—	Kentwood	11	11	—
Wilder	6	6	—	Kinder	12	12	—
Williamsburg	8	8	—	Krotz Springs	5	4	1
Williamstown	9	4	5	Lafayette	276	211	65
Wilmore	9	7	2	Lake Charles	164	160	4
Winchester	39	28	11	Leesville	28	28	—
Wingo	2	1	1	Mamou	29	18	11
Worthington	3	3	—	Mandeville	39	28	11
Wurtland	1	1	—	Mansfield	16	11	5
				Many	11	11	—
LOUISIANA				Marksville	26	20	6
Abbeville	37	36	1	Minden	31	30	1
Abita Springs	5	5	—	Monroe	232	169	63
Addis	4	4	—	Morgan City	52	43	9
Alexandria	177	146	31	Natchitoches	81	78	3
Amite	18	18	—	New Iberia	75	56	19
Baker	32	31	1	New Orleans	1,613	1,302	311

Table 78. — Number of Full-time Law Enforcement Employees, Cities, October 31, 1996 — Continued

City	Total police employees	Total officers	Total civilians	City	Total police employees	Total officers	Total civilians
LOUISIANA — Continued				**MAINE — Continued**			
New Roads	21	16	5	Damariscotta	3	3	—
Oakdale	23	23	—	Dexter	6	5	1
Olla	4	4	—	Dixfield	4	4	—
Opelousas	52	44	8	Dover-Foxcroft	5	5	—
Patterson	18	18	—	East Millinocket	4	4	—
Pineville	43	37	6	Eastport	4	4	—
Plaquemine	31	28	3	Eliot	7	7	—
Ponchatoula	18	17	1	Ellsworth	15	11	4
Port Allen	23	23	—	Fairfield	11	10	1
Rayne	22	22	—	Falmouth	18	13	5
Richwood	8	7	1	Farmington	9	8	1
Ruston	49	41	8	Fort Fairfield	6	5	1
St. Francisville	7	6	1	Fort Kent	8	4	4
St. Joseph	3	3	—	Freeport	17	12	5
St. Martinville	21	16	5	Fryeburg	4	4	—
Scott	16	15	1	Gardiner	15	10	5
Shreveport	650	496	154	Gorham	22	16	6
Simmesport	4	3	1	Gouldsboro-Winter Harbor	1	1	—
Slidell	95	65	30	Greenville	2	2	—
Sorrento	4	3	1	Hallowell	5	5	—
Springhill	14	14	—	Hampden	14	9	5
Sunset	12	12	—	Houlton	18	13	5
Tallulah	16	16	—	Jay	11	7	4
Thibodaux	56	47	9	Kennebunk	21	16	5
Vidalia	20	20	—	Kennebunkport	16	11	5
Ville Platte	30	30	—	Kittery	25	19	6
Vinton	12	12	—	Lewiston	96	79	17
Vivian	14	14	—	Limestone	4	4	—
Washington	5	5	—	Lincoln	4	3	1
Welsh	10	10	—	Lisbon	17	12	5
Westlake	18	17	1	Livermore Falls	11	6	5
West Monroe	66	62	4	Machias	4	4	—
Westwego	21	20	1	Madawaska	8	7	1
Winnfield	23	23	—	Madison	7	6	1
Zachary	27	26	1	Mechanic Falls	4	4	—
				Medway	2	2	—
MAINE				Mexico	4	4	—
Ashland	3	3	—	Milbridge	1	1	—
Auburn	56	47	9	Millinocket	15	12	3
Augusta	52	39	13	Milo	3	3	—
Baileyville	5	5	—	Monmouth	3	3	—
Bangor	78	65	13	Mount Desert	9	5	4
Bar Harbor	13	9	4	Newport	5	5	—
Bath	25	17	8	North Berwick	8	7	1
Belfast	17	13	4	Norway	8	7	1
Berwick	11	10	1	Oakland	8	7	1
Bethel	3	3	—	Ogunquit	12	7	5
Biddeford	56	42	14	Old Orchard Beach	21	16	5
Boothbay Harbor	10	6	4	Old Town	20	15	5
Brewer	19	15	4	Orono	17	12	5
Bridgton	12	8	4	Oxford	5	4	1
Brownville	2	2	—	Paris	8	7	1
Brunswick	40	31	9	Penobscot Nation	8	4	4
Bucksport	9	7	2	Phippsburg	1	1	—
Buxton	10	6	4	Pittsfield	5	5	—
Calais	12	8	4	Portland	206	149	57
Camden	15	10	5	Presque Isle	21	17	4
Cape Elizabeth	17	13	4	Richmond	4	4	—
Caribou	15	14	1	Rockland	28	21	7
Carrabassett Valley	1	1	—	Rockport	3	3	—
Clinton	4	4	—	Rumford	15	15	—
Cumberland	15	10	5	Sabattus	7	6	1

City	Total police employees	Total officers	Total civilians	City	Total police employees	Total officers	Total civilians
MAINE — Continued				**MARYLAND — Continued**			
Saco	33	27	6	Hyattsville	32	25	7
Sanford	46	32	14	Landover Hills	5	5	—
Scarborough	39	26	13	La Plata	9	9	—
Searsport	3	3	—	Laurel	65	48	17
Skowhegan	17	12	5	Luke	2	2	—
South Berwick	11	7	4	Manchester	3	3	—
South Portland	57	52	5	Morningside	5	5	—
Southwest Harbor	9	5	4	Mount Rainier	18	14	4
Thomaston	5	5	—	North East	7	6	1
Topsham	15	11	4	Oakland	7	6	1
Van Buren	4	4	—	Ocean City	110	93	17
Veazie	4	4	—	Ocean Pines	16	11	5
Waldoboro	5	4	1	Oxford	3	3	—
Washburn	1	1	—	Pocomoke City	17	13	4
Waterville	38	30	8	Preston	3	3	—
Wells	25	20	5	Princess Anne	8	7	1
Westbrook	37	31	6	Ridgely	3	3	—
Wilton	5	5	—	Rising Sun	5	4	1
Windham	25	20	5	Riverdale	19	14	5
Winslow	7	6	1	Rock Hall	4	4	—
Winthrop	13	9	4	St. Michaels	8	7	1
Wiscasset	9	8	1	Salisbury	102	77	25
Yarmouth	15	10	5	Seat Pleasant	11	9	2
York	28	21	7	Smithsburg	2	2	—
				Snow Hill	8	8	—
MARYLAND				Sykesville	8	7	1
Aberdeen	46	37	9	Takoma Park	50	42	8
Annapolis	147	118	29	Taneytown	8	8	—
Baltimore	3,658	3,081	577	Thurmont	8	8	—
Baltimore City Sheriff	116	112	4	University Park	7	7	—
Bel Air	41	30	11	Westernport	5	5	—
Berlin	19	14	5	Westminster	45	36	9
Berwyn Heights	6	6	—				
Bladensburg	22	16	6	**MASSACHUSETTS**			
Brunswick	11	9	2	Abington	28	26	2
Cambridge	53	41	12	Acton	33	29	4
Capitol Heights	9	7	2	Adams	22	17	5
Centreville	6	6	—	Agawam	54	47	7
Chestertown	11	9	2	Amesbury	32	27	5
Cheverly	13	11	2	Amherst	54	40	14
Cottage City	4	4	—	Andover	63	47	16
Crisfield	11	9	2	Arlington	69	62	7
Cumberland	65	57	8	Ashburnham	7	6	1
Delmar	12	11	1	Ashby	3	3	—
Denton	10	9	1	Ashfield	1	1	—
District Heights	8	7	1	Ashland	22	21	1
Easton	48	37	11	Athol	23	18	5
Edmonston	7	7	—	Attleboro	79	65	14
Elkton	32	25	7	Auburn	30	26	4
Federalsburg	10	9	1	Avon	18	15	3
Forest Heights	5	5	—	Ayer	21	16	5
Frederick	122	98	24	Barnstable	100	91	9
Frostburg	18	14	4	Barre	8	5	3
Fruitland	11	10	1	Bedford	24	23	1
Glenarden	9	8	1	Belchertown	20	15	5
Greenbelt	62	48	14	Bellingham	29	24	5
Greensboro	3	3	—	Belmont	57	53	4
Hagerstown	111	89	22	Berkley	3	3	—
Hampstead	1	1	—	Berlin	9	6	3
Hancock	4	3	1	Bernardston	3	3	—
Havre de Grace	31	24	7	Beverly	71	68	3
Hurlock	3	3	—	Billerica	70	65	5

Table 78. — Number of Full-time Law Enforcement Employees, Cities, October 31, 1996 — Continued

City	Total police employees	Total officers	Total civilians	City	Total police employees	Total officers	Total civilians
MASSACHUSETTS — Continued				**MASSACHUSETTS — Continued**			
Blackstone	16	13	3	Grafton	22	17	5
Bolton	12	8	4	Granby	11	9	2
Boston	2,926	2,218	708	Great Barrington	16	15	1
Bourne	37	30	7	Greenfield	41	36	5
Boxborough	7	6	1	Groton	19	14	5
Boxford	12	12	—	Groveland	13	8	5
Boylston	13	10	3	Hadley	10	7	3
Braintree	92	83	9	Halifax	14	10	4
Brewster	22	18	4	Hamilton	19	14	5
Bridgewater	33	30	3	Hampden	12	8	4
Brockton	204	178	26	Hanover	31	29	2
Brookfield	1	1	—	Hanson	22	18	4
Brookline	151	135	16	Hardwick	2	2	—
Buckland	2	2	—	Harvard	12	8	4
Burlington	64	57	7	Harwich	34	32	2
Cambridge	318	266	52	Hatfield	2	2	—
Canton	43	41	2	Haverhill	93	86	7
Carlisle	12	9	3	Hingham	54	44	10
Carver	20	15	5	Hinsdale	1	1	—
Charlton	20	13	7	Holbrook	20	19	1
Chatham	26	21	5	Holden	22	17	5
Chelmsford	69	54	15	Holliston	22	22	—
Chelsea	95	79	16	Holyoke	139	122	17
Chicopee	122	119	3	Hopedale	10	9	1
Clinton	28	27	1	Hopkinton	20	15	5
Cohasset	21	17	4	Hubbardston	7	4	3
Concord	41	34	7	Hudson	34	29	5
Dalton	11	10	1	Hull	29	23	6
Danvers	58	44	14	Ipswich	24	23	1
Dartmouth	73	60	13	Kingston	25	18	7
Dedham	62	60	2	Lakeville	19	14	5
Deerfield	7	6	1	Lancaster	8	7	1
Dennis	43	35	8	Lanesboro	5	5	—
Dighton	10	10	—	Lawrence	151	129	22
Douglas	13	10	3	Lee	11	11	—
Dover	17	17	—	Leicester	19	15	4
Dracut	44	39	5	Lenox	9	9	—
Dunstable	3	3	—	Leominster	87	71	16
Duxbury	36	31	5	Lexington	58	53	5
East Bridgewater	24	23	1	Lincoln	17	12	5
East Brookfield	3	3	—	Littleton	20	14	6
Eastham	22	16	6	Longmeadow	31	30	1
Easthampton	27	26	1	Lowell	305	246	59
East Longmeadow	23	21	2	Ludlow	35	31	4
Easton	33	32	1	Lunenburg	12	12	—
Edgartown	13	12	1	Lynn	192	174	18
Erving	1	1	—	Lynnfield	24	19	5
Essex	9	8	1	Malden	106	100	6
Everett	100	88	12	Manchester-by-the-Sea	18	14	4
Fairhaven	31	28	3	Mansfield	37	31	6
Fall River	294	251	43	Marblehead	40	36	4
Falmouth	71	61	10	Marion	12	11	1
Fitchburg	101	82	19	Marlborough	76	64	12
Foxborough	28	27	1	Marshfield	41	39	2
Framingham	121	110	11	Mashpee	36	27	9
Franklin	50	41	9	Mattapoisett	17	17	—
Freetown	19	14	5	Maynard	25	22	3
Gardner	44	35	9	Medfield	25	20	5
Gay Head	4	4	—	Medford	114	108	6
Georgetown	14	10	4	Medway	24	18	6
Gill	1	1	—	Melrose	48	46	2
Gloucester	69	64	5	Mendon	7	6	1

Table 78. — Number of Full-time Law Enforcement Employees, Cities, October 31, 1996 — Continued

City	Total police employees	Total officers	Total civilians	City	Total police employees	Total officers	Total civilians
MASSACHUSETTS — Continued				**MASSACHUSETTS — Continued**			
Merrimac	10	6	4	Salem	100	91	9
Methuen	86	72	14	Salisbury	22	17	5
Middleboro	40	32	8	Sandwich	33	32	1
Middleton	12	11	1	Saugus	67	59	8
Milford	48	47	1	Scituate	36	30	6
Millbury	23	18	5	Seekonk	37	32	5
Millis	18	14	4	Sharon	32	26	6
Millville	3	3	—	Sheffield	4	3	1
Milton	66	57	9	Shelburne	2	2	—
Monson	15	11	4	Sherborn	14	14	—
Montague	17	15	2	Shirley	10	9	1
Nahant	12	12	—	Shrewsbury	42	35	7
Nantucket	30	25	5	Shutesbury	1	1	—
Natick	68	53	15	Somerset	38	30	8
Needham	52	46	6	Somerville	141	135	6
New Bedford	315	279	36	Southampton	7	7	—
Newbury	10	9	1	Southborough	17	13	4
Newburyport	37	35	2	Southbridge	34	33	1
Newton	185	164	21	South Hadley	29	24	5
Norfolk	19	14	5	Southwick	19	14	5
North Adams	32	28	4	Spencer	8	5	3
Northampton	71	64	7	Springfield	637	542	95
North Andover	43	34	9	Sterling	15	10	5
North Attleboro	56	44	12	Stockbridge	6	6	—
Northborough	25	19	6	Stoneham	45	36	9
Northbridge	23	18	5	Stoughton	56	53	3
North Brookfield	6	6	—	Stow	15	11	4
Northfield	3	3	—	Sturbridge	16	13	3
North Reading	28	27	1	Sudbury	31	25	6
Norton	25	23	2	Sunderland	4	3	1
Norwell	22	19	3	Sutton	12	10	2
Norwood	71	61	10	Swampscott	32	31	1
Oak Bluffs	12	11	1	Swansea	35	28	7
Oakham	1	1	—	Taunton	104	100	4
Orange	12	12	—	Templeton	7	7	—
Orleans	26	20	6	Tewksbury	65	56	9
Oxford	23	18	5	Tisbury	14	12	2
Palmer	21	16	5	Topsfield	13	9	4
Paxton	8	7	1	Townsend	14	13	1
Peabody	99	86	13	Truro	16	12	4
Pelham	1	1	—	Tyngsboro	18	18	—
Pembroke	25	24	1	Upton	11	8	3
Pepperell	16	15	1	Uxbridge	19	15	4
Petersham	1	1	—	Wakefield	48	47	1
Phillipston	1	1	—	Walpole	41	38	3
Pittsfield	102	88	14	Waltham	165	141	24
Plainville	17	13	4	Ware	15	15	—
Plymouth	102	87	15	Wareham	48	42	6
Plympton	8	6	2	Warren	9	6	3
Princeton	7	4	3	Watertown	79	68	11
Provincetown	24	18	6	Wayland	30	21	9
Quincy	226	195	31	Webster	32	26	6
Randolph	59	57	2	Wellesley	53	40	13
Raynham	26	21	5	Wellfleet	15	10	5
Reading	50	40	10	Wenham	11	10	1
Rehoboth	24	19	5	Westborough	32	26	6
Revere	121	109	12	West Boylston	12	11	1
Rochester	11	9	2	West Bridgewater	22	21	1
Rockland	32	30	2	West Brookfield	4	4	—
Rockport	18	17	1	Westfield	76	71	5
Rowley	11	10	1	Westford	37	30	7
Rutland	1	1	—	Westminster	12	9	3

Table 78. — Number of Full-time Law Enforcement Employees, Cities, October 31, 1996 — Continued

City	Total police employees	Total officers	Total civilians	City	Total police employees	Total officers	Total civilians
MASSACHUSETTS — Continued				**MICHIGAN — Continued**			
West Newbury	12	7	5	Bridgeport Township	6	5	1
Weston	30	25	5	Bridgman	4	4	—
Westport	27	23	4	Brighton	15	14	1
West Springfield	88	78	10	Bronson	5	5	—
West Tisbury	6	6	—	Brooklyn/Columbia	5	4	1
Westwood	33	27	6	Brown City	2	2	—
Weymouth	109	97	12	Brownstown Township	44	35	9
Whitman	23	22	1	Buchanan	12	11	1
Wilbraham	28	27	1	Buena Vista Township	19	17	2
Williamstown	13	10	3	Burr Oak	1	1	—
Wilmington	45	40	5	Burton	42	38	4
Winchendon	17	12	5	Cadillac	21	19	2
Winchester	37	37	—	Calumet	2	2	—
Winthrop	37	35	2	Cambridge Township	2	2	—
Woburn	78	72	6	Camp Grayling	1	1	—
Worcester	524	464	60	Canton Township	86	64	22
Wrentham	16	15	1	Capac	4	3	1
Yarmouth	54	45	9	Carleton	4	3	1
				Caro	10	9	1
MICHIGAN				Carrollton Township	7	6	1
Adrian	36	29	7	Carson City	2	2	—
Albion	34	28	6	Carsonville	1	1	—
Algonac	7	6	1	Caseville	1	1	—
Allegan	12	10	2	Cass City	3	3	—
Allen Park	57	51	6	Cassopolis	5	5	—
Alma	16	15	1	Cedar Springs	7	7	—
Almont	7	6	1	Center Line	33	25	8
Alpena	19	17	2	Centreville	2	2	—
Ann Arbor	239	181	58	Charlevoix	8	7	1
Argentine Township	6	6	—	Charlotte	18	17	1
Armada	3	3	—	Cheboygan	10	9	1
Atlas Township	2	2	—	Chelsea	11	8	3
Auburn	3	2	1	Chesterfield Township	27	22	5
Auburn Hills	44	33	11	Chikaming Township	3	3	—
Augusta	1	1	—	Chocolay Township	5	4	1
Bad Axe	8	8	—	Clare	7	6	1
Bancroft	1	1	—	Clarkston	2	2	—
Bangor	5	5	—	Clawson	23	22	1
Baraga	4	4	—	Clay Township	16	12	4
Barry Township	2	2	—	Clinton	3	3	—
Bath Township	8	7	1	Clinton Township	119	87	32
Battle Creek	176	126	50	Clio	3	2	1
Bay City	80	73	7	Coldwater	18	16	2
Belding	10	9	1	Coleman	2	2	—
Bellaire	2	2	—	Coloma City	5	4	1
Belleville	11	9	2	Coloma Township	5	5	—
Bellevue	3	3	—	Colon	3	3	—
Benton Harbor	34	26	8	Concord	3	3	—
Benton Township	33	24	9	Constantine	4	4	—
Berkley	35	31	4	Corunna	5	5	—
Berrien Springs-Oronoko Township	8	7	1	Covert Township	7	7	—
Beverly Hills	29	25	4	Croswell	6	6	—
Big Rapids	19	18	1	Crystal Falls	5	5	—
Birch Run	6	5	1	Crystal Township	1	1	—
Birmingham	52	35	17	Davison	11	9	2
Blackman Township	26	25	1	Davison Township	13	11	2
Blissfield	5	4	1	Dearborn	220	198	22
Bloomfield Hills	27	23	4	Dearborn Heights	115	92	23
Bloomfield Township	86	67	19	Decatur	4	4	—
Bloomingdale	1	1	—	Deckerville	1	1	—
Boyne City	8	7	1	Denmark Township	1	1	—
Breckenridge	3	3	—	Denton Township	3	3	—

Table 78. — Number of Full-time Law Enforcement Employees, Cities, October 31, 1996 — Continued

City	Total police employees	Total officers	Total civilians	City	Total police employees	Total officers	Total civilians
MICHIGAN — Continued				**MICHIGAN — Continued**			
Detroit	4,453	3,917	536	Grosse Pointe	27	24	3
De Witt	7	6	1	Grosse Pointe Farms	41	31	10
Dewitt Township	14	13	1	Grosse Pointe Park	45	42	3
Douglas	4	4	—	Grosse Pointe Shores	20	18	2
Dowagiac	14	13	1	Grosse Pointe Woods	44	41	3
Dryden Township	2	2	—	Hamburg Township	11	10	1
Durand	7	6	1	Hampton Township	12	11	1
East Grand Rapids	34	31	3	Hamtramck	54	54	—
East Jordan	5	5	—	Hancock	7	7	—
East Lansing	86	56	30	Harbor Beach	4	4	—
Eastpointe	57	53	4	Harbor Springs	6	5	1
East Tawas	5	5	—	Harper Woods	40	35	5
Eaton Rapids	10	9	1	Hart	4	4	—
Eau Claire	2	1	1	Hartford	5	5	—
Ecorse	40	34	6	Hastings	16	14	2
Edmore-Home	3	3	—	Hazel Park	41	35	6
Elk Rapids	3	3	—	Hesperia	4	4	—
Elkton	2	2	—	Highland Park	86	71	15
Elsie	2	2	—	Hillsdale	19	15	4
Emmett Township	11	10	1	Holland	72	61	11
Erie Township	1	1	—	Holly	14	10	4
Escanaba	45	37	8	Homer	3	3	—
Essexville	8	8	—	Houghton	9	9	—
Evart	3	3	—	Howard City	1	1	—
Fair Haven Township	1	1	—	Howard Township	3	3	—
Farmington	29	22	7	Howell	17	16	1
Farmington Hills	153	109	44	Hudson	3	3	—
Fenton	19	13	6	Hudsonville	10	9	1
Ferndale	60	50	10	Huntington Woods	16	15	1
Flat Rock	27	22	5	Huron Township	14	11	3
Flint	350	306	44	Imlay City	9	8	1
Flint Township	42	39	3	Inkster	68	50	18
Flushing	12	11	1	Ionia	19	17	2
Flushing Township	8	7	1	Iron Mountain	13	13	—
Forsyth Township	8	7	1	Iron River	8	7	1
Fowlerville	6	5	1	Ironwood	19	15	4
Frankenmuth	7	7	—	Ishpeming	14	13	1
Frankfort	5	5	—	Ishpeming Township	1	1	—
Franklin	11	10	1	Ithaca	5	4	1
Fraser	54	43	11	Jackson	86	65	21
Fremont	8	7	1	Jonesville	4	4	—
Frost Township	1	1	—	Kalamazoo	317	250	67
Galesburg	2	2	—	Kalamazoo Township	38	29	9
Garden City	53	41	12	Kalkaska	7	6	1
Gaylord	10	9	1	Keego Harbor	6	5	1
Genesee Township	20	18	2	Kentwood	55	49	6
Gerrish Township	4	4	—	Kingsford	19	19	—
Gibraltar	14	13	1	Kinross Township	2	2	—
Gladstone	13	12	1	Laingsburg	3	3	—
Gladwin	3	3	—	Lake Angelus	2	2	—
Gobles	2	2	—	Lake Linden	2	2	—
Grand Beach	3	3	—	Lake Odessa	3	3	—
Grand Blanc	20	16	4	Lake Orion	9	4	5
Grand Blanc Township	34	30	4	Lakeview	2	2	—
Grand Haven	41	35	6	L'Anse	5	5	—
Grand Ledge	12	12	—	Lansing	344	254	90
Grand Rapids	448	374	74	Lansing Township	16	15	1
Grandville	22	19	3	Lapeer	20	17	3
Grayling	7	6	1	Lathrup Village	12	10	2
Green Oak Township	11	11	—	Laurium	4	4	—
Greenville	23	18	5	Lawrence	3	2	1
Grosse Ile Township	21	15	6	Lawton	5	5	—

Table 78. — Number of Full-time Law Enforcement Employees, Cities, October 31, 1996 — Continued

City	Total police employees	Total officers	Total civilians	City	Total police employees	Total officers	Total civilians
MICHIGAN — Continued				**MICHIGAN — Continued**			
Lennon	1	1	—	New Baltimore	12	11	1
Leoni Township	5	4	1	Newberry	4	4	—
Leslie	4	4	—	New Buffalo	6	6	—
Lexington	4	4	—	New Haven	5	4	1
Lincoln Park	78	60	18	New Lothrop	1	1	—
Lincoln Township	13	11	2	Niles	30	23	7
Linden	4	4	—	Niles Township	7	7	—
Litchfield	5	5	—	North Branch	1	1	—
Livonia	194	165	29	Northfield Township	9	8	1
Lowell	8	6	2	North Muskegon	7	6	1
Ludington	16	14	2	Northville	17	15	2
Luna Pier	4	4	—	Northville Township	29	21	8
Mackinac Island	6	5	1	Norton Shores	32	30	2
Mackinaw City	6	6	—	Norvell Township	2	2	—
Madison Heights	77	60	17	Norway	6	6	—
Madison Township	1	1	—	Novi	83	57	26
Mancelona	4	4	—	Oak Park	80	70	10
Manchester Township	1	1	—	Olivet	2	2	—
Manistee	16	15	1	Onaway	3	3	—
Manistique	10	9	1	Ontwa Township-Edwardsburg	8	7	1
Manton	2	2	—	Orchard Lake	9	8	1
Maple Rapids	3	3	—	Oscoda Township	11	10	1
Marcellus	2	2	—	Otisville	1	1	—
Marenisco Township	1	1	—	Otsego	8	7	1
Marine City	8	7	1	Ovid	2	2	—
Marion	1	1	—	Owosso	22	20	2
Marlette	4	4	—	Oxford	22	17	5
Marquette	43	35	8	Parchment	5	4	1
Marshall	19	14	5	Parma Sandstone	2	2	—
Marysville	16	14	2	Paw Paw	10	8	2
Mason	10	9	1	Peck	1	1	—
Mattawan	4	4	—	Pennfield Township	7	6	1
Mayville	1	1	—	Pentwater	3	3	—
Melvindale	30	28	2	Perry	5	5	—
Memphis	2	2	—	Petoskey	16	14	2
Menominee	19	17	2	Pierson Township	1	1	—
Meridian Township	50	43	7	Pigeon	1	1	—
Michiana	3	3	—	Pinckney	4	4	—
Middleville	4	4	—	Pinconning	3	3	—
Midland	52	48	4	Pittsfield Township	36	27	9
Midland Township	2	2	—	Plainwell	9	8	1
Milan	13	9	4	Pleasant Ridge	8	7	1
Milford	20	13	7	Plymouth	19	15	4
Millington	3	3	—	Plymouth Township	30	23	7
Monroe	52	46	6	Pontiac	203	166	37
Montague	5	5	—	Portage	69	55	14
Montrose Township	7	5	2	Port Austin	1	1	—
Morenci	3	3	—	Port Huron	73	53	20
Morrice	1	1	—	Portland	6	6	—
Mount Clemens	42	36	6	Port Sanilac	2	2	—
Mount Morris	6	6	—	Potterville	3	3	—
Mount Morris Township	43	40	3	Prairieville Township	1	1	—
Mount Pleasant	30	26	4	Quincy	4	4	—
Mundy Township	15	12	3	Reading	1	1	—
Munising	5	5	—	Redford Township	92	76	16
Muskegon	96	87	9	Reed City	5	5	—
Muskegon Heights	36	32	4	Reese	2	2	—
Muskegon Township	14	13	1	Republic Township	1	1	—
Napoleon Township	3	3	—	Richfield Township (Roscommon County)	3	3	—
Nashville	3	3	—	Richfield Township (Genesee County)	8	7	1
Negaunee	13	12	1	Richland	2	2	—
Newaygo	3	3	—	Richland Township	4	4	—

Table 78. — Number of Full-time Law Enforcement Employees, Cities, October 31, 1996 — Continued

City	Total police employees	Total officers	Total civilians	City	Total police employees	Total officers	Total civilians
MICHIGAN — Continued				**MICHIGAN — Continued**			
Richmond	11	8	3	Tittabawassee Township	3	3	—
Richmond Township	1	1	—	Traverse City	33	32	1
River Rouge	43	38	5	Trenton	50	47	3
Riverview	31	27	4	Troy	185	132	53
Rochester	21	15	6	Tuscarora Township	6	6	—
Rockford	12	9	3	Twin City	2	2	—
Rockwood	8	8	—	Ubly	2	2	—
Rogers City	7	7	—	Unadilla Township	3	3	—
Romeo	10	7	3	Union City	4	3	1
Romulus	71	60	11	Unionville	2	2	—
Roosevelt Park	7	7	—	Utica	17	13	4
Roscommon Township	1	1	—	Van Buren Township	26	23	3
Rose City	1	1	—	Vassar	5	5	—
Roseville	87	87	—	Vernon	1	1	—
Ross Township	2	2	—	Vicksburg	5	4	1
Royal Oak	116	97	19	Walker	40	33	7
Royal Oak Township	11	9	2	Walled Lake	19	13	6
Saginaw	157	139	18	Warren	283	238	45
Saginaw Township	47	43	4	Waterford Township	92	81	11
St. Charles	4	4	—	Watertown Township	1	1	—
St. Clair	11	10	1	Watervliet	5	5	—
St. Clair Shores	101	84	17	Wayland	5	4	1
St. Ignace	7	6	1	Wayne	54	39	15
St. Johns	14	12	2	West Bloomfield Township	91	66	25
St. Joseph	25	20	5	West Branch	5	4	1
St. Joseph Township	10	9	1	Westland	119	98	21
St. Louis	6	5	1	White Cloud	1	1	—
Saline	19	14	5	Whitehall	6	6	—
Sand Lake	1	1	—	White Lake Township	34	25	9
Sandusky	7	6	1	White Pigeon	5	4	1
Saugatuck	5	4	1	Williamston	5	5	—
Sault Ste. Marie	34	26	8	Wixom	21	17	4
Schoolcraft	5	4	1	Wolverine Lake	8	7	1
Scottville	2	2	—	Woodhaven	31	28	3
Sebewaing	3	3	—	Woodstock Township	1	1	—
Shelby	3	3	—	Wyandotte	59	46	13
Shelby Township	67	52	15	Wyoming	111	81	30
Shepherd	2	2	—	Yale	4	4	—
Somerset Township	1	1	—	Ypsilanti	58	46	12
Southfield	206	160	46	Zeeland	10	9	1
Southgate	49	42	7	Zilwaukee	3	3	—
South Haven	25	20	5				
South Lyon	15	13	2	**MINNESOTA**			
South Rockwood	3	3	—	Albert Lea	37	28	9
Sparta	8	7	1	Alexandria	19	16	3
Spaulding Township	1	1	—	Annandale	3	3	—
Spring Arbor Township	2	2	—	Anoka	37	29	8
Springfield	15	14	1	Appleton	4	4	—
Spring Lake-Ferrysburg	11	11	—	Apple Valley	53	37	16
Stanton	1	1	—	Austin	31	28	3
Sterling Heights	217	162	55	Babbitt	4	4	—
Sturgis	19	16	3	Baxter	8	7	1
Summit Township	4	4	—	Bayport	5	5	—
Sumpter Township	15	13	2	Belle Plaine	6	5	1
Sunfield	1	1	—	Bemidji	25	21	4
Swartz Creek	8	7	1	Benson	6	5	1
Sylvan Lake	5	5	—	Big Lake	6	5	1
Taylor	124	101	23	Blaine	47	39	8
Tecumseh	16	15	1	Blooming Prairie	3	3	—
Thomas Township	5	4	1	Bloomington	132	102	30
Three Oaks	4	4	—	Blue Earth	6	6	—
Three Rivers	17	14	3	Brainerd	26	21	5

Table 78. — Number of Full-time Law Enforcement Employees, Cities, October 31, 1996 — Continued

City	Total police employees	Total officers	Total civilians	City	Total police employees	Total officers	Total civilians
MINNESOTA — Continued				**MINNESOTA — Continued**			
Breckenridge	11	7	4	Kenyon	3	3	—
Brooklyn Center	58	43	15	La Crescent	6	5	1
Brooklyn Park	78	64	14	Lake City	9	8	1
Buffalo	11	10	1	Lakefield	3	3	—
Burnsville	76	62	14	Lakeville	47	35	12
Caledonia	5	4	1	Le Sueur	10	6	4
Cambridge	10	9	1	Lino Lakes	19	16	3
Canby	2	2	—	Litchfield	10	9	1
Cannon Falls	6	5	1	Little Falls	12	10	2
Champlin	22	21	1	Long Prairie	5	5	—
Chanhassen	5	2	3	Luverne	6	6	—
Chaska	18	15	3	Madison	4	4	—
Chisholm	11	10	1	Mankato	51	44	7
Circle Pines-Lexington	15	12	3	Maple Grove	52	42	10
Cloquet	20	19	1	Maplewood	54	41	13
Cold Spring	4	4	—	Marshall	21	17	4
Columbia Heights	33	25	8	Medina	6	5	1
Coon Rapids	67	57	10	Melrose	4	4	—
Corcoran	3	3	—	Mendota Heights	17	15	2
Cottage Grove	43	33	10	Minneapolis	1,081	913	168
Crookston	17	15	2	Minnetonka	64	50	14
Crosby	10	6	4	Montevideo	9	8	1
Crystal	33	27	6	Moorhead	58	47	11
Dawson	4	4	—	Mora	9	8	1
Dayton	3	3	—	Morris	9	8	1
Deephaven	8	7	1	Mound	15	13	2
Detroit Lakes	14	12	2	Mounds View	17	16	1
Dilworth	5	5	—	New Brighton	26	24	2
Duluth	159	134	25	New Hope	37	30	7
Eagan	86	57	29	Newport	8	8	—
East Grand Forks	20	19	1	New Prague	9	7	2
Eden Prairie	68	46	22	New Ulm	21	18	3
Edina	62	49	13	Northfield	23	18	5
Elk River	27	22	5	North Mankato	10	9	1
Ely	12	7	5	North Saint Paul	18	16	2
Eveleth	9	8	1	Oakdale	29	25	4
Fairmont	17	15	2	Oak Park Heights	9	8	1
Faribault	38	27	11	Olivia	5	5	—
Farmington	12	10	2	Orono	17	15	2
Fergus Falls	23	19	4	Ortonville	5	4	1
Forest Lake	13	12	1	Osseo	4	4	—
Fridley	48	36	12	Owatonna	26	24	2
Gilbert	6	6	—	Park Rapids	6	6	—
Glencoe	10	8	2	Pipestone	6	6	—
Glenwood	3	3	—	Plainview	4	4	—
Golden Valley	40	30	10	Plymouth	68	54	14
Goodview	4	4	—	Princeton	9	8	1
Grand Rapids	18	14	4	Prior Lake	20	18	2
Granite Falls	5	5	—	Proctor	6	5	1
Hallock	2	2	—	Ramsey	15	13	2
Hastings	24	21	3	Red Wing	30	25	5
Hermantown	11	10	1	Redwood Falls	10	9	1
Hibbing	30	27	3	Richfield	55	42	13
Hopkins	36	24	12	Robbinsdale	26	21	5
Hoyt Lakes	5	5	—	Rochester	137	101	36
Hutchinson	27	20	7	Roseau	5	5	—
International Falls	13	13	—	Rosemount	16	14	2
Inver Grove Heights	32	25	7	Roseville	50	44	6
Jackson	7	7	—	St. Anthony	20	18	2
Janesville	4	4	—	St. Bonifacius-Minnetrista	10	8	2
Jordan	5	4	1	St. Cloud	90	73	17
Kasson	6	6	—	St. James	7	6	1

Table 78. — Number of Full-time Law Enforcement Employees, Cities, October 31, 1996 — Continued

City	Total police employees	Total officers	Total civilians	City	Total police employees	Total officers	Total civilians
MINNESOTA — Continued				**MISSISSIPPI — Continued**			
St. Joseph	6	6	—	Fulton	9	9	—
St. Louis Park	69	51	18	Gloster	7	5	2
St. Paul	755	578	177	Goodman	2	2	—
St. Paul Park	7	7	—	Greenville	138	100	38
St. Peter	18	12	6	Greenwood	68	50	18
Sartell	9	8	1	Grenada	50	37	13
Sauk Centre	9	6	3	Gulfport	212	149	63
Sauk Rapids	11	10	1	Hattiesburg	170	104	66
Savage	22	19	3	Heidelberg	5	5	—
Scanlon	4	4	—	Hernando	14	12	2
Shakopee	22	19	3	Horn Lake	26	21	5
Silver Bay	4	4	—	Indianola	36	27	9
Slayton	3	3	—	Inverness	4	4	—
Sleepy Eye	5	5	—	Iuka	9	9	—
South Lake Minnetonka	15	14	1	Jackson	579	396	183
South St. Paul	26	25	1	Kosciusko	28	21	7
Springfield	5	5	—	Leakesville	4	4	—
Spring Lake Park	13	11	2	Long Beach	39	25	14
Staples	6	6	—	Lucedale	13	9	4
Stillwater	22	18	4	Macon	10	9	1
Thief River Falls	19	18	1	Madison	36	28	8
Tracy	4	4	—	Magee	15	12	3
Two Harbors	8	7	1	McComb	46	30	16
Virginia	23	22	1	Mendenhall	12	8	4
Wabasha	5	4	1	Meridian	136	106	30
Wadena	9	8	1	Morton	13	13	—
Waite Park	9	8	1	Moss Point	49	43	6
Warroad	5	4	1	Natchez	88	56	32
Waseca	12	10	2	Newton	16	11	5
Wayzata	10	8	2	Oxford	52	43	9
Wells	4	4	—	Pascagoula	87	56	31
West Hennepin	10	8	2	Pass Christian	22	17	5
West St. Paul	36	23	13	Petal	18	13	5
White Bear Lake	34	27	7	Purvis	9	6	3
Willmar	34	30	4	Raymond	6	6	—
Windom	7	6	1	Ridgeland	57	36	21
Winona	41	38	3	Ripley	14	13	1
Woodbury	42	36	6	Rolling Fork	5	5	—
Worthington	23	17	6	Shaw	10	6	4
Zumbrota	4	4	—	Southaven	62	50	12
				Starkville	49	36	13
MISSISSIPPI				Tupelo	115	86	29
Aberdeen	21	17	4	Vaiden	3	3	—
Ackerman	5	5	—	Verona	12	8	4
Amory	23	18	5	Vicksburg	109	89	20
Baldwyn	14	10	4	Waveland	26	20	6
Batesville	35	25	10	Waynesboro	21	15	6
Bay St. Louis	31	25	6	Wiggins	11	7	4
Belzoni	11	6	5	Winona	16	11	5
Booneville	23	21	2	Yazoo City	39	27	12
Brandon	30	20	10				
Byhalia	5	5	—	**MISSOURI**			
Clarksdale	58	48	10	Arnold	56	44	12
Cleveland	40	33	7	Aurora	16	10	6
Clinton	44	32	12	Ballwin	57	45	12
Collins	14	10	4	Bellefontaine Neighbors	24	24	—
Columbus	80	71	9	Bel-Nor	9	9	—
Corinth	44	34	10	Bel-Ridge	22	17	5
Crenshaw	5	5	—	Belton	41	31	10
Decatur	4	4	—	Berkeley	54	44	10
Edwards	4	4	—	Blue Springs	85	61	24
Flowood	27	21	6	Bolivar	20	13	7

Table 78. — Number of Full-time Law Enforcement Employees, Cities, October 31, 1996 — Continued

City	Total police employees	Total officers	Total civilians	City	Total police employees	Total officers	Total civilians
MISSOURI — Continued				**MISSOURI — Continued**			
Bonne Terre	9	9	—	Lake St. Louis	23	16	7
Boonville	26	15	11	Lamar	11	9	2
Branson	53	38	15	Lebanon	26	20	6
Breckenridge Hills	12	11	1	Lees Summit	106	74	32
Brentwood	28	22	6	Lexington	10	9	1
Bridgeton	67	56	11	Liberty	44	33	11
Brookfield	17	10	7	Louisiana	14	10	4
Buckner	6	5	1	Manchester	21	19	2
Calverton Park	9	6	3	Maplewood	29	24	5
Cameron	17	12	5	Marceline	7	6	1
Canton	9	4	5	Marshall	32	23	9
Cape Girardeau	90	66	24	Maryland Heights	77	62	15
Carterville	4	4	—	Maryville	24	17	7
Carthage	32	25	7	Mexico	36	30	6
Centralia	10	6	4	Moberly	39	34	5
Chaffee	10	6	4	Moline Acres	9	9	—
Charlack	13	11	2	Monett	27	19	8
Charleston	20	18	2	Montgomery City	5	5	—
Chesterfield	76	70	6	Neosho	26	24	2
Claycomo	10	8	2	Nevada	25	18	7
Clayton	61	48	13	Newburg	2	2	—
Clinton	17	16	1	Normandy	20	19	1
Columbia	143	113	30	North Kansas City	50	40	10
Cool Valley	8	8	—	Northwoods	19	17	2
Crestwood	38	31	7	Oak Grove	5	5	—
Creve Coeur	57	46	11	Oakview	3	3	—
Crystal City	18	14	4	Odessa	11	10	1
Dellwood	18	17	1	O'Fallon	60	45	15
De Soto	19	14	5	Olivette	27	22	5
Des Peres	41	34	7	Osage Beach	32	20	12
Edmundson	8	8	—	Overland	56	42	14
Ellisville	22	21	1	Pacific	18	13	5
Eureka	21	18	3	Pagedale	20	19	1
Excelsior Springs	33	23	10	Park Hills	16	15	1
Farmington	32	23	9	Parkville	11	10	1
Fayette	7	7	—	Pevely	17	12	5
Ferguson	58	52	6	Pine Lawn	19	18	1
Festus	30	22	8	Pleasant Hill	12	8	4
Florissant	94	75	19	Poplar Bluff	52	41	11
Frontenac	23	18	5	Potosi	17	13	4
Fulton	28	22	6	Raytown	77	58	19
Gladstone	63	51	12	Republic	18	15	3
Glendale	14	11	3	Rich Hill	4	4	—
Grandview	61	48	13	Richland	8	5	3
Hannibal	44	35	9	Richmond	14	9	5
Harrisonville	24	17	7	Richmond Heights	46	39	7
Hazelwood	66	53	13	Riverside	18	14	4
Hillsdale	12	11	1	Riverview	9	9	—
Independence	257	176	81	Rock Hill	16	12	4
Ironton	4	4	—	Rolla	46	28	18
Jackson	22	17	5	St. Ann	52	44	8
Jefferson City	93	71	22	St. Charles	129	97	32
Jennings	44	39	5	St. Genevieve	11	10	1
Joplin	82	71	11	St. George	5	5	—
Kansas City	1,849	1,179	670	St. John	22	20	2
Kearney	9	9	—	St. Joseph	145	109	36
Kennett	28	28	—	St. Louis	2,281	1,625	656
Kirksville	29	22	7	St. Peters	81	66	15
Kirkwood	69	55	14	St. Robert	14	10	4
Ladue	35	29	6	Salem	14	9	5
Lake Lotawana	6	5	1	Savannah	4	4	—
Lake Ozark	14	7	7	Sedalia	45	40	5

Table 78. — Number of Full-time Law Enforcement Employees, Cities, October 31, 1996 — Continued

City	Total police employees	Total officers	Total civilians	City	Total police employees	Total officers	Total civilians
MISSOURI — Continued				**MONTANA — Continued**			
Shrewsbury	20	17	3	Saint Ignatius	2	2	—
Sikeston	51	43	8	Sidney	11	10	1
Slater	6	3	3	Thompson Falls	3	3	—
Smithville	10	9	1	Three Forks	2	2	—
Springfield	302	233	69	Troy	3	3	—
Sugar Creek	17	15	2	West Yellowstone	10	5	5
Sullivan	20	13	7	Whitefish	15	10	5
Sunset Hills	27	21	6	Whitehall	3	2	1
Town and Country	36	32	4				
Trenton	18	12	6	**NEBRASKA**			
Union	16	14	2	Ainsworth	3	3	—
University City	98	79	19	Alliance	28	21	7
Valley Park	13	12	1	Ashland	5	5	—
Vandalia	10	6	4	Auburn	6	6	—
Vinita Park	13	12	1	Aurora	7	7	—
Warrensburg	34	31	3	Beatrice	29	20	9
Warrenton	17	13	4	Bellevue	61	53	8
Warsaw	7	7	—	Blair	12	11	1
Warson Woods	8	7	1	Broken Bow	8	7	1
Washington	25	20	5	Central City	6	5	1
Webb City	22	21	1	Chadron	18	12	6
Webster Groves	55	45	10	Columbus	34	26	8
Wentzville	30	23	7	Cozad	11	7	4
Weston	4	4	—	Crete	15	10	5
West Plains	25	19	6	David City	5	4	1
Winchester	1	1	—	Elkhorn	6	6	—
Windsor	6	6	—	Fairbury	7	6	1
Woodson Terrace	17	15	2	Falls City	13	9	4
Wright City	5	4	1	Fremont	40	31	9
				Geneva	4	4	—
MONTANA				Gering	18	15	3
Baker	3	3	—	Gordon	7	5	2
Belgrade	9	7	2	Gothenburg	10	6	4
Billings	129	108	21	Grand Island	67	60	7
Boulder	2	2	—	Hastings	55	37	18
Bozeman	45	39	6	Holdrege	12	8	4
Bridger	2	2	—	Imperial	3	3	—
Columbia Falls	14	9	5	Kearney	45	37	8
Conrad	6	5	1	Kimball	7	6	1
Cutbank	5	5	—	La Vista	26	22	4
Dillon	9	8	1	Lexington	14	12	2
East Helena	4	4	—	Lincoln	372	273	99
Eureka	3	2	1	Madison	4	4	—
Flathead Tribal	27	16	11	McCook	18	14	4
Fort Benton	3	3	—	Milford	4	4	—
Glasgow	9	8	1	Minden	6	5	1
Glendive	14	10	4	Mitchell	5	5	—
Great Falls	100	66	34	Nebraska City	12	11	1
Hamilton	14	13	1	Neligh	3	3	—
Havre	22	19	3	Norfolk	55	36	19
Helena	60	42	18	North Platte	57	37	20
Kalispell	34	26	8	Ogallala	11	10	1
Laurel	15	9	6	Omaha	879	702	177
Lewistown	18	12	6	O'Neill	12	7	5
Livingston	19	12	7	Ord	8	4	4
Manhattan	2	2	—	Papillion	23	21	2
Miles City-Custer County	19	15	4	Pierce	3	3	—
Missoula	89	73	16	Plainview	2	2	—
Plentywood	4	3	1	Plattsmouth	10	9	1
Polson	8	8	—	Ralston	12	11	1
Red Lodge	5	5	—	Schuyler	10	8	2
Ronan	5	4	1	Scottsbluff	34	29	5

City	Total police employees	Total officers	Total civilians	City	Total police employees	Total officers	Total civilians
NEBRASKA — Continued				**NEW HAMPSHIRE — Continued**			
Seward	11	7	4	Gorham	8	8	—
Sidney	13	12	1	Hampstead	3	3	—
South Sioux City	20	19	1	Hampton	39	30	9
Superior	7	5	2	Hanover	29	19	10
Syracuse	3	3	—	Henniker	7	6	1
Tecumseh	4	3	1	Hinsdale	6	5	1
Tekamah	3	3	—	Holderness	5	5	—
Valley	4	4	—	Hollis	10	9	1
Wahoo	6	6	—	Hooksett	31	17	14
Wayne	12	8	4	Hudson	43	32	11
West Point	6	6	—	Jaffrey	12	11	1
Wilber	4	4	—	Keene	57	44	13
Wymore	2	2	—	Lebanon	42	30	12
York	19	14	5	Lincoln	13	8	5
				Litchfield	9	8	1
NEVADA				Littleton	12	10	2
Boulder City	35	28	7	Manchester	245	185	60
Carlin	8	6	2	Meredith	14	11	3
Elko	52	34	18	Merrimack	44	33	11
Fallon	30	20	10	Milford	26	23	3
Henderson	219	167	52	Moultonborough	9	7	2
Las Vegas Metropolitan Police Department				Nashua	198	146	52
Jurisdiction	2,520	1,666	854	New Castle	2	2	—
Lovelock	6	5	1	Newington	10	9	1
Mesquite	29	20	9	Newport	17	12	5
North Las Vegas	211	146	65	Newton	6	5	1
Reno	447	310	137	Northfield	8	7	1
Sparks	121	79	42	Northwood	5	4	1
Wells	6	5	1	Peterborough	13	11	2
West Wendover	17	14	3	Pittsfield	6	5	1
Winnemucca	19	15	4	Plaistow	19	13	6
Yerington	10	8	2	Plymouth	16	9	7
				Portsmouth	80	60	20
NEW HAMPSHIRE				Rindge	8	7	1
Alton	10	8	2	Rochester	51	41	10
Amherst	15	14	1	Rollinsford	3	3	—
Atkinson	3	3	—	Seabrook	30	23	7
Auburn	7	5	2	Somersworth	26	19	7
Barrington	8	7	1	Tilton	10	9	1
Bedford	32	22	10	Troy	3	3	—
Berlin	22	19	3	Wakefield	9	8	1
Boscawen	5	4	1	Wilton	6	5	1
Bow	11	7	4	Winchester	5	5	—
Bristol	7	6	1	Windham	20	15	5
Candia	6	5	1	Wolfeboro	15	11	4
Charlestown	8	5	3				
Chesterfield	4	4	—	**NEW JERSEY**			
Claremont	30	25	5	Aberdeen Township	37	30	7
Concord	84	66	18	Absecon	28	26	2
Conway	29	20	9	Allendale	16	12	4
Derry	59	48	11	Allenhurst	12	8	4
Dover	58	43	15	Allentown	6	5	1
Durham	17	15	2	Alpha	5	5	—
Enfield	6	5	1	Alpine	13	13	—
Epping	7	6	1	Andover Township	13	9	4
Exeter	30	23	7	Asbury Park	74	64	10
Farmington	14	11	3	Atlantic City	553	429	124
Fitzwilliam	4	3	1	Atlantic Highlands	19	14	5
Franconia	3	3	—	Audubon	19	17	2
Franklin	25	18	7	Audubon Park	5	5	—
Gilford	19	13	6	Avalon	28	19	9
Goffstown	36	25	11	Avon-by-the-Sea	10	10	—

Table 78. — Number of Full-time Law Enforcement Employees, Cities, October 31, 1996 — Continued

City	Total police employees	Total officers	Total civilians	City	Total police employees	Total officers	Total civilians
NEW JERSEY — Continued				**NEW JERSEY — Continued**			
Barnegat Township	26	21	5	Clinton	6	6	—
Barrington	16	15	1	Clinton Township	24	21	3
Bay Head	9	8	1	Closter	19	17	2
Bayonne	219	191	28	Collingswood	30	27	3
Beach Haven	16	12	4	Colts Neck Township	17	16	1
Beachwood	18	16	2	Cranbury Township	12	11	1
Bedminster Township	16	15	1	Cranford Township	65	50	15
Belleville	108	104	4	Cresskill	23	20	3
Bellmawr	25	19	6	Deal	16	11	5
Belmar	26	21	5	Delanco Township	8	7	1
Belvidere	6	6	—	Delaware Township	7	7	—
Bergenfield	51	46	5	Delran Township	30	26	4
Berkeley Heights	31	26	5	Demarest	12	12	—
Berkeley Township	74	56	18	Denville Township	37	29	8
Berlin	17	16	1	Deptford Township	65	54	11
Berlin Township	19	17	2	Dover	40	36	4
Bernards Township	38	29	9	Dover Township	165	133	32
Bernardsville	22	16	6	Dumont	39	33	6
Beverly	6	5	1	Dunellen	18	14	4
Blairstown Township	9	8	1	Eastampton Township	16	14	2
Bloomfield	144	122	22	East Brunswick Township	116	87	29
Bloomingdale	15	14	1	East Greenwich Township	16	14	2
Bogota	19	19	—	East Hanover Township	34	27	7
Boonton	24	18	6	East Newark	9	9	—
Boonton Township	10	10	—	East Orange	304	279	25
Bordentown	11	10	1	East Rutherford	27	26	1
Bordentown Township	27	20	7	East Windsor Township	63	50	13
Bound Brook	22	17	5	Eatontown	41	33	8
Bradley Beach	23	18	5	Edgewater	24	23	1
Branchburg Township	21	20	1	Edgewater Park Township	14	13	1
Brick Township	133	103	30	Edison Township	224	174	50
Bridgeton	75	65	10	Egg Harbor City	22	14	8
Bridgewater Township	78	62	16	Egg Harbor Township	89	67	22
Brielle	15	13	2	Elizabeth	440	353	87
Brigantine	44	37	7	Elk Township	9	8	1
Brooklawn	5	5	—	Elmer	5	5	—
Buena	10	9	1	Elmwood Park	33	32	1
Burlington	35	31	4	Emerson	19	19	—
Burlington Township	43	35	8	Englewood	84	68	16
Butler	16	16	—	Englewood Cliffs	26	25	1
Byram Township	15	13	2	Englishtown	4	4	—
Caldwell	22	21	1	Essex Fells	14	11	3
Califon	2	2	—	Evesham Township	55	50	5
Camden	415	351	64	Ewing Township	93	77	16
Cape May	25	17	8	Fairfield	38	35	3
Carlstadt	30	26	4	Fair Haven	14	13	1
Carney's Point Township	23	18	5	Fair Lawn	62	54	8
Carteret	63	50	13	Fairview	32	32	—
Cedar Grove Township	33	30	3	Fanwood	22	21	1
Chatham	26	20	6	Far Hills	4	4	—
Chatham Township	27	22	5	Flemington	12	11	1
Cherry Hill Township	157	126	31	Florence Township	26	21	5
Chesilhurst	9	8	1	Florham Park	32	31	1
Chester	9	8	1	Fort Lee	112	91	21
Chesterfield Township	3	3	—	Franklin	13	12	1
Chester Township	15	14	1	Franklin Lakes	27	22	5
Cinnaminson Township	34	29	5	Franklin Township (Gloucester County)	29	22	7
Clark Township	57	46	11	Franklin Township (Hunterdon County)	4	4	—
Clayton	25	15	10	Franklin Township (Somerset County)	106	84	22
Clementon	14	13	1	Freehold	34	26	8
Cliffside Park	42	40	2	Freehold Township	57	46	11
Clifton	170	146	24	Frenchtown	3	3	—

Table 78. — Number of Full-time Law Enforcement Employees, Cities, October 31, 1996 — Continued

City	Total police employees	Total officers	Total civilians	City	Total police employees	Total officers	Total civilians
NEW JERSEY — Continued				**NEW JERSEY — Continued**			
Galloway Township	52	44	8	Kinnelon	16	15	1
Garfield	63	53	10	Lacey Township	47	37	10
Garwood	18	16	2	Lakehurst	10	9	1
Gibbsboro	3	3	—	Lakewood	123	100	23
Glassboro	48	38	10	Lambertville	13	11	2
Glen Ridge	34	27	7	Laurel Springs	10	9	1
Glen Rock	22	19	3	Lavallette	16	11	5
Gloucester City	27	25	2	Lawnside	9	8	1
Gloucester Township	93	74	19	Lawrence Township	79	64	15
Green Brook	24	17	7	Lebanon Township	9	8	1
Greenwich Township (Gloucester County)	18	14	4	Leonia	27	20	7
Greenwich Township (Warren County)	6	5	1	Lincoln Park	25	23	2
Guttenberg	27	24	3	Linden	131	122	9
Hackensack	132	111	21	Lindenwold	40	37	3
Hackettstown	20	18	2	Linwood	22	18	4
Haddonfield	29	23	6	Little Egg Harbor Township	40	30	10
Haddon Heights	21	16	5	Little Falls Township	28	24	4
Haddon Township	27	25	2	Little Ferry	30	24	6
Haledon	22	17	5	Little Silver	20	16	4
Hamburg	7	7	—	Livingston Township	68	60	8
Hamilton Township (Atlantic County)	58	44	14	Lodi	45	32	13
Hamilton Township (Mercer County)	208	169	39	Logan Township	14	13	1
Hammonton	36	29	7	Long Beach Township	42	35	7
Hanover Township	35	28	7	Long Branch	116	97	19
Harding Township	14	13	1	Long Hill Township	30	23	7
Hardyston Township	20	14	6	Longport	14	12	2
Harrington Park	11	11	—	Lopatcong Township	11	10	1
Harrison	63	61	2	Lower Alloways Creek Township	17	12	5
Harrison Township	10	9	1	Lower Township	65	49	16
Harvey Cedars	11	9	2	Lumberton Township	22	20	2
Hasbrouck Heights	34	30	4	Lyndhurst Township	48	44	4
Haworth	12	11	1	Madison	39	35	4
Hawthorne	31	30	1	Magnolia	9	9	—
Hazlet Township	49	41	8	Mahwah Township	56	50	6
Helmetta	4	4	—	Manalapan Township	61	48	13
High Bridge	6	6	—	Manasquan	24	18	6
Highland Park	34	28	6	Manchester Township	68	56	12
Highlands	17	13	4	Mansfield Township (Burlington County)	6	5	1
Hightstown	20	15	5	Mansfield Township (Warren County)	12	12	—
Hillsborough Township	53	43	10	Mantoloking	8	7	1
Hillsdale	21	18	3	Mantua Township	31	21	10
Hillside Township	83	72	11	Manville	25	23	2
Hi Nella	6	4	2	Maple Shade Township	39	31	8
Hoboken	151	141	10	Maplewood Township	72	56	16
Ho-Ho-Kus	14	14	—	Margate City	40	30	10
Holland Township	7	6	1	Marlboro Township	80	61	19
Holmdel Township	39	31	8	Matawan	27	21	6
Hopatcong	31	25	6	Maywood	26	22	4
Hopewell Township	36	29	7	Medford Lakes	10	9	1
Howell Township	82	66	16	Medford Township	42	33	9
Independence Township	6	5	1	Mendham	11	10	1
Interlaken	5	5	—	Mendham Township	14	12	2
Irvington	218	183	35	Merchantville	14	13	1
Island Heights	5	5	—	Metuchen	34	28	6
Jackson Township	78	59	19	Middlesex	34	32	2
Jamesburg	9	9	—	Middle Township	60	43	17
Jefferson Township	40	34	6	Middletown Township	121	98	23
Jersey City	964	839	125	Midland Park	14	12	2
Keansburg	42	31	11	Millburn Township	64	52	12
Kearny	116	111	5	Milltown	16	13	3
Kenilworth	27	26	1	Millville	80	68	12
Keyport	22	16	6	Mine Hill Township	10	9	1

Table 78. — Number of Full-time Law Enforcement Employees, Cities, October 31, 1996 — Continued

City	Total police employees	Total officers	Total civilians	City	Total police employees	Total officers	Total civilians
NEW JERSEY — Continued				**NEW JERSEY — Continued**			
Monmouth Beach	11	10	1	Paterson	470	386	84
Monroe Township (Gloucester County)	58	47	11	Paulsboro	22	16	6
Monroe Township (Middlesex County)	49	34	15	Peapack and Gladstone	9	8	1
Montclair	131	102	29	Pemberton	4	4	—
Montgomery Township	33	23	10	Pemberton Township	62	55	7
Montvale	22	21	1	Pennsauken	119	93	26
Montville Township	45	39	6	Penns Grove	17	13	4
Moonachie	19	16	3	Pennsville Township	33	26	7
Moorestown Township	43	33	10	Pequannock Township	31	26	5
Morris Plains	22	16	6	Perth Amboy	141	118	23
Morristown	66	58	8	Phillipsburg	37	31	6
Morris Township	50	41	9	Pine Beach	7	6	1
Mountain Lakes	16	13	3	Pine Hill	19	17	2
Mountainside	26	21	5	Pine Valley	6	5	1
Mount Arlington	10	9	1	Piscataway Township	101	85	16
Mount Ephraim	13	12	1	Pitman	18	14	4
Mount Holly	29	25	4	Plainfield	176	141	35
Mount Laurel Township	70	56	14	Plainsboro Township	38	29	9
Mount Olive Township	48	40	8	Pleasantville	57	48	9
Mullica Township	15	14	1	Plumsted Township	6	5	1
National Park	6	6	—	Pohatcong Township	7	6	1
Neptune	21	17	4	Point Pleasant	34	26	8
Neptune Township	89	72	17	Point Pleasant Beach	30	23	7
Netcong	7	6	1	Pompton Lakes	24	19	5
Newark	1,396	1,249	147	Princeton	40	32	8
New Brunswick	174	138	36	Princeton Township	38	31	7
Newfield	5	5	—	Prospect Park	12	12	—
New Hanover Township	2	2	—	Rahway	94	82	12
New Milford	36	33	3	Ramsey	36	33	3
New Providence	28	23	5	Randolph Township	45	38	7
Newton	26	19	7	Raritan	21	17	4
North Arlington	37	34	3	Raritan Township	40	35	5
North Bergen Township	133	116	17	Readington Township	20	18	2
North Brunswick Township	100	83	17	Red Bank	51	40	11
North Caldwell	18	18	—	Ridgefield	40	29	11
Northfield	29	21	8	Ridgefield Park	30	27	3
North Haledon	20	16	4	Ridgewood	47	42	5
North Hanover Township	7	6	1	Ringwood	26	20	6
North Plainfield	49	44	5	Riverdale	16	12	4
Northvale	12	12	—	River Edge	26	23	3
North Wildwood	35	27	8	Riverside	14	13	1
Norwood	14	14	—	Riverton	6	6	—
Nutley	72	64	8	River Vale	20	20	—
Oakland	32	28	4	Rochelle Park Township	20	18	2
Oaklyn	12	10	2	Rockaway	15	14	1
Ocean City	78	63	15	Rockaway Township	63	49	14
Ocean Gate	6	6	—	Roseland	29	27	2
Oceanport	20	14	6	Roselle	68	55	13
Ocean Township (Monmouth County)	70	58	12	Roselle Park	37	33	4
Ocean Township (Ocean County)	21	15	6	Roxbury Township	47	40	7
Ogdensburg	6	6	—	Rumson	17	17	—
Old Bridge	124	86	38	Runnemede	19	17	2
Old Tappan	13	12	1	Rutherford	44	39	5
Oradell	23	22	1	Saddle Brook Township	37	35	2
Orange	127	117	10	Saddle River	15	13	2
Oxford Township	5	4	1	Salem	29	23	6
Palisades Park	32	31	1	Sayreville	94	78	16
Palmyra	18	16	2	Scotch Plains Township	52	46	6
Paramus	111	86	25	Sea Bright	15	11	4
Park Ridge	20	18	2	Sea Girt	14	11	3
Parsippany-Troy Hills Township	131	108	23	Sea Isle City	28	21	7
Passaic	163	149	14	Seaside Heights	27	19	8

Table 78. — Number of Full-time Law Enforcement Employees, Cities, October 31, 1996 — Continued

City	Total police employees	Total officers	Total civilians	City	Total police employees	Total officers	Total civilians
NEW JERSEY — Continued				**NEW JERSEY — Continued**			
Seaside Park	17	13	4	Wenonah	6	6	—
Secaucus	62	53	9	Westampton Township	21	18	3
Ship Bottom	12	11	1	West Amwell Township	5	4	1
Shrewsbury	20	15	5	West Caldwell	32	30	2
Somerdale	12	11	1	West Cape May	12	11	1
Somers Point	31	26	5	West Deptford Township	39	32	7
Somerville	38	32	6	Westfield	68	59	9
South Amboy	26	25	1	West Long Branch	22	18	4
South Belmar	9	9	—	West Milford Township	51	44	7
South Bound Brook	13	13	—	West New York	116	109	7
South Brunswick Township	87	64	23	West Orange	113	100	13
South Hackensack	21	18	3	West Paterson	24	23	1
South Harrison Township	5	4	1	Westville	13	10	3
South Orange	63	55	8	West Wildwood	4	4	—
South Plainfield	68	56	12	West Windsor Township	48	37	11
South River	32	26	6	Westwood	29	25	4
South Toms River	10	9	1	Wharton	13	12	1
Sparta Township	37	30	7	Wildwood	51	42	9
Spotswood	22	18	4	Wildwood Crest	27	21	6
Springfield	47	43	4	Willingboro Township	84	70	14
Springfield Township	5	5	—	Winfield Township	9	9	—
Spring Lake	17	13	4	Winslow Township	86	71	15
Spring Lake Heights	15	12	3	Woodbridge Township	242	200	42
Stafford Township	54	42	12	Woodbury	35	27	8
Stanhope	8	7	1	Woodbury Heights	8	7	1
Stillwater Township	4	4	—	Woodcliff Lake	17	16	1
Stone Harbor	23	18	5	Woodlynne	9	8	1
Stratford	14	13	1	Wood Ridge	22	19	3
Summit	58	46	12	Woodstown	8	7	1
Surf City	14	10	4	Woolwich Township	6	5	1
Swedesboro	7	7	—	Wyckoff	29	24	5
Teaneck Township	110	95	15				
Tenafly	33	27	6	**NEW MEXICO**			
Tewksbury Township	10	9	1	Acoma	14	8	6
Tinton Falls	38	30	8	Alamogordo	92	67	25
Totowa	27	25	2	Albuquerque	1,253	895	358
Trenton	427	374	53	Artesia	37	24	13
Tuckerton	8	8	—	Aztec	21	14	7
Union Beach	16	13	3	Belen	32	21	11
Union City	184	167	17	Bloomfield	17	15	2
Union Township	163	119	44	Capitan	3	3	—
Upper Saddle River	23	18	5	Carlsbad	65	51	14
Ventnor City	47	38	9	Carrizozo	3	3	—
Vernon Township	37	29	8	Clayton	16	6	10
Verona	33	30	3	Cloudcroft	3	3	—
Vineland	144	126	18	Clovis	79	60	19
Voorhees Township	58	46	12	Corrales	21	14	7
Waldwick	25	20	5	Cuba	2	1	1
Wallington	23	22	1	Deming	35	28	7
Wall Township	62	52	10	Eunice	10	6	4
Wanaque	20	16	4	Farmington	148	96	52
Warren Township	30	23	7	Gallup	107	55	52
Washington	12	11	1	Grants	32	22	10
Washington Township (Bergen County)	22	22	—	Hatch	8	4	4
Washington Township (Gloucester County)	82	69	13	Jal	8	4	4
Washington Township (Mercer County)	25	19	6	Las Cruces	179	142	37
Washington Township (Morris County)	37	29	8	Las Vegas	60	42	18
Washington Township (Warren County)	11	10	1	Los Lunas	31	25	6
Watchung	32	24	8	Lovington	25	19	6
Waterford Township	23	21	2	Milan	12	8	4
Wayne Township	138	110	28	Moriarty	10	9	1
Weehawken Township	47	45	2	Mountainair	4	3	1

Table 78. — Number of Full-time Law Enforcement Employees, Cities, October 31, 1996 — Continued

City	Total police employees	Total officers	Total civilians	City	Total police employees	Total officers	Total civilians
NEW MEXICO — Continued				**NEW YORK — Continued**			
Portales	31	24	7	Cattaraugus Village	1	1	—
Questa	3	2	1	Cayuga Heights Village	7	6	1
Raton	26	18	8	Cazenovia Village	6	6	—
Red River	8	4	4	Centre Island Village	5	5	—
Rio Rancho	137	96	41	Chatham Village	3	3	—
Roswell	102	81	21	Cheektowaga Town	165	128	37
Ruidoso	39	25	14	Chester Town	8	7	1
Ruidoso Downs	11	7	4	Chester Village	10	8	2
Springer	4	4	—	Chittenango Village	7	7	—
Taos	33	18	15	Clarkstown Town	171	152	19
Tatum	8	4	4	Clayton Village	3	3	—
Texico	3	3	—	Clay Town	24	19	5
Truth or Consequences	16	14	2	Clifton Springs Village	2	2	—
Tularosa	13	8	5	Clyde Village	6	4	2
Zuni Tribal	34	16	18	Cobleskill Village	10	10	—
				Coeymans Town	6	3	3
NEW YORK				Cohoes	48	36	12
Addison Town and Village	2	2	—	Colchester Town	2	2	—
Akron Village	1	1	—	Cold Spring Village	2	2	—
Albion Village	14	13	1	Colonie Town	152	108	44
Alexandria Bay Village	2	2	—	Cooperstown Village	7	6	1
Alfred Village	6	6	—	Corinth Village	5	5	—
Altamont Village	2	2	—	Cornwall Town	14	10	4
Amherst Town	178	151	27	Cortland	40	37	3
Amityville Village	27	26	1	Croton-on-Hudson Village	20	19	1
Amsterdam	38	36	2	Cuba Town	4	4	—
Angola Village	3	3	—	Delhi Village	4	4	—
Arcade Village	6	6	—	Depew Village	39	31	8
Ardsley	17	17	—	Deposit Village	2	2	—
Asharoken Village	3	3	—	Dewitt Town	35	32	3
Athens Village	1	1	—	Dobbs Ferry Village	26	25	1
Avon Village	4	4	—	Dolgeville Village	5	5	—
Baldwinsville Village	15	12	3	Dunkirk	34	34	—
Ballston Spa Village	11	7	4	East Aurora-Aurora Town	19	15	4
Batavia	37	31	6	Eastchester Town	60	50	10
Bath Village	16	12	4	East Greenbush Town	25	19	6
Beacon	38	36	2	East Rochester Village	8	7	1
Bedford Town	43	39	4	East Syracuse Village	10	7	3
Bethlehem Town	51	38	13	Eden Town	5	4	1
Binghamton	152	144	8	Ellicott Town	12	11	1
Blooming Grove Town	13	12	1	Ellicottville	3	3	—
Bolivar Village	1	1	—	Elmira Heights Village	10	10	—
Bolton Town	1	1	—	Elmira Town	4	4	—
Boonville Village	2	2	—	Elmsford Village	17	17	—
Brant Town	1	1	—	Endicott Village	44	36	8
Briarcliff Manor Village	18	18	—	Evans Town	25	20	5
Brighton Town	46	40	6	Fairport Village	12	11	1
Brockport Village	11	11	—	Fallsburg Town	20	16	4
Bronxville Village	26	23	3	Floral Park Village	44	37	7
Buchanan Village	7	7	—	Florida Village	1	1	—
Buffalo	1,099	903	196	Fort Edward Village	5	5	—
Caledonia Village	2	2	—	Fort Plain Village	3	3	—
Camden Village	4	4	—	Frankfort Village	4	4	—
Camillus Town and Village	20	19	1	Freeport Village	107	90	17
Canajoharie Village	3	3	—	Fulton	38	35	3
Canastota Village	4	4	—	Garden City Village	61	48	13
Canisteo Village	2	2	—	Gates Town	36	30	6
Canton Village	11	9	2	Geddes Town	17	15	2
Carmel Town	34	31	3	Geneseo Village	8	8	—
Carroll Town	1	1	—	Geneva	38	34	4
Carthage Village	8	7	1	Glen Cove	57	52	5
Catskill Village	13	13	—	Glens Falls	39	32	7

City	Total police employees	Total officers	Total civilians	City	Total police employees	Total officers	Total civilians
NEW YORK — Continued				**NEW YORK — Continued**			
Gloversville	35	33	2	Marlborough Town	8	5	3
Goshen Village	13	12	1	Massena Village	22	21	1
Gouverneur Village	12	8	4	Mechanicville	12	12	—
Granville Village	6	6	—	Middleport Village	2	2	—
Great Neck Estates Village	14	13	1	Middletown	68	60	8
Greenburgh Town	122	104	18	Monroe Village	16	13	3
Green Island Village	6	5	1	Montgomery Town	2	1	1
Greenport Town	1	1	—	Monticello Village	31	27	4
Greenwich Village	2	2	—	Moravia Village	1	1	—
Greenwood Lake Village	14	11	3	Moriah Town	2	2	—
Groton Village	2	1	1	Mount Morris Village	5	5	—
Guilderland Town	42	29	13	Mount Pleasant Town	49	44	5
Hamburg Village	14	12	2	Mount Vernon	211	180	31
Hamilton Village	6	5	1	Nassau Village	1	1	—
Hammondsport Village	2	2	—	Newark Village	20	19	1
Harriman Village	6	6	—	Newburgh	92	78	14
Harrison Town	66	57	9	Newburgh Town	57	43	14
Haverstraw Town	30	29	1	New Castle Town	39	36	3
Hempstead Village	121	95	26	New Paltz Town and Village	24	20	4
Herkimer Village	24	23	1	New Rochelle	220	177	43
Highland Falls Village	12	8	4	New Windsor Town	44	32	12
Homer Village	5	4	1	New York	48,441	37,090	11,351
Hoosick Falls Village	3	3	—	New York Mills Village	2	2	—
Hornell	20	19	1	Niagara Falls	180	159	21
Horseheads Village	14	12	2	Niagara Town	4	4	—
Hudson	25	21	4	Niskayuna Town	40	29	11
Hudson Falls Village	16	12	4	North Castle Town	37	32	5
Huntington Bay Village	6	6	—	North Greenbush Town	14	12	2
Ilion Village	19	17	2	Northport Village	20	16	4
Inlet Town	6	3	3	North Syracuse Village	15	12	3
Irondequoit Town	62	53	9	North Tonawanda	57	53	4
Ithaca	89	73	16	Norwich	20	18	2
Jamestown	82	67	15	Ocean Beach Village	3	3	—
Johnson City Village	47	39	8	Ogdensburg	30	25	5
Johnstown	26	25	1	Old Brookville Village	49	38	11
Kenmore Village	25	24	1	Old Westbury Village	27	22	5
Kensington Village	6	6	—	Olean	40	38	2
Kent Town	23	19	4	Oneida	25	22	3
Kings Point Village	21	21	—	Oneonta	30	26	4
Kingston	81	76	5	Orchard Park Town	32	30	2
Lake Placid Village	17	14	3	Ossining Town	13	13	—
Lake Success Village	22	19	3	Oswego	55	44	11
Lakewood-Busti	11	10	1	Owego Village	13	9	4
Lancaster Town	39	33	6	Oxford Village	2	2	—
Lancaster Village	22	16	6	Oyster Bay Cove Village	12	12	—
Laurel Hollow Village	8	8	—	Painted Post Village	4	4	—
Lewiston Village	5	4	1	Palmyra Village	6	5	1
Liberty Village	19	16	3	Pelham Manor Village	28	27	1
Liverpool Village	11	10	1	Pelham Village	28	25	3
Lloyd Harbor Village	13	12	1	Penn Yann Village	11	10	1
Lloyd Town	6	6	—	Perry Village	5	5	—
Lockport	55	52	3	Philmont Village	6	6	—
Long Beach	94	80	14	Plattsburgh	52	46	6
Lowville Village	6	6	—	Pleasantville Village	23	22	1
Lynbrook Village	51	44	7	Port Chester Village	57	56	1
Lyons Village	12	10	2	Port Dickinson Village	4	3	1
Macedon Town and Village	4	4	—	Port Jervis	27	27	—
Malone Village	18	18	—	Port Washington Village	63	56	7
Malverne Village	18	18	—	Potsdam Village	20	16	4
Mamaroneck Town	40	39	1	Poughkeepsie Town	89	77	12
Mamaroneck Village	53	47	6	Pound Ridge Town	1	1	—
Manlius Town	44	39	5	Pulaski Village	2	2	—

City	Total police employees	Total officers	Total civilians	City	Total police employees	Total officers	Total civilians
NEW YORK — Continued				**NEW YORK — Continued**			
Putnam Valley Town	15	11	4	Westfield Village	5	5	—
Quogue Village	12	12	—	West Seneca Town	77	67	10
Ramapo Town	127	110	17	White Plains	242	202	40
Rensselaer	35	28	7	Windham Town	3	3	—
Riverhead Town	90	73	17	Woodstock Town	9	9	—
Rockville Centre Village	56	49	7	Yonkers	582	515	67
Rome	80	73	7	Yorktown Town	58	51	7
Rosendale Town	3	3	—				
Rotterdam Town	52	40	12	**NORTH CAROLINA**			
Rouses Point Village	3	3	—	Aberdeen	19	17	2
Rye	40	36	4	Ahoskie	22	17	5
Rye Brook Village	23	23	—	Albemarle	49	43	6
Sag Harbor Village	13	11	2	Andrews	6	6	—
St. Johnsville Village	4	4	—	Angier	6	6	—
Salamanca	14	14	—	Apex	28	22	6
Sands Point Village	20	20	—	Archdale	23	18	5
Saranac Lake Village	15	14	1	Asheboro	54	50	4
Saratoga Springs	68	61	7	Asheville	209	170	39
Saugerties Town	18	14	4	Atlantic Beach	24	19	5
Saugerties Village	12	10	2	Aulander	2	2	—
Scarsdale Village	44	39	5	Ayden	21	16	5
Schenectady	193	144	49	Bailey	2	2	—
Schodack Town	9	8	1	Banner Elk	6	6	—
Scotia Village	15	14	1	Beaufort	17	17	—
Seneca Falls Village	16	12	4	Beech Mountain	13	9	4
Shawangunk Town	3	3	—	Belhaven	13	10	3
Shelter Island Town	8	6	2	Belmont	27	25	2
Sherburne Village	1	1	—	Benson	19	15	4
Sherrill	4	4	—	Bessemer City	14	10	4
Sidney Village	9	9	—	Bethel	8	8	—
Silver Creek Village	5	4	1	Beulaville	3	3	—
Sleepy Hollow	25	25	—	Biltmore Forest	11	10	1
Solvay Village	12	12	—	Biscoe	6	6	—
Southampton Village	35	26	9	Black Creek	2	2	—
South Glens Falls Village	6	6	—	Black Mountain	16	14	2
South Nyack-Grandview	7	7	—	Bladenboro	6	5	1
Southport Town	2	1	1	Blowing Rock	13	9	4
Spring Valley Village	64	58	6	Boiling Springs	4	4	—
Stony Point Town	27	26	1	Boiling Springs Lake	7	7	—
Suffern Village	29	24	5	Bolton	1	1	—
Tarrytown Village	39	32	7	Boone	38	32	6
Tonawanda	33	30	3	Brevard	24	23	1
Tonawanda Town	153	106	47	Broadway	3	3	—
Trumansburg Village	1	1	—	Bryson City	5	5	—
Tupper Lake Village	12	11	1	Bunn	3	3	—
Tuxedo Town	12	9	3	Burgaw	6	6	—
Vernon Village	2	2	—	Burlington	129	101	28
Vestal Town	41	33	8	Butner	42	36	6
Walton Village	6	5	1	Candor	4	4	—
Wappingers Falls Village	6	4	2	Canton	17	12	5
Warwick Town	31	26	5	Cape Carteret	5	5	—
Washingtonville Village	12	11	1	Carolina Beach	28	22	6
Waterford Town and Village	13	10	3	Carrboro	35	32	3
Waterloo Village	9	8	1	Carthage	8	7	1
Watertown	62	58	4	Cary	107	86	21
Watervliet	26	26	—	Caswell Beach	4	4	—
Watkins Glen Village	4	4	—	Catawba	1	1	—
Waverly Village	15	10	5	Chadbourn	10	8	2
Wayland Village	1	1	—	Chapel Hill	114	96	18
Webb Town	4	4	—	Charlotte-Mecklenburg	1,633	1,290	343
Webster Town and Village	38	30	8	Cherryville	19	15	4
Wellsville Village	16	12	4	China Grove	8	8	—

Table 78. — Number of Full-time Law Enforcement Employees, Cities, October 31, 1996 — Continued

City	Total police employees	Total officers	Total civilians	City	Total police employees	Total officers	Total civilians
NORTH CAROLINA — Continued				**NORTH CAROLINA — Continued**			
Chocowinity	1	1	—	Henderson	67	59	8
Claremont	9	8	1	Hendersonville	46	34	12
Clayton	23	19	4	Hertford	10	9	1
Cleveland	3	3	—	Hickory	117	93	24
Clinton	35	28	7	Highlands	9	9	—
Clyde	4	4	—	High Point	208	186	22
Coats	5	5	—	Hillsborough	22	21	1
Concord	99	83	16	Holden Beach	5	5	—
Conover	21	20	1	Holly Ridge	5	5	—
Conway	1	1	—	Holly Springs	11	10	1
Cooleemee	5	5	—	Hope Mills	29	21	8
Cornelius	28	20	8	Hudson	12	11	1
Cramerton	7	7	—	Huntersville	24	22	2
Creedmoor	14	11	3	Indian Beach	4	4	—
Dallas	14	11	3	Jackson	1	1	—
Davidson	11	11	—	Jacksonville	115	92	23
Denton	6	6	—	Jefferson	3	3	—
Dobson	4	4	—	Jonesville	8	8	—
Drexel	6	6	—	Kannapolis	83	71	12
Dunn	43	34	9	Kenansville	4	4	—
Durham	413	354	59	Kenly	8	8	—
East Spencer	3	3	—	Kernersville	49	38	11
Eden	57	48	9	Kill Devil Hills	27	22	5
Edenton	18	16	2	King	14	12	2
Elizabeth City	47	40	7	Kings Mountain	32	26	6
Elizabethtown	17	16	1	Kingstown	2	2	—
Elkin	21	18	3	Kinston	89	78	11
Ellerbe	3	3	—	Kitty Hawk	16	14	2
Elm City	4	4	—	Knightdale	9	8	1
Elon College	12	11	1	La Grange	7	7	—
Emerald Isle	20	16	4	Lake Lure	9	9	—
Enfield	15	10	5	Lake Waccamaw	2	2	—
Erwin	14	10	4	Landis	4	4	—
Eureka	1	1	—	Laurel Park	5	5	—
Fair Bluff	3	3	—	Laurinburg	38	32	6
Fairmont	15	11	4	Leland	6	6	—
Farmville	24	20	4	Lenoir	60	50	10
Fayetteville	372	283	89	Lewiston	2	2	—
Fletcher	7	7	—	Lexington	72	58	14
Forest City	29	24	5	Liberty	9	9	—
Four Oaks	4	4	—	Lillington	8	8	—
Franklin	16	16	—	Lincolnton	31	26	5
Franklinton	8	7	1	Littleton	2	2	—
Fremont	5	4	1	Locust	5	5	—
Fuquay-Varina	23	18	5	Long Beach	20	16	4
Garner	44	39	5	Longview	16	16	—
Garysburg	3	3	—	Louisburg	16	13	3
Gaston	5	3	2	Lowell	7	7	—
Gastonia	211	169	42	Lucama	2	2	—
Gibson	1	1	—	Lumberton	74	64	10
Gibsonville	15	12	3	Madison	16	15	1
Glen Alpine	1	1	—	Maggie Valley	3	3	—
Goldsboro	120	99	21	Maiden	14	14	—
Graham	27	24	3	Manteo	6	5	1
Granite Falls	13	11	2	Marion	21	16	5
Granite Quarry	3	3	—	Mars Hill	5	5	—
Greensboro	582	457	125	Marshville	7	7	—
Greenville	160	128	32	Matthews	45	35	10
Grifton	5	5	—	Maxton	15	11	4
Hamlet	22	17	5	Mayodan	15	12	3
Havelock	28	23	5	Maysville	3	3	—
Haw River	8	8	—	McAdenville	4	4	—

Table 78. — Number of Full-time Law Enforcement Employees, Cities, October 31, 1996 — Continued

City	Total police employees	Total officers	Total civilians	City	Total police employees	Total officers	Total civilians
NORTH CAROLINA — Continued				**NORTH CAROLINA — Continued**			
Mebane	16	13	3	Salisbury	95	75	20
Mocksville	12	11	1	Saluda	3	3	—
Monroe	96	85	11	Sanford	88	70	18
Montreat	5	5	—	Scotland Neck	14	8	6
Mooresville	41	35	6	Seaboard	1	1	—
Morehead City	35	29	6	Seagrove	1	1	—
Morganton	95	78	17	Selma	27	22	5
Morrisville	12	11	1	Seven Devils	6	6	—
Mount Airy	46	35	11	Shallotte	9	8	1
Mount Gilead	6	6	—	Sharpsburg	5	5	—
Mount Holly	26	21	5	Shelby	70	58	12
Mount Olive	21	15	6	Siler City	20	18	2
Murfreesboro	11	7	4	Smithfield	37	30	7
Murphy	12	8	4	Southern Pines	33	27	6
Nags Head	22	19	3	Southern Shores	9	8	1
Nashville	10	9	1	Southport	11	9	2
New Bern	100	81	19	Sparta	5	5	—
Newland	4	4	—	Spencer	12	12	—
Newport	4	4	—	Spindale	13	13	—
Newton	42	33	9	Spring Hope	6	6	—
Newton Grove	3	3	—	Spring Lake	29	22	7
Norlina	5	4	1	Spruce Pine	10	10	—
North Topsail Beach	8	7	1	Stanfield	3	3	—
North Wilkesboro	25	22	3	Stanley	13	9	4
Norwood	6	6	—	Stantonsburg	3	3	—
Oakboro	3	3	—	Star	5	5	—
Ocean Isle Beach	7	7	—	Statesville	86	68	18
Old Fort	8	8	—	Sugar Mountain	6	6	—
Oxford	34	27	7	Sunset Beach	7	7	—
Pembroke	15	11	4	Surf City	10	9	1
Pine Level	3	3	—	Swansboro	5	5	—
Pilot Mountain	8	8	—	Sylva	10	10	—
Pinebluff	3	3	—	Tabor City	9	8	1
Pinehurst	27	22	5	Tarboro	33	25	8
Pine Knoll Shores	8	8	—	Taylortown	1	1	—
Pinetops	9	6	3	Taylorsville	9	9	—
Pineville	35	25	10	Thomasville	68	57	11
Pink Hill	1	1	—	Topsail Beach	5	5	—
Pittsboro	7	7	—	Trent Woods	4	4	—
Plymouth	14	13	1	Troutman	6	6	—
Princeton	3	3	—	Troy	10	10	—
Raeford	16	15	1	Tryon	13	9	4
Raleigh	640	573	67	Valdese	13	12	1
Ramseur	7	7	—	Vanceboro	2	2	—
Randleman	11	11	—	Vass	4	4	—
Ranlo	5	5	—	Wadesboro	24	18	6
Red Springs	19	15	4	Wagram	4	4	—
Reidsville	50	41	9	Wake Forest	26	21	5
Richlands	4	4	—	Wallace	16	14	2
River Bend	3	3	—	Walnut Cove	6	6	—
Roanoke Rapids	44	35	9	Warsaw	14	11	3
Robbins	8	7	1	Washington	40	32	8
Robersonville	8	8	—	Waynesville	34	29	5
Rockingham	32	27	5	Weldon	13	9	4
Rocky Mount	178	142	36	Wendell	15	11	4
Rolesville	4	4	—	West Jefferson	4	4	—
Roseboro	5	5	—	Whispering Pines	7	7	—
Rose Hill	4	4	—	Whitakers	5	4	1
Rowland	8	5	3	White Lake	4	4	—
Roxboro	31	28	3	Whiteville	30	26	4
Rutherfordton	13	12	1	Wilkesboro	18	17	1
St. Pauls	16	11	5	Williamston	19	18	1

City	Total police employees	Total officers	Total civilians	City	Total police employees	Total officers	Total civilians
NORTH CAROLINA — Continued				**OHIO — Continued**			
Wilmington	180	157	23	Amberley	17	15	2
Wilson	108	92	16	Amherst	22	17	5
Windsor	7	7	—	Archbold	8	8	—
Wingate	5	5	—	Ashland	38	30	8
Winston-Salem	579	446	133	Athens	37	24	13
Winterville	14	13	1	Aurora	25	18	7
Winton	2	2	—	Bainbridge Township	23	17	6
Woodfin	9	9	—	Barberton	53	42	11
Woodland	1	1	—	Bazetta Township	9	8	1
Wrightsville Beach	25	19	6	Beavercreek	53	41	12
Yadkinville	10	9	1	Beaver Township	13	9	4
Yaupon Beach	5	5	—	Bedford	39	30	9
Youngsville	5	5	—	Bedford Heights	46	33	13
Zebulon	20	19	1	Bellaire	14	14	—
				Bellbrook	13	9	4
NORTH DAKOTA				Bellefontaine	30	23	7
Beulah	7	6	1	Bellevue	15	11	4
Bismarck	99	75	24	Bellville	2	2	—
Bowman	3	3	—	Belpre	16	11	5
Cando	3	3	—	Berea	37	30	7
Carrington	6	6	—	Bethel	4	4	—
Casselton	2	2	—	Bexley	33	26	7
Cavalier	4	4	—	Blanchester	5	5	—
Cooperstown	1	1	—	Bowling Green	50	37	13
Crosby	3	3	—	Bradford	4	4	—
Devils Lake	17	15	2	Brecksville	33	28	5
Dickinson	34	24	10	Briarwood Beach	1	1	—
Elgin	1	1	—	Brooklyn	39	32	7
Emerado	1	1	—	Brooklyn Heights	13	13	—
Fargo	125	94	31	Brookville	14	10	4
Fessenden	1	1	—	Bryan	23	18	5
Grafton	12	11	1	Bucyrus	25	19	6
Grand Forks	77	66	11	Burton	3	3	—
Gwinner	1	1	—	Cadiz	4	4	—
Harvey	2	2	—	Cambridge	30	24	6
Hatton	2	2	—	Canal Fulton	9	8	1
Hazen	4	4	—	Carey	10	7	3
Hillsboro	2	2	—	Carlisle	9	8	1
Jamestown	33	28	5	Centerville	42	33	9
Larimore	2	2	—	Chardon	13	8	5
Linton	2	2	—	Chillicothe	57	50	7
Lisbon	2	2	—	Cincinnati	1,259	986	273
Mandan	33	27	6	Clear Creek Township	11	10	1
Mayville	3	3	—	Cleveland	2,359	1,785	574
Minot	76	54	22	Cleveland Heights	123	107	16
Northwood	2	2	—	Cleves	3	3	—
Oakes	2	2	—	Clinton Township	10	9	1
Parshall	2	2	—	Clyde	16	12	4
Powers Lake	1	1	—	Coitsville Township	3	3	—
Rugby	4	4	—	Columbiana	14	10	4
South Heart	1	1	—	Columbus	2,029	1,641	388
Stanton	1	1	—	Conneaut	25	21	4
Steele	1	1	—	Cortland	9	9	—
Thompson	1	1	—	Covington	6	5	1
Valley City	17	12	5	Crestline	14	12	2
Wahpeton	20	14	6	Cuyahoga Falls	98	80	18
Watford City	3	3	—	Dayton	678	472	206
West Fargo	27	19	8	Deer Park	11	10	1
Williston	28	20	8	Delaware	48	33	15
Wishek	2	2	—	Delhi Township	30	26	4
				Dennison	5	5	—
OHIO				Deshler	3	3	—
Akron	528	485	43				

Table 78. — Number of Full-time Law Enforcement Employees, Cities, October 31, 1996 — Continued

City	Total police employees	Total officers	Total civilians	City	Total police employees	Total officers	Total civilians
OHIO — Continued				**OHIO — Continued**			
Dover	22	20	2	Lordstown	12	8	4
Dublin	61	45	16	Louisville	15	12	3
Eastlake	44	34	10	Loveland	17	15	2
East Liverpool	26	20	6	Lowell Marshal	1	1	—
East Palestine	10	7	3	Madeira	13	12	1
Eaton	16	10	6	Madison Township (Lake County)	18	16	2
Englewood	26	17	9	Mansfield	143	100	43
Euclid	172	102	70	Mariemont	10	9	1
Fairborn	56	43	13	Marietta	37	30	7
Fairfax	9	9	—	Marion	73	52	21
Fairfield	67	50	17	Marlboro Township	2	2	—
Fairlawn	29	21	8	Mason	22	20	2
Fairport Harbor	7	6	1	Massillon	57	53	4
Fayette	3	3	—	McConnelsville	5	5	—
Forest	2	2	—	Mentor	96	66	30
Forest Park	40	33	7	Mentor-on-the-Lake	14	10	4
Fort Shawnee	4	3	1	Miamisburg	47	37	10
Franklin	25	20	5	Miami Township	30	28	2
Fremont	38	33	5	Middlefield	7	6	1
Gahanna	49	43	6	Middletown	125	84	41
Garfield Heights	71	57	14	Milford	16	13	3
Gates Mills	16	12	4	Minerva	12	8	4
Germantown	13	8	5	Mingo Junction	14	12	2
German Township	5	5	—	Mogadore	8	8	—
Gibsonburg	4	4	—	Monroe	13	9	4
Girard	25	21	4	Montgomery	19	18	1
Glendale	6	6	—	Moraine	41	34	7
Golf Manor	9	5	4	Mount Sterling	10	5	5
Goshen Township	7	6	1	Munroe Falls	8	7	1
Grandview Heights	23	18	5	Navarre	4	4	—
Granville	13	10	3	Nelsonville	10	8	2
Greenfield	12	11	1	Newark	77	67	10
Grove City	51	39	12	Newcomerstown	12	7	5
Hamilton	141	117	24	New Lebanon	8	7	1
Harrison	21	18	3	New Lexington	11	7	4
Hartville	6	6	—	New Philadelphia	24	20	4
Hicksville	11	10	1	Newtown	5	5	—
Highland Heights	27	21	6	Niles	36	31	5
Hilliard	52	38	14	North Baltimore	5	5	—
Holgate	1	1	—	North Canton	27	20	7
Holland	5	5	—	North Kingsville	4	4	—
Hubbard	17	13	4	North Ridgeville	39	30	9
Huber Heights	52	48	4	Northwood	20	15	5
Hunting Valley	14	12	2	Norton	22	16	6
Huron	16	12	4	Norwalk	26	22	4
Indian Hill	24	19	5	Norwood	47	46	1
Jackson Township	36	31	5	Oakwood	36	30	6
Jefferson	6	5	1	Oberlin	19	15	4
Johnstown	9	5	4	Olmsted Township	16	12	4
Kent	58	38	20	Ontario	21	17	4
Kettering	107	81	26	Oregon	54	44	10
Kirtland Hills	8	7	1	Orrville	19	14	5
Lakemore	9	8	1	Ottawa Hills	15	11	4
Lancaster	91	67	24	Oxford	31	22	9
Lawrence Township	5	5	—	Pataskala	9	9	—
Lebanon	30	23	7	Paulding	5	4	1
Lexington	11	7	4	Peninsula	6	5	1
Liberty Township	28	25	3	Pepper Pike	23	17	6
Lima	117	96	21	Perkins Township	22	18	4
Lockland	11	11	—	Perrysburg	29	22	7
Logan	16	11	5	Perry Township (Stark County)	23	18	5
Lorain	137	103	34	Pierce Township	12	11	1

Table 78. — Number of Full-time Law Enforcement Employees, Cities, October 31, 1996 — Continued

City	Total police employees	Total officers	Total civilians	City	Total police employees	Total officers	Total civilians
OHIO — Continued				**OHIO — Continued**			
Piqua	35	31	4	Waterville	14	13	1
Poland Township	12	11	1	Waterville Township	4	4	—
Poland Village	5	5	—	Wauseon	13	11	2
Port Clinton	16	11	5	Waverly	17	12	5
Portsmouth	48	44	4	Wellsville	7	7	—
Randolph Township	13	12	1	West Carrollton	33	26	7
Ravenna	32	24	8	Westerville	62	54	8
Reading	23	19	4	West Jefferson	11	8	3
Reynoldsburg	56	43	13	Westlake	57	43	14
Richmond Heights	24	18	6	Weston	1	1	—
Rittman	12	9	3	Whitehall	52	43	9
Salem	20	19	1	Wickliffe	37	31	6
Salineville	5	4	1	Willard	19	15	4
Seaman	3	2	1	Wilmington	23	20	3
Sebring	9	6	3	Winchester	1	1	—
Seven Hills	16	15	1	Windham	7	5	2
Shadyside	10	6	4	Woodsfield	6	6	—
Shaker Heights	100	70	30	Woodville	4	3	1
Sharonville	44	33	11	Worthington	46	34	12
Sheffield Lake	13	10	3	Wyoming	21	17	4
Shelby	18	15	3	Xenia	69	45	24
Silverton	13	10	3	Yellow Springs	12	9	3
Solon	50	40	10	Youngstown	217	192	25
South Russell	9	9	—	Zanesville	92	54	38
Spencerville	4	4	—				
Springboro	21	15	6	**OKLAHOMA**			
Springdale	39	32	7	Ada	45	32	13
Springfield	173	127	46	Altus	58	45	13
Springfield Township (Hamilton County)	43	36	7	Alva	17	9	8
Steubenville	50	41	9	Anadarko	23	18	5
Stow	35	27	8	Antlers	8	4	4
Streetsboro	27	20	7	Apache	8	4	4
Struthers	16	15	1	Ardmore	68	53	15
Swanton	6	6	—	Arkoma	7	3	4
Sylvania	36	30	6	Atoka	15	14	1
Sylvania Township	38	29	9	Barnsdall	6	4	2
Tallmadge	36	24	12	Bartlesville	80	52	28
Tiffin	43	30	13	Beggs	8	3	5
Tipp City	15	14	1	Bethany	36	24	12
Toledo	784	712	72	Bixby	17	12	5
Toronto	9	9	—	Blackwell	21	14	7
Trenton	12	8	4	Blanchard	7	4	3
Trotwood	61	50	11	Boise City	3	3	—
Troy	40	37	3	Bristow	14	12	2
Twinsburg	34	25	9	Broken Arrow	105	77	28
Uhrichsville	8	8	—	Broken Bow	17	11	6
Uniontown	6	5	1	Carnegie	9	6	3
Union Township (Butler County)	65	50	15	Catoosa	11	11	—
Union Township (Clermont County)	44	34	10	Chandler	13	9	4
University Heights	35	27	8	Checotah	14	12	2
Upper Arlington	59	49	10	Chelsea	5	5	—
Upper Sandusky	10	9	1	Cherokee	6	3	3
Vandalia	39	30	9	Chickasha	46	36	10
Van Wert	29	22	7	Choctaw	16	15	1
Vermilion	23	18	5	Chouteau	7	5	2
Village of Highland Hills	6	6	—	Claremore	49	33	16
Wadsworth	29	24	5	Clayton	8	4	4
Waite Hill	5	5	—	Cleveland	8	8	—
Walbridge	9	5	4	Clinton	28	20	8
Walton Hills	15	12	3	Coalgate	6	6	—
Warrensville Heights	37	32	5	Collinsville	8	4	4
Washington Court House	24	17	7	Comanche	4	4	—

Table 78. — Number of Full-time Law Enforcement Employees, Cities, October 31, 1996 — Continued

City	Total police employees	Total officers	Total civilians	City	Total police employees	Total officers	Total civilians
OKLAHOMA — Continued				**OKLAHOMA — Continued**			
Commerce	4	4	—	Locust Grove	8	4	4
Cordell	9	6	3	Lone Grove	8	5	3
Coweta	23	17	6	Luther	2	2	—
Crescent	7	4	3	Madill	10	10	—
Cushing	24	19	5	Mangum	14	7	7
Davis	14	10	4	Mannford	10	6	4
Del City	46	34	12	Marietta	5	5	—
Dewey	9	8	1	Marlow	10	9	1
Dibble	2	2	—	Maud	3	3	—
Drumright	5	5	—	Maysville	3	2	1
Duncan	45	39	6	McAlester	54	41	13
Durant	34	27	7	McLoud	9	5	4
Edmond	85	76	9	Meeker	4	4	—
Elk City	28	18	10	Miami	40	31	9
Elmore City	5	4	1	Midwest City	118	97	21
El Reno	33	27	6	Minco	4	4	—
Enid	116	88	28	Moore	62	43	19
Erick	3	3	—	Mooreland	3	3	—
Eufaula	12	8	4	Morris	3	3	—
Fairfax	8	5	3	Muldrow	11	7	4
Fairview	9	5	4	Muskogee	110	86	24
Forest Park	3	2	1	Mustang	22	17	5
Fort Gibson	6	6	—	Newcastle	12	8	4
Frederick	16	10	6	Newkirk	7	6	1
Geary	9	5	4	Nichols Hills	19	14	5
Glenpool	14	10	4	Nicoma Park	5	5	—
Goodwell	2	2	—	Noble	15	11	4
Gore	4	4	—	Norman	151	112	39
Granite	3	3	—	Nowata	8	6	2
Grove	21	13	8	Oilton	3	3	—
Guthrie	33	25	8	Okeene	10	2	8
Guymon	21	15	6	Okemah	12	8	4
Harrah	8	8	—	Oklahoma City	1,280	995	285
Hartshorne	5	5	—	Okmulgee	39	29	10
Haskell	7	7	—	Oologah	3	3	—
Healdton	7	4	3	Owasso	31	23	8
Heavener	10	6	4	Pauls Valley	21	15	6
Hennessey	9	4	5	Pawhuska	14	8	6
Henryetta	15	10	5	Pawnee	6	6	—
Hinton	4	4	—	Perkins	4	4	—
Hobart	16	11	5	Perry	19	14	5
Holdenville	14	10	4	Piedmont	6	5	1
Hollis	10	6	4	Pocola	11	7	4
Hominy	10	5	5	Ponca City	70	56	14
Hooker	3	3	—	Porum	3	3	—
Hugo	19	14	5	Poteau	23	16	7
Hulbert	4	4	—	Prague	9	6	3
Hydro	2	2	—	Pryor	25	19	6
Idabel	28	22	6	Purcell	22	16	6
Inola	8	2	6	Ringling	3	3	—
Jay	9	7	2	Roland	16	8	8
Jenks	17	12	5	Rush Springs	4	4	—
Jones	4	4	—	Salina	7	3	4
Keyes	1	1	—	Sallisaw	25	18	7
Kingfisher	9	7	2	Sand Springs	32	30	2
Kingston	4	4	—	Sapulpa	46	36	10
Konawa	7	5	2	Sayre	9	6	3
Krebs	4	4	—	Seiling	3	3	—
Laverne	6	2	4	Seminole	19	14	5
Lawton	170	147	23	Shawnee	72	51	21
Lexington	9	6	3	Skiatook	15	10	5
Lindsay	11	7	4	Snyder	4	4	—

Table 78. — Number of Full-time Law Enforcement Employees, Cities, October 31, 1996 — Continued

City	Total police employees	Total officers	Total civilians	City	Total police employees	Total officers	Total civilians
OKLAHOMA — Continued				**OREGON — Continued**			
Spencer	8	7	1	Coburg	3	3	—
Spiro	5	5	—	Coos Bay	43	29	14
Stigler	13	8	5	Coquille	10	8	2
Stillwater	87	59	28	Cornelius	16	14	2
Stilwell	21	14	7	Corvallis	77	53	24
Stratford	3	3	—	Cottage Grove	24	15	9
Stroud	14	10	4	Culver	1	1	—
Sulphur	13	9	4	Dallas	18	17	1
Tahlequah	30	23	7	Dundee	5	5	—
Talihina	8	5	3	Eagle Point	6	5	1
Tecumseh	15	10	5	Elgin	3	3	—
Temple	2	2	—	Enterprise	4	4	—
The Village	30	24	6	Eugene	328	165	163
Tishomingo	9	8	1	Florence	21	12	9
Tonkawa	11	7	4	Forest Grove	31	25	6
Tulsa	907	781	126	Garibaldi	3	3	—
Tuttle	12	8	4	Gaston	1	1	—
Valliant	8	4	4	Gearhart	3	3	—
Vian	4	4	—	Gladstone	18	13	5
Vinita	20	15	5	Gold Beach	7	6	1
Wagoner	18	12	6	Gold Hill	2	2	—
Walters	4	4	—	Grants Pass	39	25	14
Warner	4	4	—	Gresham	123	88	35
Warr Acres	34	23	11	Heppner	3	3	—
Watonga	11	7	4	Hermiston	27	20	7
Waukomis	3	3	—	Hines	7	3	4
Waurika	5	4	1	Hood River	14	11	3
Waynoka	3	3	—	Hubbard	7	5	2
Weatherford	28	19	9	Independence	13	12	1
Weleetka	11	4	7	Jacksonville	4	4	—
Westville	9	4	5	John Day	9	4	5
Wetumka	7	6	1	Junction City	12	8	4
Wewoka	13	10	3	Keizer	38	30	8
Wilburton	8	5	3	King City	3	3	—
Wilson	5	3	2	Klamath Falls	36	33	3
Woodward	30	21	9	La Grande	32	18	14
Wright City	2	2	—	Lake Oswego	67	43	24
Wynnewood	9	5	4	Lakeview	5	5	—
Yale	8	4	4	Lebanon	31	23	8
Yukon	44	29	15	Lincoln City	30	21	9
				Madras	11	10	1
OREGON				McMinnville	34	27	7
Albany	69	50	19	Medford	126	87	39
Amity	2	2	—	Milton-Freewater	15	11	4
Ashland	37	25	12	Milwaukie	43	31	12
Astoria	23	16	7	Molalla	12	10	2
Athena	2	2	—	Monmouth	13	11	2
Aumsville	6	5	1	Mount Angel	5	4	1
Aurora	3	2	1	Myrtle Creek	14	8	6
Baker	16	12	4	Myrtle Point	7	6	1
Bandon	7	6	1	Nehalem Bay	2	2	—
Beaverton	109	87	22	Newberg	33	22	11
Bend	65	49	16	Newport	27	23	4
Boardman	7	6	1	North Bend	23	16	7
Brookings	18	13	5	North Plains	5	4	1
Burns	10	5	5	Nyssa	10	8	2
Butte Falls	1	1	—	Oakland	2	2	—
Canby	25	19	6	Oakridge	12	7	5
Cannon Beach	8	7	1	Ontario	29	20	9
Carlton	2	2	—	Oregon City	32	26	6
Central Point	20	17	3	Pendleton	30	22	8
Clatskanie	7	6	1	Philomath	10	8	2

City	Total police employees	Total officers	Total civilians	City	Total police employees	Total officers	Total civilians
OREGON — Continued				**PENNSYLVANIA — Continued**			
Phoenix	9	8	1	Aston Township	20	18	2
Pilot Rock	5	4	1	Athens	5	5	—
Portland	1,247	979	268	Athens Township	7	7	—
Powers	2	2	—	Baldwin Borough	28	22	6
Prineville	20	12	8	Baldwin Township	5	5	—
Rainier	7	6	1	Bally	1	1	—
Redmond	28	22	6	Bangor	8	7	1
Reedsport	18	13	5	Bedford	7	6	1
Rockaway	3	3	—	Bedminster Township	5	5	—
Rogue River	3	3	—	Belle Acres	1	1	—
Roseburg	42	38	4	Bellefonte	11	10	1
St. Helens	21	18	3	Bellwood	2	2	—
Salem	266	167	99	Bensalem Township	90	75	15
Sandy	10	9	1	Bentleyville	2	2	—
Scappoose	11	9	2	Berlin	1	1	—
Seaside	23	17	6	Bern Township	7	7	—
Shady Cove	4	3	1	Berwick	11	10	1
Sherwood	12	11	1	Bethel Park	41	35	6
Silverton	14	12	2	Bethel Township (Lebanon County)	2	2	—
Sisters	7	6	1	Bethlehem	159	136	23
Springfield	90	61	29	Big Beaver	3	3	—
Stanfield	5	5	—	Birdsboro	6	6	—
Stayton	16	15	1	Birmingham Township	2	2	—
Sutherlin	14	12	2	Blair Township	3	3	—
Sweet Home	16	11	5	Blairsville	2	2	—
Talent	8	7	1	Blakely	7	7	—
The Dalles	22	20	2	Bloomsburg Town	16	12	4
Tigard	62	51	11	Blossburg	2	2	—
Tillamook	11	9	2	Bolivar	1	1	—
Toledo	13	8	5	Boyertown	7	7	—
Troutdale	18	15	3	Brackenridge	5	5	—
Tualatin	28	26	2	Braddock	24	21	3
Turner	2	2	—	Braddock Hills	1	1	—
Umatilla	8	7	1	Bradford	21	19	2
Vale	5	5	—	Bradford Township	6	5	1
Vernonia	6	5	1	Bridgeport	10	9	1
Waldport	4	3	1	Bridgeville	9	8	1
Warrenton	8	7	1	Bridgewater	2	2	—
West Linn	29	24	5	Brighton Township	4	4	—
Winston	11	7	4	Bristol	12	11	1
Woodburn	30	25	5	Bristol Township	74	65	9
Yamhill	2	2	—	Brockway	1	1	—
				Brookhaven	8	7	1
PENNSYLVANIA				Brookville	6	6	—
Abington Township	111	91	20	Brownsville	5	5	—
Adams Township (Butler County)	1	1	—	Bryn Athyn	5	5	—
Adams Township (Cambria County)	4	4	—	Buckingham Township	20	18	2
Akron	6	5	1	Bushkill Township	7	6	1
Albion	1	1	—	Butler	21	21	—
Alburtis	3	3	—	Butler Township (Luzerne County)	6	5	1
Aldan	5	4	1	California	9	7	2
Aleppo Township	9	5	4	Cambria Township	4	4	—
Aliquippa	19	18	1	Camp Hill	9	8	1
Allegheny Township (Blair County)	6	6	—	Canonsburg	17	15	2
Allegheny Township (Westmoreland County)	7	7	—	Canton	2	2	—
Allentown	223	200	23	Carlisle	36	30	6
Altoona	88	71	17	Carnegie	14	13	1
Ambler	14	12	2	Carroll Township (Washington County)	4	4	—
Amity Township	6	6	—	Carroll Township (York County)	5	5	—
Arnold	11	10	1	Castle Shannon	13	12	1
Ashland	5	5	—	Catasauqua	9	8	1
Ashley	3	3	—	Catawissa	2	2	—

Table 78. — Number of Full-time Law Enforcement Employees, Cities, October 31, 1996 — Continued

City	Total police employees	Total officers	Total civilians	City	Total police employees	Total officers	Total civilians
PENNSYLVANIA — Continued				**PENNSYLVANIA — Continued**			
Cecil Township	12	12	—	Duncansville	1	1	—
Center Township	8	8	—	Dunmore	9	8	1
Central Berks Regional	12	11	1	Dupont	1	1	—
Chalfont	5	5	—	Duquesne	15	15	—
Chambersburg	32	29	3	East Bethlehem Township	1	1	—
Charleroi	10	9	1	East Brandywine Township	9	8	1
Cheltenham Township	89	79	10	East Cocalico Township	20	18	2
Cheswick	3	3	—	East Conemaugh	2	2	—
Chippewa Township	9	8	1	East Deer Township	5	2	3
Christiana	1	1	—	East Donegal Township	12	11	1
Churchill	9	9	—	East Fallowfield Township	3	3	—
Clairton	10	10	—	East Hempfield Township	27	23	4
Clarion	9	8	1	East Lansdowne	3	3	—
Clearfield	8	8	—	East McKeesport	3	3	—
Cleona	3	3	—	East Norriton Township	25	22	3
Clifton Heights	10	9	1	Easton	61	51	10
Coatesville	29	25	4	East Pennsboro Township	17	16	1
Cochranton	2	2	—	East Pikeland Township	6	6	—
Colebrookdale Township	7	7	—	East Stroudsburg	15	13	2
Collegeville	6	6	—	Easttown Township	14	13	1
Collier Township	11	10	1	East Vincent Township	5	5	—
Collingdale	9	8	1	East Washington	2	2	—
Columbia	18	15	3	East Whiteland Township	14	12	2
Conemaugh Township (Somerset County)	6	6	—	Ebensburg	5	5	—
Conestoga Township	3	3	—	Economy	11	10	1
Conewago Township	5	5	—	Edgeworth	5	5	—
Conewango Township	4	4	—	Edinboro	9	8	1
Connellsville	16	15	1	Edwardsville	7	7	—
Conshohocken	13	12	1	Elizabeth	2	2	—
Conway	3	3	—	Elizabethtown	15	13	2
Conyngham	2	2	—	Elizabeth Township	18	17	1
Coolbaugh Township	10	9	1	Elizabethville	1	1	—
Coopersburg	5	5	—	Elkland	2	2	—
Coplay	4	4	—	Emmaus	16	14	2
Coraopolis	12	9	3	Emporium	1	1	—
Cornwall	6	5	1	Ephrata	23	20	3
Corry	16	12	4	Ephrata Township	11	10	1
Crafton	13	9	4	Erie	234	193	41
Cranberry Township	21	19	2	Etna	5	4	1
Cressona	2	2	—	Everett	2	2	—
Cresson Township	2	2	—	Fairview	1	1	—
Croyle Township	1	1	—	Fairview Township (York County)	14	13	1
Cumberland Township (Adams County)	6	6	—	Falls Township	52	46	6
Cumru Township	23	22	1	Fawn Township	2	2	—
Dale	1	1	—	Ferguson Township	15	13	2
Dallas	5	5	—	Findlay Township	19	13	6
Dallas Township	8	8	—	Fleetwood	5	5	—
Danville	9	8	1	Folcroft	9	9	—
Darby	13	11	2	Ford City	4	4	—
Darby Township	13	12	1	Forest Hills	9	9	—
Derry	4	4	—	Forks Township	12	11	1
Derry Township (Dauphin County)	36	31	5	Forty Fort	8	7	1
Dickson City	11	11	—	Foster Township	5	5	—
Donora	5	5	—	Fountain Hill	7	7	—
Dormont	14	13	1	Fox Chapel	12	12	—
Douglass Township (Berks County)	5	5	—	Frackville	7	7	—
Douglass Township (Montgomery County)	10	9	1	Franconia Township	10	9	1
Downingtown	14	12	2	Franklin (Cambria County)	2	2	—
Doylestown	21	15	6	Franklin (Venango County)	22	16	6
Doylestown Township	22	19	3	Franklin Park	10	9	1
Du Bois	14	10	4	Franklin Township (Beaver County)	1	1	—
Duboistown	1	1	—	Franklin Township (Carbon County)	3	3	—

Table 78. — Number of Full-time Law Enforcement Employees, Cities, October 31, 1996 — Continued

City	Total police employees	Total officers	Total civilians	City	Total police employees	Total officers	Total civilians
PENNSYLVANIA — Continued				**PENNSYLVANIA — Continued**			
Freeland	5	5	—	Lansdale	30	22	8
Freemansburg	1	1	—	Lansdowne	18	15	3
Gettysburg	14	12	2	Lansford	4	4	—
Girard	6	5	1	Latrobe	10	10	—
Glenolden	10	9	1	Lawrence Park Township	7	6	1
Granville Township	5	5	—	Lawrence Township	8	8	—
Greensburg	33	27	6	Lebanon	47	40	7
Greenville	13	12	1	Leetsdale	4	4	—
Grove City	6	6	—	Lehigh Township (Northampton County)	9	8	1
Hamburg	8	7	1	Lehman Township	2	2	—
Hampton Township	19	18	1	Lewisburg	8	7	1
Hanover Township (Luzerne County)	19	14	5	Ligonier Township	2	2	—
Hanover Township (Washington County)	8	8	—	Limerick Township	11	9	2
Harmar Township	4	4	—	Lincoln	1	1	—
Harmony Township	3	3	—	Linesville	1	1	—
Harrisburg	225	181	44	Littlestown	7	7	—
Harrison Township	16	12	4	Lock Haven	14	12	2
Hatboro	19	14	5	Logan Township	21	16	5
Hatfield Township	28	23	5	Lower Allen Township	21	18	3
Haverford Township	79	65	14	Lower Gwynedd Township	18	16	2
Hazleton	34	29	5	Lower Heidelberg Township	5	5	—
Heidelberg	2	2	—	Lower Merion Township	160	133	27
Heidelberg Township (Berks County)	1	1	—	Lower Moreland Township	27	20	7
Heidelberg Township (Lebanon County)	2	2	—	Lower Paxton Township	52	47	5
Hellam Township	7	7	—	Lower Pottsgrove Township	12	11	1
Hellertown	10	9	1	Lower Providence Township	32	25	7
Hemlock Township	3	3	—	Lower Salford Township	16	15	1
Hempfield Township	7	6	1	Lower Saucon Township	15	10	5
Hermitage	28	25	3	Lower Southampton Township	29	26	3
Hilltown Township	16	14	2	Lower Windsor Township	5	5	—
Hollidaysburg	13	8	5	Lower Yoder Township	3	3	—
Honesdale	6	6	—	Lykens	1	1	—
Honey Brook Township	2	2	—	Macungie	4	4	—
Hooversville	1	1	—	Malvern	6	5	1
Hopewell Township	14	14	—	Manheim	7	6	1
Horsham Township	45	37	8	Manheim Township	64	48	16
Hummelstown	6	6	—	Manor	2	2	—
Independence Township	3	3	—	Manor Township	18	16	2
Indiana	24	19	5	Marlborough Township	4	4	—
Indiana Township	8	8	—	Marple Township	36	29	7
Ingram	6	6	—	Martinsburg	2	2	—
Jackson Township (Cambria County)	1	1	—	Marysville	3	3	—
Jackson Township (York County)	8	7	1	Masontown	5	5	—
Jeannette	17	16	1	Matamoras	2	2	—
Jefferson	15	14	1	McAdoo	3	3	—
Jefferson Township	3	3	—	McCandless	34	28	6
Jermyn	1	1	—	McConnellsburg	2	2	—
Jim Thorpe	4	4	—	McDonald	3	3	—
Johnsonburg	5	5	—	McKeesport	33	31	2
Johnstown	53	44	9	McKees Rocks	13	9	4
Kane	6	6	—	McSherrystown	3	3	—
Kennedy Township	11	10	1	Meadville	29	22	7
Kennett Square	8	6	2	Mechanicsburg	15	14	1
Kidder Township	6	6	—	Media	20	13	7
Kilbuck Township	3	3	—	Meyersdale	4	4	—
Kingston	22	18	4	Mid-Cumberland Valley Regional	12	11	1
Kingston Township	10	10	—	Middlesex Township (Butler County)	6	6	—
Kittanning	9	8	1	Middlesex Township (Cumberland County)	8	7	1
Kline Township	2	2	—	Middletown	14	13	1
Laflin Boro	3	3	—	Midland	6	6	—
Lake City	3	3	—	Mifflin County Regional	23	22	1
Lancaster	149	137	12	Mifflin Town	1	1	—

Table 78. — Number of Full-time Law Enforcement Employees, Cities, October 31, 1996 — Continued

City	Total police employees	Total officers	Total civilians	City	Total police employees	Total officers	Total civilians
PENNSYLVANIA — Continued				**PENNSYLVANIA — Continued**			
Millbourne	2	2	—	North Sewickley Township	2	2	—
Millcreek Township	68	55	13	North Strabane Township	12	11	1
Millersburg	4	3	1	Northumberland	5	5	—
Millersville	13	11	2	North Versailles Township	14	12	2
Millville	1	1	—	North Wales	3	3	—
Milton	10	9	1	Norwegian Township	1	1	—
Minersville	7	6	1	Norwood	7	6	1
Mohnton	2	2	—	Oakdale	1	1	—
Monessen	12	12	—	Oakmont	8	7	1
Monongahela	12	8	4	O'Hara Township	14	13	1
Monroeville	69	54	15	Ohio Township	5	4	1
Montgomery Township	41	31	10	Old Lycoming Township	8	7	1
Moon Township	35	29	6	Oley Township	1	1	—
Moore Township	6	5	1	Olyphant	5	5	—
Moosic	2	2	—	Orangeville	1	1	—
Morrisville	12	10	2	Oxford	7	7	—
Morton	5	5	—	Paint Township	2	2	—
Mount Joy	11	9	2	Palmerton	8	7	1
Mount Joy Township	7	6	1	Palmer Township	25	21	4
Mount Lebanon	59	42	17	Palmyra	8	8	—
Mount Oliver	3	3	—	Parkside	2	2	—
Mount Pleasant	5	5	—	Patton Township	14	13	1
Mount Union	6	6	—	Paxtang	2	2	—
Muhlenberg Township	25	23	2	Pen Argyl	3	3	—
Munhall	19	15	4	Penbrook	6	6	—
Murrysville	21	17	4	Penn Hills	65	56	9
Myerstown	4	4	—	Pennridge Regional	16	14	2
Nanticoke	16	13	3	Penn Township (Butler County)	5	4	1
Narberth	6	6	—	Penn Township (Lancaster County)	6	6	—
Nazareth Area	7	5	2	Penn Township (Westmoreland County)	23	20	3
Neshannock Township	4	4	—	Pequea Township	3	3	—
Nesquehoning	3	3	—	Perkasie	12	11	1
Neville Township	8	6	2	Peters Township	22	19	3
New Britain	2	2	—	Philadelphia	7,410	6,455	955
New Britain Township	12	11	1	Philipsburg	3	3	—
New Castle	37	37	—	Phoenixville	23	21	2
New Cumberland	8	8	—	Pine Grove	3	3	—
New Hanover Township	5	5	—	Pine Township	14	13	1
New Holland	9	8	1	Pitcairn	4	4	—
New Hope	7	6	1	Pittsburgh	1,209	1,148	61
New Oxford	2	2	—	Pittston	9	6	3
Newport Township	2	2	—	Plainfield Township	7	7	—
Newtown	3	3	—	Plains Township	11	11	—
Newtown Township (Bucks County)	21	18	3	Pleasant Hills	18	14	4
Newtown Township (Delaware County)	14	13	1	Plum	24	19	5
New Wilmington	4	4	—	Plumstead Township	11	9	2
Norristown	83	65	18	Plymouth	2	2	—
Northampton	12	12	—	Plymouth Township	43	35	8
Northampton Township	42	37	5	Pocono Mountain Regional	19	17	2
North Belle Vernon	2	2	—	Pocono Township	11	11	—
North Cornwall Township	7	6	1	Portage	2	2	—
North Coventry Township	10	9	1	Port Allegany	3	3	—
North East	7	6	1	Pottstown	49	39	10
Northeastern Berks Regional	8	8	—	Pottsville	30	29	1
Northeastern Regional	7	6	1	Prospect Park	8	8	—
Northern Cambria Regional	2	2	—	Punxsutawney	15	9	6
North Fayette Township	20	14	6	Pymatuning Township	4	4	—
North Franklin Township	6	6	—	Quakertown	16	14	2
North Huntingdon Township	29	23	6	Quarreyville	2	2	—
North Lebanon Township	9	8	1	Rankin	1	1	—
North Londonderry Township	6	6	—	Reading	225	197	28
North Middleton Township	7	7	—	Red Lion	9	8	1

Table 78. — Number of Full-time Law Enforcement Employees, Cities, October 31, 1996 — Continued

City	Total police employees	Total officers	Total civilians	City	Total police employees	Total officers	Total civilians
PENNSYLVANIA — Continued				**PENNSYLVANIA — Continued**			
Redstone Township	2	2	—	South Waverly	3	3	—
Reserve Township	3	3	—	Southwest Greensburg	2	2	—
Reynoldsville	2	2	—	S.W. Mercer County Regional	15	13	2
Richland	1	1	—	South Whitehall Township	35	32	3
Richland Township (Allegheny County)	11	10	1	South Williamsport	6	6	—
Richland Township (Cambria County)	21	19	2	Spring City	5	4	1
Ridgway	6	6	—	Springdale	3	3	—
Ridley Township	43	34	9	Springfield Township (Bucks County)	4	4	—
Riverside	3	3	—	Springfield Township (Delaware County)	39	32	7
Roaring Spring	2	2	—	Springfield Township (Montgomery County)	30	29	1
Robesonia Boro	2	2	—	Spring Garden Township	18	17	1
Robeson Township	6	5	1	Spring Township (Berks County)	21	20	1
Robinson Township	22	17	5	State College	65	57	8
Rochester	13	11	2	Steelton	10	9	1
Rochester Township	1	1	—	Stoneycreek Township	3	3	—
Rockledge	4	4	—	Stowe Township	8	7	1
Ross Township	45	37	8	Strasburg	4	4	—
Rostraver Township	12	11	1	Stroudsburg	16	12	4
Royersford	7	6	1	Stroud Township	16	14	2
St. Clair	5	5	—	Sugarcreek	7	5	2
St. Marys	15	13	2	Sugarloaf Township	1	1	—
Salisbury Township	11	9	2	Summerhill Township	2	2	—
Sandy Lake	1	1	—	Summit Hill	4	4	—
Sandy Township	5	5	—	Sunbury	18	15	3
Sayre	10	8	2	Susquehanna Township (Cambria County)	2	2	—
Schuylkill Haven	12	8	4	Susquehanna Township (Dauphin County)	33	30	3
Schuylkill Township	7	6	1	Swarthmore	8	8	—
Scottsdale	7	7	—	Swatara Township	31	29	2
Scott Township (Allegheny County)	20	19	1	Swissvale	12	9	3
Selinsgrove	4	3	1	Sykesville	1	1	—
Seven Springs	7	5	2	Tamaqua	11	10	1
Sewickley	14	10	4	Tarentum	11	6	5
Sewickley Heights	8	7	1	Teleford	6	5	1
Shaler Township	29	28	1	Temple	2	2	—
Shamokin Dam	3	3	—	Tinicum Township (Bucks County)	4	4	—
Sharon	34	31	3	Tinicum Township (Delaware County)	9	8	1
Sharon Hill	8	7	1	Titusville	14	14	—
Sharpsburg	5	4	1	Towamencin Township	22	20	2
Sharpsville	6	5	1	Towanda	4	4	—
Shenandoah	7	6	1	Trafford	2	2	—
Shenango Township (Lawrence County)	4	4	—	Trainer	5	4	1
Shenango Township (Mercer County)	3	2	1	Tredyffrin Township	57	49	8
Shippingport	2	2	—	Tullytown	8	7	1
Shiremanstown	2	2	—	Tunkhannock	5	5	—
Silver Spring Township	11	10	1	Turtle Creek	7	5	2
Sinking Spring	4	4	—	Union City	5	4	1
Slatington	6	6	—	Union Township (Washington County)	6	6	—
Slippery Rock	5	5	—	Upland	2	2	—
Solebury Township	9	8	1	Upper Allen Township	15	14	1
Somerset	5	4	1	Upper Chichester Township	22	20	2
Souderton	7	6	1	Upper Darby Township	112	103	9
South Abington Township	10	9	1	Upper Dublin Township	41	36	5
South Beaver Township	3	3	—	Upper Gwynedd Township	18	17	1
South Centre Township	5	5	—	Upper Makefield Township	7	7	—
Southern	7	6	1	Upper Moreland Township	51	40	11
South Fayette Township	17	16	1	Upper Nazareth Township	3	3	—
South Fork	1	1	—	Upper Pottsgrove Township	10	4	6
South Greensburg	2	2	—	Upper Providence Township (Montgomery County)	12	11	1
South Heidelberg Township	5	5	—				
South Lebanon Township	7	6	1	Upper St. Clair Township	36	29	7
South Londonderry Township	4	4	—	Upper Saucon Township	14	13	1
South Park Township	17	16	1	Upper Southampton Township	24	21	3

Table 78. — Number of Full-time Law Enforcement Employees, Cities, October 31, 1996 — Continued

City	Total police employees	Total officers	Total civilians	City	Total police employees	Total officers	Total civilians
PENNSYLVANIA — Continued				**RHODE ISLAND — Continued**			
Upper Uwchlan Township	8	7	1	Charlestown	22	17	5
Upper Yoder Township	6	6	—	Coventry	63	50	13
Uwchlan Township	23	21	2	Cranston	176	145	31
Valley Township	6	6	—	Cumberland	51	44	7
Vandergrift	9	9	—	East Greenwich	38	33	5
Vanport Township	2	2	—	East Providence	104	85	19
Vernon Township	3	3	—	Foster	11	7	4
Verona	4	3	1	Glocester	14	10	4
Versailles	2	2	—	Hopkinton	14	9	5
Warminster Township	50	44	6	Jamestown	17	13	4
Warren	17	13	4	Johnston	85	68	17
Warwick Township (Lancaster County)	16	14	2	Lincoln	38	33	5
Washington Township (Westmoreland County)	5	5	—	Little Compton	12	8	4
Watsontown	4	4	—	Middletown	41	37	4
Waynesboro	16	15	1	Narragansett	41	34	7
Waynesburg	6	6	—	Newport	111	89	22
Weatherly	3	3	—	New Shoreham	8	3	5
Wellsboro	5	5	—	North Kingstown	57	49	8
Wernersville	2	2	—	North Providence	96	71	25
Wesleyville	4	4	—	North Smithfield	20	16	4
West Conshohocken	8	7	1	Pawtucket	175	148	27
West Deer Township	10	9	1	Portsmouth	29	27	2
West Donegal Township	6	6	—	Providence	501	435	66
West Earl Township	4	4	—	Richmond	9	6	3
Westfall Township	6	6	—	Scituate	20	15	5
West Grove	3	3	—	Smithfield	45	36	9
West Hempfield Township	16	14	2	South Kingstown	58	44	14
West Hills Regional	10	9	1	Tiverton	30	23	7
West Homestead	10	5	5	Warren	27	21	6
West Lampeter Township	10	9	1	Warwick	215	165	50
West Mifflin	42	35	7	Westerly	48	38	10
West Newton	4	4	—	West Greenwich	12	7	5
West Pottsgrove Township	7	7	—	West Warwick	68	62	6
Westtown Township	17	15	2	Woonsocket	106	98	8
West Whiteland Township	23	21	2				
West York	6	6	—	**SOUTH CAROLINA**			
Whitehall	23	18	5	Abbeville	22	16	6
Whitehall Township	52	43	9	Aiken	109	89	20
White Haven	2	2	—	Allendale	13	8	5
White Oak	11	11	—	Anderson	96	73	23
Whitpain Township	33	27	6	Andrews	18	13	5
Wiconisco Township	1	1	—	Atlantic Beach	6	3	3
Wilkes-Barre Township	16	12	4	Aynor	9	4	5
Wilkinsburg	44	39	5	Bamberg	10	9	1
Williamsport	58	55	3	Barnwell	11	10	1
Willistown Township	16	15	1	Batesburg-Leesville	24	19	5
Wilmerding	1	1	—	Beaufort	49	43	6
Windber	3	2	1	Belton	22	16	6
Wind Gap	3	3	—	Bennettsville	31	28	3
Windsor Township	9	8	1	Bishopville	18	13	5
Wrightsville	2	2	—	Blacksburg	10	9	1
Wyomissing	20	17	3	Blackville	9	8	1
Wyomissing Hills	4	4	—	Bluffton	4	4	—
Yardley	3	3	—	Bonneau	2	2	—
York	106	96	10	Bowman	6	5	1
York Springs-Latimore Township	3	3	—	Branchville	3	2	1
				Briarcliffe Acres	1	1	—
RHODE ISLAND				Burnettown	2	1	1
Barrington	27	24	3	Calhoun Falls	9	8	1
Bristol	46	35	11	Camden	25	23	2
Burrillville	27	21	6	Cameron	1	1	—
Central Falls	41	40	1	Campobello	2	2	—

Table 78. — Number of Full-time Law Enforcement Employees, Cities, October 31, 1996 — Continued

City	Total police employees	Total officers	Total civilians	City	Total police employees	Total officers	Total civilians
SOUTH CAROLINA — Continued				**SOUTH CAROLINA — Continued**			
Cayce	39	33	6	Kingstree	20	15	5
Central	6	6	—	Lake City	30	25	5
Chapin	2	2	—	Lake View	4	3	1
Charleston	418	315	103	Lamar	4	4	—
Cheraw	31	25	6	Lancaster	47	38	9
Chesnee	5	5	—	Landrum	8	7	1
Chester	28	25	3	Latta	9	7	2
Chesterfield	6	5	1	Laurens	25	19	6
Clemson	30	24	6	Lexington	22	19	3
Clinton	30	25	5	Liberty	13	9	4
Clio	3	3	—	Loris	9	5	4
Clover	11	11	—	Lyman	6	5	1
Columbia	326	288	38	Manning	15	14	1
Conway	43	33	10	Marion	30	23	7
Cowpens	5	4	1	Mauldin	37	28	9
Darlington	29	25	4	Mayesville	4	3	1
Denmark	10	9	1	McBee	2	2	—
Dillon	20	19	1	McColl	6	6	—
Due West	3	3	—	McCormick	7	7	—
Duncan	6	6	—	Moncks Corner	20	18	2
Easley	36	27	9	Mount Pleasant	104	71	33
Edgefield	8	8	—	Mullins	27	22	5
Edisto Beach	7	6	1	Myrtle Beach	162	121	41
Ehrhardt	2	2	—	Newberry	27	24	3
Elgin	3	2	1	New Ellenton	6	6	—
Elloree	4	4	—	Ninety Six	7	6	1
Estill	9	8	1	North	2	2	—
Eutawville	1	1	—	North Augusta	63	47	16
Fairfax	6	6	—	North Charleston	273	208	65
Florence	98	89	9	North Myrtle Beach	66	50	16
Folly Beach	13	8	5	Norway	5	2	3
Forest Acres	32	24	8	Orangeburg	90	78	12
Fort Lawn	1	1	—	Pacolet	5	4	1
Fort Mill	21	15	6	Pageland	16	11	5
Fountain Inn	22	16	6	Pamplico	6	4	2
Gaffney	36	29	7	Pawleys Island	2	2	—
Gaston	1	1	—	Pendleton	8	7	1
Georgetown	42	34	8	Perry	1	1	—
Goose Creek	41	32	9	Pickens	13	11	2
Great Falls	8	6	2	Pine Ridge	2	1	1
Greenville	216	176	40	Pinewood	3	3	—
Greenwood	59	52	7	Port Royal	13	12	1
Greer	51	42	9	Prosperity	3	3	—
Hampton	9	8	1	Ridgeland	9	9	—
Hanahan	28	21	7	Ridge Spring	4	4	—
Hardeeville	14	10	4	Ridgeway	2	2	—
Harleyville	3	2	1	Rock Hill	142	112	30
Hartsville	37	34	3	St. George	11	10	1
Hemingway	9	5	4	St. Matthews	7	7	—
Holly Hill	7	6	1	St. Stephens	7	7	—
Honea Path	15	11	4	Saluda	9	9	—
Inman	7	7	—	Santee	13	6	7
Irmo	18	16	2	Sellers	1	1	—
Isle of Palms	24	17	7	Seneca	36	30	6
Iva	4	3	1	Simpsonville	35	29	6
Jackson	4	4	—	Society Hill	7	4	3
Jamestown	2	1	1	South Congaree	3	3	—
Jefferson	3	3	—	Spartanburg	158	138	20
Johnsonville	5	4	1	Springdale	13	7	6
Johnston	8	7	1	Springfield	2	1	1
Jonesville	4	4	—	Sullivans Island	8	6	2
Kershaw	14	9	5	Summerton	5	5	—

City	Total police employees	Total officers	Total civilians	City	Total police employees	Total officers	Total civilians
SOUTH CAROLINA — Continued				**TENNESSEE — Continued**			
Summerville	51	48	3	Baxter	2	2	—
Sumter	123	89	34	Bolivar	24	20	4
Surfside Beach	16	11	5	Bradford	2	2	—
Tega Cay	10	6	4	Brentwood	44	35	9
Timmonsville	8	7	1	Bristol	77	63	14
Travelers Rest	19	13	6	Brownsville	34	30	4
Turbeville	2	1	1	Bruceton	5	5	—
Union	39	37	2	Carthage	11	7	4
Vance	1	1	—	Centerville	13	10	3
Varnville	6	3	3	Chattanooga	554	430	124
Wagener	4	4	—	Church Hill	9	8	1
Walhalla	12	11	1	Clarksville	181	158	23
Walterboro	36	27	9	Cleveland	89	73	16
Ware Shoals	10	9	1	Collegedale	10	10	—
Wellford	6	6	—	Collierville	61	47	14
West Columbia	43	34	9	Collinwood	4	3	1
Westminster	10	10	—	Columbia	85	76	9
West Pelzer	2	2	—	Cowan	3	3	—
West Union	1	1	—	Crossville	26	21	5
Whitmire	4	4	—	Cumberland Gap	2	2	—
Williamston	19	16	3	Dayton	14	12	2
Williston	8	8	—	Dresden	6	6	—
Winnsboro	26	21	5	Dyersburg	68	54	14
Woodruff	15	11	4	East Ridge	41	32	9
Yemassee	4	4	—	Elizabethton	30	28	2
York	27	21	6	Elkton	1	1	—
				Erwin	12	12	—
SOUTH DAKOTA				Estill Springs	5	5	—
Aberdeen	47	39	8	Etowah	19	12	7
Belle Fourche	8	7	1	Fairview	12	11	1
Box Elder	9	7	2	Fayetteville	29	22	7
Brookings	32	26	6	Franklin	82	64	18
Burke	1	1	—	Friendsville	2	2	—
Canton	5	5	—	Gallatin	52	43	9
Eagle Butte	4	3	1	Gates	2	2	—
Eureka	5	5	—	Gatlinburg	50	42	8
Harrisburg	1	1	—	Germantown	78	60	18
Hot Springs	8	7	1	Gleason	4	4	—
Madison	10	10	—	Goodlettsville	46	33	13
McLaughlin	4	2	2	Grand Junction	3	3	—
Miller	4	4	—	Greenbrier	6	6	—
Mitchell	32	22	10	Greeneville	44	42	2
North Sioux City	7	6	1	Halls	7	7	—
Parkston	2	2	—	Hartsville	10	9	1
Pierre	30	21	9	Henderson	12	12	—
Rapid City	122	96	26	Hendersonville	79	62	17
Sioux Falls	182	154	28	Hohenwald	9	9	—
Sisseton	7	7	—	Hollow Rock	3	3	—
Spearfish	20	14	6	Humboldt	29	23	6
Sturgis	14	13	1	Huntingdon	16	10	6
Vermillion	18	17	1	Jacksboro	3	3	—
Winner	17	8	9	Jackson	214	173	41
Yankton	41	25	16	Jefferson City	20	19	1
				Johnson City	167	137	30
TENNESSEE				Jonesborough	15	11	4
				Kenton	4	4	—
Adamsville	10	7	3	Kingsport	138	96	42
Algood	6	6	—	Knoxville	474	383	91
Ardmore	8	5	3	Lafayette	15	12	3
Ashland City	9	9	—	La Follette	24	18	6
Athens	29	28	1	Lake City	10	7	3
Bartlett	79	59	20	La Vergne	30	23	7

Table 78. — Number of Full-time Law Enforcement Employees, Cities, October 31, 1996 — Continued

City	Total police employees	Total officers	Total civilians	City	Total police employees	Total officers	Total civilians
TENNESSEE — Continued				**TENNESSEE — Continued**			
Lawrenceburg	45	33	12	Woodbury	9	8	1
Lexington	28	24	4	**TEXAS**			
Livingston	19	14	5	Abernathy	3	3	—
Loudon	16	15	1	Abilene	227	170	57
Manchester	29	28	1	Addison	67	52	15
Martin	31	24	7	Alamo	22	16	6
Maryville	43	39	4	Alamo Heights	26	19	7
Mason	4	4	—	Alice	47	32	15
McEwen	3	3	—	Allen	49	33	16
McKenzie	15	11	4	Alpine	18	11	7
McMinnville	38	33	5	Alto	3	3	—
Memphis	2,002	1,469	533	Alvarado	12	6	6
Millersville	10	7	3	Alvin	57	40	17
Millington	34	27	7	Amarillo	319	244	75
Minor Hill	4	2	2	Andrews	16	14	2
Morristown	72	67	5	Angleton	42	31	11
Mount Juliet	21	15	6	Anson	5	4	1
Mount Pleasant	12	11	1	Anthony	8	8	—
Nashville	1,563	1,166	397	Aransas Pass	24	18	6
Newbern	15	10	5	Argyle	5	5	—
New Johnsonville	5	5	—	Arlington	597	454	143
New Tazewell	8	8	—	Arp	3	2	1
Norris	7	7	—	Athens	30	23	7
Oak Ridge	64	49	15	Atlanta	18	13	5
Obion	3	3	—	Austin	1,352	935	417
Oliver Springs	14	9	5	Azle	31	21	10
Parsons	6	6	—	Baird	2	2	—
Pigeon Forge	50	40	10	Balch Springs	38	28	10
Pikeville	3	3	—	Balcones Heights	20	15	5
Portland	21	16	5	Ballinger	10	5	5
Pulaski	25	23	2	Bangs	2	2	—
Red Bank	25	19	6	Bastrop	13	11	2
Ripley	29	24	5	Bay City	45	36	9
Rockwood	13	13	—	Bayou Vista	5	5	—
Rutherford	4	4	—	Baytown	142	112	30
Savannah	14	14	—	Beaumont	327	259	68
Sevierville	49	39	10	Bedford	100	71	29
Sewanee	12	8	4	Beeville	28	22	6
Sharon	4	4	—	Bellaire	53	39	14
Shelbyville	39	33	6	Bellmead	20	15	5
Signal Mountain	16	14	2	Bellville	10	9	1
Smyrna	61	44	17	Belton	32	22	10
Soddy-Daisy	25	21	4	Benbrook	40	32	8
Somerville	12	9	3	Bertram	2	2	—
South Carthage	4	4	—	Beverly Hills	7	6	1
South Fulton	9	7	2	Big Sandy	3	3	—
South Pittsburg	9	9	—	Big Spring	66	44	22
Sparta	16	15	1	Bishop	9	5	4
Spring City	10	6	4	Blanco	4	4	—
Springfield	43	32	11	Blue Mound	9	5	4
Spring Hill	14	13	1	Boerne	17	15	2
Sweetwater	17	16	1	Bonham	23	17	6
Tazewell	13	7	6	Borger	27	20	7
Town of Decaturville	1	1	—	Bovina	2	2	—
Trenton	22	17	5	Bowie	17	11	6
Trimble	3	3	—	Brady	16	9	7
Union City	36	29	7	Brazoria	13	8	5
Waverly	15	10	5	Breckenridge	15	10	5
Westmoreland	10	6	4	Brenham	43	30	13
White House	17	10	7	Bridge City	18	13	5
Winchester	24	19	5	Bridgeport	12	7	5

Table 78. — Number of Full-time Law Enforcement Employees, Cities, October 31, 1996 — Continued

City	Total police employees	Total officers	Total civilians	City	Total police employees	Total officers	Total civilians
TEXAS — Continued				**TEXAS — Continued**			
Brookshire	13	9	4	De Leon	3	3	—
Brownfield	24	18	6	Del Rio	79	60	19
Brownsville	243	179	64	Denison	52	43	9
Brownwood	44	31	13	Denton	139	110	29
Bruceville-Eddy	4	4	—	Denver City	14	8	6
Bryan	119	100	19	DeSoto	73	53	20
Bullard	2	2	—	Devine	13	8	5
Burkburnett	19	15	4	Diboll	16	12	4
Burleson	47	36	11	Dickinson	24	19	5
Burnet	11	10	1	Dilley	7	6	1
Caddo Mills	1	1	—	Dimmitt	9	7	2
Caldwell	12	11	1	Donna	27	18	9
Cameron	14	9	5	Dublin	9	7	2
Caney City	5	3	2	Dumas	37	29	8
Canton	21	12	9	Duncanville	76	54	22
Canyon	18	16	2	Eagle Lake	6	5	1
Carrollton	200	134	66	Eagle Pass	67	51	16
Carthage	20	13	7	Early	6	5	1
Castle Hills	25	19	6	Earth	3	3	—
Cedar Hill	47	35	12	Eastland	10	8	2
Cedar Park	38	27	11	Edcouch	10	8	2
Celina	5	5	—	Eden	3	3	—
Center	18	12	6	Edgewood	5	5	—
Childress	16	10	6	Edinburg	88	64	24
Cisco	9	8	1	Edna	10	9	1
Clarksville	13	8	5	El Campo	32	23	9
Cleburne	53	42	11	Electra	11	6	5
Cleveland	26	17	9	Elgin	17	12	5
Clifton	5	4	1	El Paso	1,231	981	250
Clute	26	18	8	Elsa	12	10	2
Cockrell Hill	18	13	5	Ennis	34	28	6
Coffee City	1	1	—	Euless	98	72	26
Coleman	16	9	7	Everman	17	12	5
College Station	120	84	36	Fairfield	7	7	—
Colleyville	31	24	7	Fair Oaks Ranch	7	7	—
Colorado City	13	8	5	Falfurrias	10	9	1
Columbus	7	6	1	Farmers Branch	87	71	16
Comanche	8	7	1	Farmersville	5	5	—
Combes	3	3	—	Ferris	16	14	2
Commerce	17	12	5	Flatonia	2	2	—
Conroe	76	58	18	Florence	1	1	—
Converse	22	20	2	Floresville	10	9	1
Coppell	46	36	10	Flower Mound	50	36	14
Copperas Cove	58	43	15	Floydada	5	5	—
Corinth	11	10	1	Forest Hill	27	20	7
Corpus Christi	574	404	170	Forney	13	8	5
Corrigan	9	6	3	Fort Stockton	25	17	8
Corsicana	55	45	10	Fort Worth	1,479	1,166	313
Crane	11	6	5	Frankston	8	5	3
Crockett	16	14	2	Fredericksburg	18	16	2
Crowley	24	18	6	Freeport	36	26	10
Crystal City	11	8	3	Freer	8	4	4
Cuero	12	11	1	Friendswood	48	34	14
Cuney	2	2	—	Friona	11	7	4
Daingerfield	6	5	1	Frisco	31	23	8
Dalhart	18	11	7	Gainesville	40	31	9
Dallas	3,553	2,822	731	Galena Park	22	17	5
Dalworthington Gardens	9	8	1	Galveston	178	151	27
Dayton	17	12	5	Garland	399	283	116
Decatur	15	11	4	Gatesville	17	11	6
Deer Park	63	48	15	Georgetown	51	33	18
De Kalb	7	6	1	Giddings	12	8	4

City	Total police employees	Total officers	Total civilians	City	Total police employees	Total officers	Total civilians
TEXAS — Continued				**TEXAS — Continued**			
Gilmer	12	11	1	Irving	401	278	123
Gladewater	20	14	6	Itasca	3	3	—
Glenn Heights	12	7	5	Jacinto City	19	14	5
Gonzales	15	10	5	Jacksboro	8	7	1
Graham	16	14	2	Jacksonville	32	23	9
Granbury	21	18	3	Jamaica Beach	5	5	—
Grand Prairie	246	167	79	Jasper	25	17	8
Grand Saline	5	5	—	Jefferson	6	5	1
Granger	2	2	—	Jersey Village	19	13	6
Granite Shoals	5	5	—	Johnson City	3	3	—
Grapeland	2	2	—	Joshua	9	9	—
Grapevine	97	69	28	Jourdanton	6	6	—
Greenville	62	42	20	Junction	4	4	—
Groesbeck	6	5	1	Karnes City	6	5	1
Groves	17	16	1	Katy	26	18	8
Gruver	2	2	—	Kaufman	20	14	6
Gun Barrel City	17	13	4	Keene	12	7	5
Hale Center	4	4	—	Keller	35	24	11
Hallettsville	5	4	1	Kemah	14	10	4
Haltom City	83	63	20	Kemp	4	4	—
Hamlin	10	5	5	Kendleton	12	12	—
Harker Heights	38	27	11	Kennedale	18	13	5
Harlingen	130	102	28	Kermit	14	8	6
Hart	1	1	—	Kerrville	62	46	16
Haskell	4	4	—	Kilgore	36	28	8
Hawkins	2	2	—	Killeen	173	136	37
Hawley	1	1	—	Kingsville	59	45	14
Hearne	20	13	7	Kirby	17	12	5
Heath	7	6	1	Kirbyville	3	3	—
Hedwig Village	23	17	6	Knox City	2	2	—
Helotes	6	6	—	Kountze	6	5	1
Hemphill	4	4	—	Kress	1	1	—
Hempstead	11	10	1	Kyle	5	5	—
Henderson	34	28	6	Lacy-Lakeview	13	9	4
Hereford	32	26	6	La Feria	13	9	4
Hewitt	23	16	7	Lago Vista	15	9	6
Hico	3	3	—	La Grange	5	4	1
Hidalgo	31	24	7	La Joya	14	9	5
Highland Park	64	51	13	Lake Dallas	14	8	6
Highland Village	21	15	6	Lake Jackson	48	34	14
Hill Country Village	7	7	—	Lakeside	4	3	1
Hillsboro	26	20	6	Lakeview	15	12	3
Hitchcock	20	15	5	Lakeway Village	25	20	5
Holland	1	1	—	Lake Worth	26	20	6
Holliday	1	1	—	La Marque	28	22	6
Hollywood Park	7	7	—	Lamesa	23	17	6
Hondo	15	13	2	Lampasas	16	11	5
Hooks	4	4	—	Lancaster	44	36	8
Horizon City	7	7	—	La Porte	79	56	23
Horseshoe Bay	7	6	1	Laredo	324	264	60
Houston	7,335	5,252	2,083	La Vernia	4	4	—
Hubbard	4	4	—	La Villa	6	5	1
Humble	62	50	12	Lavon	4	4	—
Huntington	4	4	—	League City	79	54	25
Huntsville	51	38	13	Leander	15	9	6
Hurst	96	63	33	Leon Valley	33	25	8
Hutchins	17	11	6	Levelland	25	18	7
Hutto	3	3	—	Lewisville	130	87	43
Idalou	3	3	—	Lexington	2	2	—
Ingleside	18	12	6	Liberty	20	14	6
Ingram	6	6	—	Lindale	12	8	4
Iowa Park	15	10	5	Littlefield	17	11	6

Table 78. — Number of Full-time Law Enforcement Employees, Cities, October 31, 1996 — Continued

City	Total police employees	Total officers	Total civilians	City	Total police employees	Total officers	Total civilians
TEXAS — Continued				**TEXAS — Continued**			
Live Oak	27	20	7	Nolanville	3	3	—
Livingston	20	11	9	Northcrest	4	4	—
Llano	8	7	1	North Richland Hills	129	83	46
Lockhart	16	16	—	Oak Ridge North	10	10	—
Lockney	3	3	—	Odessa	224	178	46
Lone Oak	1	1	—	Olmos Park	11	11	—
Lone Star	3	3	—	Olney	10	6	4
Longview	195	144	51	Olton	4	4	—
Lorena	4	4	—	Onalaska	4	4	—
Los Fresnos	17	12	5	Orange	56	43	13
Lubbock	340	299	41	Orange Grove	3	3	—
Lufkin	90	68	22	Ore City	3	3	—
Luling	14	8	6	Overton	9	6	3
Lumberton	13	11	2	Oyster Creek	9	5	4
Lytle	5	5	—	Palacios	9	6	3
Madisonville	7	6	1	Palestine	44	34	10
Magnolia	5	5	—	Palmer	4	4	—
Malakoff	5	5	—	Pampa	33	28	5
Manor	7	6	1	Panhandle	5	4	1
Mansfield	45	34	11	Pantego	16	11	5
Manvel	6	6	—	Paris	78	56	22
Marble Falls	22	14	8	Parker	1	1	—
Marfa	6	4	2	Pasadena	277	219	58
Marlin	17	13	4	Pearland	69	45	24
Marshall	63	46	17	Pearsall	10	9	1
Marshall Creek	1	1	—	Pecos	25	19	6
Mart	3	3	—	Pelican Bay	3	2	1
Martindale	3	3	—	Perryton	14	8	6
Mathis	7	7	—	Pflugerville	25	18	7
McAllen	279	185	94	Pharr	77	60	17
McGregor	11	7	4	Pilot Point	5	5	—
McKinney	62	46	16	Pinehurst	8	5	3
Meadows	14	14	—	Pittsburg	10	9	1
Memphis	5	3	2	Planview	41	33	8
Mercedes	34	24	10	Plano	331	233	98
Meridian	2	2	—	Pleasanton	20	13	7
Merkel	4	4	—	Point Comfort	2	2	—
Mesquite	256	193	63	Port Aransas	16	11	5
Mexia	22	17	5	Port Arthur	137	109	28
Midland	211	159	52	Port Isabel	25	18	7
Midlothian	21	16	5	Portland	26	19	7
Mineola	12	10	2	Port Lavaca	26	20	6
Mineral Wells	34	27	7	Port Neches	20	17	3
Mission	102	82	20	Poteet	6	5	1
Missouri City	60	45	15	Pottsboro	4	4	—
Monahans	20	13	7	Premont	5	5	—
Mont Belvieu	13	8	5	Primera	3	3	—
Morgans Point Resort	5	5	—	Princeton	4	4	—
Mount Pleasant	33	25	8	Quanah	4	4	—
Muleshoe	10	5	5	Quinlan	7	6	1
Munday	2	2	—	Quitman	6	6	—
Mustang Ridge	3	3	—	Ranger	4	4	—
Nacogdoches	67	53	14	Ransom Canyon	2	2	—
Naples	2	2	—	Raymondville	22	14	8
Nassau Bay	18	13	5	Red Oak	14	8	6
Navasota	23	16	7	Refugio	5	4	1
Nederland	29	19	10	Richardson	230	142	88
Needville	6	5	1	Richland Hills	23	15	8
New Boston	11	7	4	Richmond	28	22	6
New Braunfels	74	55	19	Richwood	6	5	1
New Deal	1	1	—	Riesel	2	1	1
Nocona	9	6	3	Rio Grande City	25	19	6

City	Total police employees	Total officers	Total civilians	City	Total police employees	Total officers	Total civilians
TEXAS — Continued				**TEXAS — Continued**			
River Oaks	21	15	6	South Houston	41	32	9
Roanoke	14	10	4	Southlake	47	38	9
Robinson	16	11	5	South Padre Island	31	22	9
Robstown	29	20	9	Southside Place	11	9	2
Rockdale	16	10	6	Spearman	8	5	3
Rockport	25	19	6	Springtown	9	5	4
Rockwall	41	28	13	Spring Valley	20	15	5
Rollingwood	5	5	—	Spur	2	2	—
Roma	22	16	6	Stafford	44	31	13
Roman Forest	6	6	—	Stamford	8	8	—
Ropesville	1	1	—	Stanton	5	5	—
Roscoe	1	1	—	Stephenville	37	28	9
Rosebud	3	3	—	Stratford	3	3	—
Rose City	2	1	1	Sugar Land	109	77	32
Rosenberg	76	61	15	Sulphur Springs	46	34	12
Round Rock	96	72	24	Sunset Valley	7	7	—
Rowlett	77	47	30	Surfside Beach	4	4	—
Royse City	6	5	1	Sweeny	6	5	1
Rule	1	1	—	Sweetwater	25	20	5
Rusk	9	8	1	Taft	6	6	—
Sabinal	4	3	1	Tahoka	4	4	—
Sachse	19	14	5	Tarleton Station	12	10	2
Saginaw	26	20	6	Tatum	4	3	1
St. Jo	2	2	—	Taylor	29	20	9
San Angelo	190	164	26	Teague	6	6	—
San Angelo Park	2	2	—	Temple	131	106	25
San Antonio	2,304	1,868	436	Terrell	42	32	10
San Augustine	7	6	1	Terrell Hills	16	15	1
San Benito	58	52	6	Texarkana	90	81	9
San Diego	4	4	—	Texas City	95	78	17
Sanger	8	8	—	The Colony	37	26	11
San Juan	29	22	7	Thrall	2	1	1
San Marcos	83	64	19	Three Rivers	5	4	1
Sansom Park Village	13	9	4	Tomball	31	25	6
Santa Anna	1	1	—	Tool	6	6	—
Santa Fe	22	15	7	Trinity	9	4	5
Santa Rosa	4	4	—	Trophy Club	10	9	1
Schertz	30	22	8	Troup	5	5	—
Seabrook	28	24	4	Tulia	13	8	5
Seadrift	3	3	—	Tye	2	2	—
Seagoville	17	14	3	Tyler	222	161	61
Sealy	12	11	1	Universal City	34	26	8
Seguin	55	40	15	University Park	41	33	8
Selma	9	8	1	Uvalde	25	20	5
Seminole	12	10	2	Van	4	4	—
Seven Points	11	6	5	Vernon	28	21	7
Seymour	7	6	1	Victoria	140	102	38
Shallowater	4	4	—	Vidor	28	21	7
Shamrock	5	2	3	Village	37	31	6
Shavano Park	10	10	—	Village of Jones Creek	4	3	1
Shenandoah	8	8	—	Waco	296	221	75
Sherman	78	57	21	Wake Village	4	4	—
Silsbee	20	14	6	Waller	8	7	1
Sinton	11	9	2	Wallis	6	3	3
Slaton	14	8	6	Watauga	39	31	8
Smithville	15	9	6	Waxahachie	45	35	10
Snyder	21	18	3	Weatherford	53	36	17
Socorro	16	15	1	Webster	47	33	14
Somerset	3	3	—	Weimar	7	6	1
Somerville	4	4	—	Wells	4	3	1
Sonora	7	5	2	Weslaco	56	42	14
Sour Lake	4	4	—	West	4	4	—

City	Total police employees	Total officers	Total civilians	City	Total police employees	Total officers	Total civilians
TEXAS — Continued				**UTAH — Continued**			
West Columbia	12	8	4	Monticello	4	4	—
West Lake Hills	16	13	3	Moroni	1	1	—
West Orange	8	7	1	Mount Pleasant	6	5	1
Westover Hills	14	14	—	Murray	72	59	13
West Tawakoni	5	4	1	Naples	7	5	2
West University Place	28	21	7	Nephi	9	7	2
Westworth	9	5	4	North Park	6	5	1
Wharton	30	20	10	North Ogden	14	12	2
Whitehouse	16	10	6	North Salt Lake	11	10	1
White Oak	15	11	4	Ogden	136	111	25
Whitesboro	12	6	6	Orem	93	70	23
White Settlement	43	31	12	Park City	26	20	6
Whitney	6	5	1	Parowan	3	3	—
Wichita Falls	242	168	74	Payson	18	16	2
Willow Park	6	6	—	Perry	2	2	—
Wills Point	8	7	1	Pleasant Grove	22	21	1
Wilmer	15	11	4	Pleasant View	5	4	1
Windcrest	23	17	6	Price	18	16	2
Winnsboro	13	10	3	Provo	163	86	77
Winters	6	6	—	Richfield	12	9	3
Wolfforth	3	3	—	Riverdale	18	16	2
Woodville	7	6	1	Roosevelt	11	10	1
Woodway	29	20	9	Roy	40	31	9
Wylie	19	14	5	St. George	72	58	14
Yoakum	16	10	6	Salem	5	5	—
Yorktown	3	3	—	Salina	5	4	1
				Salt Lake City	542	385	157
UTAH				Sandy	121	98	23
Alpine	12	11	1	Santaquin	4	4	—
Alta	9	4	5	South Jordan	19	16	3
American Fork	28	24	4	South Ogden	23	19	4
Blanding	6	5	1	South Salt Lake	57	45	12
Bountiful	42	33	9	Spanish Fork	20	17	3
Brian Head	4	4	—	Springville	27	20	7
Brigham City	30	23	7	Sunset	9	8	1
Cedar City	24	21	3	Syracuse	7	6	1
Centerville	16	13	3	Tooele	24	21	3
Clearfield	30	26	4	Tremonton	9	7	2
Clinton	8	7	1	Vernal	17	15	2
East Carbon	4	4	—	Washington Terrace	14	12	2
Ephraim	5	5	—	Wellington	4	4	—
Fairview	1	1	—	Wendover	8	7	1
Farmington	13	10	3	West Bountiful	6	6	—
Garland	2	2	—	West Jordan	77	63	14
Grantsville	10	7	3	West Valley	168	143	25
Gunnison	3	3	—	Willard	2	2	—
Harrisville	5	4	1	Woods Cross	9	8	1
Heber City	9	8	1				
Helper	5	5	—	**VERMONT**			
Hildale	4	4	—	Barre	22	17	5
Hurricane	12	9	3	Barre Town	8	7	1
Kamas	2	2	—	Bellows Falls	12	8	4
Kanab	7	5	2	Bennington	30	25	5
Kaysville	15	13	2	Brandon	6	6	—
Layton	70	56	14	Brattleboro	36	24	12
Lehi	16	15	1	Bristol	3	3	—
Logan	63	49	14	Burlington	119	87	32
Mantua	1	1	—	Castleton	3	3	—
Mapleton	7	7	—	Chester	5	4	1
Midvale	28	26	2	Colchester	27	23	4
Minersville	1	1	—	Dover	4	3	1
Moab	15	13	2	Essex	28	22	6

City	Total police employees	Total officers	Total civilians	City	Total police employees	Total officers	Total civilians
VERMONT — Continued				**VIRGINIA — Continued**			
Fair Haven	2	2	—	Clarksville	6	5	1
Hardwick	8	7	1	Clifton Forge	17	11	6
Hartford	27	21	6	Clintwood	4	4	—
Ludlow	9	5	4	Coeburn	8	7	1
Manchester	13	8	5	Colonial Beach	12	8	4
Middlebury	13	11	2	Colonial Heights	56	41	15
Milton	12	11	1	Courtland	1	1	—
Montpelier	22	16	6	Covington	18	14	4
Morristown	8	7	1	Crewe	5	5	—
Newport	13	11	2	Culpeper	37	28	9
Northfield	6	5	1	Damascus	2	2	—
Norwich	5	4	1	Danville	125	119	6
Randolph	4	4	—	Dayton	4	4	—
Richmond	4	4	—	Dublin	8	7	1
Rutland	47	38	9	Dumfries	14	12	2
St. Albans	21	14	7	Edinburg	3	3	—
St. Johnsbury	17	11	6	Elkton	10	6	4
Shelburne	15	10	5	Emporia	25	19	6
South Burlington	34	29	5	Exmore	5	5	—
Springfield	21	16	5	Fairfax City	76	61	15
Stowe	10	8	2	Falls Church	40	29	11
Swanton	4	3	1	Farmville	28	19	9
Vergennes	4	4	—	Franklin	34	25	9
Vernon	5	4	1	Fredericksburg	82	59	23
Waterbury	3	3	—	Fries	1	1	—
Weathersfield	1	1	—	Front Royal	36	29	7
Williston	5	4	1	Galax	29	23	6
Wilmington	6	5	1	Gate City	4	4	—
Windsor	10	6	4	Glade Springs	3	3	—
Winhall	5	5	—	Glen Lyn	1	1	—
Winooski	17	13	4	Gordonsville	7	7	—
Woodstock	6	5	1	Gretna	2	2	—
				Grottoes	3	3	—
VIRGINIA				Grundy	6	6	—
Abingdon	19	17	2	Halifax	5	5	—
Alexandria	389	271	118	Hampton	339	245	94
Altavista	15	11	4	Harrisonburg	68	54	14
Amherst	5	5	—	Haysi	3	2	1
Appalachia	7	6	1	Herndon	51	41	10
Ashland	26	24	2	Hillsville	7	7	—
Bedford	27	21	6	Honaker	4	4	—
Berryville	8	7	1	Hopewell	61	45	16
Big Stone Gap	15	13	2	Hurt	3	3	—
Blacksburg	64	48	16	Independence	2	2	—
Blackstone	15	10	5	Jonesville	4	4	—
Bluefield	15	12	3	Kenbridge	6	6	—
Bowling Green	2	2	—	Kilmarnock	4	4	—
Boykins	1	1	—	La Crosse	3	3	—
Bridgewater	6	6	—	Lawrenceville	5	5	—
Bristol	72	53	19	Lebanon	11	10	1
Brookneal	3	3	—	Leesburg	45	41	4
Buena Vista	18	13	5	Lexington	21	16	5
Burkeville	3	3	—	Louisa	2	2	—
Cape Charles	2	2	—	Luray	14	13	1
Cedar Bluff	2	2	—	Lynchburg	191	144	47
Charlottesville	139	101	38	Manassas	87	69	18
Chase City	10	7	3	Manassas Park	21	13	8
Chatham	4	4	—	Marion	20	18	2
Chesapeake	390	315	75	Martinsville	60	54	6
Chilhowie	6	6	—	McKenney	1	1	—
Chincoteague	11	8	3	Middleburg	4	3	1
Christiansburg	40	32	8	Middletown	2	2	—

City	Total police employees	Total officers	Total civilians	City	Total police employees	Total officers	Total civilians
VIRGINIA — Continued				**WASHINGTON — Continued**			
Mount Jackson	3	3	—	Arlington	13	11	2
Narrows	6	6	—	Auburn	98	74	24
New Market	4	4	—	Bainbridge Island	22	18	4
Newport News	490	361	129	Battle Ground	15	13	2
Norfolk	854	731	123	Bellevue	245	157	88
Norton	22	16	6	Bellingham	153	96	57
Onancock	5	5	—	Bingen	2	2	—
Onley	2	2	—	Black Diamond	7	7	—
Orange	17	16	1	Blaine	15	13	2
Parksley	3	3	—	Bonney Lake	21	14	7
Pearisburg	7	7	—	Bothell	57	37	20
Pembroke	1	1	—	Bremerton	79	63	16
Pennington Gap	9	5	4	Brewster	10	8	2
Petersburg	153	107	46	Brier	7	6	1
Pocahontas	3	3	—	Buckley	17	8	9
Poquoson	23	18	5	Burlington	25	17	8
Portsmouth	352	241	111	Camas	20	16	4
Pound	4	4	—	Carnation	1	1	—
Pulaski	40	29	11	Castle Rock	6	5	1
Purcellville	7	7	—	Centralia	34	29	5
Quantico	3	3	—	Chehalis	22	18	4
Radford	37	26	11	Chelan	14	7	7
Rich Creek	1	1	—	Cheney	10	9	1
Richlands	20	15	5	Chewelah	6	5	1
Richmond	759	667	92	Clarkston	17	14	3
Roanoke	292	250	42	Cle Elum	9	6	3
Rocky Mount	14	13	1	Clyde Hill	8	7	1
Rural Retreat	1	1	—	Colfax	5	5	—
St. Paul	5	5	—	College Place	15	11	4
Salem	80	59	21	Colville	13	11	2
Saltville	6	5	1	Connell	7	7	—
Shenandoah	4	4	—	Cosmopolis	6	5	1
Smithfield	21	13	8	Coulee Dam	4	4	—
South Boston	22	19	3	Darrington	4	3	1
South Hill	21	16	5	Davenport	2	2	—
Stanley	3	3	—	Des Moines	50	39	11
Staunton	63	47	16	Duvall	7	6	1
Stephens City	3	3	—	East Wenatchee	15	13	2
Strasburg	11	10	1	Eatonville	6	6	—
Suffolk	151	117	34	Edmonds	63	46	17
Tappahannock	8	8	—	Ellensburg	26	19	7
Tazewell	12	11	1	Elma	8	7	1
Victoria	3	3	—	Elmer City	1	1	—
Vienna	49	38	11	Enumclaw	29	22	7
Vinton	24	17	7	Ephrata	19	12	7
Virginia Beach	881	678	203	Everson	5	4	1
Warrenton	20	18	2	Ferndale	13	11	2
Warsaw	3	3	—	Fife	26	19	7
Waverly	8	4	4	Fircrest	10	8	2
Waynesboro	50	46	4	Forks	13	7	6
Weber City	5	5	—	Gig Harbor	11	9	2
Williamsburg	43	30	13	Goldendale	8	7	1
Winchester	78	57	21	Grand Coulee	3	3	—
Wise	12	11	1	Grandview	21	15	6
Woodstock	13	12	1	Granite Falls	8	7	1
Wytheville	37	24	13	Harrington	1	1	—
				Hoquiam	26	21	5
WASHINGTON				Issaquah	31	20	11
Aberdeen	50	37	13	Kalama	6	5	1
Airway Heights	8	7	1	Kelso	33	29	4
Algona	8	6	2	Kennewick	96	76	20
Anacortes	33	19	14	Kent	152	105	47

Table 78. — Number of Full-time Law Enforcement Employees, Cities, October 31, 1996 — Continued

City	Total police employees	Total officers	Total civilians	City	Total police employees	Total officers	Total civilians
WASHINGTON — Continued				**WASHINGTON — Continued**			
Kettle Falls	6	5	1	Ruston	2	2	—
Kirkland	81	56	25	Seattle	1,776	1,238	538
Kittitas	3	3	—	Sedro Woolley	18	11	7
La Center	4	4	—	Selah	14	12	2
Lacey	54	40	14	Sequim	14	11	3
La Conner	5	5	—	Shelton	35	20	15
Lake Forest Park	32	24	8	Snohomish	20	17	3
Lake Stevens	8	8	—	Snoqualmie	11	9	2
Langley	3	3	—	Soap Lake	4	4	—
Long Beach	7	6	1	South Bend	5	4	1
Longview	60	53	7	Spokane	386	286	100
Lummi Tribal	18	16	2	Stanwood	10	8	2
Lynden	14	11	3	Steilacoom	12	11	1
Lynnwood	76	54	22	Sultan	7	5	2
Mabton	3	3	—	Sumner	24	17	7
Marysville	49	26	23	Sunnyside	34	23	11
McCleary	4	4	—	Swinomish Tribal	7	6	1
Medical Lake	8	7	1	Tacoma	425	370	55
Medina	9	7	2	Tekoa	2	2	—
Mercer Island	41	31	10	Tenino	6	5	1
Mill Creek	21	17	4	Tieton	3	3	—
Milton	11	10	1	Toledo	2	2	—
Monroe	23	20	3	Tonasket	5	4	1
Montesano	10	8	2	Toppenish	24	17	7
Morton	5	4	1	Tukwila	82	68	14
Moses Lake	34	25	9	Tumwater	26	22	4
Mossyrock	2	2	—	Twisp	3	3	—
Mountlake Terrace	37	31	6	Union Gap	20	15	5
Mount Vernon	45	36	9	Vancouver	118	108	10
Moxee	3	3	—	Waitsburg	2	2	—
Mukilteo	23	20	3	Walla Walla	46	39	7
Napavine	4	3	1	Wapato	16	11	5
Newport	3	3	—	Warden	5	5	—
Normandy Park	14	13	1	Washougal	13	11	2
Northport	1	1	—	Wenatchee	54	39	15
Oak Harbor	40	24	16	Westport	9	7	2
Ocean Shores	11	8	3	West Richland	14	11	3
Olympia	86	63	23	White Salmon	4	4	—
Omak	15	12	3	Wilbur	2	2	—
Oroville	8	7	1	Winlock	4	3	1
Othello	19	12	7	Winthrop	3	3	—
Pacific	10	8	2	Woodland	8	7	1
Pasco	54	44	10	Yakima	164	110	54
Pe Ell	2	2	—	Yelm	11	9	2
Pomeroy	3	3	—	Zillah	8	6	2
Port Angeles	53	29	24				
Port Orchard	14	13	1	**WEST VIRGINIA**			
Port Townsend	15	12	3	Alderson	2	2	—
Poulsbo	17	15	2	Anmoore	2	2	—
Prosser	15	10	5	Ansted	3	3	—
Pullman	36	24	12	Barboursville	16	15	1
Puyallup	69	50	19	Beckley	62	45	17
Rainier	5	5	—	Belington	3	3	—
Raymond	8	7	1	Belle	5	5	—
Redmond	82	60	22	Benwood	10	5	5
Renton	116	86	30	Bethlehem	4	4	—
Republic	2	2	—	Bluefield	32	29	3
Richland	55	50	5	Bridgeport	22	19	3
Ridgefield	5	4	1	Buckhannon	7	6	1
Ritzville	4	4	—	Cameron	4	4	—
Roslyn	2	2	—	Cedar Grove	1	1	—
Royal City	4	4	—	Ceredo	8	5	3

City	Total police employees	Total officers	Total civilians	City	Total police employees	Total officers	Total civilians
WEST VIRGINIA — Continued				**WEST VIRGINIA — Continued**			
Chapmanville	4	4	—	Parkersburg	79	64	15
Charleston	214	182	32	Parsons	2	2	—
Charles Town	12	10	2	Pennsboro	1	1	—
Chesapeake	4	4	—	Petersburg	4	4	—
Chester	5	5	—	Philippi	6	6	—
Clarksburg	44	39	5	Piedmont	2	2	—
Clendenin	3	3	—	Pineville	4	4	—
Danville	4	4	—	Point Pleasant	8	7	1
Delbarton	2	2	—	Princeton	24	22	2
Dunbar	18	13	5	Rainelle	4	4	—
Elkins	16	10	6	Ranson	9	8	1
Fairmont	42	32	10	Ravenswood	12	8	4
Fayetteville	6	5	1	Richwood	8	5	3
Follansbee	10	10	—	Ripley	9	8	1
Fort Gay	2	2	—	Romney	4	3	1
Gauley Bridge	1	1	—	Ronceverte	3	3	—
Glen Dale	6	5	1	St. Albans	27	20	7
Glenville	4	4	—	St. Marys	8	4	4
Grafton	12	8	4	Salem	3	3	—
Grantsville	2	2	—	Shepherdstown	5	4	1
Granville	2	2	—	Shinnston	5	5	—
Harpers Ferry/Bolivar	3	3	—	Sistersville	2	2	—
Harrisville	2	2	—	Smithers	5	5	—
Hinton	6	6	—	Sophia	6	6	—
Huntington	113	103	10	South Charleston	38	32	6
Hurricane	15	11	4	Spencer	7	6	1
Kenova	10	7	3	Star City	5	4	1
Kermit	4	3	1	Stonewood	3	3	—
Keyser	12	7	5	Summersville	14	13	1
Kimball	2	2	—	Sutton	3	3	—
Kingwood	6	6	—	Terra Alta	2	2	—
Lewisburg	11	9	2	Vienna	23	15	8
Logan	9	6	3	War	4	4	—
Lumberport	2	2	—	Wayne	3	2	1
Mabscott	5	5	—	Weirton	46	38	8
Madison	6	5	1	Welch	13	10	3
Man	4	4	—	Wellsburg	6	5	1
Mannington	4	4	—	Weston	9	8	1
Marlinton	3	2	1	Westover	10	8	2
Marmet	4	4	—	Wheeling	82	80	2
Martinsburg	47	41	6	White Sulphur Springs	8	7	1
Mason	3	3	—	Whitesville	2	2	—
Matewan	3	3	—	Williamson	11	9	2
McMechen	4	4	—	Williamstown	6	5	1
Milton	5	5	—				
Mitchell Heights	1	1	—	**WISCONSIN**			
Monongah	4	4	—	Algoma	6	6	—
Montgomery	9	8	1	Altoona	10	9	1
Moorefield	5	5	—	Amery	7	6	1
Morgantown	62	53	9	Antigo	20	17	3
Moundsville	18	12	6	Appleton	123	98	25
Mount Hope	6	6	—	Arcadia	4	4	—
Mullens	5	5	—	Ashland	26	20	6
New Cumberland	4	4	—	Ashwaubenon	45	36	9
New Haven	2	2	—	Bangor	3	3	—
New Martinsville	15	10	5	Baraboo	26	22	4
Nitro	18	13	5	Barron	6	6	—
North Fork	3	3	—	Bayfield	3	3	—
Nutter Fort	6	6	—	Bayside	21	15	6
Oak Hill	14	11	3	Beaver Dam	37	28	9
Oceana	5	5	—	Belleville	3	3	—
Paden City	8	4	4	Beloit	103	83	20

Table 78. — Number of Full-time Law Enforcement Employees, Cities, October 31, 1996 — Continued

City	Total police employees	Total officers	Total civilians	City	Total police employees	Total officers	Total civilians
WISCONSIN — Continued				**WISCONSIN — Continued**			
Beloit Town	10	9	1	Grand Chute	22	18	4
Berlin	17	12	5	Green Bay	241	186	55
Black Earth	3	3	—	Greendale	35	28	7
Black River Falls	10	9	1	Greenfield	92	59	33
Bloomfield	8	7	1	Green Lake	3	3	—
Brillion	6	6	—	Hales Corners	17	17	—
Brodhead	11	7	4	Hallie	7	6	1
Brookfield	84	63	21	Hartford	25	20	5
Brookfield Township	10	9	1	Hartland	16	14	2
Brown Deer	38	29	9	Hayward	7	6	1
Burlington	27	21	6	Hillsboro	2	2	—
Burlington Town	7	7	—	Holmen	8	7	1
Butler	8	7	1	Horicon	11	9	2
Caledonia	33	26	7	Hudson	20	17	3
Cedarburg	27	19	8	Hurley	7	6	1
Chenequa	9	9	—	Independence	2	2	—
Chetek	5	4	1	Jackson	6	5	1
Chilton	6	6	—	Janesville	103	91	12
Chippewa Falls	34	25	9	Jefferson	16	13	3
Clear Lake	1	1	—	Juneau	5	4	1
Clinton	5	5	—	Kaukauna	23	22	1
Clintonville	16	12	4	Kenosha	181	171	10
Colby-Abbotsford	7	6	1	Kewaskum	5	5	—
Columbus	13	9	4	Kewaunee	6	6	—
Combined Locks	4	4	—	Kiel	11	6	5
Cornell	4	4	—	Kohler	7	6	1
Cottage Grove	4	4	—	La Crosse	110	89	21
Crandon	3	3	—	Ladysmith	7	6	1
Cuba City	5	4	1	Lake Delton	11	10	1
Cudahy	42	32	10	Lake Geneva	24	17	7
Darien	6	6	—	Lake Mills	10	9	1
Darlington	5	4	1	Lancaster	8	7	1
De Forest	12	11	1	Lodi	6	5	1
Delafield	11	10	1	Madison	395	333	62
Delavan Town	9	9	—	Manitowoc	73	62	11
Delavan	19	15	4	Marinette	31	24	7
De Pere	31	27	4	Marshfield	51	38	13
Dodgeville	10	9	1	Mauston	8	7	1
Durand	4	4	—	Mayville	11	9	2
Eagle River	7	7	—	Mazomanie	3	3	—
East Troy	8	7	1	McFarland	10	9	1
Eau Claire	112	86	26	Medford	10	9	1
Edgar	1	1	—	Menasha	35	30	5
Edgerton	9	8	1	Menasha Town	25	21	4
Elkhorn	17	15	2	Menomonee Falls	70	59	11
Elm Grove	23	17	6	Menomonie	34	26	8
Elroy	4	3	1	Mequon	44	36	8
Everest	23	21	2	Merrill	26	22	4
Fall Creek	3	3	—	Middleton	34	26	8
Fennimore	5	5	—	Milton	9	8	1
Fitchburg	31	25	6	Milwaukee	2,848	2,130	718
Fond Du Lac	76	65	11	Minocqua	17	11	6
Fort Atkinson	23	18	5	Mondovi	4	4	—
Fox Lake	3	3	—	Monona	20	17	3
Fox Point	23	17	6	Monroe	33	25	8
Fox Valley	28	25	3	Mosinee	7	6	1
Franklin	50	38	12	Mount Horeb	9	8	1
Geneva Town	6	5	1	Mount Pleasant	33	25	8
Genoa City	4	4	—	Mukwonago	16	11	5
Germantown	38	28	10	Neenah	49	41	8
Glendale	48	47	1	Neillsville	7	6	1
Grafton	26	20	6	New Berlin	79	62	17

City	Total police employees	Total officers	Total civilians	City	Total police employees	Total officers	Total civilians
WISCONSIN — Continued				**WISCONSIN — Continued**			
New Glarus	5	5	—	Strum	2	2	—
New Holstein	10	6	4	Sturgeon Bay	19	18	1
New Lisbon	3	3	—	Sturtevant	12	10	2
New London	18	17	1	Summit	8	8	—
New Richmond	12	11	1	Sun Prairie	48	36	12
North Fond Du Lac	8	7	1	Theresa	1	1	—
Oak Creek	51	41	10	Thiensville	8	7	1
Oconomowoc	29	22	7	Tomah	23	18	5
Oconomowoc Town	11	10	1	Tomahawk	6	6	—
Oconto	8	8	—	Town of East Troy	7	6	1
Oconto Falls	6	6	—	Town of Madison	20	18	2
Omro	6	5	1	Twin Lakes	12	8	4
Onalaska	29	27	2	Two Rivers	29	25	4
Oregon	12	11	1	Verona	12	11	1
Osceola	4	4	—	Viroqua	11	9	2
Oshkosh	104	89	15	Walworth	7	6	1
Palmyra	4	4	—	Washburn	5	5	—
Pardeeville	3	3	—	Waterloo	7	6	1
Park Falls	8	7	1	Watertown	50	36	14
Peshtigo	6	6	—	Waukesha	132	100	32
Pewaukee	16	14	2	Waunakee	12	11	1
Pewaukee Township	11	10	1	Waupaca	17	13	4
Phillips	5	5	—	Waupun	22	15	7
Platteville	23	19	4	Wausau	72	58	14
Pleasant Prairie	21	20	1	Wauwatosa	115	87	28
Plover	13	12	1	West Allis	149	128	21
Plymouth	15	14	1	West Bend	67	51	16
Portage	29	21	8	Westby	4	4	—
Port Washington	23	17	6	West Milwaukee	24	19	5
Poynette	2	2	—	Whitefish Bay	28	24	4
Prairie du Chien	18	13	5	Whitehall	3	3	—
Prescott	6	5	1	Whitewater	32	23	9
Princeton	4	4	—	Williams Bay	7	6	1
Pulaski	7	7	—	Winneconne	5	4	1
Racine	240	207	33	Wisconsin Dells	15	15	—
Reedsburg	19	14	5	Wisconsin Rapids	48	38	10
Rhinelander	28	20	8				
Rice Lake	23	16	7	**WYOMING**			
Richland Center	12	10	2	Afton	4	4	—
Ripon	18	13	5	Baggs	1	1	—
River Falls	23	20	3	Basin	3	3	—
River Hills	14	14	—	Buffalo	12	8	4
Rome Town	3	3	—	Casper	91	76	15
Rothschild	10	9	1	Cheyenne	112	85	27
St. Croix Falls	3	3	—	Cody	18	16	2
St. Francis	20	19	1	Diamondville	4	3	1
Sauk Prairie	11	10	1	Douglas	21	14	7
Saukville	8	7	1	Evanston	29	24	5
Shawano	26	19	7	Evansville	10	6	4
Sheboygan	114	90	24	Gillette	52	35	17
Sheboygan Falls	10	10	—	Glenrock	9	6	3
Shorewood Hills	5	5	—	Green River	30	26	4
Silver Lake	4	3	1	Greybull	4	4	—
Slinger	6	5	1	Guernsey	5	5	—
Somerset	5	4	1	Hanna	6	3	3
South Milwaukee	36	32	4	Hulett	2	2	—
Sparta	23	17	6	Jackson	24	18	6
Spencer	3	3	—	Kemmerer	12	9	3
Spooner	6	5	1	Lander	18	17	1
Stanley	4	4	—	Laramie	44	35	9
Stevens Point	52	42	10	Lovell	8	4	4
Stoughton	24	19	5	Lusk	5	5	—

Table 78. — Number of Full-time Law Enforcement Employees, Cities, October 31, 1996 — Continued

City	Total police employees	Total officers	Total civilians	City	Total police employees	Total officers	Total civilians
WYOMING — Continued				**WYOMING — Continued**			
Lyman	6	5	1	Saratoga	7	4	3
Mills	8	7	1	Sheridan	43	27	16
Moorcroft	4	3	1	Sundance	4	4	—
Newcastle	13	7	6	Thermopolis	13	7	6
Pine Bluffs	6	2	4	Torrington	20	14	6
Powell	20	13	7	Upton	2	2	—
Rawlins	31	20	11	Wheatland	11	10	1
Riverton	32	22	10	Worland	11	11	—
Rock Springs	51	32	19				

Table 79. — Number of Full-time Law Enforcement Employees, Universities and Colleges, October 31, 1996

University/College	Total police employees	Total officers	Total civilians	University/College	Total police employees	Total officers	Total civilians
ALABAMA				**CALIFORNIA — Continued**			
Alabama State University	28	25	3	San Bernardino	18	13	5
Auburn University:				San Marcos	15	6	9
Main Campus	41	21	20	Stanislaus	16	10	6
Montgomery	22	13	9	College of the Sequoias	3	1	2
Enterprise State Junior College	2	2	—	Contra Costa Community College	25	19	6
Jacksonville State University	19	15	4	El Camino College	27	21	6
Talladega College	9	5	4	Foothill-De Anza College	8	7	1
Troy State University	9	8	1	Fresno Community College	12	10	2
University of Alabama:				Humboldt State University	16	11	5
Birmingham	88	54	34	Kings River Community College	15	13	2
Huntsville	13	9	4	Long Beach Community College	13	12	1
Tuscaloosa	39	34	5	Los Angeles City College	10	10	—
University of Montevallo	14	9	5	Marin Community College	11	8	3
University of North Alabama	12	11	1	Pasadena Community College	18	9	9
University of South Alabama	31	25	6	San Diego State University	29	19	10
University of West Alabama	7	5	2	San Francisco State University	39	25	14
ALASKA				San Jose State University	30	30	—
				San Jose/Evergreen Community College	9	4	5
University of Alaska:				Santa Rosa Junior College	15	10	5
Fairbanks	14	11	3	Sonoma State University	15	10	5
ARIZONA				University of California:			
				Berkeley	116	73	43
Arizona State University:				Davis	74	43	31
Main Campus	57	35	22	Irvine	35	26	9
West	17	8	9	Lawrence Livermore National Laboratory	7	2	5
Arizona Western College	8	7	1	Los Angeles	77	53	24
Central Arizona College	6	6	—	Riverside	27	20	7
Northern Arizona University	29	17	12	San Diego	47	26	21
Pima Community College	36	29	7	San Francisco	46	25	21
University of Arizona	78	46	32	Santa Barbara	38	26	12
Yavapai College	6	4	2	Santa Cruz	28	16	12
ARKANSAS				West Valley College	10	8	2
				COLORADO			
Arkansas State University	24	19	5	Adams State College	10	3	7
Henderson State University	9	8	1	Arapahoe Community College	5	4	1
Southern Arkansas University	5	5	—	Auraria Higher Education Center	28	15	13
University of Arkansas:				Colorado School of Mines	8	7	1
Fayetteville	31	24	7	Colorado State University	28	20	8
Little Rock	32	26	6	Fort Lewis College	6	2	4
Medical Science	49	37	12	Pike's Peak Community College	6	5	1
Monticello	6	5	1	Red Rocks Community College	9	8	1
Pine Bluff	18	14	4	University of Colorado:			
University of Central Arkansas	22	19	3	Boulder	70	32	38
CALIFORNIA				Colorado Springs	10	5	5
				Health Sciences Center	45	21	24
Allan Hancock College	3	2	1	University of Northern Colorado	19	12	7
Cabrillo Community College	6	4	2	University of Southern Colorado	9	3	6
California State Polytechnic University:				**CONNECTICUT**			
Pomona	33	14	19				
San Luis Obispo	13	13	—	Central Connecticut State University	27	23	4
California State University:				Eastern Connecticut State University	19	15	4
Bakersfield	13	9	4	Southern Connecticut State University	33	24	9
Chico	15	10	5	University of Connecticut:			
Fresno	26	17	9	Health Center	22	17	5
Fullerton	28	13	15	Storrs, Avery Point, and Hartford	59	48	11
Hayward	32	11	21	Western Connecticut State University	20	17	3
Long Beach	26	20	6	Yale University	85	69	16
Los Angeles	17	17	—	**DELAWARE**			
Monterey Bay	21	14	7				
Northridge	22	17	5	University of Delaware	76	47	29
Sacramento	20	15	5				

Table 79. — Number of Full-time Law Enforcement Employees, Universities and Colleges, October 31, 1996 — Continued

University/College	Total police employees	Total officers	Total civilians	University/College	Total police employees	Total officers	Total civilians
FLORIDA				**ILLINOIS — Continued**			
Florida Atlantic University	30	25	5	Morton College	10	7	3
Florida International University	46	32	14	Northeastern Illinois University	24	18	6
Florida State University:				Northern Illinois University	44	31	13
Panama City	3	2	1	Northwestern University	17	13	4
Tallahassee	83	50	33	Oakton Community College	8	7	1
Santa Fe Community College	15	13	2	Parkland College	15	9	6
University of Central Florida	53	36	17	Rock Valley College	8	7	1
University of Florida	139	86	53	Sangamon State University	16	10	6
University of North Florida	35	22	13	Southern Illinois University:			
University of South Florida:				Carbondale	55	42	13
St. Petersburg	16	12	4	Edwardsville	36	28	8
Sarasota	18	13	5	School of Medicine	11	2	9
Tampa	60	41	19	South Suburban College	13	10	3
University of West Florida	32	22	10	State Community College	9	8	1
				Triton College	13	8	5
GEORGIA				University of Illinois:			
Abraham Baldwin Agricultural College	10	9	1	Chicago	87	62	25
Agnes Scott College	26	14	12	Urbana	56	44	12
Albany State College	23	11	12	Waubonsee Community College	2	2	—
Armstrong State College	16	12	4	Western Illinois University	25	21	4
Augusta College	15	14	1	William Rainey Harper College	13	7	6
Berry College	16	12	4				
Brunswick College	7	6	1	**INDIANA**			
Clark Atlanta University	52	21	31	Ball State University	41	33	8
Clayton State College	13	11	2	Indiana State University	30	23	7
Columbus College	11	9	2	Indiana University:			
Dalton College	7	7	—	Bloomington	53	44	9
Emory University	40	25	15	Gary	13	10	3
Fort Valley State College	21	18	3	Indianapolis	51	32	19
Georgia College	19	12	7	New Albany	9	7	2
Georgia Institute of Technology	44	30	14	Purdue University	46	39	7
Georgia Southern University	33	26	7				
Georgia Southwestern College	11	10	1	**IOWA**			
Georgia State University	99	82	17	Iowa State University	30	27	3
Gordon College	6	6	—	University of Iowa	48	26	22
Kennesaw State University	28	19	9	University of Northern Iowa	26	19	7
Medical College of Georgia	88	46	42				
Mercer University	31	23	8	**KANSAS**			
Middle Georgia College	10	7	3	Emporia State University	10	9	1
Morehouse College	49	34	15	Fort Hays State University	10	10	—
North Georgia College	13	5	8	Kansas State University, Manhattan	33	20	13
Reinhardt College	4	4	—	Pittsburg State University	14	12	2
Savannah State College	27	15	12	University of Kansas:			
South Georgia College	7	7	—	Main Campus	49	28	21
Southern College of Technology	13	11	2	Medical Center	41	27	14
University of Georgia	83	70	13	Wichita State University	30	23	7
Valdosta State University	31	21	10				
Wesleyan College	6	5	1	**KENTUCKY**			
West Georgia College	31	17	14	Eastern Kentucky University	28	19	9
Young Harris College	1	1	—	Jefferson Community College	5	5	—
				Kentucky State University	16	11	5
ILLINOIS				Morehead State University	19	10	9
Black Hawk College	5	4	1	Murray State University	21	12	9
Chicago State University	30	23	7	Northern Kentucky University	25	17	8
College of DuPage	17	12	5	University of Kentucky	51	35	16
College of Lake County	14	9	5	University of Louisville	47	25	22
Eastern Illinois University	33	24	9	Western Kentucky University	30	23	7
Governors State University	15	10	5				
Illinois State University	29	24	5	**LOUISIANA**			
John A. Logan College	3	2	1	Grambling State University	24	23	1
Joliet Junior College	10	6	4	Louisiana State University:			
Loyola University of Chicago	50	21	29	Baton Rouge	62	60	2

Table 79. — Number of Full-time Law Enforcement Employees, Universities and Colleges, October 31, 1996 — Continued

University/College	Total police employees	Total officers	Total civilians	University/College	Total police employees	Total officers	Total civilians
LOUISIANA — Continued				**MICHIGAN — Continued**			
Medical Center	61	60	1	Oakland Community College	17	15	2
Shreveport	7	7	—	Oakland University	20	15	5
Louisiana Tech. University	20	18	2	Saginaw Valley State University	8	6	2
McNeese State University	13	11	2	University of Michigan:			
Nicholls State University	13	11	2	Ann Arbor	84	40	44
Northeast Louisiana University	25	21	4	Flint	17	5	12
Northwestern State University	15	14	1	Western Michigan University	57	26	31
Southeastern Louisiana University	28	21	7	**MINNESOTA**			
Southern University and A&M College,				University of Minnesota:			
Baton Rouge	33	32	1	Duluth	8	8	—
University of New Orleans	28	24	4	Twin Cities	54	41	13
University of Southwestern Louisiana	19	16	3	**MISSISSIPPI**			
MAINE				Hinds Community College	12	10	2
University of Maine:				Itawamba Community College	4	4	—
Farmington	4	4	—	Jackson State University	41	37	4
Orono	34	22	12	Mississippi State University	43	28	15
University of Southern Maine	24	18	6	University of Mississippi:			
MARYLAND				Medical Center	75	69	6
Bowie State University	22	16	6	Oxford	47	30	17
Coppin State University	16	15	1	**MISSOURI**			
Frostburg State University	20	15	5	Lincoln University	15	11	4
Morgan State University	46	32	14	University of Missouri:			
St. Mary's College	10	5	5	Columbia	47	34	13
Salisbury State University	19	17	2	St. Louis	26	17	9
Towson State University	47	33	14	Washington University	27	19	8
University of Baltimore	45	13	32	**MONTANA**			
University of Maryland:				Montana State University	16	11	5
Baltimore City	119	58	61	University of Montana	15	11	4
Baltimore County	28	19	9	**NEBRASKA**			
College Park	82	63	19	University of Nebraska:			
Eastern Shore	17	13	4	Kearney	6	6	—
MASSACHUSETTS				Lincoln	42	24	18
Boston College	55	45	10	**NEVADA**			
Boston University	52	46	6	University of Nevada:			
Brandeis University	21	20	1	Las Vegas	33	21	12
Emerson College	13	12	1	Reno	20	16	4
Framingham State College	10	10	—	**NEW HAMPSHIRE**			
Massachusetts Institute of Technology	56	53	3	University of New Hampshire	33	17	16
North Adams State College	13	8	5	**NEW JERSEY**			
Northeastern University	67	42	25	Brookdale Community College	16	11	5
Tufts University	53	38	15	Essex County College	50	17	33
University of Massachusetts:				Kean College	33	20	13
Amherst	90	54	36	Middlesex County College	16	11	5
Boston	37	26	11	Monmouth University	20	14	6
Worcester	28	14	14	Montclair State University	35	11	24
Wentworth Institute of Technology	26	10	16	New Jersey Institute of Technology	52	23	29
MICHIGAN				Rowan College	33	2	31
Central Michigan University	25	16	9	Rutgers University:			
Delta College	11	8	3	Camden	33	17	16
Eastern Michigan University	28	23	5	Newark	62	27	35
Ferris State University	21	15	6	New Brunswick	141	65	76
Grand Valley State University	9	8	1	Richard Stockton College	19	15	4
Hope College	12	7	5	Trenton State College	28	19	9
Lansing Community College	11	8	3				
Macomb Community College	34	27	7				
Michigan State University	58	53	5				
Michigan Technological University	13	9	4				
Northern Michigan University	20	15	5				

Table 79. — Number of Full-time Law Enforcement Employees, Universities and Colleges, October 31, 1996 — Continued

University/College	Total police employees	Total officers	Total civilians	University/College	Total police employees	Total officers	Total civilians
NEW JERSEY — Continued				**OKLAHOMA**			
University of Medicine and Dentistry:				Cameron University	7	6	1
Camden	20	19	1	East Central University	5	5	—
Newark	135	52	83	Murray State College	3	3	—
Piscataway	38	27	11	Northeastern State University	12	10	2
William Paterson College	31	22	9	Oklahoma State University:			
				Main Campus	35	24	11
NEW MEXICO				Okmulgee	8	8	—
Eastern New Mexico University	7	6	1	Seminole Junior College	4	4	—
New Mexico Highlands University	5	4	1	Southeastern Oklahoma State University	6	6	—
New Mexico State University	28	19	9	Tulsa Junior College	18	10	8
				University of Central Oklahoma	17	11	6
NEW YORK				University of Oklahoma:			
Cornell University	60	45	15	Health Sciences Center	22	18	4
Ithaca College	31	15	16	Norman	50	40	10
Rensselaer Polytechnic Institute	23	21	2	University of Tulsa	19	17	2
Syracuse University	48	43	5				
				PENNSYLVANIA			
NORTH CAROLINA				Bloomsburg University	17	16	1
Appalachian State University	24	18	6	California University	18	14	4
Barton College	10	4	6	Clarion University	17	12	5
Beaufort County Community College	1	1	—	East Stroudsburg University	15	14	1
Davidson College	11	9	2	Edinboro University	15	14	1
Duke University	134	56	78	Elizabethtown College	12	7	5
East Carolina University	48	33	15	Indiana University	23	18	5
Elizabeth City State University	12	10	2	Kutztown University	18	11	7
Fayetteville State University	24	16	8	Lehigh University	25	14	11
Mars Hill College	6	5	1	Lock Haven University	10	9	1
Methodist College	21	7	14	Mansfield University	11	11	—
North Carolina Agricultural and				Millersville University	20	14	6
Technical State University	57	27	30	Pennsylvania State University:			
North Carolina Central University	38	20	18	Altoona	6	5	1
North Carolina School of the Arts	10	9	1	Behrend	8	5	3
North Carolina State University	73	46	27	Harrisburg	8	7	1
Pembroke State University	13	10	3	University Park	58	46	12
Pfeiffer College	3	3	—	Shippensburg University	16	14	2
Queens College	6	4	2	Slippery Rock University	16	15	1
University of North Carolina:				University of Pittsburgh, Bradford	7	5	2
Asheville	9	7	2	West Chester University	38	20	18
Chapel Hill	54	31	23				
Charlotte	28	25	3	**RHODE ISLAND**			
Greensboro	38	23	15	Brown University	59	24	35
Wilmington	27	20	7	University of Rhode Island	26	16	10
Wake Forest University	28	12	16				
Western Carolina University	16	13	3	**SOUTH CAROLINA**			
Winston-Salem State University	13	8	5	Clemson University	44	26	18
				Columbia College	1	1	—
NORTH DAKOTA				Denmark Technical College	5	4	1
University of North Dakota	17	12	5	Erskine College	2	2	—
				Francis Marion University	11	11	—
OHIO				Lander University	11	10	1
Bowling Green State University	20	19	1	Medical University of South Carolina	112	67	45
Cuyahoga Community College	33	27	6	Presbyterian College	9	7	2
Kent State University	41	32	9	South Carolina State University	29	24	5
Lakeland Community College	11	7	4	The Citadel	13	13	—
Marietta College	4	4	—	Trident Technical College	20	18	2
Miami University	37	27	10	University of South Carolina:			
Ohio State University	54	45	9	Aiken	2	2	—
Ohio University	32	26	6	Coastal Carolina	13	9	4
University of Toledo	35	30	5	Columbia	74	60	14
Wright State University	24	16	8	Spartanburg	9	9	—
Youngstown State University	23	19	4	Winthrop University	20	13	7

Table 79. — Number of Full-time Law Enforcement Employees, Universities and Colleges, October 31, 1996 — Continued

University/College	Total police employees	Total officers	Total civilians	University/College	Total police employees	Total officers	Total civilians
TENNESSEE				**TEXAS — Continued**			
East Tennessee State University	23	17	6	Austin	166	67	99
Middle Tennessee State University	30	27	3	Brownsville and Texas Southmost College	13	7	6
University of Tennessee:				Dallas	28	11	17
Knoxville	56	49	7	El Paso	48	17	31
Martin	17	12	5	Health Science Center, San Antonio	58	19	39
				Health Science Center, Tyler	20	4	16
TEXAS				Houston	184	63	121
Alamo Community College	41	30	11	Medical Branch	91	37	54
Alvin Community College	12	10	2	Pan American	20	11	9
Amarillo College	8	5	3	Permian Basin	11	4	7
Angelo State University	11	9	2	San Antonio	66	30	36
Austin College	8	7	1	Southwest Medical School	61	21	40
Baylor University	28	19	9	Tyler	8	5	3
Baylor University Medical Center	85	49	36	West Texas A&M University	14	9	5
Central Texas College	11	10	1				
College of the Mainland	8	7	1	**UTAH**			
Eastfield College	8	7	1	Brigham Young University	36	24	12
East Texas State University, Commerce	22	14	8	College of Eastern Utah	2	2	—
Grayson County Junior College	4	3	1	Salt Lake Community College	14	12	2
Hardin-Simmons University	6	5	1	Southern Utah University	6	5	1
Houston Baptist University	8	8	—	University of Utah	45	36	9
Lamar University, Beaumont	23	14	9	Utah State University	18	12	6
Laredo Community College	8	7	1	Utah Valley State College	5	4	1
McLennan Community College	5	4	1	Weber State University	16	10	6
Midwestern State University	8	7	1				
North Lake College	9	8	1	**VERMONT**			
Paris Junior College	3	1	2	University of Vermont	26	15	11
Prairie View A&M University	24	16	8				
Rice University	39	26	13	**VIRGINIA**			
Richland College	8	7	1	Christopher Newport University	14	13	1
St. Mary's University	19	12	7	Clinch Valley College	5	5	—
Southern Methodist University	34	23	11	College of William and Mary	22	18	4
South Plains College	4	4	—	George Mason University	40	32	8
Southwestern University	6	6	—	Hampton University	37	22	15
Southwest Texas State University	45	25	20	James Madison University	22	17	5
Stephen F. Austin State University	34	17	17	Longwood College	12	11	1
Sul Ross State University	8	6	2	Mary Washington College	18	13	5
Texas A&M International University	5	4	1	Norfolk State University	55	23	32
Texas A&M University:				Northern Virginia Community College	29	29	—
College Station	114	44	70	Old Dominion University	35	29	6
Corpus Christi	21	11	10	Radford University	26	18	8
Galveston	8	7	1	Thomas Nelson Community College	9	8	1
Kingsville	21	15	6	University of Richmond	30	15	15
Texas Christian University	30	19	11	University of Virginia	110	56	54
Texas College Osteo. Med.	21	14	7	Virginia Commonwealth University	81	59	22
Texas Southern University	33	18	15	Virginia Military Institute	5	5	—
Texas State Technical College:				Virginia Polytechnic Institute and			
Harlingen	9	6	3	State University	47	33	14
Waco	13	12	1	Virginia State University	31	15	16
Texas Tech. University:				Virginia Western Community College	5	5	—
Health Science Center	43	17	26				
Lubbock	36	27	9	**WASHINGTON**			
Texas Woman's University	34	17	17	Central Washington University	12	11	1
Trinity University	22	9	13	Eastern Washington University	7	6	1
Tyler Junior College	7	3	4	University of Washington	76	51	25
University of Houston:				Washington State University	26	18	8
Central Campus	54	40	14	Western Washington University	17	12	5
Clearlake	16	9	7				
Downtown Campus	24	16	8	**WEST VIRGINIA**			
University of North Texas	47	24	23	Concord College	6	5	1
University of Texas:				Glenville State College	3	3	—
Arlington	64	31	33				

Table 79. — Number of Full-time Law Enforcement Employees, Universities and Colleges, October 31, 1996 — Continued

University/College	Total police employees	Total officers	Total civilians	University/College	Total police employees	Total officers	Total civilians
WEST VIRGINIA — Continued				**WISCONSIN — Continued**			
Marshall University	28	19	9	Madison	85	42	43
West Liberty State College	6	6	—	Milwaukee	37	33	4
West Virginia State College	12	10	2	Oshkosh	14	13	1
West Virginia Tech	7	7	—	Parkside	9	6	3
West Virginia University	63	42	21	Platteville	7	6	1
WISCONSIN				Stout	10	7	3
				Whitewater	11	10	1
University of Wisconsin:				**WYOMING**			
Eau Claire	11	10	1	Sheridan College	2	2	—
Green Bay	9	4	5	University of Wyoming	23	13	10
La Crosse	8	8	—				

Table 80. — Number of Full-time Law Enforcement Employees, Suburban Counties, October 31, 1996

County by State	Total police employees	Total officers	Total civilians	County by State	Total police employees	Total officers	Total civilians	County by State	Total police employees	Total officers	Total civilians
ALABAMA				**CALIFORNIA —**				**GEORGIA**			
				Continued							
Autauga	29	16	13	San Mateo	514	299	215	Barrow	71	41	30
Baldwin	131	64	67	Santa Barbara	583	418	165	Bartow	152	125	27
Blount	45	23	22	Santa Clara	522	403	119	Bibb	259	225	34
Calhoun	64	28	36	Santa Cruz	142	114	28	Bryan	35	23	12
Colbert	33	21	12	Shasta	236	152	84	Carroll	95	62	33
Dale	20	14	6	Solano	408	89	319	Catoosa	94	52	42
Elmore	55	21	34	Sonoma	583	401	182	Chatham Police			
Etowah	98	42	56	Stanislaus	493	179	314	Department	250	149	101
Houston	92	38	54	Sutter	70	53	17	Chattahoochee	3	2	1
Jefferson	585	461	124	Tulare	409	293	116	Cherokee	208	160	48
Lauderdale	61	24	37	Ventura	1,106	700	406	Cherokee Police			
Lawrence	36	27	9	Yolo	213	77	136	Department	6	3	3
Limestone	52	30	22	Yuba	72	49	23	Clayton	202	162	40
Madison	170	91	79					Clayton Police			
Mobile	474	145	329	**COLORADO**				Department	245	218	27
Montgomery	244	117	127	Adams	360	240	120	Cobb	407	278	129
Morgan	75	44	31	Arapahoe	488	335	153	Coweta	136	68	68
Russell	74	21	53	Boulder	317	151	166	Dade	38	15	23
Shelby	104	72	32	Douglas	144	106	38	Dekalb	550	143	407
St. Clair	38	21	17	El Paso	506	388	118	Dekalb County Police			
Tuscaloosa	167	69	98	Jefferson	531	364	167	Department	908	730	178
				Larimer	238	80	158	Dougherty	205	189	16
ARIZONA				Pueblo	229	122	107	Dougherty Police			
Maricopa	2,006	474	1,532	Weld	169	86	83	Department	49	48	1
Mohave	218	89	129					Douglas	212	147	65
Pima	1,081	395	686	**DELAWARE**				Fayette	114	84	30
Pinal	326	135	191	New Castle Police				Forsyth	105	75	30
Yuma	210	51	159	Department	309	283	26	Fulton	763	609	154
								Fulton Police			
ARKANSAS				**FLORIDA**				Department	344	214	130
Benton	99	50	49	Alachua	344	207	137	Gwinnett	295	188	107
Crawford	41	17	24	Bay	216	148	68	Gwinnett Police			
Crittenden	62	27	35	Broward	3,155	1,070	2,085	Department	530	370	160
Faulkner	54	18	36	Charlotte	398	225	173	Harris	58	33	25
Jefferson	50	44	6	Clay	258	175	83	Henry	95	55	40
Lonoke	21	14	7	Collier	800	438	362	Jones	33	18	15
Miller	40	20	20	Dade	4,070	2,856	1,214	Lee	31	28	3
Pulaski	462	373	89	Escambia	882	356	526	McDuffie	24	12	12
Saline	45	31	14	Flagler	109	53	56	Muscogee	216	127	89
Sebastian	110	27	83	Gadsden	54	34	20	Newton	70	42	28
Washington	91	42	49	Hernando	246	159	87	Oconee	41	28	13
				Hillsborough	2,490	938	1,552	Paulding	130	78	52
CALIFORNIA				Lake	249	166	83	Peach	48	20	28
Alameda	1,292	768	524	Leon	603	278	325	Pickens	35	23	12
Butte	204	99	105	Manatee	860	300	560	Richmond	639	546	93
Contra Costa	843	571	272	Marion	602	235	367	Rockdale	116	93	23
El Dorado	292	142	150	Martin	433	204	229	Spalding	112	78	34
Fresno	515	362	153	Nassau	116	54	62	Twiggs	15	11	4
Kern	942	430	512	Okaloosa	191	148	43	Walker	92	62	30
Los Angeles County	6,808	4,419	2,389	Orange	1,468	996	472	Walton	99	50	49
Madera	98	70	28	Osceola	431	231	200				
Marin	275	185	90	Palm Beach	1,665	926	739	**IDAHO**			
Merced	93	72	21	Pasco	764	311	453	Ada	193	88	105
Monterey	413	313	100	Pinellas	1,930	811	1,119	Canyon	83	50	33
Napa	90	72	18	Polk	1,126	432	694				
Orange	2,182	1,230	952	St. Johns	333	143	190	**ILLINOIS**			
Placer	343	209	134	St. Lucie	463	203	260	Boone	41	26	15
Riverside	2,215	1,176	1,039	Santa Rosa	206	151	55	Champaign	57	50	7
Sacramento	1,634	1,169	465	Sarasota	779	346	433	Clinton	22	18	4
San Bernardino	2,133	1,193	940	Seminole	590	255	335	Cook	632	528	104
San Diego	2,799	1,708	1,091	Volusia	536	351	185	De Kalb	66	52	14
San Joaquin	316	158	158					Du Page	196	142	54
San Luis Obispo	334	248	86								

Table 80. — Number of Full-time Law Enforcement Employees, Suburban Counties, October 31, 1996 — Continued

County by State	Total police employees	Total officers	Total civilians
ILLINOIS — Continued			
Grundy	40	28	12
Henry	46	43	3
Jersey	12	11	1
Kane	137	94	43
Kankakee	106	64	42
Kendall	68	61	7
Lake	371	173	198
Macon	141	47	94
Madison	85	70	15
McHenry	239	198	41
McLean	70	50	20
Menard	12	11	1
Monroe	20	11	9
Ogle	61	43	18
Peoria	182	64	118
Rock Island	122	54	68
St. Clair	59	54	5
Sangamon	219	74	145
Tazewell	62	37	25
Will	417	276	141
Winnebago	145	122	23
Woodford	28	18	10
INDIANA			
Allen	257	118	139
Boone	42	17	25
Clark	75	31	44
Dearborn	57	20	37
Delaware	99	40	59
Elkhart	154	67	87
Hamilton	130	52	78
Hancock	54	29	25
Harrison	31	11	20
Howard	98	33	65
Huntington	30	12	18
Johnson	89	44	45
Lake	289	168	121
Marion	880	407	473
Morgan	59	18	41
Porter	131	53	78
St. Joseph	202	126	76
Scott	20	8	12
Tippecanoe	119	45	74
Tipton	12	8	4
Vanderburgh	159	103	56
Warrick	61	29	32
Wells	33	12	21
IOWA			
Black Hawk	141	105	36
Dallas	35	12	23
Dubuque	48	40	8
Johnson	72	48	24
Linn	131	90	41
Polk	218	167	51
Pottawattamie	60	35	25
Scott	132	41	91
Warren	27	18	9
Woodbury	87	31	56
KANSAS			
Butler	51	46	5
KANSAS — Continued			
Douglas	69	36	33
Harvey	22	13	9
Johnson	406	332	74
Leavenworth	53	37	16
Miami	30	18	12
Sedgwick	343	154	189
Shawnee	122	103	19
Wyandotte	166	139	27
KENTUCKY			
Bell	10	6	4
Boone	24	21	3
Boone Police Department	54	50	4
Bourbon	6	6	—
Boyd	18	18	—
Bullitt	22	19	3
Campbell	11	11	—
Campbell Police Department	34	24	10
Christian	15	14	1
Christian Police Department	7	6	1
Clark	10	10	—
Daviess	36	36	—
Gallatin	2	2	—
Grant	7	5	2
Greenup	9	9	—
Henderson	21	19	2
Jefferson	198	164	34
Jefferson Police Department	567	426	141
Jessamine	17	16	1
Kenton	30	30	—
Kenton Police Department	49	33	16
Madison	15	13	2
Oldham	10	10	—
Oldham Police Department	18	16	2
Pendleton	3	2	1
Scott	20	19	1
Woodford	5	5	—
Woodford Police Department	20	19	1
LOUISIANA			
Acadia	95	62	33
Ascension	162	88	74
Bossier	149	120	29
Caddo	591	408	183
Calcasieu	506	505	1
East Baton Rouge	664	664	—
Jefferson	1,345	905	440
Lafayette	457	457	—
Lafourche	192	148	44
Livingston	117	117	—
Ouachita	293	286	7
Plaquemines	178	176	2
Rapides	286	191	95
St. Charles	240	152	88
St. James	88	48	40
LOUISIANA — Continued			
St. John The Baptist	165	160	5
St. Landry	104	104	—
St. Martin	165	130	35
St. Tammany	344	251	93
Terrebonne	257	257	—
Webster	90	30	60
West Baton Rouge	81	49	32
MAINE			
Androscoggin	17	12	5
Cumberland	60	43	17
MARYLAND			
Allegany	30	21	9
Anne Arundel	50	41	9
Anne Arundel Police Department	771	586	185
Baltimore County Sheriff	76	62	14
Baltimore County Police Department	1,832	1,545	287
Calvert	71	60	11
Carroll	32	28	4
Cecil	53	42	11
Charles	219	155	64
Frederick	108	80	28
Harford	302	173	129
Howard	47	28	19
Howard Police Department	390	318	72
Montgomery	114	102	12
Montgomery Police Department	1,248	972	276
Prince George's	255	195	60
Prince George's Police Department	1,522	1,220	302
Queen Anne's	35	31	4
Washington	157	60	97
MICHIGAN			
Allegan	96	56	40
Bay	37	31	6
Berrien	166	57	109
Calhoun	84	51	33
Clinton	61	22	39
Eaton	123	70	53
Genesee	238	132	106
Ingham	211	110	101
Jackson	102	48	54
Kalamazoo	163	130	33
Kent	157	135	22
Lapeer	62	48	14
Lenawee	60	44	16
Livingston	103	56	47
Macomb	374	177	197
Midland	55	34	21
Monroe	158	91	67
Muskegon	83	37	46
Oakland	827	563	264
Ottawa	92	81	11
Saginaw	129	88	41
St. Clair	116	62	54

Table 80. — Number of Full-time Law Enforcement Employees, Suburban Counties, October 31, 1996 — Continued

County by State	Total police employees	Total officers	Total civilians
MICHIGAN — Continued			
Van Buren	62	33	29
Washtenaw	247	134	113
Wayne	1,416	756	660
MINNESOTA			
Anoka	163	78	85
Benton	46	14	32
Carver	111	55	56
Chisago	50	25	25
Clay	54	24	30
Dakota	138	69	69
Hennepin	613	289	324
Houston	19	11	8
Isanti	33	17	16
Olmsted	53	52	1
Polk	31	21	10
Ramsey	347	275	72
St. Louis	173	88	85
Scott	91	32	59
Sherburne	80	33	47
Stearns	105	42	63
Washington	189	73	116
Wright	125	71	54
MISSISSIPPI			
Lamar	31	20	11
Madison	64	31	33
Rankin	99	46	53
MISSOURI			
Andrew	10	7	3
Boone	90	59	31
Buchanan	73	59	14
Cass	48	25	23
Christian	35	27	8
Clay	126	95	31
Franklin	96	85	11
Greene	137	116	21
Jackson	108	77	31
Jasper	94	80	14
Jefferson	201	152	49
Lafayette	31	23	8
Platte	69	53	16
Ray	24	13	11
St. Charles	160	109	51
St. Louis County Police Department	818	600	218
Warren	32	26	6
Webster	18	17	1
MONTANA			
Cascade	53	32	21
Yellowstone	128	47	81
NEBRASKA			
Cass	31	17	14
Dakota	23	10	13
Douglas	173	114	59
Lancaster	80	63	17
Sarpy	124	99	25
Washington	28	11	17

County by State	Total police employees	Total officers	Total civilians
NEVADA			
Nye	107	78	29
Washoe	540	357	183
NEW JERSEY			
Atlantic	111	85	26
Atlantic Prosecutor	159	70	89
Bergen	442	358	84
Bergen Police Department	110	84	26
Bergen Prosecutor	254	113	141
Burlington	75	59	16
Burlington Prosecutor	126	46	80
Camden	206	179	27
Camden Prosecutor	219	100	119
Cape May	121	106	15
Cape May Prosecutor	47	18	29
Cumberland	59	53	6
Cumberland Prosecutor	49	17	32
Essex	473	415	58
Essex Police Department	54	42	12
Essex Prosecutor	440	300	140
Gloucester	188	159	29
Gloucester Prosecutor	74	41	33
Hudson	192	153	39
Hudson Prosecutor	271	95	176
Hunterdon	31	23	8
Hunterdon Prosecutor	44	17	27
Mercer	120	94	26
Mercer Prosecutor	126	77	49
Middlesex	199	162	37
Middlesex Prosecutor	219	135	84
Monmouth	573	434	139
Monmouth Prosecutor	250	68	182
Morris	283	199	84
Morris Prosecutor	144	94	50
Ocean	183	78	105
Ocean Prosecutor	124	56	68
Passaic	661	512	149
Passaic Prosecutor	194	77	117
Salem	150	133	17
Salem Prosecutor	34	10	24
Somerset	162	135	27
Somerset Prosecutor	94	61	33
Sussex	119	104	15
Sussex Prosecutor	50	31	19
Union	167	150	17
Union County Police Department	424	407	17
Union Prosecutor	217	125	92
Warren	24	17	7
Warren Prosecutor	56	33	23
NEW MEXICO			
Sandoval	41	36	5
NEW YORK			
Albany	144	94	50
Broome	194	174	20
Chemung	43	33	10
Dutchess	125	108	17
Genesee	57	41	16

County by State	Total police employees	Total officers	Total civilians
NEW YORK — Continued			
Herkimer	53	43	10
Livingston	55	42	13
Monroe	327	264	63
Montgomery	35	28	7
Nassau	3,653	2,988	665
Oneida	145	99	46
Onondaga	258	231	27
Ontario	91	57	34
Orleans	44	25	19
Oswego	73	62	11
Rensselaer	38	33	5
Saratoga	102	75	27
Schoharie	25	13	12
Suffolk	173	129	44
Suffolk Police Department	3,347	2,760	587
Warren	82	63	19
Wayne	76	49	27
Westchester	283	231	52
NORTH CAROLINA			
Alamance	114	68	46
Alexander	26	17	9
Brunswick	81	73	8
Buncombe	297	182	115
Burke	80	65	15
Cabarrus	139	129	10
Caldwell	80	48	32
Catawba	110	103	7
Chatham	72	46	26
Cumberland	430	260	170
Currituck	41	30	11
Davidson	136	88	48
Davie	43	25	18
Durham	362	108	254
Edgecombe	67	38	29
Forsyth	432	224	208
Franklin	62	33	29
Gaston Police Department	173	120	53
Guilford	362	196	166
Johnston	115	59	56
Lincoln	76	56	20
Madison	15	10	5
Nash	87	52	35
New Hanover	253	187	66
Onslow	114	73	41
Orange	102	84	18
Pitt	195	93	102
Randolph	136	84	52
Rowan	132	108	24
Stokes	50	31	19
Union	129	97	32
Wake	443	203	240
Wayne	96	47	49
Yadkin	44	22	22
NORTH DAKOTA			
Burleigh	53	37	16
Cass	67	44	23
Grand Forks	27	21	6
Morton	30	18	12

County by State	Total police employees	Total officers	Total civilians	County by State	Total police employees	Total officers	Total civilians	County by State	Total police employees	Total officers	Total civilians
OHIO				**PENNSYLVANIA — Continued**				**TEXAS — Continued**			
Allen	137	60	77	Lebanon Detective	6	5	1	El Paso	673	211	462
Ashtabula	83	44	39	Washington	30	26	4	Fort Bend	294	193	101
Auglaize	35	21	14	Westmoreland Detective	54	14	40	Galveston	322	275	47
Belmont	53	43	10					Grayson	94	53	41
Clermont	160	64	96	**SOUTH CAROLINA**				Gregg	133	71	62
Columbiana	79	32	47	Aiken	108	81	27	Guadalupe	90	31	59
Crawford	38	17	21	Anderson	135	112	23	Hardin	49	27	22
Cuyahoga	1,114	151	963	Berkeley	125	74	51	Harris	3,260	2,480	780
Delaware	85	39	46	Charleston	551	227	324	Harrison	86	33	53
Franklin	695	565	130	Cherokee	51	39	12	Hays	174	65	109
Fulton	29	18	11	Dorchester	114	56	58	Henderson	73	27	46
Geauga	75	37	38	Edgefield	30	18	12	Hidalgo	314	133	181
Greene	97	87	10	Florence	217	83	134	Hood	57	22	35
Hamilton	961	274	687	Greenville	348	287	61	Hunt	54	23	31
Jefferson	47	25	22	Horry	25	14	11	Jefferson	384	85	299
Lake	176	41	135	Horry Police Department	136	124	12	Johnson	124	56	68
Licking	131	99	32	Lexington	277	174	103	Kaufman	65	28	37
Lorain	157	50	107	Pickens	84	63	21	Liberty	59	42	17
Lucas	400	254	146	Richland	361	320	41	Lubbock	243	151	92
Medina	133	87	46	Spartanburg	257	234	23	McLennan	243	117	126
Miami	70	39	31	Sumter	109	102	7	Midland	164	94	70
Pickaway	80	41	39	York	191	92	99	Montgomery	380	245	135
Portage	119	54	65					Nueces	289	73	216
Richland	109	53	56	**SOUTH DAKOTA**				Orange	127	60	67
Stark	227	119	108	Minnehaha	119	68	51	Parker	69	33	36
Trumbull	85	41	44	Pennington	111	45	66	Potter	182	71	111
Wood	97	62	35					Randall	77	62	15
				TENNESSEE				Rockwall	43	15	28
OKLAHOMA				Carter	58	49	9	San Patricio	72	33	39
Canadian	35	18	17	Hawkins	49	46	3	Smith	228	65	163
Cleveland	89	39	50	Knox	743	321	422	Tarrant	1,256	391	865
Comanche	48	28	20	Madison	65	65	—	Taylor	128	70	58
Creek	27	16	11	Marion	26	14	12	Tom Green	106	46	60
Garfield	18	9	9	Montgomery	146	134	12	Travis	1,063	396	667
Logan	15	9	6	Robertson	79	35	44	Upshur	37	18	19
McClain	17	7	10	Rutherford	160	105	55	Victoria	145	101	44
Oklahoma	488	103	385	Shelby	1,296	484	812	Waller	44	23	21
Osage	30	26	4	Sullivan	184	157	27	Webb	221	162	59
Pottawatomie	29	15	14	Sumner	122	46	76	Wichita	125	35	90
Rogers	26	14	12	Union	12	12	—	Williamson	210	130	80
Sequoyah	18	6	12	Washington	141	62	79	Wilson	57	17	40
Tulsa	391	201	190								
Wagoner	17	10	7	**TEXAS**				**UTAH**			
				Archer	10	6	4	Davis	183	67	116
OREGON				Bastrop	94	26	68	Salt Lake	866	398	468
Clackamas	240	201	39	Bell	219	71	148	Utah	177	132	45
Columbia	15	13	2	Bexar	1,447	968	479	Weber	162	55	107
Jackson	67	47	20	Bowie	187	42	145				
Lane	105	68	37	Brazoria	267	172	95	**VIRGINIA**			
Marion	104	75	29	Brazos	125	56	69	Albemarle Police Department	102	84	18
Multnomah	162	105	57	Caldwell	54	15	39	Amherst	51	40	11
Polk	29	23	6	Cameron	242	68	174	Arlington Police Department	416	336	80
Washington	207	150	57	Chambers	59	21	38	Bedford	90	90	—
Yamhill	59	45	14	Collin	312	107	205	Botetourt	54	43	11
				Comal	105	47	58	Campbell	63	53	10
PENNSYLVANIA				Coryell	40	17	23	Charles City	16	10	6
Allegheny Police Department	249	214	35	Dallas	1,598	441	1,157	Chesterfield Police Department	433	372	61
Beaver	28	23	5	Denton	399	102	297	Clarke	17	11	6
Cambria	21	15	6	Ector	152	95	57				
Chester Detective	20	17	3	Ellis	112	39	73				
Cumberland	22	20	2								

Table 80. — Number of Full-time Law Enforcement Employees, Suburban Counties, October 31, 1996 — Continued

County by State	Total police employees	Total officers	Total civilians	County by State	Total police employees	Total officers	Total civilians	County by State	Total police employees	Total officers	Total civilians
VIRGINIA — Continued				**VIRGINIA — Continued**				**WEST VIRGINIA — Continued**			
Culpeper	71	55	16	Stafford	122	90	32	Wayne	29	12	17
Dinwiddie	50	26	24	Washington	67	55	12	Wood	40	29	11
Fairfax Police				York	84	75	9				
Department	1,340	1,051	289					**WISCONSIN**			
Fauquier	88	76	12	**WASHINGTON**				Brown	198	132	66
Fluvanna	15	11	4					Calumet	33	26	7
Gloucester	72	61	11	Benton	59	47	12	Chippewa	52	48	4
Goochland	20	14	6	Clark	200	136	64	Dane	426	340	86
Greene	16	10	6	Franklin	24	21	3	Douglas	42	28	14
Hanover	148	133	15	Island	54	35	19	Eau Claire	80	52	28
Henrico Police				King	838	577	261	La Crosse	77	34	43
Department	627	454	173	Kitsap	113	90	23	Marathon	135	65	70
Isle Of Wight	26	20	6	Pierce	342	291	51	Milwaukee	806	606	200
James City Police				Snohomish	245	175	70	Outagamie	186	72	114
Department	58	55	3	Spokane	232	183	49	Ozaukee	87	66	21
King George	26	23	3	Thurston	116	79	37	Pierce	39	38	1
Loudoun	208	166	42	Whatcom	115	58	57	Racine	251	184	67
Mathews	15	9	6	Yakima	97	67	30	Rock	171	94	77
New Kent	26	17	9					St. Croix	59	28	31
Pittsylvania	85	39	46	**WEST VIRGINIA**				Sheboygan	130	74	56
Powhatan	19	16	3	Brooke	21	15	6	Washington	111	58	53
Prince George	48	37	11	Cabell	86	33	53	Waukesha	306	148	158
Prince William Police				Hancock	33	22	11	Winnebago	156	89	67
Department	412	332	80	Kanawha	85	70	15				
Roanoke Police				Marshall	25	22	3	**WYOMING**			
Department	133	106	27	Mineral	12	7	5	Laramie	123	85	38
Scott	42	33	9	Ohio	25	19	6	Natrona	49	39	10
Spotsylvania	85	63	22	Putnam	27	22	5				

Table 81. — Number of Full-time Law Enforcement Employees, Rural Counties, October 31, 1996

County by State	Total police employees	Total officers	Total civilians	County by State	Total police employees	Total officers	Total civilians	County by State	Total police employees	Total officers	Total civilians
ALABAMA				**ARKANSAS —** Continued				**CALIFORNIA —** Continued			
Barbour	28	10	18	Clay	17	7	10	Del Norte	36	25	11
Butler	14	7	7	Cleburne	19	12	7	Glenn	55	22	33
Chambers	50	16	34	Cleveland	10	6	4	Humboldt	99	71	28
Cherokee	22	13	9	Columbia	24	12	12	Imperial	111	65	46
Chilton	18	16	2	Conway	27	8	19	Inyo	63	39	24
Choctaw	17	6	11	Craighead	51	16	35	Kings	181	73	108
Clarke	18	12	6	Cross	30	11	19	Lake	70	52	18
Clay	9	3	6	Dallas	13	6	7	Lassen	89	70	19
Cleburne	6	5	1	Desha	12	7	5	Mariposa	58	47	11
Coffee	35	10	25	Drew	17	7	10	Mendocino	134	110	24
Conecuh	16	7	9	Franklin	13	7	6	Modoc	20	20	—
Coosa	11	6	5	Fulton	10	5	5	Mono	42	25	17
Covington	35	15	20	Garland	92	33	59	Nevada	172	72	100
Crenshaw	13	7	6	Grant	12	7	5	Plumas	68	38	30
Cullman	70	53	17	Greene	44	13	31	San Benito	58	20	38
Dallas	50	25	25	Hempstead	38	13	25	Sierra	15	10	5
De Kalb	38	22	16	Hot Spring	22	12	10	Siskiyou	63	48	15
Escambia	40	15	25	Howard	17	7	10	Tehama	82	53	29
Fayette	12	12	—	Independence	61	39	22	Trinity	25	20	5
Franklin	35	19	16	Izard	13	10	3	Tuolumne	72	50	22
Geneva	16	8	8	Jackson	19	12	7				
Greene	14	6	8	Johnson	15	9	6	**COLORADO**			
Hale	13	6	7	Lafayette	14	6	8	Archuleta	29	8	21
Henry	21	10	11	Lawrence	18	8	10	Baca	9	9	—
Jackson	45	26	19	Lee	7	5	2	Bent	10	5	5
Lee	80	36	44	Lincoln	14	4	10	Chaffee	26	12	14
Lowndes	22	8	14	Little River	14	7	7	Cheyenne	8	5	3
Macon	25	14	11	Logan	22	11	11	Clear Creek	34	15	19
Marion	19	10	9	Madison	19	9	10	Crowley	12	5	7
Marshall	45	23	22	Marion	16	7	9	Custer	15	7	8
Monroe	34	16	18	Mississippi	48	24	24	Delta	38	15	23
Perry	16	7	9	Monroe	13	6	7	Dolores	7	4	3
Pickens	12	7	5	Montgomery	13	6	7	Eagle	57	48	9
Pike	19	10	9	Nevada	17	6	11	Elbert	26	15	11
Randolph	8	8	—	Newton	8	5	3	Fremont	58	39	19
Talladega	56	21	35	Ouachita	27	14	13	Garfield	49	17	32
Tallapoosa	48	17	31	Perry	10	6	4	Gilpin	32	21	11
Walker	43	23	20	Phillips	28	8	20	Grand	46	27	19
Washington	12	6	6	Pike	10	6	4	Gunnison	20	10	10
Wilcox	16	8	8	Poinsett	41	11	30	Hinsdale	5	4	1
Winston	18	12	6	Polk	20	9	11	Jackson	6	3	3
				Pope	44	22	22	Kiowa	4	3	1
ARIZONA				Prairie	12	5	7	Kit Carson	20	6	14
Apache	58	29	29	Randolph	9	8	1	Lake	17	7	10
Cochise	168	63	105	St. Francis	32	14	18	Las Animas	19	12	7
Graham	32	15	17	Scott	12	5	7	Lincoln	16	5	11
Greenlee	26	15	11	Searcy	9	4	5	Logan	25	12	13
Lapaz	88	40	48	Sevier	18	9	9	Mesa	151	65	86
Navajo	104	52	52	Sharp	20	10	10	Mineral	5	3	2
Santa Cruz	57	33	24	Stone	16	6	10	Moffat	30	26	4
Yavapai	200	88	112	Union	45	21	24	Montezuma	35	31	4
				Van Buren	14	8	6	Morgan	43	37	6
ARKANSAS				White	57	26	31	Otero	19	19	—
Arkansas	8	8	—	Woodruff	12	6	6	Ouray	8	7	1
Ashley	25	11	14	Yell	14	8	6	Park	36	21	15
Baxter	31	22	9					Phillips	4	3	1
Boone	24	13	11	**CALIFORNIA**				Pitkin	39	21	18
Bradley	5	4	1	Alpine	12	9	3	Prowers	24	7	17
Calhoun	7	4	3	Amador	50	36	14	Rio Blanco	19	10	9
Carroll	23	9	14	Calaveras	75	58	17	Rio Grande	18	9	9
Chicot	8	6	2	Colusa	42	29	13	Routt	36	22	14
Clark	25	12	13								

Table 81. — Number of Full-time Law Enforcement Employees, Rural Counties, October 31, 1996 — Continued

County by State	Total police employees	Total officers	Total civilians	County by State	Total police employees	Total officers	Total civilians	County by State	Total police employees	Total officers	Total civilians
COLORADO — Continued				**GEORGIA —** Continued				**GEORGIA —** Continued			
Saguache	12	7	5	Crawford	21	11	10	Talbot	9	5	4
San Juan	5	4	1	Crisp	53	42	11	Taylor	13	9	4
Sedgwick	10	5	5	Dawson	33	20	13	Telfair	14	8	6
Summit	43	27	16	Decatur	53	21	32	Terrell	19	11	8
Teller	37	27	10	Dooly	22	12	10	Thomas	53	25	28
Washington	14	9	5	Early	20	12	8	Tift	65	35	30
Yuma	11	6	5	Echols	4	4	—	Toombs	33	10	23
				Elbert	37	22	15	Towns	13	9	4
FLORIDA				Emanuel	20	14	6	Treutlen	9	5	4
Baker	53	26	27	Fannin	21	16	5	Troup	97	51	46
Bradford	29	18	11	Floyd	81	56	25	Turner	24	10	14
Calhoun	26	13	13	Floyd Police Department	63	58	5	Union	24	13	11
Citrus	222	133	89	Franklin	37	20	17	Upson	40	28	12
Columbia	151	70	81	Gilmer	29	18	11	Ware	54	28	26
De Soto	76	64	12	Glascock	3	2	1	Ware Police Department	13	2	11
Dixie	52	20	32	Glynn	104	31	73	Warren	3	3	—
Franklin	59	25	34	Glynn Police Department	124	98	26	Washington	29	22	7
Gilchrist	36	20	16	Grady	26	11	15	Wayne	31	21	10
Glades	44	23	21	Greene	10	10	—	Webster	3	2	1
Gulf	43	31	12	Habersham	35	21	14	Wheeler	5	3	2
Hamilton	52	13	39	Hall	250	223	27	White	31	16	15
Hardee	67	55	12	Hancock	34	11	23	Whitfield	132	83	49
Hendry	108	55	53	Haralson	33	19	14	Wilcox	11	6	5
Highlands	213	99	114	Irwin	10	5	5	Wilkes	18	11	7
Holmes	14	10	4	Jackson	58	36	22	Wilkinson	16	7	9
Indian River	344	158	186	Jasper	20	9	11	Worth	28	17	11
Jackson	53	36	17	Jeff Davis	19	11	8				
Jefferson	39	15	24	Jenkins	8	4	4	**HAWAII**			
Lafayette	8	7	1	Johnson	11	9	2	Hawaii Police Department	229	205	24
Levy	118	66	52	Lamar	37	12	25	Kauai Police Department	169	128	41
Liberty	16	10	6	Lanier	11	4	7	Maui Police Department	406	310	96
Madison	57	50	7	Laurens	73	39	34				
Monroe	520	198	322	Liberty	69	42	27	**IDAHO**			
Okeechobee	121	53	68	Long	11	10	1	Adams	12	12	—
Putnam	193	92	101	Lowndes	161	69	92	Bannock	62	33	29
Sumter	54	34	20	Lumpkin	36	25	11	Bear Lake	11	5	6
Taylor	71	57	14	Macon	17	7	10	Benewah	17	17	—
Union	15	8	7	Marion	12	4	8	Bingham	40	26	14
Wakulla	74	30	44	McIntosh	29	25	4	Blaine	26	16	10
Walton	94	51	43	Meriwether	28	16	12	Boise	15	10	5
Washington	49	28	21	Miller	17	8	9	Bonner	52	43	9
				Mitchell	24	12	12	Bonneville	60	44	16
GEORGIA				Monroe	53	42	11	Boundary	16	8	8
Appling	19	13	6	Morgan	27	18	9	Butte	5	3	2
Atkinson	9	5	4	Murray	43	18	25	Camas	5	5	—
Bacon	16	7	9	Oglethorpe	14	10	4	Caribou	13	13	—
Baldwin	68	37	31	Pierce	15	9	6	Cassia	48	34	14
Banks	24	17	7	Pike	16	7	9	Clark	3	3	—
Ben Hill	21	10	11	Polk	41	7	34	Clearwater	24	16	8
Berrien	17	11	6	Polk Police Department	22	20	2	Custer	11	7	4
Bleckley	17	8	9	Pulaski	18	9	9	Elmore	15	15	—
Brantley	14	10	4	Putnam	68	20	48	Franklin	15	7	8
Bulloch	51	50	1	Quitman	3	2	1	Fremont	14	14	—
Butts	38	19	19	Rabun	21	15	6	Gem	19	10	9
Calhoun	15	6	9	Schley	8	2	6	Gooding	10	7	3
Charlton	20	8	12	Screven	18	9	9	Idaho	30	19	11
Chattooga	41	25	16	Seminole	12	8	4	Jefferson	23	14	9
Clay	6	3	3	Stephens	31	24	7				
Clinch	14	9	5	Stewart	4	4	—				
Coffee	59	38	21								
Colquitt	63	28	35								

377

County by State	Total police employees	Total officers	Total civilians	County by State	Total police employees	Total officers	Total civilians	County by State	Total police employees	Total officers	Total civilians
IDAHO — **Continued**				**ILLINOIS —** **Continued**				**INDIANA —** **Continued**			
Jerome	18	14	4	Marion	24	21	3	Wabash	29	13	16
Kootenai	101	66	35	Marshall	17	7	10	Wayne	75	28	47
Latah	32	22	10	Mason	10	9	1	White	25	11	14
Lewis	11	6	5	Massac	24	9	15				
Lincoln	4	3	1	McDonough	18	12	6	**IOWA**			
Madison	18	18	—	Mercer	17	11	6				
Minidoka	22	12	10	Montgomery	12	12	—	Adair	6	5	1
Nez Perce	31	18	13	Morgan	38	16	22	Adams	8	3	5
Oneida	9	5	4	Moultrie	16	10	6	Allamakee	13	7	6
Owyhee	18	9	9	Perry	22	14	8	Appanoose	13	8	5
Payette	22	13	9	Piatt	20	10	10	Audubon	8	5	3
Power	13	7	6	Pike	19	9	10	Benton	19	7	12
Shoshone	21	13	8	Pope	6	4	2	Boone	13	7	6
Teton	11	8	3	Pulaski	10	5	5	Bremer	15	10	5
Twin Falls	63	45	18	Putnam	11	5	6	Buchanan	25	13	12
Valley	26	14	12	Randolph	18	9	9	Buena Vista	14	9	5
Washington	14	7	7	Richland	20	13	7	Butler	13	9	4
				Saline	45	32	13	Calhoun	11	6	5
ILLINOIS				Schuyler	8	3	5	Carroll	13	10	3
				Scott	7	3	4	Cass	9	7	2
Adams	61	26	35	Shelby	24	12	12	Cedar	18	6	12
Alexander	14	12	2	Stark	10	5	5	Cerro Gordo	28	14	14
Bond	17	8	9	Stephenson	31	31	—	Cherokee	15	5	10
Brown	6	5	1	Union	12	8	4	Chickasaw	13	8	5
Bureau	32	31	1	Vermilion	76	34	42	Clarke	9	5	4
Calhoun	6	3	3	Wabash	10	5	5	Clay	13	8	5
Carroll	21	13	8	Warren	17	11	6	Clayton	13	9	4
Cass	7	6	1	Washington	11	5	6	Clinton	40	27	13
Christian	28	14	14	Wayne	9	7	2	Crawford	11	9	2
Clark	8	8	—	White	7	7	—	Davis	8	3	5
Clay	12	7	5	Whiteside	31	21	10	Decatur	9	3	6
Coles	31	25	6	Williamson	58	25	33	Delaware	11	9	2
Crawford	15	8	7					Des Moines	21	17	4
Cumberland	11	6	5	**INDIANA**				Dickinson	17	8	9
De Witt	27	17	10					Emmet	16	8	8
Douglas	21	9	12	Bartholomew	80	37	43	Fayette	18	8	10
Edgar	18	17	1	Benton	12	4	8	Floyd	13	8	5
Edwards	8	3	5	Blackford	23	7	16	Franklin	9	7	2
Effingham	35	14	21	Carroll	24	8	16	Fremont	16	6	10
Fayette	20	9	11	Daviess	22	9	13	Greene	11	6	5
Ford	11	8	3	Decatur	21	7	14	Grundy	13	9	4
Franklin	42	19	23	Dubois	24	11	13	Guthrie	9	4	5
Fulton	26	20	6	Gibson	30	11	19	Hamilton	11	9	2
Gallatin	2	2	—	Grant	89	40	49	Hancock	7	7	—
Greene	12	6	6	Henry	30	18	12	Hardin	17	10	7
Hamilton	8	4	4	Jackson	28	13	15	Harrison	15	6	9
Hancock	17	9	8	Jefferson	22	12	10	Henry	16	10	6
Hardin	5	3	2	Jennings	16	10	6	Howard	11	7	4
Henderson	13	8	5	La Grange	27	14	13	Humboldt	9	9	—
Iroquois	29	17	12	La Porte	108	52	56	Ida	12	7	5
Jackson	37	19	18	Lawrence	46	17	29	Iowa	14	11	3
Jasper	20	9	11	Martin	16	5	11	Jackson	14	8	6
Jefferson	31	17	14	Montgomery	24	13	11	Jasper	27	9	18
Jo Daviess	30	27	3	Newton	26	8	18	Jefferson	12	6	6
Johnson	12	6	6	Noble	38	16	22	Jones	17	9	8
Knox	46	43	3	Pulaski	21	9	12	Keokuk	9	5	4
La Salle	61	48	13	Putnam	26	10	16	Kossuth	11	9	2
Lawrence	9	5	4	Randolph	37	14	23	Lee	28	14	14
Lee	35	30	5	Ripley	15	9	6	Louisa	16	8	8
Livingston	42	30	12	Rush	23	10	13	Lucas	12	5	7
Logan	26	20	6	Steuben	50	19	31	Lyon	11	8	3
Macoupin	27	23	4	Switzerland	9	4	5	Madison	13	5	8

Table 81. — Number of Full-time Law Enforcement Employees, Rural Counties, October 31, 1996 — Continued

County by State	Total police employees	Total officers	Total civilians	County by State	Total police employees	Total officers	Total civilians	County by State	Total police employees	Total officers	Total civilians
IOWA — Continued				**KANSAS —** Continued				**KANSAS —** Continued			
Mahaska	23	9	14	Ford	38	15	23	Stevens	14	6	8
Marion	20	11	9	Franklin	45	19	26	Sumner	24	13	11
Marshall	29	15	14	Geary	56	22	34	Thomas	11	11	—
Mills	19	8	11	Gove	4	3	1	Trego	7	3	4
Mitchell	7	6	1	Graham	7	3	4	Wabaunsee	10	6	4
Monona	11	5	6	Grant	13	6	7	Wallace	2	2	—
Monroe	10	5	5	Gray	11	5	6	Washington	6	6	—
Montgomery	19	9	10	Greeley	6	3	3	Wichita	9	4	5
Muscatine	53	19	34	Greenwood	20	11	9	Wilson	18	6	12
O'Brien	18	10	8	Hamilton	8	5	3	Woodson	8	4	4
Osceola	15	10	5	Harper	13	5	8				
Page	9	5	4	Haskell	16	11	5	**KENTUCKY**			
Palo Alto	11	7	4	Hodgeman	9	4	5				
Plymouth	17	8	9	Jackson	16	7	9	Adair	4	3	1
Pocahontas	10	5	5	Jefferson	36	17	19	Allen	9	9	—
Poweshiek	12	8	4	Jewell	7	3	4	Anderson	7	7	—
Ringgold	7	3	4	Kearny	11	11	—	Anderson Police Department	2	2	—
Sac	9	6	3	Kingman	7	6	1	Ballard	7	7	—
Shelby	10	6	4	Kiowa	13	13	—	Barren	10	8	2
Sioux	22	12	10	Labette	27	14	13	Bath	4	4	—
Story	53	35	18	Lane	9	5	4	Boyle	7	7	—
Tama	25	12	13	Lincoln	7	3	4	Bracken	1	1	—
Taylor	8	4	4	Linn	16	9	7	Breathitt	4	4	—
Union	13	6	7	Logan	3	3	—	Breckinridge	7	7	—
Van Buren	10	5	5	Lyon	56	10	46	Butler	5	5	—
Wapello	27	8	19	Marion	12	5	7	Caldwell	1	1	—
Washington	27	19	8	Marshall	14	6	8	Calloway	14	10	4
Wayne	8	4	4	McPherson	31	31	—	Carlisle	4	4	—
Webster	29	15	14	Meade	13	4	9	Carroll	5	5	—
Winnebago	7	5	2	Mitchell	6	4	2	Casey	5	5	—
Winneshiek	16	10	6	Montgomery	26	19	7	Clay	6	6	—
Worth	10	5	5	Morris	7	3	4	Clinton	3	3	—
Wright	7	6	1	Morton	9	4	5	Crittenden	3	3	—
				Nemaha	11	5	6	Cumberland	2	1	1
KANSAS				Neosho	18	10	8	Edmonson	6	6	—
				Ness	11	6	5	Elliott	2	1	1
Allen	15	7	8	Norton	8	3	5	Estill	3	2	1
Anderson	13	12	1	Osage	31	14	17	Fleming	6	6	—
Atchison	16	10	6	Osborne	14	8	6	Floyd	20	12	8
Barber	10	5	5	Ottawa	9	5	4	Franklin	10	10	—
Barton	37	19	18	Pawnee	12	5	7	Fulton	4	4	—
Bourbon	7	6	1	Phillips	14	8	6	Garrard	4	4	—
Brown	17	6	11	Pottawatomie	31	19	12	Graves	12	9	3
Chase	9	3	6	Pratt	14	8	6	Grayson	9	9	—
Chautauqua	9	4	5	Rawlins	8	3	5	Green	4	4	—
Cherokee	22	12	10	Reno	61	51	10	Hancock	6	6	—
Cheyenne	4	3	1	Republic	10	5	5	Hardin	16	16	—
Clark	10	5	5	Rice	14	7	7	Harlan	12	11	1
Clay	13	10	3	Riley Police Department	129	87	42	Harrison	6	6	—
Cloud	15	10	5	Rooks	10	6	4	Hart	7	7	—
Coffey	21	9	12	Rush	9	4	5	Henry	5	5	—
Comanche	9	6	3	Russell	10	5	5	Hickman	3	2	1
Cowley	31	31	—	Saline	73	69	4	Hopkins	16	13	3
Crawford	51	19	32	Scott	5	4	1	Jackson	4	4	—
Decatur	7	3	4	Seward	18	12	6	Johnson	8	7	1
Dickinson	26	15	11	Sheridan	8	3	5	Knott	6	4	2
Doniphan	7	3	4	Sherman	11	5	6	Knox	8	8	—
Edwards	9	5	4	Smith	8	3	5	Larue	7	6	1
Elk	6	3	3	Stafford	8	4	4	Laurel	14	14	—
Ellis	18	11	7	Stanton	11	6	5	Lawrence	6	4	2
Ellsworth	13	8	5								
Finney	61	58	3								

379

Table 81. — Number of Full-time Law Enforcement Employees, Rural Counties, October 31, 1996 — Continued

County by State	Total police employees	Total officers	Total civilians	County by State	Total police employees	Total officers	Total civilians	County by State	Total police employees	Total officers	Total civilians
KENTUCKY — Continued				**LOUISIANA —** Continued				**MARYLAND —** Continued			
Lee	1	1	—	Beauregard	63	51	12	Wicomico	72	57	15
Leslie	6	6	—	Bienville	39	33	6	Worcester	31	26	5
Letcher	12	10	2	Cameron	72	50	22				
Lewis	8	8	—	Catahoula	29	29	—	**MICHIGAN**			
Lincoln	4	4	—	Claiborne	24	17	7				
Livingston	4	4	—	Concordia	58	55	3	Alcona	21	13	8
Logan	11	9	2	De Soto	60	52	8	Alger	13	9	4
Lyon	3	2	1	East Carroll	23	23	—	Alpena	25	14	11
Lyon Police				East Feliciana	42	18	24	Antrim	39	16	23
Department	6	5	1	Evangeline	47	47	—	Arenac	20	13	7
Magoffin	5	4	1	Franklin	65	65	—	Baraga	5	5	—
Marion	2	2	—	Grant	43	43	—	Barry	36	23	13
Marshall	17	16	1	Iberia	147	147	—	Benzie	41	16	25
Martin	8	8	—	Iberville	142	65	77	Branch	38	17	21
Mason	11	10	1	Jackson	34	34	—	Cass	64	33	31
McCracken	40	36	4	Jefferson Davis	40	15	25	Charlevoix	23	15	8
McCreary	12	10	2	La Salle	32	21	11	Cheboygan	26	14	12
McCreary Police				Lincoln	46	46	—	Chippewa	27	15	12
Department	1	1	—	Morehouse	136	30	106	Clare	32	23	9
McLean	4	4	—	Natchitoches	62	42	20	Crawford	27	16	11
Meade	6	6	—	Pointe Coupee	106	76	30	Delta	27	14	13
Menifee	2	2	—	Red River	43	40	3	Dickinson	23	12	11
Mercer	6	6	—	Richland	38	38	—	Emmet	28	16	12
Metcalfe	3	3	—	Sabine	62	62	—	Gladwin	27	21	6
Monroe	4	4	—	St. Helena	20	14	6	Gogebic	20	16	4
Montgomery	12	12	—	St. Mary	110	110	—	Grand Traverse	85	55	30
Morgan	4	4	—	Tangipahoa	203	75	128	Gratiot	37	21	16
Muhlenberg	9	9	—	Tensas	51	51	—	Hillsdale	37	23	14
Nelson	9	6	3	Tensas Basin Levee	2	2	—	Houghton	28	19	9
Nelson Police				Union	40	25	15	Huron	48	24	24
Department	6	6	—	Vermilion	102	73	29	Ionia	48	19	29
Nicholas	3	3	—	Vernon	118	118	—	Iosco	28	13	15
Ohio	14	14	—	Washington	95	65	30	Iron	10	8	2
Owen	4	4	—	West Carroll	21	21	—	Isabella	42	22	20
Owsley	3	3	—	West Feliciana	25	20	5	Kalkaska	39	19	20
Pike	30	18	12	Winn	33	33	—	Keweenaw	6	5	1
Powell	9	7	2					Lake	40	13	27
Pulaski	24	16	8	**MAINE**				Leelanau	31	15	16
Robertson	1	1	—	Aroostook	14	9	5	Livingston	103	56	47
Rockcastle	3	3	—	Franklin	23	14	9	Luce	4	3	1
Rowan	7	4	3	Hancock	14	12	2	Mackinac	17	7	10
Russell	7	3	4	Kennebec	27	20	7	Manistee	25	13	12
Shelby	9	9	—	Knox	21	15	6	Marquette	47	31	16
Simpson	8	8	—	Lincoln	19	16	3	Mason	31	20	11
Spencer	3	3	—	Oxford	20	12	8	Mecosta	41	26	15
Taylor	6	6	—	Penobscot	21	18	3	Menominee	31	14	17
Todd	3	3	—	Piscataquis	12	8	4	Missaukee	21	10	11
Trigg	6	4	2	Sagadahoc	19	16	3	Montcalm	54	23	31
Trimble	3	3	—	Somerset	18	12	6	Montmorency	25	12	13
Union	7	5	2	Waldo	15	10	5	Newaygo	24	21	3
Warren	33	28	5	Washington	16	10	6	Oceana	32	18	14
Washington	4	4	—	York	17	15	2	Ogemaw	30	18	12
Wayne	7	7	—					Ontonagon	13	10	3
Webster	7	7	—	**MARYLAND**				Osceola	30	16	14
Whitley	8	8	—	Caroline	20	18	2	Oscoda	14	8	6
Wolfe	4	3	1	Dorchester	30	22	8	Otsego	23	11	12
				Garrett	31	17	14	Presque Isle	17	12	5
LOUISIANA				Kent	20	19	1	Roscommon	23	18	5
Allen	39	21	18	St. Mary's	102	81	21	St. Joseph	51	24	27
Assumption	56	39	17	Somerset	15	13	2	Sanilac	46	25	21
Avoyelles	238	238	—	Talbot	15	13	2	Schoolcraft	7	4	3

Table 81. — Number of Full-time Law Enforcement Employees, Rural Counties, October 31, 1996 — Continued

County by State	Total police employees	Total officers	Total civilians	County by State	Total police employees	Total officers	Total civilians	County by State	Total police employees	Total officers	Total civilians
MICHIGAN — Continued				**MINNESOTA — Continued**				**MISSOURI — Continued**			
Shiawassee	57	34	23	Roseau	15	9	6	Crawford	18	16	2
Tuscola	52	30	22	Sibley	19	9	10	Dallas	18	12	6
Wexford	46	20	26	Steele	31	16	15	Daviess	5	4	1
				Stevens	10	5	5	Dent	12	9	3
MINNESOTA				Swift	12	6	6	Douglas	8	5	3
Aitkin	34	16	18	Todd	21	12	9	Dunklin	14	8	6
Becker	41	18	23	Traverse	6	4	2	Gentry	6	3	3
Beltrami	49	19	30	Wabasha	22	11	11	Grundy	8	4	4
Big Stone	7	4	3	Wadena	13	5	8	Holt	10	6	4
Blue Earth	40	19	21	Waseca	22	10	12	Howell	21	16	5
Brown	32	9	23	Watonwan	16	8	8	Johnson	32	29	3
Carlton	35	17	18	Wilkin	7	6	1	Laclede	16	15	1
Cass	48	30	18	Winona	46	18	28	Lawrence	23	22	1
Chippewa	16	7	9	Yellow Medicine	13	7	6	Linn	5	4	1
Clearwater	14	7	7					Livingston	11	11	—
Cook	13	8	5	**MISSISSIPPI**				Maries	10	8	2
Cottonwood	10	6	4	Adams	44	27	17	McDonald	13	12	1
Crow Wing	53	26	27	Attala	11	6	5	Mercer	7	3	4
Dodge	32	18	14	Chickasaw	12	12	—	Mississippi	12	11	1
Douglas	46	16	30	Claiborne	17	10	7	Moniteau	9	5	4
Faribault	16	8	8	Clarke	18	7	11	Monroe	9	6	3
Fillmore	25	14	11	Clay	10	7	3	Montgomery	15	10	5
Freeborn	33	17	16	Coahoma	11	10	1	Morgan	12	10	2
Goodhue	58	31	27	Covington	11	6	5	Nodaway	15	8	7
Grant	10	5	5	Franklin	7	5	2	Oregon	9	5	4
Hubbard	21	10	11	Grenada	30	10	20	Osage	8	3	5
Itasca	47	43	4	Holmes	19	8	11	Ozark	10	8	2
Jackson	14	7	7	Itawamba	17	7	10	Pemiscot	19	14	5
Kanabec	16	8	8	Jones	52	20	32	Perry	21	17	4
Kandiyohi	58	31	27	Lauderdale	60	25	35	Pike	31	11	20
Kittson	9	5	4	Lawrence	10	6	4	Polk	25	19	6
Koochiching	16	10	6	Lee	49	49	—	Pulaski	18	18	—
Lac Qui Parle	9	4	5	Montgomery	8	5	3	Ripley	9	8	1
Lake	18	12	6	Oktibbeha	27	14	13	St. Clair	34	12	22
Lake-of-the-Woods	8	4	4	Panola	35	12	23	Ste. Genevieve	46	36	10
Le Sueur	21	12	9	Quitman	9	5	4	Saline	14	13	1
Lincoln	8	4	4	Simpson	29	10	19	Schuyler	9	5	4
Lyon	20	9	11	Tate	22	10	12	Scotland	9	8	1
Mahnomen	14	9	5	Tippah	9	7	2	Shelby	10	4	6
Marshall	15	9	6	Tishomingo	12	7	5	Stone	28	23	5
Martin	21	7	14	Union	15	8	7	Sullivan	7	5	2
McLeod	35	17	18	Walthall	12	4	8	Vernon	19	11	8
Meeker	21	10	11	Warren	53	27	26	Washington	22	15	7
Mille Lacs	31	14	17	Washington	42	21	21	Wayne	10	6	4
Morrison	39	14	25	Wayne	9	4	5	Worth	5	4	1
Mower	40	18	22	Winston	12	6	6				
Murray	9	5	4	Yalobusha	11	6	5	**MONTANA**			
Nicollet	21	11	10					Beaverhead	14	7	7
Nobles	16	7	9	**MISSOURI**				Big Horn	27	12	15
Norman	8	5	3	Atchison	8	4	4	Blaine	13	6	7
Otter Tail	58	25	33	Audrain	21	21	—	Broadwater	9	6	3
Pennington	16	6	10	Barry	20	12	8	Carbon	10	7	3
Pine	36	20	16	Barton	11	9	2	Carter	2	2	—
Pipestone	16	6	10	Benton	15	12	3	Chouteau	15	9	6
Pope	11	5	6	Bollinger	10	6	4	Custer	11	5	6
Red Lake	10	8	2	Butler	23	19	4	Daniels	7	3	4
Redwood	18	9	9	Caldwell	9	4	5	Dawson	11	6	5
Renville	15	9	6	Cape Girardeau	43	30	13	Deer Lodge	35	23	12
Rice	36	32	4	Carroll	16	7	9	Fallon	13	2	11
Rock	11	5	6	Carter	4	4	—	Fergus	19	7	12
				Cole	47	39	8	Flathead	81	41	40
				Cooper	7	6	1	Gallatin	54	31	23

Table 81. — Number of Full-time Law Enforcement Employees, Rural Counties, October 31, 1996 — Continued

County by State	Total police employees	Total officers	Total civilians	County by State	Total police employees	Total officers	Total civilians	County by State	Total police employees	Total officers	Total civilians
MONTANA — Continued				**NEBRASKA — Continued**				**NEVADA — Continued**			
Garfield	4	3	1	Deuel	5	4	1	Churchill	41	34	7
Glacier	16	8	8	Dixon	10	6	4	Douglas	106	92	14
Golden Valley	2	2	—	Dodge	19	16	3	Elko	58	49	9
Granite	9	5	4	Dundy	7	4	3	Esmeralda	15	11	4
Hill	23	10	13	Fillmore	8	4	4	Eureka	22	16	6
Jefferson	18	10	8	Franklin	3	3	—	Humboldt	47	21	26
Judith Basin	4	3	1	Frontier	9	5	4	Lander	34	25	9
Lake	33	14	19	Furnas	15	8	7	Lincoln	17	16	1
Lewis and Clark	54	31	23	Gage	16	9	7	Lyon	76	51	25
Liberty	9	4	5	Garden	10	5	5	Mineral	32	27	5
Lincoln	31	18	13	Garfield	2	2	—	Pershing	17	12	5
Madison	14	8	6	Gosper	5	4	1	Storey	27	24	3
McCone	3	3	—	Grant	1	1	—	White Pine	37	37	—
Meagher	7	4	3	Hall	28	22	6				
Mineral	22	8	14	Hamilton	13	6	7	**NEW HAMPSHIRE**			
Missoula	88	48	40	Harlan	8	4	4	Belknap	18	9	9
Musselshell	9	5	4	Hitchcock	9	4	5				
Park	19	13	6	Holt	10	4	6	**NEW MEXICO**			
Phillips	12	8	4	Hooker	1	1	—	Catron	10	5	5
Pondera	11	8	3	Jefferson	10	5	5	Curry	17	14	3
Powder River	7	3	4	Johnson	6	2	4	Eddy	72	33	39
Powell	17	10	7	Kearney	11	6	5	Lincoln	21	14	7
Prairie	8	3	5	Keith	15	8	7	Luna	47	23	24
Ravalli	48	23	25	Keya Paha	1	1	—	McKinley	51	37	14
Richland	15	7	8	Kimball	7	3	4	Quay	8	7	1
Roosevelt	23	12	11	Knox	15	7	8	Rio Arriba	29	27	2
Rosebud	32	17	15	Lincoln	43	22	21	Roosevelt	10	9	1
Sanders	22	8	14	Logan	2	2	—	San Juan	78	64	14
Sheridan	10	5	5	Loup	1	1	—	Sierra	13	11	2
Silver Bow	73	44	29	Madison	39	20	19	Socorro	11	9	2
Stillwater	11	7	4	McPherson	1	1	—	Taos	19	15	4
Sweet Grass	10	4	6	Merrick	9	5	4	Torrance	13	12	1
Teton	11	7	4	Morrill	8	3	5				
Toole	18	11	7	Nance	9	5	4	**NEW YORK**			
Treasure	2	2	—	Nemaha	9	3	6	Allegany	8	4	4
Valley	15	7	8	Nuckolls	7	4	3	Cattaraugus	58	39	19
Wheatland	7	5	2	Otoe	16	8	8	Chenango	36	22	14
Wibaux	2	2	—	Pawnee	4	3	1	Clinton	42	33	9
				Phelps	9	4	5	Columbia	45	35	10
NEBRASKA				Pierce	8	4	4	Cortland	45	29	16
Adams	29	18	11	Platte	25	22	3	Delaware	18	11	7
Antelope	11	6	5	Polk	12	6	6	Greene	21	19	2
Arthur	1	1	—	Red Willow	6	4	2	Jefferson	111	85	26
Banner	1	1	—	Richardson	12	6	6	Lewis	23	17	6
Blaine	1	1	—	Rock	8	3	5	Otsego	17	14	3
Boone	10	6	4	Saline	14	10	4	St. Lawrence	36	33	3
Box Butte	14	4	10	Saunders	23	11	12	Steuben	41	24	17
Boyd	2	2	—	Scotts Bluff	20	15	5	Sullivan	50	34	16
Brown	7	3	4	Seward	19	9	10	Tompkins	39	29	10
Buffalo	49	20	29	Sheridan	5	4	1	Ulster	58	52	6
Burt	10	5	5	Sherman	3	2	1	Wyoming	40	29	11
Butler	7	4	3	Sioux	1	1	—	Yates	37	20	17
Cedar	9	4	5	Stanton	8	7	1				
Chase	8	2	6	Thayer	10	6	4	**NORTH CAROLINA**			
Cherry	10	4	6	Thomas	1	1	—	Alleghany	27	10	17
Cheyenne	5	4	1	Thurston	7	2	5	Anson	37	19	18
Clay	9	4	5	Valley	6	3	3	Ashe	29	16	13
Colfax	9	5	4	Wayne	5	4	1	Avery	27	22	5
Cuming	8	4	4	Webster	9	6	3	Beaufort	63	37	26
Custer	7	6	1	York	19	9	10	Bertie	20	14	6
Dawes	8	3	5	**NEVADA**				Bladen	60	38	22
Dawson	53	17	36	Carson City	106	77	29				

Table 81. — Number of Full-time Law Enforcement Employees, Rural Counties, October 31, 1996 — Continued

County by State	Total police employees	Total officers	Total civilians	County by State	Total police employees	Total officers	Total civilians	County by State	Total police employees	Total officers	Total civilians
NORTH CAROLINA — Continued				**NORTH DAKOTA —** Continued				**OHIO —** Continued			
Camden	7	7	—	Bottineau	12	8	4	Muskingum	97	56	41
Carteret	78	36	42	Bowman	1	1	—	Noble	13	8	5
Caswell	46	28	18	Burke	4	4	—	Ottawa	50	43	7
Cherokee	23	12	11	Cavalier	9	5	4	Preble	66	49	17
Chowan	30	12	18	Dickey	5	4	1	Ross	84	61	23
Clay	18	9	9	Divide	4	3	1	Scioto	50	36	14
Cleveland	98	61	37	Dunn	4	3	1	Seneca	63	19	44
Columbus	73	42	31	Eddy	5	5	—	Shelby	60	34	26
Dare	111	51	60	Emmons	3	3	—	Union	39	25	14
Duplin	67	40	27	Foster	3	2	1	Van Wert	23	17	6
Gates	4	4	—	Golden Valley	4	3	1	Williams	24	21	3
Granville	38	24	14	Grant	2	2	—	Wyandot	18	10	8
Greene	24	21	3	Griggs	2	2	—				
Halifax	74	43	31	Hettinger	3	3	—	**OKLAHOMA**			
Harnett	101	63	38	Kidder	3	2	1	Adair	14	8	6
Haywood	32	31	1	Lamoure	4	3	1	Alfalfa	8	5	3
Henderson	111	85	26	Logan	3	2	1	Atoka	9	5	4
Hertford	47	13	34	McHenry	6	5	1	Beaver	9	5	4
Hoke	52	47	5	McIntosh	3	3	—	Beckham	13	9	4
Hyde	12	8	4	McKenzie	8	5	3	Blaine	11	7	4
Iredell	109	91	18	McLean	23	22	1	Bryan	23	10	13
Jackson	34	27	7	Mercer	18	7	11	Caddo	18	18	—
Jones	14	10	4	Mountrail	8	4	4	Carter	42	11	31
Lee	57	28	29	Nelson	5	4	1	Cherokee	18	14	4
Lenoir	81	44	37	Oliver	4	4	—	Choctaw	12	5	7
Macon	31	30	1	Pembina	20	14	6	Cimarron	8	4	4
Martin	21	19	2	Pierce	7	3	4	Coal	10	5	5
McDowell	51	37	14	Ramsey	6	5	1	Cotton	11	6	5
Montgomery	41	25	16	Ransom	5	5	—	Craig	12	6	6
Moore	86	51	35	Renville	5	5	—	Custer	18	6	12
Northampton	48	16	32	Richland	17	9	8	Delaware	20	12	8
Pamlico	24	13	11	Rolette	12	9	3	Dewey	7	3	4
Pasquotank	28	24	4	Sargent	4	3	1	Ellis	8	4	4
Pender	52	33	19	Sheridan	1	1	—	Garvin	20	12	8
Perquimans	9	8	1	Sioux	1	1	—	Grady	23	12	11
Person	65	34	31	Slope	1	1	—	Grant	9	6	3
Polk	32	18	14	Stark	12	9	3	Greer	6	6	—
Richmond	49	31	18	Steele	3	3	—	Harmon	2	2	—
Robeson	182	79	103	Stutsman	10	8	2	Harper	6	3	3
Rockingham	94	77	17	Towner	2	1	1	Haskell	12	7	5
Rutherford	97	44	53	Traill	8	4	4	Hughes	12	6	6
Sampson	64	45	19	Walsh	14	8	6	Jackson	14	8	6
Scotland	54	33	21	Ward	40	17	23	Jefferson	16	8	8
Stanly	46	34	12	Wells	3	3	—	Johnston	10	5	5
Surry	66	47	19	Williams	27	22	5	Kay	27	12	15
Swain	23	10	13					Kingfisher	12	7	5
Transylvania	50	34	16	**OHIO**				Kiowa	10	10	—
Tyrrell	14	8	6	Ashland	49	23	26	Latimer	12	9	3
Vance	73	30	43	Champaign	35	21	14	Le Flore	20	9	11
Warren	54	18	36	Clinton	37	29	8	Lincoln	17	10	7
Washington	26	15	11	Coshocton	60	47	13	Love	15	6	9
Watauga	41	26	15	Darke	57	30	27	Major	8	4	4
Wilkes	80	50	30	Defiance	26	21	5	Marshall	14	7	7
Wilson	113	56	57	Erie	68	30	38	Mayes	20	17	3
Yancey	15	7	8	Hardin	20	13	7	McCurtain	26	16	10
				Harrison	10	10	—	McIntosh	13	8	5
NORTH DAKOTA				Henry	20	17	3	Murray	9	4	5
Adams	4	3	1	Huron	37	30	7	Muskogee	18	14	4
Barnes	7	7	—	Logan	55	25	30	Noble	11	11	—
Benson	4	4	—	Marion	59	39	20	Nowata	16	15	1
Billings	4	3	1	Morrow	52	31	21	Okfuskee	12	8	4

Table 81. — Number of Full-time Law Enforcement Employees, Rural Counties, October 31, 1996 — Continued

County by State	Total police employees	Total officers	Total civilians	County by State	Total police employees	Total officers	Total civilians	County by State	Total police employees	Total officers	Total civilians
OKLAHOMA — **Continued**				**SOUTH CAROLINA —** **Continued**				**TENNESSEE —** **Continued**			
Okmulgee	20	18	2	Chesterfield	35	24	11	Chester	19	7	12
Ottawa	22	12	10	Clarendon	54	26	28	Coffee	47	46	1
Pawnee	16	10	6	Colleton	105	46	59	Crockett	24	9	15
Payne	25	13	12	Darlington	40	37	3	Fentress	19	9	10
Pittsburg	29	21	8	Dillon	35	21	14	Gibson	55	29	26
Pontotoc	16	9	7	Fairfield	41	36	5	Greene	97	41	56
Pushmataha	14	6	8	Georgetown	101	51	50	Hamblen	47	23	24
Roger Mills	13	13	—	Greenwood	86	57	29	Henderson	27	16	11
Seminole	13	8	5	Hampton	26	13	13	Henry	50	47	3
Stephens	19	11	8	Jasper	43	21	22	Houston	17	8	9
Texas	15	7	8	Kershaw	39	36	3	Humphreys	15	8	7
Tillman	11	6	5	Lancaster	78	48	30	Lawrence	40	25	15
Washington	27	15	12	Laurens	68	36	32	Lincoln	45	16	29
Washita	8	5	3	Lee	25	23	2	Macon	29	16	13
Woods	8	4	4	Marion	26	21	5	Marshall	35	15	20
Woodward	15	10	5	Marlboro	23	20	3	Maury	54	27	27
				McCormick	19	9	10	McMinn	49	23	26
OREGON				Newberry	42	29	13	Meigs	19	10	9
Baker	11	7	4	Oconee	57	43	14	Monroe	31	31	—
Benton	34	29	5	Orangeburg	74	59	15	Perry	13	8	5
Clatsop	24	20	4	Saluda	27	13	14	Putnam	81	34	47
Coos	46	29	17	Union	29	25	4	Stewart	14	9	5
Crook	13	9	4	Williamsburg	45	22	23	Trousdale	15	7	8
Curry	23	14	9					Van Buren	11	6	5
Deschutes	68	54	14	**SOUTH DAKOTA**				Warren	50	35	15
Douglas	91	72	19	Aurora	4	3	1	Wayne	17	11	6
Gilliam	5	4	1	Beadle	16	5	11	Weakley	31	16	15
Grant	5	4	1	Bennett	10	6	4	White	27	24	3
Harney	5	4	1	Brookings	16	8	8				
Hood River	27	14	13	Butte	5	4	1	**TEXAS**			
Jefferson	19	14	5	Charles Mix	10	4	6	Anderson	48	20	28
Josephine	54	37	17	Clay	6	5	1	Andrews	23	14	9
Klamath	31	24	7	Corson	3	2	1	Angelina	73	41	32
Lake	6	6	—	Davison	18	4	14	Aransas	33	17	16
Lincoln	27	22	5	Day	6	3	3	Armstrong	8	3	5
Linn	79	53	26	Deuel	7	4	3	Atascosa	62	22	40
Malheur	18	11	7	Douglas	2	2	—	Austin	36	24	12
Morrow	18	11	7	Edmunds	6	4	2	Bailey	9	4	5
Sherman	6	5	1	Faulk	6	3	3	Bandera	25	15	10
Tillamook	23	21	2	Grant	9	3	6	Baylor	9	4	5
Umatilla	29	16	13	Harding	2	1	1	Bee	32	16	16
Umatilla Tribal	17	12	5	Hughes	21	6	15	Blanco	11	5	6
Union	10	9	1	Hyde	1	1	—	Borden	3	2	1
Wallowa	14	5	9	Jerauld	1	1	—	Bosque	21	9	12
Wasco	24	18	6	Kingsbury	3	2	1	Brewster	12	6	6
Wheeler	3	3	—	Lake	6	5	1	Briscoe	3	2	1
				Lawrence	32	10	22	Brooks	25	12	13
PENNSYLVANIA				Lyman	4	3	1	Brown	38	19	19
Clarion	8	8	—	McCook	3	2	1	Burleson	21	11	10
Elk	3	2	1	Meade	42	14	28	Burnet	49	28	21
Jefferson	5	5	—	Miner	4	3	1	Calhoun	36	18	18
Warren	45	32	13	Perkins	2	2	—	Callahan	11	7	4
				Potter	8	3	5	Camp	14	5	9
SOUTH CAROLINA				Sanborn	3	2	1	Carson	11	5	6
Abbeville	33	23	10	Spink	14	9	5	Cass	34	11	23
Allendale	10	9	1	Stanley	6	5	1	Castro	17	11	6
Bamberg	16	10	6	Sully	2	2	—	Cherokee	47	21	26
Barnwell	30	22	8	Yankton	7	6	1	Childress	12	5	7
Beaufort	162	150	12					Clay	15	9	6
Calhoun	12	11	1	**TENNESSEE**				Cochran	14	8	6
Chester	34	30	4	Bradley	98	84	14	Coke	5	4	1

Table 81. — Number of Full-time Law Enforcement Employees, Rural Counties, October 31, 1996 — Continued

County by State	Total police employees	Total officers	Total civilians	County by State	Total police employees	Total officers	Total civilians	County by State	Total police employees	Total officers	Total civilians
TEXAS — Continued				**TEXAS —** Continued				**TEXAS —** Continued			
Coleman	11	5	6	Jones	17	6	11	Rusk	50	26	24
Collingsworth	11	7	4	Karnes	15	8	7	Sabine	16	7	9
Colorado	28	16	12	Kendall	38	16	22	San Augustine	10	4	6
Comanche	18	9	9	Kenedy	8	8	—	San Jacinto	25	14	11
Concho	7	3	4	Kent	7	3	4	San Saba	9	4	5
Cooke	26	14	12	Kerr	57	28	29	Schleicher	9	4	5
Cottle	4	2	2	Kimble	9	5	4	Scurry	17	7	10
Crane	11	7	4	King	1	1	—	Shackelford	13	4	9
Crockett	12	9	3	Kinney	14	4	10	Shelby	28	10	18
Crosby	16	7	9	Kleberg	39	28	11	Sherman	9	4	5
Culberson	11	6	5	Knox	9	4	5	Somervell	28	18	10
Dallam	9	4	5	Lamar	60	19	41	Starr	93	32	61
Dawson	9	6	3	Lamb	14	8	6	Stephens	10	5	5
Deaf Smith	34	17	17	Lampasas	22	11	11	Sterling	4	3	1
Delta	12	6	6	La Salle	9	8	1	Stonewall	6	2	4
Dewitt	23	8	15	Lavaca	20	10	10	Sutton	14	5	9
Dickens	6	3	3	Lee	15	9	6	Swisher	10	7	3
Dimmit	22	11	11	Leon	15	9	6	Terrell	5	3	2
Donley	6	5	1	Limestone	38	18	20	Terry	15	7	8
Duval	27	15	12	Lipscomb	8	4	4	Throckmorton	5	1	4
Eastland	16	7	9	Live Oak	26	16	10	Titus	34	13	21
Edwards	11	5	6	Llano	26	15	11	Trinity	13	8	5
Erath	39	20	19	Loving	3	2	1	Tyler	27	13	14
Falls	9	4	5	Lynn	12	6	6	Upton	16	9	7
Fannin	20	11	9	Madison	20	9	11	Uvalde	27	15	12
Fayette	33	16	17	Marion	11	10	1	Val Verde	78	24	54
Fisher	10	5	5	Martin	7	3	4	Van Zandt	48	23	25
Floyd	12	6	6	Mason	3	1	2	Walker	62	23	39
Foard	5	3	2	Matagorda	66	45	21	Ward	29	14	15
Franklin	22	16	6	Maverick	34	18	16	Washington	45	32	13
Freestone	21	14	7	McCulloch	10	5	5	Wharton	55	36	19
Frio	18	9	9	McMullen	4	3	1	Wheeler	12	6	6
Gaines	18	8	10	Medina	28	16	12	Wilbarger	18	8	10
Garza	12	8	4	Menard	8	4	4	Willacy	34	21	13
Gillespie	19	12	7	Milam	25	11	14	Winkler	28	9	19
Glasscock	4	2	2	Mills	9	5	4	Wise	56	29	27
Goliad	23	8	15	Mitchell	10	4	6	Wood	47	22	25
Gonzales	29	17	12	Montague	19	8	11	Yoakum	19	9	10
Gray	28	13	15	Moore	24	11	13	Young	22	13	9
Grimes	12	10	2	Morris	20	7	13	Zapata	44	26	18
Hale	47	47	—	Motley	2	2	—	Zavala	17	9	8
Hall	9	3	6	Nacogdoches	57	26	31				
Hamilton	20	9	11	Navarro	77	46	31	**UTAH**			
Hansford	8	3	5	Newton	18	13	5				
Hardeman	8	4	4	Nolan	19	11	8	Beaver	17	12	5
Hartley	5	2	3	Ochiltree	15	7	8	Box Elder	33	23	10
Haskell	6	3	3	Oldham	10	5	5	Cache	64	45	19
Hemphill	14	9	5	Palo Pinto	45	20	25	Carbon	29	15	14
Hill	32	16	16	Panola	33	26	7	Daggett	6	5	1
Hockley	19	9	10	Parmer	12	5	7	Duchesne	20	19	1
Hopkins	43	21	22	Pecos	21	18	3	Emery	33	28	5
Houston	20	8	12	Polk	56	29	27	Garfield	10	4	6
Howard	23	14	9	Presidio	17	5	12	Grand	25	17	8
Hudspeth	30	8	22	Rains	17	10	7	Iron	19	16	3
Hutchinson	30	19	11	Reagan	10	6	4	Juab	17	6	11
Irion	8	4	4	Real	6	3	3	Kane	16	10	6
Jack	14	10	4	Red River	20	10	10	Millard	33	25	8
Jackson	23	12	11	Reeves	33	14	19	Morgan	8	7	1
Jasper	26	17	9	Refugio	34	15	19	Piute	4	3	1
Jeff Davis	4	3	1	Roberts	4	3	1	Rich	8	3	5
Jim Hogg	31	15	16	Robertson	19	7	12	San Juan	30	27	3
Jim Wells	25	16	9	Runnels	16	8	8	Sanpete	22	16	6

Table 81. — Number of Full-time Law Enforcement Employees, Rural Counties, October 31, 1996 — Continued

County by State	Total police employees	Total officers	Total civilians	County by State	Total police employees	Total officers	Total civilians	County by State	Total police employees	Total officers	Total civilians
UTAH — Continued				**VIRGINIA — Continued**				**WEST VIRGINIA — Continued**			
Sevier	57	22	35	Rockingham	42	33	9	McDowell	13	12	1
Summit	37	22	15	Russell	62	42	20	Mercer	27	21	6
Tooele	56	22	34	Shenandoah	46	41	5	Mingo	39	14	25
Uintah	42	17	25	Smyth	41	41	—	Monongalia	54	24	30
Wasatch	20	19	1	Southampton	64	21	43	Monroe	5	5	—
Washington	52	46	6	Surry	14	9	5	Morgan	9	8	1
Wayne	5	4	1	Sussex	35	33	2	Nicholas	19	14	5
				Tazewell	53	45	8	Pendleton	5	2	3
VERMONT				Warren	62	61	1	Pleasants	10	6	4
Lamoille	14	7	7	Westmoreland	24	17	7	Pocahontas	13	5	8
Orleans	7	4	3	Wise	62	46	16	Preston	25	13	12
Windham	9	9	—	Wythe	52	39	13	Raleigh	50	39	11
								Randolph	16	6	10
VIRGINIA				**WASHINGTON**				Ritchie	7	2	5
Accomack	46	43	3	Adams	19	17	2	Roane	6	6	—
Alleghany	32	29	3	Asotin	13	11	2	Summers	3	2	1
Amelia	16	10	6	Chelan	60	48	12	Taylor	12	5	7
Appomattox	25	23	2	Clallam	46	35	11	Tucker	9	4	5
Augusta	87	75	12	Columbia	14	10	4	Tyler	8	4	4
Bath	20	20	—	Cowlitz	53	46	7	Upshur	13	7	6
Bland	20	13	7	Douglas	35	25	10	Webster	4	4	—
Brunswick	29	21	8	Ferry	11	9	2	Wetzel	10	6	4
Buchanan	45	38	7	Garfield	11	4	7	Wirt	4	2	2
Buckingham	16	12	4	Grant	62	38	24	Wyoming	19	19	—
Caroline	39	31	8	Grays Harbor	81	40	41				
Carroll	38	30	8	Jefferson	38	20	18	**WISCONSIN**			
Charlotte	22	21	1	Kittitas	42	21	21	Adams	46	43	3
Craig	11	6	5	Lewis	61	46	15	Ashland	20	15	5
Cumberland	14	9	5	Lincoln	15	13	2	Barron	35	34	1
Dickenson	36	32	4	Mason	68	38	30	Bayfield	29	21	8
Essex	17	17	—	Okanogan	37	32	5	Buffalo	20	11	9
Floyd	21	14	7	Pend Oreille	26	14	12	Clark	38	38	—
Franklin	70	56	14	San Juan	26	19	7	Columbia	61	29	32
Frederick	70	58	12	Skagit	98	49	49	Crawford	20	19	1
Giles	37	26	11	Skamania	23	20	3	Dodge	74	40	34
Grayson	27	21	6	Wahkiakum	14	6	8	Door	43	41	2
Greensville	30	28	2	Walla Walla	43	19	24	Dunn	32	20	12
Halifax	62	44	18	Whitman	31	15	16	Florence	12	12	—
Henry	100	89	11					Fond Du Lac	101	92	9
Highland	16	11	5	**WEST VIRGINIA**				Forest	19	15	4
King and Queen	12	6	6	Barbour	10	5	5	Grant	42	23	19
King William	24	18	6	Berkeley	36	27	9	Green	43	34	9
Lancaster	28	23	5	Boone	20	18	2	Green Lake	29	17	12
Lee	44	42	2	Braxton	6	5	1	Iowa	19	11	8
Louisa	33	22	11	Calhoun	2	2	—	Iron	12	12	—
Lunenburg	13	7	6	Clay	4	4	—	Jackson	30	20	10
Madison	17	10	7	Doddridge	2	2	—	Jefferson	110	87	23
Mecklenburg	64	51	13	Fayette	31	29	2	Juneau	33	27	6
Middlesex	17	11	6	Gilmer	4	4	—	Kewaunee	29	26	3
Montgomery	53	43	10	Grant	9	6	3	Lafayette	21	13	8
Nelson	22	21	1	Greenbrier	26	18	8	Langlade	27	16	11
Northampton	39	34	5	Hampshire	9	3	6	Lincoln	39	26	13
Northumberland	20	20	—	Hardy	6	5	1	Manitowoc	98	53	45
Nottoway	17	16	1	Harrison	88	28	60	Marinette	50	26	24
Orange	32	21	11	Jackson	21	12	9	Marquette	27	26	1
Page	25	18	7	Jefferson	15	12	3	Menominee	11	10	1
Patrick	26	20	6	Lewis	9	9	—	Menominee Tribal Pd	46	27	19
Prince Edward	18	18	—	Lincoln	5	5	—	Monroe	42	40	2
Pulaski	67	55	12	Logan	42	19	23	Oconto	45	20	25
Rappahannock	21	20	1	Marion	49	24	25	Oneida	51	28	23
Richmond	14	8	6	Mason	23	12	11	Pepin	10	10	—
Rockbridge	23	16	7								

Table 81 — Number of Full-time Law Enforcement Employees, Rural Counties, October 31, 1996 — Continued

County by State	Total police employees	Total officers	Total civilians	County by State	Total police employees	Total officers	Total civilians	County by State	Total police employees	Total officers	Total civilians
WISCONSIN — Continued				**WISCONSIN — Continued**				**WYOMING — Continued**			
Polk	38	34	4	Waushara	27	21	6	Lincoln	35	16	19
Portage	76	41	35	Wood	69	42	27	Niobrara	16	4	12
Price	23	18	5					Park...........................	34	27	7
Richland	29	16	13	**WYOMING**				Platte	7	6	1
Rusk	26	13	13					Sheridan	27	13	14
Sauk	77	60	17	Albany	20	18	2	Sublette	24	16	8
Sawyer	28	25	3	Big Horn	16	8	8	Sweetwater	51	31	20
Shawano	81	34	47	Campbell	50	31	19	Teton	26	13	13
Taylor	28	17	11	Carbon	20	13	7	Uinta	53	36	17
Trempealeau	36	20	16	Converse	17	9	8	Washakie	13	7	6
Vernon	23	23	—	Crook	12	6	6	Weston	9	6	3
Vilas	49	31	18	Fremont	48	28	20				
Walworth	199	76	123	Goshen	9	7	2	**OTHER AREAS**			
Washburn	22	11	11	Hot Springs	11	10	1				
Waupaca	41	41	—	Johnson	7	6	1	Guam	439	315	124

SECTION VII

APPENDIX I

Methodology

The information compiled by UCR contributors is forwarded to the FBI either directly from local law enforcement agencies or through state-level UCR Programs in 44 states and the District of Columbia. Agencies submitting directly to the FBI are provided continuing guidance and support on an individual basis.

State-level UCR Programs are very effective intermediaries between local contributors and the FBI. Many of the Programs have mandatory reporting requirements and collect data beyond the national UCR scope to address crime problems germane to their particular locales. In most cases, these agencies are also able to provide more direct and frequent service to participating law enforcement agencies, to make information more readily available for use at the state level, and to contribute to more streamlined operations at the national level.

With the development of a state UCR Program, the FBI ceases direct collection of data from individual law enforcement agencies within the state. Instead, information from local agencies is forwarded to the national Program through the state data collection agency.

The conditions under which these systems are developed ensure consistency and comparability in the data submitted to the national Program, as well as provide for regular and timely reporting of national crime data. These conditions are (1) The state Program must conform to national Uniform Crime Reports' standards, definitions, and information requirements. The states are not, of course, prohibited from collecting other statistical data beyond the national requirements. (2) The state criminal justice agency must have a proven, effective, statewide Program and have instituted acceptable quality control procedures. (3) Coverage within the state by a state agency must be, at least, equal to that attained by the national Uniform Crime Reports. (4) The state agency must have adequate field staff assigned to conduct audits and to assist contributing agencies in record practices and crime reporting procedures. (5) The state agency must furnish to the FBI all of the detailed data regularly collected by the FBI in the form of duplicate returns, computer printouts, and/or magnetic tapes. (6) The state agency must have the proven capability (tested over a period of time) to supply all the statistical data required in time to meet national Uniform Crime Reports' publication deadlines.

To fulfill its responsibilities in connection with the UCR Program, the FBI continues to edit and review individual agency reports for both completeness and quality; has direct contact with individual contributors within the state when necessary in connection with crime reporting matters, coordinating such contact with the state agency; and upon request, conducts training programs within the state on law enforcement records

and crime reporting procedures. Should circumstances develop whereby the state agency does not comply with the aforementioned requirements, the national Program may reinstitute a direct collection of Uniform Crime Reports from law enforcement agencies within the state.

Reporting Procedures

Based on records of all reports of crime received from victims, officers who discover infractions, or other sources, law enforcement agencies across the country tabulate the number of Crime Index or Part I offenses brought to their attention each month. Specifically, the crimes reported to the FBI are murder and nonnegligent manslaughter, forcible rape, robbery, aggravated assault, burglary, larceny-theft, motor vehicle theft, and arson.

Whenever complaints of crime are determined through investigation to be unfounded or false, they are eliminated from an agency's count. The number of "actual offenses known" is reported to the FBI regardless of whether anyone is arrested for the crime, stolen property is recovered, or prosecution is undertaken.

Another integral part of the monthly submission is the total number of actual Crime Index offenses cleared. Crimes are "cleared" in one of two ways: (1) at least one person is arrested, charged, and turned over to the court for prosecution; or (2) by exceptional means when some element beyond law enforcement control precludes the arrest of an offender. Law enforcement agencies also report the number of Index crime clearances which involve only offenders under the age of 18; the value of property stolen and recovered in connection with the offenses; and detailed information pertaining to criminal homicide and arson.

In addition to its primary collection of Crime Index (Part I) offenses, the UCR Program solicits monthly data on persons arrested for all crimes except traffic violations. The age, sex, and race of arrestees are reported by crime category, both Part I and Part II. Part II offenses include all crimes not classified as Part I.

Various data on law enforcement officers killed or assaulted are collected on a monthly basis. The number of full-time sworn and civilian personnel are reported as of October 31 each year.

Editing Procedures

Each report submitted to the UCR Program is thoroughly examined for arithmetical accuracy and for deviations which may indicate errors. To identify any unusual fluctuations in an agency's crime count, monthly reports are compared with previous submissions of the agency and with those for similar agencies. Large variations in crime levels may indicate modified records procedures, incomplete reporting, or changes in the jurisdiction's geopolitical structure.

Data reliability is a high priority of the Program and noted deviations or arithmetical adjustments are brought to the attention of the state UCR Program or the submitting agency through correspondence. A standard procedure of the FBI is to study the monthly reports and to evaluate periodic trends prepared for individual reporting units. Any significant increase or decrease is made the subject of a special inquiry. When it is found that changes in crime reporting procedures or annexations are influencing the level of crime, the figures for specific crime categories, or if necessary, totals are excluded from trend tabulations.

To assist contributors in complying with UCR standards, the national Program provides training seminars and instructional materials in crime reporting procedures. Throughout the country, liaison with state Programs and law enforcement personnel is maintained, and training sessions are held to explain the purpose of the Program, the rules of uniform classification and scoring, and the methods of assembling the information for reporting. When an individual agency has specific problems in compiling its crime statistics and remedial efforts are unsuccessful, FBI Criminal Justice Information Services Division personnel may visit the contributor to aid in resolving the difficulties.

The *Uniform Crime Reporting Handbook*, which details procedures for classifying and scoring offenses, is supplied to all contributors as the basic resource document for preparing reports. Since a good records system is essential for accurate crime reporting, the FBI also furnishes the *Manual of Law Enforcement Records.*

To enhance communication among Program participants, letters to UCR contributors and State UCR Program "Bulletins" are utilized. They address Program policy, as well as present information and instructional material, and are produced as needed.

The final responsibility for data submissions rests with the individual contributing law enforcement agency. Although the Program makes every effort through its editing procedures, training practices, and correspondence to assure the validity of the data it receives, the statistics' accuracy depends primarily on the adherence of each contributor to the established standards of reporting. Deviations from these established standards which cannot be resolved by the national UCR Program may be brought to the attention of the Criminal Justice Information Systems Committees of the International Association of Chiefs of Police and the National Sheriffs' Association.

NIBRS Conversion

Several states provide their UCR data in the expanded NIBRS format. For presentation in this book, NIBRS data were converted to the historical summary UCR formats. The NIBRS data base was constructed to allow for such conversion so that UCR's long-running time series could continue.

Offense Estimation

Tables 1 through 5 and 7 of this publication contain statistics for the entire United States. Because not all law enforcement agencies provide data for complete reporting periods, estimated crime counts are included in these presentations. Offense estimation occurs within each of three areas: Metropolitan Statistical Areas (MSAs), cities outside MSAs, and rural counties. Using the known crime experiences of similar areas within a state, the estimates are computed by assigning the same proportional crime volumes to nonreporting agencies. The size of agency; type of jurisdiction, e.g., police department versus sheriff's office; and geographic location are considered in the estimation process.

Because of efforts to convert to the NIBRS in recent years, it has become necessary to estimate totals for some states. Also, the inability of some state UCR Programs to provide forcible rape figures in accordance with UCR guidelines and other problems at the state levels have required unique estimation procedures. A summary of state- and offense-specific estimation procedures are outlined below.

1985 through 1996 — The Illinois (1985-1996), Michigan, and Minnesota (1993 only) state UCR Programs were unable to provide forcible rape figures in accordance with UCR guidelines. The rape totals were estimated using national rates per 100,000 inhabitants within the eight population groups and assigning the forcible rape volumes proportionally to each state.

1988 and 1991 — Reporting problems at the state levels resulted in no usable data for Florida and Kentucky for 1988. In 1991, Iowa NIBRS conversion required estimation during the transition. State totals were estimated during these years by updating previous valid annual totals for individual jurisdictions, subdivided by population group. Percent changes for each offense within each population group of the geographic divisions in which the states reside were applied to the previous valid annual totals. The state totals were compiled from the sums of the population group estimates.

1993 — NIBRS conversion efforts resulted in estimations for Kansas and Illinois. Kansas totals were estimated by updating previous valid annual totals for individual jurisdictions, subdivided by population group. Percent changes for each offense within each population group of the West North Central Division were applied to the previous valid annual totals. The state totals were compiled from the sums of the population group estimates.

Since valid annual totals were available for approximately 60 Illinois agencies, those counts were maintained. The counts for the remaining jurisdictions were replaced with the most recent valid annual totals or were generated using standard estimation procedures. The results of all sources were then combined to arrive at the 1993 state total for Illinois.

1994 — State totals for Kansas and Illinois, both undergoing NIBRS conversion, were generated using only the valid crime rates for the geographic division in which the state resides. Within each population group, each state's offense totals were estimated based on the rate per 100,000 inhabitants within the remainder of the division. Montana state totals were estimated by the same method as were Kansas state totals in 1993.

1995 — The Kansas state-level UCR Program was able to provide valid 1994 state totals which were then updated using 1995 crime trends for the West North Central Division.

Concerning Illinois, valid Crime Index counts were available for most of the largest cities. For other agencies, the only available counts were generated without application of the UCR Hierarchy Rule. (The Hierarchy Rule requires that only the most serious offense in a multiple-offense criminal incident is counted.) To arrive at a state estimate comparable to the rest of the Nation, the total supplied by the Illinois State Program (which was inflated because of the nonapplication of the Hierarchy Rule) was reduced by the proportion of multiple offenses reported within single incidents in the available NIBRS data. Valid totals for the large cities were excluded from the reduction process. Montana state estimates were computed by updating the previous valid annual totals using the 1994 versus 1995 percent changes for the Mountain States.

1996 — Annual figures for Kansas were extrapolated from 1996 January-June state totals provided by the Kansas state-level UCR Program. The 1995 and 1996 percent changes within each geographic division were applied to valid 1995 state totals reported by Kentucky and Montana to generate 1996 state totals. For Florida, the state-level UCR Program was able to rpovide an aggregated state total; data received from 94 individual Florida agencies are shown in the 1996 jurisdictional figures presented in Tables 8 through 11. The 1996 Illinois state totals were estimated in the same manner as in 1995.

Crime Trends

Showing fluctuations from year to year, trend statistics offer the data user an added perspective from which to study crime. Percent change tabulations in this publication are computed only for reporting units which have provided comparable data for the periods under consideration. Exclusions from trend computations are made when figures from a reporting agency are not received for comparable timeframes or when it is ascertained that unusual fluctuations are due to such variables as improved records procedures, annexations, etc.

Care should be exercised in any direct comparison between data in this publication and those in prior issues of *Crime in the United States.* For example, upon receiving 1995 aggravated assault figures for the state of Kentucky, it was determined the 1994 aggravated assault figures previously submitted were not valid; therefore, the Kentucky aggravated assault figures were not included in Tables 12 through 15 of the 1995 edition. The 1994 estimates in certain offense categories were updated for both Kansas and Kentucky. Estimates in certain offense categories for Delaware were also updated for the year 1994. In addition, Montana figures for 1995 were updated to show the actual offense data which were received after publication of *Crime in the United States 1995.* These updates appear in the national trends.

Table Methodology

Although most law enforcement agencies submit crime reports to the UCR Program, data are sometimes not received for complete annual periods. To be included in this publication's Tables 8 through 11, showing specific jurisdictional statistics, figures for all 12 months of the current year must have been received at the FBI prior to established publication deadlines. Other tabular presentations are aggregated on varied levels of submission. With the exception of the tables which consist of estimates for the total United States population, each table in this publication shows the number of agencies reporting and the extent of population coverage.

Designed to assist the reader, this appendix explains the construction of many of this book's tabular presentations. The following key refers to the columnar headings used throughout the appendix.

Key: A) Column 1 shows the table numbers. Included are Tables 1 through 69, *Crime in the United States 1996.*

B) Column 2 indicates the level of submission necessary for an agency's statistics to be included in a table.

C) Column 3 explains how each table was constructed. Data adjustments, if any, are discussed along with various definitions of data aggregation.

D) Column 4 contains general comments regarding the potential use and misuse of the statistics presented.

(1) Table	(2) Data Base	(3) Table Construction	(4) General Comments
1	All law enforcement agencies in the UCR Program (including those submitting less than 12 months in 1996).	The 1996 statistics are consistent with Table 2. Pre-1996 crime statistics may have been updated, and hence, may not be consistent with prior publications. Crime statistics include estimated offense totals for agencies submitting less than 12 months of offense reports for each year. Population statistics represent July 1 provisional estimations for each year except 1980 and 1990, which are Bureau of the Census decennial census data (see App. III). Crime volume statistics are rounded to the nearest 10 for violent crime and the nearest 100 for property crime. Percent changes and rates are computed prior to rounding.	Represents an estimation of national reported crime activity from 1977 to 1996.
2	All law enforcement agencies in the UCR Program (including those submitting less than 12 months in 1996).	Statistics are aggregated from individual state statistics as shown in Table 5. Crime statistics include estimated offense totals for agencies submitting less than 12 months of offense reports. Population statistics represent July 1, 1996, Bureau of the Census provisional estimates. See Appendix III for UCR population breakdowns.	Represents an estimation of national reported crime activity in 1996.
3	All law enforcement agencies in the UCR Program (including those submitting less than 12 months in 1996).	Regional offense distributions are computed from volume figures as shown in Table 4. Population distributions are based on July 1, 1996, Bureau of the Census provisional estimates (see App. III).	Represents the 1996 geographical distribution of estimated Crime Index offenses and population.
4	All law enforcement agencies in the UCR Program (including those submitting less than 12 months in 1996).	The 1996 statistics are aggregated from individual state statistics as shown in Table 5. Crime statistics include estimated offense totals for agencies submitting less than 12 months of offense reports for 1995 and 1996. Population statistics represent July 1 provisional estimates for both years (see App. III).	Represents an estimation of reported crime activity for Index offenses at the: 1. national level 2. regional level 3. division level 4. state level Any comparison of UCR statistics should take into consideration demographic factors.
5	All law enforcement agencies in the UCR Program (including those submitting less than 12 months in 1996).	Crime statistics include estimated offense totals for agencies submitting less than 12 months of offense reports. Population statistics represent 1996 estimates (see App. III). Statistics under the heading "Area Actually Reporting" represent reported offense totals for agencies submitting 12 months of offense reports and estimated totals for agencies submitting less than 12 but more than 2 months of offense reports. The statistics under the heading "Estimated Totals" represent the above plus estimated offense totals for agencies having less than 3 months of offense reports.	Represents an estimation of reported crime activity for Index offenses at the state level. Any comparison of UCR statistics should take into consideration demographic factors.
6	All law enforcement agencies in the UCR Program (including those submitting less than 12 months in 1996).	Statistics are published for all Metropolitan Statistical Areas (MSAs) having at least 75% reporting and for which the central city/cities submitted 12 months of data in 1996. Crime statistics include estimated offense totals for agencies submitting less than 12 months of offense statistics for 1996. Population statistics represent July 1, 1996, Bureau of the Census provisional estimates. The statistics under the heading "Area Actually Reporting" represent reported offense totals for agencies submitting all 12 months of offense reports plus estimated offense totals for agencies submitting less than 12 but more than 2 months of offense reports. The statistics under the heading "Estimated Total" represent the above plus the estimated offense totals for agencies submitting less than 3 months of offense reports. The tabular breakdowns are according to UCR definitions (see App. II).	Represents an estimation of the reported crime activity for Index offenses at individual MSA level. Any comparison of UCR statistics should take into consideration demographic factors.
7	All law enforcement agencies in the UCR Program (including those submitting less than 12 months in 1996).	Offense totals are for all Index offense categories other than aggravated assault. Crime statistics include estimated offense totals for agencies submitting less than 12 months of offense reports for each year.	Represents an estimation of national reported crime activity from 1992 to 1996. Aggravated assault is excluded from Table 7, because if money or property is taken in connection with an assault, the offense is robbery.

(1) Table	(2) Data Base	(3) Table Construction	(4) General Comments
8	All law enforcement agencies submitting complete reports for 12 months in 1996.	"Cities and Towns" are defined to be agencies in Population Groups I through V (see App. III). The agency populations are 1996 estimates for each agency (see App. III).	Represents reported crime activity of individual agencies in cities and towns 10,000 and over in population. Any comparison of UCR statistics should take into consideration demographic factors.
9	All university/college law enforcement agencies submitting complete reports for 12 months in 1996.	The 1994 student enrollment figures, which are provided by the U.S. Department of Education, are the most recent available. They include full- and part-time students. No adjustments to equate part-time enrollments into full-time equivalents have been made.	Represents reported crime from those individual university/college law enforcement agencies contributing to the UCR Program. These agencies are listed alphabetically by state. Any comparison of these UCR statistics should take into consideration size of enrollment, number of on-campus residents, and other demographic factors.
10	All law enforcement agencies submitting complete reports for 12 months in 1996.	"Suburban Counties" are defined as the areas covered by noncity agencies within an MSA (see App. III). Population estimates of suburban counties are as of July 1, 1996, (see App. III).	Represents crime reported to individual law enforcement agencies in suburban counties, i.e., the individual sheriff's office, county police department, highway patrol, and/or state police. These figures do not represent the county totals since they exclude city crime counts. Any comparison of UCR statistics should take into consideration demographic factors.
11	All law enforcement agencies submitting complete reports for 12 months in 1996.	"Rural Counties" are those outside MSAs and whose jurisdictions are not covered by city police agencies (see App. III). Population classifications of rural counties are based on 1996 estimates for individual agencies (see App. III).	Represents crime reported to individual rural county law enforcement agencies covering populations 25,000 and over, i.e., the individual sheriff's office, county police department, highway patrol, and/or state police. These figures do not represent the county totals since they exclude city crime counts. Any comparison of UCR statistics should take into consideration demographic factors.
12-15	All law enforcement agencies submitting complete reports for at least 6 common months in 1995 and 1996.	The 1996 crime trend statistics are 2-year comparisons based on 1996 reported crime activity. Only common reported months for individual agencies are included in 1996 trend calculations. Populations represent July 1, 1996, estimates for individual agencies. See Appendix III for UCR population breakdowns. Note that "Suburban and Nonsuburban Cities" are all municipal agencies other than central cities in MSAs.	Slight decrease in national coverage for Table 15 due to editing procedure and lower submission rate.
16-19	All law enforcement agencies submitting complete reports for 12 months in 1996.	The 1996 crime rates are the ratios of the aggregated 1996 crime volumes and the aggregated 1996 populations of the contributing agencies. Population statistics represent 1996 estimates for individual agencies. See Appendix III for UCR population breakdowns. Note that "Suburban and Nonsuburban Cities" are all municipal agencies other than central cities in MSAs.	The forcible rape figures furnished by the Illinois state-level UCR Program were not in accordance with national guidelines. For inclusion in these tables, the Illinois forcible rape figures were estimated by using the national rates for each population group applied to the population by group for Illinois agencies supplying all 12 months of data. Slight decrease in national coverage for Table 19 due to editing procedure and lower submission rate.
20	All law enforcement agencies submitting Supplementary Homicide Report (SHR) data in 1996.	The weapon totals are the aggregate for each murder victim recorded on the SHRs for calendar year 1996.	The SHR is the monthly report form concerning homicides. It details victim and offender characteristics, circumstances, weapons used, etc.
21, 22	All law enforcement agencies submitting complete reports for 12 months in 1996.	The weapon totals are aggregated 1996 totals. Population statistics represent 1996 estimates.	
23, 24	All law enforcement agencies submitting complete reports for at least 6 months in 1996.	Offense total and value lost total are computed for all Index offense categories other than aggravated assault. Percent distribution is based on offense total of each Index offense. Trend statistics are based on agencies with at least 6 common months complete for 1995 and 1996.	Aggravated assault is excluded from Table 23. For UCR Program purposes, the taking of money or property in connection with an assault is reported as robbery.
25-28	All law enforcement agencies submitting complete reports for at least 6 months in 1996.	The 1996 clearance rates are based on offense and clearance volume totals of the contributing agencies for 1996. Population statistics represent 1996 estimates. See Appendix III for UCR population breakdowns.	

(1) Table	(2) Data Base	(3) Table Construction	(4) General Comments
29	All law enforcement agencies in the UCR Program (including those submitting less than 12 months in 1996).	The arrest totals presented are national estimates based on the arrest statistics of all law enforcement agencies in the UCR Program (including those submitting less than 12 months). The "Total Estimated Arrests" statistic is the sum of estimated arrest volumes for each of the 29 offenses. Each individual arrest total is the sum of the estimated volumes within each of the eight population groups (see App. III). Each group's estimate is the reported volume (as shown in Table 26) divided by the percent of total group population reporting (according to 1996 Bureau of the Census provisional estimates; see App. III).	
30, 31	All law enforcement agencies submitting complete reports for 12 months in 1996.	The 1996 arrest rates are the ratios, per 100,000 inhabitants, of the aggregated 1996 reported arrest statistics and populations. The population statistics represent July 1, 1996, estimates. See Appendix III for UCR population classifications/geographical configuration.	
32, 33	All law enforcement agencies submitting complete reports for 12 months in 1987 and 1996.	The arrest trends are the percentage differences between 1987 and 1996 arrest volumes aggregated from all common agencies. Population statistics represent July 1, 1996, estimates (see App. III).	
34, 35	All law enforcement agencies submitting complete reports for 12 months in 1992 and 1996.	The arrest trends are the percentage differences between 1992 and 1996 arrest volumes aggregated from common agencies. Population statistics represent 1996 estimates (see App. III).	
36, 37	All law enforcement agencies submitting complete reports for 12 months in 1995 and 1996.	The arrest trends are 2-year comparisons between 1995 and 1996 arrest volumes aggregated from common agencies. Population statistics represent 1996 estimates (see App. III).	
38-43	All law enforcement agencies submitting complete reports for 12 months in 1996.		Slight decrease in coverage for Table 43 due to editing procedure and lower submission of race data.
44, 45	All city law enforcement agencies submitting complete reports for 12 months in 1995 and 1996.	The 1996 city arrest trends represent the percentage differences between 1995 and 1996 arrest volumes aggregated from common city agencies. "City Agencies" are defined to be all agencies within Population Groups I-VI (see App. III).	
46-49	All city law enforcement agencies submitting complete reports for 12 months in 1995 and 1996.	"City Agencies" are defined as agencies within Population Groups I-VI (see App. III).	Slight decrease in coverage for Table 49 due to editing procedure and lower submission of race data.
50, 51	All suburban county law enforcement agencies submitting complete reports for 12 months in 1995 and 1996.	The 1996 suburban county arrest trends represent percentage differences between 1995 and 1996 volumes aggregated from contributing agencies. "Suburban Counties" are defined as the areas covered by noncity agencies within an MSA (see App. III).	
52-55	All suburban county law enforcement agencies submitting complete reports for 12 months in 1996.	"Suburban Counties" are defined as the areas covered by noncity agencies within an MSA (see App. III).	Slight decrease in coverage for Table 55 due to editing procedure and lower submission of race data.
56, 57	All rural county law enforcement agencies submitting complete reports for 12 months in 1995 and 1996.	The 1996 rural county arrest trends represent percentage differences between 1995 and 1996 volumes aggregated from contributing agencies. "Rural Counties" are defined as noncity agencies outside MSAs (see App. III).	
58-61	All rural county law enforcement agencies submitting complete reports for 12 months in 1996.	"Rural Counties" are defined as noncity agencies outside MSAs (see App. III).	Slight decrease in coverage for Table 61 due to editing procedure and lower submission of race data.

(1) Table	(2) Data Base	(3) Table Construction	(4) General Comments
62, 63	All suburban area law enforcement agencies submitting complete reports for 12 months in 1995 and 1996.	The 1996 suburban area arrest trends represent percentage differences between 1995 and 1996 arrest volumes aggregated from contributing agencies. "Suburban Area" is defined as cities with fewer than 50,000 inhabitants and all counties within MSAs (see App. III).	
64-67	All suburban area law enforcement agencies submitting complete reports for 12 months in 1996.	"Suburban Area" is defined as cities with fewer than 50,000 inhabitants and all counties within MSAs (see App. III).	Slight decrease in coverage for Table 67 due to editing procedure and lower submission of race data.
68	All law enforcement agencies submitting complete reports for 12 months in 1996.	Population statistics represent July 1, 1996, estimates for individual agencies. See Appendix III for definitions of the population classifications presented.	Data furnished are based upon individual state age definitions for juveniles
69	All law enforcement agencies submitting complete reports for 12 months in 1996.	Arrest totals are aggregated for individual agencies within each state. Population figures represent July 1, 1996, estimates (see App. III).	Any comparison of statistics should take into consideration variances in arrest practices, particularly for Part II crimes.

APPENDIX II

Offenses in Uniform Crime Reporting

Offenses in Uniform Crime Reporting are divided into two groups, Part I and Part II. Information on the volume of Part I offenses known to law enforcement, those cleared by arrest or exceptional means, and the number of persons arrested is reported monthly. Only arrest data are reported for Part II offenses.

The Part I offenses are:

Criminal homicide—a. Murder and nonnegligent manslaughter: the willful (nonnegligent) killing of one human being by another. Deaths caused by negligence, attempts to kill, assaults to kill, suicides, accidental deaths, and justifiable homicides are excluded. Justifiable homicides are limited to: (1) the killing of a felon by a law enforcement officer in the line of duty; and (2) the killing of a felon, during the commission of a felony, by a private citizen. b. Manslaughter by negligence: the killing of another person through gross negligence. Traffic fatalities are excluded. While manslaughter by negligence is a Part I crime, it is not included in the Crime Index.

Forcible rape—The carnal knowledge of a female forcibly and against her will. Included are rapes by force and attempts or assaults to rape. Statutory offenses (no force used — victim under age of consent) are excluded.

Robbery—The taking or attempting to take anything of value from the care, custody, or control of a person or persons by force or threat of force or violence and/or by putting the victim in fear.

Aggravated assault—An unlawful attack by one person upon another for the purpose of inflicting severe or aggravated bodily injury. This type of assault usually is accompanied by the use of a weapon or by means likely to produce death or great bodily harm. Simple assaults are excluded.

Burglary-breaking or entering—The unlawful entry of a structure to commit a felony or a theft. Attempted forcible entry is included.

Larceny-theft (except motor vehicle theft)—The unlawful taking, carrying, leading, or riding away of property from the possession or constructive possession of another. Examples are thefts of bicycles or automobile accessories, shoplifting, pocket-picking, or the stealing of any property or article which is not taken by force and violence or by fraud. Attempted larcenies are included. Embezzlement, confidence games, forgery, worthless checks, etc., are excluded.

Motor vehicle theft—The theft or attempted theft of a motor vehicle. A motor vehicle is self-propelled and runs on the surface and not on rails. Specifically excluded from this category are motorboats, construction equipment, airplanes, and farming equipment.

Arson—Any willful or malicious burning or attempt to burn, with or without intent to defraud, a dwelling house, public building, motor vehicle or aircraft, personal property of another, etc.

The Part II offenses are:

Other assaults (simple)—Assaults and attempted assaults where no weapon is used and which do not result in serious or aggravated injury to the victim.

Forgery and counterfeiting—Making, altering, uttering, or possessing, with intent to defraud, anything false in the semblance of that which is true. Attempts are included.

Fraud—Fraudulent conversion and obtaining money or property by false pretenses. Included are confidence games and bad checks, except forgeries and counterfeiting.

Embezzlement—Misappropriation or misapplication of money or property entrusted to one's care, custody, or control.

Stolen property; buying, receiving, possessing—Buying, receiving, and possessing stolen property, including attempts.

Vandalism—Willful or malicious destruction, injury, disfigurement, or defacement of any public or private property, real or personal, without consent of the owner or persons having custody or control.

Weapons; carrying, possessing, etc.—All violations of regulations or statutes controlling the carrying, using, possessing, furnishing, and manufacturing of deadly weapons or silencers. Included are attempts.

Prostitution and commercialized vice—Sex offenses of a commercialized nature, such as prostitution, keeping a bawdy house, procuring, or transporting women for immoral purposes. Attempts are included.

Sex offenses (except forcible rape, prostitution, and commercialized vice)—Statutory rape and offenses against chastity, common decency, morals, and the like. Attempts are included.

Drug abuse violations—State and/or local offenses relating to the unlawful possession, sale, use, growing, and manufacturing of narcotic drugs. The following drug categories are specified: opium or cocaine and their derivatives (morphine, heroin, codeine); marijuana; synthetic narcotics–manufactured narcotics that can cause true addiction (demerol, methadone); and dangerous nonnarcotic drugs (barbiturates, benzedrine).

Gambling—Promoting, permitting, or engaging in illegal gambling.

Offenses against the family and children—Nonsupport, neglect, desertion, or abuse of family and children.

Driving under the influence—Driving or operating any vehicle or common carrier while drunk or under the influence of liquor or narcotics.

Liquor laws—State and/or local liquor law violations, except "drunkenness" and "driving under the influence." Federal violations are excluded.

Drunkenness—Offenses relating to drunkenness or intoxication. Excluded is "driving under the influence."

Disorderly conduct—Breach of the peace.

Vagrancy—Vagabondage, begging, loitering, etc.

All other offenses—All violations of state and/or local laws, except those listed above and traffic offenses.

Suspicion—No specific offense; suspect released without formal charges being placed.

Curfew and loitering laws (persons under age 18)—Offenses relating to violations of local curfew or loitering ordinances where such laws exist.

Runaways (persons under age 18)—Limited to juveniles taken into protective custody under provisions of local statutes.

APPENDIX III

Uniform Crime Reporting Area Definitions

The presentation of statistics by reporting area facilitates analyzing local crime counts in conjunction with those for areas of similar geographical location or population size. Geographically, the United States is divisible by regions, divisions, and states. Further breakdowns rely on population figures and proximity to metropolitan areas. As a general rule, sheriffs, county police, and state police report crimes committed within the limits of counties but outside cities, while local police report crimes committed within city limits.

Community Types

UCR data are often presented in aggregations representing three types of communities:

1. Metropolitan Statistical Areas (MSAs)—Each MSA includes a central city of at least 50,000 people or an urbanized area of at least 50,000. The county containing the central city and other contiguous counties having strong economic and social ties to the central city and county are also included. Counties in an MSA are designated "suburban" for UCR purposes. An MSA may cross state lines. The MSA concept facilitates the analysis and presentation of uniform statistical data on metropolitan areas by establishing reporting units which represent major population centers. Due to changes in the geographic composition of MSAs, no year-to-year comparisons of data for those areas should be attempted.

New England MSAs are comprised of cities and towns instead of counties. In this publication's tabular presentations, New England cities and towns are assigned to the proper MSAs. Some counties, however, have both suburban and rural portions. Data for state police and sheriffs in those jurisdictions are included in statistics for the rural areas.

MSAs made up approximately 80 percent of the total United States population in 1996. Some presentations in this book refer to "suburban area." A suburban area includes cities with less than 50,000 inhabitants in addition to counties (unincorporated areas) within the MSA. The central cities are, of course, excluded. The concept of suburban area is especially important because of the particular crime conditions which exist in the communities surrounding the Nation's largest cities.

2. Cities Outside MSAs—Cities outside MSAs are mostly incorporated. They comprised 8 percent of the 1996 population of the United States.

3. Rural Counties Outside MSAs—Rural counties are comprised of mostly unincorporated areas. Law enforcement agencies in rural counties cover areas that are not under the jurisdiction of city police departments. Rural county law enforcement agencies served 12 percent of the national population in 1996.

The following is an illustration of the community types:

	MSA	NON-MSA
CITIES	CENTRAL CITIES 50,000 AND OVER	CITIES OUTSIDE METROPOLITAN AREAS
	SUBURBAN CITIES	
COUNTIES (including unincorporated areas)	SUBURBAN COUNTIES	RURAL COUNTIES

Population Groups

The population group classifications used by the UCR Program are:

Population Group	Political Label	Population Range
I	City	250,000 and over
II	City	100,000 to 249,999
III	City	50,000 to 99,999
IV	City	25,000 to 49,999
V	City	10,000 to 24,999
VI	City[1]	Less than 10,000
VII (Rural County)	County[2]	N/A
IX (Suburban County)	County[2]	N/A

[1] Includes universities and colleges to which no population is attributed.
[2] Includes state police to which no population is attributed.

The major source of UCR data is the individual law enforcement agency. The number of agencies included in each population group will vary slightly from year to year due to population growth, geopolitical consolidation, municipal incorporation, etc. Population figures for individual jurisdictions are estimated by the UCR Program in noncensus years. In this edition, the state and national population figures used are 1996 Bureau of the Census provisional estimates. Population figures for individual jurisdictions were updated by applying 1996 state growth rates to 1995 city and county estimates. The estimate of United States population showed a 1-percent increase from 1995 to 1996.

The following table shows the number of UCR contributing agencies within each population group for 1996.

Population Group	Number of Agencies	Population Covered
I	65	47,046,340
II	152	22,288,174
III	384	26,154,354
IV	731	25,304,786
V	1,793	28,207,132
VI[1]	8,008	25,696,924
VIII (Rural County)[2]	3,627	32,113,297
IX (Suburban County)[2]	2,038	58,472,993
Total	16,798	265,284,000

[1] Includes universities and colleges to which no population is attributed.
[2] Includes state police to which no population is attributed.

Regions and Divisions

As shown in the accompanying map, the United States is comprised of four regions: the Northeastern States, the Midwestern States, the Southern States, and the Western States. These regions are further divided into nine divisions. The following table delineates the regional, divisional, and state configuration of the country.

NORTHEASTERN STATES

New England
  Connecticut
  Maine
  Massachusetts
  New Hampshire
  Rhode Island
  Vermont

Middle Atlantic
  New Jersey
  New York
  Pennsylvania

MIDWESTERN STATES

East North Central
  Illinois
  Indiana
  Michigan
  Ohio
  Wisconsin

West North Central
  Iowa
  Kansas
  Minnesota
  Missouri
  Nebraska
  North Dakota
  South Dakota

SOUTHERN STATES

South Atlantic
  Delaware
  District of Columbia
  Florida
  Georgia
  Maryland
  North Carolina
  South Carolina
  Virginia
  West Virginia

East South Central
  Alabama
  Kentucky
  Mississippi
  Tennessee
West South Central
  Arkansas
  Louisiana
  Oklahoma
  Texas

WESTERN STATES

Mountain
  Arizona
  Colorado
  Idaho
  Montana
  Nevada
  New Mexico
  Utah
  Wyoming

Pacific
  Alaska
  California
  Hawaii
  Oregon
  Washington

REGIONS AND DIVISIONS OF THE UNITED STATES
1996

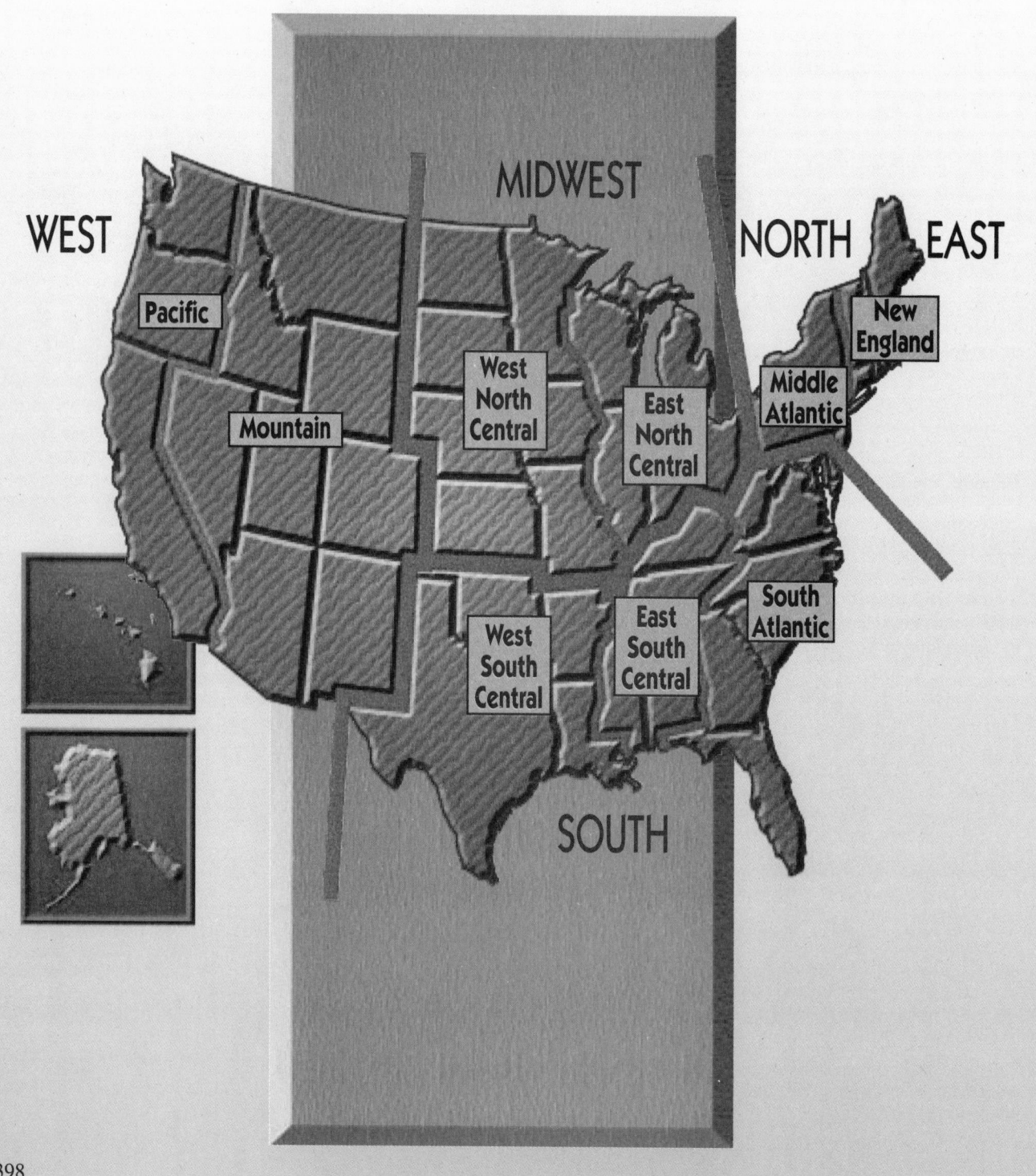

WEST

MIDWEST

NORTH EAST

Pacific

Mountain

West North Central

East North Central

Middle Atlantic

New England

West South Central

East South Central

South Atlantic

SOUTH

APPENDIX IV

The Nation's Two Crime Measures

The U.S. Department of Justice administers two statistical programs to measure the magnitude, nature, and impact of crime in the Nation: the Uniform Crime Reporting (UCR) Program and the National Crime Victimization Survey (NCVS). Each of these programs produces valuable information about aspects of the Nation's crime problem. Because the UCR and NCVS programs are conducted for different purposes, use different methods, and focus on somewhat different aspects of crime, the information they produce together provides a more comprehensive panorama of the Nation's crime problem than either could produce alone.

Uniform Crime Reports

The FBI's UCR Program, which began in 1929, collects information on the following crimes reported to law enforcement authorities: homicide, forcible rape, robbery, aggravated assault, burglary, larceny-theft, motor vehicle theft, and arson. Arrests are reported for 21 additional crime categories.

The UCR data are compiled from monthly law enforcement reports or individual crime incident records transmitted directly to the FBI or to centralized state agencies that then report to the FBI. Each report submitted to the UCR Program is examined thoroughly for reasonableness, accuracy, and deviations that may indicate errors. Large variations in crime levels may indicate modified records procedures, incomplete reporting, or changes in a jurisdiction's boundaries. To identify any unusual fluctuations in an agency's crime counts, monthly reports are compared with previous submissions of the agency and with those for similar agencies.

In 1996, law enforcement agencies active in the UCR Program represented approximately 252 million United States inhabitants— 95 percent of the total population.

The UCR Program provides crime counts for the Nation as a whole, as well as for regions, states, counties, cities, and towns. This permits studies among neighboring jurisdictions and among those with similar populations and other common characteristics.

UCR findings for each calendar year are published in a preliminary release in the spring, followed by a detailed annual report, *Crime in the United States*, issued in the following calendar year. In addition to crime counts and trends, this report includes data on crimes cleared, persons arrested (age, sex, and race), law enforcement personnel (including the number of sworn officers killed or assaulted), and the characteristics of homicides (including age, sex, and race of victims and offenders, victim-offender relationships, weapons used, and circumstances surrounding the homicides). Other special reports are also available from the UCR Program.

Following a 5-year redesign effort, the UCR Program is currently being converted to the more comprehensive and detailed National Incident-Based Reporting System (NIBRS). NIBRS will provide detailed information about each criminal incident in 22 broad categories of offenses.

National Crime Victimization Survey

The Bureau of Justice Statistics' NCVS, which began in 1973, provides a detailed picture of crime incidents, victims, and trends. After a substantial period of research, in 1993 the survey completed an intensive methodological redesign. The redesign was undertaken to improve the questions used to uncover crime, update the survey methods, and broaden the scope of crimes measured. The redesigned survey collects detailed information on the frequency and nature of the crimes of rape, sexual assault, personal robbery, aggravated and simple assault, household burglary, theft, and motor vehicle theft. It does not measure homicide or commercial crimes (such as burglaries of stores).

U.S. Census Bureau personnel interview all household members at least 12 years old in a nationally representative sample of approximately 49,000 households (about 101,000 persons). Households stay in the sample for 3 years and are interviewed at 6-month intervals. New households rotate into the sample on an ongoing basis.

The NCVS collects information on crimes suffered by individuals and households, whether or not those crimes were reported to law enforcement. It estimates the proportion of each crime type reported to law enforcement, and it summarizes the reasons that victims give for reporting or not reporting.

The survey provides information about victims (age, sex, race, ethnicity, marital status, income, and educational level), offenders (sex, race, approximate age, and victim-offender relationship), and the crimes (time and place of occurrence, use of weapons, nature of injury, and economic consequences). Questions also cover the experiences of victims with the criminal justice system, self-protective measures used by victims, and possible substance abuse by offenders. Supplements are added periodically to the survey to obtain detailed information on topics like school crime.

The first data from the redesigned NCVS were published in a BJS bulletin in June 1995. BJS publication of NCVS data includes *Criminal Victimization in the United States*, an annual report that covers the broad range of detailed information collected by the NCVS. BJS publishes detailed reports on topics such as crime against women, urban crime, and gun use in crime. The NCVS data files are archived at the National Archive of Criminal Justice Data at the University of Michigan to enable researchers to perform independent analysis.

Comparing UCR and NCVS

Because the NCVS was designed to complement the UCR Program, the two programs share many similarities. As much as their different collection methods permit, the two measure the same subset of serious crimes, defined alike. Both programs cover rape, robbery, aggravated assault, burglary, theft, and motor vehicle theft. Rape, robbery, theft, and motor vehicle theft are defined virtually identically by both the UCR and NCVS. (While rape is defined analogously, the UCR Crime Index measures the crime against women only, and the NCVS measures it against both sexes.)

There are also significant differences between the two programs. First, the two programs were created to serve different purposes. The UCR Program's primary objective is to provide a reliable set of criminal justice statistics for law enforcement administration, operation, and management. The NCVS was established to provide previously unavailable information about crime (including crime not reported to police), victims, and offenders.

Second, the two programs measure an overlapping but nonidentical set of crimes. The NCVS includes crimes both reported and not reported to law enforcement. The NCVS excludes, but the UCR includes, homicide, arson, commercial crimes, and crimes against children under age 12. The UCR captures crimes reported to law enforcement, but it excludes simple assaults and sexual assaults other than forcible rape from the Crime Index.

Third, because of methodology, the NCVS and UCR definitions of some crimes differ. For example, the UCR defines burglary as the unlawful entry or attempted entry of a structure to commit a felony or theft. The NCVS, not wanting to ask victims to ascertain offender motives, defines burglary as the entry or attempted entry of a residence by a person who had no right to be there.

Fourth, for property crimes (burglary, theft, and motor vehicle theft), the two programs calculate crime rates using different bases. The UCR rates for these crimes are per-capita (number of crimes per 100,000 persons), whereas the NCVS rates for these crimes are per-household (number of crimes per 1,000 households). Because the number of households may not grow at the same rate each year as the total population, trend data for rates of property crimes measured by the two programs may not be comparable.

In addition, some differences in the data from the two programs may result from sampling variation in the NCVS and from estimating for nonresponse in the UCR. The NCVS estimates are derived from interviewing a sample and are therefore subject to a margin of error. Rigorous statistical methods are used to calculate confidence intervals around all survey estimates. Trend data in NCVS reports are described as genuine only if there is at least a 90 percent certainty that the measured changes are not the result of sampling variation. The UCR data are based on the actual counts of offenses reported by law enforcement jurisdictions. In some circumstances, UCR data are estimated for nonparticipating jurisdictions or those reporting partial data.

Each program has unique strengths. The UCR provides a measure of the number of crimes reported to law enforcement agencies throughout the country. The UCR's Supplementary Homicide Reports provide the most reliable, timely data on the extent and nature of homicides in the Nation. The NCVS is the primary source of information on the characteristics of criminal victimization and on the number and types of crimes not reported to law enforcement authorities.

By understanding the strengths and limitations of each program, it is possible to use the UCR and NCVS to achieve a greater understanding of crime trends and the nature of crime in the United States. For example, changes in police procedures, shifting attitudes towards crime and police, and other societal changes can affect the extent to which people report and law enforcement agencies record crime. NCVS and UCR data can be used in concert to explore why trends in reported and police-recorded crime may differ.

Apparent discrepancies between statistics from the two programs can usually be accounted for by their definitional and procedural differences or resolved by comparing NCVS sampling variations (confidence intervals) of those crimes said to have been reported to police with UCR statistics.

For most types of crimes measured by both the UCR and NCVS, analysts familiar with the programs can exclude from analysis those aspects of crime not common to both. Resulting long-term trend lines can be brought into close concordance. The impact of such adjustments is most striking for robbery, burglary, and motor vehicle theft, whose definitions most closely coincide.

With robbery, annual victimization rates based only on NCVS robberies reported to the police are possible. It is also possible to remove from analysis UCR robberies of commercial establishments such as gas stations, convenience stores, and banks. When the resulting NCVS police-reported robbery rates are compared to UCR non-commercial robbery rates, the results reveal closely corresponding long-term trends.

APPENDIX V

Directory of State Uniform Crime Reporting Programs

Alabama

Alabama Criminal Justice
   Information Center
Suite 350
770 Washington Avenue
Montgomery, Alabama 36130
(334) 242-4900

Alaska

Uniform Crime Reporting Section
Department of Public Safety
   Information System
5700 East Tudor Road
Anchorage, Alaska 99507
(907) 269-5708

American Samoa

Department of Public Safety
Post Office Box 1086
Pago Pago
American Samoa 96799
(684) 633-1111

Arizona

Uniform Crime Reporting Program
Arizona Department of Public Safety
Post Office Box 6638
Phoenix, Arizona 85005-6638
(602) 223-2263

Arkansas

Arkansas Crime Information Center
One Capitol Mall, 4D-200
Little Rock, Arkansas 72201
(501) 682-2222

California

Criminal Justice Statistics Center
Department of Justice
Post Office Box 903427
Sacramento, California 94203-4270
(916) 227-3470

Colorado

Uniform Crime Reporting
Colorado Bureau of Investigation
Suite 3000
690 Kipling Street
Denver, Colorado 80215
(303) 239-4300

Connecticut

Uniform Crime Reporting Program
Post Office Box 2794
Middletown, Connecticut 06457-9294
(860) 685-8030

Delaware	State Bureau of Identification Post Office Box 430 Dover, Delaware 19903 (302) 739-5875
District of Columbia	Information Services Division Metropolitan Police Department Room 5054 300 Indiana Avenue, Northwest Washington, D.C. 20001 (202) 727-4301
Florida	Uniform Crime Reports Section Florida Crime Information Center Bureau Post Office Box 1489 Tallahassee, Florida 32302-1489 (904) 487-1179
Georgia	Georgia Crime Information Center Georgia Bureau of Investigation Post Office Box 370748 Decatur, Georgia 30037-0748 (404) 244-2840
Guam	Guam Police Department Planning, Research and Development 23909 GMF Barrigada, Guam 96921 (671) 472-8911 x 418
Hawaii	Crime Prevention and Justice Assistance Division Department of the Attorney General 1st Floor 425 Queen Street Honolulu, Hawaii 96813 (808) 586-1416
Idaho	Criminal Identification Bureau Department of Law Enforcement Post Office Box 700 Meridian, Idaho 83680 (208) 884-7156
Illinois	Uniform Crime Reporting Program Crime Studies Section Illinois State Police Post Office Box 3677 Springfield, Illinois 62708-3677 (217) 782-5791
Iowa	Iowa Department of Public Safety Wallace State Office Building East Ninth and Grand Des Moines, Iowa 50319 (515) 281-8494

Kansas	Kansas Bureau of Investigation 1620 Southwest Tyler Street Topeka, Kansas 66612 (913) 296-8200
Kentucky	Information Services Branch Kentucky State Police 1250 Louisville Road Frankfort, Kentucky 40601 (502) 227-8783
Louisiana	Louisiana Commission on Law Enforcement Room 708 1885 Wooddale Boulevard Baton Rouge, Louisiana 70806 (504) 925-4847
Maine	Records Management Services Uniform Crime Division Department of Public Safety Maine State Police 36 Hospital Street Augusta, Maine 04333-0042 (207) 624-7004
Maryland	Central Records Division Maryland State Police Department 1711 Belmont Avenue Baltimore, Maryland 21244 (410) 298-3883
Massachusetts	Crime Reporting Unit Massachusetts State Police 470 Worcester Road Framingham, Massachusetts 01701 (508) 820-2110
Michigan	Central Records Division Uniform Crime Reporting Section Michigan State Police 7150 Harris Drive Lansing, Michigan 48913 (517) 322-1150
Minnesota	Bureau of Criminal Apprehension Minnesota Department of Public Safety Criminal Justice Information Systems 1246 University Avenue St. Paul, Minnesota 55104 (612) 642-0670
Montana	Montana Board of Crime Control 303 North Roberts Helena, Montana 59620-1408 (406) 444-2077

Nebraska	Uniform Crime Reporting Section The Nebraska Commission on Law Enforcement and Criminal Justice Post Office Box 94946 Lincoln, Nebraska 68509 (402) 471-2194
Nevada	Criminal Information Services Nevada Highway Patrol 555 Wright Way Carson City, Nevada 89711 (702) 687-5713
New Hampshire	Uniform Crime Reporting Unit New Hampshire Department of Public Safety Division of State Police 10 Hazen Drive Concord, New Hampshire 03305 (603) 271-2509
New Jersey	Uniform Crime Reporting Division of State Police Post Office Box 7068 West Trenton, New Jersey 08628-0068 (609) 882-2000 x 2392
New York	Statistical Services New York State Division of Criminal Justice Services Executive Park Tower Stuyvesant Plaza 3764 Albany, New York 12203 (518) 457-8381
North Carolina	Crime Reporting and Field Services Division of Criminal Information State Bureau of Investigation 407 North Blount Street Raleigh, North Carolina 27601 (919) 733-3171
North Dakota	Information Services Section Bureau of Criminal Investigation Attorney General's Office Post Office Box 1054 Bismarck, North Dakota 58502 (701) 328-5500
Oklahoma	Uniform Crime Reporting Section Oklahoma State Bureau of Investigation Suite 300 6600 North Harvey Oklahoma City, Oklahoma 73116 (405) 848-6724
Oregon	Law Enforcement Data Systems Division Oregon Department of State Police 400 Public Service Building Salem, Oregon 97310 (503) 378-3057

Pennsylvania	Bureau of Research and Development Pennsylvania State Police 1800 Elmerton Avenue Harrisburg, Pennsylvania 17110 (717) 783-5536
Puerto Rico	Puerto Rico Police Post Office Box 70166 San Juan, Puerto Rico 00936-8166 (787) 793-1234 x 3113
Rhode Island	Rhode Island State Police 311 Danielson Pike North Scituate, Rhode Island 02857 (401) 444-1121
South Carolina	South Carolina Law Enforcement Division Post Office Box 21398 Columbia, South Carolina 29221-1398 (803) 896-7162
South Dakota	South Dakota Statistical Analysis Center 500 East Capitol Avenue Pierre, South Dakota 57501-5070 (605) 773-6310
Texas	Uniform Crime Reporting Crime Information Bureau Texas Department of Public Safety Post Office Box 4143 Austin, Texas 78765-9968 (512) 424-2091
Utah	Data Collection and Analysis Bureau of Criminal Identification Utah Department of Public Safety 4501 South 2700 West Box 148280 Salt Lake City, Utah 84114-8280 (801) 965-4445
Vermont	Vermont Crime Information Center 103 South Main Street Waterbury, Vermont 05671-2101 (802) 244-8786
Virginia	Records Management Division Department of State Police Post Office Box 27472 Richmond, Virginia 23261-7472 (804) 674-2023
Virgin Islands	Records Bureau Virgin Islands Police Department 2nd Floor Nisky Center Saint Thomas, Virgin Islands 00802 (809) 774-2211 x 206

Washington	Uniform Crime Reporting Program Washington Association of Sheriffs and Police Chiefs Post Office Box 826 Olympia, Washington 98507 (360) 586-3221
West Virginia	Uniform Crime Reporting Program West Virginia State Police 725 Jefferson Road South Charleston, West Virginia 25309 (304) 746-2159
Wisconsin	Office of Justice Assistance 2nd Floor 222 State Street Madison, Wisconsin 53702 (608) 266-3323
Wyoming	Uniform Crime Reporting Criminal Records Section Division of Criminal Investigation 316 West 22nd Street Cheyenne, Wyoming 82002 (307) 777-7625

APPENDIX VI

National Uniform Crime Reporting Program Directory

Administration .... (304) 625-3691
    Program administration; management; policy

Information Dissemination .... (304) 625-4995
    Requests for published and unpublished data; printouts, magnetic tapes, books

Training/Education .... (304) 625-2821
    Requests for training of law enforcement; information on police reporting systems;
    technical assistance

Statistical Processing .... (304) 625-4830
    Processing of summary and incident-based reports from data contributors;
    reporting problems; requests for reporting forms; data processing; data quality
        Statistical models; special studies and analyses; crime forecasting

    Send correspondence to: Federal Bureau of Investigation
                              Criminal Justice Information
                                 Services Division
                              Attention: Uniform Crime Reports
                              1000 Custer Hollow Road
                              Clarksburg, West Virginia 26306

APPENDIX VII

Uniform Crime Reporting Publications List

Crime in the United States (annual)

Law Enforcement Officers Killed and Assaulted (annual)

Hate Crime Statistics (annual)

Killed in the Line of Duty: A Study of Selected Felonious Killings of Law Enforcement Officers (special report)

Uniform Crime Reports: Their Proper Use (brochure)

National Incident-Based Reporting ystem (brochure)

UCR Preliminary Release, January-June

UCR Preliminary Annual Report

Uniform Crime Reporting Handbook:
    Summary System
    National Incident-Based Reporting System (NIBRS)

NIBRS:
    Volume 1—*Data Collection Guidelines*
    Volume 2—*Data Submission Specifications*
    Volume 3—*Approaches to Implementing an Incident-Based Reporting (IBR) System*
    Volume 4—*Error Message Manual*
    Supplemental Guidelines for Federal Participation

Manual of Law Enforcement Records

Hate Crime:
    Hate Crime Data Collection Guidelines
    Training Guide for Hate Crime Data Collection
    Hate Crime Magnetic Media Specifications for Tapes and Diskettes
    Hate Crime Statistics, 1990: A Resource Book

Age-Specific Arrest Rates and Race-Specific Arrest Rates for Selected Offenses

Periodic Press Releases:
    Crime Trends
    Law Enforcement Officers Killed
    Hate Crime

Evaluation Form For
Crime in the United States - 1996

1. For what purpose did you use this issue of *Crime in the United States?*

2. Was the publication adequate for that purpose?

    ____ Quite adequate   ____ Somewhat adequate   ____ Quite inadequate
    ____ Adequate   ____ Not Adequate

3. Are there presentations not included that you would find particularly useful?

4. What changes, if any, would you recommend for subsequent issues?

5. Can you point out specific table notes or presentations which are not clear or additional terms which need to be defined?

6. In what capacity did you use *Crime in the United States?*

    ____ Criminal justice/law enforcement   ____ Researcher
           agency employee *(specify functional area)*   ____ Student
           ____ Legislator
    ____ Other government employee   ____ Media
    ____ Private citizen   ____ Other *(specify)*
    ____ Educator

7. Add any additional comments you care to make.

OPTIONAL

Name	Telephone ( )
Number and street	
City	State	Zip Code

— — — —(Fold here)— — — —

U.S. Department of Justice
Federal Bureau of Investigation
Washington, D.C. 20535

PLACE
STAMP
HERE

Uniform Crime Reports
Federal Bureau of Investigation
1000 Custer Hollow Road
Clarksburg, West Virginia 26306

— — — —(Fold here)— — — —